THE OXFORD HANDBOOK OF

THE STUDY
OF RELIGION

THE OXFORD HANDBOOK OF

THE STUDY
OF RELIGION

Edited by

MICHAEL STAUSBERG

and

STEVEN ENGLER

OXFORD
UNIVERSITY PRESS

OXFORD
UNIVERSITY PRESS

Great Clarendon Street, Oxford, OX2 6DP,
United Kingdom

Oxford University Press is a department of the University of Oxford.
It furthers the University's objective of excellence in research, scholarship,
and education by publishing worldwide. Oxford is a registered trade mark of
Oxford University Press in the UK and in certain other countries

Published in the United States of America by Oxford University Press
198 Madison Avenue, New York, NY 10016, United States of America

British Library Cataloguing in Publication Data
Data available

Library of Congress Control Number: 2016944781

ISBN 978-0-19-872957-0

Jacket illustration: Egglant Land, 2016
© Zhana Kondratenko. Permission courtesy of the artist

CONTENTS

PART I RELIGION

PART II THEORETICAL APPROACHES

PART III MODES

PART IV ENVIRONMENTS

PART V TOPICS

PART VI PROCESSES

PART VII THE DISCIPLINE

List of Figures and Tables

Figures

Tables

LIST OF CONTRIBUTORS

Christoph Auffarth is Professor of Religionswissenschaft at the University of Bremen, Germany. He has published widely on ancient Mediterranean religions, Christianity, religion in the Middle Ages and early modern Europe, religion in the Third Reich, and the history of the study of religion.

Gustavo Benavides is an independent scholar who lives near Philadelphia, USA. Until his retirement he taught history of religions at Villanova University. A collection of essays under the title *Religion at the Intersection* is in preparation.

Jason C. Bivins is Professor of Religious Studies at North Carolina State University, USA. He is the author *of Spirits Rejoice! Jazz and American Religion* (2015); *Religion of Fear: The Politics of Horror in Conservative Evangelicalism* (2008); *The Fracture of Good Order: Christian Antiliberalism and the Challenge to Postwar American Politics* (2000).

Henrik Bogdan is Professor in History of Religions at the University of Gothenburg, Sweden. His recent book publications include *Handbook of Freemasonry* (2014, co-edited with Jan Snoek); *Sexuality and New Religious Movements* (2014, co-edited with James R. Lewis); *Occultism in a Global Perspective* (2013, co-edited with Gordan Djurdjevic); *Aleister Crowley and Western Esotericism* (2012, co-edited with Martin P. Starr).

Steve Bruce is Professor of Sociology at the University of Aberdeen, UK. He has written extensively on the nature of religion in the modern world, secularization theory, and on the links between religion and politics. Recent publications include *Secularization* (2011) and *Scottish Gods: Religion in Modern Scotland, 1900–2012* (2014).

Jeremy Carrette is Professor of Religion and Culture at the University of Kent, UK. His recent works include *William James's Hidden Religious Imagination* (2013).

Giovanni Casadio is Professor of History of Religions at the University of Salerno, Italy. He is the author of six books and more than 150 papers in Italian, English, French, German, Spanish, and Romanian on issues of ancient religions and historiography.

David Chidester is Professor of Religious Studies at the University of Cape Town, South Africa. His recent books are *Empire of Religion: Imperialism and Comparative Religion* (2014); *Wild Religion: Tracking the Sacred in South Africa* (2012).

John Corrigan is the Lucius Moody Bristol Distinguished Professor of Religion and Professor of History at Florida State University, USA. His most recent book on emotion and religion is *Emptiness: Feeling Christian in America* (2015).

Carole M. Cusack is Professor of Religious Studies at the University of Sydney, Australia. Her books include (with Katharine Buljan) *Anime, Religion and Spirituality: Profane and Sacred Worlds in Contemporary Japan* (2015); *The Sacred Tree: Ancient and Medieval Manifestations* (2011); *Invented Religions: Imagination, Fiction and Faith* (2010).

Matthew Day is Associate Professor in the History and Philosophy of Science Program at Florida State University, USA. His research focus has recently shifted from the academic study of religion to the transatlantic history of capitalism.

Albert de Jong is Professor for the Study of Religion at the Leiden University Centre for the Study of Religion of the University of Leiden, the Netherlands. He chiefly works on the premodern religious history of Iran and Central Asia, and on the history of the religious minorities of the modern Middle East.

Steven Engler is Professor of Religious Studies at Mount Royal University, Canada, Professor Colaborador at the Pontifícia Universidade Católica de São Paulo, Brazil, and Affiliate Professor at Concordia University, Canada. He is co-editor of the *Routledge Handbook of Research Methods in the Study of Religion* (2011, with Michael Stausberg) and the *Handbook of Contemporary Religions in Brazil* (2016, with Bettina E. Schmidt).

Gavin Flood is the Academic Director of the Oxford Centre for Hindu Studies, UK. His recent books include *The Truth Within: A History of Inwardness in Christianity, Hinduism, and Buddhism* (2013) and *The Importance of Religion: Meaning and Action in our Strange World* (2011).

David Garbin is Lecturer in Sociology at the University of Kent, UK. His fields of research include: migration and transnationalism; globalization, religion, and development; South Asian and new African diasporas in Europe and North America.

Mark Q. Gardiner is Associate Professor of Philosophy at Mount Royal University, Calgary, Canada. He is the author of a number of articles on intersections between semantic theory and theories of religion (many co-authored with Steven Engler).

Armin W. Geertz is Professor in the History of Religions at the Department for the Study of Religion, School of Culture and Society, Aarhus University, Denmark. He is co-founder of the Religion, Cognition and Culture Research Unit at Aarhus. His recent publications include *Origins of Religion, Cognition and Culture* (edited, 2014) and *Religious Narrative, Cognition and Culture* (2011, co-edited with Jeppe Sinding Jensen).

Rosalind I. J. Hackett is Professor and Head of Religious Studies at the University of Tennessee, Knoxville, USA. She has published extensively on religion in Africa, notably in the areas of New Religious Movements, art, gender, media, and conflict.

Olav Hammer is Professor of the Study of Religions at the University of Southern Denmark. Recent publications include *Western Esotericism in Scandinavia* (2016, co-edited with Henrik Bogdan) and *Handbook of the Theosophical Current* (2013, co-edited with Mikael Rothstein).

Manfred Hutter is Professor of Comparative Religions at the Institute of Oriental and Asian Studies, University of Bonn, Germany. His recent research focuses on pre- and non-Islamic religions of Iran and on the mythologies, rituals, and religious traditions of Ancient Anatolia in the second and early first millennium BCE.

Adrian Ivakhiv is Professor of Environmental Thought and Culture at the University of Vermont's Rubenstein School of Environment and Natural Resources (USA). He is the author of *Ecologies of the Moving Image: Cinema, Affect, Nature* (2013).

Jeppe Sinding Jensen is Senior Lecturer in the Department for Culture and Society and a research associate at the Interacting Minds Centre, both at Aarhus University, Denmark. His most recent book is *What is Religion?* (2014).

Paul Christopher Johnson is Professor of History and Afroamerican and African Studies at the University of Michigan, Ann Arbor, USA. His publications include *Spirited Things: The Work of "Possession" in Afro-Atlantic Religions* (edited, 2015).

Darlene M. Juschka teaches in Women's and Gender Studies and Religious Studies at the University of Regina, Canada. She is the author of *Political Bodies, Body Politic: The Semiotics of Gender* (2009).

Pamela E. Klassen is Professor in the Department for the Study of Religion at the University of Toronto, Canada. Her publications include *Spirits of Protestantism: Medicine, Healing, and Liberal Christianity* (2011).

Constantin Klein is Assistant Professor at the Department of Theology, Bielefeld University, Germany. His research interests include the empirical assessment of religiousness and empirical research about contemporary religiousness and spirituality, in particular the relation between religiousness and attitudes, between religiousness and gender, and between religiousness and mental and physical health.

Anne Koch is Professor of Religious Studies at the University of Salzburg, Austria. Her research focuses on the aesthetics of religion, the economy of culture and religion, religion, health, and healing, and global yoga.

Volkhard Krech is Professor of Religionswissenschaft at Ruhr-University, Bochum, Germany. He is the Director of the Käte Hamburger Kolleg "Dynamics in the History of Religions between Asia and Europe." His main research interests are related to the theory of religion and history of religions, religious pluralization and globalization, religion and violence, and history of the study of religion.

Oliver Krüger is Professor of Religious Studies at Fribourg University, Switzerland. He has published extensively on the sociology of religion and media, posthumanism, ritual studies, and research methods in the study of religion.

Lois Lee is a sociologist and research associate at the Institute of Advanced Studies UCL, UK. She is author of *Recognizing the Non-Religious: Reimagining the Secular* (2015), co-editor of *Religious Pluralism: A Resource Book* (2015) and *Secularity and Non-religion* (2013), and co-editor of the journal *Secularism and Nonreligion*.

Arvind Mandair is S.B.S.C. Associate Professor at the University of Michigan, USA. His publications include: *Sikhism: A Guide for the Perplexed* (2013); *Religion and the Specter of the West: Sikhism, India, Postcoloniality and the Politics of Translation* (2009); and *Secularism and Religion-Making* (2011, co-edited with Markus Dressler).

Craig Martin is Associate Professor of Religious Studies at St. Thomas Aquinas College, USA. His recent publications include *Capitalizing Religion: Ideology and the Opiate of the Bourgeoisie* (2014) and *A Critical Introduction to the Study of Religion* (2012).

Philip A. Mellor is Professor of Religion and Social Theory at the University of Leeds, UK. His most recent book publication is *The Sociology of the Sacred: Religion, Embodiment and Social Change* (2014, with Chris Shilling).

Axel Michaels is Professor of Classical Indology, South Asia Institute, University of Heidelberg, Germany. His publications include *Homo Ritualis: Hindu Ritual and Its Significance for Ritual Theory* (2016); *Exploring the Senses* (2014, co-edited with Christoph Wulff); *Emotions in Rituals in Performances* (2012, co-edited with Christoph Wulff).

David Morgan is Professor of Religious Studies at Duke University, USA. He has published widely on religious material culture, most recently *The Forge of Vision: A Visual History of Modern Christianity* (2015).

Alex Norman is a senior lecturer in higher education at the Graduate Research School, Western Sydney University, Australia. He is the author of *Spiritual Tourism* (2011).

Benjamin Grant Purzycki is a Senior Researcher at the Max Planck Institute for Evolutionary Anthropology. He examines religious cognition, its effects on human coordination and cooperation, and how religious systems co-evolve with social and ecological problems.

Jörg Rüpke is Permanent Fellow in Religionswissenschaft and Co-Director of the Max Weber Center for Advanced Cultural and Social Studies, University of Erfurt, Germany. His publications in English include *From Jupiter to Christ: On the History of Religion in the Roman Imperial Period* (2014); *Religion: Antiquity and its Legacy* (2013); *Religion in Republican Rome: Rationalization and Ritual Change* (2012); and several co-edited books.

William S. Sax is Professor and Head of the Department of Anthropology, South Asia Institute, Heidelberg University, Germany. He is Principal Investigator and co-leader of a number of research projects in the areas of Ethnography of India/Western Himalayas, Anthropology of Religion, and Medical Anthropology.

Benjamin Schonthal is Senior Lecturer in Asian Religions at the University of Otago, New Zealand. His first book, *Buddhism, Politics and the Limits of Law*, is forthcoming.

Peter Seele is trained in economics, philosophy, and protestant theology. He worked as Assistant Professor at the Center of Religion, Economy and Politics at the University of Basel, Switzerland and currently works as Professor of Corporate Social Responsibility and Business Ethics at the Università della Svizzera in Lugano, Switzerland.

Hubert Seiwert is Professor Emeritus of Religionswissenschaft at the University of Leipzig, Germany. His work focuses on Chinese religions, New Religious Movements, and systematic-comparative perspectives on the study of religion.

John H. Shaver is Lecturer in Religion at the University of Otago. His research is concerned with understanding intracultural variation in ritual behavior, relations between religion and fertility, and the evolution of syncretic religions.

Chris Shilling is Professor of Sociology at the University of Kent, UK. His book publications include *The Body: A Very Short Introduction* (2016) and *Sociology of the Sacred: Religion, Embodiment and Social Change* (2014, co-authored with Philip Mellor).

Richard Sosis is James Barnett Professor of Humanistic Anthropology and Director of the Evolution, Cognition, and Culture Program at the University of Connecticut, USA. His work has focused on the evolution of religion and cooperation, with particular interests in ritual, magic, religious cognition, and the dynamics of religious systems.

Michael Stausberg is Professor of Religion at the University of Bergen, Norway. His recent publications include *Religion and Tourism: Crossroads, Destinations, and Encounters* (2011) and, as co-editor, *The Wiley-Blackwell Companion to Zoroastrianism* (2015, with Yuhan S.-D. Vevaina), *Defining Magic* (2013, with Bernd-Christian Otto), and *The Routledge Handbook of Research Methods in the Study of Religion* (2011, with Steven Engler).

Heinz Streib is Professor for Religious Education at the University of Bielefeld, Germany, where he has established the Research Center for Biographical Studies in Contemporary Religion. His recent books in English include *Semantics and Psychology of Spirituality: A Cross-Cultural Analysis* (2016, co-authored with Ralph W. Hood).

Paul-François Tremlett is Senior Lecturer in Religious Studies at the Open University, UK. His publications include *Lévi-Strauss on Religion: The Structuring Mind* (2014) and *Religion and the Discourse of Modernity* (2011).

Thomas A. Tweed is the Harold and Martha Welch Professor of American Studies and Professor of History, University of Notre Dame, USA. His most recent monograph is *America's Church: The National Shrine and the Catholic Presence in the Nation's Capital* (2011).

Asonzeh Ukah is a sociologist/historian of religion affiliated with the Department of Religious Studies, University of Cape Town, South Africa. He is Director of the Research Institute on Christianity and Society in Africa (RICSA), University of Cape Town, and Affiliated Senior Fellow of Bayreuth International Graduate School of African Studies (BIGSAS), University of Bayreuth, Germany.

Hugh B. Urban is Professor in the Department of Comparative Studies, The Ohio State University, USA. His most recent monograph is *The Church of Scientology: A History of a New Religion* (2011).

Manuel A. Vásquez is Professor of Religion at the University of Florida, Gainesville, USA. He is the author of *More than Belief: A Materialist Theory of Religion* (2011) and *Living "Illegal": The Human Face of Unauthorized Immigration* (2011, co-authored with Marie F. Marquardt, Timothy J. Steigenga, and Philip J. Williams).

Laura J. Vollmer is currently working on her PhD in the comparative study of religion at the University of Groningen, the Netherlands. She researches the historical and social construction of discourses of 'religion' relative to 'science.'

Kocku von Stuckrad is Professor of Religious Studies at the University of Groningen, the Netherlands. Recent publications include *The Scientification of Religion* (2014); *Making Religion: Theory and Practice in the Discursive Study of Religion* (2016, co-edited with Frans Wijsen); *The Vocabulary for the Study of Religion* (2015, co-edited with Robert A. Segal).

Robert A. Yelle is Professor for the Theory and Method of Religious Studies and Chair of the Interfaculty Program in Religionswissenschaft at Ludwig-Maximilians-University, Germany. His recent publications include *Semiotics of Religion: Signs of the Sacred in History* (2013); *The Language of Disenchantment: Protestant Literalism and Colonial Discourse in India* (2013); *After Secular Law* (2011, co-editor).

Lucas Zapf currently is postdoctoral fellow at the Università della Svizzera italiana, Switzerland. His research revolves around the influence of market economy on its agents and how religion is involved.

INTRODUCTION
Aims, Scope, and Organization

MICHAEL STAUSBERG AND STEVEN ENGLER

THE first fifteen or so years of this century have seen the publication of various compendia consisting of commissioned chapters to survey the state of the art in the study of religion\s (in English: Braun/McCutcheon 2000; Hinnells 2005/2010; Segal 2006; Orsi 2011; in German: Figl 2003; Stausberg 2012; and in Portuguese: Usarski 2007; Passos/Usarski 2013).[1] The present volume bears the ambitious title of a handbook. This reflects its publication as part of the *Oxford Handbooks* series, whose volumes are meant to "offer authoritative and up-to-date surveys of original research in a particular subject area." More fundamentally, this *Handbook* has aimed from its inception at a greater degree of completeness and coherence than all the above books. Its far greater number of chapters is organized more coherently and systematically in seven sections, as follows.

PART I: RELIGION

Self-evidently 'religion' is the key issue of the study of religion\s. The first section addresses five major conceptual aspects of research on religion, starting with definitions and theories of religion. The study of religion\s deals with religion as a historical and cross-cultural phenomenon; the third chapter therefore addresses the historicization and translation of the concept of religion. In recent years, two developments have put the boundaries of religion into question: the emergence of spirituality and non-religion, categories discussed in one chapter each.

---

[1] The backslash (following Stausberg 2010) is intended to foreground debates over exactly what it is that our discipline studies, given a whole series of theoretical and meta-theoretical questions regarding the meaning and framing of 'religion' and 'religions.'

PART II: THEORETICAL APPROACHES

The second section surveys eleven main frameworks of analysis, interpretation, and explanation of religion. (The chapters in this and the following four sections are presented in alphabetical order.) Some of these have been with the study of religion\s since its beginnings, while others have been applied to religion in more recent times or their application has become more popular in recent times (e.g. economics). Not all of these approaches are equally well recognized: for example, semiotics is relatively well known, but the importance of semantics is often overlooked. There are separate chapters for cognitive science and evolutionary theory; though these approaches are related and coexist in much research, their genealogy and research questions are distinct. For more established theoretical approaches—such as Marxism and social theory—chapters survey recent applications and advances, not just historical perspectives, because none of these theoretical approaches are dead. Similarly, hermeneutics will remain relevant as long as interpretation remains important to the study of religion\s. Where 'critical theory' is often used as an umbrella term covering a range of theories, this book features a more specific subset: feminism/gender theory; Marxism; postcolonialism; and poststructuralism.

PART III: MODES

Reflecting recent turns in the humanities and social sciences, the third section of this *Handbook* surveys eight forms of the expression of religion. Some have been long-standing concerns in the study of religion\s: e.g. space and time, categories that have recently been theorized in new manners, with space now central to thinking about culture. Others—e.g. narrative and performance—have emerged as sites of theoretical innovation since the 1960s. Communication reflects and extends the linguistic turn. Materiality (presented here with a focus in visual materials) has emerged vigorously in this century, while the sonic qualities of culture and religion are receiving wider recognition, as witnessed by the body of research reviewed in that chapter.

PART IV: ENVIRONMENTS

In modern Western settings at least, religion is generally distinguished from other societal arenas, spheres, or (sub)systems. At the same time, religion's boundaries with these remain a matter of ongoing dispute or negotiation. For other cultures and historical periods, the meaningfulness or even the possibility of distinguishing religion from these other societal areas has been challenged. This *Handbook* considers ten such spheres and their interdependence with religion. While Part II contains a discussion of economic theory, Part IV provides a discussion of the ways societies and religions (or religious organizations) are shaped by different forms of allocation of resources, i.e. the economy. Other chapters consider law, the media, nature, medicine, politics, science, sports, and tourism.

PART V: TOPICS

Religion is typically identified by certain characteristic concerns that are sometimes studied comparatively in the study of religion\s. Salvation and gods/spirits, for example, have sometimes been held to be a defining feature of religion, but are treated here as topics for comparative analysis. Some of these topics have been particularly prominent in Protestantism and earlier Protestant-derived ways of studying religion. This is correlated with their being discredited as keys to analyzing religion in some recent scholarship. Yet, people continue to have experiences in religious terms and settings, and people continue to hold forms of belief related to religious traditions. Connected to the topic of experience, there has been an abundance of research on emotion, also in religious contexts. Readers will no doubt think of other chapters that might have been included in a book of this sort. (We listed many further potential contributions ourselves—more than one specific chapter on our wish list failed to materialize for one reason or another.) This 'topics' section is the one in which there is the largest scope for discussion regarding chapters that might have been included. That said, the other topics considered in this section are also prominent in the study of religion\s and related disciplines like anthropology and sociology and their treatment here reviews important developments, distinctions, and arguments: gift and sacrifice; initiations and traditions; and priests, prophets, and sorcerers.

PART VI: PROCESSES

As stated earlier, the study of religion\s addresses religion as a historical phenomenon. Historical change is sometimes conceptualized in terms not of contingent events but of ordered developments that follow a specific logic. The sixth section of the *Handbook* surveys seven historical processes. A key dimension of history is innovation and tradition. A popular example of a more specific historical process is secularization, which refers to the idea that history, at least in certain contexts, manifests some sort of cumulative decline, marginalization, or diminution of religion. Apart from the question of the accuracy of this linearity, on closer inspection it turns out that secularization is a composite of different processes, of which two are dealt with separately in this section: societal differentiation; and individualization/privatization. While secularization refers to the assumed modern process of a decline of the importance of religion for society and individuals in general, the historical process of the disintegration or death of religions has rarely been addressed specifically. A more recent macro-narrative of historical change is globalization. Three other chapters address additional processes of proven centrality to the recent study of religion\s: objectification/commoditization/commodification; and syncretism/hybridization.

PART VII: THE DISCIPLINE

Religion is studied in various ways by many disciplines. Some degree of internal diversity notwithstanding, we consider the study of religion\s to be an academic discipline in its own right (Engler/Stausberg 2011, 129–134). Despite some inter- or cross-disciplinary overlap in data, methods, and theories, scholars of religion are not anthropologists, economists, geographers, philosophers, political scientists, psychologists, sociologists, theologians, etc. This *Handbook* sharpens the profile of the study of religion\s as a discipline. It does not seek to characterize religious studies, which we take to be a much broader interdisciplinary field. This is why we decided against including necessarily superficial surveys of complex fields like anthropology of religion, psychology of religion, sociology of religion, etc. There are already many publications available that provide such surveys, from book chapters to other handbooks in this same *Oxford Handbook* series. The disciplinary profile of this *Handbook* is reflected in the last section, which only comprises two chapters: one on the history of the discipline; and one on its relevance, a crucial topic in times of an ongoing need for self-justification, not least in the face of understandable attempts by students, by their parents, and by governments, donors, and other funders to understand what this discipline is good for.

Notwithstanding some prominent exceptions, the study of religion\s is currently practiced in much of the world. Though not strictly global, this *Handbook* is a highly international enterprise. Contributors are affiliated with universities in twelve countries (Australia, Canada, Denmark, Germany, Italy, the Netherlands, New Zealand, Norway, South Africa, Sweden, UK, USA).

This *Handbook* emphasizes discussions of published research and seeks to advance the state of the discipline. In addition, all chapters have several features that make them reader friendly and apt for teaching purposes. Beyond detailed indices for the volume as a whole and rich bibliographies for each chapter, these features include chapter summaries, glossaries, and lists of annotated readings. In this regard, this *Handbook* follows the example set by our *Routledge Handbook of Research Methods in the Study of Religion* (2011), which can be considered an informal companion to this book. Questions of research methods are an essential aspect of the study of religion\s but, because they received extensive treatment in that other handbook, they are not addressed explicitly in this one.

REFERENCES

Braun, Willi and Russell T. McCutcheon, eds. 2000. *Guide to the Study of Religion*. London and New York: Cassell.

Engler, Steven and Michael Stausberg. 2011. "Introductory Essay. Crisis and Creativity: Opportunities and Threats in the Global Study of Religion/s." *Religion* 41(2): 127–143. doi: 10.1080/0048721X.2011.591209

Figl, Johann, ed. 2003. *Handbuch Religionswissenschaft. Religionen und ihre zentralen Themen*. Innsbruck, Wien, and Göttingen: Tyrolia/Vandenhoeck & Ruprecht.

Hinnells, John, ed. 2005. *Routledge Companion to the Study of Religion*, 2nd edition. London: Routledge, 2010.

Orsi, Robert A., ed. 2011. *The Cambridge Companion to Religious Studies*. Cambridge and New York: Cambridge University Press.

Passos, João Décio and Frank Usarski, eds. 2013. *Compêndio de Ciência da Religião*. São Paulo: Paulinas/Paulus.

Segal, Robert A., ed. 2006. *The Blackwell Companion to the Study of Religion*. Malden, MA: Blackwell.

Stausberg, Michael. 2010. "Prospects in Theories of Religion." *Method & Theory in the Study of Religion* 22(4): 223–238. doi:10.1163/157006810X531021

Stausberg, Michael, ed. 2012. *Religionswissenschaft*. Berlin: de Gruyter.

Stausberg, Michael and Steven Engler, eds. 2011. *The Routledge Handbook of Research Methods in the Study of Religion*. London: Routledge.

Usarski, Frank, ed. 2007. *O espectro disciplinar da Ciência da Religião*. São Paulo: Paulinas.

PART I

RELIGION

CHAPTER 1

··

DEFINITION

··

MICHAEL STAUSBERG AND MARK Q. GARDINER

Chapter Summary

- There are differences of opinion over whether defining religion is necessary or even possible.
- There are two common methods of defining: extension and intension; the former takes the empirical as its starting point, the latter the conceptual; these methods are not mutually exclusive.
- The relation between the expression to be defined (the *definiendum*) and the expression doing the defining (the *definiens*) can be conceived of as either an equivalence or an elucidation.
- Definitions address the word and the thing and their mutual relationships; definitional lexicalism assigns priority to the word; definitional objectualism seeks to determine the thing.
- Definitions are based on underlying theories of meaning; a crucial semantic distinction is that between meaning realism, which sees meanings as fully determinate, and meaning antirealism, which sees meanings as in principle indeterminate.
- The positions resonate with different types (as opposed to methods) of definitions (real, lexical, and stipulative).
- Substantive and functionalist definitions of religion have limitations which suggests the value of combining them.
- Similarly, both definitions requiring the necessary presence of one or several criteria (so-called monothetic definitions) and those that require only some portion of the list of criteria (so-called polythetic definitions) each have limitations; homeostatic property cluster definitions are a possible alternative.
- Definitions of religion are not value-free; they are often implicated in power structures both inside and outside of the academy (for example in legal and political contexts).

There are innumerable attempts at defining 'religion,' both in various branches of the academy and beyond. Much ink has been spilled over the topic (see the Further Reading section at the end of this chapter) and the discussion continues (see, e.g. Bruce 2011; Schilbrack 2013; Frankenberry 2014; Schaffalitzky de Muckadell 2014), though one might think that "any attempt at definition is futile" (Stringer 2008, 3). Some introductory books (see, e.g. McCutcheon 2007; Jensen 2014) and earlier handbooks or companions (see, e.g. Arnal 2000; Droogers 2009; Greil 2009) dedicate a chapter or a section to the problem. The appendix to this chapter samples some influential and noteworthy classical and contemporary definitions proposed by scholars (see Dubuisson 2003, 57–63 and Greil 2009 for larger samples). A commentator has observed there to be a "gulf . . . between those scholars who think that arguments about definitions are very important and those of us who believe that some loosely commonsensical conceptualization of religion is sufficient to allow us to get on with our primary purpose of exploring its sociologically interesting features" (Bruce 2011, 118). In fact, "[m]ost scholars of religion do not develop a definition of religion" (Platvoet 1999a, 252), and even some theoreticians of religion have failed to propose (e.g. Rappaport 1999) or refused to suggest definitions of religion. Among classical theorists, Max Weber, at the beginning of his study of religious communities, stated that a definition of religion cannot be made at the outset of such a study, but, if at all, only at the end (Weber 1993 [1920], 1).

To Define or Not to Define

Weber's case points to two distinct functions of definitions in the research process. In the first stage, one needs to delimit the subject area under investigation. This recalls the etymology of 'definition,' which derives from the Latin verb *definire* (*de+finire*), meaning 'to limit, end.' The most frequent ancient Greek term translated as 'definition' derives from ὅρισμα (*horisma*), literally a marked boundary in an earth-measuring sense. It is the origin of the English 'horizon,' that which marks off the celestial from the terrestrial, or the heavenly from the mundane. In this sense, a definition delimits the range of the subject in question. Often such definitions are made implicitly; in such cases, making them explicit increases the transparency of the study.

In contrast to the claim that a definitional delineation of religion is necessary to make religious studies possible are two opposing views: that definitions of religion are not, in fact, necessary for the study of religion; and that definitions of religion are impossible (see Bergunder 2014, 248). For the former view, one might think that religion is simpler, clearer, and more common or intuitive than suggested by any of the characteristics used to define it: there may simply be no need to define it. In response, the sheer number and diversity of attempts to define religion suggest that it is not a simple, clear, or intuitive idea. At the same time, the multitude of extant definitions has been thought to index its indefinability, at the same time showing that the expression can be defined in many ways (Smith 1998, 281). Others point out that almost no other discipline seems to feel the need to define their subject matter. Bergunder (2014, 252), for example, claims that literary scholars seldom define 'literature,' nor music scholars 'music,' nor art historians 'art.' In response it might be recognized that some disciplines do concern themselves with this question, the rise of meta-philosophy in recent years being a prominent example. Secondly, definitional questions of the sort that Bergunder mentions are certainly asked by at least non-academics, especially in the context of attempting to delineate problematic cases (Is D. H. Lawrence's *Lady Chatterley's Lover* literature or pornography? Is thrash metal music or noise? Is Duchamp's *Fountain* art or plumbing?). Such things as art, football (aka soccer), nationalism, veganism, environmentalism, and even atheism are routinely referred to as religions, and at some point scholars will be asked their views; from time to time administrators and courts also require definitions of religion (see section "After all: Why define?").

On a theoretical level, the need to define religion is challenged by some 'critical' theorists who insist that there is simply no such 'thing' as religion. This call ranges from those who hold that ultimately the religious reduces to the sociological, anthropological, economic, political, etc. (Arnal/McCutcheon 2013), to those who claim that 'religion' is primarily a creation of the academy (Smith 1998), and to those who think that while it might be applicable to a particular historical context—namely post-Reformation Protestantism and the rise of the modern nation state—its expansion beyond that is Eurocentric, imperialistic, and called into question by postcolonial critique (Dubuisson 2003; but see Casadio, "Historicizing and Translating Religion," this volume). Some conclude that instead of attempting to define religion the study of religion\s should focus its efforts elsewhere: to "focus on deconstructing the category and analyzing its function within popular discourse" (Arnal 2000, 30); to abandon "the tendency to regard religion as a relatively well-defined object" and instead examine "critically the social processes whereby certain things are counted as religious" (Beckford 2003, 2–3); to treat religion "not as a characteristic that inheres in certain phenomena, but as a cultural resource over which competing interest groups may vie" and to view religion as "a claim, made by certain groups and, in some cases, contested by others" (Greil 2009, 148); or to shift the focus to a study of "a consensus-capable, contemporary, everyday understanding of 'religion'" (Bergunder 2014, 246). While we neither oppose nor endorse those positions in this chapter, the inference from them to the impossibility of defining religion rests on a particular assumption about definitions—namely that only real things can be defined—which is somewhat controversial (see the discussion of 'real definitions' later in this chapter). In other words, even those who question the necessity or propriety of defining religion presuppose certain definitions of religion and certain definitions of definition.

Assuming that a definition of religion is possible, questions about the strategies of its construction are unavoidable. Defining something that exhibits considerable diversity in actual cases, like religion (and many other things), involves a blend of the empirical and the conceptual. Both these dimensions pose problems in their own right, i.e. which empirical materials and which concepts to draw on. This resonates with two common general strategies for constructing a definition of religion.

Taking the empirical as its point of departure, the method of extension (named from the term in logic for the range of things to which the use of a word is extended, sometimes called denotation) would identify an intuitively plausible range of observed things uncontroversially labeled as religions or qualified as religious, and distil a statement of what they appear to have in common. Starting from the conceptual, on the other hand, the method of intension (named from the term in logic for the criteria by which something is to be included in a word's extension, sometimes called connotation) builds on an intuitively plausible conception of what delimits the religious from the non-religious, and sorts through actual cases accordingly. Each of these methods, which start with intuitive preconceptions, allow for modification and re-tooling in light of further reflection and a growing body of empirical materials. For example, provisional definitions for the first can be tested against, and modified accordingly, an expanding list of examples starting from the contextual variety of religions the scholar is most familiar with from her or his own academic and non-academic experience. Provisional definitions obtained by the second method can be modified in light of how easy or difficult it is to fit cases into the model. These methods are not mutually exclusive and are typically combined.

MEANINGS OF DEFINITION: THEORETICAL POINTS OF DEPARTURE

Conceptions of the Definitional Relation: Equivalence or Elucidation

Linguistically, definitions are sentences that link a *definiendum* (expression to be defined) to a *definiens* (expression that does the defining). Because these are expressed merely as strings of words, there is nothing in a proposed definition itself that indicates whether the link is to be conceived of either (i) as an equivalence or (ii) as an elucidation. In the case of definitions as equivalences (i) the *definienda* are taken to be semantically equivalent to *definiens* in the sense that each is essentially an unequivocal stylistic variant of the other (such as defining 'sister' as 'female sibling'), whereas (ii) in the other conception *definiens* are taken to elucidate the *definienda* in the sense of clarifying, or explaining, the meaning for example to one who is not already familiar with the term, when novel, revisionary, precising, or unusual meanings are intended, or when ambiguities need to be resolved. The distinction between these two conceptions of definition can only be drawn on the basis of the underlying assumptions and intentions of the definer (not always open to view) or its pragmatic use, especially the inferences drawn from it. When a definition is conceived of as expressing an equivalence, it is assumed that the things to which the *definiendum* applies are only the things to which the *definiens* applies, and vice versa. In this way a *definiens*, usually more linguistically complex than the *definiendum*, can be seen as supplying a set of individually necessary and jointly sufficient conditions for the application of the *definiendum*. When Schilbrack's definition of religion as "forms of life predicated upon the reality of the superempirical" (2013, 313) is viewed as expressing an equivalence, it can be inferred that all religions are forms of life, that all religions are committed to the reality of the superempirical, and that anything that is a form of life committed to the reality of the superempirical is thereby a religion. This definition can be critiqued by way of a counterexample: some logicians regard the logical properties (tautological, contrary, valid, etc.) as real, knowable, but inaccessible to the senses, and assert that we have an (intellectual) duty to correctly apprehend them in order to adjust our inferential 'forms of life'; is formal logic then a religion? On the other hand when a definition is proposed and received in elucidatory terms, failure of the applicability of the *definiens* does not logically entail failure of the applicability of the *definiendum*, or vice versa. When Schilbrack's definition is viewed as elucidatory, the counterexample is not as threatening. Rather, both 'form of life' and 'reality of the superempirical' can be viewed as offering a sound and useful way of understanding religion\s, at least in the context in which the definition is advanced.

Failure of the definer, or readers, to understand which definitional conception is assumed, may lead to drawing faulty inferences and giving misdirected criticisms. For example, consider the fact that Schilbrack offers two distinct (that is, inequivalent) definitions of religion: "normative practices that at least implicitly make ontological claims in terms of which the practical norms are authorized" (2013, 306) and "forms of life predicated on the reality of the superempirical" (2013, 313). The temptation to accuse him of inconsistency seems relevant only under an equivalence conception. Seen under an elucidatory model they can be both seen as valuable within their specific contexts. Indeed, Schilbrack intends his latter definition to subsume the main insights of the former one, and so the introduction of a second definition is better understood as refining an elucidation rather than replacing an equivalence claim.

For another example, consider how definitions of religion are often used differently inside and outside of the academy. Scholarly offerings tend towards an elucidatory model in that they are often offered as contributing towards improving our understanding of the subject matter itself. On the other hand, definitions asked for outside of the academy, such as in judicial or political settings (see section "After all: Why define?"), tend towards asking for a equivalence-informed taxonomy aimed at giving a definitive (pun intended) mechanism for deciding whether this or that is or is not a religion, for example to help determine what is and is not legally protected. Academics often resent the simplifying directives, whereas non-academics may lose confidence that the academics really know what they're talking about. What is the point of studying religion for a lifetime without even knowing what it is—or is it the other way around: studying something for a lifetime makes its contours even fuzzier?

Conceptions of *Definienda*: Objectual or Lexical

A second point of potential confusion involves differing conceptions of the nature of *definienda*; do definitions define words or things? In a syntactic sense, definitions have words as their *definienda*, but from a semantic point of view, given that words have meanings, definitions may be held to refer to things. One may call these two options definitional lexicalism versus definitional objectualism. Both options have been championed by prominent contemporary philosophers. Tyler Burge, for example, insists on the priority of what he calls "metaphysical or essence-determining definitions," a variety of objectual definitions; for Burge (1993, 314) a "metaphysically correct definition" is one that "states actual necessary and sufficient conditions" for instantiations of a kind. In the study of religion\s, many would be skeptical regarding such an undertaking, since there seems to be a widespread incredulity towards the feasibility of such an operation and a suspicion of the political entanglements of essentialist claims (see Schaffalitzky de Muckadell 2014 for a discussion). Willard Van Orman Quine, on the other hand, held that lexical definitions are prior to objectual ones: "The one way of talking of definition reduces to the other, since we define men by defining 'man'" (Quine 1987, 44). By analogy, we define religions by defining the word 'religion'. Several scholars have doubted that there is such a thing as religion (see section "To define or not to define"), and that we can only speak of the word: i.e. there is no thing called religion; it is a reified product of our language or of discursive practices engaging the word. Yet, even if one insists on the discursive or cognitive construction of both religion as a thing and 'religion' as a word, discursive or imaginary entities also qualify as things in the wider sense. This is especially so when they are held to be observable entities with specific properties ascribed with an agentic quality.

Specifying the *Definiens*

Definitions are potentially undermined by the presence of vague, ambiguous, or mysterious terms in the *definiens*. For example, defining religion by reference to experiences of the holy or the numinous is in danger of explaining the complex (religion) by reference to the obscure (the holy). This is less of a problem under an equivalence model, though, since claiming the ontological identity of two notions is not challenged by their respective obscurity—it is their identity that counts. Under the elucidation model, however, which aims at epistemic relationships between two expressions, it is desirable that the *definiens* be better understood than the *definienda*. By often failing to do so, definitions have a tendency to proliferate the need for further definitions.

DEFINITIONS AND SEMANTIC THEORY

Given that *definiens* are intended to express the meanings of the *definienda*, either as an equivalence or an elucidation, definitions are theoretically impacted by the underlying theory of meaning (see Gardiner/Engler, "Semantics," this volume). One crucial distinction is that between meaning realism and antirealism.

Meaning realism is the view that meanings, at least in a given context, are fully determinate. In other words, it posits that there is an objective fact of the matter concerning what a given expression means in a given context. Meaning realist views include such positions as that meaning is fixed by the intentions of the speaker (Paul Grice), by the conventions of a linguistic community (David Lewis), by how it is used within a linguistic community (the later Ludwig Wittgenstein), or by its syntactic structure (Noam Chomsky). There are two main types of meaning realists: those who regard the determinate meanings as fixed by the relation of the expression to extra-linguistic reality (externalism) and those who regard them as independent of relations to such a reality (internalism).

Meaning antirealism, on the other hand, is the view that meanings, even in single contexts, have indeterminate, or a range of non-equivalent, meanings. There is no single fact of the matter concerning what a given expression means. Meaning antirealists need not be either meaning relativists (holding that meanings are subjectively made up) or meaning nihilists (holding that meaning is an empty or explanatorily useless notion). In contrast to these two positions, one can hold that there is no single thing that can be identified as *the* meaning of an expression, there are many things that can be eliminated as possible candidates for its meaning. Two prominent meaning antirealists, W. V. O. Quine and Donald Davidson, argue this view on the basis of a prior commitment to semantic holism, a philosophical view that sees the meaning of any linguistic expression as being a function, at least in part, of the meaning of others (as opposed to semantic atomism, which sees meaning as directly embedded in linguistic expressions themselves). Quine and Davidson argue that there will always be more than one possible meaning equally supported by all of the available interpretative evidence.

A practical difference with respect to definitions is that meaning realists will think of definitions in terms of being true or false, depending on whether they express the meaning-determining facts, whereas meaning antirealists will think of them in terms of being better or worse, depending on whether they allow for the range of interpretations supported by the evidence while excluding those precluded by it. According to the meaning realists, there can only be one correct definition of religion\s; for meaning antirealists, there can be several. Acknowledging the indeterminacy of definition runs counter to the agenda of definitions to delimit and to create semantic boundaries; on this view, definitions would be unbounded and open up semantic relations rather than closing them off.

Prior commitment, whether realized or not, to either meaning realism (and more specifically externalism or internalism) or meaning antirealism has profound implications with respect to what *types* of definitions are admissible. Even though one of the co-authors of this chapter (Gardiner) endorses antirealist and holistic semantics (while Stausberg remains uncommitted), this chapter is not meant to advocate for any philosophical position in particular, but to unpack the philosophical choices often made when engaging in reflections on definitions of religion (or of anything else).

Types of Definition

The literature suggests distinctions between different types of definitions, which to some extent similarly reflect different underlying theories of meaning.

Real, Lexical, and Stipulative Definitions

What are often called real definitions purport that the definitional criteria are satisfied by the objects in and of themselves. In other words, the objects to which the *definienda* of real definitions apply are thought to have an objective existence whose identity conditions are intrinsic to the things themselves—they are discovered, not invented—and the definition tries to state criteria which delineate them from other objects in precisely the way determined by the objective facts. This is the type of definition favored by various forms of ontological realists who tend towards meaning realism of the external variety: e.g. a real definition of biological species will attempt to state the objective criteria by which one species is ontologically distinct from another; and a real definition of moral goodness will attempt to state that which objectively distinguishes things that are morally good from those that are not. Real definitions, then, are objectively true or false.

In our context, real definitionists of religion take it to be a real thing, instantiated in the myriad religions found around the world. It is what they all have in common, their essence, which transcends any particular case (or even all of them) and which is the proper object of definition. Few scholars of religion today are tempted by such an understanding of their subject matter, though this appears to be a common way of reading Mircea Eliade. However, commitment to a real definition of religion need not be a commitment to the ontological *sui genericity* of religion. A Durkheimian reduction of the religious to the social (holding that god-talk is really society-talk in disguise) is just as committed to the reality of religion as an Eliadean one. It is also significant that many adherents seem to view their religion in such objective terms: religion is typically taken by adherents to have a transcendent reality on its own, rather than being a product of human design.

A further classical real definition is the one by Geertz (see appendix) in that religion is characterized by an objectively specified system of symbols. Real definitions have generally been conceived by adopting the Aristotelian/Scholastic rule: *definitio fi(a)t per genus proximum et differentiam specificam*; i.e. a definition points to the category of things that the thing to be defined belongs to (*genus proximum*) and the distinctive features that make it specific (*differentia specifica*). Some would agree that religion is a specific subtype of culture, system of symbols, worldview, taxonomy, or discourse. Durkheim's definition (see appendix) is an example of such a definition; if something is not a "unified system," for example, or is not "relative to sacred things," it will not qualify as a religion.

Meaning realists of the internalist variety tend towards lexical definitions, which aim at giving a description of the ways a term is used in a linguistic community. Like the real definitions favored by the externalist variety, such definitions are true or false, though unlike them they are made so by intersubjective considerations of how communities use their language. Depending on the authority ascribed to the lexicon in a given linguistic community—consider the *Oxford English Dictionary* for speakers of English or the *Duden* for speakers of German—some such collections of definitions have normative power, because different ways of using an expression can be resisted by referring to them. Bergunder suggests that scholars of religion implicitly use an "unexplained" and "contemporary, everyday understanding of religion" that is "widely regarded as capable of consensus and goes largely undisputed" (Bergunder 2014, 252). It is this implicit "consensual definition" which, he argues, delimits the "undisclosed subject matter of religious studies" (255). In other words, he claims that there is a single universally accepted implicit definition lurking behind the myriad explicit ones on offer, and that it is the one doing the real work.

Lexical definitions can be contrasted with another meaning realist form of definition—stipulative definitions—in which definers introduce novel or unusual uses for a term within a given linguistic context such as a book. Here the connection to meaning realism is most stark, as stipulations tend towards a full determination of the *definiendum*'s meaning, at least in the context of use intended by the stipulator. Here there is not so much a question of whether the definition is accurate or inaccurate as whether it does useful work in the context and whether those invited choose to accept it or not. William James's introduction of his definition of religion in *Varieties of Religious Experience* is a classic example: "Religion, therefore, as I now ask you arbitrarily to take it, shall mean for us . . ." (James 1958 [1902], 24). One danger of stipulative definitions, especially when using familiar *definienda*, is that definers or readers may equivocate between the stipulated meaning and more familiar ones.

Substantive and Functional Definitions

In the study of religion\s, a recurrent distinction is that between so-called functionalist and substantive definitions (with either type being potentially real, lexical, or stipulative). Simply put, functional definitions focus on what religions do and substantialist definitions on what religions are (what was earlier called their morphology).

Substantive definitions aim at delineating the content of the religious from that of the non-religious. A glance at the definitions in the appendix show purported reference to such things as: spiritual beings (Tylor), the holy (Otto), the sacred (Durkheim, Droogers), an unseen order (James), superhuman agents (Spiro, Jensen, Frankenberry), counterintuitive worlds (Atran). Besides the fact that these latter terms are not without ambiguity, critics have pointed out that such attempts face obvious counterexamples in two ways: for most proposed substantive criteria, (i) there are things commonly recognized as religions which lack them (such as Theravada Buddhism with respect to the ultimate importance of superhuman agents), and (ii) there are things commonly recognized as non-religions which have them (such as spiritual beings in fairy stories or counterintuitive worlds in science fiction). In other words, finding a single set of substantive features which all religions but only religions have has proven quite elusive.

That has provided impetus to those who seek to define religion in functional terms, most commonly either socially (e.g. Durkheim) or individually (e.g. Tillich), both offering classical functional definitions, which allows for "an openness to religious diversity and without limitation on or presuppositions about the nature of the religious reality" (Schilbrack 2013, 294). Tweed's definition of religions (see appendix) as organic-cultural flows that intensify joy and confront suffering is a contemporary example of a functional definition. Some have rejected functional definitions entirely as committing the 'functionalist fallacy' (inferring that y causally explains x from the fact that x may function to produce y—e.g. that the need for social cohesion can cause religions to arise as religions may cause social cohesion), though the jury is still out concerning whether there is a genuine fallacy here. Others have more specifically critiqued functionalist definitions of religion by pointing out that they (i) leave out that which practitioners often take as the most important aspects of their religion, (ii) are too static, ignoring historical change, or (iii) are far too broad in that they become unspecific, vague, and include things that many would agree would not reasonably fall into the category (see, e.g. Fitzgerald 1997, 92–93; Riesebrodt 2010, xi). Moreover it has turned out that well-known functionalist definitions in fact also comprise substantive features (Bruce 2011)—Durkheim's definition, for example, combines functional and substantive elements. Yet, there are some influential definitions—in particular by Tylor and Spiro—that are purely substantive (see also Snoek 1999; Flood 2012; Jensen 2014 for recent examples).

To overcome these limitations, some have sought a two-aspect approach, including both substantive and functional elements as aspects of their definitions of religion (see Pollack 1995 and Schilbrack 2013 for explicit strategies of this kind). To some extent this combination is a logical extension of both types of definitions: on the one hand, if religion is defined substantially, one can assume that people will only invest their resources in religion and transmit it to future generations if it does effective work, so that substantial definitions require functionality; on the other hand, functional definitions identify a problem religion is assumed to address or resolve (e.g. death, suffering, contingency, cohesion), which gives functional definitions a substantive dimension.

Monothetic and Polythetic Definitions

Monothetic definitions require satisfaction of a single criterion, whether one feature/property or a conjunction of them, for application of the *definiendum*. Tylor's definition of religion as belief in spiritual beings (see appendix) is a classic example of a simple monothetic definition, while Lincoln's definition—in which religion comprises four domains: specific types of discourse and related forms of practice, community, and institutions—is a contemporary example of a complex one (see appendix). Monothetic definitions can be objectual or lexical, substantive, or functional.

Developments in philosophy—in particular Wittgenstein's posthumously published investigations on a theory of language and his metaphor of 'family resemblance' (1972 [1953])—and in various natural sciences such as evolutionary theory, bacteriology, botany, and zoology have challenged this classical way of thinking of classification and definition. Those developments suggest an alternative to monothetic taxonomy—polythetic classification—which has also proven influential outside of their original contexts, especially social anthropology (Needham 1975), and, with some delay, the study of religion\s (Snoek 1994; Saler 2000 [1993]; 2008). Polythetic definitions are similar to complex monothetic ones in that their *definiens* mention more than one criterion, but they differ from them in that there is no necessity that the things to which *definienda* apply satisfy all of the criteria. The basic principle is that satisfaction of some portion suffices for application of the *definiendum*. For example, in Lincoln's definition of a 'proper religion' (see appendix), networks or groups that have practices and communities grounded in religious discourses but lack institutions would not be considered a 'proper' religion, while a potential polythetic revision of this definition could allow for some subset of these characteristics, be it one, two, or three of them, to index the *definiendum*. With a monothetic approach, the question of whether a thing falls under the definition is an either-or one. With a polythetic approach, it is a more-or-less one: the more of the criteria satisfied, the more secure the application of the *definiendum*.

The construction of polythetic definitions raises several problems. To begin with, how many criteria does something need to match in order to qualify: just one, some, several, many, or most? While this uncertainty may be removed by meta-criteria explicitly made in the definition itself, such as in Southwold's rather liberal "at least some" of a list of twelve quite distinct features (see appendix), any such demarcation would be arbitrary and artificial. Further, how long shall the set of criteria be and how does one generate the list? Is it practical to have a list of more than, say, ten or twenty criteria? More importantly: how does one get at the set of features? One strategy, akin to the method of extension (see section "To define or not to define"), is to select a so-called prototype, or several prototypes, which would generally be taken to exemplify the phenomenon in a paradigmatic manner; the criteria can then be derived from a morphological analysis of the prototype. Apples, for example, are prototypical fruits, dogs prototypical animals—and Christianity is often, in different parts of the world, considered a prototypical example for religion (a fact negatively noted by the 'critical' theorists). As such, a list could be prepared on the basis of an analysis of the basic formal structures of Christianity (or other candidates for prototypicality). This raises a series of problems. Is the process circular (Christianity is a religion because religion is defined on the basis of Christianity)? Who decides on the issue of prototypicality and on which ground? Can such a list of criteria be achieved at all, how, and who decides on it? Shall the list be fixed or flexible? If it is flexible, so as to include the results of further analysis and discussion, any definition becomes potentially revisable. Polythetic definitions are thereby far from unproblematic, at least from the standpoint of meaning realism (see section "Definitions and semantic theory"), and do not promise to achieve unambiguous solutions. Some have even argued that polythetic definitions are antithetical to theorizing religion; philosopher Peter Byrne argues that "No theory of the religious is appropriate if the genus of the religious is simply a collection of things connected by overlapping analogies" (Byrne 1999, 384). Yet, polythetic definitions have the appeal of avoiding essentialism, which is regarded by most scholars of religion as a pitfall and a danger (even though most anti-essentialists have a hard time completely erasing essentialism from their own critique, leaving aside the fact that some have a narrow conception of essentialism). Yet, if polythetic definitions protect against essentialism, they do so in an uncertain and costly manner. As a matter of fact, many definitions proposed by contemporary scholars of religion are monothetic ones (see, for example, Frankenberry, Jensen, Lincoln, Schilbrack, in the appendix). The only definition in our sample that is explicitly constructed as a polythetic one comes from anthropologist Martin Southwold (1978).

Polythetic definitions are neutral to the question of meaning realism or antirealism. Meaning antirealists will regard the plethora of criteria as forever open-ended and endlessly revisable; for them, addition, deletion, or revision to the criteria need not be seen as changing the meaning of an expression like religion because there is simply no such thing as *the* meaning of anything. Moreover—on at least Davidson's version of antirealistic semantic holism—any two people who use the term religion, no matter how far apart in time, space, or social position, must as a semantic precondition, agree considerably, whether they realize it or not, on much of the definitional criteria. It is that commonality that, Davidson would say, allows them to be conversing about the same subject, although their understandings need not be anywhere near equivalent: even disagreement about X presupposes a good deal of agreement on it. These implicit commonalities are seen by this semantic approach as polythetically related: i.e. speaker A's and B's respective implicit definitional criteria for the term will overlap on some points, as will speaker B's and C's, but (i) A–B's overlap needn't be the same as B–C's; and as long as A and C are far enough apart temporally, spatially, socially, institutionally, etc., their respective implicit definitional criteria may be considerably divergent. Meaning antirealist definitions, then, can be seen as an attempt to find words for capturing such commonalities, at least for those within particular placements or situational contexts.

Homeostatic Property Cluster Definitions

A relatively new type of definition, which seems promising in avoiding some of the worries raised against polythetic definitions, has arisen in ethics and the philosophy of science but has not yet received attention in the study of religion\s. American philosopher Richard Boyd developed the theory of homeostatic property clusters (HPC) in metaethics as a way of understanding how moral properties (good, right, just, etc.) may be natural ones and introduced an allied form of definition—the homeostatic cluster definition (Boyd 1988). He later extended HPC to the philosophy of science in making sense of natural kinds such as water or biological species (Boyd 1999), a move that has received wide attention. In a nutshell, a homeostatic property cluster is a family of natural properties which are non-accidentally related—i.e. the presence of one of them increases the likelihood of the presence of others—in virtue of common underlying 'mechanisms.' In Boyd's example, he argues that moral goodness is predicated of things which display a set of properties that are homeostatically clustered around an underlying mechanism of satisfying important human needs, including physical (e.g. health), psychological (e.g. the need to exercise control over one's own life), and social (e.g. the need for love and friendship) ones. Moral goodness can be polythetically defined, he says, by this homeostatically unified cluster of properties. There is one other important element of this type of definition, at least as envisioned by Boyd: the individual properties of the cluster are allowed to be hierarchically ordered, in the sense that the presence of some might provide greater weight than others for applying the *definiendum*. It is even conceivable that, in certain cases, possession of one property might be deemed necessary (though not sufficient) for the application of the *definiendum*. A modified form of Lincoln's definition of religion (see appendix), for example, might insist on the presence of a certain type of discourse as necessary for something to count as a religion, but that would not be enough for it to count; it must also display a certain type of practice, community, or institution, etc. Homeostatic-style definitions that are constructed in this manner insert quasi-monothetic elements into a polythetic framework; they are quasi-monothetic because there are no sets of properties which are both necessary and sufficient for the application of the *definiendum* in every case. On a final note, Boyd insists that there may be irresolvable uncertainty in some cases of whether the *definiendum* applies, but it is unclear whether this is because of uncertainty whether all of the properties in the cluster have been identified, whether the hierarchy has been correctly identified, how many of the properties of the cluster need to be realized, or because of a prior assumption of meaning antirealism. One advantage of homeostatic-style definitions is that particular examples can be empirically tested, at least to some degree; as the elements of the cluster must be non-accidentally related, it is predictable that the presence of one (or more) element will statistically increase the likelihood of the presence of others.

An outline of a possible homeostatic cluster definition of religion might go like this: religion is to be defined by reference to a homeostatic cluster of commonly mentioned features, e.g. actions, attitudes, behaviors, beliefs, communities, discourses, emotions, experiences, institutions, narratives, representations, signs, etc. They are clustered, it might be argued, in the sense that the presence of one of these features makes the presence of others more likely; e.g. that a social formation defined as religion not only comprises actions, attitudes, etc., but that these are predicted to co-occur; for example, that there will be relevant types of behavior where one observes a requisite form of narrative. The proposed definition would then also express (i) a hierarchical ordering of at least some of these features, some of which may be necessary and (ii) underlying mechanisms which cluster them homeostatically (e.g. anthropomorphism [Guthrie], by-products of normal evolutionary cognitive development [Barrett/Boyer], the cognitive representation of actions [Lawson/McCauley], exchange processes [Stark], ritual [Rappaport], interventionist practices [Riesebrodt], or communication [Luhmann]). One limitation to a homeostatic-style approach is that it calls for a robust theory of religion (see Stausberg/Engler, "Theories of Religion," this volume), and might not serve as a preliminary means of delineating the subject matter prior to theorizing. Whether this is a worry comes down to the relation between defining and theorizing religion: does defining precede theorizing or vice versa? From a practical point of view it is likely to be a two-way relationship: definitions are refined by theorizing, but theorizing is guided by definitional delineations. The sort of balancing we noted between the methods of extension and of intension earlier will likely resurface here.

Perhaps the most problematic feature of homeostatic-style definitions is their connection with an attempt to naturalize the thing defined: recall that, for Boyd, the defining clustered properties are natural ones. Some theorists, principally the 'critical' ones, might therefore balk at the very idea of a homeostatic-style definition of religion: religion, they often maintain, must be de-naturalized rather than re-naturalized. But, the question as to whether religion is a natural kind is a theoretical, not a definitional, problem. This question rests on the deeper theoretical question of what constitutes natural kinds. It is worth nothing that naturalism does not imply, as seems to be often assumed, staticity, non-contingency, timelessness, unconstructedness, ahistoricity, or immunity from critique or change. Moreover, despite Boyd's interest in using homeostatic-style definitions to advance forms of ontological realism (moral and scientific), there is nothing in such definitions themselves which prevents them being extended to socially constructed phenomena. 'Games'—as a general type including such specific instances as chess, baseball, or monopoly—is a paradigmatic example of a social construction, but a homeostatic-style definition does not seem impossible for them. Wittgenstein's famous injunction against defining 'game' (1972 [1953], §§65–67) is only an injunction against a real definition of it, and the general idea of family resemblances is blown out of all proportion to the argument that he actually gives for it. He mentions only three aspects around which people have tried to essentialize games—amusement, competition, and skill—and he points out, correctly enough, that not every game is amusing, or competitive, or requires skill. Yet, we recognize that the presence of these features increases the claim that a given instance will fall under the concept: i.e. an activity that was amusing and competitive would be more likely to be recognized as a game than one to which people were indifferent or which required no special abilities. Moreover, one that was amusing and required skill would be more likely than not to also be one that was competitive, suggesting a homeostatic relationship between polythetic criteria. Finally, speculations regarding underlying mechanisms by which these features are homeostatically clustered cannot be ruled out: e.g. it might be argued that those humans who go in for games have a tendency, whether as the result of evolution, enculturation, or special creation, to voluntarily set up unnecessary obstacles which they then seek to overcome (see Suits 1978). Despite Boyd's own intent to utilize homeostatic-style definitions to defend forms of realism, there is nothing in them that obviously forces that commitment.

Value-Free and Universal Definitions

Religions are a matter of public dispute, and so is the very category and definition of religion (the word and the thing). Given its disputed character, we might conclude that "[a] value-free definition of 'religion' is thus impossible" (Devine 1986, 271). This, of course, does not logically imply that the expression cannot be defined in the first place. Another issue is that of historical change and diversity. Talal Asad is an influential voice in this regard: "My argument is that there cannot be a universal definition of religion, not only because its constituent elements and relationships are historically specific, but because that definition is itself the historical product of discursive processes" (1993, 29). Remarkably, Asad seems simultaneously to deny the possibility of defining religion and to acknowledge that religions have "constitutive elements and relationships," as if those could somehow be known in the absence of some sort of, even rudimentary, definition. Moreover, Asad's argument rests on the important qualifier 'universal': it remains unclear whether he thinks that all definitions invoke timeless characteristics, or whether he thinks that non-universal definitions of religion would be possible. From the fact that particular religions are historically specific, it does not necessarily follow that they cannot share some common elements. His second point is similarly questionable: from the facts that all discourse is linguistic and that all actual languages are historically situated, it does not follow that a particular language cannot talk about things that transcend its historical location. Or perhaps Asad intends that universal definitions are impossible only when historically situated languages talk about historically situated things: i.e. perhaps universal definitions are possible for such natural entities as water, even though our speaking about water is itself part of a historically situated discursive process, but not for such things as religion? In sum, Asad's influential statement is far from clear.

The Dutch scholar of religion Jan G. Platvoet provides a more coherent argument against a "universally valid definition of religion," which he deems "most likely, unattainable" and "a recent Western idiosyncrasy" (1999a, 255, 251). Platvoet argues against such a 'universal' definition based upon several features of religion (1999a, 247–252): the diachronic and synchronic diversity of religions (polymorphism); their density and complexity (polyvalence); the variety of their meanings (polysemantics) and of their functions (polyfunctionality); the likelihood of extreme religious innovation in the future; and the Western origin and specificity of the concept of religion (on the latter problem see Casadio, "Historicizing and Translating Religion," this volume). Platvoet, however, argues that there is a pressing need for definitions of religion in order "to clarify terms, concepts, and theories" (Platvoet 1999a, 254), and he stresses the potential heuristic, analytical, and explanatory uses of a definition of religion (255).

One problem with Asad's and Platvoet's arguments is that they seem to use 'universal definitions' as shorthands for 'definition' as such under the implicit presupposition of an equivalence model (see section "Meanings of definition: Theoretical points of departure"): it is the diversity, i.e. non-equivalence, of actual religions that they present as making a universal definition covering them all impossible. Yet, if we suppose that the points made by Asad and Platvoet are really central for religion, there is no reason not to include them in a potential definition. People would probably not think that definitions of politics, or the state would necessarily be 'universal' (whatever is meant by this term) to qualify as a definition. That this should the case with religion is an example of the *reverse sui generis* rhetoric (Stausberg 2010) among scholars of religion who construct religion in a manner one would hesitate to do for any other expression.

There appears to be no single understanding of the term 'universal definition.' Writers on it are seldom explicit. The following have all been suggested at least implicitly: a universal definition of religion is one (i) that is universally accepted (by all scholars) (Platvoet 1999a, 247); (ii) that defines a concept possessed by all humans and is represented in all languages (Platvoet 1999a, 250); (iii) whose *definiens* is permanent and unrevisable (Platvoet 1999a, 261; 1999b, 465); (iv) that describes the genus to which all particular religions as species fall under (Cox 1999, 267); (v) that groups specialized academic areas/approaches (e.g. medieval Islam, pre-contact Inca, snake-handling in modern Appalachia) into a single academic unit (Hanegraaff 1999, 337–338); (vi) whose *definiendum* names an eternal and unchanging thing (Belzen 1999, 96–97); (vii) that is atemporal by delineating everything that was, is, and will be a religion, including all of the unactualized but possible religions (Platvoet 1999a, 248); and (viii) that is uniquely true or valid (Belzen 1999, 96; Platvoet 1999b, 503). There is no single element that weaves through these myriad uses: e.g. universal acceptability as per (i) operates on a very different level from the others. On the other hand, (iv) and (vii), and to a lesser extent (v), invoke the common genus-species form of real definition noted above, with (vi) falling squarely within the real definitionist camp as well. The psychological and linguistic ubiquity mentioned in (ii), whether actual or not, suggests the objectivity of the thing defined (in either an objectual or lexical manner), and so appears to be in the same general real definitional neighborhood. Finally, the unrevisability aspect of (iii) and the uniqueness (determinate) aspects of (viii) cohere with a prior, though perhaps unrecognized, commitment to meaning realism and so are also closely aligned with real definitions. In short, the predominant conceptions of universally defining religion have them take the form of real definitions that lean heavily on a presupposition of meaning realism. To take the skepticism of the possibility of a universal definition of religion as a call to abandon the attempt to define it entirely—one of the predominant themes in Platvoet's "To Define or Not to Define" (1999a)—is to limit oneself to only a small segment of the definitional and semantic spaces available. Even granted such arguments against one limited approach to defining religion, there are other approaches available. Conversely, the increasing dissatisfaction with universal definitions may perhaps signal a growing, though largely unrecognized, dissatisfaction with meaning realism.

AFTER ALL: WHY DEFINE?

Having gone through the roles, theoretical issues, and types of definitions, we conclude this chapter by considering the pragmatic functions and perils of defining religion.

One of the key practical payoffs of defining is to address or overcome ambiguities in communication. Appeals to define one's term typically arise when understanding is at risk, when misunderstandings are suspected. Definitions are also a powerful tool to enhance reflexivity: asking oneself what one means exactly by a word is always a useful exercise for achieving greater clarity (not necessarily about the object, but certainly about the nature of the respective inquiry and one's own horizon and perspective). On the other hand, definitions can also be used as a political instrument of control, coercion, and denial, a point noticed by Chidester (1996) in his study of the South African colonial frontiers. The one who defines is the one who decides what's in and what's out, who understands and who doesn't, and who speaks knowledgeably and who doesn't. This is especially true if one is committed to the admissibility of only real definitions: i.e. that once accepted, a definition expresses a fundamental truth. Definitions can substantiate real claims, and real definitions—insofar as people grant them reality—are particularly powerful in this respect.

Critics of certain studies—e.g. on religion and politics, or religion and science—may hold that the particular subject area was delimited wrongly to start with, so that the studies were misconceived right from the start. In fact, inter-, cross-, or transdisciplinary work brings to light that terms are often used in different fashions across the disciplines: disciplines such as economy, history, philosophy, political science, psychology, or theology often speak of religion in different manners than do scholars of religion\s; these differences can be measured by eliciting definitions in order to make implicit understandings explicit. In a more technical sense, definitions are crucial in academic projects that seek to measure the effects of religion, or individual religiosity (religion as transmitted, learned, acquired, and developed), on other variables (attitudes, preferences, behavior, etc.). For example, empirical investigation of relations between religion and health, including the question whether religious people are healthier than non-religious people, requires an operationalization of 'religion' or 'religious.'

Definitions of religion are of importance also beyond the purely academic sphere, especially in the realm of law (see Schonthal, "Law," this volume), public administration, and taxation. The 1948 Universal Declaration of Human Rights entitles every human to the "freedom of thought, conscience and religion" (§18). This includes the "freedom, either alone or in community with others and in public or private, to manifest his religion or belief in teaching, practice, worship and observance" (§18). Religion is not defined in this Declaration, and it is not universally clear which entities would be protected by this stipulation. On a national scale, there is legislation pertaining to religion in different spheres of law. A prominent example is the United States. The First Amendment to the United States Constitution (adopted in 1791) declares: "Congress shall make no law respecting an establishment of religion, or prohibiting the exercise thereof." While it is clear that this protection was initially offered to (Protestant) Christianity, this protection was not intended to be restricted to this religion alone: the principle author, Thomas Jefferson (1743–1826), remarked in his autobiography that it was "meant to comprehend within the mantle of its protection the Jew and the Gentile, the Christian and Mahometan, the Hindoo and infidel of every denomination" (Jefferson 2009 [1821],

37). Over the course of American history, an increasing and accelerating number of contenders for religion have arrived on the scene. In order to judge what deserves protection as religion and what does not requires a definition of religion (Greenawalt 1984; Feofanov 1994). Areas of litigation where recognition as religion is relevant in the United States include matters of tax exemption, schools and schooling, the military and conscientious objection, free speech, property, Sunday rules, land development, employment regulations, prison rules, medical procedures, adoption, and child custody (Greenawalt 2006). Other legal systems face similar challenges. The purpose for which definitions are required in this context is classificatory: does a particular group, institution, or phenomenon belong to the class of religion or not? Few definitions proposed by contemporary scholars of religion will help legislators to perform this taxonomic task. Yet, these definitions were not devised for that purpose in the first place and hence cannot be held accountable here.

As a final observation, and one seldom mentioned in similar discussions, definitions may delineate in more than one direction. Formally, definitions—insofar as they create boundaries between what is included and what is not—simultaneously create two classes: the A's and the non-A's. As a consequence, there can be no understanding of the A's without at least an implicit understanding of the non-A's and how they stand apart. A definition of religion, then, rests on some at least implicit understanding of non-religion (see also Lee, "Non-Religion," this volume, which describes phenomena for which the distinction from religion becomes a meaningful quality). In actual practice, 'non-religion' is conceived of in more specific terms: this distinction operates on two dimensions, both involving the question of the legitimate range of religion. Metaphorically speaking, in systemic terms, the first involves external (or horizontal) and the second internal (or vertical) boundaries; the former variety of 'non-religion' is delimited through (mutual) exclusion with 'non-religious,' the latter with 'wrong religion.' In the external/horizontal divide, 'secular' is the most frequent designator given to the non-religious other in the sense of 'no-religion'; it points to the limit of the legitimate expansion of religion (for instance with regard to the 'secular' state); it is the zone of no-go for religion. The internal/vertical divide has seen more variation with distinctions between religion and non-religion being drawn with regard to such things as 'idolatry,' 'magic,' 'superstition,' 'sects,' 'heresies,' 'cults,' etc. They are non-religion from the point of view of insider-discourses; they are the 'wrong religion' variety of non-religion. Both of the divides face theoretical and normative questions. Along the external/horizontal divide, 'secular religion' or 'religious secularity' is not obviously oxymoronical, though it should be if 'secular' designated the non-religious in a mutually exclusive way. Along this divide, people sometimes speak of implicit, pseudo-, or quasi-religions, suggesting that the external/horizontal delineation of religion from non-religion (e.g. sports, atheism, etc.) is not as sharp as should be required by a definitional delineation. Perhaps of more pressing concern, however, is that both distinctions/demarcations are fraught with value judgments and power structures. For instance, along the external/horizontal divide the secular has become a normative idea (Taylor 2007); or, as the basis of secularism, the category is treated as a historical set of practices that in some aspects overlaps with the religious (Asad 2003). The 'new atheists'—by defining religion in opposition to science, which they view as an inexorable force for secularization—denigrate the religious as irrational and portray religion as bad science. Conversely, many in the creationist movement, especially in the United States, use the label 'secular' as a pejorative. Some Iranian religious scholars who seek to liberate religion from the grip of the (Islamic) state, on the other hand, advocate 'religious secularity' (Ghobadzadeh 2015). Along the internal/vertical divide, Durkheim's defining of magic in opposition to religion, as 'wrong religion,' reproduces within the realm of scholarship normative ideas from within the religious field. A choice of where to place the definitional divide on the vertical axis could all too easily contribute to the suppression, denigration, or marginalization of certain groups or phenomena. This is as much a danger inside the academy as outside of it: many phenomena have been ignored by scholars of religion as a result of their not falling within predominant definitions; the new field of Western Esotericism is one counter-reaction against such exclusionary practices.

APPENDIX

SAMPLE OF ACADEMIC DEFINITIONS OF RELIGION

Classical

Kant (1960 [1793], 142): "Religion is the recognition of all duties as divine commands."

Tylor (1903 [1871], 424): "the belief in Spiritual Beings."

Durkheim (1995 [1912], 44 [italics in original]): "*A religion is a unified system of beliefs and practices relative to sacred things, that is to say, things set apart and forbidden—beliefs and practices which unite into one single moral community called a Church, all those who adhere to them.*"

James (1958 [1902], 58): "the belief that there is an unseen order, and that our supreme good lies in harmoniously adjusting ourselves thereto."

James (1958 [1902], 42 [italics in original]): "Religion, therefore, as I now ask you arbitrarily to take it, shall mean for us *the feelings, acts, and experiences of individual men in their solitude, so far as they apprehend themselves to stand in relation to whatever they may consider the divine.*"

Tillich (1960, 6): "Religion is the state of being grasped by an ultimate concern, a concern which qualifies all other concerns as preliminary and which itself contains the answer to the question of the meaning of our life."

Geertz (1973 [1966], 90 [italics in original]): "*(1) a system of symbols which acts to (2) establish powerful, pervasive, and long-lasting moods and motivations in men by (3) formulating conceptions of a general order of existence and (4) clothing these conceptions with such an aura of factuality that (5) the mood and motivations seem uniquely realistic.*"

Spiro (1966, 96): "an institution consisting of culturally patterned interactions with culturally postulated superhuman agents."

Southwold (1978, 370–371): "Roughly, then, anything which we would call a religion must have at least some of the following attributes:

(1) A central concern with godlike beings and men's relation with them.
(2) A dichotomisation of elements of the world intro sacred and profane, and a central concern with the sacred.
(3) An orientation towards salvation from the ordinary conditions of worldly existence.
(4) Ritual practices.
(5) Beliefs that are neither logically nor empirically demonstrable or highly probable . . .
(6) An ethical code, supported by such beliefs.
(7) Supernatural sanctions on infringements of that code.
(8) A mythology.
(9) A body of scriptures, or similarly exalted oral traditions.
(10) A priesthood, or similar specialist religious elite.
(11) Association with a moral community . . .
(12) Association with an ethnic or similar group."

Contemporary

Byrne (1999, 385): "[A] religion is any set of symbols (and associated actions, attitudes, feelings and experiences) providing human beings with a solution to evil by way of a theodicy . . . Religion is that propensity in human beings (however grounded) to respond to evil by seeking the kind of meaning (to engage in the kinds of actions, exhibit the kind of attitudes . . .) associated with the enterprise of theodicy."

Atran (2002, 264): "Religions are costly, hard-to-fake commitments to counterintuitive worlds. . . . There is no such entity as 'religion' . . ."

Lincoln (2003, 5–7 [italics in original]): A proper religion comprises four domains: "1. *A discourse whose concerns transcend the human, temporal, and contingent, and that claims for itself a similarly transcendent status. . . . 2. A set of practices whose goal is to produce a proper world and/or proper human subjects, as defined by a religious discourse to which these practices are connected. . . . 3. A community whose members construct their identity with reference to a religious discourse and its attendant practices. . . . 4. An institution that regulates religious discourse, practices, and community, reproducing them over time and modifying them as necessary, while asserting their eternal validity and transcendent value.*"

Tweed (2006, 54 [italics in original]): "*Religions are confluences of organic-cultural flows that intensify joy and confront suffering by drawing on human forces to make homes and cross boundaries.*"

Droogers (2009, 277): "Religion is the field of experiencing the sacred—a field in which both believers and scholars act, each category applying the human capacity for play, within the constraints of power mechanisms, to the articulation of basic human dichotomies, thus adding an extra dimension to their construction and view of reality."

Schilbrack (2013, 306): "normative practices that at least implicitly make ontological claims in terms of which the practical norms are authorized."

Schilbrack (2013, 313): "Forms of life predicated upon the reality of the superempirical."

Jensen (2014, 8): "Semantic and cognitive networks comprising ideas, behaviours and institutions in relation to counter-intuitive superhuman agents, objects and posits."

Frankenberry (2014, 195–196): "The short version is this: religion can be defined as a system of myth and ritual. The long version has three parts: (1) Religion is a communal system of propositional attitudes (i.e. beliefs, including hopes, fears, and desires) and practices that are related to superhuman agents. (2) Myth is a story with a beginning, middle, and end, which was or is transmitted orally about the deeds of superhuman agents. The salience of 'oral transmission' places certain genres, such as novels and science fiction, out of bounds as myths. (3) Ritual is a system of communal action consisting of both verbal and nonverbal interactions with a superhuman agent or agents."

GLOSSARY

Definienda/definiens the former is that which is defined; the latter is that which does the defining.

Equivalence/elucidation a basic divide in conceptions of definition: the former holds that definiens are merely stylistic variants of definienda; the latter holds that definiens advance our understanding of definienda.

Meaning realism/antirealism a basic divide in philosophical theories of meaning: the former holds that meaning (semantic content) is fully determinate in principle; the latter regards it as variable and fluid in both practice and principle.

Monothetic/polythetic definition a basic divide in types of definition: the former requires that all of the criteria mentioned in the definiens be satisfied by whatever to which the definiendum applies; the latter requires satisfaction of only some of the criteria.

Objectual/lexical definitions a basic divide in conceptions of definition: the former purport to define objects; the latter purport to define words.

Real definition a common type of definition which assumes that the thing defined has real or objective existence, often attempting to state the essential features of the thing.

Substantive/functional definition a basic divide in conceptions of definition: the former proceeds by mentioning properties of the thing defined; the latter proceeds by mentioning what the thing does.

REFERENCES

Arnal, William E. 2000. "Definition." In *Guide to the Study of Religion*, edited by Willi Braun and Russell T. McCutcheon. London and New York: Cassell, 21–34.

Arnal, William E. and Russell T. McCutcheon. 2013. *The Sacred Is the Profane: The Political Nature of "Religion."* Oxford and New York: Oxford University Press.

Asad, Talal. 1993. *Genealogies of Religion: Discipline and Reasons of Power in Christianity and Islam*. Baltimore, MD: Johns Hopkins University Press.

Asad, Talal. 2003. *Formations of the Secular: Christianity, Islam, Modernity*. Stanford, CA: Stanford University Press.

Atran, Scott. 2002. *In Gods We Trust: The Evolutionary Landscape of Religion*. New York: Oxford University Press.

Beckford, James A. 2003. *Social Theory and Religion*. Cambridge: Cambridge University Press.

Belzen, Jacob A. 1999. "Paradoxes: An Essay on the Object of the Psychology of Religion." In *The Pragmatics of Defining Religion: Contexts, Concepts and Contests*, edited by Jan G. Platvoet and Arie L. Molendijk. Leiden and Boston, MA: Brill, 93–122.

Bergunder, Michael. 2014. "What is Religion? The Unexplained Subject Matter of Religious Studies." *Method & Theory in the Study of Religion* 26(3): 246–286. doi: 10.1163/15700682-12341320

Boyd, R. N. 1988. "How to Be a Moral Realist." In *Essays on Moral Realism*, edited by G. Sayre-McCord. Ithaca, NY: Cornell University Press, 181–228.

Boyd, R. N. 1999. "Homeostasis, Species, and Higher Taxa." In *Species: New Interdisciplinary Essays*, edited by R. Wilson. Cambridge, MA: MIT Press, 141–185.

Bruce, Steve. 2011. "Defining Religion: A Practical Response." *International Review of Sociology* 21(1): 107–120. doi: 10.1080/03906701.2011.544190

Burge, Tyler. 1993. "Concepts, Definitions, and Meanings." *Metaphilosophy* 24(4): 309–325. doi: 10.1111/j.1467-9973.1993.tb00198.x

Byrne, Peter. 1999. "The Definition of Religion: Squaring the Circle." In *The Pragmatics of Defining Religion: Contexts, Concepts and Contests*, edited by Jan G. Platvoet and Arie L. Molendijk. Leiden and Boston, MA: Brill, 379–396.

Chidester, David. 1996. *Savage Systems: Colonialism and Comparative Religion in Southern Africa*. Charlottesville and London: University Press of Virginia.

Cox, James L. 1999. "Intuiting Religion: A Case for Preliminary Definitions." In *The Pragmatics of Defining Religion: Contexts, Concepts and Contests*, edited by Jan G. Platvoet and Arie L. Molendijk. Leiden and Boston, MA: Brill, 267–284.

Devine, Philip E. 1986. "On the Definition of 'Religion.'" *Faith and Philosophy* 3(3): 270–284.

Droogers, André. 2009. "Defining Religion: A Social Science Approach." In *The Oxford Handbook of the Sociology of Religion*, edited by Peter B. Clarke. Oxford: Oxford University Press, 263–279.

Dubuisson, Daniel. 2003. *The Western Construction of Religion: Myths, Knowledge, and Ideology*, translated by William Sayers. Baltimore: Johns Hopkins University Press.

Durkheim, Émile. 1995. *The Elementary Forms of Religious Life*, translated by Karen E. Fields. New York: Free Press.

Feofanov, Dmitry N. 1994. "Defining Religion: An Immodest Proposal." *Hofstra Law Review* 23(2): 309–405.

Fitzgerald, Timothy. 1997. "A Critique of 'Religion' as a Cross-Cultural Category." *Method & Theory in the Study of Religion* 92(2): 91–110. doi: 10.1163/157006897X00070

Flood, Gavin D. 2012. *The Importance of Religion: Meaning and Action in Our Strange World*. Malden, MA and Oxford: Wiley-Blackwell.

Frankenberry, Nancy. 2014. "The Study of Religion after Davidson and Rorty." *American Journal of Theology and Philosophy* 35(3): 195–210. doi: 10.5406/amerjtheophil.35.3.0195

Geertz, Clifford. 1973. *The Interpretation of Cultures: Selected Essays*. New York: Basic Books.

Ghobadzadeh, Naser. 2015. *Religious Secularity: A Theological Challenge to the Islamic State*. Oxford: Oxford University Press.

Greenawalt, Kent. 1984. "Religion as a Concept in Constitutional Law." *California Law Review* 72(5): 753–816. doi: 10.2307/3480329

Greenawalt, Kent. 2006. *Religion and the Constitution: Free Exercise and Fairness*. Princeton, NJ: Princeton University Press.

Greil, Arthur L. 2009. "Defining Religion." In *The World's Religions: Continuities and Transformations*, edited by Peter B. Clarke and Peter Beyer. London and New York: Routledge, 135–149.

Hanegraaff, Wouter J. 1999. "Defining Religion in Spite of History." In *The Pragmatics of Defining Religion: Contexts, Concepts and Contests*, edited by Jan G. Platvoet and Arie L. Molendijk. Leiden and Boston, MA: Brill, 337–378.

James, William. 1958. *The Varieties of Religious Experience*. New York: Signet. Original edition, 1902.

Jefferson, Thomas. 2009. *The Autobiography of Thomas Jefferson*. Digireads.com Publishing (www.digireads.com). Original edition, 1821.

Jensen, Jeppe Sinding. 2014. *What is Religion?* Durham: Acumen Publishing.

Kant, Immanuel. 1960. *Religion Within the Limits of Reason Alone*, translated by Theodore M. Greene and Hoyt H. Hudson. New York: Harper Torchbooks. Original edition, 1793.

Lincoln, Bruce. 2003. *Holy Terrors: Thinking About Religion after September 11*. Chicago, IL and London: University of Chicago Press.

McCutcheon, Russell T. 2007. *Studying Religion: An Introduction*. London and Oakville: Equinox.

Needham, Rodney. 1975. "Polythetic Classification: Convergence and Consequences." *Man* 10(3): 349–369. doi: 10.2307/2799807

Otto, Rudolf. 1923. *The Idea of the Holy: An Inquiry into the Non-rational Factor in the Idea of the Divine and its Relation to the Rational*, translated by J. W. Harvey. London and New York: Oxford University Press. Original edition, 1917.

Platvoet, Jan G. 1999a. "To Define or Not to Define: The Problem of the Definition of Religion." In *The Pragmatics of Defining Religion: Contexts, Concepts and Contests*, edited by Jan Platvoet and Arie L. Molendijk. Leiden and Boston, MA: Brill, 41–72.

Platvoet, Jan G. 1999b. "Contexts, Concepts & Contests; Towards a Pragmatics of Defining 'Religion.'" In *The Pragmatics of Defining Religion: Contexts, Concepts and Contests*, edited by Jan G. Platvoet and Arie L. Molendijk. Leiden and Boston, MA: Brill, 464–516.

Pollack, Detlef. 1995. "Was ist Religion? Probleme der Definition." *Zeitschrift für Religionswissenschaft* 3(2): 163–190.

Quine, W. V. O. 1987. *Quiddities: An Intermittently Philosophical Dictionary*. Cambridge, MA: Harvard University Press.

Rappaport, Roy A. 1999. *Ritual and Religion in the Making of Humanity*. Cambridge: Cambridge University Press.

Riesebrodt, Martin. 2010. *The Promise of Salvation: A Theory of Religion*. Chicago, IL and London: University of Chicago Press.

Saler, Benson. 2000. *Conceptualizing Religion: Immanent Anthropologists, Transcendent Natives, and Unbounded Categories*. New York and Oxford: Berghahn Books. Original edition, 1993.

Saler, Benson. 2008. "Conceptualizing Religion: Some Recent Reflections." *Religion* 38(3): 219–225. doi: 10.1016/j.religion.2008.03.008

Schaffalitzky de Muckadell, Caroline. 2014. "On Essentialism and Real Definitions of Religion." *Journal of the American Academy of Religion* 82(2): 495–520. doi: 10.1093/jaarel/lfu015

Schilbrack, Kevin. 2013. "What Isn't Religion?" *The Journal of Religion* 93(3): 291–318. doi: 10.1086/670276

Smith, Jonathan Z. 1998. "Religion, Religions, Religious." In *Critical Terms for Religious Studies*, edited by Mark C. Taylor. Chicago, IL and London: University of Chicago Press, 269–284.

Snoek, Jan A. M. 1994. "Classification and Definition Theory: An Overview." In *The Notion of "Religion" in Comparative Research* [. . .], edited by Ugo Bianchi. Rome: 'L'Erma' di Bretschneider, 741–754.

Snoek, Jan A. M. 1999. "Defining 'Religions' as the Domain of Study of the Empirical Sciences of Religion." In *The Pragmatics of Defining Religion: Contexts, Concepts and Contests*, edited by Jan Platvoet and Arie L. Molendijk. Leiden and Boston, MA: Brill, 313–333.

Southwold, Martin. 1978. "Buddhism and the Definition of Religion." *Man* 13(3): 362–379.

Spiro, Melford E. 1966. "Religion: Problems of Definition and Explanation." In *Anthropological Approaches to the Study of Religion*, edited by Michael Banton. London: Tavistock, 85–126.

Stausberg, Michael. 2010. "Distinctions, Differentiations, Ontology, and Non-Humans in Theories of Religion." *Method & Theory in the Study of Religion* 22(4): 354–374. doi:10.1163/157006810X531139

Stringer, Martin D. 2008. *Contemporary Western Ethnography and the Definition of Religion*. London: Continuum.

Suits, Bernard Herbert. 1978. *The Grasshopper: Games, Life, and Utopia*. Toronto and Buffalo: University of Toronto Press.

Taylor, Charles. 2007. *A Secular Age*. Cambridge, MA and London: Belknap Press of Harvard University Press.

Tillich, Paul. 1963. *Christianity and the Encounter of World Religions*. New York: Columbia University Press.

Tweed, Thomas A. 2006. *Crossing and Dwelling: A Theory of Religion*. Cambridge, MA: Harvard University Press.

Tylor, Edward B. 1903. *Primitive Culture: Researches into the Development of Mythology, Philosophy, Religion, Art, and Custom*, 4th revised edition. London: J. Murray. Original edition, 1871.

Weber, Max. 1993. *The Sociology of Religion*, translated by Ephraim Fischoff. Boston, MA: Beacon Press. Original edition, 1920.

Wittgenstein, Ludwig. 1972. *Philosophical Investigations*, translated by G. E. M. Anscombe. Oxford: Blackwell. Original edition, 1953.

FURTHER READING

Greil, Arthur L. and David G. Bromley, eds. 2003. *Defining Religion: Investigating the Boundaries between the Sacred and Secular*. Amsterdam: JAI. [*A useful volume with contributions by sociologists, whose guiding principle is that religion "is a 'category of discourse,' whose precise meaning and implications are continually being negotiated in the course of social action" (5).*]

Platvoet, J. and A. L. Molendijk, eds. 1999. *The Pragmatics of Defining Religion: Contexts, Concepts, and Contests*. Leiden and Boston, MA: Brill. [*A seminal volume. Particularly noteworthy are the contributions by Introvigne, Platvoet, Snoek, Hanegraaff, Byrne, and Jensen.*]

....

CHAPTER 2

HISTORICIZING AND TRANSLATING RELIGION

....

GIOVANNI CASADIO

CHAPTER SUMMARY

....

- The aim of this chapter is to justify the general application of the taxon 'religion' as a unitary analytical concept situated in history, and to locate religions as interculturally translatable and communicable systems of beliefs and practices related to superhuman agents.
- A series of case studies disprove the common idea that religion was an exclusive invention of modern European scholarship.
- Both ordinary people and scholars across diverse world traditions and various historical epochs not only conceptualized their religion as a specific realm but also talked about religions as a cross-cultural taxonomic category.

HISTORY

....

"History is not the past; it is an artful assembly of materials from the past, designed for usefulness in the future. In this way, history verges upon that idea of tradition in which it is identified with the resource out of which people create. History and tradition are comparable in dynamic; they exclude more than they include, and so remain open to endless revision" (Glassie 1995, 395). This feisty definition of history by prominent American folklorist Henry H. Glassie III echoes the views of British historian Edward H. Carr who sees in history a "continuous process of interaction between the historian and his facts, an unending dialogue between the present and the past" (Carr 1986 [1961], 30), in a vein that makes him, if not a precursor of postmodernist history, a supporter of epistemological relativism, stressing that the facts of history never come to us pure, but are always refracted through the mind of the historian in a delicate balance with empirically derived evidence.

To put the issue in a different perspective, since Hegel it has been conventional for historians to distinguish between *res gestae* (the *res*, things or events that have actually happened) and *historia rerum gestarum* (the story of the events that have happened); the distinction is between the data of historical events themselves and the representation of those events in the historian's report. We are used to referring to both historical events themselves and the timelines of these events as 'history' in a somewhat undifferentiated way. But even the *res gestae* are a re-presentation (a 'making present again' in a text) of what took place, and not the actual events themselves on the ground. This is not to say that those events did not take place. Of course they did: people believed in a higher power and people lived and died *in the name of God*. But how we learn about those 'things' is always 'mediated,' available to us only in indirect form in images or narratives. We of course continually experience events immediately, but when we give or read an account of those events as *historia rerum gestarum*, we are giving or reading a mediated version of them from a particular point of view, which is shaped by our own time, by the context within which the re-presenting work occurs (in this sense B. Croce said that "all history is contemporary history," meaning that all history was written from the point of view of contemporary preoccupations).

HISTORICIZING

Historicizing a topic implies interpreting it as fully embedded in its own society ("Religion without Society" does not interest a modern historian [Brown 2003, 6]) and as a product of historical development. Persons and actions conceived of as historical are mutable as the result of a process involved in the flux of time. To stress this fact a pioneer of the historical-comparative method in the history of religions, Raffaele Pettazzoni (1883–1959), used to say that every *phainomenon* ('phenomenon,' 'manifestation') is a *genomenon* ('event in formation, subject to continuous change'); in other words, every religious phenomenon is a historical occurrence located in its own spatial and temporal context (Pettazzoni 1954, 69). But Pettazzoni is far from denying the specific value of religious phenomena, and in fact he acknowledges as one of the merits of religious phenomenology the effort of "discerning the essence of religion itself," as his student Ugo Bianchi put it (1975, 199; cf. Eliade 1969, 29–30). In fact 'essences'—in the sense of the intrinsic nature or indispensable quality of something that determines its character and development—are in my opinion an inescapable component of human history, including the multifarious variety of Christian, Islamic, Hindu, and Buddhist formations.

Further, historicizing means also taking a distance, becoming aware that here and now is not like there and then, and also becoming aware that we address the past and the other from our personal contemporary point of view, trying to approach and define what things have been like and what they meant in the past and for the other. As a matter of fact, almost all of today's religions use the past (sometimes a constructed past) as a revitalizing resource in their self-understanding; in other words, they see themselves as traditions (see Engler forthcoming). Both old and new religions conceive of themselves not as innovations, "but as a 'return' to the past, as a recovery of their myth of origin" (Beyer 2006, 119).[1] In sum, it is vital for a religion to have a history, the longer the better. In the absence of a recognized tradition, founders of new religions invent it, as in the case of Mormonism (new scriptures, baptism for the dead) or Sikhism (Guru Gobind Singh molding the heritage of Guru Nanak with foundation of the *khalsa*, the Sikh church, in 1699).

TRANSLATION

Translating (lit. to 'transfer' or 'carry over' from one place to another) is a way of highlighting the similarity and preserving the difference. Religious translation is a case of broader cultural translation, a practice aiming to bridge cultural differences and to present a cultural trait to representatives of another culture. By making the 'other' understandable, translation solves some critical issues of cultural variety, in its specific aspects such as ways of speaking, ways of eating, ways of dressing, or ways of believing. The main problem—considered by some an impossible task—that cultural (religious) translation must cope with consists in giving a universal meaning to a specific cultural feature without potentially playing down the original element (for instructive examples of the difficulties involved in religious translation see Lieu 2009; Tommasi 2014). Frequently, the re-conceptualization of the original vision into a different one can produce conflicts and the persecution of minorities, as happened in eighteenth-century Korea when Confucian sages converted to Catholicism tried to pour new Christian wine into old Confucian wineskins by founding *chu-gyo*, the 'religion of the Lord' (Cawley 2012), or in nineteenth-century Iran when the Bab, by introducing messianic overtones somewhat inspired by Christian doctrines, attempted to initiate a new prophetic cycle into the Muslim system, meeting with rigid and violent clerical and political opposition.

The concept and practice of translation is particularly salient in ages dominated by human migration and globalization (Beyer 2006). Translation seems to enable mediation on a general basis while at the same time allowing individual languages to retain their own particularity, including in a certain way their own elements of untranslatability. Cultural translation thus operates as a tool which apparently succeeds in resolving tensions between universalism and relativism, cultural fixity and historical changes (see Bhabha 1994).

---

[1] Beyer finds here a historical and sociological fact that re-echoes the Eliadean phenomenological concept of the 'nostalgia for origins' (Eliade 1969).

Translating Religion

Just as cultural translation implies the notion of culture, religious translation implies the notion of religion, which thus needs to be defined (see Stausberg/Gardiner, "Definition," this volume). According to a dominant recent narrative, the concept of 'religion' (which is inappropriately confused with the term *religio* and its vernacular derivates) as a distinct and differentiated sphere of human activity and communication is a recent Western formation (dating to the middle of the eighteenth century according to Platvoet 1999, 466, 477). In spite of the overwhelming recent literature supporting this view (partially discussed in Casadio 2010, 301–304) this scholarly opinion is unfounded, as it has been empirically assessed on independent grounds and using different strategies by social scientists with a solid historical background (Beyer 2006, esp. 11, 62–79, 113–115; Riesebrodt 2010; 2013) and historians of religions (Casadio 2010; Deeg/Freiberger/Kleine 2013). Apparently, "those critiques of the modern category of religion which point out its indebtedness to theological, scientific and political interests are accurate as concerns their analysis, but incorrect in their conclusion that religion is therefore 'not real'" (Beyer 2006, 113). It must be admitted that we perceive religion as a discrete concept only when a group's explicit or implicit conceptions of a superhuman agency "are confronted, peacefully or violently, by another group's analogous representations. Religion as a concept presupposes the diversity of religions, even if those religions have not been conceptualized as such" (Benavides forthcoming). Only after a community has encountered a different religion does it begin to reflect on its own practices in relation to those of the others. The experience of difference and competition leads to the rationalization and systematization of religious practices (Riesebrodt 2004, 137–138). In other terms, the notion of religion as a distinct domain of culture can hardly be found in a preliterate society living in relative isolation from other groups. But this is true of any other realm of social life, like politics, economics, law, or science. It is in any case important to keep in mind that the lack of a clearly defined concept and univocal term for a specific phenomenon does not ipso facto indicate the absence of that to which the concept refers in more general comparative context. Ancient Greeks, for example, lacked the categories 'economy,' 'society,' 'culture,' etc., but we can study the fields covered by them using our own categories without committing any epistemological violence. In other words, we can recognize that some of the assumptions we bring to these terms in an analysis of an alien context can influence our way of understanding without implying the inexistence of the object of study, much less the claim that it is fantasy. No matter how different a religion is from 'our' concept of religion, if it were totally different it would not be possible to speak about it at all (attempts at translation would simply not work): the fact that common people (and scholars of all disciplines) continue to use the category implicitly indicates that they believe translation is possible.

As has been forcefully argued by Riesebrodt (2004; 2010) against discursive deconstructions of religion as a universal concept, the evidence of an analogous (cf. Bianchi 1975, 4–8, 200, 207, 214–215) intercultural notion of religion comes from the patterns of interactions by heterogeneous actors, and institutions that are usually referred as 'religious' by scholars and others and practically construct and recognize each other as similar. Religions mutually constitute, define, and transform each other; they compete with and borrow from each other, incorporating elements of each other's practices, ideologies, and liturgies. In short, the reality itself of these competitions, conversions, borrowings, and assimilations confirms that religions perceive each other as similar (Riesebrodt 2004, 138–142). Riesebrodt (2010) provides examples of mutual references of religions in terms of competitive demarcations as well as acculturations or identifications, showing how religious actors and institutions have related to each other as similar in kind though different in value; or how religions have claimed to be akin to other religions; or how political powers have regulated the practices of diverse religions in their legislations. At a more theoretical level, my goal is to legitimate the use of the analytical concept of religion as a 'concrete universal' (Bianchi 1975, 200; see also Shushan 2009, 9–24, for a reappraisal of universals in relationship with the issue of cultural similarities), "a universal whose connotation is so particularized that it denotes one concrete reality especially an organized unity as distinguished from a universal that denotes any one of a class" (Merriam-Webster), based on diverse evidence situated in concrete historical contexts. Thus religion becomes not just a label of convenience, but a specific operative category and a name for a commonality of style in the social world that humans have inhabited, do inhabit, and will inhabit.

The following sections present a series of historical case studies that exemplify and concretize the theoretical agenda of this introductory premise. As we will see, religions were always already there and shaped each other for centuries or even millennia before modern Western Christian-centric discourse supposedly invented, constructed, or even manufactured anything and everything under the sun. In fact, the very idea of a Western unified concept of religion is an essentialist stereotype whose flaw is demonstrated by empirical evidence (Riesebrodt 2010; 2013, xix; cf. Freiberger 2013, 24–25). We have, in any case, to resist firmly the temptation of ethnocentrism involved in positing that some human faculty may have been the sole discovery (or, even worse, invention) of Europeans from which the refined civilizations of Asia were excluded (cf. Pye 1994, pleading for an overcoming of both Westernism and Orientalism).

Classical Antiquity

Among ancient Mediterranean cultures, Greece is considered the matrix of almost all the compartments of human intellectual activity (from science to philosophy, history, and politics). Instead, the category religion is in general regarded as extraneous to its genuine 'emic' conceptions, insofar as Greek religion is conceived of as tightly embedded in other aspects of Greek culture. This is in fact the dominating paradigm adopted and circulated by the field's leading scholars (e.g. J.-P. Vernant, J. N. Bremmer, Ph. Borgeaud). Greek self-consciousness would probably not have been so acquiescent with this modern (viz. postmodern) assumption. There was a clear consciousness of the specificity of religion as an autonomous aspect of human life within the Aristotelian school (Theophrastus, composer of a treatise *Peri eusebeias*, and Eudemus, who wrote a comparative essay on the theogonies of various nations, including the Egyptians, the Assyrians, and his own compatriots, the Greeks), the Epicurean school (Philodemus, who authored another treatise *Peri eusebeias*), and especially among the followers of Plato (Plutarch and Porphyry in particular). Since the fifth century, reflections on religion as a human capacity and a universal category were central to the thought of the Sophists: Protagoras's agnosticism vis-à-vis the gods, Prodicus of Ceos, giving a rationalistic explanation of the origin of deities that foreshadowed Euhemerus's famous scholarly fiction, Critias, deeming that religion was invented to frighten men into adhering to morality and justice. Further, an examination of the semantic development of terms like *eusebeia/theosebeia* ('reverence towards the gods,' 'piety') or *threskeia* ('religious worship,' the meaning of which evolved to 'religion' *sic et simpliciter* in modern Greek) in literary and epigraphic sources (Foschia 2004) allows us to put forward a description of Greek religion "as constituting a complex and quite subtle statement about what the world is like and a set of responses for dealing with that world" (Gould 1983, 2). This confirms the existence, in the Greek linguistic domain, of a taxon corresponding to the category religion in current modern usage.

Unlike the Greeks, and since the beginnings of their history the ancient Romans had in their vocabulary a specific word to define the concept of religion: *religio*—a Latin word with a remarkable semantic history, which is attested in many literary and epigraphic documents denoting a clear consciousness of the existence of a distinct sphere corresponding to 'religion' in its later meanings (Casadio 2010). The culmination of the semantic development is evident in a document which has a remarkably practical and political relevance. Lactantius (*c*.240–*c*.320) reported in his work *De Mortibus Persecutorum* (*On the Death of the Persecutors*; Lactantius 1954, 48, 2–12) about a meeting in the year 313 CE between the emperors Constantine and Licinius in Milan, in which they decided to stop the persecution. The text of the edict is quite telling in several respects, since by attaining the status of a *religio licita* Christianity is explicitly compared to other *religiones*. Here are the salient passages:

> When I, Constantine, and I, Licinius, happily met at Milan . . . we thought that, among all the other things that we saw would benefit the majority of men, the arrangements which above all needed to be made were those which ensured reverence for the divinity, so that we might grant both to Christians and to all men freedom to follow whatever religion (*religionem*) each one wished, in order that whatever deity there is in the seat of heaven may be appeased and made propitious towards us and towards all who have been set under our power. We thought therefore that . . . we ought to follow the policy of regarding this opportunity as one not to be denied to anyone at all, whether he wished to give his mind to the observances of the Christians or to that religion (*religioni*) which he felt was most fitting to himself, so that the supreme deity, whose religion (*religioni*) we obey with free minds, may be able to show in all matters its usual favor and benevolence towards us. (Riesebrodt 2010, 39 [modified]; cf. Riesebrodt 2004, 144)

Christian Middle Ages

The importance of the medieval (cf. Biller 1985) and later historical development of the word/concept *religio* is demonstrated by the fact that in most but not all European languages (significant exceptions are three Slavic and two Finno-Ugric languages, that have all preserved their indigenous denominations) the term used to define the field of religion is directly or indirectly derived from the Latin name *religio*.

The process of historicization and demarcation of the notion of religion as a segment of culture and a category (the denomination used can be *secta, lex, fides*, or *religio*, all terms that have specific meanings but that in a certain context assume that of religion as a coherent notion defining a range of human words) through the late Christian Middle Ages is expounded through the works of three prominent members of the Catholic clergy who were also cosmopolitan men of letters with pan-European sensibilities.

French scholastic philosopher Peter Abelard (1079–1142) in the *Dialogue between a Philosopher, a Jew and a Christian* represents a Philosopher (remarkably enough a secular Arab with a Stoic education), a Jew, and a Christian arguing over the nature of humanity's ultimate happiness, and the best path to reach it (Abelard 2001). The Jew claims that the law of the Old Testament is the path to ultimate human happiness. For the Philosopher the true happiness must be achievable in this life with human means by the person who seeks virtue. The Christian argues that real happiness is attainable only in the afterlife as a spiritual bliss coming through the love and intelligence of God.

Catalan Franciscan Ramon Llull (*c*.1232–*c*.1315) in the *Llibre del gentil e dels tres savis* (the *Book of the Gentile and the Three Wise Men, c*.1274–1276) deals with the three laws or religions of the book, Judaism, Christianity, and Islam, with a minimum of apologetic implications without assuming that what happens in the other monotheistic religions is idolatry or mere fanaticism (Llull 1993). Two things draw one's attention in the *Book of the Gentile*. First, the systematic presentation of the principles of the Mosaic Law and of that of Islam, with an extensive knowledge of the contents of both, which was not common among writers of religious polemic at this time. Second, the narrative frame which informs the treatise. A Gentile, that is a pagan or non-believer who is ignorant of monotheism, consents to learn the redeeming doctrine through the teachings of three wise men, one Jewish, one Christian, and one Muslim. After instructing the disciple upon the existence of a single God, creation, and resurrection, each one presents in detail his own religion or creed (*fides, creensa* in Catalan) so that the listener and the reader might choose the good religion.

Nicholas of Kues—or Nicolaus Cusanus (1401–1464), a German Catholic cardinal and philosopher—in his *De pace fidei* (1453), written in response to the news of the fall of Constantinople under the Turks, introduces a discussion that takes place in "the heaven of reason" (*in caelo rationis*) between the Incarnate Word (*Verbum/Logos*) and several earthly "intellectual powers" representing diverse (seventeen) national competing traditions (a Greek, an Italian, an Arab, an Indian, a Chaldean, a Jew, a Scythian, a Frenchman, a Persian, a Syrian, a Spaniard, a German, etc.). Throughout this discussion, Nicholas supports the recognition by all the sages that there is one religion (*religio*) and worship (*cultus*), which is presupposed "in all the diversity of rites (*rituum*)" (Cusanus 1956, 7). So long as there are enlightened rulers and an insistence on dialogue between these representatives of the diverse religious denominations (*sectae*), peace can be lasting. Further, "since truth is one and since it is not possible that it is not be understood by every free intellect, all diversity of religions (*religionum*) will be led to one orthodox faith (*fidem*)" (Cusanus 1956, 10). In these claims, Cusanus, swinging between religious exclusivism and religious pluralism, theoretically affirms both the diversity of rites and the universality of religious expression found in a shared Logos theology, and practically defends a commitment to religious tolerance on the basis of the notion that all diverse rites are but manifestations of one true religion. While convergence and substantial unity of the religions is realized at the level of their common participation in the cosmic Word of God, distinctions are nonetheless maintained between the various differing religious and moral customs of Christians, Jews, and Muslims, in accord with Cusanus's formulation: "a unity of religion in a variety of rites" (*una religio in omni diversitate rituum*). With respect to our present concern, in Cusanus's highly influential treatise, the lemma *religio* translates both 'religion' as a metaphysical essence according to the Neo-Platonic tradition and, remarkably enough, 'religion' as a concrete and discrete historical category: "every religion, including that of the Jews, Christians, Muslims, and all the other humans" (*omnis religio—Iudaeorum, Christianorum, Arabum et aliorum plurimorum hominum* [Cusanus 1956, 40; cf. Stünkel 2013, introducing the important notion of interreligious 'topologies']).

Early European Modernity

The culmination of this semantic and conceptual process is evident in two quite different documents of early European modernity, but many more could be cited. One is the *Colloquium heptaplomeres de rerum sublimium arcanis abditis* ("Colloquium of the Seven regarding the hidden secrets of the sublime things") written around 1590 by the French statesman, and political and religious theorist, Jean Bodin (1530–1596). It is a conversation about the nature of truth between seven highly educated representatives of various religions and worldviews (collectively denominated *religiones*): a natural philosopher, a Calvinist, a Muslim, a Roman Catholic, a Lutheran, a Jew, and a skeptic. Truth, in Bodin's view, commands universal agreement; and the adepts of Abrahamic religions in the end agree with secular philosophers on the fundamental underlying similarity of their worldviews despite the diversity of their beliefs. They also agree that the freedom of conscience should be respected, because one should not be constrained in matters of religion (*religio*), and that beliefs should be voluntarily embraced, not imposed. Although the author deliberately leaves this discussion open and without a definite conclusion, the dialogue relies on the views of the adept of natural religion who states that the laws of Nature (a personalized and quasi-divine entity) and natural religion are sufficient for salvation. The conclusion is that whatever will be true religion (*vera religio*) each of them should seek it through piety and integrity of life (*pietatem ac vitae integritatem*). The other document is *Relazione della China* ("Report on China") drafted in 1666 by the Italian scientist and traveler Lorenzo Magalotti (1637–1712) after an interview with the Austrian Jesuit Johann Grueber. Magalotti, reporting Grueber's words, states that the Chinese have full freedom to profess "their ancient religions (*religioni*)" (Magalotti 1974, 47), religions that he then refers to as sects (*sette*), consisting of the Confucians (called *letterati*, i.e. literati), the Taoists (the communality of people), and the Buddhists (called *bonzi*). Clearly, in the view of two experts of intercultural relations like Bodin and Magalotti, *religio*/religion both defines a cross-cultural reality (separated from other culture segments, like economy, marriage, cookery, etc.) and a specimen of this reality.

Between Europe and Asia in the Middle Ages

This section draws attention to frequently ignored evidence of theological disputations between spokesmen of the three Abrahamic monotheist religions, each trying to demonstrate the pre-eminence of their religion with the aim of converting the sovereign, and subsequently his subjects, to that religion (Oişteanu 2009, 142–149). Between the seventh and the tenth centuries, the Khazars formed an empire in the south of Russia. This empire was in competition with two superpowers of the time: the Byzantine Empire (Christian Orthodox) and the Caliphate of Bagdad (Muslim). At some point between 740 CE and 920 CE, the Khazar royalty and nobility (originally practicing the traditional Turkic religion, i.e. Tengrism with features of shamanism) appear to have converted to Judaism, perhaps to deflect competing pressures from Arabs and Byzantines to accept either Islam or Orthodoxy. According to Arab and Hebraic sources, the Khazar King Bulan is said to have converted first to Judaism following angelic visitations exhorting him to find the true religion. Bulan is then said to have convened a theological disputation between exponents of the three Abrahamic religions. Having questioned the Muslims and the Christians as to which of the other two laws they considered the better—both chose that of the Jews—he finally decided to adopt Judaism as the religion of his nation when he was convinced of its superiority. This account attests that in those remote times both political authorities and authors of chronicles were very conscious that religious faiths and laws were something quite distinct from the cultures in which they were 'embedded' and that they could be transferred or translated into another society.

Another instructive case is that concerning the conversion to Orthodox Christianity of Vladimir, grand prince of Kievan Rus', following the theological dispute that took place in Kiev in 988. The *Chronicle of Nestor*, Russian *Povest vremennykh let*, "Tale of Bygone Years" ('Nestor' 1953), which was compiled about 1113, reports that in the year 987 Vladimir sent envoys to inquire about the forms of worship of the various nations whose representatives had been urging him to embrace their respective faiths. Of the Muslim Bulgarians of the Volga the envoys reported there was no happiness among them, only sorrow and a dreadful stench. They also reported that Islam was unattractive due to its taboo against alcoholic beverages and pork. Other sources describe Vladimir consulting with Jewish envoys, and questioning them about their religion but ultimately rejecting it as well, because their exile was evidence that they had lost the favor of God. His emissaries also visited Roman Catholic Germans, without being particularly impressed by their ceremonials. Ultimately Vladimir opted for Orthodox Christianity after his ambassadors had exalted the dazzling festival ritual of the Byzantine Church. Being both impressed by the account of his envoys and attracted by the political gains of the Byzantine alliance, Vladimir settled on being baptized, taking the Christian name of Basil. What is most remarkable for our purpose, the chronicler 'Nestor,' writing in Old Church Slavonic but familiar with Byzantine and Latin literature, demonstrates an accomplished understanding of the comparative religious topics at issue and the connected problems of terminology. In his report of the events taking place in 986–988 CE, he adopts two precise Russian terms to define individually the three Abrahamic religions, the native East Slavic paganism, and also religion as a category comprehending all the religious realities at issue. These terms used evenly with the evident meaning of religion are *věra*/вера ('faith'), translating Greek *pistis* and Latin *fides*, and *zakon*/законъ ('law,' but also 'custom'), translating Greek *nomos* as well as Latin *lex*. Two examples from the chronicle of the year 986 are by themselves quite explicit: (1) "Vladimir was visited by Bulgars of Mohammedan faith (*věra*), who said, 'Though you are a wise and prudent prince, you have no law (*zakon*). Adopt our law (*zakon*), and revere Mahomet.' Vladimir inquired what was the nature of their faith (*věra*)." (2) "Then came the Germans, asserting that they were come as emissaries of the Pope. They added, 'Thus says the Pope: Your country is like our country, but your faith (*věra*) is not as ours. For our faith (*věra*) is the right one'" (my translation).

Islamicate Western Asia

The primary source of any notion of religion in the Islamic world is not surprisingly the Qur'an. Like Judaism and Christianity, early Islam emerged through contrast and distinction from other religions. For Islam, the points of comparison are Judaism and Christianity as 'religions of the book' on the one hand, and polytheism or 'idolatry' on the other, the former representing the legitimate form of religion, the latter the illegitimate one. Besides the auto-representational concepts of *islam* (submission to God's will) and *iman* ('faith') which define Mohammed's religion and are contrasted with the other book religions, in the Qur'an we find the relational and comparative concepts of *din* and *milla* (Haussig 1999, 194–243). Regardless of its controversial etymology (Semitic or Iranian), *din* is a key term in the Qur'an where it recurs ninety-two times. It embraces the entire range of the meanings of religion in contemporary Latin Christian usage, namely that of *religio, lex,* and *fides,* including the theological, practical, and social semantic sphere of the word religion. In a series of cases *din* is used to denominate religion as a category including the *vera religio* of the Muslims contrasted to the *falsa religio*—I adopt consciously the Augustinian terminology—of both the Arab polytheists and the Jewish and Christian monotheists, such as in suras 85 and 109; the latter is particularly telling in this regard: "To you be your din, and to me mine" (trans. A. Arberry, modified). Although less frequent in the Qur'an than *din, milla* (plural *milal*) similarly conveys the meanings of religion in its practical and social aspects, and it is characteristically used in an apologetic-polemic context. Following the author of the Qur'an who, in his penchant to classify humanity into distinct categories of believers and disbelievers of two different kinds, clearly possesses a distinct notion of religion as a category, a series of Muslim scholars of the Abbasid period (750–1258) extended and generalized that notion, until it assumed a universal dimension, in erudite works verging between the genre of heresiography and that of a rudimentary kind of history of religions.

A referential, i.e. explicitly denoting or designating or naming, comparative concept of religion is first clearly expressed in the *Book of Religion and Empire* by the physician Ali Ibn Rabban Al-Tabari (838–870 CE). In the conclusion he asks the following hypothetical question: "What would you say of a man coming to this country from the regions of India and China, with the intention of being rightly guided, of inquiring into the religions found in it . . .? It will be said to him that some of its inhabitants belong to a religion (*din*) called Magianism. . . . Some of its inhabitants belong to a religion called Zindikism. . . . Some of its inhabitants belong to a religion called Christianity . . . Some of its inhabitants belong to a religion called Judaism. . . . Some of its inhabitants belong to this pure and sublime religion called Islam . . . In which of these religions and creeds would that Indian or that Chinese wish to believe . . ." (Tabari 1922, 165–166). Al-Tabari classifies and compares cultural products that appear to him as pertaining to the same class of phenomena. Although he values them differently, he has a clear idea of their resemblance and translatability (Riesebrodt 2004, 132–133).

The reasons—theological, political, and intellectual—that lead a number of Arabo-Persian scholars of medieval times to register, analyze, and classify the religious communities of the surrounding world according to Islamic perspectives have been investigated several times (Lawrence 1976; Monnot 1986; 2010; Waardenburg 2003; Latief 2006). It has been also largely recognized that at least two of these Muslim literati, Abu Rayhan al-Biruni (973–1048) and Abd al-Karim al-Shahrastani (1086–1153) revealed a genuine interest in understanding non-Islamic religions through comparison and demonstrated such skill in the investigation of other religions as to be considered forerunners if not founders of the comparative study of religions (see Stausberg, "History," this volume). The relevance of the contribution of these medieval Muslim scholars to the historical and anthropological study of religion is enormous, notwithstanding a certain theological Islamo-centric bias which shapes the modes of their classifications and evaluations of world religious traditions. It must also be noted that their approaches are different and complementary. Whereas al-Biruni focuses on the ritual practice, al-Shahrastani is more interested in the doctrinal variety of the religions and sects under examination (Al-Shahrastani 1986–1993). Thus they present different approaches to classifying world religions, but both make extensive and conscious usage of the comparative tool.

India

Political regulations through laws or edicts are, like theological competitions, informed by a referential concept of religion. Edicts seldom deal with one religion alone, but quite often regulate several religious groups and communities. The Indian king of the Maurya dynasty Asoka (304–232 BCE) who ruled almost all of the Indian subcontinent for almost forty years and converted gradually to Buddhism—regarding it as a doctrine that could serve as a cultural foundation for political unity without being a state religion—was perhaps the first sovereign to promulgate edicts of religious toleration that seem particularly relevant to current affairs. In the seventh rock edict we find a classification of groups (Buddhist, Jain, Brahman) compatible with the concept of (Indian) religions. Even more explicit is the twelfth edict:

> King Priyadarsi, Beloved of the Gods, honors men of all religions (*pasanda*) with gifts and with honors of various kinds . . . But the Beloved of the Gods does not value either the offering of gifts or the honoring of people so highly as the following, viz., that there should be a growth of the essential of Dharma among men of all religions. . . . there should be no extolment of one's own religion or disparagement of other religions on inappropriate occasions . . . On the contrary, other religions should be duly honored in every way on all occasions. If a person acts in this way, he not only promotes his own religion but also benefits other religions. But, if a person acts otherwise, he not only injures his own religion but also harms other religions. Truly, if a person extols his own religion and disparages other religions with a view to glorifying his religion owing merely to his attachment to it, he injures his own religion very severely by acting in that way. . . . This indeed is the desire of the Beloved of the Gods that persons of all religions become well informed about the doctrines of different religions. (Translation based on Pugliese Carratelli 2003, 49 and 65)[2]

Thus we have here a very ancient and non-Western attestation of a usage of a term, *pasanda*, defining social institutions that have religious experts and laypeople and specific distinguishable worldviews, in other words religions, in a context that confers to the term a classificatory value (Haussig 1999, 120–122; Riesebrodt 2004, 143; Freiberger 2013, 33–37). Dharma, instead, very seldom evolved from the original meaning of 'cosmic-social order' referring exclusively to the indigenous religion of the Arya, to a comparative concept to be used for religion in general (Haussig 1999, 78–102).

After the Mughal conquest of India in the sixteenth century and the consequent partial Islamization, we find in Urdu an umbrella term for religion, namely the Persian *din*. We have evidence of this usage in the chronicles reporting the religious experiments at the court of the Mughal emperor Akbar the Great (1542–1605 CE), which inter alia led to an increasingly clean-cut demarcation between politics and religion. In 1575, Akbar established a House of Worship in which theological and religious discussions

---

[2] Hultzsch (1925, 20–22) in a critical edition of the edicts, renders the term *pasanda* as 'sect,' a meaning that is in fact current in late Sanskrit but is not appropriate in this context.

took place every week. Originally only Islamic groups were admitted, including Sunni and Shi'a scholars, Sufi mystics, and others. Later, non-Muslim groups were included, such as Brahmans and even Jesuit missionaries and a Zoroastrian priest. Despite resistance by the exponents of Sunni orthodoxy, the emperor decided to establish a kind of 'interreligious council,' with the participation of the most illustrious representatives of every faith, among them Islam, Hinduism, Jainism, Buddhism, Zoroastrianism, and Christianity. Akbar finally went so far as to found a new universalistic ethical religion (*Dīn-i Ilāhī*, "Religion of God"), implying a complete absence of a dogmatic theology and of specific forms of worship. This entails a kind of secularism and a distinct awareness of the pluralistic nature of religious traditions (Riesebrodt 2004, 141; King 2013).

China

In classical European histories of historiography (the situation is in part different in America: see Breisach 2005, 4026) one could hardly find the name of a pioneer of universal history like the Chinese historian of the Han dynasty Sima Qian (Suma Chien; *c.*145 BCE–86 BCE) who in his work *Shiji* ("Historical Records") set himself the task of describing in narrative terms everything of significance that had happened in the known world from the earliest mythological origins to the present day. Among the five sections of which the work consists, section three, the "Treatises," is of special concern for us. This section contains eight entries on such subjects as rituals, music, astronomy, and *religious sacrificial ceremonies* (including sacrifices to Heaven and Earth). This work of Sima Qian launches a historical tradition in China that already implies a principle of classification including the category of religion, as a social segment. In another part of his encyclopaedia, Sima Qian went so far to devise even a taxonomy of these doctrinal, social, and political entities by introducing the notion of *liu-jia*, i.e. the 'six schools,' including the Yin-Yang Masters, the Confucians, the Mohists, the Logicians, the Legalists, and the Taoists (Denecke 2010, 53–54; Kleine 2013, 259–260).

The story of how the modern Chinese word for 'religion' *zongjiao* was first employed to mean religion in China during the first decade of the twentieth century (Yu 2005, 7; Meyer 2013, 361) under the influence of Japanese *shukyo* (first attested in Japanese in 1867, Kleine 2013, 258) provides an extremely instructive example of a translingual and transcultural process involving the translation and adaptation of the—originally Western but virtually universal in its irradiation—notion of religion into the Chinese specific context. *Zong-jiao* (like *shu-kyo*) is a compound consisting of *zong* (*shu*), a logogram which—from the original meaning of 'ancestor,' 'basis'—evolves in Buddhist usage to indicate both a "particular divisional lineage of the religion" and "established dogma" (Yu 2005, 11), finally denoting a 'sect' or religious denomination, and *jiao* (*kyo*), meaning "teaching." Because of this association with both native religious practices and Buddhist doctrines, *zongjiao/shukyo* resulted in an apt umbrella term to designate a general concept of religion, including Christianity, in which both praxis and doctrine are essential elements.

But this standard narrative is partial and flawed by a Euro-centrism shared even by Chinese secular scholars, and it should be improved in various ways. Long before the adoption of the new term *zongjiao*, *jiao* itself (in general rendered as 'doctrine' or 'tradition') came closest, in usage, to the meaning of 'religion'. Since at least the Ming dynasty (1368–1644), the standard rubric for classifying the religions of China was *san-jiao*, or the 'three doctrines', referring to Confucianism, Daoism, and Buddhism (Yu 2005, 13; Meyer 2013, 361). "Far from being a creation of alien traditions in modernity, *zongjiao* in its historical development had been itself fashioned by an alien religion [Buddhism] negotiating its way into China" (Yu 2005, 15).

Also, and most significantly, the term *jiao* was employed to refer to other foreign religious traditions including Nestorian Christianity (*Jingjiao*), Manichaeism (*Monijiao*), and Zoroastrianism (*Xianjiao*), that entered China in the Tang period (618–907 CE) (Yu 2005, 11–25; Deeg 2013, 213; Meyer 2013, 361; Tommasi 2014, 651, the latter based on a study of the Nestorian [Christian] Xi'an Stele [781 CE]). This is a remarkable example of cultural interaction and semantic interpenetration of theological concepts. Even earlier, the Manichaean *Hymnscroll* produced in Tang China when Manichaeism was introduced by the Uighurs in 768 CE testifies to a sinicization of the *Monijiao* (Mani religion), also denominated *Ming-jiao* (Religion of Light): *Ming* is in fact a Chinese character consisting of two ideograms for sun and moon (Yuanyuan/Wushu 2012, 235–236), a concept of Light which is absent in Manichaean Eastern sources. This *Hymnscroll* survived in spite of severe persecutions suffered by Manichaeans at the beginning of the Huichang era (840–846) of the Tang dynasty under Emperor Wuzong. Notwithstanding these persecutions, in Chinese documents of the Song Dynasty (960–1279) *Ming-jiao* is still attested as popular in present Fujian province, in addition to mainstream religions like Buddhism and Daoism.

CONCLUSION

Contrary to much of the recent social constructionist literature (for critiques, see Martin 2009, 143–152; Bergunder 2014), I have demonstrated on a rigorous historical basis that supposedly recent European words and concepts did not create and impose on non-European cultures new, extraneous, colonial configurations such as the separation of the sphere of religion from other spheres of human culture (politics, economy, etc.). That this separation was not 'invented' at all is implied by the universal process of construction of boundaries between distinct domains of social life and the consequent elaboration of cross-cultural categories. The possibility of *de-fining* and *trans-lating* religion into the most diverse historical and geographical milieus shows the panhuman character of this historical constellation. In conclusion, renouncing the chimera of a modern 'Western' Christian origin of this human reality (a claim of origin that implicitly involves a notion of guilt and a pretense of ownership and exclusivity: Bergunder

2014, 276) would result both in re-establishing the rights of history and in disposing of an ideologically charged politically divisive stereotype.

GLOSSARY

Category a class or group of things possessing some quality or qualities in common.

History history is midway between chronicle and legend.

Modernity the ensemble of particular sociocultural norms, attitudes, and practices that arose in post-medieval Eurasia and that have developed since, in various ways and at various times, around the world.

Religion a contract between humans and superhuman agents.

Tradition the transmission of cultural traits by word of mouth or by example from one generation to another without written instruction.

Translation a term for cultural processes that are profoundly dialogic and continuously 'carried across,' transformed and reinvented in practice.

Universal a pattern which is spread across all cultures.

REFERENCES

Primary Sources

Abelard, Peter. 2001. *Collationes. Dialogus inter Philosophum, Iudaeum et Christianum*. Edited and translated by John Marenbon and Giovanni Orlandi. Oxford: Clarendon Press. Original edition, 1136–1139 (or 1125–1127).

Cusanus (De Cusa), Nicolaus. 1956. *De pace fidei cum epistula ad Ioannem de Segobia*. Edited by R. Klibansky and R. Bascour. London: Warburg Institute. Original edition, 1453.

Hultzsch, Eugen. 1925. *Inscriptions of Asoka*. Oxford: Clarendon Press.

Lactantius. 1954. *De mortibus persecutorum*. Edited and translated by J. Moreau. Paris: Du Cerf. Original edition, 316–321.

Llull, Ramon. 1993. *Llibre del gentil e dels tres savis*. Palma de Mallorca: Patronat Ramon Llull. Original edition, 1274–1276.

Magalotti, Lorenzo. 1974. *Relazione della China*. Milan: Adelphi. Original edition, 1672.

'Nestor' = S. H. Cross and O. P. Sherbowitz-Wetzor, trans. and eds., 1953. *The Russian Primary Chronicle: Laurentian Text*. Cambridge, MS: Mediaeval Academy of America. Original edition, 1377 [compiled about 1113.]

Al-Shahrastâni. 1986–1993. *Livre des religions et des sectes*. Translated by D. Gimaret, Guy Monnot, and Jean Jolivet. Louvain: Peeters. Original edition, 1140–1150.

Tabari, Ali. 1922. *The Book of Religion and Empire*. Translated by A. Mingana. Manchester: Longmans. Original edition, 847–861.

Secondary Literature

Benavides, Gustavo. Forthcoming. "The Concept of Religion." In *The Wiley-Blackwell Companion to Religious Diversity*, edited by Kevin Schilbrack. Oxford: Wiley-Blackwell.

Bergunder, Michael. 2014. "What is Religion?" *Method and Theory in the Study of Religions* 26(3): 246–286. doi: 10.1163/15700682-12341320

Beyer, Peter. 2006. *Religions in Global Society*. London and New York: Routledge.

Bhabha, Homi. 1994. *The Location of Culture*. London: Routledge.

Bianchi, Ugo. 1975. *The History of Religions*. Leiden: Brill.

Biller, Peter. 1985. "Words and the Medieval Notion of 'Religion.'" *Journal of Ecclesiastical History* 36(3): 351–369.

Breisach, Ernst. 2005. "Historiography." In *The Encyclopedia of Religion*, 2nd edition, edited by Lindsay Jones. Detroit: Thomson Gale, 4024–4035.

Brown, Peter. 2003. *A Life of Learning*. New York: ACLS.

Carr, Edward Hallett. 1986. *What Is History?* 2nd edition. Harmondsworth: Penguin. Original edition, 1961.

Casadio, Giovanni. 2010. '*Religio* versus Religion.' In *Myths, Martyrs, and Modernity: Studies in the History of Religion in Honour of Jan Bremmer*, edited by Jitse Dijkstra, Justin Kroesen, and Yme Kuiper. Leiden: Brill, 301–326.

Cawley, Kevin N. 2012. "Deconstructing Hegemony: Catholic Texts in Chosŏn's Neo-Confucian Context." *Acta Koreana* 15(1): 15–42.

Deeg, Max. 2013. "Religiöse Identität durch Differenz und Abgrenzungsdiskurs als indirekte Anerkennung von Gemeinsamkeit: chinesisch-buddhistische Apologetik und ihr 'Religions'begriff." In *Religion in Asien? Studien zur Anwendbarkeit des Religionsbegriffs*, edited by Peter Schalk, Max Deeg, Oliver Freiberger, Christoph Kleine, and Astrid van Nahl. Uppsala: Acta Universitatis Upsaliensis, 203–224.

Deeg, Max, Oliver Freiberger, and Christoph Kleine. 2013. "Einleitung." In *Religion in Asien? Studien zur Anwendbarkeit des Religionsbegriffs*, edited by Peter Schalk, Max Deeg, Oliver Freiberger, Christoph Kleine, and Astrid van Nahl. Uppsala: Acta Universitatis Upsaliensis, ix–xix.

Denecke, Wiebke. 2010. *The Dynamics of Masters Literature: Early Chinese Thought from Confucius to Han Feizi*. Cambridge, MA and London: Harvard University Press.

Eliade, Mircea. 1969. *The Quest: History and Meaning in Religion*. Chicago, IL: University of Chicago Press.

Engler, Steven. Forthcoming. "The Concept of Tradition." In *The Wiley Blackwell Companion to Religious Diversity*, edited by Kevin Schilbrack. Oxford: Wiley-Blackwell.

Foschia, Laurence. 2004. "Le nom du culte, *threskeia*, et ses dérivés à l'époque impériale." In *L'hellénisme d'époque romaine: Nouveaux documents, nouvelles approches (Ier s. a. C. – IIIe s. p. C)*, edited by S. Follet. Paris: De Boccard, 15–35.

Freiberger, Oliver. 2013. "Religionen und Religion in der Konstruktion des frühen Buddhismus." In *Religion in Asien? Studien zur Anwendbarkeit des Religionsbegriffs*, edited by Peter Schalk, Max Deeg, Oliver Freiberger, Christoph Kleine, and Astrid van Nahl. Uppsala: Acta Universitatis Upsaliensis, 15–41.

Glassie, Henry. 1995. "Tradition." *Journal of American Folklore* 108(430): 395–412. doi: 10.2307/541653

Gould, John. 1983. "On Making Sense of Greek Religion." In *Greek Religion and Society*, edited by P. E. Easterling and J. V. Muir. Cambridge: Cambridge University Press, 1–33.

Haussig, Hans-Michael. 1999. *Der Religionsbegriff in den Religionen*. Berlin: Philo.

King, Richard. 2013. "The Copernican Turn in the Study of Religion." *Method & Theory in the Study of Religion* 25(2): 137–159. doi: 10.1163/15700682-12341280

Kleine, Christoph. 2013. "Religion als begriffliches Konzept und soziales System im vormod-ernen Japan—polythetische Klassen, semantische und funktionale Äquivalente und struk-turelle Analogien. In *Religion in Asien? Studien zur Anwendbarkeit des Religionsbegriffs*, edited by Peter Schalk, Max Deeg, Oliver Freiberger, Christoph Kleine, and Astrid van Nahl. Uppsala: Acta Universitatis Upsaliensis, 225–292.

Latief, Hilman. 2006. "Comparative Religion in Medieval Muslim Literature." *American Journal of Islamic Social Sciences* 23(4): 28–62.

Lawrence, Bruce. 1976. *Shahrastani on the Indian Religions*. The Hague: Mouton.

Lieu, Samuel N. C. 2009. "Epigraphica Nestoriana Serica." In *Exegisti Monumenta: FS in Honour of Nicholas Sims-Williams*, edited by W. Sundermann, Halmut Hintze, and François de Blois. Wiesbaden: Harrassowitz, 227–246.

Martin, Craig. 2009. "On the Origin of the Private Sphere: A Discourse Analysis of Religion and Politics from Luther to Locke." *Temenos* 45(2): 143–178.

Meyer, Christian. 2013. "Der moderne chinesische 'Religionsbegriff' zongjiao als Beispiel translingualer Praxis: Rezeption westlicher Religions-begriffe und -vorstellungen im China des frühen 20. Jahrhunderts." In *Religion in Asien? Studien zur Anwendbarkeit des Religionsbegriffs*, edited by Peter Schalk, Max Deeg, Oliver Freiberger, Christoph Kleine, and Astrid van Nahl. Uppsala: Acta Universitatis Upsaliensis, 351–392.

Monnot, Guy. 1986. *Islam et religions*. Paris: Maisonneuve.

Monnot, Guy. 2010. "Apports musulmans à l'histoire des religions." *Revue de la Société Ernest Renan* 45–47: 191–205.

Oişteanu, Andrei. 2009. "Jews, Christians, and Muslims in Controversy: Public Theological Disputations in Medieval Europe." *Archæus* 13(2): 137–154.

Pettazzoni, Raffaele. 1954. *Essays on the History of Religions*, translated by H. J. Rose. Leiden: Brill.

Platvoet, J. G. 1999. "Contexts, Concepts & Contests: Towards a Pragmatics of Defining 'Religion.'" In *The Pragmatics of Defining Religion*, edited by J. G. Platvoet and A. L. Molendijk. Leiden: Brill, 463–516.

Pugliese Carratelli, Giovanni. 2003. *Gli editti di Asoka*. Milan: Adelphi.

Pye, Michael. 1994. "Religion: Shape and Shadow." *Numen* 41(1): 51–75. doi: 10.2307/3270413

Riesebrodt, Martin. 2004. "Überlegungen zur Legimität eines universalen Religionsbegriffs." In *Religion im kulturellen Diskurs: FS für Hans G. Kippenberg zu seinem 65. Geburtstag*. Berlin and New York: de Gruyter, 127–149.

Riesebrodt, Martin. 2010. *The Promise of Salvation: A Theory of Religion*, translated by Steven Rendall. Chicago, IL: University of Chicago Press.

Riesebrodt, Martin. 2013. "Religion als analytisches Konzept und seine universale Anwendbarkeit." In *Religion in Asien? Studien zur Anwendbarkeit des Religionsbegriffs*, edited by Peter Schalk, Max Deeg, Oliver Freiberger, Christoph Kleine, and Astrid van Nahl. Uppsala: Acta Universitatis Upsaliensis, 1–12.

Shushan, Gregory. 2009. *Conceptions of the Afterlife in Early Civilizations: Universalism, Constructivism, and Near-Death Experience*. London: Continuum.

Stünkel, Knut Martin. 2013. *Una sit religio: Religionsbegriffe und Begriffstopologien bei Cusanus, Llull und Maimonides*. Würzburg: Königshausen & Neumann.

Tommasi, Chiara Ombretta. 2014. "'Nestorians' on the Silk Road: Some Notes on the Stele of Xi'an." In *La teologia dal V all'VIII secolo fra sviluppo e crisi. XLI Incontro di Studiosi dell'Antichità Cristiana*. Rome: Augustinianum, 645–669.

Waardenburg, Jacques. 2003. *Muslims and Others: Relations in Context*. Berlin and New York: de Gruyter.

Yu, Antony. 2005. *State and Religion in China*. Chicago and La Salle, IL: Open Court.

Yuanyuan, Wang and Lin Wushu. 2012. "New findings on the popularity of Manichaean Hymnscroll in Ming Jiao after the Tang dynasty." In *Gnostica et Manichaica: Festschrift für Aloïs van Tongerloo*, edited by Michael Knüppel and Luigi Cirillo. Wiesbaden: Harrassowitz, 233–245.

FURTHER READING

Bianchi, Ugo, ed. 1994. *The Notion of "Religion" in Comparative Research: Selected Proceedings of the XVI IAHR Congress*. Rome: L'Erma di Bretschneider. [*An invaluable resource of materials with well-grounded and balanced interpretations.*]

Budick, Sanford and Wolfgang Iser, eds. 1996. *The Translatability of Cultures: Figurations of the Space Between*. Stanford: Stanford University Press. [*The 14 essays in this volume consider a wide variety of cultures from ancient Egypt to contemporary Japan. The essays describe the conditions under which cultures that do not dominate each other may yet achieve a limited translatability of cultures, while at the same time alerting us to some of the dangers of a so-called mutual translation between cultures. The essays by Jan Assmann and Moshe Barasch are of particular value with regard to the issue of religion as a factor of cultural (un)translatability and visual syncretism respectively.*]

Father Adriano di St. Thecla. 2002. *Opusculum de Sectis apud Sinenses et Tunkinenses. A Small Treatise on the Sects among the Chinese and Tonkinese*, translated by Olga Dror and Mariya Berezovska. Ithaca: South East Asia Program, Cornell University. [*This 1750 text, written by a Catholic missionary in Tonkin, is the earliest known systematic first-hand account of Vietnamese religious practice, presented in comparison with Chinese religious traditions.*]

Feuchtwang, Stephan. 2010. *The Anthropology of Religion: Charisma and Ghosts*. Berlin and New York: de Gruyter. [*The historical transfer into China of 'religion' as a category that emerged in sixteenth-century Europe.*]

Hofer, Nathan. 2014. "Scriptural Substitutions and Anonymous Citations: Judaization as Rhetorical Strategy in a Jewish Sufi Text." *Numen* 61(4): 364–395. doi: 10.1163/15685276-12341329 [*Presenting a case of translation of a text from a religious tradition (Muslim Sufi) to another one (Jewish Rabbinic), preserving the original Linguistic medium (Arabic).*]

Krech, Volkhard and Marion Steinicke, eds. 2012. *Dynamics in the History of Religions between Asia and Europe: Encounters, Notions, and Comparative Perspectives*. Leiden: Brill. [*A series of papers on all major religious traditions in intercultural perspective mostly focused on the issue of translating religious concepts.*]

Lorenzetti, Tiziana and Fabio Scialpi, eds. 2012. *Glimpses of Indian History and Art*. Rome: Sapienza Università. [*Old terminologies, approaches and perspectives of Western origin in tension with modern and post-modern Indian views.*]

Pye, Michael. 2013. *Strategies in the Study of Religions*. Vol. 1: *Exploring Methods and Positions*. Berlin and Boston: de Gruyter. [*Asian intellectual traditions pertaining to systematic reflection on issues of typology, comparison, and transculturality of religions should be given full weight in their own right.*]

Sparks, Garry. 2014. "The Use of Mayan Scripture in the Americas' First Christian Theology." *Numen* 61(4): 396–429. doi: 10.1163/15685276-12341330 [*In the* Theologia Indorum *(1553–1554)*

Dominican Friar de Vico strategically used Mayan names and concepts from indigenous narratives to translate the Christian doctrine into eloquent Mayan discourse for a more nuanced understanding of the mutual dynamics between missionaries and the missionized.]

Waardenburg, Jacques, ed. 1999. *Muslim Perceptions of Other Religions: A Historical Survey.* New York: Oxford University Press. [*Muslim perceptions of other religions in contact and confrontation in the East and West.*]

CHAPTER 3

THEORIES OF RELIGION

MICHAEL STAUSBERG AND STEVEN ENGLER

CHAPTER SUMMARY

- There are two types of theories: top-down theories that apply a theoretical apparatus (cognition, evolution, social systems, etc.) to religion; and bottom-up theories that try to elaborate one, aiming initially to explain or interpret a given set of empirical phenomena.
- The emergence of theories of religion has two preconditions: (a) it presupposes the existence of something (or some thing) called religion; (b) that thing, from at least some perspectives, constitutes some kind of problem or puzzle worth resolving.
- Theories of religion typically address the following five questions: (a) what kind of subject matter does religion constitute?; (b) what is the structure of religion?; (c) what is distinctive/specific about religion? (d) what are the origins of religion? (e) what are the effects, functions, or products of religion?
- Theories of religion provide a shared horizon of inquiry in the study of religion\s; implicit theories underlie empirical work and the potential achievability of explicit theories is a regulative idea for the discipline.
- The distinction between data and theory is best conceived of in a relative sense; there is no qualitative abyss separating data and theory.
- There are different aims and ways of assessing theories and their use in research. Theories of different types play different roles in relation to specific constellations of theory, methods, and data, and they must be assessed in that context.

INTRODUCTION: THEORY AND THEORIES OF RELIGION

While the notion of theory continues to show "a bewildering variety of meanings" (Wiebe 1983, 295) in the study of religion\s as much as in other disciplines, in this chapter we operate with a broad notion of 'theory' as an interconnected set of ideas or statements (propositions) expressed in language that, from within a certain discursive placement and from a given point of view (which implies certain interests and values), frames cognitive claims about some phenomenon (here: 'religion').

Our focus here is one segment of theory in the study of religion\s, namely theories of religion, i.e. theories that seek to account for religion by explaining what it is, what it does, how it originates, etc. If one holds, as a reader of this chapter suggested, that scholars of religion study a peculiar domain of human thought and behavior related to assumptions about a certain kind of agents or beings, a theory of religion will address the nature of this domain. Theories of religion in this sense are distinct from more general theoretical approaches that are sometimes brought to bear on issues of religion: e.g. cognitive, evolutionary, hermeneutic, Marxist, postcolonial, (post)structuralist, semiotic, semantic, etc., as discussed in Part II of this book. These and other approaches are put to work in many kinds of research, and sometimes, albeit rarely, one finds theories of religion built on them. These by-products of more general paradigms are then labeled as cognitive, evolutionary, Marxist, critical, feminist, social systems, etc. theories of religion. Such theories are rarely proposed by scholars of religion (in a disciplinary sense), but occasionally scholars of religion (e.g. Martin Riesebrodt, Thomas Tweed) have developed theories of religion of their own, which make use of certain concepts and ideas that connect them to more general theoretical approaches but which are not an outgrowth of any of the above-mentioned paradigms.

Our focus here is on the work of scholars explicitly interested in theory with a specific focus on religion. Theory of religion in this sense is just a fraction of the theoretical output and concerns in the study of religion. Many scholars will associate theories of religion primarily with reading and 'drawing on' the works of classics such as Marx, Tylor, Durkheim, Freud, Jung, Geertz, and others. This chapter does not advocate one theory of religion, but engages in meta-theoretical reflections on the corpus of contemporary (rather than classical) theories, in order to sketch a range of issues and positions. Meta-theoretical, theoretical, and methodological pluralisms are inescapable and often healthy aspects of the study of religion\s, as they are throughout the humanities and social sciences.

THE PROBLEMATIC OF RELIGION

A precondition for the emergence of theories of religion is that religion means something worthy of theorizing. This has two implications: (a) a theory of religion presupposes the existence of something (or some thing) called religion, whether discursively constructed, ontologically distinct, or some other form of object; and (b) that thing, from at least some perspectives, constitutes some kind of problem or puzzle worth resolving. On the face of it, both features are the outcome of modern European history.

Religion—even if understood in different manners—emerged as some sort of stable object in the work of various theoreticians since the seventeenth century. For the early theoreticians—down to the nineteenth century almost exclusively philosophers—religion was largely identical with Christianity, but the scope of the term eventually broadened to include non-Christian specimens of the (presumed) genus. One the main axes of the modern concept of religion appears to be the plurality of religions that are held to exemplify the singular category (Hermann 2015).

Early theoreticians of religions addressed a number of issues, especially the following:

- the origin(s) of religion, sometimes conceived as the idea of a 'natural religion';
- forms or types of religion, e.g. public/private/positive/civil, monotheism/polytheism, etc.;
- religion's (ir)rationality;
- religion's social functions and consequences, in particular in relation to the state and morality and as causes for war and conflict.

In general terms, these earlier discussions clustered along two broad lines that continue to frame current debates: problematizing religion itself and discussing its relation to—or impact on—other aspects of society or on society as a whole. Philosophical theories of religion, in particular since the Enlightenment, have not been merely analytical and descriptive: they have often taken the form of either critique or apology. This reflects the emergence of the 'secular option,' i.e. "the move from a society where belief in God is unchallenged and indeed, unproblematic, to one in which it is understood to be one option among others, and frequently not the easiest to embrace" (Taylor 2007, 3). In this context, we can replace the philosopher's 'belief in God' by 'religion.' In this light, religion, and being religious, have lost their assumed natural status and have become negotiable. This process has taken several centuries, from intellectual critiques of religion to the spread of non-religion among broader segments of the population (see Lee, "Non-Religion" this volume). The trend to argue for or against religion (and the existence of God) continues in traditional philosophy of religion. Similarly, some of the classical social scientific or psychological theories of religion were informed by anti-religionism (Marx, Freud) or presented religion as something to be overcome (Tylor, Frazer). The idea that religion does not exist, being just a word, is a continuation and to some extent a radicalization of the de-naturalizing tradition of critique. On the other hand, there are theories sympathetic to religion, even if not explicitly apologetic with respect to specific religions (e.g. Eliade or, for contemporary theories, Stark/Finke). Theoretical approaches that hypothetically or seemingly re-naturalize religion—for example as by-products of cognitive processes (Boyer 2001), or as stimulating solutions to evolutionary problems such as the establishment of trust among strangers in the formation of large groups (Norenzayan 2013)—could be read as providing potential defenses of religion even if they were not written in that spirit.

On a different level of analysis, religion may be seen as a problem inherent in modern Western society that has 'modernity' as its founding narrative. Hans Kippenberg (2001) has argued that the emerging field of the history of religions was centrally occupied with the 'other half' of modernity, namely those aspects of life not at the service of the idea of progress. Historians of religion drew upon themes such as nature mysticism, soul, rituals, magic, mysteries, ecstasy, and salvation, in order to address forces considered obsolete and past, yet still powerfully present even in modern societies. From a theoretical point of view, standard views of religion—as something traditional, grounded in the eternal and the supernatural, operating with symbols, and committed to the ritual recovery of the mythical—seem to contradict the spirit of modernity, with its claim of relentless self-reflection (Benavides 1998)—which melts everything that is solid into air, starting with religion. In this sense, dominant narratives of modernity frame religion as the 'other' and thus as a fundamental problem or threat.

Starting Points for Theories of Religion

In general terms, there are two types of theories: those that apply a theoretical apparatus (cognition, evolution, social systems, etc.) to religion; and those that try to elaborate a theoretical apparatus based upon the study of putatively religious phenomena. The former is more top-down, aiming at a general account, and the latter is bottom-up, seeking initially to explain or interpret a given set of empirical phenomena. Here, we review selected examples of the latter sort, which results in theories that are more characteristic of the discipline, as opposed to top-down applications of more general theoretical perspectives.

Philologist Walter Burkert (1996), an expert on Greek and Near Eastern religions, employs a variety of theoretical perspectives to make sense of findings of religious behavior and integrate them in an overarching theory of religion—where religion is a strategy of human survival between biology and culture (see Benavides in Stausberg 2009b). Turning to contemporary Western societies, sociologist Rodney Stark, who has been involved in studies of American religion since the 1960s, has—first with William Sims Bainbridge then with Roger Finke—developed a theory of religion that resonates with his view of the vitality of the American religion scene or market and goes against a perceived atheist bias and focus on human irrationality in earlier social science theories of religion (Stark/Bainbridge 1987; Stark/Finke 2000). He emphasizes the rationality of religious choices, the importance of competition for religious vitality, and the relative advantages of strict or costly forms of religion, which are in tension with their environment (see Alles in Stausberg 2009b).

Fieldwork also offers a launching point in the search for more adequate theories. Thomas Tweed writes that his theory of religion arose out of dissatisfaction with available theories of religion for making sense of his observations at a shrine attended by Cuban exiles in Miami, Florida. Accordingly, he builds his own theory around the three leitmotivs of movement, relation, and position (Tweed 2006, 4–5) that emerged from his fieldwork. Just as these exiles had crossed the waters between Cuba and Florida, his theory strategically engages with aquatic tropes, and his two main axes are crossing boundaries and making homes.

Broader reviews of religious material also motivate dissatisfaction with existing theory. Sociologist of religion Martin Riesebrodt (2010 [2007]), like Tweed, reviews data for a wide range of Eastern and Western religions. For him, interventionist practices that establish and maintain contact with superhuman powers are at the core of religions, and these practices ground religions' promises to avert misfortune, overcome crises, and achieve salvation for groups and individuals (see Stausberg in Stausberg 2009b; see Flood, "Salvation," this volume, on the core concept of salvation).

With a more explicit assessment of theoretical resources in the study of religion\s, Manuel Vásquez, a trained sociologist, reports that the available theoretical 'canon' was "for the most part unhelpful" for addressing "the religious creativity, cross-fertilization, and fluidity that accompany globalization, particularly . . . the ways in which transnational immigrants transform both their countries of origin and settlement by generating hybrid identities, practices, and spaces" (Vásquez 2011, 1). Accordingly, he provides a genealogy of three fields of theoretical investigation in a variety of disciplines and fields, namely body, practice, and space. Vásquez finds that these are the "key sites where some of the most innovative and potentially influential non-reductive work on religion is taking place" (2011, 11). Vásquez's guiding framework is that of a non-reductive materialism, i.e. a position that emphasizes "the material constraints and possibilities entailed by our being-in-the world through our physical bodies" (2011, 6) without wishing to reduce everything to matter and without being andro- and anthropocentric and by remaining attentive to complexity, emergence, situatedness, and openness. By competently engaging with a vast panorama of theoretical work, Vásquez enriches readers' understanding of body, practice, and space in relation to religion, but leaves the identification of religion deliberately untouched.[1]

FIVE QUESTIONS

Theories of religion typically address the following questions, which serve as the central foci of different theories and as the motivation for the building of new theories (see also Stausberg 2009a):

1. What kind of subject matter does religion constitute?
2. What is the structure of religion?
3. What is distinctive/specific about religion?
4. What are the origins of religion?
5. What work does religion do (effects, functions, or products)?

---

[1] *More than Belief* was discussed in review symposia published in *Religion* 42(4) (2012) and *Method & Theory in the Study of Religion* 24(4–5) (2012).

Religion as Subject Matter

The word religion has a long history going back to antiquity (see Casadio 2010 for the meaning of the term in Latin sources from antiquity). Various studies have examined the trajectories of the word through European history (e.g. Despland 1979; Feil 1986–2007; Smith 1998; Fitzgerald 2007; Nongbri 2013; see Casadio, "Historicizing and Translating Religion," this volume). One reading of these works is that there has not been one single transhistorical European concept of religion. The extant studies are based on literary sources and therefore reflect the way 'religion' was used, understood, and developed by literate elites. We know virtually nothing about popular concepts of religion. Even though we might consider 'the emic' as a relatively unproblematic entry point for what counts as religion (Vásquez 2012, 660), we have no empirical studies on emic everyday concepts of religion for the modern and contemporary periods (see Bergunder 2014, who proposes that genealogies of these are the genuine subject matter of religious studies). The situation has become even more complex since 'religion'—during the course of Western expansion and colonialism—has spread to other parts of the world, where Western notions of religion have been appropriated first by literary elites and then diffused into the broader population, partly in line with further processes of Westernization. This diffusion and appropriation has occurred against the background of emic semantics and vocabularies as a process of translation (see Casadio, "Historicizing and Translating Religion," this volume, for premodern processes of intercultural interaction and semantic interpenetration). The status of religion as an object of study has been problematized by the constructionist views of what we might call 'critical' scholars of religion—Russell McCutcheon, Timothy Fitzgerald, and others—whose work resonates with that of J. Z. Smith and Talal Asad. Recognizing the historicity (and ethnocentrism) of the category of religion, such critics have concluded that "there is no such thing as 'religion'" or "no such entity as 'religion'"; in other words, "Religion as a distinct and substantive reality in the world . . . is a myth" (Arnal 2000, 32; Atran 2002, 264; Fitzgerald 2007, 9). This position denies that there is some stable, ontologically distinct domain, entity, or thing 'out there' in the world to which the word 'religion' refers. It holds that 'religion' is a discursively constructed concept, with no extra-linguistic referent: it is a word that refers to other words, not a word that refers to a thing.

On a strong interpretation, this 'no such religion' position implies that theorizing must aim at the cross-cultural or even the universal, rather than the historical and contextual and, even more radically, that the historicity and the constructed nature of an expression disqualifies its spectrum of reference from theoretical scrutiny. This would presuppose that certain concepts do in fact escape historicity and discourse, with this protection from historicity providing an Archimedean point of objectivity and innocence that would ground real theorizing. But it remains unclear what these might be, how we are to distinguish them from less stable concepts, and how they could be verifiably translated into the necessarily situated discourses of the study of religion\s.

The 'standard' line among 'critical' theorists is generally framed in more limited terms: methodological consequences stem not from the fact that religion is a construct but from the manner of its construction. The claim is not just that religion refers to words rather than things; it is that it refers to a certain set of other concepts, formed in a specific cultural and historical context. On this view, 'religion' means what it means not because it refers to religious things (there are no such things), but because it refers to such things as 'non-political,' 'non-scientific,' 'non-public,' etc. 'Religion' makes no sense apart from "what in shorthand gets called the religion-secular dichotomy" (Fitzgerald 2007, 232); another variant of this view is "that cross-cultural or non-specific characterizations of so-called religious phenomena are distorting, that the phenomenology of religion is in fact a phenomenology of the Modern state" (Arnal 2000, 32).

Claiming that there is no such 'thing' as religion raises the question what one means by 'thing' or 'entity.' The critics can hardly think of simple material objects; that would merely be stating the obvious. Probably, what they mean is that religion 'only' has a linguistic or discursive nature: there is only the word, but no related extra-linguistic thing. This would shift the focus of the theoretical endeavor from religion to 'religion,' where a theory of 'religion' would need to explain, for example, how that specific word originated and came to be connected to certain discursive positions and claims, how it allowed people to do important things with it, how its discursive efficiency works differently from that of other words, and how it is connected to other words.

In sum, clarifying the ontological status of religion is a major requirement for a theory of religion. This is not to suggest that there is some one correct view on this matter; rather, theories of religion must address this unavoidable issue. The deflationary claim that 'religion' is nothing but a word—when supplemented by the view that this is hardly unique to religion—usefully emphasizes the role of action, language, and intentionality in the creation of social reality. If we grant that social/human reality (minimally) is constructed and is not independent of human action, communication, and intentionality, this does not make it less real (Stausberg 2010; Schilbrack 2014, 89–92).

The Structure of Religion

The question of the structure of religion—its component elements and their relations to each other—has received relatively little attention in theories of religion. Many theories regard religion as an integrated unit comprising several aspects, components, dimensions, elements, facets, or parts. At the outset of his classical study, Émile Durkheim announced his intention to proceed "as if religion were to form a kind of indivisible unit"; but, at the same time, he refers to religion as "a more or less complex system of myths, teachings, rites, and ceremonies" (Durkheim 1912, 49 [trans. Stausberg]). A whole, he adds, can only be defined relative to its constituent parts (Durkheim 1912, 49).

In later sociology of religion, an influential mapping of religion along five dimensions was suggested by sociologist Charles Glock (1962) in the context of a discussion of religion in the United States; he distinguished the following dimensions: experiential, ritual, belief intellectual, intellectual, and application (Glock/Stark 1965). The model was then used and refined in a book that Glock co-published with Rodney Stark (Stark/ Glock 1968). The work of Ninian Smart has been particularly influential in the study of religion\s. Smart introduced his own dimensional model to achieve balance so that description and theory of religion are not 'lopsided' (Smart 1996, 8); the other reason is to provide an alternative to simple definitions. Smart distinguishes between 'most basic' dimensions (Smart 1996, 10): ritual or practical; doctrinal or philosophical; mythic or narrative; experiential or emotional; ethical or legal; organization or social; material or artistic. In addition, he pays attention to the political and economic dimensions of religion. This 'anatomic' model is still used in recent theoretical publications. Schilbrack, for example, while referring to Smart (Schilbrack 2014, 26), operates with a model comprising five dimensions organized around key 'interests' pursued by different religions (Schilbrack 2014, 14–18). While this kind of dimensional anatomy seeks to capture the empirical complexities of religion, the distinctions as proposed seem either commonsense or improvised; the theoretical principles underlying these distinctions await further clarification—if one wants to continue with this model at all.[2] Its value seems to reside more on its analytical and hermeneutical affordances. One problem with this model is that each of the dimensions is as complex as religion; ritual, for example, shares many conceptual and theoretical complexities and predicaments with religion and can in turn be anatomized into different dimensions.

Ann Taves proposes 'building blocks' as an alternative metaphor (2009; 2013). This implies a different perspective altogether, which could avoid a problem with dimensional theorizing. Acknowledging that religion is a complex cultural concept, she proposes to break different established definitions of religion down into more basic components. In particular, Taves proposes to address processes involving imagination, setting apart (so that some things are considered more salient than others), and valuation (so that some things are treated as more significant than others). This strategy connects religion to more basic levels of cognitive or psychological analysis that operate across cultures and historical periods. Yet, this approach is not without challenges. These different processes interconnect in an arbitrary fashion, as they were identified on the basis of a pre-selected set of definitions of religion; e.g. setting apart draws on Durkheim and valuation on Tillich. The question then becomes how one reassembles these different processes—or just what the motivation would be for attempting to do so. Having let different building blocks escape the bottle, how do we get them back in?

---

[2] In the psychology of religion, the multidimensional character of the construct religion is generally recognized: "the empirical stream of religious measurement has developed and supported a multi-dimensional model of religiousness" (Hall/Meador/Koenig 2008, 154). There have been several attempts (usually employing factor analysis) to operationalize and specify the dimensions: an early example of a study based on factor and cluster analyses was King (1967) who proposed nine dimensions. In the sociology of religion, a dimensional model was relaunched and tested with a large sample of American Mormons by Cornwall et al. (1986). Koenig (2011, 210–215) provides an unsystematic list of sixteen dimensions that have been used in psychological health/religion research.

If the specification of building blocks was based on a different initial set of definitions, other cognitive or psychological processes could be identified by the same methods. What would protect the selection of definitions and the resulting set of building blocks from the charge that they are completely arbitrary? Is it simply the label on the bottle ('religion') that contingently links these building blocks together? On this view, the real explanation for the (historical and/or conceptual) emergence of religion would occur on the level of cultural labeling; from a theory of religion we would arrive at cultural and social history.

The third strategy—fractionation—explicitly takes this step toward cultural and social contextualization. The program here is "to fractionate religion into numerous different traits, each of which must be explained on its own account," as Harvey Whitehouse (2008, 35) puts it. This program is a prominent approach in the Cognitive Science of Religion (see Geertz, "Cognitive Science," this volume). While Whitehouse has a tendency to dichotomize rather than to fractionize—for him variation typically can be assigned to two contrasting or opposite modes or processes (see, e.g., Whitehouse/Lanman 2014)—other scholars posit a variety of unrelated processes. Anthropologist Pascal Boyer is a prominent voice. He suggests "a fractionated model of religious cognition, in which different aspects of religious thought and behavior activate different mental capacities" (Boyer 2010, 28). He wishes to overcome any singular notion of religion, which he finds misleading: "We understand better all these phenomena once we stop believing that they are *sui generis* and belong together" (Boyer 2010, 23). The set of things commonly described as religions are an "amorphous mixture" that "does not really exist, either as a set of mental phenomena in anyone's heads or as a social or cultural phenomenon" (Boyer 2010, 10). He speculates that the 'illusion' that these things stem from one and the same cultural domain is the result of a clever marketing strategy of "a single institution, the guild of religious officers" (Boyer 2010, 21), but he does not provide any explanation for this strategy's tremendous success.

Another influential evolutionary anthropologist, Scott Atran (2002, 265), has produced a theory that is fractional in origin but not with regard to structure or effects. Atran claims that "Religious belief and practice involve a variety of cognitive and affective systems, some with separate evolutionary histories and some with no evolutionary history to speak of." These, he speculates, "have been culturally co-opted, or 'exapted,' in religion to new functions" (Atran 2002, 265). Yet, contrary to Boyer, Atran claims that "All religions follow the same structural contours" (2002, 266). So, even if religion is grounded in an originally heterogeneous assembly of brain and body systems, their products converge in an evolutionary landscape, and religion has powerful psychological and social effects. Contrary to Boyer, Atran's account delineates a scenario in which the different systems interact in a coherent manner, so that the initial fractionizing model is effectively overcome.

Metaphors of dimensions, building blocks, or originally independent systems generally presume that the different subunits operate in a non-hierarchical manner: one dimension, building block, or system is not more important or central than the others.[3] However, some theoreticians delineate the structure of religion in a more hierarchical manner. Historian of religions Bruce Lincoln (2003, 3–7) outlines a structure that leads from religious discourse—characterized by specific claims to authority, truth, and transcendent status—to religious practices, a community, and an institution. Lincoln refers to these four units as 'domains' (2003, 7), and he emphasizes their various cross-relations. However, the latter three all require the domain of discourse as their prerequisite, thereby creating a hierarchical structure. The late Martin Riesebrodt, who based his explanation of religion on the systematization of insider perspectives on meaningful social actions, distinguished between three sets of practices, namely interventionist, discursive, and behavior-regulating. Interventionist practices are practices, "which aim at establishing contact with superhuman powers" (Riesebrodt 2010, 75). For Riesebrodt, interventionist practices are central for religion, and while the different kinds of practices are 'interconnected,' discursive and behavior-regulating practices are of a 'derivative' significance (Riesebrodt 2010, 86). Here we find a similar hierarchical structure as with Lincoln, but with an interesting inversion of emphasis, leading to different foundational theories: for Lincoln, discourse is central and practices derive from discursive claims; whereas for Riesebrodt discourse derives its authority from practices that establish connections with the superhuman.

The Distinctiveness of Religion

Most contemporary scholars of religion reject the idea that religion is a *sui generis* entity, i.e. an isolated thing set apart, following its own rules and unexplainable in non-religious terms. Debates over this inflated notion of distinctiveness should not overshadow the question whether and how religion can be distinguished from other phenomena—as many people the world over habitually distinguish religion from other domains such as economy, politics, etc. One question is whether it is sufficient that this distinction is made by the theorist or whether this distinctiveness must be articulated by the respective data or people concerned. While concepts of 'holy' or 'sacred' served to anchor the distinctiveness of religion in some earlier theories (and continue to do so in the psychology of religion [e.g. Pargament/Magyar-Russell/Murray-Swank 2005]) several contemporary theories refer to notions of the superhuman, the supernatural, the non-empirical, the transcendent, absolute authoritativeness, immunity from falsification, etc. as the distinctive features and factors. While some theories treat the existence of these notions as given, others—such as cognitive theories—seek to explain their emergence, thus leading to the question of origins. Like most theories in the humanities

---

[3] Even on this point Atran tends to leave a purely fractionated account behind when he states (2002, 267): "it should be patent that supernatural agency is the principal conceptual go-between and main watershed in our evolutionary landscape." This would imply that supernatural agency (on which see Pyysiäinen 2009) is the main factor of religion.

and social sciences, cognitive theories explain notions of the supernatural, etc. as human creations or products of psychological processes. This anthropocentric ontology is questioned by theories that remain open towards or even affirm the existence of the meta-human. Gavin Flood, for example, claims "There is a reality that human beings encounter which shows itself to us through religion" (2012, 15).

Origins of Religion

The question of the origin(s) of religion should not be confused with that of its beginning(s). Both questions are informed by one's concept, definition, and views of the ontology, structure, and distinctiveness of religion. Is myth a dimension of religion or an independent mental structure? Depending on one's position, the putative emergence of mythic culture (Donald 2001) would have implications for the putative beginnings of religion. If one follows Rappaport's (1999) speculations that religion is ultimately grounded in the structure of human language and communication, then religion's beginnings would be identical with the dawn of human language. Sociologist Robert Bellah (2011) grounds religion in the human capacity for play and inscribes the emergence of religion into the deep history of the earth and humanity. So far, there is neither a robust debate nor a consensus concerning the beginnings of religion, probably because the question is to some extent circular and speculative, and because it involves the study of prehistory, a period investigated by few scholars of religion. Another take on the issue is to insist on the modern beginning of religion as a global system: even if religions may have antedated globalized society, religion as a globalized function system, which we take as a self-evident category, may have only emerged in conjunction with the establishment of a globalized society (Beyer 2006).

One source for the origin of religion that is referred to by several theories is human meaning-making. This is a theme that runs across different disciplines; it is central in Weberian, Mannheimian, and Cassirerian traditions in sociology and philosophy, and plays a prominent place in the late-classical theories of religion (Geertz 1973 [1966]; Berger 1967). It continues to be a major theoretical anchor for theories of religion in the psychology of religion (Park 2013), among anthropologists of religion (Droogers/ van Harskamp 2014), and scholars of religion (Jensen 2014). Meaning is addressed not only as a human capacity (Bellah 2011), but also in terms of a stipulated human need. In a phrasing that could seem to echo Mircea Eliade, Gavin Flood speaks of the "human quest for meaning," to which he adds "an impulse towards transcendence" (Flood 2012, 17). Religion, on the other hand, is assumed to provide such meaning, for example by locating human "within an ordered cosmos" (Flood 2012, 55). In a very strong sense, Flood (2012, 27) claims: "Religions bestow meaning for human communities not as illusions—although they do that too—but because they access the ontological referent that gives rise to those meanings." This can be read as an assumption of the reality of the transcendent. It is difficult to see how such a claim could be argued. Identifying human needs is part of a debate on human nature, but when speaking of meaning in language and communication, semantics and semiotics are central (see Gardiner/ Engler, "Semantics," and Yelle, "Semiotics," this volume). No theorist claims that religion is the exclusive domain of human meaning-making, but that it is one extreme form of it. While religion appears as one variety of meaning-making, some cognitive theories of religion (e.g. Boyer 2001; Pyysiäinen 2003; Atran 2002; Norenzayan 2013), which ground the origin of religions in cognitive and affective processes and systems, navigate beyond the level of explicit meaning; they seek to explain the evolutionary effectiveness of representations and practices by appealing to a variety of psychological processes, which mostly operate subconsciously. This reflects different theories of culture and human nature.

Another set of contemporary theories of religion seek to explain the origin of religion in structures of cognition and processes of evolution. E. Thomas Lawson and Robert McCauley (1990), a scholar of religion and a philosopher respectively, consider the structure of religious-ritual systems as determined by cognitive competence for the representation of action (see Engler/Gardiner in Stausberg 2009b). For anthropologist Stewart Guthrie (1993), religion results from humans' cognitive proclivity to represent the world as animated and humanlike (see Saler in Stausberg 2009b). Anthropologist Pascal Boyer (2001) and scholar of religion Ilkka Pyysiäinen (2003) explain religions as unintended by-products of brain functions that can help to solve challenges faced by humanity (see Jensen in Stausberg 2009b). Similarly, anthropologist Scott Atran (2002) theorizes religion on the basis of humanity's evolutionary landscape (see Bulbulia in Stausberg 2009b).

Functions of Religion

The functionality of religion and its constituent parts—or the lack thereof—is an important theme in many theories of religion. From this perspective, religion is not the primary target (theoretical object) of theories of religion; rather religion is held to exemplify, identify, or resolve certain problems. Explanations of society in general or modern society in particular sometimes draw on religion in a dialectical manner, where religion is necessary for society and can be explained in terms of its function for society.

This sort of discussion of 'functions' has generally taken shape within, and over against, functionalist theories. In this context, it is important to distinguish between effects and functions. An effect is a state of affairs caused by some other. A function is an effect that contributes to a larger system. 'Function' is teleological; 'effect' may or may not be. Only some effects are functional: pumping blood and making noise are two effects of the heart, but only the first of these is a function.

Functionalism—in its sociological and anthropological variants—was rooted in the nineteenth-century analogy of society-as-organism. Two conceptual elements were central: an analysis of the parts of society—or religion—and their relation to the whole; and an implicit teleology, in which the 'function' of the parts is to maintain the stability of, or contribute to the evolution of, the whole. The most common functionalist claim about religion has been that it contributes to social cohesion by creating and strength-ening interpersonal bonds, for example in Durkheim (though his work is not entirely functionalist).

Although generally considered to have been discredited as a theoretical perspective, functionalism continues to have current and potential relevance for the study of religion (Stausberg 2010, 234–236). Functionalist accounts of religion are sometimes champi-oned by non-scholars of religion in their writing on religion. The noted polymath Jared Diamond, for instance, proposes a list of seven 'functions' of religion (supernatural explanation; defusing anxiety; providing comfort about pains and death; standardized organization; preaching political obedience; moral codes of behavior towards strangers; justification of wars); Diamond claims that these functions changed as religion 'evolved' (Diamond 2012, 323–368).

Carl Hempel's 1959 critique of functional explanations set the terms of subsequent debates (1994). To simplify, Hempel argued that functionalist claims are invalid because they commit the logical fallacy of affirming the consequent. That is, functionalist claims move backwards from observing an effect—e.g. social stability—to claiming that one particular thing—e.g. religion—is its cause. This ignores the possibility that something else might have caused that particular effect. However, as Robert Segal (2010) notes, this problem can potentially be avoided if we draw on discussions of functionalism that move beyond the narrow terms of the debate as set by Hempel. Segal suggests that—instead of arguments that position religion as the sole cause of certain effects, i.e. those that fulfill certain functions or needs—religion should be placed in a different sort of context, a functional context that examines the effects of religion as part of a larger sys-tem, taking into account the effects of comparable institutions: "One would not be con-sidering religion as serving any need, be it an original need or a present need, let alone a distinctively religious need. Religion would be seen as doing something that it can do only because, however it got there, it is now part of a system far bigger than itself" (Segal 2010, 352). The function of religion is thus decoupled from its putative origins.

Communication is another function of religion prominent in functionalist theories. Roy Rappaport's analysis of religious ritual—or of religion *qua* ritual—also empha-sized the social function of communication: "In enunciating, accepting and making conventions moral, ritual contains within itself not simply a symbolic representation of social contract, but tacit social contract itself. As such, ritual . . . is *the* basic social act" (Rappaport 1999, 138; see Segal in Stausberg 2009b). Niklas Luhmann viewed reli-gion as a functionally differentiated subsystem of society, the specific function of which, as a form of communication, is to maintain the conditions of communication itself. It does so by managing the distinction between the observable and unobservable, between immanence and transcendence (Luhmann 2013 [2000]; see Krech, "Communication," this volume). For Luhmann "religion grounds the ultimate indeterminability of all meaning; it absorbs the risk of failure inherent in all social representations and determi-nations" (Beyer in Stausberg 2009b, 99).

Evolutionary theories of religion echo functionalist views in their assessment of the adaptivity of religion, especially by framing religion as an evolved adaptation with positive benefits to individuals and groups (though others argue that it is a by-product): e.g. religions function to limit individualistic and to further altruistic actions; the costliness of membership and participation in rituals functions to increase commitment and to decrease free-riders (see Shaver/Purzycki/Sosis, "Evolutionary Theory," this volume). For biologist David Sloan Wilson (2002), religion is considered as explaining the emergence of human cooperation, where human groups are understood as evolutionary superorganisms (see Bulbulia/Frean in Stausberg 2009b). Even though he does not aim to present a new theory of religion, psychologist Ara Norenzayan (2013) is among those who find one variety of religion to have played a key role in the evolution of human prosociality.[4] Of course prosocial behavior is not preselected: selections that turn out to have a recurrent functional effect are generally termed adaptations.

META-THEORY

Meta-theory addresses such issues as the nature, scope, roles, goals, and functions of theory in academic work. This chapter as a whole is meta-theoretical: it is *about* theories of religion. To conclude, we will address two meta-theoretical issues: the motivation for building or using theory; and the assessment of theories.

Do We Need Theories of Religion?

Advocating a pragmatic turn in the study of religion\s, G. Scott Davis has recently dismissed the practice of and need for theory.[5] As his critics point out (e.g. Hart 2012, 144), Davis's notion of theory is particularly narrow. Davis himself indicates that his model of theory is that of some natural sciences (2012, 2). For him, theory is only applicable to "objects and events in the natural world"; and theories are "preferably couched in mathematical form" (2012, 2). Few scholars of religion would hold such a narrow sense of theory. Pointing to the example of Tweed (2006), Davis claims: "What masquerades as theory is almost always . . . reflection on scholarly practice wrapped up in pithy metaphor. Debates about theory, at least in the study of religion\s, have typically been contests to lay bare the presuppositions that have informed one or another scholar's professional practice" (Davis 2012, 20). This is, of course, one of the functions of theory, defined more broadly. Davis suggests the following alternative to theory: "understanding religion requires nothing more than the sensitive and imaginative reading of human phenomena

---

[4] *Big Gods* was discussed in review symposia published in *Religion* 44(4) (2014) and *Religion, Brain & Behavior* (2015).

[5] The title of the chapter—"Believing and Acting: The Allure of Method in the Study of Religion"—exemplifies a widespread confusion between 'method' and 'theory' in our discipline (Davis 2012, 1).

informed by the best available ethnography set in the best available historical narrative" (2012, 3). Probably, this is an idea shared by many practitioners in the field.

Setting aside the philosophically motivated narrowness of Davis's definition of 'theory,' he in effect advocates the status quo in the academic practice of the discipline as he points to ethnography and history as paths to 'understanding' religion. Most scholars of religion study one religion, one period, or one region either ethnographically or historically, and some in both ways. For Davis, theory distracts, and methodology counts: it is not the 'best available' theory that promises to help us understand religion, but the best available use of established methods. It is exceedingly rare that a scholar who has worked empirically (e.g. ethnographically, historically, etc.) dares to take a broader stance by either extrapolating a theory of religion from her/his empirical case, or by putting one's case in a broader comparative context in order to build a theory of religion. Instead, theories are mostly advanced by scholars working in disciplines that have stronger traditions of generalization. The reluctance to engage in active theory building may be understandable, but at the same time scholars draw on general theories of religion at some point or another in teaching or research, though with a bias in favor of the classical ones. Grand theory is in demand because it provides a view on the forest, whereas scholars of religion tend to concern themselves with trees. It is helpful to realize that they form part of the same landscape—theory providing the constitutive interconnectivity that makes an observer recognize the similarity across family members. This is perhaps why new theories of religion—at least when they are launched by scholars with a sound record of empirical work—tend to attract attention. Tweed's *Crossing and Dwelling* (2006), for example, is his most often cited publication, Vásquez's *More than Belief* (2011) was discussed extensively in specialist journals (see note 2), and Bellah's *Religion in Human Evolution* (2011) was discussed widely in academic and popular journals (see Stausberg 2014).

Levels of Theory

Different disciplines and subdisciplines have customs—and individual scholars have habits—regarding the definition of 'theory.' 'Middle-range theories' are especially prominent in the study of religion\s: i.e. "theories that lie between the minor but necessary working hypotheses that evolve in abundance during day-to-day research and the all-inclusive systematic efforts to develop a unified theory that will explain all the observed uniformities" of those phenomena considered relevant to a given discipline (Merton 1967 [1949]: 39). Of course, even very broad theories can be nested within higher-level 'super-theories,' or within broad meta-theoretical positions. Evolutionary theory is the most influential theory of this sort in the natural, social, and human sciences today.

Theoretical work is not limited to the highly abstract level of fully-developed theories of religion. Categorizing and re-describing one's empirical materials, seeking correlations, defining terms, using categories and concepts to compare cases, elaborating models and general propositions, all these and many other aspects of the research process are acts of theorizing—modes of theoretical work—even if they are not cases of working with 'a theory.' Most theorizing of religion occurs below the level of abstraction of full-fledged theories of religion.

This perspective helps us to avoid the error of imagining that theory is some abstract, autonomous zone that stands apart from—or that floats freely above, as if transcending—the distinct zone of 'facts' or 'data.' It makes sense to contrast theory and data in a relative sense: e.g. insofar as theory addresses conceptual relations beyond the boundaries of a single instance of data, or in the sense that theory can be 'applied' to data. However, there is no qualitative abyss separating data and theory. Data are always already theory-laden. To give an obvious example, the data that scholars of religion choose to work with must somehow already have been identified as religious, but this presupposes a theoretical stance on the nature and scope of 'religion.' Even when not constructing theories of religion, scholars operate with implicit theories of religion. It is a mistake to think that data are simply brute facts of reality that can be directly observed. Such a view would reflect a naïve realist ontology and an anachronistic positivist view of science, both of which are untenable given the last seventy years of work on knowledge, language, meaning, science, etc. Minimally, after the linguistic turn and the demise of positivism, there is a scholarly consensus that there is no such thing as direct, unfiltered, unmediated access to reality.

Theory does not begin where data end: the two are always interwoven. Theory is always already present: it is there when any single fact, observation, event, or incident is linked in any way to any other; it is there when that first, single fact is selected out *as data*, as fodder for a given scholarly process or goal, as worthy of methodological interest. Theory, in this light, is what motivates data-collection and analysis. An 'undertheorized' case is one that takes its relevance for granted.

The entanglement of data and theory implies that theory is an inescapable element of all research. Theory is not limited to the 'theory' sections of publications. It is implicit in the treatment of empirical materials as data, as objects of study. It informs the concepts that are used (or not used) to make the data speak. It constitutes and is constituted by the relations between the concepts and categories that we use to 'make sense' of religious phenomena.

Assessing Theories

The success of a theory depends on what we think it should do. Theories that aim at explanation will be assessed more for accuracy and truthfulness, and theories that aim at interpretation will be assessed more in terms of the pragmatic value of their results in a given context. Of course, this difference is relative. There are several families or types of theories in the human and social sciences, with different histories and goals, and with distinct conceptual and normative commitments (Abend 2008; Mjøset 2012).

A basic issue determining the goal of theory, and hence how it should be assessed, is the place of theory in the research design of a given project: e.g. would it be more effective for theory to be built up from cumulative conceptual work with empirical materials, as in grounded theory, or to be brought in after the empirical materials are collected and ordered, as a sort of interpretative frame? All theories raise general evaluative issues such as the salience of the phenomena conceptualized (e.g. in relation to established problems in the relevant literature), the relative coherence and completeness of the set of concepts informing the analysis, and interrelations between theory, data, and methods. At this level, criteria used to assess theories overlap with those used to assess methods (Stausberg/Engler 2011, 7–11). More specifically, theories can be assessed relative to a variety of 'theoretical virtues': internal validity (their well-formedness as a theory of their particular type), external validity (generalizability to other cases, again varying between types of theory), breadth (subsuming and relating a large number of phenomena), non-counterintuitiveness (harmony with established theories and perspectives), correctness of implications (e.g. successful prediction in the natural sciences or doctrinal acceptability in theology), and fruitfulness (pragmatic results).

Assessing theories (our topic here) differs from assessing a given use of a given theory. The latter would raise more contextualized questions, e.g. the competence of a given analysis. On a related note, researchers sometimes make the mistake of concluding that a theory is 'falsified' by the fact that it does not fit or resonate with their particular case or data. This falls into the trap of universalizing 'theory,' as if only one true theoretical perspective can exist. Different theories of different types play different roles in relation to a specific constellation of theory, methods, and data, and they must be assessed in that context. A mismatch between a given theory and one's methods and data is a problem with that match, not with the theory.

Discussions about the value of theories have a social and political dimension: "the reception, survival and diffusion of intellectual products—whether as research programmes, theories, concepts or propositions—depends not just on the intrinsic quality of the arguments proposed or the strength of the evidence provided, but also on the range of rhetorical devices which the authors employ to locate themselves (and position others) within the intellectual and political field" (Baert 2012, 304). As discussed here, assessing theories involves rigorous, formal evaluation, as opposed to facile labeling, which often plays a tactical role in rhetorical positioning and struggles for academic capital. The use of superficial criteria devoid of specific assessment—e.g. new vs. old, 'cutting-edge' vs. 'run-of-the-mill,' philosophical vs. common sense—cuts both ways and generally tells us more about the self-perceptions of critics than about the theories that they critique.

Conclusion

There will never be a completely satisfying theory of religion. But 'theory of religion' can remain a regulative idea for the study of religion\s as a discipline, informing a collective recognition that it would be desirable and possible if not to ultimately decode at least to throw light on the fundamental themes of theories of religion: What kind of a thing is religion? How does it work and what kind of work does it do? Why does it work as it does? How does it hang together? How does it originate and develop? Even if one has no answer to such questions, they linger in the background of scholars' work—theories of religion bring out this implicit preoccupation.

GLOSSARY

Data discrete bits of qualitative or quantitative information or knowledge; the 'raw materials' that are collected, measured, compared, ordered, analyzed, etc. during the process of generating scholarly knowledge. Data are not necessarily empirical in a narrow sense: e.g. concepts and theories can serve as data for higher level conceptualizing and theorizing.

Meta-theory theory about theory—and issues of conceptualization more generally—addressing such issues as the nature, scope, roles, goals, and functions of theory in academic work.

Methods ways of collecting, organizing, and analyzing data.

Theory an interconnected set of ideas or statements (propositions) expressed in language that, from within a certain discursive placement and from a given point of view (which implies certain contexts, interests, and values), frames cognitive claims about some phenomenon.

REFERENCES

Abend, Gabriel. 2008. "The Meaning of 'Theory.'" *Sociological Theory* 26(2): 173–199. doi: 10.1111/j.1467-9558.2008.00324.x

Arnal, William. 2000. "Definition." In *Guide to the Study of Religion*, edited by Willi Braun and Russell T. McCutcheon. London and New York: Cassell, 21–34.

Atran, Scott. 2002. *In Gods We Trust: The Evolutionary Landscape of Religion*. New York: Oxford University Press.

Baert, Patrick. 2012. "Positioning Theory and Intellectual Interventions." *Journal for the Theory of Social Behaviour* 42(3): 304–324. doi: 0.1111/j.1468-5914.2012.00492.x

Bellah, Robert N. 2011. *Religion in Human Evolution: From the Paleolithic to the Axial Age*. Cambridge, MA: Harvard University Press.

Benavides, Gustavo. 1998. "Modernity." In *Critical Terms for Religious Studies*, edited by Mark C. Taylor. Chicago, IL: University of Chicago Press, 186–204.

Berger, Peter L. 1967. *The Sacred Canopy: Elements of a Sociological Theory of Religion*. New York: Anchor Books.

Bergunder, Michael. 2014. "What Is Religion?" *Method & Theory in the Study of Religion* 26(3): 246–286. doi: doi:10.1163/15700682-12341320

Beyer, Peter. 2006. *Religions in a Global Society*. London and New York: Routledge.

Boyer, Pascal. 2001. *Religion Explained: The Evolutionary Origins of Religious Thought*. New York: Basic Books.

Boyer, Pascal. 2010. *The Fracture of an Illusion: Science and the Dissolution of Religion*. Göttingen: Vandenhoeck & Ruprecht.

Burkert, Walter. 1996. *Creation of the Sacred: Tracks of Biology in Early Religions*. Cambridge, MA and London: Harvard University Press.

Casadio, Giovanni. 2010. "Religio versus Religion." In *Myths, Martyrs, and Modernity: Studies in the History of Religions in Honour of Jan N. Bremmer*, edited by Jitse Dijkstra, Justin Kroesen, and Yme Kuiper. Leiden: Brill, 301–326.

Cornwall, Marie, Stan L. Albrecht, Perry H. Cunningham, and Brian L. Pitcher. 1986. "The Dimensions of Religiosity: A Conceptual Model with an Empirical Test." *Review of Religious Research* 27(3): 226–244. doi: 10.2307/3511418

Davis, G. Scott. 2012. *Believing and Acting: The Pragmatic Turn in Comparative Religion and Ethics*. Oxford: Oxford University Press.

Despland, Michel. 1979. *La religion en occident: évolution des idées et du vécu*. Montreal: Fides.

Diamond, Jared. 2012. *The World until Yesterday: What Can We Learn from Traditional Societies?* London: Allen Lane.

Donald, Merlin. 2001. *A Mind So Rare: The Evolution of Human Consciousness*. New York: Norton.

Droogers, André and Anton van Harskamp, eds. 2014. *Methods for the Study of Religious Change: From Religious Studies to Worldview Studies*. Sheffield and Bristol, CT: Equinox Publishing.

Durkheim, Émile. 1912. *Les formes élémentaires de la vie religieuse: Le système totémique en Australie*. Paris: F. Alcan.

Feil, Ernst. 1986–2007. *Religio: Die Geschichte eines neuzeitlichen Grundbegriffs*. 4 vols. Göttingen: Vandenhoeck & Ruprecht.

Fitzgerald, Timothy. 2007. *Discourse on Civility and Barbarity: A Critical History of Religion and Related Categories*. New York and Oxford: Oxford University Press.

Flood, Gavin D. 2012. *The Importance of Religion: Meaning and Action in Our Strange World*. Malden, MA: Wiley-Blackwell.

Geertz, Clifford. 1973. "Religion as a Cultural System." In *The Interpretation of Cultures*. New York: Basic Books, 87–125. Original edition, 1966.

Glock, Charles Y. 1962. "On the Study of Religious Commitment." *Religious Education* 57(suppl. 4): 98–110. doi: 10.1080/003440862057S407

Glock, Charles Y. and Rodney Stark. 1965. *Religion and Society in Tension*. Chicago, IL: Rand McNally.

Guthrie, Stewart E. 1993. *Faces in the Clouds: A New Theory of Religion*. Oxford: Oxford University Press.

Hall, Daniel E., Keith G. Meador, and Harold G. Koenig. 2008. "Measuring Religiousness in Health Research: Review and Critique." *Journal of Religion and Health* 47(2): 134–163. doi: 10.1007/s10943-008-9165-2

Hart, William David. 2012. "What is Theory?" *Soundings* 95(2): 141–148. doi: 10.1353/sij.2012.0015

Hempel, Carl G. 1994. "The Logic of Functional Analysis." In *Readings in the Philosophy of Social Science*, edited by Michael Martin and Lee C. McIntyre. Cambridge, MA and London: MIT Press, 349–375. Original edition, 1959.

Hermann, Adrian. 2015. *Unterscheidungen der Religion: Analysen zum globalen Religionsdiskurs und dem Problem der Differenzierung von 'Religion' in buddhistischen Kontexten des 19. und frühen 20. Jahrhunderts*. Göttingen: Vandenhoeck & Ruprecht.

Jensen, Jeppe Sinding. 2014. *What Is Religion?* Durham: Acumen.

King, Morton. 1967. "Measuring the Religious Variable: Nine Proposed Dimensions." *Journal for the Scientific Study of Religion* 6(2): 173–190. doi: 10.2307/1384044

Kippenberg, Hans G. 2001. *Discovering Religious History in the Modern Age*. Translated by Barbara Harshav. Princeton, NJ: Princeton University Press. Original edition, 1997.

Koenig, Harold G. 2011. *Spirituality & Health Research: Methods, Measurement, Statistics, and Resources*. West Conshohocken, PA: Templeton Press.

Lawson, E. Thomas and Robert N. McCauley. 1990. *Rethinking Religion: Connecting Cognition and Culture*. Cambridge: Cambridge University Press.

Lincoln, Bruce. 2003. *Holy Terrors: Thinking About Religion after September 11*. Chicago, IL and London: University of Chicago Press.

Luhmann, Niklas. 2013. *A Systems Theory of Religion*, translated by David A. Brenner and Adrian Hermann. Stanford, CA: Stanford University Press. Original edition, 2000.

Merton, Robert K. 1967. *Social Theory and Social Structure*, 3rd edition. New York: Free Press. Original edition, 1949.

Mjøset, Lars. 2012. "Many Notions of Theory—Too Few Methodologies to Deal with Them." In *The Role of Theory in Educational Research*, edited by Kirsti Klette. Oslo: The Research Council of Norway, 17–25. <http://is.gd/eUzo4r>.

Nongbri, Brent. 2013. *Before Religion: A History of a Modern Concept*. New Haven, CT: Yale University Press.

Norenzayan, Ara. 2013. *Big Gods: How Religion Transformed Cooperation and Conflict*. Princeton, NJ: Princeton University Press.

Pargament, Kenneth I., Gina M. Magyar-Russell, and Nichole A. Murray-Swank. 2005. "The Sacred and the Search for Significance: Religion as a Unique Process." *Journal of Social Issues* 61(4): 665–687. doi: 10.1111/j.1540-4560.2005.00426.x

Park, Crystal L. 2013. "Religion and Meaning." In *Handbook of the Psychology of Religion and Spirituality*, edited by Raymond F. Paloutzian and Crystal L. Park. New York and London: Guilford Press, 357–379.

Pyysiäinen, Ilkka. 2003. *How Religion Works: Towards a New Cognitive Science of Religion*. Leiden: Brill.

Pyysiäinen, Ilkka. 2009. *Supernatural Agents: Why We Believe in Souls, Gods, and Buddhas*. Oxford: Oxford University Press.

Rappaport, Roy A. 1999. *Ritual and Religion in the Making of Humanity*. Cambridge: Cambridge University Press.

Riesebrodt, Martin. 2010. *The Promise of Salvation: A Theory of Religion*. Chicago, IL and London: University of Chicago Press. Original edition, 2007.

Schilbrack, Kevin. 2014. *Philosophy and the Study of Religions: A Manifesto*. Chichester: Wiley-Blackwell.

Segal, Robert A. 2010. "Functionalism since Hempel." *Method and Theory in the Study of Religion* 22(4): 340–353. doi: 10.1163/157006810X531120

Smart, Ninian. 1996. *Dimensions of the Sacred: An Anatomy of the World's Beliefs*. London: HarperCollins.

Smith, Jonathan Z. 1998. "Religion, Religions, Religious." In *Critical Terms for Religious Studies*, edited by Mark C. Taylor. Chicago, IL and London: University of Chicago Press, 269–284.

Stark, Rodney and William Sims Bainbridge. 1987. *A Theory of Religion*. New York: Peter Lang.

Stark, Rodney and Roger Finke. 2000. *Acts of Faith: Explaining the Human Side of Religion*. Berkeley, CA: University of California Press.

Stark, Rodney and Charles Y. Glock. 1968. *American Piety: The Nature of Religious Commitment*. Berkeley, CA: University of California Press.

Stausberg, Michael. 2009a. "There is Life in the Old Dog Yet: An Introduction to Contemporary Theories of Religion." In *Contemporary Theories of Religion: A Critical Companion*, edited by Michael Stausberg. London and New York: Routledge, 1–21.

Stausberg, Michael, ed. 2009b. *Contemporary Theories of Religion: A Critical Companion*. London and New York: Routledge.

Stausberg, Michael. 2010. "Prospects in Theories of Religion." *Method and Theory in the Study of Religion* 22(4): 223–238. doi: 10.1163/157006810X531021

Stausberg, Michael. 2014. "Bellah's *Religion in Human Evolution*: A Post-Review." *Numen* 61(2–3): 281–299. doi:10.1163/15685276-12341320

Stausberg, Michael and Steven Engler. 2011. "Introduction." In *The Routledge Handbook of Research Methods in the Study of Religion*, edited by Michael Stausberg and Steven Engler. London and New York: Routledge, 3–20.

Taves, Ann. 2009. *Religious Experience Reconsidered: A Building-Block Approach to the Study of Religion and Other Special Things*. Princeton, NJ: Princeton University Press.

Taves, Ann. 2013. "Building Blocks of Sacralities." In *Handbook of the Psychology of Religion and Spirituality*, edited by Raymond F. Paloutzian and Crystal L. Park. New York and London: Guilford Press, 138–161.

Taylor, Charles. 2007. *A Secular Age*. Cambridge, MA and London: Belknap Press of Harvard University Press.

Tweed, Thomas A. 2006. *Crossing and Dwelling: A Theory of Religion*. Cambridge, MA: Harvard University Press.

Vásquez, Manuel A. 2011. *More Than Belief: A Materialist Theory of Religion*. Oxford and New York: Oxford University Press.

Vásquez, Manuel A. 2012. "On the Value of Genealogy, Materiality, and Networks: A Response." *Religion* 42(4): 649–670. doi: 10.1080/0048721X.2012.721289

Whitehouse, Harvey. 2008. "Cognitive Evolution and Religion: Cognition and Religious Evolution." *Issues in Ethnology and Anthropology* n.s. 13(3): 35–47.

Whitehouse, Harvey and Jonathan A. Lanman. 2014. "The Ties That Bind Us: Ritual, Fusion, and Identification." *Current Anthropology* 55(6): 674–695. doi: 10.1086/678698

Wiebe, Donald. 1983. "Theory in the Study of Religion." *Religion* 13(4): 283–309.

Wilson, David Sloan. 2002. *Darwin's Cathedral: Evolution, Religion, and the Nature of Society*. Chicago, IL: University of Chicago Press.

FURTHER READING

Stausberg 2009b [*A collection of summaries and critical assessments of seventeen recent theories of religion.*]

Vásquez 2011 [*A genealogical overview of a wide variety of relevant theories—cumulatively making a case for greater emphasis on embodiment, practices, and emplacement within a proposed non-reductive materialist framework for the study of religion\s.*]

Wiebe 1983 [*A critical assessment of the place of 'theory' in the study of religion.*]

....

CHAPTER 4

RELIGION AND SPIRITUALITY

....

HEINZ STREIB AND CONSTANTIN KLEIN

Chapter Summary

- An enormous change in the religio-semantic field has occurred, by which 'spirituality' has emerged as a serious competitor for 'religion.'
- This geological fault in the religio-semantic field has taken place in a relatively short time, as illustrated here by recent survey data.
- Results regarding the semantics of spirituality are detailed in ten components, characterizing a variety of meanings.
- We conclude with the discussion of whether spirituality should be a concept in the scientific study of religion.
- It is our thesis that, while spirituality should not be established as scientific concept (to compete with or replace 'religion'), spirituality as self-attribution needs to be studied.

Spiritual Self-Identification as Reflected in Surveys

Many empirical findings support the growing popularity of the term 'spirituality' and of speaking of oneself as 'spiritual' (Utsch/Klein 2011). The semantics of spirituality appears to have found its most fertile soil in the United States. As presented in Table 4.1, the General Social Survey (GSS 1972–2012) documents for the year 2012 that 30.1 percent of the respondents self-identify as 'very spiritual' and 38.0 percent as 'moderately spiritual,' while only 10.5 percent indicate that they are 'not spiritual.' Thus a clear majority of two out of three US-Americans self-identify as moderately or very spiritual.

Table 4.1 Spiritual and religious self–identification in the United States (GSS 2012)

	Not religious	Slightly religious	Moderately religious	Very religious	Sum
Not spiritual	7.4%	2.1%	0.8%	0.2%	10.5%
Slightly spiritual	4.8%	11.1%	5.2%	0.3%	21.5%
Moderately spiritual	4.2%	6.0%	24.5%	3.2%	38.0%
Very spiritual	3.2%	2.7%	9.5%	14.6%	30.1%
Sum	19.7%	21.9%	40.1%	18.3%	100.0%

Note: Cross-tabulation based on *n* = 1,920 respondents.

Credit: "Investigating 'Spirituality': Between Survey Data and the Study of Biographies." In *Semantics and Psychology of Spirituality: A Cross-Cultural Analysis*, edited by Heinz Streib and Ralph W. Hood. Cham, Heidelberg, New York, Dordrecht, and London: Springer International Publishing Switzerland. © Springer International Publishing Switzerland, 2016, p. 28. With permission of Springer.

Noteworthy are the proportions between 'religion' and 'spirituality.' The number of the 'not religious' (19.7 percent) is almost twice the number of the 'not spiritual' (10.5 percent) respondents, while the number of the 'very spiritual' (30.1 percent) is considerably higher than that of the 'very religious' (18.3 percent).

The table also allows for an estimation of preferences of spirituality over religion or the other way round: over half of the US-Americans (57.6 percent) assemble in the diagonal cells, where ratings on both scales are equal; thus about 40 percent can be regarded 'equally religious and spiritual.' Correspondingly, self-rated spirituality and religion are statistically highly correlated ($r = 0.57$). However, almost a third of the US-American respondents (30.4 percent) assemble in the lighter cells below the diagonal and thus can be identified as 'more spiritual than religious,' 10.1 percent as 'clearly more spiritual than religious' (rating difference ≥ 2), while only 11.8 percent are 'more religious than spiritual' and 1.3 percent 'clearly more religious than spiritual.' Taken together, a vast majority of US-Americans self-identify as 'spiritual' ('equally' or 'more' than they self-identify as 'religious'), and the number of US-Americans who prefer 'spirituality' over 'religion' is by far greater than the number of 'more religious' or 'exclusively religious.'

For Germany, to take one European example, all of these proportions are reversed: according to the Allgemeine Bevölkerungsumfrage der Sozialwissenschaften (ALLBUS 2012), less than 6 percent self-rate as 'very spiritual,' while over 50 percent self-rate as 'not spiritual.' When half of the population can be estimated to reject 'spirituality' for themselves, there is not much room for the 'more spiritual than religious,' which amounts to 14.4 percent according to the ALLBUS; and the 'clearly more spiritual than religious' respondents are a minority of 6.3 percent in Germany.

We present these survey results to give examples of the diversity in the religious fields and the cross-cultural differences in regard to the new semantics of 'spirituality' as indicated by the most reliable data, namely self-ratings (for more details, see Streib/Klein/Hood 2016). Attending not only to single-item self-ratings, but working with a Latent Class Model, Siegers (2012) has profiled the value orientations of 'alternatively spiritual' persons using the data from the fourth wave (2008–2010) of the European Value Study. Siegers identified 'alternative spirituality' on the basis of seven questionnaire responses: church attendance = no; religious individualism = yes; spiritual interest = yes; image of God = impersonal; belief in reincarnation = yes; prayer/meditation = yes; importance of God = no. Siegers concludes that "alternative spiritualities are a relevant option in Europe, with large regional differences however" (2012, 320). According to his analyses, 'alternative spiritualties' are more frequent (between 10 percent and 15 percent) in the North and West of Europe, while less frequent in the Catholic countries in the South and Middle of Europe. Huber and Klein (2011), however, observed that people who self-identify as 'very spiritual' and as 'very religious' score significantly higher on meditation, impersonal image of God, and religious quest than persons who describe themselves as 'spiritual, but not religious.' Spirituality might thus become more visible in the religious field when expressed in terms of one's religiousness.

Investigating change toward 'spirituality' over time, Houtman and Aupers (2007) have completed an analysis in which they document a 'spiritual turn,' a 'spread of post-Christian spirituality,' in fourteen Western countries. Based on a selection of questions from the WVS data 1981–2000 regarding the image of God (personal God; some sort of spirit or life force; etc.), New Age affinity, disagreement with traditional Christian beliefs, but simultaneous disagreement with secular rationalism, Houtman and Aupers's analysis reveals that France, Great Britain, the Netherlands, Belgium, and Sweden most clearly reveal a pattern of decline of traditional values and religion. Their analysis demonstrates, for the religious fields in the United States and in Germany, a modest (United States) or recognizable (Germany) longitudinal increase of 'post-Christian spirituality' from 1980 to 2000. This interpretation has provoked critique (e.g. Popp-Baier 2009) and caused a lively discussion (Flere/Kirbis 2009a; 2009b; Houtman/Aupers/Heelas 2009).

Taken together, such survey results clearly demonstrate that, with 'spirituality,' a new semantic complementary term has emerged for 'religion'—albeit one with strong cross-cultural differences between Western countries such as the United States and Germany.[1] Survey results also indicate that this new semantic development may correspond to 'alternative' or 'post-Christian' spiritualities. On the other hand, many findings also show the clear overlap of 'spirituality' with traditional 'religion.' All in all, spirituality is a poorly defined construct, and no real consensus has been reached about how to operationalize

---

[1] The consideration and discussion of cross-cultural differences in 'spirituality' on a global scale is only beginning (see e.g. Susumu 2012) and rather difficult, because there is no consensus about how the US-American word 'spirituality' translates in other languages.

this in large-scale survey data. This raises the question what respondents may have in mind when self-identifying as spiritual.

SEMANTICS OF SPIRITUALITY

A series of studies have empirically investigated the contemporary semantics of spirituality (Zinnbauer et al. 1997; Walker/Pitts 1998; Greenwald/Harder 2003; Schlehofer/Omoto/Adelman 2008; Lindeman/Blomqvist/Takada 2012; la Cour/ Ausker/Hvidt 2012; Ammerman 2013; Berghuijs/Pieper/Bakker 2013). Thereby a variety of semantic components have been identified which are mirrored by our own results. Here we discuss current understandings of spirituality in a presentation of our own results.

The Bielefeld-based cross-cultural study of 'spirituality' (Streib/Hood 2016a) used many methods for the investigation of the semantics of spirituality: semantic differentials (Streib/Keller/Klein/Swhajor-Biesemann/Hood 2016), indirect measures (Klein/Hood/Silver/Keller/Streib 2016), free-text entries (Altmeyer/Klein 2016; Eisenmann/Klein 2016), and personal interviews (e.g. Keller/Wollert 2016). Here we present results from the analysis of the free-text entries in the questionnaire, in which 1,779 respondents from the United States and Germany gave their definitions of spirituality. A content-analytic procedure resulted in the assignment of forty-four categories; Principal Component Analysis was used to reduce dimensions to ten components (for more details, see Eisenmann/Klein 2016). Thus the following ten components for the semantics of 'spirituality' emerged from our sample:

1. *Connectedness and harmony with the universe, nature, and the whole.* Connectedness with others and universality is also reflected in Piedmont's (2001) concept of 'spiritual transcendence,' in Zinnbauer et al.'s (1997) 'feeling or experience of connectedness/relationship/oneness,' in Greenwald and Harder's (2003) 'loving connection to others,' and eventually in the experiences of introvertive and extrovertive unity described in Hood's (1975) theory of mysticism.

2. *Part of religion, or Christian beliefs.* The perception that spirituality is rooted in religion is expressed in this second component. It is a clear feature of vertical transcendence. In this semantic variant, spirituality is 'an expression of vital religiousness' (Koenig 2008). It reflects Greenwald and Harder's (2003) component 'religiosity/sacredness' and la Cour et al.'s (2012) 'integrated part of established religious life.'

3. *Search for (higher) self, meaning, inner peace, and enlightenment.* Our third component reflects a version of spirituality with an imprint of societal processes such as subjectivity and individualization. This component reflects Roof's (1993) 'highly active seekers' among the American Baby Boomers, as well as the 'subjective-life spirituality' identified by Heelas et al. (2005). More critically, la Cour et al. (2012) discovered 'selfishness and greediness' as a factor.

4. *Ethics: holding and everyday acting according to values and morality in relation to humanity.* Here spirituality is associated with the perceived value of leading a moral life. Ammerman (2013), in her study of people who associate with being spiritual, documents the obligation to practice higher ethical standards than those who are 'merely' or 'still' religious. Greenwald and Harder's (2003) factor 'self-effacing altruism' is also mirrored in this fourth component.

5. *Belief in higher power(s), higher beings (deities, gods).* This component of spirituality had already been discovered by Zinnbauer et al. (1997) to be the most typical category to describe the understanding of 'equally religious and spiritual' people. Similarly, Walker and Pitts (1998) found 'belief in a higher power' to be the most characteristic descriptor of both religion and spirituality.

6. *Intuition of something or some being(s) that are unspecified, but higher and beyond oneself.* The controversial 'fuzziness' of spirituality (Spilka 1993) seems to find its empirical reflection particularly in this component, where people refuse to further define the nature of the transcendent, but acknowledge its mere existence. This may be reflected in Greenwald and Harder's (2003) factor 'blissful transcendence.'

7. *Experience of truth, purpose, and wisdom beyond rational understanding.* This component reflects an understanding of spirituality as a resource of meaning, based for these respondents on a notion of 'higher,' non-rational truth, insight, and wisdom.

8. *Awareness of a non-material, invisible world and experience of supernatural energies and beings (spirits etc.).* This esoteric component is important for some of our respondents' understanding of spirituality. Similar to our results, la Cour et al. (2012) found 'New Age-ideology' to be one of six common understandings of spirituality. It is primarily this component for which the label 'New-Age spirituality' may be appropriate (Spilka 1993; Heelas et al. 2005; Heelas 2007; Granqvist/ Fransson/Hagekull 2009; Oman 2013; Beit-Hallahmi 2015a; 2015b).

9. *Opposition to religion, dogmatic rules, and traditions.* This component is mirrored by la Cour et al.'s (2012) factor 'vague striving, opposed to religion.' According to Zinnbauer and Pargament (2005), spirituality is often positively evaluated as subjective, experiential-based, dynamic, and functional, while religion is characterized as negative, objective, belief-based, and static. This component is clearly opposed to Component 2 and also to Component 10—and it demonstrates the extreme variety of the semantics of 'spirituality' that includes even contradictory understandings.

10. *Individual religious praxis, meditation, prayer, worship.* This component builds on the characterization of spirituality as 'experiential-based' (Zinnbauer/Pargament 2005); it also may express respondents' understanding of spirituality as a kind of 'lived religion,' as 'doing religion' opposed to mere consent to a system of beliefs.

SPIRITUALITY AS SCIENTIFIC CONCEPT?

How did—how should—the scientific study of religion react to this enormous change in the religio-semantic field? The integration of spirituality as scientific concept, as it stands to date, appears to be rather inconsistent across scientific disciplines and countries: e.g. European-based scholars of religion are reluctant to welcome such inclusion, yet spirituality is popular in the United States, especially in the psychology of religion. Examples are abundant: the number of publications in the psychology of religion with 'spirituality' in the title increased 39-fold between 1970 and 2005 (Oman 2013); the APA Division 36 'Psychology of Religion' has been renamed the 'Society for the Psychology of Religion and Spirituality' and the Division's journal is *Psychology of Religion and Spirituality*; the latest handbooks in the psychology of religion (Paloutzian/Park 2013; Pargament 2013) announce in their titles that they are about both 'religion' *and* 'spirituality.'

In contrast to the attraction for the new semantic fashion in academic discourse in the United States, the thoughtfully conceptual integration of spirituality appears to be an unfinished project. This can be seen, for example, in the *Handbook of the Psychology of Religion and Spirituality*, edited by Paloutzian and Park (2013), for which a critical scholar of religion observes that the thematic focus of the single chapters is not coherent—and, more severely, many chapters "fail to provide either conceptual clarity on the distinction between the two concepts or sufficient detail to make conceptual choices comprehensible" (Stausberg 2014, 37).

For the people on the street, spirituality, as an emic term, is not fuzzy, but is characterized by a variety of different semantic associations, as noted earlier (see also Hood/Streib 2016). But there is still considerable fuzziness in regard to the conceptualization of spirituality as an etic term. In the early times of the new spirituality discourse, some criticized the fuzziness of the term (Spilka 1993) but nevertheless identified spirituality—depreciatingly—as 'New Age religion' (Hood/Spilka/Hunsberger/Gorsuch 1996, 116) and as mainly a phenomenon of the 'baby boomer' generation. Interestingly, both critical (Spilka 1993; Granqvist et al. 2009; Beit-Hallahmi 2015b) and sympathetic observers (Heelas et al. 2005; Heelas 2007) likewise associate 'New Age' and spirituality. This, however, appears guided by pre-judgments, rather than by conceptual rigor.

Another, highly influential approach to conceptualizing spirituality is Pargament's definition of religion as "search for significance in ways related to the sacred" (1992, 204) and of spirituality as "search for the sacred" (Pargament 1997; cf. Zinnbauer et al. 1999). Pargament's proposal for defining religion and spirituality with reference to an established construct in the theory of religion (the sacred) highlights commonalities, rather than differences. But if spirituality is to be expressed in terms traditionally used to describe religion, why do we need two concepts, when their difference is so marginal? Is it not a waste of time and energy to develop special measures of spirituality, if they, as Pargament (1999, 8) himself notes, "look suspiciously like old measures of religiousness" and add little or no incremental validity to the study of religion? In fact, most measures of spirituality operate empirically as measures of religious experience (Gorsuch/Miller 1999; Hood 2003; Hood/Hill/Spilka 2009).

Streib and Hood (2011; 2016a) therefore suggest defining spirituality as 'privatized experience-oriented religion,' which gravitates toward a segment in the religious field where access to the ultimate is not mediated by tradition, institution, or clergy, but characterized by immediacy for the individual, and where the symbolization of transcendence is not necessarily vertical (heaven; God or gods), but may include horizontal transcendence (Streib/Hood 2013; Streib/Hood/Keller 2016). Conceptually, all of these characteristics would not necessitate introducing—and defining with great effort—spirituality as a separate etic term. This would imply opposing and resisting any attempts in the study of religion to use the concept of spirituality interchangeably with religion—or to substitute 'spirituality' for 'religion.' To hive off some phenomena traditionally described as 'religious' and to subsume them under 'spiritual' would be counter-productive. However, as noted earlier, it is an empirical fact that talking about spirituality and self-identifying as spiritual (and not religious) is growing in prominence. Therefore, every possible effort should be made to empirically investigate the privatized experience-oriented religion (which many people on the street today call 'spirituality').

GLOSSARY

Content analysis an analytic procedure to quantitatively or qualitatively identify categories, dimensions, or structures of meaning within a certain set of verbal data.

Emic and etic two kinds of research perspectives in the social sciences, anthropology, and ethnology. The emic approach describes a perspective of the subjects within the social group in order to comprehensively understand how they perceive the world and explain things. The etic approach describes an observer's perspective from outside of the social group, trying to abstract from the limited scope of the group members in order to draw generalized conclusions about human thinking, experience, and behavior.

Horizontal transcendence and vertical transcendence two ways of symbolizing experiences of transcending. Vertical transcendence is represented by such symbols as 'God,' deities, 'heaven,' etc., which are thought to refer to a transcendent realm somehow 'higher' or 'above' the given world. Horizontal transcendence, however, refers to concepts which represent the immanent sphere such as humanity, the world, or the universe in its entirety and to experiences of their presence or of connectedness with them.

Images of God different ways in which the divine is represented cognitively (e.g. personal or impersonal images of God: understanding God as a symbol of the greatest possible value, as an eternal law, as energy flowing through everything, or the like) or emotionally (God as benevolent and forgiving or as wrathful and punishing).

Latent Class Modeling (LCM) a statistical procedure to assign survey participants to clusters according to their profile on a selection of indicators.

Principal Component Analysis a type of factor analysis, a group of statistical procedures to identify significantly strong sets of associations (which are represented as factors) between a selection of variables.

Semantics studying meaning that is used for understanding human expression through language, e.g. the meaning that is processed when people are using the term 'spirituality' (see Gardiner/Engler, "Semantics," this volume).

REFERENCES

ALLBUS 2012. 2013. Allgemeine Bevölkerungsumfrage der Sozialwissenschaften ALLBUS 2012 [machine-readable datafile]. Köln, gesis—Leibniz Institute for the Social Sciences—Datenarchiv.

Altmeyer, Stefan and Constantin Klein. 2016. "'Spirituality' and 'Religion'—Corpus Analysis of Subjective Definitions in the Questionnaire." In *Semantics and Psychology of Spirituality: A Cross-Cultural Analysis*, edited by Heinz Streib and Ralph W. Hood. Cham, Heidelberg, New York, Dordrecht, and London: Springer International Publishing Switzerland, 105–123.

Ammerman, Nancy T. 2013. "Spiritual but Not Religious? Beyond Binary Choices in the Study of Religion." *Journal for the Scientific Study of Religion* 52(2): 258–278. doi: 10.1111/jssr.12024

Beit-Hallahmi, Benjamin. 2015a. *Psychological Perspectives on Religion and Religiosity*. London and New York: Routledge.

Beit-Hallahmi, Benjamin. 2015b. "Resisting the Match between Religion and 'Spirituality.'" In *Religion, Brain and Behavior, Book Symposium: Handbook of the Psychology of Religion and Spirituality*, 2nd edition, edited by Ray Paloutzian and Crystal Park. Abingdon: Taylor & Francis, 118–123. doi:10.1080/2153599X.2014.891250

Berghuijs, Jonantine, Jos Pieper, and Cok Bakker. 2013. "Conceptions of Spirituality among the Dutch Population." *Archive for the Psychology of Religion* 35(3): 369–397.

Eisenmann, Clemens and Constantin Klein. 2016. "Dimensions of 'Spirituality': The Semantics of Subjective Definitions." In *Semantics and Psychology of Spirituality: A Cross-Cultural Analysis*, edited by Heinz Streib and Ralph W. Hood. Cham, Heidelberg, New York, Dordrecht, and London: Springer International Publishing Switzerland, 125–151.

Flere, Sergej and Andrej Kirbis. 2009a. "Christian Religiosity and New Age Spirituality: A Cross-cultural Comparison Comment on Houtman and Aupers JSSR, September 2007." *Journal for the Scientific Study of Religion* 48(1): 169–179.

Flere, Sergej and Andrej Kirbis. 2009b. "New Age is Not Inimical to Religion and Traditionalism." *Journal for the Scientific Study of Religion* 48(1): 179–184. doi: 10.1111/j.1468-5906.2009.01435_3.x

Gorsuch, Richard L. and William R. Miller. 1999. "Assessing Spirituality." In *Integrating Spirituality into Treatment: Resources for Practitioners*, edited by William R. Miller. Washington: APA, 47–64.

Granqvist, Pehr, Mari Fransson, and Berit Hagekull. 2009. "Disorganized Attachment, Absorption, and New Age Spirituality: A Mediational Model." *Attachment and Human Development* 11(4): 385–403.

Greenwald, Deborah F. and David W. Harder. 2003. "The Dimensions of Spirituality." *Psychological Reports* 92: 975–980.

GSS 1972–2012. 2013. General Social Surveys, 1972–2012 [machine-readable data file]. Chicago, IL: National Opinion Research Center.

Heelas, Paul. 2007. "The Spiritual Revolution of Northern Europe." *Nordic Journal of Religion and Society* 19(1): 1–28.

Heelas, Paul, Linda Woodhead, Benjamin Seel, Bronislaw Szerszynski, and Karin Tusting. 2005. *The Spiritual Revolution: Why Religion Is Giving Way to Spirituality*. Oxford: Blackwell.

Hood, Ralph W. 1975. "The Construction and Preliminary Validation of a Measure of Reported Mystical Experience." *Journal for the Scientific Study of Religion* 14(1): 29–41.

Hood, Ralph W. 2003. "The Relationship between Spirituality and Religion." In *Defining Religion: Investigating the Boundaries between the Sacred and the Secular*, edited by Arthur L. Greil and David G. Bromley. Amsterdam: Elsevier Science, 241–265.

Hood, Ralph W., Peter C. Hill, and Bernhard Spilka. 2009. *The Psychology of Religion: An Empirical Approach*, 4th edition. New York: Guilford Press.

Hood, Ralph W., Bernhard Spilka, Bruce Hunsberger, and Richard L. Gorsuch. 1996. *The Psychology of Religion: An Empirical Approach*, 2nd edition. New York: Guilford Press.

Hood, Ralph W. and Heinz Streib. 2016. "'Fuzziness' or Semantic Diversification? Insights About the Semantics of 'Spirituality' in Cross-Cultural Comparison." In *Semantics and Psychology of Spirituality: A Cross-Cultural Analysis*, edited by Heinz Streib and Ralph W. Hood. Cham, Heidelberg, New York, Dordrecht, and London: Springer International Publishing Switzerland, 153–161.

Houtman, Dick and Stef Aupers. 2007. "The Spiritual Turn and the Decline of Tradition: The Spread of Post-Christian Spirituality in 14 Western Countries, 1981–2000." *Journal for the Scientific Study of Religion* 46(3): 305–320. doi: 10.1111/j.1468-5906.2007.00360.x

Houtman, Dick, Stef Aupers, and Paul Heelas. 2009. "Christian Religiosity and New Age Spirituality: A Cross-Cultural Comparison—A Rejoinder to Flere and Kirbis." *Journal for the Scientific Study of Religion* 48(1): 169–179.

Huber, Stefan and Constantin Klein. 2011. "Spirituelle und religiöse Konstrukträume: Plurale Konstruktionsweisen religiöser und spiritueller Identitäten im Spiegel der deutschen Daten des Religionsmonitors 2008." In *Spiritualität transdisziplinär: Wissenschaftliche Grundlagen im Zusammenhang mit Gesundheit und Krankheit*, edited by Arnd Büssing and Nico B. Kohls. Heidelberg: Springer, 53–66.

Keller, Barbara and Michele Wollert. 2016. "'Whether These Gifts Are from God, from Buddha, from the Universe, I Do Not Care, I Do Not Care at All . . .'—Qulit Spiritualities." In *Semantics and Psychology of Spirituality: A Cross-Cultural Analysis*, edited by Heinz Streib and Ralph W. Hood. Cham, Heidelberg, New York, Dordrecht, and London: Springer International Publishing Switzerland, 319–337.

Klein, Constantin, Ralph W. Hood, Christopher F. Silver, Barbara Keller, and Heinz Streib. 2016. "Is 'Spirituality' Nothing but 'Religion'? An Indirect Measurement Approach." In *Semantics and Psychology of Spirituality: A Cross-Cultural Analysis*, edited by Heinz Streib and Ralph W. Hood. Cham, Heidelberg, New York, Dordrecht, and London: Springer International Publishing Switzerland, 71–85.

Koenig, Harold G. 2008. "Concerns about Measuring 'Spirituality' in Research." *Journal of Nervous and Mental Disease* 196(5): 349–355.

la Cour, Peter, Nadja H. Ausker, and Niels C. Hvidt. 2012. "Six Understandings of the Word Spirituality in a Secular Country." *Archive for the Psychology of Religion* 34(1): 63–81. doi: 10.1163/157361212X649634

Lindeman, Marjaana, Sandra Blomqvist, and Mikito Takada. 2012. "Distinguishing Spirituality from other Constructs not a Matter of Well-Being but of Belief in Supernatural Spirits." *Journal of Nervous and Mental Disease* 200(2): 167–173. doi: 10.1097/NMD. Ob013e3182439719

Oman, Doug. 2013. "Defining Religion and Spirituality." In *Handbook of the Psychology of Religion and Spirituality*, 2nd edition, edited by Raymond F. Paloutzian and Crystal L. Park. New York: Guilford Press, 23–47.

Paloutzian, Raymond F. and Crystal L. Park, eds. 2013. *Handbook of the Psychology of Religion and Spirituality*, 2nd edition. New York: Guilford Press.

Pargament, Kenneth I. 1992. "Of Means and Ends: Religion and the Search for Significance." *International Journal for the Psychology of Religion* 2(4): 201–229.

Pargament, Kenneth I. 1997. *The Psychology of Religion and Coping: Theory, Research, Practice.* New York: Guilford Press.

Pargament, Kenneth I. 1999. "The Psychology of Religion *and* Spirituality? Yes and No." *International Journal for the Psychology of Religion* 9(1): 3–16.

Pargament, Kenneth I. ed. 2013. *APA Handbooks in Psychology: APA Handbook of Psychology, Religion and Spirituality, Vols. 1 and 2.* Washington: APA.

Piedmont, Ralph L. 2001. "Spiritual Transcendence and the Scientific Study of Spirituality." *Journal of Rehabilitation* 67(1): 4–14.

Popp-Baier, Ulrike. 2009. "From Religion to Spirituality: Megatrend in Contemporary Society or Methodological Artefact? A Contribution to the Secularization Debate from Psychology of Religion." *Journal of Religion in Europe* 3: 1–34.

Roof, Wade C. 1993. *A Generation of Seekers: The Spiritual Journeys of the Baby Boom Generation.* San Francisco, CA: Harper & Row.

Schlehofer, Michele M., Allen M. Omoto, and Janice R. Adelman. 2008. "How do 'Religion' and 'Spirituality' Differ? Lay Definitions among Older Adults." *Journal for the Scientific Study of Religion* 47(3): 411–425.

Siegers, Pascal. 2012. *Alternative Spiritualitäten. Neue Formen des Glaubens in Europa: Eine empirische Analyse.* Frankfurt/M.: Campus.

Spilka, Bernhard. 1993. "Spirituality: Problems and Directions in Operationalizing a Fuzzy Concept." Paper for the Annual Meeting of the American Psychological Association, Toronto 1993-VIII.

Stausberg, Michael. 2014. "The Psychology of Religion/Spirituality and the Study of Religion." In *Religion, Brain and Behavior, Book Symposium: Handbook of the Psychology of Religion and Spirituality*, 2nd edition, edited by Ray Paloutzian and Crystal Park. Abingdon: Taylor & Francis, 30–40.

Streib, Heinz and Ralph W. Hood. 2011. "'Spirituality' as Privatized Experience-Oriented Religion: Empirical and Conceptual Perspectives." *Implicit Religion* 14(4): 433–453. doi: 10.1558/imre.v14i4.433.

Streib, Heinz and Ralph W. Hood. 2013. "Modeling the Religious Field: Religion, Spirituality, Mysticism and Related World Views." *Implicit Religion* 16(3): 137–155.

Streib, Heinz and Ralph W. Hood, eds. 2016a. *Semantics and Psychology of Spirituality: A Cross-Cultural Analysis.* Cham, Heidelberg, New York, Dordrecht, and London: Springer International Publishing Switzerland.

Streib, Heinz and Ralph W. Hood. 2016b. "Understanding 'Spirituality': Conceptual Considerations." In *Semantics and Psychology of Spirituality: A Cross-Cultural Analysis*, edited by Heinz Streib and Ralph W. Hood. Cham, Heidelberg, New York, Dordrecht, and London: Springer International Publishing Switzerland, 3–17.

Streib, Heinz, Ralph W. Hood, and Barbara Keller. 2016. "Deconversion and 'Spirituality': Migrations in the Religious Field." In *Semantics and Psychology of Spirituality:*

A Cross-Cultural Analysis, edited by Heinz Streib and Ralph W. Hood. Cham, Heidelberg, New York, Dordrecht, and London: Springer International Publishing Switzerland, 19–26.

Streib, Heinz, Barbara Keller, Constantin Klein, Anne Swhajor-Biesemann, and Ralph W. Hood. 2016. "Semantic Differentials Open New Perspectives on the Semantic Field of 'Spirituality' and 'Religion.'" In *Semantics and Psychology of Spirituality: A Cross-Cultural Analysis*, edited by Heinz Streib and Ralph W. Hood. Cham, Heidelberg, New York, Dordrecht, and London: Springer International Publishing Switzerland, 87–103.

Streib, Heinz, Constantin Klein, and Ralph W. Hood. 2016. "Investigating 'Spirituality': Between Survey Data and the Study of Biographies." In *Semantics and Psychology of Spirituality: A Cross-Cultural Analysis*, edited by Heinz Streib and Ralph W. Hood. Cham, Heidelberg, New York, Dordrecht, and London: Springer International Publishing Switzerland, 27–38.

Susumu, Shimazono. 2012. "From Salvation to Spirituality: The Contemporary Transformation of Religions Viewed from East Asia." *Religious Studies in Japan* 1: 3–23.

Utsch, Michael and Constantin Klein. 2011. "Religion, Religiosität, Spiritualität: Bestimmungsversuche für komplexe Begriffe." In *Gesundheit—Religion—Spiritualität: Konzepte, Befunde und Erklärungsansätze*, edited by Constantin Klein, Hendrik Berth, and Friedrich Balck. Weinheim: Juventa, 25–45.

Walker, Lawrence J. and Russell C. Pitts. 1998. "Naturalistic Conceptions of Moral Maturity." *Developmental Psychology* 34(3): 403–419.

Zinnbauer, Brian J. and Kenneth I. Pargament. 2005. "Religiousness and Spirituality." In *Handbook of the Psychology of Religion and Spirituality*, edited by Raymond F. Paloutzian and Crystal L. Park. New York: Guilford Press, 21–42.

Zinnbauer, Brian J., Kenneth I. Pargament, Brenda Cole, Makr S. Rye, Eric M. Butter, Timothy G. Belavich, Kathleen M. Hipp, Allie B. Scott, and Jill L. Kadar. 1997. "Religion and Spirituality: Unfuzzying the Fuzzy." *Journal for the Scientific Study of Religion* 36(4): 549–564.

FURTHER READING

Heelas et al. 2005 [*This is a classic study about forms of alternative holistic spirituality among the residents of Kendall/UK.*]

Houtman/Aupers 2007 [*Though not without problems, this analysis is one of the most influential, empirically based suggestions of a spiritual turn.*]

Koenig 2008 [*This is an analysis of instruments for measuring 'spirituality' in psychology of religion and health research; it is highly critical of confounding 'spirituality' and 'well-being,' which risks tautological measurements and biased results.*]

la Cour et al. 2012 [*This article presents an analysis of the semantics of spirituality in Denmark, which may be compared to the results presented in this chapter from our own research in terms of results and, in part, with respect to its methodology.*]

Roof 1993 [*One of the historical pioneering studies about the turn to spirituality.*]

Siegers 2012 [*A study of the spiritual turn in Europe, based on the European Value Study and trying to identify the size of alternative spiritual milieus in certain countries.*]

Streib/Hood 2016a [*The comprehensive presentation of the results of and conclusions from the recently completed Bielefeld-based Cross-Cultural Study on 'Spirituality,' including conceptual and methodological chapters.*]

CHAPTER 5

···

NON-RELIGION

···

LOIS LEE

CHAPTER SUMMARY

···

- The study of religion's various 'others' is receiving increasing attention from scholars of religion.
- The major empirical foci of these overlapping fields are the studies of (i) non-religious populations, or the 'nones'; (ii) 'religious-like' phenomena such as non-religious lifecycle ceremonies and worldviews; (iii) dialectics between the religious and non-religious or secular; and (iv) secularist regimes of power.
- Theoretical issues at stake include postcolonial versus multiple accounts of secularism/s; new ways of investigating and challenging secularization theory; and 'egalitarian' approaches to religion which critique the idea that religion is unique—a sole example of a type.
- As young fields, conceptual resources and distinctions are works in progress. This chapter's glossary provides one way of disentangling related phenomena.

There are lots of phenomena in the world that are not religious and most of these are not intrinsically of interest to the study of religion, nor do they require dedicated attention in a volume such as this. Be it public transport and children's cartoons, science syllabi or vintage wines—the world is full of things that the study of religion can happily ignore, at least until such a time as they become implicated in religious life—when cartoons depict religious actors or experiences, when science teaching is, or is perceived to be, at odds with religious instruction, when wine is rendered sacred. There are, however, a particular set of ostensibly areligious phenomena that are in fact central to the study of religion. These are those that are identified and made meaningful specifically through their being understood in explicit contrast to the religious.

These are the things I term 'non-religious' in my work (Lee 2015), so that 'non-religiosity' denotes the quality of being differentiated from religion. This sense of 'non-religion' as meaningful difference from religion is then distinguished from 'areligion', which denotes the absence of religion, or 'secularity,' which denotes a turn away from religion so that the religious becomes a secondary concern. Phenomena with non-religious characteristics are diverse, and combine with religious, spiritual, and secular characteristics in numerous configurations. They can include forms of anticlerical protest; a- and non-theistic worldviews; the irreligious emotion experienced by someone performing a religious ritual from which they feel alienated; diverse forms of identification which may or may not be combined with other forms of non-religious belief and practice ('secular humanist' and 'spiritual but not religious' are both examples of non-religious identification, but each combines with different religious, spiritual, and non-religious practices [for the religious/spiritual distinction see Streib/Klein, "Religion and Spirituality," this volume]). Non-religious phenomena may be created by secularist institutions that delineate specific roles for religious actors and cultures, and by any other form of secularist ideology—articulated or enacted—that distinguishes between the religious and the non-religious. As several scholars have observed in relation to the specific expressions of non-religion that interest them, non-religious phenomena are fundamentally bound up with the religious, to the extent, some argue, that the concept of 'religion' is only meaningful in relation to these 'others' (see, e.g., Asad 2003; see also Stausberg/Gardiner, "Definition," this volume). The study of the non-religious is not, therefore, a diverting addition to the study of religion, but is inseparable from it.

This chapter introduces the burgeoning study of the non-religious, distinguishes between some of the main non-religious phenomena that have interested scholars, and indicates key theoretical debates that this work contributes to. It concludes by outlining the pressing theoretical, empirical, and methodological questions facing scholars and students in these areas.

The Emerging Study of Non-Religion

The relevance of non-religious phenomena to engagements with religion has a long history, and the use of terms like 'secular,' 'secularism,' 'irreligion,' and 'atheism' to identify things that are comparable to but differentiated from religion is established and familiar in many places in the world. Yet it is only in recent years that scholars have started to give non-religion dedicated attention. This began with a focus on 'secularism' in the mid-1990s and extended to the study of 'secularity,' 'atheism,' and 'irreligious' and 'non-religious' cultures from the mid-2000s onwards.

Proto-Studies of the Non-Religious

These sometimes parallel projects build on and often challenge previous traditions of engaging with non-religious phenomena. Much new work engages with the more established scholarship of secularization, testing and contesting the particular and narrow notion of non-religion involved in that paradigm. In focusing on the declining role of religion in mental and social life, secularization-focused approaches adopt an exclusive understanding of religion as a sole example of a type of human experience, thought, and action. These approaches assume that all aspects of religion can either be replaced by functional equivalents and simply dissolved without harm, or, on the contrary, that religion either does or should continue in some form. Philosopher Charles Taylor (2007) has described secularization researchers as telling a 'subtraction story,' one consequence of which is that those researchers have tended to assume rather than explicate and investigate the nature of the secular itself (Lee 2015).

Another precedent for non-religion research is in debate about what counts as 'real religion'—an argument that normally relies on designating some other phenomena as non-religious (see Stausberg/Gardiner, "Definition," this volume). The identification of superstition, magic, idolatry, cults, animism, and alternative or rival religious traditions and practices as not truly religious are, like any process of boundary-making, controversial and contested; and the shifting focus from one or other of these 'others' itself tells researchers something significant about contemporaneous understandings of religion.

New Approaches

In a sense, contemporary interest in 'atheism' and 'secularism' is heir to both of these traditions in that these are the 'others' most favored by the secularization paradigm and the concepts most used to demarcate the 'really religious' within it. This interest continues, but is also joined by new, inclusive or 'egalitarian' approaches to religion (Laborde 2014) that search for equivalents to religion that have properties which seem to make them meaningfully distinct from religion yet comparable in some way, too. For example, scholars in the study of anti-religious and other non-religious cultural movements or of the subjectivities of 'godless' people in their godlessness are interested in the 'religion-related' (Quack 2014) and the 'religious-like' (Lee 2015). Egalitarian approaches are also pursued by Western policy-makers and lawyers who increasingly concern themselves with 'all faiths *and none*'—and attempt to include the non-religious in spaces previously demarcated for the religious through, for example, directives that refer to 'religion and belief' or 'religion and conscience' (e.g. in the Universal Declaration of Human Rights, art. 18). Alternatively, the egalitarian theories that Laborde (2014) has in mind are those that seek to subsume religion within a broader category of human interest such as 'conscience,' particularly in relation to liberal political theory.

This focus on more thoroughly or principally non-religious phenomena is what distinguishes the new study of non-religion from the old. The attributed non-religious characteristic of 'alternative spirituality' or 'secularity' represents one, rather minor aspect of phenomena that can be described quite richly apart from their relation to 'religion'—according to individualistic and 'questing' approaches to the cosmos or to some material practice or concern, respectively. By contrast, phenomena that are identified largely in terms of their relation to religion—secularism; secularity as an experienced and lived position; implicitly and explicitly non-religious humanisms and rationalisms; atheism; irreligion; and non-religion itself—are much more amenable to study *qua* their non-religiosity.

But new research into non-religion is also transforming how such phenomena are understood and conceptualized. It begins by attending to the concrete characteristics of phenomena identified according to their non-religiosity—the workings of atheists' cognition, the detailed ideological content and contingencies of political secularisms, the cultural construction of secularity, the nature and variety of philosophies and philosophical cultures like non-religious humanism, naturalism, and materialism that shape people's lives and are expressed in symbolic and ritual forms. As a consequence of this work, however, scholars are increasingly able to describe these same phenomena in other ways, rather than merely in their contrast to religion. Being able to describe such phenomena independently of religion then opens up new questions about the relationship between the two, including a return to deep questions about the exclusivity and singularity of religious experience itself (see Martin, "Experience," this volume). In this way, the study of the non-religious *qua* their non-religiosity can be a means to an end, a methodological tool for making neglected forms of experience, practice, and other phenomena visible.

INCLUDING THE 'NONES'

One of the major research programs into the non-religious underway is the study of the 'nones,' which is by now one of the most established. Originating primarily in US research, the notion of the 'nones' is used to identify non-affiliates, that is, people who say that they are not religious. While secularization-focused research was only really concerned to provide head-counts of the nones, scholars have become more deeply interested in this population, as well as in related and to some extent overlapping populations such as those who do not hold religious beliefs or participate in religious rituals and other practices, variously identified as 'atheists,' 'secularists,' 'the secular,' and the 'non-religious.'

In the first place, this work involves a major and ongoing task of profiling and mapping the non-religious. Demographers have begun to provide more detailed accounts of non-affiliates, atheists, and non-theists, noticing that, despite accounting for hundreds of millions of people worldwide, such populations are concentrated in certain parts of the world (including but not limited to Northern Europe, Japan, and post-socialist regions) and are frequently more likely to be young, male, and educated compared to general populations (Keysar/Navarro-Rivera 2013, 553). Using their different methodologies, cognitive scientists also explore what it means to be a 'none,' investigating similarities and differences between the cognitive processes of theists and atheists and of religious and non-religious people (see Lanman 2013). Such research helps flesh out our understanding of people who are not religious, humanizing a category that was hitherto residual (Campbell 2013 [1971]) or purely analytical.

Non-Religious Activity and Experience

Taking proper account of non-religious people and phenomena in research is associated with two areas of debate in particular. One is interested to work with non-religious populations in order to test or demonstrate secularization theories in new ways. In this vein, scholars have debated the extent to which non-affiliates and non-believers are really non-religious: rational choice theorists wonder if they are latently religious, just waiting for satisfying religious 'products' to come available again; others suggest that these populations might be vicariously religious, still participating in religious culture but indirectly (Davie 2015). One objective for researchers working with non-religious populations is to test these claims more extensively. Phil Zuckerman's (e.g. 2008) research is a significant example of this sort of work. His pioneering work with non-affiliates investigates whether these people really experience the absence of religion in a negative way—as a conspicuous absence or a lack—as many propose. In relation to this, Zuckerman explores levels of contentment, well-being, and health associated with non-religious populations.

Secondly, the study of non-religious populations pays attention to 'religious-like' phenomena that have been excluded from research as a result of religion-centered conceptual frameworks and subdisciplines. This type of research is interested in an array of beliefs, rituals, and practices that are typically identified in relation to religion and yet also take place outside of religious settings and in forms that are markedly unlike religious versions. An important example is the study of lifecycle rituals like civil, Humanist, or other non-religious ceremonies, such as baby naming celebrations, weddings, and funerals. In some parts of the world, these ritual practices are instituted in established communities and cultures, seen in mainstream Norwegian Humanism, for example, or in French republicanism and its focus on civil ceremonies. Another, related example is the study of existential philosophies, worldviews, and cultures (Lee 2015) that are developed outside of religious traditions but which give people meaning as well as symbolic resources with which to negotiate life: naturalism, naturalist forms of humanism, or skepticism, for example.

Such practices and beliefs have attracted little research not only because they have, in some cases, only emerged in recent years and decades, but also because, on the one hand, they do not slot easily into spaces marked out for the study of religion and, on the other, they do not obviously belong elsewhere. In fact, understanding how these religious-like but non-religious phenomena relate to religion raises new possibilities beyond narrower approaches to the study of religion, in which broader categories are developed within which religious phenomena are incorporated as one set of options among many. This brings the study of religion into line with the other, typically inclusive, general categories used to demarcate areas of social life such as age, gender, class, and political orientation; indeed, the notion of the 'nones' is only viable as a short-hand for the non-*religious* because there is no equivalent in these other areas—no idea of established and unproblematic 'non-aged', 'non-classed', or 'non-political' populations (Lee 2015). In this way, inclusion of the non-religious in the study of religion is a basis for interrogating religion-focused and religion-centric theories, concepts, and methodologies. Like women's studies as an aspect of gender studies or sports studies as one approach to the study of physical disciplines, so religious studies remains relevant as an area of specialism; at the same time, the study of the non-religious has renewed scholars' interest in identifying religion in relation to broader or 'parent' anthropological categories—soteriology or culture, in Fitzgerald's (2000) work, for example; existential culture, in my own; or world-view and lifestance in academic work (e.g. Droogers/Harskamp 2014) and policy-related discussions.

Non-Religious Institutions and Domains

Alongside the study of individuals and populations identified as non-religious in these different ways, another often-parallel set of scholarly engagements concern the designation of domains of social life as religious or not. While today many people take it as self-evident that some practices are 'religious' and others are not, critics contend that this cannot be taken for granted. Instead, they point to the ways that overlapping differentiations—between religious and secular, private and public, personal and political—emerge in relation to particular historical contexts. They also argue that being able to understand some domains as religious relies on a concomitant sense of other ones as non-religious, and they explore the co-construction of these domains. This work then opens up questions about when, how, and why differentiations between the religious and the non-religious take place, as well as about the kinds of action and interaction that are made possible by how the religious and non-religious are conceived of as a result of these processes.

Secularism and Modernity

These inquiries into the 'formation of the secular' (Asad 2003) began with work from anthropologists such as Talal Asad and Webb Keane (2007). Influenced by Foucault, this work uses genealogical methods to trace the influences and interests that shape the discursive trajectory of the 'religious'/'non-religious.' It points to the development of the categories 'religion' and 'secular' in relation to Western processes of modernization, via which religion changed from being something woven through all of life into a single, clearly demarcated, and segregated aspect of it. For Asad, Keane, and others, 'secularism' is a more or less single historical form, part of a constellation of phenomena—the Westphalian nation state system, liberal politics, materialist philosophy, humanistic ideology, and scientific epistemology—that make up Western modernity. An understanding of 'secularism' as intrinsic to the cultural condition of Western modernity is also found in critical studies of religion, from Timothy Fitzgerald (2000) and others, who draw particular attention to capitalism as the crucial feature of this modernity.

Multiple Secularities

Other scholars have built on these historical approaches by arguing that—though secularist notions of religious and non-religious domains may have emerged in the West at a certain moment in time—these concepts can be abstracted from those contexts and used to describe phenomena found elsewhere. Thus, 'secularity' can be used to indicate that the religious is a secondary authority or concern, while 'secularism' can be used to indicate any theory that specifies which domains are religious, which are secular, and in what ways (Lee 2015).

More limited, analytical understandings of 'secularity' and 'secularism' enable scholars to attend to variation in the way that religious and secular domains are differentiated from one another in particular cases and the specific secularist ideologies underpinning this. So, for example, Monica Wohlrab-Sahr and Marian Burchardt's (Burchardt et al. 2015) 'multiple secularities' project explores the manifestation of secularist differentiations in diverse cultural settings that have received much less attention than Western ones in relation to the study of any form of non-religion, including regions in Africa, Asia, and post-socialist contexts. Other scholars distinguish between secularist political arrangements and present normative arguments in favor of certain ones of these, as in work by Tariq Modood (2010) on 'radical' and 'moderate' secularism. In contrast with the idea that secularism denotes a *particular* arrangement of religious and non-religious domains then, this scholarship contends that secularism may denote several possible arrangements.

Religious and Non-Religious Interactions

In the sociological study of religion in particular, scholars have been interested to provide detailed accounts of the mechanics of exchange between actors and domains designated as religious and secular. As well as noticing the religious inflections to broadly secular contexts, this work considers how interaction between religious and non-religious actors and cultures may lead to the reconfiguration of either or both. Some argue that the decreasing relevance of religion to many domains of public life seen in many parts of the world leads to the intensification of religious experience and is implicated in the emergence of fundamentalist forms of religion; others argue that excluding religious language, arguments, and sentiments from politics enables the rise of theocratic movements and regimes. Yet others see more diffuse effects: Charles Taylor (2007) argues that the emergence of unbelief as a viable option alters the 'conditions of belief' in general and the nature and experience of religion. Theist cultures are thereby relocated (with non-theistic ones) to 'the immanent frame' and cease to support the same experiences of transcendence that they once did.

FUTURE PROSPECTS

Closer attention to different types of non-religiousness over the past two decades is associated with fundamental theoretical and methodological shifts in the study of religion. This work calls existing conceptualizations of 'religion' and its boundaries into question. It sensitizes scholars to differentiations between religion and the secular that are far more diverse and multi-dimensional than in the classical secularizationist notion of secularism as 'separation of church and state.' It historicizes taken-for-granted Western and colonial norms relating to religion, enabling new empirical and critical approaches to those norms. And it encourages the application of concepts and methods from the study of religion to ostensibly areligious phenomena, opening up new ways of understanding these phenomena as well as new avenues for critiquing and refining those concepts and methods for the study of religion itself.

As a relatively young field of inquiry, the study of the non-religious is already experiencing major shifts—in its core concepts, theoretical concerns, and empirical foci—and this is likely to continue for some time. Empirically, one new priority is the anthropological exploration of how non-religious and secularist cultures, political and everyday, manifest outside the West (with which most research has been occupied, alongside a limited number of non-Western cases that have aroused particular interest, such as India and Turkey). Another pressing concern that scholars have identified is the need to better understand how sociological factors such as class, ethnicity, and gender impact upon secularist ideologies and non-religious belief and ritual practice. Scholars from a number of disciplines are engaging with the psychological, social, and cultural processes that contribute to the formation of different kinds of non-religious and secular subjectivities, providing more detailed micro-level accounts of what would have been called 'secularization' processes but which are now undergoing a dynamic period of analysis and re-theorizing.

Methodologically, the study of non-religion combines with the study of non-traditional forms of religion in the need for and development of innovative research methods, capable of handling sociocultural experiences and formations that are often highly decentralized and not therefore amenable to the kinds of methods used to study congregational and other centralized forms of religion. Finally, theoretically (and conceptually, too) the study of the non-religious continues to contribute to big questions about the nature of religion, as well as to theories about the nature and causes of religious change in relation to industrialization, urbanization, globalization, and other processes of social and religious transformation.

Non-Religion and Secularity

One intriguing set of theoretical and empirical questions that have come into view concerns the relationship between non-religion and secularity (Lee 2015). A common pitfall in engagements with secularization theory is the tendency to fudge distinctions between (i) the absence of religion, or 'areligion,' (ii) the presence of anti- and other irreligious cultural movements, and (iii) the presence of non-religious alternatives to religious belief, practice, and culture. At the same time, postcolonial and poststructural critiques of secularism also tend to conflate different non-religious phenomena—postreligious experience, for example—with anti-religious stances. By contrast, new studies of non-religion distinguish more clearly between these things and thereby open up questions about the relationships between them (see Lee 2015).

Making these distinctions draws attention to different theories about these relationships that are already in circulation. These include the view from secularization theory that irreligion and non-religious worldviews are different from secularity, which itself involves indifference to religious matters; thus, both non-religion and religion are at odds with secularity (e.g. Bruce 2011). In direct contrast, others see the endpoint of secularization as rampant irreligion (Casanova 2011). Different again is Taylor's (2007) view that secularity involves the reconfiguring of religion as a result of the pluralization of both belief and, crucially, non-belief. Non-religion and secularity are also bound together but differently again in Colin Campbell's (2013 [1971]) pioneering work with irreligious movements. This proposes that agitation against religion may play a significant role in bringing the secular into being—and, by implication, keeping it going. My own work (Lee 2015) sees non-religion and secularity as antithetical to each other but in yet another sense, arguing that what many countries have experienced is not declining engagement with the existential and the transcendent, but the reforming of this engagement particularly into materialist and naturalist forms.

Each of these accounts provides markedly different ways of theorizing 'not religious' phenomena and would interpret the emergence of the New Atheism and any other non-religious cultural movement in strikingly different ways. Being able to distinguish between these different accounts is itself, however, one of the earlier achievements of the study of non-religion—and demonstrates how understandings of religion and society may be improved by the careful study of the non-religious.

GLOSSARY

This glossary presents one way of allocating terms to different phenomena that are relational to religion (derived from Lee 2015). Significant alternative definitions are also provided. Note that all of these concepts are relational and are therefore contingent upon an understanding of 'religion' or 'theism.' These concepts require, therefore, that users outline the sense of 'religion' and 'theism' employed in using and presenting these terms.

Anti-religion hostility toward religion.

Anti-theism hostility toward theism.

Areligion the absence of religion.

Atheism the absence of theism. Alternatively called 'negative atheism.'

Irreligion the rejection of religion. Alternatively defined as 'hostility or indifference towards religion' (e.g. Campbell 2013 [1971]), though Lee (2015) argues that both are forms of rejection.

Non-religion a phenomenon primarily identified in contrast to religion; including but not limited to rejections of religion, or irreligion. The 'non-' prefix here is used as in 'non-violence' to indicate something meaningfully unlike the phenomena at hand[1] and contrasts with areligion.

Non-theism a phenomenon primarily identified in contrast to theism; including but not limited to rejections of theistic claims. Alternatively called 'positive atheism' and as one sense of the term 'atheism' used in common speech.

Post-secular the term has several senses, but may generally be said to imply a critical stance towards areligious and anti-religious modes of secularity. Sometimes called 'post-secularity' or 'post-secularism.'

Secular immanence or 'this-worldliness'; also characterized by the subordination of the transcendent and religion as cultural or political authorities or concerns (though they may be important secondary authorities or concerns). There are numerous alternative understandings of the term in circulation, though these core ideas are often present.

Secularism a theory or ideology demarcating the secular from the religious and prioritizing the secular in some regard. Secularism is notably but not only advocated by the state. Alternatively, some scholars provide thicker historical understandings of secularism (see discussion).

Secularity the state of being secular. Alternatively, authors contrast 'secularity' with 'secularism' to distinguish personal existential philosophies that are alternative to religious ones or the absence of any such philosophy, religious or otherwise, from political secularism.

REFERENCES

Asad, Talal. 2003. *Formations of the Secular: Christianity, Islam, Modernity*. Stanford, CA: Stanford University Press.

Bruce, Steve. 2011. *Secularization: In Defense of an Unfashionable Theory*. Oxford: Oxford University Press.

Burchardt, Marian, Monika Wohlrab-Sahr, and Matthias Middell, eds. 2015. *Multiple Secularities Beyond the West*. Berlin and Boston: de Gruyter.

Campbell, Colin. 2013 [1971]. *Towards a Sociology of Irreligion*. No place: Alcuin Academics. Original edition, 1971.

Casanova, José. 2011. "The Secular, Secularizations, Secularisms." In *Rethinking Secularism*, edited by Craig Calhoun, Mark Juergensmeyer, and Jonathan Van Antwerpen. Oxford: Oxford University Press, 54–74.

Davie, Grace. 2015. *Religion in Britain: A Persistent Paradox*, 2nd edition. Chichester: Wiley-Blackwell. Original edition, 1994.

---

[1] I am indebted to Nonreligion and Secularity Research Network co-director Stacey Gutkowski for this analogy.

Droogers, André and Anton van Harskamp, eds. 2014. *Methods for the Study of Religious Change: From Religious Studies to Worldview Studies*. Sheffield: Equinox.

Fitzgerald, Timothy. 2000. *The Ideology of Religious Studies*. Oxford: Oxford University Press.

Keane, Webb. 2007. *Christian Moderns: Freedom and Fetish in the Mission Encounter*. Berkeley: University of California Press.

Keysar, Ariela and Juhem Navarro-Rivera. 2013. "A World of Atheism: Global Demographics." In *The Oxford Handbook of Atheism*, edited by Stephen Bullivant and Michael Ruse, Oxford: Oxford University Press, 553–586.

Laborde, Cécile. 2014. "Equal Liberty, Nonestablishment, and Religious Freedom." *Legal Theory* 20(1): 52–77. doi: 10.1017/S1352325213000141

Lanman, Jonathan. 2013. "Atheism and Cognitive Science." In *The Oxford Handbook of Atheism*, edited by Stephen Bullivant and Michael Ruse, Oxford: Oxford University Press, 483–496.

Lee, Lois. 2015. *Recognizing the Non-religious: Reimagining the Secular*. Oxford: Oxford University Press.

Modood, Tariq. 2010. "Moderate Secularism, Religion as Identity and Respect for Religion." *The Political Quarterly* 81(1): 4–14.

Quack, Johannes. 2012. *Disenchanting India: Organized Rationalism and Criticism of Religion in India*. New York: Oxford University Press.

Quack, Johannes. 2014. "Outline of a Relational Approach to 'Nonreligion.'" *Method & Theory in the Study of Religion* 26(4–5): 439–469.

Taylor, Charles. 2007. *A Secular Age*. Cambridge, MA: Belknap Press of Harvard University Press.

Zuckerman, Phil. 2008. *Society Without God: What the Least Religious Nations Can Tell Us About Contentment*. New York: New York University Press.

FURTHER READING

Asad 2003 [*Establishes the Foucauldian, 'genealogical' approach to the secular.*]

Bruce 2011 [*An accessible and comprehensive overview of secularization theory from the leading 'secularizationist' of the twenty-first century, updated to take account of recent critiques of that theory.*]

Bullivant, Stephen and Michael Ruse, eds. 2013. *The Oxford Handbook of Atheism*. Oxford: Oxford University Press. [*A compendium of forty-six essays considering philosophical and conceptual issues relating to atheism, as well as case studies from around the world.*]

Burchardt/Wohlrab-Sahr/Middell 2015 [*Book-length exploration of Wohlrab-Sahr and Burchardt's 'multiple secularities' program, with essays focusing, atypically, on non-Western contexts.*]

Lee 2015 [*Based on UK-based fieldwork, presents theory, methodology, and vocabulary for dealing with the non-religious and disaggregating different approaches to the secular, as well as a glossary of core terms.*]

Quack 2012 [*A pioneering ethnographic study of rationalist, atheist, and materialist movements and cultures outside of the West and challenging the idea of India as comprehensively religious.*]

Taylor 2007 [*A seminal text in the program of re-engaging with and reformulating secularity.*]

Zuckerman 2008 [*The first major qualitative study of everyday secularity, which is methodologically pioneering and provides rich data on post-religious life in Scandinavia.*]

PART II

THEORETICAL APPROACHES

···

CHAPTER 6

COGNITIVE SCIENCE

···

ARMIN W. GEERTZ

CHAPTER SUMMARY

··

- The cognitive revolution reinstated the mind as a central unit of empirical and theoretical analysis.
- There is an ongoing debate on whether cognition is simply individual mental representations or broader interactions of minds in bodies negotiating natural and
  social environments.
- The cognitive science of religion (CSR) produced significant foundational hypotheses during the 1990s.
- Since then, the field has expanded exponentially in terms of themes, methods, and
  theories.
- There are at present five significant new directions in CSR, namely neuropsychology, experimental science of religion, field experiments, history, and big data.

THE COGNITIVE REVOLUTION: PROMISING BEGINNINGS

··

The cognitive sciences emerged as a reaction to the behaviorism of American psychology in the middle of the twentieth century. The following were the key features of the
new cognitive science (Gardner 1987, 38–44): mental representations as a separate level
of analysis; computers as models of thought and as tools in analyses; "a de-emphasis
on affect, context, culture, and history," all of which were considered to be murky concepts; "belief in interdisciplinary studies"; and "rootedness in classical philosophical
problems."

The cognitive science of religion (CSR) also signaled a revolution. It arose as a reaction against the cultural disciplines that studied religion, i.e. history of religions, philosophy of religion, anthropology of religion, and so on. The reaction was against the Blank Slate hypothesis, which—according to evolutionary psychologists John Tooby and Leda Cosmides—was promoted by anthropologists in the so-called 'Standard Social Science Model.' The alternative was to be the 'Integrated Causal Model,' which avowed that our cognitive capacities evolved during the Stone Age as domain-specific modules or mini-computers already programmed to deal with environmental challenges, thus ensuring swift and intuitive responses to those challenges (Tooby/Cosmides 1992, 24).

Despite criticisms (Geertz 2013a; Laland/Brown 2002, 194; Fodor 2000, 55ff.), this view had a significant impact on the new CSR. Two of its founding fathers, scholars of religion E. Thomas Lawson and Robert N. McCauley (1990), proclaimed the new science as an alternative to the mostly postmodern and anti-science cultural studies that had come to dominate religious studies first in the United States and later in Europe. They argued that the CSR is an explanatory rather than an interpretative endeavor (Lawson/McCauley 1990, 2). They were convinced that symbolic-cultural systems could be explained in terms of innate cognitive constraints (Lawson/McCauley 1990, 3).

Thus, like the cognitive revolution of the 1950s, the CSR was a strident reaction to the 'mind-blindness' of comparative religion, sociology, and anthropology. There were, of course, scholars in anthropology and sociology who did, in fact, take both cognition and psychology seriously, but they were a minority.

What is Cognition? Mental Representations

One of the key factors in the cognitive sciences is identifying what cognition is. There are very few definitions of cognition, but most cognitivists would agree that the central aspect of cognition is 'mental representation.' One of the other founding fathers of CSR, anthropologist Pascal Boyer, was interested in the religious ideas that occur in the minds of actual people, are stored in their memories and passed on to other people (1994, 51). More importantly, he was concerned with the 'cognitive constraints' that evolutionary selection imposes on the types of representations that survive and are passed on transgenerationally (1994, 11). Boyer argues that religious representations are constrained by schematic assumptions from four cognitive domains (also termed 'repertoires'): the ontological, the causal, the episodic, and the social (1994, 42–43). He then posits the ways in which these domains are violated and/or concepts are transferred from one domain to another, but also, and more importantly, are stimulated by default in religious concepts. The concepts that survive selection through generations are minimally counterintuitive: i.e. they are easier to remember because they draw on default assumptions without being overly bizarre.

Although cognitive scientists may agree that knowledge is stored in the brain as mental representations, there is no consensus on the nature of the mind or on what is actually occurring in the brain (Thagard 1996, 134–136).

What is Cognition? Brain, Body, and Sociality

But what, then, is cognition, if it is not primarily about individual mental representations? Many of the 'cognitive constraints' that psychologists have demonstrated experimentally, and that many of the founders of CSR have based their groundbreaking hypotheses on, are properties that we share with virtually every other animal in the vertebrate, arthropod, and cephalopod phylas (Trestman 2013, 90).

The question, then, is what is *human* cognition? Mental representations are indeed a part of that cognition, but they are hardly the whole story. Human cognition, like that of other animals, is bodily-driven and sense-dependent. Neuropsychologists have argued that cognition is thoroughly 'embrained.' In other words, the mind consists of an emotional brain intertwined in a web of neural networks that allows intelligent and experiential interaction with the world around us. Recently, neuropsychologists such as Chris Frith (2007) and Moshe Bar (2009) have demonstrated that the brain is a predictive organ, constantly imagining the next instant and creatively filling in all the gaps that our senses and experiences carry with them.

There is, in fact, much more to human cognition. As neuropsychologist Merlin Donald has argued:

> Human cognitive evolution is characterized by two special features that are truly novel in the primate line. The first is the emergence of "mindsharing" cultures that perform cooperative cognitive work, and serve as distributed cognitive networks. The second is the emergence of a brain that is specifically adapted for functioning within those distributed networks, and cannot realize its design potential without them. (Donald 2007, 214)

On the basis of these and other such insights, I argue, in my appeal for the development of a biocultural approach to religion, that cognition is embrained, embodied, encultured, extended, and distributed (Geertz 2010, 304).

What has CSR Explained?

All CSR founders share the mentalistic, individualistic, representational paradigm and consider culture and religious behavior to be by-products of other more fundamental processes. Ultimately, however, almost any feature or function, such as noses, thumbs, and sex, can be seen as by-products. Although the by-product argument is trivial and the understanding of cognition limited, CSR pioneers have introduced hypotheses that have fired the imaginations of scholars and have been used in many ways in the academic study of religion as well as in other disciplines. Whether these hypotheses constitute 'explanations' can be contested.

There are basically six foundational hypotheses in CSR. They are as follows:

- Epidemiology of representations (Dan Sperber)
- Animism and anthropomorphism (Stewart Guthrie)
- Hyperactive Agency Detection Device—HADD (Justin Barrett)
- Ritual representations (E. Thomas Lawson and Robert N. McCauley)
- Counterintuitive ideas (Pascal Boyer)
- Modes of religiosity (Harvey Whitehouse)

Since these hypotheses are widely known, I will not discuss them here.

NEW DIRECTIONS

Most CSR work was published in the *Journal of Cognition and Culture* (Brill), established in 2001, but CSR research has grown significantly since then. To accommodate this growth, the International Association for the Cognitive Science of Religion (IACSR) was established in 2006, and, in 2013, it launched the *Journal for the Cognitive Science of Religion* (Equinox). The journal also has a supplement book series, *Advances in the Cognitive Science of Religion* (incorporating an earlier series called *Religion, Cognition and Culture*). Another important journal is *Religion, Brain and Behavior* (Routledge) which was established by the Institute for the Biocultural Study of Religion.

The exponential growth of CSR has paved the way for a wide variety of research interests and a growing body of data that do not necessarily concern themselves with the above-mentioned foundational hypotheses. Current studies use at least five different methodologies, i.e. neuroscience technologies, laboratory experiments, fieldwork, history, and large databases. All five approaches are crucial to the development of what has come to be called experimental anthropology, the experimental science of religion, and experimental humanities.

Neuropsychology

The neuropsychology of religion has been plagued by sensationalist accounts published by scholars self-designated as 'neurotheologians'—or who can be identified as such, e.g. Eugene d'Aquili, Andrew Newberg, Michael Persinger, Mario Beauregard, Vincent

Paquette, and many if not most meditation researchers—who are searching for special areas of the brain dedicated to 'religious experience' (in the singular) through the methodological use of 'mature contemplative introspection' and brain scans. Many of these studies are poor science and/or driven by confessional agendas (Geertz 2009). Unfortunately, scholars of religion who are interested in these approaches, but who have little or no insight in the problems of the field, sometimes fall prey to neurotheology. CSR scientist Uffe Schjoedt has argued in his review of the neuropsychology of religion that the search for God modules and dedicated areas of the brain rests on faulty assumptions about the brain and 'religious experience' and ignores their complexity (Schjoedt 2009, 328).

In a series of fMRI experiments, Schjoedt and his teams have demonstrated that even simple religious behavior, such as Christian prayer, draws on at least two different domains that involve formalized and improvised behavior. Formalized prayers such as the Lord's Prayer activate the striatal reward system (Schjoedt et al. 2008; cf. Neubauer 2013). Improvised prayers, other the other hand, activate the classic areas of social cognition: those areas that are active when we communicate with each other. Thus praying to God in the latter sense is "an intersubjective experience comparable to 'normal' interpersonal interaction" (Schjoedt et al. 2009, 199). A final experiment showed the influence of top-down cognitive governance and supported the predictive coding hypothesis. It showed that authority is an important mechanism in facilitating top-down charismatic influence (Schjoedt et al. 2011).

During the first decade of the second millennium, a growing number of neuropsychological studies have appeared which should prove to be promising for the future. One of the foremost neuroscientists in promoting neuropsychological studies of religion is Patrick McNamara. In a single-author volume and two anthologies, he has introduced the subject to a general academic audience (McNamara 2004; 2006; 2011). In another book (2009), he has provided a systematic overview based on empirical neurological studies.

Experimental Science of Religion

In 2008, psychologists Nicholas Gibson and Justin Barrett argued persuasively that what CSR needed was more psychological experimentation (Gibson/Barrett 2008). Judging by the growing numbers of papers read at conferences and published papers, this call is being met. There is little room for a detailed discussion here, but mention can be made of five centers of such research founded between 2003 and 2010.

The team at the Religion, Cognition and Culture Research Unit (RCC) in Aarhus, Denmark has focused on the mutual causal dynamics between brain, social interaction, and culture. Thus researchers have studied top-down cultural and social mechanisms (Geertz 2010; Jensen 2002; 2013) as well as bottom-up neural and cognitive mechanisms. The latter studies have been driven by the neuropsychological paradigms of predictive coding and cognitive resource depletion as a way of explaining ritual behavior (Schjoedt et al. 2013a; 2013b; Nielbo/Sørensen 2011; Nielbo et al. 2013; Sørensen 2007).

The Institute of Cognition and Culture at Queen's University Belfast was founded by Harvey Whitehouse, who is well-known for his groundbreaking hypothesis on modes of religiosity. Since Whitehouse left Belfast for Oxford, his successor Jesse Bering has conducted experiments on ideas about death among children and adults (Bering et al. 2005) and on what he has called "an organized cognitive 'system' dedicated to forming illusory representations of (1) psychological immortality, (2) the intelligent design of the self, and (3) the symbolic meaning of natural events" (Bering 2006, 453). Bering's successor, Paulo Sousa, has conducted experiments on moral psychology (Piazza et al. 2013) and his colleague Jon Lanman on atheism (2012).

In Oxford at the Institute of Cognitive and Evolutionary Anthropology, founded by Harvey Whitehouse, a sustained study of rituals has been pursued in both the lab and the field. Special mention can be made of their recent work on religion, morality, and guilt (McKay/Whitehouse 2015; McKay et al. 2013), ritual and mood (Russell et al. 2016), and ritual and social cohesion (Whitehouse/Lanman 2014).

In Vancouver, at the Centre for Human Evolution, Cognition, and Culture (HECC), Joseph Henrich has contributed to evolutionary accounts of religion both theoretically and experimentally, especially his work on costly displays and prestige (Henrich 2009). Psychologist Ara Norenzayan has done important work on prosociality, and his recent publication *Big Gods* (2013) summarizes much of the experimental literature which may indicate that belief in moralizing gods played a key role in the growth of agriculturally based civilizations. His hypothesis has been criticized (Atkinson et al. 2015; Stausberg 2014; Watts et al. 2015), but it remains an important contribution to a crucial topic. CSR scholar Edward Slingerland has applied an experimental approach to testing hypotheses about ancient Chinese texts (Slingerland/Chudek 2011).

A recent player in the experimental science of religion—at the Department for the Study of Religions, Masaryk University in Brno, Czech Republic—is the Laboratory for Experimental Research of Religion (LEVYNA) directed by Dimitris Xygalatas and William W. McCorkle Jr. A number of publications have appeared: McCorkle on corpses and burial (2010), Aleš Chalupa on Mithras (2011), and Radek Kundt on evolutionary theories (2015).

Field Experiments

Perhaps the most exciting and promising development in CSR is the application of experimental approaches in the field. The idea is to transform fieldwork into a more scientific endeavor. This is of course not new, but the new direction here is a reinvigorated experimental anthropology of religion. One of the leading figures in this development is Dimitris Xygalatas, currently developing the Experimental Anthropology Lab at the University of Connecticut. According to Xygalatas, the lab is dedicated to developing a paradigm for studying human culture scientifically in real-life settings. The lab promotes methodological innovation and integration in the study of human behavior through a combination of in-depth qualitative field research, experimental methods, and advanced technological tools (personal communication June 28, 2015). During the past few years, Xygalatas and colleagues have established a field site in Mauritius, called the Mauritian Laboratory for Experimental Anthropology (MALEXA), which has an extensive network of local assistants, collaborators, gatekeepers, and field sites, and serves as an ideal setting for naturalistic studies, which in turn generate new questions and a need for new methodological tools.

Xygalatas's earlier fieldwork in San Pedro Manrique, Spain, was very successful in drawing widespread public interest. The most spectacular study concerned the heart rates of firewalker participants during the annual summer solstice event in San Pedro. To test Émile Durkheim's classic theory of 'collective effervescence' as a result of communal rituals, participants were equipped with transmission belts around their chests which recorded their heart rate averaged over five-second intervals. The results showed that the walkers, their partners (who are carried on the backs of the firewalkers), and related spectators—but not non-related spectators—showed synchronized arousal, thus partially supporting Durkheim's theory (Konvalinka et al. 2011; Fischer et al. 2014).

In a series of studies of the Thaipusam celebration on Mauritius, Xygalatas and teams have been testing whether extreme rituals promote prosociality as is claimed by many (Xygalatas et al. 2013a; Xygalatas 2013), whether extreme rituals affect autobiographical memory in the manner claimed in Whitehouse's modes of religiosity hypothesis (Xygalatas et al. 2013b), whether moralizing and punishing high gods increase moral behavior (Xygalatas et al. forthcoming), and whether anxiety leads spontaneously to ritual behavior (Lang et al. 2015). A number of scientists have been involved in these studies, and others have made interesting contributions to CSR through their fieldwork (Cohen 2007; Hoverd et al. 2015).

History

It is not an exaggeration to say that history and archaeology are crucial to the success of CSR hypotheses and methodologies. Not only are they essential to discussions on the origins of religion, cognition, and culture (Geertz 2013b), but also to testing central hypotheses with prehistorical and historical data and sources. In the following, I will present one CSR hypothesis that has stimulated research in archaeology, history, biblical studies, history of religions, simulation approaches, and big data approaches.

As already mentioned in passing, Harvey Whitehouse developed an important hypothesis concerning two types of religiosity, namely the doctrinal and the imagistic modes. It is common knowledge that the ethnographic record reveals routinized and charismatic forms of religious behavior. Whitehouse hypothesizes that these two types of behavior arose through the ritual stimulation of two types of memory, namely, the episodic and the semantic (Whitehouse 1995). In the imagistic mode, episodic memory is stimulated by infrequent, but high-arousal rituals, which lead to intense cohesion of local groups, a diversity of religious representations due to spontaneous exegetical reflection, and subsequent lack of orthodoxy (Whitehouse

2002, 303–308). In the doctrinal mode, semantic memory is stimulated by frequent, repetitive rituals accompanied by religious teachings that lead to implicit memory for religious rituals, centralized authority, and orthodoxy checks (Whitehouse 2002, 296–303). It is evident that Whitehouse's hypothesis is the very strong claim that psychological features are the cause of sociopolitical features (Whitehouse 2002, 309). His claim of causality is, however, impossible to demonstrate unless there is some way to test the hypothesis.

Whitehouse has been criticized by a number of scholars, but his hypothesis has also led to creative attempts by historians of religion to apply and/or test his and other CSR theories and hypotheses. A central figure in this field is historian of religions Luther H. Martin. A specialist in Greco-Roman Hellenistic religions and firm proponent of naturalistic methodologies, Martin worked closely with Whitehouse on applying the modes theory to historical sources (Whitehouse/Martin 2004). His recent publication on Mithraism is an excellent example of applying CSR theories to historical sources (Martin 2015). Martin is a prime instigator of the new field of 'cognitive historiography' and has established the *Journal of Cognitive Historiography* (Equinox) together with classicist Esther Eidinow from the University of Nottingham in England (Eidinow/ Martin 2014; Martin/Sørensen 2011). Martin's and Whitehouse's research has inspired a number of other scholars of religion as well (Chalupa 2009; Martin/Pachis 2009; Panagiotidou 2014).

Scholars of biblical studies have also found Whitehouse's and other CSR theories to be useful in opening up new ways of studying ancient sources. One of the leading scholars in this field is Hungarian New Testament scholar István Czachesz, who has worked with colleagues in various countries, especially Risto Uro in Finland (Czachesz/Uro 2013) in developing CSR approaches to biblical studies (Czachesz 2011; Czachesz/Biró 2011).

Big Data

An exciting development, likely to impact all sciences dealing with history and prehistory, concerns 'big data.' CSR scientists are in need of ways to test major hypotheses not only on the origins of religion, cognition, and culture, but also on social evolution, religious ideas, and other crucial factors in human history.

Whitehouse has been deeply involved in this development and has joined forces with two other major players in developing big databases, namely, theoretical biologists Peter Turchin and Edward Slingerland. In a groundbreaking collective article, they introduced the 'Historical Database of Sociocultural Evolution' (Turchin et al. 2012). The database is designed to bring historical and archaeological data together so that competing hypotheses can be tested against one another. They argue that this approach will offer a "rapid discovery science" to prehistoric and historic study, which will complement history and archaeology and "extend their intellectual scope and explanatory power" (Turchin et al. 2012, 271).

Peter Turchin and colleagues developed a mathematical model of cultural evolution (Turchin et al. 2013, 16384) in line with the growing field of computer simulations in the study of history. Scholar of religion Donald Braxton and colleagues Kristoffer Nielbo and Afzal Upal have argued that computer simulations can be used to test not only CSR hypotheses, but also hypotheses and theories in the comparative study of religion (Nielbo et al. 2012). Others, under the guidance of psychologist Russell D. Gray, have applied mathematical models to political complexity in the Pacific region (Currie et al. 2010), the ecology of religious beliefs (Botero et al. 2014), and moralizing gods in Austronesia (Watts et al. 2015). Whitehouse has also applied modeling together with Quentin Atkinson on religious forms (Atkinson/Whitehouse 2011).

Moving beyond computer simulations, Peter Turchin established 'Sheshat: the Global History Databank' under the auspices of the Evolution Institute, directed by David Sloan Wilson, to bring

> together data on social complexity, warfare, ritual, religion, institutions, and resources from across the globe and for the past 10,000 years, allowing systematic statistical analysis that will enable us to discover new patterns in world history and to test novel hypotheses about the evolution of social complexity. (<https://evolution-institute.org/project/seshat/contributors/letter-to-experts/#down>, accessed July 7, 2015)

Former collaborator, Edward Slingerland, has established his own database called 'The Database of Religious History (DRH).' Based at the University of British Columbia in Vancouver and the Cultural Evolution of Religion Research Consortium, the DRH is a "quantitative encyclopedia of religious cultural history" (Slingerland/Sullivan in press). The website notes that the DRH was "built to explore and rigorously test functionalist theories of religion by collecting hundreds of variables on past societies that are clearly located in space and time" (<http://www.religiondatabase.org/landing/>, accessed July 6, 2015).

These two major databases are a much-needed improvement on existing anthropological databases, which although still in use today are inadequate for the 'big history' approach needed in contemporary studies of religion and society.

CONCLUSION

The CSR is an ever-expanding field of inquiry drawing on the methodologies from the natural and social sciences and using new methods and technologies to answer age-old questions about human consciousness, social and cultural behavior, and the origins of religion, cognition, and culture. Although the field is not without its challenges, it is without doubt essential to the holistic ambitions of comparative religion.

GLOSSARY

Blank slate hypothesis (tabula rasa *hypothesis)* the assumption that human beings are born without innate knowledge and are solely the products of their societies and cultures.

Cognitive constraints innate universal properties of the human mind-brain that handle particular kinds of information in certain ways and determine or influence human behavior.

Cognitive resource depletion when attentional demands are made on the brain's frontal executive network in critical situations, its limited resources are depleted.

Distributed cognition cognition is distributed in networks outside of individual brains.

Domain-specific modules innate neural structures in the brain that help the organism survive in specific circumstances.

Embodied cognition human cognition is strongly influenced by the body and emotions.

Embrained cognition the mind consists of a brain intertwined in a web of neural networks that allows intelligent and experiential interaction with the world around us.

Encultured cognition human cognition is integrated in mind-sharing networks that are fundamentally cultural.

Extended cognition external objects in the world support cognitive processes, whereby the mind and environment act as a 'coupled system.'

Hypersensitive Agency Detection Device (HADD) a categorizing mental tool that searches for evidence of animate beings in the environment and automatically influences response patterns.

Predictive coding the brain makes sense of the world by generating predictive models which are then subjected to monitoring for prediction errors in relation to input from the senses.

REFERENCES

Atkinson, Quentin D., Andrew J. Latham, and Joseph Watts. 2015. "Are Big Gods a Big Deal in the Emergence of Big Groups?" *Religion, Brain & Behavior* 5(4): 266–274. doi: 10.1080/2153599X.2014.928351

Atkinson, Quentin D. and Harvey Whitehouse. 2011. "The Cultural Morphospace of Ritual Form: Examining the Modes of Religiosity Cross-Culturally." *Evolution & Human Behavior* 32(1): 50–62. doi: 10.1016/j.evolhumbehav.2010.09.002

Bar, Moshe. 2009. "The Proactive Brain: Memory for Predictions." *Philosophical Transactions of the Royal Society B: Biological Sciences* 364(1521): 1235–1243. doi: 10.1098/rstb.2008.0310

Bering, Jesse M. 2006. "The Folk Psychology of Souls." *Behavioral and Brain Sciences* 29(5): 453–498. doi: 10.1017/S0140525X06009101

Bering, Jesse M., Carlos Hernández-Blasi, and David F. Bjorkland. 2005. "The Development of 'Afterlife' Beliefs in Secularly and Religiously Schooled Children." *British Journal of Developmental Psychology* 23(4): 587–607. doi: 10.1348/026151005X36498

Botero, Carlos A., Beth Gardner, Kathryn R. Kirby, Joseph Bulbulia, Michael C. Gavin, and Russell D. Gray. 2014. "The Ecology of Religious Beliefs." *Proceedings of the National Academy of Sciences of the USA* 111(47): 16784–16789. doi: 10.1073/pnas.1408701111

Boyer, Pascal. 1994. *The Naturalness of Religious Ideas: A Cognitive Theory of Religion.* Berkeley, Los Angeles, and London: University of California Press.

Chalupa, Aleš. 2009. "Religious Change in Roman Religion from the Perspective of Whitehouse's Theory of the Two Modes of Religiosity." In *Imagistic Traditions in the*

Graeco-Roman World: A Cognitive Modeling of History of Religions Research, edited by Luther H. Martin and Panayotis Pachis. Thessaloniki: Vanias Editions, 113–135.

Chalupa, Aleš. 2011. "What Might Cognitive Science Contribute to Our Understanding of the Roman Cult of Mithras?" In *Past Minds: Studies in Cognitive Historiography*, edited by Luther H. Martin and Jesper Sørensen. London: Equinox Press, 107–123.

Cohen, Emma. 2007. *The Mind Possessed: The Cognition of Spirit Possession in an Afro-Brazilian Religious Tradition*. Oxford: Oxford University Press.

Currie, Thomas E., Simon J. Greenhill, Russell D. Gray, Toshikazu Hasegawa, and Ruth Mace. 2010. "Rise and Fall of Political Complexity in Island South-East Asia and the Pacific." *Nature* 467(7317): 801–804. doi: 10.1038/nature09461

Czachesz, István. 2011. "Explaining Magic: Earliest Christianity as a Test Case." In *Past Minds: Studies in Cognitive Historiography*, edited by Luther H. Martin and Jesper Sørensen. London: Equinox, 141–165.

Czachesz, István and Tamas Biró, eds. 2011. *Changing Minds: Religion and Cognition Through the Ages*. Leuven: Peeters.

Czachesz, István and Risto Uro, eds. 2013. *Mind, Morality and Magic: Cognitive Science Approaches in Biblical Studies*. Durham: Acumen.

Donald, Merlin. 2007. "The Slow Process: A Hypothetical Cognitive Adaptation for Distributed Cognitive Networks." *Journal of Psychology* 101(4–6): 214–222. doi: 10.1016/j.jphysparis.2007.11.006

Eidinow, Esther and Luther H. Martin. 2014. "Editors' Introduction." *Journal of Cognitive Historiography* 1(1): 5–9. doi: 10.1558/jch.v1i1.5

Fischer, Ronald, Dimitris Xygalatas, Panagiotis Mitkidis, Paul Reddish, Penny Tok, Ivana Konvalinka, and Joseph Bulbulia. 2014. "The Fire-Walker's High: Affect and Physiological Responses in an Extreme Collective Ritual." *PLOS ONE* 9(2): e88355, 1–6. doi: 10.1371/journal.pone.0088355

Fodor, Jerry. 2000. *The Mind Doesn't Work That Way: The Scope and Limits of Computational Psychology*. Cambridge, MA and London: MIT Press.

Frith, Chris D. 2007. *Making Up the Mind: How the Brain Creates Our Mental World*. Oxford: Blackwell.

Gardner, Howard. 1987. *The Mind's New Science: A History of the Cognitive Revolution. With a New Epilogue by the Author: Cognitive Science after 1984*. New York: Basic Books.

Geertz, Armin W. 2009. "When Cognitive Scientists Become Religious, Science Is in Trouble: On Neurotheology from a Philosophy of Science Perspective." *Religion* 39(4): 319–324. doi: 10.1016/j.religion.2009.08.001

Geertz, Armin W. 2010. "Brain, Body and Culture: A Biocultural Theory of Religion." *Method and Theory in the Study of Religion* 22(4): 304–321. doi: 10.1163/157006810X531094

Geertz, Armin W. 2013a. "The Meaningful Brain: Clifford Geertz and the Cognitive Science of Culture." In *Mental Culture: Classical Social Theory and the Cognitive Science of Religion*, edited by Dimitris Xygalatas and William W. McCorkle, Jr. Durham: Acumen, 176–196.

Geertz, Armin W., ed. 2013b. *Origins of Religion, Cognition and Culture*. Durham: Acumen.

Gibson, Nicholas J. S. and Justin L. Barrett. 2008. "On Psychology and Evolution of Religion: Five Types of Contribution Needed from Psychologists." In *The Evolution of Religion: Studies, Theories, & Critiques*, edited by Joseph Bulbulia et al. Santa Margarita: Collins Foundation Press, 333–338.

Henrich, Joseph. 2009. "The Evolution of Costly Displays, Cooperation and Religion: Credibility Enhancing Displays and Their Implications for Cultural Evolution." *Evolution & Human Behavior* 30(4): 244–260. doi: 10.1016/j.evolhumbehav.2009.03.005

Hoverd, William James, Joseph Bulbulia, Negar Partow, and Chris G. Sibley. 2015. "Forecasting Religious Change: A Bayesian Model Predicting Proportional Christian Change in New Zealand." *Religion, Brain & Behavior* 5(1): 15–23. doi: 10.1080/2153599X.2013.824497

Jensen, Jeppe Sinding. 2002. "The Complex Worlds of Religion: Connecting Cultural and Cognitive Analysis." In *Current Approaches in the Cognitive Science of Religion*, edited by Ilkka Pyysiäinen and Veikko Anttonen. London and New York: Continuum, 203–228.

Jensen, Jeppe Sinding. 2013. "Normative Cognition in Culture and Religion." *Journal for the Cognitive Science of Religion* 1(1): 47–70. doi: 10.1558/jcsr.v.lil.47

Konvalinka, Ivana, Dimitris Xygalatas, Joseph Bulbulia, Uffe Schjødt, Else-Marie Jegindø, Sebastian Wallot, Guy Van Orden, and Andreas Roepstorff. 2011. "Synchronized Arousal between Performers and Related Spectators in a Fire-Walking Ritual." *Proceedings of the National Academy of Sciences of the USA* 108(20): 8514–8519. doi: 10.1073/pnas.1016955108

Kundt, Radek. 2015. *Contemporary Evolutionary Theories of Culture and the Study of Religion.* London: Bloomsbury.

Laland, Kevin N. and Gillian R. Brown. 2002. *Sense and Nonsense: Evolutionary Perspectives on Human Behaviour.* Oxford: Oxford University Press.

Lang, Martin, Jan Krátký, John H. Shaver, Danijela Jerotijević, and Dimitris Xygalatas. 2015. "Effects of Anxiety on Spontaneous Ritualized Behavior." *Current Biology* 25(14): 1892–1897. doi: 10.1016/j.cub.2015.05.049

Lanman, Jonathan A. 2012. "The Importance of Religious Displays for Belief Acquisition and Secularization." *Journal of Contemporary Religion* 27(1): 49–65. doi: 10.1080/13537903.2012.642726

Lawson, E. Thomas and Robert N. McCauley. 1990. *Rethinking Religion: Connecting Cognition and Culture.* Cambridge: Cambridge University Press.

McCorkle, William W., Jr. 2010. *Ritualizing the Disposal of the Deceased: From Corpse to Concept.* New York: Peter Lang.

McKay, Ryan, Jenna Herold, and Harvey Whitehouse. 2013. "Catholic Guilt? Recall of Confession Promotes Prosocial Behavior." *Religion, Brain & Behavior* 3(3): 201–209. doi: 10.1080/2153599X.2012.739410

McKay, Ryan and Harvey Whitehouse. 2015. "Religion and Morality." *Psychological Bulletin* 141(2): 447–473. doi: 10.1037/a0038455

McNamara, Patrick. 2004. *An Evolutionary Psychology of Sleep and Dreams.* Westport, CT and London: Praeger.

McNamara, Patrick, ed. 2006. *Where God and Science Meet: How Brain and Evolutionary Studies Alter Our Understanding of Religion,* 3 vols. Westport, CT and London: Praeger.

McNamara, Patrick. 2009. *The Neuroscience of Religious Experience.* Cambridge and New York: Cambridge University Press.

McNamara, Patrick. 2011. *Spirit Possession and Exorcism: History, Psychology, and Neurobiology,* 2 vols. Santa Barbara, Denver, and Oxford: Praeger.

Martin, Luther H. 2015. *The Mind of Mithraists: Historical and Cognitive Studies in the Roman Cult of Mithras.* London: Bloomsbury Academic.

Martin, Luther H. and Panayotis Pachis, eds. 2009. *Imagistic Traditions in the Graeco-Roman World: A Cognitive Modeling of History of Religions Research.* Thessaloniki: Vanias Editions.

Martin, Luther H. and Jesper Sørensen, eds. 2011. *Past Minds: Studies in Cognitive Historiography*. London: Equinox.

Neubauer, Raymond L. 2013. "Prayer as an Interpersonal Relationship: A Neuroimaging Study." *Religion, Brain & Behavior* 4(2): 92–103. doi: 10.1080/2153599X.2013.768288

Nielbo, Kristoffer L., Donald M. Braxton, and Afzal Upal. 2012. "Computing Religion: A New Tool in the Multilevel Analysis of Religion." *Method and Theory in the Study of Religion* 24(3): 267–290. doi: 10.1163/157006812X635709

Nielbo, Kristoffer L., Uffe Schjoedt, and Jesper Sørensen. 2013. "Hierarchical Organization of Segmentation in Non-Functional Action Sequences." *Journal for the Cognitive Science of Religion* 1(1): 71–97. doi: 10.1558/jcsr.v1i1.71

Nielbo, Kristoffer L. and Jesper Sørensen. 2011. "Spontaneous Processing of Functional and Non-Functional Action Sequences." *Religion, Brain & Behavior* 1(1): 18–30. doi: 10.1080/2153599X.2010.550722

Norenzayan, Ara. 2013. *Big Gods: How Religion Transformed Cooperation and Conflict*. Princeton, NJ and Oxford: Princeton University Press.

Panagiotidou, Olympia. 2014. "The Asklepios Cult: Where Brains, Minds, and Bodies Interact with the World, Creating New Realities." *Journal of Cognitive Historiography* 1(1): 14–23. doi: 10.1558/jch.v1i1.14

Piazza, Jared, Pascale Sophie Russell, and Paulo Sousa. 2013. "Moral Emotions and the Envisioning of Mitigating Circumstances for Wrongdoing." *Cognition and Emotion* 27(4): 707–722. doi: 10.1080/02699931.2012.736859

Russell, Yvan I., Fernand Gobet, and Harvey Whitehouse. 2016. "Mood, Expertise, Analogy, and Ritual: An Experiment Using the Five-Disk Tower of Hanoi." *Religion, Brian & Behavior* 6(1): 67–87. doi: 10.1080/2153599X.2014.921861

Schjoedt, Uffe. 2009. "The Religious Brain: A General Introduction to the Experimental Neuroscience of Religion." *Method and Theory in the Study of Religion* 21(3): 310–339. doi: 10.1163/157006809X460347

Schjoedt, Uffe, Jesper Sørensen, Kristoffer Laigaard Nielbo, Dimitris Xygalatas, Panagiotis Mitkidis, and Joseph Bulbulia. 2013a. "Cognitive Resource Depletion in Religious Interactions." *Religion, Brain & Behavior* 3(1): 39–55. doi: 10.1080/2153599X.2012.736714

Schjoedt, Uffe, Jesper Sørensen, Kristoffer Laigaard Nielbo, Dimitris Xygalatas, Panagiotis Mitkidis, and Joseph Bulbulia. 2013b. "The Resource Model and the Principle of Predictive Coding: A Framework for Analyzing Proximate Effects of Ritual." *Religion, Brain & Behavior* 3(1): 79–86. doi: 10.1080/2153599X.2012.736714

Schjoedt, Uffe, Hans Stødkilde-Jørgensen, Armin W. Geertz, Torben E. Lund, and Andreas Roepstorff. 2011. "The Power of Charisma: Perceived Charisma Inhibits the Frontal Executive Network of Believers in Intercessory Prayer." *Social Cognitive and Affective Neuroscience* 6(1): 119–127. doi: 10.1093/scan/nsq023

Schjoedt, Uffe, Hans Stødkilde-Jørgensen, Armin W. Geertz, and Andreas Roepstorff. 2008. "Rewarding Prayers." *Neuroscience Letters* 443: 165–168. doi: 10.1016/j.neulet.2008.07.068

Schjoedt, Uffe, Hans Stødkilde-Jørgensen, Armin W. Geertz, and Andreas Roepstorff. 2009. "Highly Religious Participants Recruit Areas of Social Cognition in Personal Prayer." *Social Cognitive and Affective Neuroscience* 4(2): 199–207. doi: 10.1093/scan/nsn050

Slingerland, Edward and Maciej Chudek. 2011. "The Prevalence of Mind–Body Dualism in Early China." *Cognitive Science: A Multidisciplinary Journal* 35(5): 997–1007. doi: 10.1111/j.1551-6709.2011.01186.x

Slingerland, Edward and Brenton Sullivan. In press. "Durkheim with Data: The Database of Religious History (DRH)." *Journal of the American Academy of Religion.*

Sørensen, Jesper. 2007. *A Cognitive Theory of Magic.* Lanham. MD: AltaMira Press.

Stausberg, Michael. 2014. "*Big Gods* in Review: Introducing Ara Norenzayan and His Critics." *Religion* 44(4): 592–608. doi: 10.1080/0048721X.2014.954353

Thagard, Paul. 1996. *Mind: Introduction to Cognitive Science.* Cambridge, MA and London: MIT Press.

Tooby, John and Leda Cosmides. 1992. "The Psychological Foundations of Culture." In *The Adapted Mind: Evolutionary Psychology and the Generation of Culture,* edited by Jerome H. Barkow, Leda Cosmides, and John Tooby. Oxford and New York: Oxford University Press, 19–136.

Trestman, Michael. 2013. "The Cambrian Explosion and the Origins of Embodied Cognition." *Biological Theory* 8(1): 80–92. doi: 10.1007/s13752-013-0102-6

Turchin, Peter, Thomas E. Currie, Edward A. L. Turner, and Sergey Gavrilets. 2013. "War, Space, and the Evolution of Old World Complex Societies." *Proceedings of the National Academy of Sciences of the USA* 110(41): 16384–16389. doi: 10.1073/pnas.1308825110

Turchin, Peter, Harvey Whitehouse, Pieter François, Edward Slingerland, and Mark Collard. 2012. "A Historical Database of Sociocultural Evolution." *Cliodynamics: The Journal of Theoretical and Mathematical History* 3(2): 271–293.

Watts, Joseph, Simon J. Greenhill, Quentin D. Atkinson, Thomas E. Currie, Joseph Bulbulia, and Russell D. Gray. 2015. "Broad Supernatural Punishment but Not Moralizing High Gods Precede the Evolution of Political Complexity in Austronesia." *Proceedings of the Royal Society B: Biological Sciences* 282(1804): 1–7. doi: 10.1098/rspb.2014.2556

Whitehouse, Harvey. 1995. *Inside the Cult: Religious Innovation and Transmission in Papua New Guinea.* Oxford: Oxford University Press.

Whitehouse, Harvey. 2002. "Modes of Religiosity: Towards a Cognitive Explanation of the Sociopolitical Dynamics of Religion." *Method & Theory in the Study of Religion* 14(3–4): 293–315. doi: 10.1163/157006802320909738

Whitehouse, Harvey and Jonathan A. Lanman. 2014. "The Ties That Bind Us: Ritual, Fusion, and Identification." *Current Anthropology* 55(6): 674–695. doi: 10.1086/678698

Whitehouse, Harvey and Luther H. Martin, eds. 2004. *Theorizing Religions Past: Archaeology, History, and Cognition.* Walnut Creek, CA: AltaMira Press.

Xygalatas, Dimitris. 2013. "Effects of Religious Setting on Cooperative Behavior: A Case Study from Mauritius." *Religion, Brain & Behavior* 3(2): 91–102. doi: 10.1080/2153599X.2012.724547

Xygalatas, Dimitris, Silvie Kotherová, Peter Maňo, Radek Kundt, Jakub Cigán, Eva Kundtová Klocová, and Martin Lang. Forthcoming. "The Random Allocation Game in Mauritius."

Xygalatas, Dimitris, Panagiotis Mitkidis, Ronald Fischer, Paul Reddish, Joshua Skewes, Armin W. Geertz, Andreas Roepstorff, and Joseph Bulbulia. 2013a. "Extreme Rituals Promote Prosociality." *Psychological Science* 24(8): 1602–1605. doi: 10.1177/0956797612472910

Xygalatas, Dimitris, Uffe Schjoedt, Joseph Bulbulia, Ivana Konvalinka, Else-Marie Jegindø, Paul Reddish, Armin W. Geertz, and Andreas Roepstorff. 2013b. "Autobiographical Memory in a Fire-Walking Ritual." *Journal of Cognition and Culture* 13(1): 1–16. doi: 10.1163/15685373-12342081

FURTHER READING

Atran, Scott. 2002. *In Gods We Trust: The Evolutionary Landscape of Religion.* Oxford: Oxford University Press. [*A detailed and critical discussion of the major CSR theories.*]

Gardner 1987 [*A history of cognitive science.*]

Geertz, Armin W. 2004. "Cognitive Approaches to the Study of Religion." In *New Approaches to the Study of Religion.* Volume 2: *Textual, Comparative, Sociological, and Cognitive Approaches,* edited by Peter Antes, Armin W. Geertz, and Randi R. Warne. Berlin and New York: de Gruyter, 347–399. [*An overview of CSR theories and other approaches.*]

Geertz 2013 [*An anthology on new approaches to the subject of origins.*]

Slingerland, Edward and Joseph Bulbulia. 2011. "Introductory Essay: Evolutionary Science and the Study of Religion." *Religion* 41(3): 307–328. doi: 10.1080/0048721X.2011.604513 [*Introductory essay to a special issue on evolutionary theories of religion.*]

CHAPTER 7

··

ECONOMICS

··

PETER SEELE AND LUCAS ZAPF

Chapter Summary

- The history of the economic discipline is replete with connections to religion, including religious objectives, language, and incentives. Religion is integral yet under-researched.
- The discipline's paradigms and axioms are socially constructed thought models, not ultimate truths.
- Economists analyze religious organizations and behavior using neoclassical theories and methods.
- Assumptions of rational, self-interested actors (*Homo oeconomicus*) have normative implications and consequences. Religious practice becomes the subject of economic considerations, e.g. optimizing the time allocated to religion by an individual.
- The New Institutional Economy (NIE), systematically including non-economic insight in its theory, appears as an adequate approach for researching the economic influence of religion and vice versa.

Introduction

This chapter provides a thematic overview of economics as an academic discipline, particularly emphasizing its relation to the study of religion. The first part presents the emergence of the discipline in antiquity. Economic thought from medieval times and current theoretical streams in the literature are then considered. Finally, we present an overview of theories extending the economic perspective to religion. Only economic viewpoints are addressed in this chapter. Sociological (e.g. the Weber thesis), theological (e.g. Christian business ethics), and historical (e.g. economic development and religion) perspectives are not considered due to space limitations.

Historical Overview: From Aristotelian *Oeconomica* to Smithian Classics and the Present Neoclassic

Antiquity: Economics as Part of the Practical Sciences

The term 'economics' is rooted in the ancient Greek 'Oikos,' best translated as 'household.' Writers like Xenophon (430–354 BCE) and Aristotle (384–322 BCE) discussed the economy in a premodern sense under the title of 'Oeconomica'. The household is seen as the basic economic structure for families as well as for city-states (*poloi*). Productive and provisional tasks are described. These processes are then applied outside the household. Parallels to national economics are drawn, particularly in the second book of the Aristotelian *Oeconomica*. Other important topics described in Aristotle's *Politics* are money and its use in particular economic settings: Aristotle called the sheer accumulation of money *chrematistics*. He condemned this absolutizing of economic means and argued the need to focus on the ends. Thus, money is a means to ethical ends, a means to enable living a good life, not an end in itself (Seele 2011, 116).

Aristotle offered practical guidance for economic behavior beyond these ethical considerations. He focused on two areas of life. First for the household itself (*Oeconomica*, books I and III), he describes processes within the household that apply to the householder, his wife, children, and servants. The proper organization and management of this economic organism are presented. The second area of economic guidance concerns the state (book II), with the allocation of public money figuring centrally due to the constant wars between city-states, which had drained public treasuries.

Between Church and Money: Economics of the Middle Ages

The economics of European medieval times oscillated between two poles: the new possibilities of a monetized economy, and the rigid rules of the church.

In feudal society, few owned land and many worked on this land. Economic and social status depended on property. The church declared itself a caretaker of this property in the Middle Ages. Control of the cultivation of the land and the distribution of its products was the consequence. Monkish austerity was the spiritual and economic ideal. Spiritual betterment was encouraged throughout the estates of the realm, but economic betterment for peasants was blocked. The church prohibited earning an income from trade or monetary operations (Pirenne 1986, 16–19).

A new economic development challenged this status quo: the monetized economy. Labor, property, land, and commodities were now measured by price. As everything had a price, economic thought began to adapt to new circumstances. Interest was claimed on loans, challenging the sinfulness of monetary profit declared by the church (Wood 2002, 206–208).

Economic thought of the time integrated the new economic possibilities with established ethical-ecclesiastical considerations. Thomas Aquinas (1225–1274), for example, considered exaggerated prices as theft and therefore a vice. However, he accepted private monetary income. In his writings, based on theological arguments, he argued for just prices: the sale of a product must cover the producer's living expenses (Koehn/Wilbratte 2012, 512).

Adam Smith: Division of Labor, the Market, and the Divine

Adam Smith (1723–1790) is a central figure in modern economics. He developed his theories in a time of economic change: the invention of the steam engine opened new possibilities for production. Smith liberated economic thought from the medieval religious restraints that hindered monetary trade and interest and from the excessive feudal authorities.

Smith's *Inquiry into the Nature and Causes of the Wealth of Nations* was published in 1776. Two of his ideas continue to influence economic models today: the division of labor, and the positive social effect of the market (Cameron 2008).

Smith proposed specialized and divided labor in the production of goods, suggesting that this organization of production would lead to growth in the economy and a subsequent rise in wealth. Production costs would fall and mass production be facilitated. Labor no longer dominated the value of a product but was treated as a commodity itself, and the value of commodities depended only on supply and demand.

According to Smith, the free market is where supply and demand meet. Competition leads the way; the allocation of goods follows. The market realizes productive efficiency. It only works if it is unhindered by governmental interference. Smith's strong stand against mercantilism—where the state systematically interferes with the economy as a political instrument—reflects this conviction (Eecke 2013). Smith described the mechanism underlying this free market exchange of goods as follows: "Give me that which I want, and you shall have this which you want, is the meaning of every such offer. [. . .] It is not from the benevolence of the butcher, the brewer, or the baker, that we expect our dinner, but from their regard to their own interest" (Smith 2007, 9–10).

The free market that emerges with repeated exchange is based on self-interest, but this act of self-interest leads to unintended social benefit. The individual only sees his or her interest, but the combined result of all the exchanges is increased wealth for all. The actor in the market is "[. . .] led by an invisible hand to promote an end which was no part of his intention" (Smith 2007, 293). The market has a benevolent force in the background: it leads self-interested behavior to a greater good.

The 'invisible hand' has become a well-known metaphor in economics. Smith mentioned the concept only once in his *Wealth of Nations* and he specifically limited it to economic activity, e.g. investments, inventions, hard work: self-interest in these fields improves individuals' social and economic conditions (Bishop 1995).

Smith's economic thought escaped the religious restraints of medieval scholastics. It relied on naturalistic and rational analysis. However, Smith was neither an atheist nor a secularist. The belief in a divine hand maintaining social order was still present. The 'invisible hand' hints at this divine providence. Its revelation is the market mechanism (Oslington 2012). Thus, religion is not just an underlying theme with Smith. He applied the rules of the market to religion itself and condemned the political preference of the state for one religious group, labeling it an impermissible intrusion into the market mechanism, due to its hindering religious competition, efficiency, diversity, and free choice. For Smith, this was true for every commodity in the market, religion included (Smith 2007, 513).

Paradigms and Axioms of Current Neoclassical Economics

Current mainstream economics in modern market economies is labeled *neoclassical economics* because it draws upon classic economics. Models are updated but still rely on the paradigms of Smith and his successors. The common idea is that of the utility-maximizing, autonomous individual. Positive effects of free markets are assumed (Aspromourgos 2008). Two men coined the term 'neoclassical economics' in the middle of the twentieth century during the turbulence of the great economic crisis of the 1920s: John Maynard Keynes (1883–1946) and Friedrich von Hayek (1899–1992). Keynes defended a central role for the state in organizing an economy. Politics had to back the economy by creating work and jobs. Hayek, on the other hand, argued for total economic freedom. The state was reduced to one economic actor amongst many others. Hayek proposed a liberal, even libertarian, organization of the state (Emmett 2008). These are two ends of an economic spectrum: a well-regulated economy versus the free market. As is often the case with ideal types, they are hardly ever found. Accordingly, economic practice and theory incorporate elements of both traditions.

These ideas of economic organization are not the only contenders. Other economic models have been proposed but failed. Marxian economics is an example for this (see also Day, "Marxism," this volume). Karl Marx (1818–1883) proposed a form of economic organization that differs from the assumptions of classical economics. He emphasized a centralized market and no private ownership. His definition of value draws on the labor used to produce economic goods. The distribution of wealth accordingly is tied to productive power, significantly reducing the influence of capital. Marxian economics organizes the economy under a communitarian paradigm, and a different form of social organization is the result. With the end of Soviet Union, the political and practical implementation of this economic alternative ceased.

Marx's alternative model illustrates that economic theories are not natural laws. They are open to critique, development, and change. The theories rest on fundamental convictions and theoretical premises, paradigms, and axioms. Neoclassical economics is one specific outline for economic organization. The following paradigm and axioms are used to model neoclassical economics (e.g. Nicholson/Snyder 2010, 301–374):

- The central paradigm and starting point is the existence of a free market. Actors voluntarily and repeatedly meet and engage in transactions.

Further to this paradigm, several axioms define the object of study:

- For modeling economic processes, a *perfect market* is assumed. Participation is free, and there are no transactional costs, no unintended side-effects of market-related actions (externalities), and no constraints.
- *Symmetric and perfect information*: The traded goods on this market are interchangeable and standardized. The characteristics of the goods are completely transparent to the traders.
- *Real-time adjustments*: Adaptation to new conditions occurs instantly.
- In this market, only *rational choices* apply. All decisions are made to maximize utility driven by self-interest. Individuals are viewed as autonomous, atomized creatures. The actor is a *homo oeconomicus*.
- Within the market, actors create constitute a *general equilibrium*. There is an infinite number of suppliers and consumers. Supply and demand are balanced. One-sided markets are ruled out.

Economists do not consider these axioms to be ends or goals. They are a starting point for constructing models. When applied, some of the ideal assumptions are substituted by empirical data while the other assumptions remain (*ceteris paribus*). The effect on the system then is analyzed with the goal of describing the principles and regularities of economic processes (Binswanger 1993, 18).

Expanding the Economic Framework toward Religion

Economics Beyond the Economy

Classical economics following Smith concentrates on labor, production, and trade. It analyzes the exchange behavior in markets. Seemingly non-productive topics such as religion are not considered.

In the 1930s, British economist Lionel Robbins (1898–1984) found economics conceptually too narrow. He opened the discipline to a broader range of issues. Robbins observed the importance of leisure to economic activity. Time spent for non-economic activity is economically relevant (Robbins 1945, 11). This thought may seem trivial to non-mainstream economists, but it dissolves the boundaries of economics. If there is no distinction between economic and non-economic action, no action is beyond the scope of economics. Gary Becker (1930–2014) built on this thought in the 1960s. He considered non-economic activities even more relevant for economists: "[. . .] the allocation and efficiency of non-working time may now be more important to economic welfare than that of working time; yet the attention paid by economists to the latter dwarfs any paid to the former" (Becker 1965, 493).

Becker—a professor of the Chicago School, the center of gravity for neoclassical economics after World War II—realigned economics. He opened the discipline to new areas of research, including family life, education, marriage and divorce, and criminality. Each and every aspect of life became economically relevant. How much time is spent on various aspects of life? What is the influence on spending and making money? The private life of *homo oeconomicus* was no longer private. Becker's disciplinary expansion was rewarded with the Nobel Prize in Economics in 1992.

In 1975, it was religion's turn for economic examination. Corry Azzi and Ronald Ehrenberg described the actions of a household in the form of goods. Relationships, labor, education, everything is produced with scarce time and means. The household evaluates and prioritizes production based on maximizing personal benefit. Attending religious activities is described as the production of religious goods. This production competes with the production of other goods within the household. The household demand for religious goods determines the optimum between production of religious goods and other goods (Azzi/Ehrenberg 1975). A Christian or Muslim who faces death is inclined to invest more in the production of religious goods, as an afterlife payoff is expected. For a healthy young atheist it may be the other way round. The household-production perspective makes the individually perceived benefits of religion visible. By equating religion and economic activities, cost–benefit calculations of religious activities are possible. Azzi and Ehrenberg's work can be considered a milestone as they introduced religion to the rational choice framework—and the study of religion into the field of economics.

Religious Supply, Religious Demand: Rational Choice and Market Theory of Religion

Neoclassical economists assume that people always seek rewards. In doing so, they act in their own self-interest. They maximize profits and avoid costs. They have stable preferences with which they evaluate rewards; their resources are scarce. The resulting behavior is then called *rational*, and this rationality is predictable.

Religion is analyzed within this rational-choice framework. Religious rewards are seen as both inner- and extra-mundane. Life is structured and oriented toward a goal in this world. Social benefits derived from belonging to a religious group are one reward. Hope for a paradise is another, directed to the extra-mundane: adherents engage in religious behavior because they expect an afterlife payoff. People choose religious affiliation along these different forms of religious rewards. The goal is maximum outcome with regard to the inner- and extra-mundane aspects of religious practice (Stark/Bainbridge 1987).

Individual 'religiosity' within this framework is modeled as the production of religious goods. Laurence Iannaccone described these goods as a form of human capital. By attending religious activities, religious human capital is both applied and produced: knowledge of the rituals and forms is a prerequisite. As rituals are learned, mastered, and perfected, and as bonds and dependencies within the community are strengthened, a gain in religious human capital ensues. Religious human capital empowers individuals to carry out religious activities efficiently. Thus, the benefits of religious activities are maximized (Iannaccone 1990; 1995).

Rational choice in religion and the production of religious human capital describe the demand side of religion: the individual selection of a religion and the following individual production of religious human capital are analyzed. The framework also allows for the supply-side perspective, modeled as 'the market of religions'. A rational actor is assumed for the formation of these markets. The possibility of seeking and changing religious offers is necessary for religious supply and demand to form a market. The commodity is the religious good. Its production is embedded in an institutionalized religious context. The supply side provides the infrastructure necessary for producing religious goods. A market-driven supplier will try to differentiate from other offers, engage more actively in attracting adherents, and endeavor to keep adherents once they join. The offers will become diverse. Specialization and orientation consistent with the wants of religious consumers will follow (Witham 2010). Further areas of research have included the effects of church-state regulations and disturbed—i.e. hindered or disabled—markets (Stolz 2006; Berger 1963).

New Institutional Economics: Systematic Theoretical Inclusion of Religion

New Institutional Economics (NIE) reaches beyond the neoclassical axioms by enriching them. According to the theory of Douglass North (awarded a Nobel Prize in 1990), economic action is determined by institutions such as laws and contracts (formal institutions) or customs and religions (informal institutions). Their historical development is conceptualized as 'institutional change', with both formal change and informal change affecting the respective institutions. Understanding the institutions involved in the exchange means better understanding the exchange. Possibilities of improving performance become visible.

In NIE the basic methodological setup of neoclassical economics remains, but the axioms are modified. The actor is not seen as atomistic. She or he is embedded in social contexts and processes. The absolute *rational choice* is substituted by a concept called *bounded rationality*, where economic decision-making is bounded by inner and outer circumstances. The institutional framework influences and limits choices. It reduces the infinite number of possible actions and reduces uncertainty (North 1990). The market is described as a regulated space. Participation is costly as taking part in the exchange results in informational and transactional costs. Market regulations are considered when modeling transactions. The perfect market with complete and symmetric information is replaced by path-dependent institutional change guided by the insight that 'history matters.'

To adequately describe these extended axioms, extra-economic factors are systematically integrated. The studies of law, culture, history, and society are included in order to understand the context of individuals. Political sciences and law are included in order to understand the formal institutions shaping behavior, and religious studies and theology are included in order to capaciously describe religion. Hence, NIE is open to the insights of non-economic disciplines. Non-economic contributions are a vital part of the economic model. The context of the actors and the peculiarities of the markets enrich the theory (Williamson 2000).

NIE allows for systematic consideration of religion as a factor in the economy. Earlier, rationality and markets were applied to religion. An economic perspective on religion was the result. Now, religion can be included as a primary aspect in economic theory. The religious impact on the economy can be modeled, as can the economic impact on religion (Zapf 2014). This still results in an economic perspective on religion but one where the theoretical frameworks better fit the objects of research.

CONCLUSION: RESEARCH APPROACH AND INTERDISCIPLINARY ECONOMICS OF RELIGION

The history of economic thought reveals some of the discipline's driving forces, including (a) the household and its productions, (b) the market and its miraculous workings, and (c) the self-interested *homo oeconomicus* and her/his actions. We have seen that these principles are not limited to the economy. In addition, we have seen the shortcomings of these broadened economics. Scholars in the tradition of Gary Becker have applied this paradigm and its axioms to religion, and the change in perspective has yielded new insights. However, the rational-choice approach has been criticized as reductionist, even imperialist: it imposes a certain logic on its subject and thereby shapes it (Söderbaum 2008). As economics adapted slowly and parts of the discipline opened up, a less simplistic conceptualization of economic processes was the result.

The application to religion benefits from this expanded perspective while the underlying interests remain compact: the systematic description of economic impacts on and of religion. Rachel McCleary (2007; 2011) has proposed the following formal division of the economics of religion:

1. *Religion as an independent variable.* The influence of religion on economic processes is the central object of study: e.g. the influence of religious structures on interpretations of economic behavior is researched, especially religious attitudes toward inner-worldly activities and rewards.
2. *Religion as a dependent variable.* The influence of economic circumstances on religion—e.g. variances in religious supply and demand—is studied using market and choice models as well as institutional analysis of religious environments (see also Koch, "Economy," this volume).

The economics of religion covers a multitude of topics. Theoretical and methodological diversity is the consequence. Particular research questions and designs determine and are determined by disciplinary emphases (Seele/Gatti/ Lohse 2014). The objects of economic analysis are multifactorial and religion is a good example of this. The discipline's perspective broadens, the approach becomes interdisciplinary, and research design becomes more flexible.

Glossary

Economics of religion an emerging research program to investigate influences of religion on economy and influence of economic thought and organization on religion.

Externalities non-intended consequences of economic action. The results exceed the reach of the initial actor. Externalities can be positive (e.g. colonies of threatened species thriving in abandoned industrial facilities) or negative (e.g. environment-changing effects of cars). The actor does not gain benefit from or have to pay for the externality.

Market the fulcrum of economic activity in market economies. A structure used by buyers and suppliers for exchange when repeatedly entering into trade relationships. Notoriously hard to grasp: it is a physical (e.g. weekly markets) as well as a metaphysical (e.g. 'the global market') space, a technical as well as a social structure aiming at organization and allocation.

Neoclassical economics a disciplinary approach to economics that relies on assumptions of eighteenth- and nineteenth-century scholars focusing on utility-maximizing and a central role of the market.

Paradigm and axioms both explain the starting point of scientific disciplines. A paradigm— e.g. the existence of a free market—is a normative setting that is not disputable. Based on the paradigm, axioms specify the interpretation of the setting, e.g. the nature of the market (perfect, cost-neutral, etc.)

Rational choice generally, every action is led by a certain reason or logic: in the economic context, the maximizing of utility by self-interested, autonomous actors.

The invisible hand a metaphor used to describe the positive, market-driven impact of aggregated, self-interested behavior. Coined by Adam Smith, it has been used since then to explain the benevolence of market-structures.

REFERENCES

Aspromourgos, Tony. 2008. "Neoclassical." *The New Palgrave Dictionary of Economics Online.* <http://www.dictionaryofeconomics.com/article?id=pde2008_N000038>. Last accessed Nov. 22, 2014. doi: 10.1057/9780230226203.3160

Azzi, Corry and Ronald Ehrenberg. 1975. "Household Allocation of Time and Church Attendance." *Journal of Political Economy* 83(1): 27–56. doi: 10.1086/260305

Becker, Gary S. 1965. "A Theory of the Allocation of Time." *The Economic Journal* 75(299): 493–517. doi: 10.2307/2228949

Berger, Peter. 1963. "A Market Model for the Analysis of Ecumenicity." *Social Research* 30(1): 77–93.

Binswanger, Hans Christoph. 1993. "Das Menschenbild der herkömmlichen Nationalökonomie." *Zeitschrift für Sozialökonomie* 97: 18–26.

Bishop, John D. 1995. "Adam Smith's Invisible Hand Argument." *Journal of Business Ethics* 14(3): 165–180. doi: 10.1007/bf00881431

Cameron, Gavin. 2008. "Classical Economics and Economic Growth." *The New Palgrave Dictionary of Economics Online.* <http://www.dictionaryofeconomics.com/article?id=pde2008_C000603>. Last accessed Oct. 1, 2014. doi: 10.1057/9780230226203.0244

Eecke, Wilfried Ver. 2013. "Adam Smith and the Free Market." In *Ethical Reflections on the Financial Crisis 2007/2008*, edited by Wilfried Ver Eecke. Heidelberg: Springer, 5–21. doi: 10.1007/978-3-642-35091-7_2

Emmett, Ross B. 2008. "Chicago School (new perspectives)." *The New Palgrave Dictionary of Economics Online.* <http://www.dictionaryofeconomics.com/article?id=pde2008_C000576>. Last accessed Oct. 7, 2014. doi: 10.1057/9780230226203.0227

Iannaccone, Laurence R. 1990. "Religious Practice: A Human Capital Approach." *Journal for the Scientific Study of Religion* 29(3): 297–314. doi: 10.2307/1386460

Iannaccone, Laurence R. 1995. "Household Production, Human Capital, and the Economics of Religion." In *The New Economics of Human Behavior*, edited by Laurence R. Iannaccone. Cambridge: Cambridge University Press, 172–187. doi: 10.1017/cbo9780511599040.013

Koehn, Daryl and Barry Wilbratte. 2012. "A Defense of a Thomistic Concept of the Just Price." *Business Ethics Quarterly* 22(3): 501–526. doi: 10.5840/beq201222332

McCleary, Rachel. 2007. "Salvation, Damnation, and Economic Incentives." *Journal of Contemporary Religion* 22(1): 49–74. doi: 10.1080/13537900601114503

McCleary, Rachel. 2011. "The Economics of Religion as a Field of Inquiry." In *The Oxford Handbook of the Economics of Religion*, edited by Rachel McCleary. Oxford: Oxford University Press, 3–36. doi: 10.1093/oxfordhb/9780195390049.013.0001

Nicholson, Walter and Christopher Snyder. 2010. *Intermediate Microeconomics and Its Application*, 11th edition. Mason: South-Western. doi: 10.4337/9781781002452.00063

North, Douglass C. 1990. *Institutions, Institutional Change, and Economic Performance.* Cambridge: Cambridge University Press. doi: 10.1017/cbo9780511808678

Oslington, Paul. 2012. "God and the Market: Adam Smith's Invisible Hand." *Journal of Business Ethics* 108(4): 429–438. doi: 10.1007/s10551-011-1099-z

Pirenne, Henri. 1986. *Sozial- und Wirtschaftsgeschichte Europas im Mittelalter.* Tübingen: Francke.

Robbins, Lionel. 1945. *An Essay on the Nature and Significance of Economic Science*, 2nd edition. London: Macmillan.

Seele, Peter. 2011. "Ethik der Existenzsicherung: Über die soziale Verantwortung des Unternehmertums bei Aristoteles." In *Ökonomie, Politik und Ethik in der praktischen Philosophie der Antike*, edited by Peter Seele. Berlin: de Gruyter, 115–132. doi: 10.1515/9783110268621

Seele, Peter, Lucia Gatti, and Aline Lohse. 2014. "Whose Economics of Religion?" *Journal of Religion in Europe* 7(1): 51–79. doi: 10.1163/18748929-00701003

Smith, Adam. 2007. *An Inquiry into the Nature and Causes of the Wealth of Nations*, edited by Jonathan Wight. Petersfield: Harriman House. Original edition, 1776.

Söderbaum, Peter. 2008. "Economics as Ideology." In *Pluralist Economics*, edited by Edward Fullbrook. London: Zed Books, 117–127.

Stark, Rodney and William Sims Bainbridge. 1987. *A Theory of Religion.* New York: Peter Lang.

Stolz, Jörg. 2006. "Salvation Goods and Religious Markets: Integrating Rational Choice and Weberian Perspectives." *Social Compass* 53(1): 13–32. doi: 10.1177/0037768606061575

Williamson, Oliver E. 2000. "The New Institutional Economics: Taking Stock, Looking Ahead." *Journal of Economic Literature* 38(3): 595–613. doi: 10.1257/jel.38.3.595

Witham, Larry. 2010. *Marketplace of the Gods: How Economics Explains Religion.* Oxford: Oxford University Press. doi: 10.1093/acprof:oso/9780195394757.001.0001

Wood, Diana. 2002. *Medieval Economic Thought.* Cambridge: Cambridge University Press. doi: 10.1017/cbo9780511811043

Zapf, Chr. Lucas. 2014. *Die religiöse Arbeit der Marktwirtschaft: Ein religionsökonomischer Vergleich.* Baden-Baden: Nomos. doi: 10.5771/9783845256924

FURTHER READING

Azzi/Ehrenberg 1975 [*Azzi and Ehrenberg present "the first systematic attempt by economists to analyze the determinants of individuals' participation in religious activities" (p. 27). In the tradition of economist Gary Becker and his theory of household production, religious behavior is described as competing with non-religious behavior. The allocation of time and money to these activities by households is described as a function of utility-maximizing.*]

Berger 1963 [*Sociologist Peter Berger offers one of the first market-models of religion. He describes Christian denominations as specializations within an environment, where religious offers compete for adherents. Religion is described as one player in an economic field: "It has been pointed out that economically speaking, religion in our society is a typical consumer product. It is consumer patterns that determine its marketing process. It should not, therefore, be surprising if this religious economy bears further resemblance to the first systematic attempt by economists to analyze the determinants of individuals' participation in religious activities" (88–89).*]

McCleary 2007 [*Harvard economist Rachel McCleary describes a method-driven approach to the economics of religion. She suggests a comparative program, using authoritative religious documents in order to distinguish the different positions and influences of religion on the economy and economic behavior.*]

North 1990 [*Nobel Prize-winning economist Douglass C. North wrote this central work of the New Institutional Economics. He lays out and defines the cornerstones of the discipline. The institutions that limit and steer economic behavior are described: "Institutions are the rules of the game in a society or, more formally, are the humanly devised constraints that shape human interaction" (3). Historic change and path-dependencies are explored and the effects on the market described.*]

Smith 2007 [1776] [*A central work in the history of the economic discipline. Smith lays out the principles of modern economic organization: the division of labor, the significance of a market for efficient allocation, and the role of self-interest and its positive impact on society:* "Give me that which I want, and you shall have this which you want, is the meaning of every such offer; and it is in this manner that we obtain from one another the far greater part of those good offices which we stand in need of. It is not from the benevolence of the butcher, the brewer, or the baker, that we expect our dinner, but from their regard to their own interest. We address ourselves, not to their humanity, but to their self-love, and never talk to them of our own necessities, but of their advantages" *(9–10).*]

CHAPTER 8

EVOLUTIONARY THEORY

JOHN H. SHAVER, BENJAMIN GRANT PURZYCKI,
AND RICHARD SOSIS

CHAPTER SUMMARY

- People in all cultures engage in ritual behaviors and hold beliefs in supernatural agents. This universality suggests that religion is a product of a shared evolutionary history.
- Although there has been a recent surge in the evolutionary study of religion, this has not been a unified endeavor.
- Currently researchers employ three major evolutionary frameworks to study religion—evolutionary psychology, behavioral ecology, and dual inheritance theory—each with different assumptions, methods, and areas of focus.
- Two of the largest sources of disagreement between evolutionary scholars of religion are: (1) religion as cognitive by-product vs. manifestation of adaptive behavioral plasticity; and (2) individual- vs. group-level selection processes as forces shaping religion.
- Integrative frameworks that incorporate aspects of all perspectives offer the best potential for real progress.

THE EVOLUTIONARY SCIENCE OF RELIGION

Evolutionary theorists generally view religion as ritual behavior that is motivated and/ or rationalized by appeals to supernatural agents (e.g. Purzycki/Sosis 2013).[1] Both rituals

[1] During the preparation of this chapter, Shaver was supported by a Templeton World Charity Foundation Grant (ID: 0077) and a Royal Society of New Zealand Marsden Fund Grant (ID: VUW 1321);

and supernatural beliefs exist in nearly all known human societies, and across cultures religions are structurally quite similar (Boyer 2001; Bulbulia 2005; Rappaport 1999). The universality and shared structure of religions beg evolutionary investigation. It is thus perhaps unsurprising that evolutionary approaches to the study of religion have flourished in recent years, as part of a general rise of evolutionary thinking across the sciences, and continue to inspire considerable empirical work. However, efforts to apply Darwinian theory to the study of religion do not represent a single unified endeavor or research program.

The focus of study is often a critical factor in determining how researchers interpret the effects of natural selection on religion. When, for instance, researchers concentrate on the cognitive requirements of religious thought, they typically conclude that religious beliefs are merely by-products of psychological adaptations designed for other purposes (e.g. Boyer 2001; Guthrie 1993). On the other hand, when researchers examine the social consequences of ritual behavior, the adaptive benefits of religion become quite clear (e.g. Alcorta/Sosis 2005). And when research emphasizes individual variation in religious behavior, it is obvious that these adaptive benefits are not equally achieved; some benefit more than others (e.g. Cronk 1994). However, research focused on group-level dynamics reveals that some religious groups are more successful than others, and this may be, in part, because they are better able to minimize individual self-interested behaviors and instead motivate behaviors that result in benefits for the group. Scholars pursuing such research argue that religious groups function as adaptive units that are subject to cultural group selection (e.g. Norenzayan 2013; Wilson 2002).

These differences in research foci roughly correspond to three relatively distinct evolutionary approaches to the study of human behavior: evolutionary psychology, human behavioral ecology, and dual inheritance theory (Smith 2000). Here we describe how each of these evolutionary subfields has approached the study of religion. We then suggest that viewing these approaches as complementary, rather than contradictory, offers the greatest potential to explain the complex phenomenon of religion (Sosis 2009; Sosis/Bulbulia 2011). Since evolved cognitive faculties, memory and its organization, behavioral expression, interpersonal social psychological responses, and the social and natural environments are all at play in the formation of religious systems, diverse approaches are necessary if we wish to uncover the evolutionary origins and development of religion.

EVOLUTIONARY PSYCHOLOGY OF RELIGION

Evolutionary psychologists use the theory of natural selection to generate hypotheses about panhuman psychological design; they contend that the human mind consists of

Purzycki was supported by the Cultural Evolution of Religion Research Consortium (CERC) which is supported by grants from SSHRC and the John Templeton Foundation; Sosis was supported by the James Barnett Endowment in Humanistic Anthropology.

several cognitive systems designed to solve specific adaptive problems that ancestral human populations faced (Tooby/Cosmides 1992; cf. Barrett et al. 2014; Samuels 1998). Because the human brain consists of cognitive adaptations to solve ancestral problems, and because modern environments often differ substantially, cognitive adaptations can produce thoughts and behaviors that are now neutral, maladaptive, or even unrelated to the problems they arose to solve. Indeed, the majority of evolutionary psychologists of religion hold that the human tendency for supernatural beliefs is an evolutionary by-product of cognitive systems that evolved to solve adaptive problems unrelated to religion (Bulbulia 2004; Sosis 2009). That is, the human proclivity for belief in the supernatural is the result of an evolved panhuman psychological design, but the cognitive architecture that supports supernatural belief did not arise because believing in supernatural agents itself was adaptive. The research questions evolutionary psychologists address include the developmental trajectories of the cognitive abilities assumed to contribute to supernatural belief, their presence in adults, and their cross-cultural prevalence, and they generally test their assumptions with laboratory experiments and/or survey research.

Evolutionary psychologists of religion assume that several cognitive systems contribute to our propensity for belief in the supernatural. Notably, Guthrie (1993) argues that the human tendency to anthropomorphize arose as a result of selection pressures that favored the ability to perceive agents and agency in the environment and that these abilities contribute the human propensity to interpret events in terms of supernatural agency. He suggests that perceiving agents, even when there are none, is advantageous insofar as *not* detecting agents that are present would be deleterious (e.g. not detecting a nearby mountain lion). While this promiscuous agency detection did not emerge for purposes relating to religion, and the evolutionary roots of this capacity run quite deep, it is nonetheless the ability to perceive unseen agents that gives rise to religious perceptions and explanations of the mysterious (Barrett 2004). Furthermore, myths, spirits, and god perceptions are the natural by-product of such a sensitive system; we explain the world in terms of agency, and frequently believe that events are caused by supernatural agents.

Human social interactions require the ability to understand and appreciate what others are thinking and feeling. Indeed, human sociality is built on the cognitive ability to interpret other individuals as having their own distinct perceptions, desires, and beliefs. This capacity, known as theory of mind (ToM—Premack/Woodruff 1978), arose for reasons unrelated to religion, but now contributes to the human propensity to believe that supernatural agents have minds with their own wishes and desires. But perceiving and thinking about such entities would contribute little to human sociality without tapping into moral cognition as well (see Haley/Fessler 2005; Nettle et al. 2013). Some evidence suggests that they do, even when the gods are not thought of as concerned with moral behavior (Purzycki 2013).

Other work suggests that humans are primed from an early age to accept teleological explanations. Deborah Kelemen, for example, suggests that children are 'intuitive theists' who believe that things in the natural world have been purposefully designed

(Kelemen 2004). Her studies show that children readily assert that both natural objects and artifacts exist for a reason. Moreover, this bias is not limited to children; less educated adults show this same tendency (Casler/Kelemen 2007), and under conditions of high cognitive load, even scientifically trained adults exhibit these same biases (Kelemen/Rossett 2009). Although 'promiscuous teleology' is thought to be the result of cognitive modules that evolved to reason about the biological world (e.g. Atran 1995), it also renders belief in a creator intuitive, and leads to interpretations that events happen for a purpose, an interpretative framework that many religions share.

While the mainstream view among evolutionary psychologists is that religious representations are evolutionary by-products, a few scholars have proposed that selection processes have resulted in psychological adaptations for religion specifically. For example, Bering (2006) and Bloom (2009) have shown that humans are intuitive dualists, and unless formally taught otherwise, they exhibit a tendency to conceptually separate minds from bodies. This propensity leads to the belief that minds and/or souls can continue to exist after death (Bering 2006). Additionally, Johnson and Bering (2006) argue that the human tendency to fear supernatural punishment is an adaptation that arose because those individuals who feared supernatural punishment were able to inhibit self-interested behavior and social transgressions that would have been punished by other group members. As god-fearing individuals were more successful at reaping the benefits of cooperation in ancestral environments, selection favored these propensities. Others argue that religions evolved, at least in part, to support mate discrimination, or finding other individuals who prefer monogamous long-term relationships and high fertility (Slone 2008; Weeden et al. 2008). Indeed, several authors interpret the lower promiscuity and higher fertility levels of religious people as an outcome of such strategies (Blume 2010; Bulbulia et al. 2015; Frejka/Westoff 2008; Kaufmann 2010).

HUMAN BEHAVIORAL ECOLOGY OF RELIGION

Whereas the majority of evolutionary psychologists of religion speculate that religious beliefs and behaviors are a by-product of cognitive systems that evolved to respond to selection pressures in ancestral environments (and that these selection pressures were unrelated to those that now motivate religious beliefs and behaviors), behavioral ecologists assume that selection has produced behavior-generating mechanisms that enable individuals to respond optimally to diverse environmental conditions, and that cross-cultural variation in behavior represents a manifestation of this behavioral plasticity. Contrary to the majority of cognitive approaches, behavioral ecologists begin their analyses by assessing how behaviors are adapted to current ecological settings. For the behavioral ecologist, determining adaptiveness means measuring the costs and benefits of a behavior, given available alternatives, in an effort to understand the selection pressures at work in any given environment. In general, behavioral ecologists of religion start by testing hypotheses derived from models that assume an individual's behavior is adaptive in its current environment. Human behavioral ecologists are typically anthropologists who engage in long-term ethnographic research and use data derived from field experiments and systematic behavioral observation to test hypotheses. They attempt to address research questions about the adaptiveness of individuals' religious behavior in a particular environment. While the behavioral ecology of religion is still in its infancy (Sosis/Bulbulia 2011), research to date has been both diverse and fruitful. Here we focus on just a few of these research programs.

At first glance, religious behavior appears maladaptive; it is often materially, energetically, and temporally expensive and thus superficially appears to be detrimental to individuals' immediate somatic and reproductive self-interest. However, behavioral ecologists interpret these costs as investments that return material benefits which positively impact fitness. To explain the adaptive benefits of ritual behavior, behavioral ecologists borrow two key insights from social theorists. First, Durkheim (2001 [1915]) speculated that the effervescent nature of collective rituals serves to bond group members and increase within-group cohesion. Second, Rappaport (1999) argued that rituals are able to increase social solidarity because they communicate adherence to a moral code and commitment to a social order, which in turn promotes trust, and hence cooperation.

Like all collectivities, religious groups are prone to exploitation by freeriders, or those who reap the benefits of group cooperation without pulling their own weight. Irons (2001) argued that the costliness of ritual behavior functions as a commitment device and serves to minimize the freerider problem because only those who are truly committed to the group would be willing to incur such costs. In other words, individuals who engage in costly ritual behavior communicate, or signal, their commitment to the group, in turn benefit from increased cooperation, and these material benefits are ultimately translated into reproductive success.

This theoretical framework, known as the costly signaling theory of religion, suggests that religious groups that require costly ritual behaviors of their members will exhibit high levels of cooperation. For example, Sosis and Bressler (2003) found that nineteenth-century United States religious communes that demanded more costly behaviors of group members out-survived those with fewer costly obligations. Moreover, the ritual costs associated with group membership vary across environments and increase as a function of the risks of exploiting these resources via freeriding. Perhaps the greatest risks of freeriding occur amongst groups engaged in warfare, where shirking on one's commitment to the group might mean death to other group members. Indeed, Sosis et al. (2007) found that cultures engaged in endemic warfare have the most taxing religious rites. In general, a significant body of empirical research now provides support for the premise that costs paid in ritual performance return high levels of cooperation (e.g. Ruffle/Sosis 2007; Soler 2012; Sosis/Ruffle 2003; 2004).

Behavioral ecologists have also explored the socio-ecological conditions that have favored specific religious behavioral patterns. For example, Strassmann's work with the Dogon of Mali (1992; 1996) examines the manner in which religious taboos and rituals surrounding sexual activity, such as attending menstrual huts, reduce the risks of cuckoldry. Specifically, she and colleagues have shown how the various religions practiced by the Dogon differentially impact cuckoldry rates (Strassmann et al. 2012).

In other studies, Fincher and Thornhill (2008; 2012) demonstrate that religious diversity varies as a function of environmental variance in disease prevalence. In every environment organisms are constantly engaged in an evolutionary arms race between greater virility and greater immunity. In high disease environments, such as the tropics, selection acts to reward limited dispersal and infrequent interaction with out-group members, as both represent increased risk for encountering novel diseases. Religions, Fincher and Thornhill argue, can provide the social barriers to limit social engagement with outside groups. Over time, in high disease environments, limited interaction with outsiders results in increased religious diversity. Conversely, in environments with relatively low disease levels, interaction with outsiders is not as deleterious. These environments therefore allow for greater dispersal, which ought to result in a decrease in religious diversity. Consistent with their predictions, in a cross-cultural analysis Fincher and Thornhill (2008) found religious diversity to be positively correlated with disease prevalence.

DUAL INHERITANCE THEORIES OF RELIGION

While the aforementioned evolutionary approaches to the study of religion focus on the individual-level evolutionary forces that led to the emergence of religious belief and behavior, a third group of scholars place emphasis on how selection that operates at the level of groups might explain the appearance and proliferation of religions. Specifically, dual inheritance theory (DIT) posits that genes and culture provide separate, but interacting, forms of inheritance. These theorists suggest that cultures, like genes, exhibit the three necessary conditions for evolution by natural selection: variation, inheritance, and fitness consequences. Because people acquire a significant amount of information from other group members, and cultures differ, the information accumulated by some groups allows them to better overcome adaptive problems, and thus spread at the expense of less successful ones (Boyd/Richerson 1985). Proponents of DIT are typically evolutionary biologists, anthropologists, and economists who rely upon computer simulations to test their mathematical models of cultural evolutionary processes. Many DIT scholars suggest that religious groups are subject to these cultural evolutionary processes.

Notably, evolutionary biologist D. S. Wilson (2002) argues that because religious groups limit self-interested behavior, but provide secular utility to members, religious groups function as adaptive units. When groups of individuals function as units, they are subject to the forces of cultural group selection; better adapted religions spread at the expense of those less equipped to overcome socio-environmental challenges. In support of his model, Wilson shows how religions, such as Calvinism and Jainism, provide material benefits for their members, while limiting self-interested behaviors and encouraging altruism toward other group members.

Other cultural evolutionary theorists share with evolutionary psychologists the assumption that supernatural beliefs are by-products of cognitive systems such as HADD (Hyperactive Agency Detection Device), ToM, and teleological reasoning, but also argue that variants of supernatural belief, and religious groups, are subject to cultural selection (e.g. Atran/Henrich 2010; Norenzayan 2013; Shariff et al. 2010). These theorists note that groups committed to omniscient high gods who intervened in human affairs and punished non-cooperators were more successful than groups whose belief systems did not promote cooperation as effectively. Thus, cultural evolutionary processes led to the current global pattern of limited religious diversity—more than half of the world's population practice Christianity or Islam, which center around belief in an omniscient high god that can punish uncooperative behavior. In support of these assertions, DIT theorists use the results of experimental studies that show that people are more cooperative under perceived social monitoring (e.g. Bering et al. 2005), that religious primes decrease cheating behavior and increase generosity, fairness, cooperation, and the punishment of non-cooperators (Norenzayan/Shariff 2008), and that religious individuals are trusted more than non-religious individuals (Purzycki/Arakchaa 2013; Tan/Vogel 2008).

Norenzayan (2013), who has most extensively developed this argument, recognizes that the widespread cooperation among non-kin in large-scale human societies is a significant evolutionary puzzle. He speculates that Big Gods, and their ability to promote prosocial behavior, enabled large-scale societies to emerge. Specifically, Norenzayan posits that through processes of cultural evolution, groups that embraced watchful and omniscient gods were able to cooperate and out-compete other groups that were unable to extend cooperation beyond kin and reciprocal relations.

Dual inheritance theorists also assume that humans are endowed with psychological adaptations for general-purpose learning, which allow for rapidly gathering fitness-relevant information from other group members. These evolved abilities contribute to the cultural accumulation of solutions to significant fitness concerns, such as techniques for tool construction or methods of agricultural production. These strategies work by biasing an individual's attention toward group members who ought to hold fitness enhancing information and then copying their strategies (Boyd/Richerson 1985; Richerson/Boyd 2005). One of these biases is the 'frequency bias' which increases the probability of learning information insofar as it appears frequently throughout the social environment. In terms of religious beliefs, the more people believe something and express that belief, the more likely one is to learn this belief and act upon it as well. Another such bias is the 'prestige bias', which focuses on the specific source of informational transfers. Like parents and successful hunters, priests, rabbis, shamans, lamas, mullahs, and other religious leaders are likely to transfer information with high fidelity, as it is assumed that selection has favored learning mechanisms that encourage us to copy the behavior of successful individuals.

Toward Synthesis

Two of the largest sources of disagreement among evolutionary scholars of religion, then, are: (1) whether or not religion is a cognitive by-product, or a manifestation of adaptive behavioral plasticity, and (2) whether or not individual- or group-level selection processes are a more potent evolutionary force in shaping the significant features religion. We contend that these are not insurmountable disagreements and conclude this chapter by briefly describing some ways to unite multiple evolutionary perspectives.

As stated above, evolutionary psychologists largely focus on how evolved cognitive systems produce, retain, and transmit religious thought. Conversely, behavioral ecological approaches emphasize variation in the costs and benefits to ritual behavior. Thus, these two perspectives differentially emphasize some features of religions while largely neglecting others. However, religions are comprised of both features—and a host of others—including emotionally evocative symbols, myths, and taboos. Some recent evolutionary approaches recognize that these core elements of religion constitute an adaptive system designed for promoting cooperation (Sosis 2009). Such an approach views beliefs as highly flexible, though constrained, cognitive processes that motivate adaptive responses to diverse environments (Alcorta/Sosis 2005; Purzycki/Sosis 2009; 2010). Moreover, these researchers seek to understand how selection favored the coalescence of religion's core features into an adaptive system. This approach incorporates the insights from all three evolutionary perspectives and aims to explain the central elements of religion with consideration of the local environment in which people operate.

A second major difference between evolutionary approaches is that some focus on individual-level selection pressures, while others focus on group-level evolutionary processes. It is likely, however, that both forces have shaped and continue to influence contemporary religions. We suggest that one of the most significant ways to reconcile evolutionary approaches is to collect data that can assess the effects of both levels of selection in a particular environment (Richerson/Newson 2008; Shaver 2015). Sober and Wilson (1998) outline a multilevel selection model that involves detailing phenotypic variation both within and between groups, and the heritability and fitness consequences of this variation. What is promising about such an approach is that it will enrich our understanding of the ways that religious behavior varies within and between populations. When combined with the view that religion is an adaptive system, such a research program will help to unify the perspectives and goals of all evolutionarily approaches. Indeed, all evolutionary scholars are united in their belief that Darwinian theory is a powerful framework for analyzing religion; the differences between approaches ought to be seen as offering complementary tools for advancing our understanding of the complex phenomenon of religion.

GLOSSARY

Adaptation process of phenotypic modification by natural selection, as well as the products of that process.

Adaptive a trait is adaptive if it confers reproductive benefits upon its bearer in a particular environment.

By-product a feature of an organism not designed for functional purpose, but one that exists because of the constraints and designs of the organism's adaptations.

Group selection natural selection that operates on groups of individuals.

Individual selection natural selection that operates on individual organisms.

Multilevel selection natural selection that operates on both individuals and groups simultaneously.

Natural selection evolutionary change that occurs when individuals vary, variation is heritable, and some variants are more likely to survive and reproduce.

Trait the quantifiable features of organisms.

REFERENCES

Alcorta, Candace S. and Richard Sosis. 2005. "Ritual, Emotion, and Sacred Symbols: The Evolution of Religion as an Adaptive Complex." *Human Nature* 16(4): 323–359.

Atran, Scott. 1995. "Causal Constraints on Categories." In *Causal Cognition: A Multi-Disciplinary Debate*, edited by Daniel Sperber, David Premack, and A. J. Premack. Oxford: Clarendon Press, 263–265.

Atran, Scott and Joseph Henrich. 2010. "The Evolution of Religion: How Cognitive By-products, Adaptive Learning Heuristics, Ritual Displays, and Group Competition Generate Deep Commitments to Prosocial Religions." *Biological Theory* 5(1): 18–30.

Barrett, Justin, L. 2004. *Why Would Anyone Believe in God?* Walnut Creek, CA: AltaMira Press.

Barrett, Louise, Thomas V. Pollet, and Gert Stulp. 2014. "From Computers to Cultivation: Reconceptualizing Evolutionary Psychology." *Frontiers in Psychology* 5. doi:10.3389/fpsyg.2014.00867

Bering, Jesse. 2006. "The Folk Psychology of Souls." *Behavioral and Brain Sciences* 29(5): 453–498.

Bering, Jesse M., Katrina McLeod, and Todd K. Shackelford. 2005. "Reasoning about Dead Agents Reveals Possible Adaptive Trends." *Human Nature* 16(4): 360–381.

Bloom, Paul. 2009. "Religious Belief as an Evolutionary Accident." In *The Believing Primate: Scientific, Philosophical, and Theological Reflections on the Origin of Religion*, edited by Jeffrey Schloss and Michael Murray. Oxford: Oxford University Press, 118–127.

Blume, Michael. 2010. "Von Hayek and the Amish Fertility: How Religious Communities Manage to be Fruitful and Multiply—A Case Study." In *The Nature of God: Evolution and Religion*, edited by Ulrich Frey. Marburg: Tectum Verlag, 159–175.

Boyd, Robert and Peter J. Richerson. 1985. *Culture and the Evolutionary Process*. Chicago, IL: University of Chicago Press.

Boyer, Pascal. 2001. *Religion Explained: The Evolutionary Origins of Religious Thought*. New York: Basic Books.

Bulbulia, Joseph. 2004. "The Cognitive and Evolutionary Psychology of Religion." *Biology and Philosophy* 19(5): 655–686.

Bulbulia, Joseph. 2005. "Are There Any Religions? An Evolutionary Exploration." *Method and Theory in the Study of Religion* 17(2): 71–100.

Bulbulia, Joseph A., John H. Shaver, Lara Greaves, Richard Sosis, and Chris Sibley. 2015. 'Religion and Parental Cooperation: An Empirical Test of Slone's Sexual Signaling Model.' In *The Attraction of Religion: A Sexual Selectionist Account*, edited by D. Slone and J. Van Slyke. London: Bloomsbury Press, 29–62.

Casler, Krista and Deborah Kelemen. 2007. "Reasoning about Artifacts at 24 Months: The Developing Teleo-Functional Stance." *Cognition* 103(1): 120–130.

Cronk, Lee. 1994. "Evolutionary Theories of Morality and the Manipulative Use of Signals." *Zygon* 29(1): 81–101.

Durkheim, Émile. 2001. *The Elementary Forms of Religious Life*. New York: Oxford University Press. Original edition, 1915.

Fincher, Corey L. and Randy Thornhill. 2008. "Assortative Sociality, Limited Dispersal, Infectious Disease and the Genesis of the Global Pattern of Religion Diversity." *Proceedings of the Royal Society B: Biological Sciences* 275(1651): 2587–2594. doi: 10.1098/rspb.2008.0688

Fincher, Corey L. and Randy Thornhill. 2012. "Parasite-Stress Promotes In-Group Assortative Sociality: The Cases of Strong Family ties and Heightened Religiosity." *Behavioral and Brain Sciences* 35(2): 61–79.

Frejka, Tomas and Charles F. Westoff. 2008. "Religion, Religiousness and Fertility in the US and in Europe." *European Journal of Population* 24(1): 5–31.

Guthrie, Stewart E. 1993. *Faces in the Clouds: A New Theory of Religion*. Oxford: Oxford University Press.

Haley, Kevin J. and Daniel M. Fessler. 2005. "Nobody's Watching? Subtle Cues Affect Generosity in an Anonymous Economic Game." *Evolution and Human Behavior* 26(3): 245–256.

Irons, William. 2001. "Religion as a Hard to Fake Sign of Commitment." In *Evolution and the Capacity for Commitment*, edited by R. M. Neese. New York: Russell Sage Foundation, 292–309.

Johnson, Dominic D. P. and Jesse M. Bering. 2006. "Hand of God, Mind of Man: Punishment and Cognition in the Evolution of Cooperation." *Evolutionary Psychology* 4(1): 219–233.

Kaufmann, Eric. 2010. *Shall the Religious Inherit the Earth?* London: Profile Books.

Kelemen, Deborah. 2004. "Are Children 'Intuitive Theists'? Reasoning about Purpose and Design in Nature." *Psychological Science* 15(5): 295–301.

Kelemen, Deborah and Evelyn Rosset. 2009. "The Human Function Compunction: Teleological Explanation in Adults." *Cognition* 111(1): 138–143.

Nettle, Daniel, Zoe Harper, Adam Kidson, Rosie Stone, Ian S. Penton-Voak, and Melissa Bateson. 2013. "The Watching Eyes Effect in the Dictator Game: It's Not How Much You Give, It's Being Seen to Give Something." *Evolution and Human Behavior* 34(1): 35–40.

Norenzayan, Ara. 2013. *Big Gods: How Religion Transformed Cooperation and Conflict*. Princeton, NJ: Princeton University Press.

Norenzayan, Ara and Azim F. Shariff. 2008. "The Origin and Evolution of Religious Prosociality." *Science* 322(5898): 58–62.

Premack, David and Guy Woodruff. 1978. "Does the Chimpanzee Have a Theory of Mind?" *Behavioral and Brain Sciences* 1(4): 515–526.

Purzycki, Benjamin G. 2013. "The Minds of Gods: A Comparative Study of Supernatural Agency." *Cognition* 129(1): 163–179.

Purzycki, Benjamin G. and Tayana Arakchaa. 2013. "Ritual Behavior and Trust in the Tyva Republic." *Current Anthropology* 54(3): 381–388.

Purzycki, Benjamin G. and Richard Sosis. 2009. "The Religious System as Adaptive: Cognitive Flexibility, Public Displays, and Acceptance." In *The Biological Evolution of Religious Mind and Behavior*, edited by Eric Voland and Wulf Schiefenhövel. New York: Springer-Verlag, 243–256.

Purzycki, Benjamin G. and Richard Sosis. 2010. "Religious Concepts as Necessary Components of the Adaptive Religious System." In *The Nature of God: Evolution and Religion*, edited by Ulrich Frey. Marburg: Tectum Verlag, 37–59.

Purzycki, Benjamin G. and Richard Sosis. 2013. "The Extended Religious Phenotype and the Adaptive Coupling of Ritual and Belief." *Israel Journal for Ecology and Evolution* 59(2): 99–108.

Rappaport, Roy A. 1999. *Ritual and Religion in the Making of Humanity*. Cambridge: Cambridge University Press.

Richerson, Peter J. and Robert Boyd. 2005. *Not by Genes Alone: How Culture Transformed Human Evolution*. Chicago, IL: University of Chicago Press.

Richerson, Peter J. and Lesley Newson. 2008. "Is Religion Adaptive? Yes, No, Neutral, but Mostly, We Don't Know." In *The Evolution of Religion: Studies, Theories, and Critiques*, edited by Joseph Bulbulia, Richard Sosis, Erica Harris, Russell Genet, Cheryl Genet, and Karen Wyman. Santa Margarita: Collins Foundation Press, 73–78.

Ruffle, Bradley and Richard Sosis. 2007. "Does It Pay to Pray? Costly Ritual and Cooperation." *The B.E. Journal of Economic Analysis and Policy* 7(1): 1–35.

Samuels, Richard. 1998. "Evolutionary Psychology and the Massive Modularity Hypothesis." *British Journal for the Philosophy of Science* 49(4): 575–602.

Shariff, Azim, Ara Norenzayan, and Joseph Henrich. 2010. "The Birth of High Gods." In *Evolution, Culture, and the Human Mind*, edited by Mark Schaller, Ara Norenzayan, Steven J. Heine, Toshio Yamagishi, and Tatsuya Kameda. London: Psychology Press/Taylor & Francis, 119–136.

Shaver, John H. 2015. "The Evolution of Stratification in Fijian Ritual Participation." *Religion, Brain & Behavior* 5(2): 101–117. doi: 10.1080/2153599X.2014.893253

Slone, D. Jason. 2008. "The Attraction of Religion: A Sexual Selectionist Account." In *The Evolution of Religion: Studies, Theories, and Critiques*, edited by Joseph Bulbulia, Richard Sosis, Erica Harris, Russell Genet, Cheryl Genet, and Karen Wyman. Santa Margarita, CA: Collins Foundation Press, 181–187.

Smith, Eric A. 2000. "Three Styles in the Evolutionary Study of Human Behavior." In *Human Behavior and Adaptation: An Anthropological Perspective*, edited by Lee Cronk, William Irons, and Napoleon Chagnon. Hawthorne, NY: Aldine de Gruyter, 27–46.

Sober, Elliot and David S. Wilson. 1998. *Unto Others: The Evolution and Psychology of Unselfish Behavior*. Cambridge, MA: Harvard University Press.

Soler, Monserrat. 2012. "Costly Signaling, Ritual and Cooperation: Evidence from Candomblé, an Afro-Brazilian religion." *Evolution and Human Behavior* 33(4): 346–356.

Sosis, Richard. 2009. "The Adaptationist-Byproduct Debate on the Evolution of Religion: Five Misunderstandings of the Adaptationist Program." *Journal of Cognition and Culture* 9(3): 315–332. doi: 10.1163/156770909X12518536414411

Sosis, Richard and Eric Bressler. 2003. "Cooperation and Commune Longevity: A Test of the Costly Signaling Theory of Religion." *Cross-Cultural Research* 37(2): 211–239.

Sosis, Richard and Joseph Bulbulia. 2011. "The Behavioral Ecology of Religion: The Benefits and Costs of One Evolutionary Approach." *Religion* 41(3): 341–362. doi: 10.1080/0048721X.2011.604514

Sosis, Richard, Howard Kress, and James Boster. 2007. "Scars for War: Evaluating Alternative Signaling Explanations for Cross-Cultural Variance in Ritual Costs." *Evolution and Human Behavior* 28(4): 234–247.

Sosis, Richard and Bradley Ruffle. 2003. "Religious Ritual and Cooperation: Testing for a Relationship on Israeli Religious and Secular Kibbutzim." *Current Anthropology* 44(5): 713–722.

Sosis, Richard and Bradley Ruffle. 2004. "Ideology, Religion, and the Evolution of Cooperation: Field Tests on Israeli Kibbutzim." *Research in Economic Anthropology* 23: 89–117.

Strassmann, Beverly I. 1992. "The Function of Menstrual Taboos among the Dogon: Defense Against Cuckoldry?" *Human Nature* 3(2): 89–131.

Strassmann, Beverly I. 1996. "Menstrual Hut Visits by Dogon Women: A Hormonal Test Distinguishes Deceit from Honest Signaling." *Behavioral Ecology* 7(3): 304–315.

Strassmann, Beverly I., Nikhil T. Kurapati, Brendan F. Hug, Erin E. Burke, Brenda W. Gillespie, Tatiana M. Karafet, and Michael F. Hammer. 2012. "Religion as a Means to Assure Paternity." *Proceedings of the National Academy of Sciences of the USA* 109(25): 9781–9785.

Tan, Jonathan H. and Claudia Vogel. 2008. "Religion and Trust: An Experimental Study." *Journal of Economic Psychology* 29(6): 832–848.

Tooby, John and Leda Cosmides. 1992. "The Psychological Foundations of Culture." In *The Adapted Mind: Evolutionary Psychology and the Generation of Culture*, edited by Jerome Barkow, Leda Cosmides, and John Tooby. New York: Oxford University Press, 19–136.

Weeden, Jason, Adam B. Cohen, and Douglas T. Kenrick. 2008. "Religious Attendance as Reproductive Support." *Evolution and Human Behavior* 29(5): 327–334.

Wilson, David S. 2002. *Darwin's Cathedral: Evolution, Religion, and the Nature of Society.* Chicago, IL: University of Chicago Press.

FURTHER READING

Alcorta/Sosis 2005 [*This paper describes religion as an adaptive complex comprised of supernatural beliefs, communal ritual, the separation of the sacred and profane, and adolescence as an experience expectant period for ritual the conditioning of sacred symbols.*]

Boyer 2001 [*This book argues that supernatural beliefs are a by-product of cognitive modules designed for purposes such as agency detection, and that supernatural concepts in all religious systems share a similar structure due to their cognitive appeal.*]

Bulbulia 2004 [*A paper that describes both by-product and adaptationist explanations of religious cognition and argues in favor of the latter.*]

Frey, Ulrich, ed. 2011. *The Nature of God: Evolution and Religion.* Marburg: Tectum Verlag [*This edited volume is comprised of works that employ a Darwinian perspective to address questions about cognitive origins, the development of religious cognition of children, and reproduction in religious communities, among others.*]

Guthrie 1993 [*One of the first applications of a cognitive and evolutionary approach to the study of religion, Guthrie argues that religion is a result of the human tendency to anthropomorphize the world.*]

Norenzayan 2013 [*Written from the perspective of both evolutionary psychology and dual inheritance theory, this book attempts to explain the rise of large-scale cooperative human societies, and the reasons for the success of the world's major religions.*]

Sosis 2009 [*The paper surveys and responds to criticisms of adaptationist approaches to religion that have been levied by by-product theorists.*]

Voland, Eckhart and Wulf Schiefenhövel, eds. 2009. *The Biological Evolution of Religious Mind and Behavior.* New York: Springer-Verlag. [*An edited volume that describes the selection pressures that may have given rise to the physiological, cognitive, and emotional processes that contribute to religion.*]

Watts, Fraser and Leon Turner, eds. 2014. *Evolution, Religion, and Cognitive Science: Critical and Constructive Essays.* Oxford: Oxford University Press. [*This edited volume, with contributions from authors of multiple disciplines, describes major controversies in evolutionary and cognitive approaches to religion.*]

CHAPTER 9

FEMINISM AND GENDER THEORY

DARLENE M. JUSCHKA

CHAPTER SUMMARY

- In the study of religio-cultural systems, gender was and continues to be a central component to organization and therefore requires the attention of scholars.
- Two distinct understandings of gender—gender as social construct and sex as biological reality vs. the social construction of both gender and sex—have shaped discussions of gender.
- Three significant theoretical developments in feminisms and gender studies have been intersectionality (analysis of interrelations between race, class, and gender), gender performance (as a central aspect of the social construction of gender, e.g. in rites of passage), and sexualities (recognizing that there is no single normative or universal sexuality).

INTRODUCTION

Gender is a central and primary concept—fluid, constructed, and ever changing—deployed in and through human signifying systems toward establishing epistemological and metaphysical narratives of existence. Some might argue such a claim is immoderate, but many would not. Gender plays a key role in all aspects of human existence be it language, education and knowledge production, social organization, or systems of belief and practice (aka religions). It is no surprise, then, that gender is hotly contested subject.

Within the frame of Euro-Western science, gender was (and continues to be by some) taken to be a biological reality insofar as penis and testicles = the male, and vagina (which includes the uterus and ovaries) and breasts = the female. In this biological narrative of human being there are only two genders, female and male. If a being lands outside of this male/female dichotomy, then medicine will intercede and alter the infant with surgeries and pharmaceuticals to fit one or the other gender: s/he cannot remain both or neither. As Ann Fausto-Sterling has argued concerning twentieth-century medicine: "Indeed, we have begun to insist upon the male–female dichotomy at increasingly early ages, making the two-sex system more deeply a part of how we imagine human life" (2000, 31). Why such extreme interventions? In Euro-Western ways of thinking about the body there can be only two kinds of gender, female and male, and furthermore these two kinds are taken to be opposite; a designation that establishes a firm boundary between the 'two' producing concrete social outcomes.

Feminists, among others, having identified gender as a primary category that suffuses all aspects of life, extended studies of gender in the academy beginning in the 1980s and continuing until the present (2014). Studies of gender emerged from numerous disciplines with anthropology having an early start, seen in the works of Margaret Mead (2001 [1928]) and Catherine Berndt (1950) among others. Across disciplines, studies pushed thinking on gender beyond the normative view that gender is simply and utterly a biological truth; rather, feminist theorists argued sex, that is sexual difference, may be a biological category and unchangeable, but gender is not. Gender, it was argued, is a social category and consequently subject to vagaries of social and historical change.

The view that only gender was theorizable was questioned in the late 1980s. Called the 'sex-gender dimorphism' by Gilbert Herdt (1996), and challenged by a number of feminists like Monique Wittig (1992) and Christine Delphy (1996), sex, they argued, does not precede gender; rather, gender precedes sex and defines and shapes it. Furthermore, understanding sex as a fixed biological reality and gender as its social interpretation simply perpetuated the current Euro-Western gender ideology. Sex, they argued, is as much a social category as gender and therefore equally subject to the vicissitudes of time and space. As Thomas Laqueur (1992) convincingly argued, the biological conceptualization of female and male as opposite sexes and genders is a relatively new phenomenon arising about 1800, and replaced the Aristotelian model (see *On the Generation of Animals*, II, iii, 737a) of one sex and two genders; that is the female and male are the same sex, but different genders. Views of gender, then, give rise to views of sex and not the other way around.

These two distinct understandings of gender—(1) gender as the social construct and sex as a biological reality of female and male sexual difference, and (2) the social construction of both gender and sex—have shaped thinking, discussions, representations, and identities pertaining to gender. In the study of systems of belief and practice (aka religions) these distinct understandings have also come into play and have shaped scholars' work therein.

GENDER AND THE STUDY OF SYSTEMS
OF BELIEF AND PRACTICE

Throughout the 1980s and early 1990s the view that gender is a social category, with biological sex hived off, dominated especially those texts organized around 'women and religion.' Gathering information and documentation, feminists in multiple areas produced texts that tracked the activities of women operating within and actively shaping systems of belief and practice. Equally, feminists also critically engaged systems of belief and practice, along with scholarly tellings, noting how those humans marked as women and girls were simply written out of existence. Joan Breton Connelly's study of priestesses in the Ancient Greek world (2007) engages both of these feminist efforts showing how ancient authors and modern scholars ignored, dismissed, or simply didn't acknowledge women's ritual work and expertise. Challenging the view that all the women were locked up in the *gynaeceum*, Connelly draws on multiple kinds of data including textual sources to convincingly show that women indeed were vibrant and constant participants of city-states throughout their lives. Indeed it had been recently argued by Simon Price that there appears to have been a remarkable equality between men and women as priest and priestess in ancient Greece (in Connelly 2007, 2).

Both of these approaches to the study of gender adhere to the view that gender is a social category, but it is less clear how sex fares. Left unaccounted for, sex occupies the default position of a biological reality that supports gender. This formulation of gender and sex, however, came under criticism for its assumptions concerning the stability of the category 'women.' These critiques of gender (and women) came largely from postmodernist and poststructuralist theorists who challenged the essentialization of these concepts, arguing they were not things in themselves but constructed in and through language, representation, and discourse. Furthermore, for poststructural theorists in feminisms and gender studies, destabilizing modernity's conceits of guaranteed truth and subject did not mean replacing 'man' with 'woman' as the privileged subject of knowledge.

An example of this kind of analysis of modernist assumptions (that is gender and sex are fixed and unchangeable) is Todd Penner and Caroline Vander Stichele's "Scripturing Gender in Acts" from their edited volume *Mapping Gender in Ancient Religious Discourses* (2006). Their contribution examines the authorization of speakers and texts in ancient Rome of the early first centuries of the Common Era and the implication for the Book of Acts in the New Testament. They note how the narrative of Acts draws on a gendered mythic past in order to legitimate the apostolic role of the protagonist Paul. For example, they argue that the text situates Paul as an heir of a "male lineage of power brokers" (Penner/Stichele 2006, 266) following in the line of Moses: Paul, like Moses, had seen the face of deity, and like Moses would authoritatively carry forth the message of deity (Acts 13:16–42). In Penner and Stichele's analysis of Acts, gender is taken to be a concept, developed and deployed in signifying systems and used for many purposes not the least of which is social power.

How gender signifies in the study of systems of belief and practice varies, but the two poles of gender analyses, that is gender as a social category, and gender and sex as both socially constructed, have tended to inform these studies. However, the 1990s saw further thinking on the subject of gender, and in what follows I discuss some of these important developments that have been taken up by scholars in the study of systems of belief and practice, aka religion.

BLACK FEMINIST STANDPOINT
AND INTERSECTIONALITY

Black feminist standpoint epistemology was developed in several Euro-Western locations (the United Kingdom, the United States, and Canada) alongside White feminist standpoint epistemology, the latter typifying the dominant feminist view of what is called second-wave feminism. Both Black and White feminist standpoint drew on Marxian social theory in order to think about women's relations to, and within, the state; the state named as patriarchal and capitalist. But in White feminist standpoint, the state was unraced as were the women the state ruled. Indeed, racism (and its social effect race) was eerily absent from mainstream feminist and gender analyses throughout much of the 1970s and 1980s.

In the United States, bell hooks (1981), Cherrie Moraga and Gloria Anzaldúa (1983), and Barbara Smith (1998), and, in the United Kingdom, Hazel Carby (1997) and Kum-Kum Bhavnani and Margaret Coulson (1997) pointed to this absence and named the feminist center as White, while its margins were populated by those other women who were equally defined racially. And although the White feminist center stood accountable for this and 'race' was added to their analyses, Black feminist standpoint's epistemological demand that experience be a primary site for the production of knowledge (as it is for White standpoint feminist standpoint) meant a separation from White feminism and the development of tools that could appropriately expose and challenge systems of oppression that included race, class, and gender, all of which impinge on the bodies and lives of women of color.

In the challenge to White feminisms, Black feminist standpoint proposed concepts like 'double jeopardy' (Beale 1969), that is the combination of racial and gender oppression, while Angela Davis (1981) and Patricia Hill Collins (1990) combined the analysis of gender, race, and class in their work. Called a 'matrix of domination' by Hill Collins, race, class, and gender interlocked to produce systems of oppression. Analysis of the deployment of race, class, and gender and how they intersected to shape and be shaped by each other was named 'intersectionality' by American Kimberlé Crenshaw (1991). In her work she argues that intersectionality is a means to get at the complexity of oppression and the lives it affects. For example, Crenshaw demonstrates that in the racialized and gendered social context of the United States there is a general perception that the darker one's skin the more one is sexualized and, as a result, that Black women are seen as less likely to be unwilling victims of rape. To support this she points to a study of dispositions in Dallas, Texas that "showed that the average prison terms for a man convicted of raping a Black woman was two years, as compared to five years for the rape of a Latina and ten years for the rape of an Anglo woman" (1991, 1269). What we see, she argues, is how gender, race, and class intersect to make Black women's lives more precarious.

Nira Yurval-Davis has argued that intersectionality is "the most valid contemporary sociological theoretical approach to stratification" (2011, 156). It is a tool of analysis that requires theorists to keep in mind both the big picture, or macrocosm, which allows for the analysis of structural oppression operating as part of our social systems, and the smaller picture, or microcosm, wherein analysis focuses on how structural oppression shapes lives and identities. For example, a masculine, white-settler, and elitist government in Canada proposed and defined 'Status Indian' in the Indian Act of 1876. In this Act, Status was conferred through the father's line and by doing this the government disenfranchised tens of thousands of Aboriginal women and their children (Green 2007). Contestation came in 1989 from self-identified Aboriginal women who successfully sued the Canadian government for its gender discrimination against Aboriginal women.

In the study of systems of belief and practice, intersectionality has come into play particularly among those who do ethnographic and sociological work. Aihwa Ong, for example, regularly intersects gender, age, religion, colonialism, and capitalism in her work. Her 1987 text *Spirits of Resistance and Capitalist Discipline: Factory Women in Malaysia* is a robust example of intersectionality wherein Ong shows the interplay between structural oppression represented by gender, age, and ethnicity, and the young, female factory workers who resist it. Situated in a free-trade zone in Malaysia, Japanese managers of the factory demanded obedience and compliance from young female factory workers, including making themselves sexually available. Unable to directly challenge men, as masculine hegemonic relations were taken to be normative, some of the young female factory workers began to complain of being harassed by displaced forest demons that had come to occupy the factory. Scoffed at and dismissed by management, the workers went on strike and demanded Shamanic intervention. The factory owners and managers were forced to exorcise the factory. As Ong notes, the demons were the means by which the young, female workers challenged managers and demonstrated their collective power.

In "State versus Islam: Malay Families, Women's Bodies, and the Body Politic in Malaysia" (1995) Ong examines how both state Islam and emergent revivalist Islam use women's reproductive bodies as a discursive means to "maintain (or rework) race, class, and religious boundaries between social groups" (159). Ong's analysis shows how both the Malay state's and Islamic revivalist's narratives use women's reproductive bodies as a means to distinguish insiders from outsiders, that is Malays and non-Malays. In time, however, the Malay state adopted the Islamic revivalist's narrative that linked Islam to what was deemed proper Malay identity. To ensure this purity of Malay identity, then, brothers, fathers, and sons set and then policed the boundaries around the bodies of wives, sisters, and daughters. Such boundaries were signified by clothing.

Notions of proper Malay identity and proper Islamic identity were joined and seen to be synonymous; Malaysia became Islamic and Malaysian people Muslims, as defined by and with the Islamic revivalist narrative. In this narrative, to evince the proper Islamic, Malay identity requires proper masculinity and proper femininity or a gender ideology that defines female and male as separate and different and requires this signification to be visible. However, as Ong notes, this gender ideology was not taken up by all segments of society; rather, it was taken up predominantly by the newly emergent middle class. It was this group that signaled its proper Malaysian-Islamic identity in dress, daily practices, gestures, and affectations. Following the prescriptions of the state and revivalist Islam, they created the 'imagined community' of proper Islamic Malaysians divided by genders (Ong 1995, 160–163).

Such interplay between the larger social structure and the individual is also central to the gender analyses of R. W. Connell. Rejecting the earlier sex role theory as the point of departure for gender studies, Connell instead combines psychoanalytic and sociological theories. Connell seeks to address the complexity of gender and its deployment in the social field focusing on 'hegemonic masculinities' (2005).

FEMINIST POSTSTRUCTURALISM, GENDER STUDIES, AND THE PERFORMANCE OF GENDER

The intersection of race, gender, class, geopolitical location, and other important social and political divisions is also part of feminist poststructuralism, but the intersecting concepts are understood to be discursive and not concrete things in the world. In this formulation, gender is an effect of language (language understood as all forms of representation including, but not limited to, image, gesture, and narrative of all kinds). Gender, race, and class—all forms of difference and social division—come into play in our systems of relations, and although they are heavily naturalized in most treatments, be they legal, economic, philosophical, biological, or metaphysical (religious), they do not exist outside of our representational systems.

Equally sex is considered a concept constructed in and by language, rather than a biological truth. In Euro-Western knowledge systems and mainstream culture the body is taken to be a passive object upon which sex is written: first there is the unsexed or androgynous human body and then sex is written upon it establishing a gendered future for this passive body (Salih and Butler 2004, 103–104). However, as feminist poststructural theorists have convincingly argued, gender precedes sex, and indeed it is gender that reads sex onto the body; and if the body does not conform to the named gender, then it will be made to conform.

Once gender ideology has been used to sex the body, humans are prescribed a gendered future in their social locations, and securing that gendered future, for good or ill, requires the proper gender performance. If this performance is not done properly (or done differently) then there can be concrete consequences. Deuteronomy 22:5 of the Hebrew Bible reads: "A woman must not wear a man's apparel, nor shall a man put on women's garments, for whosoever does such things is abhorrent to the LORD your God." This passage assumes as normative, and therefore redraws and reinforces, a boundary between two so-called kinds of humans, male and female, much as Islamic revivalism in Malaysia. As such, then, the text presents to the reader a prescription regarding the normative performance of gender: women and men are different genders; clothing is an 'outward' signifier of that difference; women and men must wear the clothing that properly signifies sexual difference. Since the text of Deuteronomy is concerned with boundaries—boundaries which keep chaos at bay—one of its concerns was to affirm and secure a boundary between the kinds it creates, female and male. To do this, the text locates this distinction of kinds, that is, female and male, with deity and in so doing gives this distinction metaphysical certitude.

The performance of gender is enacted in many ways and clothing, as evidenced in Deuteronomy, is one of the more obvious examples. Wearing gender-coded apparel allows the wearer to perform the gender, while the constant repetition of this performance, both with and without awareness, as in all habits, manifests the appropriate (or not) gender. As Judith Butler has written, "[g]ender ought not to be construed as a stable identity or locus of agency for which various acts follow; rather, gender is an identity tenuously constituted in time, instituted in an exterior space through a *stylized repetition of acts*" (2004, 114, author's italics).

The work of anthropologists and ritual studies scholars has long paid attention to the idea of the performance of gender, particularly when examining rites of passage. Rites of passage are used to transit participants from one way of being to another. So, for example, genital cutting, often one part of a rite of passage into (pre)adulthood, is a ritual that takes its mark, the cut that produces blood, to signify the body as now properly gendered. Over participants' lives, other myths, symbols, and ritual will come into play to reinforce the gender ideology of the initial rite of passage.

For example, Gilbert Herdt's (1987) ethnographic work with the Sambia people of New Guinea examines the rites that males enact over an extended period of time toward transforming the child-youth-bachelor into a proper Sambian warrior able to marry, have children, and protect what is his. The rite began with the removal of potentially-male children from the proximity of females and spaces marked as feminine (the back half of the living space, women's gardens, village paths, and a section of the river bank for example). With much noise and lamentation, 'proper' men take the participants out of the village to the men's house where they are to live until after the birth of their first child many years later. During the initial days of the ritual the children are thrashed with branches and rubbed with stinging nettles, and regularly frightened by the haunting sounds of the flute in the dense forest, a flute linked to the phallus/penis. Due to having spent their first years in feminine space with females, the participants have been contaminated and need to be purified of their contamination. Whipping and rubbing the flesh with nettles stretches the boys and purifies their bodies of feminine taint. Sharpened grass is used to initiate nose bleeding in order to expel contaminated blood, while vomiting allows the participants to rid their body of female food. With this they are ready to ingest the semen of older males—youths who have been in the men's lodge for several years—which will effectively transit these feminine boys to properly masculine men, warriors who fear neither pain nor death (Herdt 1987, 221ff.).

In this system of belief and practice, semen is seen to contain the essence of masculinity, and it is the continual ritual purification, ingestion of semen, and physical distance from all things female and feminine that allows for the making of proper men. Through these steps and the pain they must stoically endure, the children learn to perform, and perform properly, their Sambia warrior masculinity. Their mothers, sisters, aunties and all female relations are set at a distance; boys will learn that men and women have their different gendered paths to the gardens, forest, and water (Herdt 1987, 89–128). In the context of Sambia, then, men learn that pain and 'proper' masculinity are intimate bedfellows.

SEXUALITIES AND QUEER STUDIES

Gilbert Herdt's work with the Sambia evidences that there is no single normative sexuality, and nor is there a universal sexuality. Like the concepts of gender, and sex, sexuality too had been naturalized, but like them, it too is a concept, one that comes to meaning in discourse. As Michel Foucault has written, sexuality appears as

> an especially dense transfer point for relations of power: between men and women, young people and old people, parents and offspring, teachers and students, priests and laity, an administration and a population. Sexuality is . . . endowed with the greatest instrumentality: useful for the greatest number of manoeuvres and capable of serving as a point of support, as a linchpin, for the most varied of strategies. (1988–1990, 103)

Queer and sexualities studies share the view that sexuality is multiple and constituted in and through discourse. And, as with poststructural and postcolonial analyses, the play of power is important to analyze; indeed, it is by following the play of power that the analysis is able to expose and engage the ideology that anchors and shapes the discourse. In the twentieth century of the Euro-West, shaped in many ways by variant versions of Christianity deployed through colonization, a gender ideology of opposite sexes and genders (that is, the female is the opposite of the male in body, mind, and psyche) intersects with and upholds an ideology of sexuality wherein sexual acts between opposite sexes and genders is the only natural and proper form of sexuality. Sexual acts between those deemed the same sex, in other words homosexuality, was criminalized and treated as a sign (symptom) of moral and mental weakness/illness. Such criminalization continues in 2014 in countries like Egypt, Uganda, India, or Singapore, while in the Euro-West attitudes in general have been tempered, but pockets of resistance remain. However, although many countries like the United States, Canada, China, and the United Kingdom have removed laws against same-sex relations, many religious institutions continue to propose the view that same-sex relations are morally wrong and against divinely designed nature.

Queer and sexualities studies, like poststructuralism, are interested in challenging the fixing of identities, for example, female, male, homosexual, and heterosexual, deconstructing what are seen to be binaries and in so doing destabilizing these binaries. Binaries are concepts, for example, homosexuality and heterosexuality, that are oppositionally related with one concept carrying negative value (–), homosexuality, when binarily linked to its so-called opposite, heterosexuality, carrying positive value (+). Poststructuralism, postcolonialism, and queer and sexualities studies deconstruct such binaries, exposing the ideologies that support and legitimate a narrow construction and understanding of sexuality, gender, and race, and arguing for a more complex analysis that sees identities and concepts as fluid and shifting. Eve Sedgwick's *Epistemology of the Closet* set the stage to challenge the binary of homosexual/heterosexual arguing that "many of the major nodes of thought and knowledge in the twentieth-century Western culture as a whole are structured—indeed, fractured—by a chronic, now endemic crisis of homo/heterosexuality definition, indicatively male, dating from the end of the nineteenth-century" (1990, 1). David Halperin wrote that to be queer is to be at odds with what is taken to be normal (in Wilcox 2012, 228), while queer theory is, writes Melissa Wilcox, "a theoretical approach that positions itself outside of and against dominant discourses, critically examining the normative from a standpoint beyond it" (Wilcox 2012, 228).

Like most critical theories, queer theory challenges normative assumptions, although, initially at least, it tightly focused on sexuality, leaving gender to feminisms and gender studies. Considering how gender and sexual ideologies are intimately linked, however, queer theorists like Judith Butler asked:

> Can sexual practices ever fully be divorced from questions of gender, or do questions of gender persist as the 'unconscious' of sexual play? Such a question is not meant to return us to the pathos of an irrefutable 'sexual difference,' but to suggest that the 'break' with gender always comes at a cost and, perhaps also, with its spectral return. (1997, 3)

Following Butler's recommendation and intersecting gender/sex and sexuality, along with other social concepts that create social divisions and inequalities, studies of sexualities are made richer and avoid caricaturing subjects and their contexts. For example, many narratives of the Indigenous peoples of Turtle Island reference the figure of the Two-Spirit, once called the *berdache* (French meaning male prostitute and therefore derogatory) by anthropologists. This individual crossed boundaries and this capacity was recognized and legitimated through ritual and ceremony wherein the Two-Spirit became either a man-woman or a woman-man with attendant gender roles. This ritual intervention ensured that the Two-Spirit person had a place within the social body. And, as the Two-Spirit was a 'changing one', always in flux and equally balancing the masculine and the feminine, such persons often became specialists in communities acting as healers, shamans, weavers, storytellers, or warriors.

When encountering the numerous peoples of Turtle Island (North America), Europeans encountered differing sexualities and gender relations including two new genders; named variously depending on the peoples, but called the *Lhamana* among the A:shiwi (Zuni). The A:shiwi have an emergence myth whereby the people ascend up through four underground worlds to reach the surface world, the centre of which will be their home. During the A:shiwi's journey to find their home, the rain priest's children, a boy and a girl, commit incest from which ten supernatural beings are born, and one of these is the *Lhamana*. The supernatural *Lhamana* embodied both genders and was fully male and fully female, "like a single ear of corn with two hearts" (Roscoe 1991, 153). The *Lhamana* corrected the imbalance the children's incest had occasioned.

Understanding the figure of the Two-Spirit requires understanding how sexuality and gender/sex intersect and work in tandem as part of the 'world' proposed by the social group.

CONCLUSION

The variation of performances of gender/sex and sexuality, of readings of the body, of shaping and reshaping of bodies, and of categories of social formations all speak of multiplicity. The multiplicity of manifestations of race, gender, sex, and sexuality also demonstrate historicity and sociality telling us they are neither natural categories, nor God-given. Rather, they are socially constructed, discursive, and embedded in the structures that give rise to our narratives, representations, and practices, something boundary-crossers like Two-Spirit, gay, lesbian, transgender, transsexual, or intersexed folks make very apparent.

GLOSSARY

Class the conceptualization of humans in multiple kinds with accompanying roles, expectations of performance, and life limitations based on economics and social status.
Gender the conceptualization of humans into kinds with accompanying roles, expectations of performance, and life limitations based on genitalia.
Gender ideology the naturalization of gendered social relations locating them in nature or with deity(ies) which are used to legitimate roles, expectations of performance, and life limitations.

Gender performance as Judith Butler names it, a styling of the flesh—an act—that is in accordance with social-historical demands.

Intersectionality a methodological tool wherein analysis understands social categories to be working together rather than individually.

Queer an appropriated term wherein the negativity of being different is given positive meaning; as an aspect of identity queer speaks to the rejection of normative gender, sex, and sexuality seeing these as ideologically driven through binarism.

Race the conceptualization of humans into multiple kinds with accompanying roles, expectations of performance, and life limitations based on melanin.

Sex often treated as biological reality, a bodily configuration in accordance with gender ideologies.

Sexualities multiple kinds and forms of intimate desire many of which have been erased and oppressed by heteronormativity or the ideology that all sexualities are under the sign of reproduction.

REFERENCES

Beale, Francis. 1969. *Double Jeopardy: To Be Black & Female*. Detroit, MI: Radical Education Project. Reprinted in *The Sixties: Primary Documents and Personal Narratives, 1960 to 1974*. Alexandria, VA: Alexander Street Press. <http://alexanderstreet.com/products/sixties-primary-documents-and-personal-narratives-1960-1974>.

Berndt, Catherine. H. 1950. *Women's Changing Ceremonies in Northern Australia*. Paris: Hermann.

Bhavnani, Kum-Kum and Margaret Coulson. 1997. "Transforming Socialist Feminism: The Challenge of Racism." In *Black British Feminism: A Reader*, edited by Heidi Safia Mirza. New York: Routledge, 59–62.

Butler, Judith. 1997. "Against Proper Objects." In *Feminism Meets Queer Theory*, edited by Elizabeth Weed and Naomi Schor. Bloomington: Indiana University Press, 1–30.

Carby, Hazel. 1997. "White Women Listen! Black Feminism and the Boundaries of Sisterhood." In *Black British Feminism: A Reader*, edited by Heidi Safia Mirza. New York: Routledge, 45–53.

Collins, Patricia Hill. 1990. *Black Feminist Thought: Knowledge, Consciousness, and the Politics of Empowerment*. Boston, MA: Unwin Hyman.

Connell, Raewyn. 2005. *Masculinities*, 2nd edition. Berkeley: University of California Press. Original edition, 1995.

Connelly, Joan Breton. 2007. *Portrait of a Priestess: Women and Ritual in Ancient Greece*. Princeton, NJ and Oxford: Princeton University Press.

Crenshaw, Kimberlé. 1991. "Mapping the Margins: Intersectionality, Identity Politics, and Violence against Women of Color." *Stanford Law Review* 43(6): 1241–1299.

Davis, Angela Y. 1981. *Women, Race & Class*. New York: Random House.

Delphy, Christine. 1996. "Rethinking Sex and Gender." In *Sex in Question: French Materialist Feminism*, edited by Diana Leonard and Lisa Adkins. London: Taylor & Francis, 30–41.

Fausto-Sterling, Ann. 2000. *Sexing the Body: Gender Politics and the Construction of Sexuality*. New York: Basic Books.

Foucault, Michel. 1988–90. *The History of Sexuality*, Vol. 1: *An Introduction*, translated by Robert Hurley. New York: Vintage.

Green, Joyce. 2007. "Balancing Strategies: Aboriginal Women and Constitutional Rights in Canada." In *Making Space for Indigenous Feminism*, edited by Joyce Green. Winnipeg/London: Fernwood Publishing/Zed Books, 140–159.

Herdt, Gilbert. 1987. *The Sambia: Ritual and Gender in New Guinea*. New York: Holt, Rinehart and Winston.

Herdt, Gilbert, ed. 1996. *Third Sex, Third Gender: Beyond Sexual Dimorphism in Culture and History*. New York: Zone Books.

hooks, bell. 1981. *Ain't I a Woman: Black Women and Feminism*. Boston, MA: South End Press.

Laqueur, Thomas. 1992. *Making Sex: Body and Gender from the Greeks to Freud*. Cambridge, MA and London: Harvard University Press.

Mead, Margaret. 2001. *Coming of Age in Samoa: A Study of Adolescence and Sex in Primitive Societies*. New York: Perennial Classics. Original edition, 1928.

Moraga, Cherrie and Gloria Anzaldúa, eds. 1983. *This Bridge Called My Back: Writings by Radical Women of Color*. Watertown, MA: Kitchen Table Press/Persephone Press.

Ong, Aihwa. 1987. *Spirits of Resistance and Capitalist Discipline: Factory Women in Malaysia*. Albany: SUNY Press.

Ong, Aihwa. "State versus Islam: Malay Families, Women's Bodies, and the Body Politic in Malaysia." In *Bewitching Women, Pious Men: Gender and Body Politics in Southeast Asia*, edited by Aihwa Ong and Michael G. Peletz. Berkeley: University of California Press, 159–194.

Penner, Todd and Caroline Vander Stichele, eds. 2006. *Mapping Gender in Ancient Religious Discourses*. Leiden: Brill.

Roscoe, Will. 1991. *The Zuni Man-Woman*. Albuquerque: University of New Mexico Press.

Salih, Sara, ed., with Judith Butler. 2004. *The Judith Butler Reader*. Malden, MA and Oxford: Blackwell.

Sedgwick, Eve Kosofsky. 1990. *Epistemology of the Closet*. Berkeley: University of California Press.

Smith, Barbara. 1998. *The Truth That Never Hurts: Writings on Race, Gender, and Freedom*. New Brunswick, NJ: Rutgers University Press.

Wilcox, Melissa. 2012. "Queer Theory and the Study of Religion." In *Queer Religion: LGBT Movements and Queering Religion*, edited by Donald Boisvert and Jay Emerson. Santa Barbara, CA: Praeger, 227–252.

Wittig, Monique. 1992. *The Straight Mind and Other Essays*. Boston, MA: Beacon Press.

Yurval-Davis, Nira. 2011. "Beyond the Recognition and Redistribution Dichotomy: Intersectionality and Stratification." In *Framing Intersectionality: Debates on a Multi-Faceted Concept in Gender Studies*, edited by Helma Lutz, Maria Teresa Vivar, and Linda Supik. Farnham: Ashgate, 155–170.

FURTHER READING

Armour, Ellen T. and Susan M. St. Ville, eds. 2006. *Bodily Citations: Religion and Judith Butler*. New York: Columbia University Press. [*A selection of essays engaging the intersection of religion, gender, and sexuality drawing on Butler's theories of materiality, the body, gender performance, and heteronormativity.*]

Banerjee, Pompa. 2003. *Burning Women: Widows, Witches, and Early Modern European Travelers in India*. New York: Palgrave Macmillan. [*A postcolonial comparative study of*

European witch burning and Sati in the early modern period demonstrating how the first is erased even as the second is used to demonstrate 'Western civility' over and against 'Eastern barbarity'.]

Hennen, Peter. 2005. 'Bear Bodies, Bear Masculinity: Recuperation, Resistance, or Retreat?' Gender & Society, 19 (1): 25–43. doi: 10.1177/0891243204269408 [A study of the intersection of American white working class masculinity and sexualities in the gay Bear subculture.]

Herdt, ed. 1996 [A collection of historical and anthropological essays critically engaging the concepts of gender, sex, and sexuality demonstrating their unnaturalness.]

Jacobs, Janet Liebman. 2000. "Hidden Truths and Cultures of Secrecy: Reflections on Gender and Ethnicity in the Study of Religion." Sociology of Religion 61(4): 433–441. [A self-reflection on how gender, race, and ethnicity were developed and then intersected in the author's oeuvre in the study of new religious movements.]

CHAPTER 10

HERMENEUTICS

GAVIN FLOOD

CHAPTER SUMMARY

- Hermeneutics is the act of interpretation.
- Theological Hermeneutics interprets sacred texts, as illustrated here using examples from the histories of Christianity and Hinduism.
- Historical-Critical Hermeneutics developed in the context of the critical, philological examination of Classical texts and was then applied to Christian scriptures.
- Philosophical Hermeneutics is a tradition in philosophy concerned with the interpretation not only of text but of existence, as we see in the work of Schleiermacher, Gadamer, Ricoeur, and feminist philosophers.
- Contemporary developments, like Comparative Theology, underline the ongoing importance of Hermeneutics.

Hermeneutics is the act of interpretation. It inquires into the ways meaning is formed in texts and is also a philosophical inquiry into human experience. In addressing broad philosophical and textual questions it recognizes that there are many kinds of meaning in human communities, and that judgments need to be made about those meanings. Hermeneutics raises questions about meaning and truth that are directly relevant to religions and highly pertinent in contemporary culture. Being concerned with meaning and truth Hermeneutics also interfaces with the related fields of Semantics (theories of meaning—see Gardiner and Engler, "Semantics," this volume), Pragmatics (the use of language in specific contexts), and Semiotics (theories of signs—see Yelle, "Semiotics," this volume). The overarching concern of Hermeneutics is therefore with language, with text as the record of language, and with the importance of language in human life. We reflect and communicate through language, and as language changes through history so does our understanding of language and the need to constantly update our interpretations of both texts and of who we are.

Hermeneutics has ramifications beyond the immediate act of interpretation. While it necessarily recognizes multiple meanings of texts, it may also make judgments about particular readings being true or superior to other readings, and making such judgments can have consequences beyond the immediate reading of the text. Hermeneutics in its widest sense is germane to all areas of culture—e.g. to Literature, to History, and to Law—but here we focus on Hermeneutics in relation to the study of religions.

We can identify three main branches of Hermeneutics: Theological Hermeneutics, interpreting Scripture for theological purposes; Historical-Critical Hermeneutics, studying the history of a text in its context; and Philosophical Hermeneutics, interpreting human life more broadly. Each of these branches raises different questions. For example, Theological Hermeneutics might address the issue of gay marriage in the Anglican Church and how we interpret Scripture in this context. Text Historical Hermeneutics might raise philological questions about the reading of particular manuscript sources and their broader historical significance. Philosophical Hermeneutics might raise questions about the nature of language and the nature of the human person as the user and bearer of language. In this chapter we will examine each of these branches as they relate to the contemporary study of religions and show how and why Hermeneutics remains a relevant approach.

THEOLOGICAL HERMENEUTICS

Theological Hermeneutics is the interpretation of religious texts regarded as sacred, born out of theological inquiry. Important Christian theologians such as Rudolf Bultmann (1884–1976) regarded themselves as doing Theological Hermeneutics, but the term can now be more broadly applied to include other religions. Thus we have Islamic Theological Hermeneutics with thinkers such as Abdolkarim Soroush referring to their own work as Hermeneutics (Dahlén 2003), and the term can be used in an ascriptive sense to Jewish, Hindu, or Sikh Theological Hermeneutics or even Buddhist Hermeneutics (although we need to be hesitant about using the adjective 'theological' because Buddhism disclaims a creator God). Traditionally, Christian Theological Hermeneutics as the theological interpretation of Scripture can be distinguished from Biblical Hermeneutics as the principles of interpreting the Bible (Jeanrond 1994), although Christian Theological Hermeneutics must assume Biblical Hermeneutics as its base.

The term 'hermeneutics' is a Latinized version derived from the Greek verb *hermeneuein*, to explain, with *hermeneia* as interpretation or translation of a text (Seebohm 2004, 11–12). The term itself evokes Hermes the winged messenger of the Greek gods who mediates between the human and divine worlds. It is attested in early Greek sources, in Plato, and particularly in Aristotle who wrote a book *Peri Hermeneias*, better known under its Latin title *De Interpretatione*, "On Interpretation." On Aristotle's view Hermeneutics is not about the interpretation of texts but rather about the nature of language, about how language forms categories, and the relation of language to logic (Modrak 2001). Here *hermeneia* simply means a statement or proposition rather than 'interpretation,' as later became the case.

To understand the practice of Hermeneutics in the history of religions it is probably best to take two examples that exemplify the process of textual reading and understanding and to illustrate what is at stake. These examples will be taken from (a) Hinduism and (b) Christianity.

Interpreting the *Bhagavad Gītā* in Hinduism

The *Bhagavad Gītā*, the "Song of the Lord," is an influential Hindu scripture. It is a dialogue between the hero Arjuna and his charioteer Krishna, who in fact turns out to be an incarnation of God (Vishnu). As the text unfolds, Krishna gradually reveals his divinity to Arjuna.

The general style of Indian philosophy is hermeneutical in that philosophers present their ideas through writing commentaries on sacred texts, and Indian philosophy develops as an interpretative tradition. Various commentaries espousing different philosophies have been written on the *Bhagavad Gītā*. One verse in particular that has been subject to various interpretations—depending upon the metaphysics of the interpreting school—is known as the *carama śloka*, the "last verse," in which Krishna as God addresses Arjuna directly: "Relinquishing all your duties, / vow to take refuge just in me! / I will cause you to be released from / every evil; do not grieve" (Flood/Martin 2013, 18.66). The first to offer an interpretation was Śaṅkara (d. *c.*722 CE), the famous philosopher of non-dualism (*advaita*) who wished to promote his view that reality is really 'one' and that all distinctions are illusions due to ignorance. His interpretative strategy is to divide sacred texts into two levels: one speaking about an absolute truth in which all distinctions are illusions; and the other a relative level of truth in which distinctions seem real. He reads this verse in terms of the former: i.e. the self (*ātman*) realizes its identity with the absolute (Brahman). The verse is attempting to guide the reader to realize that knowledge of the truth is the path to follow, not ritual action ("relinquishing all your duties"), and furthermore that this truth is that of the non-distinction between self and absolute reality.

The later thinker Rāmānuja (*c.*1017–1137 CE) interprets the verse in a radically different way: "relinquishing all your duties" means that one should continue to perform one's obligatory duties according to one's social class and stage of life, but renounce the fruits of those acts. That is, the practitioner should continue to act but become detached from action and its results, placing all trust in the transcendent Lord (Mumme 1992, 71–73). In ordering Arjuna "to take refuge in me," Krishna is saying that he should practice devotion (*bhakti*) rather than seek knowledge. Only devotion leads to liberation.

We can see from this simple example how different interpretations of a single verse can reflect and reinforce divergent philosophical and theological views. Indeed, the ramifications of interpretation such as this are not simply confined to philosophy but in this case had more concrete social and political consequences. By a hundred years or so after Rāmānuja, the tradition had divided into northern and southern cultures: Pillai Lokācārya (*c.*1205–1311 CE) of the southern culture interpreting the *carama śloka* to mean that there is a secret path to God open to all, namely surrender (*prapatti*) (Mumme 1992, 74–76), and Vedānta Deśika (1268–1369) of the northern school disclaiming any hidden meaning.

Interpreting the Gospels in Christianity

The interpretation of the Christian Bible, in particular the New Testament, has always been motivated by religious and political concerns: differentiating theological positions and buttressing views of Church authority. The formation of the canon entailed a process of selection and highlighting in the service of the vision of the redactors. Creating the New Testament involved a reinterpretation of Jewish custom and text by the New Testament writers and later redactors. Christian theologians re-read the Hebrew Bible proleptically, turning it into the "Old Testament," read as a precursor of the New, and the redactors of the New Testament offered new interpretations of the Old. Matthew, the author of a gospel, presents Jesus' Sermon on the Mount (Matthew 5–7) as an interpretation of the ten commandments of the Old Testament in a new, ethical way. Thus interpretation has been at the heart of Christianity since its beginning.

The early Church Fathers, such as Origen and Clement of Alexandria, developed new readings of Scripture, particularly in reference to the problem of who Jesus was. But Augustine of Hippo (354–430 CE) was the most important interpreter for early Christianity. Like his predecessors, Augustine developed allegorical readings of Scripture in books 11 to 13 of his *Confessions*: e.g. interpreting the darkness of Genesis as the darkness of the soul bereft of God's light, and "in the beginning" to indicate "in the co-eternal word," which is Christ. Christ is the true meaning of Scripture and the meaning of life on earth. To understand this truth, the Holy Spirit must guide our interpretation (Williams 2000, 117–118). On this view Hermeneutics is of fundamental importance to Christianity because the life of the sacred text in its ritual use parallels the life of Christ and becomes a material sign of Christ. Through reading and engaging with the text in a way passed down by tradition, we are participating in the life of Christ.

In the pre-Protestant, Catholic, and Orthodox world, Scripture was allegorical and metaphorical, in contrast to the later Protestant understanding. Martin Luther (1483–1536 CE) thought that there is no need for interpretation at all, as Scripture is self-interpreting, with the literal sense privileged over the spiritual senses of medieval exegesis. (Yet this itself is an interpretation.) There is a perspicuity (*perspicuitas*) to Scripture that allows it to stand alone, outside of traditional Church authority: thus Scripture and not tradition becomes the only source for Theology. The Christian must read Scripture to experience faith and to apply the teachings of the Gospels to his contemporary problems; through faith Scripture is understood (Burrows 1997, 231).

HISTORICAL-CRITICAL HERMENEUTICS

Closely linked to Theological and Biblical Hermeneutics is what we might call Historical-Critical Hermeneutics or the 'historical-critical method' that seeks to understand the historical origins and trajectory of a text. As such, it has sometimes been regarded with suspicion from the perspective of faith, because it seeks to explain texts in their context and to discern different elements or layers within the text.

For example, earlier interpreters of the Bible perceived inconsistencies and contradictions in the texts and attempted to explain these through a process of harmonization, claiming that different readings of the Bible are compatible. For example, that the angel appears inside Jesus' tomb according to Mark but outside according to Matthew is not a contradiction according to Augustine as there were two angels (Barton 2007, 15). Modern text critical scholarship eschews harmonization and concludes that different layers of text have different origins and relate to each other in complex ways. Through a text-historical method we can gain a picture—an accurate one according to the methodological norms of this hermeneutical approach—of how the text came to be as it is.

This close attention to the language of the text and to the text's genre and historical context is generally called Philology, originating in Classics in the study of Greek and Latin texts. This involves establishing a critical edition of the text based on two or more manuscripts (where only one manuscript exists the edition is called 'diplomatic'). The text critic creates a lineage or *stemma* of the manuscripts used, notes peculiarities of language, and establishes which manuscripts are older. For example, historical-critical scholarship might argue that most of the psalms were composed by many generations who reshaped them as a worshipping community, as argued by Mowinckel in the 1960s (Barton 2007, 73). Although there is a high degree of objectivity to this process in the collation of manuscripts, subjective judgments must be made regarding particular readings, alternative readings usually being noted in the critical apparatus that records variants. This kind of text criticism declined in the late twentieth century, partly due to the rise of postmodern textual approaches that disclaimed objectivity, emphasizing multiple readings instead.

Behind the quest for the earliest or authentic text is the idea that a text is the expression of an author's intention and that the purpose of the text critic, and the task of establishing a critical edition, is to understand that intention. With poststructuralism the idea of an author's intention was questioned. Several schools of literary criticism arose in the wake of "the death of the author" (Barthes 1977). Stanley Fish explored the effect of the text on the reader or community of readers (Fish 1980) and reader-response theory emphasized the aesthetic response to the text in the reader's mind (Iser 1978). In the context of religion, Paul Griffiths has emphasized the place of reading in the practice of religion and the way a community receives and enacts its sacred scriptures (Griffiths 1999). Against the perceived relativism of Hermeneutics as found in Gadamer (discussed in the following section), some scholars in literary studies such as Hirsch (1967) have defended the importance of the author and of discovering the intended meaning of a text.

What is important is what historical-critical scholarship can tell us about how the meaning of a text changes through time. Establishing the history of the religious texts such as the Bible or the Qur'an independently of the concerns of the believing community has been a task of philology in all fields of textual scholarship about religion. In particular the work of Alexis Sanderson and his students in Hinduism is important here (e.g. Sanderson 2001) along with the recent development of philology in a global context, or 'world philology,' making sense of texts across times and histories (Pollock/Elman/Chang 2015).

PHILOSOPHICAL HERMENEUTICS

Philosophical Hermeneutics is the explanation not only of how we understand texts but more broadly of how we understand life. Although Hermeneutics began as a textual discipline, it quickly broadened, particularly since Schleiermacher, to an interpretation of history and of life in general, especially as linked to Phenomenology.

Schleiermacher

We cannot understand contemporary Hermeneutics of religion without reference to the founding father of modern Hermeneutics in the nineteenth century, the theologian Friedrich Schleiermacher (1768–1834). For Schleiermacher, reading is at the heart of Theology, driven by the desire of an author to be understood and the desire of a reader to understand. He held that Hermeneutics comprises both a psychological element, concerned with the relationship between reader and text, and a grammatical element, concerned with the correct analysis of language in order to arrive at understanding. Language and thought are completely intertwined, with thought as the 'inside' of language and language as the 'outside' of thought (Vial 2009, 32). Interpretation is the art of understanding, and to understand a text we have to interpret the particular in the light of the whole, and to understand the whole we need to pay attention to the particular. In re-reading a text we come to it with new questions and can understand it in a wider context. This is the hermeneutic circle: the part is understood in relation to the whole and the whole through the parts. In this way, by careful reading and interpretation, we might even be able to understand a text better than the author himself (Mueller-Vollmer 2000, 72–97).

Schleiermacher's general theory of Hermeneutics, as applicable to different linguistic contexts, manifests a concern about the nature of human life. At the heart of thought is language, and language by its very nature is social, forming customs (*Sitten*) in human communities. Through language we attain clarity of thinking and cultivation or development (*Bildung*) that defines who we are. Hence, understanding a speaker in the context of their community of other speakers is important for understanding human beings

(Sockness 2004). In the wake of Schleiermacher we have a philosophical concern developing alongside a textual concern, both influencing modernity.

Gadamer

Perhaps the most important figure in the recent history of Hermeneutics is Hans Georg Gadamer, who is generally associated with the phrase 'philosophical hermeneutics.' Gadamer (1900–2002) was a student of Heidegger, and he developed Heidegger's idea that pre-understanding or 'prejudice' is a precondition for any understanding. How we can distinguish between 'correct' and 'distorted' interpretations—or what the epistemological criteria are for judging between conflicting interpretations—is a question concerning the legitimacy of a discourse and the source of its authority. For Gadamer, method does not give rise to truth but rather understanding, that is modified in the light of further inquiry. As regards texts, there is an anticipation of completeness on the part of the interpreter. This completeness is the text's truth. The meaning of the text, and indeed life in general, only arises because of preconception and the circular route of the hermeneutic circle. Language is our fundamental way of being in the world, and the being that can be understood is language (Gadamer 2004). We can understand in no other way.

Although Gadamer does not directly address religion and religious questions, his work is important for the Hermeneutics of religion in highlighting a form of presupposition or foreknowledge that implicitly argues against a scientific reductionism. While science gives us a certain kind of knowledge, it has to be brought into the realm of meaning and so interpretation. Perhaps one of the most important understandings that Gadamer brings to religion is that we are subject to effective history. That is, we are subject to the historical conditions in which we find ourselves and cannot escape them: we cannot step out of where we are in historical location and our prejudices constitute the historical reality of our being (Grondin 1994, 114). In reading a text we are reading how it speaks to us (a position that contrasts to the view by Hirsch cited earlier that the text contains the author's intention).

Ricoeur

Another important hermeneutical philosopher is Paul Ricoeur (1913–2005) who, like Gadamer, recognizes the importance of historical location for understanding not only text, but also who we are. Unlike Gadamer, however, he develops the full force of Philosophical Hermeneutics in relation to religious questions. For Ricoeur, Hermeneutics is how to do philosophy and this entails understanding how language works, especially in stories, and how language relates to text and social action. Firstly, actions, argues Ricoeur, are like texts insofar as they exceed the intention of their author and need to be interpreted. Actions have effects beyond the agent who performs them

and Hermeneutics has the task of interpreting significant actions in a manner comparable to the interpretation of texts. Secondly, as we have a pre-understanding of action
and can anticipate an action's effects, so we have a pre-understanding of narrative plot
in text; we understand the representation of action in the text (both fact and fiction);
and we understand the way the text connects to the world or the way the reader interacts with the text. This work brings history and fiction closer together, both necessarily
being subject to interpretation. Furthermore, the texts of religion are also like this, and
Ricoeur has written on Biblical Hermeneutics where a 'hermeneutics of faith' has pre-
dominated over a 'hermeneutics of suspicion.'

Postmodern and Feminist Hermeneutics

Our survey cannot be complete without some mention of poststructuralism and postmodern Hermeneutics. Partly in response to Philosophical Hermeneutics, philosophers such as Jacques Derrida offered readings of texts—philosophical and literary as
well as religious—that attempted to reveal or deconstruct their implicit assumptions
about the nature of the world, about God, and about the self. While Derrida's work can
be understood as fundamentally critical of religion, his deconstruction nevertheless
shares something with negative or apophatic Theology. In apophatic Theology all language is inadequate to describing God, as a reality that can only be expressed in denials,
negating all positive statements about transcendence. Derrida is sometimes close to this
position in that anything that can be said in a sense misses the truth of the world: the
truth can only be approximated through languages of the unsayable (Derrida 1987, 3–
70). Deconstruction was a kind of Hermeneutics that easily came to be adopted by critical theorists of culture, particularly feminists and postcolonialists who read history in
terms of hegemony and the oppression of women or the West's 'others.'

Feminist Hermeneutics is the interpretation of Scripture from a feminist perspective
or in interests of women. Such perspectives are sometimes called 'advocacy' perspectives
(Barton 2007, 150–151). The Bible is seen as a patriarchal document; but through a feminist
hermeneutical lens we can uncover the hidden voices of women in the text, reveal patriarchal structures of power, and point to how the Bible can be a resource for contemporary Feminist Theology. For example, the cultural critic Mieke Bal interpreted the book of
Judges from a perspective that deconstructs the male orientation of the text and reveals the
structures of power present that have, in effect, occluded women's voices (Bal 1997, 179).

SOME CONTEMPORARY DEVELOPMENTS

All of the above styles of Hermeneutics have continued into the present. Close, philological reading of religious texts has become important once again; the concerns
of Philosophical Hermeneutics transform into new discussions in Hermeneutical

Phenomenology that are rooted in Heidegger and Ricoeur; and drawing on this herit-age new forms of religious Hermeneutics have arisen that we can classify as Scriptural Reasoning, theologians of Judaism, Christianity, and Islam, reading together texts from each other's traditions (Ford/Pecknold 2006), and Comparative Theology that seeks to read scriptures across traditions, while standing within a particular religion (Clooney 2010).

Every religious practitioner comes to practice Hermeneutics in some sense. This bears witness to the centrality and importance of sacred texts in many religions, which are constantly enacted through ritual, prayer, and meditation and constantly rethought by practitioners in their own situations. We might even understand religion as partly the construction of a ritual sphere within which a text received from the past is realized within the present moment and brought to life in the here and now for a community of reception. This is generally true for historical religions in which a sacred scripture is important. The mantras from the Veda are regularly recited in rites, and verses from the Qur'an are recited and used in preaching, as are verses from the Bible in Christian liturgies. The text in its liturgical use is appropriated or internalized by practitioners through participation in the ritual act and furthermore enacted beyond the ritual sphere in daily life (Flood 2008). There are other developments in which Hermeneutics is central such as Oliver Davies's transformational theology (Davies 2013), but it is in the religious life of communities that Hermeneutics will continue to live and for as long as religions persist, so will the necessity of interpretation.

GLOSSARY

Hermeneutic arc the movement from a position of trust in the text (the first naïveté), to critical distance, to a recovery of meaning in the text (the second naïveté).

Hermeneutic circle the idea that the parts of a text are understood in relation to the whole and the whole in relation to the parts.

Hermeneutics of suspicion the critical stance toward religious texts that questions their ideological assumptions (such as by Nietzsche, Freud, and Marx on Christianity).

Intentionality firstly the idea in phenomenology that consciousness always has an object (it is always 'consciousness of . . .') and secondly that texts themselves contain an intentionality. For Ricoeur this goes beyond the intention of the author.

Philology the scientific or systematic knowledge of texts based on the analysis of language and a hypothesis that texts undergo historical development that can be reconstructed in the stemma or genealogy of the text.

Prejudice the idea developed by Gadamer that there is a pre-understanding of text and world that is necessary for any understanding.

REFERENCES

Augustine. 1991. *Confessions*, translated by James J. O'Donnell. Oxford: Oxford University Press.

Bal, Mieke. 1997. *Narratology: Introduction to the Theory of Narrative*, 2nd edition. Toronto: University of Toronto Press.

Barthes, Roland. 1977. *Image, Music, Text*. London: Fontana Press.

Barton, John. 2007. *The Nature of Biblical Criticism*. Louisville and London: Westminster John Knox Press.

Burrows, Mark S. 1997. "Selections from Martin Luther's Sermons on the Sermon on the Mount." In *The Theological Interpretation of Scripture*, edited by Stephen E. Fowl. Oxford: Blackwell, 248–261.

Clooney, Francis X. 2010. *Comparative Theology: Deep Learning across Religious Borders*. Oxford: Wiley-Blackwell.

Dahlén, Ashk P. 2003. *Islamic Law, Epistemology and Modernity: Legal Philosophy in Contemporary Iran*. London: Routledge.

Davies, Oliver. 2013. *Theology of Transformation: Faith, Freedom, and the Christian Act*. Oxford: Oxford University Press.

Derrida, Jacques. 1987. "How to Avoid Speaking: Denials." In *Languages of the Unsayable: The Play of Negativity in Literature and Literary Theory*, edited by Sanford Budick and Wolfgang Iser. New York: Columbia University Press, 3–70.

Fish, Stanley. 1980. *Is There a Text in this Class? The Authority of Interpretive Communities*. Cambridge, MA: Harvard University Press.

Flood, Gavin. 2008. "Dwelling on the Borders: Self, Text and World." *Temenos: Nordic Journal of Comparative Religion* 44(1): 13–34.

Flood, Gavin and Charles Martin. 2013. *The Bhagavad Gita: A New Translation*. New York: Norton.

Ford, David and Chad Pecknold, eds. 2006. *The Promise of Scriptural Reasoning*. Oxford: Blackwell.

Gadamer, Hans-Georg. 1976. "The Universality of the Hermeneutical Problem." In *Philosophical Hermeneutics*. Berkeley and Los Angeles: University of California Press, 3–17.

Gadamer, Hans Georg. 2004. *Truth and Method*, translated by Joel Weisheimer and Donald G. Marshall (revised 2nd edition). London: Bloomsbury.

Griffiths, Paul. 1999. *Religious Reading: the Place of Reading in the Practice of Religion*. Oxford: Oxford University Press.

Grondin, Jean. 1994. *Introduction to Philosophical Hermeneutics*. New Haven, CT: Yale University Press.

Hirsch, Eric D. 1967. *Validity in Interpretation*. New Haven: Yale University Press.

Iser, Wolfgang. 1978. *The Act of Reading: A Theory of Aesthetic Response*. Baltimore, MD and London: Johns Hopkins University Press.

Jeanrond, Werner. 1991. *Theological Hermeneutics: Development and Significance*. London: SCM Press.

Modrak, Deborah. 2001. *Aristotle's Theory of Language and Meaning*. Cambridge: Cambridge University Press.

Mueller-Vollmer, Kurt, ed. 2000. *The Hermeneutics Reader*. New York: Continuum.

Mumme, Patricia. 1992. "Haunted by Śaṅkara's Ghost." in *Texts in Context: Traditional Hermeneutics in South Asia*, edited by J. R. Timm. Albany: SUNY Press, 69–84.

Pollock, Sheldon, Benjamin A. Elman, and Ku-ming Kevin Chang, eds. 2015. *World Philology*. New York: Columbia University Press.

Sanderson, Alexis. 2001. "History Through Textual Criticism in the Study of Śaivism, the Pāñcarātra and the Buddhist Yoginītantras." In *Les Sources et le temps*, edited by F. Grimal. Pondicherry: Institut Français d'Extrême-Orient, 1–47.

Seebohm, Thomas M. 2004. *Hermeneutics: Method and Methodology*. Dordrecht: Kluwer.

Sockness, Brent. 2004. "Schleiermacher and the Ethics of Authenticity." *Journal of Religious Ethics* 32(3): 477–517. doi: 10.1111/j.1467-9795.2004.00175.x

Vial, Theodore. 2009. "Schleiermacher." In *The History of Western Philosophy of Religion*, vol. 4, edited by Graham Robert Oppy and Nick Trakakis. Oxford: Oxford University Press, 3–8.

Williams, Rowan. 2000. *On Christian Theology*. Oxford: Blackwell.

FURTHER READING

Barton 2007 [*This book presents an overview of biblical criticism, detailing the recent scholarship and the history of the issues: a strong and eloquent advocacy of the value of biblical criticism.*]

Dalferth, Ingolf U. and Marlene A. Block, eds. 2015. *Hermeneutics and the Philosophy of Religion: The Legacy of Paul Ricœur*. Tübingen: Mohr Siebeck, 2015. [*This collection of essays contains up-to-date material, including an interesting article by the hermeneutical theologian David Tracey.*]

Jasper, David. 2004. *A Short Introduction to Hermeneutics*. Louiseville and London: Westminster John Knox Press. [*This is a short and accessible historical survey of Hermeneutics, giving accounts of the most important thinkers and a clear exposition of the issues.*]

Jeanrond 1991 [*More advanced than Jasper, this book gives an account of the history of theological Hermeneutics up to the end of the twentieth century, including an account of Schleiermacher.*]

Mueller-Vollmer, Kurt, ed. 2000 [*This is an excellent reader that includes short extracts from the works of major thinkers in Hermeneutics from Chaldenius to Habermas.*]

Ramberg, Bjørn and Kristin Gjesdal. 2013. "Hermeneutics." In *The Stanford Encyclopedia of Philosophy*, edited by Edward N. Zalta. <http://plato.stanford.edu/archives/sum2013/entries/hermeneutics/>. [*This is an authoritative online text that offers a philosophical account of Hermeneutics.*]

Thistelton, Anthony C. 1992. *New Horizons in Hermeneutics: The Theory and Practice of Transforming Biblical Reading*. Grand Rapids, MI: Zonervan [*This is a very thorough and detailed text on theological and biblical Hermeneutics that covers the main ground and also presents an account of Semiotics and Postmodern Hermeneutics.*]

CHAPTER 11

···

MARXISM

···

MATTHEW DAY

CHAPTER SUMMARY

···

- Several of the most prominent approaches to the contemporary study of religion are barely imaginable without Marx.
- Instead of treating Marx's corpus as a uniform whole, it is more productive to distinguish between an early and a late constellation of theoretical positions regarding religion.
- For much of the twentieth century, intellectuals were often more interested in determining whether Marxism itself was a religion than strategically drawing upon the Marxist vocabulary to explain specific religious discourses and practices.
- Successful Marxist strategies for analyzing religion as something more than *an opiate of the people* include: (a) a mode of anti-capitalist protest; (b) a form of non-elite reflection on capital; (c) a mythologizing ideological discourse.

Much as the ghostly, bloodied dagger troubles Macbeth, Karl Marx discomfits the academic study of religion. By this I mean that many of the contemporary field's dominant approaches—from postcolonialism and feminism to poststructuralism and critical theory—have assumed their privileged position only by struggling to depose him. "Marxism exists in nineteenth century thought like a fish in water," Michel Foucault hissed in *The Order of Things*, "that is, it is unable to breathe anywhere else" (1973, 262). Yet, regardless of how diligently they scrub, the mandarins of 'post-Marxist' theorizing cannot fully erase the signs of their own dependence upon Marx (Wolff/Cullenberg 1986). As a case in point, despite his best efforts to distinguish a postmodern incredulity toward meta-narratives from the vaulting ambition of Marxist historiography, Jean-François Lyotard's critique of the 'commodification of knowledge' makes little sense without Marx's analysis of commodity production in the background (Lyotard 1984).

In what follows, rather than treating Marx as a prelude to the contemporary study of religion—as a sort of conceptual ladder that serious theorists may safely throw away after climbing—I want to demonstrate how Marx and Marxism have been central to theorizing religion for more than a century. The first section offers a brief overview of Marx's writings on the topic. The second section surveys the initial waves of Marxist reflections on religion in the twentieth century and their latter-day descendants. The third section highlights the best work from three different genres of contemporary Marxist scholarship on religion.

A TALE OF TWO MARXES

Louis Althusser argued that Marx passed through a decisive 'epistemological rupture' in 1845, separating the early 'humanist' texts from the mature 'anti-humanist' work (1965). Although one can obviously make heavy weather of this sort of thing—fretting about the devious machinations of the 'author-function,' for example—the suggestion that we avoid treating the Marxist corpus as a single homogeneous mass makes good sense (Foucault 1977). After all, the pre-eminent theorist of contradiction is sure to harbor one or two of his own. Thus, rather than trying to isolate *the* Marxist stance on the subject, I will distinguish between a fairly stable early set of positions and a later, less stable but more intriguing suite of attitudes.

Marx on Religion: 1843–1850

The young Marx was a dissatisfied Hegelian, a restless philosopher *cum* journalist committed to extending the materialist 'inversion' of Hegel initiated by Ludwig Feuerbach (Van Harvey 1995). Feuerbach rejected Hegel's elaborate cosmic opera—whereby the abstract potentiality of pure Being (*Sein*) converts itself into the actual, but limited particularity of existing beings (*Dasein*) along the way to becoming fully self-conscious of itself as Being (*Bei-sich-selbst-sein*)—for its upside-down priorities. His response was to outline a new philosophical project that viewed the gods as inventions through which human beings achieved self-consciousness. "The personality of God is thus the means by which man converts the qualities of his own nature into the qualities of another being—of a being, external to himself," Feuerbach argued. "The personality of God is nothing else than the projected personality of man" (Feuerbach 1989 [1841], 226).

A Feuerbach-inflected version of materialism provided the necessary conceptual scaffolding for Marx's earliest analyses of religion. It is there in *On the Jewish Question* (1843) when he observes: "As long as man is imprisoned within religion, he only knows how to objectify his essence by making it into an alien imaginary being" (Marx 2000, 69). So, too, it shoulders a good deal of the weight behind his well-known assertion in *Towards a Critique of Hegel's 'Philosophy of Right'* (1844):

Religion is the general theory of this world, its encyclopedic compendium, its logic in popular form, its spiritual *point d'honneur*, its enthusiasm, its moral sanction, its solemn complement, its general basis of consolation and justification. It is the *fantastic realization* of the human being inasmuch as the *human being* possesses no true reality. Thus, the struggle against religion is indirectly a struggle against *that world* of which religion is the spiritual aroma. (Marx 1994, 57)

For the early Marx, there are genuine empirical facts to be gleaned from these spirit-haunted discourses—so long as one knows how to decode theological reflection as both an *echo of* and *answer to* the specific, material conditions of human misery. "The wretchedness of religion is at once an *expression of* and a *protest against* real wretchedness," he continues: "Religion is the sigh of the oppressed creature, the heart of a heartless world and the soul of soulless conditions" (Marx 1994, 57). Religious assertions about the nature of human existence are not true, of course—but neither do they lie. In this way, religion is the 'symptom' of a disordered social existence (cf. Žižek 1989).

Marx on Religion: 1850–1883

Althusser located the decisive 'epistemic break' in Thesis Six of *Theses on Feuerbach* (1845), where Marx recommends that all portraits of a transhistorical, 'essential' human nature should be reduced to a contingent ensemble of social relations (Marx 2000, 172). Although I find it more illuminating to think of the crucial shift in Marx's corpus emerging in response to the messy and unsuccessful revolutionary uprisings that spread across Europe in 1848, the fact remains that his interest in religion had shifted gears by the early 1850s.

To be sure, there are moments when the mature Marx can sound like his much younger self. "The religious world is but the reflex of the real world," he judges in *Capital* (1867): "The religious reflex of the real world can, in any case, only then finally vanish, when the practical relations of everyday life offer to man none but perfectly intelligible and reasonable relations with regard to his fellow-men and to Nature" (Marx 1976, 91). Nevertheless, what we find after 1850 is a move away from philosophy and toward critical political economy. One indicator of this new orientation is that his 1853 reading notes on Thomas Stamford Raffles's *The History of Java* (1817)—a book which informed his understanding of precolonial India's socio-economic structures—indicate that Marx skipped the chapters on religion (cf. Anderson 2010, 24–28).

Marx was convinced that capitalism's historical distinctiveness could not be understood apart from the commodity-form. He was not foolish enough to argue that commodities only exist within the capitalist mode of production. Rather, his hunch was that we must wrestle with commodities because capitalism's most fundamental and historically distinct social relation—between those who sell their labor-power in order to secure the means of subsistence (i.e. wage-laborers) and those who buy labor-power in the pursuit of surplus-value (i.e. capitalists)—is structured by and for their creation: "The fact that it produces commodities does not in itself distinguish it from other modes of production, but that the dominant and determining character of its product is that it is a commodity certainly does so' (1981 [1883], 1019).

This observation does not exhaust the issue for Marx, however. Among other things, it cannot explain how the commodity-form is able to present itself as both an *object of subjective utility* (i.e. a thing with use-value) and a *bearer of objective value* (i.e. a thing with exchange-value). The first trait is dealt with easily enough: use-value is a function of some particular thing's ability to satisfy a perceived human need. To drive nails, a hammer must be hard. To skin hides, a knife must be sharp. In this way, he writes: "usefulness does not dangle in mid-air. It is conditioned by the physical properties of the commodity, and has no existence apart from the latter" (Marx 1976, 126). Yet, Marx thinks it is more difficult to account for the second trait since it is not a natural property of matter that one thing is 'equivalent' to a certain amount of another thing. Five hundred and thirty pounds of coffee beans do not resemble an ounce of gold any more than an ounce of gold looks or behaves like eighteen barrels of crude oil. Yet, when we consider these three commodities from the standpoint of exchange, each is equivalent to the others.[1] "Not an atom of matter enters into the objectivity of commodities as values," he observes: "in this it is the direct opposite of the coarsely sensuous objectivity of commodities as physical objects" (Marx 1976, 138). Exchange-values seem to exist as sensibly supra-sensible spirits, shape-shifting beings that call out to us in the language of price.

According to Marx, the only possible source for the limitlessly convertible values preserved and conveyed by the commodity-form is human labor itself.[2] That is to say, the relationships that seem to obtain between things—that one ounce of gold can be converted into five hundred and thirty pounds of coffee beans without loss or remainder—are actually bundles of labor-mediated relationships between human beings. If this tale of woeful misrecognition sounds vaguely familiar, it is because a minimalist rendition of the old, Feuerbach-inflected portrait of religion is lurking just beneath the surface:

> the existence of the things *qua* commodities, and the value relation between the products of labour which stamps them as commodities, have absolutely no connection with their physical properties and with the material relations arising therefrom. There it is a definite social relation between men that assumes, in their eyes, the fantastic form of a relation between things. In order, therefore, to find an analogy, we must have recourse to the mist-enveloped regions of the religious world. In that world the productions of the human brain appear as independent beings endowed with life, and entering into relation both with one another and the human race. So it is in the world of commodities with the products of men's hands. (Marx 1976, 165)

---

[1] When this essay was composed, the market prices for these commodities were: (a) $2.20/lb (coffee beans); (b) $1166/oz (gold); and (c) $66/barrel (crude oil).

[2] Whether this commitment to the labor theory of value is an essential feature of Marxian economics—or even makes sense—has occasionally been a matter of rigorous debate. For a sense of the basic issues at stake, see: Sraffa 1960; Robinson 1962; Howard/King 1992.

With a knowing anthropological wink, Marx christened this misrecognition *the fetishism of commodities.*

Marx had flirted with a version of this approach a quarter century before, but his allegiance to the post-Hegelian philosophical vocabulary left him ill equipped to do much more. "As in religion the human imagination's own activity, the activity of man's head and heart, reacts independently on the individual as an alien activity of gods or devils," he ventured in 1844, "so the activity of the worker is not his own spontaneous activity. It belongs to another and is the loss of himself" (Marx 2000, 89). Back then, the best he could do to advance this line of thought was to protest that when human beings must sell their labor-power to secure the means of their subsistence they are reduced to mere animals. With the turn toward critical political economy, however, the old 'theological' examination of commodity fetishism productively fans out to confront the metaphysical strangeness of things like interest-bearing capital and the gold standard. By the end of his life, Marx was no longer interested in explaining religion per se. Rather, he strategically drew upon analogies from the religious world in order to demythologize the metaphysically spooky forces of capital accumulation that haunted the marketplace. These were the only gods that mattered for a world that lives under the thumb of capital apotheosized—a mode of production that had become an Anselmian limit of the human imagination.

Religion after Marx: Is Communism a Religion?

Throughout the second half of the nineteenth century, materialist accounts of religion were more or less content to remain on the paths Marx blazed. Consider *The Peasant War in Germany* (1850), written by Marx's loyal friend, partner, and patron Friedrich Engels while the disappointments about 1848 still ached. The organizing thesis is that one could "see the classes and fractions of traitors which everywhere betrayed 1848 and 1849 in the role of traitors, though on a lower level of development, already in 1525" (Engels 2006 [1850], xvi). Engels insisted that the sixteenth-century theological controversies that erupted between, say, the church and the Reformers, or between Luther and Müntzer, reveal and reflect the class struggles of the day. The key was adopting a Marxist stance and reading early modern 'religious thought' as thinly veiled political discourses advancing or combating real, material interests. "Even the so-called religious wars of the sixteenth century mainly concerned very positive material class interest," he advised: "Although the class struggles of those days were clothed in religious shibboleths, and though the interests, requirements, and demands of the various classes were concealed behind a religious screen, this changed nothing at all and is easily explained by the conditions of the times" (Engels 2006 [1850], 13).

The same lesson even applies for many of Marx's left-wing rivals. While Marx and Mikhail Bakunin crossed swords over the need of a revolutionary vanguard, for example, they arrived at very similar conclusions when it came to religion. Thus, in *God and State* (*c.*1871) Bakunin writes that religion is an essential weapon in the bourgeoisie's war against the proletariat: "That is the eternal mirage; which leads away the masses in a search for divine treasures, while much more reserved, the governing class contents itself with dividing among all its members—very unequally, moreover and always giving most to him who possesses most—the miserable goods of earth and the plunder taken from the people, including their political and social liberty" (Bakunin 1970 [*c.*1871], 70).

Things began to change after the October Revolution of 1917. In the wake of events such as the bloody suppression of the Kronstadt Rebellion (1921) and the Moscow show trials of the 1930s, intellectuals sympathetic to Marx's analyses of capital accumulation and its cultures of exploitation were forced to reckon with Soviet brutality. Bakunin had noted this potential early on, condemning Sergei Nechayev's lethal blend of moral idealism and strategic violence as an essentially "Jesuitical system" (Jensen 2014, 14). What many observers found particularly worrying was the way that the Revolution had acquired an absolute value, resulting in a Marxist version of Kierkegaard's 'teleological' suspension of the ethical: in the name of class struggle, it appeared as though all things were permitted. The socialist revolution, an exiled but resolute Trotsky wrote in *Their Morals and Ours* (1938), "must be completely free from the fictions of religion, 'democracy' and transcendental morality—the spiritual chains forged by the enemy to tame and enslave it. Only that which prepares the complete and final overthrow of imperialist bestiality is moral, and nothing else. The welfare of the revolution, that is the supreme law!" (Trotsky 1969, 72).

By the mid-1930s, many left-leaning intellectuals found themselves agreeing with Bakunin's initial assessment. Soviet-style communism had, somehow, morphed into a religion. Although this charge emerged from various theoretical camps, there were two basic versions of the claim.

Revolutionary Politics, Dangerous Religion

One faction argued that, by virtue of its eschatological, prophetic, soteriological, and even mythical characteristics, Marxist theorizing shared a common architectural structure with religious thought. In *Capitalism, Socialism and Democracy* (1942), his now-classic work on the creative instability of capital accumulation, Joseph Schumpeter noted:

> In one important sense, Marxism *is* a religion. To the believer it presents, first, a system of ultimate ends that embody the meaning of life and are absolute standards by which to judge events and actions; and, secondly, a guide to those ends which implies a plan of salvation and the indication of the evil from which mankind, or a chosen section of mankind, is to be saved. (1942, 5)

Yet, as far as this group was concerned, this was not a point in Marx's favor. Reinhold Niebuhr consistently argued that communism represented a dangerously flawed form of religion because its mix of political romanticism and moral certainty resulted in fanaticism (Niebuhr 1935, 465). Marxism was dangerous for Niebuhr because—as Trotsky illustrated—it permitted the demonic "to enter into human life through the religious sanctification of partial and relative values" (Niebuhr 1934, 379). Again and again, we find intellectuals troubled by the creeping absolutism that distinguished the Bolshevik school of Marxism. "Marxism is eschatology without God," Frederick Augustus Voigt announced in *Unto Caesar* (1938): "It demands unquestioning faith in the coming of the Kingdom of Heaven on Earth and imposes a dogmatic atheism. The Marxist is not even allowed to be an agnostic" (1938, 42).

Over time, this line of thought eventually made its way into the religious studies curriculum through widely used textbooks like Ninian Smart's *The World's Religions* (1989), James Livingston's *Anatomy of the Sacred* (1993), and Richard Charles Zaehner's *Encyclopedia of World Religions* (1997) (cf. Fitzgerald 1999 for a critique of this trend).

Marxist Hope and Religious Faith

The other bloc argued that the homologies between Marxism and religion created a unique opportunity for a *rapprochement* between progressive politics and religious commitment. Prior to his exile from Nazi Germany, for example, Paul Tillich spent considerable effort fashioning a brand of 'religious socialism' that drew equally upon the work of Marx and the Christian New Testament. As he explained in the "Introduction" to *The Protestant Era* (1948):

> Religious socialism was always interested in human life as a whole and never in its economic basis exclusively. In this it was sharply distinguished from economic materialism, as well as from all forms of "economism." It did not consider the economic factor as an independent one on which all social reality is dependent. It recognized the dependence of economy itself on all other social, intellectual, and spiritual factors, and it created a picture of the total, interdependent structure of our present existence. We understood socialism as a problem not of wages but of a new theonomy in which the question of wages, of social security, is treated in unity with the question of truth, of spiritual security. (Tillich 1992, 293)

By the 1960s, this sort of thing had become a staple of high cultural theorizing. "There is only one political problem in our world today," Norman O. Brown decreed in *Love's Body*: "the unification of mankind. The Internationale shall be the human race. That they should be one—*ut unum sint*. This was Christ's last prayer before the Crucifixion" (1966, 81). While figures like Tillich and Brown were primarily interested in closing the gap between *The Communist Manifesto* and *The Sermon on the Mount*, others stressed the correlations between Marxism and the Hebrew Bible. "It is hardly possible to talk about Marx's attitude toward religion without mentioning the connection between his philosophy of history, and of socialism, with the Messianic hope of the Old Testament prophets," Erich Fromm advised in *Marx's Concept of Man* (1961): "They show man a vision of how he ought to be, and confront him with the alternatives between which he must choose. Most of the Old Testament prophets share the idea that history has a meaning, that man perfects himself in the process of history, and that he will eventually create a social order of peace and justice" (2003, 52). For the first time, Marx's own Jewishness was an asset rather than a liability.

This sort of grand meta-historical enterprise began to look bloated and lifeless when the poststructuralist moment arrived. It belonged to a bygone era of philosophical grandeur in which, as Foucault put it dismissively, "a philosophical text, a theoretical text, finally had to tell you what life, death, and sexually really were, if God existed or not, what liberty consisted of, what one had to do in a political life, how to behave in regard to others, and so forth" (1989, 51). As a result, these projects were quickly swept out to sea with the changing tide. Yet, the desire to synthesize Marxist hope and religious faith managed to hang around for a little while longer, eventually finding a home in the hothouse of liberation theology throughout the 1970s and 1980s.

Both of the *Marxism as religion* camps should now seem hopelessly antiquated. One reason for this is that each side treats 'religion' as a natural kind rather than a contingent feature of a particular socio-taxonomic order. By safeguarding the category itself from critical scrutiny, the debate eventually dissolved into a series of uninspiring exchanges regarding the apparent metaphysical foundations of modern democratic life (e.g. liberalism vs. communitarianism). Nevertheless, their trajectories through the academy underscore something absolutely decisive about Marx's place in the study of religion.

Some scholars now insist that *pouvoir/savoir* relationships are more complicated than Marx could have imagined. Others argue that meta-narratives of transnational proletarian revolution are forms of tyranny that eventually end in the national horrors of Stalin's gulags or Pol Pot's killing fields. Still others maintain that Marx is fatally Eurocentric, surreptitiously naturalizing the West's domination of the rest. However, it is worth pointing out that each one of these anti-Marxist claims would be barely conceivable apart from the Marxist strategy of treating our intellectual and moral lives as inextricable aspects of economic and political structures. In other words, unless one is willing to talk about human beings as solitary brains in vats—a challenge that some cognitive theorists often seem eager to accept—there is no avoiding Marx.

MORE THAN AN OPIATE: MARXISM AND RELIGION TODAY

While Marxists have spent the last quarter-century or so beating against the winds of academic fashion, they nevertheless managed to find several paths forward. In the space remaining I would like to identify three genres of Marxist scholarship that illustrate its continuing analytic potential.

Religion as the Protest against Wretchedness

The first genre views religion as a latent form of *popular protest against wretchedness*. Looking back on the ruined promise of 1848, Marx had isolated England's lack of a revolutionary uprising as a key ingredient in the continental bourgeoisie's ascent. "England, the country that turns whole nations into her proletarians, that spans the whole world with her enormous arms," he sighed: "England seems to be the rock which breaks the revolutionary waves, the country where the new society is stifled before it is born" (2000, 299). It is thus a mark of history's cunning that the most productive uses of Marx to analyze the revolutionary potential of god-talk emerged from England. Taking on the canonical Marxist imperative to write history as the history of class struggle, a small band of scholars—including Rodney Hilton, Christopher Hill, Eric Hobsbawm, and E. P. Thompson—began to regard the kaleidoscopic variety of non-conforming Christian communities in seventeenth- and eighteenth-century England as anti-capitalist provocateurs. Arguably, the greatest scholarly achievement from this genre is Christopher Hill's *The World Turned Upside Down* (1972).

The book's organizing principle is that the English Civil Wars were shadowed by a "revolution which never happened, though from time to time it threatened. This might have established communal property, a far wider democracy in political and legal institutions, might have disestablished the state church and rejected the protestant ethic" (1972, 15). The agitators for this would-be revolution were groups like the Diggers, Levelers, Quakers, and Ranters, Christian radicals who drew upon the unprecedented accessibility of the English Bible to resist the legal and extra-legal means through which the landed gentry was creating a new social order after its own interests. What catches Hill's eye in particular about these groups is that their theologically-informed resistance to the privatization of common lands through enclosure and the concomitant sanctification of private property in law was, in hindsight, a struggle against the coercive forces that would oblige the rural peasantry to either submit to the degradations of wage labor or starve to death. When read in this way, for example, the writings of the Digger Gerrard Winstanley begin to resemble a Marxist critique of capital *avant la lettre*. "In the beginning of Time, the great Creator Reason, made the Earth to be a Common Treasury, to preserve Beasts, Birds, Fishes, and Man, the lord that was to govern this Creation; for Man had Domination given to him, over the Beasts, Birds, and Fishes; but not one word was spoken in the beginning, That one branch of mankind should rule over another," Winstanley proclaims in *The True Levellers Standard Advanced* (1649). Yet, human sinfulness upended this righteous order:

> And hereupon, The Earth (which was made to be a Common Treasury of relief for all, both Beasts and Men) was hedged in to In-closures by the teachers and rulers,

and the others were made Servants and Slaves: And that Earth that is within this Creation made a Common Store-house for all, is bought and sold, and kept in the hands of a few, whereby the great Creator is mightily dishonoured, as if he were a respector of persons, delighting in the comfortable Livelihoods of some, and rejoycing in the miserable povertie and straits of others. (Quoted in Hill 1972, 132)

Instead of religion merely providing the moral sanction for the exploitation of labor by capital, Hill presents Christian radicalism as a revolutionary movement struggling against the injustices of early modern capitalism (cf. Corfield 2004). Centuries before Lenin and Trotsky, there were men like Winstanley and Edward Sexby who responded to the crucible of capitalism by dreaming of smashing social hierarchies and ending oppression.

Religion as Popular Logic

The second genre of Marxist analysis treats religious discourses on gods, ghosts, and spirits as *modes of popular logic*, non-elite discourses that fight to make sense of capitalism's metaphysical spookiness. Although his theoretical debt to Marx remains insufficiently acknowledged, Marshall Sahlins helpfully explains the basic anthropological premise of this stance when he observes: "Western capitalism has loosed on the world enormous forces of production, coercion and destruction. Yet precisely because they cannot be resisted, the relations and goods of the larger system also take on meaningful places in local schemes of things" (1988, 4; cf. Comaroff/Comaroff 2000). In other words, the kinds of agents and forces that typically appear in religious ontologies become the terms through which a homegrown understanding of capital accumulation is assembled. In my judgment, the finest example of a distinctly Marxist approach to these topics is Michael Taussig's *The Devil and Commodity Fetishism in South America* (1980).[3]

Painted in broad strokes, Taussig's ambition is to document how the introduction of capitalist modes of production in Columbia and Bolivia triggered far-reaching social disruptions that were conceptualized, by those living through the tumult, as the work of the devil. "In two widely separated areas of rural South America, as peasant cultivators became landless wage laborers, they invoke the devil as part of the process of maintaining or increasing production," we learn: "However, as peasants working their own land according to their own customs they do not do this. It is only when they are proletarianized that the devil assumes such importance" (1980, 13). His specific focus is on the stories these newly proletarianized laborers tell of short-sighted *compañeros* who—in a bid to game the system of piece-rate compensation—make pacts with the devil to increase their productivity and thus maximize their wages. What these workers soon discover is that the existential costs of the contracts, paid to the devil in the form

---

[3] Other noteworthy examples include Carlo Ginzburg's *The Cheese and the Worms* (1980) and Sumanta Banerjee's *Logic in Popular Form* (2002).

of blood, sweat, and tears, always outstrip their marginal fiscal benefits. In Taussig's estimation:

> the fabled devil contract is an indictment of an economic system which forces men to barter their souls for the destructive powers of commodities. Of its plethora of interconnected and often contradictory meanings, the devil contract is outstanding in this regard: man's soul cannot be bought or sold, yet under certain historical conditions mankind is threatened by this mode of exchange as a way of making a livelihood. In recounting this fable of the devil, the righteous man confronts the struggle of good and evil in terms that symbolize some of the most acute contradictions of market economies. (Taussig 1980, xvi)

That is to say, although the legends of *un pacto con el Diablo* represent an unmistakably non-elite discourse, they nevertheless manage to articulate the Marxist portrait of commodity production as an inexorably exploitative social relationship between labor and capital in the pursuit of profit (cf. Marx 1981, 232). Considered in this light, these diabolical tales represent what might be called—with a tip of the cap to Claude Lévi-Strauss—a critical political economy of the concrete.

Religion as Ideological Discourse

The third genre regards religion as a *type of ideological discourse*. In many ways, this approach represents the most obvious articulation of an orthodox Marxist attitude toward religion. It is also one of the most difficult exercises to pull off given the muddled nature of what Marx had to say about *ideology*. The enduring problem, Raymond Williams observed, is that in Marx's writings ideology "hovers between 'a system of beliefs characteristic of a specific class' and 'a system of illusory beliefs—false ideas or false consciousness—which can be contrasted with true or scientific knowledge.' This uncertainty was never really resolved" (Williams 1977, 66). Throw in the fact that it is always the *other* guys who suffer from ideological misconceptions, and soon ideology begins to look like a useful polemical weapon but a useless analytic device.

In the academic study of religion, no one has done a better job of saving standard Marxist *Ideologiekritik* from its own shortcomings than Bruce Lincoln. By selectively incorporating the work of theorists such as Antonio Gramsci, Roland Barthes, and Pierre Bourdieu, Lincoln has charted a fruitful course forward by a twofold substitution. First, rather than viewing *ideology as false ideas*, Lincoln prefers to speak of *socio-taxonomic naturalization* to describe the process whereby socially constructed differences come to be taken for granted as neither constructed nor arbitrary. As Lincoln makes the point, a socio-taxonomic system "renders its operations invisible, since one is so consistently immersed in and bombarded by its products that one comes to mistake them (and the apparatus through which they are produced and disseminated) for nothing other than 'nature'" (Lincoln 2012, 2). Thus, what makes the manufactured catalogue of distinctions between men and women (e.g. active vs. passive, violent vs.

nurturing, promiscuous vs. chaste) so difficult to perceive *as socially constructed* is that this set of differences makes constant reference to another set of anatomical differences that are virtually non-negotiable (cf. Bourdieu 2001).

In this way, the work of *naturalization* is abetted by *misrecognition*—the second Lincolnian substitution. Where Marx endowed ideology with the power to mystify or distort reality, Lincoln chooses instead to stress how a socio-taxonomic order's apparent naturalness encourages actors to misrecognize or overlook its strategic role in establishing and reproducing asymmetries (cf. Bourdieu 1989). Symbolic systems of classification are expressions of both the will to knowledge and the will to power. "Taxonomy is thus not only a means of organizing information," he explains, "but also—as it comes to organize the organizers—an instrument for the classification and manipulation of society, something that is facilitated by the fashion in which taxonomic trees and binary oppositions can conveniently recode social hierarchies" (Lincoln 1989, 137). Taxonomic practices and the social register of distinctions they exploit, like politics itself, represent the continuation of war by different means.

With these two substitutions in hand, Lincoln is able to treat religion as a more or less distinct ensemble of ideological discourses, practices, and institutions. On the one hand, religion is ideological inasmuch as it tends to naturalize a socially constructed and thus arbitrary order of things by anchoring it in the eternal structure of the cosmos or the transcendent will of the gods. On the other hand, religion is intrinsically ideological insofar as it expects us to misrecognize a merely human discourse as more than merely human. Considered in this light, the academic study of religion's mandate is to "insist on discussing the temporal, contextual, situated, interested, human, and material dimensions of those discourses, practices, and institutions that characteristically represent themselves as eternal, transcendent, spiritual, and divine" (Lincoln 2012, 1). Whether one is prepared to self-identify as a Marxist or not, it is difficult to imagine a better agenda for this particular corner of the academy.

Conclusion

Bourdieu argued that the key to academic success was charting a middling trajectory that was neither too innovative nor too traditional. On the one hand, genuine innovation threatens the material and symbolic capital of those who have conscientiously climbed their way up the established institutional hierarchy. On the other hand, explicit conservatism jeopardizes the illusion of scholarly 'progress' which both organizes and legitimates these institutionalized relationships of authority and dependency. The dispositions which constitute this tepid ideal of *academica mediocritas*, Bourdieu insisted, "which implies the refusal of all kinds of excesses, even in questions of intelligence and originality, are no doubt inherent in the intermediate position, of double negation, which the academic holds between the artist and the bourgeois" (Bourdieu 1989, 224).

In other words, academics want the existential freedom of bohemia and the cozy comforts of suburbia. The antinomies that exist between creativity and inertia, between bohemia and suburbia, are crucial for understanding why Marx should never stop being an essential theorist for the academic study of religion.

For the past quarter-century or so, generations of ambitious scholars have judged that Marx was too traditional, too old-fashioned, too 'crude' to take seriously. It was only the Marx left standing after someone like Deleuze or Derrida roughed him up a bit that deserved our attention. The world had changed. The sort of industrial capitalism that preoccupied Marx was a thing of the past. We now lived in a postmodern, post-industrial, postcolonial, and perhaps even post-capitalist epoch. It was time to move on. All the while, as academics were busying themselves with this expanding catalogue of *posts*, the dynamics of capital accumulation pressed on in the relentless pursuit of a solid return on investment. This indifference toward material interests is understandable. "How could one not believe that capitalism has dissolved in a 'flux of signifiers detached from their signifieds,'" Bourdieu observes, "when one lives in a little social and electronic paradise from which all trace of work and exploitation has been effaced?" (Bourdieu 2000, 41). It was only when their own economic contingency became painfully obvious—including, among other things, the rise of adjunct professors, the demise of tenure, and a financial crisis that destroyed home equity and retirement portfolios—that many academics 'rediscovered' Marx.

Marx continues to be relevant to the study of religion because, on some absolutely key points, he was right. As Engels complained in *The Peasant War*, when scholars begin to talk about religion they all too often become naïve ideologists "so gullible that they accept unquestioningly all the illusions that an epoch makes about itself or that ideologists of an epoch make about an epoch" (Engels 2006 [1850], 12). In my estimation, the Marxist refusal to treat religion as an independent or 'irreducible' cultural sphere, combined with its commitment to finding what is materially at stake in theological discourses, are the only things that might make the study of religion an academically relevant enterprise. Here again, Bruce Lincoln reliably points the way forward.

> When one permits those whom one studies to define the terms in which they will be understood, suspends one's interest in the temporal and contingent, or fails to distinguish between "truths", "truth-claims", and "regimes of truth", one has ceased to function as historian or scholar. In that moment, a variety of roles are available: some perfectly respectable (amanuensis, collector, friend and advocate), and some less appealing (cheerleader, voyeur, retailer of import goods). None, however, should be confused with scholarship. (Lincoln 2012, 2–3)

All I can add to this is: *hear, hear!* So, until human beings abandon the practice of trafficking in extra-human authority—or capitalism finally surrenders to its own, ever-shifting contradictions—the best scholars of religion will continue to find an ally in Marx.

Glossary

Capital denotes a particular mode of money rather than money per se. It is money invested in commodity production (e.g. purchasing labor-power) or financial instruments (e.g. money lending) in order to realize surplus value. In other words, capital is money used in the process of making more money.

Capitalism gestures toward the larger cultural, political, and social arrangements that facilitate capital accumulation. Like near-kin terms such as *market society*, it implies a comprehensive vision of individual and collective life that is organized around and imagined through the associated practices of buying and selling.

Commodity something made in order to be sold. In this way, a commodity can be described as representing both a temporary 'metamorphosis' of capital (i.e. from the *money-form* into the *commodity-form*) and a material 'crystallization' of the labor required to produce it.

Fetishism a fundamental misperception about the nature of a given artifact. For Marx, it signifies a mistake about the nature of value by insisting that things have *objective value* the same way they have *objective weight*. As a case in point, rather than recognizing the social constellation of needs and relationships in which commodities are produced and exchanged as the ultimate source of their value, fetishism generates theories of a commodity's 'intrinsic value' (e.g. gold).

Ideology a central category in Marx and Marxism, but one that is notoriously difficult to pin down. At bottom, the concept attempts to highlight how cognitive orders, webs of belief, socio-taxonomic systems, etc. tend to actively misrepresent particularities as universals in ways that benefit some and injure others.

Marxism the constellation of theorists and texts for which Marx's writings—more than any other figure—provide an intellectual center of gravity. It is far less complicated to identify constituent figures and texts (e.g. Engels, Gramsci) rather than themes (e.g. revolutionary proletariat, labor theory of value). To be considered a 'real' or 'genuine' Marxist is, like any identity, the outcome of countless political and social challenges.

Materialism a fundamental methodological commitment in Marx and Marxism, but one that comes in a variety of strengths (e.g. weak vs. strong) and types (e.g. inclusive vs. restrictive). If there is one intuition around which all of these varieties gather, however, it is that human intellectual activities must be understood as both products of and strategic responses to the material conditions of existence within a historically particular social order.

Post-Marxism contemporary bundles of theorists and texts which, for countless reasons and motivations, contend that Marxism's general orientation around—and continuing engagement with—Marx's corpus is mistaken.

References

Althusser, Louis. 1965. *For Marx*. London: Verso.

Anderson, Kevin. 2010. *Marx at the Margins*. Chicago, IL: University of Chicago Press.

Bakunin, Mikhail. 1970. *God and State*. New York: Dover.

Banerjee, Sumanta. 2002. *Logic in Popular Form*. Calcutta: Seagull Books.

Bourdieu, Pierre. 1989. *The State Nobility*. Stanford, CA: Stanford University Press.

Bourdieu, Pierre. 2000. *Pascalian Meditations*. Stanford, CA: Stanford University Press.

Bourdieu, Pierre. 2001. *Masculine Domination*. Stanford, CA: Stanford University Press.

Brown, Norman O. 1966. *Love's Body*. Berkeley: University of California Press.

Comaroff, Jean and John Comaroff. 2000. "Millennial Capitalism: First Thoughts on a Second Coming." *Public Culture* 12(2): 291–343.

Corfield, Penelope J. 2004. "We are All One in the Eyes of the Lord: Christopher Hill and the Historical Meanings of Radical Religion." *History Workshop Journal* 58(1): 110–127.

Engels, Friedrich. 2006. *The Peasant War in Germany*, 3rd edition. New York: International Publishers. Original edition, 1850.

Feuerbach, Ludwig. 1989. *The Essence of Christianity*. New York: Prometheus Book.

Fitzgerald, Timothy. 1999. *The Ideology of Religious Studies*. New York: Oxford University Press.

Foucault, Michel. 1973. *The Order of Things*. New York: Vintage.

Foucault, Michel. 1977. "What Is An Author?" In *Language, Counter-Memory, Practice*. Ithaca, NY: Cornell University Press, 113–138.

Foucault, Michel. 1989. *Foucault Live*. New York: Semiotext(e).

Fromm, Erich. 2003. *Marx's Concept of Man*. New York: Continuum. Original edition, 1961.

Ginzburg, Carlo. 1980. *The Cheese and the Worms*. Baltimore, MD: Johns Hopkins University Press.

Harvey, Van. 1995. *Feuerbach and the Interpretation of Religion*. New York: Cambridge University Press.

Hill, Christopher. 1972. *The World Turned Upside Down*. New York: Vintage.

Howard, Michael and John King. 1992. *A History of Marxian Economics: Volume Two, 1929–1990*. Princeton, NJ: Princeton University Press.

Jensen, Richard. 2014. *The Battle Against Anarchist Terrorism*. New York: Cambridge University Press.

Lincoln, Bruce. 1989. *Discourse and the Construction of Society*. New York: Oxford University Press.

Lincoln, Bruce. 2012. *Gods and Demons, Priests and Scholars*. Chicago, IL: University of Chicago Press.

Livingston, James. 1993. *Anatomy of the Sacred*, 2nd edition. New York: Macmillan.

Lyotard, Jean-François. 1984. *The Postmodern Condition*. Minneapolis: University of Minnesota Press.

Marx, Karl. 1976. *Capital: A Critique of Political Economy, Volume One*. New York: Penguin.

Marx, Karl. 1981. *Capital: A Critique of Political Economy, Volume Three*. New York: Penguin.

Marx, Karl. 1994. *Early Political Writings*. New York: Cambridge University Press.

Marx, Karl. 2000. *Karl Marx: Selected Writings*, 2nd edition, edited by David McLellan. New York: Oxford University Press.

Niebuhr, Reinhold. 1934. "The Problem of Communist Religion." *The World Tomorrow* 17: 378–379.

Niebuhr, Reinhold. 1935. "Christian Politics and Communist Religion." In *Christianity and the Social Revolution*, edited by John Lewis, Karl Polanyi, and Donald K. Kitchin. Freeport, NY: Books for Libraries Press, 442–472.

Raffles, Thomas Stafford. 1817. *The History of Java*. London: Black, Parbury, and Allen.

Robinson, Joan. 1962. *Economic Philosophy*. Chicago, IL: Aldine Transaction.

Sahlins, Marshal. 1988. "Cosmologies of Capitalism: The Trans-Pacific Sector of the World System." *Proceedings of the British Academy* 74: 1–51.

Schumpeter, Joseph. 1942. *Capitalism, Socialism and Democracy*. New York: Harper & Brothers.

Smart, Ninian. 1989. *The World's Religions*. New York: Cambridge University Press.

Sraffa, Piero. 1960. *The Production of Commodities By Means of Commodities*. New York: Cambridge University Press.

Taussig, Michael. 1980. *The Devil and Commodity Fetishism in South America*. Chapel Hill: University of North Carolina Press.

Tillich, Paul. 1992. *The Protestant Era*. Chicago, IL: University of Chicago Press.

Trotsky, Leon. 1969. *Their Morals and Ours*. New York: Pathfinder Press.

Voigt, Frederick Augustus. 1938. *Unto Caesar*. New York: G. P. Putnam's Sons.

Williams, Raymond. 1977. *Marxism and Literature*. New York: Oxford University Press.

Wolff, Richard D. and Stephen Cullenberg. 1986. "Marxism and Post-Marxism." *Social Text* 15 (Autumn): 126–135.

Zaehner, Richard Charles. 1997. *Encyclopedia of World Religions*. New York: Barnes & Noble.

Žižek, Slavoj. 1989. *The Sublime Object of Ideology*. London: Verso.

FURTHER READING

Blair, Jennifer, ed. 2009. *Frontiers of Commodity Chain Research*. Stanford, CA: Stanford University Press. [*Any contemporary interest in what Marx called the 'theological niceties' of commodity fetishism must begin with an appreciation for the ways international production networks have grown more complex and more distributed since the nineteenth century. A crucial point of entry for that work.*]

Cohen, Gerald. 1978. *Karl Marx's Theory of History: A Defense*. New York: Oxford University Press. [*A central text for the British school of 'analytical Marxism,' which virtuously tried to scrape away some of the philosophical excesses that are par for the course when discussing Marx. Cohen's bid to fashion an empirically useful notion of fetishism remains a model of precision and clarity.*]

McLellan, David. 1987. *Marxism and Religion*. New York: Harper & Row. [*Despite its vintage and relatively narrow purview, this remains the standard survey of Marx and Marxism on religion. Early chapters on Marx and Engels are complemented by subsequent discussions of Karl Kautsky, Antonio Gramsci, and the 'neo-Marxists' of the Frankfurt School.*]

Postone, Moishe. 1993. *Time, Labor and Domination*. New York: Cambridge University Press. [*A robust attempt to reinterpret Marx after the collapse of Soviet-style communism. Its centerpiece is an exhaustive presentation of the 'critical social theory' embedded in* Grundrisse *and* Capital, *something Postone believes 'traditional' Marxists have neglected or distorted. A demanding book that rewards patience and stamina.*]

Rediker, Marcus and Peter Linebaugh. 2000. *The Many-Headed Hydra*. Boston: Beacon Press. [*A stirring look at the transatlantic and maritime cultures of capitalism 'from below.' The focus on capitalism's voracious demand for labor—and its punishing brutality—is deftly organized around the biblical mytheme of "hewers of wood and drawers of water" (Joshua 9:23).*]

Thompson, E. P. 1966. *The Making of the English Working Class*. New York: Vintage. [*Essential reading in every sense. Thompson's portrait of Methodism as a reactionary institution—advancing the bourgeoisie's interests in a disciplined workforce while offering the proletariat a space to express libidinal energies and ungovernable emotions in non-revolutionary ways—still has the power to upset some and inspire others.*]

CHAPTER 12

....

POSTCOLONIALISM

....

ARVIND MANDAIR

CHAPTER SUMMARY

- Postcolonialism attempts to shift dominant ways of seeing relations between Western and non-Western societies created by European imperialism, thereby facilitating a politics of the 'subaltern,' or subordinated, classes and peoples.
- Two major critical points of reference for postcolonialism are the critique of Orientalism and the critique of Occidentalism.
- Limitations of postcolonialism include reliance on an ontological model of agency and cultural difference based on a causal negativity and reliance on an explicitly secular model of social reality which posits 'religion' as a cause of the negative.
- Postcolonial studies has largely missed the strategic importance of new developments in the study of religion due to the un-interrogated nature of 'religion' as an analytic category, a limitation remedied to some extent by recent developments in the study of religion.
- The case of Hinduism shows that *if* scholars of postcoloniality are able to take critiques of the relation between the categories of religion and the secular seriously, then far from undermining postcolonial studies, it has the potential to further evolve the field.

WHAT IS POSTCOLONIALISM?

Postcolonialism is the discourse that attempts to shift dominant ways of seeing relations between Western and non-Western societies which came about as a result of European imperialism. One of the enduring legacies of European imperialism is that we inherit an unequal world, and much of this inequality is reflected in the division between peoples of the West and the non-West. This division was concretized in the nineteenth century by the global expansion of European empires. European control over colonized societies developed in complex and often unforeseen ways. As a result, imperial cultures inadvertently found themselves appropriated in active and passive counter-colonial resistance which drew upon many different indigenous local and hybrid processes of self-determination to resist and sometimes replace European dominance (Ashcroft et al. 1995).

Towards the end of the nineteenth century such resistance developed into nationalist struggles for independence. Although many former colonies in Asia, Africa, and Latin America achieved national sovereignty, moving from colonial to autonomous postcolonial status, decolonization represented little more than a transition from direct to indirect rule and dependence on former colonizers, thereby re-establishing a relationship of subordination and economic inequality. Insofar as it actively contests this continued disparity, postcolonialism is a politically motivated discourse. At the same time postcoloniality calls attention to the interaction and mutual imbrications of the European/American metropole and its postcolonies in Asia, Africa, and America. Postcolonialism has developed into a sophisticated form of cultural analysis concerned with generating theoretical models that contest previously dominant Western ways of seeing things. Also known as 'postcolonial theory', such analysis facilitates a politics of the 'subaltern', or subordinated, classes, and peoples.

DEBATES AND FAULT LINES

Despite its rapid rise to prominence in the North American academy, the rubric 'postcolonial' has been hotly debated by cultural critics. This is partly because of confusion over the meaning of the prefix 'post' and partly because some scholars prefer the term 'decolonial' as opposed to 'postcolonial' in as much as it is possible to trace a different geo-history for each of these terms. It is helpful to consider these debates as they give us purchase into the intellectual genealogies of postcolonialism.

Direct criticism of the term postcolonial has come mostly from Marxist scholars who portray postcolonial studies as having taken over a domain which was theirs prior to the end of the Cold War. Such critics are troubled by the implications of the prefix 'post' which, for them, suggests the 'end of colonialism' with a clean break from colonial exploitation (Sagar 1997, 423). Others regard 'post' as a more ambiguous term that can mean 'since colonialism began' thereby temporally encompassing the end of one phase of Western imperialism with the formal dismantling of colonial political-administrative machinery, only to enter the next phase, where Western imperialism reorganizes itself in the form of late-capitalist economies.

A second objection is that the term 'post' elides geographical and cultural differences between formerly colonized peoples in Asia, Africa, North America, and the rather different cases of internally colonized European communities such as Ireland or the

European-settled ex-colonies of Australia, New Zealand, and North America where indigenous non-European populations have been reduced to minority status or herded into reservations. In reply, protagonists of the postcolonial remind us that postcolonial studies is structured on the ground of difference and is therefore under obligation to constantly examine the relationship between various formations of the postcolonial without assuming they can either be reduced to a general category or that there is a radical discontinuity. Postcolonial theory undertakes the task of theorizing these differences and identities (Sagar 1997, 424).

A third and interrelated set of objections to the term 'postcolonial' is that (i) it continues to designate the relation to former colonizers rather than allowing relations between colonized peoples or nations to come to the fore, and (ii) it overemphasizes the power and role of former imperialisms in Third World countries or cultures. The counter-argument to this is that if the term postcolonial defines ex-colonized in relation to European imperial centers, it does so partly because of the material homogenization that resulted from past and present imperial control, and that this control or homogenization will not disappear if left un-named, and partly because of the non-material (psychological, social, affective) aspects of past imperialisms that continue to remain in play today, though some may choose to ignore this.

A possible theoretical fault line in the broader field can be detected in the work of scholars who prefer the term decolonial studies as opposed to postcolonial studies and argue that there is more at stake here than mere semantics (Mignolo 2011). Decolonial and postcolonial studies trace their origins to different points of emergence. Postcolonial studies originates in the experiences of decolonization in British India, Egypt, and Palestine and owes much to Edward Said's influential work *Orientalism* (1993 [1978]) and at a later stage to the writings of the Subaltern Studies collective, a group of Indian scholars (Ranajit Guha 1997; Ashis Nandy [1994; 1998], Dipesh Chakrabarty 2000; Gayatri Spivak 1999; Gyan Pandey 1990) who eventually crossed over into the American academy and were formative in the establishment of postcolonial studies. The intellectual influence behind early postcolonial studies is French poststructuralism, especially figures such as Antonio Gramsci, Michel Foucault, Jacques Derrida, and Gilles Deleuze, who provided alternatives to the Marxist theory of revolution. However, the vocabulary of postcolonial studies was and remains colonial English (Mignolo 2011, xxvi).

Decolonial studies, on the other hand, originated in the writings of Afro-Caribbean and Latin American intellectuals and activists such as Frantz Fanon, Aime Cesaire, and C. L. R. James, whose writings emerged long before poststructuralist and postmodernist movements. Influenced by Marx and Jean-Paul Sartre, Fanon's acclaimed works *Wretched of the Earth* (1986 [1961]) and *Black Skin/White Masks* (1969) take the black body as a point of departure for thinking and can be seen as responses to the long history of enslavement of Africans, racism, the conditions of the Cold War, and the struggle of Africans to decolonize.

However, the main difference between postcolonial and decolonial boils down to different readings of colonialism itself. Whereas postcolonial studies emerges from a critique of Orientalism (the thesis that the Orient was invented by Europeans in the late eighteenth century as its other), scholars of the decolonial point out that the idea of Orientalism in the eighteenth or nineteenth century is unthinkable without first taking into consideration the European invention of the West Indies after the 'discovery' of America by the Spanish (Venn 2000). In other words, in order to imagine Orientalism, it is necessary to posit Occidentalism as a point of reference. Simply defined, Occidentalism is the 'becoming-West' of Europe and boils down to a "conceptual and historical space in which an ego-logical narrative of the subject and a mono-linear narrative of history is constituted" (Venn 2000, 2). Unlike Orientalism, Occidentalism is a sixteenth-century invention.[1]

The stakes in this debate are nothing less than the story of modernity itself. Modernity does not go directly from Greece/Rome to France, England, and Germany as imagined by Protestant thinkers (Hegel, Mill), but takes a detour—via the Atlantic—and it is in this Atlantic detour, from which Catholicism cannot be removed, that Occidentalism was invented (Mignolo 2011). As this particular debate makes clear, the rapid institutionalization and oppositional charge of postcolonial studies has been based not only on its ability to define the 'post' in a way that encompasses questions of nation, class and caste, gender, race, sexuality, and ethnicity, but as far as this chapter is concerned, in a way that marginalizes the question of religion. In ways that are rarely understood, the question of religion provides a useful pointer to the limits of postcolonial theory.

Limits of Postcolonial Theory I: Dialectics, Negation, Recognition

Since the late 1980s postcolonial studies has consciously inserted itself into the gap left by the demise of Marxism in the industrialized West and its satellites. By doing so it was able to position itself as a form of radical critical theory and in so doing acquired major visibility in the academy particularly in the hands of two of its most influential practitioners, Homi Bhabha and Gayatri Spivak. Migrating quickly beyond its initial entry point of literary and cultural studies, it was able to find a home in other disciplines, notably anthropology, history, sociology, and more recently in the study of religions. Its Marxist critics have argued that one reason for its rapid institutionalization in the 1990s is the conceptually nebulous nature of postcolonial theory, a characteristic drawn from poststructuralist and postmodernist critique that made it difficult for its critics to pin down.

Nevertheless in recent years prominent members of the Subaltern Studies group, widely considered to be the exemplary form of postcolonial theorizing, have produced

---

[1] My use of 'Occidentalism' follows the work of decolonial theorists such as Couze Venn and Walter Mignolo. The use of that term to refer to demonizing and dehumanizing images and constructions of 'the West' (Buruma/Margalit 2004) is unhelpful and potentially confusing.

statements outlining something close to a set of core theses that go beyond Said's critique of Orientalism. The central thesis is that there are deep-seated cultural differences that separate East and West, and this structural chasm undermines any Western framework that claims to be universally applicable (Chibber 2013). This core assumption is related to three observations. First, although political modernization in the West was a consequence of the universalization of capital (via the modern European elites), the elite classes in the non-West (especially India) resisted capital's universalizing drive, leading at best to partial success. Second, this resistance to capital's universalization derives from forms of power and authority within indigenous cultures that are inconsistent with the logic of capital. Third, the political agency of the colonized operates with an entirely different psychology than Western agency. That is to say, while the East is broadly subject to the project of nationalization, indigenous cultures at the local everyday level continue to resist the full force of historicization and rationalizing logics even as they insert themselves into the narratives of capitalization (Chibber 2013, 22). For example, as Dipesh Chakrabarty explains, the lives of ordinary people, both elites and peasants, "including their politics, are replete with practices that could seem 'superstitious'", and a "polytheism that marks everyday life," with its "tendency to treat gods, spirits, and other supernatural entities as agential beings in the worlds of humans" (Chakrabarty 2000, 237). By labeling such practices and lived existences as anachronistic or irrational, social scientists fail to discern the nature of the present, or of rationality, as 'irreducibly not-one,' as allowing multiple modes of coexistence, which is central to postcolonial criticism.

While advocating forms of difference, the narratives of postcolonial theory nevertheless fall short of actually showing how alternative modes of logic/consciousness can and do operate, or why they appear to be forbidden from manifesting alongside modern consciousness. As is evident from Chakrabarty's language, his attempt to narrate this difference comes uncomfortably close to the sphere occupied by 'religion,' a term which he and other postcolonial theorists are deeply hesitant to adopt. Part of the reason for this reluctance, as we shall see in the following sections, is that any use of the term religion as a signifier of cultural and ontological difference risks exposing a fundamental problem with the very mode of critique itself, and exposes a flaw within the way that postcolonial theory has conceptualized its politics of difference. In general terms, poststructuralist thought can be considered an attack on Enlightenment traditions that exalt a universality of reason only to sustain a supremacy of the white, male, Euro-Christian subject (Hardt/Negri 2004, 140). Politically, it is an attack on the tradition of modern sovereignty that emerges from it. Conceptually the attack is directed formally towards the dialectic as the central logic of modern domination, exclusion, and command, and nominally towards the figure of G. W. F. Hegel as chief architect of the modern dialectical process based on the master–slave relationship. Thus, if modern power is dialectical (the argument goes) then postcolonialism speaks for displaced, marginalized, and exploited peoples by targeting the dialectical form of modern sovereignty thereby dissolving the power structure that supports the binary opposition. As Hardt and Negri put it, "if the modern is the field of power of the white, male, the European, then in perfectly symmetrical fashion the postcolonial/postmodern will be the field of liberation of the non-white, the non-male and the non-European" (2004, 144–145).

But despite its anti-Hegelian rhetoric, postcolonial theory remains oblivious of a deeper complicity between its critical framework and the Hegelian dialectic, a complicity which actually impedes the process of postcolonialism, or at least imposes limits on what it can achieve in practice and theory. The problem stems from the fact that postcolonial theory in its conventional form continues to utilize two of the most influential organizing concepts in modern political and social theory. First the concept of negation, also known as dialectical negativity, which privileges a form of critique in which a given identity is established only by its opposition to that which it is 'not' or from which it is different. The effect of negation is that difference itself is determined as a function of the negative. For example, the non-West is different from the West because it is determined by a lack that it seeks to remedy by desiring the apparent fullness of the West. To take this one step further, India is essentially religious (it lacks secularism) whereas the West has been able to overcome religion through secularization. Second, there is the concept of recognition, which underlies forms of identity politics and claims for equality. By tacitly accepting negation as the driving force of desire and transformation at the personal and social level, and that recognition of identity is the basis of equality, postcolonial theory at best remains ambiguous, and this ambiguity results in a conceptualization of subjectivity, agency, and process that are problematic and finally unsuitable to the work of decolonization. As a result postcolonial theory remains complicit with an imperial philosophy of difference when it tacitly accepts that negation is the motive force of change (Bignall 2010).

Limits of Postcolonial Theory II: The Problem of Religion

If conventional postcolonial theory is indeed complicit with a form of difference that remains imperialistic, this complicity reveals itself most clearly in its somewhat hesitant and confused engagement with the phenomenon and question of religion. A cursory glance at some of the leading introductions to postcolonialism shows that the theme of religion hardly, if ever, gets a mention. On the one hand this is understandable given that postcolonialism frames itself as an explicitly secular discourse, which tacitly identified at the outset that decolonization implies de-religionization which in turn implies secularization. On the other hand it is surprising given that the rise of postcolonial studies happened against the backdrop of a very loud and visible resurgence of 'fundamentalisms' (a code word for religious nationalisms) following the demise of the Soviet Union and a shift towards a global capitalist order underpinned by the ideology of the free market (Hardt/Negri 2004, 146–150). By and large, although postcolonial studies found it easier to marginalize or ignore religion as a vehicle of anti-modernism, out of joint with the times, postcolonial theorists have had a harder time accounting for the fact that what goes by the name of 'religion' has in equal measure provided a language of resistance for the colonized, and a language of colonial oppression. And postcolonial theorists have had even greater difficulty explaining how the dominant form of nationalism in many of the former colonies is not secular nationalism but religious nationalism which drew as much from indigenous cultural sources as it did from the colonizing West, even as both secular and religious nationalism are being accosted by the forces of global capitalism.

A crucial reason for this lacuna in postcolonial studies is that its main exponents have tended to operate within a narrow definition of religion based on the Marxist premise that 'the criticism of religion is the premise of all criticism.' Within postcolonial theory religion has been treated as a primitive conceptual category synonymous with the very Orientalism that they are trying to decolonize, a conceptual category that should have been exorcized by modernity yet continues to haunt scholarship. Thus through its Marxist inheritance postcolonial discourse has tended to adopt a universalist or *sui generis* definition of religion (see Stausberg/Gardiner, "Definition," this volume), one defined by opposition to reason rather than a relation to 'the sacred.' That is to say, in order to define the proper nature of critique they rely on a definition of religion as the negation of true critical thinking. By doing so, however, they cannot avoid inheriting the three main attributes of the concept of religion as a universal: (i) that religion retains the same essence over time, (ii) that it retains the same essence over space, and (iii) that it is theoretically separable from secular realities and political institutions.

This gap in the narrative of postcolonialism has been indirectly addressed by scholars working in several key areas of the study of religion, including: (i) the construction of religion as a *sui generis* category and the development of religious studies as an academic discipline in the modern university (Balagangadhara 1994; McCutcheon 1997; King 1999; Masuzawa 2005; Fitzgerald 2007); (ii) critiques of the religion–secular binary (Connolly 1999; Asad 2003; Taylor 2008; Anidjar 2008; Cavanaugh 2008; Fitzgerald 2011); (iii) the history of colonial cultural formations categorized as religion or religious in geographical areas as diverse as Africa, Latin America, and Asia (Asad 1993; Chidester 1996; Lopez 1998; Mandair 2009). Armed with detailed empirical analyses, and theoretical insights based on Derrida's deconstruction of Western metaphysics or Foucault's genealogical analysis of power/knowledge, scholars associated with this influential field of research (which might usefully be called 'critical religion studies') have been able to explore the ideological construction of the category religion in the Western knowledge and political system.

A key insight of critical religion studies is to target the move whereby scholars, media spokespersons, and politicians identify a transhistorical, transcultural, and essentially interior concept of religion, and then separate this concept from secular phenomena. This move points to a particular configuration of power, namely, the rise and development of the modern liberal nation state in the West which is paralleled by the history of invention of the category of religion in the modern West by figures such as Nicholas of Cusa, Marsilio Ficino, Herbert of Cherbury, and John Locke. This concept of religion as universal "justifies the liberal state's self-presentation as an apparatus concerned with the wholly negative function of preventing the incursion of substantive collective ends into the public sphere" (Cavanaugh 2008, 84). Rather religion needs to be regarded as a political category that marginalizes and domesticates forms of collective social action that challenge this segregative model of society and politics (Fitzgerald 2011). Consequently the category of religion is not simply descriptive but prescriptive—it acts as a normative category.

If the weight of historical evidence indicates that the genus religion does not extend over time, there is even less evidence for the belief that religion extends spatially across the world, or that it is a worldwide concept in the form of 'World Religions.' An entire generation of scholarship, arguably going back to W. C. Smith's *The Meaning and End of Religion* (1959), has shown that the concept of religion was introduced into non-Western contexts through European colonization and it primarily served the interests of colonizing powers (but see Casadio, "Historicizing and Translating Religion," this volume, for an alternative account). Notwithstanding the diversity of areas being covered (the Americas, Africa, Pacific Islands, and Asia), a coherent narrative emerges which goes something like this.

Initially, prior to conquering a particular culture, European explorers routinely reported that the local peoples had no religion at all. Denying religion was a way of denying them rights. If they were shown to lack a basic human characteristic such as religion, then the natives could be treated as less than human and deprived of legitimate rights to law, land, and property. But once the natives were conquered and colonized, scholars and administrators suddenly began to 'discover' that they did in fact have religion, although it was a primitive version of Christianity. After annexation and colonization, attributing religion to indigenous peoples was a way of depoliticizing their cultures and entering them into a comparative framework. The standard for the comparative framework was of course Christianity which served both as the norm of religion-in-general, and as the unique religion which had historically overcome religion giving rise to secularism. So if religion gave some hope for comparing West and East, the comparison became meaningless, because it was secularism that the practices and thinking of the indigenous cultures essentially lacked. This operation of comparison (or the attribution of lack/negativity resulting from comparison) followed a fairly consistent pattern in the colonization of various peoples: Maya and Peruvians (Blume 2006); Zulus in South Africa (Chidester 1996); Native American Indians (Venn 2000; Fessenden 2008); Buddhists in Tibet, Burma, China, Japan, etc. (Lopez 1998); Gikuyu in Kenya (Peterson/Walhof 2002); Hinduism and Sikhism in India (Balagangadhara 1994; King 1999; Zavos 2002; Mandair 2009); Shinto in Japan (Ichi Isomae 2014; Maxey 2014).

Though not immediately obvious, this pattern of reversals in colonial observations about the native cultures (God/Religion doesn't exist → God/Religion exists) is less indicative of changes in the empirical findings of scholars, missionaries, and travelers during the colonial period, than it is of an increasingly coherent discourse of 'religion-making' (Dressler/Mandair 2011). Broadly conceived, the discourse of religion-making derives from a particular configuration of power, the power of the modern liberal state, and refers to a logic of governmentality through which the state's functionaries (scholars, administrators, politicians, etc.) conceptualized and institutionalized ideas, sociocultural formations, and practices that were discursively reified and objectified as essentially 'religious.' By the early nineteenth century it is possible to distinguish two levels of religion-making: macropolitical versus micropolitical. In order to understand how these two levels of religion-making work in conjunction with each other, and to further underscore the importance of the question of religion to postcolonialism, it will be helpful to focus on a specific example. A useful example that is in many ways illustrative of what is happening in other colonized societies around the world, is the construction of Hinduism as a religion in late nineteenth- and early twentieth-century India. The discussion will try to show the continued relevance of this constructed entity Hindu-*ism* to the question of postcoloniality.

Religion-Making and (Post)Coloniality

Macropolitics

The macropolitical level refers to a 'religion-making from above' (Mandair/Dressler 2011, 21), that is, authoritative discourses and practices that defined and confined things (an entity, culture, social group, symbols, language) as 'religious' or 'secular' through the disciplining means of the modern state and its institutions (law-making, the judiciary, state bureaucracies, state media, and the public education systems). Thus cultures, social groups, or entities labeled as either 'religious' or 'secular' became instruments of government, a means to legitimize certain politics and positions of power. By the early nineteenth century, the modern state manifested itself physically in the form of empire and discursively through invisible structures of power associated with the imperial state's 'logic of governmentality'—structures such as law, language, and the specifically 'Western code' of political theology. Taken together these structures constituted a formidable conceptual apparatus that helped the colonizer to consolidate power by reproducing knowledge of colonized cultures through a globally secured epistemology which had the ability to manufacture and insert universals such as the concept of religion or the secular into contexts where it may not previously have been present.

A good example of a globally secured epistemological apparatus driven by imperial governance was Hegel's comparative schema of world systems such as world history, religions, philosophies, and aesthetics. Hegelian theories changed the hermeneutic of modernity by centralizing the structure of human consciousness (or self-representation) around the operations of metaphysical logic, and re-embedding consciousness within the dialectical movement of historical time. Hence, what has come to be known as 'historical consciousness,' central to which is the movement of dialectic, becomes the defining mark of modernity. From here it was but a short step to suggest that critical thinking or critique is secular insofar as it dialectically overcomes religion. Accordingly the relationship between 'religion' and 'the secular' is seen as dialectical. By thus implementing a circular relationship between (i) historical consciousness, (ii) critique, and (iii) secularity, Hegel was able to identify tangible and threatening 'others' (e.g. Asia, Africa, etc.) as 'religions' while arguing that Christianity is 'Religion' because it provides the cultural constituents necessary for overcoming its particularity (that Christianity is also a 'religion' like others) and inexorable movement towards secularity, which non-Western 'religions' lacked (Hegel 1827).

Aspects of this schema were incorporated into explanations about the essential nature of non-Western cultures that would eventually become seamlessly incorporated into the system of the emerging human sciences. Within an emerging World Religions discourse, the schema provided an intuitive comprehension of the 'meaning-value' of cultures through a principle of 'generalized translation'—a mechanism for bringing different cultures into a taxonomic system of equivalence, in which the relative meaning-values could be assigned to each culture in order for them to be exchanged/compared (Liu 1999). By bringing the meaning-value of different cultures into a system of exchange-comparison, this approach effectively replaced the tangible problem of translation (and hence the anxiety of real encounter) with the work of representation proper to the political economy of the sign. Within the context of cultural exchange and comparison that begins to parallel commodity exchange in the political economy of empire, the system of exchange-comparison that is intrinsic to the comparative cultural imaginary of the West, can be seen as a precursor of the system of global monetary exchange which, as Marx pointed out, developed at roughly the same time (Taylor 2008).

The results of this new comparative epistemology were far-reaching. It enabled Orientalists, missionaries, philosophers, anthropologists, historians, economists, sociologists, and religionists, to *make religion*, albeit imaginatively, by applying a model that recognized the diversity of world cultures in terms of an imperializing difference. Non-Western cultures could be recognized as *religions* (and therefore similar to 'our own,' i.e. Christianity and as part of a broad human unity) but at the same time the designation of religion served to differentiate between humans/cultures precisely on the basis of their lack of elevation/progress towards 'true' religion (Christianity) and secularity (the ability to separate culture from religion) which as a tendency could only emerge from Christianity (Dressler/Mandair 2011).

Micropolitics: 'Reform,' Agency, and Religion-Making

The implications of this global comparative epistemology were not lost on imperial policy-makers, law-makers, educators, and administrators who deployed its universalizing tendencies to full effect in colonial government. But it is in the micropolitics of native elite resistance and accession to colonial rule, at the level of agency, that we see the tangible results of this epistemological apparatus. It is well known that modern indigenous elites were educated in new school systems implemented by European colonizers (Guha 1997). Through colonial systems of education, modern native elites developed a new kind of agency which on the one hand allowed them to resist the colonial project, by organizing social movements motivated by the desire to improve the status of the colonized through social, political, and religious reform. On the other hand, paradoxically, these new elites were essential for the success of the imperial mission, becoming the very instrument by which the dominant symbolic order, arguably the most important structure of colonization, was internalized by the native psyche (Mandair 2009).

For many postcolonial theorists the troubling aspect of this paradox is how to account for the way that an identifiable imperialist technology in the past (religion-making by native elites) continues to strongly influence the present in the shape of interlinked crises: e.g. the return of religion and/or the crisis of secularism at the heart of Indian democracy. The key to this paradox lies in understanding the complex nature of 'reform' and its role in constructing a form of agency that derived its generative force from a negative ontology, an ontology based on lack, that feeds the production of identity through the colonial, neocolonial, and postcolonial periods. More specifically, the nature of reform is dependent not only on the project of religion-making, but on a process that had to become instituted before any religion-making as such could begin in the first place—the project of language-making.

Thus, when the British first arrived in India what they expected to find was a simple correspondence between religion and language (i.e. Sanskrit to Hinduism, Arabic/Persian to Islam, etc.). Derived from the ideology of deism, this expectation was based on a belief in a direct correspondence between monotheism and monolingualism (respectively represented by Christianity as national religion and English as national language) through the natural light of reason. One of the main proponents of this isomorphism between monotheism/monolingualism/reason was Sir William Jones, also known as the founder of Indology. Jones believed that the natural correspondence between religion and language would be proven by native enunciation or self-identification with one of India's diverse religions. Instead they found Hindus and Muslims using a common spoken language (Moors or Hindustanee) composed of several vernaculars with varying admixtures of Sanskrit, Braj, Persian, Arabic, etc. depending on region and social context (Dalmia 1997). The heterogeneity of this spoken language made it difficult for the natives to register a satisfactory response to the question 'What is your religion?' which the British considered a serious impediment to both secular administration of Indians, and to the possibility of converting them to Christianity. The Orientalist explanation for this was that the spoken languages had degenerated from their original purity due to mixing with foreign Muslim languages such as Arabic and Persian, which in turn led to a degeneration of the original religions of the Hindus. The linguistic and religious culture of Indians therefore needed to be reformed from their 'fallen' state. To remedy this 'lack' in the native cultures the British set about re-codifying the spoken languages of North India using English as a grammatical standard (Cohn 1996). The result was the creation of two separate languages based on religious identification (Hindi for Hindus, and Urdu for Muslims) the teaching of which was institutionalized initially in language seminaries such as Fort William College, Calcutta, and eventually through a large network of Anglo-Vernacular schools spread throughout much of North India. Within such schools it is possible to identify regimes of translation that effectively replaced the prior heterolingual frameworks of native speech with a monolingual form of address between colonizer and colonized. The multiple effects of this new mode of address included the production of a seamless exchange of linguistic categories and concepts between English as the first idiom (or dominant symbolic order) of empire and the imagined, and newly fabricated, vernaculars represented by the figure of the mother tongue (Hindi, Urdu, Punjabi, etc.) as the monolingual other of English. Once the linguistic structure of the native mindset was reframed as monolingual, it became receptive to foreign categories such as religion, the secular, etc. The category of religion was thereby internalized by native elites, and consequently their habits of enunciation were also transformed such that they begin to enunciate their identity as a specifically religious identity. Having internalized the category of religion, the native elites could be considered to be reformed and accorded some degree of recognition by the colonizer insofar as they showed evidence of having 'improved' their language and religion according to the imperial standard. By doing so the native elites became the essential agents of reform movements which in turn were precursors of later religious and secular nationalist movements of independence. Reform movements such as these were not limited to India. Similar movements emerged in other areas of European colonization such as the Middle East, Africa, as well as Southeast and East Asia. What makes the thesis of the reform process generalizable to other cultures and geographical areas is its logic based on causal negativity. Though rarely acknowledged, the logic of reform is as relevant to the Indian context as it is to similarly colonized areas in the Middle East, Southeast Asia, parts of East Asia, and the Americas, precisely because of the dual and simultaneous role of a Christian–secular continuum, that is, Christianity in combination with European languages. It is this continuum that Derrida identifies through his neologism *mondialatinisation*. Translated as globalatinization this neologism suggests a worldwide spreading of a particular way of 'speaking religion' according to the Latin, and therefore Christian imprint, which still "speaks today through the new lingua franca of the world, namely, English, or rather Anglo-American, which is attempting to spread its empire . . . across the globe" (Naas 2012, 57). As Derrida notes:

> For everything that touches religion in particular, for everything that speaks "religion", for whoever speaks religiously or about religion, Anglo-remains Latin. *Religion* circulates in the world, one might say, like an *English word* that has been to Rome and taken a detour to the United States. Well beyond its strictly capitalist or politico-military figures, a hyper-imperialist appropriation has been underway now for centuries. It imposes itself in a particularly palpable manner within the conceptual apparatus of international law and of global political rhetoric. Wherever this apparatus dominates, it articulates itself through a discourse on religion. (Derrida 1998, 29)

The reform process thus produces one of the intractable aporias of (post)coloniality: that prior to the encounter with European imperialism the category of religion (and the secular, as well as the opposition between then) did not exist in the lexicons of

Indian cultures, but then, at a certain stage of the colonizing process when Anglophone consciousness was internalized by native elites, the category of religion emerged and took shape within nationalist enunciation as if it had been an indigenous category all along (Dalmia 1997; Mandair 2009). Scholarly awareness of the function of translation-enunciation has shifted debates about the nature of agency from an earlier focus on the overt violence of macropolitical structures in coercing native elites, towards a more interactionist or dialogical model of agency, suggesting that native elites adapted to colonial power structures through a process of 'intercultural mimesis.' Yet even these theories fail to explain why, in a supposedly postcolonial era, elites in India and elsewhere continue to be chained to mechanisms that reproduce imperialist technologies, either in the form of religious nationalism or as secular state nationalism. What is it about the contemporary world that keeps imperial technologies (language-making/religion-making/reformism) in place, rather than dissipating them?

Symbolic Violence: Or, How a Foreign Concept ('Religion') is Internalized

The problem with theories of dialogue or intercultural mimesis is that they obfuscate the key mechanism in the colonizing process. What we understand as 'internalization' is actually a psycho-linguistic operation that exerts a form of violence that normally passes under the radar of epistemological or political scrutiny. We can call this symbolic violence—a violence embodied in the socially dominant language and reproduced in our customary forms of speech, i.e. at the moment when a subject chooses words (enunciates) or formulates conceptual thought (Žižek 2008). At this moment the subject's ability to choose indigenous concepts is interdicted by a law inherent in the dominant language (Derrida 1992). This law quite literally prohibits (refuses recognition to) certain kinds of indigenous words or concepts from coming to expression in the public sphere, while permitting (recognizing) others. What tends to be interdicted, forbidden from appearing in the public space governed by the colonial idiom, hence not recognized, are non-modern articulations of concepts associated with forms of logic and ways of organizing temporality that might challenge the universalist pretensions of European modernity. Again, using the case of Hinduism in the Indian context as a generalizable example, enunciations such as "Hinduism is my religion" or "I am Hindu (because I am *not* Muslim)" etc., can only happen because this particular identification is granted recognition while older and alternative logics of identification are not recognized. This dialectic of recognition/non-recognition is responsible for the translation-transformation of indigenous concepts into the category 'religion.' And this generalized logic of translation—hence the apparent universality of religion—is inextricably related to the task of reforming one's 'religion' according to an imagined past exemplar from which it had apparently fallen. Through such reform it enters the hermeneutic of modernity whose essential characteristic is an explicitly representational form of consciousness that becomes the *modus operandi* of the modern social imaginary which in turn stakes its dominance on the 'fundamental translatability' of its linguistic categories, notably 'religion' and 'the secular' (Derrida 2004). Because our 'secular age' remains tied to an Anglophone consciousness and therefore to a Christian–secular continuum, Hindus who present themselves within this modern social imaginary as a 'religious' identity, as Hindu nationalism, foreclose themselves from enunciating in other ways.

What symbolic violence of language makes visible is the operation of the interdict as an event that didn't just happen in the colonial past, but which continues to be repeated each time Hindus identify as a 'religion.' And this repetition continues ad nauseam because the agency of elites continues to be shaped by an imperial or possessive incli-nation of self to other that is inherited from the comparative relation to the colonizer, which in turn is shaped by a negative form of difference. Because of this causal onto-logical negativity, the reform movements and their contemporary political incarnations (Hindu nationalism and Indian secular nationalism) are driven by a politics of nega-tion—"I am Hindu because I am not Muslim, Christian, Sikh etc.," or, "I am an Indian nationalist but not religious"—which consistently positions bearers of difference (Sikh, Hindu, Muslim) as active agents of change, yet simultaneously marked by a problem-atic negativity. If the negating class (Hindu nationalists/Indian secular nationalists) alone assumes responsibility for transformative action, inevitably the accountability of the dominant class is elided, with the result that the apathy of privileged former colo-nizers (European-American) is excused (Bignall 2010). There is therefore little or no motivation for yesterday's colonizing class, or those today who identify themselves as upholders of the modern social imaginary, the secular age, to engage in any postcolonial transformation (or even to recognize postcoloniality as a perspective), when "this is not presented as a common task responsibly shared by all within the postcolony" (Bignall 2010, 231).

What Bignall calls the 'common task' can be stated more simply. Given that the domi-nant symbolic order of the colonial period continues to exert its influence through the modern social imaginary of our secular age, non-Western discourses are still faced with the burden of translating into a dominant Western conceptuality. Hence the two basic questions facing postcolonials today: How to introduce a 'genuine discontinuity' in the repetitions driven by the negative dialectic of religion and the secular? What might be the benefits of such a discontinuity for the future of postcolonialism?

Scholars of critical religion have provided a variety of answers to these questions. The more productive responses (e.g. by Asad 2003; McCutcheon 1997; Fitzgerald 2007; Goldenberg 2015; King 1999; Cavanaugh 2008; Balagangadhara 2013; Abeyesekara 2008; Dressler/Mandair 2011) to these questions acknowledge that while, on the one hand, it is necessary for scholars to critically distance themselves from the idea that religion is universal, on the other hand, we can neither simply receive the heritage of secularism nor abandon its legacy. So while many recognize that the experience of postcoloniality is essentially *aporetic* (a contradiction that cannot be resolved by recon-ciling opposites), there is less enthusiasm about developing a method of critical inquiry attuned to the nature of *aporia* itself. Such a method might be able to address the major limitation of conventional postcolonial theory discussed earlier. In part, the issue here is that the currently dominant method favored by scholars of religion remains restricted to a form of genealogical critique derived from Foucault which remains tethered to the notional practice and logic of historical consciousness driven by a problematic casual negativity.

A rather different move would be to grasp the *aporia* itself. But to do this one has to accept that scholarly positions based on genealogical critique are limited. They are "animated by the belief that answers to the problems of our political present are available within our present, within shouting distance of our modernity" (Abeyesekara 2008, 46–47). In other words, the problem with genealogical critique is that it remains tied to an *imperialism of the present* whose temporality continues to be determined by an image of thought that closes off alternative temporalities which may otherwise be capable of tapping past and future as possibilities for living. This may require scholars who work at the intersection of religious studies and postcolonial theory to strive for approaches that can work productively with the contradictions of the present rather than succumbing to the 'dogmatic image of thought' based on the law of non-contradiction (Deleuze 1995 [1968]) whose continuing legacy is that different entities, persons, and concepts are not allowed to coexist or mutually contaminate each other. Bearing this in mind, a more productive path for postcolonial theory in relation to the question of religion may be to adopt a strategy that allows scholars to simultaneously inherit and un-inherit the legacy of the religion–secular nexus. The notion of un-inheriting suggests a path of thinking that treats any heritage (e.g. religion, the secular, democracy, etc.) as an impossible inheritance (Abeyesekara 2008, 9). To give an example of impossible inheritance, it would not be enough to simply desire the post-secular or post-religious, but to desire something like the *post-secular-religious* so that secular and religious epistemes are treated as mutually contaminated and contaminating. By grasping this *aporia* it may be possible for postcolonial theory to come closer to glimpsing its holy grail, namely, the idea of a present infused by multiplicity, a present that enables concepts of different cultures to coexist, to embrace and make love, in order to change the future.

Glossary

Aporia an irresolvable contradiction, e.g. between religion and the secular.

Dialectical negativity a mode of thought that aims to reconcile contradictions whose driving force is negativity.

Enunciation discourse of the postcolonial subject not bound to fixed referents or significations due to experiences of exile, marginalization, colonization, etc.

Interdiction a force that prohibits or privatizes certain words or speech from coming to mind or being enunciated in public, whilst allowing others access to the public realm.

Internalization in the context of this chapter, the incorporation and integration of 'foreign' words, categories, or concepts into one's 'native' lexicon.

Religion-making the idea that religion is not simply a natural thing out there waiting to be found and researched, but a social construct produced in complex contexts, e.g. social, political, and economic.

Symbolic violence this is a violence that normally goes undetected because it is embodied in language, present in forms of social domination that are reproduced in our customary forms of speech. As such it is the form of violence that underpins the distinction between religion and the secular.

References

Abeyesekara, Ananda. 2008. *The Politics of Postsecular Religion*. New York: Columbia University Press

Anidjar, Gil. 2008. *Semites: Race, Religion, Literature*. Stanford, CA: Stanford University Press.

Asad, Talal. 1993. *Genealogies of Religion: Discipline and Reasons of Power in Christianity and Islam*. Baltimore: Johns Hopkins University Press.

Asad, Talal. 2003. *Formations of the Secular: Christianity, Islam, Modernity*. Stanford, CA: Stanford University Press.

Ashcroft, Bill, Gareth Griffiths, and Helen Tiffin, eds. 1995. *The Postcolonial Studies Reader*. London and New York: Routledge.

Balagangadhara, S. N. 1994. *The Heathen in His Blindness: Asia, the West and the Dynamic of Religion*. Leiden: Brill.

Bignall, Simone. 2010. *Postcolonial Agency: Critique and Constructivism*. Edinburgh: University of Edinburgh Press.

Blume, Anna. 2006. *A Pre-Columbian World*. Cambridge, MA: Harvard University Press.

Buruma, Ian and Avishai Margalit. 2004. *Occidentalism: The West in the Eyes of Its Enemies*. New York: Penguin.

Cavanaugh, William. 2008. *The Myth of Religious Violence*. New York: Oxford University Press.

Chakrabarty, Dipesh. 2000. *Provincializing Europe: Postcolonial Thought and Historical Difference*. Princeton, NJ: Princeton University Press.

Chibber, Vivek. 2013. *Postcolonial Theory and the Specter of Capital*. London: Verso.

Chidester, David. 1996. *Savage Systems: Colonialism and Comparative Religion in Southern Africa*. Charlottesville, VA: University Press of Virginia.

Cohn, Bernhard. 1996. *Colonialism and its Forms of Knowledge*. Dehli: Oxford University Press.

Connolly, William. 1999. *Why I Am Not a Secularist*. Minneapolis: University of Minnesota Press.

Dalmia, Vasudha. 1997. *The Nationalization of Hindu Traditions*. Delhi: Oxford University Press.

Deleuze, Gilles. 1995 [1968]. *Difference and Repetition*, translated by Paul Patton. New York: Columbia University Press.

Derrida, Jacques. 1992. "Force of Law: The 'Mystical Foundation of Authority.'" In *Deconstruction and the Possibility of Justice*, edited by Drucilla Cornell, Michel Rosenfeld, and David G. Carlson. London: Routledge, 3–67.

Derrida, Jacques. 1998. "Faith and Knowledge: The Two Sources of 'Religion' at the Limits of Reason Alone." In *Religion*, edited by Jacques Derrida and Gianni Vattimo. Cambridge: Polity Press, 1–78.

Derrida, Jacques. 2004. "Theology of Translation." In *Eyes of the University: Right to Philosophy 2*, translated by Jan Plug et al. Palo Alto, CA: Stanford University Press, 64–79.

Dressler, Markus and Arvind-Pal S. Mandair, eds. 2011. *Secularism and Religion-Making*. New York: Oxford University Press.

Fanon, Franz. 1969. *Black Skin/White Masks*. London: Pluto Press.

Fanon, Franz. 1986. *The Wretched of the Earth*. Harmondsworth: Penguin. Original edition, 1961.

Fessenden, Tracy. 2008. *Culture and Redemption*. Princeton, NJ: Princeton University Press.

Fitzgerald, Timothy. 2007 *Discourse on Civility and Barbarity*. New York: Oxford University Press.

Fitzgerald, Timothy. 2011. *Religion and Politics in International Relations*. London: Continuum.

Goldenberg, Naomi. 2015. "The Category of Religion in the Technology of Governance." In *Religion as a Category of Governance and Sovereignty*, edited by Trevor Stack, Tim Fitzgerald, and Naomi Goldenberg. Leiden: Brill, 280–292.

Guha, Ranajit. 1997. *Dominance Without Hegemony*. Delhi: Oxford University Press.

Hardt, Michael and Antonio Negri. 2004. *Empire*. Cambridge, MA: Harvard University Press.

Hegel, G. W. F. 1827. *Lectures on the Philosophy of Religion*, translated by Peter Hodgson. Berkeley: University of California Press.

Isomae, Jun Ichi. 2014. *Religious Discourse in Modern Japan*. Leiden: Brill.

King, Richard. 1999. *Orientalism and Religion*. London: Routledge.

Liu, Lydia, ed. 1999. *Tokens of Exchange*. Durham, NC: Duke University Press.

Lopez, Donald S. 1998. *Prisoners of Shangri La: Tibetan Buddhism and the West*. Chicago, IL: University of Chicago Press.

McCutcheon, Russell. 1997. *Manufacturing Religion: Sui Generis Discourse and the Politics of Nostalgia*. New York: Oxford University Press.

Mandair, Arvind-Pal S. 2009. *Religion and the Specter of the West: Sikhism, India, Postcoloniality and the Politics of Translation*. New York: Columbia University Press.

Mandair, Arvind-Pal S. and Markus Dressler. 2011. "Introduction: Modernity, Religion-Making and the Postsecular." In *Secularism and Religion-Making*, edited by Markus Dressler and Arvind-Pal S. Mandair. New York: Oxford University Press, 3–36.

Masuzawa, Tomoko. 2005. *The Invention of World Religions*. Chicago, IL: University of Chicago Press.

Maxey, Trent E. 2014. *The "Greatest Problem": Religion and State Formation in Meiji Japan*. Cambridge, MA: Harvard University Press.

Mignolo, Walter. 2011. *The Darker Side of Western Modernity*. Durham, NC: Duke University Press.

Naas, Michael. 2012. *Miracle and Machine: Jacques Derrida and the Two Sources of Religion, Science and the Media*. New York: Fordham University Press.

Nandy, Ashis. 1994. *The Illegitimacy of Nationalism*. Delhi: Oxford University Press.

Nandy, Ashis. 1998. *Exiled at Home*. Delhi: Oxford University Press.

Pandey, Gyan. 1990. *The Construction of Communalism in Colonial North India*. Delhi: Oxford University Press.

Peterson, Derek and Darren Walhof. 2002. "Rethinking Religion." In *The Invention of Religion: Rethinking Belief in Politics and History*, edited by Derek R. Peterson and Darren R. Walhof. New Brunswick, NJ: Rutgers University Press, 1–16.

Sagar, Aparajita. 1997. "Postcolonial Studies." In *A Dictionary of Cultural and Critical Theory*, edited by Michael Payne and Jessica R. Barbera. Oxford: Blackwell, 423–427.

Said, Edward. 1993. *Culture and Imperialism*. London: Chatto & Windus.

Said, Edward. 1993. *Orientalism*. London: Routledge & Kegan Paul. Original edition, 1978.

Smith, W. C. 1959. *The Meaning and End of Religion*. New York: Macmillan.

Spivak, Gayatri. 1999. *A Critique of Postcolonial Reason*. Cambridge, MA: Harvard University Press.

Taylor, Mark C. 2008. *After God*. Chicago, IL: University of Chicago Press.

Venn, Couze. 2000. *Occidentalism: Modernity and Subjectivity*. London: Sage.

Zavos, John. 2002. *The Emergence of Hindu Nationalism in India*. Delhi: Oxford University Press.

Žižek, Slavoj. 2008. *Violence*. New York: Picador.

FURTHER READING

Asad 2003 [*Key work in 'critical religion studies' which deconstructs the religion–secular binary in the context of comparative study of Islam and Christianity.*]

Bhabha, Homi. 1994. *The Location of Culture*. London and New York: Routledge. [*A classic in the field of postcolonial theory that draws on Lacan and Derrida to define many of the field's key terms and neologisms such as mimicry, ambivalence, hybridity, etc.*]

Chakrabarty 2000 [*Important work that develops some of the core theses of conventional postcolonialism, especially historical difference as a key Western notion.*]

King 1999 [*One of the first works to bring the field of religious studies into contact with postcolonialism.*]

Mandair 2009 [*Brings conventional postcolonial theory into contact with 'critical religion studies' and simultaneously develops a form of postcolonial agency by operationalizing non-Western concepts through alternative modes of translation.*]

Said 1978; 1993 [*Two classics which develop the notion of Orientalism in detail and provide a critique of nationalism.*]

CHAPTER 13

....

SEMANTICS

....

MARK Q. GARDINER AND STEVEN ENGLER

CHAPTER SUMMARY

....

- Semantics—the study of meaning, in the sense of linguistic content rather than existential significance—asks various questions of relevance for the study of religion\s, especially a recent turn toward the intentions of speakers and actors.
- Two basic positions are representationalism (identifying the meaning of linguistic expressions with that which they supposedly represent) and interpretationalism (attributing meaningfulness to anything that can be understood by a neutral 'interpreter').
- Semantics has had significant impact on two areas directly related to the study of religion\s: the philosophy of religion and cognitive science.
- Paying attention to semantics sheds useful light on a variety of issues: for example, the relation between religious and other types of languages (e.g. scientific); whether text and ritual should be studied in radically different ways; the viability of *sui generis* views of religion; and the 'insider/outsider problem.'
- Because some stance regarding the nature of meaning—if only implicit—is unavoidable, scholars of religion should acquire a minimal working knowledge of semantics.

WHAT IS SEMANTICS AND WHY DOES IT MATTER?

....

Semantics is the study of meaning, in the sense of linguistic content rather than existential significance. It asks a variety of questions:

- What is meaning? Is it a 'thing' that is somehow 'out there' to be found; a product of the intentions of language users; a construct of the acts of interpretation that people engage in in specific contexts?
- Are there distinct types of meaning—e.g. religious and scientific—or only one?
- Is meaning associated with individual words or with broader groupings of language units?
- Is the purpose of language to represent the world or something else, like prescribing or emoting?
- Do words and actions—e.g. texts and rituals—mean in the same or in different ways?

These questions and many related ones have direct relevance for the study of religion\s. As scholars of religion, we should be aware of semantics because our work is shaped and constrained by implicit semantic stances, whether we admit it or not. At one level, this is because the phenomena that we study, and the ways we choose to study them, have semantic dimensions. For example, contrasting positions in many debates in the discipline stand or fall as a direct consequence of their semantic presuppositions: e.g. the translatability of sacred scriptures; 'correct' methods for studying ritual; the insider/outsider problem; *sui generis* views of 'religion'; the status of symbolic or metaphorical language; and the alleged ineffability of mystical experience. At another level, semantics is relevant for all scholarly work of any sort, given that it is shaped and constrained by implicit semantic stances, whether we recognize it or not. All objects and results of study—more generally all meaningful phenomena and all acts of communication—*mean what they mean* in certain ways, and asking well-informed questions about this has significant practical implications for how we do scholarship. A stumbling block that prevents many people from taking philosophical questions seriously—e.g. epistemological debates about 'truth' and semantic debates about 'meaning'—is that they are so essential and so basic to almost every aspect of our personal and professional lives that we necessarily act on the basis of implicit assumptions that, as a result, are hard to reflect on formally and hard to let go of when proven untenable. In terms of epistemological and semantic views, to offer an analogy that is more appropriate than it might seem at first, most people think that the earth is flat and the sun revolves around it.

A baseline view of semantics sees it as the study of how language is related to the extra-linguistic world, i.e. the study of the relation between our abstract symbol systems and that which they were intended to represent. This would have intrinsic importance to scholars of religion for a number of reasons. Most basically, the religious 'world' postulated by the adherent differs from the empirical one that is accessed by both scholars and adherents. The 'insider' typically considers the religious 'world' to be just as real as (and often coextensive with) the empirical one, but the scholarly 'outsider' typically doesn't. This talk of different 'worlds' is meant to represent a commonly held attitude, which this chapter problematizes. This common attitude largely assumes a representationalist semantics: i.e. it is assumed that talk about these 'worlds' is fixed by word–world relations, from which it follows that the different ways that insiders and outsiders talk about these 'worlds' indicate that they are indeed different. Our point is that interpretationalism—a different semantic view clarified further in the following— doesn't lead to that conclusion: if 'meaning' means something different, the differences between insiders and outsiders are cast in a new light.

In other words, a broader attention to semantics forces us to pay attention to the intentions of speakers and actors in more nuanced ways. Some scholars hold that 'world' is a social construction whose basic building materials are the mythological narratives and ritual performances of social groups. A fuller understanding of religions would include what those narratives and performances are supposed to mean. Even to realist scholars—e.g. many theologians who, like adherents, typically regard the religious 'world' as objectively real—and to 'critical' theorists—who are quite happy to regard it as illusory or even delusionary—understanding and explaining religious phenomena would be greatly advanced by exploring what it is that adherents *intend* to be representing in their narratives and performances. Empirically grounded approaches that ignore issues of meaning can provide evidence only of the structure and function of religious practices, leaving out what adherents typically take as the most significant or important aspects of their religious lives. Readers might respond at this point that the study of religion\s almost always looks at or takes into account what religious practitioners mean. That is our point precisely—though formal analyses that leave aside issues of meaning in the sense we are discussing here are prominent, e.g. functionalism and syntactical analyses of ritual—and that is why it is important to take semantics seriously. Our point is that methodology, theory, and meta-theory in the study of religion\s could often proceed more effectively and defensibly if pursued in the light of current 'best practices' in philosophical thinking about the nature of meaning.

Semantics (the study of linguistic meaning) has traditionally been understood in contrast to syntactics (emphasizing grammar or the rules for combining symbols) and pragmatics (emphasizing how the language is used). In religion, narratives and rituals typically have recognizable syntactic patterns as well as more or less clear pragmatic forces (e.g. functionalist views of religion), but limiting the study of religion to either or both of these impoverishes it. In addition, the distinction between semantics, syntactics, and pragmatics is complicated by advances in the philosophy of language. For one thing, many contemporary philosophers of language challenge whether any significant distinction can be drawn between syntactics, pragmatics, and semantics (as per many of the essays in Ezcurdia/Stainton 2013). On the one hand, the 'formal' semanticists regard meaning as a function of syntax (as, for example, the intuitive meaning differences between "Muslims worship only Allah" and "Only Muslims worship Allah"), but pure formalism is incompatible with the fact that communication often succeeds despite improper syntactic construction; on the other hand, 'use' theorists regard meaning as determined entirely by how the language is pragmatically used (Davidson 1984), but pure 'use' approaches are unable to explain how a never-before-used sentence can be immediately understood (Cappelen/LePore 2006). In a nutshell, language needs compositional syntactic resources, but meaning cannot swing entirely free of its capacity to be understood. Meaning (semantics), structure (syntactics), and use (pragmatics) come as a package.

More challenging to semantics is a split between philosophers of language over whether the role of language is to represent an extra-linguistic world. In other words, many philosophers of language reject a *representationalist* semantics which sees the meaning of linguistic expressions identified with that which they supposedly represent. For some representationalists, individual words are taken to be signs or symbols, in the sense that they refer to or pick out purported elements of the world. As a variant, some have taken individual words to be signs of inner mental states ('affections of the soul' for Aristotle or 'internal conceptions' for Locke) but generally have still regarded those mental states as having a representational content. On this view sentences are descriptions of 'states-of-affairs' built up out of the objects and properties that its individual words pick out, either directly or as mediated through the mind. The meaning of a sentence is identified with that description: reference determines meaning, and truth—correspondence between these descriptions and the world—becomes a central semantic concept.

Philosopher J. L. Austin's *How to Do Things with Words* (1962) fundamentally challenged this approach by bringing to the forefront the fact that we do many more things with words than just describe (see Michaels/Sax, "Performance," this volume). He drew a distinction between linguistic *statements* and *performances*, noting two predominant—but not mutually exclusive—types of linguistic performance: *locution* (the act of making a statement, as in uttering "I do") and *illocution* (achieving some purpose by means of making the statement, such as getting married). However, for Austin it was the *statement* issued in the locutionary act, not its performance, which carried semantic content, and he continued to think of that content in representational terms (1962, 100).

Non- or anti-representationalists take a much more radical approach, arguing that (i) not all locutionary acts issue statements whose semantic content is given by what they purport to represent, yet (ii) they may still be linguistically meaningful (and so *have* semantic content). Religions provide powerful examples of (i). The logical positivists' critique that religious language is meaningless—rejecting (ii)—rests on an assumption of representationalism (e.g. Ayer 1936; Klemke 1960), and so can be easily avoided by taking an alternative semantic stance. The most influential form of anti-representationalism, dubbed 'interpretationalism' (see Schilbrack 2014), attributes meaningfulness to anything that can be understood by a neutral 'interpreter.'

This move has three important elements. First, semantic content would not be limited to linguistic usage that is purely descriptive or truth-evaluable. Types of religious language—prayer, exhortation, incantation, metaphor, etc.—can be analyzed as meaningful even if they lack obvious truth-conditions. For interpretationalists, semantic content shifts from what an expression purports to describe to how the interpreter understands what the linguistic performer is doing. For interpretationalists like Davidson (1984), this involves attributing a range of propositional attitudes to the linguistic performer (e.g. beliefs and desires), that are expressible in the interpreter's own scholarly language and that would maximally explain why the former is acting the way they act in that context.

Second, meaningfulness need not be limited to 'language' narrowly understood in terms of familiar patterns of phonemes and morphemes (e.g. identifiable as such things as English, Cantonese, or Sanskrit). Social-scientifically oriented scholars point out that we can understand—even explain—human behavior generally, and so the number and type of meaning-bearers expand: e.g. including ritual, whether accompanied or unaccompanied by words. Under an interpretationalist semantics, ritualistic behavior, at least that which is intentional, is meaningful. Interpretationalists think of language and linguistic activity in very broad terms, not limited to the familiar morphemes and phonemes of discursive language. This provides a significant philosophical foundation for the shift from belief- to practice-centric conceptions of religion (e.g. Vásquez 2011).

Finally, the shift from representational content (of individual syntactic strings of symbols) to interpretation (of contextually placed and spatio-temporally extended behavior) allows for a *holistic* rather than *atomistic* approach to meaning. For interpretationalists like Davidson, linguistic acts, conceived broadly as any instance of intentional behavior, can only be arbitrarily circumscribed: their semantic content is given by a considerable and open-ended range of propositional attitudes attributed by the interpreter to the performer. Such performances always take place in wider contexts, and the more complete the scholar's awareness of the contextual placement of a linguistic act, the fuller will be her grasp of its semantic content. This implies the inseparability of religion from such things as economy, law, media, nature, medicine, politics, science, sports, and tourism, thus justifying the range of entries in the "Environments" section of this volume.

As an approach to studying religion, the basic framework of any semantic theory is the same: empirically grounded knowledge of the medium (either bits of text for formalists and representationalists or bits of behavior—including text—for interpretationalists), coupled with a philosophically informed *theory* of what fixes meaning (internal logical structure for formalists, representation of extra-linguistic reality for representationalists, or maximal rationality of overall behavior for interpretationalists), will yield an understanding of the meaningfulness of religious phenomena.

SEMANTICS IN THE STUDY OF RELIGION\s

Semantics has had a significant impact on at least two areas directly related to the study of religion\s, namely the philosophy of religion and cognitive science. The typical entities (gods, spirits, fairies, etc.) and attributes (transcendence, omniscience, atemporalness, etc.) of religion parallel the unobservable entities (e.g. electrons) and attributes (e.g. gravity) of science, in that they are postulated rather than directly perceived. A 'problem of reference' in the philosophy of science emerges as to what, exactly, terms such as 'electron' or 'gravity' refer to: are they objectively real objects/attributes that fall outside of our direct observational power (as per scientific realism), or only things that we can directly observe, such as trails in cloud chambers or the acceleration of dropped objects (as per scientific instrumentalism)? A similar, though much older, 'problem of reference' emerges in the philosophy of religion, including Aquinas's analogical approach and Maimonides's negative theology, as well as, more recently, Ayer's (1936) denial of meaningfulness, and Alston's (1988) thesis of univocality. Mysticism provides another nice example in that mystical experiences are often said to be purely private and hence literally indescribable (see Katz 1978). Philosophers of religion have asked whether such experiences could then even be genuine, or if so how it could be verified that two mystics undergo the same experience. These theologically-oriented problems within the philosophy of religion re-emerge as methodological problems in the academic study of religion\s: e.g. on what basis can the 'outsider' scholar determine the referents of the language of 'insider' adherents (see the following section)?

The cognitive science (CS) 'revolution' has stormed the humanities and social sciences, with scholars of religion making important contributions (see Geertz, "Cognitive Science," this volume). At its core this approach analyzes religious phenomena in terms of cognitive structures housed in the evolutionarily developed human brain. Emerging from an original partnership between psychology, computer science, and philosophy, CS largely views those structures in representational terms and hence as semantically charged. The biggest philosophical contribution to the partnership has been investigation into how cognitive mental states have semantic content. Proponents of 'embodied,' 'embedded,' and 'distributed' cognition argue instead that it is only bodies embedded in social relations that are capable of cognition (e.g. Jensen 2010). This important development has a semantic foundation: the 'standard' model tends to assume a representationalist semantics in which the semantic contents of cognitive states are fixed only in their relation to the mind-independent objective world, whereas the newer challenging models think of them in more holistic and socially contextual ways. The standard model makes it difficult to see how the cognitive states are to be accessed by social scientists, or how their content may be sensitive to the contingencies of cultural or historical context. The newer models, on the other hand, better harmonize the obvious advances of CS with the more traditional approaches to studying religion (Gardiner/Engler 2015).

Attempts to define 'religion' provide another example of semantics' centrality to the study of religion\s (see Stausberg/Gardiner, "Definition," this volume). Not only do differing conceptions of the nature of definition themselves rest on more basic assumptions about meaning, but some scholars have attempted to explicitly define religion as a certain type of semantic structure, the most influential being that of Clifford Geertz: "*(1) a system of symbols which acts to (2) establish powerful, pervasive, and long-lasting moods and motivations in men by (3) formulating conceptions of a general order of existence and (4) clothing these conceptions with such an aura of factuality that (5) the mood and motivations seem uniquely realistic*" (1973, 90; original emphasis). Notice the emphasis of representationalism in elements (3) through (5), though Geertz does include non-representational factors in element (2) in his definition.

Despite the importance of such issues, semantics is off the radar for most scholars of religion. But there are notable exceptions, scholars fully aware of and explicit about their underlying semantic assumptions: e.g. Lawson/MacCauley (1990) on ritual structures and content along with Stout (1988), Frankenberry (2014), and Davis (2012) on religious practice; Penner (1995) on the role of the 'truth' question for scholars of religion; Proudfoot (1985) on religious experience; Godlove (1989; 2014) on religious concepts; and Schilbrack (2014) and Jensen (2003; 2004; 2014) on the subject matter and methodologies of religious studies in general.

What Issues does Semantics Help Us Address?

More explicit awareness and discussion of semantics in the study of religion\s would move debates on a number of issues to a more fruitful level. For example, if we adopt semantic interpretationalism, then we need not think of religious language as attempting to represent. Rather, on most common accounts, it may be taken principally to prescribe or emote, and as such would not be truth-evaluable. Interpretationalists warn that, once meaning is broken from syntax, we cannot infer that, say, a sentence expressed in declarative grammatical form is necessarily descriptive in its pragmatic force. Even if religious language is declarative in outward form, this tells us very little about what it *means*. In more radical ways, this opens up the range of relationships between the descriptive and the prescriptive, particularly in allowing prescription to be seen not as something 'added' on top of description, but as something that can be quite independent of it. In other words, interpretationalism allows that religious language may be exclusively affective and non-descriptive. For such language, the question of its truth or falsehood need not arise: the 'truth' question of religious language is minimized, if not entirely sidestepped. As a corollary, methodological agnosticism, insofar as this is seen as a bracketing of religious truth claims, is largely unnecessary. Furthermore, on non-representational semantics, reference is a function of meaning, not the other way around; i.e. instead of asking what entity a particular name picks out, interpretationalists ask how or whether a range of sentences using a name have overlapping meanings. What is being talked about, then, is determined by what the talk has in common with other talk—with respect to how they can be understood, not their relationship to what exists. As a result, there is little or no 'problem of religious reference,' or at least the problem of determining what religious language refers to is no more or less difficult than in the case of any other linguistic expression.

To give another example, if meaning depends upon the pragmatic contexts of language use then, as those contexts vary, there is no such thing as 'the' meaning of any religious text, nor does text stand over against ritual as a special site of meaning: rather, meaning reflects context, and intentional actions come to the fore as crucial aspects of those contexts. As a methodological corollary, scholars should take the basic approach whether studying texts or rituals: interpreting them as forms of intentional behavior.

We conclude with three further examples that draw on a specific type of semantic holism, interpretationalism. The holistic perspective on the nature of meaning is dominant among scholars of religion who explicitly discuss semantics (those mentioned at the end of the previous section). Where semantic atomism locates meaning at the level of words, semantic holism locates it in *relations* between parts of language, from an indefinite network of linked units to an entire language. For example, Lévi-Strauss's basic insight—that the meaning of mythical classifications is to be found in binary semantic oppositions—is holistic (see Tremlett, "(Post)structuralism," this volume). Following Saussure's insistence that language works through semantic difference, Lévi-Strauss shifted emphasis from words or motifs on their own—as if meaning were something to be found in these—to relations between concepts. Structuralism has a holistic view of language: "the linguistic system is not a system of separate items between which certain extrinsic relations hold, but a system wherein the elements of the system are themselves constituted by the differences and relationships between them" (Malpas 1992, 59–60).

One implication of this holistic view of meaning is that it undermines prominent *sui generis* views of religion. Religion could be argued (if not necessarily cogently) to be a *sui generis* phenomenon ('of its own unique kind') in several senses. We refer here to the most commonly discussed conception (or bugbear) that religion is characterized by something (often a specific type of experience) that is irreducible to non-religious phenomena. The relevant point here is the implication that the meaning of religion is thus methodologically tied to making sense of this irreducible phenomenon on its own terms, not in the same terms used to make sense of non-religious phenomena: e.g. "the *meaning* of religion . . . is that it is the inevitable, though by definition inadequate, interpersonal statement and institutionalization of a prior feeling or faith" (McCutcheon 1997, 14–15; original emphasis, paraphrasing W. C. Smith). Because the set of relations that constitute meaning depends on the particular context of a given utterance or bit of text, there is no *thing* which can be identified as *the meaning* of any particular portion of language. Judgments regarding meaning are always tentative and open to revision: the interpreter must always concede that there are other, just as well evidenced, ways of understanding a given meaningful expression or act. Many semantic holists take this further by rejecting the possibility of fundamentally different types of meaning or interpretation. Davidson, one of the most influential of holists, famously rejected the idea that there can be such a thing as metaphorical meaning distinct from literal meaning; and the same critique applies to the possibility of some form of distinctly transcendent or symbolic meaning that supposedly emerges from some special relation between religious language and its 'sacred' referents (Davidson 1984; Frankenberry 2002; Penner 2002). In sum, if there is only one type of meaning, then *sui generis* views of religion (in the above sense) are non-starters.

A second implication of a holistic view of meaning is that religious language cannot be sharply distinguished between other types of language, e.g. scientific, moral, aesthetic, or political. The meaning of religious terms and concepts is cashed out in terms of their relation to others, and these others are those that happen to appear along with the religious ones:

> Semantic holism explicates meaning by reference to positions or roles in a vast web of interconnected points whose portions do not admit of discrete dissection. Understanding the claim that Yahweh called to Moses from a burning bush blends items from traditionally different subject matters, e.g., Jewish scriptural tradition, botany, and pyrogenics. The meaning of each those nodes is given by relation to still others, and so on. (Engler/Gardiner 2010, 289)

Whether one accepts semantic holism or not, there is an important general question here that can only be answered by paying attention to semantics: "The question seems to be whether there really is any such specific entity as 'religious language' and/or whether the semantics of religious systems are just 'plain' semantics of an order similar to other specialized terminological systems, those of, say, politics, sports or economics" (Jensen 2004, 220).

A third implication is that there can be no strong insider/outsider problem (Gardiner/Engler 2012). A holistic view of meaning leaves scholars with a weak or relative problem—the methodological challenge of studying groups that have subject matters and vocabularies that are relatively inaccessible to outsiders—but not an absolute one—the claim that religious insiders have unique and monopolistic access to religious knowledge. The latter is associated with *sui generis* views of religion (see earlier discussion). If the meaning of expressions is a function of their relations to the meaning of others (as in semantic holism), then the meaning of insider language is arrived at in part through easier-to-interpret non-religious language, which is shared by outsiders. In other words, because religious language is not some distinct, walled-off sphere of meaning, because it necessarily overlaps into other types of language that are shared by non-insiders, scholars may have to work hard in their attempt to understand insider discourse (a relative challenge), but that is a practical hurdle not an inescapable dead-end (not an absolute barrier to research and interpretation).

CONCLUSION

The study of religion\s has been little informed by semantic approaches. The 'linguistic turn' in early twentieth-century Western philosophy—in both the 'analytic' branch (e.g. Frege, Russell, Wittgenstein, Austin, Carnap, Quine, Davidson, Rorty) and the 'continental' one (e.g. Saussure, Heidegger, Gadamer, Derrida, Ricouer, Foucault, Habermas)—explored how philosophical reflection on meaning constrains approaches to philosophy's traditional concerns, especially epistemology, metaphysics, and ethics. A predominant debate in ethics, for example, concerns whether ethical language points us to objective moral truths or only to expressions of subjective inner sentiments;

when a vegetarian declares "Eating meat is wrong," is she best understood as stating a moral truth (or falsehood) or only expressing, in verbal terms, her love of animals, or something else entirely? A significant debate in the philosophy of science is over what specialized scientific vocabulary actually means: can scientists really refer to unobservable entities, like the Higgs boson, and if not can they really be thought to exist? Do biological species-terms pick out natural kinds, or are they rather to be understood as pragmatically fruitful shorthands for ultimately amorphous groupings? Our very conceptions of ethics and science are tied to our conceptions of what we are doing when we use language ethically and scientifically, and those conceptions are inseparable from an understanding of how those uses might be meaningful. Analogously, the scholar of religion cannot separate a conception of religion from a conception of what adherents are doing when they use religious language (either narrowly as per the formalists/representationalists or broadly as per the interpretationalists). Contrary to Frits Staal's contention that much religious ritual is 'meaningless' (1979), adherents clearly intend their religious language to *mean* something, and the nature of that meaning should guide the scholar's theoretical reflections and methodological practices.

The importance of semantics to the study of religion is manifold. On an object level, approaching religious phenomena as being either analogous to or describable in linguistic terms has proven very fruitful for scholars of religion. This approach has opened up many interdisciplinary doors and methodologies (e.g. linguistics, generative grammars, linguistic anthropology, cognitive science, semiotics, discourse analysis, etc.). Ignoring the semantic side—that linguistic expressions *mean* something—impoverishes the field. At a theoretical level, it is important to understand (i) that there are a range of divergent but philosophically respectable semantic positions, and (ii) that the choices that one makes between them, either implicitly or explicitly, have implications with respect to general theoretical frameworks that should guide one's research. On a meta-theoretical level, the admissibility and plausibility of this-or-that bit of research will stand or fall with the admissibility and plausibility of the semantic assumptions it makes.

While scholars of religion needn't engage in direct philosophical defense or critique of semantic frameworks, they should be aware of at least the main contours of different positions and to acquire a minimal working knowledge of what's happening in the philosophy of language. Every scholar of religion—regardless of their academic home, cultural/historical focus, or theoretical preference—makes semantic assumptions that constrain which ways of thinking are in and which are out of bounds.

Glossary

Atomism/holism a basic divide in semantic theories; atomists hold expressions have their meanings intrinsically, whereas holists hold that those meanings depend on their relations to the meanings of other expressions.

Contextualism/formalism a basic divide in semantic theories; contextualists hold that the meaning of linguistic expressions is largely determined by the pragmatic contexts of its usage, whereas formalists regard them as largely determined by their internal syntactic structure.

Interpretationalism an influential holistic and non-representationalist semantic theory that identifies meaning with the range of propositional attitudes attributable to some subject by a neutral interpreter, in order to maximally explain the subject's overall intentional behavior.

Meaning semantic content, information conveyed (as opposed to personal or subjective importance).

Monism/pluralism a basic divide in the theory of meaning; monists hold that all meaningful expressions are meaningful in virtue of sharing the same underlying property, whereas pluralists hold that there are several and distinct *types* of meaning.

Reference the relation between a name and its bearer (= referent); theories of reference are theories of what fixes that relation, including descriptive theories (reference is fixed by whatever satisfies an implicit description), ostension (reference is fixed by pointing at the referent), and causal theories (in which the referent stands in a direct causal relation to its name, as in a case of baptism).

Representationalism/non-representationalism a basic divide in conceptions of the basic function of language; representationalists regard language inherently as a system of representing or describing non-linguistic 'states-of-affairs,' whereas non-representationalists deny that this is the central or even a significant function of language.

Semantics the study of meaning, in the sense of linguistic content rather than existential significance.

References

Alston, William P. 1988. "Referring to God." *International Journal for Philosophy of Religion* 24(3): 113–128. doi: 10.2307/40024800

Austin, John L. 1962. *How to Do Things with Words*. Oxford: Clarendon Press.

Ayer, A. J. 1936. *Language, Truth and Logic*. London: Victor Gollancz.

Cappelen, Herman and Ernest LePore. 2006. "Shared Content." In *The Oxford Handbook of Philosophy of Language*, edited by Ernest LePore and Barry C. Smith. Oxford: Clarendon Press, 1020–1055.

Davidson, Donald. 1984. *Inquiries into Truth and Interpretation*. Oxford: Clarendon Press.

Davis, G. Scott. 2012. *Believing and Acting: The Pragmatic Turn in Comparative Religion and Ethics*. Oxford: Oxford University Press.

Engler, Steven and Mark Q. Gardiner. 2010. "Ten Implications of Semantic Holism for Theories of Religion." *Method & Theory in the Study of Religion* 22(4): 283–292. doi: 10.1163/157006810X531067

Ezcurdia, Maite and Robert J. Stainton, eds. 2013. *The Semantics–Pragmatics Boundary in Philosophy*. Peterborough, ON: Broadview Press.

Frankenberry, Nancy K. 2002. "Religion as a 'Mobile Army of Metaphors.'" In *Radical Interpretation in Religion*, edited by Nancy K. Frankenberry. Cambridge: Cambridge University Press, 171–187.

Frankenberry, Nancy K. 2014. "The Study of Religion after Davidson and Rorty." *American Journal of Theology & Philosophy* 35(3): 195–210. doi: 10.5406/amerjtheophil.35.3.0195

Gardiner, Mark Q. and Steven Engler. 2012. "Semantic Holism and the Insider–Outsider Problem." *Religious Studies* 48(2): 239–255. doi: 10.1017/S0034412511000205

Gardiner, Mark Q. and Steven Engler. 2015. "The Philosophy and Semantics of the Cognitive Science of Religion." *Journal for the Cognitive Science of Religion* 3(1): 7–35. doi:10.1558/jcsr. v3i1.21033

Geertz, Clifford. 1973. "Religion as a Cultural System." In *The Interpretation of Cultures*. New York: Basic Books, 87–125.

Godlove, Terry F., Jr. 1989. *Religion, Interpretation, and Diversity of Belief: The Framework Model from Kant to Durkheim to Davidson*. Cambridge and New York: Cambridge University Press.

Godlove, Terry F., Jr. 2014. *Kant and the Meaning of Religion: The Critical Philosophy and Modern Religious Thought*. London and New York: I. B. Tauris.

Jensen, Jeppe Sinding. 2003. *The Study of Religion in a New Key: Theoretical and Philosophical Soundings in the Comparative and General Study of Religion*. Aarhus: Aarhus University Press.

Jensen, Jeppe Sinding. 2004. "Meaning and Religion: On Semantics in the Study of Religion." In *New Approaches to the Study of Religion*. Volume 1: *Regional, Critical and Historical Approaches*, edited by Peter Antes, Armin W. Geertz, and Randi R. Warne, 219–252.

Jensen, Jeppe Sinding. 2010. "Doing it the Other Way Round: Religion as a Basic Case of 'Normative Cognition.'" *Method & Theory in the Study of Religion* 22(4): 322–329. doi: 10.1163/157006810X531102.

Jensen, Jeppe Sinding. 2014. *What is Religion?* Durham: Acumen Publishing.

Katz, Steven T. 1978. "Language, Epistemology, and Mysticism." In *Mysticism and Philosophical Analysis*. New York: Oxford University Press, 22–74.

Klemke, E. D. 1960. "Are Religious Statements Meaningful?" *Journal of Religion* 40(1): 27–39.

Lawson, E. Thomas and Robert N. McCauley. 1990. *Rethinking Religion: Connecting Cognition and Culture*. Cambridge and New York: Cambridge University Press.

McCutcheon, Russell T. 1997. *Manufacturing Religion: The Discourse of Sui Generis Religion and the Politics of Nostalgia*. Oxford and New York: Oxford University Press.

Malpas, Jeff E. 1992. *Donald Davidson and the Mirror of Meaning: Holism, Truth, Interpretation*. Cambridge and New York: Cambridge University Press.

Penner, Hans H. 1995. "Why Does Semantics Matter in the Study of Religion?" *Method & Theory in the Study of Religion* 7(3): 221–249.

Penner, Hans H. 2002. "You Don't Read a Myth for Information." In *Radical Interpretation in Religion*, edited by Nancy K. Frankenberry. Cambridge: Cambridge University Press, 153–170.

Proudfoot, Wayne. 1985. *Religious Experience*. Berkeley: University of California Press.

Schilbrack, Kevin. 2014. *Philosophy and the Study of Religions: A Manifesto*. Oxford: Wiley-Blackwell.

Staal, Frits. 1979. "The Meaninglessness of Ritual." *Numen* 26(1): 2–22.

Stout, Jeffrey. 1988. *Ethics after Babel: The Languages of Morals and Their Discontents*. Boston: Beacon Press.

Vásquez, Manuel. 2011. *More Than Belief: A Materialist Theory of Religion*. Oxford: Oxford University Press.

FURTHER READING

Engler/Gardiner 2010 [*A brief overview of ways in which the acceptance of semantic holism would have practical import in the study of religion\s.*]

Ezcurdia/Stainton 2013 [*A collection of influential classic and contemporary essays in philosophical semantics. A valuable collection for those wanting to explore the philosophical terrain first hand.*]

Frankenberry, Nancy K. and Hans H. Penner, eds. 1999. *Language, Truth, and Religious Belief: Studies in Twentieth-Century Theory and Method in Religion.* Atlanta: Scholars Press. [*A collection of classic philosophical and study-of-religion\s texts dealing broadly with semantics. In their framing and contributions, the editors make cases against positivism, functionalism, and relativism.*]

Jensen 2004 [*A rich compact overview of the relevance of 'meaning' and semantic theory for the study of religion\s.*]

CHAPTER 14

··

SEMIOTICS

··

ROBERT A. YELLE

Chapter Summary

···

- The study of religion was influenced most heavily by semiotics during the heyday of structuralism (*c.*1960–1975), and recent decades have seen a shift toward the pragmatic and performative dimensions of discourse.
- Roman Jakobson's analysis of the poetic function of language has been extended to ritual, which in some cases deploys poetry to enhance rhetorical performance.
- Ritualization, as a form of semiosis, involves such factors as the deployment of poetry, reflexivity, and metricalization.
- The ability of the sign to figure something absent intersects with the general problem in religion concerning how (and whether) to represent transcendence.
- The semiotic ideology of modernity reflects an inheritance from Protestant iconoclasm: a bias against metaphysical and poetic language.
- Differences in semiotic ideology were on display in various colonial encounters between Europeans and indigenous peoples.
- Semiotics is shifting attention from universalizing and formalist approaches to a study of cultural and historical differences, including differences in semiotic or linguistic ideologies, meaning the emic theories of language that inform a particular culture.

Structuralism and the Origins of A Semiotics of Religion

···

Semiotics is the study of processes of signification and communication, and encompasses both language and non-linguistic signs. Broader than linguistics, semiotics emerged within the past century or so as a subfield of that parent discipline before developing into a relatively independent approach within the human sciences. There are now semiotic analyses of film, of pictures, of gesture and bodily movement ('kinesiology'), of music, of oral discourse, of literary texts—and also of religion. Much of semiotics remains concerned with the analysis of forms of language, whether written or oral; and a thorough grounding in semiotics requires a study of the linguistic theories that laid the foundations for the study of signs in general.

The application of semiotics within the study of religion has been derived largely from applications in anthropology and literary theory. That said, there is good reason to believe that religion offers a rich field for semiotic analysis. Religious traditions have

- mythological and other narratives;
- canons of scripture and interpretation;
- systems of encryption and decryption;
- examples of multi-sensorial expression in the context of ritual performances, including in the more extreme forms that some have called 'sensory pageantry' (McCauley/Lawson 2002, 7, 114, 123);
- various types of ritual language, from incantations and charms to glossolalia;
- plastic and pictorial images, such as statues, relics, and icons.

Many religious traditions deploy symbols, metaphors, and poetry in measures greater than are commonly found elsewhere. Of course, for a semiotics of religion, as well as for the study of religion in general, the basic question of how to identify any phenomenon as 'religious,' as distinct from the merely non-religious or secular, remains important; but it does not pose an insuperable barrier to analysis. Semiotics does not presume any absolute qualitative difference between religious and other phenomena. It applies perspectives gained from the study of ordinary language, and it seeks to identify structures and processes within the religious domain that are also found elsewhere. This follows not only from the linguistic origins of semiotic analysis, but also from natural constraints on human behavior. Scholars in subfields adjacent to or overlapping with semiotics, such as aesthetics and material religion, have recognized increasingly that human beings are embodied creatures, who must experience and communicate with each other, if at all, through the medium of matter, beginning with bodies. Sound, including language, is a less tangible yet still perceptible medium (see Hackett, "Sound," this volume).

Saussurean Semiology and the Study of Myth

One important branch of contemporary semiotic theory is commonly traced to the Swiss linguist Ferdinand de Saussure (1857–1913), whose posthumously published lecture notes, the *Cours de linguistique générale* (1966), have become essential reading for all further semiotic endeavors. A fundamental axiom of Saussure, anticipated by John Locke, is that signs, including the sounds of the different languages, have only an arbitrary connection with their referents. In the absence of a one-to-one connection between a word, on the one hand, and a concept or thing, on the other, language succeeds in creating an order of signification by representing distinctions in concepts or things through phonic distinctions. Even minimal differences in sound, such as that between the English words 'hero' and 'zero', can signal profound differences in meaning. Rather than a single word in isolation, it is the system or structure of language as a whole that creates meaning.

Saussure predicted the advent of a 'sémiologie' that would encompass very nearly the entire domain of culture, including religious phenomena, in its analysis. The approach he inaugurated has had significant influence on the study of religion, most notably in the heyday of the structuralist movement (roughly, 1960–1975). Claude Lévi-Strauss's (1908–2009) four-volume study of Native American mythologies (1964–1971) may be regarded as the high point of the application of a rigorous structuralist methodology to culture. The possibilities and limitations of such a semiotics were thereby clearly established. Insofar as Lévi-Strauss aimed to reveal a universal underlying structure in myth, that moreover was shared with other genres and with language in general, his approach proved less able to account for historical and cultural differences. The thrust of Lévi-Strauss's analyses was to show that myths and related types of narrative constitute forms of rhetoric that respond to the ever present gap between nature and culture. Myths attempt to negotiate psychological conflicts that arise from a subliminal awareness of the arbitrariness of cultural institutions, or from the conflict between these institutions and individual impulse.

Following Lévi-Strauss, scholars of religion applied similar techniques to the analysis of the Bible (e.g. Mary Douglas 1966 and Edmund Leach 1969), ancient Hindu mythology (Wendy Doniger 1973), and other traditions. Such analyses continued with, for example, Seth Kunin's (1995) structuralist approach to the stories of the Hebrew Bible, or even Carlo Ginzburg's (1991, 227–240, 267–279) update of Lévi-Strauss's analysis of the Oedipus myth.

Reacting against the arid intellectualism of structuralism, later scholars, often called poststructuralists, emphasized the flexibility (rather than psychological or cultural determinacy) of signification, and its embeddedness in networks that reflect social relations and strategic interests (see Tremlett, "(Post)structuralism," this volume). Despite the continuity of rigorous semiotic analysis in some disciplines, such as linguistic anthropology, the turn away from formalism has exerted a decisive influence in religious studies.

Peircean Semiotic and the Shift to Pragmatics

Another important source for modern semiotics was the American philosopher Charles Sanders Peirce (1839–1914), whose 'semeiotic' was part of a broader project to replace traditional metaphysics with pragmatism or, as Peirce later called his approach, 'pragmaticism.' Peirce's focus on how signs work, both in allowing probabilistic knowledge and effective communication, attempted to go beyond a narrow focus, in the disciplines of logic and epistemology, on the truth-value of utterances. In terms of his contributions to semiotics, Peirce is perhaps best known for his tripartite division of signs into icons, indexes, and symbols: roughly, signs based on resemblance, physical or causal connection, and convention, respectively. (Peirce's system has many more categories and subcategories of sign types; see Parmentier 1994, 3–22.)

Peirce has exerted a tremendous influence on semiotics. His influence has been less visible in the study of religion, with some notable exceptions, including the work of semiotic anthropologists such as Richard Parmentier (1994) and Michael Silverstein (1998).

Meanwhile, paralleling Peirce in some respects, the English philosopher J. L. Austin (1911–1960), in his famous lectures on *How to Do Things with Words* (1975), attempted to describe pragmatic effects of language not accounted for in standard logic. Certain words—called variously 'illocutionary' (as opposed to merely declarative) statements or 'performative utterances' (or, in John Searle's later formulation, 'speech acts'), bring about a state of affairs, rather than merely describing said state. Words may thus become forms of action. An example used by Austin is the statement "I do" uttered in the course of a marriage ceremony.

Austin's ideas were adapted by some scholars of religion, such as Wade Wheelock (1989), who applied it to Indian mantras, and Stanley Tambiah, especially in his article "A Performative Approach to Ritual" (1985). Rather than dismissing the formal features of magical language and related types of effective ritual as meaningless, Tambiah argued, we should regard them as powerful modes of cultural performance. He explicitly invoked Peirce and Austin in advocating this shift of approach (see Michaels/Sax, "Performance," this volume).

Recall that Peirce recognized a special role for signs based on resemblance ('icons') or co-occurrence ('indexes'). Both Tambiah (1985, 35) and Thomas Sebeok (1976, 31–32, 76–77, 131–132) cited Peirce in noting that magical operations often construct sign-relations based on either resemblance, contiguity, or both. For example, using yellow objects to cure jaundice is a common form of what James G. Frazer called 'sympathetic magic,' which can be found in ancient Vedic texts as well as more recent European folk magic (Yelle 2013a, 27). The voodoo doll both resembles (= icon) and, often, is physically connected to (= index) the intended victim, by incorporating part of his or her body or possessions. Frazer argued that magic consists of mistaking such ideal associations for a real, causal connection. As Mary Douglas pointed out (1966, 23), this is not however a simple mistake—not a mere lapse of judgment on the part of so-called primitives—but rather demonstrates the power of signification.

Within contemporary biblical studies, Bernard Jackson (2000) has made noteworthy attempts to apply a pragmatic approach to the analysis of the Hebrew Bible, although he cites the structuralist Algirdas Julien Greimas (1917–1992) rather than Peirce as a primary inspiration.

One can argue that, with such approaches, semiotics has returned to, and begun to map, part of the terrain that was occupied previously by the discipline of classical rhetoric. Semiotics is as much the study of culturally effective illusions as the key to a universal science of communication. Or perhaps it must be both at the same time.

Jakobson's Poetics and the Analysis of Ritual Language

The Russian linguist Roman Jakobson (1896–1982) played a key role in disseminating knowledge of structuralist ideas and techniques of analysis as his career moved from Moscow, to Prague, to France, then finally to the United States. Jakobson (1960) focused particularly on the 'poetic function' of language, which he identified as distributed far beyond the confines of poetry itself. The poetic function is characterized by the repetition of similar sounds (which Jakobson called 'metaphors'; cf. Peircean 'icons') in a sequence of language, and is exemplified by such common phenomena as parallelism, or the restatement of the same basic idea, often in only slightly different terms. Jakobson was interested also in the phenomenon of sound symbolism, such as onomatopoeia and other apparent cases of iconicity in language, which appear to violate the principle of the arbitrary nature of the sign.

Jakobson argued that one purpose of such poetic devices was to highlight the communicative event, by bringing attention to language: the "set toward the message as such" (1960, 356). This coincides with the emphasis of later scholars, such as Catherine Bell (1997, 81), on ritual as an event of 'ritualization,' which operates by establishing a distinction from ordinary discourse or behavior. Jakobson's poetics has obvious application to religious language, which often augments the poetic function, especially in repetitive chants. Parallelism as well has been noted as an important feature of some religious uses of language; already in the eighteenth century, Robert Lowth (1787) pointed to this feature in the Psalms of the Hebrew Bible.

In the later, American, phase of his career, Jakobson combined structuralism with an emphasis on the role of 'deictics,' or pointing words such as 'this' and 'that,' as well as other types of linguistic indexicals. Indexicals are, as mentioned previously, important in Peirce's classification of signs. They signal, among other things, co-occurrence or causation. Jakobson's student, Michael Silverstein (2004, 626–627), has developed an account of how the proliferation of icons in a sequence of discourse—a phenomenon he refers to as 'metricalization,' in a clear nod to the poetic function—reinforces the indexical function of this discourse. This helps to explain why so many effective rituals, particularly magical utterances, deploy various types of poetry, as well as numerous direct indexes including imperative verbs and deictics such as 'now!' and 'immediately!'

Building from Silverstein's general linguistic theory, I have developed an account of the role played by such 'indexical icons' across a range of ritual languages (Yelle 2003; 2013a, 23–60). Hindu mantras, for example, often contain quasi-palindromic patterns consisting of apparently nonsensical vocables. Similar patterns had been noted previously, for example by Frits Staal, who declared them meaningless (1996, 253–293), and by Agehananda Bharati (1993, 128–131). As I showed, the structure of such utterances diagrams multiple forms of creation, such as the in-and-out cycle of the cosmogony, of life-and-death (or emerging from and returning to the womb), of breath, and even of speech itself, as it exits the mouth (Yelle 2003, 23–48). By diagramming events of physical creation, these mantras represent the virtual 'causation' of such events by speech.

Such cases illustrate how rituals may augment the poetic function to a degree that marks such events as something special, indeed as 'rituals.' Beyond merely announcing an event of ritualization, however, these uses of the poetic function also motivate or strengthen the ritual as a sign of its goal, reinforcing rhetorically a belief in the causal efficacy of this sign. Although signs are arbitrary, as Saussure argued, this belief is not shared by all traditions, which may use poetic devices to lend the appearance of naturalness or verisimilitude to ritual signs (Yelle 2013a, 32–34, 61–68).

Reflexivity and the Figuration of Transcendence

As highlighted already in Jakobson's definition of the poetic function as the "set toward the message as such," semiotics is concerned ineluctably with reflexivity. The manner in which certain ritual discourses—such as Hindu Tantric mantras—diagram the process of coming-into-being of what lies beyond discourse—i.e. in the domain of reality—marks such rituals as a form of virtuality (see Kapferer 2006). Such cases offer one illustration of a more general semiotic phenomenon called 'recursion.' Another example of this phenomenon is *mise-en-abyme*, in which the whole is contained within a part: for example, there is a play within the play (e.g. *Hamlet*), or a portrait contains a smaller image of itself, and so on, potentially *ad inifinitum*. Recursiveness of structures is prominent in Vedic ritual, for example, in the sense of repeated patterns of embedding that facilitate the indefinite extension of a ritual sequence. (Recursion involves reflexivity, not simply mindless repetition as Staal 1996 would have it.) The use of back-and-forth or chiastic patterns to diagram events of dialogical communication—mirroring the function of language in its very form—represents another example (Yelle 2013a, 46–50). As Peirce diagnosed, semiosis is unavoidably reflexive, given that it requires, in addition to a sign and referent, an 'interpretant': roughly, someone for whom the sign-relation presents itself.

From Peirce and Saussure onward, semiosis has been recognized as a relational phenomenon, a property of structures and systems rather than of nature itself (see Tremlett's discussion of systems theory in the chapter "(Post)structuralism," this volume). Within the domain of religion, semiotic figuration can be observed notably when it comes to that which cannot be observed or characterized directly: namely, the transcendent. In the two mystical paths, cataphatic and apophatic, described by Pseudo-Dionysius (c.500 CE), an approach to the representation of the divinity was made alternatively either by the use of epithets emphasizing the magnitude of God's goodness or power, or by the denial of the representative power of all descriptive terms to capture the deity's nature. Whereas many texts and traditions (e.g. the Hindu *Upanisads*, the fourteenth-century English *Cloud of Unknowing*, and various strands of iconoclasm within Jewish, Christian, and Islamic traditions) have emphasized the impossibility of figuring transcendence, what remains noteworthy is the apparent impulse to find some image that may serve to represent the divine. As Webb Keane describes this problem:

> For all its specificity, the Christian doctrine of incarnation bears on a general problem faced by those who want to deal with a spirit world … in just what way can any being that transcends the material world actually be available to perception? The idea of *Logos* is a highly abstract answer to this question. (2013, 6; see Volli 2014, S24; for Müller's similar view see Yelle 2013b, 67)

This is only one demonstration of Massimo Leone's claim that "there is no representation of transcendence without semiosis" (2014, S49). Semiotics, reconceived as a rhetoric of cultures rather than a prescriptive science of communication, must concern itself with the virtual rather than, or in addition to, the actual. There is no question here of reigniting a fruitless debate over the existence of the deity or of the soul. Yet what may be given only a virtual existence through the medium of representation, or the indirection of the sign, is then amenable to study by the semiotician.

An illustration is afforded by Leone's (2013) tracing of the symbolization of the self or soul in classical pagan and succeeding Christian traditions. He shows how something as subtle as the vital breath came early on to be identified with an interior spirit, one that leaves the body at death and was often symbolized in earlier times by a small bird. It may be just a coincidence that such images connected the soul with the mouth as the organ of speech. However, in Hindu Tantric traditions also, the breath, and the speech that it carried, were viewed as the bearers of the vital spirit, so that mantras that symbolically represented these forces were deployed in order to invest life into plastic images of the gods, in a ritual called "establishing the vital breath" (*prāṇapratiṣṭhā*) (Yelle 2003, 52–53). Does this signal an awareness of the power of speech and its role in the constitution of a stable image of the self (see Carr 2013)?

Iconoclasm and the Triumph of the Literal

Within the Baconian tradition, the power of such verbal images to call into life, as it were, specters, ghosts, and chimeras—what Bacon called the "idols of the marketplace"—was both recognized and attacked (Yelle 2013b, 33–70). Thomas Hobbes rejected, on linguistic grounds, the inference from the Bible that supernatural beings exist. The literal meaning of the Latin *spiritus* (or the Hebrew *ruach*) is "breath," while that of the Greek *angelos* is "messenger." Yet people have reasoned falsely from such words and asserted the existence of 'incorporeal beings,' which Hobbes regarded as an oxymoron. Even God, he reasoned, must be corporeal. Hobbes's attack on such metaphysical language borrowed not only from Francis Bacon, but also from a tradition of literal interpretation of the Bible within English Protestantism (Yelle 2013b, 33–50). Both traditions influenced the linguistic iconoclasm of thinkers as diverse as Jeremy Bentham and Friedrich Max Müller, one of the founders of the comparative study of religion. Indeed, it is arbitrary to separate Reformation from Enlightenment in this regard. Both colluded in producing a certain regimentation of language that paralleled the regimentation of knowledge and society.

Leone argues that the delicate balance by which a sign, such as a relic, presents itself effectively as a mediator of transcendence depends on an erotics of distanciation: the image must be capable of both holding out the promise of direct contact with the sacred, and of deferring such contact. The sign must represent simultaneously 'presence' and 'absence.' To overemphasize one or the other would mean, on the one hand, to convert the sign into a fetish—by asserting complete presence, or collapsing the sign into its referent—and, on the other, to deny any possibility of mediation—by asserting complete absence, or severing any connection between sign and referent. (Keane [2013] describes a related phenomenon of 'transduction,' meaning the power generated by the shift from one semiotic modality to another, especially through the de- or rematerializing of religious language.) Leone formulates this in the following terms: "there is no revealing without re-veiling, and no re-veiling without revelation" (2014, S52).

> A paradoxical consequence of transcendence being evoked as shadow, as the hidden face of the moon, is that no representation of transcendence is possible without materiality, that is, without an immanent counterpart. . . . Transcendence can, therefore, be intuited, or perhaps only emotionally experienced, as the light that is promised beyond the screen of a material, immanent, actual sign. The paradox is that nothing promises this light to us if not the sign itself. (Leone 2014, S50)

Leone's formulation echoes traditional Christian theology, specifically St. Paul's argument that the 'veil' of the Mosaic law (referring both to the veil worn by Moses when descending Sinai, and also perhaps to the veil of the Temple that was supposedly rent upon Christ's death) was merely a shadow that obscured the full light of the Gospel (Yelle 2013b, 23–24). Such ideas were eventually elaborated into a system of typological interpretation of Scripture, which read in the Old Testament precisely the 'veiled revelation' that foreshadowed the New Testament. The traditional Christian interpretation of the Bible recognized multiple layers of signification in the Bible beyond the literal sense, and gave certain events or images, particularly in the Hebrew Bible, a symbolic interpretation, as 'types' that pointed to and predicted other events—'antitypes'—occurring in the New Testament, as for example the near-sacrifice of Isaac foreshadowed the accomplished sacrifice of Jesus on the Cross. Although these ideas belonged to supersessionism, and indeed to messianism, they were nonetheless semiotic.

From this perspective, a disruption of the traditional dialectic occurred when certain movements within the Protestant tradition—in the name of securing the immediacy, transparency, and referential power of (sacred) discourse—denied revelation altogether. The deist John Toland, partly following John Locke's linguistics, utterly rejected the whole system of typological interpretation since, with the Crucifixion, all such 'mysteries' had already been removed, together with the Mosaic law that veiled them, upon the promulgation of the Gospel (1696, 115).

SEMIOTIC IDEOLOGIES, CULTURAL SEMIOTICS, AND THE COMPARATIVE STUDY OF RELIGION

As such historical examples illustrate, a semiotics of religion must be sensitive not only to those apparently general principles of communication that are deployed across cultural traditions, but also to the differences among cultures that shape and influence ideas and practices of language (see Rambelli 2013 for an exemplary study). In recent decades, the term 'semiotic ideology' (or 'linguistic ideology') has come into use to describe this dimension of cultural systems (for a recent account, see Lambek 2013). The anthropologist Webb Keane (2007) has traced the difference in semiotic ideologies between Dutch Calvinists and indigenous inhabitants of Sumba in the Indonesian archipelago. The Dutch attacked the formulaic or stereotyped practices of the Sumbans as 'fetishes,' in a manner resembling Hobbes et al.'s attack on linguistic 'idols.' Keane shows how the attack on such forms of speech coordinated with an emphasis on sincerity and spontaneity as the hallmarks of a modern, Protestant self.

I have traced a similar phenomenon in colonial India, where many British administrators, scholars, and missionaries expressed a linguistic ideology inherited from both Baconianism and Protestant literalism in agitating against indigenous Hindu ideas and practices (Yelle 2013b). For example, the Calvinist critique of 'vain repetitions' in prayer (based on Matthew 6:7) that had originally been deployed against Roman Catholic chants such as the Hail Mary, was directed against various types of Hindu mantras. The theological root of this complaint was a Protestant view that such forms of poetic ritual were illicit rhetoric, magic, and idolatry.

In the colonial context, such complaints against poetic chants were associated with the widespread introduction of printed texts as well as with efforts to impose either the English language or at least Romanized transliteration. In this connection, it is interesting to note that the disappearance of more poetic forms of the marriage oath, such as "for fairer for fouler" (replaced by "for better or for worse"), coincided in England with the introduction of the Book of Common Prayer (1549), a uniform printed liturgy that replaced older, Catholic versions of the liturgy in manuscripts (Yelle 2013a, 127–132). A study of these developments must therefore attend to the role played by transformations in the media of communications themselves. Austin's failure to account for such historical transformations in the context of his analysis of the marriage oath, and of illocutionary utterances in general, underscores the need for a cultural semiotics. It is clear that what is allowed to stand as both performative and legitimate speech has not remained constant.

CONCLUSION

The semiotics of religion has come very far from the days of formalism and the structuralist analysis of myth. With the concept of 'semiotic ideologies,' and the greater awareness of cultural and historical variations implied by that concept, semiotics has the potential to serve as a useful rubric for describing the differences (as well as similarities) between cultures, and to contribute to our understanding of the historical transformations grouped together under the label of 'secularization.' It remains to be seen whether more scholars of religion will choose to make use of these tools, apart from the very vibrant field of linguistic anthropology (e.g. Kreinath 2006 and the work of the Anthropology of Christianity collective), and a few intrepid scholars working under the rubrics of either cultural or cognitive semiotics (e.g. Sørensen 2006). A general bias against comparison has combined with a specific allergy to formalism to inure many scholars of religion to the attractions and possibilities of a semiotic approach. Given recent theoretical advances and the semiotic richness of much of the data of the study of religion, however, the prospects for a semiotics of religion appear brighter now than they have for quite some time.

GLOSSARY

Arbitrariness the fundamentally arbitrary nature of linguistic and other human signs, as recognized by both Saussurean structuralism and the Peircean concept of the symbol.

Icon the name in Peircean semiotics for a type of sign relation based on resemblance.

Index the name in Peircean semiotics for a type of sign relation based on co-occurrence or physical connection.

Indexical icon a concept developed in Peircean semiotic analysis to describe a type of sign, the indexicality of which is reinforced by iconism, particularly by diagrams or metricalization (see Silverstein 2004: 626–627).

Performance the pragmatic dimension of verbal and ritual expression, including both the orchestration of the expression itself and its range of effects such as intersubjective communication, cultural transmission, social influence, and rhetorical persuasion.

Poetic function the deployment of metricalization, repetition, or metaphor in the syntactic sequence of language and other behaviors, with attendant semantic and pragmatic effects.

Pragmatics the branch of linguistics and semiotics that focuses on the interaction between discourse and context; as contrasted with semantics and syntactics.

Recursion the use of self-referential devices, such as *mise-en-abyme* or the embedding of patterns within patterns, which demonstrates reflexivity as a general property of semiotic systems.

Semiosis the process of signification.

Semiotic (or linguistic) ideology the more or less articulated theories of signification in a culture that affect the semiotic forms produced and their interaction with other domains of culture.

References

Austin, John Langshaw. 1975. *How to Do Things with Words*. Cambridge, MA: Harvard University Press.

Bell, Catherine. 1997. *Ritual: Perspectives and Dimensions*. New York: Oxford University Press.

Bharati, Agehananda. 1993. *Tantric Traditions*, revised edition. Delhi: Hindustan Publishing Corp.

Carr, E. Summerson. 2013. "'Signs of the Times': Confession and the Semiotic Production of Inner Truth." *Journal of the Royal Anthropological Institute* 19(1): 34–51.

Doniger, Wendy. 1973. *Siva: The Erotic Ascetic*. New York: Oxford University Press.

Douglas, Mary. 1966. *Purity and Danger: An Analysis of Concepts of Pollution and Taboo*. London: Routledge & Kegan Paul.

Ginzburg, Carlo. 1991. *Ecstasies: Deciphering the Witches' Sabbath*. Chicago, IL: University of Chicago Press.

Jackson, Bernard. 2000. *Studies in the Semiotics of Biblical Law*. Sheffield: Sheffield Academic Press.

Jakobson, Roman. 1960. "Closing Statement: Linguistics and Poetics." In *Style in Language*, edited by Thomas Sebeok. Cambridge, MA: MIT Press, 350–377.

Kapferer, Bruce. 2006. "Virtuality." In *Theorizing Rituals: Issues, Topics, Approaches, Concepts*, edited by Jens Kreinath, Jan Snoek, and Michael Stausberg. Leiden: Brill, 681–684.

Keane, Webb. 2007. *Christian Moderns: Freedom and Fetish in the Mission Encounter*. Berkeley: University of California Press.

Keane, Webb. 2013. "On Spirit Writing: Materialities of Language and the Religious Work of Transduction." *Journal of the Royal Anthropological Institute* 19(1): 1–17.

Kreinath, Jens. 2006. "Semiotics." In *Theorizing Rituals: Issues, Topics, Approaches, Concepts*, edited by Jens Kreinath, Jan Snoek, and Michael Stausberg. Leiden: Brill, 429–470.

Kunin, Seth D. 1995. *The Logic of Incest: A Structuralist Analysis of Hebrew Mythology*. Sheffield: Sheffield Academic Press.

Lambek, Michael. 2013. "Varieties of Semiotic Ideology in the Interpretation of Religion." In *A Companion to the Anthropology of Religion*, edited by Janice Boddy and Michael Lambek, 2nd edition. London: Wiley-Blackwell, 137–153.

Leach, Edmund. 1969. *Genesis as Myth and Other Essays*. London: Jonathan Cape.

Leone, Massimo. 2013. "Signs of the Soul: Toward a Semiotics of Religious Subjectivity." *Signs and Society* 1(1): 115–159. doi: 10.1086/670169

Leone, Massimo. 2014. "Wrapping Transcendence." *Signs and Society* 2(S1): S49–S83. doi: 10.1086/674314

Lévi-Strauss, Claude. 1964–71. *Mythologiques*. 4 vols. Paris: Plon.

Lowth, Robert. 1787. *On the Sacred Poetry of the Hebrews*. London: J. Johnson.

McCauley, Robert N. and E. Thomas Lawson. 2002. *Bringing Ritual to Mind: Psychological Foundations of Cultural Forms*. Cambridge: Cambridge University Press.

Parmentier, Richard. 1994. *Signs in Society: Studies in Semiotic Anthropology*. Bloomington: Indiana University Press.

Rambelli, Fabio. 2013. *A Buddhist Theory of Semiotics: Signs, Ontology, and Salvation in Japanese Esoteric Buddhism*. London: Bloomsbury.

Saussure, Ferdinand de. 1966. *Course in General Linguistics*, translated by Wade Baskin. New York: McGraw-Hill.

Sebeok, Thomas. 1976. *Contributions to the Doctrine of Signs*. Bloomington: Indiana University Press.

Silverstein, Michael. 1998. "The Improvisational Performance of Culture in Realtime Discursive Practice." In *Creativity in Performance*, edited by R. Keith Sawyer. Greenwich, CT: Ablex Publishing Corp., 265–311.

Silverstein, Michael. 2004. "'Cultural' Concepts and the Language–Culture Nexus." *Current Anthropology* 45(5): 621–652.

Sørensen, Jesper. 2006. *A Cognitive Theory of Magic*. Lanham, MD: Rowman & Littlefield.

Staal, Frits. 1996. *Ritual and Mantras: Rules without Meaning*. Delhi: Motilal Banarsidass.

Tambiah, Stanley. 1985. *Culture, Thought, and Social Action*. Cambridge, MA: Harvard University Press.

Toland, John. 1696. *Christianity Not Mysterious*. London: Samuel Buckley.

Volli, Ugo. 2014. "Cherubim: (Re)presenting Transcendence." *Signs and Society* 2(S1): S23–S48.

Wheelock, Wade. 1989. "The Mantra in Vedic and Tantric Ritual." In *Understanding Mantras*, edited by Harvey Alper. Albany, NY: SUNY Press, 96–122.

Yelle, Robert. 2003. *Explaining Mantras: Ritual, Rhetoric and the Dream of a Natural Language in Hindu Tantra*. London: Routledge.

Yelle, Robert. 2013a. *Semiotics of Religion: Signs of the Sacred in History*. London: Bloomsbury.

Yelle, Robert. 2013b. *The Language of Disenchantment*. New York: Oxford University Press.

FURTHER READING

Eco, Umberto. 1995. *The Search for the Perfect Language*, translated by James Fentress. Oxford: Blackwell. [*Examines European varieties of the quest for a universal medium of communication, a quest that historically has intersected with Christian soteriology.*]

Keane, Webb. 2002. "Sincerity, Modernity, and the Protestants." *Cultural Anthropology* 17(1): 65–92. [*A succinct statement of the influence of Protestantism on the semiotic ideology of modernity and the constitution of modern subjectivity and agency.*]

Leach, Edmund. 1976. *Culture and Communication: The Logic by which Symbols are Connected*. Cambridge: Cambridge University Press. [*Still one of the best introductions to semiotic anthropology in the structuralist tradition; engages with a range of religious phenomena.*]

Lévi-Strauss, Claude. 1967. "The Structural Study of Myth." In *Structural Anthropology*, vol. 2, translated by Claire Jacobson and Brooke Grundfest Schoepf. New York: Doubleday, 206–231. [*One of the most accessible accounts of the master's structuralist analysis of mythology, and of the theory underlying that analysis.*]

Parmentier, Richard. 1997. "The Pragmatic Semiotics of Cultures." *Semiotica* 116(1): 1–114. [*A cogent argument for the application of semiotics as a general methodology for studying culture, including religion.*]

Sebeok, Thomas. 1964. 'The Structure and Content of Cheremis Charms.' In *Language in Culture and Society*, edited by Dell Hymes. New York: Harper & Row, 356–371. [*Key techniques in the poetic study of ritual.*]

Yelle, Robert. 2011. "Semiotics." In *Handbook of Research Methods in Religious Studies*, edited by Michael Stausberg and Steven Engler. London and New York: Routledge, 355–365. [*An overview of contemporary methodologies in the semiotic study of religion from a Peircean/Jakobsonian perspective.*]

CHAPTER 15

(POST)STRUCTURALISM

PAUL-FRANÇOIS TREMLETT

CHAPTER SUMMARY

- Structuralism and poststructuralism should be understood as part of a 'turn' in social theory and philosophy to 'systems.'
- Lévi-Strauss's approach to myth entwines linguistics and dynamic systems theory, pointing 'back' to formalism and 'forward' to poststructuralism.
- Lévi-Strauss's critique of evolutionist and functionalist accounts of 'primitive' religion undermine notions of progress and accounts of the regulatory role of religion in the closed social system described by functionalism.
- Derrida's account of language and deconstruction privileges the idea of the open system and has significant implications for textual, historical, and sociological studies of religion.

INTRODUCTION

Distributed at the intersections of sociology, philosophy, anthropology, psychoanalysis, linguistics, folklore, history, and political science (but also and probably more importantly cybernetics, mathematics, biology, art, and music), structuralism and poststructuralism have conventionally been associated with a turn to language in social theory (Callinicos 1999, 266) and with a rejection of humanism including the death of the author (Barthes 1977, 148) and the erasure of 'Man' (Lévi-Strauss 1966, 247; Foucault 1970, 387). Indeed, structuralism and poststructuralism were distilled, according to skeptical Anglo-Saxon commentators, in a Parisian laboratory somewhere on the Left Bank from the work of a Swiss linguist whose key book seemed to suggest that the meaningfulness of words resided in language rather than the intentions of any putative speaker (which was ironic given that it was composed, after his death, from the notes taken by his students during his lectures), and a Viennese doctor who was convinced that the dreams and verbal slips of his bourgeois patients did not mean what they appeared to mean on the surface. There was also the work of the German philologist— work which was comprehensively ignored until long after his death in the madhouse. That structuralism and poststructuralism are purported to have exposed the illusion of meaning's guarantee under the fiduciary signs of the author, Man, and God bears all the hallmarks of that German's furious tirade against metaphysics.

Yet, structuralism and poststructuralism are more than exquisite deliberations on language. Beyond the writings of Ferdinand de Saussure, Sigmund Freud, and Friedrich Nietzsche, the structuralist approach which convulsed anthropology and the study of religion in the 1960s and 1970s was very much an intervention in debates initiated by evolutionist thinkers such as James G. Frazer on totemism (1910) and functionalist thinkers such as Bronislaw Malinowski on myth (1984). Within Frazer's evolutionist framework, totemism evolved into religion and religion into science. Societies were ordained to progress—implicitly either under Western tutelage (colonialism) or within parameters established according to the Western experience of modernity—stage by stage, away from religion and towards science, industry, and democracy in a journey towards 'civilization.' This linear theory of historical transformation was challenged by structuralism and later poststructuralism, which posed a series of non-linear models whereby change occurred not as the result of any theory of progress but according to contingent and complex interactions of elements. According to Malinowski's functionalist framework, myths functioned homeostatically to sustain social order in 'primitive' societies. However, reframed according to structuralist and poststructuralist logics, myths and societies were transformed into complex forms subject not to functionalist laws of closed-system equilibrium but to open-system dynamics and non-linear processes of transformation. In this chapter I will focus predominantly on the writings of the French anthropologist Claude Lévi-Strauss (1908–2009) and the French philosopher Jacques Derrida (1930–2004). I will argue that structuralism and poststructuralism form part of a decisive and interdisciplinary 'turn' in social theory and philosophy towards 'systems' conceived as open and unstable. The consequences of this 'turn' for the study of religion remain undecided.

THE STRUCTURALIST APPROACH TO MYTH

Structuralism has been characterized as a mode of analysis that privileges invariant structures (or structuring structures) said to function like grammar in language—that is, like an unconscious set of rules that determines sequences of words although these rules remain largely hidden to ordinary language speakers. This opposition of grammar (*langue*) to speech (*parole*) and of a hidden depth to a visible surface is a key feature of Saussure's linguistics. Saussure developed a series of oppositions—diachronic to synchronic, signifier to signified, and syntagmatic to paradigmatic—to capture the sense of language as a system of (ordinarily hidden) rules and relationships for which the focus of analysis was not individual words as carriers of meaning but the structuring relations between words. Fredric Jameson has described this as a "movement from a substantive way of thinking to a relational one" (1972, 13).

For Saussure then, the structural study of language concentrated not on speech as it unfolded in time (diachronically) but on grammar as a closed system that might be caught in an analytical 'snapshot' (synchronically). According to Saussure, language was a system of differences—acoustic differences of sound and ideational differences of meaning (for an overview see Sturrock 1993). Words (signs) signify or point, but meaning resides not in signs/words as containers of meaning—there is no essential tie between signs and that to which they point—but is generated according to horizontal, syntagmatic relations of combination (e.g. the positioning of personal pronouns in relation to verbs in a sentence) and vertical, paradigmatic relations of substitution (e.g. the use of a word in a sentence always implies the potential use of other words that are related either semantically or phonetically).

Claude Lévi-Strauss's work has been summarized very much in these terms: that is, as a search for unconscious and therefore hidden structuring structures that are analytically comparable to a grammar in that they generate variable (religious and cultural) forms that are in turn analytically comparable to speech. For Lévi-Strauss the structures in question are cognitive. That is, they are the species-specific, cognitive structuring structures—the mental architectures that every single member of *Homo sapiens* is born with—that lie behind all the varied products of human culture and religion (to study culture and religion is therefore to study the mind at work).

In Lévi-Strauss's work on myth (1993a) the influence of Saussure is immediately apparent: the myth is not to be read simply as a narrative that unfolds diachronically. Instead, the narrative is suspended and key events ('bundles of events' or, elsewhere, 'mythemes') are extracted as the proper subject matter of the analysis:

> It is impossible to understand a myth as a continuous sequence. This is why we should be aware that if we try to read a myth as we read a novel or a newspaper article, that is line after line, reading from left to right, we don't understand the myth, because we have to apprehend it as a totality and discover that the basic meaning of the myth is not conveyed by the sequence of events but—if I may say so—by bundles of events although these events appear at different moments in the story. Therefore, we have to read the myth more or less as we would read an orchestral score, not stave after stave, but understanding that we should apprehend the whole page and understand that something which was written on the first stave at the top of the page acquires meaning only if one considers that it is part and parcel of what is written below on the second stave, the third stave, and so on. That is, we have to read not only from left to right, but at the same time vertically, from top to bottom. We have to understand that each page is a totality. And it is only by treating the myth as if it were an orchestral score, written stave after stave, that we can understand it as a totality, that we can extract the meaning out of the myth. (Lévi-Strauss 2001, 40)

Lévi-Strauss's method of 'reading' horizontally and vertically draws upon Saussure's model of language with its syntagmatic and paradigmatic dimensions, but also Vladimir I. Propp's formalism and his earlier work on fairy tales (see Hawkes 1983, 67). It also points to Lévi-Strauss's fascination with music (Tremlett 2008a, 58–61) and a more general but important eclecticism: structuralism, as will be seen momentarily, cannot be reduced to its linguistic inheritances. Once extracted, the 'bundles of events' or 'mythemes' are re-composed into binary oppositions that are then compared to other versions of the same myth or other myths from the same cultural area: "to study a myth is to study the relationships of 'transformation' ... between the different versions of the myth and between the myth and other myths. With this approach, neither a single version nor a synthesis of several versions is an appropriate object of study. A myth should be considered, rather, as the set of all its versions" (Sperber 1996, 27).

In the study of myth advocated by Lévi-Strauss, it is the shifts in pattern of the key 'bundles of events' across differing versions of the myth that are significant. For example, in *The Raw and the Cooked* (1992 [1970]) Lévi-Strauss demonstrates that a number of apparently distinct myths collected from different South American cultures are structurally interrelated: myths about the origins of fire, the origins of wild pigs, and the origins of tobacco turn out to be variations or transformations of one another (Lévi-Strauss 1992, 107). But, once we have our "permutation group" (Lévi-Strauss 1993a, 223), what then? And what of meaning?

Myth and Meaning

Structuralism challenges traditional theories of meaning. For example Carl Jung and Joseph Campbell assumed, like Lévi-Strauss, that to study myth was to study the mind (Capps 1995, 236). However, whereas for Jung and Campbell the study of myth revealed universal, psychological archetypes pointing to deep and profound meanings about human existence and possibilities for well-being, Lévi-Strauss's structuralist analysis transformed myth into a mathematical formula (see Lévi-Strauss 1993a, 228). But, Lévi-Strauss never claimed that myths were without meaning: at the end of *The Raw and the Cooked* he stated that

> Each matrix of meanings refers to another matrix, each myth to other myths. And if it is now asked to what final meaning these mutually significant meanings are referred—since in the last resort and in their totality they must refer to something—the only reply to emerge from this study is that myths signify the mind that evolves them by making use of the world of which it is itself a part. Thus there is simultaneous production of myths themselves, by the mind that generates them and, by the myths, of an image of the world which is already inherent in the structure of the mind. (Lévi-Strauss 1992, 340–341)

In an interview he went further and said "in everything I have written on mythology I have wanted to show that one never arrives at a final meaning" (Lévi-Strauss and Eribon 1991, 142). As Derrida has pointed out, Lévi-Strauss abandons "all reference to a *centre*, to a *subject*, to a privileged *reference*, to an *origin*, or to an absolute *archia*" (Derrida 2002, 361). Saussure's signs were always routed to a real world through the idea that they signified objects, states, and phenomena. The poststructuralist twist was to claim that signs did not point beyond language to an 'outside' world but only to other signs in a process of infinite deferral or *différance* (meaning both to differ and to defer). Myths, it turns out, are thoroughly poststructuralist: they signify other myths as one myth turns into another, the series assuming complex non-linear forms in the process (Lévi-Strauss 1996, 157).

But of course myths are also supposed to be windows onto the human mind. How is it that myths can turn into other myths seemingly all by themselves? Lévi-Strauss claims to be able to show "how myths operate in men's minds without their being aware of the fact and, as I have already suggested, it would perhaps be better to go still further and, disregarding the thinking subject completely, proceed as if the thinking process were taking place in the myths, in their reflection upon themselves and their interrelation" (Lévi-Strauss 1992, 12).

Dynamic Systems

Earlier I suggested that structuralism could not be reduced to its linguistic inheritances. The mathematician and philosopher Jean Petitot (2009) has persuasively demonstrated that Lévi-Strauss's work is intersected by other influences and thinkers, undermining claims that "structuralism is of formalist, logicist and linguistic descent" or that it celebrates exclusively "a static, algebraic and combinatory concept of structure" (Petitot 2009, 276). Indeed, Petitot indicates an alternative or additional genealogy for Lévi-Strauss's writings which includes the biologist D'Arcy Wentworth Thompson for whom structures are "morphodynamically (self-) organised and (self-)regulating wholes" (Petitot 2009, 276). The theory of self-organizing structures (dynamic systems theory) also derives from Norbert Wiener's cybernetics and points to an active rather than static notion of structure as summarized by Frank Capra:

> To understand the phenomenon of self-organization, we first need to understand the importance of pattern. The idea of a pattern of organization—a configuration of relationships characteristic of a particular system—became the explicit focus of systems thinking in cybernetics and has been a crucial concept ever since. . . . Is there a common pattern of organization that can be identified in all living systems? . . . Whenever we look at life, we look at networks . . . The first and most obvious property of any network is its non-linearity—it goes in all directions . . . Because networks of communication may generate feedback loops, they may acquire the ability to regulate themselves . . . The pattern of life . . . is a network pattern capable of

self-organization … we can say that self-organization is the spontaneous emergence of new structures and new forms of behaviour in open systems far from equilibrium, characterized by internal feedback loops and described mathematically by non-linear equations. (1996, 80–85)

According to Christopher Johnson (2003, 92–103), Lévi-Strauss's approach to myth was informed by these ideas of self-organizing patterns of life. So, what of the mind—the "uninvited guest" (Lévi-Strauss 1993b, 80)—and the deep grammar lying behind myth and religion/culture more generally?

When dynamic systems theory is deployed to frame the question of cognition, a picture of the human mind emerges that is at odds with recent work in the cognitive theory of religion (see Sperber 1996; Boyer 2001). Cognition or thinking—for Boyer and Sperber—is the translation of sensory experiences into information about an independently existing, outside world, a view which privileges the idea of a fixed and unchanging cognitive architecture. By contrast, dynamic systems theory claims that the mind "does not react to environmental stimuli through a linear chain of cause and effect, but responds with structural changes in its nonlinear, organizationally closed, autopoietic network" (Capra 1996, 269; see also Ingold 2001; Fodor/Piattelli-Palmarini 2011, 72–92; Tremlett 2011). If the mind is a non-linear, dynamic system—a claim that may be inferred from products of the mind such as myths which 'grow' or self-organize, proliferating in spiral fashion like a 'crystal' to form an "intermediary entity between a statistical aggregate of molecules and the molecular structure itself" (Lévi-Strauss 1993a, 229)—then key assumptions of cognitive theory such as the modularity thesis appear suspect.

'Primitive' Religion: Evolutionism, Functionalism, and Entropy

At the centre of early theories of so-called primitive religion are two explanatory frames—evolutionism and functionalism. These rival theoretical positions were staked out in the study of religion around arguments regarding totemism, magic, and animism and what Lévi-Strauss would later call "*la pensée sauvage*." Evolutionism posits a model of linear, developmental progress, allegedly measurable in terms of technology and the correspondence of ideas (as mental representations) to the external environment. According to this model, religion is explanatory in character and will wither away as scientific (accurate, mental) representations of the world proliferate. For evolutionists such as Frazer, the question of religion was a question of representation—a question of the correspondence of a religious truth-claim with the actually existing world. It was for this reason that evolutionists predicted the demise of religion in the face of the advance of science. Functionalism emerged as a rival to evolutionism. It ignored the truth content of religion to concentrate on the function of religion in society. Functionalists posited an equilibrium model of society that de-privileged history and ruled out change. For functionalists such as Malinowski, religion was primarily an element in a complex, closed, homeostatic system. Both evolutionism and functionalism rendered non-Western societies outside of history, either because they had become stuck in some backward stage of development (evolutionism) or because they were insulated against historical change by a range of homeostatic mechanisms/institutions including religion (functionalism). The structuralist intervention placed key elements of evolutionist and functionalist theories of religion and society in doubt.

According to Lévi-Strauss, the evolutionist hypothesis accounts for cultural diversity by ranking cultures on a scale of developmental progress. He argues that this method of classification cancels out the diversity of cultures by transforming non-Western cultures and societies into stages of the West's own past. The rationalist critique of religion and religious thought played a key role in this ranking procedure. For example, near the beginning of *The Golden Bough* (1987 [1922]) Frazer set out the thesis that magical beliefs and practices are founded upon mistaken assumptions regarding causality, specifically that homeopathic magic applies the "Law of Similarity" and contagious magic the "Law of Contact or Contagion" (Frazer 1987, 11). For Frazer, magical thought as representational thought is remarkable because of the lack of correspondence between it and the actually existing world. This lack renders it, for Frazer, empty. Magic is a childlike fantasy and a flight of fancy which the modern, scientific mind has surpassed. By contrast, for Lévi-Strauss, magic and science sit side by side as "two parallel modes of acquiring knowledge" (Lévi-Strauss 1966, 13). He states that the "thirst for objective knowledge is one of the most neglected aspects of the thought of people we call 'primitive'. Even if it is rarely directed towards facts of the same level as those with which modern science is concerned, it implies comparable intellectual application and methods of observation" (Lévi-Strauss 1966, 3). As such, Lévi-Strauss applies the notion of bricolage to allow for a kind of empathic or imaginative reconstruction of *la pensée sauvage*. Bricolage is a form of assembling which works with whatever comes to hand, but *la pensée sauvage* also suggests that the assemblages of the 'bricoleur' emerge from cognitive operations qualitatively different to those of the scientist or engineer. The evolutionist premise of ranks is thereby rejected and replaced by the idea of "two strategic levels at which nature is accessible to scientific enquiry: one roughly adapted to that of perception and the imagination: the other at a remove from it" (Lévi-Strauss 1966, 15).

Johnson (2003, 116) has claimed that the "thermodynamic or informational concept of entropy"—including game theory and Norbert Wiener's work on cybernetics, communication patterns, and feedback loops—influenced Lévi-Strauss's attempt to think against the grain of linear change posited by the evolutionists but also against the hermetic, cryogenic chambers imagined by the functionalists. Lévi-Strauss's idea of 'hot' and 'cold' societies—the latter existing in a Rousseau-esque relation with 'nature' and the former rapaciously consuming their resources and those of other cultures, before finally falling subject to entropic collapse—is evidence of this influence:

I have suggested ... that the clumsy distinction between 'peoples without history' and others could with advantage be replaced by a distinction between what
for convenience I called 'cold' and 'hot' societies [*les sociétés froides et les sociétés
chaudes*]: the former seeking, by the institutions they give themselves, to annul the
possible effects of historical factors on their equilibrium and continuity in a quasi-
automatic fashion; the latter resolutely internalizing the historical process and making it the moving power of their development. (Lévi-Strauss 1966, 233–234)

In *The Savage Mind* (1966) and the essay "The Scope of Anthropology" (1994, 29–
30) Lévi-Strauss fabricates a series of binary associations: egalitarian vs. hierarchical,
'cold' vs. 'hot' and elsewhere, clocks vs. steam engines (Johnson 2003, 122). According to
Lévi-Strauss, egalitarian, cold, clockwork societies require a minimum amount of initial
input energy to get them going and are characterized by a negative feedback loop where
"information on the output of the system is fed back to its input, to ensure that subsequent output is maintained within a limited set of parameters" (Johnson 2003, 123). By
contrast, hierarchical, hot, steam-powered societies generate energy through exploitation ("differentiations between castes and between classes are emphasized unceasingly
in order to draw from them change and energy" [Lévi-Strauss 1994, 29]) and are characterized by a positive feedback loop whereby "the system is subject to an exponential
growth that knows no limits" (Johnson 2003, 123). Lévi-Strauss deployed these chains of
metaphor to reimagine societies as different types of system. Whereas the hot societies
of the West are characterized by exploitation as a means of guaranteeing a rapid pace of
change, the cold societies of the Amazon 'chose' stasis and, as such, engage the environment in a manner guaranteeing "both a modest standard of living and the conservation of natural resources" (Lévi-Strauss 1994, 28). In the classic functionalist theories of
religion, the role of religion was to act as a stabilizing body of practices and ideas against
potentially pathological complexes. However, for Lévi-Strauss totemism, magic, and
animism offer rather a window onto "different solutions to common problems in the
organization of social life" (Doja 2008, 93).

Poststructuralism, Derrida, and Deconstruction

Where does structuralism end and poststructuralism begin? In everything I have discussed so far, the suggestion has been that a clear boundary between them is difficult to
draw. According to Johnson (1993, 7), structuralism privileges "the 'closed-system' models of linguistics and mathematics," although arguably Lévi-Strauss's work has always
gone beyond the closed-system to explore "forces of interaction and change, both within
and between systems" such as in his definition of 'hot' society. Nevertheless it is here at
the tendentious border identified by Johnson (1993) that I will locate poststructuralism
and Derrida's *oeuvre*.

Derrida's basic contention is that Western philosophy has been structured by what
he calls the metaphysics of presence. In *Of Grammatology*, Derrida suggests that the

privileging of speech (presence) over writing (absence or distance) constitutes a strategy to guarantee that meaning is stabilized and crystallized, thus ensuring the possibility of communication and understanding between speakers. According to Derrida, speech has traditionally been seen as a natural act that facilitates direct or unmediated communication between speakers. For Aristotle for example, "spoken words . . . are the symbols of mental experience . . . and written words are the symbols of spoken words' and this is because, for Aristotle, "the voice, [as] producer of *the first symbols*, has a relationship of essential and immediate proximity with the mind" (Derrida 1997, 11). The presence of speech to mind is the guarantee of reason's transparency to itself in the proximity of thought to speech and then on to speaker to speaker. This intimacy and immediacy allows speakers to know what they mean, to mean what they say, and to understand what has been said. This speech community is disrupted by writing (in much the same way that in sociology, modernity disrupts the communing community of the *Gemeinschaft*) because writing requires interpretation and interpretation contaminates understanding with all kinds of temporal and spatial distortions. Derrida seeks to unravel this metaphysics of presence by arguing that writing is not corrupted speech but rather both speech and writing are instances of systems that, in their instability, must always fall prey to interpretation. Importantly, Derrida situates this claim beyond philosophy in relation to biology and cybernetics (Derrida 1997, 9), suggesting a relationship with structuralism that, according to Johnson (1993), aligns Derrida's conception of writing "with the metamorphic and adaptational ('open-system') models found in systems theory," that is "models which were never properly assimilated and applied by structuralist theory" (1993, 8; see also 1993, 191). It is this notion of the open system that provides a point of departure for exploring Derrida's idea of deconstruction.

According to Derrida, deconstruction is not a method or a procedure and he provides a definition of sorts in *Of Grammatology*:

> The movements of deconstruction do not destroy structures from the outside. They are not possible and effective, nor can they take accurate aim, except by inhabiting those structures. Inhabiting them *in a certain way*, because one always inhabits, and all the more when one does not suspect it. Operating necessarily from the inside, borrowing all the strategic and economic resources of subversion from the old structure, borrowing them structurally, that is to say without being able to isolate their elements and atoms, the enterprise of deconstruction always in a certain way falls prey to its own work. (Derrida 1997, 24)

For Derrida, language exceeds and overwhelms. Deconstruction is a process through which this excess and overwhelming can be glimpsed. In *Memoires for Paul de Man* Derrida writes that "there is always already deconstruction, at work in works, especially in literary works. Deconstruction cannot be applied, after the fact and from the outside, as a technical instrument of modernity. Texts deconstruct *themselves* by themselves" (Derrida in Moran 2000, 452). Derrida's insight is that texts weave the illusion of possessing a central meaning. A deconstructive reading reveals that such a core mean-ing is never in fact attained and indeed is subverted by other meanings within the text. Derrida's claim that *"there is no outside-text"* [*il n'y a pas de hors-texte*] (1997, 158) sug-gests that a text can never be set apart as a discrete object either from the contexts of its production or from the contexts of its interpretation, which, in any case, generate only more text. Thus textual meaning is always an effect or function of context and there is no possibility for predicting or indeed controlling further contextualization. Translation is especially susceptible to deconstruction, as translation is never the generation of a copy but always, for Derrida, an alteration (see Derrida 2004). What is the significance of such alterations?

> As the catastrophe of disturbance and seasonal differentiation could not be logically produced from within an inert system, one must imagine the unimaginable: a little push entirely exterior to Nature. This apparently "arbitrary" explanation responds to a profound necessity and thus reconciles many exigencies. Negativity, the origin of evil, of society, of articulation, comes from without. Presence is surprised by what threatens it. On the other hand, it is imperative that this exteriority of evil be nothing or nearly nothing. The little push, the "slight movement" produces a revolution out of nothing . . . A nearly non-existent force is a nearly infinite force when it is strictly alien to the system it sets going. (Derrida 1997, 256–257)

Derrida's work has immense significance for those working with sacred texts as trans-lators and interpreters and for those studying religions more generally. For example, if translation and interpretation have become techniques for fixing meaning, then decon-struction can operate in the other direction by providing emancipatory routes out from traditional or canonical interpretations of texts designated 'sacred.' As such, it has been claimed that deconstruction offers *"play*, with its connotations of free experimentation and endless alternatives" (Bible and Culture Collective 1995, 131). However, deconstruc-tion can problematize both 'repressive' and 'progressive' interpretations, not just hegem-onic readings but radical readings as well.

Jürgen Habermas has suggested an affinity between Derrida's notion of decon-struction and Jewish mysticism (Callinicos 1989, 78–79; Habermas 1987, 181–184). According to Habermas, the undecidability of language becomes a confirmation of what in Judaeo-Christian thought is known as 'the Fall'—the moment that reg-isters the exile of human beings from God. Without that comforting (metaphys-ics of) presence there is only the cacophony of language, de-centered and forever subject to deconstruction. Bryan Rennie has extended this insight a step further to claim that Derrida's work expresses "a longing for a centre" (Rennie 2001, xiv; see also Permenter 2001). This opens sufficient space for Rennie to argue for an affin-ity between Derrida's thought and that of Mircea Eliade. Sherwood and Hart (2005, 24) have even claimed an affinity between Derrida and Rudolf Otto indicating per-haps the implication of poststructuralism in the very essentialisms it seeks to break down (see Tremlett 2008b).

Deconstructing Social Systems

For those keen to apply Derridean insights to sociological rather than textual and philo-logical questions (see also Mandair, "Postcolonialism," this volume), Ernesto Laclau's poststructuralist intervention in Marxist thought offers a pertinent point of departure. Laclau begins with conceptions of historical agency and argues that Marx articulates two different theories of history: the first is history as the linear unfolding of a prede-termined journey to communism; however, Laclau rejects the idea of history as already being decided. The second is history as struggle. According to Laclau, when history is conceived as struggle it means that the social system must always remain open, but this is "not as the result of the empirical impossibility of its specific coherence being fulfilled, but as something which 'works' within the structure from the beginning" (1990, 29). In other words, in the same way that deconstruction is always already at work in texts, it is also always at work in social systems meaning that they are always prey to deconstruc-tion and therefore, to change. The zero-sum game of the secularization thesis—with its either/or binary of secular/religious for the identity of the social—would appear to be particularly vulnerable to a deconstructive reading.

CONCLUSIONS

In this chapter I began by demonstrating that Lévi-Strauss's structuralism emerged as a critique of evolutionist and functionalist thought in anthropology. Thinkers includ-ing Frazer and Malinowski were interested in questions concerning the origins of reli-gion through the postulation of a linear theory of progress and the function of religion through the postulation of a closed, equilibrium model of society. Lévi-Strauss's struc-turalist interventions offered a completely novel way to begin to understand religion, not merely through the imaginative exploration of *la pensée sauvage* but also because Lévi-Strauss's experiments in anthropology and linguistics but also music, philosophy, cybernetics, biology, and art opened out new problems and questions, the ramifications of which are still being explored today. His work on myth in particular, with its elision of the subject through the suggestion that it's the myths that 'think,' constitutes a fun-damental challenge for a field of study operating according to a humanist and subject-centered epistemology. Derrida's work has similarly performed a radical challenge for the study of religion. His approach to language as an open system marked by *différance* and deconstruction poses difficult questions both for those working on religious texts and their translations and for those interested in sociological questions of religion. Most of all, I hope this chapter has demonstrated that structuralism and poststructuralism constitute much more than a 'linguistic turn' and draw together influences and strands of thought that are part of a wider and ongoing interdisciplinary-epistemic shift in social theory and philosophy.

GLOSSARY

Bricolage in French, it means DIY or do-it-yourself (the 'bricoleur' is the odd-job-person). The implication in Lévi-Strauss's work is of a mode of thinking that assembles connections with whatever materials are to hand rather than according to any predetermined schema or plan. Elsewhere the term has been used to refer, metaphorically, to qualitative research methods where it "denotes . . . practices explicitly based on notions of eclecticism, emergent design, flexibility and plurality. Further, it signifies approaches that examine phenomena from multiple, and sometimes competing, theoretical and methodological perspectives" (Rogers 2012, 1).

Cybernetics "The study of artificial or natural systems which store information and use feedback mechanisms to guide and control their behaviour" (Honderich 1995, 173).

Deconstruction deconstruction for Derrida is not a method but the assumption that texts—in effect all assemblages be they linguistic, cultural, or historical—are composed of unstable articulations of elements.

Différance meaning both to differ and to defer, Derrida's neologism points to the endless slippage of meaning from word to word in a potentially endless regress.

Dynamic systems theory the idea that systems—language systems, social systems, religious systems, biological systems—are self-organizing and can change in unpredictable ways according to both endogenous and exogenous logics or factors.

Entropic "A measure of *un*available energy in a physical system. Since usable energy is lost in irreversible energy transfers, entropy increases in closed systems (the second law of thermodynamics)" (Honderich 1995, 238).

Evolutionism the idea that social, religious, political, and economic systems develop uniformly from simple to complex forms in a manner said to resemble the evolution of biological forms and systems according to principles of selection, fitness, and adaptation.

Formalism perhaps more accurately designated as Russian Formalism, this refers to the ideas of a circle of early twentieth-century Russian scholars including V. I. Propp and Roman Jakobson whose work on linguistic and literary forms would influence the thought of Lévi-Strauss (during World War II, Lévi-Strauss and Jakobson met in New York—both had fled Europe to escape the Nazis).

Functionalism in anthropology and sociology, the idea that institutions such as religion can be studied as 'parts' contributing to the maintenance of the social whole.

Linear refers to the representation of a set of relationships or events by a straight line.

Metaphysics of presence Derrida claims that this idea has structured much of the Western philosophical tradition. The idea itself privileges the notion of a foundational point which anchors meaning and reference through binary oppositions such as speech and writing. It is precisely this metaphysics that Derrida seeks to open out to deconstruction.

Pensée sauvage has been translated in English as "savage thought," although in French the phrase is also a pun on "wild pansies." According to Lévi-Strauss, this type of thinking is wild (as in untamed), natural, and universal. The phrase represents a departure from the ranking of cognitive operations constitutive of evolutionist thought.

REFERENCES

Barthes, Roland. 1977. "The Death of the Author." In *Image Music Text*, translated by Stephen Heath. London: Fontana Press, 142–148.

Bible and Culture Collective. 1995. *The Postmodern Bible*. New Haven, CT and London: Yale University Press.

Boyer, Pascal. 2001. *Religion Explained: The Evolutionary Origins of Religious Thought*. New York: Basic Books.

Callinicos, Alex. 1989. *Against Postmodernism: A Marxist Critique*. Cambridge: Polity Press.

Callinicos, Alex. 1999. *Social Theory: An Historical Introduction*. Cambridge: Polity Press.

Capps, Walter, H. 1995. *Religious Studies: The Making of a Discipline*. Minneapolis: Fortress Press.

Capra, Fritjof. 1996. *The Web of Life: A New Scientific Understanding of Living Systems*. New York: Anchor Books.

Derrida, Jacques. 1997. *Of Grammatology*, translated by Gayatri Chakravorty Spivak. Baltimore, MD and London: John Hopkins University Press. Original edition, 1976.

Derrida, Jacques. 2002. "Structure, Sign and Play in the Discourse of the Human Sciences." In *Writing and Difference*, translated by Alan Bass. London and New York: Routledge, 351–370. Original edition, 1978.

Derrida, Jacques. 2004. "Plato's Pharmacy." In *Dissemination*, translated by Barbara Johnson. London and New York: Continuum, 67–186. Original edition, 1981.

Doja, Albert. 2008. "From Neolithic Naturalness to *Tristes Tropiques*: The Emergence of Lévi-Strauss's New Humanism." *Theory, Culture & Society* 25(1): 77–100. doi: 10.1177/0263276407085154

Fodor, Jerry and Massimo Piattelli-Palmarini. 2011. *What Darwin Got Wrong*. London: Profile Books.

Foucault, Michel. 1970. *The Order of Things: An Archaeology of the Human Sciences*. London and New York: Routledge.

Frazer, James, G. 1910. *Totemism and Exogamy: A Treatise on Certain Early Forms of Superstition and Society, Volume 1*. London: Macmillan.

Frazer, James, G. 1987. *The Golden Bough: A Study in Magic and Religion*, abridged edition. London: Papermac. Original edition, 1922.

Habermas, Jürgen. 1987. *The Philosophical Discourse of Modernity*, translated by Frederick Lawrence. Cambridge: Polity Press.

Hawkes, Terence. 1983. *Structuralism and Semiotics*. London: Methuen.

Honderich, Ted, ed. 1995. *The Oxford Companion to Philosophy*. Oxford and New York: Oxford University Press.

Ingold, Tim. 2001. "From Complementarity to Obviation: On Dissolving the Boundaries Between Social and Biological Anthropology, Archaeology, and Psychology." In *Cycles of Contingency: Developmental Systems and Evolution*, edited by Susan Oyama, Paul E. Griffiths, and Russell D. Gray. Cambridge, MA: MIT Press, 255–279.

Jameson, Fredric. 1972. *The Prison-House of Language: A Critical Account of Structuralism and Russian Formalism*. Princeton, NJ: Princeton University Press.

Johnson, Christopher. 1993. *System and Writing in the Philosophy of Jacques Derrida*. Cambridge: Cambridge University Press.

Johnson, Christopher. 2003. *Claude Lévi-Strauss: The Formative Years*. Cambridge: Cambridge University Press.

Laclau, Ernesto. 1990. *New Reflections on the Revolution of our Time*. London and New York: Verso.

Lévi-Strauss, Claude. 1966. *The Savage Mind*. London: Weidenfeld & Nicolson.

Lévi-Strauss, Claude. 1992. *The Raw and the Cooked: Introduction to a Science of Mythology 1*, translated by John Weightman and Doreen Weightman. Harmondsworth: Penguin. Original edition, 1970.

Lévi-Strauss, Claude. 1993a. "The Structural Study of Myth." In *Structural Anthropology Volume 1*, translated by Claire Jacobson and Brooke Grundfest Schoepf. Harmondsworth: Penguin, 206–231. Original edition, 1963.

Lévi-Strauss, Claude. 1993b. "Linguistics and Anthropology." In *Structural Anthropology Volume 1*, translated by Claire Jacobson and Brooke Grundfest Schoepf. Harmondsworth: Penguin, 67–80. Original edition, 1963.

Lévi-Strauss, Claude. 1994. "The Scope of Anthropology." In *Structural Anthropology Volume 2*, translated by Monique Layton. Harmondsworth: Penguin, 3–32. Original edition, 1976.

Lévi-Strauss, Claude. 1996. *The Jealous Potter*, translated by Bénédicte Chorier. Chicago, IL and London: University of Chicago Press. Original edition, 1988.

Lévi-Strauss, Claude. 2001. *Myth and Meaning*. London and New York: Routledge. Original edition, 1978.

Lévi-Strauss, Claude and Didier Eribon. 1991. *Conversations with Claude Lévi-Strauss*, translated by Paula Wissing. Chicago, IL and London: University of Chicago Press.

Malinowski, Bronislaw. 1984. "Myth in Primitive Psychology." In *Magic, Science and Religion and Other Essays*. Westport, CT: Greenwood Press, 93–148. Original edition, 1948.

Moran, Dermot. 2000. *Introduction to Phenomenology*. London and New York: Routledge.

Permenter, Rachela. 2001. "Romantic Postmodernism and the Literary Eliade." In *Changing Religious Worlds: The Meaning and End of Mircea Eliade*, edited by Bryan Rennie. New York: SUNY Press, 95–116.

Petitot, Jean. 2009. "Morphology and Structural Aesthetics: From Goethe to Lévi-Strauss." In *The Cambridge Companion to Lévi-Strauss*, edited by Boris Wiseman. Cambridge: Cambridge University Press, 275–295.

Rennie, Bryan. 2001. "Introduction." In *Changing Religious Worlds: The Meaning and End of Mircea Eliade*, edited by Bryan Rennie. New York: SUNY Press, ix–xxiv.

Rogers, Matt. 2012. "Contextualizing Theories and Methods of Bricolage Research." *The Qualitative Report* 17(48): 1–17. <http://www.nova.edu/ssss/QR/QR17/rogers.pdf>.

Sherwood, Yvonne and Kevin Hart. 2005. "Other Testaments." In *Derrida and Religion: Other Testaments*, edited by Yvonne Sherwood and Kevin Hart. London and New York: Routledge, 3–26.

Sperber, Dan. 1996. *Explaining Culture: A Naturalistic Approach*. Oxford: Blackwell.

Sturrock, John. 1993. *Structuralism*. London: Fontana.

Tremlett, Paul-François. 2008a. *Lévi-Strauss on Religion: The Structuring Mind*. London: Equinox.

Tremlett, Paul-François. 2008b. *Religion and the Discourse on Modernity*. London and New York: Continuum.

Tremlett, Paul-François. 2011. "Structure Amongst the Modules: Lévi-Strauss and Cognitive Theorizing about Religion." *Method and Theory in the Study of Religion* 23(3–4): 351–366. doi: 10.1163/157006811X608421

FURTHER READING

Belsey, Catherine. 2002. *Poststructuralism: A Very Short Introduction*. Oxford: Oxford University Press. [*A very accessible introductory text.*]

Critchley, Simon and William R. Schroeder, eds. 1998. "Part IX: Structuralism and After." In *A Companion to Continental Philosophy*. Oxford: Blackwell, 507–612. [*Part IX offers excellent overviews of individual thinkers associated with structuralism and poststructuralism including*

Lévi-Strauss and Derrida but also Althusser, Deleuze, Irigaray, and Kristeva among others. For more advanced readers.]

Sturrock, John, ed. 1980. *Structuralism and Since: From Lévi-Strauss to Derrida*. Oxford: Oxford University Press. [*This excellent volume consists in essays summarizing the thought of scholars including Lévi-Strauss and Derrida, but also Foucault and Lacan.*]

CHAPTER 16

....

SOCIAL THEORY

....

PHILIP A. MELLOR AND CHRIS SHILLING

CHAPTER SUMMARY

- The category of the sacred was central to 'problems' of order and meaning in classical sociology; it remains key to understanding the distinctive contribution of social theory to the study of religion and society.
- Durkheim and Weber each proposed two contrasting modalities of the sacred, yielding four overall.
- First, the 'socio-religious' sacred (Durkheim): other-worldly cosmologies and practices sanctify social life as a whole, characteristically bringing all ideas, actions, and social spaces under religious direction and control.
- Second, a 'bio-economic' modality of the sacred in capitalist economies and highly differentiated social contexts (Durkheim): anything can be 'set apart' from, and emotionally experienced as 'special' in relation to, mundane life. This modality is characteristic of the consumerization of the sacred.
- Third, the 'transcendent sacred' (Weber), in which forces experienced as extraordinary and other-worldly coexist with a social sphere differentiated as secular. Though those who are 'religious' may seek to steer society via other-worldly directed norms and disciplines, the social and the sacred are essentially distinct.
- Fourth, a 'bio-political' modality of the sacred (Weber): forces of rationalization and bureaucratization—bereft of religious, other-worldly orientations—have a de-differentiating impact upon the varied sectors of society and even redefine life and death itself.
- Taken together, these four modalities can be used to provide new insights into a range of contemporary sacred phenomena, including resurgent forms of Islam and Christian Pentecostalism, the fetishization of commodities, and the increasingly powerful bio-political governance of bodies.

INTRODUCTION

Social theory is located at the philosophical end of the spectrum of sociological activity. It operates conceptually at a high level of generality and is focused on the systematic analysis and explanation of social phenomena. From its late nineteenth-century origins, it developed a diverse set of analytical models and approaches designed to highlight and explain a wide range of issues associated with structural and cultural change, the substantive and functional features of meaning and behavior, the relationships between selves and societies, and human agency and constraint. From the late twentieth century onwards, this diversification of social theory intensified further through the emergence of general accounts of a variety of issues: e.g. gender; race; ethnicity; postcolonialism; developments in critical and cultural theory; structuralism and poststructuralism; actor-network theory; and the 'new' materialism. Alongside this proliferation of concerns, social theorists have engaged in disputes concerning the relationship between theoretical and empirical matters, normative or 'scientific' authority claims, and methodological priorities (Coleman 1990; Hedström/Swedberg 1998; Wagner 2001). Though the sheer scope of its inquiries has sometimes blurred what distinguishes social theory from cognate approaches, we can identify questions concerning social order and meaning as core concerns from the start through to the present. Not only are these key to understanding the emergence of influential synthetic or integrative approaches aiming to bridge divergent philosophical and theoretical traditions (Parsons 1968; 1991; Berger 1967; Habermas 1984; 1987), they are also the ones that have enabled several of its perspectives to have a major impact on the study of religion. This is particularly evident among those writings that have utilized the notion of the 'sacred' to interrogate the demarcation of the religious relative to the secular.

The background to these developments returns us to social theory's origins, wherein perceptions of religion's implication in problems of order and meaning were central to the writings of classical sociological thinkers. At stake here were questions about how social and cultural orders could operate in modern contexts characterized by the decline of absolutist governments and the fracturing of those 'sacred canopies' provided by notions of divine order. For Auguste Comte, Émile Durkheim, and Max Weber, traditional forms of Christianity had been damaged by the corrosive impacts of rationalization and pluralization sweeping Europe. The decline of these particular forms was not usually taken to be indicative of the obsolescence of religious forces altogether, however, and most classical theorists suggested that there existed religious forces possessing continued (if variable) efficacy in processes of group formation and meaning making. At their most effective, indeed, such forces not only harnessed a range of cognitive and 'non-rational' bodily affects and practices to collective norms, providing a basis on which social order could be secured, but also provided individuals with answers to fundamental questions regarding life and death (Shilling/Mellor 2001).

These classical accounts were highly influential (Wrong 1994), but have been criticized for what is perceived to be their inherent tendency toward functionalist understandings of religion that fail to account for its complexity and diversity (McCauley/Lawson 1984). Subsequent writings have also identified in this work a Western bias that universalizes what some view as a specifically Christian and European demarcation of the 'religious' from the 'secular', and privileges the secular as the sphere within which religions operate as human constructions possessed of social functions (Milbank 1990; Asad 1993).

Such critiques may hold with regard to crude functionalist models based upon partial readings of classical social theorists, but possess limited relevance for the actual accounts developed in these earlier writings. For Durkheim, Weber, and others, the social directionality of religion—the capacity of religious activity to reshape social norms and redirect social action through a range of cognitive, emotional, and experiential phenomena—is of far greater interest than some essentially conservative functional contribution to social order. This concern with the directionality of religion, moreover, remains relevant to issues that range far beyond the differentiated and privatized contexts that have been viewed as culturally specific to post-Reformation Western modernity, and it is in this regard that classical theorists attributed such importance to the category of the sacred.

The Category of the Sacred

In hailing the development of the category of the sacred as *the* distinctive contribution of social theory to the social sciences, Robert Nisbet (1993, 221) highlights its socially creative connotations, as well as its explanatory breadth. It deserves recognition as social theory's key 'unit-idea', he suggests, because it enables us to analyze the reshaping and redirecting of social forms across the totality of myth, dogma, and ritual in religious life as well as in relation to a range of "ostensibly non-religious phenomena such as authority, status, community and personality." In facilitating such analyses, conceptions of the sacred also enable us to interrogate interactions between the religious and the secular that have a socially productive character—thereby implicating it in questions concerning the economy, state, society, and personal identity—without reducing religion to its social functions or assuming that it is fated to struggle for survival within an increasingly dominant secular sphere.

Nisbet's concern is with the philosophical underpinnings of sociological thought, but there is a strong case for arguing that the category of the sacred continues to underpin social theory's distinctive contribution to the study of religion and society. In pursuing this, we ground our analysis in the writings of two key classical theorists. Weber's and Durkheim's accounts of religion and society are routinely portrayed as opposed, reflecting broader oppositions between the methodological individualism of much German social thought and the methodological holism characteristic of the French philosophical tradition. What conventional accounts overlook, however, is that they converge in suggesting that the embodied experience of certain phenomena as 'extraordinary' relative to mundane day-to-day life, irrespective of the religious or secular enframing of such phenomena, influences social action in potentially transformative ways (Mellor/ Shilling 1997; 2014).

Durkheim, Weber, and the Sacred

Durkheim insists there are things considered sacred, 'set apart' from egoistic organic life, accessed through 'positive' and 'negative' rites that stimulate effervescent experiences possessing the capacity to join individuals to a collectivity imbued with forms of collective consciousness (Durkheim 1995, 138, 212). In a distinct yet related analysis, Weber also explores how phenomena encountered as 'sacred,' 'enchanted,' and 'charismatic' stimulate in people a socially creative experience of distance between extraordinary life and routinized existence (Weber 1978, 789–90, 818–828, 1111–1157; 1948, 328, 155). Extraordinary phenomena steer society by influencing the practical techniques through which bodies are trained: adjusting the 'psycho-physical apparatus' of humans rouses in them a propensity to intervene in their environment on the basis of priorities that are felt as, and thought to be, 'special' (Weber 1978, 1156). Focused on the relational, socially constructed, and embodied character of extraordinary phenomena (Anttonen 2000; Taves 2009), such accounts contrast with more restrictive, arguably neo-theological, understandings of the sacred sometimes found in religious studies—including Eliade's (1963) conception of 'hierophany' (confined to this-worldly experiences of something 'wholly other'), and James's (1983 [1902]) psychological account (confined to ineffable as well as noetic experiences generative of exceptional *knowledge*)—and highlight the broad terrain addressed by 'the sacred' as conceived of within social theory.

If the convergences between Durkheim and Weber highlight the analytical significance of the sacred in terms of its impact upon societies, cultures, and embodied subjects, it is their internally divergent assessments of the precise direction of sacred forces that help develop our understanding further. First, both, in different ways, are attentive to the fact that experiences of phenomena as sacred may possess strong or weak/non-existent other-worldly dimensions, with implications for whether we categorize them as 'religious' or not. Here, 'other-worldly' refers to social constructions of a supernatural or theological character, which are taken to characterize religious rather than non-religious constructions of the sacred. The term therefore has primarily a relational, rather than ontological or metaphysical, character. Second, again in different ways, both recognize the divergent implications of distinct forms of the sacred in relation to patterns of differentiation and de-differentiation, with implications for debates about secularization. Taking these divergent positions together, we suggest that their work provides us with a basis for identifying four distinct modalities of the sacred which can be termed the socio-religious, bio-economic, transcendent, and bio-political.

MODALITIES OF THE SACRED

It is Durkheim who provides us with a conception of the 'socio-religious' modality of the sacred. Developed in his account of the universal significance of religion and the sacred, the socio-religious sacred is constructed and maintained through an other-worldly cosmology and practices that sanctify society as religious (Durkheim 1995). Centered on tribal groups, but concerned with the basic processes informing all societies, *The Elementary Forms of Religious Life* reveals a pervasive intermingling of religious and social phenomena. Social life can only exist as a result of it being permeated by strong other-worldly elements (other-worldly in that they transpose individuals from natural organic existence to what is constructed and experienced as a supernatural social and moral existence). These are elements that impart a de-differentiating quality to society.

Elsewhere in his writings, however, Durkheim provides grounds for conceptualizing the sacred in what we can call 'bio-economic' terms. This modality is evident in modern societies possessed of an advanced capitalist economy and division of labor in which anything, including worldly phenomena, can be 'set apart' from, and emotionally experienced as 'special' in relation to mundane life. Here, individuals' physical, biological properties become subject to patterns of attraction, stimulation, and manipulation by commercial products and processes: forms of the extraordinary persist, but they have weak or non-existent other-worldly elements and develop on the basis of personal preferences operating within segmented societies that prize 'the cult of the individual' (Durkheim 1984, 122). This is quite distinct from the socio-religious sacred, and it is suggestive of the consumerization of the sacred: incorporating non-religious and—insofar as they retain some other-worldly relational referents—religious forms, within a market of lifestyle options that appeal directly to the biologically grounded, yet commercially shaped, emotions of individuals.

While Durkheim provides us with a platform on which to investigate socio-religious and bio-economic modalities of the sacred, it is Weber (1991) who accounts for what we term the 'transcendent sacred,' a central explanatory device in his account of the Protestant ethic, secularization, and disenchantment. Here, forces experienced as extraordinary are construed in supernatural terms but, in contrast to Durkheim's account of the socio-religious sacred, these are deemed to be distinct from the organic or 'immanent' processes that constitute social life, not only in origin but in their ongoing personal or communal significance. While Durkheim emphasizes the pervasive, all-encompassing social influence of the sacred and religion, Weber's analysis of the transcendent sacred highlights a modality wherein it is accepted that there exists a worldly existence, a 'secular' sphere, distinct from religious forms, even though those who identify themselves as religious may seek to steer secular society in particular directions via other-worldly directed norms and disciplines.

Having identified a transcendent modality of the sacred bonded to a major form of religion, Weber was nonetheless insistent that the forces of rationalization and bureaucratization embedded within modern law and governance were bereft of religious, other-worldly orientations. These forces not only eroded religion, but also extended subsequently into the realm of bio-politics, stretching across the varied sectors of society and effecting a de-differentiating impact upon them through their pervasive social influence and power. Weber himself did not see such phenomena as sacred, but he did highlight the experiential impact of the extraordinary scope and power of the technological domination of science in the management of life. Indeed, Giorgio Agamben's (1998) association of the sacred with a system of this-worldly governmentality that reduces human existence to 'bare life'—a reduction that cuts across social differentiations and even defines life and death itself—suggests a 'bio-political' modality of the sacred that builds on Weber's attentiveness to the extraordinary power that modern law and governance have over our lives and bodies.

In short, Durkheim and Weber enable us to utilize the category of the sacred not as a referent for a substantive phenomenon wholly 'other' to day-to-day life, but for a number of analytically distinct modalities, competing 'sacreds', wherein experiences of certain relationally constructed phenomena as 'extraordinary' relative to mundane life enframe, shape, and direct social life and action in specific ways—some of which may be called religious and some of which may not. The socio-religious and the transcendent modalities have a religious character, which we can define as being characterized by other-worldly orientations towards worldly activity. The bio-economic and the bio-political, in contrast, are associated with secular, non-religious developments, possessing weak or non-existent other-worldly aspects. It is the transcendent and bio-economic modalities that share an acceptance of, or accommodation to, social differentiation, however, with the socio-religious and bio-political possessing a de-differentiating orientation. This can be presented diagrammatically (Fig. 16.1).

Condensed and abstract though this typology is, we shall now explicate its utility by illustrating how the sacred remains core to the study of religion and society in social theory today.

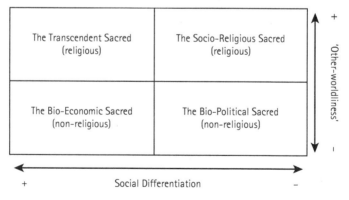

FIGURE 16.1 Modalities of the sacred.

The Socio-Religious Sacred

Durkheim (1995) argued that the socio-religious sacred was a modality elementary to all societies, although his development of his analysis through anthropological data on 'primitive' aboriginal beliefs and practices led many to question its contemporary relevance. Indeed, Durkheim's (1952 [1897]) own emphasis in other writings on the key role of Protestant individualism in shaping modern life implies a poor fit between the socio-religious sacred and modernity. In the context of the global resurgence of Islam, however, we can utilize this modality to cast fresh light on the socio-religious sacred in the current era, particularly in the context of widespread anxieties about the incorporation of Islam into Western culture and politics evident in debates today (Turner 2010, 655), as well as the often tumultuous responses of some Muslim communities to perceived profanations of those material emblems of the sacred that are the foundations for a distinctively Muslim social and bodily existence (D'Souza 2012).

Islam and the Socio-Religious Sacred

We are not suggesting that Durkheim's model can account for the diverse and complex traditions of belief and practice characteristic of one of the world's major religions. Nevertheless, insofar as some Islamic forms exhibit a commitment to a 'total' socio-religious society, they are expressive not only of the moral force Islam can exercise over those who constitute the community of the *umma*, but also the ways in which this form of the sacred challenges conceptions of social life as differentiated in religious and non-religious terms. Islam's strong focus on the primacy of bonds with other Muslims above local particularities, cultures, and institutional variables is, for example, embodied in the enactment of obligations to other followers encoded within *salat* and in the way that these signal patterns of social inclusion or exclusion relative to believers and non-believers, rather than the construction of a social sphere that embraces both (Henkel 2005, 489, 492). It is also evident in the fact that the key functionaries of *sharia* are not priests but interpreters of law, thus revealing the close link between legal regulation, social solidarity, and constructions of other-worldly authority that Durkheim identifies as central to the socio-religious sacred.

A recognition of the centrality of law to Islam, and the anxieties about the potential conflict with macro-level and meso-level differentiation it implies, is reflected in Bruce's (2003, 234) suggestion that desires for secession from, or moves to overcome, alternative systems of law are endemic to Islam. Certainly, the relative severity of many punishments encoded into some formulations of this law, in comparison to secular systems, echoes Durkheim's account, most notably with regard to penalties for apostasy (Rahman 2006). This is not only the ultimate offense against the divine, but also a challenge to what Durkheim called the 'naturalization' of the sacred, i.e. the social construction of human embodiment that defines its 'natural' character and identity in other-worldly terms, through the construction of a 'Muslim body' (a process that reveals the centrality of the socio-religious sacred to the organic realm of embodiment as well as to society). This importance placed on the naturalization of the sacred is also evident in widespread concerns within many Islamic communities about the permissibility of organ transplants between Muslim and non-Muslim bodies (Hayward/Madill 2003, 397). The conception of the purity of Muslim bodies signals both a powerful differentiation against impure, non-Muslim, bodies and a defense *against* the differentiation of the religious from the social or the organic. It is an insurance against the body being aligned with or containing the potential to generate anything that might profane the strictures of Islam.

These dimensions of the socio-religious sacred associated with Islam indicate how this modality offers a potent means for imparting a particular directionality to social life, since constructions of other-worldly sacred norms, values, bodily experiences, and symbolic systems come to have a pervasive influence on identity, action, and the relative positioning of communities in normative terms. It is, in consequence, a directionality that can exist in a relationship of tension and conflict with other cultural values. This potential for conflict is emphasized in Durkheim's (1995) argument that threats of profanation to the socio-religious sacred are received as a danger so great that they can warrant acts of deadly violence. Recognition of this is central to Ivan Strenski's (2003) discussion of the violent expenditure of human life amongst Palestinian 'suicide bombers.' For Strenski (2003, 19, 26), 'sacrifice' rather than 'suicide' best captures the actions of these bombers: they 'become holy' within their community through the effervescent sacrifice of themselves and their victims (sacrifices that reveal subordination to greater socio-religious imperatives); a process that spills over into the sacralization of the sites of their violence, the circulation of heroic stories about their lives, the offerings given to their bereaved families, the commemoration of them in prayer, and the revitalization of their communities in the face of conflict. The assertively religious nature of such other-worldly legitimations of violent sacrifice operates in conflict with a wider societal/international context experienced as antagonistic to that religion's normative expressions of effervescence and associated conceptions of ultimate importance.

THE TRANSCENDENT SACRED

Rather than categorizing all social life and bodily experience as an engagement with the sacred or with what threatens to profane the sacred and undermine society, the Weberian transcendent modality highlights the possibility that religion may coexist with a 'secular' realm. Indeed, the transcendent sacred is operationalized through a 'lifting' of people and their experiences out of existing social identities and bonds, predicated upon an emergent individualism in which ultimate religious meaning is found above and beyond the 'immanent' ethnic or cultural loyalties of social communities. This conception of the transcendent sacred contrasts with that of the socio-religious sacred; there is no sense that it is 'diffused' and naturalized into the bodies of all through collective symbols and mythologies. It characteristically gives rise to new forms of collectivity, but these are associational and actively chosen rather than emergent from or expressive of immanent bonds.

The 'reaching beyond' the boundaries and limitations of the secular central to the transcendent sacred is key to how it imparts directionality to society. As Niklas Luhmann (2000, 77) suggests, the contribution of religion informed by this modality to the development of complex social systems rests on its capacity to 'call out' individuals from their immanent lives, and to provide them with the space to judge society critically from the standpoint of an infinite, transcendent order. For Georg Simmel (1971, 173, 311, 362), this capacity simultaneously imparts a directionality to individuals, enabling them to reframe rather than negate secular experiences on the basis of an other-worldly source of personally authentic truth and to steer their lives in particular directions.

Weber's transcendent modality of the sacred can illuminate important features of a number of religions: David Martin, for example, notes the significance of polarizations of notions of the 'transcendent' and the 'immanent' in various major religions, while Charles Taylor utilizes these same polarizations in relation to Buddhism, Taoism, and Hinduism (Martin 2011, 43; Taylor 2007, 15, 18–19, 676). Both, however, note their particular significance in Christianity, though it is in its Protestant forms that this transcendent sacred is most significant, with studies of charismatic, Pentecostal, and evangelical Christianity across the world highlighting its continuing vitality.

Pentecostalism and the Transcendent Sacred

The evangelical emphasis on the individual freedom to respond to the call of God encourages an 'opting out' of social 'sacred canopies' and promotes reflexive engagements with social and political pluralism based upon transcendent considerations (Freston 2007, 224). This opting out also sometimes involves 'leaping above' local communities, in contrast to the socio-religious sacred which involves the religious enframing of the collectivity, especially in the case of ethnic-minority Christians linking themselves to "evangelicalism as an expression of transnational modernity" (Martin 2005, 277). Indeed, it has been suggested that conversion in this context is not only a conversion to modern forms of these religions, but also to religious forms of modernity (Van der Veer 1996, 2–4). This is because conversion to a religion that incorporates within it a transcendent sacred can facilitate assimilation, on religious grounds, into contexts marked by modern patterns of differentiation, and modern valuations of mobility and voluntarism. The ambiguity here concerning whether Pentecostalism is a modern form of religion or a religious form of modernity can be explored further in relation to the notion of 'elective affinity'.

Just as Weber's (1991) and Troeltsch's (1976) discussions of Puritanism's 'elective affinity' with modern capitalism suggested an interactive and mutually constitutive relationship between religious culture and economic conditions, a number of analysts have indicated that Pentecostalism promotes practices uniquely well adapted to contemporary global conditions, but they are resistant to viewing it as "a mere reflex of the modern," arguing that it continues to exert an independent effect on capitalism's development (Robbins 2004, 137). Pentecostalism's success, on this view, rests on its capacities for crafting a mode of being that locates human action, feeling, and thought at an embodied intersection of constructions of worldly and other-worldly realities where traffic flows both ways. This is evident in a range of analyses that identify the astonishing growth of Pentecostalism in South Korea as an important factor in that country's modernization (e.g. Baldacchino 2012), and studies that identify the cultivation of Pentecostal orientations in 'mega-churches' as a method which utilizes 'commercialized' places of worship to facilitate a systematic cultivation of distance from prevailing, non-Christian cultural mores and practices (e.g. Maddox 2012). Here, the particular beliefs and practices of Protestantism (including hard work, honesty, and clean living) become the means through which worldly economic activity is not only promoted but also infused with other-worldly significance via framing activities, experiences, and identities within the lens of biblical interpretation and via constructions of the transformational agency of the Holy Spirit.

THE BIO-POLITICAL SACRED

While the global vitality of Pentecostalism suggests the ongoing utility of Weber's account of the transcendent sacred, his analysis of the 'elective affinity' between earlier Protestant forms and modern capitalism understood this as a historically and culturally contingent phenomenon emergent from a specific stage in the development of modern societies. Most critical commentators of Weber's work would agree that this stage has now been superseded by the radically disenchanting impetus of rationalized culture which controls and defines the secular realm so completely that society is removed from any link to religion, and where nothing is considered ultimate apart from the power and reach of this instrumentalist mode of governance and activity. Far from resulting in a complete disappearance of the sacred, however, the implications of Weber's (1968, 24–25, 1156; 1991) analyses suggest that the extension of technological culture itself constitutes an exceptionally powerful and prized incarnation of the extraordinary. In clarifying the nature and scope of this technologically informed bio-political modality of the sacred, Agamben has done most to explore and extend the implications of Weber's analysis.

Homo Sacer

Contrary to socio-religious and transcendent legitimations of worldly activity and being with reference to other-worldly authorities, Agamben (1998, 1, 3–12, 80) traces the origins of modern bio-political management to ancient Greece and archaic Roman law, focusing on the sacred as a category of juridico-political governance. Specifically, Agamben turns to the ambiguous figure of *homo sacer* within archaic law. Homo sacer, or 'sacred man,' is an exceptional and ambiguous figure not because of the potentially volatile energies Durkheim associated with effervescent gatherings of the collective, but because of a particular relationship to the law. Acquiring this status once legally condemned to exile, homo sacer is august because expulsion precludes the possibility of being sacrificed in accordance with divine law, but also accursed because of exclusion from the safeguards guaranteed by human law (and liable to be killed, with impunity) (Agamben 1998, 8, 73). Homo sacer thus becomes sacred by being placed in a space that is 'exceptional' relative to others in that removal from the auspices of both state authority and divine power reduces this figure to the status of 'bare life,' i.e. a basic, minimal, organic form of life set apart from collective representations of ways of living valued by the group.

In contrast to Foucault's exclusive association of bio-politics with the modern era, then, Agamben traces the sacralization of bare life back to those exceptional acts that occurred during the institution of political sovereignty—acts that signaled what might be called a type of secularization insofar as the sacred was cut adrift from religion and became expressive of sovereign power over individual bodies. What is different about modernity, however, is that rather than being an exception, this sovereign power over bodies has become the norm. We are all homines sacri now, with the sacred being foundational to the modern age through the state's 'totalizing' power to manage embodied subjects on the basis of life and death via a somatic individuality in which the prized value of sustaining life as an object of management has been internalized through an obsession with 'health' and productivity (Agamben 1998, 111; Rose 2007).

Evidence for the pervasiveness and power of the bio-political sacred in contemporary society and its impact upon action and experience can be seen in various areas. In legal debates about euthanasia the notion of a 'life unworthy of being lived' reminds us of the state's power over 'bare' ('sacred') life, while technological interventions into the bodies of coma patients have facilitated new legal definitions of life, death, or liminal states between these (Agamben 1998, 139, 186). Bare life has also been extended to research and policy initiatives ranging from the pursuit of control over the building blocks of human life via the human genome project, to the management of the unborn foetus (having reached a stage in the United States where pregnant women classified as having 'at risk' lifestyles can be incarcerated in order to safeguard future life). These and related initiatives involve weakening the boundaries between humans, machines, and rationalities of control that complement Heidegger's (1993) account of the technological 'enframing' of humans. For Heidegger, humans become positioned as a 'standing reserve' for technologically driven demands for efficiency within the 'immanent frame,' vacated by the transcendent sacred, and forced to yield their properties and potential to any efficiency-based demand placed upon them.

The Bio-Economic Sacred

Despite Durkheim's focus on the socio-religious sacred, his writings, like those of Weber, also allow us to identify a secular modality of the sacred wherein that which is deemed extraordinary is dislocated from any conception of society as religious and any notion that it is connected to a transcendent realm. This modality of the *bio-economic* sacred is not involved in the degree of control of people's actions associated with socio-religious or bio-political modalities, or representative of the other-worldly, religious characteristics of the transcendental sacred. Instead, it is grounded in the consumerization of the sacred in which there exists a proliferation of re-enchantment options available to individuals and groups within a broad, socially differentiated market.

Spirituality and the Fetishism of Commodities

This idea that the experience of the sacred can possess a this-worldly as well as an other-worldly character has been explored widely. Michel Maffesoli's (1996) analysis of the 'return of the sacred' as an emotionally constituted tribalism, for example, identifies the power of extraordinary experiences to shield people from modern disenchantment, without this effervescence being linked to institutional religion. In a contrasting but related discussion, Stjepan Meštrović's (1997) *Postemotional Society* is one of a range of studies that focus on an instrumentally rational manipulation of emotional experiences of the extraordinary for economic (as well as political) ends. Here, human feelings become 'post-emotional' through being enframed by commercial worldviews that harness intimations of the extraordinary to a modality of the sacred that joins together human biological and neurological responses and economic instrumentalism.

Meštrović's concerns have been complemented by other explorations of how 'affective energy' is utilized within as well as outside consumer culture (Thrift 2004), identifying a secular, commercial exploitation of emotions stimulated by religious symbols (Gauchet 2002, 344–345; 1985). Drawing upon Marx's depiction of capitalism's 'fetishism of commodities,' Vásquez (2011) develops this argument about the commercial potentialities of the sacred by drawing attention to the material aspects of its incorporation into the cycle of production, circulation, and consumption of cultural goods. This is not the materialization of the socio-religious sacred outlined by Durkheim; it is aestheticization for gain. In this context, consumer products such as Coca-Cola and McDonald's become invested with transcendence, omnipotence, and omnipresence. Even capitalism itself is sacralized as "a this-worldly eschatology in which endless consumption is the mark of grace" (Chidester 2005, 34).

For Bryan Turner (2010), such developments highlight how the contemporary sacred has become 'hollowed out' via its incorporation into markets promoting multiple 'spiritualities' in books, the Internet, TV, and elsewhere. Not only has it become clear that anything can be identified and experienced as sacred, but it is also the case that multi-national corporations spend increasing resources on market research seeking to identify and control the mechanisms implicated in people's affectual responses to signs and images of 'extraordinary' products in consumer culture. To the extent that governmental and market pressures are able to 'reach down' to control the physiological responses, feelings, and reflections of embodied subjects, there is here a dissemination of the sacred into the bodies of individual subjects very different from the naturalization evident in Durkheim's socio-religious sacred.

This analysis of the bio-economic sacred has particular implications for 'holistic' or 'New Age' forms of 'spirituality' that self-consciously mark themselves out from contemporary capitalism in pursuing what they perceive to be truths antithetical to it. Richard Fenn's (1978, 70–71) suggestion that these spiritualities have such weak otherworldly referents that they operate entirely harmoniously with the secular, differentiated imperatives of modern societies is supported by recent writings that reinforce the sense that these spiritualities are more part of, than set aside from, commercialism. This is because they enable individuals to consume cultural phenomena that may enable experiential transformations of various sorts, but only in forms and combinations facilitated by the marketplace. In this regard, New Age spirituality's acceptance of differentiation and consumerism may manifest what Philip Hammond (2000, 3–11) has called the 'extravasation' of the sacred though, contrary to his focus on this as a multidirectional process, it frequently involves rechanneling the sacred in the direction of the economy (Gauchet 2002, 344–345). Here, religious traditions can be ransacked selectively with no expectation that they will be adopted as cosmological and practice-oriented wholes able to shape individuals' experiences in a comprehensive manner (Wood 2010, 277). Instead, New Age fashions reinforce the sense that there exists a bio-economic modality of the sacred in which commercial interests stimulate a 'combination of somatic effects' in searching for economic advantage (Bennett 2001, 4–5).

INTERACTIONS OF THE SACRED

Exploring social theory's distinctive contribution to the study of religion, we have outlined how Weber and Durkheim offered contrasting frameworks for identifying and assessing phenomena experienced as sacred, and how their expressions might be socially and religiously significant today. Each modality of the sacred can be associated with the attempt to enframe bodily experiences in particular ways in order to impart directionality to social life, with significant implications for those questions concerning secularization and de-secularization prominent within sociology of religion. It is only by taking these modalities together, furthermore, that we can gain an understanding of the considerable potential of social theory for the study of such issues today.

In both socio-religious and transcendent modalities, the enframing of experience is centered on strongly polarized conceptions of the sacred and profane, wherein other-worldly sources of authority serve to steer worldly life, though with different consequences in terms of whether their cohabitation with the secular and with structural differentiation is likely to be marked by conflict or accommodation. The socio-religious sacred is opposed to any secularization insofar as this would interfere with its consecration of phenomena as sacred or as potential profanations of the sacred, and would open a sphere of existence in which experiences are cosmologically meaningless. The transcendent sacred is also opposed to wholesale secularization, but its equation of society with an immanent, this-worldly sphere that contrasts with an other-worldly realm presupposes and even valorizes differentiation and at least a degree of social space characterized by non-religious phenomena.

Both socio-religious and transcendent modalities of the sacred, however, are associated closely with cosmologies that consecrate respectively society—or a realm that exists outside society—as *religious*. Bio-political and bio-economic modalities, in contrast, involve a weakening or collapse of the sacred/profane polarity and its links to institutional forms of religion, and a displacement of other-worldly legitimations of authority in favor of this-worldly political or economic foci. As such, these are suggestive of a secularization of the sacred manifest respectively as either a de-differentiating technologically driven bio-political materialization of the sacred as 'bare life,' or a bio-economic identity-based consumerism that fits comfortably into the wider patterns of differentiation affecting global societies.

These four modalities are ideal-types intended to outline possible relationships between the structural level of society and those meso-level feelings and experiences of the sacred that circulate outside the formal institutional spheres of modern states, but we have suggested it is possible to identify elements of them in the modern world. Not only is it the case that the major global religions exhibit elements of more than one of these modalities contemporarily as well as historically, it is also evident that global migration can encourage their intermingling and the development of novel interactions and combinations (Vásquez 2011; Orsi 1999). Similarly, broader patterns of globalization can facilitate varying degrees of accommodation or conflict between these modalities across diverse contexts.

We have indicated that Islam, for example, has many features suggestive of the socio-religious sacred, including the fact it allows no space for a differentiated sphere of the secular. This would indicate a marked antipathy to the secular modalities of the sacred that we have outlined, which is certainly evident in a number of contexts, and which is a common theme in contemporary assessments of Islam. Godazgar's (2007, 391, 407) study of consumerism in Iran, nonetheless, finds what we have called the bio-economic sacred to be as deeply embedded there as religion: even while Islamic authorities unequivocally condemn it and seek to eradicate it, global trends towards consumerism reinforced through the Internet and (illegal) satellite television increasingly make Islam one part of a differentiated existence. Similarly, Gökariksel's (2009, 665) exploration of Muslim women's adoption of the veil in Turkey can be said to suggest a strong, socio-religious challenge to the bio-economic sacred in modernity, but it is also of note that these women often take advantage of the specialist fashion outlets catering for the veiling market, introducing preference, choice, and consumer culture into their decisions.

Despite this intermingling, however, these modalities of the sacred indicate analytically distinct ways of enframing bodily experiences and cognitive systems of meaning, a range of implications in terms of their capacities for imparting directionality to a society, and divergent outcomes in terms of their consequences for religion in society more generally. This provides a useful context, moreover, for assessing the potentially partial character of some of the other social theoretical analytical models—touched on at the beginning of this chapter—that have been applied to questions of religion and society. We have already noted Luhmann's (2000) focus within his social systems theory on the capacity of religion to provide a critical standpoint on society, but we have located this specifically within a broadly Weberian transcendent modality of the sacred. The influential 'reflexive modernization' thesis of the 1990s (Giddens 1991)—wherein individualism becomes more prominent as religious traditions (and sociocultural structures more broadly) dissolve into 'liquidity'—has a similar partiality. In this latter case, the analysis of religion (which is simply conflated with the 'sacred') is more reductive than Luhmann's account, signaling a thoroughgoing reflexive reconstruction of religion subject to individual life projects, but offering an analogous presentation of it as a set of cognitive resources for individuals in the broader context of secular modernity.

Margaret Archer's (2012) recent focus on the increased importance of individual reflexivity in the context of rapid social change—wherein religion, along with other social and cultural forms, faces mutually reinforcing cultural and socio-structural changes that continually confront individuals with novel circumstances, necessitating internal conversations about alternative courses of action—is rather different. There is for Archer no *one* course mapped out for the development of global societies, only a set of circumstances wherein different traditions, cultural resources, experiences, and values must interact with each other and adapt to accelerating patterns of change. In these circumstances, the 'problems' of order and of meaning central to classical social theory take on a more complex character, but the foregoing discussion suggests the continued relevance and utility of interrogating the evolving demarcation of the religious and the secular within analytically distinct modalities of the sacred. These modalities may seek to shape and steer social action in contexts that are marked by increasingly diverse patterns of interaction, reflexivity, and change, but they alert us to the continuing significance of variable, religious and secular, forms, and experiences of the sacred, and their divergent impacts upon social life. As such, they also suggest the ongoing utility of social theory's distinctive contribution to the study of religion and society.

Glossary

Bio-economic sacred a conception and experience of extraordinary forces involving the consumerization of non-religious and—insofar as they retain some other-worldly relational referents—religious forms, within a market of lifestyle options that appeal directly to the biologically grounded, yet commercially shaped, emotions of individuals.

Bio-political sacred a conception and experience of extraordinary forces involving the scope and power of the technological domination of science in the management of life.

Enframing the capacity of a modality of the sacred (or faith, economic system, technological arrangement, or set of customs and ritual practices) to structure the meaning and significance of human experience.

Other-worldly social constructions of a supernatural or theological character, which are taken to characterize religious rather than secular constructions of the sacred. The term has primarily a relational, rather than ontological or metaphysical, character.

Problem of order the classical philosophical and sociological concern for questions of how social and cultural orders could operate in modern contexts characterized by the decline of notions of divine order, embracing issues of group formation, meaning making, and a range of rational and non-rational processes related to the internalization of collective norms.

Reflexivity the capacity of individuals to treat their thoughts, feelings, and identities as objects that can be deliberated on through the medium of 'internal conversations.' Reflexivity is inherently temporal, involving a time delay between thinking and feeling, on the one hand, and cogitating upon those thoughts and feelings, on the other.

Sacred the conception and experience of certain relationally constructed phenomena as 'extraordinary' relative to mundane life, and which come to enframe, shape, and direct social life and action in specific ways—some of which may be called 'religious' and some of which may not.

Social differentiation the process where social life is divided into semi-autonomous spheres with their own character and rationale, and is used here to signal broad differentiations between phenomena deemed 'secular' or 'religious,' and further differentiations of the social covering phenomena such as law, commerce, education, and so on, which may be construed as having complete, relative, or no autonomy from these broader differentiations.

Social theory the systematic analysis and explanation of social phenomena focused upon the significance of supra-individual processes for patterns of human interdependence spanning across local groups, societies, nations, and the globe.

Socio-religious sacred a conception and experience of extraordinary forces constructed and maintained through an other-worldly cosmology and practices that sanctify society as religious.

Transcendent sacred a conception and experience of extraordinary forces constructed and maintained in supernatural terms and deemed to be distinct from the organic or 'immanent' processes that constitute social life.

REFERENCES

Agamben, Giorgio. 1998. *Homo Sacer*, translated by Daniel Heller-Roazen. Stanford, CA: Stanford University Press. Original edition, 1995.

Anttonen, Veikko. 2000. "Sacred." In *Guide to Study of Religion*, edited by W. Braun and R. T. McCutcheon. London and New York: Cassell, 271–282.

Archer, Margaret S. 2012. *The Reflexive Imperative*. Cambridge: Cambridge University Press.

Asad, Talal. 1993. *Genealogies of Religion*. Baltimore, MD: Johns Hopkins University Press.

Baldacchino, Jean-Paul. 2012. "Markets of Piety and Pious Markets: The Protestant Ethic and the Spirit of Korean Capitalism." *Social Compass* 59(3): 367–385. doi: 10.1177/0037768612449721

Bellah, Robert N. 2011. *Religion in Human Evolution: From the Paleolithic to the Axial Age*. Cambridge, MA: Harvard University Press.

Bennett, Jane. 2001. *The Enchantment of Modern Life*. Princeton, NJ: Princeton University Press.

Berger, Peter L. 1967. *The Sacred Canopy*. New York: Doubleday.

Bruce, Steve. 2003. *Politics and Religion*. Cambridge: Polity Press.

Chidester, David. 2005. *Authentic Fakes*. Berkeley, CA: University of California Press.

Coleman, James S. 1990. *Foundations of Social Theory*. Cambridge, MA: Harvard University Press.

D'Souza, Shanthie M. 2012. "Quran Copy Burning in Afghanistan and the US 'Exit' Strategy." *Institute of South Asian Studies* 158(5), March 5. <http://ssrn.com/abstract=2150757>.

Durkheim, Émile. 1952. *Suicide*, translated by John A. Spaulding and George Simpson. London: Routledge. Original edition, 1897.

Durkheim, Émile. 1984. *The Division of Labour in Society*, translated by W. D. Halls. London: Macmillan. Original edition, 1893.

Durkheim, Émile. 1995. *The Elementary Forms of Religious Life*, translated by Karen E. Fields. New York: Free Press. Original edition, 1912.

Eliade, Mircea. 1963. *Myth and Reality*. New York: Harper & Row.

Fenn, Richard K. 1978. *Toward a Theory of Secularization*. Society for the Scientific Study of Religion, Monograph Series, no. 1.

Freston, Paul. 2007. "Evangelicalism and Fundamentalism: The Politics of Global Popular Protestantism." In *The Sage Handbook of the Sociology of Religion*, edited by J. A. Beckford and N. J. Demerath III. London: Sage, 205–226.

Gauchet, Marcel. 1985. *Le Désenchantement du Monde*. Paris: Gallimard.

Gauchet, Marcel. 2002. *La Démocratie contre Elle-Même*. Paris: Gallimard.

Giddens, Anthony. 1991. *Modernity and Self-Identity*. Cambridge: Polity Press.

Godazgar, Hossein. 2007. "Islam Versus Consumerism and Postmodernism in the Context of Iran." *Social Compass* 54(3): 389–418.

Gökariksel, Banu. 2009. "Beyond the Officially Sacred: Religion, Secularism, and the Body in the Production of Subjectivity." *Social and Cultural Geography* 10(6): 657–674.

Habermas, Jürgen. 1984. *The Theory of Communicative Action*, vol. 1, translated by Thomas McCarthy. Boston: Beacon Press. Original edition, 1981.

Habermas, Jürgen. 1987. *The Theory of Communicative Action*, vol. 2, translated by Thomas McCarthy. Boston: Beacon Press. Original edition, 1981.

Hammond, Philip E. 2000. *The Dynamics of Religious Organizations: The Extravasation of the Sacred and Other Essays*. Oxford: Oxford University Press.

Hayward, Clare and Anna Madill. 2003. "The Meanings of Organ Donation: Muslims of Pakistani Origin and White English Nationals Living in Northern England." *Social Science and Medicine* 57(3): 389–401.

Hedström, Peter and Richard Swedberg. 1998. *Social Mechanisms: An Analytical Approach to Social Theory*. Cambridge: Cambridge University Press.

Heidegger, Martin. 1993. "The Question Concerning Technology." In *Martin Heidegger: Basic Writings*, edited by David F. Krell. London: Routledge, 311–320. Original edition, 1954.

Henkel, Heiko. 2005. "Between Belief and Unbelief Lies the Performance of Salat: Meaning and the Efficacy of a Muslim Ritual." *Journal of the Royal Anthropological Institute* 11(3): 487–507.

James, William. 1983. *The Varieties of Religious Experience*. Harmondsworth: Penguin. Original edition, 1902.

Luhmann, Niklas. 2000. *Die Religion der Gesellschaft*. Frankfurt: Suhrkamp.

McCauley, Robert N. and E. Thomas Lawson. 1984. "Functionalism Reconsidered." *History of Religions* 23(4): 372–381.

Maddox, Marion. 2012. "In the Goofy Parking Lot: Growth Churches as a Novel Religious Form for Late Capitalism." *Social Compass* 59(2): 146–158. doi: 10.1177/0037768612440954

Maffesoli, Michel. 1996. *The Time of the Tribes*, translated by Rob Shields. London: Sage. Original edition, 1988.

Martin, David. 2005. *On Secularization: Towards a Revised General Theory*. Aldershot: Ashgate.

Martin, David. 2011. *The Future of Christianity*. Aldershot: Ashgate.

Mellor, Philip A. and Chris Shilling. 1997. *Re-forming the Body: Religion, Community and Modernity*. London: Sage.

Mellor, Philip A. and Chris Shilling. 2014. *Sociology of the Sacred: Religion, Embodiment and Social Change*. London: Sage.

Meštrović, Stjepan. 1997. *Postemotional Society*. London: Sage.

Milbank, John. 1990. *Theology and Social Theory*. Oxford: Blackwell.

Nisbet, Robert. 1993. *The Sociological Tradition*. New Brunswick, NJ: Transaction Publishers. Original edition, 1966.

Orsi, Robert. 1999. *Gods of the City*. Bloomington: Indiana University Press.

Parsons, Talcott. 1968. *The Structure of Social Action*. New York: Free Press. Original edition, 1937.

Parsons, Talcott. 1991. *The Social System*. London: Routledge. Original edition, 1951.

Rahman, S. A. 2006. *Punishment of Apostasy in Islam*. Malaysia: The Other Press.

Robbins, Joel. 2004. "The Globalization of Pentecostal and Charismatic Christianity." *Annual Review of Anthropology* 33: 117–143.

Rose, Nikolas. 2007. *The Politics of Life Itself*. Princeton, NJ: Princeton University Press.

Shilling, Chris and Philip A. Mellor. 2001. *The Sociological Ambition*. London: Sage.

Simmel, Georg. 1971. "The Transcendent Character of Life." In *Simmel on Individuality and Social Forms*, edited and translated by Donald N. Levine. Chicago, IL: University of Chicago Press. Original edition, 1918.

Strenski, Ivan. 2003. "Sacrifice, Gift and the Social Logic of Muslim 'Human Bombers.'" *Terrorism and Political Violence* 15(3):1–34.

Taves, Ann. 2009. *Religious Experience Reconsidered: A Building Block Approach to the Study of Religion and Other Special Things*. Princeton, NJ: Princeton University Press.

Taylor, Charles. 2007. *The Secular Age*. Boston, MA: Harvard University Press.

Thrift, Nigel. 2004. "Intensities of Feeling: Towards a Spatial Politics of Affect." *Geografiska Annaler* 86(1): 57–78.

Troeltsch, Ernst. 1976. *The Social Teaching of the Christian Churches*, translated by Olive Wyon. Chicago, IL: University of Chicago Press. Original edition, 1912.

Turner, Bryan S. 2010. "Religion in a Post-Secular Society." In *The New Blackwell Companion to the Sociology of Religion*, edited by Bryan S. Turner. Oxford: Blackwell, 649–667.

Van der Veer, Peter, ed. 1996. *Conversion to Modernities*. London: Routledge.

Vásquez, Manuel A. 2011. *More Than Belief: A Materialist Theory of Religion*. Oxford: Oxford University Press.

Wagner, Peter. 2001. *A History and Theory of the Social Sciences*. London: Sage.

Weber, Max. 1948. "Religious Rejections of the World and their Directions." In *From Max Weber*, edited and translated by H. H. Gerth and C. W. Mills. London: Routledge, 323–363. Original edition, 1919.

Weber, Max. 1978. *Economy and Society: An Outline of Interpretive Sociology*, edited by Guenther Roth and Claus Wittich. 2 vol. Berkeley: University of California Press. Original edition, 1922.

Weber, Max. 1991. *The Protestant Ethic and the Spirit of Capitalism*, translated by Talcott Parsons. London: Collins. Original edition, 1930.

Wood, Matthew. 2010. "The Sociology of Spirituality: Reflections on a Problematic Endeavour." In *The New Blackwell Companion to the Sociology of Religion*, edited by Bryan S. Turner. Oxford: Blackwell, 267–285.

Wrong, Dennis H. 1994. *The Problem of Order*. Cambridge, MA: Harvard University Press.

FURTHER READING

Beckford, James A. 2003. *Social Theory and Religion*. Cambridge: Cambridge University Press. [*This is a comprehensive discussion and assessment of how a broad range of social theoretical perspectives have shaped the contemporary study of religion, with a focus on how these contribute to a social-constructionist account of religion.*]

Levine, Donald. 1995. *Visions of the Sociological Tradition*. Chicago, IL: University of Chicago Press. [*This is an authoritative account of the diverse philosophical traditions that have contributed to the development of the sociological tradition and of their complex interrelations across the last two centuries.*]

Mellor/Shilling 2014 [*This is a systematic and comprehensive account of the evolving nature of the concept of the 'sacred' in social theory and its contemporary implications for making sense of a range of religious and non-religious phenomena.*]

Nisbet 1993 [*This is a highly influential discussion of the interaction of Enlightenment and counter-Enlightenment philosophical influences on the development of sociology, most notably with regard to the focus on the sacred as one of sociology's 'unit-ideas,' a focus that places the study of religion at the heart of sociology and social theory.*]

Turner, Bryan S. 1991. *Religion and Social Theory*. London: Sage. [*This was the first book-length study to address the key role of the body in social theories of religion, specifically with regard to the governmental regulation of bodies relative to problems of order.*]

PART III

MODES

CHAPTER 17

···

COMMUNICATION

···

VOLKHARD KRECH

CHAPTER SUMMARY

···

- Studying religion as communication is relevant, because in empiricism as well as in the study of religion something can only be identified as religious if it is communicatively addressed as such.
- Communication consists of the three elements of information, utterance, and understanding.
- Specifics of religious communication consist in ultimately coping with contingency on the basis of the distinction between immanence and transcendence.
- Religious semantics and the institutional framework of religious communication have to be analytically distinguished and synthetically related to each other.
- Inner and outer boundaries of religious communication have to be distinguished. Religious communication constitutes a self-referential societal system and at the same time differentiates from other forms of communication such as politics, economics, science, and arts. Differentiation is the basis for interaction between various forms of communication including religion.

INTRODUCTION

···

Choosing a communication theoretical approach is both plausible and difficult when treating the subject of religion. On the one hand, we would not know anything about the world of religious ideas if they were not communicated; similarly, experiences and actions would not be revealed to us as being religious, if their religious aspects had not been mentioned as such.[1] On the other hand, religion frequently claims that its contents

---

[1] Regarding the attribution of the senses by religious communication, cf. Pace 2011, 47ff.

cannot be communicated, or at least stresses the incommensurability between the subject of reference and the signification used to refer to it. Due to this ambiguity, approaching religious matters from the perspective of communication theory is not the most obvious choice to make. While the notions of experiencing and acting are paramount to established theories of religion, the notion of communication still has to assert itself.

The greatest asset of conceptualizing religion as a communicative phenomenon is the ability to avoid scientific sterility, i.e. avoiding a tendency to disregard religious self-description. Insofar as it follows a communicative approach, the study of religion is able to observe the procedure of religious communication, the ways in which this communication reflects upon and describes itself, and the means by which it sets itself apart from other kinds of communication. Thereby, correspondences between religious self-descriptions and scientific meta-language can be established without having to set into stone a fixed scientific understanding of religion in advance and thus enabling reflexivity between scientific observation and religious self-description.

Conceptualizing Communication

Communication theories are developed in the sciences (information theory, cybernetics, biology), as well as in the humanities and in social sciences (philosophy, psychology, sociology, ethnology, linguistics, semiotics, etc.). They are just as diverse as the disciplines from which they stem. Some theories are oriented towards the sender or utterance, while others focus on contents or center on the medium of communication. Marshall McLuhan (1911–1980), for example, regards the medium as the message (McLuhan 1964). By contrast, Paul Watzlawick (1921–2007) and others (Watzlawick/Beavin/Jackson 1967) hold that meanings are constituted through interpretation of the semantic dimension and the relational (syntactic) dimension of the message. One common feature of current communication theories is the conceptualization of the communicative process as tripartite. The long-prevailing sender–receiver model as advocated by older communication theories (Bühler 1934; Shannon/Weaver 1949) has been proven to be insufficient by semiotic and cybernetic findings. Rather than focusing on the sender and the receiver, the process of communication itself has moved to the fore.

Since the linguistic turn in philosophy, the social sciences, and cultural studies, there has been a minimum consensus among advocates of different communication theories that communication is to be understood as an interaction of information, utterance, and understanding. The core question, however, is what 'understanding' means. In this context, two important theories should be mentioned. The theory of communicative action (*kommunikatives Handeln*) outlined by Jürgen Habermas (1929–) conceptualizes communication as an intersubjective process, in which subjects try to understand each other, and each others' intentions and goals (Habermas 1981). By contrast Niklas Luhmann's (1927–1998) sociological systems theory sees understanding as a process within a communicative system, which proceeds by its own and has psychic systems (of individual and collective actors) as its environment. From this perspective, understanding means successful connection of a communicative operation to another. For a communicative operation to be successful, it needs to succeed in maintaining the system. Drawing on speech-act theory, Habermas defines communication as a form of intentional action (oriented towards understanding and consensus), whose felicity is dependent on conditions that have to be negotiated. Luhmann, on the other hand, defines actions as instances of communication, namely, as a kind of communication that is attributed socially—and thus also communicatively—to a person or to a collective entity.

Given the interplay of three different components—information, utterance, and understanding—communication is to be seen as conditioned by the contingent and unlimited range of possibilities, which have to be limited by social factors:

- Information has a specific, although polysemic content, which becomes clear through the process of understanding by distinguishing between information and utterance.
- An utterance can or cannot (as in the case of secrets or hegemonic knowledge) be conveyed and may take different shapes (e.g. delivered as speech-act, as written text, or as topicalized action).
- Understanding reflects the actually recognized difference between utterance and information and is a selection, insofar as there can be multiple ways of understanding something (a statement made by one person, for example, may be understood differently from the meaning intended and claimed by the speaker in the ensuing communication).[2] Understanding therefore does not mean grasping another person's feelings, motivation, and thoughts. Rather, understanding is part of communication itself, and psychic processes belong to its environment.

Communication is successful if it creates connections and if it is not hampered by conditions in its respective environment (e.g. by sleepiness or the lack of concentration of the psychic systems in face-to-face interactions). Generally, connections can be realized from an infinite number of possibilities; but not every context is an occasion for every content. For example, justifying a murder on religious grounds in court would fail to connect appropriately: in court, only arguments grounded in law and adhering to the corresponding rules and regulations are considered valid. An attempt to justify a crime on religious grounds would therefore likely not be successful in the legal context. Beyond the sender–receiver model, the self-reference of communication has to be considered.

The sociocultural context of the carriers involved in communication is determined by:

- language;
- worldview, forms of knowledge;

---

[2] On the difference between expression and meaning see Austin 1962; Searle 1979.

- experiences and the ways in which these are processed;
- ethos (norms, habitus, conduct of life);
- social status (social class);
- political events;
- social points of reference (such as group, associations, ethnicity, society, nation, mankind).

The institutional frame is shaped by the social forms in and through which communication takes place. There is a difference, for example, between communication as an informal face-to-face interaction (in the sense of an ephemeral encounter) and communication in a formal organization. Different contents usually overlap in different social forms. For instance, under certain sociocultural conditions persons usually chat on intimate issues only in a communication in the context of a friendship and not in a formalized framework—say between a customer and a clerk at a cashier's desk in a bank. Every social form (with the exception of fleeting face-to-face interaction), however, is subordinate to the primacy of a certain function. For example, monetary problems can be discussed within a religious group. However, this will usually be done in relation to the religious interpretative framework that unites the group.

The functional context of a given act of communication also determines the manner of threefold selection between information, utterance, and understanding. A customer telling a clerk in a bank about a religious revelation, during the process of making a deposit, will have a hard time creating conditions of understanding for successful religious communication. These would more likely be given in a sacred building, in a religious group, or in lifeworld communication about existential issues (e.g. death).

The communicative process is also influenced by the choice of signs used. In this respect, it is important to keep in mind that the sign relation also is tripartite. This is due to the fact that the interpretant—here in the sense of a certain communicative process rather than in the sense of a human actor—determines what is the case. This is done by connecting a quality (firstness) to an object (secondness) through ascription (thirdness). According to Charles Sanders Peirce (1839–1914), firstness covers everything that exists and how it exists insofar as it exists as it is regardless of anything other than itself; firstness stands for the quality of everything within the spectrum of rule and varying adaption, possibility and reality. Secondness covers everything that exists and how it exists insofar as it exists in relation with one or more others; secondness stands for development, connection, and actuality within the spectrum of identity and difference. Thirdness covers everything that exists and how it exists insofar as it constitutes mediating representation between a first and a second; thirdness stands for mediating existence within the spectrum of facticity and contingency. Furthermore, Peirce differentiates several ways of semiotically constructing meaning that are related to the three categories of firstness, secondness, and thirdness: *icons* as signs that express something by virtue of their qualities and properties (perceived, e.g. as impressions); *indices* as signs that have a spatial and temporal relation to their object; and *symbols* as conventional signs that establish a relation between the object and the quality attributed to it.

The three elements of a sign correspond to the three classes of signs, namely the means, which are used to denote something, the object that is referred to, and the interpretant, which establishes the relationship between means and object. The portrait of a person (means), for example, points to a certain person (object), but as a means of designation, it also conveys qualities, which are associated with the person by the interpretant. Someone looking at a painting of the crucifixion painted by Velázquez may for example say of this painting (which functions as the semantic interpretant) that it underlines the powerlessness (quality) of Jesus (object). Iconicity, indexicality, and symbolicity are by no means mutually exclusive classes. Rather, they represent aspects of the use of signs that can be realized within the framework of different media (speech-acts, texts, images, artifacts, etc.). A sign is characterized by iconic, indexical, and symbolic facets simultaneously; which one of these aspects is foregrounded is dependent on the communication process. Another person seeing the same painting by Velázquez (means) of the crucifixion of Jesus (object) might for example say that it stresses fortitude (quality) in the face of death. When these two persons discuss this one painting, religious communication in the form of a face-to-face interaction may be established (as the social interpetant). Here, it is not the two persons with their individual perceptions of the painting (as shaped by their respective religious attitudes) who act as interpretants, but rather the religious interaction itself.

Religious Communication

In the following, some particularities of the above-mentioned constituents, conditions, and contexts of communication will be discussed. This involves aspects of religious semiotics (see Yelle, "Semiotics," this volume) and semantics (see Gardiner/Engler, "Semantics," this volume), as well as the institutional frame. Religious communication is understood as an interplay of semantics and certain social forms, in which communication proceeds. Communication always consists of the interplay between semantics and social structures. Despite the heterogeneity involved, the perspective of a 'sociology of knowledge' has been a common feature of analyses in the study of religion since its beginnings: e.g. research into the relationship between myth (stressing its semantics) and ritual (as a specific social form). And in classics of the sociology of religion, both Max Weber (1864–1920), with his attention to the interplay of ideas and interests, and Ernst Troeltsch (1865–1923)—besides the representatives of the *Religionsgeschichtliche Schule*—figure here.[3]

---

[3] Since Karl Mannheim (1893–1947), this approach is termed *Wissenssoziologie* (sociology of knowledge); this term has been given different theoretical and methodological characteristics by Robert Merton (1910–2003), Thomas Luckmann, Peter L. Berger, Niklas Luhmann, and others.

Religiously Denoted Signs and Semantics

In order to identify religious communication—i.e. to differentiate it from other forms of communication—its semiotic and semantic particularities have to be scrutinized. Above all, this includes the analytically reconstructed distinction between immanence and transcendence. This is at work in formal respects where culture generally and religion in particular are taken into consideration. Both culture and religion are concerned with transcending. A relation to transcendence is not to be understood in the sense of Christian or other religious semantics of transcendence. Rather, it is given in a general, modal, and experience theoretical sense, namely as reference to something that is not part of awareness of the daily here and now, and as a reference to something that is not experienced as a genuine part of the self. This approximately corresponds to social phenomenologists' (Alfred Schütz [1899–1959], Peter L. Berger [1929–], and Thomas Luckmann [1927–]) understanding of transcending. According to this definition, there are many ways of transcending: ranging from religion and history to sociality (awareness of *alter ego*), ideals of order, imagining future, dreams, surprising experiences and events, the entire realm of art, and many more. If no distinction is made between the principle of transcendence as such and its religious shape—as second-order transcending—then everything outside of immediate experience of the here and now is religious, resulting in inflationary use of the term 'religion' (as illustrated by the reception of Luckmann's concept of 'invisible religion'; cf. Luckmann 1991).

From the perspective of communication theory, specifically religious relations to transcendence are differentiated from other such relations in the following ways: in their religious shape, immanent relations to transcendence are concerned with the problem of designating transcendence—which in principle cannot be conveyed—using immanent means. In other words: ways by which unavailable things and issues can be transformed into available ones and in which inexpressible things can be rendered expressible. 'Availability' in this context means that communication has access to conventionlized—i.e. immanent—ways of making sense of occurrences that do not evidentially make sense—i.e. that are transcendent. Of course, this is contradictory and cannot be achieved directly without any mediation. If heralding inexpressible transcendence were its only goal, religion would have to remain silent forever and thus would volatilize more and more out of the sociocultural reality, so that ultimately it would no longer exist—at least not as a social fact. Therefore, religion has to present transcendence by means of immanent (publicly available and well-known) signs in order to transform that which is unavailable into the semantically accessible. Religion has to denote the inexpressible through immanent means. Thereby, the paradox of attempting to speak of the inexpressible or to observe that which cannot be observed is concealed. This is done by using terms such as 'god' (set apart from 'world'), 'nothing' or 'emptiness' (as different from 'being'), *nirvāṇa* (as opposed to *saṃsāra*), 'divine kingdom' or 'paradise' (as different from the earthly realm), 'the end of the world' or 'apocalypse', καιρός as 'filled' or 'favorable time' (as different from 'ordinary time'), 'experience of the innermost self' (as a counterpart to the outside world), and so forth. These and other expressions are used to refer to spatial, temporal, and conceptually symbolized transcendence.

This task inevitably gives religious communication a tropic character, i.e. recourse to certain rhetoric figures such as metaphors, metonymy, and irony, on which religious communication is dependent to a greater degree than are other forms of communication. Religious communication allows seemingly novel and strange issues to be communicated through reference to familiar things and phenomena. Subjective experiences or exceptional events that escape communication by means of established communicative schemata can be conveyed: the unknown can be translated into familiar terms through religious communication. It usually hides its underlying paradoxes or—if the contradictions are explicit—solves them in a way that is evident for religious self-reflection. However, the solutions still remain paradoxical for other forms of communication such as politics, law, economics, arts, or science; the contradictions may appear once more within religion and have to be coped with over again. In religious communication, socially determined—and therefore observable—issues receive additional value that is not attributed to them in the context of other forms und circumstances of communication. "Forms of meaning are experienced as religious if their meaning refers back to the unity of the difference between observable and unobservable, if *for that* a form is found" (Luhmann 2013, 21). The choice of concrete sense of reference to transcendence (temporal, spatial, material, action, and cognitive-conceptual) is dependent on the cultural conditions and is determined by demarcation from—i.e. in relation to—other interpretations of the world, such as politics, economy, law, art, education, and medicine.

Religious communication is concerned with the particular interplay of iconicity (representation), indexicality (reference), and symbolicity (concept) of signs in the context of conveying mental states and social meaning. This interplay is condensed in certain religious icons, which hide the arbitrary relation between the means and objects of signs. But religious icons may also be unfolded again in the communicative process. The dynamics of religious communication is grounded in the fact that the relationship of iconicity, indexicality, and symbolicity can be modified time and again in various and extraordinary ways. Transferred to our previous example of the painting by Velázquez: two people may thoughtfully ponder the crucifixion scene. They may quarrel over its salvatory value or judge its display of light and shadow. The first debate would constitute a case of religious communication on a religious icon which is observed as the presence of salvation (i.e. as the congruence between means and meaning of the picture), the second would be an art-related discussion which constitutes the picture as an aesthetic icon stressing the communicated sense-perception. Apart from this, there are also other interpretants, such as texts that interpret the symbol of the cross or of the crucifixion with regard to Christology. In this case, the arbitrary relation between the means of depicting and the reference of the picture becomes obvious. Or the painting might be offered in an auction catalogue making it the subject of economic considerations. In this case, the index of the picture would consist of an economic item.

This example also reveals that there is no such thing as religion per se and that nothing exists only by virtue of its capacity of being religiously relevant. When examining the analytical disambiguation of a situation or an issue, possible polysemyic meaning and ambiguity always has to be considered; there is no single event, no material object, and no sense-perception whose meaning is exclusively determined by religion. 'The church' for example is not only a religious organization—there are always other tasks in the realms of, for example, administration, economy, politics, education, and occasionally art that have to be attended to. Nor is it a physical structure dedicated solely to religious services, but rather a public space that may also be used in relation to museum and tourism matters, etc. Similarly, no word, phrase, text, image, or act is per se and exclusively religious. It is only through such ascription within the framework of self-referential religious communication (i.e. communication referring to itself as religious and prevailing as such) that issues, events, and objects are determined and disambiguated as religious.

The Institutional Framework of Religious Communication

Besides the semantic particularities, religious communication is characterized by a peculiar interplay of extension and limitation (Luhmann 1989, 271ff.). On the one hand, its tropic (in rhetoric respects 'embellishing') character generates excess of meaning that transcends the meaning of everyday language and is largely detached from the realm and control of sensual perception and of practical requirements. But in order for it to be conveyable, intelligible, and acceptable—to function as a means of legitimation and reassurance and thus to have the status of a 'social fact'—this excess of meaning has to be limited socially.

This is done, for example:

- through socially regulated modes of interpretation which qualify certain facts, events, acts, objects, times, and places as religious—for instance by means of reading entrails or observing the flight of birds, astrology and other mantic practices, or through visions and audition;
- through specification of certain signs and their use (such as kneeling before a cross or covering one's head inside a sacred building);
- through the development of fixed patterns and figures of speech (e.g. formulas), myths, texts, and their compilation (e.g. Talmud, Hebrew Bible, New Testament, and Qur'an);
- by establishing certain social forms, which—if not exclusively, then predominantly—are devoted to religious communication (such as religious groups, movements, schools, orders, organizations, rituals, conduct of life);
- by processing topics from lifeworld communication which lend themselves to religious communication (e.g. biographical or collective crises and their resolution, death being the most common topic).

The limitations that are imposed on the excess of meaning generated in religious communication contribute to the creation of memory, of traditions, of a sense of origin, and belonging or identity. They constitute a kind of institutionalization and may be solidified or liquefied again over time. Paradoxically, these forms of limitations imposed on religious communication—in serving their purpose of dealing with contingency—throw into sharp relief this same contingency: other religious traditions make different choices, and this becomes apparent where religions make contact. Furthermore, the limitations are dependent on context and lead to semantic solidification, which may be rendered incompatible with social and cultural developments and altered conditions of reception as time passes. For these reasons—not least through diachronic and synchronic contacts between religions—there is recurring semantic extension of the excess of meaning, generation of new (or amalgamated) signs, patterns of speech, visualizations, and texts. The extension may trigger processes of deinstitutionalization, or it may change existing social forms: e.g. through glosses, commentaries, and new approaches to interpretation. These glosses, commentaries, etc. may also generate new social forms, such as new strata, groups, schools, teacher–pupil connections, and corresponding genealogical chains (classified as 'heterodox' or 'heretical' by religious object language). For certain kinds of religious communication, however, deliberate anachronism is a defining feature; for them, unchanging constancy (of a language [e.g. in the King James Bible], of a text, or a sacred building) is considered as 'tradition,' involving a meta-claim of authentic continuity with the past.

The Functional Context of Religious Communication

The primary function of religious communication consists in addressing and dealing with contingency, i.e. the realization that everything is as it is but could be different or decided differently at any time. The fact that religious communication topicalizes and deals with contingency, however, does not mean that this contingency is necessarily overcome. Religion may also produce contingency. For example, only those who actually believe in hell's existence can fear it. Where religious communication overcomes contingency, it translates the unfamiliar into the well known and closes open spaces of interpretation and action. It addresses the difference between a finite consciousness and a world of boundless communication and mediates by means of its signs.

Religious communication treats the difference in handling that which is unavailable and has to be considered unchangeably valid as opposed to that which is available, be it by attempting to make the unavailable available (as through sacrifice or prayer) or by expressly leaving the unavailable in an unresolvable tension with the available (as in 'mystical' communication). The distinction between transcendence and immanence is presupposed to be stable. The reification of the semantic concretion of this difference, however, varies diachronically and across cultures. These variations are at the heart of religious concern (diachronically and synchronically, interreligious, and intrareligious) and can be highlighted through research into religious history.

Inner and Outer Boundaries of Religious Communication

For religious communication to be identifiable as religious, it has to be set apart from other kinds of communication such as political, legal, economic, and scientific communication. This distinction does not mean that religious forms of communication should be analyzed in isolation. This pertains to both religious self-description and other kinds of communication (such as political, legal, economic, and scientific communication); social differentiation does not mean separation. This precondition is valid both for religious self-description and for scholarly reconstruction. One prominent option is differentiating between system and environment. With regard to systems theory, this means, first of all, that a system organizes itself in order to delineate itself from its surroundings; such auto-organization constitutes the inner boundaries of a system. But secondly, no system can exist without constant adaption to its environment, through which the outer boundaries of a system are generated. Thus, inner boundaries are those which religion constitutes by self-reference, while outer boundaries are the other side of the coin, namely those boundaries that religion constitutes in relation to other societal systems such as politics, economics, science, law, arts, education, and medicine. Religious communication is identifiable as a system through considering the distinction between immanence and transcendence as its special code (with semantic concretions such as available/unavailable, blessed/cursed, etc.), without neglecting connections to other social phenomena, such as religious processing of political communication and vice versa. The criteria of topicalization of contingency, as well as the differentiation between transcendence and immanence are relevant to the religious system. Other social systems, such as politics, economy, law, science, medicine, social aid, or art may, on the other hand, take recourse to religious elements without turning into religious communication. A political speech, for example, may contain eschatological motifs while still remaining part of political communication, as it is based on the distinction between power and powerlessness and primarily concerned with votes and not with, for example, questions of salvation in the face of 'the end of all things.' Self-referential religious communication and processes of sacralization—where religious elements are used for non-religious purpose—should be distinguished analytically, in order to determine the inner and outer boundaries of religion as opposed to other kinds of communication, and to simultaneously allow for consideration of the use of religious elements in other contexts (cf. Krech 2011). At the same time the study of religion, as is inspired by systems theory, assumes that this differentiation is also empirically at work. In addition, this differentiation can be useful where—historically or in intercultural comparison—there is not yet or no longer any systemically differentiated social structure.

The inner boundaries can best be elucidated scientifically if one keeps as closely as possible to empirical self-description and reflection in object language. Inner-religious reflection is amplified whenever (a) anachronistic traditions are addressed, meaning they are compiled, reformed, or rejected (diachronically stimulated religious reflection), or (b) solidified or solidifying religious traditions come into contact with others (synchronically stimulated religious reflection). This generates discursive fields that are

designated by object-language concepts such as εὐσέβεια, δεισιδαιμονία (Greek), *fides,*
pietas, superstitio, religio (Latin—and the words derived from these terms in Roman languages and in German), *dhamma, sāsana* (Pali), *dharma* (Sanskrit), *sanjiao* (Chinese),
śaśin (Mongolian), *dāt* (Hebrew), *dīn* (Arabic), and *shūkyō* (Japanese) (Schmitz 1996;
Haußig 1999; see Casadio, "Historicizing and Translating Religion," this volume).

Family resemblance can be used in identifying basic religious terms in which religious semantics are compressed. Such similarities are defined by Ludwig Wittgenstein
(2008) as properties of terms that evade sufficient description through categorial and
hierarchical systematics, since terms have blurred boundaries and may tend to evade
categorization. Thus, family resemblance means that words and their references that are
considered as being connected by essential common features may in fact be related by a
series of overlapping similarities, where no one feature is common to all. From a logical
point of view, such family resemblance is a relation of equivalence that generates classes:

1. reflexive (consequently, we cannot simply map different terms onto each other
   and subsume them categorially);
2. symmetrical (similarities can nonetheless be discerned);
3. transitive (the act of translating respective semantics or setting them into relation,
   e.g. via commentaries, is directional and may entail adjustments).

The process of drawing family resemblance both in religious self-description and in
scientific reconstruction oscillates between categorization and typification. It is suitable
for identifying certain terms diachronically, without having to employ one single understanding of religion. But it is also suitable for observing the ways in which religious traditions synchronically identify one another as religious. A representative (e.g. a person,
a text, or a collective) of a certain cultural entity for which it/(s)he does not have an
explicit and precise notion of religion may in a situation of contact be able to construct a
notion in the sense of a family resemblance, namely through contact with a representative of a cultural entity which has established a certain notion of religion. On the other
hand, the representative who has an understanding of 'religion' may also adapt it to the
adequate term generated by the other representative and to its mode of usage.

One example for the first of the above-mentioned cases is the introduction of the term
shūkyō (literally: "religious teaching") to Japan (Josephson 2012). On the one hand, the
term was generated as a translation of the Western notion of religion and is oriented
towards the notion of a religion grounded in certain dogmas. On the other hand, it also
has a certain independence. The second case described above is exemplified by *De vera
religio*. In his writing, Augustine of Hippo (354–430 CE) takes the term *religio*—which
he first took over from Roman use (e.g. by Cicero [106–43 BCE])—and first applies it
to Manichaeism and then connects it to Christianity after his own conversion. These
developments of object language have to be examined in order to gain meta-language
terminology, so that the latter is in correspondence with religio-historical object language. This is a way in which sterile scientism that neglects religious self-description
through object language can be avoided. In this sense, science, as well as law and

politics—each in its own way and communicative context—partake in the identification of religious communication. Ideally, this is done through interaction with object-level self-description of religious communication.

The outer boundaries of religious communication—i.e. the identification of religion in relation to other societal systems—are *inter alia* constituted through ranges of terms, whose meanings are closely related, but nonetheless are characterized by specific semantic differences that point towards specifically religious meaning. Among such ranges of terms are, for example:

- belief, faith, certainty, wisdom, knowledge;
- superstition, error, nonsense;
- looking, theoretical and mystical seeing, recognition;
- rite, liturgy, routine, habit;
- prophecy, divination, prognosis;
- providence, law, order.

With this process, it is important to consider the context in which the terms are used to grasp possible semantic differences or polysemy of one and the same term. After all, as mentioned previously, no word can be defined by itself as exclusively religious. An unexpected utterance, for example, may be put to different uses in different contexts: within a newly established religious movement, it may be considered prophetical; in another context—namely from a distinct perspective that claims religious truth—it may be seen as superstition; in a third context, say by a psychologist, it may be interpreted as psychopathological; or in a fourth context, such as a political speech, it might be used to refer to an ideal order or to foster a political attitude. In the first two cases, the boundaries of the religious field are determined from the inside, namely as 'true' or 'false' religion. In the third and fourth contexts, the outer boundaries are constituted by differentiation between religion and other forms of communication.

Even if intense scrutiny should reveal the absence of such chains of terms or of the mentioned semantic differentiation of the same term for different times or cultural contexts, this would be a valuable result in itself. Where such markers of differentiated religious communication cannot be discerned, this might be taken to indicate that—in these cases—there is no social differentiation and thus no existence of religion.[4]

GLOSSARY

Boundary the distinguishing structure between a system and its environment. It has an inner side, from which the system perceives 'environmental noise', transforming it into self-referential meaning, and an outer side, which constitutes itself through relations between one system and another observed by a third position in another system.

---

[4] I would like to thank Vivian Strotmann for translating the text. The chapter is based on Krech 2012.

Environment within systems theory 'the other side' of a system, on which the system is dependent, but to which it can only refer through external reference that has to be balanced with self-reference. For the system the environment contains only noise that has to be transformed into meaning via the system's self-reference.

Immanence/transcendence distinction the basic code of religious communication. Each side of the distinction only has meaning if it refers to the other side. While immanence consists of everything of the sociocultural reality that is perceivable, effable, conceivable, and thus available, transcendence hints at the opposite, namely at the unperceivable, ineffable, inconceivable, and thus unavailable. Transcendence therefore has to be indicated with immanent means. This constitutes the main religious paradox which has to be solved within religious communication and, since it appears again and again, to be hidden once more. The immanence/transcendence distinction is a formal one and is semantically filled within religious communication—e.g. through heaven and earth, the future (or past) of salvation and the baleful presence, etc.

Object language a meta-language makes statements about statements in an object language. In the study of religion, object language is the language of the empirical material in the history of religion, while scientific concepts belong to the meta-language of the study of religion.

Religious communication sorry, you have to read the chapter to understand this notion.

Sacralization in contrast to self-referential religion, other societal forms of communication refer to religious elements used for non-religious purpose in order to auratize the respective rationale. For example, a certain position in the political system can refer to religious elements such as an apocalyptic worldview to gain more political power.

System within systems theory the basic entity. It emerges and reproduces itself by (a) system-reference and (b) by constituting a boundary between the system and its environment to which it constantly has to adapt in order to survive.

REFERENCES

Austin, John L. 1962. *How to Do Things with Words*. Cambridge, MA: Harvard University Press.

Bühler, Karl. 1934. *Sprachtheorie: Die Darstellungsfunktion der Sprache*. Jena: G. Fischer.

Habermas, Jürgen. 1981. *Theorie des kommunikativen Handelns*, 2 vols. Frankfurt a.M.: Suhrkamp.

Haußig, Hans-Michael. 1999. *Der Religionsbegriff in den Religionen: Studien zum Selbst- und Religionsverständnis in Hinduismus, Buddhismus, Judentum und Islam*. Berlin: Philo.

Josephson, Jason Ānanda. 2012. *The Invention of Religion in Japan*. Chicago, IL and London: University of Chicago Press.

Krech, Volkhard. 2011. *Wo bleibt die Religion? Zur Ambivalenz des Religiösen in der modernen Gesellschaft*. Bielefeld: Transcript.

Krech, Volkhard. 2012. "Religion als Kommunikation." In *Religionswissenschaft* (De Gruyter Studium), edited by Michael Stausberg. Berlin and New York: de Gruyter, 49–62.

Luckmann, Thomas. 1991. *Die unsichtbare Religion*. Frankfurt a.M.: Suhrkamp. Original edition: *The Invisible Religion: The Problem of Religion in Modern Society*. New York: Macmillan, 1967.

Luhmann, Niklas. 1989. "Die Ausdifferenzierung der Religion." In *Gesellschaftsstruktur und Semantik: Studien zur Wissenssoziologie der modernen Gesellschaft*, vol. 3. Frankfurt a.M.: Suhrkamp, 259–357.

Luhmann, Niklas. 2013. *A Systems Theory of Religion*. Stanford, CA: Stanford University Press.

McLuhan, Marshall. 1964. *Understanding Media: The Extensions of Man*. New York: McGraw-Hill.

Pace, Enzo. 2011. *Religion as Communication: God's Talk*. Farnham and Burlington, VT: Ashgate.

Schmitz, Bertram. 1996. *"Religion" und seine Entsprechungen im interkulturellen Bereich*. Marburg: Tectum.

Searle, John. 1979. *Expression and Meaning: Studies in the Theory of Speech Acts*. Cambridge and New York: Cambridge University Press.

Shannon, Claude Elwood and Warren Weaver. 1949. *The Mathematical Theory of Communication*. Urbana: University of Illinois Press.

Watzlawick, Paul, Janet H. Beavin, and Don D. Jackson. 1967. *Pragmatics of Human Communication: A Study of International Patterns, Pathologies, and Paradoxes*. New York: Norton.

Wittgenstein, Ludwig. 2008. *Philosophische Untersuchungen* [*Philosophical Investigations*], 4th edition. Frankfurt a.M.: Suhrkamp. Original edition, 1953.

FURTHER READING

Beyer, Peter. 2006. *Religions in Global Society*. London and New York: Routledge. [*An (unconventional) application of Luhmann's systems theoretical approach to the study of religion.*]

Luhmann, Niklas. 1995. *Social Systems*, translated by John Bednarz Jr. and Dirk Baecker. Stanford, CA: Stanford University Press. [*A general approach to sociology as systems theory. Difficult to read, but worth the effort. The book does not concentrate on the sociology of religion, but occasionally refers to religious issues from the perspective of sociological systems theory (e.g. 63, 114, 123, 155, 185, 191, 200f., 211, 237, 301f., 311, 343, 400f., 454, 461).*]

Merrell, Floyd. 2001. "Charles Sanders Peirce's Concept of the Sign." In *The Routledge Companion to Semiotics and Linguistics*, edited by Paul Cobley. London: Routledge, 28–39. [*Merrell provides an overview of the semiotic approach of Charles Sanders Peirce, more approachable than the original writings.*]

Morris, Charles W. 1946. *Signs, Language, and Behavior*. New York: Prentice-Hall. [*The book further develops Peirce's semiotic approach. The book's distinction between semantics (meaning), syntactics (relation between elements of meaning), and pragmatics (the use of language) is its most important contribution to semiotics.*]

Pace 2011 [*Pace applies systems theory to the study of religion, mainly Roman Catholicism, and paradigmatically conceptualizes religion as communication.*]

Wittgenstein, Ludwig. 1974. *Philosophical Grammar*, edited by Rush Rhees and translated by Anthony Kenny. Oxford: Blackwell. [*A philosophical approach to language; useful for understanding the interplay between semantics, syntactics, and pragmatics.*]

CHAPTER 18

MATERIALITY

DAVID MORGAN

CHAPTER SUMMARY

- Beginning with the material turn in the study of religions, this chapter explores the relevance of the study of materiality in recent developments in the study of religion.
- Arguing that material culture studies is actually as old as the modern study of religion, the chapter traces the development of the material turn as a response to post-structuralism's focus on textuality.
- Merleau-Ponty's phenomenology of perception leads us to a more productive study of embodiment and works effectively with network studies as a way of robustly grounding the study of religion in the configuration of human and non-human agencies.
- Three examples illustrate how material analysis draws attention to the materiality of enacting the presence of saints; the materiality of prayer; and embodiment as a primary medium of religious formation.

Study of the materiality of religion is nothing new. Archaeology, art history, architectural studies, and physical anthropology have long contributed to the study of religions as material phenomena. Each of these approaches has shaped the study of religion through the work of several important scholars such as Austen Henry Layard, Lewis Henry Morgan, Augustus Henry Fox-Lane Pitt-Rivers, and James Henry Breasted (Layard 1853; Morgan 1897 [1879]; Pitt-Rivers 1906; Breasted 1912). It is impossible to imagine the study of the ancient Near East without the generations of important archaeological excavations; Greek and Roman religion without the attention of art and architectural historians over the last several centuries; or prehistoric and Neolithic peoples without the work of physical anthropologists and paleontologists scrutinizing garbage heaps, burial remains, ancient latrines, and village and encampment ruins; or aboriginal peoples without their architecture, hunting, textile, and ceramic technologies. Much of this kind of material culture continues to haunt the modern imagination.

Think only of the long afterlife of Stonehenge, the Pyramids at Giza, the Great Wall of China, or the Incan stone structures of Cuzco. So it is neither novel nor difficult in this respect to argue for the relevance of the study of the materiality of religions. Yet it remains true that the discipline in the twentieth century was most distinctively shaped by philological studies of scriptures, by analysis of kinship, by structuralist interpretations of myth, and by philosophical studies of cosmology and religious ontology. Still, there is substantial precedent for material analysis of objects and sites as primary evidence for the study of religious history. And the broad shift in the discipline in the later twentieth century toward the study of gender, sexuality, media, ritual, performance, and sacred space is the setting for what has been widely called 'the material turn' in the study of religion.

The Material Turn (from Textualism)

In view of the much older interest in material culture, what does it mean to speak of the more recent 'material turn' in the humanities in general and the study of religion in particular? The study of ancient material culture is typically occasioned by need: quite often this is some of the only evidence that has survived. And what can be gleaned from pottery fragments, garbage, amulets, decorative schemes, technological devices, and iconography is often enough to corroborate, challenge, or completely reframe what the venerable textual sources such as the Bible have been taken to mean about ancient history and culture. More recent material culture studies have expanded the scope of material evidence to include not only what materials do and evince, but how materiality as a range of cultural activities is formed. This has meant that the study of religious materiality applies equally to modern religious life as to ancient. And it means that the materialization of the study of religion portends far more than marshaling evidence of material artifacts. The task of the so-called material turn is to explore how religions are material phenomena even while they are also spiritual, ethical, intellectual, metaphysical, and linguistic at the same time.

Also relevant is the way in which material culture studies have always focused on the material artifact, the physical object, as the principal evidence and subject of interpretation. But the materiality of religion is about more than objects alone. It is embodied, emplaced, and enacted, to use the categories offered by Vásquez (2011). Studying the materiality of religion means examining the production of beliefs, practices, ideas, institutions, persons, groups, states, artifacts, and bodies as the ongoing work of social organization and cultural rites and imaginaries. The materiality of religion consists of how feeling, gathering, teaching, learning, punishing, celebrating, hating, adoring, speaking, dressing, eating, breathing, seeing, hearing, touching, and tasting make religion happen. The material turn in the study of religion entails the development of methods that will yield accounts of the materialization of religion.

Semiology and Poststructuralism

In the context of the recent history of cultural interpretation, the material turn in the study of culture and society means the turn away from structuralism's and deconstructionism's tendency to regard everything as a text, as a discursive formation of one sort or another. Whether it is the semiology of Ferdinand de Saussure or Jacques Derrida's grammatology, the notion that signifiers bear no other than arbitrary relations to signifieds means that knowledge is a play of signs and that power is a discursive formation that enforces certain connections and ignores or censures others. What matters is the difference between signifier and signified. Human knowledge never transcends this field of semiological play (see Tremlett, "(Post)structuralism" and Yelle, "Semiotics," this volume). Language is the stuff life is made of. In the study of religion, one finds the implications of this approach most fully and influentially operationalized in the work of Jonathan Z. Smith, where all talk of place and space is ultimately a metaphor for the relations among arbitrary signifiers. "Ritual is, above all," as he puts it succinctly, "an assertion of difference" (1987, 109). Smith's approach assumes that the sacred is defined largely, if not entirely by cognitive distinctions. There is no sacred without the ritual that consecrates a difference as definitive of sacred and profane. Sacrality is a way of knowing how the world is or works in a particular way. At heart, the sacred is an epistemological structure with immediate social or communal consequences.

But textuality or the difference machine is only one way to know the world. When ritual is seen as a statement or assertion of the way the world ought to be, it becomes a map that is different from what it describes, as Smith has pointed out. In practice, however, such a distinction often does not hold. Things have a way of becoming what they refer to. Christians stroke the images of their saints, kiss them, rub their hands and clothing against shrines, make pilgrimage to the place where a martyr died, pray before relics, collect the dirt around a monument or tomb, drink holy water, consume the Eucharistic body of their deity. In each case, people are not content to have 'meaning' mediate their relationship to what they regard as sacred or holy. What they do is not about or does not merely signify or symbolize the sacred, but embodies it. Materialization is the intermingling of sign and referent. Contact with the sacred is what matters. In the case of saints and ancestors, relationship is enduring contact. Devotees of a saint maintain an ongoing relationship that may not be unilateral or prescribed by the normative strictures of an official cult. It is not the stipulation of an ideal, but itself a living relationship replete with disappointment, frustration, intimidation, forgetfulness, adoration, and compassion, all going both ways (Orsi 1996; 2005).

Beyond Textualism: Semiotics

The limits of the textualist approach became evident as scrutiny of practice and lived religion recovered the body as a process of formation. Embodiment has become a new focus of interest among many scholars, influenced by a range of intellectual dispositions, from ethnography to Merleau-Ponty's phenomenology of perception (in contrast to the much criticized tradition of the phenomenology of religion), feminist and gender studies, the history and anthropology of the senses, and more recently the study of affect and emotion (e.g. Csordas 1994; Hermkens 2005; Schmidt 2000; Atran 2002; Corrigan et al. 2000; see Taylor 1998). Bodies, animals, and objects, their complex and integral relations, and their relation to speech and textuality pressed the investigation of religion in new directions. In his study of Dutch Calvinism in Indonesia, anthropologist Webb Keane (2007) has shown that the Protestant project was dedicated to sorting out and asserting the strong difference between signs, things, and people as a way of establishing the Protestant faith among the Sumba people. The indigenous culture, in their view, failed to make the requisite distinctions, which were evident in what they considered the idolatrous idea of animated things, talking animals, and humans influenced unduly by them. The Protestant missionaries sought to 'modernize' the culture by disenchanting it, separating signs and referents such that signifier and signified would be clearly distinguished.

Keane sought to expand the register of his cultural analysis beyond language, which was of course the focus of Dutch Calvinist missionaries in Indonesia. He shifted from the semiological model, which privileges language as textuality, to the semiotic approach of Charles Sanders Peirce. For Peirce, the symbol or arbitrary sign was only one among many other semiotic phenomena to be catalogued and studied. Two other forms of signs composed a major triad along with the symbol: icon and index. Both of these were in some sense materially motivated signs: the icon participates in its referent, bearing likeness; and the index bears a causal relation to what it signifies, as with a bullet hole in a window or the strokes of paint on a canvas and the brush and movement of the painter's arm that created them. Both icon and index introduce modes of presence in the experience of the sign, whereas the symbol stands in the place of its referent and therefore turns on absence. Written words mark the loss of sound, one might say, whereas icons and indices more than recall the referent, but seem to body it forth. Whether they actually do or not is another question: after all, pictures can be made up to appear to resemble referents that were never actually pictured and the hole in a window might actually have been caused by a stone or arrow. In any case, semiotics re-embodies the study of culture.

Others have found this approach helpful in the study of religion in other parts of the world (Engelke 2007; 2012; Meyer 2011; Yelle 2013), and the semiotic approach certainly helps turn a corner on the long dominance of structuralism and many forms of post-structuralism. It also helpfully stresses that materiality is about more than objects. It is about embodiment and sensation, social relations, devotion, taxonomies of cultural classification, epistemology, and the social nature of speech utterances and texts as artifacts.

MATERIAL CULTURE AND PHENOMENOLOGY

All this has worked importantly toward recognizing the materiality of religions as a field of study. Another major source of influence has been material culture studies. This approach has developed since the 1980s and has drawn on work beyond the study of religion. In the United States scholars of domestic and industrial culture had developed a broad literature by the 1980s, which examined landscaping, the built environment, furniture, tools, machinery, and product design. Cultural geography and archaeology contributed to this research in significant ways. Thomas Schlereth was a leading figure and edited a useful research guide in 1985, gathering the work of some of the most influential authors in the United States. In his examination of definitions of material culture studies, Schlereth points out that definitions of 'material culture' treat it as a synonym for 'artifacts,' 'objects,' or 'things.' And he recognized the usefulness of the term 'material culture' to consist of its suggestion of, "at least among its current students, a strong interrelation between physical objects and human behavior" (1985, 3). Moreover, he wrote, the term "simultaneously refers to both the subject of the study, material, and to its principal purpose, the understanding of culture" (1985, 3). But he continued to understand 'culture' as a prior intellectual or volitional state that is expressed in objects "since material culture is not actually culture but its product" (1985, 4). He defined material culture as "that segment of humankind's biosocial environment that has been purposely shaped by people according to culturally dictated plans" (1985, 5). Things express mind, which comports with the view of the nineteenth-century archaeologist who pioneered the collection, study, and display of material artifacts, Augustus Pitt-Rivers, and whose definition of material culture in an essay of 1875 Schlereth quoted: "outward signs and symbols of particular ideas in the mind" (Schlereth 1985, 1; Pitt-Rivers 1906, 23).

This distinction between mind and objecthood is problematic for many reasons. Some have wanted to mark the distinction of the material turn from the older model of material culture studies by the term 'materiality,' suggesting that material culture is a conceptual focus that remains on humanity whereas materiality refers to the much broader domain of non-human material conditions (Hazard 2013). This is plausible, although it is important to assert that the study of material culture hardly need endorse the older dualism that Pitt-Rivers and Schlereth maintain. Blurring their stark inner/outer difference seems desirable in order to topple the ontological prejudices that invariably sneak into the study of human culture. Thinking is embodied, relying on what has been called 'distributed cognition' in the study of external devices that assist computation or memory (Hollan/Hutchins/Kirsh 2000; Sutton 2010) or the role of feeling, intuition, imagination, or aesthetic judgment as non-rational faculties that shape cognition (Schusterman 2012). A strong distinction between matter and spirit does not comport with the neurological or aesthetic study of cognition. The idea of outward signs and inner ideas urges a dualism that locates human beings, or at least their abstract consciousness, at the center of reality and places everything else in orbit about them. It also forfeits the agency of objects, and it conforms to the traditional definition of religion as a cluster of creeds, doctrines, and beliefs that shortchanges the material reality of practice and embodiment. If the study of the materiality of religions can offer anything concrete and unique to understanding a religion, it should begin with the powers attributed to objects by religious devotees. No account of a religion should ignore the allure of place, the ability of objects to heal or protect, the investment of memory in images and objects, the presence of ancestors, saints, spirits in masks or portraits, the transformative capacity of ceremonial dress, or the importance of eating (see, for example, Garnett and Rosser 2013; Hahn 2012; Bynum 2011; Swearer 2004; Kohl 2003; Brown 2003). These material practices and others rely on things to do powerful cultural work that is inseparable from religion. Regarding them as no more than symbols or illustrations of ideas or beliefs succeeds only at splitting a human being into a mind and body. A number of important theorists have offered accounts dedicated to overcoming this dualist split (see, for instance, Vásquez 2011). Perhaps of greatest influence for the study of religion have been Maurice Merleau-Ponty's phenomenology of perception and the sociology of actor-network theory developed by Bruno Latour and a host of colleagues in Britain and France.

Merleau-Ponty took issue with the idea of a transcendental ego posited by Husserl as the overarching organizer of consciousness and knowledge, choosing instead to explore the overlooked share that perception contributed to the awareness of the world.[1] He dismantled the distance of mind and matter as well as body and world in order to understand in their continuity the intimate connectedness that is the matrix of consciousness. Sensation is not a coding of the world, not a transformation of sense-data into abstract information, but a communion, and one that Merleau-Ponty portrayed in mystical terms. He described looking at color in the following way:

> I give ear, or look, in the expectation of a sensation, and suddenly the sensible takes possession of my ear or my gaze, and I surrender a part of my body, even my whole body, to this particular manner of vibrating and filling space known as blue or red. Just as the sacrament not only symbolizes, in sensible species, an operation of Grace, but also the real presence of God ... in the same way the sensible has not only a motor and vital significance, but is nothing other than a certain way of being in the world suggested to us from some point in space, and seized and acted upon by our body ... so that sensation is literally a form of communion. (1962, 246; see Morgan 2012a)

---

[1] On the difference of Merleau-Ponty from Husserl regarding the distance of thinking from what is thought versus their fusion see Kwant (1967).

Network Theory

Actor-network theory has aimed at removing from human beings the centrality and exclusive claim to agency, arguing instead that any social event is the result of an extended network of actors (Latour 1992; see Day 2010; Stausberg 2010; Morgan 2014). The result breaks down subject–object dualism. The role of the actant includes human and non-human agents. For example, Alfred Gell considered the agency of artifacts in his anthropological study of art (1998, 16–19), and his ideas have influenced discussions of religious material culture (Kendall/Tâm/Hu'o'ng 2010; McDaniel 2011).

Even within the domain of human agency, the self is not understood to be sealed off or enclosed. Humans create technologies whose purpose is to have delegated to them the duties and behaviors that humans are very good at forgetting or neglecting. The result has been a redefinition of human selfhood as distributed rather than concentrated in the encapsulated interiors of the mind. Our bodies do not end at the fingertips, but continue in the diverse tools or technologies that extend our actions and link us to the world around and within us. In this way of thinking, a religion can be understood as a system of technologies for the body's interface with complex networks that join human and non-human actors in practices of exchange and interaction. These matrices of fields of interaction become invested in the authority of social relations that want to persist, resulting in standing orders of social arrangements. "Every established order," Bourdieu once observed, "tends to produce the naturalization of its own arbitrariness" (1977, 164). The resulting misrecognition freezes a configuration of forces and agents into an enduring ideology that subordinates one party to another's dominance.

This practice of power is what network theory, deeply influenced by Michel Foucault's work, can be understood to destabilize, contending that no system of domination is natural, but is made 'natural' in an artificial manner by investing a particular set of relations into the engineered environment of palaces, shrines, monuments, city plans, uniforms and dress keyed to station, sumptuary laws, and the display of authority or wealth in image, dwelling, and ritual. Latour has repeatedly argued that 'nature' is inseparable from culture, is indeed the work of culture, modernity's invention of a domain of inactive resources awaiting exploitation through the mind-controlled technologies that do humanity's bidding. Actor-network theory is a sociological project of showing how in fact this ideology misrecognizes causality and misses thereby the robust collaboration of human and non-human actors in the assemblages that are sociality. This allows us to begin to take *things* very seriously, recognizing that they are not inert or impotent or dead, but active in their own way in ecologies that envelop human beings even when they do not recognize their place in encompassing networks of action (Hodder 2012; Bennett 2010; Latour 2009). The implications for the study of religions and for the materiality of religions are considerable since a network approach encourages scholars to focus on the relations that structure religious experience and which some have recently stressed as a defining feature of religion (Orsi 2005, 5–6). Religion becomes understood not as a web of meanings, but of embodied relations among people, things, gods, saints, ancestors, places, and times.

The study of how a variety of agencies assemble in an interactive network has also helped scholars rethink the nature of medium. Things take their place within ecologies that accommodate their *affordances*, a term coined in 1986 by James Gibson to designate what an environment furnishes to organisms that thrive in it (1986, 127–130). He lists 'medium' as a primary instance of affordance since perception relies on the medium in which it occurs (130–131). By focusing on the material relations among agents, the material culture study of religions scrutinizes how the physical characteristics of objects, places, and human viewers shape the construction of what people experience as sacred. These characteristics afford certain possibilities, and therefore enable religions to happen the way they do.

THE EMBODIMENT OF DEVOTION

The operation of a network is visible in the devotional cult of the saints in Roman Catholicism. An image such as Our Lady of the Immaculate Conception shown here (Fig. 18.1), a solid cast of plaster about 14 inches tall, is displayed in bedrooms and on mantles in private homes, and on the altars of shrines and churches and monasteries, or in niches in Catholic institutions such as orphanages, schools, and hospitals. Faint writing on the bottom of Figure 18.1 indicates that it was a gift in the year 1955. Devotees encounter the statue in formal devotion, worship settings, or in passing. The figure presents itself for quiet contemplation. Her downcast gaze and outspread hands invite the viewer's inspection. The face is long, slender, and smooth, and shares the smooth surface of the entire piece. Her chest is slight, perhaps indicating her age, which appears late teenage, but surely also signaling her non-sexual character. The image resembles several other types of Mary. The iconography is unmistakable: a blue mantle over a white robe and a head draped in a white cloth are the most common dress of Mary. The hands spread at the sides recall the medieval portrayal of the Protective Madonna, spreading her cope wide to receive and guard the faithful, who were shown on a much smaller scale huddling in masses beneath her outspread hands. But the snake, stars, and globe on which she stands in Figure 18.1 are the iconography of the Immaculate Conception, a visual formula first developed in the middle of the seventeenth century in Spain. The doctrine asserted Mary's special role in the plan of salvation: since she was conceived without the taint of original sin, she was able to triumph completely over the serpent that had originally introduced sin or the fall from grace. The design derives from the revelation of Our Lady of the Immaculate Conception to Sister Catherine Labouré in 1830 (Fig. 18.2), in whose vision Our Lady appeared in a three-dimensional frame that included stars and a monogram, with rings on her fingers radiating light as favors sent from her to earth. It was a picture come to life as we might say Figure 18.1 is a medal

FIGURE 18.1 Our Lady of the Immaculate Conception, plaster, 1955. Photo by author.

morphed into a three-dimensional figure. The inscription on the medal refers to the Immaculate Conception: "O Mary, conceived without sin, pray for us who have recourse to you" (on the imagery of the Immaculate Conception and especially the Miraculous Medal see Seland 2010, 41–43).

The writhing snake at Mary's feet in Figures 18.1 and 18.2 invokes a primary biblical touchstone of the Immaculate Conception, Genesis 3:15, as it is rendered in the Vulgate, where God says to the serpent that has succeeded in urging Eve to disobey divine command, "I will put enmity between you and the women, and between your seed and her seed; she will crush your head" (*ipsa conteret caput tuum*). Mary reverses the fault of the first mother, and the Immaculate Conception, which freed her of the original sin caused by Eve, secures her capacity to do so. In the nineteenth century, the Immaculate Conception had become closely associated with a triumphalist view of Mary as vindicating divine will in a world that had become rebellious, hence the development of the

FIGURE 18.2 Miraculous Medal revealed to Catherine Labouré, 1830. With petition to Our Lady ("Oh Mary, conceived without sin, pray for us, who have recourse to you") in Portuguese. Photo by author.

iconography of standing on the globe, which was not an original aspect of the seventh-century visual formula. The Marian apparitions to Catherine Labouré and at Lourdes and later at Fatima (1917) affirmed the doctrine of the Immaculate Conception, which was officially promulgated in 1854 by Pius IX, whose enmity with modernity was highly charged. So Mary conducts what Catholic exegesis ascribed to her as the Mother of God who, from her high perch on the globe, showed her majestic triumph over evil in a world that seemed to many Catholics to have forgotten the prophecy of Genesis 3:15.[2]

---

[2] <http://buffaloah.com/a/east/149/2010nmural/nmural.html>, accessed July 23, 2014. On the use of the image in regard to the National Shrine of the Immaculate Conception in Washington, DC, see Tweed (2011, 158, 185–186, 211).

Some modern portrayals of the Immaculate Conception even show the continents on the globe as a way of signaling the special message of the Immaculate Conception. In 1847 Pius IX made the Blessed Virgin the patroness of the United States, which accounts for the appearance of North America in a 1920 painting of Maria Immaculate by the Benedictine monk, F. Raphael Pfisterer, in the church of St. Francis Xavier in Buffalo, New York.

As in Catherine Labouré's vision, Mary's outspread hands are sometimes shown streaming rays of light from the palms. Occasionally she even bears the marks of the crucifixion. The suggestion is that she participated in the work of redemption accomplished by her son, and indeed, this is work credited to her by those who regard Mary as the co-redemptrix. (The Medal of the Immaculate Conception received official approval by the Sacred Congregation of Rites on April 19, 1895.) For those going to Mary in prayer, beseeching her intercession on their behalf, she ably undertakes their requests because Jesus is her son and is devoted to her, but also because some have accorded Mary the special role of co-redemptrix in charge of the treasury of spiritual merits, which she may dispense at her discretion. The eighteenth-century Marian devotee, St. Louis Marie de Montfort, wrote:

> Because God gave her his Son, it is his will that we should receive all gifts through her, and that no heavenly gift should come down upon earth without passing through her as through a channel.
>
> Of her fullness we have all received, and any grace or hope of salvation we may possess is a gift which comes to us from God through Mary. So truly she is mistress of God's possessions that she gives to whom she wills, all the graces of God, all the virtues of Jesus Christ, all the gifts of the Holy Spirit, every good thing in the realm of nature, grace and glory. (Montfort 1988, 108)

The Material Culture of Enactment

The devout address Mary standing or kneeling before this statue, confident that she hears their prayers and will respond. Their act of engagement is not an intellectualized formulation of ideas, but utterances shaped by the tradition of piety and the affordances of the statue itself, that is, by the rhetorical disposition it presents to them, tenderly encouraging their response to her. The statue enacts their relation to Mary. The elements of the statue are not experienced as abstract symbols or emblems, as arcane meanings to be decoded, but as the miniature parts of a sacred theatre, a dramaturgy of a deeply felt relationship. The words inscribed about the medal are the utterance of bodies and breath, hope wrapped about the image of the one who will help. Standing on the globe, having defeated Satan, the Virgin showers graces on the earth. The iconography of the statue is not, therefore, a message bullet targeting the minds of the devout and impacting with prescribed contents, but is rather a gesture of invocation and an indication of what to expect. The faithful position themselves before her, hands in prayer, head bowed, body placed in the posture of intercession. They enact prayer with the statue. She is the interface for access to a celestial hierarchy, entry into an order of being that acts like a channel to Our Lady, to Jesus, and to the Heavenly Father beyond her. The structure of intercession consists of the entire history of dogma, liturgy, devotion, imagery, and practice that has shaped it down to the present moment. But all of this vanishes in the sweetness and delicacy of the statue, the interfacial node that brings the devotee to Our Lady.

An especially important implication of network theory is the recognition of the human body's integration into the surrounding and enabling ecology of objects, forces, and actions (on embodiment see, in the study of religion, Weiner 2014; Promey 2014; Morgan 2010; 2012b; Bynum 2011; Meyer 2006; and, more generally, Noland 2009; Howes 2005; Strathern 1996). The body is not alone, complete, or finished, but forever developing in practices and interactions that connect it to the broader world. Embodiment is a process, not a static mode of existence. The body is a plastic, adaptive, highly complex bio-technology that learns what Marcel Mauss called 'techniques of the body' for every sort of routine, from eating, sitting, running, swimming, and throwing a ball, to the more dedicated behaviors that constitute religious practices such as concentration, gestures of prayer and veneration, meditative breathing, stillness, and various ways of seeing, hearing, and touching (Mauss 1973). The body's plasticity and trainability as well as its perceptual faculties constitute a number of affordances that make it a diverse bio-technology. The world is made to look, sound, taste, and smell the way it does in concert with the regimentation of practices that parents, teachers, clergy, and worship styles impart to children, pilgrims, devotees, and converts. People learn to dress, sit, listen, walk, and perform devotional gestures in ways that enable them to participate viscerally in social bodies, the shared appearance and felt-knowledge that organizes people into corporeal kinship. A religious believer is what the believer does, and doing means more than prescribed action.

The Materiality of Prayer

One of the most common practices of believers in Christianity, Islam, Judaism and other religions is prayer. Although composed of words, prayers are highly formulaic, structured practices that position the body in particular postures that are widely practiced within individual traditions. Bowed heads, kneeling, prostration, folded hands, hands held upward and open, seated in church, kneeling in mosque, individual or group, before meals, at prescribed times of the day—the conventions are varied, but nevertheless carefully observed. Departure from the convention easily disrupts the state of mind and feeling that are deliberately cultivated as proper to the practice of prayer.

The embodied nature of prayer is evident, for example, in the Shi'a Muslim use of the *turbah*, which means earth or dirt, and traditionally consists of a molded disc or other shape of pressed but not baked clay (Fig. 18.3). The tablet generally carries Arabic

FIGURE 18.3 Turbah, Shi'ite clay prayer disc, c.2000. Photo by author.

text embossed on the surface and sometimes such schematic imagery as shown in the illustration here, a depiction of a mosque at Karbala, which enshrines the memory of Husayn ibn Ali, grandson of the Prophet, whom Shi'ites honor as the third imam, the heir of Mohammad, and therefore as the legitimate leader of the Islamic community. He was killed by a rival. Turbahs are customarily made of earth, but those composed of earth from Karbala are preferred. The turbah is placed on the ground before the devout, who in the course of prayer kneels and places the head down in prostration, touching the clay disc. The turbah receives the forehead, which is pressed against it and held in position there, resulting in a round mark in the flesh. On many turbahs the raised text is high enough to leave a clear indention in the skin. Around the central image of the mosque's dome and two minarets in Figure 18.3 are the names of the twelve imams, the successors of the Prophet who form the genealogy of spiritual rulers from Ali, son of Mohammad and father of Husayn, to the last imam, the Mahdi, a messianic figure who has entered occultation but will one day reappear with Jesus and re-establish righteousness and peace. Thus, the turbah shapes the act of prayer by enfleshing devotion to Shi'ism's leaders. Touching their names, touching the soil into which the prophet's slain grandson bled, is the somatic medium of prayer, of praising Allah. Prayer takes place on the earth and in the cosmology of Allah's creation of the world from earth, and in the sacred genealogy of Allah's servants, the lineage of his Prophet. And by bearing the mark of the earthen disc, those praying imitate the Prophet, imaging in their bodies the one who delivered God's words.

Embodiment as Religious Formation

The body is the medium of the most basic religious formation. In fact, the bodies of children are among the most lasting modes of religious learning since their formation installs practice in the memory of muscles and nerves that become the enduring register of religious feeling. Before abstract ideas are invested in the language of creeds and doctrines that are committed to memory, they are recited and performed in the movements, breathing, rhythmic recitation, and adjunct sensations that powerfully structure the minds and bodies of children. A few years ago I watched a teacher assemble a bustling group of young boys at the Temple Mount in Jerusalem. The boys were dressed alike in black pants and white shirt, the signature dress of Ultra-Orthodox Jewish males. Their teacher was clad entirely in black and wore the familiar hat, long beard, and curling locks of the Chabad Hasid. The boys gathered on this day to receive their first *siddur*, or prayer book. They also sported paper Torah crowns to celebrate the day. And each of them wore the *tzitzit*, a tassel or twisted length of threads that hung from their waists. The *tzitzit* is part of a garment worn beneath the shirt. Scripture commands Jewish men to wear garments bearing twisted or knotted threads from their corners (Deuteronomy 22:12; Numbers 15: 38–40) in order to remind them of the Exodus and to call attention to their religious duties. But these as well as their dress and common practices also signaled to others that they were Jews who were mindful of religious obligations. The assembly of boys, lining up as a single group in similar dress, fashioned a social body to which they belonged, from which they drew identity, and to which they contributed their person and future. Doing things together is not the same as doing them singularly. The effect of collective action on the individual is profound and something that cannot be achieved otherwise.

EVERYDAY LIFE, MATERIALITY, AND THE DEFINITION OF RELIGION

At work in a great deal of scholarship on materiality in religion over the last few decades have been theories of religion that foreground human relations, exchange, the body, and the performance of ritual and practice (Vásquez 2011). This took shape in direct response to the long-standing view that any religion is a particular scheme of beliefs, creeds, dogmas, or doctrines, and akin to a system of philosophical principles. This is probably the joint legacy of the Enlightenment and the dominance of Protestantism, which sorted out differences among religions in terms of prevailing beliefs. But as early as 1757, in his *Natural History of Religion*, David Hume suggested that religion had deeper roots in the human organism. He considered one of the most universal features of religion to be the "tendency among mankind to conceive all beings like themselves, and to transfer to every object, those qualities, with which they are familiarly acquainted, and of which they are intimately conscious. We find human faces in the moon, armies in the clouds" (Hume 2008, 141). This is a point that has not been missed by some advocates of the cognitive sciences as well as others for whom religion arises in part from a sense of the agency of objects. Hume's observation certainly serves to demonstrate that the study of religion has a genealogy that is larger than definition by rational argument or confessional formulae.

While Hume dismissed the 'natural propensity' of such animism as a mistake best "corrected by experience and reflection" (2008, 141), we can recover something of its vivacity and relevance through the models of agency that network studies provide, allowing us to take the power of objects more seriously. Understood as practices, religion can be said to happen materially—not merely to be signified by symbols and objects as representations of an inherently immaterial reality. Certainly, religions rely on such signage as symbolic devices to encapsulate beliefs and to signify important differences. But the material life of practice relies on much more than signs. Religion may be defined in concrete terms as the spaces, objects, clothing, food, sound, and other forms of sensation that organize relations among people and other beings—gods, demons, angels, saints— and the forces that surpass human control but are nevertheless accessible to negotiation of one sort or another. All of these material things consist of media that allow or afford a range of uses and experiences that organize and characterize religious practices, making any religion as much sensation as thought, as much feeling as abstract idea. Defined in this way, it is clear that religion is for many practitioners a thoroughgoing form of world-maintenance (Berger and Luckmann 1966). It is how people assemble and sustain their worlds, but do so in the medium of material practice. If, like many other approaches, social constructivism stresses discourse and language, material culture studies focus on things, enacted relations, and the dynamics of embodiment in order to understand how people put together their sense of reality and keep it in working order. Accordingly, the study of material religion scrutinizes felt-life, environment, practice, and embodiment, without which a religion would be no more than a floating cloud of ideas.

Glossary

Embodiment rather than treating the body as a biologically determined or fixed entity, embodiment casts attention on the processes of formation of the senses, of feeling, of gender and sexuality, techniques of using the body, and of concepts of purity, shame, and human relatedness. This approach regards the body as a complex and evolving medium in which religion takes shape.

Material culture not only the physical things and spaces that produce value in human life, but the practices and categories of sensation, imagination, feeling, perception, taste, and intuition that put things to work to form cognition within the matrix of the body.

Material turn the development in the 1980s and 1990s in the interpretation of culture that came to look beyond the textualism of poststructuralist thought, regarding things, spaces, food, dress, and bodies as the means of forming the body as a matrix or medium for religious practice and the production of value.

Network a key focus in work since the 1990s, inspired by the writings of Michel Foucault and Gilles Deleuze, and shaped most famously by Bruno Latour, which argues for understanding social phenomena as assemblages of human and non-human agencies.

Phenomenology of perception the key work of French philosopher Maurice Merleau-Ponty, who set out to recover the primary role of perception in human cognition. Opposed to the notion of mind as a separate 'thinking substance', Merleau-Ponty demonstrated the degree to which the body is enfolded into the world around it, thus subverting the dualist framework that has dominated the study of knowledge in modern philosophy.

References

Abt, Jeffrey. 2011. *American Egyptologist: The Life of James Henry Breasted and the Creation of His Oriental Institute*. Chicago: University of Chicago Press.

Atran, Scott. 2002. *In Gods We Trust: The Evolutionary Landscape of Religion*. Oxford: Oxford University Press.

Bennett, Jane. 2010. *Vibrant Matter: A Political Ecology of Things*. Durham, NC: Duke University Press.

Berger, Peter L. and Thomas Luckmann. 1966. *The Social Construction of Reality: A Treatise in the Sociology of Knowledge*. New York: Anchor, Doubleday.

Bourdieu, Pierre. 1977. *Outline of a Theory of Practice*, translated by Richard Nice. Cambridge: Cambridge University Press.

Breasted, James Henry. 1912. *Development of Religion and Thought in Ancient Egypt: Lectures*. New York: Charles Scribner.

Brown, David H. 2003. *Santería Enthroned: Art, Ritual, and Innovation in an Afro-Cuban Religion*. Chicago, IL: University of Chicago Press.

Bynum, Caroline Walker. 2011. *Christian Materiality: An Essay on Religion in Late Medieval Europe*. New York: Zone Books.

Corrigan, John, Eric Crump, and John Kloos. 2000. *Emotion and Religion: A Critical Assessment and Annotated Bibliography*. Westport, CT: Greenwood Press.

Csordas, Thomas J. 1994. *The Sacred Self: A Cultural Phenomenology of Charismatic Healing*. Berkeley: University of California Press.

Day, Matthew. 2010. "How to Keep It Real." *Method & Theory in the Study of Religion* 22(4): 272–282. doi: 10.1163/157006810X531058

Engelke, Matthew. 2007. *A Problem of Presence: Beyond Scripture in an African Church*. Berkeley: University of California Press.

Engelke, Matthew. 2012. "Material Religion." In *The Cambridge Companion to Religious Studies*, edited by Robert A. Orsi. Cambridge: Cambridge University Press, 209–229.

Garnett, Jane and Gervase Rosser. 2013. *Spectacular Miracles: Transforming Images in Italy from the Renaissance to the Present*. London: Reaktion.

Gell, Alfred. 1998. *Art and Agency: An Anthropological Theory*. Oxford: Clarendon Press.

Gibson, James J. 1986. *The Ecological Approach to Visual Perception*. New York: Psychology Press, Taylor & Francis.

Hahn, Cynthia. 2012. *Strange Beauty: Issues in the Making and Meaning of Reliquaries, 400–circa 1204*. University Park: Pennsylvania State University Press.

Hazard, Sonia. 2013. "The Material Turn in the Study of Religion." *Religion and Society* 4: 58–78. doi:10.3167/arrs.2013.040104

Hermkens, Anna-Karina 2005. "Engendering Objects: Barkcloth and the Dynamics of Identity in Papua New Guinea." PhD dissertation, University of Nijmegen.

Hodder, Ian. 2012. *Entangled: An Archaeology of the Relationships between Humans and Things.* Malden, MA: Wiley-Blackwell.

Hollan, James, Edwin Hutchins, and David Kirsh. 2000. "Distributed Cognition: Toward a New Foundation for Human–Computer Interaction Research." *ACM Transactions on Computer–Human Interaction* 7(2): 174–196.

Howes, David, ed. 2005. *Empire of the Senses: The Sensual Culture Reader.* Oxford: Berg.

Hume, David. 2008. *Principal Writings on Religion,* edited by J. C. A. Gaskin. Oxford: Oxford University Press.

Keane, Webb. 2007. *Christian Moderns: Freedom and Fetish in the Mission Encounter.* Berkeley: University of California Press.

Kendall, Laurel, Vũ Thị Thanh Tâm, and Nguyễn Thị Thu Hương. 2010. "Beautiful and Efficacious Statues: Magic, Commodities, Agency and the Production of Sacred Objects in Popular Religion in Vietnam." *Material Religion* 6(1): 60–85. doi: 10.2752/174322010X12663379393378

Kohl, Karl-Heinz. 2003. *Die Macht der Dinge: Geschichte und Theorie sakraler Objekte.* Munich: C. H. Beck.

Kwant, Remy C. 1967. "Merleau-Ponty and Phenomenology." In *Phenomenology: The Philosophy of Edmund Husserl and Its Interpretation,* edited by Joseph J. Kockelmans. Garden City, NY: Doubleday & Company, 375–392.

Latour, Bruno. 1992. "Where are the Missing Masses? The Sociology of a Few Mundane Artifacts." In *Shaping Technology/Building Society: Studies in Sociotechnical Change,* edited by Wiebe E. Bijker and John Law. Cambridge, MA: MIT Press, 225–258.

Latour, Bruno. 2009. "Will Non-Humans be Saved? An Argument in Ecotheology." *Journal of the Royal Anthropological Institute* 15(3): 459–475. doi: 10.1111/j.1467-9655.2009.01568.x

Layard, Austen Henry. 1853. *Discoveries in the Ruins of Nineveh and Babylon.* London: John Murray.

McDaniel, Justin Thomas. 2011. "The Agency between Images: The Relationships among Ghosts, Corpses, Monks, and Deities at a Buddhist Monastery in Thailand." *Material Religion* 7(2): 242–267. doi: 10.2752/175183411X13070210372706

Mauss, Marcel. 1973. "Techniques of the Body." *Economy and Society* 2(1): 70–88.

Merleau-Ponty, Maurice. 1962. *Phenomenology of Perception,* translated by Colin Smith. London: Routledge.

Meyer, Birgit. 2006. *Religious Sensations: Why Media, Aesthetics, and Power Matter in the Study of Contemporary Religion.* Amsterdam: Vrije Universiteit.

Meyer, Birgit. 2011. "Mediation and Immediacy: Sensational Forms, Semiotic Ideologies and the Question of the Medium." *Social Anthropology/Anthropologie Sociale* 19(1): 23–39. doi: 10.1111/j.1469-8676.2010.00137.x

Montfort, St. Louis Marie de. 1988. *The Love of Eternal Wisdom.* In *God Alone: The Collected Writings of St. Louis Marie de Montfort.* Bay Shore, NY: Montfort Publications.

Morgan, David, ed. 2010. *Religion and Material Culture: The Matter of Belief.* London: Routledge.

Morgan, David. 2012a. "The Look of the Sacred." In *The Cambridge Companion to Religious Studies,* edited by Robert A. Orsi. New York: Cambridge University Press, 296–318.

Morgan, David. 2012b. *The Embodied Eye: Religious Visual Culture and the Social Life of Feeling.* Berkeley: University of California Press.

Morgan, David. 2014. "The Ecology of Images: Seeing and the Study of Religion." *Religion and Society* 5(1): 83–105. doi: http://dx.doi.org/10.3167/arrs.2014.050106

Morgan, Hon. Lewis H. 1897. *On the Ruins of a Stone Pueblo on the Animas River in New Mexico, with a Ground Plan.* Salem: Salem Press. Original edition, 1879.

Noland, Carrie. 2009. *Agency & Embodiment: Performing Gestures/Producing Culture.* Cambridge, MA: Harvard University Press.

Orsi, Robert A. 1996. *Thank You, St. Jude: Women's Devotion to the Patron Saint of Hopeless Causes.* New Haven, CT: Yale University Press.

Orsi, Robert A. 2005. *Between Heaven and Earth: The Religious Worlds People Make and the Scholars Who Study Them.* Princeton, NJ: Princeton University Press.

Pitt-Rivers, Augustus Henry Fox-Lane. 1906. *The Evolution of Culture, and Other Essays,* edited by J. L. Myres. Oxford: Clarendon Press.

Promey, Sally M., ed. 2014. *Sensational Religion: Sensory Cultures in Material Practice.* New Haven, CT: Yale University Press.

Schlereth, Thomas J. 1985. "Material Culture and Cultural Research." In *Material Culture: A Research Guide,* edited by Thomas J. Schlereth. Lawrence: University Press of Kansas, 1–34.

Schmidt, Leigh Eric. 2000. *Hearing Things: Religion, Illusion, and the American Enlightenment.* Cambridge, MA: Harvard University Press.

Schusterman, Richard. 2012. *Thinking Through the Body: Essays in Somaesthetics.* Cambridge: Cambridge University Press.

Seland, Eli Heldaas. 2010. "Traveling Images: Our Lady of Lourdes in Popular Piety and Art." In *Mind and Matter: Selected Papers of Nordik 2009 Conference for Art Historians,* edited by Johanna Vakkari. Helsinki: Helsingfors, 33–49.

Smith, Jonathan Z. 1987. *To Take Place: Toward Theory in Ritual.* Chicago, IL: University of Chicago Press.

Stausberg, Michael. 2010. "Distinctions, Differentiations, Ontology, and Non-Humans in Theories of Religion." *Method & Theory in the Study of Religion* 22(4): 346–366. doi: 10.1163/157006810X531139

Strathern, Andrew J. 1996. *Body Thoughts.* Ann Arbor: University of Michigan Press.

Sutton, John. 2010. "Memory." *Stanford Encyclopedia of Philosophy.* <http://plato.stanford.edu/entries/memory/#MemDisCogSocSci>.

Swearer, Donald K. 2004. *Becoming the Buddha: The Ritual of Image Consecration in Thailand.* Princeton, NJ: Princeton University Press.

Taylor, Mark C. ed. 1998. *Critical Terms for Religious Studies.* Chicago, IL: University of Chicago Press.

Tweed, Thomas A. (2011). *America's Church: The National Shrine and Catholic Presence in the Nation's Capital.* New York: Oxford University Press.

Vásquez, Manuel A. 2011. *More Than Belief: A Materialist Theory of Religion.* Oxford: Oxford University Press.

Weiner, Isaac. 2014. *Religion Out Loud: Religious Sound, Public Space, and American Pluralism.* New York: New York University Press.

Yelle, Robert A. 2013. *Semiotics of Religion: Signs of the Sacred in History.* London: Bloomsbury.

FURTHER READING

Fleming, Benjamin J. and Richard D. Mann, eds. 2014. *Material Culture and Asian Religions: Text, Image, Object*. London: Routledge . [*A collection of essays that examine the materiality of several religions in Asia by focusing on the materiality of texts, images, and objects used in a variety of practices.*]

Keane 2007 [*A rich investigation of the cultural encounter of Calvinist missionaries in Indonesia that reveals the modern enterprise of distinguishing bodies, things, and animals deployed by the Christian critique of idolatry. Keane demonstrates the material richness of Peirce's semiotics in contrast to the textualism of semiology.*]

McDaniel 2011 [*A compelling example of the study of the agency of images, drawing on Gell (1998), that examines the relation of images to one another as well as to other human and non-human agents such as ghosts, corpses, monks, and deities in a Thai Buddhist monastery.*]

Meyer 2011 [*A study of media and religion in African Pentecostalism that focuses on the senses and the formation of sensory routines.*]

Morgan 2012b [*An argument for linking the sense of vision to the entire bodily sensorium in the study of religion.*]

Orsi 2005 [*A series of case studies of lived Catholicism that explore the understanding of religion as relationships among humans and saints.*]

Vásquez 2011 [*A theoretical genealogy of materializing the study of religion that focuses on embodiment, practice, and emplacement.*]

CHAPTER 19

NARRATIVE

JEPPE SINDING JENSEN

CHAPTER SUMMARY

- Narrative is essential in human life, culture, and society, and in the formation and maintenance of religious worlds.
- The study of narrative is interdisciplinary. The history of the study of narrative is crucial for the understanding of narrative theory.
- Narrative plays a fundamental role in religion and (other) social constructions. Narratives are crucial in individual and social integration. Human imagination and meaning-making depend on narrative. Origins of narrative, phylogenesis, and ontogenesis are interrelated.
- Narratives play a central role in creating religious worlds.

DEFINITIONS

The definition of narrative can be quite simple, as in *The Oxford English Dictionary*: "A spoken or written account of connected events; a story." As trivial as this may seem at first glance, the definition highlights a crucial point about the nature of narratives: that they are about 'connected events' and as such they provide the means for communicating ideas and experiences about the world, real or imagined. Definitions may of course also be more fine-grained and problem-oriented; a 'fuzzy-set' definition would include multiple dimensions such as the spatial, temporal, mental, and formal or pragmatic dimensions (Ryan 2011, 28–29). When narratives connect events, across such dimensions, they also provide the relations between actors, events, and objects and so make sense of 'what happens.' The relations between what happens, events and their causes and effects are not given simply by perception and impression; they need to be interpreted. Especially when it comes to human (and human-like) actions, it is essential to grasp the modes of intentionality and rationality involved. It is unlikely that humans would understand much of their worlds (natural, mental, and social) without narrative competence, and they certainly would have difficulties in communicating jointly without narratives.

Narrative is Essential in Human Life, Culture, and Society

Humans use language and narratives to organize their thoughts and impressions into more comprehensive patterns in order to construct and participate in worldviews. Narratives serve as conceptual scaffolding that makes the world (seen, unseen, experienced, and/or imagined) understandable and shareable between individuals and groups. Values and norms are crucial for human life, and narrative is a capable medium for distributing these in the social dimension. For similar reasons, narratives are fundamental in religious worlds, whether as universes of thought or networks of practices (with related sociocultural institutions). When humans use narratives, they are able to 'connect' events, real or imagined, to group them together, to provide them with value and importance, and so provide the rationales for action and thought. In religious traditions, narratives abound in the countless myths and legends that are involved in how rituals and institutions 'talk' and 'tell stories' (explicit and implicit). Narrative is involved in even the most abstract or terse dogmas, as these are often condensed versions of what would otherwise be longer narrative sequences; and, conversely, narratives are used when the meaning of dogma needs to be explained and interpreted. Narratives are in the centre of a "matrix of relations between individuals, groups, cultural repertoires and social institutions" (Geertz 2011, 23). Thus, narrative is the primary medium of making sense, also in the worlds of religious traditions (Paden 1994, 69–92).

THE INTERDISCIPLINARY STUDY
OF NARRATIVE

Several academic disciplines contribute to the interdisciplinary study of narrative Herman et al. 2005). Most of these belong to the humanities. *Narratology*, that is, the general study of narrative, is now closely connected to literary theory and visual media (Ryan 2004; 2006; Herman 2005). *Discourse analysis* also studies narratives, especially their functions in the social world, in the formation of individual and social identities as well as the use of narrative(s) in the construction and maintenance of social and political power and influence. Both these fields owe inspirations to and have a theoretical legacy from the field of semiotics (see Yelle, "Semiotics," this volume), that is, from the study of how meaning is produced and organized through the use of signs and symbols. In turn, these theoretical inspirations trace back to the groundbreaking influences of structuralism from the mid-twentieth century (Jensen 2000; 2005). These influences have accumulated and diversified over time and so, now, countless fields take an interest in narrative, from anthropology to discourse psychology, political theory to philosophy and theology. The study of religion, in turn, is so broad that it may benefit from the findings of these disciplines.

The History of 'Narratology': The Study of Narrative

The study of narrative can be said to have a long history if one includes ideas and theories (from Plato and onwards) about stories, myth, fairy tales, and other kinds of narratives (Herman 2005). However, the more strictly scholarly study of narrative can be said to have begun with Vladimir Propp's 1928 study of the morphology (i.e. the composition) of folk tales (Propp 1958). This type of study paved the way for the later structuralist approaches that came to dominate the field. In the 1940s Claude Lévi-Strauss took inspiration from formal linguistics in his structuralist analyses of how myths were composed and how they (as narratives) conveyed various kinds of culturally important messages. Scholars began to take an interest in how elements and functions of narrative were combined and structured so as to make cohesive stories with plots. One general ambition was to discover the 'grammar' of story-telling as there seemed to be hidden rules involved in the composition of narratives—hence the value of the inspiration from formal linguistics. The point of the analysis is that narratives not only have surface presentations of actors and actions, but also 'deeper' structures that convey messages and analyze how they do so (e.g. the fairy tale "The Ugly Duckling" is *not* about birds). Slightly later, Roland Barthes used structuralist analyses on the 'hidden' narratives of modern culture, from racism to fashion. Barthes introduced the important distinction between narrative 'functions,' the sequence or elements of action that constitute the narrative, and 'indices' that 'point' to values (positive or negative) in the narrative (Barthes 1975; Jensen 2009, 290–307). For instance, the Exodus story in the Bible is composed of numerous functions that point to positive ('ten commandments') or negative (the 'golden calf') values. The legends of the Buddha's enlightenment contain similar constructions. In fact, most myths do. Thus, from the 1960s the field of semiotics (the study of signs and symbols) began to flourish with analyses of various kinds of cultural and religious phenomena *as if* they were stories (Jensen 2009, 251–320; Yelle 2013). As a result of this development ('semiotic turn'), it has now become common to 'read' human action as if it were narrative. In fact, social and religious institutions may be 'read' for what they 'are about.' For instance, a wedding (or any ritual) can be 'read' as narrative when considering its 'aboutness': there are always stories 'hidden' in rituals and institutions (Jensen 2014, 95–154). In 1966 the semiotician A. J. Greimas designed the 'actantial model' as a tool for analyzing all kinds narratives, as the 'actant' is an abstract role that may be cast with specific agents (human or non-human) (Greimas 1970, 249–270). In light of the discussion here, it proves useful also in the analysis of rituals and institutions. The 'project' axis displays

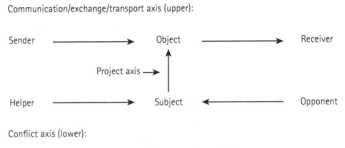

Communication/exchange/transport axis (upper):

Sender ⟶ Object ⟶ Receiver

Project axis ⟶

Helper ⟶ Subject ⟵ Opponent

Conflict axis (lower):

FIGURE 19.1 A. J. Greimas's 'Actantial Model'.

a subject's desire of gaining an 'object' (a goal of any kind) and how this project is surrounded by positive and negative agents or circumstances (Fig. 19.1).

Entire religious traditions may be plotted into the model as 'cosmic dramas' about salvation or bliss, where there are helpers as well as opponents. The model is deliberately simplistic, which only extends its utility. It is also a *universal* model in the sense that all cultures have stories that engage the actantial positions of the model. Narratives generate messages because of the structural relations and dynamics between the actantial roles. As an example, consider the hero who typically has to pass two tests: first the 'qualifying' test that demonstrates his competence and then the 'glorifying' test, which proves him the conqueror. Greimas also drew attention to the importance of modalities in narrative, where the analysis can include scrutiny of 'be,' 'can,' 'do,' 'know,' 'ought,' 'will,' and their negations, which characterize the action structures in the narratives. Such classifications of modalities facilitate the exploration of who does what, when, and why as well as the distribution of duties, possibilities, abilities, etc. in the universe of the narrative.

At the same time, the semiotician Claude Bremond added a theory concerning the logic of narratives and defined the basic narrative chain as consisting of three links: an opening situation with a possibility, i.e. a virtuality, where things can go well or wrong; the occurrence of the possibility (or not); and finally the achievement or failure of the project of the story. Bremond developed a complex classification of roles in stories. Here the distinction between agents and patients is important: agents start processes, influence the patients, and turn them into either victims or beneficiaries. The characters encounter difficulties that they may overcome (or not); there may be traps and deceit, seduction and threats. The relations between characters may rely on conventions (parents help children); they may negotiate and make alliances, either in solidarity relations (among equals) or in unequal relations (as between debtors and creditors). Bremond's theory offers a careful analysis of the logic of tales (Bremond 1980). It explains why a story may appear unfinished because it did not reach the equilibrium that seemed inherent in the plot.

Later, the literary theorist Gerard Genette (1990) added a number of terms and concepts for the study of narrative. Among these are *order, frequency, duration, voice,* and *focus*. Although intended for literary analysis, they may also be deployed in work on religious narrative(s) as they focus on the syntax of narratives and not the interpretation of contents. 'Order' may include flash-back or flash-forward, prolepsis, discovery, conflict, resolution, or anachrony (i.e. the disarrangement of events in unfamiliar ways). 'Frequency' or redundancy (continuous repetition) is often encountered in religious narratives, functioning mainly as a mnemonic tool. 'Duration' concerns narrative and discourse time: "From Adam and Eve until Resurrection" is a very long narrative time but only a short discourse time (taking one second to pronounce). Genette's idea of 'voice' is fourfold and concerns 'who speaks': from inside or outside the text, and whether the narrator is a character in the story or not. Narrative 'focus' (or 'mood') concerns the 'perspective' of the narrator, as this changes in narrated speech, transposed speech, and reported speech. The perspective of the narrator is called focalization: who sees, perceives, or imagines? The perspective can be fixed, variable, multiple, or collective. Multiple voices may also be present in single narratives as may be indicated by the theoretical concepts of 'polyphony' (multiple voices) or 'heteroglossia' (conflicting discourses). All these aspects of fiction and literature apply equally well to religious narratives, with the added emphasis on existential importance: religious narratives are typically about the narrators' and receivers'/listeners' own life-worlds and are normative for thought and behavior. Religious narratives can be entertaining but more often they are engaging and socially important.

Currently, the study of narrative ('narratology') has developed into a variety of theories, concepts, and methods concerning the human ability to produce and process narratives in various forms, media, contexts, and practices (Ryan 2008; Herman 2011). As that human ability to take impressions and perceptions (along with ideas and imagination) and turn them into stories has its roots in human cognitive 'fluidity,' scientists in such fields as psychology and cognitive science are now also involved in the investigation of the origin, properties, and functions of narrative (Donald 2001; Herman 2013). The human ability to make sense depends profoundly on the properties and functions of narrative(s) and the human mind's literary character (Turner 1996). Humans understand things when they are able to talk about them. Narrative organizes basic epistemic functions, as linguistic constructions and event cognition converge (Tomasello 1999, 134–160; Herman 2013, 225–251).

Theories from cognitive semiotics also contribute insights that expand knowledge about how (religious) narratives work and what they are composed of. They frequently contain *metaphors*, where meaning from one domain is used to make sense in another, such as "my love is a rose," or "God is our father." Narratives include *scripts* that order sequences of events and the thoughts about them, for instance going to the supermarket, going on a date, participating in a wedding, or attending a funeral. One's behavior will be shaped according to *frames*, that is, existing cultural and mental models of such situations. Religious discourse is often about a world unseen, and so there is frequent use of metaphors, scripts, and frames taken from one domain onto another in order to produce *mappings* of the imaginable onto the known, e.g. paradise depicted as a 'garden.' When thinking in such ways—universal in religious life—humans apply mental space *blending* (Fauconnier 1997).

Narratives are always embedded in discourse because narratives configure discourse. Discourse can be defined as a 'manner of speaking' about things. Thus, discourse consists of narrative(s) that (for example) speak(s) about humans in a certain manner: a medical discourse is different from a legal one, and these differ from a religious discourse that may talk about humans as created, sinners, un-enlightened, or divine. Narratives *about* religion may be religious, scholarly, and scientific, or public media discourse. These modes of discourse all differ in perspective and are at times incommensurable and incompatible (Murphy 2000).

Origins of Narrative in a Phylogenetic Perspective

Undoubtedly, the origins of the human narrative capacity are to be found in the human capacity for mimesis, the ability to imitate and demonstrate objects, subjects, actions, and perhaps even thoughts and intentions. During human cultural evolution, with the appearance of language and other symbolic means of communication, it became possible to imitate and demonstrate not only existing but also imagined objects, actions, and intentions (Donald 2001). Through imagination, humans could cognize ('represent') matters that were non-existing in the physical world, and they could talk about these matters. The ensuing narrative competence has been fundamental for human social and cultural evolution: narrative is important for remembering, for sharing information, and, most importantly, it makes planning ahead possible, insofar as it represents the future as already existing ('prolepsis'). In cultural and religious evolution, myth-making and story-telling concerning actors, actions, and intentions in imaginary worlds became the means of providing paradigms for the narrative governance (action, cognition, emotion) of human life and the all-important 'collectivity of mind.' Whereas the development of narrative(s) in oral and prehistorical societies is almost impossible to investigate, the advent of literate culture (and so historical sources) provided definitive turns in cultural technology. First, the narratives (e.g. myths) could be written down; the meaning ('semantic contents') could then become fixed, being debated and, perhaps, even rejected. (For a discussion of 'meaning' in the study of religion, see Jensen 2004). The invention of literacy allowed for reflection and so for reflexivity and meta-cognition, that is, thinking about thoughts and expressing such thinking in ways that allowed others to take part in them, even if the narrators (i.e. writers) were not themselves present (Donald 2001, 305–315). In that manner, the contents of the narrative may be fictive, and the presence of the story-teller is no longer mandatory. Narratives about anything imaginable may then begin to circulate on their own. With the latest explosion of electronic and visual media, narrative(s) can be produced, stored, and distributed in cyber-space at immense speed, independent of distance in space. The evolution and history of narrative are thus closely interwoven with the growth of available technologies in culture and society. The functions of narrative in the evolution of language and the human mind and in the evolution of culture and society are closely related, and so studies of narrative have now become tightly linked with the sciences of mind (Herman 2013).

Narrative(s) in Individual Integration

In many ways, narratives function as devices to process information 'in and out of the brain' and they likewise make possible the transmission of mental contents between brains. Add to this the technologies that make it possible to store mental contents (such as beliefs, ideas, intentions, and knowledge) in *external* media for later use or for dissemination, and the importance of narrative becomes obvious. Narrative is a technology for linking individual brains in mental networks. Narratives are instruments of mind. This may also (at least partly) explain why narratives look the way they do: cognitive processes of conceptualization 'surface' as dimensions of narrative and semantic structures that enable humans to organize representations of actions in temporal, spatial, perspectival, subject, and object networks (Herman 2013, 169–174). Language and narrative actually mirror mental processes: narratives generally resemble processes of perception and action, but they may exceed factual experience and 'fire off' the imagination. Narratives may then connect the individual with fictive action representations, orders, temporalities, and perspectives that are only imaginable. Narratives such as parables may situate the listening subject ('receiver') in normative cognition imageries where the potentialities and consequences of imagined actions can be played out. In literate religious traditions, the biographies of the lives of exemplary persons (e.g. hagiographies) demonstrate this function of narrative. The construction of fictional worlds may also be considered the 'really real' as when religious traditions assert 'truth pretentions,' and here narrative can transport the individual from the mundane to a sphere of special value to the tradition.

Individual Imagination and Meaning-Making

Humans live and act in constructed worlds. The 'myths of modernity' convey the impression that humans mostly live by rationality, but in fact they live as much by their (i) conceptual ecologies and (ii) imagined worlds (Bruner 1986). These are the major constituents of religious worlds. In managing one's own identity, thought, and action, a measure of imagination is necessary, and that is generally supported by the individual's capability to enter imaginative realms. The Delphic maxim 'know thyself' is possible only through mental mirroring mechanisms that fundamentally rely on imagination (Harris 2000). Meaningful narrative integration of the individual (i.e. 'becoming a whole person') demands imagination: you need to be able to imagine who you are and might be (Modell 2003). Human experience of self and other is mediated in and through narratives that allow for imagining, simulating, and having vicarious experiences with others and their mind products: "Narratives, especially shared life narratives, are the basis of autobiographical memory itself. Stories and myths can completely reshape our semantic spaces, leading to a consensual definition of a shared virtual reality that is the core of oral culture" (Donald 2001, 296). Individual integration is a fundamental ontogenetical achievement. For the child and adolescent, narrative universes provide 'scaffolding' for playing, learning, remembering, and developing. How these complex processes expand in ontogenesis is becoming increasingly clear (e.g. Nelson 2006). Armin W. Geertz states that "The primary function of narrative is to maintain the illusion of an individual, controlling agent on the one hand and a member of the group who can be identified, held responsible and made predictable on the other" (2011, 23).

Narrative(s) in Social Integration

Narratives are crucially important in social integration where they contribute collective perspectives, reasoning, and courses for action as well as common knowledge, norms, and values. Culture may be considered a hyper-social network ('a collective brain') consisting of a sum of narratives that support collective internalization and integration into a cultural order (Jensen 2011, 47). Narrative offers shared identities and memories, the creation of collective representations (as proposed by Émile Durkheim), and stable social and cultural institutions. Collective imagination and meaning-making are above all encountered in the narratives of myths and mythologies. In 1964, Claude Lévi-Strauss stated that myths are narratives with objectified thought. Ingeniously, he set out to demonstrate "not how men think in myths, but how myths operate in men's minds without their being aware of the fact" (Lévi-Strauss 1986, 12). Since then, philosophers and psychologists have pointed out how human individual life is thoroughly social and cultural and mediated by narrative(s) (e.g. Bruner 1986; Clark 2001; Tomasello 2010). Being the 'ultimate artefact,' language and so also narrative make humans 'smart' and allow them to share experiences, perspectives, and thoughts for joint decisions and actions through the functions of their social institutions (Douglas 2012, 128). The construction and maintenance of social institutions are products of collective intentionality and are primarily language-dependent (Searle 2010). Tomasello (2010, 343) notes: "Language, or better linguistic communication [e.g. narratives], is not just any kind of object, formal or otherwise; rather it is a form of social action constituted by social conventions for achieving social ends, premised on at least some shared understandings and shared purposes among users." Edwin Hutchins introduced the notion of 'distributed cognition' (1995). Here again, language and narrative are a medium for externalizing and distributing complex cognitive loads among members of a collective working on a joint project. Religious traditions offer multitudes of concepts, models, norms, and values that go into such cognitive distribution: the complex staging of elaborate rituals is a case in point. Thus, narratives have important social functions in that they support collective intentionality in groups and simultaneously augment individual cognition (and emotion) as an extension of mind. Collective narrative(s) in sociocultural traditions thus not only function to make groups work but also to help individuals function. Cognitive governance, that is, the general functions of consciousness, depend on social and cultural creations with narrative governance of action, cognition, and emotion. Humans depend on social and cultural universes and on tradition in order to become fully functioning social beings. Religious traditions offer (or impose) 'life scripts' consisting of roles, conditions, and stages for participants. In that sense, religious traditions play a dominant role in normative cognition. Additionally, most languages are saturated with religious terminologies. With language, and so narratives, humans are given certain ways of acting, because all languages come with built-in norms, values, symbols, and an implicit ideology: "A whole mythology is deposited in our language" (as once pointed out by Ludwig Wittgenstein in his comments on Frazer's *Golden Bough*).

Special Features of Religious Narrative(s)

In addition to the aesthetic and literary perspectives prevalent in general narratology (e.g. Fludernik 2009), there are interesting factors that are distinctive and crucial in the study of religious narratives. A conspicuous quality of religious narratives is their crossing of borders. Religious narratives go between and unite ('mediate') what is individual with the collective, the human with the super-human, the natural with the supernatural, and religious narratives may collapse time and eliminate space. From a non-religious or agnostic perspective, religious narratives are products of the human imagination and as such comparable to fiction. However, religious narrative(s) claim to be about the real—or, even more, about what is 'really real'—and as such they differ from the stories that are told from aesthetic or entertaining perspectives. Religious narratives claim authority and have importance for social and cultural universes of meaning. They regularly have world-making and world-ordering qualities; that is, they are foundational stories about the world and how it came to be the way humans think it is and how they should accordingly behave. The power of religious narratives consists precisely and proportionally in the power they have over human minds. Religious narratives are the products and the bearers of reflective beliefs as these are the beliefs that are derived from the communication with others (Jensen 2014, 71–76). Remarkably, and in some contrast to the modern common-sense view, humans have a tendency to believe more in beliefs derived from others than in their own intuitive beliefs that are derived from their own experience (Frith 2012). This may go a long way toward explaining the survival and success of many religious convictions, especially as these are backed with the authority of narratives embedded in traditions.

Religious worlds are worlds of human imagination and as such, they share many of the properties of other kinds of fictive or possible worlds. Religious worlds are 'multi-person worlds' with specific kinds of 'narrative modalities' that can be used or manipulated to different purposes. In Lubomir Dolezel's model, these are *alethic* (about what is possible, impossible, or necessary), *deontic* (about what is permitted, prohibited, or obligatory), *axiological* (about what is good, bad, or indifferent), and *epistemic* (about what can be known or believed) (Dolezel 1998, 113–132). Any test of a set of religious narratives will attest to the existence and functions of these four modalities. One may note here, how the recent genre of 'fantasy' often relies heavily on motifs and schemata from religious narratives.

A peculiar aspect of religious narrative or discourse is that it often speaks in the second person, that is, it speaks 'to you.' Whether expressed in imperatives, wishes, or prohibitions, such second-person speech 'speaks' directly to its reader or addressee as in a dialogue. This kind of communication in religious narratives bears similarity to the concept of interpellation in 'discourse psychology,' where the receiver is hailed or summoned by the narrative or discourse. In condensed form, it addresses the receiver with a 'Hey you!' and then the contents of the message, e.g. 'reform,' 'rejoice,' or 'repent.' Most religious narrative(s) have explicit social functions focusing on behavior, and so religious narratives are often moralizing, instructive, normative, and prescriptive. Religious narrative(s) and discourse(s) encode normative cognition in members of the group according to the tradition.

When religious narratives or discourse appear as plainly descriptive, it is often in order to set the stage for a normative message. For instance, if the world is being described as a miserable place, this then makes room for another message that glorifies a different world to be achieved by changes in mind and behavior. In his studies of myths, Claude Lévi-Strauss stressed these functions of simultaneously separating and uniting the 'world lived-in' with the 'world thought-of' (Lévi-Strauss 1955; 1963). Religious narrative and discourse link together the ontologies of the two worlds: one 'real' and very difficult to change; the other imagined and 'wished-for.' It is noteworthy that many religious narratives carry messages that resemble a doctor's diagnosis, such as when the Buddha taught the 'Four Noble Truths': the truth of suffering; the truth of the cause of the suffering; the truth of the end of suffering; and the truth of the path (to end the suffering). This model form of narrative may be termed the 'prophetic model'—it is the kind of message that all prophets and reformers convey. Once such messages have been adopted, then change must be avoided and the modes of religious communication tend toward 'auto-communication,' that is, repeating and confirming the same messages continually. 'Auto-communication' introduces no new meaning because the important dimension is the confirmation of what is already known and the ultimate sacrality of existing meaning.

Importance of Religious Narratives in the Formation and Maintenance of Religious Worlds

In religion, the fundamental importance of narrative derives precisely from the 'power' of story to 'connect things' in words. All known religions are made of narrative, and so without narratives there would be no religions. The process of 'putting things into words' is called *narrativization*. Myths talk about how and why the world and all that is relevant in it was created. Narratives imbue the present world with meaning and value. Narratives provide identity and perspective, put things in their proper place, and give humans explanations and interpretations of existence, of why they live, act, think, and feel the way they do. Even when ritual participants are unable to present a reasonable narrative of what they do or why they have a specific social institution, they will, minimally, make up stories like 'this is what we do' and that may be story enough (e.g. when a priest speaks in a different language). Thus, rituals and institutions are 'narrate-able' in many ways when they are provided with references and sources in sacred narratives. Examples range from the many legends about the Buddha, Muslim stories from the biography (Seerah) of the prophet Mohammad, the Exodus narrative in the Hebrew Bible, pious legends about the doings of saints, to Japanese stories of the country's origin in the ancient collection, Kojiki. Religious world-making narratives often have a 'from A to B' shape: the Maori have narratives about their legendary origins in Hawaiki and the Parsi (Zoroastrian) community has its story, *Qissa–i Sanjan*, about how they fled from Iran and settled in Gujarat, India. Religious narratives are important because they are able to posit imaginary worlds in relation to this present physical world. Whether the narrated world is imagined as a distant past, a displaced present, or a far future, the present is always compared to the narrated world as an exemplary blueprint for what goes on in the present world. Religious narrative plays a crucial role in producing, organizing, and maintaining shared, collective, and imaginary worlds. This is what myths do.

Religious ritual often provides similar functions. In rituals, the overarching religious narratives are often broken down into small units that apply to or are recited in the ritual context and process. To understand the meaning of the bits presented in ritual, the whole story must be familiar to the participant. Through the use of narratives, rituals may be imbued with traditional meanings and intentionality, and so the 'aboutness' of a ritual can be secured by the narrative anchoring of the event. Narratives permit a multitude of transformations of meaning such as decoupling ritual imitative behavior from actual events, thus playing out alternative and imagined scenarios. 'Anything is possible' in ritual where roles can be inverted or substituted: patients and instruments may act as agents etc. Narrative changes non-instrumental ritual actions into the ritual play with order, efficacy, action representations, temporality, and perspectives (Jensen 2014, 95–131).

Diverging scholarly views of 'religious narrative' not only depend upon definitions of narrative but they will necessarily also involve and draw on theories of religion (see Stausberg/Engler, "Theories of Religion," this volume) in any assessment of the character and function of narrative. According to whether theories of religion emphasize a social, cultural, individual, or collective dimension, they will accordingly emphasize different but compatible dimensions of religious narratives, dimensions that correspond to what is being highlighted by the theory. For instance, whoever works from a theory of religion that stresses the functions of religion in emotion regulation or political hegemony will most likely study similar dimensions in the religious narratives, the theory in question being responsible for what emerges as the core thematic material. The foci of narrative analyses are always theoretically determined, and it is evident that even a simple or 'innocent' interest also involves a specific perspective for hearing, reading, and interpreting narrative. Apologetic and deconstructive interpretations may have directly opposing ideas of interpreting narratives. In modern and postmodern analyses of religious narrative(s), there is often a perceptible trace of a 'hermeneutics of suspicion'; that is, religious narratives are not taken at face value, but considered to be loaded with social, political, or economic interests. Also, the same narratives can be used very differently, in different contexts and discourses, so that narratives that signify salvation for some could mean domination, persecution, and perhaps even extinction for others. These cultural, social, and political dimensions only serve to underscore the importance of narrative in human life.

GLOSSARY

Discourse a manner of speaking about a subject, e.g. the human body, related to (e.g.) health, nutrition, appearance, or biology.
Mode, modality can be either (a) grammatical mode, such as indicative, subjunctive, and imperative, or (b) modality of being: real, virtual, prohibited, wished-for, etc.
Narrative story or account of connected events, mostly with a specific plot.
Ontogenesis the development of the individual from new-born to adult.
Phylogenetic the evolution of the human species in general.
Semiotics the general theory and study of signs and symbols, how they are produced and organized.

REFERENCES

Barthes, Roland. 1975 [1966]. "An Introduction to the Analysis of Narrative." In *The Semiotic Challenge*. Berkeley: University of California Press, 95–136.
Bremond, Claude. 1980 [1966]. "The Logic of Narrative Possibilities." *New Literary History* 11(3): 387–411.
Bruner, Jerome. 1986. *Actual Minds, Possible Worlds*. Cambridge, MA: Harvard University Press.
Clark, Andy. 2001. *Being There: Putting Brain, Body, and World Together Again*. Cambridge, MA: MIT Press.

Dolezel, Lubomir. 1998. *Heterocosmica: Fiction and Possible Worlds*. Baltimore, MD: Johns Hopkins University Press.

Donald, Merlin. 2001. *A Mind So Rare: The Evolution of Human Consciousness*. New York: Norton.

Douglas, Mary. 2012. *How Institutions Think*. London: Routledge. Original edition, 1986.

Fauconnier, Gilles. 1997. *Mappings in Thought and Language*. Cambridge: Cambridge University Press.

Fludernik, Monika. 2009. *An Introduction to Narratology*. London: Routledge.

Frith, Chris D. 2012. "The Role of Metacognition in Human Social Interactions." *Philosophical Transactions of the Royal Society B: Biological Siences* 367(1599): 2213–2223.

Geertz, Armin W. 2011. "Religious Narrative, Cognition and Culture: Approaches and Definitions." In *Religious Narrative, Cognition and Culture: Image and Word in the Mind of Narrative*, edited by Armin W. Geertz and Jeppe Sinding Jensen. Sheffield: Equinox, 9–29.

Genette, Gérard. 1990. *Narrative Discourse Revisited*. Ithaca, NY: Cornell University Press.

Greimas, Algirdas J. 1970. *Du Sens*. Paris: Seuil.

Harris, Paul. 2000. *The Work of the Imagination*. Oxford: Blackwell.

Herman, David. 2005. "Histories of Narrative Theory (I): A Genealogy of Early Developments." In *A Companion to Narrative Theory*, edited by J. Phelan and P. J. Rabinowitz. Malden, MA: Blackwell, 19–35.

Herman, David, ed. 2011. *The Cambridge Companion to Narrative*. Cambridge: Cambridge University Press.

Herman, David. 2013. *Storytelling and the Sciences of the Mind*. Cambridge, MA: MIT Press.

Herman, David, Manfred Jahn, and Marie-Laure Ryan, eds. 2005. *The Routledge Encyclopedia of Narrative Theory*. London: Routledge.

Hutchins, Edwin. 1995. *Cognition in the Wild*. Cambridge, MA: MIT Press.

Jensen, Jeppe Sinding. 2000. "Structure." In *Guide to the Study of Religion*, edited by Willi Braun and R. N. McCutcheon. London: Cassell, 314–333.

Jensen, Jeppe Sinding. 2004. "Semantics in the Study of Religion." In *New Approaches to the Study of Religion*, vol. 1, edited by Peter Antes, Armin W. Geertz, and Randi Warne. Berlin and New York: de Gruyter, 219–252.

Jensen, Jeppe Sinding. 2005. "Structuralism: Further Considerations." In *The Encyclopedia of Religion*, revised edition, vol. 13, edited by Lindsay Jones, Mircea Eliade, and Charles J. Adams. Detroit: Macmillan Reference, 8757–8768.

Jensen, Jeppe Sinding. 2009. *Myths and Mythologies: A Reader*. London: Equinox.

Jensen, Jeppe Sinding. 2011. "Framing Religious Narrative, Cognition and Culture Theoretically." In *Religious Narrative, Cognition and Culture: Image and Word in the Mind of Narrative*, edited by Armin W. Geertz and Jeppe Sinding Jensen. Sheffield: Equinox, 31–50.

Jensen, Jeppe Sinding. 2014. *What is Religion?* London: Routledge.

Lévi-Strauss, Claude. 1955. "The Structural Study of Myth." *Journal of American Folklore* 68(270): 428–44.

Lévi-Strauss, Claude. 1963. *Structural Anthropology*. New York: Basic Books. Original edition, 1958.

Lévi-Strauss, Claude. 1986. *The Raw and the Cooked: Introduction to a Science of Mythology*. Chicago, IL: University of Chicago Press. Original edition, 1964.

Modell, Arnold H. 2003. *Imagination and the Meaningful Brain*. Cambridge, MA: MIT Press.

Murphy, Tim. 2000. "Speaking Different Languages: Religion and the Study of Religion." In *Secular Theories of Religion: Current Perspectives*, edited by Tim Jensen and Mikael Rothstein. Copenhagen: Museum Tusculanum Press, 183–192.

Nelson, Katherine, ed. 2006. *Narratives from the Crib*. Cambridge, MA: Harvard University Press.

Paden, William E. 1994. *Religious Worlds: The Comparative Study of Religion*. Boston, MA: Beacon Press.

Propp, Vladimir. 1958. *Morphology of the Folktale*. Bloomington: Indiana University Press. Original edition, 1928.

Ryan, Marie-Laure, ed. 2004. *Narrative across Media: The Languages of Storytelling*. Lincoln: University of Nebraska Press.

Ryan, Marie-Laure. 2006. *Avatars of Story*. Minneapolis: University of Minnesota Press.

Ryan, Marie-Laure. 2008. "Transfictionality across Media." In *Theorizing Narrativity*, edited by J. Pier and J. Á. García Landa. Berlin: de Gruyter, 385–417.

Ryan, Marie-Laure. 2011. "Towards a Definition of Narrative." In *The Cambridge Companion to Narrative*, edited by David Herman. Cambridge: Cambridge University Press, 22–35.

Searle, John R. 2010. *Making the Social World: The Structure of Human Civilization*. Oxford: Oxford University Press.

Tomasello, Michael. 1999. *The Cultural Origins of Human Cognition*. Cambridge, MA: Harvard University Press.

Tomasello, Michael. 2010. *Origins of Human Communication*. Cambridge, MA: MIT Press.

Turner, Mark. 1996. *The Literary Mind*. New York: Oxford University Press.

Yelle, Robert A. 2013. *Semiotics of Religion: Signs of the Sacred in History*. London and New York: Bloomsbury Academic.

FURTHER READING

Dolezel 1998 [*This volume spans wide and is theoretically sophisticated. It indicates how fictive narrative universes are organized and articulated. While it does not cover religion (like most works on literary theory), the concepts, models, methods, and theories are easily transposed to the study of religion.*]

Geertz, Armin W. and Jeppe Sinding Jensen, eds. 2011. *Religious Narrative, Cognition and Culture: Image and Word in the Mind of Narrative*. Sheffield: Equinox. [*The volume—the first of its kind—deals with religious narrative in both culture (society) and cognition (human mind).*]

Herman 2011 [*An indispensable collection of contributions for anyone interested in narrative.*]

Herman 2013 [*A cutting-edge work on narrative that engages the sciences of the mind, such as psychology, cognitive science, narratology, and semiotics.*]

Jensen 2009 [*A collection of classical and contemporary readings (analyses and interpretations) of myth(s) and mythologies with critical introductions.*]

Ryan 2006 [*Insightful work on the many ways and media in which narrative are expressed.*]

Turner 1996 [*A turning point in the history of the study of narrative as a basic principle of mind.*]

CHAPTER 20

···

PERFORMANCE

···

AXEL MICHAELS AND WILLIAM S. SAX

Chapter Summary

- Ritual has a great deal in common with various kinds of linguistic and theatrical performance.
- Performative approaches to social and cultural phenomena tend to emphasize embodiment over cognition, situated communication over linguistic structure, and contextual meaning over propositional content.
- Austin's theory of 'performativity' in speech has been influential, as have pragmatic approaches to language—emphasizing meaning and communication over grammatical and syntactical structures.
- Formality and repetition are important components of both performance and ritual.
- Most forms of Indian popular theatre take a ritual form, and major strands of Indian theology are based on a theatrical ontology.
- Ritual performance is not simply based on 'belief'. Rather, the performance of ritual often leads to certain 'beliefs.'

Introduction

The terms 'performance' and 'performativity' have been used to denote a number of different approaches to language, gender, and sociocultural phenomena generally, as well as to religion and ritual in particular. Although they differ significantly in their theoretical assumptions and methodological implications, they all tend to emphasize embodiment over cognition, situated communication over linguistic structure, and contextual meaning over propositional content. A performative approach to religion thus emphasizes the embodied 'doing' of religion in particular contexts, and gives rather less attention to religious belief, doctrine, and history. It also downplays traditional mind/body and thought/action dichotomies. Performative acts in religions are therefore mostly staged, mediatized (scripted, liturgical), embodied, and public events. Questions about whether ritual action is a subcategory of performance or vice versa, and whether the two, performance and ritual, are distinguishable or not are still being actively debated.

THE ROOTS OF PERFORMANCE THEORY

Modern performance theory might be said to have begun with J. L. Austin (1911–1960), one of the 'ordinary language philosophers' at Oxford who, in the 1950s, mounted a challenge to logical positivist views of language according to which a sentence expresses a 'proposition' analyzable in terms of its truth-conditions. In classical Aristotelian logic, a proposition affirms or denies the predicate of a subject, so that in the sentence "Aristotle is a man" a predicate ("is a man") is affirmed of a subject ("Aristotle").

By contrast, Austin and his colleagues focused on the 'doing' of language, rather than its propositional content. To analyze the sentence "I promise you that I will come tomorrow" in terms of its propositional content is not only illogical, it also fails to notice what is arguably the most important aspect of the sentence: namely, that it is what Austin called a 'speech-act'; in this case, a promise. Austin introduced a threefold division of speech-acts: illocutionary acts (the semantic force of the utterance, its intended meaning), locutionary acts (the utterance itself), and perlocutionary acts (the actual effect, whether intended or not). The theory applies most obviously to overt performative utterances: a judge sentencing a prisoner, a chairperson opening a meeting, an official christening a ship, and so on. For all such utterances, it makes little sense to ask the question, "Is it true?" The more appropriate question is, "Was it effective?": i.e. was the accused person really sentenced, the meeting actually opened, the ship effectively christened? Efficacy therefore has become a crucial notion in the analysis of performances and rituals (Quack/Sax/Weinhold 2010). Austin argued, however, that performativity applied to all forms of speech. Even to say "It is raining" makes no sense if one does so in an inappropriate context.

Austin coined the term 'performative', which he found to be more adequate than 'performatory': "Formerly I used 'performatory': but 'performative' is to be preferred as shorter, less ugly more tractable, and more traditional in formation" (Austin 1962, 6 fn. 3). In addition, he introduced the term 'felicity' to denote the effectiveness or non-effectiveness of such performative speech-acts (and to distinguish his approach from that of the logical positivists, who were interested in 'truth'), and it has often been noticed that judgments of felicity point to antecedent social conditions. The judge must make his utterance at a particular time and place, and be acting in his official capacity, a quorum must be present in the room where the meeting is opened, and the person holding the champagne bottle must be authorized to name the ship, before their respective speech-acts can be judged to be felicitous. Many such 'performative speech-acts' resemble rituals, or have ritual-like properties, which is why speech-act theory later came to be so important in the development of performative approaches to religion and ritual (see the following section). More broadly, speech-act theory consistently emphasized the social and contextual preconditions for the generation of linguistic meaning, and the performance of language in particular contexts. Generally speaking, performative approaches to language stress its communicative and transformative potential, as opposed to its grammatical and syntactical structures.

Speech-act theory thus resembles pragmatic approaches to language in general, and differs radically from other well-known linguistic paradigms that seek to discover the formal (grammatical, syntactical) characteristics of all language, as for example exemplified by Noam Chomsky's 'generative grammar' (1988 [1965]). Such approaches often claim to have discovered universal logical or cognitive structures, and are scarcely concerned with how language is used to communicate, which would require attention to specific contexts. On the other hand are pragmatic approaches to language, beginning with the American philosopher Charles Saunders Peirce (1839–1914), and continuing through the Chicago linguist Edward Sapir (1884–1939), his student Benjamin Lee Whorf (1897–1941), and more recently Michael Silverstein and his students, also from the University of Chicago (Manning 2003; Silverstein 2000; 2009; forthcoming). All of these linguists, philosophers, and anthropologists stress not only the grounding of the linguistic production of meaning in particular historical and cultural contexts, but also its communicative and transformative potential (as opposed to its grammatical and syntactical structure). This potential is consistently and dramatically illustrated by religious and ritual uses of language to bless, curse, sanctify, vow, swear, transform, exorcize, excommunicate, dedicate, baptize, marry, and many other uses as well.

Performance and Ritual

Many prominent scholars (e.g. Asad 1993; Kapferer 1983; Smith 1964) have argued that the emphasis on religious 'belief' characteristic of modern theology and religious studies is a late, Protestant development, and that a more adequate understanding of religion requires greater attention to religious practices, especially ritual (see also Bivins, "Belief," this volume). Performative approaches to language have been especially fruitful for the analysis of religious rituals and other public events, because they directed scholars' attention away from an exclusive focus on beliefs and religious dogma and in the direction of embodied and mostly public performance. Performative approaches to religion and ritual have been even more directly informed by Performance Studies, a term that refers to a set of heterogeneous academic approaches that often compare conventional genres of performance like theatre, dance, and opera with neighboring genres like news, sports, and of course ritual and religion. One of the earliest theorists to write in this vein was Erving Goffman (1967; 1969) who analyzed 'the presentation of self in everyday life' as a kind of performance. Milton Singer extended the term 'cultural performance' to denote not only theatrical events like plays or concerts, but also "prayers, ritual readings and recitations, rites and ceremonies, festivals, and all those things we usually class under religion and ritual rather than with the cultural and artistic" (1972, 71). Dell Hymes (1975, 11) even argued that such a notion of performance was a 'breakthrough' that might reintegrate the humanities and social sciences. It was, however, difficult for those working with historical sources to incorporate the performative turn, since it relies very heavily on observation and visual documentation (Buc 2001; Boute/Småberg 2012).

Also important was Richard Bauman's (1975) attempt to revitalize the study of folklore by shifting attention away from the then-dominant identification and classification of motifs, toward context-based performance. In an influential article that should be read against the background of Chomsky's then-emerging paradigm of linguistic competence (something that Chomsky and his followers think of as a structural feature of the human brain), Bauman defined 'performance' as "the assumption of responsibility to an audience for a display of communicative competence" (1984, 11), thus contributing to an understanding of 'performance' as particular and context-based, rather than universal and abstract.

Another influential figure in Performance Theory was Richard Schechner (1934–), an avant-garde theatre director from New York who wrote a series of influential books and articles on the topic, many of them based on his collaboration with the anthropologist Victor Turner (1920–1983), who had developed a theory of ritual as 'social drama.' Schechner used his long-term editorship of *The Drama Review* to advance a Performance Studies agenda within theatre circles, and established a degree program in Performance Studies at New York University, of which he was the first chair holder.

Schechner argued that modern theatre is characterized by a radical distinction between performer and audience (the so-called 'fourth wall'), and by a focus on commercial entertainment. Members of the audience rarely expect to be directly involved in the action on stage, nor do they think that they (or their society) will be transformed by the play. They simply pay their money and expect to be entertained. Schechner argues that many traditional forms of drama (for example European passion plays, North Indian Ramlilas, the Noh theatre of Japan) are, by contrast, highly ritualized, or even indistinguishable from ritual. Such traditional dramatic performances do not involve a radical distinction between performers and audience: members of the audience frequently join in the work of dramatic representation, while those on stage may join the audience for periods of varying length. Moreover, the performances themselves are meant to accomplish something: bring a successful harvest or a victory in war, initiate young people into the next stage of their lives, please the god or the sovereign and thus obtain his/her benevolence and mercy (Schechner 1985). Schechner noted, however, that this distinction was far from constant, and that even 'Western' theatre had oscillated between the 'ritualized' and the 'secular' poles of this spectrum many times in the course of its history. Indeed, with the benefit of hindsight it can be argued that the period in which Schechner wrote his influential essays was the beginning of a 'turn' in Western theatre back in the direction of more ritualized forms; a turn to which he himself contributed.

This view has been extended by theatre studies scholar Erika Fischer-Lichte (2004) in her theory of the aesthetics of the performative. In her view, artistic and ritual performances share certain features like script, improvisation, the constitution of a reality, entertainment, the involvement and exchange of roles of actors and audience, and a weak framework. But ritual differs from theatre because of the transformations evoked by threshold experiences and the collapse of the distinction between art and reality. According to her, although both rituals and theatre involve repetition, they are nevertheless unique events, even though staged dramatizations often become items in a repertoire that are performed many times. Gavin Brown points out that there is "a significant unscripted dimension in all performances," since they are "susceptible to contingency and indeterminacy" (2003, 6). Embodiment, spatiality, materiality, and acousticality are expressed performatively (Fischer-Lichte 2004, 18), and all these components are ephemeral, existing only in the moment of the performance. No script can determine such dimensions of performance, because they only come into existence during the event itself. For Fischer-Lichte, the aesthetic experience of participation in a performance is thus similar to the experience in a transformative *rite de passage*.

As Schieffelin (1996, 80) has noted, both rituals and other kinds of performance are therefore inherently risky, since the factors leading to their success or failure (varying competencies of the performers, the attitude of the audience, as well as contingency and blind luck) cannot be controlled. But the failure of performances and rituals is often masked as a kind of radical change: Balzani attempts to reveal "the whole drama of ritual and change in a form of writing that masks change and silences disputes and which often records events, however new they may actually be, as though they formed part of a long tradition" (2003, 27; cf. Hüsken 2007).

Performance and ritual thus have much in common, including formality and repetition, which are important components of both. Formality may be defined as action based on repetitive rules, which are laid down and transmitted by means of rule-governed structures, and often codified in ritual handbooks. Repetition lives from imitation and mimesis, and is an essential part of any ritual performance. Ritual formality even encompasses emotions and other forms of bodily expressions, such as weeping (Michaels 2012), dancing, and music. In both ritual and performance (e.g. theatre, opera, ballet, television, film), performers tend to suppress or control their emotions or other internal feelings since these might interfere with the ritual order, script, or choreography. Both performers and audience are in a sense reduced to the rules prescribed for them by the ritual or the performative format, and to the "purpose and theory embedded in it. If a ritual allows spontaneity and chaos, it does so 'in prescribed times and places', manners and styles" (Platvoet 1995, 29). In short, and as Humphrey and Laidlaw have pointed out (1994; cf. Sax 2006), participants in most forms of ritual transfer their individual agency to the ritual itself.

However, the variability of ritual and performance manifests in the performative aspects of ritual because—pace Humphrey and Laidlaw—the ritual specialists and participants do not entirely renounce their individual agency. Instead, because of conflicts of interests of the performers and participants, different interpretations of ritual elements and their sequences, variant exegeses of texts, or the malleability of memory of the rules, there remains a certain vagueness in the ritual performance. Thus, even though ritual performances include a great deal of formality, they are nevertheless contingent. Even failed or disordered performances, which often cause amusement and jokes among the participants, do not inevitably invalidate the ritual as a whole (Hüsken 2007).

Several of these themes were summed up in Stanley Tambiah's "A Performative Approach to Ritual," first published in 1979 as the Radcliffe-Brown lecture in social anthropology and subsequently republished in Tambiah (1985). In this very influential essay, Tambiah seeks to integrate the analysis of rituals as formal, rule-bound events on the one hand, and as contextually embedded on the other. His method for doing so is the 'performative approach,' and he distinguishes between three different senses in which ritual is performative: in the Austinian sense of a performative speech-act, in the sense of dramatic or theatrical performance, and in the sense of its 'duplex' structure, whereby it "symbolically and/or iconically represents the cosmos and at the same time indexically legitimates and realizes social hierarchies" (Tambiah 1979, 153) by performatively representing them.

RITUAL AND THEATRE

In the 1970s and 1980s, Schechner collaborated with Linda Hess and others on a series of publications based on the Ramlila of Ramnagar, arguably the largest and best-known dramatic performance in India of the great epic *Ramayana*. Along with India's second great epic *Mahabharata*, it has been 'exported' to nearly all parts of Asia, where both have been transformed and 'indigenized,' resulting in new forms of religious dance, drama, puppetry, and much more (Brandon 1993; Cadet 1971; Flueckiger/Sears 1991; Phalgunadi 1990; 1994; 2000; Raghavan 1980). The literature on religious (and sometimes politicized) drama in India is vast indeed, and it has been argued that nearly all forms of Indian popular theatre take a ritual form (Sax 2009). Major strands of Indian theology are based on a theatrical ontology (Haberman 1988; Gnoli 1985; Wulff 1986). Perhaps the most fundamental term here is the Sanskrit word *līlā*, which means "God's play: it refers not only to the supreme being's playful actions but also to the dramatic 'plays' staged by human beings in memory of those actions" (Sax 1995, 33).

Schechner's sometime-collaborator Victor Turner also wrote a great deal about the relationship between ritual and theatre. Turner's writings on ritual, and on 'social dramas,' were very positively received, not only in anthropology but also theology, religious studies, history, and related disciplines, making him one of the most influential anthropologists of the late twentieth century. Throughout his career, Turner maintained a strong interest in the study of ritual, seeing it as a powerful instrument of personal and social transformation. His early works, which mostly drew on his ethnographic research amongst the Ndembu of Zambia, focused on the ritual healing of both persons and societies (Turner 1969a) and on how rituals with their symbolic forms mediated certain kinds of human experience, for example in initiation rituals (Turner 1969b). He went on to develop the concept of 'social drama,' a self-consciously theatrical metaphor suggesting that when social groups are faced with conflicts that might result in schism, they tend to pass through a series of steps following a drama-like sequence: breach, crisis, and redress, where the third stage resulted either in resolution or formal separation (1974). Although this model had been prefigured in some of Turner's earliest work (1957), it was only later that he went on to apply it to social phenomena—predominantly religious and ritual forms—throughout the world, and some of his most influential essays deal with religions like Islam (1973) and Christianity (1978).

Recently, Grimes (2014, 223–230) has proposed using 'action' as a parent term and a distinctive verb for what is done in rituals: "When speaking strictly, I prefer to say that ritualists 'enact' rituals, whereas actors 'perform' plays" (2014, 228). He thus hopes that distinctions between ritual and performance are not occluded.

Clearly, both religion and ritual have important performative elements, and that is why there is such considerable overlap between ritual displays and various forms of drama. Extensive evidence is provided by hundreds of ethnographic descriptions from virtually every known culture area in the world, where cosmological truths and moral precepts have typically been conveyed by means of dramatic performances. But such performances are hardly limited to non-literate cultures: the Christian Eucharist also has important performative aspects, with the blessing and transformation of the host taking on a dramatic form; the performance of gender exemplified by the priest's elevated position; the relationship between priest, host, and congregation performatively enacted through practices of standing, sitting, kneeling; and so on. The performative dimensions of Muharram processions of Shi'a Muslims have often been noted, and it has even been argued that the Taziyeh displays associated with them led directly to the Islamic revolution in Iran (Chelkowski 1979; 1980).

Mind, Body, and Performance

Performative approaches to religion and ritual focus on physical participation and embodiment. For example, most people would probably say that Christians kneel in church in order to demonstrate (or 'perform') their subordination to God. But as Catherine Bell (1952–2008) points out, it might just as well be argued (bearing in mind that children are socialized into such forms of embodied action long before they have developed much of an awareness of religious doctrine), that Christians feel themselves to be subordinate to God *because* they engage in practices like kneeling (Bell 1992, 100). In a similar way, Connerton (1989) has argued that although traditional hermeneutics privileges text over embodiment, the embodied practices of ritual have a greater power than texts in creating and maintaining collective memories—primarily by means of ritual. Rituals and performances indeed draw, to a large extent, on implicit procedural knowledge, which can only be made conscious up to a point. This 'background knowledge' is important for the performances but it also seems that—spontaneously, accidentally, emotionally, atmospherically—*something* more than the participants' intentions is imparted through them.

Most of the theorists discussed so far argue that the ideational and theological aspects of religion have been overemphasized, and seek to correct this by focusing on embodiment. But such a focus can lead to ignoring cognition altogether. Still newer approaches to performance reintegrate it by also including emotional aspects. The question therefore arises how performativity and emotions are linked (cf. Michaels/ Wulf 2012). The most prominent theory in this regard stems from Harvey Whitehouse, who—perhaps too simplistically—differentiates between doctrinal and imagistic modes of religiosity:

> Semantic memory consists of 'general knowledge' about the world (e.g. how to behave in restaurants, or what is the capital city of France, etc.). We can seldom recall how or when we acquired this sort of knowledge. By contrast, episodic memory consists of specific events in our life experience (e.g. our first kiss, the death of a beloved relative, the day war broke out, etc.). These types of memory are activated very differently in doctrinal and imagistic modes of religiosity. (Whitehouse 2004, 65)

Victor Turner also paid attention to the fact that some (ritual) performances include 'liminality', i.e. non-ordinary, ludic, paradoxical, ambiguous, sometimes hilarious and playful moments. Whitehouse suggests that:

> some religious practices are very intense emotionally; they may be rarely performed and highly stimulating (e.g. involving altered states of consciousness or terrible ordeals and tortures); they tend to trigger a lasting sense of revelation, and to produce powerful bonds between small groups of ritual participants. Whereas, by contrast, certain other forms of religious activity tend to be much less stimulating: they may be highly repetitive or 'routinized', conducted in a relatively calm and sober atmosphere; such practices are often accompanied by the transmission of complex theology and doctrine; and these practices tend to mark out large religious communities—composed of people who cannot possibly all know each other (certainly not in any intimate way). (Whitehouse 2004, 63)

CONCLUSION

Performative approaches to social and cultural phenomena generally, and to religion and ritual in particular, emphasize embodied communication and participation rather than formal structure or propositional content. They see social action as emergent, contingent, creative, dynamic, and embodied rather than specifiable in terms of rules or propositional content. Just as Austinian 'felicity' implies antecedent social conditions, so performativity in religion implies collective forms, and the presence of an audience. It also implies shared aesthetics for appreciating any given performance.

But there is a more profound point that is consistently made by studies of religion as performance, which is that religious 'belief' is not necessarily primary, as is often assumed, that it might indeed be generated and perpetuated by embodied action. What the study of religion and performance shows us is that religious faith, attitudes, and even 'beliefs' are not necessarily the direct results of teaching, doctrinal inculcation, or some other cognitive process, but can instead be understood as things that are *achieved* by means of embodied action, especially ritual. In this sense, one can regard prayer as a kind of performance, not simply in the sense that one performs it in order to please god, or to come closer to him, but rather in the sense already identified by Clifford Geertz, who argued that rituals were 'plastic dramas' in which "men attain their faith as they portray it" (1973, 114).

In sum, performative approaches to human language and social life see them as involving emergent, contingent, creative, dynamic, embodied, open-ended, and above all context-dependent strategies for achieving human ends, rather than as processes that can predominantly be specified in terms of rules, propositional content, or determining structures.

GLOSSARY

Felicitous a speech-act is felicitous when it achieves its object.
Līlā "divine play," dramatization of mythological narratives in India.
Performance generally the execution of an action, more specifically the enactment and staging of a (scripted or liturgical) play or event.
Performative according to Austin who coined this term, a quality of certain kinds of actions that are done with words. Later, any kind of ritualized or staged action.
Performativity a term deduced from 'the performative' (q.v.).
Ritual variously defined, and influentially as "the performance of more or less invariant sequences of formal acts and utterances not entirely encoded by the performers" (Rappaport 1999, 24).
Speech-act theory the theory according to which the meaning of linguistic expressions can be explained in terms of the rules governing their performative use.

REFERENCES

Asad, Talal. 1993. *Genealogies of Religion: Disciplines and Reasons of Power in Christianity and Islam*. Baltimore, MD: Johns Hopkins University Press.
Austin, John L. 1962. *How to Do Things with Words*. Oxford: Clarendon Press.
Balzani, Marzia. 2003. *Modern Indian Kingship: Tradition, Legitimacy & Power in Rajasthan*. Oxford: James Currey.
Bauman, Richard. 1984. *Verbal Art as Performance*. Long Grove, IL: Waveland Press.
Bell, Catherine. 1992. *Ritual Theory, Ritual Practice*. New York: Oxford University Press.

Boute, Bruno and Thomas Småberg, eds. 2012. *Devising Order: Socio-Religious Models, Rituals, and the Performativity of Practice*. Leiden and Boston: Brill.

Brandon, James R. 1993. *On Thrones of Gold: Three Javanese Shadow Plays*. Honolulu: University of Hawaii Press.

Brown, Gavin. 2003. "Theorizing Ritual as Performance: Explorations of Ritual Indeterminacy." *Journal of Ritual Studies* 17(1): 3–18.

Buc, Philippe. 2001. *The Danger of Ritual: Between Early Medieval Texts and Social Scientific Theory*. Princeton, NJ: Princeton University Press.

Cadet, J. M. 1971. *The Ramakien: The Thai Epic*. Nagayama: Kodansha International.

Chelkowski, Peter. 1979. *Ta'ziyeh: Ritual and Drama in Iran*. New York: New York University and Soroush Presses.

Chelkowski, Peter. 1980. "Iran: Mourning Becomes Revolution." *Asia* 3(1): 30–37, 44–45.

Chomsky, Noam. 1988. *Aspects of the Theory of Syntax*. Cambridge, MA: MIT Press. Original edition, 1965.

Connerton, Paul. 1989. *How Societies Remember*. Cambridge: Cambridge University Press.

Fischer-Lichte, Erika. 2004. *Ästhetik des Performativen*. Frankfurt am Main: Suhrkamp (*The Transformative Power of Performance: A New Aesthetics*. London and New York: Routledge, 2008).

Flueckiger, Joyce Burkhalter, and Laurie Jo Sears. 1991. *Boundaries of the Text: Epic Performances in South and Southeast Asia*. Ann Arbor: Center for South and Southeast Asian Studies, Univ. of Michigan.

Geertz, Clifford. 1973. *The Interpretation of Culture: Selected Essays*. New York: Basic Books.

Gnoli, Raniero, ed. 1985. *The Aesthetic Experience According to Abhinavagupta*, 3rd edition. Varanasi: Chowkhamba Sanskrit Series Office. Oiginal edition, 1956.

Goffman, Erving. 1967. *Interaction Ritual*. Chicago, IL: Aldine.

Goffman, Erving. 1969. *The Presentation of the Self in Everyday Life*. London: Allen Lane.

Grimes, Ronald L. 2014. *The Craft of Ritual Studies*. Oxford and New York: Oxford University Press.

Haberman, David. 1988. *Acting as a Way of Salvation: A Study of Raganuga Bhakti Sadhan*. New York: Oxford University Press.

Humphrey, Caroline and James Laidlaw. 1994. *The Archetypal Actions of Ritual: A Theory of Ritual Illustrated by the Jain Rite of Worship*. Oxford: Clarendon Press.

Hüsken, Ute, ed. 2007. *When Rituals Go Wrong: Mistakes, Failure, and the Dynamics of Ritual*. Leiden and Boston: Brill.

Hymes, Dell. 1975. "Breakthrough into Performance." In *Folklore: Performance and Communication*, edited by Dan Ben-Amos and Kenneth S. Goldstein. The Hague: Mouton, 11–20.

Kapferer, Bruce. 1983. *A Celebration of Demons: Exorcism and the Aesthetics of Healing in Sri Lanka*. Bloomington: Indiana University Press.

Manning, P., ed. 2003. "Indexical Order and the Dialectics of Sociolinguistic Life." *Language and Communication* 23(3–4): 193–229. [Special issue on the work of M. Silverstein and students: *Words and Beyond: Linguistic and Semiotic Studies of the Sociocultural Order*.]

Michaels, Axel. 2012. "Performative Tears: Emotions in Rituals and Ritualized Emotions." In *Emotions in Rituals and Performance*, edited by Axel Michaels and Christoph Wulf. London, New York, and New Delhi: Routledge, 29–40.

Michaels, Axel. 2016. *Homo Ritualis: Hindu Ritual and its Significance to Ritual Theory*. Oxford and New York: Oxford University Press.

Michaels, Axel and Christoph Wulf, eds. 2012. *Emotions in Rituals and Performances*. London, New York, and New Delhi: Routledge.

Phalgunadi, I. Gusti Putu, ed. 1990. *Indonesian Mahabharata. Adiparva—The First Book*. International Academy of Indian Culture and Aditya Prakashan.

Phalgunadi, I. Gusti Putu, ed. 1994. *The Indonesian Mahābhārata: Udyogaparva*. Vol. 5. International Academy of Indian Culture and Aditya Prakashan

Phalgunadi, I. Gusti Putu, ed. 2000. *The Indonesian Brahmāṇḍapurāṇa: Translated From the Original Classical Kawi text*. Sundeep Prakashan.

Platvoet, Jan G. 1995. "Ritual in Plural and Pluralist Societies." In *Pluralism and Identity: Studies in Ritual Behaviour*, edited by Jan G. Platvoet and Karel van der Toorn. Leiden: Brill, 25–51.

Quack, Johannes, William Sax, and Jan Weinhold, eds. 2010. *The Problem of Ritual Efficacy*. New York: Oxford University Press.

Raghavan, Venkatarama, ed. 1980. *The Ramayana Tradition in Asia: Papers Presented at the International Seminar on the Ramayana Tradition in Asia, New Delhi, December 1975*. New Delhi: Sahitya Akademi.

Rappaport, Roy. 1999. *Ritual and Religion in the Making of Humanity*. Cambridge: Cambridge University Press.

Sax, William. 1995. "Introduction." In *The Gods at Play: Lila in South Asia*, edited by William Sax. New York: Oxford University Press, 3–12.

Sax, William. 2002. *Dancing the Self: Personhood and Performance in the Pandav Lila of Garwhal*. Oxford and New York: Oxford University Press.

Sax, William. 2006. "Agency." In *Theorizing Rituals*. Vol. I: *Issues, Topics, Approaches, Concepts*, edited by Jens Kreinath, Jan Snoek and Michael Stausberg. Leiden and Boston, MA: Brill, 473–482.

Sax, William. 2009. "Ritual and Theatre in Hinduism." In *Religion, Ritual, Theatre*, edited by Bent Flemming Nielsen, Bent Holm, and Karen Vedel. Frankfurt: Peter Lang, 79–105.

Schechner, Richard. 1985. *Between Theatre and Anthropology*. Philadelphia: Pennsylvania University Press.

Schechner, Richard. 2003. *Performance Theory*, 2nd edition. New York and London: Routledge. Original edition, 1977.

Schieffelin, Edward L. 1996. "On Failure and Performance." In *The Performance of Healing*, edited by Carol Laderman and Marina Roseman. London: Routledge, 59–90.

Silverstein, Michael. 2000. "Whorfianism and the Linguistic Imagination of Nationality." In *Regimes of Language: Ideologies, Polities, and Identities*, edited by P. Kroskrity. Santa Fe: School of American Research Press, 85–138.

Silverstein, Michael. 2009. "Private Ritual Encounters, Public Ritual Indexes." In *Ritual Communication*, edited by Gunter Senft and Ellen B. Basso. Oxford: Berg, 271–291.

Silverstein, Michael. Forthcoming. "Performative Risks in Risking Performance." In *Translating the Social World for Law*.

Singer, Milton. 1972. *When a Great Tradition Modernizes: An Anthropological Approach to Modern Civilization*. New York, Washington, DC, and London: Praeger.

Smith, Wilfred Cantwell. 1964. *The Meaning and End of Religion*. New York: New American Library. Original edition, 1962.

Tambiah, Stanley. 1979. "A Performative Approach to Ritual." *Proceedings of the British Academy* 65: 113–169.

Tambiah, Stanley. 1985. *Culture, Thought, and Social Action: An Anthropological Perspective*. Cambridge, MA and London: Harvard University Press.

Turner, Victor. 1957. *Schism and Continuity in an African Society: A Study of Ndembu Village Life*. Manchester: Manchester University Press.

Turner, Victor. 1969a. *The Forest of Symbols: Aspects of Ndembu Ritual.* Ithaca, NY: Cornell University Press.

Turner, Victor. 1969b. *The Ritual Process: Structure and Anti-Structure.* Berlin: de Gruyter.

Turner, Victor. 1973. "The Centre Out There: Pilgrim's Goal." *History of Religions* 12(3): 191–230. [Also printed as "Pilgrimages as Social Processes," in *Dramas, Fields and Metaphors: Symbolic Action in Human Society.* Ithaca, NY: Cornell University Press, 1974, 166–230.]

Turner, Victor. 1974. *Dramas, Fields and Metaphors: Symbolic Action in Human Society.* Ithaca, NY and London: Cornell University Press

Turner, Victor. 1978. *Image and Pilgrimage in Christian Culture: Anthropological Perspectives.* New York: Columbia University Press.

Whitehouse, Harvey. 2004. *Modes of Religiosity: A Cognitive Theory of Religious Transmission.* Walnut Creek, CA: AltaMira Press.

Wulff, Donna M. 1986. "Religion in a New Mode: The Convergence of the Aesthetic and the Religious in Medieval India." *Journal of the American Academy of Religion* 54(4): 673–688.

FURTHER READING

Austin 1962 [*This is the locus classicus for Austin's theory of performativity in language. The book has had a tremendous influence on the philosophy of language as well as ritual studies.*]

Bell 1992 [*Drawing upon the sociologist Pierre Bourdieu's theory of practice, Bell develops a theory of 'ritual mastery' that finds its paradigmatic expression in the performance of ritual.*]

Fischer-Lichte 2004 [*In this book, Erika Fischer-Lichte traces the emergence of performance as 'an art event' in its own right. In setting performance art on an equal footing with the traditional art object, she heralds a new aesthetics.*]

Michaels 2012 [*This article discusses the difference between 'natural' emotions and ritual or staged emotions, especially weeping.*]

Michaels 2016 [*This book deals with various Hindu rituals and Hindu ritual theory, as exemplified in the Purvamimamsa theory, the only elaborate non-Western theory of ritual.*]

Michaels/Wulf 2012 [*This volume contains a number of articles focusing on emotions in rituals and festivals, private and public performances, and fine and performing arts.*]

Sax 1995 [*A brief summary of the Indian concept of 'lila,' which denotes 'play' in both senses of the English term: theatre as well as playful activity. In India, dramatic lilas often take a highly ritualized form.*]

Sax 2002 [*Analyzes a popular ritual performance that takes the form of a dramatization of India's great epic Mahabharata.*]

Schechner 1985 [*A collection in which Schechner explicitly addresses the relationship between ritual and performance.*]

Schechner 2003 [*A collection of Schechner's earliest essays, several of which relate performance to ritual.*]

Tambiah 1979 [*Perhaps the most sophisticated—and certainly the most influential—attempt to apply 'performance theory' to rituals.*]

Turner 1974 [*A very accessible collection of mid-career essays from Turner, in several of which he develops his theory of 'ritual drama.'*]

Whitehouse 2004 [*In this book, Harvey Whitehouse presents a testable theory of how religions are created, passed on, and changed. At the center of his theory are two divergent 'modes of religiosity': the imagistic and the doctrinal.*]

CHAPTER 21

....

SOUND

....

ROSALIND I. J. HACKETT

CHAPTER SUMMARY

....

- Whether through singing, chanting, reciting, preaching, wailing, shouting, or whispering, the voice is a primary mode of expression in religious contexts.
- Its delivery and modulation, as well its silencing, can be analyzed in relation to performance, gender, identity, embodiment, affect, imagination, and spatial context.
- Using a sound-based methodology in studying religion relates to broader interest in sound studies, as well as multi-sensoriality and materiality.
- The use of sound-producing instruments in rituals raises salient questions about the materiality of sound in relation to listening experiences and healing.
- New emphasis on the spatiality of sound offers fresh understanding of the interplay between sight, sound, and religious ideas as well as the use of acoustic design, material, and/or natural features to optimize the sensual, especially the acoustic, experience of ritual spaces.
- A more sonically aware religious studies would provide new analytical insights into forms of religious mediation, expression, and communication, notably in those cultures that do not privilege visuality.
- New forms of technological mediation have transformed the capacity to amplify, record, transmit, modify, and repurpose religiously or spiritually significant sounds.

It is often said that communication is at the heart of most forms of religious activity, whether it is prayer, ritual, symbolic expression, musical performance, meditation, or healing (see Krech, "Communication," this volume). In reaching out to perceived divine or spiritual powers and to each other, humans draw on various types of sonic expression, such as singing, chanting, shouting, preaching, crying, clapping, and drumming, which in turn may be heard by others.[1] They may also engage in forms of silent meditation and

---

[1] For related discussions of sound and religion see my chapters "Sounds Religious," in *Contemporary Views on Comparative Religion*, edited by Peter Antes, Armin W. Geertz, and Mikael Rothstein (Sheffield:

deep listening to connect with their inner being. Spirit forces may be identified with particular sounds, manifesting independently or through human or natural agents. In some traditions, sound is believed to be the creative, vibrational energy of the universe itself.

This chapter explores the significance and potential of a sound-based approach to the study of religion using the themes of voice, ritual instruments, and spatiality. Such an approach is timely given the growing attention to the phenomena of sound, noise, and silence in a range of academic disciplines from ethnomusicology to ecology, and physics to phenomenology. The focus on aurality also dovetails well with the efforts of those seeking to promote studies of the materiality and multi-sensoriality, and not just the textuality, of religion (see the *Journal of Material Religion*; Promey 2014; Plate 2014; Meyer 2009; 2012; Morgan 2005).[2] By the same token, it seeks to open up more space in sound studies for religious considerations and examples, particularly beyond the liturgical realm.

In part because of the tendency of Western thought to privilege sight over other senses, and in part because of the challenges of studying the acoustic and auditory dimensions of religion (Hackett 2011), there is a relative dearth of scholarship on sound in or as religion (Beck 2009 [1993]; 2006, cf. Samuels et al. 2010; Weiner 2014). Isaac Weiner trenchantly refers to this as our "disciplinary deafness" (Weiner 2009, 897). Happily, there now exists a critical mass of scholars in religion, history, anthropology, and ethnomusicology, along with sound artists and filmmakers, who have been foregrounding sound in their studies of religion, and engaging the burgeoning literature on sound studies (Sterne 2012). Variously, they explore the production, transmission, and reception of sound in different religious and cultural contexts, as well as broader conceptual and methodological questions. They consider religion in terms of the temporal, affective, and experiential qualities of the sonic, and think about the myriad ways that sound constitutes, structures, and affords particular sensory experience to religion—and vice versa.

DEFINITION AND SCOPE

From the outset it is important to recognize the complexity of the phenomenon of sound. This is well captured by Douglas Kahn, a historian and theorist of the media arts and experimental music:

> By sound I mean sounds, voices, and aurality—all that might fall within or touch on auditive phenomena, whether this involves actual sonic or auditive events or ideas

Equinox, 2016) and "Aural Media" in *The Wiley-Blackwell Companion to Material Religion*, edited by Manuel Vásquez and Vasudha Narayan (Chichester: John Wiley, 2016).

  [2] We should not forget the pioneering work of William A. Graham, who in his landmark book, *Beyond the Written Word: Oral Aspects of Scripture in the History of Religion* (Graham 1993), reminded us that scriptures were as much spoken and performed as read.

about sound or listening: sounds actually heard or heard in myth, idea, or implication; sounds heard by everyone or imagined by one person alone; or sounds as they fuse with the sensorium as a whole. (Kahn 1999, 3)

It is important to note the emphasis on sounds made and sounds heard, as well as sounds imagined. Certain sounds could be classified as 'music' in some instances (cf. John Blacking's seminal definition, 'humanly organized sound'), but the broader categorization has greater cross-cultural purchase and takes us beyond more formal ritual settings into private and public soundscapes.[3] Ethnomusicologist Peter McMurray, whose own research on Sufi rituals in the Balkans takes him to the "margins of music studies," is thus inclined to propose that the basic premise of sound studies is that "sound, and not just music, can serve as a stable and rich object of study" (McMurray 2012, 235). He offers a cogent summary of this emergent field, with plenty of resonances for those coming from the study of religion:

> More specifically, questions of the voice, of amplification, of vocal and instrumental timbre, of intersections between architecture and sound, of recitation and speaking as sonic matter, of presence and nearness, of "desirability" of sound and "noise," of body movement and breathing, of theologies of sacral uttering, of materialities of sound production and resonance, and many others can and should be addressed, and indeed may be understood as priorities in sound studies. (McMurray 2012, 235)

This new attentiveness to sonic culture, which may matter more for different historical periods, is ably demonstrated by one of the earlier authors writing on sound and hearing in (American) religious history, Leigh Eric Schmidt, in his landmark study *Hearing Things: Religion, Illusion, and the American Enlightenment* (2002). A study of the auditory, he contends, must take into account "the whole of the devotional soundscape," namely "attentiveness to noises, joyful and awful" that might comprise "sobbing, sighing, groaning, and laughing," as well as "psalms, bells, and trumpets" (Schmidt 2002, 35). Likewise, it must recognize the corporeal, dialogic, and participatory aspects of hearing through examination of the historical accounts and representations of the "rituals, disciplines, performances, and commodities" in particular cultural settings (Schmidt 2002, 36). Importantly, his work examines how auditory experiences and hallucinations of people 'hearing God' were reimagined and marked with illusion during the American Enlightenment and its aftermath.

VOICE AND VOCALIZATION

Using the human voice as a form of religious expression and communication is common to many religious traditions, and privileged in some. In her review of anthropological

---

[3] But, see Novak/Sakakeeny (2015) for critiques on the limitations of sound and soundscape theory and the need for more integration of 'sound studies' and 'music studies.'

approaches to voice and voicing, Amanda Weidman underscores the need to be attentive to the multiple registers of the voice—it is a sonic phenomenon, with timbre or
vocal quality that is socially meaningful, as well as being material in the sense that vocal
sounds are produced through bodily actions and particular practices (Weidman 2014,
235). This is well instanced in Greg Urban's study of Amerindian ritual wailing in Brazil,
where he provides interesting physical details on how the various vocal sounds, such as
cry break, voiced inhalation, creaky voice, and falsetto vowels, are produced to signal
sadness and grief (Urban 1988). For those in the field of sound healing, the vibrations
generated through chanting, singing, and singing bowls are the means of recalibrat-
ing the diseased body.[4] As emphasized by musician and philosopher Marcel Cobussen,
"[m]usic as well as sound in general needs bodies and bodily action; only through interacting bodies does air start to vibrate and becomes able to transmit sounds" (Cobussen
2012, 436).[5]

The embodied nature of the voice is well evidenced in the case of the German medieval mystic and musician Hildegard of Bingen (1098–1179) who believed her body to
be the vestment of the spirit, which has a living voice. She thus considered it proper for
the body, with its soul, to use its voice to sing praises to God. Singing for Hildegard was
an embodied performance that reflected both the pleasures and suffering of devotion
(Holsinger 2002, 131). Relying too much on a strictly formalistic analysis of this medieval mystic's compositions and musical expression, Holsinger contends, would miss her
understanding of musical sound as a somatic, erotic, and often gendered aspect of her
visionary life (Holsinger 2002, 102).

Vocalized forms of expression mediate natural and historical contexts. Tuvan throat-
singers draw on the natural sound sources of their "overtone-rich ambient environment"
in Central Asia to please the local spirits (Levin 2006, 38). Jeff Todd Titon has studied
the way special sounds signify a spiritual presence through chanted and sung sermons
and prayers in both the black and white Baptist traditions in the American South (see,
for example, Titon 1988). Linguistic anthropologist Nicholas Harkness examines how
Korean Christians "strive through vocalization to exhibit certain idealized qualities of
contemporary Christian personhood, using European-style classical singing as their
model" (Harkness 2014, 6). He describes how they cultivate a 'clean,' healthy voice that
is associated with a Christian aesthetic of peace and progress, and suppress sounds of
suffering and hardship heard in the voices of older generations. Based on her study of
nineteenth-century Colombian primary sources (hearing, writing, speech, and song),
ethnomusicologist Ana María Ochoa Gautier finds that "ideas about sound, especially
the voice, were central to the very definition of life" and that the question of how to

---

[4] See, for example, the work of the late Dr. Mitchell Gaynor: <http://gaynoroncology.com/services/
mind-body-spirit/> (accessed April 16, 2015).

[5] Marleen de Witte's call for a more embodied, tactile approach to African religious life and its
sonic dimensions, rather than the more symbolic interpretations of religious sounds, is apposite here
(2008, 692).

distinguish between human and non-human sounds took on greater importance in a colonial context (Gautier 2014, 5).

Anne Rasmussen's ethnomusicological study of Islamic performance in Indonesia also addresses how vocal sounds, in this case, Qur'anic recitation, index Arab-influenced Islamic musical styles and genres, notably from Egypt (Rasmussen 2010). This Arab aesthetic combines with local musical discourses and practices in the archipelago, mediating the interplay of multiple Islamic identities. The voices of women are a distinctive feature of Indonesia's rich soundscape and Rasmussen's rich research focuses on how women embody, encode, and enact the sound of the recited Qur'an in public and private settings. Despite the apparently transient nature of recorded music in this context, Rasmussen discusses how audiocassettes "created significant space for women as composers, performers, and producers in the field of Islamic musical arts" (Rasmussen 2010, 192). She suggests that the process of making the music may be more important than a lasting product; moreover, the material media could serve as souvenirs of live music events and become a commodity of exchange (Rasmussen 2010, 188–189).

Further examples demonstrate the salience of aural media technologies not just for the reproduction and amplification of ritual vocal performance but because they may also be considered as ritual instruments. Vicki Brennan (2012) conducted ethnographic research on the musical recordings done by the members of a branch of the Cherubim and Seraphim Church Movement in Nigeria. She examines how these 'religious sound artifacts'—in the form of record albums and music videos—play an important role in the everyday religious practices of this Nigerian independent church community.[6] The 'recontextualized' recordings do not supplant live musical performance but they reproduce and circulate ethical and aesthetic values, nurturing "disciplined forms of emotion and embodiment" (413). Along with Birgit Meyer (2011) and Patrick Eisenlohr (2007), Brennan is interested in the paradox of how processes of mediation are rendered invisible by the materiality of technology and generate immediacy in religious settings. She pays particular attention to what she calls the "labor of immediacy" (Brennan 2012, 411) or the practical techniques that go into allowing choir members to achieve "affective and effective spiritual experiences" (Brennan 2012, 425).

Devotional songs were able to become a prominent feature of daily village life in a predominantly Hindu village in Tamil Nadu thanks to the advent of low-cost audiocassette technology in the 1980s. Ethnomusicologist Paul Greene writes about how such technological mediation allowed villagers to select songs suitable for a particular deity's festival or an important family event, or that marked the beginning of a day for a business, such as a teashop (Greene 1999). In some instances, women went into a trance when listening to a song about a goddess approaching, even though they were aware it was not live music. Greene notes that the villagers treated this 'refunctioned' cassette music as a type of 'auspicious sound' or offering to the deities (Greene 1999, 465). Its amplification during festival days meant that the presence of the goddess, Muttumariamma, became

---

[6] Brennan's article on hymns and the hymnal in Cherubim and Seraphim churches reminds us that material technologies are not solely electronic (Brennan 2013).

"especially palpable and inescapable" (Greene 1999, 465) and, over time, increasingly central to goddess-worship in the village in general, and even further afield.

Ritual Instruments

After singing, chanting, and reciting, ritual (sounding) instruments constitute a productive area of inquiry for those interested in the interrelationship of sound and religion. R. Murray Schafer proposes that this type of sound-producing object has a complex function (Schafer 2003, 26). For example, the church bell can be centrifugal in that it is believed to scare off evil spirits and centripetal in the sense that it draws people together for religious observance to maintain the ritual regimen. Historian Alain Corbin's study of bells in nineteenth-century France demonstrates how they served as auditory and defensive markers (Corbin 1998). He notes that no sounds in the rural setting could compete with the bell. In addition to their apotropaic virtue, bells were also believed to have the power to summon angels. Steven Feld was also interested in how village bells, like rainforest birds, "habituate local listeners to a sense of place and produce consciousness of space and time" (Feld 2012, xxviii). This turned into a multi-CD project on the worldwide culture of bells that sought to counter the notion of sound as ephemeral, such as how one can hear history and transformation in European bells.[7]

The 'supernatural' power of bells in many cultures stems from both from their sheer size and their "peculiar and somewhat dissonant sound" (Marsh 2013, 465). Bells were regularly baptized and given names in medieval England. Their music was believed to be able to carry prayers to heaven, where they might facilitate the passage of departed souls through purgatory (Marsh 2013, 466). Historian Christopher Marsh attributes the persistence of church bells to their "unmistakable loudness" (Marsh 2013, 499) and the fact that their messages could be received and interpreted in various ways. This meant that "[o]lder beliefs in the power of bells were in practice permitted to coexist with more rigorous reformist attitudes" (Marsh 2013, 501). In his masterly study of bells across history and cultures, Percival Price traces the earliest use of bells to ancient China. Early writings discuss the tone qualities of the bells and the marvelous powers ascribed to them, based on theories of the essence of sound as a transcendental power (Price 1983, 3).[8]

Being attentive to the particular sounds and material properties of sound-making instruments may provide deeper understanding of their symbolic, mythic, aesthetic, and ritual significance more generally. For example, the metal objects—mainly bells and rattles—used in ritual in ancient West Mexico were valued because of both their sound and color (Hosler 1994). Archaeologist Dorothy Hosler notes that the proportion of metal ritual objects is unusually high compared to other zones in Mesoamerica. She

---

[7] See his CD series, 'The Time of Bells' with VoxLox.

[8] Price cites Laurence Picken in D. P. Walker, *Spiritual and Demonic Magic from Ficino to Campanella* (London: Warburg Institute 1958, 86).

links the belief that metal was sacred and animate to their creation myth that the first humans were formed by the creator out of ash and particular metals, and to the linguistic connections between bell sounds and metallic colors. Golden and silvery colors were associated with the solar and lunar deities in many regions of the Americas. The sounds of bells and composite bell instruments played a major role in rituals celebrating human and agricultural fertility and regeneration, in warfare as protective devices, and in the sacred paradise, created through song and sound. They also were believed to replicate the sounds of thunder, rain, jaguars, and rattlesnakes. While evidence is incomplete, Hosler suggests that rattles, bells, and other rattling instruments are used presently or in the recent past in the context of shamanic activity.

The Tibetan singing bowl provides another example of an ancient sound-producing instrument that is used in contemporary healing practices. Long used as a signal to begin and end periods of silent meditation in Tibetan Buddhism, it is now the subject of publications, websites, and blogs. According to tradition, the bowls are made of seven metals—one metal for each of the planets (Jansen 2002, 23). Each metal produces an individual sound, including harmonics, and together these sounds produce the unique singing sound of the bowl as the rim is struck or rubbed by a padded mallet. They also produce a physical vibration that can be felt. For some sound healers, it is the somatic rather than the auditory quality of the vibrations that is paramount. The emphasis is on finding a bowl that harmonizes with each individual and his or her body. For experts in or purveyors of these sounding objects, materiality matters in accounting for the perceived spiritual and healing powers of the bowls. The majority of singing bowls are made from similar high quality bell metal bronze which is difficult to make, very hard to work with, and expensive, according to Joseph Feinstein, and whose wonderful tone some would claim is "another secret to the special sound of singing bowls."[9] For others, the authenticity of these objects is linked to the belief that prayers or mantras were recited as the metals were hammered into the ancient bowls, emerging later when the bowls were played. New discourses of authentication now come from the scientific world with studies of the bowls' natural vibrational modes (Terwagne/Bush 2011).[10] These types of valuations of sonic material efficacy point to new avenues of research in the study of religion.

Spatiality

Sound and space are mutually constitutive of each other, whether from the perspective of audition or vibration (Eisenberg 2015). Yet the spatial turn in religious studies has generally failed to draw on the rich array of works in sound studies that explore the intimate relationship between sound and space. These works have served to question the

---

[9] <http://www.himalayanbowls.com> (accessed April 15, 2015).
[10] <http://www.bbc.com/news/science-environment-13976598> (accessed April 15, 2015).

privileging of temporality over spatiality in descriptions of auditory experience and the binary oppositions between the visual and the auditory (Eisenberg 2015).

The 'soundscape' concept that has featured prominently in several studies derives from the work of R. Murray Schafer on sonic environments (Schafer 1994). Along similar lines, but with greater emphasis on emplacement (Eisenberg 2015), anthropologist and ethnomusicologist Steven Feld developed the concept of an 'acoustic ecology' or 'acoustemology'. Based on his field experiences in the rich aural environments of the Bosavi people in Papua New Guinea during the 1970s (Feld/Brenneis 2004), he understood this as a sonic way of knowing place, a way of attending to hearing, a way of absorbing that would do justice to the layered complexity of the human and environmental world of sound.[11] In his discussion of how sonic practices territorialize, Andrew Eisenberg (2015) is interested in how Islam mediates the public/private distinction in relation to the sacred, and the sacred in relation to sound. His own research using 'participant-audition' on the acoustic ecology of a Muslim neighborhood in Mombasa demonstrates how the residents enact a sonorous 'communitarian privacy' through their pious acts of audition, movement, and vocalization (2015; see also 2013). In a similar vein, Charles Hirschkind's landmark book on listening practices among Muslim communities in Egypt demonstrates how the soundscapes produced through the circulation of the Qur'an and sermon tapes reshape moral aptitudes and the moral economy of revival in Cairo (Hirschkind 2006).

Art historian Nina Ergin is particularly attentive to the acoustic and material qualities of mosques and their religious significance. In her study of the soundscape of sixteenth-century Istanbul mosques, she uses archival documents to demonstrate that Ottoman architects used acoustic technology and design to optimize the sensual, especially the acoustic, experience of the performance space of the Qur'anic 'text-as-event' (Ergin 2008, 212–214). In that connection, she cites the sixteenth-century master architect Mimar Koca Sinan who creatively used domed ceilings and structural and decorative elements, such as sounding vessels, tiled walls, and soft carpets, to balance sound reflection and absorption (Ergin 2008, 214). He even factored in the sound-absorbing qualities of the worshipper's bodies in the quest for a "very reverberant, 'live' space that gives the audience a feeling of majesty and grandeur" (Ergin 2008, 215). Ergin makes a persuasive case for closer analysis of sonic phenomena by architectural historians, maintaining that this could explain the physical appearance of some mosques (Ergin 2008, 218) and do more justice to the mosque as an experiential space. Since sound is integral to many buildings in the Islamic world, she contends that such a sonically aware approach would be more sensitive to the original cultural context. Moreover, it would also bring new understandings to studies of space in relation to Middle Eastern gender history, as attested to by her research on Ottoman royal women's spaces (Ergin 2014).

Relatedly, the work of medieval art historian Bissera Pentcheva explores the way sight and sound work together in the sixth-century interior of the church of Hagia Sophia in

---

[11] <http://acousticecology.org>. See also <http://www.earthear.com>.

Constantinople to afford the worshipper a multi-sensory aesthetic experience (Pentcheva 2011). Using a combination of liturgical texts, Byzantine ekphrasis or poetic language, and modern digital technology, particularly computer auralizations, she uncovers how the optical shimmer of the marble (together with gold sheaths) is linked to its acoustical capacity to reflect sound waves. Marble was also linguistically and culturally linked to water adding to the sensual materiality of the space (Pentcheva 2011, 96). Pentcheva contends that the psychoacoustics of the distant, non-intimate type of sound generated by human breath in the reverberant acoustical space of Hagia Sophia could be perceived in metaphysical terms. Worshippers experienced the 'bodiless voice' of Hagia Sophia as 'indwelling spirit' or *pneuma* through the building's dynamic optical and aural effects.

An exciting new direction for sonically aspirational religion scholars is Isaac Weiner's *Religion Out Loud: Religious Sound, Public Space, and American Pluralism* (2014), which analyzes the politics of religious pluralism in the United States through a series of case studies that involve disputes about religious sound and noise in the public realm. Contending that religion is not just about beliefs and values but more so about expressive practices that extend into the public realm, Weiner's research raises important questions about the regulation and accommodation of religious sounding in American urban spaces. Along similar lines, in an article that explores the 'sonic sacralization' of urban space in Accra, Ghana, Marleen de Witte (2008) describes the clashes between Ga traditionalists and born-again Christians over the traditional "ban on drumming and noisemaking" (Witte 2008, 690). She is interested in the conflicting ways of conceptualizing sound in relation to space, personhood, and spiritual power (Witte 2008, 707). In the increasingly competitive urban soundscape, Pentecostal and charismatic groups have succeeded in creating an auditory sacred space beyond that of physical religious territory through their effective, and at times, aggressive, use of modern sound technologies (Witte 2008, 706).

CONCLUSION

It has been the contention of this chapter that greater attention to the acoustic and auditory is called for in studies of religion, whether as a primary or complementary focus. That sound is a critical component of religious world-making is well attested to by the range of scholarly contributions discussed here. Greater engagement by religion scholars of the broader interdisciplinary turn to sound promises to be one of the more exciting prospects of the field of religious studies.

GLOSSARY

Auditory relating to the sense or organs of hearing.
Hearing the sense by which sound is perceived. As in the case of the other senses, hearing mediates cultural and religious experience.

Listening the act of hearing attentively.

Music organized or patterned types of sounds that are meaningful within a particular cultural setting. Musical sounds are generally described as having four components: timbre, pitch, duration, and dynamics. Religions vary in whether they have a concept of 'music' or 'sacred music' and whether they distinguish between vocal and instrumental music.

Sonic of or relating to audible sound.

Sound mechanical vibrations that have auditory effects. Sound involves propagation, transmission, and perception.

Soundscape a term coined by the Canadian composer R. Murray Shafer. It refers to an atmosphere or environment created by or with sound (musical or non-musical).

REFERENCES

Beck, Guy, ed. 2006. *Sacred Sound: Experiencing Music in World Religions*. Waterloo, ON: Wilfred Laurier University Press.

Beck, Guy. 2009. *Sonic Theology: Hinduism and Sacred Sound*, 2nd edition. Columbia, SC: University of South Carolina Press. Original edition, 1993.

Brennan, Vicki L. 2012. "Take Control: The Labor of Immediacy in Yoruba Christian Music." *Journal of Popular Music Studies* 24(4): 411–429. doi: 10.1111/jpms.12001

Brennan, Vicki L. 2013. "'Up Above the River Jordan': Hymns and Historical Consciousness in the Cherubim and Seraphim Churches of Nigeria." *Studies in World Christianity* 19(1): 31–49. doi: http://dx.doi.org/10.3366/swc.2013.0037

Cobussen, Marcel. 2012. "Towards a Material Spirituality (and Beyond)." *Die Tonkunst* 4(6).

Corbin, Alain. 1998. *Village Bells: Sound and Meaning in the 19th-Century French Countryside*. New York: Columbia University Press.

Eisenberg, Andrew J. 2013. "Islam, Sound, and Space: Acoustemology and Muslim Citizenship on the Kenyan Coast." In *Music, Sound, and Space: Transformations of Public and Private Experience*, edited by Georgina Born. Cambridge and New York: Cambridge University Press, 186–202.

Eisenberg, Andrew J. 2015. "Sound." In *Keywords in Sound*, edited by David Novak and Matt Sakakeeny. Durham, NC: Duke University Press, 193–207.

Eisenlohr, Patrick. 2007. "Technologies of the Spirit: Devotional Islam, Sound Reproduction and the Dialectics of Mediation and Immediacy in Mauritius." *Anthropological Theory* 9(3): 273–296.

Ergin, Nina. 2008. "The Soundscape of Sixteenth-Century Istanbul Mosques: Architecture and Qur'an Recital." *Journal of the Society of Architectural Historians* 67(2): 204–221. doi: 10.1525/jsah.2008.67.2.204

Ergin, Nina. 2014. "Ottoman Royal Women's Spaces: The Acoustic Dimension." *Journal of Women's History* 26(1): 89–111. doi: 10.1353/jowh.2014.0003

Feld, Steven. 2012. *Sound and Sentiment: Birds, Weeping, Poetics, and Song in Kaluli Expression*, 3rd edition with a new introduction by the author. Durham, NC: Duke University Press. Original edition, 1982.

Feld, Steven and Donald Brenneis. 2004. "Doing Anthropology in Sound." *American Ethnologist* 31(4): 461–474. doi: 10.1525/ae.2004.31.4.461

Gautier, Ana Maria Ochoa. 2014. *Aurality: Listening and Knowledge in Nineteenth-Century Colombia*. Durham, NC: Duke University Press.

Graham, William A. 1993. *Beyond the Written Word: Oral Aspects of Scripture in the History of Religion*. New York: Cambridge University Press.

Greene, Paul D. 1999. "Sound Engineering in a Tamil Village: Playing Audio Cassettes as Devotional Performance." *Ethnomusicology* 43(3): 459–489.

Hackett, Rosalind I. J. 2011. "Auditory Materials." In *The Routledge Handbook of Research Methods in the Study of Religion*, edited by Michael Stausberg and Steven Engler. London and New York: Routledge, 447–458.

Harkness, Nicholas. 2014. *Songs of Seoul: An Ethnography of Voice and Voicing in Christian South Korea*. Berkeley and Los Angeles: University of California Press.

Hirschkind, Charles. 2006. *The Ethical Soundscape: Cassette Sermons and Islamic Counterpublics*. New York: Columbia University Press.

Holsinger, Bruce W. 2002. *Music, Body and Desire in Medieval Culture: Hildegard of Bingen to Chaucer*. Stanford, CA: Stanford University Press.

Hosler, Dorothy. 1994. *The Sounds and Colors of Power: The Sacred Metallurgical Technology of Ancient West Mexico*. Cambridge, MA: MIT Press.

Jansen, Eva Rudy. 2002. *Singing Bowls: A Practical Handbook of Instruction and Use*. Havelte, Holland: Binkey Kok Publications.

Kahn, Douglas. 1999. *Noise, Water, Meat: A History of Sound in the Arts*. Cambridge, MA: MIT Press.

Levin, Theodor. 2006. *Where Rivers and Mountains Sing: Sound, Music, and Nomadism in Tuva and Beyond*. Bloomington, IN: Indiana University Press.

McMurray, Peter. 2012. "Urban Heterophony and the Mediation of Place." *Urban People* 14(2): 227–254.

Marsh, Christopher. 2013. *Music and Society in Early Modern England*. New York: Cambridge University Press.

Meyer, Birgit, ed. 2009. *Aesthetic Formations: Media, Religion, and the Senses*. New York: Palgrave Macmillan.

Meyer, Birgit. 2011. "Mediation and Immediacy: Sensational Forms, Semiotic Ideologies and the Question of the Medium." *Social Anthropology* 19(1): 23–39. doi: 10.1111/j.1469-8676.2010.00137.x

Meyer, Birgit. 2012. *Mediation and the Genesis of Presence: Towards a Material Approach to Religion*. Utrecht: Universiteit Utrecht.

Morgan, David. 2005. *The Sacred Gaze: Religious Visual Culture in Theory and Practice*. Berkeley and Los Angeles: University of California Press.

Novak, D. and M. Sakakeeny, eds. 2015. *Keywords in Sound*. Durham, NC: Duke University Press.

Pentcheva, Bissera V. 2011. "Hagia Sophia and Multisensory Aesthetics." *GESTA* 50(2): 93–111.

Plate, Brent. 2014. *A History of Religion in 5½ Objects: Bringing the Spiritual to Its Senses*. Boston, MA: Beacon Press.

Price, Percival. 1983. *Bells and Man*. Oxford: Oxford University Press.

Promey, Sally, ed. 2014. *Sensational Religion: Sensory Cultures in Material Practice*. New Haven, CT: Yale University Press.

Rasmussen, Anne K. 2010. *Women, the Recited Qur'an, and Islamic Music in Indonesia*. Berkeley and Los Angeles: University of California Press.

Samuels, David W., Louise Meintjes, Ana Maria Ochoa, and Thomas Porcello. 2010. "Soundscapes: Toward a Sounded Anthropology." *Annual Review of Anthropology* 39: 329–345. doi: 10.1146/annurev-anthro-022510-132230

Schafer, Murray. 2003. "Open Ears." In *The Auditory Culture Reader*, edited by Michael Bull and Les Back. New York: Berg, 25–39.

Schafer, R. Murray. 1994. *The Soundscape: Our Sonic Environment and the Tuning of the World*. Rochester, VT: Destiny Books.

Schmidt, Leigh Eric. 2002. *Hearing Things: Religion, Illusion, and the American Enlightenment*. Cambridge, MA: Harvard University Press.

Sterne, Jonathan, ed. 2012. *The Sound Studies Reader*. New York: Routledge.

Terwagne, Denis and John W. M. Bush. 2011. "Tibetan Singing Bowls." *Nonlinearity* 24: R51–R66.

Titon, Jeff Todd. 1988. *Powerhouse for God: Speech, Chant, and Song in an Appalachian Baptist Church*. Austin, TX: University of Texas Press.

Urban, Greg. 1988. "Ritual Wailing in Amerindian Brazil." *American Anthropologist* NS 90(2): 385–400.

Weidman, Amanda. 2014. "Anthropology and Voice." *Annual Review of Anthropology* 43: 37–51. doi: 0.1146/annurev-anthro-102313-030050

Weiner, Isaac A. 2009. "Sound and American Religions." *Religion Compass* 3(5): 897–908. doi: 10.1111/j.1749-8171.2009.00164.x

Weiner, Isaac. 2014. *Religion Out Loud: Religious Sound, Public Space, and American Pluralism*. New York: New York University Press.

Witte, Marleen de. 2008. "Accra's Sounds and Sacred Spaces." *International Journal of Urban and Regional Research* 32(3): 690–709. doi: 10.1111/j.1468-2427.2008.00805.x

FURTHER READING

Beck 2006 [*The current textbook of choice for anyone wanting to teach a course on sound and music in religion, or simply gain a comparative and historical overview of this neglected dimension of religious studies. The focus is on liturgical music, mainly chant, in the major religious traditions. Each chapter is written by someone who has both academic and performing skills in a particular tradition, and musical samples can be heard on the accompanying CD.*]

Cobussen, Marcel. 2008. *Thresholds: Rethinking Spirituality Through Music*. Aldershot: Ashgate. [*A philosophically and theoretically rich analysis of the relationship between music and spirituality. Cobussen focuses on the current movement within contemporary classical music known as New Spiritual Music to reflect critically on definitions of music and spirituality and their affinities.*]

Ergin 2008 [*A magnificent study of the acoustic and material qualities of mosques and their religious significance.*]

Erlmann, Veit, ed. 2004. *Hearing Cultures: Essays on Sound, Listening and Modernity*. London: Bloomsbury. [*This book richly demonstrates the merits of the cultural and historical contextualization of auditory perception. Focusing on extramusical sounds (mainly nonreligious), the contributions are theoretically sophisticated and diverse. They make a cogent case that research on sound offers new ways to examine culture and social issues.*]

Feld/Brenneis 2004 [*Essential reading for anyone wanting to conduct research on the sonic dimensions of religious worlds. Takes the form of an interview with the father of the anthropology of sound, Steve Feld. Engaging and methodologically rich.*]

Hirschkind 2006 [*An exemplary ethnographic study of Islamic listening practices in Egypt. Methodological contributions of this book include the importance of sensitive field research and* participant-observation/audition, and relating auditory experience to ethical dispositions and changing social and political contexts.]

Novak/Sakakeeny 2015 [*A definitive resource for sound studies, with twenty compelling essays on why studying sound matters. Topics covered include noise, acoustics, music, and silence with each author addressing the philosophical debates and core problems in defining, classifying, and conceptualizing sound.*]

Schmidt 2002 [*A highly influential study of spiritual hearing practices in a particular historical and cultural setting. An impressive range of examples with brilliant interdisciplinary analysis.*]

Sterne 2012 [*An essential collection of essays on the key debates and discussions in sound studies. The Reader touches on key themes like noise and silence; architecture, acoustics and space; media and reproducibility; listening, voices, and disability; culture, community, power and difference; and shifts in the form and meaning of sound across cultures, contexts and centuries.*]

Weiner 2014 [*This landmark study traces the story of religious 'noise' through multiple historical eras and diverse American religious communities. By taking seriously the sonic disputes over the appropriate and inappropriate public expressions of religious presence, Weiner is able to make the case that religious pluralism is more about styles of practice and use of body and space than beliefs and values. Moreover, this important work encourages scholars to pay much greater attention to the publicly contested sensory cultures, especially the sonic worlds, of American religious life.*]

CHAPTER 22

···

SPACE

···

DAVID CHIDESTER

Chapter Summary

···

- Theories of religious space can be divided between those that focus on poetic meaning, political power, or material production.
- Examples from Africa illustrate how religious space can be based on structural oppositions, such as the indigenous opposition between home and wild space and the colonial opposition between land and sea.
- The production of religious space commonly establishes barriers, but instances of shared religious space can be found in Africa, India, and elsewhere.
- Competition over the ownership of a place is a recurring feature of the dynamics of religious space, as illustrated by the conflict over the site in Ayodhya identified by Hindus as the birthplace of Rama and by Muslims as a historically significant mosque.
- With the rise of modern nations, religious space is increasingly managed by state apparatuses, such as courts, and at the same time dispersed through transnational social networks in diaspora.

Religious space is produced through the labor of ritualization and interpretation. Although spatial orientations, special places, and embodied disciplines might be imagined as given by God or handed down by tradition, religious space is created in and through the performance of ritual in set apart times and places and the interpretative work of making meaning. This religious labor generates a surplus of meaning and power that is inevitably subject to competing claims on its ownership. In struggles over the ownership of space, crucial questions are raised about access and control. In the dynamics of inclusion and exclusion, who is allowed in? Who is kept out? Often symbolized in terms of purity, this issue of access is entangled in the dynamics of power: Who owns the means of spatial production? How are spatial resources distributed? What are the material locations, networks, and oppositions of spatial orientation?

After a brief review of theoretical literature on space in the study of religion, this chapter illustrates the production of space through examples drawn from Africa and India. By exploring these cases, we will encounter recurring features of the production of space in the history of religions.

POETICS, POLITICS, AND PRODUCTION

Scholars of religion have tended to emphasize either the poetics or the politics of religious space. While the poetics of space is all about meaning, the politics of space is the dynamics in which people, along with their meanings, are positioned as above or below, as inside or outside, within the structure of a prevailing regime of power. Developing a Romantic poetics of religious meaning, Mircea Eliade held that the sacred irrupted, manifested, or appeared in certain places, causing them to become powerful centers of meaningful worlds (Eliade 1958, 367–385; 1961, 20–65). By contrast, Jonathan Z. Smith has shown how place is sacralized through the cultural labor of ritual, in specific historical situations and political conditions, involving the hard work of attention, memory, design, construction, and control of place (Smith 1978, 88–103; 1987). This clash between the poetics of meaning-making and the politics of power relations marks a recurring divide in theories of religious space.

Can poetics and politics be combined? In his landmark text on the phenomenology of religion, *Religion in Essence and Manifestation* (1986 [1933]), Gerardus van der Leeuw explored the implications of his substantial definition of the sacred—'power'—in spatial terms. In a chapter on sacred space, he outlined an inventory of typical sacred places that have appeared in the history of religions. That inventory, however, was also a series of homologies in which van der Leeuw asserted the metaphoric equivalence of home, temple, settlement, pilgrimage site, and human body. A home was a temple, a temple a home. The city of Jerusalem, identified by van der Leeuw as sacred space in its most 'typical form', was a temple in the beginning and would be a temple in the end. The pilgrimage site, as a home, temple, or sacred settlement away from home, could ultimately be found at the center of the body in the human heart. Sacred places, therefore, formed a recursive series of metaphoric equivalences. In addition, van der Leeuw tracked a second series of homologies, identifying the core of each item in the first series, which linked the hearth (of the home), the altar (of the temple), the sanctuary (of the settlement), the shrine (of the pilgrimage site), and the heart (of the human body). These two series of equivalences established van der Leeuw's basic vocabulary for an analysis of sacred places. As they recurred in his analysis, they provided a poetics of sacred space.

At the same time, van der Leeuw laced his analysis with hints of a politics of sacred space. First, he identified a politics of position. In some moments, like Eliade, he attributed sole, transcendent, and ultimate agency to sacred power, even holding that sacred power actually positioned itself in the world. However, this mystifying of power was tempered by his recognition that the positioning of a sacred place was also a political act, whether that positioning involved, in his terms, selection, orientation, limitation, or conquest.

Second, van der Leeuw suggested another political aspect of sacred space by paying attention to the politics of exclusion. A sacred place, such as a home, was a space in which relations among persons could be negotiated and worked out. Some persons, however, were left out, kept out, or forced out. In fact, the sanctity of the inside was certified by maintaining and reinforcing boundaries that kept certain persons outside the sacred place. By recognizing this process of excluding persons, van der Leeuw raised the possibility that a politics of exclusion might be an integral part of the making of sacred space.

Third, van der Leeuw linked sacred space with a politics of property. A sacred place was not merely a meaningful place; it was a powerful place because it was appropriated, possessed, and owned. In several important passages of his text, van der Leeuw referred to the sacred power of property, asserting that property was the "realization of possibilities" (1986, 210). As the ultimate realization of possibilities, sacred space was inevitably owned by someone as property.

Fourth, and finally, van der Leeuw ultimately positioned sacred space in the context of a politics of exile. He insistently highlighted a 'modern' loss of the sacred, or alienation from the sacred, or nostalgia for the sacred, in his interpretation of basic data of religion. Van der Leeuw repeatedly noted that 'primitives' had the sacred; some common peasant folk have retained it; but 'moderns' have entirely lost it. The historical and essentially political situation of exile from the sacred entailed two theoretical implications for van der Leeuw's phenomenology of religion: the most sacred places were remote and the most authentic religious experience in relation to sacred space was homesickness. In the politics of exile, the sacred was positioned in relation to human beings who found themselves to be out of position.

In recent years, the study of the poetics and politics of space has been supplemented by theoretical work on the production of religious space. Following the philosopher Henri Lefebvre (1991), Kim Knott (2005) has focused on the production of space. Beginning with the body, which provides the primary source of space, Knott has analyzed the importance for religion of spatial dimensions, properties, aspects, and dynamics. The embodied bilateral contrast between right and left hands, for example, can structure general orientations in space as well as spatial oppositions. In developing a general theory of religion, Thomas A. Tweed has analyzed spatial strategies of dwelling and crossing, proposing that religious actors endeavor to "make homes and cross boundaries" (2006, 54). In this respect, Tweed has attended to productions of both domestic space, which is anchored in a specific place, and the transitional spaces of movement, migration, and diaspora in the spatial dynamics of religion. Emphasizing the material constraints on dwelling and crossing, Manuel A. Vásquez (2011, 260–319) has developed a theory of spatial networks for analyzing the production of space. Whether situated at home or moving on roads, deserts, or oceans, the production of religious space depends upon dealing with specific material conditions and shifting social networks.

HOMES AND CAVES, LAND AND SEA

Moving from theory to practice, we will consider specific cases of the production of religious space in Africa and India. As reconstructed in the anthropological literature (Hammond-Tooke 1975; Comaroff 1981), the cosmology of indigenous religion in southern Africa is based on a structural opposition between 'home space' and 'wild space.' Among the Xhosa-speaking people of the Eastern Cape, for example, the home is a sacred space, a domestic order that is built up not only through social relations of production and reproduction but also through ongoing ritual relations with ancestors. As the "people of the home" (*abantu bekhaya*), the ancestors perform vital functions—guiding, protecting, and sometimes chastising their descendants; reinforcing the authority of elders; and representing a spiritual reality beyond death—in a domestic religion designed "to make the homestead right" (*ukulungisa umzi*). While certain parts of the home, such as the hearth, the back wall, and the top of the door, are particularly associated with the spiritual presence of ancestors, the entire homestead is marked out through regular rituals as an ordered space of communication and exchange with ancestral spirits, with the cattle enclosure, or *kraal*, representing the most important site in this sacred architecture of the homestead.

The sacred space of the home, however, is also marked out in opposition to the wild, chaotic, and potentially dangerous region of the forest. In stark contrast to the space of the home, with its ancestral spirits, structured human relations, and domesticated animals, the forest contains not only wild animals but also witch familiars, the dangerous spirits deployed by witches, those anti-social agents who act to disrupt the harmony or stability of the home. The sacred space of the home, therefore, must be sustained by rituals that both invoke ancestors and protect against witches who draw their power from the wild space.

In between the home space and the wild space, the river represents a liminal space—sometimes good, sometimes evil—in which the spiritual "people of the river" (*abantu bomlambo*) play an ambiguous role in mediating between the domestic order of the homestead and the wild forces that threaten to disrupt it. Diviners, healers, and other ritual specialists have a distinctive relationship with this liminal space of the river, since they also mediate between the spiritual order of the home and the dangers associated with the wild space (Hammond-Tooke 1975; Chidester 2014, 9–13).

By this account, therefore, the indigenous Xhosa religion of the Eastern Cape is based on a kind of symbolic mapping, a spiritual geography grounded in the dichotomy between home space and wild space. A similar symbolic mapping has been identified in Tswana religion in the Northern Cape in the distinction between the domestic order of the human settlement (*motse*), which is organized and reinforced through ritual relations with ancestors, and the wild, chaotic, and dangerous forces associated with bush (*naga*), the domain of wild spirits and witch familiars (Comaroff 1981). Under colonial conditions, however, this mapping was altered by new relations between land and sea.

For both alien and indigenous people in colonial contact zones, a new orientation to the land was often articulated precisely in terms of an opposition between the land and the sea. In Africa, this opposition goes back at least to the contacts of the seventeenth century. "It is well-documented from missionary reports," as Wyatt MacGaffey has observed, "that in the seventeenth century white people were believed to live under the ocean." MacGaffey concludes that this belief "is not derived from experience but is a fundamental postulate in terms of which experience is interpreted" (1994, 257). Drawing on earlier mythic themes, this identification of Europeans with the sea became a symbolic template for interpreting the colonial encounter. Using this symbolic framework, Africans could reconfigure the encounter in terms of the spatial opposition between sea and land.

Under the impact of British colonization in nineteenth-century southern Africa, myths of the sea were reworked to make sense of the military incursions, dispossession of land, and new relations of power. In response to the British incursions and depredations of the early nineteenth century, for example, the Xhosa chief Ngqika (r. 1775–1829) observed that since the Europeans were people of the sea—the "natives of the water"— they should have stayed in the sea. They had no business coming out of the sea onto the land (Campbell 1815, 526). The Xhosa religious visionary and war-leader Nxele (d. 1819), also known as Makana, the Lynx, developed this observation about sea and land into an indigenous theology that identified two gods: Thixo, the god of the white people, who had punished white people for killing his son by casting them into the sea, and Mdalidiphu, the god of the deeps, who dwelled under the ground but had ultimate dominion over the sea (Peires 1979). Similarly, during the first half of the nineteenth century, a Zulu emergence myth was reconfigured in terms of this colonial opposition between land and sea. In the beginning, according to an account recorded in the 1850s, uNkulunkulu created human beings, male and female, but also black and white. While black human beings according to this myth were created to be naked, carry spears, and live on the land, white human beings were created to wear clothing, carry guns, and live in the sea (Bleek 1952, 3–4). For these African religious thinkers, therefore, the mythic origin of the world was clearly located in the new colonial era that produced the crucial spatial opposition between people of the sea and people of the land.

After the advent of postcolonial and post-apartheid democracy in 1994, South Africans still struggled over the ownership of religious space. In the Caledon Valley of the Free State, in a region known as the Conquered Territory, a chain of cave shrines formed a spatial network for new forms of religious coexistence (Coplan 2003).

Displaced and denied land ownership in the territory, Africans had also been prevented from visiting ancestral graves or sites associated with powerful chiefs and diviners of the past. After 1994, however, pilgrims began traveling to the caves overhanging streams and springs in the territory, marking out a series of sites that stretched over 60 kilometers. Although the caves were located on white-owned farms, neither the landowners nor the government prevented the pilgrims from gaining access to the cave shrines. White farmers might assert their claims to ownership, based on the sanctity of property, by charging admission fees. But ritual also asserted a claim to ownership.

Overcoming decades of exclusion, Africans pursued religious pilgrimage as an avenue for performing spiritual rituals of healing, purification, possession, and empowerment while implicitly asserting African claims on ownership of the land.

In the largest site, Badimong, "among ancestors," the caves above a river bed became locations for building altars, small enclosures, and temporary housing for pilgrims. A diverse array of religious practices coexisted at Badimong, with adherents of ancestral religion, initiates of traditional divination, and members of independent and mainline Christian churches all sharing the same space. Displaying fluidity in which a Christian feast of thanksgiving could shift into ancestral divination or possession, religious practices mixed and merged in the ritual observances of the cave shrines. As a vortex drawing together diverse rituals, Badimong was a rare instance of a shared religious space.

Mosques and Temples, Nation and Diaspora

Although rare, sharing religious space has occurred elsewhere in history (see, for example, Bigelow 2010; Cormack 2013). During the fourth century in Palestine, the shrine of the sacred oak at Mamre, near Hebron, was a place for regular ritualization and intensive interpretation by Jews, Christians, and pagans. Mamre, which was identified by Jews as the place where three angels visited the patriarch Abraham (Gen. 18:1–22), was interpreted by Christians as a site at which Christ, the second person of this trinity, appeared in the world. While Mamre attracted Jewish and Christian pilgrims, the sacred oak was also a pagan shrine, the site of an annual festival at which pagan celebrants invoked the angels, poured out wine, burned incense, and sacrificed animals. Although the Christian emperor Constantine tried to assert an exclusive Christian ownership of Mamre, alternative claims on the site continued to be advanced by Jews and pagans through ritual (Chidester 2000, 105–106).

India also holds examples of shared religious sites. Thomas Christians, tracing their lineage back to the apostle Thomas from Syria, who according to tradition moved to India in the first century, found a home within a broadly Hindu environment in southern India. Christians and Hindus shared temple precincts, street processions, and ritual regalia. The Christian shrine of Mylapore, the site of the martyrdom of Thomas, was also revered by Hindus and Muslims. Until captured by the Portuguese in 1517, Mylapore was an interreligious site for adherents of different religions (Chidester 2000, 454–457). In the city of Ayodhya in northern India, Muslims and Hindus worshiped together in the Babri Masjid, the mosque built in 1528 on the site of the presumed birthplace of the Hindu deity Rama, an avatar or manifestation of Vishnu. Under the impact of British colonialism, conflict between Muslims and Hindus developed at this site, inspiring the British administrators to erect a fence separating Muslims worshiping in the mosque from Hindus worshiping on a raised platform (van der Veer 1994, 153). Although divided by a barrier, Hindus and Muslims continued to perform rituals within the same sacred precinct of Ayodhya.

As a production of space, the fence was as much a part of the religious built environment of the precinct as the architecture of the mosque or the platform for ritual observances. Certainly, Muslims and Hindus developed different interpretations of the precinct's significance within larger sacred geographies. For Muslims, the Babri Masjid, like any mosque, was as an inviolable sacred site for prayers, sermons, and devotion to Allah. Although directing prayer to God toward Mecca, the mosque established a spatial orientation, which might be called a utopian orientation, which revolves around a God who is everywhere. By contrast, Hindus interpreted the site not only as the birthplace of Rama but also as the 'head' of the body of Vishnu that formed a geographical network made up of seven pilgrimage sites, or *tirthas*, distributed throughout India (Eck 2012). In this spatial orientation, which might be called a locative orientation, God might ultimately be everywhere but also necessarily anchored in specific sites or particular places of a sacred geography (see Smith 1978, 100–103; 1990, 121–142). The fence reinforced the division between these two religious orientations in space, a division further entrenched by British colonial administration, the partition of India and Pakistan, and religious rivalry over contested territory.

For Hindus, the network of *tirthas*, the dwellings of deities and the crossings between worlds, created a symbolic map of a unified India linked together by pilgrimage sites. Taking up this ritual construction of space, Hindu nationalists advanced the ideology of *hindutva*, the sacred bond between Hindus and Bharat Mata, Mother India. During the 1980s, Hindu nationalist campaigns focused on Ayodhya. Securing a secular court decision over Muslim objections in 1986, Hindu nationalists were granted the right to enter the Babri Mosque to perform ritual *puja* to Rama. In 1989, during a national election, Hindu nationalists focused on Ayodhya for political mobilization by asserting ritual claims to the space in laying the foundation stone for a new temple to Rama. Placed next to the mosque, the foundation stone was consecrated by water from all the sacred rivers and earth from all the pilgrimage sites of India. On December 6, 1992, in an extraordinary act of desecration, as many as 150,000 Hindus participated in the demolition of the mosque, brick by brick, to claim ownership of the space. In this ritualized destruction, the Muslim mosque became a locative space, a specific, highly charged location for the sacred, while the Hindu temple proposed for this location, remaining unbuilt for decades, became a utopian space for Hindu national aspirations (see Friedland and Hecht 1998).

A nation, which Ernst Renan (1990 [1882], 19) characterized as "a soul, a spiritual principle," can be based on utopian religious space, but a modern state in Max Weber's (1948 [1918], 78) classic definition is the monopoly on the exercise of legitimate violence over a territory. What counts as 'legitimate', of course, is the crucial problem in this definition of the state, but the spatial demarcation of territory is also at stake in the formation of the modern state system. In the production of religious space within this system, ritual rights are increasingly subject to the jurisdiction of state functions such as secular courts, civil administration, and public policing. In the case of

Ayodhya, secular courts tried to adjudicate religious space for Hindu nationalists by ruling for their ritual access to the mosque in 1986 but ruling against their plans for the ritual destruction of the mosque in 1992. As events unfolded, the state clearly did not hold a monopoly on the exercise of violence in the production and destruction of religious space.

While modern secular states have been involved in producing religious space, adjudicating ritual rights, access, and ownership, transnational circulations of people have produced new spatial orientations. Diaspora, or dispersion, has generated new interpretations and ritualizations of a sacred home that can only be engaged away from home. In the African diaspora, practitioners of Haitian Vodou, descendants of Africans who underwent the middle passage across the Atlantic Ocean into slavery, perform rituals that link Haiti with Africa, pouring libations on the ground, for example, that will cross the ocean to the motherland (Brown 1999). For the Hindu diaspora, which extends throughout the world, domestic rituals connect practitioners with Bharata Mata, Mother India (Vertovec 2000). In these ritual transactions in diaspora, local space, whether in Haiti or Trinidad, is reproduced as the utopian sacred space of a lost but recoverable home in Africa or India.

Religious Spacing

Although we have considered cases from Africa and India, we can draw more general conclusions from these illustrations about the production of space in the history of religions.

First, as we have seen, structured oppositions, such as the oppositions between home and wild or sea and land, are important features of the production of meaningful and powerful religious space. Perhaps derived from the left–right axis of the human body (Hertz 1973 [1909]; see Knott 2005, 133–228), the primary space of religious production, structural oppositions—inside and outside, up and down—are deployed in producing spatial orientations of religious purity and power, religious purity through rituals of exclusion and religious power through rituals of subordination, subjection, and extraction of human and material resources.

Second, in between structured oppositions, liminal space, like the river that is neither home nor wild, signals the importance of possibility in the religious production of space. Not fixed in place on one side or the other, the liminal space is open to new things. In the colonial relations between sea and land in southern Africa, the liminal space was the frontier zone, the contact zone, in which anything might happen. As religious resources were drawn into configuring the meaning and power of this in-between space of intercultural contact, new spatial orientations toward the land and sea emerged. These reconfigurations of space in liminality, contact, and mediation between land and sea have been crucial to the production of religious space in colonial and postcolonial worlds (see Johnson 2007).

Third, religious space is directional, directing attention, but also directing people to move. Space is a medium for motion. The directionality of religious space, its *deictic* quality (Fernandez 1986), shows how space is a medium for motion. People move through space, whether pushed or pulled, in ways that produce space. Characteristically, religious motion in space is centripetal, drawing into a center, or centrifugal, moving out from a center, which suggests that people move between centers and peripheries in a kind of Newtonian social physics of religious space. However, in religious diasporas we find a post-Newtonian field of circulations in which relations between centers and peripheries are constantly being renegotiated.

Fourth, in a Newtonian social physics, since no two points can occupy the same space, conflict is inevitable between any two or more religious groups who try to inhabit the same site. Certainly, we can find instances of mutual coexistence, but conflict seems to be the norm. Although conflicts might not be primarily or exclusively religious (Cavanaugh 2009), fighting over space seems to be a recurring feature of the production of space in the history of religions. Not merely meaningful, space is also powerful as an arena for asserting claims to access, control, and ultimately ownership of the sacred.

As the ongoing religious work of ritualization and interpretation produces a surplus of meaning and power, significance and energy, which arises out of space but also overflows any place, no assertion of privileged ownership of the sacred can ever be final. Inviting and resisting assertions of ownership, the materiality of space confounds all religious claims. Nevertheless, the production of religious space, in all of its meaning, power, and inherent materiality, is the production and reproduction of religion.

GLOSSARY

Abantu bekhaya "people of the home," an isiXhosa phrase in South Africa referring to ancestors.

Abantu bomlambo "people of the river," an isiXhosa phrase in South Africa referring to ambiguous spirits who work sometimes for good and sometimes for evil.

Avatar Hindu, a manifestation or incarnation of God, such as the avatar, Rama.

Badimong seSotho meaning "among ancestors," a pilgrimage site of cave shrines in South Africa.

Centrifugal in physics, a force moving out from a center.

Centripetal in physics, a force drawing into a center.

Diaspora from the Greek, "dispersion," a population dispersed from an original homeland while developing ways, especially through narrative and ritual, of remaining connected to home.

Kraal in indigenous religion in South Africa, a cattle enclosure, the center of the sacred space of the home.

Locative in linguistics, indicating location; in spatial analysis an orientation that is attached to a specific place.

Motse seTswana in South Africa, a human settlement produced as a sacred space through ritual relations with ancestors.

Naga seTswana in South Africa, the "bush," a wild space associated with dangerous forces.

Puja Sanskrit term for acts or processes of ritual worship.

Tirthas Sanskrit term, literally "crossings," for pilgrimage sites.

Ukulungisa umzi an isiXhosa phrase in South Africa, "to make the homestead right" through ritual relations with ancestors.

Utopian derived from the Greek for "no place"; in spatial analysis an orientation that encompasses the totality of space, everywhere, and is not dependent upon any specific place.

REFERENCES

Bigelow, Anna. 2010. *Sharing the Sacred: Practicing Pluralism in Muslim North India.* Oxford: Oxford University Press.

Bleek, W. H. I. 1952. *Zulu Legends*, edited by J. A. Engelbrecht. Pretoria: Van Schaik. Original edition, 1857.

Brown, Karen McCarthy. 1999. "Staying Grounded in a High-Rise Building: Ecological Dissonance and Ritual Accommodation in Haitian Vodou." In *Gods of the City: Religion and the American Urban Landscape*, edited by Robert A. Orsi. Bloomington: Indiana University Press, 79–102.

Campbell, John. 1815. *Travels in South Africa.* London: Blackwell.

Cavanaugh, William T. 2009. *The Myth of Religious Violence: Secular Ideology and the Roots of Modern Conflict.* New York: Oxford University Press.

Chidester, David. 2000. *Christianity: A Global History.* San Francisco: Harper.

Chidester, David. 2014. *Religions of South Africa.* London: Routledge.

Comaroff, Jean. 1981. "Healing and Cultural Transformation: The Case of the Tswana of Southern Africa." *Social Science and Medicine* 15(2): 367–378.

Coplan, David. 2003. "Land from the Ancestors: Popular Religious Re-appropriations along the Lesotho–South African Border." *Journal of Southern African Studies* 29(4): 977–993. doi: 10.1080/0305707032000135923

Cormack, Margaret, ed. 2013. *Muslims and Others in Sacred Space.* Oxford: Oxford University Press.

Eck, Diana L. 2012. *India: A Sacred Geography.* New York: Random House.

Eliade, Mircea. 1958. *Patterns in Comparative Religion*, translated by Rosemary Sheed. New York: Harper & Row.

Eliade, Mircea. 1961. *Sacred and Profane*, translated by Willard R. Trask. New York: Harcourt Brace.

Fernandez, James W. 1986. "Location and Direction in African Religious Movements: Some Deictic Contours of Religious Conversion." *History of Religions* 25(4): 352–367.

Friedland, Roger and Richard D. Hecht. 1998. "The Bodies of Nations: A Comparative Study of Religious Violence in Jerusalem and Ayodhya." *History of Religions* 38(2): 101–149.

Hammond-Tooke, W. D. 1975. "The Symbolic Structure of Cape Nguni Cosmology." In *Religion and Social Change in Southern Africa*, edited by M. G. Whisson and M. West. Cape Town: David Philip, 15–33.

Hertz, Robert. 1973. "The Pre-eminence of the Right Hand: A Study of Religious Polarity." In *Right and Left: Essays on Dual Symbolic Classification*, edited by Rodney Needham. Chicago, IL: University of Chicago Press, 3–31.

Johnson, Paul Christopher. 2007. *Diaspora Conversions: Black Carib Religion and the Recovery of Africa.* Berkeley: University of California Press.

Knott, Kim. 2005. *The Location of Religion: A Spatial Analysis*. London: Equinox.

Lefebvre, Henri. 1991. *The Production of Space*, translated by Donald Nicholson-Smith. Oxford: Blackwell.

MacGaffey, Wyatt. 1994. "Dialogues of the Deaf: Europeans on the Atlantic Coast of Africa." In *Implicit Understandings: Observing, Reporting, and Reflecting on the Encounters between Europeans and Other Peoples in the Early Modern Era*, edited by Stuart B. Schwartz. Cambridge: Cambridge University Press, 249–267.

Peires, J. B. 1979. "Nxele, Ntsikana, and the Origins of the Xhosa Religious Reaction." *Journal of African History* 20(1): 51–61. doi: http://dx.doi.org/10.1017/S0021853700016716

Renan, Ernest. 1990. "What is a Nation?" In *Nation and Narration*, edited by Homi Bhabha. London: Routledge, 8–22.

Smith, Jonathan Z. 1978. *Map is Not Territory: Studies in the History of Religions*. Leiden: Brill.

Smith, Jonathan Z. 1987. *To Take Place: Toward Theory in Ritual*. Chicago, IL: University of Chicago Press.

Smith, Jonathan Z. 1990. *Drudgery Divine: On the Comparison of Early Christianities and the Religions of Late Antiquity*. Chicago, IL: University of Chicago Press.

Tweed, Thomas A. 2006. *Crossing and Dwelling: A Theory of Religion*. Cambridge, MA: Harvard University Press.

van der Leeuw, Gerardus. 1986. *Religion in Essence and Manifestation*, translated by J. E. Turner, foreword by Ninian Smart. Princeton, NJ: Princeton University Press. Original edition, 1933.

van der Veer, Peter. 1994. *Religious Nationalism: Hindus and Muslims in India*. Berkeley: University of California Press.

Vásquez, Manuel A. 2011. *More than Belief: A Materialist Theory of Religion*. Oxford: Oxford University Press.

Vertovec, Steven. 2000. *The Hindu Diaspora: Comparative Patterns*. London: Routledge.

Weber, Max. 1948. "Politics as a Vocation." In *From Max Weber: Essays in Sociology*, edited and translated by H. H. Gerth and C. Wright Mills. London: Routledge & Kegan Paul, 77–128.

FURTHER READING

Chidester, David and Edward T. Linenthal, eds. 1995. *American Sacred Space*. Bloomington: Indiana University Press. [*A theoretical introduction, emphasizing the situational production of sacred space, leads into a series of case studies in American space.*]

Jones, Lindsay, 2000. *The Hermeneutics of Sacred Architecture: Experience, Interpretation, Comparison*, 2 vols. Cambridge, MA: Harvard University Press. [*A theoretically informed and comparative analysis of the spatial dynamics of built environments in the history of religions.*]

Knott 2005 [*A systematic examination of the spatial dimensions, properties, aspects, and dynamics of religion.*]

Lefebvre 1991 [*A broadly Marxist, materialist analysis of spatial practice, representations of space, and representational space.*]

Smith 1987 [*A landmark study of the ritual production of sacred space.*]

Tweed 2006 [*A general theory of religion giving special attention to spatial dynamics of building homes and crossing boundaries.*]

CHAPTER 23

....

TIME

....

DAVID CHIDESTER

CHAPTER SUMMARY

....

- Classic theories of religious time emphasize subjective experience, social cohesion, or sacred renewal.
- Ritual produces regularities—simultaneous, sequential, and hierarchical—that are coordinated by clocks and calendars.
- Ancestral time, relying on memory, establishes continuity between human generations of ancestors and offspring.
- Mythic time, transmitted in narratives of origin and destiny, establishes continuity through underlying moral, legal, or forensic relations between actions and consequences.
- While establishing temporal continuity, mythic time can also signal temporal ruptures in a past crisis, a present conflict, or a future apocalypse.

Religious time is produced through the labor of ritualization and interpretation, but it is also subject to regulation by clocks, calendars, and other instruments for coordinating different temporalities. In time, embodied rhythms such as inhaling and exhaling, stillness and motion, might be spontaneous or accidental. Integrated into religious disciplines, however, these rhythms can be coordinated with temporal regularities and regulations that merge personal subjectivities, lived in time, with social collectivities that evoke a sense of timelessness. By enacting traditions supposedly handed down from time immemorial—for example, rites of passage that turn death into new birth, or liturgies that transform temporal succession into a succession of eternities—ritual and interpretative labor can be orchestrated in producing religious time.

Embodied time and social time come together in religious time. Adapting terms from the philosopher John Locke (1959 [1690], 1:466–468), we can distinguish between two basic types of religious time—ancestral time that establishes *cognitive* continuity through memory and mythic time that establishes *forensic* continuity by linking actions with consequences.

While cognitive continuity is based on remembering, forensic continuity can be established, even if no one remembers, by linking actors with the effects of their actions. Although the term *forensics* is familiar from modern criminal investigations, following Locke, who proposed that personal identity is a forensic term (Locke 1959 [1690], 1:467), we can see how religious discourse and practice often establish forensic links between actions and consequences. Myth, in particular, relies on forensic continuity to draw personal identity into social narratives that no one personally remembers because these stories are situated in time immemorial. Nevertheless, in mythic time, everyone is implicated. In the absence of personal memory, the basis for cognitive continuity, myth provides forensic terms and conditions for holding everyone accountable. Religious time, therefore, does not merely take place in time. Through ritual regularities and mythic narratives, through cognitive continuity and forensic continuity, religion produces time.

Ritual, Regularities, and Regulation

By contrast to the philosopher Henri Bergson (1910 [1889]), who analyzed the subjective experience of time as an indivisible flow, theorists of religion have argued that myth and ritual break up the flow of time. A student of Émile Durkheim, Henri Hubert, undertook a preliminary study of religious representations of time by outlining the ways in which rituals create intervals and interventions in time. As a result, the sacred "seeds itself within time" (Hubert 1999 [1905], 50; see Miller 2000). Interrupting the flow of everyday, ordinary, or profane time, sacred time marks out a field of temporal regularities that are also collective representations of society. Sharing sacred time, in this rendering, is sharing social cohesion.

Adopting this distinction between profane and sacred time, Mircea Eliade developed a theory of religion as the repetition of paradigmatic or archetypal events that happened in the beginning, as re-enacting a sacred model initiated by gods or ancestors in a time of origins. Religious practices, according to Eliade, enable people to break out of ordinary time into a mythic world, "periodically becoming contemporary with the gods" (1959, 91). As a religious interruption of ordinary time, sacred time in Eliade's theory is placed in opposition not only to the everyday temporal flow but also to history or the "terror of history" (1954, 139–162). In a formulation that has been generally rejected in subsequent scholarship (see Smith 1990, 105), Eliade contrasted the circular time of myth, which enables renewal, reactualization, and eternal return, with the linear time of history. If religion provides ways in which "time can be overcome" (1963, 75–91), Eliade's notion of transcendence involved overcoming both profane time and historical time.

Against history, Eliade nevertheless developed a kind of theory of religious history based on erasure and nostalgia. As an example of historical erasure, when considering 'primitive' millenarian movements, he found that historical factors and forces could be neglected by scholars of religion because "there is no need to dwell on the political, social, and economic character of these movements" (1963, 71). As an example of historical nostalgia, when reflecting on the loss of the sacred in modern politics, society, and economy, he asserted that "the secularization of work is like an open wound in the body of modern society" (1978, 178). Eliade's poetics of sacred time, based on a metaphoric equivalence between now and then, between ritual and origins, also bore traces of a politics of nostalgia.

Without sharing Eliade's nostalgia for the sacred, many anthropological theorists of religious time have based their analysis on distinguishing between two different kinds of time (see Gell 1992; Munn 1992). In his analysis of time reckoning among the Nuer, E. E. Evans-Pritchard (1939, 201; 1940, 95–108) distinguished between natural oecological time and social structural time. Claude Lévi-Strauss (1953, 530) opposed statistical or historical time to mechanical or structural time. Clifford Geertz contrasted quantitative time to the qualitative time cycles he observed in Bali, where "They don't tell you what time it is. They tell you what kind of time it is" (Geertz 1973, 393). Maurice Bloch (1977) distinguished between 'durational' time and the 'static' or 'cyclic' time derived from ritual. In a significant theoretical intervention in these dualisms, Edmund Leach argued that two kinds of time—the irreversible processes of aging, entropy, and death and the repetition observed in rain falling, clocks ticking, rhythmic drumming, and the recurrence of days, months, and seasons—are only brought together under the same term, 'time,' because of religion (Leach 1961, 125). By turning irreversible processes into regularities, religious ritual produces not only sacred time but also the very notion of time that has been inherited in West.

Temporal regularities include the simultaneous, the sequential, and the hierarchical (see Rappaport 1999, 169–276).

First, simultaneous regularities are produced by everyone doing the same thing at the same time. Whether the activity is prayer, meditation, chanting, listening, singing, drumming, or dancing, the synchronization of bodies in time creates a sense of presence in the present. Simultaneity depends upon rhythm and repetition, moving in time, but its coordinated timing evokes a sense of timelessness by staying on the beat.

Second, sequential regularities are produced by moving through prescribed stages in a liturgical ordering of time, attending to each stage, step by step, in a temporal progression. A single ritual, a series of rituals, or a large ritual cycle can create sequential regularity. Paying attention to each stage in the sequence, enacting the ritual choreography in its proper timing, duration, and transitions, officiants and participants enact not only a temporal sequence but also a connection with previous enactments. In the process, sequential regularities produce a link between present and past.

Third, hierarchical regularities are produced in many rituals by marking transitions between lower and higher status. A recurring feature of religion, rites of passage mark transitions in the lifecycle—birth, adulthood, marriage, and death—as a production of time that mediates between past and future. Following the pattern identified by Arnold van Gennep (1960 [1909]), rites of passage enact a symbolic death, a liminal period of seclusion, and a symbolic rebirth, but they are also a hierarchical ordering of time. Although the in-between or liminal stage of transition might be a time of uncertainty, the timing of the ritual process links an abandoned past with a better future.

All of these regularities, which can overlap and intersect in any ritual production of time, inevitably come under the jurisdiction of the owners of clocks and calendars, those instruments of temporal regulation (Aveni 1994). Although many ancient societies developed methods of time keeping, the clock in the West arose directly from religious ritual as an instrument for regulating the observance of monastic prayer (D. Landes 1983; Rossum 1996). For Roman Catholic monasteries in the European Middle Ages, the clock was a technique of religious regulation, timing the observance of a daily cycle of prayers to which monks or nuns were bound. Under the auspices of an ecclesiastical hierarchy, the monastic clock regulated a division of time into prayer, work, and leisure. As the historian E. P. Thompson (1967) argued, this division of time became a division of labor in the rise of capitalism. The owners of capital found that time is money, but workers were subjected to a temporal discipline in which all of their time was regulated by the clock.

Owners of calendars, as well, have been instrumental in regulating religious time (Richards 1999; Zerubavel 1985). Every calendar is authorized—the Julian calendar by an emperor, the Gregorian calendar by a pope—in order to regulate observance and obedience in time. The diversity of calendrical calculations, which might place this year in relation to the birth of Christ, the creation of the world, the *hijrah* of the Prophet, or the Mayan apocalypse (Restall/Solari 2011), is never merely a matter of mathematics. By appropriating the religious production of time, with its simultaneous, sequential, and hierarchical regularities, political agents can regulate time and thereby entrench the regulation of people in time.

ANCESTRAL TIME

In religious time, continuity is crucial. Ritual enactments establish a sense of continuity. They generate sensory experiences and practical repertoires that can be retained in memory. Following Endel Tulving (1983, 184–185), we can distinguish between two kinds of memory, the episodic memory of distinct events, full of sensory content, and the schematic memory of basic patterns, recalling the way things usually happen. While episodic memory might be intense, fleeting, or even lost, schematic memory is relatively stable. The anthropologist Harvey Whitehouse has drawn upon this analysis of memory in distinguishing between two types of rituals, those of high sensory intensity that are infrequently performed and those of low intensity that are frequently performed. Rituals of high intensity and low frequency, such as many rites of passage, tend to be retained in episodic memory; rituals of low intensity and high frequency, such as daily prayer or weekly liturgy, are held in schematic memory as general patterns (Whitehouse 1995; 2000; 2004).

Schematic memory is essential for performing rituals for the dead. In Hindu *śrāddha* rituals, memory is activated not only by recalling episodes from the life of the deceased but also in following the sequential timing of prescribed ritual observances. According to one account, on the day after sacrificing the body through cremation the son of the deceased began a ritual sequence designed to form a new spiritual body by shaping a ball of cooked rice, a *piṇḍa*, which was treated with reverence as the temporary body of the deceased. Placed on an altar of dirt about half an inch high by a small lamp, the *piṇḍa* was honored with prayers, incense, flowers, and white threads symbolizing clothing. While offering prayers for the deceased, the son poured a mixture of water and sesame seeds from a clay cup over the rice ball, signifying the nourishment and strengthening of a new body for the deceased. For ten days this *piṇḍa* service, the *sapiṇḍikaraṇa*, was repeated. Each day, however, the number of cups of sesame seed water was increased, until on the tenth and final day of the sequence ten cups were poured out over the rice ball. Although the process was interpreted as producing a new body for the deceased, creating the head on the first day, the neck and shoulders the second day, then the heart and chest, the back, the stomach, the thighs and bowels, the lower legs and skin, the knees and hair, the genitals, and finally on the tenth day the power of digestion, the sequential regularity of the ritual also produced a temporal continuity between present and past.

During the ten days after death, the deceased lingered in an interim state as a ghost (*preta*) who had not yet become an ancestor (*pitṛ*). On the eleventh and final day of the ritual, sequential timing culminated in a hierarchical transition from ghost to ancestor. In that final ceremony, attended by priests representing ancestors, the son laid out rice balls representing the lineage of the deceased's father, grandfather, and great-grandfather. Reciting prayers, the son performing the ritual cut the rice ball representing the deceased into three portions and blended each into the rice balls of the ancestors. Calling on each by name, the son invited the deceased to join his ancestors. Finally, as all rice balls were blended into one, the ritual marked the integration of the deceased as a revered ancestor in heaven (Knipe 1977). Replicating the Hindu lunar calendar's tenth-month gestation period for human birth, the ten-day ritual sequence turned death into rebirth, culminating in a hierarchical transition from an abandoned past to an ancestral future.

In Zulu tradition in South Africa, ancestral time was also produced out of ritual sequencing and transformation. The great Zulu dramatist H. I. E. Dhlomo compared the indigenous Zulu ritual of death to the sequencing of a five-act play. "In this great ceremony," he observed, "there are five divisions or five 'acts': Death, Burial, Mourning, Ihlambo (Cleansing), and Ukubuyisa (the bringing back of the spirit of the deceased)" (Dhlomo 1977 [1939], 30). In this "great, tragic performance," ritual timing involved simultaneity in sharing temporal regularities of silence, wailing, humming, fasting, sharing in a sacrifice, and refraining from work, while the entire sequence extended over one year between death and *ukubuyisa*, the final bringing back of the deceased as an ancestor in the household. The beginning of the sequence was marked by reversals of conventional behavior, such as walking backwards when carrying the corpse, wearing clothing inside out, using the left hand, and adopting a special language in which 'no' means 'yes' and 'yes' means 'no,' which signaled a disruption of the conventional structure of ordinary time. As in the Hindu *śrāddha* ritual, the deceased lingered in an interim status, suspended in time, until the ritual sequence culminated in the final integration of the deceased into the generations of ancestors. The Zulu ritual of *ukubuyisa*, a festive occasion of sacrifice, feasting, and celebration, marked the presence of the ancestor in the ongoing life of a household. Ultimately, therefore, ancestral time links the past with an unbroken continuity, unbroken by death, which extends into the future.

In ancestral ritual, time is regulated by clocks and calendars, by hours, days, months, and years, but time is also produced as dynamic relations between past, present, and future. The primary medium of time-keeping in ancestral ritual is food—preparing, cooking, and eating food. Ritual recipes take time and make time. While *śrāddha* rituals marked sacred time by preparing rice balls and pouring sesame water, Zulu rituals of death marked sacred time by eating sacrificial meat and drinking sanctified beer. In ongoing relations with an ancestral spirit, food is essential. The ritualized feeding of the ancestor is the crucial link between generations in many religious traditions. In this regard, the end of a funeral cycle can mark the beginning of an ongoing commitment to nourishing and sustaining ancestors through the ritual timing of offering and sharing food, suggesting that religion is often more like cooking than like philosophy.

MYTHIC TIME

Mythic time is narrative time, the temporal ordering of sacred stories about universal creation and destruction, human origin and destiny, and dramatic disruption and redemption. These powerful narratives produce a sense of continuity that is different than the continuity entailed by the ritual observances of ancestral time. While memory establishes continuity in ancestral time, mythic time is ruled by forensics, by legal accountability and moral responsibility, by acts and their consequences. As the temporal subtext of myth, a forensic dimension runs like a unifying thread through religious stories about time.

The Hindu conception of time related in the ancient *Laws of Manu* moves from infinitesimally small units—the twinklings of an eye that make a second, the seconds that make a minute, the minutes that make an hour, and the hours that make a cycle of day and night—to extraordinarily vast ages, the *yugas*, that are the day and night of Brahma. Encompassing a time span of 4,320,000 human years, the four *yugas* mark a sequence of degeneration from the golden Krita age to the current Kali age of iron in which the human condition has worsened dramatically. When the current age ends in destruction, the creative process begins again, as Manu observed, because "the creations and destructions (of the world, are) numberless; sporting [or playing], as it were, Brahman repeats this again and again" (Manu 1886, 22).

The forensic subtext in this mythic time is *karma*, the consequences of past actions, which bind a person, as the same person, to the cycle of birth, death, and rebirth through eternity. Shared by Hindus, Buddhists, Jains, and others, this understanding of temporal continuity does not depend upon the cognitive capacity of memory; it is fashioned out of a forensic link between past actions, present consequences, and future prospects. Liberation from the cycle of rebirth, from the eternity of creations and destructions, promises timelessness. In the meantime, however, temporal continuity is measured by the enduring karmic law governing acts and consequences (Trautmann 1995, 186–190).

A Christian conception of the temporal duration of the world, drawn from biblical tradition, can encompass a comparatively brief time span, extending perhaps less than 6,000 years, following Augustine of Hippo (1950, 390–392), from the original creation of the world to its final destruction in the apocalypse. Although Christian mythic time is often regarded as linear, directional, and even historical, it can also be circular, based on a single temporal cycle of fall and redemption. Here the forensic thread linking past, present, and future in a temporal continuity is sin, which, like *karma*, measures time by connecting actions with consequences. Even if sin is not inherited unconsciously as original sin, human acts, desires, and dispositions are embedded in a mythic time that extends from origin to eventual redemption or damnation. In this understanding of time, which is generally shared by Christians, Jews, and Muslims, mythic time is again driven by forensic continuity.

In counterpoint to temporal continuity, mythic time also deals with dramatic ruptures in time.

First, myth can focus on a rupture in the past. In the beginning, according to a Nuer myth, God gave cattle to the good human being, Nuer, but the cattle were stolen by the wicked human being, Dinka. This original theft, which disrupted the divine order instituted by God in the beginning, justified Nuer warriors in raiding cattle from the neighboring Dinka people. In the moral economy of mythic time, cattle-raiding was not stealing but restoring. For their part, the Dinka told the same story, except with the roles reversed (Evans-Pritchard 1940, 125–126; Lincoln 1981, 13–48; 1989, 21–22). Focusing on a rupture in the past, mythic time can provide a warrant for actions in the present.

Second, myth can focus on a rupture in the present. Under colonial conditions in South Africa during the 1860s, the Zulu Christian convert Mpengula Mbande related the "account which black men give white men of their origin" (Callaway 1970 [1868–1870], 77). According to this creation myth, black men emerged first from the *uhlanga*, the place of the origin of all nations, coming out, however, with only a few things. They emerged with some cattle, corn, spears, and picks for digging the earth. Arrogantly, with their few possessions, the black men thought that they possessed all things. When the white men emerged, however, they came out with ox-drawn wagons, bearing abundant goods, and able to traverse great distances. By displaying this new, unexpected use for cattle, the whites demonstrated a superior wisdom that had been drawn from the *uhlanga*. In relation to the power and possessions of white men, black men recognized that they were defenseless. The wisdom, wealth, and virtue that whites had drawn from the *uhlanga* were sufficient to overpower the black people, who reflected among themselves, as Mbande reported, that "these men who can do such things, it is not proper that we should think of contending with them, as if because their works conquer us, they would conquer us by weapons" (Callaway 1970 [1868–70], 79–80). In this mythic account, Mpengula Mbande recorded an indigenous religious rationale for submission to the colonial government and its Christian mission. Obviously, this myth was not an ancient Zulu cosmogony. It was a critical reflection on the contemporary Zulu colonial situation.

Third, myth can focus on a rupture in the future. Millenarian myths, anticipating an imminent, dramatic, and collective redemption, are recurring features of mythic time. In the Eastern Cape of South Africa during 1856, a millenarian movement arose on the basis of the prophecy of a young woman, Nongqawuse, that the ancestors were returning. Against the background of decades of British colonial warfare, this prophecy was a promise of future redemption, a vision of an ancestral return that would drive away the white invaders and restore land, cattle, and prosperity to the people. Mediated by her uncle, Mhlakaza, who had spent time with the Christian mission, and adopted by the Xhosa chief Sarhili, Nongqawuse's visionary promise came at a price: all surviving cattle that had not been taken by the British or lost to an epidemic of lungsickness had to be killed to open the way for the return of the ancestors. In this millennial ritual of destruction, the majority of Xhosa homesteads responded to the prophecy by sacrificing their cattle and destroying their crops. An estimated 400,000 head of cattle were sacrificed in expectation of the imminent return of the ancestors. In the failure of the prophecy, which brought death, indentured labor, and the destruction of any political independence for the Xhosa, many observers labeled the Xhosa cattle-killing as national suicide or suicidal millennialism (Peires 1989; R. Landes 2011). However, with its focus on temporal rupture in the immediate future, this millenarian movement can also be seen as an attempt, perhaps a desperate attempt, to restore a just order in the moral accounting of mythic time.

Religious Timing

Ritual practices and mythic narratives generate religious time, but religious timing is also crucial in other spheres of human activity, such as politics, economics, and aesthetics.

First, in the politics of religious time, political power can be legitimated by privileged claims on origins, whether those claims are certified through ancestral or mythic time. Like the Nuer myth that asserted an original ownership of cattle, religious timing can be engaged in underwriting claims on territory, resources, and people. Originality, in these assertions of power, is inevitably contested. Although the Christian convert Mpengula Mbande developed a mythic rationale for the political subordination of the Zulu, the participants in the Xhosa millenarian movement anticipated an imminent return of their ancestors that would restore their original political sovereignty. In the politics of religious time, beginnings and endings are negotiated in the present, an expanded present that embraces memories of an origin and anticipations of a future. Since those memories and anticipations are multiple, conflict arises over who can establish claims on being there first and being there in the end.

Second, in the economy of religious time, temporality is measured by money, debt, and credit. Although the science of economics defines money as a unit of accounting, a store of value, and a medium of exchange, money is also a system of symbols that generates profound moods and motivations and cloaks those dynamics of desire and agency in an aura of factuality to make them seem uniquely real (Chidester 2005, 112). Money is time—the timing of debt and its repayment, credit and its duration, interest and its multiplication of value. In an economy of religious time, the term for 'sin' can be derived from debt, the term for 'merit' can be derived from credit, and the accumulation of interest can be transformed from the sin of usury to the virtue of capital investment. While the term 'redemption' is derived from the process of paying a debt, millenarian movements generally anticipate the destruction of the prevailing system of accounting (Graeber 2011, 59–60, 248–250). Religious time, therefore, can be embedded in a religious economy.

Finally, the aesthetics of religious time cultivates the embodied, sensory engagement with the lights and colors, the bells and music, the incense, flavors, and rhythms of time. Not only regulated by clocks and calendars, religious time is mediated by the senses, drawing personal subjectivity into the temporal regularities of a social collectivity. Although the discipline of the senses in focusing attention is crucial for religious timing, the derangement of the senses through synesthesia, trance states, or spirit possession can create a sense of timelessness in productions of religious time.

Religious time, therefore, is not only or merely religious. With its regularities and regulations, its ancestral and mythic constructions of continuity, religious time is also the aesthetics, economics, and politics of time.

Glossary

Ancestral time temporal continuity from generation to generation mediated by ritual.
Episodic memory recalling specific events with sensory details.
Forensics a legal term for linking actions to consequences.
Ihlambo Zulu death ritual performed for cleansing the family and the household.
Itongo Zulu ancestral spirit.
Kali yuga in Hindu mythic time the last of four ages, the current iron age of the worsening human condition.
Karma Hindu, Buddhist, and Jain concept of actions and consequences establishing forensic continuity in the cycle of birth, death, and rebirth.
Krita yuga in Hindu mythic time the first of four ages, the golden age at the beginning of a cycle of universal creation and destruction.

Mythic time temporal continuity, mediated by narrative, which links past actions with future consequences.

Piṇḍa rice ball, used in Hindu death rituals to represent the deceased in successive stages in the transition to becoming an ancestor.

Pitṛ in Sanskrit, an ancestor.

Preta in Sanskrit, a ghost.

Regularity a recurring repetition of temporal events.

Regulation a disciplinary management of temporal events.

Schematic memory recalling basic patterns of the way things happen or are done.

Śrāddha Hindu rituals of death and transition to the status of ancestor.

Synesthesia the mixing or merging of the senses.

Uhlanga Zulu place of origin in traditional emergence myths.

Ukubuyisa Zulu ritual performed one year after a death to bring the deceased back home as an ancestor.

Yugas Hindu ages of the world.

REFERENCES

Augustine of Hippo. 1950. *The City of God*. New York: Modern Library.

Aveni, Anthony F. 1994. *Empires of Time: Calendars, Clocks, and Cultures*. New York: Kodansha America.

Bergson, Henri. 1910. *Time and Free Will: An Essay on the Immediate Data of Consciousness*, translated by Frank Lubecki Pogson. London: S. Sonnenschein. Original edition, 1889.

Bloch, Maurice. 1977. "The Past and the Present in the Present." *Man* 12(2): 278–292.

Callaway, Henry. 1970. *The Religious System of the Amazulu*. Cape Town: Struik. Original edition, 1868–1870.

Chidester, David. 2005. *Authentic Fakes: Religion and American Popular Culture*. Berkeley: University of California Press.

Dhlomo, H. I. E. 1977. "Nature and Variety of Tribal Drama." *English in Africa* 4(2): 23–36. Original edition, 1939.

Eliade, Mircea. 1954. *The Myth of the Eternal Return*, translated by Willard R. Trask. New York: Pantheon.

Eliade, Mircea. 1959. *The Sacred and the Profane: The Nature of Religion*, translated by Willard R. Trask. New York: Harcourt, Brace & World.

Eliade, Mircea. 1963. *Myth and Reality*, translated by Willard R. Trask. New York: Harper & Row.

Eliade, Mircea. 1978. *The Forge and the Crucible*, translated by Stephen Corrin. Chicago, IL: University of Chicago Press.

Evans-Pritchard, E. E. 1939. "Nuer Time Reckoning." *Africa* 12(2): 189–216.

Evans-Pritchard, E. E. 1940. *The Nuer: A Description of the Modes of Livelihood and Political Institutions of a Nilotic People*. Oxford: Clarendon Press.

Geertz, Clifford. 1973. *The Interpretation of Cultures*. New York: Basic Books.

Gell, Alfred 1992. *The Anthropology of Time: Cultural Constructions of Temporal Maps and Images*. Oxford: Berg.

Graeber, David. 2011. *Debt: The First 5,000 Years*. New York: Melville House.

Hubert, Henri. 1999. *Essay on Time: A Brief Study of the Representation of Time in Religion and Magic*, translated by Robert Parkin and Jacqueline Redding. Oxford: Durkheim Press. Original edition, 1905.

Knipe, David M. 1977. "*Sapiṇḍīkaraṇa*: The Hindu Rite of Entry into Heaven." In *Religious Encounters with Death: Insights from the History and Anthropology of Religions*, edited by Frank E. Reynolds and Earle H. Waugh. University Park, PA: Pennsylvania State University Press, 111–124.

Landes, David. 1983. *Revolution in Time: Clocks and the Making of the Modern World*. Cambridge, MA: Harvard University Press.

Landes, Richard. 2011. "Suicidal Millennialism: Xhosa Cattle-Slaying (1856–1857 CE)." In *Heaven on Earth: The Varieties of the Millennial Experience*. Oxford: Oxford University Press, 91–122.

Leach, Edmund R. 1961. *Rethinking Anthropology*. London: Athlone Press.

Lévi-Strauss, Claude. 1953. "Social Structure." In *Anthropology Today: An Encyclopedic Inventory*, edited by A. L. Kroeber. Chicago, IL: University of Chicago Press, 524–553.

Lincoln, Bruce. 1981. *Priests, Warriors and Cattle: A Study in the Ecology of Religions*. Berkeley: University of California Press.

Lincoln, Bruce. 1989. *Discourse and the Construction of Society: Comparative Studies of Myth, Ritual, and Classification*. New York: Oxford University Press.

Locke, John. 1959. *An Essay Concerning Human Understanding*, 2 vols. New York: Dover. Original edition, 1690.

Manu. 1886. *The Laws of Manu*, translated by Georg Bühler. Oxford: Clarendon Press.

Miller, William Watts. 2000. "Durkheimian Time." *Time & Society* 9(1): 5–20. doi: 10.1177/0961463X00009001001

Munn, Nancy. 1992. "The Cultural Anthropology of Time: A Critical Essay." *Annual Review of Anthropology* 21: 93–123.

Peires, J. B. 1989. *The Dead Will Arise: Nongqawuse and the Great Xhosa Cattle-Killing Movement of 1856–7*. Johannesburg: Ravan Press.

Rappaport, Roy A. 1999. *Ritual and Religion in the Making of Humanity*. Cambridge: Cambridge University Press.

Restall, Matthew and Amara Solari. 2011. *2012 and the End of the World: The Western Roots of the Maya Apocalypse*. Lanham, MD: Rowman & Littlefield.

Richards, E. G. 1999. *Mapping Time: The Calendar and its History*. Oxford: Oxford University Press.

Rossum, Gerhard Dohrn-van. 1996. *History of the Hour: Clocks and Modern Temporal Orders*, translated by Thomas Dunlap. Chicago, IL: University of Chicago Press.

Smith, Jonathan Z. 1990. *Drudgery Divine: On the Comparison of Early Christianities and the Religions of Late Antiquity*. Chicago, IL: University of Chicago Press.

Thompson, E. P. 1967. "Time, Work-Discipline, and Industrial Capitalism." *Past and Present* 38 (December): 56–97.

Trautmann, Thomas R. 1995. "Indian Time, European Time." In *Time: Histories and Ethnologies*, edited by Diane O. Hughes and Thomas R. Trautmann. Ann Arbor: University of Michigan Press, 167–197.

Tulving, Endel. 1983. *Elements of Episodic Memory*. New York: Oxford University Press.

van Gennep, Arnold. 1960. *The Rites of Passage*, translated by Monika B. Vizedom and Gabrielle L. Caffee, with an introduction by Solon T. Kimball. Chicago, IL: University of Chicago Press. Original edition, 1909.

Whitehouse, Harvey. 1995. *Inside the Cult: Religious Innovation and Transmission in Papua New Guinea*. Oxford: Oxford University Press.

Whitehouse, Harvey. 2000. *Arguments and Icons: Divergent Modes of Religiosity.* Oxford: Oxford University Press.

Whitehouse, Harvey. 2004. *Modes of Religiosity: A Cognitive Theory of Religious Transmission.* Walnut Creek, CA: AltaMira Press.

Zerubavel, Eviatar. 1985. *The Seven Day Circle: The History and Meaning of the Week.* New York: Free Press.

FURTHER READING

Eliade 1959 [*Accessible account of a classic romantic theory of the return of the sacred time of origins in religious myth and ritual.*]

Gell 1992 [*A useful overview of anthropological analysis and case studies of the construction of time.*]

Hubert 1999 [*Classic analysis in the Durkheimian tradition of the social significance of relations between sacred and profane in representations of time.*]

Hughes, Diane O. and Thomas R. Trautmann, eds. 1995. *Time: Histories and Ethnologies.* Ann Arbor: University of Michigan Press. [*Important cross-cultural collection of research on the historical anthropology of time, with special attention to religious time.*]

Rappaport 1999 [*Excellent analysis of temporal regularities in religious ritual.*]

Ricoeur, Paul 1984. *Time and Narrative,* 3 vols. Chicago, IL: University of Chicago Press. [*Philosophical reflection on the temporal dynamics of narrative, with attention to mythic time.*]

Stausberg, Michael. 2003–2004. "Approaches to the Study of 'Time' in the History of Religions." *Temenos* 39–40: 247–268. [*A useful analysis of classical and contemporary approaches to the problem of time in the history of religions.*]

PART IV

ENVIRONMENTS

CHAPTER 24

....

ECONOMY

....

ANNE KOCH

CHAPTER SUMMARY

....

- Economy is significant for religion both as a co-system and for its permeating religious structures.
- Economy, in the historical form of capitalism, shapes present contemporary societies and governs politics.
- The political economy of liberalism in varying forms provides the ideological and ethical foundation of most capitalist societies.
- Markets are interactional arenas of exchange, investment, and speculation.
- Religious organizations are engaged in various sectoral markets.
- Religious organizations produce all kinds of private and public goods, entailing products and services.

INTRODUCTION: THE CULTURAL AND SOCIAL EMBEDDEDNESS OF ECONOMY

....

Like any cultural phenomenon, religion and economy are interdependent and may oppose, intensify, counter-caricature, stabilize, or delegitimize each other across societal subsystems. This interaction of society, politics, and economy is and has been described with the concept of political economy, but views vary as to which of these (sub)systems is dominant. In recent times, economy has again been seen as embedded in social relationships and especially as culturally conditioned and varying across cultures. Previously—within neoclassical economic theory (see Seele/Zapf, "Economics," this volume)—culture was seen as an exogenous factor, meaning that culture is a stable framing condition and therefore outside the theory and irrelevant to economic analysis. The same goes for individual preferences. Change of preferences was not a relevant explanatory factor partly due to the smaller period of time that was of interest. This differs from today's economic theory that takes the history of institutions, path dependencies, and changes of mental models into account, for example in market research, which sometimes even considers the religious affiliation of consumers. Towards the background of social embeddedness (Coleman 2005), de-constructivist critics allege the societal disembeddedness of transnational and finance markets today and understand this as a reason for contemporary gaffes of bubble economies, highly virtual finance market products, and the barely controlled power of transnational corporations.

Religion is in many ways an economic phenomenon and can be analyzed as such. By economy most economists understand systems for the allocation of resources. Religious organizations act as employer and supplier, providing and demanding several kinds of capital (cultural, financial, social), goods (e.g. public, private, club), and services (e.g. consulting, care, development). Demands for financial means and knowhow differ widely, depending on the kind of organization—charitable association, hospital, school, brewery, print house, shop, tourist office, bank, kindergarten, consulting office, etc. Organizations that are charitable or legally recognized as 'religious' are often economically privileged. Such organizations engage in a variety of economic activities: administering property, fundraising, investment of employees' retirement fund contributions, or pricing of services. Religious organizations are sometimes wealthy owners of real estate or of artworks that are valued as 'cultural heritage'. Profits stem from sources like capital income, membership taxes or fees, rents, product or property sales, donations, and property rights. Religions produce, distribute, and market all kinds of goods: public goods like a vision of the meaning of life, a moral system, a worldview, or the interpretation of present occurrences; as well as private goods like workshops, talismans, and access rights to rituals.

Economic Governance from Social Obligations to Market Capitalism

Throughout history, cultural institutions like social obligations, gift economies, theft, and sacrifice have exerted powerful influence on the regulation of social life. Theft and conquest have had the effect of undermining the hoarding of riches, returning them to circulation and often removing them again. But with the predominance of today's finance market capitalism, the market has become the most powerful regulator and has spread its influence to social subsystems including the religious institutional field. Throughout economic history, different types of economy and of correlated societies have superseded each other or coexisted: subsistence agriculture, feudal, mercantile, industrial, and planned economies, etc. The historic origin of the currently dominant economic system of capitalism can be traced back at least to eighteenth-century thinking in central Europe. For classical liberalism, the market is a moral system of social regulation. One of liberalism's prevailing strategies is the naturalization of elements like market forces, economic growth, and efficiency. This is consequential for the most recent varieties of liberalism that permeate all segments of social interaction in family, friendships, and religion.

Capitalism is based on the right of property; the accumulation of capital in its diverse forms is a main goal. Current debates note that capitalisms are legion, differing in their degree of industrialization and institutionalization, their political economy of welfare provision, their legal system, their degree of transition to a knowledge society, etc. (Marshall/Ramsey/Mitchell 2008). To create ever-new values, capitalism is compelled to increase commercial efficiency, to invent ever-new products, and to reach out for as well as create ever-new (emotional) needs. One recent example is the open-ended product—or half-finished frame—to which consumers bring their own meanings and uses, thus making the product a tool for identity-building, in addition to whatever primary purpose(s) it might have (e.g. meditation timer apps). Forcing the self into entrepreneurship is part of this reinventing its means (Foucault 2008) and has left its trace in the spiritual marketplace (see the following section). In this vein, economic processes are also very successful in imposing their needs on the political system, sometimes in cooperation with secularist and religious institutions providing the moralization of basic economic principles. Ethics and economics are two evaluative perspectives on human action. Economic ethics is therefore confronted with many issues known from other domains of action, like conflict of interests, majority dominance, opportunism, and altruism.

Since the mid-1970s capitalism in post-industrial countries is no longer growing through production but through the marketing machinery and consumption of mass-produced goods. This reversal of early capitalism which aimed at rationalizing production processes has resulted in far-reaching consequences for the religious field: new forms of regulation aim at triggering consumer wants and needs to create demand and growth in a circular way. Knowledge and service societies expand their array of products to include accompanying services and a correlated surplus in education opportunities and attainments. The body is increasingly immersed in modern media and marketing as a site of knowledge, where perfection or prevention are created as a new demand side. Pre-existent cultural values and meanings are attached to objects of use. It is the object-as-consumed through which the subject gains reality and signals a specific consumer identity. Our mediated selves live in a re-enchanted world of meaningful everyday objects surrounded by religious events, theme parks, self-discovery tourism, and pilgrimage (Stausberg 2011; Norman, "Tourism," this volume). All this can be observed on a global scale (see Kitiarsa 2008 on commodification and Fisher 2008 on the spiritual entrepreneur), which adds to these economic changes a remarkable intensity and a series of tensions.

Markets as Social Arenas of Capitalism

'Market' is the pivotal concept for economic performance. Economies consist of markets but are also regulated by institutions outside the market, like regulatory political institutions. Regulation through non-market institutions is necessary to implement moral, ecological, national, or humanitarian goals, to protect consumers' health, or to preserve resources for future generations from exploitation and fraud. A market is not only a place for the exchange of goods; it also fulfills further essential tasks of investment, insurance, or value-determination through pricing and speculation. Markets are networks of private persons and companies that reduce the cost of transaction and realize optimum gain for users; that is why some see the market as the greatest private good. Beyond mere exchange, markets are interactional arenas for symbolic production, future engagement, and speculation. Market phases with their specific challenges and transaction costs are also highly significant for religiously plural markets. There is an economic difference between founding a yoga studio in Berlin in 1916 and founding one today. The fact that markets are opaque, with complex, unforeseeable, and inaccessible information (so-called hidden characteristics), underlines the need to bring a cultural and action theoretical approach and to analyze specific cases in their historical and national contexts.

Religion can hardly escape from neoliberalization, as seen for example in the field of charitable action of religious organizations in the field of migrant work: the privatization of public services and the stimulus to public–private partnerships driven by efficiency and competition affect the involved religious institutions (Gray 2013). The shape of New Age markets is also a result of market dynamics: with the economic recession during the 1970s, the human growth movement shrank and the only lowly organized scene bifurcated into professionalized commercial providers on the one side and clients on the other (Redden 2005). With accelerated economic globalization, the fall of the Iron Curtain and the postcolonial emergence of independent national states, some societies were catapulted into 'turbo capitalism.' Not familiar with the rules, people had to live under its conditions and somehow adapt, and within a few years they invented folk explanations for some of the inscrutable aspects of capitalism. In the case of post-apartheid South Africa, a 'millennial capitalism' emerged, characterized by 'occult economies' of working zombies, bewitched credit cards, and further hybrids of indigenous and capitalist practices (Comaroff/Comaroff 2001).

The Spiritual Marketplace and the Spiritual Entrepreneur

The spiritual service market at the interface of alternative therapy, healthcare, sports, tourism, consulting, and science may serve as an example of a recent partial market in knowledge societies. Different organizational solutions address a range of spiritual demands: from extensive face-to-face services, incorporating intermediate structures, to industries responsive to mass demands. This market is characterized by under-regulation, increasing division of labor, hybrid products (like mixing cosmetic, thera-peutic, and spiritual dimensions in aromatherapeutic oils—Barcan 2014) and new professions (like angel therapist and aurasoma cleanser). The pluralistic and competi-tive spiritual market follows well-known market dynamics. Organizations employ strategies to reduce information asymmetries between supply and demand sides and to produce efficiently. Most suppliers are sole traders, but smaller companies, especially distributors, are also multiplying as a consequence of online business opportunities. Smaller entities are increasing, like educational or event centers, for example in the field of neo-kabbalah or in the provision of alternative treatments. The rapidly growing new industry of eco-friendly products, services, and consulting is expressed in the 'lifestyle of health and sustainability' that sells the moral properties of sustainability and holism (Emerich 2011).

Spiritual entrepreneurs can reduce uncertainty in their relationships with current cli-ents and may attract future clients by investing in professional training and certificates (for example from the Academy of Astrology or Matrix™) in order to display reputation capital. By doing so, they build up specific human and cultural capital. They also invest in virtual self-representations on homepages to inform potential clients about their worldview, products, and services (Hero 2014). Client-centered services may compen-sate for anonymous and bureaucratic customer relationships. Under conditions of com-petition, the market diversifies and niche markets evolve: for example yoga offers health improvement, counseling, business, Indian philosophy, and rituals for gender identity.

RELIGIOUS ECONOMIES AS EXPLICIT ECONOMIC SYSTEMS

Religious economies take various forms. Some emerge as niche markets and rely on the consumer for whom profit is not the highest goal: religiously affiliated mutual funds provide higher asset stability in terms of price changes, return, and general volatility compared with conventional, and even with ethical-like ecological, funds (Peifer 2011). Findings like this make religious finance market products interesting for investors. Many religious suppliers of holiday trips and devotional objects sell only to particular market segments and are often influenced by pop cultures. Other religious economies are propagated through firms or more general worldviews that act as cultural institu-tions engaging in political and moral fields. One such example is theologies of pros-perity: the idea of blessed wealth and open efforts to stimulate powers that offer riches can be found in East Asian popular religion in urban spaces, in street-corner deity cults and the new talisman boom in Thailand, in Chinese Confucian temples, and in Neo-Pentecostalisms all over the globe. Gurus and new-religious-group leaders are savaged by critics for conspicuously displaying their riches or simply enjoying a lavish lifestyle. Fleets of Rolls Royces, stud farms, or deep-sea vessels can symbolize power and blessing, thus reinforcing the alleged value of faith.

Temple Economies in the Mediterranean and Contemporary China

Temple economies thrive and diminish with economic but also political waves of renewal or recession. Ancient temple economies, like those of the Jerusalem temple or Greek and Roman temple institutions, fulfilled various economic tasks: they delivered services (administration, counseling, legislation, etc.), produced goods (agricultural goods, handicrafts), engaged in education, stored riches, and collected taxes as intermediaries for communal principals or the emperor (Assmann et al. 2009). In the Roman Empire, the riches and immense real estate of temples in conquered areas were often not confiscated but received further donations through the new sovereign. Local priests were respected as political and entrepreneurial forces. The highest-ranking temples in centralized organizational fields fulfilled further important functions by producing cultural as well as political capital through conspicuous displays of riches, art, and the imperial program through ritual and aesthetic performances.

During recent decades, China's temple economy has revived, despite a high degree of state regulation, offering services that were performed in premodern China (Chan/ Graeme 2010). Temples of Taoism, Chinese popular religion, and Buddhism engage in semi-professional marketing efforts to raise their visibility and to attract pilgrims, devotees, and tourists (Stausberg 2011, 83–86). The reinvigorated religious economy in China is primarily based on inclusivist polytheism, so that worship at one temple need not exclude worship at another. Under these conditions temples may even compete with each other, particularly if their main income consists of revenue from worshipers. In larger temples, focused on tourism, temple managers employ clergy and other staff (Lang/Chan/Ragvald 2005). Such temples often conduct market research, copy innovations from other temples, actively promote their offers, and cooperate with local officials who support the emerging economy with the expectation that tourists will spend money, thus creating new jobs due to temple activity.

Religious Organizations as Firms: The Roman Catholic Church in the Middle Ages

In the feudal economy of the Middle Ages, the Latin Catholic Church in Rome was supported by a dense hierarchical institutional network throughout central Europe. Rational choice theory (see Seele/Zapf, "Economics," this volume) speaks of dense and vertically integrated institutions. The medieval church can be regarded as a vertically integrated firm in this sense (Ekelund et al. 1996). With its key product, the salvation of souls, it enjoyed a near monopoly, and it was very creative in arousing consumer needs, for instance by selling relics and fostering pilgrimages, even to the distant 'Holy Land'. During the thirteenth century this firm went through severe changes and became unstable. A papal catalogue of sins introduced fixed prices for indulgences to meet the price slump arising from competition between the clergy and religious orders. From the perspective of new institutional economics (see Seele/ Zapf, "Economics," this volume), the question of the principal–agent relation arises. The principal denotes the orderer, purchaser, customer, or contractee whereas the agent is the contractor. The question now becomes: How can the principal, in this case the pope, control the agent, in our case the clergy who have to collect and deliver the pope the charges? A strategy to solve this problem is to establish a market balance (Pareto optimum) between the clergy and the newly founded franchised entrepreneurship of monastic orders, like the begging friars (Schmidtchen/Mayer 1997). This competition between agents exerts control among the agents (dioceses and orders). It realizes an optimal incentive structure: every agent would put himself in a worse position if he defeated the competitors, thus risking their failing to cooperate in the future. In this way the institutional net gain reaches a maximum. In a more complex elaboration of vertical integration, the firm had then a competitive double structure of dioceses and orders.

Islamic Economy

The Islamic economy consists of a conglomerate of fields that include banking, halal products, and an economic ethics. An overall principle is risk-and-loss-sharing between principal and agent. This has some severe effects on the risk management of 'lending' and acquisition in Islamic banking. Some of the principles refer to Qur'anic authority, such as the prohibition of usury (*zakat*), gambling, or speculation, but most have been invented for economic and legal contexts unknown in Qur'anic times, such as leasing, hire-purchase, and other modern finance products. Even Qur'anic principles are controversial among Islamic traditions, especially as formalized in theological and law schools, for example the question whether the prohibition of interest only addresses the problem of excessive interest. 'Sharia-conformity', 'halal', and 'Muslim-friendly' are symbolically constructed product qualities counting as unique selling properties (Waarden/Dalen 2013), sometimes enlarged to an morally acceptable lifestyle (Arab. *tayyib*—"good"), parallel to the widening of eco-friendly seals to indicate general sustainability (Housby 2013). Thus, Muslim-ness gains an ethical quality in late-modern consumer markets. Nevertheless, the Islamic economy's outreach is limited by the small proportion of Muslims in most capitalist countries in the West and the even smaller proportion that demand such specialized products.

CONCLUSION

Economy matters for religion insofar as religious organizations act in this field of material as well as symbolic value creation. In addition, religious worldviews and ethics contribute to conceptions of value, fair exchange, and legitimate economic returns as an important part of the cultural framing of economies. More specifically, at certain points in history religions have developed explicitly religious economies, either in opposition to mainstream economies (e.g. through asceticism or collectivist goals) or by implementing religious firms, distribution networks, and banks with moral agendas of their own. Over the course of different processes in late modernity—e.g. economization, commoditization, and lifestyle aesthetization—economy has become a strong structural element in the religious field, with neoliberalism and consumerism as its cultural ideologies. Communication processes, identity-building, and charitable work, for example, are performed in the environment of commoditized action. This is an influence from which religion can hardly stand aloof; rather, it becomes a mode of performance and a reference point for religious messages and goods.

GLOSSARY

Capitalism capitalism has a long history prior to its conceptual formation in the late eighteenth century, including extra-European roots and surviving thanks to its adaptive capacity starting from merchant capitalism that superseded feudalism to industrial, colonial, and newer forms of corporate, welfare, or finance market capitalism. In classical capitalism, capital ownership conditions the power of disposition used for profit maximization and steered by market laws. Today this type of capitalism is said to give place to shareholder-value capitalism.

Consumerism consumerism characterizes most of today's post-industrial societies where social positioning, communication, and identity-building are deeply entangled with practices of consuming. As a consequence, suppliers are most successful when they narrate an attractive product story, trigger positive emotions, and associate extraordinary experiences with the consumption of their products.

Cultural capital the result of efforts to gain knowledge, titles, or reputation in order to better realize one's general interests. It may be amplified by or offset by the display of religious symbols or behavior.

Markets interactional arenas of exchange, investment, and speculation of goods, resources, and services. They influence and are influenced by particular cultural and political frameworks. Markets are divided into types of markets (labor, resources, finance, service, insurance) and various sectoral markets.

Neoliberalism this political economy—originating in the United States and influencing further countries from the 1980s onwards—involves the global dispersal of labor processes, an intense time–space compression, highly segmented markets, and flexible modes of production in a networked society. However one conceives of neoliberalism—a political economy, a practice, a political technology, a mode of governmental regulation, or an ideology—it is discursively linked to the freedom of the individual (entrepreneurship), deregulation, high individual risk taking, and a credo of flexibility in the work force.

Transaction cost according to New Institutional Economics, costs derive from keeping companies running (internal) and selling and positioning products in markets (external). This concept corrects the neoclassical neglect of cost that arises, for example, from procuring materials, controlling employees, negotiating treaties, and building human capital. In neoclassical theory all those activities were either cost-neutral or negligible.

REFERENCES

Assmann, Jan, Fritz Graf, Tonio Hölscher, Ludwig Koenen, Jörg Rüpke, and John Scheid, eds. 2009. "Part I. Thematic Issue on Temple Economies." *Archiv für Religionsgeschichte* 11: 1–120.

Barcan, Ruth. 2014. "Aromatherapy Oils: Commodities, Material, Essences." *Cultural Studies Review* 20(2): 141–171.

Chan, Selina and Graeme Lang. 2010. "Temples as Enterprises." In *Religion in Contemporary China: Religion and Innovation*, edited by Adam Yuet Chau. London: Routledge, 133–153.

Coleman, Simon. 2005. "Economy and Religion." In *A Handbook of Economic Anthopology*, edited by James G. Carrier. Cheltenham: Edward Elgar, 339–352.

Comaroff, Jean and John Comaroff. 2001. *Millennial Capitalism and the Culture of Neoliberalism*. London: Duke University Press.

Ekelund, Robert, Robert D. Tollison, Gary M. Anderson, Robert F. Hébert, and Audrey B. Davidson. 1996. *Sacred Trust: The Medieval Church as an Economic Firm*. New York: Oxford University Press.

Emerich, Monica M. 2011. *The Gospel of Sustainability: Media, Market, and LOHAS*. Urbana: University of Illinois Press.

Fisher, Gareth. 2008. "The Spiritual Land Rush: Merit and Morality in the New Chinese Buddhist Temple Construction." *Journal of Asian Studies* 67(1): 143–170. doi: 10.1017/S0021911808000053

Foucault, Michel. 2008. *The Birth of Biopolitics. Lectures at the Collège de France, 1978–79*. Basingstoke and New York: Palgrave Macmillan.

Gray, Breda. 2013. "Catholic Church Civil Society Activism and the Neoliberal Governmental Project of Migrant Integration in Ireland." In *Religion in the Neoliberal Age: Political Economy and Modes of Governance*, edited by Tuomaas Martikainen and François Gauthier. Farnham: Ashgate, 69–90.

Hero, Markus. 2014. "The Marketing of Spiritual Services and the Role of the Religious Entrepreneur." In *Religions as Brands: New Perspectives on the Marketization of Religion and Spirituality*, edited by Jörg Stolz and Jean Claude Usunier. Aldershot: Ashgate, 75–87.

Housby, Elaine. 2013. *Islamic and Ethical Finance in the United Kingdom*. Edinburgh: Edinburgh University Press.

Kitiarsa, Pattana, ed. 2008. *Religious Commodifications in Asia: Marketing Goods*. London and New York: Routledge.

Lang, Graeme, Selina Chan, and Lars Ragvald. 2005. "Temples and the Religious Economy." In *State, Market, and Religions in Chinese Societies*, edited by Fenggang Yang and Joseph B. Tamney. Leiden: Brill, 149–179.

Marshall, Shelley, Ian M. Ramsay, and Richard Mitchell, eds. 2008. *Varieties of Capitalism, Corporate Governance and Employees*. Carlton: Melbourne University Press.

Peifer, Jared L. 2011. "Morality in the Financial Market? A Look at Religiously Affiliated Mutual Funds in the USA." *Socio-Economic Review* 9(2): 235–259. doi: 10.1093/ser/mwq024

Redden, Guy. 2005. "The New Age: Towards a Market Model." *Journal of Contemporary Religion* 20(2): 231–246. doi: 10.1080/13537900500067851

Schmidtchen, Dieter and Achim Mayer. 1997. "Established Clergy, Friars and the Pope: Some Institutional Economics of the Medieval Church." *Journal of Institutional and Theoretical Economics* 153(1): 122–149.

Stausberg, Michael. 2011. *Religion and Tourism: Crossroads, Destinations and Encounters*. London and New York: Routledge.

Waarden, Frans van and Robin Dalen. 2013. "Halal and the Moral Construction of Quality: How Religious Norms Turn a Mass Product into a Singularity." In *Constructing Quality: The Classification of Goods in Markets*, edited by Jens Beckert and Christine Musselin. Oxford: Oxford University Press, 197–222.

Further Reading

Boltanski, Luc and Eve Chiapello. 2005. *The New Spirit of Capitalism*. London: Verso. Original edition, 1999. [*A rich, critical, and often cited work that, among other things, offers empirical evidence of a new managerial societal organization—rooted in project-based selves—that can be considered 'the new spirit of capitalism.' One might say that instead of the Weberian Protestant spirit it is alternative spirituality, seeking for human growth and self-realization, that resonates with today's capitalism and masters the moral crisis of the emergent technocracy.*]

Demerath III, Jay N., Peter D. Hall, Terry Schmitt, and Rhys H. Williams, eds. 1998. *Sacred Companies: Organizational Aspects of Religion and Religious Aspects of Organizations*. New York and Oxford: Oxford University Press. [*This analysis of the US-American religious organizational field and its interface with secular organizations draws on Paul DiMaggio and Walter W. Powell's organizational sociology.*]

Gray 2013 [*Drawing on Foucault, Gray shows how religious organizations under neoliberal governance become civil society agents: they employ social workers, apply for public funding, treat 'cases,' and invoice local communities. The consequence is a new portfolio of human capital, financial dependence, communicational forms, and competitors.*]

Meyer, Birgit. 2007. "Pentecostalism and Neo-liberal Capitalism: Faith, Prosperity and Vision in African Pentecostal-Charismatic Churches." *Journal for the Study of Religion* 20(2): 5–28. [*(Neo-)Pentecostal organizations may change from a neoliberalism affirmative theology to critique especially when social injustice increases, e.g. in Brazil, whereas other cases develop a consumerist retro-gender theology, e.g. Australia's Hillsong Megachurch.*]

CHAPTER 25

··

LAW

··

BENJAMIN SCHONTHAL

CHAPTER SUMMARY

- One cannot assume an easy and unproblematic distinction between religion and law. The two categories remain deeply intertwined in their functions, structures, histories, and even in their ambiguousness as analytical categories.
- Complex political histories and motivations inform the creation and interpretation of laws governing religion, including the laws protecting religious freedom.
- It is helpful to look at four aspects of the law–religion nexus: links between state law and religious law; the religious history of state laws; religious presuppositions inherent in state law; and the politics associated with creating and litigating laws concerning religion.
- Scholars of religion and practitioners of law tend to differ in their attitudes towards the question of law's perfectibility; that is, the question of whether state law can ever be perfectly separated from and neutral towards religion.
- Legal and religious traditions adapt and respond to each other. Religious traditions alter themselves to conform to the categories of state law. Judges and legislators periodically alter the parameters of what counts as religion.

INTRODUCTION

Studies of religion and law often come pre-loaded with assumptions. They assume that religion and law are obvious, stable, bounded social phenomena. They assume that religion and law are readily separable and that each one has its own domains of influence and authority. They assume that law is synonymous with state law and that state law sits above religion, regulating it from afar. If these assumptions sound familiar and logical, it is because they are frequently built into the texts of court decisions, the transcripts of constituent assemblies, and the briefs of lawyers. It is the story of religion and law as told by the agents and institutions of state law.

While influential, this framing of the encounter between religion and law should not be treated by scholars of religion as an accurate description of reality. It is, rather, part of the reality that scholars of religion study. Studying religion in the environment of law requires a balancing act. One must repeatedly de-activate and reactivate an attitude of critical incredulity. On the one hand, one must engage fully with a discursive universe that presupposes many things about religion and law and their encounter. On the other hand, one must remain vigilant so as not to naturalize those presuppositions for oneself.

In this chapter, I try to engage in just such a balancing act in order to illuminate some of the different considerations that one should bring to examining religion in contexts of state-legal institutions and processes. To do so, I examine how pre-loaded assumptions about law and religion (such as those just described) sit alongside other ways of viewing the links between the two categories. To illustrate this, I examine a particular case of religion in the environment of law, the case of *Hodkin v. Registrar* from the UK Supreme Court in 2012. With reference to this case, I analyze four aspects of the law–religion nexus: the links between state law and religious law; the religious history of state laws; the religious presuppositions inherent in state law; and the politics associated with creating and litigating laws concerning religion.

Hodkin v. Registrar

In 2011, a London office of the Registrar-General for Births, Deaths and Marriages refused to recognize the marriage of two Scientologists, Alessandro Calcioli and Louisa Hodkin, by a local Scientology minister. In explaining the office's refusal, the Registrar-General insisted that she was simply following long-standing legal principles: UK law only recognized marriages conducted in churches that were registered under the Places of Worship Registration Act (PWRA) of 1855; since the Church of Scientology was not registered as a place of worship, marriages conducted there were not legally valid. The Registrar noted further that the UK Court of Appeals had ruled explicitly on the matter in its judgment in *R. v Registrar General, ex parte Segerdal* in 1970. In *Segerdal*, the court had argued that because Scientology didn't involve "reverence or veneration of God or of a Supreme Being" it could not be classified as religion; therefore Scientology buildings could not be classified as places of worship under the PWRA.[1]

In response, Hodkin and the minister of Scientology petitioned the courts to review the Registrar-General's decision. Two years later, after failing in the Court of Appeal,

---

[1] *R v. Registrar General, ex parte Segerdal* [1970] 2 QB 697 (herein: *Segerdal*).

Hodkin and the minister won a remarkable victory in the UK Supreme Court.[2] Overturning *Segerdal*, the United Kingdom's highest judicial body ruled unanimously that relying on theistic definitions of religion such as that used in *Segerdal* would be "a form of religious discrimination unacceptable in today's society" (*Hodkin*, paragraph 51). Lord Toulson, writing for the court, offered a new description of religion which, although "not a definitive formula," could serve as a guide in the administration of the PWRA (*Hodkin*, paragraph 57):

> I would describe religion as a spiritual or non-secular belief system, held by a group of adherents, which claims to explain mankind's place in the universe and relationship with the infinite, and to teach its adherents how they are to live their lives in conformity with the spiritual understanding associated with the belief system. By spiritual or non-secular I mean a belief system which goes beyond that which can be perceived by the senses or ascertained by the application of science. . . . Such a belief system may or may not involve belief in a supreme being, but it does involve a belief that there is more to be understood about mankind's nature and relationship to the universe than can be gained from the senses or from science.

Under Toulson's new definition, Scientology qualified as a religion. Accordingly, the court ordered the Registrar-General to list the Church of Scientology as a registered place of worship. Hodkin and Calcioli registered their marriage shortly thereafter.

The *Hodkin* case contains many features common to the analysis of religion in the environment of state law. It involved a point of friction between the perceived requirements of religious law (marriage by a Scientology minister according to a Scientology ceremony) and the enforced protocols of state law (only recognized places of worship can solemnize marriages). It called into question the secularity of existing law and its ability to remain impartial to diverse religious traditions. It involved creating a definition of religion that would permit law to continue its regulatory function.

STATE LAW AND RELIGIOUS LAW

From one perspective, the core of the *Hodkin* case is one of conflicting mandates: Scientology mandates that marriages ought to be performed by Scientologist ministers; the Office of the Registrar-General—acting in its capacity as a representative of the state—mandates that only marriages performed in state-recognized places of worship ought to receive official validation. Revealed in this conflict of mandates are the deep overlaps and similarities between the ways in which religion and state law function. Both involve structures of rules and sanctions. Both are heavily involved in

[2] *R (on the Application of Hodkin and Another) (Appellants) v. Registrar General of Births, Deaths and Marriages (Respondent) [2013] UKSC 77* (herein: *Hodkin*).

influencing the decisions made by persons and families. Both claim absolute authority over particular aspects of life. Both reflect historically and culturally specific conceptions of human agency and of social norms

The similarities between religion and state law form one part of the broader overlap between the categories of religion and law. Scholars of religion have long observed that religion has its own structures of law. From the *Laws of Manu* in India (*manavadharmasastra*) to the Jewish legal codes of *halakhah* to the prescriptions of Islamic *sharia*, scholars regularly acknowledge the importance of collections of rules or commandments for shaping religious cultures.

In many religious traditions, a single word covers the same semantic range of both law and religion as used by contemporary Anglophones. For example, the Arabic term *din* can be used to refer both to (divine) law and justice as well as to the communities and institutions of practice dedicated to interpreting and enforcing that law. Jewish writers used the Hebrew term *dat* in the early Middle Ages to cover a similar range of meanings (Novak 2008). Law (*lex*) was used alongside sect (*secta*) in early modern Europe as a standard term to refer to other religions (Feil 1997). Analogous dynamics can be seen in the ancient Indian world, where a variety of words that might be translated as 'law' carry with them both the idea of rules that one ought to follow as well as notions of cosmology, soteriology, and ritual. The Sanskrit term *dharma* has been important to many Indian religions since the first millennium BCE. Frequently translated as 'law,' the term refers simultaneously to the ideal ordering of the universe, the specific moral and social duties incumbent on various groups of people to uphold and protect that order, and the total systems of practice and belief in which people participated. In the most famous ancient Indian treatise (*sastra*) on *dharma*, the *manavadharmasastra*, the author brings together in one collection stories about the creation of the cosmos, rules of ritual purity for priests (*brahmins*), standards of conduct for kings and judges, appropriate types of punishments for various crimes, rules about the proper height of village fences, and the maximum reasonable tolls to be levied at ferry crossings and on highways, among many other things. Translated into modern parlance, the science of *dharma* in this text would be said to incorporate myth, liturgy, ethics, penal law, administrative law, and even zoning ordinances (O'Flaherty 1992).

An interesting equivalent can be seen in the Buddhist world. Building upon the genre of *dharmasastra*, the premodern polities of mainland Southeast Asia developed their own *dhammsattha-s* (Pali for *dharmasastra*). Here too, myth, ritual, and cosmology mixed with rules detailing the proper types of behavior and conventions of royal rule. A story about the origin of *dhammasattha* that appears at the beginning of many *dhammasattha* texts describes Manu—the hero of Hindu *dharmasastra*, but here cast as a royal advisor to the world's first king, Mahasammata—as discovering the words of *dhammasattha* inscribed on the boundary wall of the universe in letters the size of elephants. Manu writes the rules down and delivers them to the king, who then uses them as a guide for virtuous rule. In this founding narrative one sees immediately the binding together of cosmic law and state law: the timeless and universal *dhammasattha* becomes the template par excellence for developing royal edicts. Also interesting here is the fact that—at least according to one seventeenth-century Burmese manuscript—early modern Buddhist authors appeared to struggle in determining how to categorize *dhammasattha* alongside other genres of literature: should it be grouped alongside canonical collections of the Buddha's saying which ultimately lead to enlightenment—what could be called religious texts—or alongside other genres such as treatises on alchemy, astrology, and the pragmatics of royal rule (Lammerts 2013)? In short, one sees in pre- and early-modern Southeast Asian Buddhism debates over the parameters of what we might today call religious law and state law, as well as evidence that those distinctions were often blurry and contested.

Religious law also plays a central role in Judaism, Islam, and Christianity. The history of Judaism remains in large part a history of wrestling with, clarifying, codifying, and elaborating the commandments of God as revealed in *Torah*, a term that is often translated as law. As with *dharmasastra*, the commandments attributed to the *Torah* link together practices of daily life (e.g. what one ought to eat, how property ought to be controlled) with Jewish soteriology. The role of rabbis in interpreting and applying those commandments to the lives of Jews living in different places and times has been seen as analogous to the work of civil court judges in applying state laws. A similar dynamic can be seen to apply to the work of *muftis*, i.e. Muslim jurists who interpret and apply principles from *Qur'an* and *Hadith* to the everyday situations of Muslims. Their opinions, called *fatwas*, attempt to harmonize the everyday conduct of individuals with a not-fully-knowable divine plan (Hallaq 2009). As will be discussed in what follows, despite the Pauline emphasis on love over law (according to which many thinkers distinguish early Christianity from its Jewish roots), later Christian traditions developed highly elaborate systems of rules and norms for governing the church and religious life.

Despite these close structural and historical links between law and religion, one can identify over the last two hundred years a growing record of conflicts between the rules elaborated by religious clerics and texts and the rules set by governments. This is due in large part to the spread of the nation-state model of political organization, in which a single central government is expected to exercise monopolistic power over the lives of individuals living within its borders through instruments of state-made and state-enforced law. In this context, the presence of varying systems of religious law and other forms of law may be seen to threaten the assumed legal hegemony of the state.

One solution to this predicament, seen in the *Hodkin* case, has been simply to assert the primacy of state legal structures. According to this logic, when state law and religious norms conflict, the former should always trump the latter. However, this solution—which forms the basis of most 'secular' legal systems—is not as simple or problem-free as it might seem. As Hussein Agrama has shown recently, "secular power" actually generates and perpetuates the very problems that it claims to resolve (2012, 29). Rather than separating religion from politics, secular legal doctrines and practices continuously render those categories unstable, while at the same time demanding their demarcation. The result is not the subordination of religion to state law, but the creation of an endless cycle of unsolvable questions about the nature of religious and legal norms and how they ought to be distinguished.

Other solutions are also proposed. Today, a variety of states employ special state-legal structures that purport to minimize the possibility of conflict between religious and civil norms (even if their origins are grounded in more dubious projects of political control or domination [e.g. Mahmood 2012]). This is true particularly for norms regarding 'personal' matters such as marriage, divorce, and inheritance. The most common way this is done is through the creation of separate legal codes, procedures, and/or courts within which in which religious principles, texts, or clerics are vested with the authority to contract agreements, make judgments, or decide penalties. In India, for example, Muslim citizens have recourse to a separate body of Muslim Personal Law—embodied in special statutes and distinct from the rest of the civil code—under which they are expected to contract marriages, execute divorces, and dispute inheritances. Separate systems of religion-based personal law also exist in India for Hindus, Christians, Parsis, and, most recently, Sikhs.

Personal law systems, such as those seen in India, exist in a variety of countries and are often a legacy of colonial rule, especially in Asia and Africa. Yet, to see them simply as religious law is somewhat misleading. Although declaredly religious in substance, religious personal law codes frequently represent highly abbreviated and artificially formalistic renderings of religious law. Rather than containing a ready-made legal system plucked from an already-existing religious legal canon, in almost all cases personal law codes were generated by state authorities or colonial officers in consultation with a limited group of religious elites. In attempting to give religious law a separate jurisdiction within state law, colonial and contemporary drafters have tended to take what are often fluid, context-specific systems of reasoning and adjudication and to give them a fixed and rigid meaning (Moustafa 2013; Anderson 1993). Scott Kugle, writing about the creation of Muslim Personal Law in colonial India, has highlighted the ways in which drafters rendered broad, ambiguous theological principles and contextual jurisprudence into a new, "reified and static entity" which could be applied to all Muslims irrespective of their specific different schools of practice, traditions, or customs (2001, 258).

THE RELIGIOUS HISTORY OF SECULAR LAW

In the previous section, I examined what one might loosely call the 'legal' aspects of religion: the tendencies for religious traditions to draw upon collections of rules and sanctions. Yet, the relationship of religious law to state law is not merely one of structural similarity. According to many scholars, the characteristic institutions and concepts of modern law root themselves in religious principles. A clue to this in the *Hodkin* case was in the UK Common Law's easy equation of religion and "belief in God or a Supreme Being." It is not difficult to see how this established principle of 'secular' law in fact bore the traces of Abrahamic religious history and thought.

Far from being a marginal view, the idea that modern law has religious roots is one of the founding insights of modern socio-legal studies. Three of the most important early historians/sociologists of law, Henry Maine (1963 [1861]), Émile Durkheim (1964 [1893]), and Max Weber (1968 [1922]) explained the development of modern legality as a process of secularizing and displacing regimes of order and solidarity in which gods, totems, spirits, and ancestors played a central role. An early example of a strong theory of modern law's roots in religion was proposed by the German political and legal theorist, Carl Schmitt in a 1922 essay entitled "Political Theology." In it, Schmitt insisted that "[a]ll significant concepts of the modern theory of the state are secularized theological concepts" (1985 [1922], 36). These included concepts in law: notions of God's omnipotence were equivalent to notions of legal supremacy; notions of divine miracles were analogous to the idea of the exception in jurisprudence.

Since Schmitt a number of scholars have offered more elaborate arguments about the Christian origins of contemporary Euro-American law. One of the most thorough is Harold Berman's classic work *Law and Revolution* (1983), which narrates in some detail the development of late-modern European law from the time of the papal revolution in the eleventh and twelfth centuries. It was during this time that Pope Gregory VII introduced a robust form of centralized, formalized Canon Law to govern the Roman Catholic Church. From this revolutionary moment in the history of religions, Berman argues, one can find the origins of the modern rule of law (1983). In a follow-up volume (*Law and Revolution II*), published two decades later, Berman adds to his argument by examining the impacts of a second revolution—the Protestant revolution in Germany and England—on German and English legal structures and organization (2006). Concurrently with and since Berman's work, the idea of contemporary legal culture having religious roots has been largely accepted. Historian Brian Tierney has argued that developments in theology made possible "the rise of constitutionalism" (1982). Legal scholar John Witte Jr. has written and edited a number of significant works about the links between Christian thought and contemporary law (2007; Witte/Alexander 2010). Political philosopher Jeremy Waldron has argued that even the formative liberal theory of John Locke has its basis in notions of Christian theism (2002).

An interesting corollary to publications that underscore the Christian foundations of modern Western legality are a variety of studies, mainly coming from the field of anthropology, that shine light on alternate systems of contemporary legality, which have their own distinctive types of relationship with non-Christian religious traditions as well as their own fully fledged ideas of justice, jurisprudence, evidence, arbitration, punishment, law, etc. Two good examples of this type of scholarship are Rebecca French's examination of Buddhist legal culture in Tibet (1995) and Lawrence Rosen's exploration of Islamic judicial culture in Morocco (1989). French and Rosen, both legal anthropologists, offer detailed analyses of Buddhist and Islamic protocols and concepts for arbitrating disputes and defining justice. The *locus classicus* for this type of work can be found in the early anthropology of Bronislaw Malinowski who famously argued that in the Trobriand Islands origin-myths functioned as the "legal charter of the community" (1926, 56). For Malinoswki religion wasn't just law-like in its structure and rules or the historical seedbed for modern law, it functioned itself as a kind of legal order (1989 [1926]). These insights were taken up and amplified in the work of anthropologists such as E. E. Evans-Pritchard (1991 [1937]) and Max Gluckman (2012 [1965]) both of whom wrote about the ways in which rituals involving magic, witchcraft, and oracle reading served as full-blown modes of dispute resolution for African tribal groups.

Yet, alternative legal cultures that are blended with religious worldviews are not exotic curiosities that thrive only in the absence of contemporary regimes of law. In many cases, religious modes of understanding injury, remedy, dispute, and justice thrive alongside and even supplant the centralizing structures of modern rights-based law. This is precisely the point that David and Jaruwan Engel highlight in their detailed study of personal injury law in Chiang Mai, Thailand (2010). Rather than modern legality displacing religion-based ways of imagining injury and responsibility, as theories of globalization would predict, Engel and Engel demonstrate how northern Thai people have increasingly turned to forms of Buddhism (rather than tort law) to deal with personal injury. In other words, principles of karma, merit, and kindness are the *de facto* tort laws for many Thai who live in Chiang Mai.

THE RELIGIOUS ASSUMPTIONS OF SECULAR LAW

Scholarship on the religious roots of modern law highlights an important fact about state law in places like England: modern state law shows traces of its historical links with Christianity. However, these traces may be more significant than scholars such as Maine, Durkheim, and Weber would have cared to admit. In the work of these formative theorists of law—as well as in the work of many contemporary scholars of law and politics—theories about the religious roots of modern law work to solidify a story about the transition from ancient to modern forms of law: in the history of legal development law becomes progressively freed of its religious influences until it emerges in the modern (European) context in the form of a formal, rationalized, secular system. One of the things that distinguish modern law, in this view of things, is the absence of the substantive theological commitments that gave rise to it; the story of modern law becomes a story of law's progressive sloughing off of theology until it achieves a posture of aloof neutrality towards all religions.

This presumption of law's aloofness from religion has today become a core tenet of many modern rights-based legal systems, not only in Europe and North America but around the world in places like India, Japan, South Africa, and elsewhere. In these systems, law-makers, judges, and government agents assume that state law is religiously impartial—or ought to be made so through adjusting its language and interpretation. Thus, in the *Hodkin* case, Lord Toulson explained that the court overturned the earlier *Segerdal* in order to make the law more religiously impartial. In its opinion, the court presented the new description of religion as a step towards sanitizing law of its theological taints and achieving a more perfect (*qua* perfectly secular) law.

Scholars of religion and practitioners of law tend to differ in their attitudes towards the question of state law's perfectibility, i.e. whether state law can ever be perfectly aloof from and neutral towards all religious traditions. To a large extent, contemporary scholars of religion—who have imbibed the critiques of religion as a category mounted by Talal Asad (1993; 2003), J. Z. Smith (1982), and others—reject the idea that state law can ever be fully and permanently isolated from some stable and universal entity called religion. The rationale for this follows from the arguments against the possibility of a translocal, trans-temporal definition of religion: in order to separate religion from law, one first has to define what religion is; in the absence of a universal definition of religion, one cannot have a religion-less law; law therefore always retains normative biases in its treatment of those practices, persons, and things it categorizes as religion. This dynamic can be seen vividly in one of the first books to apply debates over the category of religion in religious studies directly to the domain of state law, Winnifred Sullivan's *The Impossibility of Religious Freedom* (2005). Sullivan exposes competing and irreconcilable assumptions about the nature of religion that complicated legal disputes over the decoration of gravesites in Boca Raton, Florida. Undertaking a legal ethnography of a court case in which she served as an expert witness, Sullivan—both a trained lawyer and a PhD in the academic study of religion—illuminates the ways in which legal reasoning in a US federal courtroom required judges to define the nature and essence of religion. That act of definition granted freedom to some forms of religiosity but not to others. For Sullivan, the forms of religion protected by US law are those that show generically Protestant features: "legal religion" in America is that which is primarily believed (rather than enacted), personal (rather than communal), textual (rather than oral), and voluntary (rather than obligatory) (2005, 8).

In the past decade, scholars have applied Sullivan's insights—or similar ones—to examine broader ranges of purportedly secular legal formations. Through a close analysis of US government Muslim-outreach initiatives, anthropologist Saba Mahmood has excavated the religiously partial assumptions that underlie what officials take to be 'moderate' forms of religion consistent with modern secular governance. Mahmood insists that ideologies of secularism do not simply work to separate off the religious from the political, but rather redefine and reconfigure the subjectivities of religious individuals to fit the conceptual categories, anthropology, and even hermeneutics of political liberalism (2006). Two important ideas emerge from the work of Sullivan and Mahmood. One point is that religion as it is practiced, lived, and understood in day-to-day life often differs dramatically from the assumptions about religion that animate secular politics and law. The other point is that secular politics and law exert a coercive, governmentalizing influence on religious lives, one that actively impinges upon the abilities of individuals and communities to live out their religious commitments. In other words, the religious biases of secular law don't simply misconstrue religion; they act upon religion in order to bring religion in line with the expectations of law. In other cases, these biases leave religious actors voiceless, unable to express their convictions in a way that is intelligible to law. A vivid portrayal of this last dynamic can be seen in the work of anthropologist Mayanthi Fernando (2010), who describes the inability of Muslim women in France to explain fully in a legal setting the significance of wearing the veil. For Fernando's interviewees, wearing the veil represents both an individual choice and a religious obligation, a voluntary act of submission to certain Islamic norms. French and European Union law, however, render volition and obligation as logical opposites in a way that makes these women's religious convictions inexpressible in law.

These examples gesture towards a broader point concerning the situation of religion in the environment of state law. State law, like religion, has its own approach to reality, its own epistemology, hermeneutics, even its own aesthetics. Rather than serving as a superstructure which sits above religion and other social and cultural formations, law exists as another cultural formation. The interaction of law and religion can therefore be interpreted as a kind of cross-cultural encounter. This idea has been explored intensively by Benjamin Berger, a Canadian legal theorist, whose recent works bring the insights of critical legal studies (particularly the work of Paul Kahn) to bear on religion. Berger has called for scholars to reject the "conventional story" about the interaction of law and religion in which "law is a means of managing or adjudicating cultural difference but enjoys a strong form of autonomy from culture . . . [one in which l]aw is the curator, rather than a component, of cultural pluralism" (2010, 99–110; 2015). Berger calls upon scholars to reject this view and, as a consequence, to moderate their expectations about state law and its ability to manage impartially the various interests of differing religious populations.

But how does one characterize the culture of law when it comes to religion? Is law's culture the product of many different quanta of theological preference, or is there a more general religious worldview to state law, a full-blown theology? Carl Schmitt suggested something like this when he referred to the political theology of modern states. Since Schmitt, scholarship on political theology has taken on even more varied forms, with academics from a variety of disciplines highlighting the importance of soteriology, cosmology, and theology to what purport to be non-religious political projects (Vries/ Lawrence 2006). In some ways the recent academic fascination with political theology has been anticipated by writing on 'civil religion,' a phrase coined by Rousseau but popularized by sociologist of religion Robert Bellah in the 1960s. For Bellah, and those who have taken inspiration from him, civil religion refers to the structures of mythological, ritual, theological, and soteriological elements that can be seen within political and institutional culture in America and, by extension, other countries. In his classic article "Civil Religion in America," Bellah reads the symbolism in US presidential speeches, public holidays, and national histories as revealing the presence of a "national faith" that recodes "Biblical archetypes"—salvation, exodus, death and resurrection, the promised land, and others—as national values (1967, 18). Although Bellah's arguments remain largely impressionistic, his conclusions nonetheless provide another suggestive category for considering the religious inclinations of purportedly secular state law.

The Legal Regulation of Religion and its Politics

If nothing else, the earlier sections will hopefully persuade readers that one cannot assume an easy and unproblematic distinction between religion and law. The two categories remain deeply intertwined in their functions, structures, histories, and even in their ambiguousness as analytical categories. (Although I've been treating law as a stable category, definitions of law remain just as contested as definitions of religion.) Approached from this perspective, the dilemma of the *Hodkin* case now appears less as a story about conflict regarding how to properly manage religion through secular law and more as a story about the deeper complexities associated with assessing and analyzing religion in the environment of a UK courtroom.

Of course, what appears to be a story of confusions and complexities from the vantage point of the academic looks like a story of success from the vantage point of Scientologists and others. After all, the court decision was a victory for Hodkin and her fiancé. Moreover, in the eyes of many observers, the Hodkin case was taken to be a triumph for religious freedom: by expanding the definition of religion to fit the new circumstances of religious diversity in the United Kingdom, the court appeared to be expanding the ambit of religious liberties for non-Christians. How does religious freedom fit into the conjuncture of religion and law? To answer this question, one must put politics back into the encounter and zoom out, historically and geographically, from the events in London.

It is important to recall that, in his description of religion, Lord Toulson rejected a theistic requirement, but he did not abandon altogether any definition for religion. In the court's logic, religions were assumed to have ministers and places of worship; they engaged in spiritual reflections and had belief systems. These belief systems, the court insisted, stood in necessary contrast to those of science. Looked at in this way, what is striking about the practices and doctrines of Scientology was less the absence of a notion of God, than the apparent presence of numerous other aspects—ministers, churches, beliefs, spiritual reflections—which made possible their recognition as religion by Toulson and the court. Put differently, what many in the media took to be a sea change in the law's definition of religion amounts essentially to the jettisoning of one relatively minor element, the importance of a Supreme Being. Looking at the *Hodkin* case this way, encourages us ask another question: How was it that Scientologists were able to secure the liberty to solemnize marriages—and be recognized as religious—so *easily* within UK civil law?

Asking the question this way helps us to put politics back into our consideration of religion in the environment of law. Legal processes—law-making, litigation, legal reform—always exist as one part of a broader social and political story. Politicians create laws protecting religion according to a variety of motivations. Deep concern for religion may be just one among many factors. The history of US laws governing religion is instructive here. Drafters of the US First Amendment seem to have been as concerned with states' rights as with protecting religion when it came to drafting the nonestablishment clause (Curry 1986). Similarly, when interpreting the First Amendment, US courts and lawyers have at times been more concerned with defending a *de facto* Protestant hegemony than with safeguarding all religious communities (Hamburger 2002). Since the end of World War II, US government actions to protect religious freedom abroad arguably have had less to do with ecumenical motives than with a desire to battle 'godless Communism,' or 'radical Islam,' or to give special protection to Christian communities (Hurd 2015; Castelli 2005).

To treat the design and interpretation of laws governing religion as existing within and reflecting broader currents of local and international politics is to look at decisions such as *Hodkin* in a new light. Instead of the quasi-Hegelian story of liberal secularism working itself out over time, one might look at other reasons why Scientology won this particular legal victory, in this venue, at this point in time. One part of the answer can be found in the sphere of the United Kingdom's domestic politics. As social and religious life in the United Kingdom becomes more diverse (through immigration, the development of new religious groups, and demographic changes), there are new pressures for legal and political elites to change statutory and common law. These pressures may come from lobbyists and constituents, as well as from the personal experiences of judges. Other parts of the answer must be sought elsewhere, outside of Britain. In addition to domestic politics, UK courts and law-makers also find themselves under pressure from without. One obvious point of external pressure comes from the European Union, and its Convention on Human Rights, to which the United Kingdom is a signatory. (In fact, the UK Human Rights Act of 1998 was designed to make the Convention a part of UK domestic law.) Were the court to have denied Scientologists status as a religion, they might have opened themselves up to criticisms for violating the terms of the Convention. A less obvious pressure has undoubtedly come from the international Scientology movement itself. Like other new religious movements worldwide—particularly the Jehovah's Witnesses—Scientologists have been prolific litigators, using the courts and other legal pathways to help defend their own status, liberties, and wealth within a variety of countries. In the United States, France, Australia, Germany, and elsewhere, the Church of Scientology has adopted legal action as strategy not simply to defend the group's religious rights, but also to make sure that they are able to claim the financial privileges and exemptions that come along with official status as a 'religion' (Richardson 2009).

But the story does not end here. The above political factors have been described as direct pressures on law itself, stimuli that lead to adjustments in the language and interpretation of state law. However, in the same way that law changes to meet the demands of religious groups and politics, religion also changes to meet the demands of law and to gain the favor of political regimes. Buddhists in Sri Lanka developed Sunday religious services and marriage ceremonies to fit the legal categories of British colonialism (Gombrich and Obeyesekere 1989, 202–273). Balinese Hindus under Suharto deliberately gave their practices an ethical, textual, monotheistic flavor so that they would better conform to Indonesian state-legal definitions of religion, and the protections and perquisites that came with official recognition as *agama* (religion) (Picard 2000). The history of Scientology provides an especially striking example of this process. The obvious presence of ministers, churches, and systems of belief in Scientology, which inclined Lord Toulson to treat it as a religion, did not develop naturally or arbitrarily. In the late 1960s and early 1970s, L. Ron Hubbard, the founder of Scientology, ordered a deliberate and comprehensive program of institutional reform that required Scientologists to give prominence to these categories. In his history of Scientology, scholar of religion Hugh Urban quotes from a memo from February 1969 which directs Scientologists to publicize "visual evidences that Scientology is a religion," steps which include displaying crosses on Scientology premises, advertising the "Creed of the Church," and wearing clerical garb designed to look like that worn by Christian ministers (black suits and vests, with white clerical collars) (2011, 163). The goal was less theological than political: to make the movement appear more 'religious' in order to secure the religion-based tax exemptions and religious freedom protections in the United States, Australia, the United Kingdom, and other places.

CONCLUSION

This chapter has showed the ways in which studying religion in the environment of law is not quite as straightforward as it might seem at first glance. Law and religion are not necessarily opposed and opposing categories: religions have laws; laws have theologies; each remains a contested and ambiguous category, which often bleeds into the other. At the same time, in most state courtrooms, the two categories are treated as if they were necessarily separate and separable; all the while, a variety of political and social forces (motivated by a variety of reasons) press on state law to accommodate religion and press on religion to conform to the categories of state law. Although the categories of religion and law often conjure in the minds of people an impression of timelessness and stability, in most cases scholars are in fact dealing with active and moving conceptual targets.

To study religion in the environment of law is to confront head-on the importance of questions about religion for modern governance. It is also to confront the distance between the academic study of religion and the legal and political management of religion. Definitions of religion matter in state law. Whether Scientology is classified as 'religion' has real effects on people's personal lives, finances, and abilities to exercise civil liberties. At the same time, the attentiveness to the fuzziness and instability of religion as an analytical category that is cultivated in the academy often feels frustratingly at odds with the confident assertions about religion made by legislators and judges. To study religion in the environment of law is to immerse oneself in that tension and to embrace the challenges and contradictions that it brings.

Glossary

Civil religion a phrase coined by Rousseau but popularized by sociologist of religion Robert Bellah; similar to the idea of political theology, it refers more directly to what might be called a 'state cult' visible in given country's public holidays, national myths, and political discourse.

Legal pluralism the existence of multiple normative and/or state-legal systems in a single place.

Liberalism a term with many definitions; when it comes to discussions of religion and law it tends to refer to the idea that law should be (1) neutral towards religion and (2) protect the rights of individuals.

Personal law systems structures and provisions within state law designed to allow particular (religious) communities to regulate matters of marriage, inheritance, and divorce—and sometimes other things—according to their own customs and norms.

Political theology a term most-often associated with the German philosopher and legal theorist Carl Schmitt; it refers to the idea that politics, law, and government have within them implicit or explicit religious concepts or structures.

References

Agrama, Hussein Ali. 2012. *Questioning Secularism: Islam, Sovereignty, and the Rule of Law in Modern Egypt.* Chicago, IL: University of Chicago Press.

Anderson, M. R. 1993. "Islamic Law and the Colonial Encounter in British India." In *Institutions and Ideologies: A SOAS South Asia Reader*, edited by P. Robb and D. Arnold. London: Curzon Press, 165–185.

Asad, Talal. 1993. *Genealogies of Religion: Discipline and Reasons of Power in Christianity and Islam.* Baltimore, MD: Johns Hopkins University Press.

Asad, Talal. 2003. *Formations of the Secular: Christianity, Islam, Modernity.* Stanford, CA: Stanford University Press.

Bellah, Robert N. 1967. "Civil Religion in America." *Dædalus: Journal of the American Academy of Arts and Sciences* 96(1): 1–21.

Berger, Benjamin L. 2010. "The Cultural Limits of Legal Tolerance." In *After Pluralism: Reimagining Religious Engagement*, edited by Courtney Bender and Pamela E. Klassen. New York: Columbia University Press, 98–125.

Berger, Benjamin L. 2015. *Law's Religion: Religious Freedom and the Constitutional Rule of Law.* Toronto: University of Toronto Press.

Berman, Harold J. 1983. *Law and Revolution: The Formation of the Western Legal Tradition.* Cambridge, MA: Harvard University Press.

Berman, Harold J. 2006. *Law and Revolution, II: The Impact of the Protestant Reformations on the Western Legal Tradition.* Cambridge, MA: Harvard University Press.

Castelli, Elizabeth A. 2005. "Praying for the Persecuted Church: US Christian Activism in the Global Arena." *Journal of Human Rights* 4(3): 321–351.

Curry, Thomas J. 1986. *The First Freedoms: Church and State in America to the Passage of the First Amendment.* New York: Oxford University Press.

Durkheim, Émile. 1964. *The Division of Labor in Society.* Glencoe, IL: Free Press. Original edition, 1893.

Engel, David and Jaruwan Engel. 2010. *Tort, Custom, and Karma: Globalization and Legal Consciousness in Thailand.* Stanford, CA: Stanford Law Books.

Evans-Pritchard, Edward Evan. 1991. *Witchcraft, Oracles, and Magic among the Azande.* Oxford: Clarendon Press. Original edition, 1937.

Feil, Ernst. 1997. *Religio. Zweiter Band. Die Geschichte eines neuzeitlichen Grundbegriffs zwischen Reformation und Rationalismus (ca. 1540-1620).* Göttingen: Vandenhoeck & Ruprecht.

Fernando, Mayanthi. 2010. "Reconfiguring Freedom: Muslim Piety and the Limits of Secular Law and Public Discourse in France." *American Ethnologist* 37(1): 19–35.

French, Rebecca Redwood. 1995. *The Golden Yoke: The Legal Cosmology of Buddhist Tibet.* Ithaca, NY: Cornell University Press.

Gluckman, Max. 2012. *Politics, Law and Ritual in Tribal Society.* New Brunswick, NJ: Transaction Publishers. Original edition, 1965.

Gombrich, Richard and Gananath Obeyesekere. 1989. *Buddhism Transformed: Religious Change in Sri Lanka.* Princeton, NJ: Princeton University Press.

Hallaq, Wael B. 2009. *An Introduction to Islamic Law.* Cambridge: Cambridge University Press.

Hamburger, Philip. 2002. *Separation of Church and State.* Cambridge, MA: Harvard University Press.

Hurd, Elizabeth Shakman. 2015. *Beyond Religious Freedom.* Princeton, NJ: Princeton University Press.

Kugle, S. A. 2001. "Framed, Blamed and Renamed: The Recasting of Islamic Jurisprudence in Colonial South Asia." *Modern Asian Studies* 35(2): 257–313.

Lammerts, D. Christian. 2013. "Narratives of Buddhist Legislation: Textual Authority and Legal Heterodoxy in Seventeenth Through Nineteenth-Century Burma." *Journal of Southeast Asian Studies* 44(01): 118–144.

Mahmood, Saba. 2006. "Secularism, Hermeneutics, and Empire: The Politics of Islamic Reformation." *Public Culture* 18(2): 323–347.

Mahmood, Saba. 2012. "Religious Freedom, the Minority Question, and Geopolitics in the Middle East." *Comparative Studies in Society and History* 54(2): 418–446.

Maine, Henry Sumner. 1963. *Ancient Law.* Boston, MA: Beacon Press. Original edition, 1861.

Malinowski, Bronislaw. 1926. *Myth in Primitive Psychology.* London: Kegan Paul.

Malinowski, Bronislaw. 1989. *Crime and Custom in Savage Society.* Totowa, NJ: Rowman & Littlefield. Original edition, 1926.

Moustafa, Tamir. 2013. "Liberal Rights Versus Islamic Law? The Construction of a Binary in Malaysian Politics." *Law & Society Review* 47(4): 771–802.

Novak, David. 2008. "Law and Religion in Judaism." In *Christianity and Law: An Introduction,* edited by John Witte and Frank F. S. Alexander. Cambridge: Cambridge University Press, 33–52.

O'Flaherty, Wendy Doniger. 1992. *The Laws of Manu: With an Introduction and Notes.* New Delhi: Penguin Books.

Picard, Michel. 2000. "Agama, Adat, Budaya: The Dialogic Construction of 'Kebalian.'" *Dialog* 1(1): 85–124.

Richardson, James T. 2009. "Scientology in Court: A Look at Some Major Cases from Various Nations." In *Scientology,* edited by James R. Lewis. Oxford: Oxford University Press, 283–294.

Rosen, Lawrence. 1989. *The Anthropology of Justice: Law as Culture in Islamic Society.* Cambridge: Cambridge University Press.

Schmitt, Carl. 1985. *Political Theology: Four Chapters on the Concept of Sovereignty.* Cambridge, MA: MIT Press. Original edition, 1922.

Smith, Jonathan Z. 1982. *Imagining Religion: From Babylon to Jonestown*. Chicago, IL: University of Chicago Press.

Sullivan, Winnifred F. 2005. *The Impossibility of Religious Freedom*. Princeton, NJ: Princeton University Press.

Tierney, Brian. 1982. *Religion, Law, and the Growth of Constitutional Thought, 1150–1650*. Cambridge: Cambridge University Press.

Urban, Hugh B. 2011. *The Church of Scientology: A History of a New Religion*. Princeton, NJ: Princeton University Press.

Vries, Hent de and Lawrence Eugene, eds. 2006. *Political Theologies: Public Religions in a Post-Secular World*. New York: Fordham University Press.

Waldron, Jeremy. 2002. *God, Locke, and Equality: Christian Foundations of John Locke's Political Thought*. Cambridge: Cambridge University Press.

Weber, Max. 1968. *Economy and Society: An Outline of Interpretive Sociology*, edited by Claus Wittich and Guenther Roth. New York: Bedminster Press. Original edition, 1922.

Witte, John. 2007. *The Reformation of Rights: Law, Religion, and Human Rights in Early Modern Calvinism*. Cambridge: Cambridge University Press.

Witte, John and Frank Alexander, eds. 2010. *Christianity and Human Rights: An Introduction*. Cambridge: Cambridge University Press.

Further Reading

Benda-Beckmann, Franz von, Keebet von Benda-Beckmann, Martin Ramstedt, and Bertram Turner. 2013. *Religion in Disputes: Pervasiveness of Religious Normativity in Disputing Processes*. Basingstoke: Palgrave Macmillan. [*A recent edited volume containing chapters from important scholars of religion and law in a variety of disciplines. The volume considers numerous examples from Asia, Africa, North America, and Israel.*]

Comaroff, John L. 2009. "Reflections on the Rise of Legal Theology: Law and Religion in the Twenty-First Century." *Social Analysis* 53(1): 193–216. [*A highly thought-provoking and original article by one of the most important legal anthropologists in the world on the growing inter-penetration of the legal and the religious in the modern world.*]

Cover, Robert M. 1983. "The Supreme Court, 1982 Term—Foreword: Nomos and Narrative." *Harvard Law Review* 97(4): 4–68. [*An important article that has deeply influenced the study of religion and law by exploring the parallels between religious law and US constitutional law as well as the importance of acknowledging law's embedding within broader narratives of mankind's present and future.*]

Davis, Donald, R. 2010. *The Spirit of Hindu Law*. Cambridge: Cambridge University Press. [*A sophisticated yet very readable examination of the dimensions and idea of 'law' in the ancient Indian context, particularly within the Dharmasastra genre. Essential reading for anyone interested in South Asian legal traditions.*]

French, R. and M. Nathan, eds. 2014. *Buddhism and Law: An Introduction*. Cambridge: Cambridge University Press; Lubin, T., Jr., D. R. Davies, and J. K. Krishnan, eds. 2010. *Hinduism and Law: An Introduction*. Cambridge: Cambridge University Press; Witte, J. and F. S. Alexander, eds. 2008. *Christianity and Law: An Introduction*. Cambridge: Cambridge University Press. [*These three works are part of a Cambridge University Press series and, collectively, constitute a solid starting point for anyone interested in the specific historical and contemporary links between Buddhism, Hinduism, Christianity, and law.*]

Huxley, A. ed. 2002. *Religion, Law and Tradition*. London: Routledge. [*A broad and illuminating comparative volume—edited by one of the world's leading scholars of Buddhism and law—that brings together essays on religious law in a variety of traditions.*]

Sullivan, Winnifred, M. Taussig-Rubbo, and Robert Yelle, eds. 2011. *After Secular Law*. Palo Alto, CA: Stanford University Press. [*One of the best and most comprehensive reassessments of modern, positivist assumptions about law's separation from religion. Brings together chapters from leading scholars of religion, law, history, and anthropology to trace discrete historical genealogies of how law came to be understood as aloof from religion as well as to highlight the inadequacies of the 'separatist' assumption for understanding and explaining contemporary life.*]

CHAPTER 26

....

MEDIA

....

OLIVER KRÜGER

CHAPTER SUMMARY

- Research on media and religion can focus on three distinct dimensions: the production, the program/contents, and the reception/consumption of media.
- The modern notion of media, termed by Marshall McLuhan, has roots in a long history of conceptions of the 'medium' in Western philosophy and nineteenth-century spiritualism.
- Religious traditions express a need for the 'spiritualization' of media technology. This chapter shows this process of perception or rejection with regard to images/photography, telephony, film, radio broadcasting, and television.
- For religious texts Wilfred Cantwell Smith claims that "scripture is a human activity" (1993, 18) taking into account the relation that texts have with different groups of interpreters over time.
- The Internet multiplies the traditional modes of communication and expression for religious communities and individuals.
- Besides its functions as a communication tool, the Internet is a symbol for social, technological, and religious utopias.

MEDIA AND RELIGION:
A SYSTEMATIC APPROACH

Entering the complex field of religion and media requires some epistemological reflections. That means, on the one hand, we have to consider the normative impact and history of key terms and concepts such as 'media' and 'Internet' and, on the other, to reflect critically on the far-reaching assumptions of media theory, in religious matters and beyond, in light of empirical evidence. The empirical field itself requires identifying key dimensions of research. These are (1) production, (2) program/contents, and (3) reception/consumption of media.

The first dimension focuses on media institutions and individual producers. What is the legal, economic, and institutional framework and who are the players in media production? Do certain religious traditions and denominations benefit from privileges in public broadcasting networks, as in many European states? In what manner do publishing houses and media enterprises owned by religious communities offer media products for the general market? Christoph Markschies (2007, 331–335) demonstrates, for example, that theological interests depended on the media infrastructure (libraries, book stores) in Christian antiquity, which had a large impact on the processes of canonization of the New Testament.

The second dimension is the media content itself. At this point, we have to differentiate between explicit religious contents (e.g. by religious broadcasters), reporting and documentation *about* religions, and references on religious issues, topics, and symbols in fictional formats.

The third dimension relates to the consumer's side, the use of media, and the reception of media content. The assumption that media consumers simply receive and adapt to attitudes and values presented in the media has been largely challenged by qualitative media research in recent years (Ayaß 2012). On the contrary, we have to assume that media users perceive media contents in manifold and creative ways.

Combining these three dimensions allows us to tackle intersecting issues. In this manner we may establish a profile of a specific religious tradition (or topic) in a cross-media perspective, e.g. the coverage of Islam in Swiss radio, television, and newspapers in 2009–2010 (parallel to the plebiscite on the prohibition of minarets). On the other hand, we could scrutinize the media profile of a specific religious community. How does a certain religious group use a medium such as television as a means of communication for their religious purposes? A cross-media perspective offers insights on the mutual interplay of production and reception of religious contents in the media.

Last but not least, the convenient availability of digital media permits new modes of presentation for the study of religion. Beyond the conventional publication of printed texts, online resources, audio and video broadcasting, blogs, and websites are gaining significance. Brief PowerPoint presentations including film clips, images, or animated graphics have widely replaced the simple 'public reading of texts' at conferences, thereby causing major changes in academic oral discourse.

MEDIA AND THE STUDY OF RELIGION

Interest in media as an object for the study of religion is twofold: traditional and electronic media are means of representation of religious iconography, texts, sounds, films, etc. Thus, the history of religion is based exclusively on media artifacts, and contemporary research can hardly ignore them. In addition, nearly all religious traditions have developed 'theories' regarding these media artifacts. From a religious perspective the existence of media touches upon epistemological questions of authenticity and truth regarding the mainly visual and auditory experience that media make possible, for example, the 'true' image and word of god. Media technology is always embedded in certain cultural and social patterns of reception. Media are—apart from their contents—received differently in diverse social, cultural, historical, and religious settings: they are 'socially shaped' and need to be 'spiritualized': i.e. new media are evaluated by a religious community in light of their set of beliefs (Campbell 2010a, 1–7).

Academic scholarship is not immune to this religious evaluation of media. Although many classic authors in the study of religion such as Mircea Eliade, Gerardus van der Leeuw, and Friedrich Heiler were contemporaries of the electronic media revolution (radio, TV) and witnessed the extensive media use by religious institutions, the role of modern media has been largely neglected until recently. Apparently, this is no accident but is due to a marginalization of media in the theoretical conception of religion that focused on the immediacy of experiences of the 'holy.' It was Friedrich Schleiermacher who introduced a hierarchy in the possible experience of god's presence in his work *On Religion: Speeches to its Cultured Despisers* (*Über die Religion: Reden an die Gebildeten unter ihren Verächtern*, 1799). The immediate experience of god figures as central, then comes the mystic's silence, the spoken word of the gospel, and lastly the 'dead written letters.' This hierarchy proved to be influential for the phenomenological school in the study of religion, which defined the immediate experience of the holy as the heart of all religion (Krüger 2012, 11–21).

The History of the Term 'Medium' in Philosophy and Spiritualism

In dealing with media we are facing a long history of the term *medium* (Latin "middle"). The medieval translation of Aristotle's work Περι Ψυχής into Latin (*De anima*) introduced the notion of the medium into Western philosophy as an ontological means of perception that has a power by its own. Later Immanuel Kant, Georg C. Lichtenberg, Friedrich W. J. Schelling, and particularly Johann G. Herder in his *Aethermetaphysik* refined this term as a matter and means of the true knowledge of the world (Hagen 2008). Thus, eighteenth-century philosophical discourse established the 'medium' as a powerful entity of cognition.

Nineteenth-century encyclopedias list the term 'medium' predominantly for persons who act as a means of contacting spirits of the dead and otherworldly entities in American and European spiritualism. Today, this obscure past of the term 'medium' is presented as strictly separate from the technical notion of media (in the plural), although the two lexemes were indeed closely linked. From the mid-nineteenth until the early twentieth century, photography was widely used to produce images of spirits (William H. Mumler) and of paranormal phenomena (Hippolyte Baraduc, Albert von Schrenck-Notzing). In this discourse, photography was considered as a technical, objective means to prove the existence of otherworldly entities, as a personal medium did in séances. Hence, photography catalyzed the development of Western spiritualism and esoteric para-psychology (Fischer/Loers 1997; Krüger 2012, 16–20).

The Concept of 'Media'

At first, we have to take into account that the modern notion of *media*, as a general term for all technical media, is a recent phenomenon, coined by Marshall McLuhan with a pejorative connotation: "Is not the essence of education civil defence against media fallout?" (2002 [1962], 246). Since the 1970s and 1980s *media* then figures as a key term in the new disciplines of media and communication studies for all kinds of broadcasting and storage media in English, German, French, etc.

McLuhan (1994 [1964]) proposed—blatantly intending to establish media studies as a key discipline of the twentieth century—to understand all extensions of the body (its senses and memory) as media: scripture, numbers, clothing, houses, money, watches, books, bicycles, airplanes, photographs, newspapers, cars, games, typewriters, telephones, movies, television, radios, weapons, and computers. Likewise postmodern philosophers such as Jean Baudrillard, Paul Virilio, and Vilém Flusser define even a football, a waiting room, a horse, and a street as media, while sociologists Talcott Parsons and Niklas Luhmann perceive money, power, art, belief, and love as social media. All focus on the social function of media as space, means, and frame of communication. However, in the study of religion the concept should be used in a more narrow sense so that specific methods and theories can be put to practical use. In a narrow sense, media are means of representation, storage, and transmission of texts, images, sounds, and audiovisual materials (Campbell 2010a, 41–63).

The difference between 'old' and 'new' media is vague: "The term new media has achieved the kind of widespread cultural dissemination that seems to strip away all specificity. 'New' media is everywhere around us, in the gadgets and devices we used to keep organized, to do our work, to play, to access information, and to communicate with friends and acquaintances" (Hansen 2010, 172). On this view, 'new media' is a relational concept—for societies as a whole or, for example, for academic disciplines—instead of a fixed set of media technologies.

Media Theory and the Study of Religion

Religion played a certain role in early media theory when the Toronto School of Communication was established. Media as crucial instruments of the human perception of the world were not seen as objective means for observation or communication, but, according to McLuhan and Harold Innis, they contain within themselves the conditions of a certain perception of reality. Elisabeth Eisenstein in *The Printing Press as an Agent of Change* (1979) and McLuhan in *The Gutenberg Galaxy: The Making of Typographic Man* (1962) demonstrated the impact of the printing press on the emergence of humanism, reformation, and democracy:

> Print is the extreme phase of alphabetic culture that detribalizes and decollectivizes man in the first instance. Print raises the visual features of alphabet to highest intensity of definition. Thus print carries the individuating power of the phonetic alphabet much further than manuscript culture could ever do. Print is the technology of individualism. (McLuhan 2002, 158)

Although these strong claims could be challenged by pointing to divergent uses of the printing press in early modern Europe (hard censorship in Catholic countries, liberal policies in the Netherlands, etc.) this approach gained much attention placing media (and media theory) at the center of analysis of social and cultural change.

Currently, the theory of mediatization of religion and culture in late modern societies initiated by Stig Hjarvard postulates fundamental changes of mediatized religion: "By the mediatization of society, we understand the process whereby society to an increasing degree is submitted to, or becomes dependent on, the media and their logic" (2008a, 113). According to Hjarvard, media have taken over ritual elements and social functions of religion (2008b, 10–13, 18–20; 2013, 84–101). However, the empirical translation of 'the logic of the media' remains diffuse, and surprisingly Hjarvard's own analyses of popular movies (*Harry Potter, Lord of the Rings*) show only marginal influence of these movies on the viewers' 'spiritual interest' (Hjarvard 2008b, 19–23). This strong mediatization thesis proposed by Hjarvard and other scholars lacks an historical and intercultural perspective and is mainly based on the situation in Scandinavian churches (Hjarvard 2013; Hjarvard/Lövheim 2012). In contrast to Hjarvard, Andreas Hepp and Friedrich Krotz point out that mediatization has to be understood as a relational concept, covering the complex dynamics between media, communication, and culture. They analyze the social, spatial, and temporal consequences of new media (Hepp/Krotz 2012, 11).

The sociological tradition in media research pointed early on to the other side of the coin: for example, "the question (is) not 'what do the media do to people?' but, rather, 'What do people do with the media'" (Katz/Foulkes 1962, 378). This implies rejecting claims that a certain medium has a determined effect on society or 'religion', searching rather for different modes of use and reception among social groups (age, gender, education, cultural/religious background), and taking historical dynamics into account. Here, media research figures as social science (Ayaß 2012; Keppler 2005), and it benefits from innovative approaches in media anthropology, which covers media use in the context of social, ritual, and corporeal practices (Meyer 2009; 2012).

THE VARIETY OF 'RELIGIOUS MEDIA'—A ROAD MAP

The oldest sources in the history of religion are figurines, petroglyphs, and cave paintings in the upper Paleolithic era; the first mass production of amulets, rings, and small deity sculptures starts at Egyptian pilgrimage centers in the third millennium (Herrmann/Staubli 2010). From as early as the sixth century BCE, coins were the first highly circulated mass media, displaying images of gods or temples in Greece and Minor Asia, and from the Hellenistic period onwards these religious elements join the rulers' portraits. In modern times, candles, pendants, pastries, beakers, calendars, lapel pins, stickers, T-shirts, caps (and potentially all kinds of clothing) bear the emblem of their original pilgrimage center or personal religious testimonial (Staubli 2003). Posters, license plates (United States), and paintings on buses (South Asia) are used for religious testimonials or for apotropaic aims. In addition to coins, stamps pick up religious motifs in modern times. Likewise from earliest times until today funerary art shows an enormous diversity of textual and visual art pieces with its headstones, aristocratic and patrician tomb monuments, decorated sarcophagi, photographs of the dead, different forms of the obituary, and eventually virtual memorials. Among modern media, the gramophone record (and its artistic covers), the compact cassette (significant even today for listening to Qur'an recitations), the videocassette, and the DVD play a crucial role for the distribution of religious instruction and propaganda. In Christian church services, Power Point presentations often replace the use of traditional hymnbooks (Krüger 2012, 215–222).

The following briefly introduces topics and studies in the main fields of images and photography, telephony, film, and radio and television broadcasting, before focusing in depth on the religious use of texts and the Internet.

Images and Photography

In Christianity the tension between images of the divine and textual presentations has long been a contentious theological issue: e.g. in early Judaism, Islam, and the periods of Byzantine and Protestant iconoclasm. The predominance of philological approaches in Christian (and especially Lutheran) theology as well as in the earlier study of religion (*Religionswissenschaft*) is probably a consequence of this theological bias. This problem has evoked a critical consideration of philological limits in the history of religion and hence a new emphasis on the iconic turn and the agenda of visible religion (Kippenberg et al. 1982–1990; Uehlinger 2007). Here, the study of religion was inspired by art and ancient history, which already had acknowledged the importance of religious art (sculpture, relief, painting, mosaics, numismatics, miniature art) and developed sophisticated systematizations (e.g. *Lexicon Iconographicum Mythologiae Classicae*). Recent approaches such as the aesthetics of religion include the reception and cultic practice of religious artifacts (Belting 1994) and take into consideration popular media such as posters, postcards, missionary photography, and illustrations in devotional literature, etc. (McLeod 1992; Morgan 2005; Meyer 2009).

Although photography has been closely linked to the early notion of the spirit *medium*, it has been largely ignored in the contemporary history of religion. This fact is astonishing as photography played a crucial role in constructing ethnic, cultural, and religious otherness from the nineteenth century onwards. Great collections of ethnographic photography—such as John F. Watson's and John W. Kaye's *The People of India* (1868–1875) or Edward S. Curtis's *North American Indian* (1907–1915), as well as oriental portraits and scenes for popular postcards—figured as an important element of orientalist, colonial, and missionary discourses (Hight/Sampson 2002). Apart from portrait photography of religious leaders and contemporary saints, photography quickly became popular to record rituals of passage (weddings, baptism, confirmation, first communion, pilgrimage), religious places, and to portray the dead in nineteenth-century Europe (Ruby 1995). Today, press photography is crucial for illustrating reports in printed and online newspapers and television news. Just as with textual information, the selection of certain images may establish an emotional bias towards the topics or people presented, especially when violence is imaged (Mitchell 2012b).

Telephony

Apart from marginal phenomena—like the telephone as a tool for spirit communication (Fischinger 2003, 39) and specific processes of domestication of the telephone among contemporary ultra-Orthodox Jews and Amish (Campbell 2010a, 162–179; Zimmermann-Umble 1992)—the telephone is of interest for the religious mainstream as a means of counseling in personal crisis. In 1895 the Baptist pastor Harry Warren founded the first 24-hour crisis hotline in New York City, and in 1953 the Anglican priest Edward Chad Varah established the organization The Samaritans, in order to prevent people from committing suicide. Today, there are crisis hotlines (including e-mail and SMS-counseling) in about sixty countries worldwide, some with a church affiliation, most without any religious or political affiliation. For Muslims so-called fatwa-hotlines and e-mail counseling were established in the late 1990s by individual Muslim authorities and Cairo's Al-Azhar University (Richter 2009). In addition, commercial 'spiritual' counseling providers have offered their services by phone since the 1980s, mainly astrology and 'magic' for business or marriage, defense against demons, etc.

The micro blogging service Twitter, launched in 2006, is used for the distribution of short religious messages (up to 140 characters), especially in the United States. Here, prominent pastors have at present up to 40,000 'followers': Pope Benedict XVI started to tweet in December 2012 and Pope Francis began shortly after his inauguration. It appears that getting messages directly from religious leaders on the mobile phone is attractive for the sender and receiver: it provides the feeling of a personal relation to the church leader (Krüger 2012, 294–304).

Film

The field of religion and film covers movies with explicit religious content (stories, characters), the religious interpretations of popular movies, documentaries on religion, and films targeted explicitly for mission. Religion was part of movie culture since the earliest days of cinema in works by Georges Méliès, Alice Guy, Jyotish Bannerjee, and David Wark Griffith around 1900. Movies have contained religious references as narratives/mythologies, as hagiographic stories, or as melodrama in a religious setting since the golden era of silent movies after World War I, as in the first monumental biblical drama *Der Galiläer* (Germany 1921 by Dimitri Buchowetzki), in *I.N.R.I* (Germany 1923 by Robert Wiene), or in the first Indian adaption of the Mahabharata (1920 by Jyotish Bannerjee). In the same period, religion also became the object of communist or atheistic criticism as in Sergei Eisenstein's *Octobre* (1928) or Luis Buñuel's and Salvador Dali's *L'Âge d'or* (1930).

Despite this evident presence of religion in film, the disciplines of theology and the study of religion have focused mainly on the interpretation of general art house movies and popular cinema. Often with reference to Paul Tillich's *Theology of Culture* (1959), the study of religion aimed to identify the implicit religious meaning of films. There are two main approaches: the first emphasizes the aesthetics of movies; the other understands the story of a film as a parable (Sitney 1987; Plate 2005).

It was the French Jesuit Amédée Ayfre who suggested in his influential book *Dieu au cinéma* seeing film as an experience of the holy (*le sacré*): "the religious quality of a work depends much less on its contents, in the strict sense—on its background context, on its subject matter—than on its form, or rather on its 'forms'. There is an extremely close relation between aesthetic values and religious values" (1953, 30). Later the US author and art director Paul Schrader (1972) searched for this apparently intercultural transcendental style. While Schrader and Ayfre applied their aesthetic perspective exclusively to a selection of art house movies, recent authors take popular movies into account as well (Campani 2007; Knauß 2008).

The second approach seeks to understand film as another way to promote meaning and values, and as therefore functioning like religion. Stories told—regardless of the absence or presence of religious references—are received as parables with existential meaning for life, death, and love as ancient mythologies did in the past (Bergesen/Greeley 2003; Herrmann 2007). With this agenda in mind the philosophers William Blizek and Ronald Burke initiated the online open access *Journal of Religion and Film* (1997ff.; Blizek/Desmaraisa 2011).[1] However, without empirical consideration of the

---

[1] See <http://www.unomaha.edu/jrf/purpose.htm> (04.08.2016).

movies' reception among audiences, these are questionable undertakings, often based upon theological premises. An important exception that considers film as filmic medium rather than text is S. Brent Plate's *Religion and Film: Cinema and the Re-Creation of the World* (2008).

Worth distinguishing is the category of documentary films. Visual anthropology was initiated by Gregory Bateson and Margaret Mead (*Trance and Dance in Bali*, 1952), Jean Rouch (*Au pays des mages noirs*, 1947), John Marshall (*The Hunters*, 1957), Tim Asch (*Magical Death*, 1974), and others. Today, visual anthropology covers a global range of ethnographic studies as exemplified by the specialized journals *Visual Anthropology Review* (since 1991) and *Visual Anthropology* (since 1987).

With regard to films of religious propaganda, American evangelist Billy Graham started the first film ministry in 1951 in order to multiply the scope of his crusades and revival meetings. Beginning in 1979, *The Jesus Film Project* has shown their Jesus-movie, based on the Gospel of Luke and translated into more than thousand languages, to an alleged audience of 5.6 billion (and counting). But today, religious propaganda by film has shifted mainly to video-sharing websites on the Internet, due to lower costs and greater accessibility.

Radio Broadcasting

With the beginning of regular radio broadcasting in the early 1920s, Christian churches in Europe and North America launched Sunday services on air. The liberal US and Canadian radio markets allowed several churches and pastors (e.g. Paul Rader, Charles E. Fuller, William Aberhart) to develop proper formats for the radio mission such as bible drama hours, healing hours, answering letters, and phone-in shows. On the side of the Catholic church Pope Pius XI initiated Radio Vatican in 1931 (Goethals/Lucas 2005). The journal *Medien aktuell: Kirche im Rundfunk*[2] covers the worldwide activities of Christian churches. Today, the air around the globe is filled with numerous religious radio broadcasters of major and minor traditions (Hangen 2002). Furthermore, the Internet offers the opportunity to establish global religious radio programs at low cost for even small communities and new religious movements. As with television, the journalistic programs of public radio often include news, reports, features, and magazines on religious issues. In the face of this omnipresence of religious radio broadcasting, Udo Tworuschka calls for an *auditive turn* in the study of religion (2008).

Television

There exists a certain bias towards television as a kind of rival to worship attendance (so-called 'media religion') among mainstream theologians in Europe and the United States (Krüger 2012, 354–372). Christian broadcasting started as early as the 1950s in both

---

[2] See http://www.addx.de/textarchiv/archiv-kir.php.

continents. In Europe, religious television was limited for a long period to the transmission of church services on Sundays and Christian holidays and, for example, brief weekly sermons on German and Swiss public television. In the United States single pastors and networks were successful from the 1950s in offering counseling, sermons, talk shows, prayers, worship, and music as 'televangelism'. Fulton J. Sheen, Rex Humbard, Oral Roberts, Billy Graham, Kathryn Kuhlman, Benny Hinn, and Joel Osteen were, and in some cases still are, prominent figures on the screen, partly with their own mega churches as stage (Melton/Lucas/Stone 1997). Televangelism was mainly covered by research in communication studies that was launched by Stewart M. Hoover in the 1980s (1988; 2005). The liberalization of the TV market in Europe and South America in the 1980s, in the Arab world in the 1990s, and recently in some Asian countries facilitated the development of specialty channels dedicated to religious mission and sporadic religious programs on general private channels (Goethals/Lucas 2005). Thus, for example, televangelism became a widespread phenomenon in the Islamic media world with renowned preachers such as the Egyptians Amr Khaled and Moez Masoud or Abdullah Gymnastiar in Indonesia (Thomas/Lee 2012; Day Howell 2008; Richter 2009).

More than religious specialty channels, which are still marginal in Europe, the display of religion in news, reports, and documentaries appears to be most influential for the general audience. Here, images and narratives of otherness—e.g. Muslims in US news—are presented in an apparently 'objective' manner. The competition for viewing ratings causes a significant focus on conflicts and scandals and a noticeably dramatized and emotionalized display of contents by use of cinematic tools (camera shots, music) and journalistic means (personalization, simplification) (Mitchell 2012a; 2012b; Hoover 1998; Tyson 2005). It would be a promising undertaking to analyze the impact on religious ideas by fictional formats as TV dramas and series as well (Schofield Clark 2003).

TEXTS

In its history (see Stausberg, "History," this volume), the study of religion has privileged one medium as a universal comparative topos among the variety of media: these are the 'holy scriptures' (*Heilige Schriften/textes sacrés*) as linked to the concept of 'religions of the book' (*Buchreligionen*). Why did this medium gain such a dominant position in the study of religion? Historically, this is due to the philological enthusiasm that resulted from the Reformation and the European Enlightenment, which sought to collect all knowledge of humankind, partly to dominate foreign peoples culturally (not only politically and economically) and partly to critically undermine the significance of Christianity. Beginning with the translation of the Zend-Avesta (1771) and the Upanishads (1786) by Abraham Anquetil-Duperron and the decryption of the Egyptian hieroglyphs (1822) by Jean-François Champollion, the early academic study of religion was based on the Rosetta stone and culminated in the monumental edition of the 50-volume *Sacred Books of the East* (1879–1910) by Friedrich Max Müller and his collaborators (Girardot 2002). On the other hand, the Protestant socialization of many classical thinkers in the study of religion with its Lutheran dictum *sola scriptura* may have caused the dominance of philological approaches (Vollmer 2009, 647). The larger context of the early comparative study of religions was an emerging interest in the origin and structure of language and scripture in general—a question far from innocent but with a long history of controversy in occidental philosophy and theology.

'Holy Scriptures' and the 'Religions of the Book'

From an emic perspective the category of 'holy scriptures' dates back to the Ptolemaic era (third to first century BCE) when Egyptian ritual texts were named in Greek as *hiera grammata* and Hebrew texts as 'holy scriptures' (*kitvei ha qodesh*). In the first and second centuries CE it was common to link the general terms for scriptures *scriptura* (Lt.), γραφή (Gr.), and *ketav* (Hebr.) with the adjectives ἱερός, ἅγιος, or *sanctus* (Gr./Lt., "holy"), θεῖος or *divinus* (Gr./Lt., "divine"), and θεόπνευστος (Gr., "inspired by god"). First, the term was related to the Jewish Tanakh, then to the Christian gospels and other texts of the New Testament. No earlier than the twelfth century, the Latin term *biblia* (feminine singular) became accepted as common expression for the Old and New Testament in many European languages (Graham 2005, 8196f.).

The academic category of 'holy scriptures' as a comparative item for various traditions was coined by Max Müller in his famous lecture *Introduction to the Science of Religion* (delivered at Oxford in 1870). Müller presents the "aristocracy of real book-religions" (1882, 53), which are centered around a canonical 'sacred book' with supposedly 'divine' origin: in his list, Judaism, Christianity, Islam, Hinduism, Buddhism, Zoroastrianism, Taoism, and Confucianism. The Dutch historian of religion Pierre Daniël Chantepie de la Saussaye, points out that the concept of Müller's 'eight bibles of humankind' has serious problems, since a large number of other texts are also considered to have great authority, such as the writings of Luther (1887, 137–141). Despite these difficulties the concept of 'holy scriptures' was widespread among the German phenomenological school (van der Leeuw, Lanczkowski, Mensching, Heiler, Colpe) and to some extent persists today. Often, traditions which are based on a book are considered to have a higher level of rationality and a greater sense of mission than oral traditions, claims that are empirically questionable (Krüger 2012, 166–203).

Wilfred Cantwell Smith (1993, 21–44) and William A. Graham (2005, 8197–8200) fundamentally challenged the notion of 'holy scriptures,' claiming that the difference between them and other religious texts makes no sense, apart from the case of Christianity: e.g. in Judaism the Talmud and in Islam the Hadith have as much significance for religious life as the Torah and the Qur'an. Therefore, Cantwell Smith argues for a relational paradigm: "I suggest: scripture is a human activity . . . On close inquiry, it emerges that being scripture is not a quality inherent in a given text, or type of text, so much as an interactive relation between that text and a community of persons (though such relations have been by no means constant)" (1993, 18). This concept focuses on the actual processes of reception—the written and oral communication about these texts as human interaction—that give meaning to these texts. The rejection of an essentialist and universal category of 'holy scriptures' also undermines the (theological) idea that a text has a constant meaning across time and different cultures. Understanding religious texts as a human activity underlines the dynamics of (re-)production, reception, interpretation, and the changing status of a given text in a certain community. Michael Bergunder (2006, 203–211) showed, for example, how the Bhagavadgita could emerge as the central 'holy scripture' of 'Hinduism' not earlier than the late nineteenth century. It was the first Sanskrit text translated into a European language in 1785. Therefore, it is not surprising that the Theosophical Society, initiated by Helena P. Blavatsky and Henry Steel Olcott, took the Gita as a crucial text of reference for Indian traditions. Influenced by these theosophical discourses, the Gita gained its acknowledgment as the most important Hindu text by Indian intellectuals and neo-Hindu reformers such as Swami Vivekananda, Aurobindo Ghose, and Gandhi (Bergunder 2014).

Finally, the relational paradigm proposed by Cantwell Smith and Graham opens our eyes to other texts beyond a defined religious canon and beyond religious institutions with particular significance for religious orientation. Historically, the *Narrenschiff/Ship of Fools* by Sebastian Brant (1494) or John Bunyan's *Pilgrim's Progress* (1678) have been as influential as the works of twentieth-century theologians such as Teilhard de Chardin or Leonardo Boff, who address contemporary problems of life and society from a religious perspective. A look at the bookshelves of a randomly selected bookstore in a Western country shows that the popular literature on religion, spirituality, and well-being far outnumbers the 'proper holy scriptures.' Furthermore, fictional literature can have an impact on religious ideas: e.g. *The Mists of Avalon* (1979) by Marion Zimmer Bradley on Neopaganism or Hermann Hesse's *Siddhartha* (1922) on the reception of Asian religions in the US hippie movement. Last but not least, the book market displays only a part of religious publications—an immense number of religious and spiritual journals are published by religious communities and institutions as well as on the general magazine market as commercial undertakings, such as the international journal *Happinez*.

The interactionist paradigm may help us to grasp the pluralist development of religious media products since early modern times. While Max Müller aimed to essentially identify the 'eight bibles of humankind,' the analysis of complex processes of reception and production of texts is more promising in a (Western) world with a nearly unlimited access to religious sources.

INTERNET

In his famous work, *The Consequences of Modernity* (1990), Anthony Giddens speaks of the disembedding of social interaction from temporal and spatial conditions as a distinguishing feature of modernity. With the beginning of the modern era, he says, social space becomes increasingly independent of concrete places. Social interaction involves partners who do not share the same geographical space and whose communication is realized over spatial distances. The Internet appears to be the high point of this development to date. For mediatization theory it is the strongest empirical evidence since the Internet offers access globally to seemingly all people by mobile or fixed communication devices. Before entering the analysis of specific tools and formats on the Internet, these 'big theories' urge us to ask for the 'myths' of the Internet and their normative or even religious impact. The euphoria over the dawn of the World Wide Web as a hypertext information system has cooled down recently in the light of worldwide censorship, spying, commercialization, and the emergence of strong new hierarchies on the Web. A new 'protestantization', the realization of a liberal and egalitarian spirit, even the generation of a new form of *communitas* in Victor Turner's sense was expected. The 'myths' of the Internet unify widespread ideas of 'techgnosis', 'cybergnosis', and 'cyberplatonism' which point to a metaphysical interpretation of the Internet as a virtual counterworld. Linked with James Lovelock's notion of Gaia—the earth as an organic whole—the Internet is perceived as forming a new layer of collective, higher consciousness for humankind (Krüger 2015). Perhaps due to these grandiose claims regarding fundamental change, the academic study of religion was fascinated since the early days of the World Wide Web (Dawson/Cowan 2004; Hojsgaard/Warburg 2005). Specialized online journals cover various topics of religion on the Internet, such as *Online—Heidelberg Journal of Religions on the Internet* (OA, from 2005) and *Cyberorient* (from 2006).

Today, it is evident that the celebrated experiments of online churches (such as the *Church of Fools*) proved to be of marginal impact in the contemporary religious world. Religious presentations and activities online will not replace the face-to-face religious life, but they form in some cases a significant complement for the social construction of identity and trans-local community and for opinion-making, mission, and networking (Campbell 2010a).

Beyond these general perceptions of the Internet we have to distinguish several analytical layers, especially three 'textual' dimensions of websites: their (1) pragmatics, (2) syntax, and (3) semantics.

First, in terms of pragmatics, we can distinguish at least four fundamental functions of religious websites. The first function is the emic and etic *presentation* of religious institutions, individuals, ideas, practices, and of contemporary issues (on homepages, newsletters, encyclopedias, video sharing websites, profiles on social networks, blogs, journals, etc.). The second function is *interactive communication* on religious themes (through chat rooms, guest books, FAQs, discussion forums, comments, profiles of social networks). The third function is the offering and performance of *religious services* (online or offline), such as pastoral care, horoscope predictions, or the ordering and performance of rituals. The last function is mostly *commercial*: the advertisement and sale of books, music, ritual items, or spiritual counseling, workshops, E-learning, etc. All these functions may appear on one website, blog, or personal profile, but in most cases, one aspect dominates.

Second, syntax refers to the format of presentation and communication on the Internet. The following are most relevant for the study of religion: (i) websites, (ii) discussion forums, (iii) blogs, (iv) online encyclopedias, (v) online ritual services, and (vi) video sharing websites. The section on television already referred to newspapers and journals. The religious effect of computer games remains to be scrutinized, although they often build on religious symbols, characters, and stories (Bainbridge 2013; Steffen 2012; special issue of *Online—Heidelberg Journal for Religions on the Internet* 5/2014). Since the Internet began in the early 1990s, there have been homepages and discussion forums for personal and institutional expression.

(i) The measure of interactivity on websites (contact, comments, counseling, ordering) varies with the aims of the site, from mere provision of information and establishing an offline contact up to community building. The fact that interactivity and transparency have developed as an aim for religious self-representation can be seen on the homepage of the Roman Catholic Church. It started as a hermetic information site on its institutional facilities in the 1990s (the library, the pope, the buildings) providing basic aspects of its doctrines. Today, it functions as a transparent multimedia center with daily news, prayers, meditations, links to Catholic radio and TV broadcasting, and various form of contact info for all its chapters (<http://www.vatican.va>).

(ii) Discussion forums offer (textual) information and debates usually in a specific religious tradition: this can be controversial (<http://www.baptistboard.com>), instructive, or commercialized (<http://www.wiccantogether.com>) (for Muslim forums see, for example, Larsson 2013).

(iii) Blogs—sequential posts by individuals and (more recently) professional multi authors—became popular around 2000, usually covering a specific topic. In terms of religion some bloggers have come to be acknowledged as renowned voices in contemporary debates of theology and church; others use their blogs simply for personal testimony (see, for example, the hundreds of Quaker blogs [<http://quaker.zebby.org/>; Campbell 2010b]).

(iv) The future of encyclopedias is online, due to accessibility and the potential for updates on the one hand and to the enormous costs of establishing a printed lexicon edition on the other. Wikipedia started in 2001 as a free encyclopedia with (mostly) anonymous authors, and others followed, such as Scholarpedia or the Encyclopedia Britannica with experts as writers. The challenge of the often quoted 'swarm intelligence' of Wikipedia in the realm of religion is the confrontation between academic and religious readings of history, persons, and doctrines (see for example the articles related to the Hindu Swaminarayan movement, for which the edit war reflects a succession conflict). Content in encyclopedias without editorial staff and experts is more a result of negotiations or scholars being outnumbered by non-scholars than the academic state of the art.

(v) The submission of prayers, online pujas at virtual Hindu temples, lighting virtual candles, virtual pilgrimages, and online worship illustrate some of the many possibilities of online ritual interaction. Here, pastoral and spiritual care via e-mail and SMS seem to be more significant than liturgical offers.

(vi) Video sharing websites (VSW) offer podcasts by private and commercial users as videos or (animated) images with music or speech. In addition to YouTube (since 2005) with its more than 2 billion views per day, more than another fifty providers worldwide make professional or amateur videos available. VSW appear to be a strong tool for mission and support of religious traditions in general, both for certain branches or single religious leaders and for specific religious and moral issues (e.g. the question of abortion). Preaching and interviews by evangelical pastors such as Reinhard Bonnke and Benny Hinn are available, as well as mission videos with prominent American Muslims. Emotionally moving videos on abortion demonstrate that VSW create a completely new discursive space for religious propaganda. In 2007 the Salem Web Network launched GodTube to provide Christian and family-friendly videos (Pasche 2008).

Third, for the study of religion, VSW exemplify the new research perspectives on the Internet and on our third analytical axis: semantics. What meaning does the displayed content have and how is it received by media users? The first aspect relies on the new means of online network analysis in addition to the established tools for analyzing images, texts, and films. The second aspect points to new research opportunities on the Internet. While radio and television enable us to perceive only the supplier and the supplies 'on the air,' the Internet—as an interactive medium—now opens up the possibility of studying the consumer's perspective as well. We can compare statistically how many views a certain film had and we can analyze the viewers' comments, which are present on many VSW such as YouTube. For example, a famous TV discussion with Malcolm X, as one of the leading figures of the Nation of Islam, has been posted on YouTube (Malcolm X: Our History was Destroyed by Slavery, 17/03/1963): it has been viewed about 4 million times with more than 18,000 comments (8/2016). Such data can be downloaded and scrutinized easily for keywords, topics, and arguments.

GLOSSARY

Media in a narrow sense, media are means of representation, storage, and transmission of texts, images, sounds, and audiovisual material. In a broad sense—as proposed by Baudrillard, Flusser, Virilio, Parsons, and Luhmann—media are the bases and frame of all kinds of communication. However, in the study of religion the concept should be used firstly in a more narrow sense so that specific methods and theories can be put to practical use in research.

Mediatization a theoretical approach that assumes an overall change of the world by 'the logic' of modern media.

Spiritualization of media the way a religious community integrates the use of a specific medium.

REFERENCES

Ayaß, Ruth. 2012. "Introduction: Media Appropriation and Everyday Life." In *The Appropriation of Media in Everyday Life*, edited by Ruth Ayaß and Cornelia Gerhardt. Amsterdam: John Benjamins, 1–15.

Ayfre, Amédée. 1953. *Dieu au cinéma: Problèmes esthétiques du film religieux*. Toulouse: Presses Universitaires de France.

Bainbridge, William Sims. 2013. *eGods: Faith versus Fantasy in Computer Gaming*. Oxford: Oxford University Press.

Belting, Hans. 1994. *Likeness and Presence: A History of the Image Before the Era of Art*. Chicago, IL: University of Chicago Press.

Bergesen, Albert J. and Andrew M. Greeley. 2003. *God in the Movies*. New Brunswick, NJ: Transaction.

Bergunder, Michael. 2006. "Die Bhagavadgita im 19. Jahrhundert." In *Westliche Formen des Hinduismus in Deutschland*, edited by Michael Bergunder. Halle: Franckesche Stiftungen, 187–216.

Bergunder, Michael. 2014. "Experiments with Theosophical Truth: Gandhi, Esotericism, and Global Religious History." *Journal of the American Academy of Religion* 82(2): 398–426. doi: 10.1093/jaarel/lft095

Blizek, William and Ronald Burke, eds. 1997ff. *Journal of Religion and Film* (online: <http://www.unomaha.edu/jrf/purpose.htm>).

Blizek, William L., Michele Marie Desmaraisa, and Ronald R. Burke. 2011. "Religion and Film Studies through the Journal of Religion and Film.". *Religion* 41(3): 471–485. doi: 10.1080/0048721X.2011.590698

Campani, Ermelinda M. 2007. *Le sacré au cinéma: Divinité et mystère sur grand écran*. Rome: Gremese.

Campbell, Heidi. 2010a. *When Religion Meets New Media*. London: Routledge.

Campbell, Heidi. 2010b. "Religious Authority and the Blogosphere." *Journal of Computer-Mediated Communication* 15(2): 251–276. doi: 10.1111/j.1083-6101.2010.01519.x

Cantwell Smith, Wilfred. 1993. *What is Scripture? A Comparative Approach*. London: SCM Press.

Chantepie de la Saussaye, Pierre D. 1887. *Lehrbuch der Religionsgeschichte*, vol. 1. Freiburg: Mohr.

Dawson, Lorne L. and Douglas E. Cowan, eds. 2004. *Religion Online: Finding Faith on the Internet*. New York: Routledge.

Day Howell, Julia. 2008. "Modulations of Active Piety: Professors and Televangelists as Promoters of Indonesian 'Sufisme.'" In *Expressing Islam: Religious Life and Politics in Indonesia*, edited by Greg Fealy and Sally White. Singapore: ISEAS Press, 40–62.

Eisenstein, Elizabeth. 1979. *The Printing Press as an Agent of Change: Communications and Cultural Transformations in Early Modern Europe*, 2 vols. Cambridge: Cambridge University Press.

Fischer, Andreas and Veit Loers, eds. 1997. *Im Reich der Phantome: Fotografie des Unsichtbaren*. Ostfildern-Ruit: Cantz.

Fischinger, Lars A. 2003. *Der Blick ins Jenseits: Was wir über das Leben nach dem Tode wissen*. Kreuzlingen: Hugendubel.

Girardot, N. J. 2002. "Max Müller's 'Sacred Books' and the Nineteenth-Century Production of the Comparative Science of Religions." *History of Religions* 41(3): 213–250.

Goethals, Gregor T. and Phillip C. Lucas. 2005. "Religious Broadcasting." In *Encyclopedia of Religion*, 2nd edition, edited by Lindsay Jones. Detroit: Macmillan, vol. 11: 7709–7716.

Graham, William A. 2005. "Scripture." In *Encyclopedia of Religion*, 2nd edition, edited by Lindsay Jones. Detroit: Macmillan, vol. 12, 8194–8205.

Hagen, Wolfgang. 2008. "Metaxy. Eine historiosemantische Fußnote zum Medienbegriff." In *Was ist ein Medium?* edited by Stefan Münker and Alexander Roesler. Frankfurt: Suhrkamp, 13–29.

Hangen, Tona. 2002. *Redeeming the Dial: Radio, Religion and Popular Culture in America*. Chapel Hill: North Carolina University Press.

Hansen, Mark B. 2010. "New Media." In *Critical Terms for Media Studies*, edited by W. J. T. Mitchell and Mark B. Hansen. Chicago, IL: University of Chicago Press, 172–185.

Hepp, Andreas and Friedrich Krotz. 2012. "Mediatisierte Welten: Forschungsfelder und Beschreibungsansätze—Zur Einleitung." In *Mediatisierte Welten*, edited by Andreas Hepp and Friedrich Krotz. Wiesbaden: Springer VS, 7–23.

Herrmann, Christian and Thomas Staubli, eds. 2010. *1001 Amulette. Altägyptischer Zauber, monotheisierte Talismane, säkulare Magie*. Freiburg: Bibel + Orient Museum.

Herrmann, Jörg. 2007. *Medienerfahrung und Religion: Eine empirisch-qualitative Studie zur Medienreligion*. Göttingen: Vandenhoeck & Ruprecht.

Hight, Eleanor M. and Gary D. Sampson, eds. 2002. *Colonialist Photography: Imag(in)ing Race and Place*. London: Routledge.

Hjarvard, Stig. 2008a. "The Mediatization of Society: A Theory of the Media as Agents of Social and Cultural Change." *Nordicom Review* 29(2): 105–134.

Hjarvard, Stig. 2008b. "The Mediatization of Religion: A Theory of the Media as Agents of Religious Change." *Northern Lights* 6: 9–26. doi: 10.1386/nl.6.1.9_1

Hjarvard, Stig. 2013. *The Mediatization of Culture and Society*. London: Routledge.

Hjarvard, Stig and Mia Lövheim, eds. 2012. *Mediatization and Religion: Nordic Perspectives*. Göteborg: Nordicom.

Hojsgaard, Morten T. and Margit Warburg, eds. 2005. *Religion and Cyberspace*. London: Routledge.

Hoover, Stewart M. 1988. *Mass Media Religion: The Social Sources of the Electronic Church*. Newbury Park, CA: Sage.

Hoover, Stewart M. 1998. *Religion in the News: Faith and Journalism in American Public Discourse*. Thousand Oaks, CA: Sage.

Hoover, Stewart M. 2005. "Media and Religion." In *Encyclopedia of Religion*, 2nd edition, edited by Lindsay Jones. Detroit: Macmillan, vol. 9, 5805–5810.

Katz, Elihu and David Foulkes. 1962. "On the Use of Mass Media as 'Escape': Clarification of a Concept." *Public Opinion Quarterly* 26(3): 377–388.

Keppler, Angela. 2005. "Medien und soziale Wirklichkeit." In *Mediensoziologie. Grundfragen und Forschungsfelder*, edited by Michael Jäckel. Wiesbaden: Springer VS, 91–106.

Kippenberg, Hans G. et al., eds. 1982–1990. *Visible Religion: Annual for Religious Iconography*, 4 vols. Leiden: Brill.

Knauß, Stefanie. 2008. *Transcendental Bodies: Überlegungen zur Bedeutung des Körpers für filmische und religiöse Erfahrung*. Regensburg: Pustet.

Krüger, Oliver. 2015. "Gaia, God, and the Internet—revisited: The History of Evolution and the Utopia of Community in Media Society." *Heidelberg Journal for Religions on the Internet* 8.

Krüger, Oliver. 2012. *Die mediale Religion: Probleme und Perspektiven der religionswissen-schaftlichen und wissenssoziologischen Medienforschung.* Bielefeld: Transcript.

Larsson, Göran. 2013. *Muslims and the New Information and Communication Technologies: Notes from an Emerging and Infinite Field.* Dordrecht: Springer.

Lövheim, Mia and Knut Lundby. 2013. "Mediated Religion across Time and Space: A Case Study of Norwegian Newspapers." *Nordic Journal of Religion and Society* 26(1): 25–44.

McLeod, William H. 1992. *Popular Sikh Art.* Oxford and New York: Oxford University Press.

McLuhan, Marshall. 1994. *Understanding Media: The Extensions of Man.* Cambridge, MA: MIT Press.

McLuhan, Marshall. 2002. *The Gutenberg Galaxy: The Making of Typographic Man.* Toronto: University of Toronto Press.

Markschies, Christoph. 2007. *Kaiserzeitliche christliche Theologie und ihre Institutionen: Prolegomena zu einer Geschichte der antiken christlichen Theologie.* Tübingen: Mohr.

Melton, J. Gordon, Philipp C. Lucas, and Jon R. Stone. 1997. *Prime-Time Religion: An Encyclopedia of Religious Broadcasting.* Phoenix, AZ: Oryx Press.

Meyer, Birgit, ed. 2009. *Aesthetic Formations: Media, Religion, and the Senses.* Basingstoke: Palgrave Macmillan.

Meyer, Birgit. 2012. *Mediation and the Genesis of Presence: Towards a Material Approach to Religion.* Utrecht: Universiteit Utrecht.

Mitchell, Jolyon, ed. 2012a. *Religion and the News.* Farnham: Ashgate.

Mitchell, Jolyon. 2012b. *Promoting Peace, Inciting Violence: The Role of Religion and Media.* London: Routledge.

Morgan, David. 2005. *The Sacred Gaze: Religious Visual Culture in Theory and Practice.* Berkeley: University of California Press.

Müller, F. Max. 1882. *Introduction to the Science of Religion.* Oxford: Longman, Green & Co.

Pasche, Florence. 2008. "Some Methodological Reflections about the Study of Religions on Video Sharing Websites." *Marburg Journal of Religion* 13(1): 1–10. <http://archiv.ub.uni-marburg.de/mjr/pdf/2008/pasche2008.pdf>, accessed February 3, 2016.

Plate, Brent. 2005. "Film and Religion." In *Encyclopedia of Religion*, 2nd edition, edited by Lindsay Jones. Detroit: Macmillan, vol. 5, 3097–3103.

Plate, Brent. 2008. *Religion and Film: Cinema and the Re-Creation of the World.* New York: Wallflower Press.

Richter, Carola. 2009. "Fernsehprediger, Online-Counselling und Fatwa-Hotlines: Zur Medialisierung des Islams." In *Religion und Massenmedien*, edited by Maud E. Sieprath. Berlin: Weißensee, 99–128.

Ruby, Jay. 1995. *Secure the Shadow: Death and Photography in America.* Cambridge, MA: MIT Press.

Rüpke, Jörg. 2007. *Historische Religionswissenschaft: Eine Einführung.* Stuttgart: Kohlhammer.

Schofield Clark, Lynn. 2003. *From Angels to Aliens: Teenagers, the Media, and the Supernatural.* Oxford: Oxford University Press.

Schrader, Paul. 1972. *Transcendental Style in Film: Ozu, Bresson, Dreyer.* Berkeley: University of California Press.

Sitney, P. Adams. 1987. "Cinema and Religion." In *Encyclopedia of Religion*, edited by Mircea Eliade. Detroit: Macmillan, vol. 3, 498–505.

Staubli, Thomas, ed. 2003. *Werbung für die Götter: Heilsbringer aus 4000 Jahren.* Freiburg: Universitätsverlag Freiburg.

Steffen, Oliver. 2012. "Introduction: Approaches to Digital Games in the Study of Religions." In *Religions in Play: Games, Rituals, and Virtual Worlds*, edited by Philippe Bornet and Maya Burger. Zürich: Pano, 249–259.

Thomas, Pradip N. and Philip Lee, eds. 2012. *Global and Local Televangelism*. Basingstoke: Palgrave Macmillan.

Tillich, Paul. 1959. *Theology of Culture*. Oxford: Oxford University Press.

Tworuschka, Udo. 2008. "Vom 'Visible' zum 'Auditive Turn' in der Praktischen Religions-wissenschaft." In *Praktische Religionswissenschaft: Ein Handbuch für Studium und Beruf*, edited by Michael Klöcker and Udo Tworuschka. Cologne: UTB, 76–83.

Tyson, Ruel W. 2005. "Journalism and Religion." In *Encyclopedia of Religion*, 2nd edition, edited by Lindsay Jones. Detroit: Macmillan, vol. 7: 4960–4967.

Uehlinger, Christoph. 2007. "Visible Religion: le champ du visuel comme objet d'étude en science des religions." *Asdiwal* 2: 17–39.

Vollmer, Ulrich. 2009. "Religionswissenschaft als akademische Disziplin im Kontext katholisch-theologischer Fakultäten." In *Wege und Welten der Religionen*, edited by Jürgen Court and Michael Klöcker. Frankfurt: Lembeck, 647–653.

Zimmerman-Umble, Diane. 1992. "The Amish and the Telephone: Resistance and Reconstructions." In *Consuming Technologies: Media and Information in Domestic Spaces*, edited by Roger Silverstone and Eric Hirsch. London: Routledge, 183–194.

FURTHER READING

Belting 1994 [*Belting presents the relation to Christian images in the European Middle Ages as a cultural practice, as interaction between image, painter, and viewer.*]

Campbell 2010a [*Campbell shows how religious communities have to 'spiritualize' new media within their religious framework: the religious-social shaping of technology.*]

Cantwell Smith 1993 [*Cantwell Smith criticizes the essentialist definition of 'holy scriptures' and proposes a new interactionist paradigm.*]

Eisenstein 1979 [*In this classic study of media history Eisenstein analyzes the social and religious impact of the printing press since the fifteenth century.*]

Hepp, Andreas and Veronika Krönert. 2009. *Medien—Event—Religion: Die Mediatisierung des Religiösen*. Wiesbaden: Springer VS. [*Analyzing the 2005 Catholic World Youth Day in Germany, Hepp and Krönert observe a general mediatization of religion.*]

Hjarvard/Lövheim 2012 [*This anthology assembles studies on the increasing significance of media in Scandinavian churches.*]

Hojsgaard/Warburg 2005 [*Hojsgaard and Warburg present a good introduction to the field of religion on the Internet.*]

Krüger 2012 [*Krüger offers a contemporary outline of media studies in the field of religion based on the sociology of knowledge.*]

McLuhan 1994 [*This book presents the starting point of media studies in 1964, considering mainly the turn from printed media to electronic media.*]

Meyer 2009 [*Meyer proposes an innovative approach combining the aesthetics of religion with media studies.*]

Mitchell 2012a [*Journalists and religious leaders reflect on their interactions with one another and their experiences of creating news.*]

Uehlinger 2007 [*Uehlinger argues for a visual turn in the study of religion.*]

CHAPTER 27

MEDICINE

PAMELA E. KLASSEN

CHAPTER SUMMARY

- Medicine and religion are both techniques of intervention in the lives of others, with intervenors almost always claiming to be doing so for the good of the person on the receiving end.
- Medicine is not necessarily 'scientific', but instead denotes a wide variety of therapeutic systems that people have invented to cure or comfort others in bodily distress, including systems that emerged within religious traditions.
- Among these therapeutic systems, biomedicine (or Western scientific medicine), has accrued particular authority through an historical process of 'medicalization'; in doing so, biomedicine has drawn on the organizational effectiveness of religious groups in Europe and North America, especially within Judaism and Christianity.
- The religion/medicine relation takes place within wider contexts of colonialism and postcolonialism, the capitalist commodification of medicine, and the ways the body is 'cultured' through such formative norms as gender, class, and race.
- Examples focused on children (e.g. home birth and vaccine hesitancy) and those focused on religious and medical exchange (e.g. Christian Yoga and scientific Ayurveda), reveal links between different understandings of healing and of what makes human bodies frail and vulnerable.

Medicine, or the various therapeutic systems that people have invented to cure or comfort others in bodily distress, is an important 'environment' in which to consider the problem of religion. Medical knowledge and techniques have often emerged directly from religious traditions, making the line between these two admittedly unstable categories—religion and medicine—particularly hard to draw with any certainty. For example, Ayurvedic medicine, which draws on humoral theories and bodily disciplines such as Yoga, claims a history rooted in ancient Vedic texts, and in which "science and religion are joined" (Langford 2002, 93). Acupuncture, or inserting needles into the skin to release pressure points, is rooted in Chinese conceptions of *qi*, which refers to "both energy and matter, and . . . to the vital stuff/force that both makes up and infuses the cosmos" (Barnes 2005, 240). Even scientific biomedicine, often thought to be 'not-religious,' emerged from modern hospitals and schools of medicine, many of which were founded by Christian and Jewish groups in Europe and North America, as well as in missionary 'fields' in India, China, and elsewhere (Klassen 2011).

Questioning the intersection of religion and medicine requires a comparative perspective on the human body and human relationships that can reveal many things: that there is more than one way to explain how the body works; that defining or measuring healing does not necessarily require the latest biomedical technologies; that there are many ways of making sense of pain and suffering; and that thinking about healing requires thinking about the social and political obligations of human beings to each other in light of the frailty and vulnerability of bodily existence. Many theorists of religion, including the nineteenth-century Quaker and Oxford anthropologist Edward Tylor, have claimed that religion emerged precisely from human contemplation of the puzzle of mortality—of how a fully alive, communicative, 'ensouled' person becomes a limp and silent corpse at death, and what happens to their spirit or soul in the process. In answer to this puzzle, Tylor posited a theory of 'animism,' namely that there was a wide human propensity to understand human beings, and often nature more broadly, as bodies animated by spirits. For Tylor, thinking of the human being as made up of both bodies and souls/spirits that needed care explained why peoples across the earth sought to heal their loved ones, neighbors, and even strangers with the use of both physiological and spiritual therapies (Tylor 1871).

Not all theorists of religion would still place health, illness, and the mortal body at the center of their thinking in the way that Tylor did. I wager, however, that human frailty and vulnerability—and the ways that people harm each other and care for each other in the face of such frailty—are still at the heart of the problem of what religion is and what religion does (Orsi 1998; Riesebrodt 2010). The idea that bodies are animated by more than physiological or neurological processes—i.e. that bodies are animated by spirits—also remains a widespread conviction, or "anthropology of the spiritual body" across many communities around the world (Klassen 2014, 69). Some may opt for a vaguely environmental attunement of 'spiritual equilibrium,' while others are committed to the healing effects of direct 'spiritual intervention' from a deity. Across traditions of Christianity, Haitian Vodou, 'metaphysical' religion, and many others, however, spiritually-animated bodies are key to the practice and promise of healing (Opp 2007; Brown 2001; Bender 2010; Behrend 2003).

The fact that religion and medicine are historically intertwined at the level of both bodily practices and the narratives told about their relationship makes the *study* of religion and medicine in the twenty-first century particularly fascinating, and perhaps especially tricky. As fields of practice that have been deeply interconnected, religion and medicine are now often posited as institutionally distinct, with people who speak in their name often suspicious or openly critical of each other. A Jehovah's Witness refuses a blood transfusion in a life-threatening situation; a medical doctor turns to legal channels to enforce chemotherapy as treatment for a patient under the age of consent who would rather turn to 'alternative' medicines. Such stories of conflict often make the news. But the academic study of the relationship between religion and medicine often tells a more complicated story, starting with considerable debate about what counts as religion and what counts as medicine.

Working Definitions of Religion and Medicine

Many of the contributors to this volume have successfully shown how religion, when paired with another orienting mode, environment, or process, such as 'media,' 'nature,' or 'commoditization,' is a concept that requires careful deliberation and elaboration. Here, I focus on the two concepts of religion and medicine as they have developed in tandem within the "muddle of modernity," shaped by three main historical processes: the rise of scientific authority, capitalist commodification of medicine, and colonialism and postcolonialism (Chakrabarty 2011). Provisionally, I use the terms religion and medicine in the following ways, keeping in mind that if the debate about the category of religion is politically fraught in both scholarly and popular contexts, the politics of the category of 'medicine' are equally contentious.

By medicine I do not only mean 'biomedicine,' the dominant mode of scientific 'evidence-based' medical practice in many parts of the world, embodied in such institutions as the World Health Organization or the emergency relief organization Doctors without Borders (Redfield 2013). As historian of Asian medicine Joseph Alter has argued, medicine must be understood as much broader than Western-based biomedicine: "medicine as a conceptual category can be thought of as a pragmatic, body-oriented copy of techniques designed to transform nature itself" (Alter 2005, 18). In line with Alter, my working definition of medicine refers to ways of treating or intervening in the human body with the aim of curing disease or alleviating suffering. Religion, for my purposes here, means social communities of memory and practice that orient people's sense of embodiment, including as spiritually-animated bodies, that convey moral and metaphysical significance to bodily pain and suffering, and that frame obligations to attend to the bodily pain of others as a form of 'social suffering' (Kleinman/Das/Lock 1997). In this sense, both medicine and religion are techniques and traditions through which people understand their own bodily states and intervene in the bodily suffering of others for the purposes of curing or removing such suffering, or at the very least understanding, recognizing, and relieving it.

Medicalization, Power, and the Rise of Scientific Authority

As techniques of intervention in the lives of others, medicine and religion are both political. That is, they are both engaged in negotiations and contests over power as it moves through institutions with long histories, systems of authoritative knowledge, and various levels of human social interaction. We can see this most clearly in the concept of 'medicalization', understood as a process by which the authority of biomedicine expands outside of conventional medical settings of the hospital, doctor's office, or laboratory, and sets and enforces wider cultural norms about what makes for 'healthy' individuals or 'healthy' populations. Occurring over the course of the nineteenth and twentieth centuries, especially in North America and Europe, medicalization gave to medical doctors increasing power in legal, social, and even ritual settings such that some even likened them to modern-day 'priests' (Opp 2007; Starr 1984). Biomedicine's overwhelming social, political, and economic authority—and many would argue, its bodily efficacy—is what transforms other, non-biomedical therapeutic approaches into 'alternative' or 'complementary' therapies.

Sometimes, this biomedical authority is challenged, as shown by the recent rise in 'vaccine hesitancy': the reluctance of North American parents, many of whom are middle- to upper-class, to have their children immunized. Opposed to vaccines that biomedical science shows have a very high chance of protecting children from potentially deadly diseases such as measles, these parents are oriented by a range of interrelated convictions: 'religious' views that God should decide who lives and who dies; 'holistic' concerns about the over-medicalization of the human body; and 'anti-science' views that consider medical researchers and doctors to be conspiring in concealing the negative health effects of vaccines (Dubé et al. 2013). Vaccine-hesitant or vaccine-refusing parents are not only questioning the medicalization paradigm, but are also rejecting the public health paradigm, in which healthcare decision-making is a collective concern and not simply an obligation of parent to child. In this regard, vaccine hesitancy or vaccine refusal shows the tension between understanding 'health' as an issue that operates at the individual level of the body or family and understanding health to be a complicated process of both individual and community-wide practices and norms. More generally, parents who choose to remove their children from biomedical care for religiously-informed reasons are at the center of a highly conflict-ridden arena in which biomedicine exerts its authority through legal, political, scientific, and social scientific authority all at once (Peters 2007; Beaman 2008; Opp 2007).

Medicalization and Bio-Politics

The concept of medicalization is at the center of the wider theoretical frame of 'bio-politics', as articulated by Michel Foucault. For Foucault, medicalization was one form of bio-political "power that has taken control of both the body and life, or that has taken control of life in general—with the body as one pole and the population as the other" (2003, 253). By this, Foucault meant, on one hand, that medicalization must be understood to work at the level of individual experiences of embodiment—how people understand and experience their choices around diet, exercise, sexuality, vaccination, etc. as making them into 'healthy' or 'unhealthy' people. But, he insisted, medicalization also operates at a much broader level of the population, through what he called 'governmentality' as states make choices about how to regulate, finance, and enumerate healthcare in their quest to create and administrate 'healthy' citizens (Foucault et al. 2009).

Scholars have often used Foucault's theories of bio-politics and medicalization as tools for revealing how state power and religious authority combine to make people willing collaborators in disciplining or medicalizing themselves both as intimate bodies and as bodies scaled-up into populations (Hacking 1986). As the vaccine example shows, however, medicalization also provokes resistance from people who do not want to join in with collective health practices that epidemiologists, medical doctors, and scientific experts would argue are bio-political in a more positive sense of 'life-giving power.' As we will see, debates about how systems of health insurance—whether state-supported or market-based—shape access to biomedical healthcare are another realm in which this tension between individual and collective understandings of medicine are refracted with 'religious' considerations.

The Mindful Body

Another approach to thinking about medicalization and religion, informed in part by Foucault, can be found in the concept of the 'mindful body' as framed by Nancy Scheper-Hughes and Margaret Lock, medical anthropologists who have each accomplished groundbreaking work on the intersection of gender, reproductive health, class, racialization, culture, and religion (Scheper-Hughes 1993; 2001; Lock 1995; Scheper-Hughes/Lock 1987). Scheper-Hughes and Lock wrote their article "The Mindful Body" as a counterpoint to what they call the "biological fallacy." By this, they meant a kind of hyper-somatization in which biology trumps everything else: "Medicalization inevitably entails a missed identification between the individual and the social bodies, and a tendency to transform the social into the biological" (Scheper-Hughes/Lock 1987, 10). Their approach, in contrast, begins from "an assumption of the body as simultaneously a physical and symbolic artefact, as both naturally and culturally produced, and as securely anchored in a particular historical moment" (1987, 7).

Offering a compendium of ethnographic examples from around the world, Scheper-Hughes and Lock recommended understanding the body on three scales: (1) the individual body, or the "lived experience of the body-self"; (2) the social body in its networks of relationships; and (3) the body politic, or the scale at which we notice "regulation, surveillance, and control of bodies (individual and collective) in reproduction and sexuality, in work and in leisure, in sickness and other forms of deviance and human difference" (1987, 7–8). Arguing that emotions mediate among all three bodies, at the levels of individual feelings, collective morality, and ideology, Scheper-Hughes and Lock posited that people are mindful bodies who have agency at the same time that they are constrained by the necessities of biology, and who can creatively interpret their experiences of illness and health at the same time that they are shaped by larger cultural or religious interpretations.

The idea of the mindful body was particularly helpful for my own research on childbirth and religion in North America, where I found that women understood what was 'natural' about childbirth with recourse to a remarkable diversity of religious, or what some called spiritual, narratives (Klassen 2001; see also Jensen, "Narrative," this volume). Focusing on women who had chosen to give birth at home, mostly with midwifery care, I found that women told birth stories that were rooted in their bodily, social, and emotional experience of giving birth, often overlaid with religious interpretations, such as Christian and Jewish women who considered that God had designed their birthing bodies. Others felt that childbirth was ideally left as a bodily process that unfolded in its own time, as a 'natural' event. These women also preferred to think of birth as a *spiritual* turning point in a woman's life that did not require the sanction or ritualization of a traditional religious authority (see Streib/Klein, "Religion and Spirituality," this volume).

The natural body, as a cultural body, is shaped not only by categories of religion and spirituality, but also those of race, class, gender, and sexuality. In the United States, the post-1970s home birth movement has been a largely—but not entirely—middle-class movement. For example, this movement developed with little connection to traditions of African-American midwifery in the southern United States, for reasons to do with racism, medicalization, and class (Fraser 1998). For the most part, the women I interviewed had homes that offered them the security and comfort in which they wanted to give birth. At the same time, most of these women had access to more conventional obstetrical care should they have wanted it, or needed it, in an emergency; they were what I called 'postbiomedical bodies.' By this, I meant that the ability to selectively choose one's level of interaction with medicalization, and to make 'alternative' or 'complementary' healthcare choices, is often grounded on the implicit knowledge that one has access to biomedical care if one changes one's mind, or mindful body.

Childbirth is perhaps one of the most powerful antidotes to the biological fallacy. Though birth is seemingly a universal biological process, babies emerge from their mother's wombs the world over with a remarkable diversity of techniques, rituals, and beliefs shaping the process; the cultural and social properties of birth cannot be extracted from its biological aspects. Considering practices of healing more generally, the biological fallacy obscures how norms and practices of biomedicine, while rooted in scientific evidence, are also socially and culturally mediated responses to treat the body. The tenacious strength and ever-present frailty of the human body is a balance that is at once measurable and mysterious; this varying balance of the body's strength and frailty is also one that many people around the world attribute to both material and spiritual forces.

THE CAPITALIST COMMODIFICATION OF HEALING

In addition to being political, medicine and religion also often share another common trait: they both come at a price. Put another way, one needs to pay to access their interventions. The commodification of medicine—whether in North American bio-medicine or South Asian Ayurvedic medicine—means that analyzing the intersection of religion and medicine cannot focus only on questions of what kinds of therapy are more efficacious than others, or which ones 'really work.' Poised at the nexus of care and cost, love and money, altruistic blessing and limited resources, medicine and religion both promise to heal, but not everyone has access to the promise of either.

Access to healthcare is shaped by what it costs and who has to pay for it. Comparative studies of models for healthcare funding reveal that choices about how to structure access to biomedical care are not simply economic choices, but are also oriented by visions of the collective good and the moral person, inflected by issues of race, religion, gender, and citizenship status (Craig 2014; Siddiqi 2009). Putting the largely state-funded Canadian model alongside the predominantly market-based model of the United States reveals that access to healthcare is both a physiological and an existential concern. Despite the best efforts of the Affordable Care Act in the United States, the dread and anxiety that the structure of healthcare funding and payment produces in the lives of Americans occurs at both personal and collective levels (Sered/Fernandopulle 2007). In most US states, and other jurisdictions in which healthcare is not state-funded, any turn away from expensive biomedical treatments to cheaper—but usually still costly—forms of 'spiritual' or 'alternative' healing is informed by infrastructures of access to biomedical healing, or the lack of them. Similarly, the very meanings and emotions that people draw from illness, health, and death, are fundamentally shaped by the political economies in which they live.

Nancy Scheper-Hughes demonstrates this most powerfully in her brave—and controversial—book, *Death Without Weeping: The Violence of Everyday Life in Brazil* (1993 [1992]). Based on many years of ethnographic research with extremely poor women in the 'Alto do Cruzeiro,' a shantytown in the northeast of Brazil with very high rates of infant mortality, *Death Without Weeping* was a challenge to conventional gendered understandings of 'mother-love.' At the same time, it was a call for the study of religion and medicine to be firmly rooted in a 'materialist,' or class-based, analysis of the conditions of everyday life. Scheper-Hughes's primary argument was that these poor women, many of whose children died as infants, did not react to their children's deaths with the same kinds of emotions expected of grieving parents living in wealthier conditions. At first surprised by and even resistant to the ways that these women would allow their sickly children to waste away instead of seeking heroic measures to save them, Scheper-Hughes came to see that these Brazilian women made choices about their children's survival that were profoundly shaped by their experiences of extreme poverty, high birth rates, and the repeated loss of their babies to early deaths. These severely marginalized women were not post-biomedical bodies. They did not have the 'option' to turn to heroic biomedical care for their babies, as they had no access even to basic healthcare in their everyday lives. Although this virtually complete lack of access to bio-medical healthcare changed somewhat when Brazil instituted nationalized healthcare in 1989, 'zones of social abandonment' still persist today in Brazil and around the world (Scheper-Hughes 1993; Biehl and Eskerod 2005).

Scheper-Hughes's analysis, however, is not merely a materialist account: she evocatively tells the stories of many women whose children died far too young. These stories reveal how many of the women of the Alto reacted with pity, and not grief, at their babies' deaths because of a mix of cultural and economic conditions that brought them to bear this human frailty not with weeping, but with dry-eyed fortitude. In part, these women's reactions were shaped by views of spiritually-animated bodies within their own traditions of Catholic-inflected 'folk piety.' Many of these women thought that a good mother would check her own tears in order to ensure that her dead infant's voyage to the next world was not made too difficult: "A mother's tears can impede the way, make the road slippery so that the spirit-child will lose her footing, or the tears will fall on her wings and dampen them so that she cannot fly" (Scheper-Hughes 1993, 429–430). Scheper-Hughes's ability to bring together women's stories with wider religious and cultural traditions and economic realities allowed her to show that the 'health' of the embodied spirit is just as subject to the ravages of class injustice as it is to healing powers of biomedical or spiritual techniques.

Colonialism and Postcolonialism

As a good deal of the world's present conditions of economic inequity can be traced back to long patterns of colonial exploitation and dispossession, thinking about religion and medicine also requires an historical understanding of the ongoing significance of colonialism for the very idea of what it means to heal and be healed. Though modern colonialism has a much longer history, the nineteenth and early twentieth centuries were the heyday of European and North American colonial aggression. As European nations sought out colonial domains that they could exploit for natural resources and human labor, they spread throughout India, Africa, Asia, and the Americas, bringing along their own systems of religion, usually Catholic or Protestant Christianity, and medicine, or what was then the relatively new, scientifically-based, biomedicine.

Especially by the late nineteenth century, Christianity and scientific medicine were firmly joined in the medical missionary movement, which sought to convert colonial subjects to Christianity *and* to cure them of their illnesses. The line between disease/illness and culture/religion was confused in the interaction of missionaries and their 'patients,' as missionaries often considered traditional diets and bodily practices, especially those related to childbirth or death, to be both unsanitary and heathen (Vaughan 1991; Hardiman 2006; Kelm 1999; Lux 2001; Boddy 2007).

Most of these European and North American nurses and doctors—including many 'lady doctors' who could not find work in their home countries due to sexism—traveled around the world with an understanding that they were devoting themselves to what might now be called a 'humanitarian' cause (Burton 1996; Bornstein and Redfield 2011). They performed cataract surgery, dispensed healing medicines, facilitated opium withdrawal, and helped to deliver babies. Many among them went even further to establish medical and nursing colleges for local women and men, to enable their colonized hosts to extend biomedical care to their communities on their own (Brouwer 2002).

While many Christian medical missionaries continued to understand their role as scientific saviors enabling a 'conquest by healing' (and some still do so today), by the mid-twentieth century a significant number of such missionaries had come to question the triumphalism and injustice of their colonial endeavor (Klassen 2011, 105). Often, these missionaries came to a new awareness of the cultural and physical violence of their healing missions with the help of the colonized peoples with whom they worked.

Indian Interactions of Biomedicine and Yoga

India provides a fascinating example for thinking about the unpredictable significance of colonialism for modern-day intersections of religion and medicine. Supported by the colonial power of the British Empire, many medical missionaries made their way to India convinced that their medical skills could enable them to cure disease, transform cultural practices such as caste-based inequities or *sati* (or the self-immolation of a widow), and bring the vast population of the Indian subcontinent to a relationship with Jesus Christ. Sometimes this did happen, albeit in unexpected and small-scale ways.

For example, Dewan Bahadur Appasamy, a Indian convert to Christianity, found that his relationship to Jesus Christ was best expressed and experienced not through biomedical practices or holy communion, but through the Indian tradition of Yoga. In a book published by a Christian press in 1926, and entitled *The Use of Yoga in Prayer*, Appasamy argued that Yoga had "healing properties" that brought powerful forms of "energy" into the human body. Confident that Yoga was a "spiritual exercise" that was entirely complementary to Christianity, he backed up his claim with references both to biblical texts and to Christian rituals of prayer (Klassen 2011, 115). Appasamy's Christian Yoga is one modest example of the complex legacy of Christian missions for medicine and healing in India; the mid-twentieth-century drive for 'family planning' is another (Brouwer 2010). Perhaps most significant, however, was the revitalization and recombination of Indian healing traditions, such as Ayurveda, in response to the rise of biomedicine in colonial India.

By the late twentieth century, after decades of a 'postcolonial' India no longer under British rule, it was not only the physical positions and spiritual exercise of Yoga, but also the therapeutic tradition of Ayurvedic medicine that had effected a transformation of the colonizer's healing interventions. As Jean Langford has shown in her book *Fluent Bodies: Ayurvedic Remedies for Postcolonial Imbalance*, Ayurvedic practitioners have accomplished a selective appropriation of the techniques and authority of Western biomedicine in establishing themselves as a powerful alternative medical tradition (Langford 2002; Engler 2003).

Based on ethnographic research with Ayurvedic practitioners in contemporary India, Langford's book shows that post-Independence Ayurveda is a form of medicine that sought to 'cure' India of its colonized history. As a nationalist therapy that seeks to 'spiritually enliven' traditional Indian medical paradigms, Ayurveda also diagnoses and treats the afflictions of the Western former colonizers. Langford provides the example of an Ayurvedic doctor, Dr. Vijayan: "For him, the bodies of Europeans and North Americans are overflowing with culturally aggravated dosa. With his not-too-spicy pancakarma, he treats their late-capitalistic illnesses of excess consumerism and troubled childhoods" (Langford 2002, 269). Ironically, other scholars have argued that Ayurveda has in turn commodified and globalized itself, marketing its virtues for middle-class Indians and North Americans requiring relief from the stresses of modern living (N. Islam 2012; M. N. Islam 2012; Reddy 2002). Taking a longer view, the 'post-colonial imbalance' that Langford discusses was addressed even in the earlier hybrid movement of Christian Yoga, as British missionaries considered Christians back home to be overly materialistic and not sufficiently spiritual, and proposed Yoga as the cure.

CONCLUSION

Medicine and religion are concepts *and* political projects shaped by national contexts, economic infrastructures, and histories of colonialism, racialization, and gender. As such, for scholars of religion to study 'medicine' requires constant attention to how both concepts are defined. We must ask ourselves how processes such as medicalization, commodification, and legacies of colonialism and violence shape what questions we ask and what kinds of 'healing' we can measure and 'see.'

As bodily practices such as Yoga, Ayurveda, *curanderismo*, and organ transplantation continue their criss-crossing journey around the globe, their practitioners and advocates will continue to make culturally located claims about the efficacy and authority of their healing systems, which others will debate (Hendrickson 2014; MacDonald 2006). While a common frame for such debates is that of an ongoing conflict between 'scientific medicine' and 'religion,' it is worth being mindful that the line between curing and harming, or drug and toxin, can sometimes be very hard to draw. The very theoretical and categorical elusiveness of religion in conjunction with the category of medicine makes the work of thinking about their relation an important and exciting theoretical, methodological, and political undertaking.

GLOSSARY

Anthropology of the spiritual body this concept is a frame for analyzing how different medical and religious traditions understand the human body, especially in relation to material and/or spiritual forces that they consider to animate and affect it.

Ayurvedic medicine an ancient South Asian therapeutic practice rooted in Sanskrit Vedic texts and that literally means the 'knowledge of life.' Based on both material remedies or therapies and anthropologies of the spiritual body, Ayurveda is a fascinating contemporary example of a medical tradition shaped by imperial modernity, commodification, and religious revival.

Biological fallacy a concept used by medical anthropologists to argue against reducing our understanding of the human body solely to biological, 'scientific' frames. The fallacy, or mistake, in this case would be to ignore how human flourishing or suffering is also shaped by political, economic, cultural, religious, and environmental conditions.

Biomedicine the term used by medical anthropologists, and others, to denote scientific, Western-based (but now globalized) medicine. As a highly materialist understanding of how the body works, biomedicine does not leave much room for the effects of spirits. Biomedicine, however, as a Western-based medical tradition, was very much shaped by Christianity, colonialism, and the development of capitalism.

Medicalization the process by which biomedicine came to have increasing political, cultural, and economic authority outside of its own particular realm of science.

REFERENCES

Alter, Joseph S., ed. 2005. *Asian Medicine and Globalization*. Philadelphia: University of Pennsylvania Press.

Barnes, Linda L. 2005. "American Acupuncture and Efficacy: Meanings and Their Points of Insertion." *Medical Anthropology Quarterly* 19(3): 239–266. doi: 10.1525/maq.2005.19.3.239

Beaman, Lori G. 2008. *Defining Harm: Religious Freedom and the Limits of the Law*. Vancouver: UBC Press.

Behrend, Heike. 2003. "Photo Magic: Photographs in Practices of Healing and Harming in East Africa." *Journal of Religion in Africa* 33(2): 129–145. doi: 10.1163/15700660360703114

Bender, Courtney. 2010. *The New Metaphysicals: Spirituality and the American Religious Imagination*. Chicago, IL: University of Chicago Press.

Biehl, João and Torben Eskerod. 2005. *Vita: Life in a Zone of Social Abandonment*. Berkeley: University of California Press.

Boddy, Janice Patricia. 2007. *Civilizing Women: British Crusades in Colonial Sudan*. Princeton, NJ: Princeton University Press.

Bornstein, Erica and Peter Redfield. 2011. *Forces of Compassion: Humanitarianism Between Ethics and Politics*. Santa Fe: SAR Press.

Brouwer, Ruth Compton. 2002. *Modern Women Modernizing Men: The Changing Missions of Three Professional Women in Asia and Africa, 1902–69*. Vancouver: UBC Press.

Brouwer, Ruth Compton. 2010. "Ironic Interventions: CUSO Volunteers in India's Family Planning Campaign, 1960s–1970s." *Histoire sociale/Social History* 43(86): 279–313. doi: 10.1353/his.2010.0033

Brown, Karen McCarthy. 2001. *Mama Lola: A Vodou Priestess in Brooklyn*. Berkeley: University of California Press. Original edition, 1991.

Burton, Antoinette. 1996. "Contesting the Zenana: The Mission to Make 'Lady Doctors for India,' 1874–1885." *Journal of British Studies* 35(3): 368–397. doi: 10.1086/386112

Chakrabarty, Dipesh. 2011. "The Muddle of Modernity." *American Historical Review* 116(3): 663–675. doi: 10.1086/ahr.116.3.663

Craig, David M. 2014. *Health Care as a Social Good*. Washington, DC: Georgetown University Press.

Dubé, Eve, Caroline Laberge, Maryse Guay, Paul Bramadat, Réal Roy, and Julie A. Bettinger. 2013. "Vaccine Hesitancy: An Overview." *Human Vaccines & Immunotherapeutics* 9(8): 1763–1773. doi: 10.4161/hv.24657

Engler, Steven. 2003. "'Science' vs. 'Religion' in Classical Ayurveda." *Numen* 50(4): 416–463. doi: 10.1163/156852703322446679

Foucault, Michel. 2003. *"Society Must Be Defended": Lectures at the Collège de France, 1975–1976*, translated by David Macey. Reprint edition. New York: Picador.

Foucault, Michel, 2009. *Security, Territory, Population: Lectures at the Collège de France 1977–1978*, translated by Graham Burchell, edited by Michel Senellart, François Ewald, and Alessandro Fontana. New York: Picador.

Fraser, Gertrude Jacinta. 1998. *African American Midwifery in the South: Dialogues of Birth, Race, and Memory*. Cambridge, MA: Harvard University Press.

Hacking, Ian. 1986. "Making Up People." In *Reconstructing Individualism: Autonomy, Individuality, and the Self in Western Thought*, edited by Thomas C. Heller and Christine Brooke-Rose. Stanford, CA: Stanford University Press, 222–236.

Hardiman, David. 2006. *Healing Bodies, Saving Souls: Medical Missions in Asia and Africa*. Amsterdam: Rodopi.

Hendrickson, Brett. 2014. *Border Medicine: A Transcultural History of Mexican American Curanderismo*. New York: New York University Press.

Islam, Md. Nazrul. 2012. "Repackaging Ayurveda in Post-Colonial India: Revival or Dilution?" *South Asia: Journal of South Asian Studies* 35(3): 503–519. doi: 10.1080/00856401.2012.682967

Islam, Nazrul. 2012. "New Age Orientalism: Ayurvedic 'Wellness and Spa Culture.'" *Health Sociology Review* 21(2): 220–231. doi: 10.5172/hesr.2012.21.2.220

Kelm, Mary-Ellen. 1999. *Colonizing Bodies: Aboriginal Health and Healing in British Columbia, 1900–50*. Vancouver: UBC Press.

Klassen, Pamela E. 2001. *Blessed Events: Religion and Home Birth in America*. Princeton, NJ: Princeton University Press.

Klassen, Pamela E. 2011. *Spirits of Protestantism: Medicine, Healing, and Liberal Christianity*. Berkeley: University of California Press.

Klassen, Pamela E. 2014. "The Politics of Protestant Healing: Theoretical Tools for the Study of Spiritual Bodies and the Body Politic." *Spiritus: A Journal of Christian Spirituality* 14(1): 68–75. doi: 10.1353/scs.2014.0006

Kleinman, Arthur, Veena Das, and Margaret M. Lock, eds. 1997. *Social Suffering*. Berkeley: University of California Press.

Langford, Jean. 2002. *Fluent Bodies: Ayurvedic Remedies for Postcolonial Imbalance*. Durham, NC: Duke University Press.

Lock, Margaret M. 1995. *Encounters with Aging: Mythologies of Menopause in Japan and North America*. Reprint edition. London: University of California Press.

Lux, Maureen Katherine. 2001. *Medicine That Walks: Disease, Medicine and Canadian Plains Native People, 1880–1940*. Toronto: University of Toronto Press.

MacDonald, Arlene. 2006. "Immortal Organs: Spirituality in the Resurrected Lives of Organ Transplant Recipients." *OMEGA: Journal of Death and Dying* 53(1): 51–67.

Opp, James. 2007. *The Lord for the Body: Religion, Medicine, and Protestant Faith Healing in Canada, 1880–1930*. Montreal: McGill-Queen's University Press.

Orsi, Robert A. 1998. *Thank You, St. Jude: Women's Devotion to the Patron Saint of Hopeless Causes*. New Haven, CT: Yale University Press.

Peters, Shawn Francis. 2007. *When Prayer Fails: Faith Healing, Children, and the Law*. New York: Oxford University Press.

Reddy, Sita. 2002. "Asian Medicine in America: The Ayurvedic Case." *Annals of the American Academy of Political and Social Science* 583(1): 97–121. doi: 10.1177/0002716202583001007

Redfield, Peter. 2013. *Life in Crisis: The Ethical Journey of Doctors Without Borders*. Berkeley: University of California Press.

Riesebrodt, Martin. 2010. *The Promise of Salvation: A Theory of Religion*. Chicago, IL: University of Chicago Press.

Scheper-Hughes, Nancy. 1993. *Death Without Weeping: The Violence of Everyday Life in Brazil*. Berkeley: University of California Press.

Scheper-Hughes, Nancy. 2001. *Saints, Scholars, and Schizophrenics: Mental Illness in Rural Ireland*. Berkeley: University of California Press. Original edition, 1979.

Scheper-Hughes, Nancy and Margaret M. Lock. 1987. "The Mindful Body: A Prolegomenon to Future Work in Medical Anthropology." *Medical Anthropology Quarterly* 1(1): 6–41. doi: 10.1525/maq.1987.1.1.02a00020

Sered, Susan Starr and Rushika J. Fernandopulle. 2007. *Uninsured in America: Life and Death in the Land of Opportunity*. Berkeley: University of California Press.

Siddiqi, Arjumand. 2009. "The Role of Health Insurance in Explaining Immigrant versus Non-Immigrant Disparities in Access to Health Care: Comparing the United States to Canada." *Social Science & Medicine* 69(10): 1452–1459. doi: 10.1016/j.socscimed.2009.08.030

Starr, Paul. 1984. *The Social Transformation of American Medicine: The Rise of a Sovereign Profession and the Making of a Vast Industry*. New York: Basic Books.

Tylor, Edward Burnett. 1871. *Primitive Culture: Researches Into the Development of Mythology, Philosophy, Religion, Art, and Custom*. London: J. Murray.

Vaughan, Megan. 1991. *Curing Their Ills: Colonial Power and African Illness*. Stanford, CA: Stanford University Press.

FURTHER READING

Alter 2005 [*This book is a fascinating collection of essays that consider how tradition, authenticity, commodification, religious revitalization, and nationalism shape the interplay of Asian and Western forms of medicine in global contexts.*]

Barnes, Linda L. and Susan S. Sered, eds. 2004. *Religion and Healing in America*. Oxford and New York: Oxford University Press. [*Another collection of essays, this book focuses on a wide diversity of healing traditions in the United States, using both ethnographic and historical approaches. The essays all address ongoing adaptations and tensions in the interaction of biomedical and religious forms of healing.*]

Brown 2001 [*A classic ethnography of a Haitian Vodou priestess who emigrated to Brooklyn, this book is an excellent—and very readable—introduction to the ways that religion and medicine must be understood in particular communities with their own constraints and histories. Brown shows that in Haitian Vodou, healing is a practice that draws on memory, story, family history, ritual, and bodily techniques, all of which are shaped by wider political and historical forces of slavery, colonialism and religious conflict.*]

Kleinman/Das/Lock 1997 [*This edited collection draws together leading social theorists, medical anthropologists, and anthropologists of religion who use the concept of 'social suffering' to* demonstrate how the vulnerability and suffering of human bodies is always framed, addressed, or exacerbated within broader cultural and political contexts.]

Opp 2007 [*This book is an historical account of the North American debates—and even battles— between early Holiness and Pentecostal 'faith healers' and their opponents, who were both 'mainstream' Protestants and medical doctors. Highly readable, and with excellent use of both historical sources and theorists such as Michel Foucault, this book is an excellent introduction to the complicated, and ongoing, tensions between healing practices rooted in spiritual author- ity and those rooted in scientific authority.*]

van der Veer, Peter. 2007. "Global Breathing: Religious Utopias in India and China." *Anthropological Theory* 7(3): 315–328. [*This essay, by a leading scholar of religion and coloni- alism, discusses how Yoga and Qigong are religious techniques of bodily discipline that have become globally commodified, but that remain politically influential—and volatile—in their original, national settings. In particular, this essay shows how the spread of 'spiritual' tech- niques of bodily healing takes place via networks developed through 'imperial modernity,' including those of capitalist globalization.*]

CHAPTER 28

....

NATURE

....

ADRIAN IVAKHIV

CHAPTER SUMMARY
....

- 'Nature' is a complex concept, with a variety of meanings that vary historically.
- Relations between religious belief/practice and the natural world vary widely, in both symbolic and practical terms.
- The recent growth of the 'religion and ecology' field reveals the 'greening' of traditional forms of religion as well as internal and external critiques of religions' relations to the natural world.
- Nature religion, environmental religiosity, and environmentalism as religion or spirituality are trends outside traditional forms of religion that have the potential to provide integrative and 'implicitly religious' meaning systems.
- A recent development is religio-environmental concepts or movements that span different faith traditions.

NATURE IN ITSELF
....

Like God, nature is a 'trump card,' as anthropologist Mary Douglas argued (1975, 209). It is a vague but weighty word customarily deployed to win arguments. Calling it "perhaps the most complex word in the [English] language," Raymond Williams (1976, 219) traced out three general 'areas of meaning' of nature: "(i) the essential quality and character of something; (ii) the inherent force which directs either the world or human beings or both; (iii) the material world itself, taken as including or not including human beings." Evernden (1992, 20–21) pointed out that once we have articulated a concept of 'nature' as distinct from 'all things' or 'the world as a whole,' it becomes possible to speak of some things as belonging to nature or being natural and others as being unnatural (thus devalued) or supernatural (and privileged). Nature has come to function as a boundary term demarcating a primary realm—which can be elevated or downgraded—from a secondary realm of the human, cultural, or otherwise non-natural. While the relative valence of nature versus culture remains open, the nature–culture duality has become foundational to many modern conceptual constructs, not least of them the division of academe into sciences and humanities, *Naturwissenschaften* and *Geisteswissenschaften*.

A genealogy of Western notions of nature in its aggregate (Williams's third meaning) would include: nature conceived as a divinely ordained system of norms and rules, rights and obligations; a book to be read, divined, and studied; a motherly female, nurturing and providing for her children's needs (or punishing them at her whim); a body-like organism, whose features mirror those of the human body; a clock-like object or machine to be analyzed, taken apart, and put to human use; a storehouse of resources; a ruthless and harsh kingdom from which humans should distance ourselves through the social contract of civilization; a flourishing web of life; an Edenic garden to be protected and visited periodically for personal replenishment; a museum, theme park, or open-air gymnasium for trials of masculinity or superhuman achievement; a cybernetic system or databank of circulating genetic information; or a divinity, Gaia, which, when pressed, may become an avenging angel meting out justice to a humanity that has transgressed her order (Glacken 1967; Gold 1984; Ivakhiv 2002).

Each of these concepts and images carries assumptions about actions appropriate in relation to nature: for instance, subjugation, control, measurement, prediction, management, aesthetic contemplation, protection, mystical union with, or active resistance on behalf of it (Ivakhiv 2001, 36–43). In the environmental era launched by Rachel Carson's (1962) *Silent Spring*, ideas of nature have become a touchstone for environmental advocates, who argue that nature tends toward a dynamic balance or equilibrium among species, leading to ecosystems of maximum diversity, harmony, and stability, which humans jeopardize with our heedlessness. This image of nature has been all but rejected within the ecological science of the last four decades, so that instead of a balance of nature, the natural world is more typically seen as unstable and non-linear, a patchwork quilt characterized by ceaseless movement of individual organisms, species, and communities, whose overall trajectory is directionless, unpredictable, and perhaps chaotic (Botkin 2012; Lodge/Hamlin 2006). Some have taken this as *carte blanche* for human activities, but others note that a nature as complex and unpredictable as this needs all the more careful treatment: in situations not fully controllable, we must apply the precautionary principle and 'adaptively manage' both our 'resources' and ourselves.

If nature presents uncertainties as a guide to human behavior, so does the science that seemingly deciphers nature for us. As a form of inquiry, field of practices, community of practitioners, set of established and accepted truths, array of popular understandings, and congeries of trappings (gadgets, science museums, and so on), science is multiple and its relations with other domains—such as religion, colonization, political programs, cultural paradigms, and popular wisdom—are historically variable. Nature, in consequence, is something to be studied by scientists; sought and appreciated by tourists, mystics, and overworked urban souls; manufactured (the less conspicuously, the better) by tourist industries; and deconstructed by postmodern academics. But it is also, perhaps above all, something understood by many people to be *there* in the world—in advance of what humans do with it. To what extent it is *threatened* by human activities is a recurrent question of our time.

NATURE IN AND WITH RELIGION—RELIGION IN AND WITH NATURE

Study of the role of nature in religious and folk practices was a feature of ethnographic and folkloristic research in the nineteenth century. Romantic and evolutionist scholars sought explanations for myths, rituals, and folk practices in human mental constructs, as, for instance, in the analogical mind's predilection to associate the world above with the world below—e.g. stars and constellations with plants and herbs, physical symptoms, and the shapes of wax figures and other divinatory signs. Traditional ideas, such as the doctrine of correspondences—popularized in medieval European bestiaries, manuals of alchemical and Renaissance magic, Hermetic texts, and other sources—provided plentiful evidence for such analogical thinking, by which nature and humans were seen to mirror and reflect each other.

As in Europe, so in China, where medicine, philosophy, landscape architecture, physical and spiritual cultivation, and other ideas and practices revolved around a set of correspondences between heaven and earth, *Yin* and *Yang*, and a small number of elements—typically earth, water, fire, metal, and wood—considered to be universally distributed in dynamically variable configurations. Chinese religion and cosmology have been characterized as forms of 'anthropocosmism', 'organic holism', 'dynamic vitalism', and 'cosmic ecology' (Miller 2006; Tucker/Berthrong 1998; Wei-Ming 1989). African, Australasian, and North and South American indigenous cosmologies have been similarly depicted as holistic, organismic, animist, or otherwise rooted in conceptions of cosmic relatedness and temporal or existential continuity—between the ancestral past and the multi-generational future, or between upper worlds, underworlds, and human worlds, as in the worldviews of some nomadic or shamanistic cultures (Grim 2001; Callicott 1997).

At stake here, commonly, is the effort to distinguish Western conceptions of the universe from non-Western and indigenous conceptions. As an all-embracing term for the world accessible to the senses, 'nature' in monotheistic, Abrahamic, or 'creationist' traditions has frequently taken on secondary status, either in relation to the creator and his plan for the world's unfolding, or to the world as it could be. At the same time, the identification of an autonomous 'nature', often credited to the twelfth and thirteenth centuries in Europe, whetted the appetite for new forms of study of nature, which led to the development of the natural sciences, *scientiae naturalis*. Some have seen this as a nature purified of most of its qualities (Latour 1993; Whitehead 1964). On the other hand, in traditions which place little credence in the notion of divine creation—where, instead, the universe may be seen as eternal, perpetually unfolding, cyclically revolving or renewing, or some combination of these—concepts akin to 'nature' come adumbrated with other qualities. For instance, they may be accompanied by some principle underlying the movement of the whole—such as the Chinese *li*, often translated as ritual or appropriate action, or *ren*, referring to goodness, virtue, or harmonious relationship—and understood as an interplay of forces—whether two, four (earth, fire, water, air), five (as in the Chinese scheme mentioned above), or another number. Indigenous worldviews, when studied collectively, continue to be depicted by comparative religionists as centered around notions of kinship and relatedness: "The pervasive cosmology of traditional societies may be characterized as a 'community of beings' world view in which humans are part of an interacting set of living things" (Berkes/Colding/Folke 2000, 1259). Nature, in this understanding, is hardly separable from culture, community, sociality, meaning, or the value-ladenness of relationships involving humans and non-human entities.

Some basic distinction between creationist, transcendental, or 'otherworldly' cosmologies and more 'immanent' worldviews has characterized intellectual debates over the environmental implications of religion at least since medieval historian Lynn White's (1967) article "The Historic Roots of Our Ecological Crisis." White famously argued that the Judeo-Christian tradition shared a heavy burden of responsibility for the crisis in relations between humans and nature. In the article's aftermath, theologians, historians, and social scientists responded in one of three predominant ways: by trying to prove White wrong, whether about the ecological dis-virtues of Christianity or Judaism, the presumable virtues of other religions, or the assumptions he made about religion vis-à-vis economic, political, and other factors; by agreeing with him and calling for an alternative to replace the Judeo-Christian worldview; or by taking up the charge to research the matter in greater depth (Livingstone 1994; Minteer/Manning 2005). The third of these responses gave birth to the field of 'religion and ecology', while the former two contributed to the movement that Nash (1996) called the 'greening of religion.'

The field of religion and ecology has featured two main forms of scholarly research. The first has focused on ideas, beliefs, and cultural resources—texts, narratives, rituals, images and iconographies, psalms and sutras, and so on—with an eye to interpreting their ecological significance or using them to generate ecologically productive meanings. Such efforts can be called 'ecotheological', 'religio-ecological', or 'confessional' in that they interpret inherited elements of religion in the direction of a reconstructive project of helping religious communities meet the ecological needs of our time. They constitute a "religious turn to ecology" (Ivakhiv 2012, 215). The practical result of this trend became evident in a series of international meetings and publications, including the gathering of religious leaders sponsored by World Wildlife Fund (WWF) in Assisi, Italy, in 1986 (WWF 1986); the Religions of the World and Ecology conferences held at Harvard in the late 1990s, with ensuing book volumes (e.g. Foltz/Denny/Baharuddin 2003; Grim 2001); the publication of *The Encyclopedia of Religion and Nature* (Taylor 2005); initiatives like the Earth Charter, a global values statement endorsed by thousands of organizations around the world; and publishers' efforts to cater to the audience of religiously inclined environmentalists (e.g. *Green Bible* 2008). If religion had earlier been a broad category whose relevance to ecology was unknown, by the early 2000s it was clear that foundational religious texts included numerous prescriptions, proscriptions, and principles concerning the proper relations between humans and animals, plants, and other parts of the natural world. Taken together, it was possible to argue that 'religions of the book' prescribed a 'stewardship' ethic for 'tending to creation,' and some theologians and scholars eagerly set upon describing what such an ethic implies for believers today.

The other type of scholarly response to White's thesis has been to undertake empirical assessments of the ecological practices of particular societies to determine how those societies' beliefs and worldviews shaped their environmental practices (Taylor 2005). Analogous empirical inquiries motivated the quantitatively focused work of 'cultural ecologists' (Rappaport 1984; Vayda 1969), but recent research has shown the relationship between beliefs and ecological outcomes to be complicated. Indigenous peoples and others with seemingly organic or holistic worldviews have overhunted, deforested, eroded, and otherwise altered their habitats to their own detriment (Denevan 1992; Harkin/Lewis 2007; Krech 1999; Redman 1999; Snodgrass/Tiedje 2008; Tuan 1968). The relationship between worldviews and behavior is less predictable than social scientists had hoped, since besides religious motivations, behavior depends on a host of economic, sociological, technological, and other factors. Some examples suggest a connection between religion and a society's ability to respond to environmental challenges: for instance, both the Classic Mayan and Greenland Norse cultures might have declined in part through the maladaptive role played by culturally sanctified and ritualized practices and the vested, institutional interests associated with them (Diamond 2005). On the other hand, the discourse of 'traditional ecological knowledge,' or TEK, makes a reasonable *prima facie* case that locally based, adaptively evolved 'knowledge–practice–belief complexes' (Berkes 1999) result in relative sustainability. Research on the roles of religion, ritual, belief, mythic narrative, and the like, within institutions of cultural-ecological practice remains important, but the precise relationships between these elements remain elusive (e.g. Veldman/Szasz/Haluza-Delay 2012).

All the same, a proliferation of religious-environmental efforts and alliances in the last two decades gives substance to the claim that a 'greening of religion' is occurring. These range from broad-based international efforts to local grassroots initiatives: they include the World Wide Fund for Nature's (WWF) Network on Conservation and Religion, the Alliance for Religions and Conservation (ARC), Conservation International's Faith-Based Initiatives Program, the International Union for the Conservation of Nature (IUCN) task force on cultural and spiritual values of protected areas, the Green Pilgrim Cities Network (launched in late 2010), and groups like the Redwood Rabbis, the Sisters of Earth, the African Earthkeepers of Zimbabwe, the Sarvodaya Movement of Sri Lanka, the Tzu-Chi Foundation of Taiwan, the Interfaith Global Climate Change Network, and the Evangelical Environmental Network, famous for its 'What would Jesus drive?' anti-SUV campaign (ARC 2010; Daneel 2001; Dudley/Higgins-Zogib/Mansourian 2009; Gardner, 2006; Gottlieb 2006a; Lee/Schaaf 2003; Posey 2002). Religious leaders, including Ecumenical Orthodox Patriarch Bartholomeos I of Constantinople, Tibetan Buddhist leader Tenzin Gyatso, His Holiness The Dalai Lama, and Catholic popes John Paul II, Benedict XVI, and most famously Francis have issued statements of what in other contexts would be called environmental policy. At the same time, religious organizations can be notoriously slow to change, and resistance to environmentalism remains a powerful force among major faith traditions, for a host of reasons.

NATURE RELIGION, ECOLOGICAL RELIGION

Aside from the 'greening' of traditional forms of religion referred to earlier, we also see the development of new forms of religion, religiosity, or spirituality associated with natural, ecological, and environmental themes. Historically, connections between religious practice and the conservation of nature have been numerous. As mentioned, indigenous societies developed forms of 'traditional ecological knowledge' (TEK) that mixed observational knowledge, mythic narratives and cosmological constructs, and collective social and ritual practices. In medieval and early modern times, explicit forms of nature conservation were initiated by rulers to preserve lands for their own recreational pursuits. By the late eighteenth and nineteenth centuries, artists, writers, and philosophers associated with the Romantic movement heralded the values of nature and traveled on journeys to experience its purifying or rejuvenating qualities. An argument can be made that the entirety of modern Romanticism—from the poetry and prose of Wordsworth, Coleridge, Blake, and Goethe to the philosophical speculations of Fichte, Schelling, and Herder—shades into a nature-oriented religiosity, an attempt to retrieve values perceived to be threatened by industrial civilization (Bate 1991; Rigby 2004). As Albanese (1990, 7) argued, religious creativity has surrounded the 'symbolic center' of some concept of 'nature' for centuries. As forms of 'American nature religion,' Albanese identified the writings and legacy of the New England Transcendentalists, the nineteenth-century metaphysical religiosity focused around notions of Mind and Reason, the 'physical religion' of natural health and healing movements, the 'ecstatic religion' of hunters, naturalists, and early wilderness and scouting advocates, and more recent self-conscious reinventions by pagan revivalists and goddess devotees. Analogous forms of nature religiosity can be discerned within intellectual as well as popular culture in nineteenth-through twenty-first-century Germany, Russia, England, the Scandinavian countries, and beyond.

With the popularization of environmental movements since the 1960s, the concept of 'civil religion' becomes relevant. Civil religion refers to something between the 'folk religion' of a society and the accepted ritual expressions of patriotism in a given country or nation. The term was popularized by sociologist Robert Bellah (1967), who speculated about the outlines of a possible 'world civil religion,' a "viable and coherent world order" which he thought would require "a major new set of symbolic forms" (2007, 244). Forty years later, Bellah (2007) recognized how little progress had been made to this end and how naïve the proposal may sound. Yet somewhere in the contours between transnational institutions—such as the United Nations and its various legal and jurisdictional affiliates and counterparts—and today's many forms of 'lived globality,' it is possible to identify nascent, plural, and often contradictory forms of global civil religiosity. Candidates for such civil religion may include the 'post-traditional' and non-denominational 'spiritualities' that have emerged in developed Western countries, where surveys show a growing preference for identifying as 'spiritual' rather than 'religious' (see Streib/Klein, "Religion and Spirituality," this volume) or as poly-confessional, multi-religious, non-denominational, 'evolving,' religious but of no single persuasion, and so on (Roof 2000; Marler/Hadaway 2002). Scholars have proposed related terms such as 'diffuse' or 'implicit religion' (Bailey 1983; *Social Compass* 1990), 'cultural religion,' and 'designer religion,' the latter for the individualistic and somewhat consumerist streak within so-called New Age religion (Heelas 1996; Ivakhiv 2001).

In this context, ideas from the natural sciences and from popular environmentalism are often taken to fill the gap left by the apparent disintegration of traditional meaning-systems. The conservation movements of the late nineteenth century, which led to the preservation of emblematic landscapes as national parks, were linked to the expression of religious as well as nationalist sentiments. In the United States, the creation of the national park system in 1912 was considered a way to display the natural bounty, richness, and beauty of a nation whose relative youth would otherwise compare unfavorably with the historic monuments and treasures of the Old World. For leading promoters of national parks, such as John Muir, nature was conceived in religious terms. In the fight to protect the Hetch Hetchy Valley in Yosemite National Park from the construction of a dam, Muir wrote: "Dam Hetch Hetchy? As well dam for water-tanks the people's cathedrals and churches, for no holier temple has ever been consecrated by the heart of man" (in Worster 2008, 425). Similar language was used by other writers of the time (Ross-Bryant 2012). Conservationists and environmentalists past and present have paid homage to Muir, Thoreau, Wordsworth, Goethe, Whitman, John Burroughs, Sigurd Olson, Aldo Leopold, Rachel Carson, Wendell Berry, Annie Dillard, and other nature writers and advocates by visiting the places where they lived or those memorialized in their names—such as Walden Pond (Thoreau), Muir Woods and Yosemite National Park (Muir), or Dove Cottage and Grasmere in the Lake District (Wordsworth)—and by turning these into sites of environmental pilgrimage.

Some have argued that contemporary environmentalism has become a quasi-religion, one based on more or less sound scientific ideas, if not on scientific practice (Dunlap 2004; Ronnow 2011; Ross-Bryant 2012; Szerszynski 1997, 2002; Taylor 2010). Today, such eco-religiosity includes practices that serve as ritual ways of expressing environmental identity: visits to the wilderness, nature writing, landscape photography, participation in political demonstrations, recycling, community gardening and farmers' markets, environmental organizations, and green consumerism and conspicuous under-consumption. Deepening Albanese's notion of 'nature religion,' Taylor (2010) identifies a biocentric variant that he labels 'dark green religion'; and Gottlieb (2006a) has written of 'religious environmentalism' as a growing international trend. Gottlieb

(2006a, 160) notes that environmentalism "can function as a religion because it begins with religious emotions and connects them to an articulated set of beliefs about our place in the universe."

One prominent trend linking scientists, scholars, and theologians is the effort to identify a new cosmological narrative—variously called the New Story, the Universe Story, the Epic of Evolution, the Journey of the Universe, Big History, and so on—by which to 're-enchant' both nature and humanity and to link the epistemological authority of science with the emotional draw of religious language (Sideris 2013). Taylor (2010, 155) sees such movements as part of an ecological 'parareligion,' a scientifically informed worldview of "awe and reverence before the universe" that expresses itself in diverse forms including nature writing and the visual arts; the activities of participants as well as producers at science museums, zoos, aquariums, and protected areas; and artistic, theatrical, and activist events surrounding the global environmental meetings and 'earth summits' that have come to mark international deliberation on global environmental issues. Travel to national parks, world heritage sites, biosphere reserves, and other protected areas is sometimes treated as quasi-sacred pilgrimage (Ivakhiv 2013). Engel (2005, 193) sees in UNESCO's biosphere reserves and world heritage sites "the outlines of a global religious vision" that would "transmit to future generations the 'universal values' of our evolutionary origins (Galapagos World Heritage site), the worst of human history (Auschwitz Concentration Camp World Heritage site) and the promise of world justice, peace, and ecological sustainability (Amistad International Peace Park in Central America)." Taken together, these trends show environmentalism and ecology providing, for a growing number of people, the kind of integrative and 'implicitly religious' meaning systems that might make up an emerging civil religion.

RELIGIOUS ECOLOGIES IN PRACTICE

Concepts of 'religious ecology,' 'spiritual ecology,' 'religio-environmentalism,' and 'eco-spirituality' arise today from a fluid discursive milieu in which conceptual innovators work both within and across multiple cultural, religious, and intellectual traditions (Gottlieb 2006a; Sponsel 2012). While the existence of a single religio-environmental movement can be debated, religio-environmental groups and orientations display an array of 'family resemblances' that show a growing convergence among faith-based groups and environmental groups on parallel themes and practices. According to these convergent articulations, the environment, or creation, or the earth and its ecosystems are to be treated with care; and religious traditions, to one degree or another, are or can be consonant with efforts to do that. The following concepts or movements present a sample of activities within this broader religio-environmental milieu.

Creation Care

Aside from rare publications by theologians such as Schaeffer (1970), environmentalism has not always been welcomed by Christian evangelicals. But once articulated in the form of 'care for God's creation,' or 'Creation Care,' green activism took on new force. With its 1992 Au Sable Forum on Evangelical Christianity and the Environment, which established the Evangelical Environmental Network (EEN), the World Evangelical Fellowship began demonstrating strong interest in environmental matters. In 1993, the EEN co-founded the National Religious Partnership for the Environment, alongside partner organizations the US Catholic Conference, the National Council of Churches, and the Coalition on Jewish Life and the Environment. In 2003, the EEN made waves with its 'What would Jesus drive?' campaign, which elicited over 4,000 national and international media stories. Groups like Christians for the Mountains (opposed to mountaintop removal coal mining in Appalachia) and the Evangelical Climate Initiative have negotiated a series of tensions among evangelicals to take prominent and sometimes controversial stances on environmental issues (Billings/Samson 2012; Simmons 2009).

Eco-kosher

First proposed in the 1980s by Rabbi Arthur Waskow, the concept of Eco-kosher, or Eco-kashrut, extends traditional Jewish dietary regulations to human relations with the natural environment. Waskow has written that if the rules of *kashrut* affirmed that "what and how we ate was holy," then today those rules ought to extend to how we live on this earth: "For shepherds and farmers, food was what they ate from the earth. For us, it is also coal, oil, electric power, paper, plastics, that we take from the earth" (Waskow 2010). This extension of the concept leads to asking if it is kosher "to destroy great forests, to ignore insulating our homes, synagogues, and nursing homes, to become addicted to automobiles so that we drunkenly pour carbon dioxide into the atmosphere, there to accelerate the heating of our globe?" (Waskow 2010).

Sacred Groves in India

The concept of 'sacred groves,' associated with specific presiding deities, has for centuries allowed for the protection of forest fragments of varying size across India. In Kerala and Karnataka provinces, there are thousands of sacred groves associated with several hundred deities, which are often ritualized and commemorated in local art forms and folk traditions. While hunting or logging are typically disallowed in sacred groves, the gathering of fruit, honey, and medicinal herbs has contributed to the groves' perceived value (Malhotra et al. 2001; Nutgeren 2005). Today the Indian government recognizes their usefulness for protection against soil erosion, desertification, and biodiversity loss. Ecologists have touted sacred groves, mountains, and ponds as viable accompaniments to the protection of ecological 'refugia' believed necessary for biodiversity protection around the world (Berkes 1999).

Green Pilgrim Cities Network

Proposed at a meeting of the Alliance of Religions and Conservation (ARC) hosted by Prince Philip at England's Windsor Castle in 2009, the Green Pilgrim Cities Network was launched in Assisi, Italy, in 2011, with the participation of UN Secretary-General Ban Ki-Moon. Renamed the Green Pilgrimage Network, the association today includes faith groups and municipalities representing over twenty major pilgrimage destinations around the world. The Network has sponsored the development of guidelines and implementation of 'best practices' for greening religious pilgrimage. It has issued a "Green Guide" for the Muslim Hajj and promoted extensive greening initiatives in many sites: including Amritsar, India; Etchmiadzin, Armenia; Trondheim, Norway; Louguan, China; and Santiago de Compostela, Spain.

The Earth Charter

This civil society initiative arose at the instigation of Maurice Strong, Secretary-General of the 1991 UN Conference on Environment and Development (the Rio 'Earth Summit'), and Mikhail Gorbachev, former Soviet Secretary-General and founder of Green Cross International. Modeled on the International Declaration of Human Rights and earlier interfaith statements of collective values, the charter underwent an international drafting process during the 1990s. Proposing "an ethical framework for building a just, sustainable, and peaceful global society in the 21st century," the current 'consensus' version of it was finalized in March 2000 at UNESCO's Paris headquarters and formally launched at the Peace Palace in The Hague that year. The document has since been endorsed by over 6,000 organizations, including local and state governments and international NGOs (Earth Charter Initiative 2012).

Eco-Paganism

The concept of 'nature religion' has been taken up eagerly and explicitly by many contemporary followers of Wicca, Druidry, Ásatrú, Heathenism, goddess spirituality, and other forms of Neo-paganism. For them, nature, conceived broadly and often inclusively of humans, is the primary source of value and is worthy of reverence in itself. Rituals and practices focused on natural cycles and time-honored relationships between human communities and their natural environments take precedence over those associated with purely human initiatives or historical events and personages. For some of these religionists, deities are considered coextensive with the natural world; alternatively, deities may be considered both supernatural and immanent within the world. Inspired by efforts to 'return to' or 'reconstruct' ancient beliefs and practices more closely rooted in nature, Pagans have worked alongside environmental activists to protect forests, groves, and green spaces in urban and rural settings in Britain, the United States, continental Europe, and elsewhere (Harvey 1997; Letcher 2001; Taylor 1995).

GLOSSARY

Eco-spirituality contemporary forms of spiritual belief or practice that draw their central reference points from an awareness of and desire to improve ecological relations.

Greening of religion the movement among some religious adherents toward proactive responses to the global environmental crisis, inclusive of the 'greening' of pilgrimage, building (church, temple, mosque) infrastructure, and so on. Alternatively, the term may refer to the thesis that religious communities in general are moving toward greater recognition of the environmental crisis as a defining contemporary challenge.

Nature religion any form of religion that draws its central reference points from the natural world.

Religion and ecology the field that has emerged since the 1970s to study the various interrelations between religious beliefs and practices and ecological awareness or sensitivity.

Religious environmentalism forms of environmental activism outwardly identified with specific religious traditions, communities, or congregations.

REFERENCES

Albanese, Catherine. 1990. *Nature Religion in America: From the Algonkian Indians to the New Age*. Chicago, IL: University of Chicago Press.

ARC (Alliance of Religions and Conservation). 2010. "Green Pilgrim Cities." <http://www.arc-world.org/downloads/Green-Cities-Leaflet.pdf>, accessed February 3, 2016.

Bailey, Edward Ian. 1983. "The Implicit Religion of Contemporary Society: An Orientation and a Plea for Its Study." *Religion* 13(1): 69–83.

Bate, Jonathan. 1991. *Romantic Ecology: Wordsworth and the Environmental Tradition*. London and New York: Routledge.

Bellah, Robert N. 1967. "Civil Religion in America." *Daedalus* 96(1): 1–21.

Bellah, Robert N. 2007. "Is a Global Civil Religion Possible?" *The Immanent Frame*. <http://blogs.ssrc.org/tif/2007/12/24/is-a-global-civil-religion-possible/>, accessed February 3, 2016.

Berkes, Fikret. 1999. *Sacred Ecology: Traditional Ecological Knowledge and Resource Management*. Philadelphia, PA: Taylor & Francis.

Berkes, Fikret, Johan Colding, and Carl Folke. 2000. "Rediscovery of Traditional Ecological Knowledge as Adaptive Management." *Ecological Applications* 10(5): 1251–1262.

Billings, Dwight B. and Will Samson. 2012. "Evangelical Christians and the Environment: 'Christians for the Mountains' and the Appalachian Movement against Mountaintop Removal Coal Mining." *Worldviews* 16(1): 1–29. doi: 10.1163/156853511X617786

Botkin, Daniel J. 2012. *The Moon in the Nautilus Shell: Discordant Harmonies Revisited.* New York: Oxford University Press.

Callicott, J. Baird. 1997. *Earth's Insights: A Multicultural Survey of Ecological Ethics from the Mediterranean Basin to the Australian Outback.* Berkeley: University of California Press.

Daneel, Martinus L. 2001. *African Earthkeepers: Holistic Interfaith Mission.* Maryknoll, NY: Orbis.

Denevan, William. 1992. "The Pristine Myth: The Landscape of the Americas in 1492." *Annals of the Association of American Geographers* 82(3): 369–385. doi: 10.1111/j.1467-8306.1992. tb01965.x

Diamond, Jared. 2005. *Collapse: How Societies Choose to Fail or Succeed.* New York: Penguin.

Douglas, Mary. 1975. *Implicit Meanings: Selected Essays in Anthropology.* London: Routledge.

Dudley, Nigel, Liza Higgins-Zogib, and Stephanie Mansourian. 2009. "The Links between Protected Areas, Faiths, and Sacred Natural Sites." *Conservation Biology* 23(3): 568–577. doi: 10.1111/j.1523-1739.2009.01201.x

Dunlap, Thomas. 2004. *Faith in Nature: Environmentalism as Religious Quest.* Seattle: University of Washington Press.

Earth Charter Initiative. 2012. *The Earth Charter.* <http://www.earthcharterinaction.org/content/pages/Read-the-Charter.html>, accessed December 6, 2014.

Engel, J. Ronald. 2005. "Biosphere Reserves and World Heritage Sites." In *Encyclopedia of Religion and Nature*, edited by Bron Taylor. London: Thoemmes Continuum, vol. 1, 192–194.

Evernden, Neil. 1992. *The Social Creation of Nature.* Baltimore, MD: Johns Hopkins University Press.

Foltz, Richard C., Frederick M. Denny, and Azizan Baharuddin, eds. 2003. *Islam and Ecology: A Bestowed Trust.* Cambridge, MA: Harvard University Press.

Gardner, Gary T. 2006. *Inspiring Progress: Religion's Contributions to Sustainable Development.* New York: Norton.

Glacken, Clarence. 1967. *Traces on the Rhodian Shore: Nature and Culture in Western Thought from Ancient Times to the End of the Eighteenth Century.* Berkeley: University of California Press.

Gold, Mick. 1984. "A History of Nature." In *Geography Matters!*, edited by D. Massey and J. Allen. London: Macmillan, 12–32.

Gottlieb, Roger S. 2006a. *A Greener Faith: Religious Environmentalism and Our Planet's Future.* New York: Oxford University Press.

Gottlieb, Roger S. 2006b. *The Oxford Handbook of Religion and Ecology.* Oxford: Oxford University Press.

Grim, John, ed. 2001. *Indigenous Traditions and Ecology: The Interbeing of Cosmology and Community.* Cambridge, MA: Harvard University Press/Harvard University Center for the Study of World Religions.

Harkin, Michael E. and David Rich Lewis, eds. 2007. *Native Americans and the Environment: Perspectives on the Ecological Indian.* Lincoln: University of Nebraska Press.

Harvey, Graham. 1997. *Contemporary Paganism: Listening People, Speaking Earth.* New York: New York University Press.

Heelas, Paul. 1996. *The New Age Movement.* Oxford: Blackwell.

Ivakhiv, Adrian J. 2001. *Claiming Sacred Ground: Pilgrims and Politics at Glastonbury and Sedona.* Bloomington: Indiana University Press.

Ivakhiv, Adrian J. 2002. "Toward a Multicultural Ecology." *Organization and Environment* 15(4): 389–409. doi: 10.1177/1086026602238169

Ivakhiv, Adrian J. 2012. "Religious (Re-)Turns in the Wake of Global Nature: Toward a Cosmopolitics." In *Nature, Science, and Religion: Intersections Shaping Society and the Environment*, edited by Catherine M. Tucker. Santa Fe: School of Advanced Research Press, 213–230.

Ivakhiv, Adrian J. 2013. "Green Pilgrimage: Problems and Prospects for Ecology and Peace-Building." In *Pilgrims and Pilgrimages as Peacemakers in Christianity, Judaism and Islam*, edited by Antón M. Pazos. Farnham: Ashgate, 85–103.

Krech, Shepherd, III. 1999. *The Ecological Indian: Myth and History*. New York: Norton.

Latour, Bruno. 1993. *We Have Never Been Modern*, translated by Catherine Porter. Cambridge, MA: Harvard University Press.

Lee, Cathy and Thomas Schaaf, eds. 2003. *The Importance of Sacred Natural Sites for Biodiversity Conservation*. Paris: United Nations Educational, Social and Cultural Organization.

Letcher, Andy. 2001. "The Scouring of the Shire: Fairies, Trolls, and Pixies in Eco-Protest Culture." *Folklore* 112(2): 147–161. doi: 10.1080/00155870120082209

Livingstone, David N. 1994. "The Historical Roots of Our Ecological Crisis: A Reassessment." *Fides et Historia* 26: 38–55.

Lodge, David M. and Christopher Hamlin, eds. 2006. *Religion and the New Ecology: Environmental Responsibility in a World of Flux*. Notre Dame, IN: University of Notre Dame Press.

Malhotra, Kailash C., Yogesh Ghokale, Sudipto Chatterjee, and Sanjeep Srivastavi. 2001. *Cultural and Ecological Dimensions of Sacred Groves in India*. Bhopal: Indian National Science Academy.

Marler, Penny Long and C. Kirk Hadaway. 2002. "'Being Religious' or 'Being Spiritual' in America: A Zero-Sum Proposition?" *Journal for the Scientific Study of Religion* 41(2): 289–300. doi: 10.1111/1468-5906.00117

Miller, James. 2006. "Daoism and Nature." In *Religion and Ecology*, edited by Roger Gottlieb. New York: Oxford University Press, 220–235.

Minteer, Ben A. and Robert E. Manning. 2005. "An Appraisal of the Critique of Anthropocentrism and Three Lesser Known Themes in Lynn White's 'The Historical Roots of Our Ecologic Crisis." *Organization & Environment* 18(2): 163–176. doi: 10.1177/1086026605276196

Nash, Roderick. 1996. "The Greening of Religion." In *This Sacred Earth: Religion, Nature, Environment*, edited by Roger S. Gottlieb. New York: Routledge, 194–229.

Nutgeren, Albertina. 2005. *Belief, Bounty, and Beauty: Rituals Around Sacred Trees in India*. Amsterdam: Brill.

Posey, Daniel A., ed. 2002. *Cultural and Spiritual Values of Biodiversity*. Reading, UK: UN Environment Programme and Intermediate Technology Publications.

Rappaport, Roy A. 1984. *Pigs for the Ancestors: Ritual in the Ecology of a New Guinea People*. New Haven, CT: Yale University Press. Original edition, 1968.

Redman, Charles. 1999. *Human Impact on Ancient Environments*. Tucson: University of Arizona Press.

Rigby, Kate. 2004. *Topographies of the Sacred: The Poetics of Place in European Romanticism*. Charlottesville: University Press of Virginia.

Ronnow, Tarjei. 2011. *Saving Nature: Religion as Environmentalism, Environmentalism as Religion*. Münster: LIT Verlag.

Roof, Wade Clark. 2000. *Spiritual Marketplace: Baby Boomers and the Remaking of American Religion*. Princeton, NJ: Princeton University Press.

Ross-Bryant, Lynn. 2012. *Pilgrimage to the National Parks: Religion and Nature in the United States*. New York: Routledge.

Schaeffer, Francis. 1970. *Pollution and the Death of Man*. Chicago: Tyndale House.

Sideris, Lisa. 2013. "Science as Sacred Myth? Ecospirituality in the Anthropocene Age." In *Linking Ecology and Ethics for a Changing World: Values, Philosophy, and Action*, edited by Ricardo Rozzi, S. T. A. Pickett, Clare Palmer, Juan J. Armesto, and J. Baird Callicott. New York: Springer, 147–162.

Simmons, J. Aaron. 2009. "Evangelical Environmentalism: Oxymoron or Opportunity?" *Worldviews* 13(1): 40–71. doi: 10.1163/156853508X394508

Snodgrass, Jeffrey and Kristina Tiedje. 2008. "Indigenous Nature Reverence and Conservation: Seven Ways of Transcending an Unnecessary Dichotomy." *Journal for the Study of Religion, Nature and Culture* 2(1): 6–29. doi: 10.1558/jsrnc.v2i1.6

Social Compass. 1990. Special Issue on "Implicit Religion." *Social Compass* 37(4).

Sponsel, Leslie E. 2012. *Spiritual Ecology: A Quiet Revolution*. Santa Barbara, CA: ABC-CLIO.

Szerszynski, Bron. 1997. "Varieties of Ecological Piety." *Worldviews: Global Religions, Culture, and Ecology* 1(1): 37–55. doi: 10.1163/156853597X00209

Szerszynski, Bron. 2002. "Ecological Rites: Ritual Action in Environmental Protest Events." *Theory, Culture & Society* 19(3): 51–69. doi: 10.1177/026327602401081521

Taylor, Bron R. 1995. "Resacralizing Earth: Pagan Environmentalism and the Restoration of Turtle Island." In *American Sacred Space*, edited by David Chidester and Edward T. Linenthal. Bloomington: Indiana University Press, 97–151.

Taylor, Bron R., ed. 2005. *Encyclopedia of Religion and Nature*, 2 vols. London: Thames Continuum.

Taylor, Bron R. 2010. *Dark Green Religion: Nature Spirituality and the Planetary Future*. Berkeley: University of California Press.

The Green Bible. 2008. New York: HarperCollins.

Tuan, Yi-Fu. 1968. "Discrepancies between Environmental Attitude and Behaviour: Examples from Europe and China." *Canadian Geographer* 12(3): 176–191. doi: 10.1111/j.1541-0064.1968.tb00764.x

Tucker, Mary Evelyn and John H. Berthrong, eds. 1998. *Confucianism and Ecology: The Interrelation of Heaven, Earth, and Humans*. Cambridge, MA: Harvard University Press/Harvard University Center for the Study of World Religions.

Vayda, Andrew. 1969. "An Ecological Approach to Cultural Anthropology." *Bucknell Review* 17: 112–119.

Veldman, Robin Globus, Andrew Szasz, and Randolph Haluza-Delay. 2012. "Introduction: Climate Change and Religion—A Review of Existing Research." *Journal for the Study of Religion, Nature and Culture* 6(3): 255–275. doi: 10.1558/jsrnc.v6i3.255

Waskow, Arthur O. 2010. "Eco-Kashrut: Environmental Standards for What and How We Eat." <http://www.myjewishlearning.com/article/eco-kashrut-environmental-standards-for-what-and-how-we-eat/>, accessed February 3, 2016.

Wei-Ming, Tu. 1989. "The Continuity of Being: Chinese Visions of Nature." In *Nature in Asian Traditions of Thought: Essays in Environmental Philosophy*, edited by J. Baird Callicott and Roger T. Ames. Albany: SUNY Press, 67–78.

White, Lynn, Jr. 1967. "The Historical Roots of Our Ecologic Crisis." *Science* 155(3767): 1203–1207. doi: 10.1126/science.155.3767.1203

Whitehead, Alfred North. 1964. *Concept of Nature*. Cambridge: Cambridge University Press. Original edition, 1920.

Williams, Raymond. 1976. *Keywords: A Vocabulary of Culture and Society*. London: Fontana.

Worster, Donald. 2008. *A Passion for Nature: The Life of John Muir*. Oxford: Oxford University Press.

WWF (World Wildlife Fund). 1986. *The Assisi Declarations: Messages on Man and Nature from Buddhism, Christianity, Hinduism, Islam and Judaism*. Gland: WWF International.

FURTHER READING

Albanese 1990 [*A definitive historical overview of 'nature religion' in the American context.*]

Gottlieb 2006b [*Of the many overviews of the topic, this one strikes an admirable balance between comprehensive scope and rigorous depth.*]

Ivakhiv 2001 [*A study of the cultural politics of nature within the context of places sanctified by contemporary earth spirituality.*]

Snodgrass/Tiedje 2008 [*An excellent starting point for understanding recent debates over aboriginality, 'ecological Indians,' and Traditional Ecological Knowledge.*]

Taylor, Bron R. 2005. "Introduction." In *The Encyclopedia of Religion and Nature*, edited by Bron R. Taylor. London: Thoemmes Continuum, vii–xxi. [*A concise summary of the discourses of religion and/with/against nature.*]

Taylor 2010 [*A detailed and provocative study of contemporary nature-based spiritualities.*]

Tucker, Catherine, ed. 2012. *Nature, Science, and Religion: Intersections Shaping Society and the Environment*. Santa Fe: School of Advanced Research Press. [*An insightful collection of empirical (and international) case studies where these three 'trump cards' intersect in interesting and novel ways.*]

White 1967 [*The classic article that elicited great debate and launched the 'greening of religion.'*]

CHAPTER 29

....

POLITICS

....

HUBERT SEIWERT

CHAPTER SUMMARY

- The relationship between religion and politics is a subject of both the study of religion and political science.
- The separation of state and religion or politics and religion reflects a normative idea in modernity, whereas religion and politics are interrelated in empirical and practical terms.
- Religions can provide legitimation and support for the existing political order, or they can oppose and delegitimize it.
- The public sphere is the arena where religion and politics regularly overlap and where their influence on social life is negotiated.
- The sacralization of the state and politics is a recurrent phenomenon in the twentieth century.
- During the past two decades the role of religion in international politics and conflicts has become obvious and accordingly has become a research field of political scientists.

Politics and religion are both concepts whose meaning is disputed. The history of both terms goes back to classical antiquity, with 'politics' deriving from Greek *politikós*, which refers to what concerns the public affairs of the *pólis*, the community of free citizens. Both concepts evolved in early modern Europe to become key concepts for classifying different aspects of social reality. However, just as in the case of 'religion,' the meaning of 'politics' varies depending on philosophical and sociological theories as well as practical concerns (Sellin 2004 [1975]). Hence, both are fuzzy concepts without clear demarcations and definitions but with a reasonable degree of applicability in academic and everyday discourses.

While the problem of defining 'religion' is a recurrent issue in the study of religion, political scientists are much less concerned with the definition of 'politics.' There are two main approaches to understanding the latter. First, the "spatial concept of politics" (Palonen 2011, 1300), sees politics as a sphere of social reality that can be distinguished from other spheres such as economics, science, or religion. The political sphere is then usually understood as the sphere of governments, political parties, and other groups participating in the formation of state policies as well as interstate relations. However, "politics as a sphere has remained both diffuse in its borders and vague in its core" (Palonen 2011, 1300). The second approach conceives of politics as a particular form of social action. Paradigmatic is Weber's understanding of 'politics' as striving for power or for influencing the distribution of power both between states or between social groups within states (Weber 1972 [1922], 822). In this case, the concept of politics can be extended to formations that do not belong to the sphere of states and governments such as the distribution of power in religious communities.

POLITICAL SCIENCE AND
THE STUDY OF RELIGION

Ecclesiastical politics and internal power relations of religious communities are, of course, not what comes first to mind when one thinks of politics and religion in the early twenty-first century. Contemporary interest in the subject has been mainly fueled by historical events and developments during the past decades that were perceived as a growing influence of religious factors on international relations and domestic politics. Key events have been the Iranian revolution of 1979 and the terrorist attacks of September 11, 2001. At the same time such developments as the rise of the Christian Right in the United States, the resurgence of religion in some former communist states in Europe and China, and the political involvement of religions in other countries such as India and Sri Lanka made it obvious that it is not just the Islamic world and less developed countries where religion and politics influence each other. Thus, by the beginning of the twenty-first century, religion as a political factor had been rediscovered by political scientists as a field of research after many decades of neglect (Wald/Wilcox 2006).

Still, religion is only slowly entering the mainstream of political science, and it is difficult to integrate it with available theories of politics (Bellin 2008). Like most social scientists, political scientists assumed that religion could be largely ignored in the analysis of modern societies because secularization would continuously reduce its role in public life. Religion accordingly is not one of the variables usually considered for explaining political processes and structures. Wuthnow (1991) was a prominent early voice to the contrary, questioning conventional theories and called for greater attention to the cultural dimensions of politics, which would allow for a better understanding of religious influences.

In the study of religion, politics has traditionally been treated from a historical and comparative perspective, focusing more on past societies than on modern developments (e.g. Stackhouse 1987). However, scholars of religion were more inclined than political scientists to study the political role of religions in contemporary societies as well (Bechert 1967–1973; Benavides/Daly 1989; Smith 1978). Given the tradition of historical and comparative studies as well as theoretical reflection on the concept of religion, the relation between religion and politics can be put in more complex theoretical contexts (Urban 2005). On the other hand, the study of religion is less occupied with the analysis of current political developments than with the influence of religions on political cultures.

The Paradigm: Separation of Religion and State

To distinguish religion and politics as two separate spheres of social activity might appear natural in everyday discourse; however, the distinction is based on classifications that developed in Western Europe largely as a product of the Enlightenment and the formation of new theories of the state. The emergence of the modern state can be described as a process of secularization in which the state was increasingly conceived of as being independent from religious authority and legitimation (Böckenförde 1992 [1967]). From a Western perspective, the modern state is a secular state and, since the state represents the core institution of the political sphere, politics and religion appear to be two separate domains. The separation between state and religion can therefore be taken as the paradigm from which the idea of institutional and functional differentiation of religion and politics is derived.

This idea, however, reflects more a normative understanding of religion and politics than a description of the real situation. We just have to turn to states not classified as 'Western democracies' to see that the separation of religion and state is far from universal in modern times. Religion and state are closely connected not only in many Muslim countries, such as Saudi Arabia, Iran, or Pakistan: according to Barro and McCleary's calculations (2005, 1339) about one third of all countries in the world had a state religion at the end of the twentieth century, most of them Christian (Catholic, Protestant, and Orthodox). Furthermore, there is hardly any state in which the government is not involved in religion either by supporting, regulating, or repressing religious life in some way. Only in the United States does there appear to be a total separation between religion and state, according to the parameters used by Fox (Fox 2006; 2008; Fox/Sandler 2005). But even though the US government may rarely interfere in religion, it cannot be denied that religious actors do interfere in politics and religion is a political issue.

The 'spatial' concept of politics, which takes politics and religion as two separate spheres or fields of human activity, does not adequately grasp the complexity of social formations and human interactions. Rather than referring to different forms of social actions and institutions, religion and politics refer to different aspects of them. Take for example the American Declaration of Independence, whose formulation certainly can be classified as a political act that laid the foundation for an independent state. Yet, this political act is introduced with a religious argument: "We hold these truths to be self-evident, that all men are created equal, that they are endowed by their Creator with certain unalienable Rights, that among these are Life, Liberty and the pursuit of Happiness" (US National Archives & Records Administration 2013 [1776]). Thus, the legitimation of fundamental political rights is based on a religious belief.

This does not make the American state a religious institution, but it shows that the political and the religious do not exclude each other but can be different aspects of the same thing. When talking about politics and religion, it is convenient to focus on states and governments, on the one hand, and institutionalized religions, on the other. But there are many constellations where states have religious dimensions and religions political ones.

POWER AND RULERSHIP

The modern state is the political institution par excellence. In the present context, the question can be left open whether earlier forms of political rule can be classified as 'states', but there is no doubt that in historical times there have been many social formations that share the minimal requirements specified by Weber: "The state, like its historical precursors, is a system of domination based on the legitimate (which means: regarded as legitimate) exercise of power" (Weber 1972 [1922], 822).[1] In Weber's explication the intimate connection between state and politics appears in the concept of power, as for him "doing politics is striving for power" (822). Since the state and comparable forms of political rule imply that humans dominate others, they are based on social inequality. Whatever the constitution of a state may be, the rulers dominate the ruled.

Legitimation

In the last resort, the power of the state rests on the exercise of or the threat to exercise physical force. Although the use of brute force to secure or acquire power is common in interstate and civil wars, power structures are less volatile if they are accepted by those over whom power is exercised. If the ruled recognize the right of the ruling individual, groups, or institutions to demand obedience, rulership is regarded as legitimate and power is based on authority (Ponton/Gill/Bretherton 1993, 26–27). It is at this point where religion comes into play, because the legitimation of power has historically often taken religious forms. In many ancient and traditional societies the authority of the

---

[1] All translations from German and French are by the author.

rulers was grounded on their special relationship with the gods, be it by genealogy (the Japanese Tenno) or heavenly mandate (the Chinese emperor), by considering them to be a god or godlike (the Egyptian pharaoh and Roman emperors), or ruling by the grace of God (the Queen of England) (Brisch 2008; Erkens 2002). It is, however, not only the power of rulership that demands legitimation but the whole power structure of a state or society, which includes the uneven distribution of privileges and material resources. Bourdieu argues that it is a central function of religion to "absolutize the relative" and to "legitimate the arbitrary" (1971, 310), which means obscuring the arbitrariness of a given social and political order by consecrating or sacralizing it.

There are two caveats to Bourdieu's view. The first concerns the question of whether religion can be said to have particular functions. A theory of religion and politics would be misleading if it considered legitimation the political 'function' of religion, because this suggests a uniform relationship between religion and politics. A functionalist approach ignores that religion may have different effects, with the legitimation of political order being just one of them. The opposite effect is delegitimation, as in cases where the existing social and political conditions contradict the ideals maintained by the adherents of a religion. The existing political order can be seen as being based on injustice and therefore doomed to destruction. This is common in millenarian and messianic movements hoping for the advent of a savior to usher in a new and perfect time (Arjomand 1993b; Seiwert 2014).

The second caveat touches on the distinction between religious and secular legitimation. The problem of legitimation exists for any system of political rule and it always demands solutions, for example by explaining the arbitrary by offering reasons why things are as they are, although they could be different. The arbitrary is—to use Bourdieu's expression—the relative, and any legitimation of the relative requires its de-relativization. Relativism is a hazardous attitude if it comes to the legitimation of political order. To admit that the foundations of democracy such as individual freedom and human rights are relative values that depend on social preferences and historical coincidence runs the risk of making them appear disposable. To justify them as being not negotiable demands transforming them from relative to absolute values. There is therefore a tendency to sacralize fundamental values of the political constitution even if no recourse is made to particular religious beliefs. The French *Declaration of the Rights of Man and of the Citizen* of 1789—a foundational document of the modern secular political order—declares human rights to be "natural, inalienable and sacred" (Conseil Constitutionnel 2014 [1789], preamble). Both 'sacredness' and 'naturalness' legitimate the arbitrary by grounding it in a normative order that transcends the realm of human disposability. This need not be considered a religious legitimation, as some scholars argue (Spickard 1999), but it certainly is a form of absolutization of the relative. Because any form of legitimation demands rhetorical arguments and explanations, it is embedded in narratives providing the background against which the explanations appear as persuasive. As Margaret Canovan (1990) has shown, even in the case of secular liberal constitutions such legitimizing narratives often take the forms of myths—a literary genre common in religious contexts.

Laws and Rules

The ultimate legitimation of power and political order is a theoretical problem that occupies political philosophers but has little bearing on practical politics. Even if the legitimacy of political rule is based on religious explanations, the exercise of power and the art of government are worldly affairs. Ruling means setting rules to be followed by subordinates. In modern states, legislation is the most important means of implementing political objectives.

As the relationship between religion and law is treated elsewhere (see Schonthal, "Law," this volume), it suffices to point to differences and possible tensions between religious and state law. In modern democratic states the validity of laws depends on the observance of legal procedures, which makes legislation an autonomous act of the legitimate political authorities. In autocratic states legislation is usually less transparent. In both cases, however, the binding force of state law is based on political power, which makes it to a certain extent arbitrary. State law can be changed; it depends on human decisions and on the idea that humans are autonomous in setting the rules that regulate social life. In this sense, state law is secular law and the state is a secular order.

By contrast, religious law is understood as not depending on human decisions but as being grounded in some form of absolute authority that restricts human autonomy. It therefore cannot be abrogated but only interpreted. In the context of politics, religious law has to be mentioned because there might be conflicts between the demands of state law and religious obligations. Historical examples are the refusal of Christians to participate in the imperial cult of Rome or the question whether Buddhist monks were obliged to bow down before the Chinese emperor (Zürcher 1972 [1959], 160–163). A modern parallel in the United States would be Jehovah's Witnesses' refusal to salute the flag and pledge allegiance (Manwaring 1962).

THE POWER OF THE STATE
AND RELIGIOUS POWER

Conflicts between the demands of the state and religious obligations are political conflicts insofar as their outcome depends on power. At first sight, the power of the state being backed by the use of physical force seems to be stronger than the power of religions. Stalin's famous question: "The Pope? How many divisions has he got?" (Churchill 1948, 135) reflects this view. But things are not as simple as that. Religions may develop sufficient political power to change even the constitution of states. In late antiquity the Christian institutions proved to be more powerful than the defenders of the pagan state and its religious legitimation (Barceló 2013; Hahn 2011). And the medieval conflict between *sacerdotium* and *regnum*, the Roman pope and the Roman emperor (Blumenthal 1988), is as much a historical paradigm for the political power of religious institutions as it is an illustration of the fact that the institutional differentiation of religion and state does not per se imply a separation of religion and politics.

What is the base of religious power? As power is not free-floating but always bound to some actor who wields it, religious power is usually attributed to persons or institutions that are deemed 'religious.' Chaves (1994) uses the term 'religious authority' for institutions that may exercise power. For him, the power of religious authorities—if they have any—is the same as that of any other institution. In 'modern' societies, religion is seen as just one of many other "mundane institutional sphere[s]" (1994, 751), which would exclude the possibility of a specific 'religious power' and reduce it to the political power of religious institutions.

Dialectics of Politics and Religion

Because in modern states political power is concentrated in state institutions, politics consists mainly in getting control of or influencing these. Religious actors can be involved in politics in an attempt to gain influence over legislation and political decisions. Representatives of the main religions usually maintain relations with the politically powerful and are in some way or another concerned with politics, and not only in countries with state religions. In the United Kingdom, twenty-six archbishops and bishops of the Church of England are as 'members spiritual' of the House of Lords directly involved in legislation. To be sure, the influence of religious representatives on political decisions may vary considerably in different countries, but so does the influence of other political actors such as parties and parliaments.

Arguably, the political influence of religious authorities depends on the same factors as the influence of 'mundane' institutions, which include networks of personal and institutional relations, economic resources, lobbying, and public relations. Although these factors must not be ignored, the relationship between religion and politics is more complex than the relations between religious and state institutions. Political power ultimately relies on the use of force, but to sustain its legitimacy it needs public support. If public support is lost, even autocratic governments may lose power. The Iranian revolution of 1979 happened despite the means of repressive violence available to the regime of the Shah, and it could not have been realized without the mobilization of large parts of the lower-class population. The Shi'ite clerics with their mosque networks were able to mobilize the poorer social groups using religious rhetoric invoking the Karbala paradigm of martyrdom in the battle against an unjust ruler (Kippenberg 2005, 64–82; Martin 2003, 149–150). The leading figure, however, was Ayatollah Khomeini, whose charisma proved to be more powerful than the secular power of the Shah. Although charisma is not confined to the field of religion—being also a potential source of political authority (Weber 1972 [1922], 654–661)—it is obvious that in Khomeini's case it could only emerge in a social environment that was permeated by the religious tradition of Shi'ism. As the Iranian revolution was a political event resulting in a constitutional change, from a political science point of view religion appears as belonging to the cultural environment affecting political processes. If a study of religion perspective is adopted, however, politics is part of the environment of religion. The political events had significant repercussions on the further development not only of Shi'ite institutions and law (Arjomand 1993a, 233–235) but also of Islamic movements worldwide.

The dialectical relationship between religious and political perspectives can also be illustrated with the example of the Christian Right in the United States. Obviously, the constitutional and religious differences between US and Iranian societies are enormous. The constitutional separation between state and religion in the United States seems to prevent any intermingling of religion and politics. Yet since the 1970s a strong alliance has developed between conservative politicians of the Republican Party and evangelical Christian movements labeled the 'Christian (or Religious) Right.' A major part of the Christian Right was represented by the Southern Baptist Convention (SBC), the country's largest Protestant denomination. Internal power struggles led to a takeover by a more conservative leadership that was closely connected with Republican politicians, who were striving to build a 'moral majority' as a counterweight to the Democratic Party and liberal ideologies. The blending of religious and party politics not only resulted in the emergence of the Religious Right as a political pressure group with considerable influence in the Republican Party; it also engendered a shift in the dominant theological orientation of the SBC. Most significant was the change from a pacifist tradition to the fierce support of American military intervention. During the Vietnam War the SBC had issued several resolutions condemning participation in the conflict (Mergenschroer-Livingston 2009). However, in 2002 leaders of the SBC defended and demanded a pre-emptive military strike on Iraq with theological arguments, while the leaders of most other denominations opposed the war (Marsden 2009, 79–80).

The two examples from Iran and the United States illustrate the difficulty of separating religion and politics. It depends largely on the perspective whether the rise of the Christian Right and the Iranian revolution are considered religious or political processes. In both cases politics and religion influenced each other. Such a dialectical relationship seems to be the normal case, even if the degree and forms of interaction vary considerably. Religions do play a role in politics for the simple reason that state power cannot exist without citizens or subjects, many of which as a rule have some form of religion.

However, the role that religions play in politics is not always as obvious as in the cases just mentioned. They often appear to play a passive rather than an active role. Such is the case when states or governments attempt to control the influence of religion in public life. Policies to regulate religion and to submit it to state control can take different forms ranging from granting privileges to persecution. Particularly religious minorities are often subjected to various forms of discrimination by state authorities including Western democracies (Richardson 2004; Seiwert 2015). In countries with atheist state ideologies, such as the People's Republic of China and the Soviet Union, all religious activities are usually discouraged and under close supervision and control of the state (Conquest 1968; Theodorowitsch 1970).

The religious policy of the Chinese Communist government after 1949 illustrates that even in a state with atheist ideology religion may be a major political concern. Realizing the influence religions have on large parts of the population, the Communist Party and government have adopted various policies to restrict them during the past sixty-five years. Shortly after the founding of the People's Republic severe measures were taken to destroy the material base of temples and monasteries and to exterminate popular religious societies (Goossaert/Palmer 2011, 146–165; Welch 1972, 42–83). The suppression and persecution of religions reached their climax during the Cultural Revolution (1966–1976) when most religious sites were destroyed and all religious activities outlawed. Whereas these measures then seemed to be successful in eradicating religion in mainland China, it turned out to be only a temporary victory. To win popular support for its policy of economic reform and development, the government had to lessen restrictions, which resulted in an unexpected revival of traditional religions including Christianity and Islam. Although religious believers and institutions seem to play only a passive role in these political processes, they are in fact actively negotiating their position in society, particularly on the local level (Ashiwa/Wank 2009; Yang 2012). Furthermore, some religions such as Tibetan Buddhism, Islam, the underground varieties of Protestantism and Catholicism, as well as various traditional and new religious formations not belonging to the officially recognized religions represent a serious political challenge for the government because they resist all attempts to submit them to state control.

RELIGION IN THE PUBLIC SPHERE

Because religion, the state, and politics are all products of human activity, they necessarily meet at the level of individual and collective convictions, values, and forms of life. In democratic states the competition of political parties to gain the support of voters urges them to pay attention to value orientations that may be influenced by religious socialization or belonging. In many European countries with significant Catholic populations, Christian Democratic parties have been or still are major political forces (Kalyvas 1996; Van Hecke/Gerhart 2004). Although the extent to which their policies today depend on official church teachings is arguably limited in most cases, they correspond to the more conservative values prevailing in Catholic milieus. Statistical correspondence between certain religious and political orientations manifests in voting behavior and can also be found in the United States and Canada (Ang/Petrocik 2012). The degree to which religion is a causative factor in political orientations is methodologically difficult to assess because many other factors come into play.

Petrocik (1998) has argued that, in the United States, the Republican Party has acquired a support profile that is highly similar to Christian Democratic parties in Europe. Although its supporters are mainly white Protestants, he observes a tendency to form coalitions with other religiously oriented voters. However, a major difference from Christian Democratic parties in Europe is American opposition to social welfare issues. It is tempting to explain this difference by the influence of Catholic social teachings on European Christian Democracy. Although this influence is less direct than may be supposed at first sight (Leitner 2003), Manow has convincingly argued that religious traditions are in fact important variables in the development of different approaches to the welfare state. According to his findings, differences exist not only between Catholic and Protestant traditions but also within the latter. Countries with Lutheran majorities appear to be much more supportive of state intervention to secure social welfare than are countries with strong Calvinist and free-church traditions (Manow 2002).

From a wider perspective, this issue touches on the demarcation of religion and politics. It is questionable whether and to what extent caring for the poor, sick, homeless, or otherwise disadvantaged is the obligation of the state. Is charity a political or a religious issue? Different answers to this question seem to be responsible for different concepts of the state and for the extent to which the state is expected to interfere in social and individual life. The significant differences existing in this respect between the United States and most European countries are possibly connected with the latent influence of diverse religious traditions.

Privatization Thesis

One widely shared interpretation of modern religion is the privatization thesis, which holds that religions are considered the private affair of individuals who are free to choose a religion or not. Privatization is one aspect of the separation of state and religion and in this context can also be seen as an aspect of secularization. This may be true as far as individual religious freedom is concerned, but it ignores the fact that religion plays a role in public as well as private life.

The public presence of religion has two aspects: the use of religious symbols and arguments in public discourses; and the public activities of religious organizations or organizations connected with religious institutions. Both aspects must be considered separately and neither depends directly on the influence of religious authorities.

Casanova (1994) was probably the first to doubt the connection between the secularization of the state and the privatization of religion. His thesis of the de-privatization of religion was mainly based on the observation that the Catholic Church significantly contributed to political discourses and developments in such countries as Poland and Spain after World War II. Yet the use of religious symbols and arguments in public and political discourses does not need to be backed by clerical institutions or sophisticated theology. Chidester (1988) has shown that religious symbols have been central from the beginning in American political discourses and are used not only in the context of particular religious denominations but also in the formally secular context of what Bellah (1967) has called 'American civil religion.'

Paradoxically, in Western Europe, where the institutional separation between state and religion is usually stressed less emphatically than in the United States, religious rhetoric in politics is rare. The public presence of religion is, however, visible in the activities of organizations connected with religious institutions. Thus, for instance, in Germany the Catholic and Protestant churches with their welfare organizations, hospitals, kindergartens, and other enterprises are—taken together—the second largest employers after the state (Köllen 2011). Their welfare activities are an indispensable element of the public sector and are overwhelmingly financed by taxpayers. The institutional and economic strength of the churches gives them political influence that cannot be measured by such standards as church attendance, declared belief in God, or other parameters usually taken to quantify the social influence of religion. Nor is there a direct correlation with the acceptance of religious authority.

Religious rhetoric in public discourses and the involvement of religious organizations in public projects show that the privatization of religious belief does not necessarily amount to the restriction of religion to the private sphere. Nevertheless, it remains an open question whether and when the public sphere is part of politics. The Social Gospel movement in North America, which originated in the late nineteenth century, can be seen as primarily a religious movement engaging in charitable work and advocating social reform (White/Hopkins 1976), but social reform at the same time is a highly political issue. It concerns ideas and ideals of how society and social relations should be, and such issues are politically controversial. On the other hand, they touch on value orientations, anthropological and sociological views that might be deeply rooted in religious convictions. Such religious convictions are privately maintained, but if they motivate social activism they become political factors.

Religion and Democracy

For some social scientists and philosophers the involvement of religion in politics poses a theoretical problem because it apparently stands in tension with the secular constitution of modern democratic states. Casanova argued that the de-privatization of religion can only be 'justified' under certain conditions: "from the normative perspective of modernity, religion may enter the public sphere and assume a public form only if it accepts the inviolable right to privacy and the sanctity of the principle of freedom of conscience" (1994, 57). This is a normative perspective that reflects the high esteem for secular political values in words ('inviolable rights,' 'sanctity') reminiscent of the French *Declaration of the Rights of Man and the Citizen* (Conseil Constitutionnel 2014 [1789], preamble). The implication is that there might be contradictions between religious ideas about the constitution of state and society and the achievements of modern democratic constitutions. In this case, religion would be a threat to the secular state that has to be contained. The matter is, of course, not a purely academic one.

Jürgen Habermas—who in recognition of the public presence of religions coined the term 'post-secular society'—refers particularly to Islam in his reflections on the participation of religions in political processes. Like Casanova he demands that religions accept the secular legitimation of the state and integrate its normative premises in their belief systems. While he advocates the right of religious citizens to articulate their beliefs and political views publicly, he insists at the same time that they have to be 'translated' into secular arguments if they are to enter the political agenda of state institutions (Habermas 2008, 44–45).

As politics is about power and legitimacy, normative points of view easily come into play. The desire to 'tame' the political impact of religions by demanding their submission to the non-negotiable values of the secular constitution is a fundamental political issue because it is about the legitimacy of power. Talal Asad has criticized this as a secularist position that aims at excluding religion from politics and power because religion is not allowed to "enter political debates *on its own terms*" (2003, 185, italics in original). By forcing religion to submit to the rules of secular political discourses, religious actors are in fact just one voice among many other secular participants, and religious authority— whether transcendental or institutional—is deprived of its specific power, which rests upon other than secular arguments.

Asad's argument targets the normative assumptions underlying the privatization thesis and the conditions made for allowing 'de-privatized' religion to enter political discourses in a 'post-secular' society. Although such theoretical considerations may have some practical impact on policies to defend the secular order of democratic states against the perceived or real threat of religiously motivated political activism, they perhaps overestimate the role of discourses in politics. In democracies, the way to win political power is to convince a majority of voters, and if voters like religious arguments politicians will tend to use them. This might explain why religious rhetoric is more common in US politics than in European countries.

When possible conflicts between religion and democracy are discussed, it is usually Islam that is implicitly or explicitly referred to. Political scientists do not agree as to whether or not the lack of democracy in most Muslim-dominated countries is due to an inherent incompatibility of Islamic law traditions and democratic governance. It is obvious that democracy is strongest in countries with a Western Christian tradition but weak in those with a Muslim majority, but it remains unclear whether there is any causal relationship (Anderson 2009, 202).

To highlight the theoretical problems, it is useful to consider the relationship between Christianity and democracy. The support of democratic government by Christian churches is historically a fairly new development. Neither the Roman popes and Orthodox patriarchs nor Luther and Calvin were democrats. There is certainly no inherent tendency for democracy in the Christian tradition. On the other hand, Christianity proved to be compatible with democratic developments, although history shows that it is equally compatible with authoritarian, racist, and undemocratic regimes (Freston 2009, 32–33). This is not to deny that religious institutions and believers often play a significant role in political developments. But religions traditions such as Buddhism, Christianity, Islam, or Hinduism are much too complex, diversified, and adaptive to changing cultural and political environments to allow for generalizations about their compatibility with particular forms of political organization.

POLITICAL RELIGIONS AND IDEOLOGIES

While the majority of recent scholarship on religion and politics concentrates on the political implications of traditional religions, some authors take a different approach by considering the religious dimension of politics. As early as 1926 Hayes (2014) observed that nationalism shares many features with religion. In 1938, Voegelin (1996) coined the term 'political religions,' which gained some currency in the study of totalitarian ideologies such as fascism and communism (Bärsch 2005; Maier 2007; Riegel 2005). The common denominator of such analyses is the 'sacralization of politics' (Gentile 2000), which goes hand in hand with the adoption of many elements typically connected with religions including rituals, myths, promises of salvation, and collective emotions. Goossaert and Palmer (2011, 167–198) have presented an intriguing analysis of the sacralization of the state and 'political religiosity' in twentieth-century China, which suggests that outwardly secular regimes, despite their rejection of traditional religions, might have spiritual and moral dimensions that have more affinities with religious beliefs than they are ready to admit.

There are some theoretical problems with the concept of political religions. One is negative connotations due to the concept's association with totalitarian regimes. Furthermore, many authors who dealt with the religious dimension of political ideologies considered them a distortion of 'true' religion and in particular a challenge to Christianity (Koenker 1965). A more serious theoretical objection is the fact that political ideologies are usually seen as 'secular' ideologies since they do not refer to God or gods and are not directly connected with traditional religions. The idea of 'secular religions' seems to be a contradiction in terms. The problem involves the definition of 'religion' and the distinction between religious and secular (see Stausberg/Gardiner, "Definition," this volume). Suffice it to note here that approaches calling attention to the religious dimensions of 'secular' political ideologies usually subscribe to a Durkheimian understanding of religion, which does not refer to supernatural agents but to the sacred (*sacré*). In this context the sacralization of secular values such as the nation can be interpreted as religious.

Less controversial than 'political' or 'secular religion' is the term 'civil religion,' which goes back to Rousseau (2014 [1762], 109–117). For Rousseau, *la religion civile* was a political program to secure the integration of the state and the loyalty of its citizens by replacing 'superstitious' religions, i.e. Christianity. Bellah (1967; Hase 2001) avoided Rousseau's critique of traditional religions and analyzed American civil religion as the shared beliefs, myths, and rituals that integrate the nation despite the plurality of existing religions and without replacing them.

Empirically, the relationships between political ideologies and traditional religions are multifarious and preclude generalizations. The problem is similar to the compatibility of particular religions with democracy. Many scholars have pointed to the fact that the fascist regimes in Italy and Spain as well as most authoritarian governments in Latin America have been backed by the Catholic Church (Anderson 2009, 195; Bruce

2003, 95–111). In Nazi Germany, a majority of Protestant churches enthusiastically supported the regime and its racist ideology, culminating in the movement of the *Deutsche Christen* ('German Christians') that attempted to purify German Protestantism of all Jewish elements and traces (Arnhold 2010a; 2010b). There are many more examples of the merging of political and religious ideologies including evangelical Protestantism in the United States (Brouwer/Gifford/Rose 1996, 13–46), Hinduism in India (Jaffrelot 1996), Buddhism in Sri Lanka (Tambiah 1992), and Shinto in Japan (Kleine 2002). Although there are many differences in detail, it must be concluded that all major religious traditions can under certain circumstances be used to promote or support political ideologies.

Religion in International Politics

The merging of political and religious movements and ensuing political activism underpinned by religious symbols and identities attracted growing attention after the Iranian revolution of 1979. As long as social movements combining religion and politics appeared as internal developments mainly in Third World countries, they could be interpreted as reactions against modernity contravening the general process of modernization. Commonly labeled 'fundamentalisms', they were studied as religious movements (Marty/Appleby 1991; Riesebrodt 1998). At the same time, the implications of religious nationalism and politicized religion for international conflicts were observed (Juergensmeyer 1993). Huntington's theses on the remaking of the world order based on civilizations (1993; 1996) brought religion into the field of vision of international relations theory, although they were discussed controversially (Fox/Sandler 2007, 115–135; Müller 2003).

The terrorist attacks of September 11, 2001, their connection with the international Islamist network Al Qaeda, and the following wars in Afghanistan and Iraq unexpectedly forced scholars of international relations to abandon their former reluctance to include religion in their analyses (Philpott 2002). It is above all the terrorism and militancy of some extremist Islamic groups and their attempt not only to destabilize states and interstate relations in the Near East and Africa but also to build international networks by mobilizing supporters all over the world that have provoked an ever increasing number of publications on religion in international politics during the past decade. At the same time it became obvious that traditional theories of international relations have difficulties in accounting for religious factors (Toft 2012). Political actors motivated by religious convictions and values often do not seem to act rationally in the sense expected by political theorists. They may be prepared to sacrifice their own life and disregard mundane values such as security or economic benefits in order to reach goals that are not included in models of political rationality. Furthermore, militant international networks based on religious identities and challenging the political order both domestically and internationally are political actors that are not consistent with the post-Westphalian understanding of international relations, which concentrates on sovereign states as the agents of international politics (Miles 2004).

There is no shortage of empirical evidence for religions having multiple influences on international politics (Fox 2008). One may consider the role of religious institutions such as the Catholic Church and its global networks (Hertzke 2009), religious non-governmental organizations (Lehmann 2013), the connection of religious identities with nationalisms in many post-socialist countries in Europe (Schulze Wessel 2006), or the religious reframing of international conflicts in the Near East (Kippenberg 2007). After having been long neglected, religion has vigorously surfaced in global politics and some therefore believe we have entered 'God's century' (Toft/ Philpott/Shah 2011).

Glossary

Ideology in a broad sense, 'ideology' can refer to any publicly propagated system of ideas and values. More specifically, it is applied to systems of ideas and values that form the basis of political theories and legitimate political actions.

Legitimation the act of explaining things as conforming to recognized principles and in this way justifying their existence.

Politics in a narrow sense 'politics' refers to activities relating to influencing the policies of state governments or getting control over them. In a broader sense 'politics' can refer to all activities of striving for power or for influencing the distribution of power either between states or between social groups within states.

Power in the social sciences, 'power' refers to the ability to control and influence other people even contrary to their will.

Sacralization explaining and treating certain ideas, things, or persons as being sacred, i.e. of ultimate value and therefore inviolable. Sacralization is used in religious contexts, where the 'sacred' is often equated with the 'holy,' but it can refer to contexts not deemed religious such as the sacralization of the nation.

State a political organization of people occupying a definite territory, claiming legal sovereignty and the legitimate use of force.

References

Anderson, John. 2009. "Does God Matter, and If So Whose God? Religion and Democratisation." In *Routledge Handbook of Religion and Politics*, edited by Jeffrey Haynes. London: Routledge, 192–210.

Ang, Adrian and John R. Petrocik. 2012. "Religion, Religiosity, and the Moral Divide in Canadian Politics." *Politics and Religion* 5(1): 103–132.

Arjomand, Saïd Amir. 1993a. "Millennial Beliefs, Hierocratic Authority, and Revolution in Shi'ite Iran." In *The Political Dimensions of Religion*, edited by Saïd Amir Arjomand. Albany, NY: SUNY Press, 219–239.

Arjomand, Saïd Amir. 1993b. "Religion and the Diversity of Normative Orders." In *The Political Dimensions of Religion*, edited by Saïd Amir Arjomand. Albany, NY: SUNY Press, 42–68.

Arnhold, Oliver. 2010a. '*Entjudung'—Kirche im Abgrund: Die Thüringer Kirchenbewegung Deutsche Christen 1928–1939*. Berlin: Institut Kirche und Judentum.

Arnhold, Oliver. 2010b. '*Entjudung'—Kirche im Abgrund: Das 'Institut zur Erforschung und Beseitigung des jüdischen Einflusses auf das deutsche kirchliche Leben' 1939–1945*. Berlin: Institut Kirche und Judentum.

Asad, Talal. 2003. *Formations of the Secular: Christianity, Islam, Modernity*. Stanford, CA: Stanford University Press.

Ashiwa, Yoshiko and David L. Wank, eds. 2009. *Making Religion, Making the State: The Politics of Religion in Modern China*. Stanford, CA: Stanford University Press.

Barceló, Pedro. 2013. *Das Römische Reich im religiösen Wandel der Spätantike. Kaiser und Bischöfe im Widerstreit*. Regensburg: Verlag Friedrich Pustet.

Barro, Robert J. and Rachel M. McCleary. 2005. "Which Countries Have State Religions?" *Quarterly Journal of Economics* 120(4): 1331–1370. doi: 10.1162/003355305775097515

Bärsch, Claus-Ekkehard. 2005. "Der Nationalsozialismus als 'politische Religion' und die 'Volksgemeinschaft.'" In *Politische Religionen und Religionspolitik: Zwischen Totalitarismus und Religionsfreiheit*, edited by Gerhard Besier and Hermann Lübbe. Göttingen: Vandenhoeck & Ruprecht, 49–78.

Bechert, Heinz. 1967–1973. *Buddhismus, Staat und Gesellschaft in den Ländern des Theravāda-Buddhismus*. 3 vols. Göttingen: Seminar f. Indologie und Buddhismuskunde der Univ. Göttingen.

Bellah, Robert N. 1967. "Civil Religion in America." *Daedalus* 96(1): 1–27.

Bellin, Eva. 2008. "Faith in Politics: New Trends in the Study of Religion and Politics." *World Politics* 60(2): 315–347. doi: 10.1353/wp.0.0007

Benavides, Gustavo and M. W. Daly, eds. 1989. *Religion and Political Power*. Albany: SUNY Press.

Blumenthal, Uta-Renate. 1988. *The Investiture Controversy: Church and Monarchy from the Ninth to the Twelfth Century*. Philadelphia: University of Pennsylvania Press.

Böckenförde, Ernst-Wolfgang. 1992. "Die Entstehung des Staates als Vorgang der Säkularisation." In *Recht, Staat, Freiheit: Studien zur Rechtsphilosophie, Staatstheorie und Verfassungsgeschichte*, 2nd edition. Frankfurt am Main: Suhrkamp, 92–114.

Bourdieu, Pierre. 1971. "Genèse et structure du champ religieux." *Revue Française de Sociologie* 12(3): 295–334.

Brisch, Nicole, ed. 2008. *Religion and Power: Divine Kingship in the Ancient World and Beyond*. Chicago, IL: Oriental Institute of the University of Chicago.

Brouwer, Steve, Paul Gifford, and Susan D. Rose. 1996. *Exporting the American Gospel: Global Christian Fundamentalism*. New York: Routledge.

Bruce, Steve. 2003. *Politics and Religion*. Cambridge: Polity Press.

Canovan, Margaret. 1990. "On Being Economical with the Truth: Some Liberal Reflections." *Political Studies* 38(1): 5–19.

Casanova, José. 1994. *Public Religions and the Modern World*. Chicago, IL: University of Chicago Press.

Chaves, Mark. 1994. "Secularization as Declining Religious Authority." *Social Forces* 72(3): 749–774.

Chidester, David. 1988. *Patterns of Power: Religion and Politics in American Culture*. Englewood Cliffs, NJ: Prentice-Hall.

Churchill, Winston. 1948. *The Second World War*. Vol. 1: *The Gathering Storm*. Boston, MA: Houghton Mifflin.

Conquest, Robert, ed. 1968. *Religion in the USSR*. London: Bodley Head.

Conseil Constitutionnel. 2014 [1789]. 'Déclaration des Droits de l'Homme et du Citoyen de 1789.' <http://www.conseil-constitutionnel.fr/conseil-constitutionnel/root/bank/print/5076.htm>, accessed April 13, 2014.

Erkens, Franz-Reiner, ed. 2002. *Die Sakralität von Herrschaft: Herrschaftslegitimierung im Wechsel der Zeiten und Räume*. Berlin: Akademie Verlag.

Fox, Jonathan. 2006. "World Separation of Religion and State into the 21st Century." *Comparative Political Studies* 39(5): 537–569. doi 10.1177/0010414005276310

Fox, Jonathan. 2008. *A World Survey of Religion and the State*. Cambridge: Cambridge University Press.

Fox, Jonathan and Shmuel Sandler. 2005. "Separation of Religion and State in the Twenty-First Century: Comparing the Middle East and Western Democracies." *Comparative Politics* 37(3): 317–335. doi: 10.2307/20072892

Fox, Jonathan and Shmuel Sandler. 2007. *Bringing Religion into International Relations*. Basingstoke: Palgrave Macmillan.

Freston, Paul. 2009. "Christianity: Protestantism." In *Routledge Handbook of Religion and Politics*, edited by Jeffrey Haynes. London: Routledge, 26–47.

Gentile, Emilio. 2000. "The Sacralisation of Politics: Definitions, Interpretations and Reflections on the Question of Secular Religion and Totalitarianism." Translated by Robert Mallett. *Totalitarian Movements & Political Religions* 1(1): 18–55. doi: 10.1080/14690760008406923

Goossaert, Vincent and David A. Palmer. 2011. *The Religious Question in Modern China*. Chicago, IL and London: University of Chicago Press.

Habermas, Jürgen. 2008. "Die Dialektik der Säkularisierung." *Blätter für deutsche und internationale Politik* 4: 33–46.

Hahn, Johannes, ed. 2011. *Spätantiker Staat und religiöser Konflikt: Imperiale und lokale Verwaltung und die Gewalt gegen Heiligtümer*. Berlin: de Gruyter.

Hase, Thomas. 2001. *Zivilreligion: Religionswissenschaftliche Überlegungen zum einem theoretischen Konzept am Beispiel der USA*. Würzburg: Ergon.

Hayes, Carlton J. H. 2014 [1926]. "Nationalism As a Religion." <http://www.panarchy.org/hayes/nationalism.html>, accessed July 3, 2014.

Haynes, Jeffrey, ed. 2009. *Routledge Handbook of Religion and Politics*. London: Routledge.

Hertzke, Allen D. 2009. "The Catholic Church and Catholicism in Global Politics." In *Routledge Handbook of Religion and Politics*, edited by Jeffrey Haynes. London: Routledge, 48–63.

Huntington, Samuel P. 1993. "The Clash of Civilizations?" *Foreign Affairs* (Summer): 22–49.

Huntington, Samuel P. 1996. *The Clash of Civilizations and the Remaking of World Order*. New York: Simon & Schuster.

Jaffrelot, Christophe. 1996. *The Hindu Nationalist Movement and Indian Politics, 1925 to the 1990s: Strategies of Identity-Building, Implantation and Mobilisation (with Special Reference to Central India)*. London: Hurst & Co.

Juergensmeyer, Mark. 1993. *The New Cold War? Religious Nationalism Confronts the Secular State*. Berkeley: University of California Press.

Kalyvas, Stathis N. 1996. *The Rise of Christian Democracy in Europe*. Ithaca, NY: Cornell University Press.

Kippenberg, Hans G. 2005. *Gewalt als Gottesdienst: Religionskriege im Zeitalter der Globalisierung*. Munich: Beck.

Kippenberg, Hans G. 2007. "Die Entsäkularisierung des Nahostkonflikts: Von einem Konflikt zwischen Staaten zu einem Konflikt zwischen Religionsgemeinschaften." In *Säkularisierung und die Weltreligionen*, edited by Hans Joas and Klaus Wiegandt. Frankfurt am Main: Fischer Taschenbuch, 465–507.

Kleine, Christoph. 2002. "Religion im Dienste einer ethnisch-natioalen Identitätskonstruktion. Erörtert am Beispiel der 'Deutschen Christen' und des japanischen Shinto." *Marburg Journal of Religion* 7: 1–17.

Koenker, Ernest Benjamin. 1965. *Secular Salvations: The Rites and Symbols of Political Religions.* Philadelphia: Fortress Press.

Köllen, Katja. 2011. "Großkonzern Kirche." *Wirtschaftswoche*, December 25. <http://www.wiwo.de/unternehmen/dienstleister/finanz-riese-grosskonzern-kirche/5220262.html>, accessed August 21, 2014.

Lehmann, Karsten. 2013. "Shifting Boundaries between the Religious and the Secular: Religious Organizations in Global Public Space." *Journal of Religion in Europe* 6(2): 201–228. doi: 10.1163/18748929-00602004

Leitner, Sigrid. 2003. "Katholizismus und Sozialpolitik: Zur Entstehung der Sozialversicherungen in Kontinentaleuropa." In *Politik und Religion*, edited by Michael Minkenberg and Ulrich Willems. Wiesbaden: Westdeutscher Verlag, 369–390.

Maier, Hans. 2007. *Politische Religionen*. Munich: Beck.

Manow, Philip. 2002. "The Good, the Bad, and the Ugly: Esping-Andersens Sozialstaats-Typologie und die konfessionellen Wurzeln des westlichen Wohlfahrtsstaates." *Kölner Zeitschrift für Soziologie und Sozialpsychologie* 54(2): 203–225.

Manwaring, David R. 1962. *Render Unto Caesar: The Flag Salute Controversy*. Chicago, IL: University of Chicago Press.

Marsden, Lee. 2009. "God, War, and Iraq." In *Religion, Conflict and Military Intervention*, edited by Rosemary Durward and Lee Marsden. Farnham: Ashgate, 71–87.

Martin, David. 2014. *Religion and Power: No Logos Without Mythos*. Farnham: Ashgate.

Martin, Vanessa. 2003. *Creating an Islamic State: Khomeini and the Making of a New Iran.* London: I. B. Tauris.

Marty, Martin E. and R. Scott Appleby, eds. 1991. *Fundamentalisms Observed*. Chicago, IL and London: University of Chicago Press.

Mergenschroer-Livingston, Sandy. 2009. "Trust Me! Jesus Would Go to War Too." In *Religion, Conflict and Military Intervention*, edited by Rosemary Durward and Lee Marsden. Farnham: Ashgate, 88–107.

Miles, Jack. 2004. "Religion and American Foreign Policy." *Survival* 46(1): 23–37. doi: 10.1080/00396330412331343633

Müller, Harald. 2003. "Kampf der Kulturen: Religion als Strukturfaktor einer weltpolitischen Konfliktformation?" In *Politik und Religion*, edited by Michael Minkenberg and Ulrich Willems. Wiesbaden: Westdeutscher Verlag, 559–580.

Palonen, Kari. 2011. "Politics." In *The Encyclopedia of Political Science*, edited by George Thomas Kurian, 5 vols. Washington, DC: CQ Press, vol. 4, 1299–1301.

Petrocik, John R. 1998. "Reformulating the Party Coalitions: The 'Christian Democratic' Republicans." <http://escholarship.org/uc/item/27r0t4k4>, accessed July 20, 2014.

Philpott, Daniel. 2002. "The Challenge of September 11 to Secularism in International Relations." *World Politics* 55(1): 66–95. doi: 10.1353/wp.2003.0006

Ponton, Geoffrey, Peter Gill, and Charlotte Bretherton. 1993. *Introduction to Politics*, 3rd edition. Oxford and Cambridge, MA: Blackwell.

Richardson, James T., ed. 2004. *Regulating Religion: Case Studies from Around the Globe*. New York: Kluwer Academic/Plenum Publishers.

Riegel, Klaus-Georg. 2005. "Der Marxismus-Leninismus als 'politische Religion.'" In *Politische Religionen und Religionspolitik: Zwischen Totalitarismus und Religionsfreiheit*, edited by Gerhard Besier and Hermann Lübbe. Göttingen: Vandenhoeck & Ruprecht, 15–48.

Riesebrodt, Martin. 1998. *Pious Passion: The Emergence of Modern Fundamentalism in the United States and Iran*. Berkeley: University of California Press.

Rousseau, Jean-Jacques. 2014 [1762]. "Du contract social ou Principes du droit politique." <http://classiques.uqac.ca/classiques/Rousseau_jj/contrat_social/Contrat_social.pdf>, accessed May 10, 2014.

Schulze Wessel, Martin, ed. 2006. *Nationalisierung der Religion und Sakralisierung der Nation im östlichen Europa*. Stuttgart: Steiner.

Seiwert, Hubert. 2014. "Wilde Religionen. Religiöser Nonkonformismus, kulturelle Dynamik und Säkularisierung in China." In *Religiöse Minderheiten und gesellschaftlicher Wandel*, edited by Edith Franke. Wiesbaden: Harrassowitz, 11–27.

Seiwert, Hubert. 2015. "Religiöser Nonkonformismus in säkularen Gesellschaften." *Zeitschrift für Religionswissenschaft* 23(1): 35–66. doi: 10.1515/zfr-2015-0008

Sellin, Volker. 2004 [1975]. "Politik." In *Geschichtliche Grundbegriffe: Historisches Lexikon zur politisch-sozialen Sprache in Deutschland*, edited by Otto Brunner, Werner Conze, and Reinhart Koselleck, 8 vols. Stuttgart: Klett-Cotta, vol. 4, 789–874.

Smith, Bardwell L., ed. 1978. *Religion and the Legitimation of Power in South Asia*. Leiden: Brill.

Spickard, James V. 1999. "Human Rights, Religious Conflict, and Globalisation: Ultimate Values in a New World Order." *International Journal on Multicultural Societies* 1(1): 2–19.

Stackhouse, Max L. 1987. "Politics and Religion." In *The Encyclopedia of Religion*, edited by Mircea Eliade, 17 vols. New York: Macmillan, vol. 11, 408–423.

Tambiah, Stanley Jeyaraja. 1992. *Buddhism Betrayed? Religion, Politics and Violence in Sri Lanka*. Chicago, IL and London: University of Chicago Press.

Theodorowitsch, Nadeshda. 1970. *Religion und Atheismus in der UdSSR: Dokumente und Berichte*. Munich: Claudius.

Toft, Monica Duffy. 2012. "Religion in International Relations Theory." In *Handbook of International Relations*, edited by Walter Carlsnaes, Thomas Risse, and Beth A. Simmons. London: Sage, 673–691.

Toft, Monica Duffy, Daniel Philpott, and Timothy Samuel Shah. 2011. *God's Century: Resurgent Religion and Global Politics*. New York: Norton.

Urban, Hugh B. 2005. "Politics and Religion: An Overview." In *Encyclopedia of Religion*, 2nd edition, edited by Lindsay Jones, 14 vols. Detroit: Macmillan Reference USA, vol. 11, 7248–7260.

US National Archives & Records Administration. 2013 [1776]. "The Declaration of Independence. A Transcription." <http://www.archives.gov/exhibits/charters/declaration_transcript.html>, accessed March 28, 2013.

Van Hecke, Steven and John Gerhart, eds. 2004. *Christian Democratic Parties in Europe Since the End of the Cold War*. Leuven: Leuven University Press.

Voegelin, Eric. 1996. *Die politischen Religionen*. 2nd edition. Munich: Fink. Original edition, 1938.

Wald, Kenneth and Clyde Wilcox. 2006. "Getting Religion: Has Political Science Rediscovered the Faith Factor?" *American Political Science Review* 100(4): 523–529. doi: 10.1017/S0003055406062381

Weber, Max. 1972. *Wirtschaft und Gesellschaft: Grundriß der verstehenden Soziologie* (Fünfte, revidierte Auflage, besorgt von Johannes Winckelmann). Tübingen: J. C. B. Mohr (Paul Siebeck). Original edition, 1922.

Welch, Holmes. 1972. *Buddhism under Mao*. Cambridge MA: Harvard University Press.

White, Ronald C. and Howard C. Hopkins. 1976. *The Social Gospel: Religion and Reform in Changing America*. Philadelphia: Temple University Press.

Wuthnow, Robert. 1991. "Understanding Religion and Politics." *Daedalus* 120(3): 1–20.

Yang, Fenggang. 2012. *Religion in China: Survival and Revival under Communist Rule*. New York: Oxford University Press.

Zürcher, Erik. 1972. *The Buddhist Conquest of China*, 2 vols. Leiden: Brill. Original edition, 1959.

FURTHER READING

Bruce 2003 [*A comprehensive treatment of religion and politics in the contemporary world with many examples from a vast variety of countries and a sociological perspective.*]

Haynes 2009 [*One of many relevant edited volumes, which unlike most others contains not only chapters on many themes discussed in political studies but also on the major religious traditions and their connection with politics.*]

Martin 2014 [*The book presents an in-depth analysis of the relationships between religion, power, and politics, which includes historical perspectives and provocative theoretical reflections.*]

Toft/Philpott/Shah 2011 [*An equally comprehensive volume with many examples, but focusing more on the global political implications of contemporary religions.*]

Urban 2005 [*A systematic and condensed introduction from a religious studies point of view, where the complexity of the relationship between religion and politics as well as various theoretical approaches are discussed.*]

CHAPTER 30

··

SCIENCE

··

LAURA J. VOLLMER AND KOCKU VON STUCKRAD

CHAPTER SUMMARY

··

- Religion and science have been systematically related to one another since the nineteenth century, partly due to contemporary debates on the role of the church in society and to the professionalization of science.
- There are at least four different positions on how to conceptualize the relationship: the conflict thesis, the complexity thesis, the dynamism thesis, and the discursive perspective.
- Most discussions of the relationship between religion and science operate with a conceptual distinction that defines 'religion' and 'science' as clear, separate categories, which then are related to each other, creating rigid dichotomies.
- Discursive approaches are presented as a suitable way to capture the complexity of meanings of 'religion' and 'science,' as they move beyond problematic dichotomous constructions.
- Two case studies, one focusing on the genealogy of nature-based spirituality and one on Buddhism and neuroscience, demonstrate the usefulness of discursive approaches for the study of religion and science.

'RELIGION,' 'SCIENCE,' AND CULTURAL ENVIRONMENTS

··

The relationship between religion and science is a much-debated topic today. Issues regarding the nature and scope of relations between religious and scientific claims repeatedly arise in public discourse, occupying journalists, politicians, and lawyers alike. Scientists and representatives of religious traditions also enter the debate; their arguments reveal a huge spectrum of possible ways to mutually position religion and science. If scholars of religion want to arrive at a sound theoretical analysis of the issues at stake, all possible ways of relating religion and science will have to be addressed, historically explained, and incorporated in a larger conceptual framework. This is a huge challenge, which is further complicated by the fact that scholars of religion themselves are not only observers of the field but active participants, making claims based on what they present as rational 'scientific', rather than religious, argumentation.

Many ways of relating religion and science have one thing in common: they first define 'religion' and 'science' and then position these definitions with reference to one another to conclude a relationship between them. While this seems to be theoretically necessary at first glance, it is problematic because such a maneuver tends to essentialize 'religion' and 'science' in a way that obscures the historicity of both concepts. It suggests that there are static entities like 'religion' and 'science' that can be related to each other, while in fact these concepts are subject to constant change and ever-new attributions of meaning in diverse situations and historical contexts. It should be noted that positioning religion and science with respect to one another is a quite recent phenomenon in European and North American history of culture. While 'science' (Latin *scientia*) has been in use in philosophy for a long time, it was only in the nineteenth century that juxtaposing 'science' as rational and experimental knowledge to 'religion' became a common way of approaching those systems (see the following section on the 'invention' of science in the nineteenth century; see also Schaffer 1986; Cunningham/Williams 1993). Not surprisingly, then, William Whewell coined the English term 'scientist' only in 1840 (Ross 1962; Yeo 1993); without such a concept, it would have been impossible to polemically marginalize scholars and knowledge claims outside the new paradigm as 'non- or pseudo-scientific' (Gieryn 1983; McKnight 1992; Rupnow et al. 2008). Of course, this was a gradual process, with roots that many trace back to the Enlightenment era during which natural philosophy was being differentiated from science based on the former's religious concerns and theological considerations (Byrne 1996; Zafirovski 2011, 107–128; see also Cunningham 1991). In such boundary work, specifically demarcating science as 'not religion' and 'religion' as 'not science' played a large role, setting a precedent for defining the two in relative perspective (Turner 1978; Gieryn 1983, 785–786; Gieryn 1999, 43–46).

These introductory remarks make it clear that the concepts of religion and science are embedded in cultural environments, and, moreover, that there are notions of religion in the environment of science, science in that of religion, and a religion-and-science environment of its own. While religion and science can still be related to one another, analysis will need to leave behind the typical approach just outlined to reflect the fluid nature of the concepts under analysis. These concepts do not carry meaning in themselves but receive their meaning in changing cultural and social contexts. Consequently, for the study of religion to provide a rigorous analysis of religion and science, it is important to take a step back and look at the various ways of positioning religion and science from a meta-perspective, which is open to other 'groupings' of terms (on which see Foucault

2010 [1972], 29), and at the same time to historicize the concepts used in contemporary discourse.

HISTORICIZING RELIGION AND SCIENCE

After much debate, a consensus has emerged that 'religion and science' constitutes a specialized field of study. There are thousands of references to date, with hundreds of monographs and articles added to the pool each year, in addition to an increasing number of conferences, academic journals, domestic and international research societies, and a prominent presence of religion–science dialogue on the Internet (Clayton 2006; van Huyssteen 2003).

As to when this field arose, the literature is inconsistent, typically ranging from the mid-1800s to the mid-1900s. Some place the date much earlier, as many of the issues discussed in what is today considered the field of religion and science have been analyzed since antiquity, such as the relation between pathology and religious experience; however, before the nineteenth century these ideas were not considered in a specifically religion and science context, but rather were explored in terms of philosophy or medicine, for example (Brooke 2003, 749).

The Warfare Thesis

Putting periodization issues to the side, the publication of *History of the Conflict Between Religion and Science* (1875),[1] by English-born American John William Draper (1811–1882), was certainly a key moment in the development of the field. Draper studied medicine and chemistry and was an enthusiast of many subjects, including science, philosophy, and history, which he brought together in this influential book. According to Draper:

> The history of Science is not a mere record of isolated discoveries; it is a narrative of the conflict of two contending powers, the expansive force of the human intellect on one side, and the compression arising from traditionary [sic] faith and human interests on the other. *No one has hitherto treated the subject from this point of view.* (Draper 1875, vi–vii; emphasis added)

Draper accurately predicted that "this [work] is only as it were the preface, or forerunner, of a body of literature, which the events and wants of our time will call forth" (1875, ix).

---

[1] Some sources date this work to 1874; the primary source itself has 1875; it entered the Library of Congress in 1874.

Draper's work spread the notion that science was associated with freedom and progress, while religion was aligned with repression and superstition, becoming conventional wisdom and adding momentum to the trend of defining religion and science as dichotomous constructs (Burton Russell 1997, 38). Draper supported the theses of Andrew Dickson White (1832–1918), co-founder of Cornell University (Ferngren 2000, xiii), whose earlier work in the form of pamphlets and lectures was later published as *A History of the Warfare of Science with Theology in Christendom* (c.1895).[2] White saw conflict in many matters, such as creation and evolution, as well as geocentrism and heliocentrism, for example, and argued for a separation of religion and academia, contrary to the norm at this time (White 1896, ix).

During the period in which the influential Draper–White thesis, also known as the 'warfare thesis,' was put forward, the relationship between religion and science was in the public eye across many countries, partly due to the Ecumenical Council convened in December 1869 under Pope Pius IX. These sessions debated "in conspicuous prominence" the infallibility of the Roman pontiff and the relations of religion—specifically Catholicism—to science (Draper 1875, 330; see also Burton Russell 1997, 36–48). Though the church made many positive remarks on science and their relationship with it (Dogmatic Constitution on the Catholic Faith 1870), according to warfare advocates these topics led to much dispute between the Catholic Church and various European states, to disagreement and dissension within the church, to the restriction of Catholic publications in some societies, to the labeling of the pope as a heretic, and even to war between Italy and Rome (see Draper 1875, 330–339). While these disputes did indeed occur, all the blame cannot be placed on the church, as religion–science differentiation created an opportunity for conflict-based boundary work that was in the interests of advocates of science. Religion–science conflict was a useful rhetorical tool to carve out interpretative, professional, and authoritative space for science in a world where religious interests and theological explanations were predominant. Engaging with religion in a conflictual way was a means to distinguish and define the emerging professional group (Turner 1978; Gieryn 1983). This was in a larger context of wide-sweeping changes that were occurring across Europe and the Americas regarding the place of religion in politics and governance, in academia and education, and in science (see Draper 1875, 330–340; Wilson 2000, 4). Also during this period the debates surrounding English naturalist Charles Darwin (1809–1882) came to prominence, highlighting tensions between evolutionary theory and creationism, and echoing through the years to this very day as one of the key issues in the field.

One aspect that was drawn upon by both Draper and White to demonstrate religion–science warfare was the conflicting views of the Christian notion of a flat earth versus the scientific view of sphericity. History texts prior to 1870 rarely mention the flat-earth

---

[2] We could not confirm this date, as the text is also cited as published in 1896, 1897, and 1898 in the relevant literature. Consultation of the text itself could not clarify the publication year, as later editions do not state the original publication date and, unfortunately, an original is not available. The earliest cited publication date of 1895 is a likely candidate.

cosmology, whereas nearly all those following 1880 do. It is likely not a coincidence therefore that presenting this old cosmology as a myth gained currency at the same time as the warfare thesis did (Burton Russell 1997, x, 43, 90–91 n. 84). Physicist John Tyndall (1820–1893), an active participant in the professionalization of science and its accompanying boundary work, summed up the (both apparent and real) tensions of this time in his famous Belfast Address in 1874: "We [representing science] claim, and we shall wrest from theology, the entire domain of cosmological theory" (Tyndall 1874; see also Gieryn 1983).

Some have suggested that *actual* religion–science warfare has been the exception, not the rule (Brooke 2003, 749; Burton Russell 1997, 48); nonetheless notions of conflict have dominated the majority of discussions on the topic, even featuring as a major theme in those works that propose alternative relations (Wilson 2000, 4; Harrison 2010, 4–5).

Challenges to the Warfare Thesis

Since the Draper–White thesis, there has been a growing movement to systematically re-evaluate the religion–science relationship and an increasing acknowledgment that the relations have been more positive, cooperative, and integrative and the histories more entangled than previously thought. American philosopher E. A. Burtt (1892–1989) in *Metaphysical Foundations of Modern Physical Science* (1924), for example, argued that science often rests on theological foundations, and English mathematician and philosopher Alfred North Whitehead (1861–1947) in *Science and the Modern World* (1926) suggested that the origins of modern science lie in the medieval theological idea of God's rationality and rational creation. He emphasized the position of science within culture. This growing approach, however, was in sharp contrast to the noise surrounding and following the 1925 Scopes Trial (*The State of Tennessee v. John Thomas Scopes*), regarding the teaching of human evolution in US public schools, which fueled perceptions of religion–science warfare for decades to come. While ubiquitously cited in relevant literature of all kinds as evidence of religion–science antagonism, in reaction to the anti-evolution movements following the Scopes Trial, many members of the scientific community voiced their support for evolution–Christianity harmony (Numbers 2007, 355; see also Livingstone 1987).

Challenges to the warfare thesis continued to grow. Robert K. Merton in *Science, Technology and Society in Seventeenth Century England* (1938) posited that the Puritan ethic was a major driving force in the growth of science, commonly referred to as the 'Merton thesis', which continues to appear in scholarship today. With the work of historian Herbert Butterfield (1900–1979), a contextualist approach came to be more widely applied to the history of science, including the religion–science relationship, as can be found in Butterfield's *Origins of Modern Science* (1949). While this shift of focus supports the rejection of the Draper–White thesis, this did not directly feature as a theme in his work.

The movement toward a more cooperative stance and an explicit rejection of religion–science warfare was finally firmly formulated in the field of religion and science by professor of physics and religion Ian Barbour (1923–2013)—some sources even claiming that the emergence of the academic field did not occur until the publication of his *Issues in Science and Religion* (1966) (e.g. Peters 2004, 8191). Barbour further developed the field in later publications in which he proposed a fourfold contextualized typology of relationships: conflict, independence, dialogue, and integration (Barbour 1990). To give some specific examples, he saw conflict in scientific materialism and biblical literalism, independence in distinct methodologies and unrelated 'languages' of description and prescription, dialogue in nature-centered spirituality, and integration in a comprehensive metaphysics that systematically synthesizes religion and science, such as in process philosophy. Although he critiqued the warfare thesis, he was later criticized as falling prey to the very thing he was challenging, since his perspective assumed a kind of conflict of its own—an inherent, fundamental separation of the two concepts—and ignored the historical contingencies of how the terms 'religion' and 'science' have been used, often entangled to the point where distinction can only be anachronistically applied (Cantor/Kenny 2001). Thus Barbour has been sometimes associated with the 'conflict thesis,' although he opposed the warfare thesis as the sole basis for analysis, emphasizing context and complexity. (Notably, some scholars do not distinguish between these theses.)

Besides Barbour, some authors in the early 1970s, reminiscent of Merton, not only rejected the warfare thesis, but turned it upside-down, claiming that Christianity was the central causal factor in the rise of modern science, including historian of science Reijer Hooykaas (1906–1994) in *Religion and the Rise of Modern Science* (1972) and priest and physicist Stanley L. Jaki (1924–2009) in *Science and Creation* (1974). However, science and the history of science were popularized by philosopher, historian, and scientist Stephen Jay Gould (1941–2002) (Wilson 2000, 8) who argued that religion and science constitute "non-overlapping magisteria" (abbreviated as NOMA) (Gould 1999) while remaining "natural antagonists" (Gould 1977, 141). In this way Gould seemed to emphasize an independence model, which was, however, still based on notions of inherent conflict. So while the academic tide of religion–science relations was shifting away from essentialized models, through Gould's popularization, ideas of conflict remained in the public eye.

It was also around this time, from the 1960s to 1980s, that centers, societies, and academic journals for the study of religion and science were established around the world.

A New Direction: The Complexity Thesis, Integrations, and Counter-Movements

With the field in full bloom, other alternatives to the warfare and conflict theses emerged, such as the 'complexity thesis,' largely associated with John Hedley Brooke's seminal work *Science and Religion: Some Historical Perspectives* (1991), which pointed out both that the terms 'religion' and 'science' have been used in different ways and that "not only have the boundaries between them shifted with time, but to abstract them from their historical contexts can lead to artificiality as well as anachronism" (Brooke 1991, 16). For example, it would be misleading to refer to Isaac Newton's 'science' when he understood his activity as 'natural philosophy.' Brooke stated, "There is no such thing as *the* relationship between science and religion. It is what different individuals and communities have made of it in a plethora of different contexts" (Brooke 1991, 321, emphasis original). Brooke's view is widely accepted in the field of the history of science (Ferngren 2000, xiii).

Already in the 1970s an increasing number of publications arguing for a correspondence between religion and science were enjoying popular acceptance, such as the best-selling *Tao of Physics* (1975) by physicist and systems theorist Fritjof Capra (b. 1939). However, the 1980s and 1990s saw an explosion of publications suggesting that modern scientific thinking—especially cosmology and physics, although more recently the cognitive sciences—"is consonant with, if not actually supportive of, a religious position" (Campbell 1998, 450). To give some examples, quantum non-locality has been cited as evidence for collective consciousness, sometimes identified with God, and the quantum uncertainty principle—as well as quantum entanglement—has been interpreted as a potential source for divine influence. A notable work that popularized this movement is mathematical physicist Paul Davies's (b. 1946) *God and the New Physics* (1983); the movement gained further momentum (though unintentionally) with the hugely successful *A Brief History of Time* (1988) by theoretical physicist Stephen Hawking (b. 1942). Hawking's work concludes with the statement "If we find the answer [a complete theory of the universe] . . . it would be the ultimate triumph of human reason—for then we would truly know the mind of God" (Hawking 1988, 191), planting the idea into the minds of a wide audience that physics might be the method for gaining knowledge of and even contact with the divine. The above-mentioned works, among many others, contributed to the growth of a specific popular genre, and a very successful one in terms of media coverage and sales, that integrated religion and science. Despite the large popular impact, this genre is typically rejected in academic circles as misrepresenting the 'religion' and especially the 'science' involved (e.g. Lewis/Hammer 2011, 6–8).

Other avenues, such as integrative research—e.g. in terms of interdisciplinarity, cross-consultation, or the advancement of common goals—however, have enjoyed a lot more success in professional communities. One reason is that representations and reformulations of 'religion' and 'science' are viewed as innovative, based on constructive dialogue conducted in the interest of society. That this involves changes for both the religious and scientific communities is not viewed as somehow 'inauthentic,' but rather as adapting to the needs of the time. Thus, this time period also saw the establishment of many institutions with aims and actions that evidence integrative movements, including the Mind & Life Institute (f. 1987), pairing Buddhism with the latest scientific research (<http://www.mindandlife.org>), and the John Templeton Foundation (f. 1987), with the mission to gain "new spiritual information" in collaboration with rigorous scientific inquiry (<http://www.templeton.org>).

Such integration gave rise to a counter-movement asserting atheistic science, such as can be found in the works of the notorious atheist and biologist Richard Dawkins (b. 1941), including *The Selfish Gene* (1976), *The Blind Watchmaker* (1986), and *The God Delusion* (2006). Once again the question of conflict became prominent, as science was identified with evolution, empirical improbability of God's existence, and rationality, while religion was equated with creationism, uninformed belief, and irrationality, perceptions that persist today. Yet, this time around, although the popular view seems to be that this question is still in need of an answer, the answer proposed is now much more often that there is no conflict.[3]

The empirical branch of the field of religion and science regarding the religion–science relationship remains underdeveloped, however, with contradictory data and analyses that are full of rhetoric. This includes data regarding the religiosity of scientists, the scientific expertise of the religious, the attitudes of scientists toward religion and of the religious toward science, and more direct inquiries into the perceptions on the religion–science relationship. There are disputes as to whether some of those surveyed about their religious convictions can be considered scientists as is claimed, in addition to missing citations in the data, factual mistakes, taking quotes out of context, and other examples of poor scholarship (McCabe 1948, 530; Dawkins 2006, 123–130). While there have been exceptions, older empirical work has been argued to support religion–science conflict, based on reifications regarding their principles or knowledge systems or via the 'secularizing force' of scientific education (see Howard Ecklund/Sheitle 2007, 291; Leuba 1921; 1934; Larson/Witham 1997; 1998; Stark 1963; 2003). Yet, other researchers have found that scientists are not necessarily irreligious (Wuthnow 1985; Paiva 2000). In contrast to the earlier studies, a newer study found very different results, in which nearly 50 percent of scientists surveyed (in the United States) identified as 'religious' and 20 percent identified as 'spiritual' (Howard Ecklund 2010; cf. Stirrat/Cornwell 2013). And the largest survey of American attitudes toward religion and science ever conducted found that only about 25 percent of scientists surveyed viewed religion and science as in conflict (Howard Ecklund/Sheitle 2014).

STATE OF THE ART AND THEORETICAL IMPLICATIONS

Today, the field has grown into several subfields: for example, method and theory covering a wide range of typologies of the relationships; specialized literature relating

---

[3] This claim is based on daily readings of Internet news on 'religion and science' and 'spirituality and science' that we have been doing for several years now.

specific religious and scientific traditions, like Daoism and physics; interdisciplinary studies utilizing religious answers to scientific questions and vice versa; and, more recently, tendencies to examine science in the context of specific religions and societies, like general science in medieval Islamic society, for instance. Courses in religion and science are now available at educational institutions worldwide (van Huyssteen 2003, vii), not only within the humanities and social sciences, but also for medical professionals and for those in the hard sciences (e.g. Lake 2012). Despite the diversity of the field, there are some key issues that regularly appear in the literature. Besides the aforementioned issues of evolution and creationism/intelligent design, along with other conflicts between the scientific worldview and biblical literalism, methodologies, domains of inquiry, etc., this includes the intersection of science, ethics, and society; scientific materialism and brain–mind dualism (or dualism involving other immaterial aspects like spirit, soul, and subjective experience); determinism and free will; the nature of knowledge and truth; and the boundaries between systems of knowledge.

Overviewing the development of the field, we can conclude that neither synthesizing nor dichotomizing religion and science is a given and neither can attest to anything fundamental about the religion–science relationship. So where does that leave us in terms of what can we say about the relationship between religion and science? Indeed, what the field needs is a dynamic model of that relationship that can capture the range of possible constructs, encompassing various perspectives, but that also has the analytical tools to maintain stability across various contexts, allowing for historical comparison. Some scholars have attempted to do just that, with varying degrees of success, in what might be referred to as the 'dynamism thesis.' Like the complexity thesis, this thesis claims that 'religion' and 'science' are dynamic concepts; at the same time, it takes the expansion or restriction of these terms as the basis of analysis, which leads to the development of various perspectives, like independence, contact, and monist views, according to Mikael Stenmark (2004). This model is dynamic because it takes into account previous situations so that restriction and expansion are contextualized, expressing historical changes in the relationship; thus, it does not rely on essentialized 'starting points' for religion and science to expand or restrict from.

Another approach that has turned out to be fruitful in capturing the complexities of processes without essentializing their components is the discursive study of religion (von Stuckrad 2014, 1–18; von Stuckrad/Wijsen forthcoming). Instead of defining concepts such as 'religion' and 'science,' this approach analyses the specific attributions of meaning to such concepts in their historical development. 'Discourses' are defined here as:

> communicative structures that organize knowledge in a given community; they establish, stabilize, and legitimize systems of meaning and provide collectively shared orders of knowledge in an institutionalized social ensemble. Statements, utterances, and opinions about a specific topic, systematically organized and repeatedly observable, form a discourse. (von Stuckrad 2014, 11)

A discourse on religion and science, then, consists of many different strands that are 'entangled' and form a 'discursive knot' that is open to scholarly investigation. The basis for such an analysis consists of the terms and concepts that are used in the historical sources, as well as in iconography, material expression, and other forms of communication and types of data about the same topic. This is not a simple identification of subject matter, issues, and ideas. Such a thematic analysis would simplify the data by identifying certain religious themes and certain scientific themes, but a discursive perspective shows that what are thought of as particularly religious or scientific ideas are in constant flux. The boundaries of these knowledge systems shift via associations regulated through communication, legitimized through social institutions, and materialized through social practices and products. These are the elements that operationalize the methodology. Such an approach, which combines the analytical instruments of historical discourse analysis and of sociology-of-knowledge approaches to discourse (abbreviated as SKAD; see Keller 2011; von Stuckrad 2016), is able to capture the various meanings that are attributed to concepts like 'religion' and 'science,' and it is able to historicize these attributions of meaning. To elaborate this approach by example, two case studies are presented here.

APPLICATIONS

Case 1: Gaian Spirituality and its Discursive History

On August 12, 2014 a video was released on YouTube under the title 'The Earth—A Living Creature (The Amazing NASA Video)' (<http:?/www.youtube.com/watch?v=JZXErLns1mM>). The film was prepared by 'NASA's Scientific Visualization Studio,' using real data to predict the movement of a category-4 typhoon off the coast of China in 2005. It shows the Earth, all in blue, with white clouds moving rapidly around it, in a very animate fashion. To underscore the understanding of the Earth as a 'living creature' (as given in the film's title), we hear the sound of breathing along with the visualization of the Earth as a living being. Examples like this—and thousands of similar ones—show the difficulty of distinguishing clearly between religion and science. What we see, instead, is a close entanglement of discourses on religion (including animistic interpretations of the cosmos) with discourses on science, in this case even legitimized by the involvement of a respected institution of 'hard science.' What is more, hundreds of online comments on "the Amazing NASA Video" demonstrate that the themes of animistic cosmologies and even the veneration of nature are closely tied to a discourse on religion.

Bron Taylor has described this discursive knot as 'Gaian spirituality,' and he argues that it is one of the most important religious developments at the beginning of the twenty-first century. It is part of a larger movement of 'nature-based spirituality,' or in Taylor's parlance, 'dark green religion.'

> Dark green religion (which some call dark green spirituality) involves perceptions that nature is sacred and has intrinsic value; beliefs that everything is interconnected and mutually dependent; and deep feelings of belonging to nature. Dark green religion is usually rooted in, or at least coheres with, an evolutionary understanding that all life shares a common ancestor, and it generally leads to kinship ethics because all life is, therefore, literally related. (B. Taylor 2011, 13; for the full argument see B. Taylor 2010)

How can we, as scholars of religion, make sense of this complex phenomenon? It is apparent that simple interpretations that relate religion and science as opposites, or even as intrinsically distinct, will not help here. Rather, it is more fruitful to study the 'ingredients,' i.e. the strands, of this discursive knot, and to analyze how these strands have taken shape in a specific constellation. A close look at the data set reveals that there is a very prominent and influential discursive knot operative in the contemporary field of religion and science that consists of terms such as nature, life, sacredness, evolution, science, biology, values, spirituality, etc. This discursive constellation gains further legitimization by the fact that not only religious communities apply the concepts but also political organizations (e.g. the United Nations), scientific institutes (e.g. NASA), and the media (journals, films, etc.; on the phenomenon of 'Avatar' see B. Taylor 2013).

In the next step of the analysis, we can reconstruct the genealogy of the discourse strands and their specific constellation or 'grouping.' Hence, we do not just look at the terms 'science' and 'religion' but at the more complex constellation of discourse strands, which together constitute the meaning of 'religion' and 'science' and their relationship. In the case of Gaian spirituality, a historical reconstruction reveals that the origin of this discursive knot goes (at least) back to nineteenth-century Romanticism, in a period that already used the respective terms in a similar combination. A prominent example of this discourse is Ernst Haeckel (1834–1919) who coined the term 'ecology' in 1866 and linked this to a strong Darwinian biological theory. Interestingly, however, Haeckel was also influential in setting up an organization that propagated the veneration of nature as a result of scientific research, the *Deutscher Monistenbund* (German Monist League, f. 1906). In 1911, Wilhelm Ostwald (1853–1932), who was awarded the Nobel Prize for Chemistry in 1909, became the president of the Monist League and continued the work of Haeckel. Their books were very successful and we can argue that their discursive impact was large. And what we read is a prefiguration of the discursive grouping that has gained further momentum during the twentieth century. To provide just one example here: "*All substance possesses life*, inorganic as well as organic; *all things are animated*, crystals as well as organisms. The ancient conviction of the inner, unified linkage of all events, of the unlimited dominion of generally valid laws of nature reasserts itself as an unshakeable truth" (Haeckel 1917, viii; emphasis original; translation ours). With these concepts, Haeckel clearly crossed the boundaries of 'scientific' claims based on experimental knowledge and included discourses on an animated cosmos that—in a dichotomous setting—would belong to the field of religion.

Tracing the genealogy of all related discourse strands and their groupings in the twentieth century would be a huge project (for a more detailed analysis of the Monist League and its discursive impact see von Stuckrad 2014, 76–93). But this brief explanation should have made clear that a discursive analysis is very helpful if we want to overcome the theoretical and conceptual problems of dichotomous constructions such as 'religion' and 'science.'

Case 2: Buddhism from Mount Meru to the Modern God of Science

The cover of *National Geographic* of March 2005 features a Tibetan monk, in traditional robes, serenely gazing at the reader, the slightest hint of a smile on his face, with electrodes covering his head, measuring his brain activity. The cover story explores various developments in the cognitive sciences, one case study demonstrating quantifiably that the Buddhist meditator featured was "the happiest man in the world" compared with previous test subjects (Shreeve 2005). The study showed that meditation resulted in a remarkable shift in brain activity toward the left prefrontal cortex, associated with positive temperaments, as well as a pronounced boost in immunity response. This example, along with multitudes of other similar studies,[4] again complicates the religion–science distinction, with its entanglement of discourses on religion and discourses on science.

For example, there is a clear interplay between these discourses that occur in the cover photo, with the juxtaposition of a stereotypical depiction of a contemplative and contemporary scientific equipment, while maintaining an otherworldly feel, as the meditator seemingly floats upon a stark black background. Moreover, there is specific emphasis on mental states in the article, rather than the physical as is the typical accepted domain of science, and these states are suggested to be accessible by scientific method. This can be seen in the entanglement of quantifiable subjective states and religious practices (i.e. happiness achieved through contemplation) and experimental results said to suggest that meditation can "literally change the mind," not the *brain* as one might expect in scientific discourse. Further to this point that the discourse is not limited to physical observations, themes of transcendence are in play, as the subtitle for this case study is "Spiritual State" in an article titled "Beyond the Brain." The entanglement of these discourses is legitimized by the neuroscientific data, as well as the influential magazine it is featured in—*National Geographic*, with an international readership of over thirty million and publications in over thirty languages (*National Geographic* 2012).

---

[4] For example, meditators featured on the cover of *Time* (US) magazine in August 2003 and *Time* (Europe) magazine in October 2003, and *Time* (US, Asia, and Europe) magazine in February 2014, as well as on *Scientific American* in November 2014. All stories involved elements of the 'science of meditation,' as well as notions of non-physical well-being.

The analysis in this example is accomplished by taking seriously the combination of terms in the discourse, like mind and brain, meditation and neuroscience, mindfulness and brain fitness, and, even more persuasive as to the emergence of new constellations of meaning, neologisms like 'contemplative science' (discussed further on in this chapter). These discursive knots exhibit meaning-making in the works and feature prominently in contemporary discourses on Buddhism and neuroscience, at both the academic and popular levels. A look at the general discourse on Buddhism and neuroscience will demonstrate that indeed these discursive knots have been solidified so as to change constellations of meaning.

It has been argued that Buddhism—reduced to its meditative practices, specifically 'mindfulness'—backed by science "will change the world" (S. Taylor 2012; Gregoire 2014a) and that the present era can be characterized as an age of a 'mindful revolution' (Pickert 2014; Gregoire 2014b; Wilson 2014), which demonstrates a great level of influential solidification. And that Buddhism-and-science is an acceptable knowledge system is legitimized by the academic community as well. Hundreds of peer-reviewed studies confirm the benefits of meditation, and there are over 1,000 empirical research publications (for a literature overview, see Cahn and Polich 2006; Ospina et al. 2007; Hussain and Bhushan 2010; see also Fraser 2013). In this discourse, meditation is commonly framed as a way of being both religious—or 'spiritual' (often constructed as a religious worldview minus institutionalization)—and scientific at the same time or, at the very least framed as religion–science congruence. This demonstrates that knowledge is organized in ways alternative to a strict religion–science differentiation.

The solidification of this discourse is further demonstrated by its societal impact, which can be found in various contexts, such as in influential media, as noted earlier (also in *Time, Scientific American, The Huffington Post,* and *The New York Times* to name a few), and among celebrities and CEOs (Gregoire 2013) and even former American president Bill Clinton (Lam 2012). This is not a marginal movement, evidenced by the discussion of these practices in terms of their 'integration' into the sciences and the increased acceptance of 'alternative medicines,' largely meditation, now considered a legitimate approach by many (Moodley and West 2005; *My Health News Daily* 2011). That 'integration' and 'acceptance' of Buddhism and science is an explicit topic of discussion—rather than an implicit understanding—shows this is meaning-making in the works. Its development is also evident in the growing number of institutions dedicated to such work, including governments. For instance, the US government has funded studies of meditation (broadly integrative medicine) through the National Center for Complementary and Alternative Medicine; in the United Kingdom similar work is being done by The Prince's Foundation for Integrated Health and by the College of Medicine. In these various venues, the same combinations and interrelations of the discursive knots identified in the opening remarks of this section are present.

However, this is not wholesale religion–science 'integration'—as Buddhism is more than mindfulness and the discourses on science expand beyond the hard data and make non-physical claims, as mentioned. As in the previous case study, analysis is more fruitful when examining the discursive knots that are operative in this constellation.

This discourse gained a lot of momentum when people from Asia actively presented Buddhism to Europeans and Americans—during the World Parliament of Religions in Chicago (1893)—and highlighted aspects of scientific compatibility while de-emphasizing the broader cultural contexts of the religious tradition. This specifically modern discursive shift, drawing parallels between Buddhism and science, was inextricably connected to the discourse on Christianity at the time, during which the mythological and irrational elements were regularly being called into question by nineteenth- and twentieth-century skeptics and proponents of scientific naturalism and of historicism in Christian theology. Hitching Buddhist rhetoric to these discussions, Buddhism was presented as a specific negation of Christianity and thus as the answer to the problem of religion–science conflict. Projecting modern attitudes, Buddhism was demythologized, suggested to be without a personal god, with a belief in a universe directed by natural law—leaving all notions of Mount Meru as the cosmic center behind—and based on reasoning and skepticism rather than blind faith. Thus, Buddhism was strategically positioned between two major discourses of modernity, that of scientific naturalism and Christianity, constructing a socially relevant interpretative space for the religion (McMahan 2008, 61–69; Lopez 2008, 32–33, 115; see also Heine/Prebish 2003).

Over time, this discourse on Buddhism–science congruence gained momentum. While many scientists were resistant at first, contemplative science—the science of contemplative techniques such as meditation and prayer—is now researched at top universities around the world and utilized in medicine and therapy.[5] Although various meditative techniques from a variety of religious traditions are being explored, Buddhist approaches are the most widely used and the pairing of Buddhism and the cognitive sciences is the greatest Buddhism–science success story. Notably, Buddhist notions have been paired with many other branches of science as well, including biology and physics. The pairings often coincide with the intellectual current of the day—thus when early discussions of Darwin's theories brought religion–science conflict to the fore, some claimed that the Buddha himself had accepted the doctrine of evolution (Dharmapala 1965, 9), and with the rise of quantum physics, Buddhist belief was said to prefigure the science with its doctrine of dependent origination (Capra 1975, 129; Badiner 1990, xvi).

The success of Buddhism–science entanglement can be partly attributed to the appropriation of scientific terminology and techniques—'karma' was translated in terms of 'cause and effect,' Buddhist notions of life, death, and rebirth were assimilated to the theory of evolution, and meditative insight was said to be akin to observation and experimentation (McMahan 2008; Lopez 2008). The pairing of Buddhism and science was further legitimized through professionalization in the form of research institutions and projects, such as the aforementioned Mind & Life Institute, chaired by the widely respected (14th) Dalai Lama (Tenzin Gyatso, b. 1935); the institute brings together top

---

[5] See, for example, the SSRC project on prayer, <http://www.ssrc.org/programs/component/religion-and-the-public-sphere/new-directions-in-the-study-of-prayer/>. For an extensive list of prominent affiliates involving a single project on contemplative science see, for example, Fraser 2013, 195–196 fn. 5.

scientists and eminent Buddhists for discussions of compatibility and directions for research. The Dalai Lama has also contributed to this entanglement of scientific and Buddhists concepts himself: "It is my view," he states, "that generally Buddhism ... is very close to a scientific approach" and the authority for both can be reduced to "reasoning" and "logic" (quoted in Hayward and Varela 2001, 31–32). While in the past this pairing has been largely contained in American and European communities, the role of science in this religious tradition is now being emphasized in Asia as well, through the implementation of scientific courses at Buddhist monasteries in Tibet, for example, as part of the Science for Monks project (<http://www.scienceformonks.org>).[6]

Over time, the attribution of scientific meaning to Buddhism has become stabilized through these above-mentioned materializations of the discourse so that today many regard the tradition as a scientific one with or without regard to the historical contingencies. As one scholar suggests, this could be interpreted as simply *upaya*, or "skillful means" to bring Buddhism to the modern world and the modern world to Buddhism—just as Buddhism came to incorporate Vedic gods in India and *kami* in Japan, perhaps the god of science has now been added to the pantheon as well (Lopez 2008, 37).

CONCLUSION

These brief examples show that what is meant by 'religion' and 'science' is always changing. The process does not consist of a simple mixing of themes but of the attribution of new meanings to religion and science. As demonstrated in the second example, contemplative science is regarded as a serious scientific discipline, whereas in the past studying meditation was associated with pseudo-science, fringe science, and superstition. The repetition of Buddhism–science associations and the systematic treatment of Buddhist contemplation in neuroscience have established a system of meaning whereby elements previously perceived (in large part) as outside of science and within religion are no longer organized as such. Meditation was once reserved for the realm of religion; now it is within science. The same is true for the notion of the Earth as a 'living being,' discussed in the first example. Science is often regarded as secular; in this context, among others, it is also often regarded as a source for spiritual growth or religious experiences. And these changes occur via our communications about religion and science—how we use the terms, what other terms are associated with them, what themes come into play regularly, etc.—and via social practices—such as institutional support, scientific practices, and government involvement. These communicative and social processes stabilize and legitimize the organization of knowledge and are open to an analysis sensitive to historical contingencies.

---

[6] Though it is worth mentioning, Buddhists have long been involved with medicine as part of the monastic curriculum. Medicinal training includes, but is not limited to, etiology, nosology, pharmacology, physiology, and dietetics. See, for example, Salguero 2014.

The two cases discussed are exemplary for the way a modern study of religion can fruitfully analyze the relationship between religion and science. The hints of the many levels of a discourse also make it clear that a full analysis can go in various directions and needs the collaboration of many scholars. The two case studies serve here to point to this approach's potential in problematizing religion–science disparity and grappling with the mutability of meanings and the porous perimeters of knowledge systems. Simple dichotomies will no longer suffice. What we need is a theoretical framework that critically reflects on the contingency of concepts in their historical development, but at the same time is rigorous in its conceptual argumentation and the use of data to prove its interpretation.[7]

Glossary

Complexity thesis the argument that the religion–science relationship is fluid and complex, such that a single thesis, such as conflict or harmony, cannot analytically capture the range of possible constructs and thus individual cases must be rigorously contextualized.

Conflict thesis the notion that religion and science are fundamentally distinct conceptually speaking.

Discourse communicative structure that organizes knowledge in a given community; it establishes, stabilizes, and legitimizes systems of meaning and provides collectively shared orders of knowledge in an institutionalized social ensemble; statements, utterances, and opinions about a specific topic, systematically organized and repeatedly observable, form a discourse.

Discursive entanglement an alternative way of describing a 'discursive knot,' this term expresses the presence of various discourse strands, which can be found in an interrelated manner within one text.

Discursive knot constellation of individual discourses (manifest in terms that are used) that are 'entangled' with one another in the data set under analysis.

Discursive study of religion and science theoretical approach that focuses on the construction, attribution, and legitimization of meaning, rather than on definitions of religion and science.

Draper–White thesis an alternative name for the warfare thesis.

Dynamism thesis the argument that religion and science are dynamic concepts, resisting essentialist definitions and analytical categories and thus must be analyzed according to the expansion and restriction of these terms compared with alternative contexts.

Warfare thesis the thesis proposing that religion and science are intellectually, socially, and historically opposed; it can perhaps be understood as a radical variant of the conflict thesis.

---

[7] Parts of this chapter have been posted before on Laura J. Vollmer's blog "Knowledge Unbound: Religion, Science, & Philosophy"; for online discussion about the arguments presented here, as well as many other related topics, see <http://www.knowledgeunbound.com>.

References

Badiner, Allan Hunt, ed. 1990. *Dharma Gaia: A Harvest of Essays in Buddhism and Ecology*. Berkeley, CA: Parallax Press.

Barbour, Ian. 1990. *Religion in an Age of Science*. San Francisco, CA: Harper & Row.

Brooke, John Hedley. 1991. *Science and Religion: Some Historical Perspectives*. Cambridge: Cambridge University Press.

Brooke, John Hedley. 2003. "Science and Religion, History of the Field." In *Encyclopedia of Science and Religion*, edited by J. Wentzel Vrede van Huyssteen. New York: Macmillan Reference, 748–755.

Burton Russell, Jeffrey. 1997. *Inventing the Flat Earth: Columbus and Modern Historians*. Westport, CT: Praeger.

Byrne, James M. 1996. *Religion and the Enlightenment: From Descartes to Kant*. Louisville, KY: Westminster John Knox Press.

Cahn, B. Rael and John Polich. 2006. "Meditation States and Traits: EEG, ERP, and Neuroimaging Studies." *Psychological Bulletin* 132(2): 180–211. doi: 10.1037/0033-2909.132.2.180

Campbell, Colin. 1998. "Science and Religion." In *Encyclopedia of Religion and Society*, edited by William H. Swatos, Jr. Walnut Creek, CA: AltaMira Press, 449–450.

Cantor, Geoffrey and Chris Kenny. 2001. "Barbour's Fourfold Way: Problems with His Taxonomy of Science-Religion Relationships." *Zygon* 36(4): 765–781.

Capra, Fritjof. 1975. *The Tao of Physics: An Exploration of Parallels Between Modern Physics and Eastern Mysticism*. New York: Bantam.

Clayton, Philip. 2006. "Introduction." In *The Oxford Handbook of Religion and Science*, edited by Philip Clayton. Oxford: Oxford University Press, 1–4.

Cunningham, Andrew. 1991. "How the *Principia* Got Its Name; Or, Taking Natural Philosophy Seriously." *History of Science* 29(4): 377–392.

Cunningham, Andrew and Perry Williams. 1993. "De-centring the 'Big Picture': *The Origins of Modern Science* and the Modern Origins of Science." *British Journal for the History of Science* 26(4): 407–432.

Dawkins, Richard. 2008. *The God Delusion*. New York: Houghton Mifflin.

Dharmapala, Anagarika. 1965. *Return to Righteousness: A Collection of Speeches, Essays and Letters of the Anagarika Dharmapala*, edited by Ananda W. P. Guruge. Ceylon: Government Press.

Dogmatic Constitution on the Catholic Faith. 1870. "The Dogmatic Decrees of the Vatican Council Concerning the Catholic Faith and the Church of Christ." <http://www.ccel.org/ccel/schaff/creeds2.v.ii.i.html>, accessed April 22, 2015.

Draper, John William. 1875. *History of the Conflict Between Religion and Science*. The International Scientific Series, vol. XII. New York: D. Appleton and Company.

Ferngren, Gary B. 2000. "Preface." In *The History of Science and Religion in the Western Tradition: An Encyclopedia*, edited by Gary B. Ferngren et al. New York: Garland Publishing, xiii–xiv.

Foucault, Michel. 2010. *The Archaeology of Knowledge & The Discourse on Language*. New York: Vintage Books. First English edition 1972.

Fraser, Andy, ed. 2013. *The Healing Power of Meditation*. Boston, MA: Shambhala Publications.

Gieryn, Thomas F. 1983. "Boundary-Work and the Demarcation of Science from Non-Science: Strains and Interests in Professional Ideologies of Scientists." *American Sociological Review* 48(6): 781–795.

Gieryn, Thomas F. 1999. *Cultural Boundaries of Science: Credibility on the Line*. Chicago, IL: University of Chicago Press.

Gould, Stephen Jay. 1977. *Ever Since Darwin: Reflections in Natural History*. New York: Norton.

Gould, Stephen Jay. 1999. *Rocks of Ages: Science and Religion in the Fullness of Life*. New York: Ballantine Books.

Gregoire, Carolyn. 2013. "The Daily Habits of These Outrageously Successful People." *The Huffington Post*, July 5. <http://www.huffingtonpost.com/2013/07/05/business-meditation-executives-meditate_n_3528731.html>, accessed September 25, 2014.

Gregoire, Carolyn. 2014a. "Why 2014 Will Be the Year of Mindful Living." *The Huffington Post*, January 2. <http://www.huffingtonpost.com/2014/01/02/will-2014-be-the-year-of-_0_n_4523975.html?ncid=edlinkusaolp00000003>, accessed September 25, 2014.

Gregoire, Carolyn. 2014b. "Actually TIME, This Is What the 'Mindful Revolution' Really Looks Like." *The Huffington Post*, February 4. <http://www.huffingtonpost.com/2014/02/04/this-is-proof-that-mindfu_n_4697734.html>, accessed September 25, 2014.

Haeckel, Ernst. 1917. *Kristallseelen: Studien über das anorganische Leben*. Leipzig: Kröner.

Harrison, Peter. 2010. "Introduction." In *The Cambridge Companion to Science and Religion*, edited by Peter Harrison. Cambridge: Cambridge University Press, 1–18.

Hawking, Stephen. 1988. *A Brief History of Time*. New York: Bantam Books.

Hayward, Jeremy W. and Francisco J. Varela, eds. 2001. *Gentle Bridges: Conversations with the Dalai Lama on the Sciences of Mind*. Boston, MA: Shambhala.

Heine, Steven and Charles S. Prebish, eds. 2003. *Buddhism in the Modern World*. Oxford: Oxford University Press.

Howard Ecklund, Elaine. 2010. *Science vs. Religion: What Scientists Really Think*. Oxford: Oxford University Press.

Howard Ecklund, Elaine and Christopher P. Sheitle. 2007. "Religion Among Academic Scientists: Distinctions, Disciplines, and Demographics." *Social Problems* 54(2): 287–307. <http://www.owlnet.rice.edu/~ehe/doc/Ecklund_SocialProblems_54_2.pdf>, accessed June 25, 2014.

Howard Ecklund, Elaine and Christopher P. Sheitle. 2014. "Religious Communities, Science, Scientists, and Perceptions: A Comprehensive Survey." Paper presented at the Annual Meetings of the American Association for the Advancement of Science. <http://rplp.rice.edu/uploadedFiles/RPLP/RU_AAASPresentationNotes_2014_0220.pdf>, accessed June 25, 2014.

Hussain, Dilwar and Braj Bhushan. 2010. "Psychology of Meditation and Health: Present Status and Future Directions." *International Journal of Psychology and Psychological Therapy* 10(3): 439–451.

John Templeton Foundation. <http://www.johntempleton.org>, accessed April 30, 2015.

Keller, Reiner. 2011. "The Sociology of Knowledge Approach to Discourse (SKAD)." *Human Studies* 34(1): 43–65.

Lake, James. 2012. "Spirituality and Religion in Mental Health: A Concise Review of the Evidence." *Psychiatric Times*, March 20, 34–38.

Lam, Andrew. 2012. "Buddhas in the West: Even Bill Clinton Turns Toward Meditation." *The Huffington Post*, August 22. <http://www.huffingtonpost.com/andrew-lam/buddhism-in-america-bill-clinton-meditation_b_1813179.html>, accessed September 25, 2014.

Larson, Edward J. and Larry Witham. 1997. "Scientists Are Still Keeping the Faith." *Nature* 386: 435–436.

Larson, Edward J. and Larry Witham. 1998. "Leading Scientists Still Reject God." *Nature* 394: 313.

Leuba, James Henry. 1921. *The Belief in God and Immortality: A Psychological, Anthropological, and Statistical Study*. Chicago: Open Court. Original edition, 1916.

Leuba, James Henry. 1934. "Religious Beliefs of American Scientists." *Harper's Magazine* 169: 291–300.

Lewis, James R. and Olav Hammer, eds. 2011. *Handbook of Religion and the Authority of Science*. Leiden: Brill.

Livingstone, David N. 1987. *Darwin's Forgotten Defenders: The Encounter Between Evangelical Theology and Evolutionary Thought*. Grand Rapids, MI: W. B. Eerdmans.

Lopez, Donald S., Jr. 2008. *Buddhism and Science: A Guide for the Perplexed*. Chicago, IL: University of Chicago Press.

McCabe, Joseph. 1948. "Scientists and Religion." In *A Rationalist Encyclopedia: A Book of Reference on Religion, Philosophy, Ethics, and Science*, edited by Joseph McCabe. London: Watts & Co., 529–531.

McKnight, Stephen A., ed. 1992. *Science, Pseudo-Science, and Utopianism in Early Modern Thought*. Columbia, MO: University of Missouri Press.

McMahan, David L. 2008. *The Making of Buddhist Modernism*. Oxford: Oxford University Press.

Mind & Life Institute. <http://www.mindandlife.org>, accessed April 30 2015.

Moodley, Ray and William West, eds. 2005. *Integrating Traditional Healing Practices Into Counseling and Psychotherapy*. Multicultural Aspects of Counseling and Psychotherapy. Thousand Oaks, CA, London, and New Delhi: Sage.

My Health News Daily. 2011. "Trend: More Doctors Prescribing Yoga & Meditation," May 9. <http://www.myhealthnewsdaily.com/1271-complementary-alternative-medicine-yoga-mediation-doctor-referral.html>, accessed May 25, 2013.

National Geographic. 2012. "National Geographic Shows 30.9 Million Worldwide Audience via Consolidated Media Report." Press release, September 24. <http://press.nationalgeographic.com/2012/09/24/national-geographic-shows-30-9-million-worldwide-audience-via-consolidated-media-report/>, accessed September 25, 2014.

Numbers, Ronald L. 2007. "Epilogue: Science, Secularization, and Privatization." In *Eminent Lives in Twentieth-Century Science & Religion*, edited by Nicolaas A. Rupke. Frankfurt am Main: Peter Lang, 349–362.

Ospina, M. B. et al. 2007. "Meditation Practices for Health: State of the Research." *Evidence Report/Technology Assessment* 155: 1–263.

Paiva, Geraldo J. de. 2000. *A religião dos cientistas: uma leitura psicológica*. São Paulo: Edições Loyola.

Peters, Ted. 2004. "Science and Religion." In *Encyclopedia of Religion*, 2nd edition, edited by Lindsay Jones. New York: Macmillan Reference, 8180–8192.

Pickert, Kate. 2014. "The Mindful Revolution." *Time*, January 23. <http://time.com/1556/the-mindful-revolution/>, accessed September 25, 2014.

Ross, Sydney. 1962. "Scientist: The Story of a Word." *Annals of Science* 18: 65–85.

Rupnow, Dirk, Veronika Lipphardt, Jens Thiel, and Christina Wessely, eds. 2008. *Pseudowissenschaft: Konzeptionen von Nichtwissenschaftlichkeit in der Wissenschaftsgeschichte*. Frankfurt am Main: Suhrkamp.

Salguero, C. Pierce. 2014. "Buddhism & Medicine in East Asian History." *Religion Compass* 8(8): 239–250.

Schaffer, Simon. 1986. "Scientific Discoveries and the End of Natural Philosophy." *Social Studies of Science* 16(3): 387–420.

Science for Monks. <http://www.scienceformonks.org>, accessed October 8, 2014.

Shreeve, James. 2005. "Beyond the Brain." *National Geographic* 207(3): 2–31. <http://science.nationalgeographic.com/science/health-and-human-body/human-body/mind-brain/#page=1>, accessed September 25, 2014.

Stark, Rodney. 1963. "On the Incompatibility of Religion and Science." *Journal for the Scientific Study of Religion* 3(1): 3–20.

Stark, Rodney. 2003. *For the Glory of God: How Monotheism Led to Reformations, Science, Witch-hunts, and the End of Slavery*. Princeton, NJ: Princeton University Press.

Stenmark, Mikael. 2004. *How to Relate Science and Religion*. Grand Rapids, MI: William B. Eerdmans.

Stirrat, Michael and R. Elisabeth Cornwell. 2013. "Eminent Scientists Reject the Supernatural: A Survey of the Fellows of the Royal Society." *Evolution: Education and Outreach* 6(33). <http://evolution-outreach.springeropen.com/articles/10.1186/1936-6434-6-33>, accessed August 11, 2014.

Taylor, Bron. 2010. *Dark Green Religion: Nature Spirituality and the Planetary Future*. Berkeley and Los Angeles, CA: University of California Press.

Taylor, Bron. 2011. "Gaian Earth Religion and the Modern God of Nature." *Phi Kappa Phi Forum* 91(2): 12–15.

Taylor, Bron, ed. 2013. *Avatar and Nature Spirituality*. Waterloo, ON: Wilfrid Laurier University Press.

Taylor, Steve. 2012. "Can Meditation Change the World?" *Psychology Today*, December 10. <http://www.psychologytoday.com/blog/out-the-darkness/201212/can-meditation-change-the-world>, accessed September 25, 2014.

Turner, Frank M. 1978. "The Victorian Conflict Between Science and Religion: A Professional Dimension." *Isis* 69(3): 356–376.

Tyndall, John. 1874. *Address Delivered Before the British Association Assembled at Belfast*. London: Longmans, Green, and Co. <https://archive.org/details/addressdelivere03tyndgoog>, accessed July 2, 2014.

van Huyssteen, J. Wentzel Vrede. 2003. "Preface." In *Encyclopedia of Science and Religion*, edited by J. Wentzel Vrede van Huyssteen. New York: Macmillan Reference, vii–viii.

von Stuckrad, Kocku. 2014. *The Scientification of Religion: An Historical Study of Discursive Change, 1800–2000*. Berlin and Boston, MA: de Gruyter.

von Stuckrad, Kocku. 2016. "Religion and Science in Transformation: On Discourse Communities, the Double-Bind of Discourse Research, and Theoretical Controversies." In *Making Religion: Theory and Practice in the Discursive Study of Religion*, edited by Frans Wijsen and Kocku von Stuckrad. Leiden and Boston, MA: Brill: 203–224.

von Stuckrad, Kocku and Frans Wijsen, eds. Forthcoming. *The Making of Religion: Theory and Practice in the Discursive Study of Religion*. Leiden and Boston, MA: Brill.

White, Andrew Dixon. 1896. *A History of the Warfare of Science with Theology in Christendom*. New York: D. Appleton and Company.

Wilson, David B. 2000. "The Historiography of Science and Religion." In *The History of Science and Religion in the Western Tradition: An Encyclopedia*, edited by Gary B. Ferngren. New York: Garland Publishing, 3–11.

Wilson, Jeff. 2014. *Mindful America: The Mutual Transformation of Buddhist Meditation and American Culture*. Oxford: Oxford University Press.

Wuthnow, Robert. 1985. "Science and the Sacred." In *The Sacred in a Secular Age*, edited by Phillip E. Hammond. Berkeley: University of California Press, 187–203.

Yeo, Richard R. 1993. *Defining Science: William Whewell, Natural Knowledge and Public Debate in Early Victorian Britain*. Cambridge: Cambridge University Press.

Zafirovski, Milan. 2011. *The Enlightenment and Its Effects on Modern Society*. New York: Springer.

FURTHER READING

Barbour, Ian. 1966. *Issues in Science and Religion*. Englewood Cliffs: Prentice-Hall. [*This work is considered one of the founding texts in the academic field of religion and science. It contains four historical chapters ranging from the seventeenth to the twentieth centuries, four chapters on religion and scientific methodology, and four chapters on religion and scientific theory.*]

Barbour, Ian. 1997. *Religion and Science: Historical and Contemporary Issues*, revised and expanded edition of *Religion in an Age of Science*. San Francisco: Harper. [*The most important and influential contribution here is the chapter "Ways of Relating Science and Religion," in which Barbour outlines his fourfold typology of conflict, independence, dialogue, and integration. Nearly every religion–science academic publication makes reference to Barbour's proposed methodology.*]

Brooke 1991 [*This seminal work has become a standard-bearer for how to approach the field of religion and science in historical perspective. This work explores religion–science relationships from the sixteenth to the twentieth centuries and examines notions of religion and science in context, analyzing political, social, biographical, and intellectual influences.*]

Brooke, John Hedley and Ronald L. Numbers, eds. 2011. *Science and Religion Around the World*. Oxford: Oxford University Press. [*This anthology fills a lacuna in the literature with its broad examination of different traditions and cultures, including those of China, India, and Africa. There are many contributions dedicated to the Abrahamic religions as well. The meaning and significance of scientific knowledge are examined in various contexts and locations, and the role of science in the loss of religious belief is also explored.*]

Ferngren, Gary B. 2002. *Science and Religion: A Historical Introduction*. Baltimore, MD: Johns Hopkins University Press. [*The strength of this contribution lies in the expanse of time covered—ranging from the beginning of the Christian era to the late twentieth century—as well as the diverse topics discussed, including geology, paleontology, cosmology, physics, ecology, and biology in the thirty essays it consists of, though restricted to the Western religious traditions. Various approaches are considered, such as environmentalism, gender studies, the social construction of knowledge, and postmodernism.*]

Harrison, Peter, ed. 2010. *The Cambridge Companion to Science and Religion*. Cambridge: Cambridge University Press. [*This volume provides a useful introduction to the recent discussions about the relationship between religion and science. The contributions, written by historians, philosophers, scientists, and theologians, reflect on the latest developments in the natural sciences and the neurosciences. Issues discussed in detail include religious responses to Darwinism, questions of secularization, and bioethics.*]

Lewis/Hammer 2011 [*The role of scientific authority in religion is the focus of this anthology. Conceptualizations of 'scientific authority' are diverse, including terminological/rhetorical, methodological, and worldview-based, while drawing on 'mainstream,' 'alternative,' and 'borderline' scientific research, for example. This work also offers an analysis of a wide variety of religious traditions, including Asian religions, the Abrahamic traditions, spiritualism and spiritism, and New Age and occult religions, with a particular focus on alternative—as opposed to mainstream—religious groups.*]

Stenmark 2004 [*Stenmark argues that there are at least four different dimensions of religion and science that need to be taken into account in order to relate them: the social (interactions of practices and practitioners), the teleological (aims of religion and science), the epistemological (beliefs, methods, theories, and concepts), and the theoretical (subject matter and content). His model includes three possible interactions between religion and science—totally separated, overlapping, or a unity of domains—while putting forth notions of scientific/religious expansionism/restrictionism to express the fluctuating boundary work between religion and science.*]

CHAPTER 31

··

SPORTS

··

CAROLE M. CUSACK

CHAPTER SUMMARY

··

- This chapter details five significant intersections between sport and religion.
- Premodern societies often viewed sports feats as ritual or worship directed to the gods.
- Physical exertion may act as a trigger for altered states of consciousness, explaining why trials of sporting prowess merit consideration as religious acts or spiritual experiences.
- In the modern world, famous sportsmen and women frequently profess religious faith, and credit their success to divine intervention.
- Fan devotion to sporting stars and teams can resemble religious devotion.
- Sports may function as a substitute for religion, or as a 'secular religion,' for certain people in the contemporary, deregulated spiritual marketplace.

INTRODUCTION

··

Both 'sport' and 'religion' are complex phenomena and the focus of contested definitional debates. Herein 'sport' refers to physical activities that have rules, an element of competition, and extrinsic measures of excellence, reflecting the etymology of *athlete* "from the Greek word *athlos* ('contest') and *athlon* ('prize')" (Guttmann 1978, 5). The discipline of 'sport studies' dates to the late 1960s. Soon after, African-American sociologist Harry Edwards identified parallels between sport and religion. He noted that sport had saints (deceased champions who embodied the sport's code in their playing lives), patriarchs (coaches, managers, and administrators who run sports clubs, etc.), gods ('stars' worshiped by fans), high councils (organizations that interpret the rules of competition), scribes (journalists and historians), shrines (museums, halls of fame, and trophy rooms), churches or temples (playing fields and stadia), sacred symbols (club logos and memorabilia), and what he called "seekers of the kingdom" (devoted fans) (Edwards 1973, 261). These striking parallels might be mere resemblances; one way to uncover deeper connections between religion and sport is through use of the sociological categories of 'sacred' and 'profane'.

In 1978 sports historian Allen Guttmann delineated the ways that modernity had transformed sports from 'ritual' to 'record.' Modern sport is characterized by: being secular and distinct from religion; competition being open to all, and not only those from a particular social class; professional athletes and specialized roles within sports; rationalization through rules and training regimes; bureaucratization of competitions, interpretation of rules, and so on; an emphasis on quantification and the measurement of performance; and finally, the keeping of records (Guttmann 1978, 16–55).

Religion(s) have arguably undergone comparable changes in the modern post-Enlightenment West, in which religion has become institutionalized and rationalized, and "there are no [longer] mysterious incalculable forces that come into play, but rather that one can, in principle, master all things by calculation . . . the world is disenchanted" (Weber 2001 [1948], 139). It is the secular context in which the Christian narrative has lost power that enables previously 'profane' phenomena such as sports to become 'sacred.' In a society lacking a unifying religious, civil, or cultural meta-narrative, individuals are free to accord absolute significance to a range of human cultural products, including sports, rock music, television and film, art, family, and politics. Thus, as acts of meaning-creation people elevate personal concerns to ultimate concerns. The social determination of sacred and profane, applied to popular culture, results in religious concerns being treated as trivial, routine, and/or mundane (profane), whereas the subtleties of sport are attributed ultimate value (sacred).

Sport and Religion in Ancient Rome: The Ritual of the October Equus

Sport and religion have deep historical connections. Classical Greece and Rome were cultures in which physical exertions were understood, in certain contexts, to be acts of worship to the gods. The best-known instance is the four-yearly games in honor of Zeus Olympios, held near Elis in the Peloponnese, the introduction of which is dated to 776 BCE by Hippias (Cusack 2010, 920). The Olympian gods were capable of great feats, and mythology chronicles contests such as the musical duel between Apollo and the satyr Marsyas and Athena's weaving competition with the human Arachne, who after losing to the goddess was turned into a spider. The Roman pantheon was largely imported from Greece, and the ritual analyzed here is the sacrifice of the 'October Equus' to the war god Mars, which followed a chariot race on the Campus Martius between champions of two neighborhoods of ancient Rome, the Subura and the Sacra Via, held on October 15 (the Ides). Charioteers competed for the head of the right-hand horse from the victorious pair, and it was displayed publicly in the winning district.

The meaning underlying this annual event is unclear. The festival's name has not survived, despite it being mentioned by Plutarch, Polybius, and several other ancient authors, and the presiding priest is similarly unknown. Modern scholars have suggested three interpretations of the October Equus: first, the horse, a military animal, is an appropriate offering to Mars; second, the ritual preserves an Indo-European tradition best exemplified by the Vedic *Aśvamedhá* (horse sacrifice); and third, that "the horse is the personification of the Corn Spirit . . . who is ritually killed at each harvest" (Pascal 1981, 264). The status of the horse as a sacrificial victim was high, and explanations linking the October Equus to the Indian *Aśvamedhá* stress the *Aśvamedhá*'s closeness to the *Purushamedhá* (human sacrifice), arguing that the two rituals stand in an analogous relation to each other. After the race, the horse was killed with a spear, and then dismembered. The severed head was taken by the victorious charioteer and prominently displayed, either on the wall of the Regia, a shrine in the Forum Romanum, or on the Mamilian Tower in the Subura.

The other important part of the horse was the tail, which was cut off and taken to the Regia, where the blood was sprinkled on the hearth (Pascal 1981, 268). An agricultural interpretation of the rite is supported by the horse's head being adorned with grains and loaves, and also by a plausible suggestion that the 'tail' (Latin *cauda*) is actually the horse's penis. It was suggested that the "tail trophy is an attenuated phallic trophy" (Devereux 1970, 300), due to the tail being unlikely to yield sufficient blood to cover the hearth of the Regia. As Mars was the chief god worshiped in the Regia and the chariot race took place on the Campus Martius ("field of Mars"), there is some support for the horse as an appropriate military animal to sacrifice to Mars, despite the rather minor role played by the Roman cavalry. In conclusion, the October Equus is a religious rite that involved a sporting competition, the chariot race, which also featured as an event in the ancient Olympics, as an act of devotion to Mars.

Sport and Religio-spiritual Experience: Sailing, Surfing, and Running

William James's *The Varieties of Religious Experience* (1902) sparked an ongoing debate about religion, mysticism, and religious experience. James defined religion as "the feelings, acts, and experiences of individual men [sic] in solitude, so far as they apprehend themselves to stand in relation to whatever they may consider the divine" (James 2008 [1902], 31). Shirl J. Hoffman observed that such feelings are deemed 'religious' depending on the experiencer's perspective, that is, if she or he *says* they are religious. He asked whether "there really is something inherent in sporting activities capable of evoking religious experiences," and if "the human experience of sport per se induces . . . states that meet the criteria for religious experience or is the experience of sport merely incidental to their occurrence?" (Hoffman 1992, 70).

Physical and mental discipline enables sportsmen and women to have 'peak' experiences as they push their bodies to the limit. Richard Hutch's study of solo yachting as spiritual practice accepts James's 'individualist' definition of religion: solo yachtsmen and women are alone, engaging in a life and death struggle that may be an aesthetically pleasing activity but equally may be an ordeal, such as they have never before experienced. Hutch pits what he calls "moral presence," an ethical and spiritual quality, against "technical self-reliance," an orientation that is human-centered and profane. Moral presence manifests in athletes when faced with loss and failure, and in solo yachtsmen and women when the boat's technology breaks down, and can result in three types of spiritual experience, which Hutch terms technical finesse, cosmic quest, and personal test (Hutch 2005, 13–17).

Bron Taylor's analysis of surfing spirituality reinforces the notion that individual spiritual experiences may be regarded as equivalent to religion or spirituality in secular modernity. Taylor asserts that "there is a mysterious magic in surfing that can only be apprehended directly through the experience; that surfing fosters self-realization; that commercialization of the practice is a defiling act but that even such acts cannot obviate its spiritual power; [and] that surfing can lead to a life characterized by compassion toward other living beings" (Taylor 2010, 104). He views surfing as a manifestation of "dark green religion," and provides examples of mythology, holy figures including Duke Kahanamoku (1890–1968), a Hawaiian shamanic figure and Olympic champion, and points to the spiritual connections between surfing, the counterculture, and environmentalism (Taylor 2010, 105–116). Similar religio-spiritual claims have been made about running: Jeffrey P. Fry says that, "the key is the *intention* of the runner . . . almost any experience can take on a religious quality, depending on how one approaches it" (Fry 2007, 57–58). This reinforces both Hoffman and James, cited earlier, confirming that individuals craft their spirituality and religious orientation from the experiences they value—be they of sport, nature, art, or other cultural products—deeming them sacred and according them religio-spiritual value.

Sports Stars and Religious Faith: Eric Liddell, Olympic Champion and Christian 'Martyr'

Athletes who attribute their sporting prowess to divine favor are found the world over. American professional sport has perhaps the greatest number, due to the prominence of religion in American public life. Historically, Christianity has been suspicious of sport, for its celebration of the body and its associations with leisure and pleasure. Yet, contemporary Christian sports stars have become effective evangelists, as the dedication needed to achieve athletic success is seen as analogous to the dedication required to develop spiritual strength and virtue (Nesti 2007, 161). An historical example of a Christian athlete is Eric Liddell (1902–1945), who won a gold medal in the 400 meters race in the Paris Olympic Games on July 11, 1924, after refusing to run in his specialist race, the 100 meters, as the heats were scheduled on Sunday. His wife Florence Liddell stated that he felt keenly being called "a traitor to his country," but that he viewed his athletic skills as a gift from God, and that reverence for the Sabbath had been inculcated in him since childhood (Magnusson 1981, 41).

After the Olympic Games, in which he also won a bronze medal for the 200 meters, Liddell completed his studies in Edinburgh and departed to teach science, supervise athletics, and participate in missionary work at the Anglo-Chinese College in Tientsin (Watson/Weir/Friend 2005, 8). Liddell was bade farewell by huge crowds at church meetings in Glasgow and Edinburgh, and he boarded the train at Waverley Station surrounded by crowds of well-wishers. Biographer Sally Magnusson notes that he began to sing "Jesus Shall Reign," and the "entire station belted out hymn after hymn as the train gathered steam and finally pulled out" (Magnusson 1981, 86). Liddell worked as a missionary in China for twenty years, and in 1943, after his wife and children left for Canada, he was interned in a camp at Weishien, where he died on February 21, 1945. He was deeply mourned in Scotland, was immortalized by Ian Charleson's performance in the film *Chariots of Fire* (1981), and has been the subject of several popular biographies by Christian authors.

DEVOTION TO FOOTBALL TEAMS: THE TARTAN ARMY AS A RELIGIOUS PHENOMENON

Passionate fan devotion to sporting teams illustrates certain themes in the post-traditional West.[1] Fan groups are neo-tribal organizations in which people with a shared focus of devotion "are affectively committed to the team and proactively engaging in sustained behaviours" (Dionisio/Leal/Moutinho 2008, 20). Group identity is reinforced by ritual activities and consumption behaviors that are focused on the fandom object. The Scottish national football team's fans, the Tartan Army, may be viewed a form of devotional 'cult' expressed through "a formal series of public and private rituals requiring a symbolic language and space deemed sacred by its worshipers" (Dionisio/Leal/

---

[1] This section owes a debt to Tancred Fergus, my former student and now friend, who first drew my attention to the Tartan Army over ten years ago, when he submitted an essay on "The Tartan Army as Secular Religion" as part of his Studies in Religion major at the University of Sydney.

Moutinho 2008, 23). Football is Scotland's most popular sport, and in recent decades the Tartan Army have become a popular global phenomenon, due to "their enthusiasm and fervour for their team, large numbers travelling, and a willingness to party wherever they go" (Bradley 2011, 820).

Joseph Bradley interviewed Tartan Army members about religion and football; some interviewees identified national team fandom as a means to heal the Protestant–Catholic sectarian divide, particularly in matches between Glasgow teams Celtic and Rangers. Jason, from the Armadale Sons of Wallace branch, stated that, "If the rest of Scotland had the same belief and used the Tartan Army as a sort of standard, Scotland would be a better place, far better place. I really believe that" (Bradley 2011, 821). The research demonstrated that the Tartan Army explicitly rejected Catholic and Protestant individual member identities, and affirmed a secular, nationalist identity. These findings reverse the classic insider–outsider divide in scholarly research, in which believers often assert a *sui generis* account of religion (as seen in the following section in the case of Iglesia Maradoniana), and academics identify secular motivations or explanations for behaviors termed 'religious.' In fandom studies fans often assert that they are secular, yet scholars identify 'religious' elements in their collective beliefs and behaviors.

Popular culture contributes to Tartan Army rituals. Mel Gibson's portrayal of the Scottish nationalist hero William Wallace in *Braveheart* (1995) is important for Scottish–English relations. The night before the Scotland–England Euro 1996 match at Wembley on June 15, "some of the Tartan Army's hard core made a ceremonial visit to the London site of Wallace's execution by the English in 1304" (Finn/Giulianotti 1998, 193–194). An England victory ended Scottish hopes, and later Trafalgar Square hosted "Tartan Army fans, defiantly drinking and singing their elegies to a beaten team" (Finn/Giulianotti 1998, 197). Legendary players, including Denis Law and Dave Mackay (featured on UK stamps in 2013) are venerated, and relics of historic matches (like ticket stubs, scarves, and jerseys) are cultural capital traded within the Army. Within fandoms, the profane may become sacred, and spirituality "flourishes outside traditional religious contexts, in the activities of everyday life" (Cusack 2010, 916). Sport, when elevated to an 'ultimate concern,' may function as religion for some people.

Sport as Religion: Iglesia Maradoniana

In the contemporary West, celebrities are powerful figures. Ellis Cashmore argues that fans have extraordinary psychological relationships with celebrities; regard celebrities as role models; and adopt the perceived attributes of celebrities (Cashmore 2006, 83). Churches dedicated to celebrities have emerged in the late twentieth century, including the First Presleyterian Church of Elvis the Divine and the Saint John Coltrane African Orthodox Church. It is often difficult to determine *when* sport becomes religion, but with Iglesia Maradoniana (Church of Maradona) there is no doubt. It was founded in Rosario, Argentina in 1998 by two fans, Alejandro Verón and Hernán Amez, and worships Diego Maradona (b. 1960). Maradona emerged from the Buenos Aires slums and had a brilliant career in soccer, which ended due to cocaine addiction, an increasingly erratic personal life, and health and weight problems. His dark and light sides are exemplified by the two goals he scored for Argentina against England in the 1986 World Cup: the first due to a hand-ball foul, which he later attributed to the 'Hand of God,' and the second, only minutes later, which was voted 'Goal of the Century' in a 2002 FIFA poll (Free 2014, 199).

The Iglesia Maradoniana has developed an ecclesiastical calendar around the dates of Diego Maradona's life: Christmas is October 30, his birthday; Easter is June 22, "the day new disciples get baptized by recreating the *Mano de Dios*, jumping in front of a life-size cardboard Peter Shilton [England goalkeeper] and trying to recreate, by means of a punchy left hand, that perfect parabola loop over his head and into a net" (Chadband 2014); his autobiography *I am El Diego of the People* (2005) is their scripture; and the years are reckoned from his birth in 1960, thus 2016 is 56 AD (After Diego). Just as Christ suffered, died, and was resurrected, members of Iglesia Maradoniana celebrate Maradona's sufferings, which are interpreted both romantically as indicative of his integrity in the face of exploitation by the corrupt international sporting establishment, and as "a fan fantasy concerning the tragedy of the commodification of sport's finest talents" (Free 2014, 203). Three films about Maradona also testify to his power as a focus of fan devotion that shades into religious dimensions: the British documentary *In the Hands of the Gods* (2007), which features five British fans on a pilgrimage to Maradona's home; *El Camino de San Diego* (2007), an Argentinian 'road movie' that follows one obsessed fan; and director Emir Kusturica's *Maradona by Kusturica* (2008), which focuses on Maradona's status as a contradictory, enigmatic figure, in which fans invest and seek redemption (Free 2014, 197). Iglesia Maradoniana is a religion focused on a celebrity, but sport is central to the church, and members come to faith through fandom.

The founders estimate the membership of Iglesia Maradoniana at over 80,000, from approximately fifty-five countries (Chadband 2014). The Church has Ten Commandments, which include: "3. Declare unconditional love for Diego and the beauty of football . . . 5. Spread the news of Diego's miracles throughout the universe . . . 8. Preach and spread the principles of the Church of Maradona. 9. Make Diego your middle name. 10. Name your first son Diego' (Franklin 2008). A ludic spirit pervades Iglesia Maradoniana, yet it has been in existence since 1998 and continues to grow, even as Maradona the individual is gradually eclipsed. Journalist Ian Chadband observes that newer Argentine stars like Lionel Messi "do not inspire the same mad love" (Chadband 2014). When another journalist, Jonathan Franklin, asked if the church would die out in a generation, convert José Gabino demurred, responding, "One fan dies, one hundred are born" (Franklin 2008). Sports are a prime site for the formation of popular-culture-based religions (Possamai 2005; Cusack 2010), but to date Iglesia Maradoniana is the only significant example of formal, church-like institutionalization.

CONCLUSION

This chapter has argued that sport and religion have manifold interactions, from the ancient world to the present. In the modern era, as Christianity lost power in the West, sport became (along with other entertainment spectacles and popular cultural phenomena) a source of ultimate concern for people seeking meaning and spirituality. The emergence of personal spiritualities and the pervasive nature of communications technologies, combined with the transformation of sport into mass entertainment spectacles, means that sports have the potential to function as, and "feel like" religion for many (Norman/Cusack 2012, 130).[2]

GLOSSARY

Celebrity "The attribution of glamorous or notorious status to an individual within the public sphere" (Rojek 2001, 10).

Fandom "Fandom was more than simple enthusiasm for a TV program or film; it was a form of collective interpretation of popular culture that created a powerful sense of group cohesion" (Sullivan 2013, 194).

Religion "one's way of valuing most intensively. Religious valuing, in a famous phrase, involves 'ultimate concern'" (Ferré 1967, 69).

Sport "[A]ny physical activity for the purposes of competition, recreation, education, or health" (Jarvis, 1999, 1).

REFERENCES

Bradley, Joseph M. 2011. "In-Groups, Out-Groups, and Contested Identities in Scottish International Football." *Sport in Society: Cultures, Commerce, Media, Politics* 14(6): 818–832. doi: 10.1080/17430437.2011.587298

Cashmore, Ellis. 2006. *Celebrity/Culture*. Abingdon and New York: Routledge.

Chadband, Ian. 2014. "World Cup 2014: Diego Maradona Still Worshipped 28 Years After the 'Hand of God' Goal Against England." *The Telegraph*, 21 June. <http://is.gd/1ddk16>, accessed February 3, 2016.

Cusack, Carole M. 2010. "Sport." In *Religion & Everyday Life and Culture*, edited by Richard D. Hecht and Vincent F. Biondo III, Vol. 3. Santa Barbara, CA: Praeger, 915–943. (Reprinted in *Religion and Culture: Contemporary Practices and Perspectives*, edited by Richard D. Hecht and Vincent F. Biondo III. Minneapolis: Fortress Press, 2012, 307–326.)

[2] The School of Letters, Art and Media (SLAM) at the University of Sydney provided funds for a research assistant, Will Noonan, whom I thank for his skill at library and database searches, and note-taking abilities. I am also grateful to Don Barrett, who has been an invaluable support to me for nearly twenty years.

Devereux, George. 1970. "The 'Equus October' Ritual Reconsidered." *Mnemosyne*, Fourth Series 23(3): 297–301.

Dionisio, Pedro, Carmo Leal, and Luiz Moutinho. 2008. "Fandom Affiliation and Tribal Behaviour: A Sports Marketing Application." *Qualitative Market Research* 11(1): 17–39. doi: 10.1108/13522750810845531

Edwards, Harry. 1973. *Sociology of Sport*. Belmont, CA: Dorsey Press.

Ferré, Frederick. 1967. *Basic Modern Philosophy of Religion*. New York: Scribner.

Finn, Gerry P. T. and Richard Giulianotti. 1998. "Scottish Fans Not English Hooligans! Scots, Scottishness, and Scottish Football." In *Fanatics: Power, Identity & Fandom in Football*, edited by Adam Brown. London and New York: Routledge, 189–202.

Franklin, Jonathan. 2008. "He Was Sent From Above." *The Guardian*, November 13. <http://is.gd/Kk2x2Z>, accessed February 3, 2016.

Free, Marcus. 2014. "Diego Maradona and the Psychodynamics of Football Fandom in International Cinema." *Celebrity Studies* 5(1–2): 197–212. doi: 10.1080/19392397.2013.828458

Fry, Jeffrey P. 2007. "Running Religiously." In *Running & Philosophy: Marathon for the Mind*, edited by Michael W. Austin. Malden, MA and Oxford: Blackwell, 57–69.

Guttmann, Allen. 1978. *From Ritual to Record: The Nature of Modern Sport*. New York: Columbia University Press.

Hoffman, Shirl J. 1992. "Sport as Religious Experience." In *Sport and Religion*, edited by Shirl J. Hoffman. Champaign, IL: Human Kinetic Books, 63–75.

Hutch, Richard. 2005. "Under Sail Alone at Sea: A Study of Sport as Spiritual Practice." *Australian Religion Studies Review* 18(1): 3–24. doi: 10.1558/arsr.2005.18.1.3

James, William. 2008. *The Varieties of Religious Experience: A Study in Human Nature*. Rockville, MD: ARC Manor. Original edition, 1902.

Jarvis, Matt. 1999. *Sport Psychology*. London and New York: Routledge.

Magnusson, Sally. 1981. *The Flying Scotsman: A Biography*. London, Melbourne, and New York: Quartet Books.

Nesti, Mark. 2007. "Suffering, Sacrifice, Sports Psychology and the Spirit." In *Sport and Spirituality: An Introduction*, edited by Jim Parry, Simon Robinson, Nick J. Watson, and Mark Nesti. London and New York: Routledge, 151–169.

Norman, Alex and Carole M. Cusack. 2012. "The Religion in Olympic Tourism." *Journal of Tourism and Cultural Change* 10(2): 124–136. doi: 10.1080/14766825.2012.683956

Pascal, C. Bennett. 1981. "October Horse." *Harvard Studies in Classical Philology* 85: 261–291.

Possamai, Adam. 2005. *Religion and Popular Culture: A Hyper-Real Testament*. Brussels: Peter Lang.

Rojek, Chris. 2001. *Celebrity*. London: Reaktion Books.

Sullivan, John L. 2013. *Media Audiences: Effects, Users, Institutions, and Power*. Los Angeles, CA and London: Sage.

Taylor, Bron. 2010. *Dark Green Religion: Nature Spirituality and the Planetary Future*. Berkeley, Los Angeles, and London: University of California Press.

Watson, Nick, Stuart Weir, and Stephen Friend. 2005. "The Development of Muscular Christianity in Victorian Britain and Beyond." *Journal of Religion & Society* 7: 1–21.

Weber, Max. 2001. *Max Weber: Essays in Sociology*, translated by Hans H. Gerth and C. Wright Mills. Abingdon and New York: Routledge. Original edition, 1948.

FURTHER READING

Birrell, Susan. 1981. "Sport as Ritual: Interpretations from Durkheim to Goffman." *Social Forces* 60(2): 354–376. [*This classic article analyzes the interrelationship and potential identity of sport and ritual in social scientific methodologies from Émile Durkheim's focus on the ritual collective, to Erving Goffman's analysis of the ritualizing individual.*]

Cusack 2010 [*This chapter proposes a fivefold relationship between sport and religion, and examines these five associations through detailed case studies of the ancient Olympic Games and sumo wrestling in Japan.*]

Scholes, Jeffrey and Raphael Sassower. 2014. *Religion and Sports in American Culture.* Oxford and New York: Routledge. [*This brief monograph investigates religion and sports through chapters focused on key terms. These are: belief, sacrifice, relics, pilgrimage, competition, work, and redemption.*]

CHAPTER 32

TOURISM

ALEX NORMAN

CHAPTER SUMMARY

- The interaction of tourism and religions is more than one of sacred and profane, and demonstrates remarkable variety.
- Tourist–pilgrim dichotomies are analytically unhelpful.
- The prominence of leisure in Western societies drives interactions between tourists and religions.
- Changes brought by secularization mean tourists interact with religions for their own purposes, rather than institutional ones.

INTRODUCTION

The meeting points of religious practices and tourism have significant appeal to travelers, media writers, and tourism promoters alike. More importantly, however, despite a slow start, scholarship has demonstrated that instances of travel that are imbricated with religious identities and structures are ubiquitous and significant, and have implications for all elements of society. Indeed, tourism can be thought of as a social sphere, or space in which certain dramas are staged and social norms maintained (Lii 1998). As a field of study the interactions between religion and tourism encompass phenomena as varied as traditions concerned with rites of passage, the social and economic infrastructure around a sacred site, marketing strategies for acts of piety and penitence, and family vacations. We can find tourism and religions interacting regularly and everywhere, and in large numbers. Recently, Stausberg (2011) published a state-of-the-scholarship text for the field, in which the staggering complexity of the tourism–religions matrix is laid out, and it is worth noting that the United Nations World Tourism Organization (WTO) regards 'religion/pilgrimages' as one of eight basic reasons human beings might take a trip (United Nations World Tourism Organization 2010). For this reason we now find tourism being included as a topic of import for scholars interested in religious phenomena generally. Care must be taken, however, with the terms applied in the quest to gain greater understanding of the great hydra of religions and tourism. At the outset, it is worth noting that, taken collectively, the scholarship that examines points of intersection between travel phenomena and religious phenomena presents a picture too plural and diverse to allow us to refer to a single type of human experience called 'religious travel.' One could argue that all tourism is ultimately religious, as indeed some have (e.g. Graburn 1989) and with interesting reasons discussed in the following. The intention of this chapter, however, is to highlight that many religious traditions involve tourism in a variety of ways, and that they do so in many more ways than scholars originally realized.

More than the Sacralization of Space

Human beings, it seems, have always been interested in traveling, and for a variety of reasons. Identities, whether cultural, national, or religious are fabricated in contrast with an 'Other.' This is true for the construction of landscape and geography too, with certain space demarcated as 'special' (see Greider/Garkovich 1994; Taves 2012) and thus worthy of visitation, or, conversely, avoidance. Indeed, insofar as many religious traditions are concerned with the construction of society, and that society itself is seen as at least potentially problematic, we find a great many traditions sectioning off parts of the world that are not near to the everyday footfalls of social actors. This is most easily observable in traditions of travel that seek to remove the individual or group from their everyday environment and towards a less humanly populated landscape, such as the climbing of sacred mountains in China (Yü 1992). In contrast, we can also see instances of society itself recast in the context of being away from home in heavily populated settings. Thus, for example, traditions of travel such as the Kumbh Mela or the Hajj both draw participants to their locales (themselves normal space for their inhabitants) en masse as celebrations and a way to sacralize and re-enforce social bonds (Haq/Jackson 2009).

This sacralization of space can, however, appear to imply that the field of religions and travel is limited to sacred–profane dichotomies. This is not the case. Rather 'the religious' in acts of travel encompasses a wide swathe of human behaviors including missionary activity, the travels of religious trainees to centers of learning, and the travels of nomadic tribes, such as Australian Aboriginal peoples in ancestral lands (Swain 1993), among many others. Getting further away from the sacred–profane dichotomy we can include the participation of individuals in meditation retreats, travel to attend events such as Mind, Body, Spirit conventions, and the global touring of leaders in order to give lectures, including world famous figures such as the Dalai Lama or the Pope, in addition to less well-known teachers such as Candice O'Denver (e.g. Norman 2010) and John of

God (e.g. Rocha 2013). It is worth noting that these tours can have significant economic and cultural impact. For example, the Chinese government has routinely threatened to reconsider its trade relations with any state that sends officials to meet with the Dalai Lama (Fuchs/Klann 2013). More broadly, Urry (2002) noted that peoples being visited altered their sense of self and authenticity in order to align with the gaze cast upon them by travelers from a hegemonic visiting culture (be they 'tourists,' 'pilgrims,' or anything else). This gaze is a social mechanism, so Urry argued, by which acts of travel may alter and destabilize host cultures.

The Pilgrimage vs. Tourism Debate

The realization that the field of religions and tourism extends far beyond pilgrimage and 'sacred travel' has helped to develop what is, to date, the most important conceptual hurdle the field has had to negotiate: the infamous tourist vs. pilgrim debate. The notion that there can be a firm distinction between tourist and pilgrim, between tourism and pilgrimage, has long been dismissed in certain scholarly realms, yet it persists elsewhere regardless. The argument is that tourism involves sightseeing and the pursuit of hedonic concerns, whereas pilgrimage is penitential, serious, and eudaimonic, and in its 'highest form' soteriological in motivation (e.g. Turner/Ash 1975). This normative model of travel is largely informed by reinterpretation of medieval Christian pilgrimage traditions (Taylor 2010), but was also pushed along by the early writings on pilgrimage by Victor and Edith Turner (Turner 1973; Turner/Turner 1978). In their groundbreaking work, a model of pilgrimage was developed that linked it with mysticism and ritual, and suggested a coherence and unity of tradition that subsequent studies have not been able to replicate reliably (e.g. Aziz 1987; Collins-Kreiner 2010). But even the Turners recognized that a hard distinction between pilgrims and tourists was impossible, as, at best, "a tourist is half a pilgrim, if a pilgrim is half a tourist" (Turner/Turner 1978, 20). Indeed, travelers who self-identify, or are identified by religious traditions, as 'pilgrims' go sightseeing and shopping, visit museums, stay in hotels, walk the streets, take photographs, and take airline seats in much the same way as all other tourists (e.g. Collins-Kreiner 2010; Stausberg 2011; Norman 2011; Reader 2013), which will be discussed further in what follows.

In the same period as the Turners were publishing their explorations of pilgrimage, Dean MacCannell published his book *The Tourist* (1976) that repositioned tourists as seekers of authenticity. This work, along with Erik Cohen's (1979) phenomenological typology, and a decade later Nelson Graburn's (1989) positioning of tourism as a sacred journey, reconfigured scholarly understanding of tourism phenomena and demanded they receive greater attention. They also laid the groundwork for understanding that the combination of tourism and religious practice goes well beyond institutional sanction. These texts, and a number of others, positioned tourism as a normal part of contemporary Western society. Indeed Graburn's work goes so far as to suggest that the routinization of tourism results in it being a norm; an expectation for social actors, the outcomes of which are valorized: "mental and physical health, social status, and diverse, exotic experiences" (Graburn 1989, 24). This has some important implications for understanding the intersections of religions and tourism, for, as an expected behavior in social contexts characterized by complex and plural religious landscapes, religious traditions cannot possibly be the only sources of sanction for all religious travel. Furthermore, the disembedding of meaning, purpose, and identity concerns from the putatively exclusive domain of religious traditions (see Lyon 2000; Giddens 1991) means that people travel for personal, so-called 'spiritual' reasons, that may not connect with, and indeed may contradict, any religious traditions to which they might claim belonging.

Dismissing Pilgrim–Tourist Dichotomies

Analytically, the suggested distinction between tourist and pilgrim is misleading, and recent scholarship has sought to progressively distance itself from this debate over the last twenty years. As Collins-Kreiner (2010) notes, scholarly discussion has moved from typologization to de-differentiation wherein scholars have characterized pilgrims and tourists as similar travelers. Accordingly, and following from the WTO (United Nations World Tourism Organization 2010, 9–10), it is best, for the purposes of religious studies, to think of the terms thus: a tourist is a visitor to a place outside his/her usual environment; a pilgrim is a tourist who is referred to in an emic discourse (either theirs or someone else's) as a pilgrim. Social sciences scholars would do well to adopt this simple framework for three reasons. Firstly, it accords with a simple international standard of definition and understanding, making discussion and collaboration much easier. Secondly, it shifts social scientific discussion away from normative and towards descriptive and analytical frameworks. Thirdly, it renders the discussion of pilgrimage tractable, insofar as it then becomes one of discourse analysis, rather than attempting to measure intractable elements like piety and belief.

Any pilgrim–tourist dichotomy is contextual and only useful for scholarly purposes if we understand what is intended by the deployment of the terms in a particular context. There exist good measures of tourist activity: an informational infrastructure consisting of visa numbers, hotel occupancy, travel ticket purchase data, site visitor numbers, and so on. As 'pilgrim' tends to be defined as serious, institutionally sanctioned, part of a tradition of travel, or 'traveller with meaning' (Digance 2006), measurement proves to be difficult. It is hard to quantify the conditions of 'pilgrim' as opposed to 'tourist' without interrogating individual tourists; there are few, if any, outwardly visible signs of meaning pilgrims might display that tourists do not. In this respect, the term 'pilgrim' becomes a shorthand or symbol for the meanings and expectations of the practices being undertaken by travelers in the context in question.

An interesting case study to examine this conceptual problem is the tradition of the Camino de Santiago, Spain; a collection of walking and cycling routes that converge on Santiago de Compostela from all over Europe. Over the last twenty years, the tradition, which usually involves walking at least 100 km, has seen a rapid increase in interest, with official pilgrim arrivals in Santiago rising from just under 5,000 in 1990 to 215,880 in 2013 (Oficina de Acogida al Peregrino 2014). While pilgrims are overwhelmingly Catholic, their motivations (as listed in their official documentation) are dominated by "religious and other" (54.6 percent) over simply "religious" (40 percent) and "not religious" (5.4 percent). A number of scholarly investigations of the Camino have been undertaken (e.g. Frey 1998; Slavin 2003; Norman 2011), with most finding that what draws and propels tourists to undertake the pilgrimage are a variety of reasons including folklore about the experience, the rural setting, popular literature on the routes (Norman 2009), and the desire for time for reflection, even for those stating explicit religious motivations. Indeed, ethnographic accounts like Frey's (1998) note that Catholicism, or even Christian identity more broadly, rarely enters the field of concern or practice for many Compostela pilgrims.

Tourism and Leisure as Religious Practice

Unsurprisingly, we now find leisure as the primary location of religious practice and activity in the West. Following from this, religious beliefs and practices have increasingly been informed by leisure activities (e.g. Jafari/Scott 2014). Indeed, certain religious practices are now being analyzed as leisure activities with interesting results. For example, Choe, Chick, and O'Regan (2014) compared the similarities and differences between meditative practice and other 'passive leisure' forms in general in a Zen meditation group in the northwestern United States, and found strong similarities in terms of reported outcomes. Furthermore, what we might call 'religious leisure,' as either the engagement with religions as sources of leisure, or the religious engagement with leisure pursuits, is widely observable in touristic contexts. For example, Olsen (2003) notes that religious sites are commodified by tourists such that the cultural products and experience of associated religious traditions can be purchased by tourists. Religious sites or experiences are thus approached for enjoyment or relaxation in such touristic settings. Meanwhile, Gilmore (2006) notes that the experiential dimensions for many attendees of the Burning Man festival in Nevada, United States, are strongly religious. Similarly, Shinde (2012) found Braj-yatra tourists in northern India to frequently be concerned with outcomes usually classified as leisure (sightseeing, enjoyment, luxury) rather than with 'religious' concerns (piety, duty, experiencing the sacred/divine). Indeed, more formally recognized instances of religious tourism can be concerned mostly with leisure for the participant (Rinschede 1992).

The intersectionality of religions and tourism is noteworthy for its complexity and variety (Stausberg 2011), and demands further scholarly investigation. As Jafari and Scott (2014) note regarding Muslim travelers and travel in 'the Muslim world,' one can, with some legitimacy, limit the scope of investigation to pilgrimage and other closely related forms of travel that are institutional or orthodox. This, however, would be to miss the real value in looking to travel as it is shaped religiously, with the resulting implications for government policy, marketing, and services catering to tourists. As MacCannell (1973) argued, tourism phenomena are arranged, overwhelmingly, for the tourists engaging with them, and thus reflect the worldviews and concerns of those tourists. Accordingly, we should focus our research wherever tourism and religions mix in any way, even if it is simply the touristic practices of a particular religious group.

SECULARIZATION, RELIGIONS, SPIRITUALITIES, AND TOURISM

While many early formulations of secularization characterized it as the death of religion (Wallace 1966), secularization, in the sense of a removal of religious domination and control of public power (Berger 1967), has instead resulted in the radical increase of interest in religious sites and traditions, and religious practices in the context of tourism. In the wake of this, as numerous scholars have noted, came a drive to privatize and individuate religious ideas and practices (Lambert 1999; Campbell 1972), and to re-label them 'spiritual.' Indeed, as secularization involved the removal of control over individuals from the hands of religious traditions, it has been argued that this results in the transfer of autonomy to individuals (Houtman/Aupers 2007). This de-traditionalization results in a 'spiritual turn' that promotes sacralization of the self (Heelas 2008), and increases emphasis on experiential and emotional dimensions of life (Ezzy 2014). These changes are visible in tourist practices, and have variously been characterized as New Age pilgrimage (Rountree 2006), wellness tourism (Voigt/Pforr 2013), and spiritual tourism (Coats 2008; Norman 2011). What is clear among these studies is that tourists often engage for reasons of personal betterment either with religious practices or with practices that have purposive well-being, meaning, and identity concerns that mimic those found in religious traditions.

FUTURE AREAS OF RESEARCH

Despite its richness, the field of religion and tourism is surprisingly understudied, though recent scholarly interest has begun to give the field momentum. The publication of a number of edited volumes in the mid-2000s (Badone/Roseman 2004; Dann 2002;

Eade/Coleman 2004; Swatos 2006; Timothy/Olsen 2006) signaled the beginning of the current surge in scholarly interest, with the chapters included taking a pluralistic turn, understanding the normative qualities as part of the phenomena being studied. Much of what is needed to begin with are richly detailed and systematically interrogated ethnographies, from which other research questions can begin to be asked. Areas of particular interest are the economic impacts on host communities, especially of the newer forms of religious/spiritual travel; environmental concerns both for host communities and in terms of global warming; underlying currents in religious practice and identity in tourist-generating societies other than Western; whether religious/spiritual tourism results in any positive outcomes for tourists; and the responses found at specific religious sites to tourism practices they find themselves host to. Also needing to be addressed are phenomena concerning the arrangement of goods and services for the particular religious identities of tourists. Future research in the field will need to be cognizant of the competing demands of religious institutions, tourist promoters and operators, local communities, and of tourists themselves.

GLOSSARY

Holiday/vacation a period of time spent away from normal routines of work and social commitments.

Leisure respite from work, thus leisure time often coincides with holidays/vacations and is typically mapped onto pleasure, relaxation, and freedom. May also be called recreation. Can take hedonic or eudaimonic forms, and be regarded as serious or casual.

Pilgrim a subset of tourist; a pilgrim is a person who identifies themselves, or is identified by a certain group or institution, as taking part in an established tradition of travel and/or some kind of journey "redolent with meaning" (Digance). It is typically a highly normatively loaded emic term.

Pilgrimage a subset of tourism; a tradition of travel, either formally or informally described by a social group. Most often this will be a religious tradition, but it also includes secular and civil religious traditions such as battlefield memorial travel.

Tourism a subset of travel that involves journeying away from everyday routines to visit another place and, typically, stay at least one night. It is also the industry that springs up to support and profit from this phenomenon.

Tourist a traveler is defined as a tourist if their trip includes an overnight stay away from their usual environments.

Travel the activity of a traveler, someone who moves between geographic locations for any reason. However, in vernacular usage it is often contrasted as the 'serious' alternative to the 'frivolous' or 'selfish' tourism.

REFERENCES

Aziz, Barbara Nimri. 1987. "Personal Dimensions of the Sacred Journey: What Pilgrims Say." *Religious Studies* 23(2): 247–261. doi: 10.1017/S0034412500018758

Badone, Ellen and Sharon R. Roseman, eds. 2004. *Intersecting Journeys: The Anthropology of Pilgrimage and Tourism*. Urbana: University of Illinois Press.

Berger, Peter L. 1967. *The Social Reality of Religion*. London: Faber.

Campbell, Colin. 1972. "The Cult, the Cultic Milieu and Secularization." *A Sociological Yearbook of Religion in Britain* 5: 119–136.

Choe, Jaeyeon, Garry Chick, and Michael O'Regan. 2014. "Meditation as a Kind of Leisure: The Similarities and Differences in the United States." *Leisure Studies* 34(4): 420–437. doi:10.1080/02614367.2014.923497

Coats, Curtis. 2008. "Is the Womb Barren? A Located Study of Spiritual Tourism in Sedona, Arizona, and Its Possible Effects on Eco-Consciousness." *Journal for the Study of Religion, Nature and Culture* 2(4): 483–507. doi: 10.1558/jsrnc.v2i4.483

Cohen, Erik. 1979. "A Phenomenology of Tourist Experiences." *Sociology* 13(2): 179–201. doi: 10.1177/003803857901300203

Collins-Kreiner, Noga. 2010. "Researching Pilgrimage: Continuity and Transformations." *Annals of Tourism Research* 37(2): 440–456. doi:10.1016/j.annals.2009.10.016

Dann, Graham, ed. 2002. *The Tourist as a Metaphor of the Social World*. Wallingford: CABI Publishing.

Digance, Justine. 2006. "Religious and Secular Pilgrimage: Journeys Redolent with Meaning." In *Tourism, Religion and Spiritual Journeys*, edited by Dallen J. Timothy and Daniel H. Olsen. London: Routledge, 36–48.

Eade, John and Simon Coleman, eds. 2004. *Reframing Pilgrimage: Cultures in Motion*. European Association of Social Anthropologists. London: Routledge.

Ezzy, Douglas. 2014. "Religion, Aesthetics and Moral Ontology." *Journal of Sociology*. doi: 10.1177/1440783314521884

Frey, Nancy Louise. 1998. *Pilgrim Stories: On and Off the Road to Santiago*. Berkeley: University of California Press.

Fuchs, Andreas and Nils-Hendrik Klann. 2013. "Paying a Visit: The Dalai Lama Effect on International Trade." *Journal of International Economics* 91(1): 164–177. 10.1016/j.jinteco.2013.04.007

Giddens, Anthony. 1991. *Modernity and Self-Identity: Self and Society in the Late Modern Age*. Stanford, CA: Stanford University Press.

Gilmore, Lee. 2006. "Desert Pilgrimage: Liminality, Transformation, and the Other at the Burning Man Festival." In *On the Road to Being There: Studies in Pilgrimage and Tourism in Late Modernity*, edited by William H. Swatos. Leiden: Brill, 125–158.

Graburn, Nelson H. H. 1989. "Tourism: The Sacred Journey." In *Hosts and Guests: The Anthropology of Tourism*, edited by Valene L. Smith. Philadelphia: University of Pennsylvania Press, 21–36.

Greider, Thomas and Lorraine Garkovich. 1994. "Landscapes: The Social Construction of Nature and the Environment." *Rural Sociology* 59(1): 1–24. doi: 10.1111/j.1549-0831.1994.tb00519.x

Haq, Farooq and John Jackson. 2009. "Spiritual Journey to Hajj: Australian and Pakistani Experience and Expectations." *Journal of Management, Spirituality and Religion* 6(2): 141–156. doi: 10.1080/14766080902815155

Heelas, Paul. 2008. *Spiritualities of Life: New Age Romanticism and Consumptive Capitalism*. Oxford: Blackwell.

Houtman, Dick and Stef Aupers. 2007. "The Spiritual Turn and the Decline of Tradition: The Spread of Post-Christian Spirituality in 14 Western Countries, 1981–2000." *Journal for the Scientific Study of Religion* 46(3): 305–320. doi: 10.1111/j.1468-5906.2007.00360.x

Jafari, Jafar and Noel Scott. 2014. "Muslim World and Its Tourisms." *Annals of Tourism Research* 44: 1–19. doi:10.1016/j.annals.2013.08.011

Lambert, Yves. 1999. "Religion in Modernity as a New Axial Age: Secularization or New Religious Forms?" *Sociology of Religion* 60(3): 303–333. doi: 10.2307/3711939

Lii, Ding-Tzann. 1998. "Social Spheres and Public Life: A Structural Origin." *Theory, Culture & Society* 15(2): 115–135. doi: 10.1177/026327698015002005

Lyon, David. 2000. *Jesus in Disneyland: Religion in Postmodern Times*. Cambridge: Polity Press.

MacCannell, Dean. 1973. "Staged Authenticity: Arrangements of Social Space in Tourist Settings." *American Journal of Sociology* 79(3): 589–603. doi: 10.1086/225585

MacCannell, Dean. 1976. *The Tourist: A New Theory of the Leisure Class*. New York: Schocken Books.

Norman, Alex. 2009. "The Unexpected Real: Negotiating Fantasy and Reality on the Camino de Santiago." *Literature & Aesthetics* 19(2): 50–71.

Norman, Alex. 2010. "Great Freedom and the Concept of Awareness: Reading an Ambiguous New Religious Movement through the Lenses of Gergen, Giddens and Lyon." *International Journal for the Study of New Religions* 1(2): 161–181. doi: 10.1558/ijsnr.v1i2.161

Norman, Alex. 2011. *Spiritual Tourism: Travel and Religious Practice in Western Society*. London: Continuum.

Oficina de Acogida al Peregrino. 2014. *Informe Estadístico: Ano Santo 2013*. Santiago de Compostela: Catedral de Santiago. <http://www.peregrinossantiago.es/esp/wp-content/uploads/informes/peregrinaciones2013.pdf>, accessed February 3, 2016.

Olsen, Daniel H. 2003. "Heritage, Tourism, and the Commodification of Religion." *Tourism Recreation Research* 28(3): 99–104. doi: 10.1080/02508281.2003.11081422

Reader, Ian. 2013. *Pilgrimage in the Marketplace*. London: Routledge.

Rinschede, Gisbert. 1992. "Forms of Religious Tourism." *Annals of Tourism Research* 19(1): 51–67. doi:10.1016/0160-7383(92)90106-Y

Rocha, Cristina. 2013. "Building a Transnational Spiritual Community: The John of God Movement in Australia." In *The Diaspora of Brazilian Religions*, edited by C. Rocha and M. A. Vásquez. Leiden and Boston: Brill, 291–312.

Rountree, Kathryn. 2006. "Journeys to the Goddess: Pilgrimage and Tourism in the New Age." In *On the Road to Being There: Studies in Pilgrimage and Tourism in Late Modernity*, edited by William H. Swatos. Leiden: Brill, 33–60.

Shinde, Kiran. 2012. "From Route to Road and Body to Car: Changing Aesthetics of Religious Tourism in a Sacred Landscape." *Literature & Aesthetics* 22(1): 88–107.

Slavin, Sean. 2003. "Walking as Spiritual Practice: The Pilgrimage to Santiago de Compostela." *Body & Society* 9(3): 1–18. doi: 10.1177/1357034X030093001

Stausberg, Michael. 2011. *Religion and Tourism: Crossroads, Destinations and Encounters*. New York: Routledge.

Swain, Tony. 1993. *A Place for Strangers: Towards a History of Australian Aboriginal Being*. Cambridge: Cambridge University Press.

Swatos, William H., ed. 2006. *On The Road to Being There: Studies in Pilgrimage and Tourism in Late Modernity*. Leiden: Brill.

Taves, Ann. 2012. "Special Things as Building Blocks of Religions." In *The Cambridge Companion to Religious Studies*, edited by Robert A. Orsi. Cambridge: Cambridge University Press, 58–83.

Taylor, L. 2010. *Encyclopedia of Medieval Pilgrimage*. Leiden: Brill.

Timothy, Dallen J. and Daniel H. Olsen, eds. 2006. *Tourism, Religion and Spiritual Journeys*. London: Routledge.

Turner, Louis and John Ash. 1975. *The Golden Hordes: International Tourism and the Pleasure Periphery*. London: Constable.

Turner, Victor. 1973. "The Center Out There: Pilgrim's Goal." *History of Religions* 12(3): 191–230.

Turner, Victor Witter and Edith Turner. 1978. *Image and Pilgrimage in Christian Culture: Anthropological Perspectives*. New York: Columbia University Press.

United Nations World Tourism Organization. 2010. "International Recommendations for Tourism Statistics 2008." United Nations Statistics Division. <http://unstats.un.org/unsd/publication/Seriesm/SeriesM_83rev1e.pdf>, accessed February 3, 2016.

Urry, John. 2002. *The Tourist Gaze*, 2nd edtion. London: Sage.

Voigt, Cornelia and Christof Pforr. 2013. *Wellness Tourism: A Destination Perspective*. Abingdon: Routledge.

Wallace, Anthony F. C. 1966. *Religion: An Anthropological Perspective*. New York: Random House.

Yü, Chün-fang. 1992. "P'u-t'o Shan: Pilgrimage and the Chinese Creation of Potalaka." In *Pilgrims and Sacred Sites in China*, edited by Chün-fang Yü and Susan Naquin. Los Angeles: University of California Press, 190–245.

FURTHER READING

Graburn 1989 [*This provocative article attempts to map out an anthropology of tourism. It is the "rituals and ceremonials, human play, and cross-cultural aesthetics" (Graburn 1989, 17) that most interest the author. More so, Graburn attempts to demonstrate how tourism is characterized as the 'best' type of Western life.*]

MacCannell 1976 [*A landmark publication that set in motion the reconsideration of tourism as a field of serious inquiry. The phenomenon of tourism is explicitly linked and problematized with a quest for authenticity. Its more recent editions include new introductions by the author in which he clarifies certain controversial points.*]

Stausberg 2011 [*This book functions as a 'state of the art' for studies of religious and touristic phenomena. The sheer scope and depth of the intersectionality of these practices is laid bare in this book.*]

Timothy/Olsen 2006 [*This edited volume was one of a group of similar volumes published around the same time. While each of these (cited above) is worth reading, this volume is marked by its deliberate attempt to weave multi-disciplinary and mixed methods research together.*]

Turner 1973 [*An iconic journal article that marks the symbolic beginning of serious conceptual and theoretical treatment of pilgrimage. Turner explains pilgrimage as the convergence of ritual semiotics, antistructure, and processual units, and goes on to detail how he sees liminality as a core experiential element. Despite its age it continues to have relevance.*]

PART V

TOPICS

CHAPTER 33

....

BELIEF

....

JASON C. BIVINS

CHAPTER SUMMARY

....

- Owing to its continued scrutiny, belief is a both an analytic device and a conceptual prism through which to assess changes in the study of religion.
- While it is difficult to write about 'belief' outside the category's well-known critical interrogation, engagement with the complexities of lived religion shows ineluctably how belief takes numerous and multivalent shapes that point beyond such critiques.
- In its imbrications with materiality, the senses, and the political, among other areas, we see that—even when not explicitly foregrounded—belief is a central shaping category in the study of religion.

'SINCERELY HELD' RELIGION

....

William James (1842–1910) remains one of the most oft-cited authors in the study of religion. He asserted the protean quality of reality and observation, an insight that holds true not just for some religious practitioners but also for those who study them. In *The Will to Believe* (1896), James sought to understand under what conditions one chooses to believe something. Beyond conditions obtaining to scientific method, James wrote, humans must frequently make decisions about belief without evidence, and such decisions often necessarily involve gambles. He famously illustrated this with his example of choosing which path to follow through a mountain pass buffeted by a dangerous snowstorm. We are aware of two as yet uncertain outcomes: we could die or we could make it beyond the storm to safety (James 1992 [1896]). Believers, James reasoned, often act on the basis of claims about reality without any extrinsic validation of their veracity.

Because the political and institutional context in which the study of religion has taken shape (see Stausberg, "History," this volume) is a predominantly liberal-constitutional one, the contemporary vexations of 'religion' in and around public defenses of 'sincerely held beliefs' resonate suggestively with belief's history in the field. The relationship between religion and the law has long been fraught in liberal constitutional polities which seek to guarantee the rights of conscience and religious belief (see Schonthal, "Law," this volume). Here 'religion,' a category often unconsciously linked with interiority, is seen as a register of identity worthy of special protection. Politically, debates about identity and participation turn regularly on considerations of whether religion ought mostly to inhabit its 'proper' sphere and deserves particular recognition and protection. In important locations where these issues come to the fore—in the realization of French laïcité, the German condemnation of Scientology, demands for religious exemptions from science curricula in the United States, or violent demands for recognizing the rights of religious minorities in Sri Lanka, India, or Iraq—the recognition of legal and political authenticity turns often on the ability of the petitioners to establish that they have a 'belief system.'

Such recognitions resonate, with considerable complication, in the study of religion. Long central to the field and often held under suspicion, belief is both an analytic device and a conceptual prism for assessing changes in the field. It is difficult to write about belief outside the widely-known critical interrogation of the category in recent decades. Yet it is a key claim of this chapter that any investigation of belief shows that, at each stage of disciplinary development, it has been identified as central but simultaneously challenged. It is through these very critical interrogations, though, that the category has facilitated new questions and orientations central to the field's changing shapes. This chapter chronicles these moments of interrogation and reassessment so as to contend that belief is still central to the study and the experience of religion. That it takes more forms than was once customarily acknowledged only underscores this point, since at each moment of critical challenge belief has showed its many and complicated dimensions.

To chronicle this, I look first at the range of experiences with which belief has historically been associated, locating its polyvocal qualities with an eye towards the possibilities this manyness may yield. I describe three traditions of religious practice so as to delineate belief's limits and its interpretative richness. I use these cases to survey the history of the category's uses in the study of religion, and to suggest that the scrutiny and the reconfigurations of the category are held together in its very conceptual difficulties. Thus we see in the category's recent conceptual returns that belief is, even when not explicitly foregrounded, a central shaping category in the study of religion, since the category's formations are always doubling back on themselves in ways that illuminate and complicate.

BELIEF'S FUZZY CONTENTS

The study of religion long assumed the primacy of belief as the lens through which to explore and understand experience, ritual, history, and more. The story of this place of privilege and its subsequent interrogation is in many ways the story of the field itself. Belief has been used as a general category whose varied elements contain far more difference than the singular term often suggests. But because belief as a discursive category and an epistemological claim is not exclusive to religion, the category has often taken shape in conversation with traditions of philosophical skepticism and questions about what religious beliefs do for believers, since they are not tangible to outsiders. Existing in a dynamic relationship with doubts, beliefs can be understood as announcements of resolution, of a definitive relation between persons and/or beings, and as statements of clarification. But because belief can never achieve anything like certainty, it has often been presumed distinct from knowledge's emphasis on verification and evidence. Belief thus would be either 'volitional' (a faith in or assent to the order of things) or 'intellectual' (first- or second-order affirmations of said volitions, situating them in a larger systematic architecture in which traditions render these claims intelligible) (MacGregor 1995, 426). While analytic philosophers admit that there are relatively stronger and weaker expressions of belief, religious beliefs are often regarded as particularly difficult cases for verification and defense; a claim about signs of an imminent apocalypse, for example, may make sense contextually in particular religious traditions, but few outside these traditions would posit such a claim as knowledge (Duchesne-Guillemin 1995, 343). Acknowledging the centrality of proclamations, professions, and affirmations of religious beliefs—including the political rights to do so—is thus distinct from asserting that a belief is a knowable fact (even granting that no fact-assertions are infallible).

Belief has also been confused or conflated with 'faith,' with formulations of the former term regularly accompanied by "intellectual conviction alongside the notion of trust" (MacGregor 1995, 426). This conflation has kept alive questions about whether belief is or can be an epistemological category, "differing from ordinary knowledge by its superior claims: an arcane character, a transcendent content, privileged channels of communication, or divine certainty" (Pelikan 1995, 255). Even leaving aside such substantive characterizations, belief is described in multiple ways. It has sometimes been understood doxologically, referring to the formal body of creeds, affirmations, and confessions (from the Nicene Creed to the Muslim *Shahadah*), the well-known formulation *credo* (which refers not just to the term meaning 'I believe,' but also to the Credo as a liturgical element and to creeds as legitimizing strategies) which is used to confer analytical and legal legitimacy on traditions. Yet it has just as regularly been presumed that belief dwelled inside the believer: in the affective register, in the internalization of particular religious judgment or knowledge, or in contemplation. Further still, belief frequently takes a relational state, where the inwardness of prayer and meditation is made manifest in the I–Thou relation famously described by Martin Buber, the establishment of what Paul Tillich called an "ultimate concern," or Saint Augustine's description of the vision that he shared with his mother, just before she died, of "the flight of the alone to the alone" (Buber 2000 [1923]; Tillich 2009 [1957]; Augustine 1998 [398], 188).

The study of religion has focused on these complexities, sometimes engaging philosophical literatures but more regularly chronicling the role of belief in religious experience and practice, as well as analyzing the category's limitations. Aside from questions about evidence or about whether the range of experiences noted earlier can be adduced to a single category, belief has been shown to be partial in its comparative reach (since belief is not always as central as it is in the Protestant cultures in which the study of religion historically emerged) (Asad 1993; Bell 2008; Ruel 1997; J. Z. Smith 1982; W. C. Smith 1991). But while disciplinary self-inventory remains valuable, I submit that recent methodological troubling of belief's limits may have partly obscured its possibilities as well as its clear centrality to the self-understandings and practices of religious persons. Taking into account the earlier observations about belief (which include the propositional, affirmational, and epistemological modes), I define belief in order to unpack the aforementioned further dimensions and possibilities. I thus describe it as an intersectional phenomenon, shaped by three factors: the self-articulations and self-understandings of religious practitioners; its uses in understanding the particular modalities of religious practices or experiences; *and* its scholarly interrogation. To reiterate, the questions posed of belief in its history of continued scrutiny have also been the occasions for the study of religion to recalibrate its analytical presumptions: since belief takes unpredictable forms, limits can become possibilities, and conundrums may illuminate. As I note in the following, the study of lived religion reveals not that belief is the antithesis of practice but that belief is articulated through relations with unseen beings, an amplification of the affective, and practices indebted to a sensorial and perceptual ordering of experience usually distinct from that of the 'everyday.' The avowals and assents formed in the indeterminate space where knowledge cannot be certain can also be, to religious practitioners, experiences of emotional intensity in response to what practitioners recognize as sacred presence; actions, places, and times understood to be qualitatively different from non-religious ones; and confirmations of participation in a network linking earthly, material bodies, and communities with heavenly ones.

THREE TRADITIONS

Consider, at the outset, the following religious traditions, selected because of factors—geographic difference, materiality, and a wide range of practitioners—that collectively exemplify this polyvocal understanding of belief. Contemporary metaphysical practitioners in Western Europe and North America are often grouped under the designation 'New Age,' referring to a loose-knit movement that sees itself as reviving ancient esoteric or mystical traditions in the name of human transformation. Its practices are combinative, aiming at transformation through bodily disciplines like yoga or reiki, environmental consciousness, or more esoteric practices like crystal rubbing or chan-neling. Defined by the self-conscious affirmation of a worldview rather than by fixed membership, common ritual, or canon, 'New Age' balances reflections on the nature of selfhood and consciousness with activities thought to participate in some larger 'spir-itual' harmony. Most metaphysical practitioners are united in their belief that nature, or the universe, is the most important touchstone in guiding actions, containing an evident order to which we must fit. Practitioners acknowledge many paths to transformation, all of which lead to this-worldly effects like peace of mind, positive self-image, physical health, personal empowerment, and insight. These practitioners eschew formal, creedal religiosity, even as their discourse of knowledge, insight, and awareness is often framed by the profession of metaphysical beliefs (even if their amalgamation of practices from across traditions problematizes the idea that they 'believe' any one thing in particular).

Other traditions articulate themselves in public performances or rituals that are emphatically singular in their religiosity. Once a year, Tamil Hindus in Malaysia and surrounding regions travel to Kuala Lumpur. Just outside the city at the Batu Caves is a shrine to Lord Muragan, where the annual celebration of Thaipusam is held. The son of Parvati and the brother of Ganesha, Saraswati, and Lakshmi, Muragan is something of a regional deity thought to oversee the fortunes of local practitioners. At Batu, the devout climb steep stairs to arrive at a crowded gathering of celebrants whose bodies are adorned and altered in multiple ways. Some have pots of milk on their heads. Others have large metal frames constructed over their bodies, and many of these come with dense sets of hooks that penetrate the flesh and are then weighed down with offerings of fruit and the like. Still others push skewers through their cheeks or tongue. With milk, ash, and lime juice covering their skin, they claim to feel no pain, the disciplining of the flesh putting them instead in a kind of trance state. At a different annual festival, in Brooklyn, approxi-mately one hundred males carry a sixty-three-foot statue of Our Lady of Mount Carmel through crowded streets. Her veneration dates back to the thirteenth century when Saint Albert (then patriarch of Jerusalem) wrote a 'formula of life' for the Carmelite order, whose devotion focused on Mount Carmel (known for its association with Elijah). Those carrying her statue strive to recreate the lives of devotion lived by the holy men on that mountain over the centuries. They believe that Mary has promised that those faithful to the Carmelite order will receive a special dispensation of grace in exchange for their devotion (Franco 2007).

These two festivals mark different, but no less trenchant articulations of belief, each freighted with associations, narratives, histories, and communities. In general, these three traditions clearly involve the kinds of relationality, affect, and epistemol-ogy that are clearly not self-evidently distinct from belief. And it is also through their complex formations of belief that their differences and specifics emerge more clearly. We might use these religions to think through how belief's many interrogations in the study of religion have been posed, and how the category's resonance has been deepened through them.

DISCIPLINARY DEVELOPMENT

Prehistory

In each historical phase of the study of religion, belief figures centrally as a conceptual fundament. It is because of this simultaneous recurrence and changing valence that belief has given rise over time to such multiple interpretations. I trace a disciplinary genealogy in order to suggest that belief is *not* simply the alternative to practice but a more fluid, responsive way of accounting for how both believers and scholars orient themselves. Jonathan Z. Smith suggests that a "shift to belief" was what made possible non-confessional investigations of religion (Smith 1998, 271). The emergence of modern understandings of belief as "a personal sentiment or private disposition" facilitated the identification of 'religion' itself as distinctive analytical category (McCutcheon/Arnal 2013, 5). Samuel Preus showed how doubt and certainty regarding the tangibility of belief was integral to the early lineage of the study of religion, helping shape an analytical orientation to interiority that cemented belief as foundational to the comparative mindset (Preus 1996). In this germinal phase, then, one imagines the street ritual of Thaipusam or Our Lady of Mount Carmel as being adduced to an early, inferior mode of religiosity or as being pronounced inessential to the authentic, interiorized core of religion. The contemplative dimensions of metaphysical religion might be recognizable, but its eclectic embodiment would doubtless have bemused or scandalized early theorists.

As Preus and others show, David Hume's empiricist scrutiny of belief was instrumental in the field's development, effectively solidifying an early comparative mode by which supposed 'natural' inclinations to piety were put in conversation with a philosophical scrutiny against which it also had to defend its own rationality and, perhaps ironically, believability. The bodily mortifications at the Batu Caves would be judged arbitrary without substantive, observable links to the deity they honored; the transformative energies of metaphysicals would require measurement. It is in this period that emerged what Donald Lopez (1998) identifies as the unquestioned assumption that religious practitioners understand themselves in terms of belief (the foregrounding of which in the study of religion is routinely acknowledged to be a residue of Christian history). It was the anchor of 'religion' that, between the eighteenth and twentieth centuries, became a tool for comparing cultures. This occurred not only in 'geneticist' accounts of religion tracing the development of monotheist belief from ostensibly crude polytheistic origins; it also shaped encounters between, say, Native Americans in Massachusetts and Puritans who judged their purported lack of a belief system as heathenism, a conclusion that likely would have obtained at Thaipusam despite belief's central role in practitioners' relationship with Muragan.

Reductionism to Phenomenology

Throughout the nineteenth century, philosophical interrogations of belief made way for sociological and psychological functionalisms. In the transition from Ludwig Feuerbach (who located the object of religious belief squarely in humanity itself) to Marx's materialist reading of belief as a tool of legitimation (see Day, "Marxism," this volume), the study of religion drifted to the simultaneous psychologization and sociologization of belief (notably in Freud) and the category's use in constructing anthropological taxonomies of religion in the work of Edward B. Tylor, James Frazer, and Friedrich Max Müller, among others (Feuerbach 2011 [1841]; Raines 2011; Gay 1995; Tylor 2010 [1871]; Frazer 2009 [1890]). Through these transformations, belief remained integral in understanding: how religious persons related to supernatural beings (in animism, for example); how religion articulates the distinction between sacred and profane (in Frazer's investigation of 'magic,' say); what is being enacted in ritual, and for what purposes; how the transformation, or salvation, of the practitioner is understood; how various modes of inwardness (reflection, prayer, meditation) serve to revivify beliefs; and how communities identify the constitutive elements of their shared worldview or 'way of life.' This expansion and proliferation of understandings, though not without biases, yielded a framework for understanding the relation between belief and human intersubjectivity, ritual practice, institutionalization, and relationality.

Following this period, Durkheim and Weber offered more precise, less reductionistic accounts of belief (Durkheim 2008 [1912]; Weber 2001 [1905]). While Durkheim elucidated the degree to which religious beliefs are accepted and experienced in terms of their social milieu (as with the regional Hinduism in Malaysia or the consumerist approach to metaphysical religiosity in North America), Weber attended to the interplay between personality, intention, and collective meaning in particular societies, making room for motivational and psychological factors in his examination of beliefs. The inheritance of the contemporary study of religion was shaped in this dynamic between interiority and exteriority, meaning and function, with belief either a sturdy or shaky connection between elements.

Subsequent developments, including the institutionalization of the study of religion, were reckonings with this inheritance. Each subsequent disciplinary phase and methodological orientation depended still on a formulation of belief, whether part of what phenomenologists like Rudolf Otto had begun to refer to as 'the sacred' experienced by medieval mystics or renunciants; of Mircea Eliade's cartography of the relation between sacred and profane, ranging from ritual re-enactments of cosmogonic myths to the experience of hierophany in heightened sacred times; or, negatively, in the growing understanding that purportedly universal theories of religion favored Western, interiorized expressions of religiosity ill-suited to delineating the complexities of collective displays like Thaipusam or the expressive combinations of metaphysicals (Otto 1958 [1917]; Eliade 1957).

The Anthropological Turn

The flowering of cultural anthropology from Victor Turner to Clifford Geertz opened up the turn to practice that challenged extant understandings of belief (Turner 1969; Geertz 1973). Classificatory schemes began to loosen in favor of flexible interpretations of religion focused on the complex intersubjectivity of lived, local religion. Consequently, the abstract (and highly polymorphous) keyword 'culture' came to the fore, as scholars of religion no longer focused on theories of religious 'causation' among societies like the Azande but instead engaged more consistently the specificity of social location and structures of kinship, comportment, and ritual among, say, the Balinese or among the practitioners venerating Our Lady of Mount Carmel. Belief was thus engaged via its lived experience and its complex social embeddedness. Belief's own disciplinary history was also central to the methodological self-interrogation that became commonplace in the 1980s and thereafter. We can see in this complex moment the incipient shapes of our own. On the one hand, 'religion' has been the subject of renewed interrogation and once-ubiquitous comparative categories like belief have suffered withering critique.

Scholars of religion came to focus increasingly, following the flowering of cultural anthropology beginning in the 1970s, on the 'doing' of religion, and in particular on the range of practices, creations, and relationships thriving outside of theological discourse or settled institutional formations. The work of Wilfred Cantwell Smith (1991), Malcolm Ruel (1997), Catherine Bell (2008), and Talal Asad (1993) marked key stages in this developing critique, resulting in a body of critical literature finding collectively that 'belief' as a category is not only not central to all traditions, but many traditions lack an analogue altogether; its centrality in the study of religion reflects a Protestant bias and orientation that obscures different emphases throughout religions in practice. Bell, Asad, Webb Keane (2007), and others have explored the analytical biases in the category, and have urged greater attention to its expressions in practice and community, and its dialogic relationship with its socio-cultural milieus. Vásquez, in his recent genealogical contextualization of this critique, suggests that not only has a focus on belief obscured practice but that it has enshrined an understanding of religion focused on "representation and communication" (2011, 2) and that "religion as private belief" has disdained other elements as "imperfectly represented by 'external' manifestations such as symbols, rituals, and institutions—an approach heavily shaped by the Protestant origins of the *Religionswissenschaft*" (2011, 3). More recently, scholarly attention has focused on how this focus is predicated on an assumed political conception linked to the instantiation of the rights-bearing subject at the center of Western political discourse, with its focus on negative liberty and rights of immunity.

Despite the ubiquity of these critical moves, the field still takes shape in light of these very central, albeit de-privileged, categories. So while belief frustratingly contains multitudes in terms of its historical uses and lived articulations, this brief genealogy suggests that in these very changes and challenges—from suspicion of religious beliefs to its use in cross-cultural comparison, from its presumed interiority to its situatedness in cultures—belief's complexities and conceptual tangles have produced its reassessments as possibilities.

BELIEF TODAY

Culturally in the West, belief is still the central, largely unconscious index of religiosity. It is at the heart of demography, jurisprudence, and the self-understanding of religious practitioners. Belief is thus both an obvious medium of disciplinary self-analysis and a vector of possibility that scholars still pursue. The category's entanglements with a field that is aware of its biases and genealogies are greater in number and reach than one might expect. Because of the conceptual fuzziness of the study of religion, it is perhaps easier to overlook how closely the disciplinary caution around belief coexists with institutional and cultural conceptions of religiosity that continue to privilege the scorned category.

So if belief is no longer a kind of magnetic true north, it helps vividly to articulate religion's multiplicity and elusiveness, since it is also clearly integral to the study of religion despite its regular criticism. Above I posited an understanding of belief as a mode by which religionists recognize and articulate their own identities and experiences, and as a conceptual habitus which facilitates the pursuit and understanding of particular practices and social locations. This polyvalent understanding of belief as more than propositional resonates with several major interpretative possibilities emerging from the interrogation of belief.

Many contemporary studies embody these conceptual reorientations by focusing on material religion, the senses, religious presence, or the legacies of colonialism. We see in the work of Courtney Bender (2010), Webb Keane (2007), Saba Mahmood (2011), David Morgan (1999), Sarah Pike (2001), Thomas Tweed (2002), Manuel Vásquez (2011), and others how focus on the textures of situated religiosities yield complex portraits of, say, metaphysicals or visual culture that cannot merely be adduced to 'meaning' or 'belief' as conventionally construed. With different methodological emphases and different data sets, scholars now look not only to new subjects like the complex sensorial experience of Thaipusam or the Brooklyn festa, but focus on space, objects, and intersubjectivity, the kinds of fluid, often combinative religiosity articulated by contemporary metaphysicals who interpolate multiple texts, traditions, and personalized rituals. These orientations have been exemplified by authors like Stewart Guthrie (1995), Robert Orsi (2011), and Greg Schopen (1996), all of whom make explicit that their work is premised on belief being part of a more complicated lived religiosity.

Perhaps in response to scholarly investigations of anthropology and materiality, investigations of religious language and epistemology have also flourished since the critical turn in the study of religion. In philosophy, these range from the rich field of religious ethics to the post-Austinian scrutiny of religious truth-claims. Some of this work, as with Robert Brandom or Donald Davidson, assesses the semantic properties of religious propositions and belief statements, focused on the rational coherence of religious 'language games' or expressions of 'preference' (Frankenberry 2002). With no stake in the alleged cultural or epistemic superiority or veracity of such claims, scholars of religion like Nancy Frankenberry focus on how beliefs facilitate the organization of experience and perception. Benson Saler's critical anthropology represents an alternate way of exploring the distinction between belief as a statement of verification and belief as the expression of mystery or folk psychology (Frankenberry 2002; Saler 1999 [1993]). These latter two examples show clear possibilities for exploring culturally situated practices such as those woven throughout this piece.

One encounters elsewhere a more robust cognitivism, embodied noticeably by recent appropriations of cognitive theory in anthropology of religion. For Maurice Bloch, a belief is that which permits the understanding of situatedness, with particular semantic content that avoids judgments about rationality or intuition by focusing on belief's capacity to solve 'problems' for believers (Bloch 2005). Authors like Pascal Boyer or Daniel Sperber propose a kind of naturalism which posits religious beliefs as characterized by a degree of counterintuitiveness but epistemologically coherent within their cultural and epistemic contexts, as with the links between bodily transformations and local divinity at Thaipusam, or the affirmation of the universe's healing energies by bourgeois meditation practitioners (Boyer 2002; Sperber 1996). Boyer—even as he seeks to displace conventional formulations of belief with a focus on memes and cognitive toolkits—focuses on belief as the repository of practical knowledge which functions smoothly with evolved human mental systems. Uninterested in the representational capacity of beliefs, or their historical origins, Boyer's analysis facilitates understanding of how cultural factors like metaphysicals' access to leisure time and exposure to religious pluralism make particular beliefs more likely than others. Ann Taves's focus on ascriptions of religious belief and experience resonate similarly in the sense that she is concerned with *how* things *seem* true to believers (Taves 2009).

These convoluted transformations are reflected in disciplinary histories and methodological anthologies, most of which reflect the category only indirectly. Several volumes, like Mark Taylor's *Critical Terms for Religious Studies*, contain important treatments of the category, which is distinguished from 'body,' 'value,' and 'rationality,' among others (Taylor 1998). Braun and McCutcheon's *Guide to the Study of Religion* posits 'cognition,' 'intellect,' or 'projection' as modes of 'explanation' (distinct from 'locations' like 'discourse') (Braun and McCutcheon 2000). *The Routledge Companion to the Study of Religion* distinguishes approaches from issues (a laundry-list of 'religion ands'), while *The Blackwell Companion to the Study of Religion*'s list of thematic orientations does not engage belief (instead focusing on myth, body, mysticism, and the like) (Hinnels 2009; Segal 2008). Thus, even when it is not explicitly named as a fundamental category in the study of religion, belief remains part of efforts to understand the formation of current conceptions of religiosity and it also suffuses other categories: as justification, as experiential description, as a kind of binding agent in ethics or views of the afterlife.

Taking these developments in stock, recall the earlier suggestion that the practice and experience of belief usually involves relations between religious practitioners and

unseen being(s), what is described (often *ex post facto*) as a heightening or transformation of emotional experience in and around the object of religious belief, and participation in disciplines or habits aligned with these avowals. Contemporary scholarship
uncovers pathways for continuing to engage belief's multiple dimensions. Flowing
from the aforementioned orientations, I here identify a series of interlocking angles
that harvest from the category's oft-avowed constraints some fresh possibilities.
(1) Anthropology of belief focuses on the ongoing elaboration of belief's doings, in relation to culture, human intersubjectivity, and symbolic expression. In addition to evoking in detail the cultural habitus framing street religious processions in North America
and Malaysia—the generations-long co-development of Italian-American families
and changing borough, or the religious negotiation of architecture and landscape outside Kuala Lumpur—scholars might follow the recent work of Manuel Vásquez (2011),
David Morgan (1999), and Thomas Tweed (2002) in attending to how belief's materiality (see Morgan, "Materiality," this volume) emerges at the intersection of objects,
images, geographic settings, and bodily or emotional experiences. (2) Investigations of
belief in/as politics refer not just to law, the differentiation of social spheres, or petitions
for rights of recognition, often focused on belief as the register of 'authentic' religiosity,
but also to relations between different groups of believers regarding access to shared
spaces, discrepant institutional arrangements or distributions of power, and the politics of representation. Here the relation between Tamil Hindus and Malaysia's Muslim
majority is recognized as integral in fashioning the self-understanding of those honor-
ing Muragan; here one explores not just the socio-economic status of metaphysicals,
but the centrality of religio-political convictions about gender and ecology in the constitution of belief. (3) Attention to belief's languages goes beyond simply investigations
of confessionalism and inscrutable avowals, and focuses on attributions and discursive
performances as central to the constitution not just of habits of judgment and conceptual coherence but of religious selves broadly speaking (Boyer 2002; Taves 2009). The
careful interpolation of varied traditions and practices in the self-articulation of metaphysicals becomes a lens through which to understand the combinative qualities of this
orientation, just as the narrations of Our Lady of Mount Carmel and the continued orientation to the monastic rule she enshrines reveal the textures of this collective practice
of belief.

CONCLUSION

To paraphrase Asad (2012), the emergence of the study of religion is related first to scrutiny of belief, second to the parsing of religion's constitutive elements, and third to the
emergence of a political order which not only relies on the avowed clarity of relation
between things secular and things religious but on particular conceptions of what counts
as acceptable, authentic religiosity. The problems of legitimation—both in the scholarly
and in the public or juridical sense—hang on such questions of boundary-drawing.

'Belief' is an archive of disciplinary change, establishing a record around a category which continues to enshrine the very things the field abjures, its enduring power partly sustained by its centrality to the public acrimony fueling cultural interest in religion as such.

Because the political cultures surrounding the discipline are framed by liberal/identitarian conceptions of religion, the study of religion is necessarily (even if negatively) imbricated in that which it suggests is historically, culturally contingent: a stand-alone category requiring specific intellectual disciplines which mirror the special protections it warrants in the liberal polis. Belief is what permits 'religion' to be identified disciplinarily and juridically alike; and while the study of religion rejects the simple identification of belief with 'worldviews' or 'meanings,' its caution about misrepresentation suggestively evokes cultural assumptions about sincerity and authenticity that, outside the academy, turn on professions or identifications of belief.

James's icy mountain pass, however, looms not just as a central moment in disciplinary history but as a metaphor for contemporary study. The concept of belief remains indispensable, precisely because the questions its complexities demand of scholars have led so regularly to fresh ways of thinking about religion. It is a practice, a category facilitating recognition, and a discourse, among many other elements constituting its polyvocality. In its continued intermingling with other areas of human communication and practice, it helps forge paths between the concrete and the abstract, difference and singularity, and, above all, interpretative constraint and possibility.

GLOSSARY

Epistemology referring to 'knowledge' or 'understanding,' epistemology is a branch of philosophical inquiry and also a term that forms a background presumption about phenomena like belief (as with the sometime presumption that a belief involves knowledge, propositions, or truth-claims).

Genealogy the term, which generically refers to an account of the emergence and development of a species or object, has a particular academic definition that stems first from Friedrich Nietzsche and subsequently from Michel Foucault. This is the assumption that in tracing the development of a category like 'belief,' one will inevitably uncover certain elements—presumptions, advantages, and so on—that have been forgotten or covered over, and which the genealogist contends merit exposure.

Lived religion this term refers to both a scholarly focus on the anthropological setting for religions (everyday practices and interactions as part of a cultural whole) and to popular religious expressions outside the formal parameters of tradition.

Reductionism in the study of religion, as in other disciplines, several phases of analytical development were characterized by the tendency to explain religion's complexity by reducing the phenomenon to a single element such as economy or eros. While some reductionist writings clarified the role or function of religion in human cultures, the field subsequently judged that reductionism distorted more than it clarified categories like 'belief.'

REFERENCES

Asad, Talal. 1993. *Genealogies of Religion: Discipline and Reasons of Power in Christianity and Islam*. Baltimore, MD: Johns Hopkins University Press.

Augustine, Saint. 1998. *The Confessions*. New York: Oxford University Press. Original edition, 398.

Bell, Catherine. 2008. "Belief: A Classificatory Lacuna and Disciplinary 'Problem.'" In *Introducing Religion: Essays in Honor of Jonathan Z. Smith*, edited by Willi B. Braun and Russell T. McCutcheon. London: Equinox Publishing, 85–99.

Bender, Courtney. 2010. *The New Metaphysicals: Spirituality and the American Religious Imagination*. Chicago, IL: University of Chicago Press.

Bivins, Jason C. 2012. "Ubiquity Scorned: Belief's Strange Survivals." *Method and Theory in the Study of Religion* 24(1): 1–9. doi: 10.1163/157006812X632883

Bloch, Maurice. 2005. *Essays on Cultural Transmission*. Oxford: Berg.

Boyer, Pascal. 2002. *Religion Explained: The Evolutionary Origins of Religious Thought*. New York: Basic Books.

Braun, Willi and Russell McCutcheon, eds. 2000. *Guide to the Study of Religion*. London: Bloomsbury Academic.

Buber, Martin. 2000. *I and Thou*. New York: Scribner. Original edition, 1923.

Duchesne-Guillemin, Jacques. 1995. "Knowledge and Ignorance." In *The Encyclopedia of Religion*, edited by Mircea Eliade. New York: Macmillan, vol. 5, 343–356.

Durkheim, Émile. 2008. *The Elementary Forms of Religious Life*. New York: Oxford University Press. Original edition, 1912.

Eliade, Mircea. 1957. *The Sacred and the Profane: The Nature of Religion*. New York: Harcourt Brace Jovanovich.

Feuerbach, Ludwig. 2011. *The Essence of Christianity*. Cambridge: Cambridge University Press. Original edition, 1841.

Franco, Philip A. 2007. "Educating Toward Communion: The Traditional Italian Festa as a Means of Christian Religious Education." *Religious Education* 102(1): 25–43. doi: 10.1080/00344080601117648

Frankenberry, Nancy K., ed. 2002. *Radical Interpretation in Religion*. Cambridge: Cambridge University Press.

Frazer, James George. 2009. *The Golden Bough: A Study in Magic and Religion*. New York: Oxford University Press. Original edition, 1890.

Gay, Peter, ed. 1995. *The Freud Reader*. New York: W. W. Norton.

Geertz, Clifford. 1973. *The Interpretation of Cultures*. New York: Basic Books.

Guthrie, Stewart Elliott. 1996. *Faces in the Clouds: A New Theory of Religion*. New York: Oxford University Press.

Hinnels, John, ed. 2009. *The Routledge Companion to the Study of Religion*. New York: Routledge.

Keane, Webb. 2007. *Christian Moderns: Freedom and Fetish in the Mission Encounter*. Berkeley, CA: University of California Press.

McCutcheon, Russell and William Arnal. 2013. "Introduction." In *The Sacred Is the Profane: The Political Nature of "Religion"*, edited by Russell McCutcheon and William Arnal. New York: Oxford University Press, 1–16.

MacGregor, Geddes. 1995. "Doubt and Belief." In *The Encyclopedia of Religion*, edited by Mircea Eliade. New York: Macmillan, vol. 4, 424–430.

Mahmood, Saba. 2011. *Politics of Piety: The Islamic Revival and the Feminist Subject*. Princeton, NJ: Princeton University Press.

Morgan, David. 1999. *Visual Piety: A History and Theory of Popular Religious Images*. Berkeley: University of California Press.

Orsi, Robert A., ed. *The Cambridge Companion to Religious Studies*. Cambridge: Cambridge University Press.

Orsi, Robert A. 2011. "Belief." *Material Religion* 7(1): 10–16. doi: 10.2752/175183411X 12968355481773

Otto, Rudolf. 1958. *The Idea of the Holy*. New York: Oxford University Press. Original edition, 1917.

Pelikan, Jaroslav. 1995. "Faith." In *The Encyclopedia of Religion*, edited by Mircea Eliade. New York: Macmillan, vol. 5, 250–255.

Pike, Sarah. 2001. *Earthly Bodies, Magical Selves: Contemporary Pagans and the Search for Community*. Berkeley: University of California Press.

Preus, J. Samuel. 1996. *Explaining Religion: Criticism and Theory from Bodin to Freud*. New York: Oxford University Press.

Raines, John, ed. 2011. *Marx on Religion*. Philadelphia: Temple University Press.

Ruel, Malcolm. 1997. *Belief, Ritual, and the Securing of Life: Reflexive Essays on a Bantu Religion*. Leiden: Brill.

Saler, Benson. 1999. *Conceptualizing Religion: Immanent Anthropologists, Transcendent Natives, and Unbounded Categories*. New York: Berghahn Books. Original edition, 1993.

Schopen, Gregory. 1996. *Bones, Stones, and Buddhist Monks: Collected Papers on the Archaeology, Epigraphy, and Texts of Monastic Buddhism in India*. Honolulu: University of Hawaii Press.

Segal, Robert A., ed. 2008. *The Blackwell Companion to the Study of Religion*. Oxford: Blackwell.

Smith, Jonathan Z. 1982. *Imagining Religion: From Babylon to Jonestown*. Chicago, IL: University of Chicago Press.

Smith, Jonathan Z. 1998. "Religion, Religions, Religious." In *Critical Terms for Religious Studies*, edited by Mark C. Taylor. Chicago, IL: University of Chicago Press, 269–284.

Smith, Wilfred Cantwell. 1991. *The Meaning and End of Religion*. Minneapolis: Fortress Press.

Sperber, Daniel. 1996. *Explaining Culture: A Naturalistic Approach*. Oxford: Blackwell.

Taves, Ann. 2009. *Religious Experience Reconsidered: A Building-Block Approach to the Study of Religion and Other Special Things*. Princeton, NJ: Princeton University Press.

Taylor, Mark C., ed. 1998. *Critical Terms for Religious Studies*. Chicago, IL: University of Chicago Press.

Tillich, Paul. 2009. *The Dynamics of Faith*. New York: HarperOne. Original edition, 1957.

Turner, Victor. 1969. *The Ritual Process: Structure and Anti-Structure*. New York: Routledge.

Tweed, Thomas. 2002. *Our Lady of the Exile: Diasporic Religion at a Cuban Catholic Shrine in Miami*. New York: Oxford University Press.

Tylor, Edward Burnett. 2010. *Primitive Culture: Researches into the Development of Mythology, Philosophy, Religion, Language, Art, and Custom*. Cambridge: Cambridge University Press. Original edition, 1871.

Vásquez, Manuel A. 2011. *More Than Belief: A Materialist Theory of Religion*. New York: Oxford University Press.

Weber, Max. 2001. *The Protestant Ethic and the Spirit of Capitalism*. New York: Routledge. Original edition, 1905.

FURTHER READING

Asad, Talal. 2012. "Thinking about Religion, Belief, and Politics." In *The Cambridge Companion to Religious Studies*, edited by Robert A. Orsi. Cambridge: Cambridge University Press, 36–57. [*Asad builds on his previous genealogical interrogations of 'religion' and 'the secular' to underscore the development of the study of religion in and around discrete categories like belief. Taking as his point of departure the upsurge of contemporary interest in religious belief as a political 'problem,' he demonstrates how conventionally liberal orientations to citizenship and agency have underpinned the study of religion. In criticizing the well-known historical accounts of Charles Taylor, he concludes that scholars must look not only to the institutional embeddedness of beliefs but to their felt, sensorial experiences as well.*]

James, William. 1992. "The Will to Believe." In *Writings 1878–1899: Psychology, Briefer Course/ The Will to Believe/Talks to Teachers and Students/Essays*. New York: Library of America, 457–479. Original edition, 1896. [*In this essay, James investigates long-standing philosophical traditions seeking to understand when, and under what conditions, a person chooses to believe something (and how belief is different from knowledge, from perception, from faith). Whereas in the scientific method, James writes, we wait for experiments or investigations to be concluded and are thus compelled by evidence to believe or disbelieve something, beliefs operate in considerable conceptual indeterminacy. Aside from questions of proof and rationality, James opens the door to a consideration of not just epistemology but to the totality of human ways of knowing as these shape the formation and experience of beliefs.*]

Lopez, Donald. 1998. "Belief." In *Critical Terms for Religious Studies*, edited by Mark C. Taylor. Chicago, IL: University of Chicago Press, 21–35. [*Lopez traces the simultaneous cultural and disciplinary developments in the category 'belief.' Focused especially on belief's centrality to emerging modern formulations of 'religion' as a universal category, Lopez's genealogy explores travel writings, nascent comparative studies, and philosophical inquiry as contributors to this consolidation. Lopez also highlights the inevitably exclusionary consequences of these understandings, tracing them through the realms of political rights and conceptual analysis alike.*]

CHAPTER 34

EMOTION

JOHN CORRIGAN

CHAPTER SUMMARY

- In the West, theorizing of emotion and theological writing historically have been intertwined.
- The study of emotion in religion often has been part of a parochial project of investigating 'religious experience.'
- The academic turn to historical *mentalités* helped spark an academic reorientation to the study of religion and emotion.
- Researchers have developed a spectrum of approaches ranging from strict constructivism to biological universality.
- Philosophical investigation of emotion that emphasizes its linkages with cognition advanced the study of religion and emotion.
- The emergence of theoretical perspectives on 'embodiment' has influenced the study of religion and emotion.
- Emotion is an important aspect of religious practice.

EMOTION AND RELIGION TOGETHER

The study of religion and emotion has deep roots. Aristotle (d. 322 BCE) wrote about emotion, particularly in relation to the practice of virtue. Over the course of two millennia his ideas were challenged, altered, and enlarged by St. Augustine (d. 430 CE), Thomas Aquinas (d. 1274), Baruch Spinoza (d. 1677), and others. Most writing about emotion was intertwined with theological ideas, so that the vocabulary for talking about one was deployed to talk about the other. Theological writing drew upon theories about emotion. Investigations of emotion borrowed theological perspectives and arguments. The production of ideas about religion and of theories about emotion accordingly developed as conjoined enterprises for most of Western history. The academic study of religion in the West developed against such a background, and especially in its specifically Christian expressions.

The area of inquiry in which emotion and religion most often were intertwined was in discussion of how persons judged good from bad, or practiced virtue while avoiding vice. In attempting to describe the dynamics of those processes, Christian writers, especially, invoked emotion. Origen, Gregory of Nyssa, Augustine, Bonaventure, Hildegard of Bingen, and Teresa of Ávila, among many others, provided vocabularies for describing and analyzing emotion. Many writers took feelings to be wellsprings of motivation, shaped through divine assistance to play a central role in the ethical life of the believer. Emotion in such a scheme of things was considered an irreducible datum. Writers assumed that the emotional aspects of religious life were susceptible to only superficial analysis. At bottom, feelings were givens, and could not be broken down into their component parts. As such, they were resistant to analysis. If love, or fear, or anger, for example, were thought to be motivations for certain kinds of actions—ethical or unethical—they could not be investigated as if they were constituted by multiple elements, each of which had its own distinct origin or character. Some of the mystery of feeling in religion thus was conserved and protected, and some emotion, inasmuch as it was associated with religion, likewise was insulated from deeper probings. Although since Hippocrates (d. 370 BCE) writers regularly described human temperament with reference to bodily 'humors' such as bile, phlegm, and blood, investigations of emotion rarely drifted from a view of the essential impenetrability of emotions. A sense of the mystery of emotion reinforced a sense of the mystery of religion, and vice versa.

Religious Experience

The Enlightenment of the long eighteenth century promoted analytical reductions in the study of the natural world and, eventually, in the study of human experience. A leading emblem of the Enlightenment was the microscope, a tool that revealed how everything in the natural world was constituted by tiny objects unseen by the naked eye. Lake water teemed with minuscule life, human blood was a mixture of various odd elements, and even the air itself was no longer a singular 'thing' but rather was constituted by different kinds of small particles, including the oxygen discovered by Joseph Priestley (1774). Emergent empirical science influenced thinking about how humans breathed air—and existed in the world in many other ways. Drawing support for their position from Enlightenment treatises purporting to lay bare the truths and laws of the cosmos, critics of religion argued that the claims of religion were dubious. They criticized especially religious claims to special kinds of knowledge unavailable to non-religious persons. Religion's refusal to investigate itself signaled to *philosophes* that it had something to hide. The site of that concealment, according to many, was emotion. Critics accordingly pressed for clarifications about how feeling played a role in religion, and opined that emotion, when viewed closely, would be revealed as an amalgam of various constituent parts. Defenders of religion conversely dug in to defend its special place.

In answering the 'cultured despisers' of religion, the German pastor Friedrich Schleiermacher (1768–1834) proposed in 1799 that the essence of religion was a specific, extraordinary feeling. In so doing he made explicit a notion about how humans are religious that had been embedded in Christianity for centuries. Schleiermacher argued that religious experience was the starting point for discussing religion, and he defined that experience as emotional (see Martin, "Experience," this volume). He proposed that the specific "feeling of absolute dependence" was qualitatively different from other emotions and defined the experience of the Christian (Schleiermacher 1960, §4). Schleiermacher made gestures towards integrating the feeling of absolute dependence with culture. His writing, however, instead served further to remove emotion—as religious experience—from investigation, from the microscopes of critics of religion who sought analytical reductions in their investigations of religion. In short, Schleiermacher's approach preserved something of the mystery of religion—and its seeming insusceptibility to critical probing by its critics—by making a mysterious emotion, and one that purportedly could be compared to no other, the basis of 'religious experience.' Such a notion of religious experience thus functioned as attempted protection for a certain idea of emotion as much as religion, rendering both, through their essential intertwining, allegedly unreachable by science (Schleiermacher 1960; 1996).

During the nineteenth century the study of emotion was advanced across a number of fronts. Some of those efforts drew upon the notion of 'religious experience' that Schleiermacher and the Methodist founder John Wesley (1703–1791) had popularized as the core of religious life. Towards the end of the century the American psychologist William James (1842–1910), as well as the first president of the American Psychological Association, G. Stanley Hall (1846–1924), sought to investigate such religious experience by studying what appeared to be its emotional components. James developed a qualified empiricism that probed religious experience for emotional patternings while avoiding outright analysis. His approach remained influential in the academic study of religion through much of the twentieth century. More importantly, Schleiermacher's definition of religious experience as emotion was resurrected by the German theologian Rudolf Otto (1869–1937). In *Das Helige* (1917) Otto argued that a certain class of feeling in religion was 'non-sensory' and 'non-rational.' Religious experience, claimed Otto, consisted in a feeling of the 'numinous' (i.e. the sacred, minus its ethical aspects) which was indefinable and unexplainable, except by crude analogy. Otto compared the experience of the numinous to a sense of 'creeping flesh,' among other things, and offered examples drawn from religious literature to illustrate his claims. In approaching religion in such a way, he followed Schleiermacher's lead in characterizing emotion in religious life as ineffable and irreducible. While he wrote as if to offer a means by which religious experience and literary culture could be related, his theory, like Schleiermacher's, eventually had the effect of isolating emotion in religious life from new currents of scholarly study of religion that were taking a more analytic approach (Otto 1973).

HISTORICAL MENTALITIES

The academic study of religion and emotion began to change in important ways in the mid-twentieth century. New understandings of emotion coalesced. Some arose as by-products of scholarly study of emotional adaptations that Charles Darwin (1809–1882) proposed in *The Expression of the Emotions in Man and Animals* (1872). Others emerged from biological sciences and social psychology. At the same time, the historical study of religion changed in ways that made the investigation of emotion a clearer object of historical analysis. In "Histoire et psychologie" (1938) and other writings French historian Lucien Febvre (1878–1956) proposed that one of the goals of the historian was "to reconstitute the emotional life of the past" (1973a; 1973b). His contemporary Marc Bloch (1886–1944)—arguing that "historical facts, are, in essence, psychological facts"—likewise contributed to the formation of a historical program (within the *Annales* school) that would lead to the historicization of emotion (1953, 194). At the same time, the broad project of *annalistes* such as Fernand Braudel (1902–1985) and Emmanuel Le Roy Ladurie (1929–) to explore *mentalités*, or collective casts of mind, enabled the framing of emotional life as historically contingent human activity (Braudel 1972–1973; Le Roy Ladurie 1978).

In the latter half of the twentieth century there emerged a body of historical scholarship focused on everyday life that eventuated in a determination to study popular culture. The study of social life and popular culture in early modern Europe, especially, nudged the study of religion away from an exclusive focus on institutional and doctrinal histories. Historians instead took up the study of 'unofficial religion,' often called popular religion, or, eventually, vernacular religion, or, in an already shopworn expression, 'lived religion.' The study of popular religion, in writings by Natalie Zemon Davis (1975), Keith Thomas (1971), Carlo Ginzburg (1982), and Peter Burke (1978), among others, focused attention on harvest festivals, moonlit devil hunts, astrologies, and local notions about the terrain of the afterlife. They also called attention to emotional expression in tears, singing, visual culture, and mourning rituals. William Christian (1982), analyzing the emotional behavior of participants in popular Passion Week rituals in early modern Spain, pointed out how persons were guided by ingrained cultural understandings of what was proper to feel during the occasion, and how that feeling should be expressed. As a view of the subject matter of religion broadened to include popular religion, the emotional performances that characterized many forms of popular religion increasingly came to the forefront of study.

CULTURE AND BIOLOGY

Historical research on feeling in popular religion was an important step in the development of new approaches to studying religion and emotion. Since the late nineteenth century, however, the study of religion has been undertaken on many fronts, not just through historical analysis. While historians were making strides in researching religion and emotion, scholars working in the social and behavioral sciences also were contributing substantially to the development of new approaches to the topic. The most important development was the articulation of a constructivist position with regard to emotion. In the wake of anthropologist Clifford Geertz's presentation of a view of the self as culturally constructed (1973), Michelle Rosaldo (1980), Catherine Lutz (1988), and other anthropologists pressed the case for the cultural construction of emotion. Given that Geertz's definition of religion emphasized the emotional component ("moods and motivations") (Geertz 1973, 90), the research of those who carried forward the constructivist view of emotion immediately became relevant to the study of religion. Rosaldo and Lutz, reporting on fieldwork in remote Pacific societies, concluded that emotions were not *sui generis*, were not 'given' in nature, Lutz expressing that claim cogently in the title of her book on the subject, *Unnatural Emotions.* Such a view corresponded with the work of sociologist Arlie Hochschild (1983) and social psychologist James Averill (1980), who at about the same time had proposed constructivist understandings of emotion: Hochschild coining the phrase 'feeling rules' to refer to socially-constructed guidelines for feeling. Such perspectives prompted important rethinking of religious life among religious studies researchers.

The constructivist understanding of emotion directly challenged much of what had been written about religion and emotion up until the latter part of the twentieth century. The view that religion was largely about religious experience and that ineffable and irreducible feelings constituted religious experience was untenable if constructivists were right. Rather than setting the study of religion on a radical course, however, constructivist theories of emotion instead stimulated the search for a middle ground that might allow for some acknowledgment of cultural derivation of emotionality while at the same time preserving a measure of subjectivity in emotional life. In short, researchers sought ways to work around the traditional view that there was something fundamentally different about the emotion that persons expressed in religious settings. They began to approach feeling in religion as they would study feeling in everyday relationships between persons, or the feeling of persons for nature, or otherwise as feeling that arose from one's experience of the small and large things of daily life. Cultural frameworks for feeling became more important, and the historicity of emotion in religion—Is fear of God in ancient Israel the same as seventeenth-century Puritans' fear of God?—increasingly mattered. At the same time, scholars did not erase the probing of subjectivities from their research agendas. It immediately was clear that constructivist theories had difficulty in addressing the problem of seeming similarities in emotional life across cultures and in answering questions about the origins of emotion.

Towards the end of the twentieth century several streams of research directed the study of religion and emotion towards fresh perspectives. New approaches enabled progress in the search for a position that was neither radically constructivist nor indebted to a view of religion as religious experience that was constituted by ineffable and irreducible emotion.

The rapid development of neuroscience, made possible in part by the refinement of technologies for measuring brain activity, led to claims for the centrality of biological process in emotional experiences. The grounding of emotional life in the amygdala, hippocampus, brain lobes, the endocrine system, and other parts of the physical body—a project based upon compelling scientific evidence—led to new theories about the universality of emotional life. Inasmuch as neuroscientific theories were able to demonstrate commonalities in feeling across cultural lines, they forced interpretation away from radically constructivist approaches. While welcomed by many as a corrective, understandings of emotion that rested wholly on biological data also were criticized as dismissive of culture. In the case of the study of religion and emotion, when researchers focused on brain function and other biological aspects of feeling, the problem of relating feeling to religious cultures again became visible. Researchers, for example, might resist the notion that a Buddhist religious culture—a society in which Buddhist doctrines, practices, material cultures, and institutions profoundly shaped collective life— was in essence grounded in the same emotional registers as a Christian one. Defenders of the centrality of doctrine to religious life were especially concerned about any theory that challenged the influence of doctrine on the emotional lives of religious persons. For some of those defenders, certain religious doctrines, or doctrinal systems, remained linked to the experiencing of certain emotions. The question of how and why they were linked subsequently became more pressing.

COGNITION

One emergent body of interpretation that attended closely to brain science and its evolutionary development in relation to religion coalesced in the late twentieth century as the cognitive science of religion (see Geertz, "Cognitive Science," this volume). Religion researchers E. Thomas Lawson and Robert McCauley (1990), along with Pascal Boyer (1994), Armin Geertz (2004), and others loosely connected across a range of disciplines, contributed to a notion of religion as an outcome of evolution. In such a view, the emotions associated with religion were evolved responses to certain kinds of stimuli within the natural environment. While not disregarding the role of culture, this approach was inclined to a view of feelings in religion as derivations from human cognitive processes that operate outside of religion itself. But because the cognitive science of religion so far has not been as concerned specifically with emotion in religion as with religious ideas and practices, it is too early to assess its potential usefulness for understanding emotion and religion. Its framework for taking religion as natural remains useful, however, as a provocation for research in this area.

The work of philosophers in assessing the relationship between emotion and cognition has been important to the study of religion for several decades. It is related to some discussions within cognitive science but has a broader importance as well. The character of scholarship in this area is reflected in the title of philosopher Robert Solomon's synthesis of research in the area, *Thinking About Feeling* (2004). For Solomon, Amélie Rorty (1980), and other philosophers working in the late twentieth century, emotions were not an aspect of human experience set aside from thinking. Rational cognition was not to be distinguished from irrational or non-rational emotion. Moreover, the cutting edge of discussion pressed the case that the two in fact were dynamically intertwined. Emotional experiences involved thinking, and much thinking involved feeling.

The philosophical effort to demonstrate the linkage between feeling and thinking made possible important new research in the study of religion. In monotheistic religions, and especially in Christianity, there are long traditions of viewing the interrelatedness of feeling, thinking, and doing as crucial to theological ethics. As philosophical investigation of emotion and cognition advanced, ethicists increasingly were equipped to revisit ethical traditions, such as those associated with Thomas Aquinas, in ways that led to fresh insights. The centrality of emotion to ethics accordingly was forcefully restated by scholars such as Martha Nussbaum (2001), Diana Cates (2009), Mark Wynn (2005), and others who demonstrated the trust among classical and medieval writers that God intervened in human determinations of good and evil by directing the mind through the prompting of feelings. Other researchers noted how the idea that 'affect,' or feeling, influenced the will was a central part of the faculty psychology of eighteenth-century Scottish Common Sense philosophers such as Dugald Stewart (1753–1828), Thomas Reid (1710–1796), and Thomas Brown (1778–1820). In the nineteenth century, and especially in American evangelicalism, that idea of feeling being involved in setting the direction of the will took root. The deep roots of nineteenth-century theories about feeling, thinking, and doing consequently became more visible to researchers because of new directions taken in philosophical writings that reframed emotion and cognition as collaborative elements in religious life. The study of emotion as a crucial part of religious ethics consequently has developed strong momentum in Western scholarship and not only among those who study monotheism.

EMBODIMENT

One of the most important developments in the study of religion and emotion at the end of the twentieth century was the joining of research on several fronts into a comprehensive study of embodied religion. Drawing on material studies, biological research, cutting-edge philosophical and anthropological studies, and historical inquiries, scholars began to fashion approaches that brought to the forefront of analysis the experience of the embodied human. Such scholarship rejected the view that thinking and feeling, words and physical practice, culture and subject had to be marked out as fully distinct aspects of experience. The goal instead has been, in most such research, a qualified materialism that takes the study of religious life as investigation of all of the activities of the human body in physical space, including the ways in which cultural settings, various discourses, gender, ethnicity, biological processes, and the structuration of power all shape religious life. Such an approach has claimed to view emotional expression in religious settings as both a performance of cultural scripts and a matter of personal and biological factors, but limited progress has been made in actually explaining how that process takes place. The importance of this development for the study of religion and emotion, nevertheless, is that researchers are better positioned to understand that the feeling of solemnity before an altar, for example, has much to do with the fact of the bowing or genuflection that persons perform before it, the sights and smells of the setting, the remembering of doctrine sparked by the sound of music, the physical experience of a gender line or the marking of the places reserved for authorities, the feeling of emptiness or longing prompted by the experience of fasting or weeping before approaching the altar, and emotional and cognitive aspects of other bodily experiences. To speak of embodiment—as have scholars such as Manuel Vásquez, Armin Geertz, A. M. Pedersen, Thomas Csordas, and J. M, Belzen—in the study of religion and emotion is to propose that feeling has much to do with seemingly mundane physical activities of everyday life.

One important development in studies of embodied feeling, and one with potential for the study of religion and emotion, comes not from the study of religion but from literary and media studies. 'Affect theory' has some similarities to cognitive science, but differs in that it places the feelings of persons clearly at the forefront of analysis (Berlaner 2010; Ahmed 2004). Affect theory is about what the psychologist Silvan Tompkins and his followers call 'affects,' or specific feelings that are non-verbally but physically expressed by persons (Tompkins 1962). One of those followers, Paul Ekman, who developed the 'facial expression' training sought by police and corporate human resource officers looking for frauds and fakers, refined Tompkins's thinking to identify nine distinct affects: joy, excitement, surprise, anger, disgust, anguish, fear, shame, and dissmell (an impulse to avoid) (Ekman 1982). Those affects are understood to be evolutionary adaptations hard-wired in humans.

Affect theory attends to impulsive physical expression. Affect theorists see in the smile a sign of an affective 'fact,' the affect of joy. Affects are detectable through visible physical display. It is harder to say why they occur. Affect theory seeks to discover in affect something of the "pre-discursive materiality of bodies" (Schaefer 2015). Interpreting writings of affect theorists, Gail Hamner suggests that the shedding of tears, for example, can be "related to but not determined by language and memory," and she offers the neologism, 'affecognitive' to refer to such events (Hamner 2015). As a kind of embodied approach to understanding human behavior, affect theory, as it has been developing, aims to explore possibilities of speaking about feeling and thinking, biology and culture, together. Its distinct contribution to that project is its focus on the prediscursive 'signs' of affect that humans display. From there, the task, as it is in all approaches that aim to take seriously human embodiedness, is to determine what prompted such signs. For scholars of religion, then, it is possible to talk about emotion without necessarily talking about doctrine, about cultural traditions of religious experience, or about transcendence. Nevertheless, this approach leaves open possibilities for fluid and open-ended analyses of religion and emotion that can incorporate a great range of cultural and biological factors.

ANALYTIC PRACTICE

Humanities researchers and social scientists have learned much about religion by drawing judiciously on recent theory. For most who study religion, the broader project is not primarily to theorize it but to examine specific clusters of religious ideas, practices, institutions, and communities and to draw conclusions about how history and culture shape and have been shaped by religion. Researchers view their data from perspectives that are informed by theory; that is, they apply it. Scholars seek to understand why members of one religion war with members of another, how power comes to be wielded by religious authorities and located in religious institutions, how religions arise, decline, and are altered, and how persons make religious lives in the interstices between traditional elements of religious thought and practice.

An example of how academic study of religion and emotion enables fresh syntheses of scholarship is historian Susan Karant-Nunn's *The Reformation of Feeling: Shaping the Religious Emotions in Early Modern Germany* (2010). Karant-Nunn explores what she terms the 'religious tenors' of Catholics and Protestants in the sixteenth century, and she addresses various disruptions in emotional cultures during the Reformation. For Lutherans, it meant that "emotion-oriented piety was at an end" (65), an interpretation that she evidences through analysis of emotional language in sermons and the shifting aesthetics of Lutheran material culture. She explains how the representation of the suffering body, such as in the tribulations of martyrs or the crucifixion of Jesus, gave way in Lutheran churches to artistic prompts to reflect on atonement and salvation, a solemn and tranquil tenor replacing one characterized by fright and anxious foreboding. The model of that tranquillity was the mood expressed by the serene gaze of Jesus in the Wittenberg altarpiece. Karant-Nunn likewise, by focusing on emotion, is able to analyze the gendering of Lutheranism in the sixteenth century, pointing out how female personages, artistically depicted as examples of loss of emotional control, became less common in Lutheran churches over the course of a period of interior redesign. Lutheranism distinguished itself from Roman Catholicism through its elaboration of an emotional culture that was more masculinized and less terrified than the Catholic emotional tenor.

By the same token, historian Phyllis Mack's study of the emotional culture of early Methodism enables a clearer understanding of Methodism through its analysis of the feelings of some of the men and women who constituted the group's core membership (Mack 2008). Demonstrating how early Methodists' habits of emotional expression arose from their critical engagement of Puritan, pietist, and Enlightenment discourses about emotion, Mack is able to identify Methodists' active resistance to Enlightenment notions of the beauty and usefulness of the body. Early Methodists endeavored to feel the suffering of Jesus, to experience sadness, grief, and fear, and they cultivated those feelings through ascetic practice. By foregoing food, drink, sleep, and other necessities in the interest of prompting certain feelings, they practiced their distancing from the religious perspectives that were being shaped by the Enlightenment.

In some cases, researchers have been able to identify how cultures of emotion among certain groups influence the religious lives of persons. In so doing, the linkage of religion to various other aspects of social life—work, leisure, politics, courtship, sports, education, legal matters, parenting—becomes apparent through the common thread of an emotion present in all of those areas. For example, a view of the history of revivalism in America is made possible through attention to emotion in the Businessmen's Revival of the late 1850s. Analyzing the behavior of participants in the revival as part of a broader white middle-class Protestant culture of emotional expression, I showed how emotion came to be conceptualized as a commodity and exchanged in contractually framed transactions between actors. Just as there were expectations for actual exchange of feeling between husband and wife, parents and children, teachers and students, with friends and others, so also did revival-goers conceptualize their relationship with their God as an exchange of their deepest feelings in return for favors. Prayer meeting participants wrote requests for divine favor on pieces of paper in noontime gatherings: a better job, cure of a sick child, peace of mind, meeting a potential spouse. In praying their hearts, the currency of emotion, to God in exchange for those favors, they performed transactionally as would persons engaged in emotional transactions in other areas of life. Religion, like other aspects of life, accordingly was a business. Prayer manuals and religious publications in the mid-nineteenth century commented on the "business of religion," revival organizers issued "stock certificates" for "mansions in the sky" to persons who vowed to "give the heart" to God, and newspapers taught that the "business men's *prayer meetings are simply prayer meetings, on business principles*" (Corrigan 2002, 220).

The objectification of emotion plays a role in organizing the religious lives of persons in other traditions. Historian of religions June McDaniel has observed it in Bengali *bhakti* traditions. Paying close attention to the conceptualization of emotion, she is able to clarify how the cultivation of emotion in *bhakti* is imagined by devotees as a pathway to union with God. She points out that emotion is understood to be a substance, *rasa*, an essence similar to 'juice' or 'sap.' Emotion accordingly can be tasted. It can be hot or cold. It can be cooked, processed. It is not ineffable and hidden (McDaniel 2004). Recognizing this Bengali conceptualization of emotion allows scholars to more effectively explore, for example, the relationship of feeling to the vast material culture of Hinduism. It invites comparisons with other things that are experienced as hot or cold, with other objects or essences, and in so doing presents opportunities to clarify the emotional experiences of religious persons within a broader Hindu culture. By enabling more extensive analytical integration of emotional experiences with the vast material environment of Hinduism, it serves as a framework for a clearer and more robust picture of religious life. Mark M. Toomey, analyzing the religious behavior of Hindus at Mount Govardhan, observed the identification of certain emotions with specific foods. By paying attention to the ways in which those foods were prepared, presented, and consumed, he was able to draw conclusions about the cultivation and management of emotion among Hindu worshipers. He then was equipped to read those understandings back into analysis of social life for a richer understanding of ritual performances (Toomey 2004).

Analysis of emotion in religion affords opportunities for clearer understandings of how moral orders are constructed and maintained. When Anna M. Gade, in the course of analyzing feelings in Sufism, detects an "affective understanding of the moral order," she calls attention to how emotion can be experienced as a blending of cognitions and raw feelings (Gade 2007, 43). She describes how in early Islam a body of writings that included the Qur'an and the literature of *hadiths*, together with a collection of Muslim hagiographies, were engaged as illustrations of the role of emotions in aesthetic judgments. In Sufism, this process was manifest in the cultivation of sentiment through recitation of poetry. The feelings associated with such performances were understood by Sufis as inclusive of cognitive elements. Recitation accordingly was undertaken with a sense of such feelings as guides to the moral order, to the integration of the individual with the social. Analysis of emotion in this case, then, leads to deepened understanding of how morality was learned and practiced.

In his study of a community of Buddhist monks in Sri Lanka, Jeffrey Samuels likewise explores linkages between emotion and aesthetics. With an eye to the cultural frameworks that guide emotional experiences, he discusses how the feelings of an individual actor might not concord with those guidelines. He takes aesthetics as a set of benchmarks or principles that prompt and channel emotion but that also are shaped by the emotional experiences of individuals, as those individuals are drawn together in community. Drawing on his ethnographic data, he observes that emotions in the community of monks "function strategically in influencing and determining the types of bonds and commitments that people make to each other, to particular monastic institutions, and to the Buddhist religion" (Samuels 2010, xxvi). Such analysis furnishes the insight that monks are formed not simply by a process that teaches them conformity to ideals represented in canonical texts but through an open-ended process involving ongoing negotiation between individuals' emotional experiences and the emotional tenor of the group.

PROSPECT

The study of religion and emotion has developed as an interdisciplinary project within the humanities. Its prospective contributions to the academic study of religion rest in part on its capability to deepen its engagements with the cutting edges of interpretation across and beyond the humanities. By focusing on emotion, scholars already have been able to contribute to better understandings of ethnicity, gender, and sexuality in religion. Researchers, however, will need to address the role of emotion and especially collective emotion in religion in connection with a broader scholarly agenda that includes discussion of postcolonialism, capitalism, violence, and global projections of national and corporate power. Such conversations have been difficult because so much study of religion and emotion has been framed with respect to specifics of time and place that the conceptual expansiveness and fluidity required to move through widely varying regional contexts, especially, is not as practiced.

The study of religion and emotion should not shy from investigating emotions that seem strange. Current research on emotion has revolved around a fairly standard listing of familiar emotions. It may be, however, that emotions or emotional clusters in religion are not easily placed on such lists. It is unlikely, for example, that researchers would recognize Friedrich Schleiermacher's "feeling of absolute dependence" as a legitimate object of investigation because of its parochial character. And while it is not likely that further study of that feeling as defined by Schleiermacher will yield important insights, it might be the case that investigation of other unfamiliar feelings, experienced by persons in religious communities that have been understudied, will prove useful.

Research is likely to advance by investigating not only the expression of emotion but the concealment and repression of emotion in religion. Just as scholars in recent decades—following the leads of Allan Megill, Maria Lewicka, and Michael Fischer—have been able to build important interpretations of ethnic communities and nations by focusing on repressed memory, so also might study of repressed emotion lead to new interpretations of religious life. The repression of anger and hatred is important in many religions, and is linked to what cultural commentators since Sigmund Freud (1989 [1930]) and Norbert Elias (1978 [1939]) have thought of as the 'civilizing' influence of religion. The cultivation of sorrowful and guilty feelings in some religions can be associated with the diminishment of feelings of happiness. Such emotional dynamics represent a kind of emotional repression, or forgetting, that should be investigated as part of a developing project of the study of religion and emotion.

GLOSSARY

Affect theory focuses on how the biology of emotion is evidenced in physical response to stimuli, such as facial reactions that are associated with specific feelings (fear, surprise, etc.).

Cognition mental life that includes reasoning, knowledge, memory, judgment, language, and other abilities.

Culture knowledge, morals, beliefs, law, emotionology, art, and customs associated with a human population at a particular time and in a particular place.

Embodiment the grounding of thinking and feeling in the body.

Emotion a complex and intense state of feeling linked to physiological arousal, judgment, pleasure/pain, and thinking.

REFERENCES

Ahmed, Sarah. 2004. *The Cultural Politics of Emotion*. London: Routledge.

Averill, J. R. 1980. "A Constructivist View of Emotion." *Emotion: Theory, Research and Experience*. Vol. 1: *Theories of Emotion*, edited by R. Plutchik and H. Kellerman. New York: Academic Press, 305–339.

Bloch, Marc. 1923. *The Royal Touch*, translated by J. E. Andersen. New York: Dorset Press.

Bloch, Marc. 1953. *The Historian's Craft*, translated by Peter Putnam. New York: Knopf.

Boyer, Pascal. 1994. *The Naturalness of Religious Ideas: A Cognitive Theory of Religion.* Berkeley: University of California Press.

Braudel, Fernand. 1972–1973. *The Mediterranean and the Mediterranean World in the Age of Philip II*, translated by Sian Reynolds. New York: Harper & Row.

Burke, Peter. 1978. *Popular Religion in Early Modern Europe.* New York: New York University Press.

Cates, Diana Fritz. 2009. *Aquinas on the Emotions: A Religious-Ethical Inquiry.* Washington, DC: Georgetown University Press.

Christian, William A. Jr. 1982. "Provoked Religious Weeping in Early Modern Spain." In *Religious Organization and Religious Experience*, edited by John Davis. London: Academic Press, 97–114.

Corrigan, John. 2002. *Business of the Heart: Religion and Emotion in the Nineteenth Century.* Berkeley: University of California Press.

Davis, Natalie Zemon. 1975. *Society and Culture in Early Modern France.* Stanford CA: Stanford University Press.

Ekman, Paul. 1982. *Emotion in the Human Face.* Cambridge: Cambridge University Press.

Elias, Norbert, 1978. *The Civilizing Process*, translated by Edmund Jephcott. New York: Untzen. Original edition, 1939.

Febvre, Lucien. 1973a. "Histoire et Psychologie." In *A New Kind of History and Other Essays*, edited by Peter Burke and translated by K. Folca. New York: Harper & Row, 1–11.

Febvre, Lucien. 1973b. "How To Reconstitute the Emotional Life of the Past." In *A New Kind of History and Other Essays*, edited by Peter Burke and translated by K. Folca. New York: Harper & Row, 12–26.

Freud, Sigmund. 1989. *Civilization and Its Discontents*, edited and translated by James Strachey. New York: Norton. Original edition, 1930.

Gade, Anna M. 2004. *Perfection Makes Practice: Learning, Emotion, and the Recitation of the Qur-an in Indonesia.* Honolulu: University of Hawai'i Press.

Gade, Anna M. 2007. "Islam." In *The Oxford Handbook of Religion and Emotion*, edited by John Corrigan. New York: Oxford University Press, 35–50.

Geertz, Armin W. 2004. "Cognitive Approaches to the Study of Religion." In *New Approaches to the Study of Religion.* Vol. 2: *Textual, Comparative, Sociological, and Cognitive Approaches*, edited by P. Antes, A. W. Geertz, and R. R. Warne. Berlin: de Gruyter, 347–399.

Geertz, Clifford. 1973. *The Interpretation of Cultures.* New York: Basic Books.

Ginzburg, Carlo. 1982. *The Cheese and the Worms: The Cosmos of a Sixteenth-Century Miller*, translated by John and Anne Tedeschi. New York: Penguin. Original edition, 1976.

Hamner, M. Gail. 2015. "The Salience of Affect Theory for Studying 'Religion in the Public Sphere': Religion in Recent Documentary Films." Unpublished paper, delivered at the National Humanities Center, Durham, North Carolina, February 20, 2015.

Hochschild, Arlie R. 1983. *The Managed Heart: Commercialization of Human Feeling.* Berkeley: University of California Press.

Karant-Nunn, Susan. 2010. *The Reformation of Feeling: Shaping the Emotions in Early Modern Germany.* New York: Oxford University Press.

Lawson, E. Thomas and Robert N. McCauley. 1990. *Rethinking Religion: Connecting Cognition and Culture.* New York: Cambridge University Press.

Le Roy Ladurie, Emmanuel. 1978. *Montaillou: Cathars and Catholics in a French Village, 1294–1324*, translated by Barbara Bray. London: Scolar. Original edition, 1975.

Lutz, Catherine A. 1988. *Unnatural Emotions: Everyday Sentiments on a Micronesian Atoll and Their Challenge to Western Theory*. Chicago, IL: University of Chicago Press.

McDaniel, June. 2004. "Emotion in Bengali Religious Thought: Substance and Metaphor." In *Religion and Emotion: Approaches and Interpretations*, edited by John Corrigan. New York: Oxford University Press, 249–270.

Mack, Phyllis. 2008. *Heart Religion in the British Enlightenment: Gender and Emotion in Early Methodism*. New York: Cambridge University Press.

Nussbaum, Martha. 2001. *Upheavals of Thought: The Intelligence of Emotions*. New York: Cambridge University Press.

Otto, Rudolf. 1973. *The Idea of the Holy: An Inquiry into the Non-Rational Factor in the Idea of the Divine and its Relation to the Rational*, translated by John W. Harvey. New York: Oxford University Press. Original edition, 1917.

Rorty, Amelie, ed. 1980. *Explaining Emotions*. Berkeley: University of California Press.

Rosaldo, Michelle Z. 1980. *Knowledge and Passion: Ilongot Notions of Self and Social Life*. New York: Cambridge University Press.

Samuels, Jeffrey. 2010. *Attracting the Heart: Social Relations and the Aesthetics of Emotion in Sri Lankan Monastic Culture*. Honolulu: University of Hawai'i Press.

Schaefer, Donovan. 2015. "Beautiful Facts: Religion, Secularism, and Affect." Unpublished paper, delivered at the National Humanities Center, Durham, North Carolina, February 20, 2015.

Schleiermacher, Friedrich. 1960. *The Christian Faith*, English translation of the second German edition, edited by H. R. Mackintosh and J. S. Stewart. London: T. & T. Clark. Original edition, 1830–1831.

Schleiermacher, Friedrich. 1996. *On Religion: Speeches to Its Cultured Despisers*, edited and translated by Richard Crouter. Cambridge and New York: Cambridge University Press. Original edition, 1799.

Solomon, Robert C. 1976. *The Passions*, Garden City, NY: Anchor/Doubleday.

Solomon, Robert C. 2004. *Thinking About Feeling: Contemporary Philosophers on Emotions*. New York: Oxford University Press.

Thomas, Keith. 1971. *Religion and the Decline of Magic*. New York: Scribner's.

Tomkins, Silvan S. 1962. *Affect Imagery Consciousness*. Vol. 1: *The Positive Affects*. New York: Springer.

Toomey, Paul M. 2004. "Krishna's Consuming Passions: Food as Metaphor and Metonym for Emotion at Mount Govardhan." In *Religion and Emotion: Approaches and Interpretations*, edited by John Corrigan. New York: Oxford University Press, 223–248.

Wynn, Mark. 2005. *Emotional Experience and Religious Understanding: Integrating Perception, Conception and Feeling*. Cambridge: Cambridge University Press.

FURTHER READING

Corrigan, John, ed. 2007. *The Oxford Handbook of Religion and Emotion*. New York: Oxford University Press. [*This is a collection of extended essays each of which discusses an aspect of religion and emotion. It is organized in four parts: Traditions, Religious Life, Emotions (specific emotions), and Historical and Theoretical Perspectives.*]

Fuller, Robert C. 2009. *Wonder: From Emotion to Spirituality*. Chapel Hill: University of North Carolina Press. [*This a study of the ways in which persons frame their experience of wonder in religious or spiritual ways. There is a particular emphasis on the experience of nature.*]

McNamer, Sarah. 2009. *Affective Meditation and the Invention of Medieval Compassion*. Philadelphia: University of Pennsylvania Press. [*This is a literary analysis of medieval cultivation of affect in religious practice.*]

Scheer, Monique. 2012. "Are Emotions a Kind of Practice (And Is That What Makes Them Have a History)? A Bourdieuian Approach to Understanding Emotion." *History and Theory* 51(2): 193–220. [*Scheer argues that emotions ought to be understood as a practice and that the historical study of emotion benefits from approaching emotion in that way.*]

Wynn 2005 [*Wynn argues that cognition and feeling are intertwined in religious experience.*]

CHAPTER 35

···

EXPERIENCE

···

CRAIG MARTIN

CHAPTER SUMMARY

···

- 'Religious experience' is a concept attributed to a wide variety of phenomena, including mystical states, altered states of consciousness, spirit possessions, etc.; theorists variously attribute the causes of experience to divine sources, social or cultural prompting, or natural, biological processes.
- Classic theorists—such as Friedrich Schleiermacher, William James, and Rudolf Otto—employ a normative paradigm that authorizes some experiences as superior to others.
- These normative approaches have been called into question by contemporary theorists who expose normative baggage in the classic works, often implicitly tied to European colonialism or assumptions of Christian superiority.
- Contemporary theorists—such as Wayne Proudfoot and Ann Taves—offer more critical, analytical paradigms for analyzing special experiences cross-culturally without reifying them or presuming their universality.
- However, even these more analytical paradigms are subject to a number of possible criticisms.

INTRODUCTION

···

The concept of 'religious experience' has been used variously to denote everything from visions of gods, goddesses, or saints to experiences of being possessed by spirits, the sense of being 'awestruck' before the infinity of the universe, or even so-called 'altered states of consciousness' that take place during intense meditation. Many scholars who write about such experiences take it for granted that they are universal or transhistorical;

in addition, some of these scholars assume that the sources or causes of experience are objectively real supernatural entities or forces. Other scholars, who challenge these ambitious claims on empirical or theoretical grounds, present religious experience as merely hallucinatory or as having natural, biological, linguistic, or social causes. There are also scholars whose positions lie somewhere in between: they may be agnostic about the causes of religious experience and may focus, instead, on how religious practitioners describe them.

This chapter will first consider three classic frameworks for thinking about religious experience—those of Friedrich Schleiermacher, William James, and Rudolf Otto—before turning to criticisms that suggest their approaches are inescapably normative and ethnocentric. Then I will focus on the works of Wayne Proudfoot and Ann Taves, which provide a more critical, analytical framework. Before concluding, I will draw attention to Robert Sharf's suggestion that at times 'experience' may be entirely fictional.

Normative Frameworks

Friedrich Schleiermacher and the Intuition of the Infinite

Christian theologian Friedrich Schleiermacher's *On Religion: Speeches to its Cultured Despisers* (1996 [1799]) is framed as a defensive response to critics who have reduced religion to propositional content (i.e. a set of doctrines or truths) or to a moral code: "Religion's essence is neither thinking nor acting" (22). Schleiermacher argues that these reductions have mistaken outward religion and its empirical trappings for the real thing, an inward experience or intuition of the divine. He does not reject doctrines or morality as completely irrelevant to religion: these finite forms may be important, but they must not be confused with true religion in and of itself; "religion's essence has remained hidden under this mask" (22). He therefore sets out to delimit the essence of religion from secondary characteristics or aspects, in order to protect the former from the criticisms leveled at the latter.

Schleiermacher defines true religion as an overwhelming intuition of the infinite. "Religion's essence is . . . intuition and feeling" (22), and "[t]o have religion means to intuit the universe" (52). This intuition is passive: "All intuition proceeds from an influence of the intuited on the one who intuits" (24); as such, the infinite is the active source of religion, and humans are mere recipients. In addition, true religion begins and ends with this intuition of the infinite: "it stops with the immediate experiences of the existence and action of the universe" (26).

On this view, those empirical trappings of outward religion are useful only insofar as they can elicit the inward intuition essential to religion. Revelation, ritual, or doctrine are for the "restoration of a religious intuition," or for transferring that intuition from one individual subject to others (49). As such, religious beliefs "must be renounced by those who would penetrate into [religion's] sanctuary" (50). At bottom, "[e]very holy writing is merely a mausoleum of religion, a monument that a great spirit was there that no longer exists" (50).

Having saved true religion from its non-religious critics, Schleiermacher uses the distinction between living experience and dead empiricism to criticize non-Christian religions. "Judaism is long since a dead religion, and those who at present still bear its colors are actually sitting and mourning beside the undecaying mummy and weeping over its demise and sad legacy" (114–115). Long since deprived of life, "its external parts were preserved ... the unpleasant appearance of a mechanical movement after the life and spirit had long since departed" (115). By contrast, "The original intuition of Christianity is more glorious, more sublime, more worthy of adult humanity, more deeply penetrating into the spirit of systematic religion, and extending farther over the whole universe" (115).

William James, Experience, and Institutional Religion

In *The Varieties of Religious Experience* (1985 [1902]), William James writes from a background in psychology and philosophy rather than theology. While James's intellectual goals were rather different from Schleiermacher's, his schema for understanding religion was nevertheless very similar.

James characterizes religious experience by using a similar inward/outward distinction, although the terms he uses are 'personal' and 'institutional':

> On the one side of it lies institutional, on the other personal religion. ... Worship and sacrifice, procedures for working on the dispositions of the deity, theology and ceremony and ecclesiastical organization, are the essentials of the institutional branch. ... In the more personal branch of religion it is on the contrary the inner dispositions of man himself. (28–29)

James sees the purpose of the outward things as secondary, as prompting the inner things, which are primary. Institutional religion 'prompts' personal experiential transactions, which in themselves are "direct from heart to heart, from soul to soul, between man and his maker" (29). James is persuaded that the personal, inward things deserve priority in his analysis: "I propose to ignore the institutional branch entirely, to say nothing of the ecclesiastical organization, to consider as little as possible the systematic theology and the ideas about the gods themselves, and to confine myself as far as I can to personal religion pure and simple" (29).

For James, personal religious experience is fundamentally a matter of feeling. In the conclusion to *Varieties* he claims to have intended to "rehabilitat[e] the element of feeling in religion and subordinat[e] its intellectual part" (501). These feelings, as with Schleiermacher, are something that can only be understood by those who have personally experienced them. Third-person knowledge is not the same as first-person experience: "to understand the causes of drunkenness . . . is not to be drunk' (488). For this reason the 'science of religion' is an intellectual endeavor with limits that cannot be surmounted without the researcher undergoing the experience of religion for herself. However, unlike Schleiermacher, the existence of these feelings does not necessarily confirm the truth of their objects for James—i.e. a religious feeling is insufficient to warrant the claim that the gods about which religions talk actually exist. Instead, James concludes that even if the claims religions make may be false, they may nevertheless be practically useful. Religions foster positive changes in human conduct, and it is on these grounds that he argues that religion may serve a "permanent function . . . whether . . . true or false' (507).

After subordinating institutional religion to religious experience, James makes a number of deprecating claims about the former. He affiliates "institutional religion" with the following negative terms: "corporate ambitions," "the spirit of politics and the lust of dogmatic rule," "hypocrisy and tyranny and meanness and tenacity of superstition" (335), "bigotries," "the spirit of dogmatic dominion" (337), "corruption by excess" (339), and "fanaticism" (340). Religious experience is positively valued, but institutional religion is seen as a degraded abomination of personal religion. "A genuine first-hand religious experience" can be turned into a new orthodoxy; "when a religion has become an orthodoxy, its day of inwardness is over: the spring is dry; the faithful live at second hand exclusively . . . The baseness so commonly charged to religion's account are thus, almost all of them, not chargeable to religion proper, but rather to religion's wicked practical partner, the spirit of corporate dominion" (337).

A Protestant Conversion Experience

One of James's central empirical examples of a religious experience is Stephen H. Bradley's nineteenth-century Protestant Christian conversion narrative. According to Bradley, during the sermon at a Methodist revival meeting the "powers" of his mind were "awakened," and he "trembled involuntarily," despite the fact that his "heart" was "unmoved" (190). After leaving the revival meeting, he claims to have had an experience of the "Holy Spirit": "I began to feel my heart beat very quick all on a sudden . . . though I was not alarmed for I felt no pain. My heart increased its beating, which soon convinced me that it was the Holy Spirit from the effect it had on me" (191). According to Bradley, he said aloud that he did not deserve this happiness, and at that point "there was a stream (resembling air in feeling) came into my mouth and heart in a more sensible manner than that of drinking . . . which appeared to be the cause of such a palpitation of my heart" (191). Then a passage from the Bible appeared to him, "as if the New Testament was placed before me" (191). Later, Bradley concluded that his "soul was full of the Holy Spirit" (192), and that he was now fully converted to Christianity.

For James, Bradley's episode exemplifies what he takes to be the core characteristics of conversion experiences. Crucially, subjects feel themselves to be passively taken by a force outside their voluntary control. The experiences bring about a "loss of all the worry," a "sense of perceiving truths not known before," and an "objective change which the world often appears to undergo" (248). What causes such experiences? James claims that the theology on which one is raised may color one's conversion experience; thus the experience of a Catholic might differ from that of a Protestant (200–201). Despite this, he insists on a non-doctrinal core to conversion experiences, which is "in no essential need of doctrinal apparatus or propitiatory machinery" (211). James assumes the universality of experience is made possible by the biological or cognitive makeup of human nature: "the elementary mechanisms of our life are presumably so uniform that what is shown to be true in a marked degree of some person is probably true in some degree of all" (233). More specifically, James argues that these experiences are caused by subconscious forces in the human mind, before which we are passive and of which we are largely unaware—much like "post-hypnotic suggestions" implanted in subjects and later activated by a hypnotist (234). Nevertheless, James resists a purely naturalist explanation and remains agnostic about the prior causes of these subliminal forces; "it is logically conceivable that *if there be* higher spiritual agencies that can directly touch us, the psychological condition of their doing so *might* be our possession of a subconscious region which alone should yield access to them" (242).

Rudolf Otto and the Holy

Rudolf Otto's *The Idea of the Holy* (1958 [1917]) is written from a Christian theological perspective, and his view is in many ways closer to Schleiermacher's. However, unlike either Schleiermacher or James, Otto employs a Kantian philosophical framework that saturates his account of religious experience at every level.

In *The Critique of Pure Reason*, Kant claims that there are intrinsic limits to human knowledge. Because humans process the world through universal, a priori categories, we can have objective scientific knowledge of natural phenomena in time and space; however, objective knowledge does not extend to noumena—things in and of themselves, independent of human cognition and categories. Noumena such as God, free will, immortality of the soul, etc. lie outside the bounds of knowledge, and although we must assume they exist, our claims about them are analogical at best. Theological contradictions or paradoxes that appear when we attempt to speak about supernatural matters are therefore not evidence against the existence of God, but rather evidence of the limits of human knowledge. As Kant famously put it, "I had to deny knowledge in order to make room for faith" (1998, 117).

Otto similarly claims that we cannot have objective knowledge about God through the categories that structure our experience; the greatest mystery of the universe is "inexpressible," "ineffable" (1958, 5), or "hidden and esoteric" (13). "The truly 'mysterious' object is beyond our apprehension and comprehension, not only because our knowledge has certain irremovable limits, but because in it we come upon something inherently 'wholly other,' whose kind and character are incommensurable with our own, and before which we therefore recoil in a wonder that strikes us chill and numb" (28).

Although we cannot 'know' this mystery, we can nevertheless experience it, and experience provides the evidence for God that knowledge cannot. These experiences of the "numinous," the "holy," and the "*mysterium tremendum*" are "perfectly *sui generis* and irreducible to any other" (7). Otto describes it as one of complete "impotence" (21): "the emotion of a creature, submerged and overwhelmed by its own nothingness in contrast to that which is supreme above all creatures" (10). Although it "cannot be rendered explicit in conceptual terms," this feeling designates or corresponds with a "reality" (30) that is the "ultimate and highest part of our nature" (36). Where words fail, experience saves.

This feeling of the infinite can be "induced, incited, and aroused" by various means, such as reading the scriptures, preaching, or singing (60). In addition, Otto assumes that humans universally have a capacity to induce and experience the numinous (177); this provides him with a foundation for the comparative study of religions. "Every religion . . . springs from personal assurance and inward convincement" (175). Otto suggests that Buddhists' experience of 'emptiness' is actually of the numinous, and 'emptiness' is just another term for the *mysterium tremendum* (30).

Not all religions are created equally, however. Some religions invoke experiences of the numinous better than others. Christianity best puts into words what cannot be put into words, and does so with "unique clarity and abundance"; as such, Christianity enjoys a "superiority over religions of other forms" (1). Crucial for Otto is the fact that the numinous makes us feel like nothing before the divine—and therefore in need of salvation—and "No religion has brought about the mystery of the need for atonement or expiation to so complete, so profound, or so powerful expression as Christianity. And in this, too, it shows its superiority" (56). The Old Testament (representing "Semitic religion") induces experiences of the numinous, but errs in tending toward an anthropomorphic representation of God. Islam too can induce experiences of the holy, but unfortunately lacks the rational component present in Christianity, resulting in a "fanatical" religion "that runs to frenzy" (91). There is something of the numinous in the magic and ancestor worship of "primitives" and "savage tribes," but it is "rudimentary" (117). It is only in Christianity that "we see the consummation of that process tending to rationalize, moralize, and humanize the idea of God"; Christianity is "unsurpassable" (82).

Although the concept of 'the holy' has largely fallen out of favor, it is not without his defenders. In "The Problem of the Holy" (2012), Robert Orsi attempts to rescue the concept from its normative baggage. He first acknowledges its problematic legacy: "As it was developed at the turn of the twentieth century . . . the concept of 'the holy' was implicated in the European ideology of Western superiority that underwrote the colonial project" (85). However, Orsi adds:

> the holy still seems to me to name both a reality and an approach to religion that scholars of religion ought to think about. For one thing, people all over the world and in different historical periods have experienced something out of the ordinary in person, places, or things, and they know what they mean, or enough of what they mean, to use the word 'holy' . . . as the only possible word for what they have experienced. (85–86)

Thus Orsi hopes to "rehabilitate" this word that points to what is "experienced as 'objective' ... [and] known as objectively real" (100), even if experiences of the holy call "into question the absolute authority of naturalistic explanations" (99).

ANALYTICAL FRAMEWORKS

Against the Normative Approach

In the works of Schleiermacher, James, and Otto, the concept of religious experience is embedded in a normative discourse that permits them to sort and rank social institutions and cultural traditions, authorizing some and sanctioning others. Each employs an authenticity rhetoric that suggests some experiences or institutions are closer to the origin and others too primitive, degraded, or impure to be of use.

In the last few decades a number of scholars have explicitly criticized discourses on 'experience' for this normative baggage. In "The Evidence of Experience," Joan Wallach Scott suggests that appeals to authentic experience function to authorize particular first-person perspectives and simultaneously discourage researchers from investigating the social conditions or power relations that make those first-person perspectives possible:

> When [experience] is defined as internal, it is an expression of an individual's being or consciousness ... Talking about experience in these ways leads us to take the existence of individuals for granted (experience is something people have) rather than to ask how conceptions of selves (or subjects and their identities) are produced. It operates within an ideological construction that not only makes individuals the starting point of knowledge, but that also naturalizes categories such as man, woman, black, white, heterosexual, and homosexual by treating them as given characteristics of individuals. (1991, 782)

Although Scott is referring to scholarship on the 'experiences' of men and women, blacks and whites, etc., the same critique could be extended to scholarship on religious experience: appeals to first-person 'experiences' of Buddhists take for granted the existence of Buddhism and Buddhist subjects, and as such likely naturalize those Buddhists' ideological construction of the world. Scott suggests that scholars should, instead, historicize particular identities, experiences, and the social relations that condition them: our task is "to understand the operations of the complex and changing discursive processes by which identities are ascribed, resisted, or embraced, and which processes themselves are unremarked and indeed achieve their effect because they are not noticed" (792). In practice this could mean, for instance, that rather than naturalizing the ideological construction Otto assumes, we could instead interrogate the 'Christian' identity he takes for granted, the identities or communities with which he, as a social actor, is in competition, and how asserting an authentic 'Christian' experience of the holy could award him or his community social, material, or symbolic capital.

This is precisely what Tim Murphy attempts to accomplish in *The Politics of Spirit: Phenomenology, Genealogy, Religion* (2010). Murphy's book is systematic: he historicizes, step by step, the work of phenomenologists of religion, including Otto, Joachim Wach, Mircea Eliade, and others. In each case he outlines their claims about religious experience, the social and political contexts of their claims, and how their scholarly productions are normatively tied up with Eurocentrism, colonialism, and the assertion of Christian superiority. Murphy concludes that phenomenology of religion—and its insistence on experiences of 'spirit'—"pretends toward a universalism but, in the end, time and time again, uses that very same universalism to marginalize the already marginal . . . and denigrate the already denigrated . . . When its core, constitutive, structural oppositions are analyzed, it is seen to be the vicious, self-aggrandizing, and monstrously narcissistic ideological formation that it is" (297).

Despite these criticisms, a number of contemporary scholars hope to save the concept of 'experience' from its normative baggage by embedding it within a new theoretical framework. Writing from a much more rigorous philosophical perspective, Wayne Proudfoot and Ann Taves provide scholars with a framework for analyzing experience that eschews authenticity rhetoric and the taken-for-granted authority of experience. Both Proudfoot and Taves are interested in how practitioners both actively produce and variously interpret experience, and neither leaves much room for a transcendent force that stamps subjects with a self-evidently divine power. For them, religious experience is a much more human phenomenon.

Wayne Proudfoot and the Causes of Experience

Both Schleiermacher and Otto took for granted the causes of religious experience: as theists, they assumed experience is produced when the divine touches humans. By contrast, in *Religious Experience* (1985), Wayne Proudfoot argues that the sources of experience are quite possibly far more mundane.

Schleiermacher insisted that true religious experience is completely unmediated by human language or discourse. While he accepted that experiences can be put into words after the fact—although descriptions of experience will always be incapable of grasping the essence of the experience itself—the primordial experience is assumed to be entirely pre-conceptual. By contrast, Proudfoot argues that "moments of experience are clearly dependent on the availability of particular concepts, beliefs, and practices" (xv–xvi). Proudfoot shows that Schleiermacher explicitly defines religious experience as an experience in which the person undergoing the experience *identifies* its cause as divine in origin. For Schleiermacher, an experience is not religious unless the practitioner *employs a set of concepts* to distinguish between mundane and divine causes—in which case religious experience cannot be entirely pre-conceptual. A religious experience "cannot be independent of concepts and beliefs and at the same time [be] an intentional state that can only be specified by reference to objects of thought" (15).

Having opened the door to the idea that our language and culture contributes to the experiences we have, Proudfoot looks at research done on subjects using, for instance, hallucinogens. One study showed that, given hallucinogens, Christian subjects at a worship service would report having had religious experiences that made sense on a Christian theological interpretation. However, during the study one participant "seems to have been immune to the religious effects of the hallucinogen because of a firmly held naturalistic interpretation. The subject was skeptical from the outset, and . . . did not report any of the characteristics of religious experience" (106). For Proudfoot,

> Any bodily changes or feelings may be accounted for in religious terms when the subject's past experience and present contexts makes such an account plausible and compelling. The common element in religious experience is likely to be found, not in a particular physiological or even mental state, but in the beliefs held by the subject about the causes of that state. (107)

It is on these grounds that Proudfoot revisits Bradley's conversion account; Proudfoot argues that Bradley explained the palpitations of his heart in terms of Protestant theology—rather than, for instance, attributing his increased heart rate to an illness— because that was the framework of interpretation immediately available to him. "Bradley, like so many prospective devotees before and since, could not understand his feelings in naturalistic terms. Religious symbols offered him an explanation that was compatible both with his experience and with his antecedent beliefs. He did not con- sider explanations involving Krishna, Zeus, or the Qur'an" (104). Another scholar, Peter Antes, puts it more bluntly: while Hindus in India might experience Kali, Catholics in North America are more likely to experience St. Mary, and as such it seems that prac- titioners are not "passive spectators" but rather that "there is a considerable amount of constructive investigation based on what has been learnt from the traditions about what is appearing" (2002, 340). In sum, "we experience very deeply what we have learnt" (341). In *Religious Experience, Justification, and History* (1999), Matthew Bagger simi- larly defends Proudfoot's claims, adding that subjective experience is active rather than passive, and that the active mechanisms which produce experience are informed by the cognitive habits encouraged by our local culture. "Presented with sensory stimuli, the mind always supplies the associations habitually aroused by similar stimuli" (36).

Some scholars of experience resist naturalistic explanations on the grounds that reli- gious experience appears to be or feels like it has been caused by supernatural rather than natural causes, at least by those undergoing the experience; when such experiences are described as having natural causes, the experience itself is distorted or "the distinctive character of religious experience and belief is lost" (216). Proudfoot argues that this type of argument is a protectionist strategy designed to exempt from criticism both religious experiences and the beliefs apparently derived from them. He allows that when dealing with experience, we must of course begin with the perspective of the subject, including the causes to which he or she attributed the experience. However, first-order description is only the first stage of a responsible analysis, and we need not stop there; there is no intrinsic reason why scholars cannot pass from first-order description to second-order attribution of causes, which may include causes not recognized by whoever underwent the experience. Thus Proudfoot rejects descriptive reductionism—that is, descriptions of what is experienced that ignore or supplant first-order causal accounts with an outsider's view—but accepts reductionism at the second-order, explanatory level, wherein scholars may advance arguments for alternative causes.

In sum, Proudfoot does not deny that subjects have religious experiences, but he insists that we as scholars must be careful about the causes we ascribe to such experiences. Contrary to Schleiermacher or Otto, who claim that some experiences are unmediated, Proudfoot insists that our culture and cognitive expectations may be constitutive and irreducible elements of experience. If so, experience is neither pure nor unmediated, and as such cannot be used to warrant the authority of claims about divine sources presumed to lie behind religious experience.

Hui-neng and the Experience of Enlightenment

In *Zen and the Unspeakable God: Comparative Interpretations of Mystical Experience* (2015), Jason N. Blum provides us with a historical study of mystical experience that separates first-order description from second-order explanation in precisely the way Proudfoot recommends. Whatever our theoretical framework, we must be attentive to "the mystic's own experience and understanding of it" (4). Toward this end, Blum offers a careful description of the mystical experiences of seventh-century Chinese Zen Buddhist, Hui-neng. According to the biographies of Hui-neng and *The Sutra of Hui-neng*, while one day delivering firewood to a client in a marketplace, Hui-neng—an illiterate man—overheard monks reciting *The Diamond Sutra* and immediately became enlightened. Contrary to a case such as Bradley's, wherein the subject had a great deal of prior familiarity with the religious doctrines at hand prior to his experience, Hui-neng did not "require long and arduous study of Buddhist doctrine" and was not dedicated to the "performance of iconic Buddhist practices such as meditation"; "Hui-neng's enlightenment is sudden, without premeditation, training, or precursor" (125). After this immediate enlightenment experience, Hui-neng joins a nearby monastery, where he subsequently undertakes a study of Buddhist texts under the monastery's patriarch. During one of his sessions, Hui-neng undergoes another enlightenment experience, whereupon he realizes the nature of the universe and the "essence of mind itself" (126).

Blum elaborates at length how Hui-neng describes this experience. Hui-neng reports a lack of distinction between self and universe; he claims to have experienced the world as essentially empty or void of distinctions, such that there was a continuity between what we normally take to be subject and object. Insofar as subject and object were mutually deconstituted in this experience, Hui-neng claimed that "[a]wakening has two meanings. One is outward awakening, seeing the emptiness of all things. The other is inward seeking knowing the emptiness and silence of the mind" (134).

Blum notes that Hui-neng refuses to attribute the cause of his initial experience of this sort of enlightenment to training in Buddhist scriptures or doctrines; rather, Hui-neng insists that any illiterate or untrained man is capable of such experiences. A "similar potential . . . is in fact inherent in all persons, regardless of background or formal training" (140). Consistent with this, Hui-neng ridicules traditional doctrinal training and emphasizes the dispensability of intellectual inquiry. Much like Schleiermacher or Otto, for Hui-neng the enlightenment experience involves "neither knowing things by their concepts nor believing them to be unknowable; it is the nondiscursive and unfettered engagement with them as merely transient phenomena" (148). For Blum, if we are to avoid descriptive reductionism, first-order description of Hui-neng's experience must attend to the fact that he himself described it both as uncaused by religious training and as direct, ineffable, and beyond concepts, labels, or distinctions.

Ann Taves and the Experience of Things Deemed Religious

Ann Taves's first major work—*Fits, Trances, and Visions* (1999)—was historical in its approach. Taves surveyed how Americans spoke about and evaluated religious enthusiasm, mesmerism, clairvoyance, spiritualism, etc. She reveals that Americans' views of these different types of experiences were deeply contested; some people viewed them as markers of true religion, while others viewed them as aberrant, pathological, or delusional. Similar to Proudfoot, one of Taves's central points is that, insofar as language is to some extent constitutive of reality, changing the language used to talk about experience may in fact have produced different experiences. "Theories of experience . . . inform the making and unmaking of experience," and thus Taves hopes that researchers will shift their focus from analyses of experience in-itself to "the *processes* by which religious and nonreligious phenomena are made and unmade" (361)—that is, including the language we use that constitutes 'religion' and 'experience.'

In her second major work—*Religious Experience Reconsidered* (2009)—Taves shifts away from history and toward providing an analytical framework that would allow us to bring together, for the purposes of scientific cross-cultural comparison, both 'religious' and 'non-religious' special experiences. Taking into account the critical work done on the concept of 'religion' in the last few decades, Taves grants that the term 'religion' is flexible and frequently loaded with a variety of essentialist norms and presuppositions—often those of Protestantism or liberal ecumenism. However, "[m]any scholars of religion, eager to deconstruct an essentialist understanding of religion and religious experience, abandoned the focus on religious experience and recast the study of religion in light of critical theories that emphasize the role of language in constituting social reality in the context of relationships of power and inequality" (5). Rather than abandon the study of religious experience altogether, Taves hopes to build a bridge between these critiques of 'religion' and the expansive work being done in the fields of psychology, evolutionary biology, cognitive science, etc.

Taves thus proposes analyzing not *sui generis* religious experiences but rather any kind of experience that practitioners deem 'religious' or special in some way. In this manner, Taves turns away from an essentialist understanding of religion and toward the social or linguistic means by which people designate experiences as 'religious'. In addition, her approach allows researchers not to ignore the experiences themselves—for Taves, we can study both the cognitive experiences and the social or linguistic conditions that constitute those experiences and make them special:

> we need to turn our attention to the processes by which people sometimes ascribe the special characteristics to things that we (as scholars) associate with terms such as 'religious,' 'magical,' 'mystical,' 'spiritual,' et cetera. . . . [This] will allow us to focus on the interaction between psychobiological, social, and cultural-linguistic processes in relation to carefully specified types of experiences sometimes considered religious and to build methodological bridges across the divide between the humanities and the sciences. (8)

In Hui-neng's case, this might mean looking not only at his reported experiences but also at the social context that made possible (or necessary) the identification of his experience *as* one of 'enlightenment' or 'awakening.' Had Hui-neng lived in another sociocultural context, he might have identified his experience using a completely different theoretical or discursive framework, and therefore a consideration of his context must be an essential part of our analysis of his experience.

In sum, much like Proudfoot, Taves allows that we may be able to offer naturalistic, reductionist accounts of the causes of atypical states of consciousness, although her view differs from his in that she recommends using both social constructionism—i.e. culture contributes to experience—and more scientific apparatuses such as those from psychology or cognitive science—i.e. not just culture but also universal biological conditions contribute to experience.

Beyond 'Experience'

While the approaches of Proudfoot and Taves are more rigorous and sophisticated than the blatantly normative paradigms considered earlier, they are not without their criticisms. In his essay on "Experience" (1998), Robert Sharf—a scholar of Asian religions—contests the centrality of 'meditation' leading to altered states of consciousness frequently attributed to Hinduism or Buddhism:

> while meditation may have been esteemed in theory, it did not occupy the dominant role in monastic and ascetic life that is sometimes supposed. . . . Even when practiced, it is by no means obvious that traditional forms of meditation were oriented toward the attainment of extraordinary "states of consciousness." . . . This is not to deny that religious practitioners had "experiences" in the course of their training, just that such experiences were not considered the goal of practice, were not deemed doctrinally

authoritative, and did not serve as the reference points for their understanding of the path. (99)

Despite the presumed centrality of 'experience' to religion, our emphasis as scholars on the experiences of those we study could be both anachronistic and distorting. Sharf goes on to point out that some famous Buddhist practitioners themselves emphasized the importance of 'experience' only after exposure to the works of William James.

Sharf also calls into question the assumption that talk of 'experience' necessarily has a referent. Going beyond the claim that experiences are mediated or constituted by language and culture rather than 'pure,' he suggests that perhaps talk about 'experience' is like talk of alien abduction:

> many abductees have no memory of the event until it is "recovered" by therapists who have made a specialty out of treating victims of alien abductions. . . . [In addition,] many central elements and motifs in the abduction narratives . . . [can be traced] to popular science fiction comics, stories, and films of the past fifty years. The scholarly consensus would seem to be that the abductions simply did not take place; there is no *originary event* behind the memories. (109)

Sharf concludes that we may be warranted not only in saying that experiences are culturally produced, but that perhaps in some instances they are not "determinative phenomenal events at all" (110). On such a view, the biographies that recount Hui-neng's enlightenment experience might be simply fictional or hagiographical.

It is for this reason that some scholars have moved away from analyzing experiences in-themselves and toward analyzing the social functions of the rhetoric of experience. For instance, in "Interiorizing Islam: Religious Experience and State Oversight in the Islamic Republic of Iran" (2015), Kathleen Foody suggests that appeals to private experience can function to carve out a depoliticized space independent of state control; in such a case, a claim to experience "is itself overtly political—a claim to make safe and retake space overwhelmed by the authoritarian stat apparatus of the Islamic Republic and its claims to religious authority" (601). In *Selling Spirituality: The Silent Takeover of Religion* (2005), Jeremy Carrette and Richard King demonstrate a connection between politics and claims to experience; they argue that the fiction of an independent, private, inner realm of experience is part of a modern, neoliberal form of governmentality that fragments society and pacifies individualized subjects by obscuring the extent to which so-called 'interior' experience is in fact constituted by exterior social structures. For these authors, 'experience' is less interesting as an object of study than the social function of *claims* about experience.

CONCLUSION

As should be clear, the legacy of the concept of 'experience' in religious studies is deeply contested. The claim that humans have access to an essential, *sui generis* 'religious experience' is at this point no longer a viable option for scholars attempting to move beyond the uncritical, normative paradigms. On the other hand, few scholars today are willing to go as far as Sharf does when he discusses alien abductions; although some experience narratives might be entirely fabricated, most scholars accept that there is sufficient evidence to demonstrate that people—religious or otherwise—do sometimes have 'special' experiences outside normal, everyday consciousness. Who among us hasn't experienced a quickening of the heart like Bradley's, whatever causes we might attribute to it? Two options appear to remain for mainstream scholarship. On the one hand, with Proudfoot and Taves we as scholars could analyze the social, discursive, and biological conditions that make certain extraordinary experiences possible, as well as the social or discursive conditions that permit us to designate those experiences as 'extraordinary.' On the other hand, we could take Scott and Murphy's central insights—that discourses on 'experience' can function as authorizing tools—and combine them with Sharf's agnosticism about the referents of experience narratives; in this case we could devote ourselves to analyzing not the 'experiences' themselves—which may or may not be real—but rather the social work that is accomplished by appeals to experience. Whatever direction we take, the study of 'experience' must now take into account the very discourses we use to talk about 'experience.'

Glossary

Authenticity rhetoric authenticity claims depict some experiences or forms of culture as more true, more pure, than others.

Essentialism the assumption of an abiding core or essence in a thing, a person, or a form of culture, which doesn't change over time, even as secondary characteristics change.

Ethnocentrism a form of cultural prejudice; viewing one's own culture or ethnicity as superior to others'.

Experience the interior stream of consciousness in a mind, often—but not always—related to an external object.

First-/second-order scholars distinguish between texts or discourses that are objects of study for them (i.e. first-order objects) and scholarly texts about those objects (i.e. second-order writings about first-order objects).

Intuition the reception of sensory data, either natural or supernatural, to a mind, prior to any cognitive processing.

Inward/outward religion many scholars demarcate between inward religion (within a body or mind), including thought, experience, sentiment, intentions, etc., and outward religion (outside bodies), including texts, rituals, worship services, habitual practices, sacred sites, etc.

Mysticism forms of culture (including reading of texts, practices of meditation, etc.) that encourage altered states of consciousness that participants claim allows them to dissolve subject–object identities and become one with a god or the universe as a whole.

REFERENCES

Antes, Peter. 2002. "What Do We Experience If We Have Religious Experience?" *Numen* 49(3): 336–342. doi: 10.1163/156852702320263954

Bagger, Matthew C. 1999. *Religious Experience, Justification, and History*. Cambridge: Cambridge University Press.

Blum, Jason N. 2015. *Zen and the Unspeakable God: Comparative Interpretations of Mystical Experience*. University Park, PA: Pennsylvania State University Press.

Carrette, Jeremy and Richard King. 2005. *Selling Spirituality: The Silent Takeover of Religion*. London: Routledge.

Foody, Kathleen. 2015. "Interiorizing Islam: Religious Experience and State Oversight in the Islamic Republic of Iran." *Journal of the American Academy of Religion* 83(3): 599–623. doi: 10.1093/jaarel/lfv029

James, William. 1985. *The Varieties of Religious Experience*. New York: Penguin Books. Original edition, 1902.

Murphy, Tim. 2010. *The Politics of Spirit: Phenomenology, Genealogy, Religion*. Albany, NY: State University of New York Press.

Orsi, Robert A. 2012. "The Problem of the Holy." In *The Cambridge Companion to Religious Studies*, edited by Robert A. Orsi. Cambridge: Cambridge University Press, 84–106.

Otto, Rudolf. 1958. *The Idea of the Holy*, translated by John W. Harvey. Oxford: Oxford University Press. Original edition, 1917.

Proudfoot, Wayne. 1985. *Religious Experience*. Berkeley: University of California Press.

Schleiermacher, Friedrich. 1996. *On Religion: Speeches to its Cultured Despisers*, translated by Richard Crouter. Cambridge: Cambridge University Press. Original edition, 1799.

Scott, Joan Wallach. 1991. "The Evidence of Experience." *Critical Inquiry* 17(4): 773–797. doi: 10.1086/448612

Sharf, Robert. 1998. "Experience." In *Critical Terms for Religious Studies*, edited by Mark C. Taylor. Chicago, IL: University of Chicago Press, 94–116.

Taves, Ann. 1999. *Fits, Trances, and Visions: Experiencing Religion and Explaining Experience from Wesley to James*. Princeton, NJ: Princeton University Press.

Taves, Ann. 2009. *Religious Experience Reconsidered*. Princeton, NJ: Princeton University Press.

FURTHER READING

Derrida, Jacques. 2011. *Voice and Phenomenon*, translated by Leonard Lawlor. Evanston, IL: Northwestern University Press. Original edition, 1967. . [*Derrida provides a thorough and devastating critique of phenomenological appeals to direct experience.*]

Kapstein, Matthew. 2004. "Rethinking Religious Experience: Seeing the Light in the History of Religions." In *The Presence of Light: Divine Radiance and Religious Experience*, edited by Matthew Kapstein. Chicago, IL: University of Chicago Press, 265–299. . [*A valuable overview of 'religious experience' in light of cross-cultural studies.*]

Katz, Stephen T., ed. 1978. *Mysticism and Philosophical Analysis*. Oxford: Oxford University Press. [*This collection offers several criticisms of theories of mysticism and religious experience.*]

Murphy, Tim. 2007. *Representing Religion*. London: Equinox. [*Murphy offers a sustained critical analysis of 'experience' in James's work and the phenomenology of religion.*]

Smart, Ninian. 1973. *The Science of Religion and the Sociology of Knowledge*. Princeton, NJ: Princeton University Press. . [*Smart offers a defense of phenomenology of religious experience that attempts to remain agnostic toward the causes of experience.*]

Wach, Joachim. 1951. *Types of Religious Experience: Christian and Non-Christian*. Chicago, IL: University of Chicago Press. . [*Wach's work is a classic in the phenomenology of religious experience.*]

....

CHAPTER 36

GIFT AND SACRIFICE

....

CHRISTOPH AUFFARTH

CHAPTER SUMMARY

....

- Gift exchange constitutes social relationships.
- The absent but imagined third party (god) is part of an asymmetrical exchange, which is performed in a symbolic act (ritual).
- The economic investment of offerings has both incalculable effects, e.g. a loss or return in an imagined other world, and economic effects.
- Gifts and sacrifices foster craftsmen or artists and the priesthood.
- For donors, conspicuous offerings yield prestige, higher status in society, and they do the same for exchange-partners (e.g. temple estate, god).
- Sacrifices should not be reduced to acts of blood and violence. There are also offerings as a more delimited type of sacrifices.

RELEVANCE OF 'GIFT' AND 'SACRIFICE' FOR THE STUDY OF RELIGION

....

If one regards 'sacrifice' as the fundamental ritual of religions, one gets a very different perspective on the meaning of religion and the relation between humans (and animals) and gods conceptualizing religion as exchange of gifts among humans and in the interaction between gods and humans. Are these perspectives mutually exclusive? Indeed, Christian and subsequent Western attitudes to modern religion as a religion without sacrifice limited the meaning of cult and rituals. The sacred realm is concentrated on a sacral place (temple, altar, image of god) and was reduced in favor of a spiritual meaning; after the end of sacrificial practice (in Jewish, Christian, and Muslim religions) became more individualistic (Rüpke 2013a), more a matter of households, more intellectual, more focused on metaphors in theological discourses (Stroumsa 2005/2010), but nevertheless that practice remained expressed in a cultic idiom in which sacrificial ritual is replaced by other rituals. The 'end of sacrifice,' where 'sacrifice' refers to blood sacrifices performed at sacred spots, is the central issue in the transformation of religion in modern Western civilizations.

The argument of the present chapter begins with the fascination with and repudiation of sacrifice by modern Western observers who are part of cultures that did not sacrifice any more, yet who nevertheless regarded the sacrificial ritual as the core of religion. In an earlier phase of the study of religion, scholars narrated a history of progress from primitive and barbarian ritual to a more spiritual and bloodless religion. Given the Christian theory of the 'sacrifice' of (the son of) God, the study of sacrificial ritual was burdened with exceptional meanings and connotations. W. Robertson Smith in 1889, however, argued that, by celebrating the ritual of the Eucharist, modern Christian congregations still continued with a 'barbarian' ritual: killing and eating the god, or the totem. That means that the dark side of religion was by no means superseded in modern spiritual religious practice. The experience of World War I reframed death in war as meaningful acts, as sacrificial offerings of one's own life for the nation, family, etc. (Despland 2009). The discussions lead to an impasse. A later generation of scholars, still fascinated by the ritual of violence, looked for an evolutionary background of sacrifice in the era of mankind as hunters. The impasse has been overcome only in the last few years: if sacrifice is no longer regarded as a ritual of its own—but is rather to be read in the context of symbolic action and in connection with other rituals, as one form of communication with gods—then sacrifice is one form of giving and taking gifts, an exchange between gods and humans.

SACRIFICE AS THE ESSENTIAL AND CENTRAL RITUAL IN RELIGION

The end of sacrificial ritual: Protestant identities

In the modern West a fundamental distinction is made between religions with and religions without sacrifices. This distinction was forged by the Protestant reformation: the end of Jewish sacrificial ritual was regarded as God's punishment for the murder of his son, and the Romans destroyed the temple in Jerusalem on behalf of god (see Bugenhagen 2013 [1524]). The reformed theologians reconstructed an image of history which was told as early as in Early Christian writings: established religions try to obliterate the vivid and life-giving word of God spoken by his prophets by killing these prophets. The so-called *Prophetenanschlusstheorie* sketches a theory of an interrupted 'evangelical' chain of prophets to which first Jesus, then Luther, added new links

(Auffarth 2012a). From their point of view, the Roman church did the same as the Jewish Pharisees and scribes: they murdered Zekhariah (Matthew 23:29–36; see also Mark 12:1–9; Qur'an, Sura 5:70), sentenced Jesus to death, burned Jan Hus, and now threaten Luther as well. In place of God's word they put written laws, rituals, and authority. But God punishes them by destroying their temples, thus making sacrificial ritual impossible. The end of sacrifice is therefore God's will: the Jews and the Roman Catholics are forced to abandon the central part of their cult, whereas the Protestant Christians maintain that they perform a bloodless cult out of inner persuasion fulfilling, by their free will, Christ's will—he expelled the money changers and vendors of sacrificial victims from the temple (Matthew 21:12–17 and parallels). Modern evangelical religion repudiates 'dead' rituals and those claiming 'magic' effects for the receivers (*ex opere operato*).

Though animals continue to be killed and to form an increasing part of the human diet, in modern Western self-fashioning the end of sacrifice is regarded as the decisive step from primitive to modern life.

Fascination and Repudiation: Sacrifice in the View of Modern (Western) Observers

Evolutionists (especially British scholars of Victorian times) regarded sacrifice as a ritual of primitive humanity, in historical times and among the subalterns of the Empire. W. Robertson Smith interpreted the Christian ritual of Eucharist as a survival of the primitive ritual in modern Western religion by quoting an odd source (Maier 2009): the tale of Pseudo-Nilus about a group of wild nomads, who, threatened by starvation, killed and ate a camel, a necessary means to survive in the desert and therefore tabooed as a 'totem.' James George Frazer and Sigmund Freud took this as an essential and existential model: killing the totem is for Freud the model of the Oedipus complex. Modern culture has to overcome by sublimation the anal wish to kill the father: religion itself reproduces the original scene; the ritual in religion turns out to be the compulsion to repeat the *Urscene* again and again.

Turning upside down evolutionary progress since the *fin de siècle*, we find a fascination with sacrifice: war as the black feast, which demands victims for the great sacrificial ritual. "The Nazi use of sacrifice defined their relationship to death to the extent that one of their primary goals was to grant meaning to the otherwise senseless deaths of German soldiers during World War I" (Pan 2012, 113). This was, however, not an invention of the Nazis; they continued a common notion of World War I (Cancik-Lindemaier 1991). The German language does not distinguish between (active) sacrifice and (passive) sacrificial victims, but has the same word ("Opfer") for both active and passive. Thus killing to prevent being killed and the soldierly death are designated by the same sacral and morally loaded term. As David Pan pointed out, the Nazi interpretation of sacrifice is distinct from genocide conceived as cleansing the body of the Aryan race. They distinguished the self-referential 'sacrifice' for the sake of the Aryan/German *Volk* as the dedication of one's own life (soldierly sacrifices). For the genocide of the Jews, the Sinti, the Roma, and the euthanasia of handicapped people, however, the Nazis used different, 'scientific' language that stressed the need for hygiene and the prevention of contamination by evil genetic influences (Pan 2012, 113–147, esp. 113–114, 118).

After Auschwitz another sacrificial term was used to make sense of the inhuman crime of genocide and the question: if God did not prevent the murder of his chosen people, is there a god at all? Elie Wiesel, who survived the genocide, proposed to call it 'holocaust': in contrast to *shelamim*, the meat of which is consumed after sacrifice in a communal meal, in a *holocaust* the offerings are consumed totally by the flames, as a gift to God, with nothing left for the sacrificers. On this view, the dead Jews ascended directly to God through the chimneys of Auschwitz. This Jewish attempt to make sense of the genocide by going back to biblical language failed: Wiesel recanted his proposal; Jews call it '*the* catastrophe', *ha-shoah*. But the sacrificial term holocaust is still prominent.

Homo necans: The Evolutionary Legacy of the Hunter's Behavior

In 1946 the Swiss classicist Karl Meuli proposed a new interpretation of Greek sacrifice. Meuli compared the pattern of offering the bones, skin, and tail of the sacrificial animal to god—while retaining the best, edible parts for the men—to the behavior of hunters in prehistoric times: having eaten the meat they reconstruct the animal with scull, bones, skin, and tail as if it were still alive, having lost only some mass, namely the edible parts. Meuli called this the "comedy of innocence." Walter Burkert (1972) picked up the theory in his famous book. Referring to Sigmund Freud, he conceived the *homo necans* (the killing man, man as hunter) not as a comedy, but as the primordial scene of killing a substitute instead of men or god, a behavior repeated again and again during thousands of years in human ethology: to prevent intraspecies aggression. Critics responded: "Sacrifices are invariably of domesticated animals in contrast to wild ones (and hence from a different sphere than religious practices associated with hunters or palaeolithic man)" (Smith 2004, 154; see Gladigow 1971).

Contrary to the self-fashioning of Christian religion as epitomizing peace and love, the discourse on sacrifice established a link between religion and violence. Whereas Burkert and Girard (see the following section) argued that sacrificial ritual resolved the problem of aggression among humans, the discussion about monotheism turned evolutionary progress upside down: peaceful polytheism may serve as a model for pluralism and tolerance in modern societies in opposition to monotheism, which produces violence by constructing an antithetic world of evil which must be annihilated (Assmann 1997; Angenendt 2011).

God Demands Sacrifices: A Blood-Thirsty Tyrant? Intruding Christian Concepts

In the same year as Burkert's book, René Girard, a French scholar of literature, published a book that presents sacrifice by assessing (Catholic) Christianity (Girard 1972; Pan 2012, 79–111). As Ivan Strenski showed (1993, 202–216; see also Despland 2009, ch. 4), Girard's view is based on the French ('black' Catholic reactionary) Romantic image of sacrifice, e.g. in Chateaubriand and Joseph de Maistre (1821). This Catholic image recalls the medieval concept of the satisfaction theory of Anselm of Canterbury, not the different and plural conceptions explaining the violent death of Christ found in early Christianity. Anselm extended the idea of atonement such that God demands satisfaction: every man, by being a sinner, deserves his death. Atonement can be granted only by shedding blood (Angenendt 2005). According to Anselm, God accepted the death of his son, once and for all, thus liberating Christians from the endless spiral of sacrifices: animal sacrifice had become the accepted substitute for human sacrifice (Isaac); the sacrifice of God's son ended both sacrifice and its substitute; he became the ultimate scapegoat; Christianity declared the end of sacral violence.

Taking a broader historical perspective, one can find critique and dismissal of sacrifice as early as the beginning of literary reflection. In the ancient Oriental and Greek myths on the origin and evolution of culture, men were vegetarians and only later learned to hunt animals and cook their flesh (e.g. *Gilgamesh* III 32f.; Genesis 2:16–17; 8:20; 9:3; Theophrast, de pietate fr. 13 [ed. Pötscher]). But as a rule, ancient societies performed sacrifices, including those of animals. The exceptions were the Pythagoreans (living separately in their own towns), who refused to eat meat and rejected bloody sacrifice (Ovid, *Metamorphoses* 15: 72–142; Philostratos, *Life of Apollonios of Tyana* 1: 31–32). In myth one could imagine what would happen if humans refused to sacrifice to the gods (Auffarth 1994). And, vice versa, people reconstructed in narratives why a god refused to accept a sacrifice directed to him (Naiden 2013). Sacrifices were performed until late antiquity and ended less due to the victory of Christianity than because of their cruelty. When the emperor Julian tried to reintroduce the bloody sacrifice even pagan supporters did not endorse him in that respect (see Ammianus, *History* 22,12,6; for the context see Barchiesi/Rüpke 2004); and, because sacrifice was accompanied by divination, it was perceived as threatening the authority of the emperor.

Religion without sacrifice was transformed not only after the end of sacrifice but also parallel to it. In addition to the Pythagoreans, consider the Jewish Nazirites (Judges 13; 16:7; Numeri 6:1–7: Simson; John the Baptist) or Asian religions, but also the rituals in the synagogues and in Christianity. Even where slaughtering of animals takes place in religio-cultures, it is not done in the sacral realm as a sacral action; in Jewish and Muslim culture, it is nevertheless framed by religious rules (*kosher; halal*).

The First (Primordial) Sacrificial Ritual: Myths

Mythic narratives about the sacrifice performed for the first time maintain that the ritual is fundamental either as the cosmogonic act itself or to sustain the world. The myth of Marduk and Tiamat narrates sacrifice as the cosmogonic act: Tiamat, the dragon of sweet water, threatened the world and no one of the gods was brave enough to resist her except Marduk. He kills her and divided her meat as the material for heaven and earth (*Enuma elish*).

After having destroyed every creature by the deluge of sweet water, in the Hebrew Bible God requests the just man Noah to sacrifice animals. If men will do this from now on, God assures, in form of a covenant, conditions for the continued existence of fruits, flocks, and men for ever (Genesis 8:20–22). Similar stories are told in Ancient Near Eastern epics (*Atra-hasis; Gilgamesh*) and in Greek tradition (Lucian, *de dea Syria* 12f., 48).

Two other narratives touch upon different issues. The one is Prometheus's trick, told by Hesiod in his *Theogony* and in *Works and Days*. Before the day of Mekone, gods and men cultivated a familiar intercourse. Prometheus, however, sought to outwit the gods. He invited them to a common meal; he slaughtered animals and distributed the portions: the one for the gods contained bones, which were hidden under the skin of the animal and decorated above with sheer fat, the tail, and a delicate but small part of the meat. The portion for men contained the meat. Though Zeus was aware of the trick, he accepted. Since then Greek sacrifice is divided in the same manner. Simultaneously Prometheus's trick constituted the divide between men and gods. (For negative reciprocity see later discussion in this chapter.)

Another feature of sacrifice is addressed in the myth of the near-sacrifice of Isaac (Genesis 22). God demands that Abraham sacrifice his only son. At the last moment God prevents the father from killing his son and sends a sheep which should be slaughtered instead of the human being. Similar narratives (e.g. Jephthah's daughter: Judges 10:6–12:7) of sparing men and slaughtering animals instead of them, are told, for example the myth of Iphigeneia (Bremmer 2001, 21–43). Human sacrifice as an historical fact is very rare; it occurred only in extreme crises, but is a well-known prejudice against strangers (Bremmer 2007; Arens 1979).

The reception history of the myth of Isaac is very different in Jewish, Christian, and Muslim traditions. The Christian one tied it together as an allegory with the death of Jesus, the unique son of God. Hence the crucifixion of Jesus gets a new meaning: not as death penalty against a pretended king of the Jews, but as a sacral ritual given to God and as a substitute 'for many/all mankind' by suffering the atonement, especially in the soteriology of Paul in his letter to the Romans (with reference to the classical background see Bendlin 2006, 9–41; Versnel 2005, 213–294).

All these interpretations reduced sacrifice to bloody sacrifice and reframed the ritual as blood and violence, guilt, meaningful and sacral death, or life given in substitution for others. It is time to reopen the field to a comprehensive religio-historical analysis of this domain of ritual actions—of sacrificial ritual in its contexts and in relation to other rituals—given the traps into which modern interpreters have fallen. This leads us to consider sacrifice as communicative gift in a gift economy.

Dividing the Sacrificial Meat: Commensality as Performance of Social Order and Power

Slaughtering an animal in a sacrificial ritual establishes ritual commensality: eating together a delicious meal imagining that god takes part. A portion put aside for an absent person can be handed over to the priests or to another representative of god. The portion of perishable food can, however, be substituted by money, candles, etc. and the addressee substituted by poor people. This is an established aspect of almsgiving: in Judaism (Mischna: *sera͑im pe'a*); in Islam *saqat*; in medieval Christianity part of *memoria* (Hauck 1950; Weijert 2011) or by young people in the form of a foundation for education (e.g. a madrasa), by paying taxes for equity and democracy as the highest (religious or not) values. In the study of religion, a theory was discussed by those who stressed the evolutionary aspect of religion: dividing sacrificial meat is a behavior inherited from other primates living in social groups, where the alpha-male receives the first and the best share. Dividing food acknowledges and rehearses the hierarchy of the society. God as the very highest gets the first fruits and the best portion; the priests, the prince and the noble men, women, children, and the weaker men in the group get their share in the given social order.

From Ideology to the Lived Ritual of Sacrifice

From a comparative anthropological perspective, which provides thick descriptions of sacrifice in specific cultures and contexts, one finds different evidence and genres:

1. Representations, pictures, ex votos (see: sacrifices, in *ThesCRA* 1 (2004), 59–134; Weihgeschenke, in *ThesCRA* 1 (2004), 269–450). For Greek antiquity, Folkert van Straten could show that the high ranking of slaughtering bulls is not reflected in representations of sacrifices on votive-tables (Straten 1995; Ekroth 2005; 2009).
2. Regulations, norms, systematic handbooks for specialists and the public. In India the Vedas give scrupulous rules for the correct sacrifice. The Hebrew Bible (Leviticus) provides a detailed systematic handbook regulating sacrifices, which mentions different forms, aims, animals, etc. The classification (why sheep, no pigs?) was a challenge for semiotics of religion (see Steiner 1956, ch. 7; GT 2008, 297–444; Douglas 1966, chapter 3; GT 1985, 60–78; Yelle 2013, 137–156). Greek *Leges sacrae* mostly explain what is forbidden or different. Greek priests, not trained professionally, did not know a precise set of sacrificial norms, e.g. the difference between Olympic and Chthonian sacrifices (Ekroth 2002; Auffarth 2005).
3. Architecture, spaces, archaeological findings (Ekroth 2011).

Historians of Greek religion distinguish between sacrifice and pre-sacrifice. On this view, sacrifice means slaughtering animals, the bloody sacrifice (Stengel 1910; Eitrem 1915). But many so-called pre-sacrifices are performed independently as well, not just before bloody sacrifices. They must be counted as a distinct form of offerings (see Table 36.1; developed from Auffarth 2008). Table 36.1 shows as well that Jewish and Christian religions in antiquity refused one set of offerings, but continued most of the others.

GIFT, EXCHANGE, AND COMMUNICATION

Other conceptions avoid problems raised by the divide between sacrificial and non-sacrificial religions, and modern (Western, Christian) vs. archaic and/or Asian religions. Sacrifice can be regarded as part of a comprehensive view of communications between men and god. Side by side with verbal communication (prayer, hymns, curses, incantations, etc.) and gestures in ritual, the transmission of material gifts is a common feature of religions. Sacrifice and offerings are thus a specific form of this exchange of material communication. Is it, however, an exchange from both sides? Is there a gift in return from the side of god? If so, how can the handing over of this return-gift be imagined? Since Marcel Mauss's *Essai sur le don* (1924), which relied on the field research of Bronislaw Malinowski, gift exchange has been discussed as a form of self-organization of archaic societies. In modern societies, the social bonding by gifts is framed by the rules of the market and capitalism, but not entirely substituted (Parry/Bloch 1989). (Continuity and difference between archaic and modern donors is discussed with South Asian examples in Heim 2004; see also Wagner-Hasel 2000). Redistribution of wealth by the welfare state stands side by side with generational transfer/gifting of wealth to heirs, by rearing children and attending parents when they become old. The family (and only in second stance the individual member) is both donator and receiver of accumulating wealth.

Some well-known examples show how gift societies function: Malinowski described obligatory circulation of the *kula* not as an exchange between two parties, but as a broader circuit of exchange, with the gift ultimately returning to the original donor. Other models are centralized redistribution (e.g. temple re-gifting) or the potlatch of indigenous nations of the Pacific northwest coast of North America, in which wealth is exposed and distributed to visitors in a show of economic power that converts material goods into social capital. The study of such exchange-procedures of gifts led Alvin Gouldner and Marshall Sahlins (2004 [1965]) to distinguish three types of exchange that constitute relations between the donor and the donated. (1) In balanced reciprocity, the value of gifts is reckoned closely, with an equivalent counter-gift given back with little delay. (2) In generalized (or indefinite) reciprocity the receiver is of higher rank. She or he will not pay back a similar gift, but in the long run the donator can expect reciprocation from the donated in form of pulling strings, to act as an guarantor, a precious gift for the marriage of the daughter, etc. This type can involve more than two partners.

Table 36.1 Types of offerings to the gods

Action	With which essence	Classical antiquity	Christian antiquity	Further developments in Judaism and Christianity
Killing animals	Bulls Sheep/goats piglets Chicken/birds Fish	In the sanctuary: they are slaughtered and eaten (Olympian sacrifice) or fully burnt or drowned (Chthonian s.)		[Chr. Slaughtered profanely Jew. Slaughtered according to religious rules ('kosher'), but not sacrificed on an altar]
Offerings/votives	Models of animals Figures in adoration Human limbs Something to eat	arranged near the god		Limbs modeled in wax
Set up votives	Images (wood, metal) Jewelry Coins	Images Jewelry Coins	Coins	Icons, Images on the walls Ex votos Coins 'for the poor people'
Libation (liquids) poured/drunk	Wine Milk Honey	Wine Milk Honey	Wine [metaphorical: blood]	Wine and bread
Sharing food	Bread, meat, olives	Bread, meat, olives	Bread [metaphorical: meat]	
Lighting candles	Lamps with oil Torches	Lamps with oil Torches	Lamps with oil Candles	Lamps with oil Candles
To raise scents	Incense Scent of barbeque	Frankincense in front of images, esp. of the emperor	Frankincense	Frankincense

And the period of give-and-take may last longer. (3) In negative reciprocity, gifts range from a toxic gift (given to harm the exchange partner) to the intention to get something for nothing or to the exclusion of outsiders. "This typology draws upon two separate sets of criteria: (a) the motivations and intentions of the participants (fostering solidarity and/or making a profit etc.), (b) the degree of indeterminacy of the exchange in value and time."[1] Given these typological tools for analyzing the social role of gifts, 'gift' is a relational term: "Gifts . . . do not constitute in themselves a coherent and well-defined object of study, because they owe their most salient properties to their relative position within given repertoires of transaction modes. It is by being modeled on other available templates or in contrast to other models within specific cultural repertoires, and not by virtue of inherent uniform properties, that they acquire their particular shape and potential effects" (Algazi et al. 2003, 101; see Algazi 2003, 13–14). Against this model the gift exchange between humans and gods has to be analyzed.

Gift or Bribery?

From a Protestant point of view, in the communication between men and god two suspicions arise: material donations may be given with neither devotion nor justice. This echoes prophetic critics in the Hebrew Bible (e.g. Amos 5:21–27) and Jesus's actions against the money-changers and vendors (Mark 11:15–18). In Greek imagination the gods live in the luxury of their wealth, even if they do not act in justice (e.g. they rape women and do not pay alimony, see Euripides, *Ion* 436–451, Auffarth 2012b, 25–30). Lack of devotion occurs where a donation is given only in order to induce god to fulfill a wish or an urgent request of the donator: the so-called *Do ut des* principle. In terms of reciprocity a gift is part of a chain of mutual ties of friendship and if I give a valuable thing to you, appreciating that I and my family have received so much from your side: *Do, quia dedisti*—generalized reciprocity.

Communication with Absent Persons: Handing Over the Gift

In the circulation of goods in a society, a temple economy builds a distinctive form and institution. A part of the economic exchange is excepted and follows different rules. As a rule, a representation or a representative of the divine person receives the gift: an image of the god or another marker of his presence, a table in his house or in front of it, the priest, the warden, etc.

---

[1] Thanks to Steven Engler for this summation, cited from an email from him, and for his drawing my attention to the following Algazi citation.

For handing over to a person not present and/or imagined as different to a human person, one needs a plausible symbol for transportation and transformation of the gift (Gladigow 2000, 86–87). As for the meat of sacrifice, both in Israel (Leviticus 17:6 and *passim*) and in Greece, god loves and is satisfied with the smell of roasted meat. Greek terminology distinguishes between holy things (*ἱερά/hierá*) and sacred things (*ὅσια/hósia*). God lends the latter one to his people especially if they prepare a war: the goddess allows the money stored in the temple of Athena to be used for building new ships for the Peloponnesian war (Thucydides, *History* 2, 13); in the—expected—case of success, the Athenians would donate to her an even bigger gift (Auffarth 2013, 13–21).

Gifts to the gods are often different from gifts exchanged between men in quality and quantity. They can differ in size (monumental or tiny) and in value (precious material as gold, but also a lot of cheap fictile vessels or figurines donated to the god are a symbol for the popularity of a god); most items are inscribed with an owner's mark, so one cannot use it outside the sanctuary. Labels prohibit taking something away (*οὐ φορά ou phorá*). And such objects should not have been used before.

Asymmetrical Communication: The Gift in Return and Reciprocity

One issue can neither be proved nor disproved: is there a counter-gift in exchanges with the gods? Religious reciprocity works regardless if there is a god or not; if there is a success or a failure these can be interpreted as god-sent or mere accident or the fruit of one's own effort. "Sacrifice may depend on a certain dissimulation: although the god may be the one to whom the sacrifice is nominally addressed, the fact that the benefit of the sacrifice is distributed to the priests or the congregants shows that the circuit of communication is located elsewhere" (Yelle 2013, 2). I would like to rephrase this remark, since a dissimulation would in reality be something different.

We rather find complementary effects in the same action: the distribution of meat and food or the handing over of precious material into god's house, which is administrated by priests, is regarded from an emic point of view as a gift to the god. It is also clear for the emic participants that it has economic and social effects for men as well. In gift societies such exchanges appreciate, maintain, or weaken the social status of the giver and the receiver. For some types of exchange, the inferiority of the donor is presupposed: "the merit of *dāna* is a direct function of the worth and caste of the recipient, making brahmins the normative recipients of this category of religious gifts" (Kane 1962–1975, 3: 115–116). Some types of exchange present a certain duality: in the gift of alms to Christian monks in medieval Europe and to Buddhist monks in Sri Lanka, the exchange is structured around a symmetrical inequality (Silber 1995). Donors are superior to recipients in worldly terms but inferior in spiritual terms. The Hindu *dharmashastras* note that donors earn the merit that results from *dāna* but only if recipients accept; the ideal is that Brahmins accept all offerings, but practicality demands caution, in that gifts bring with them the spiritual impurities of the donors, and only the purest of Brahmins can deal with especially grievous sin so absorbed:[2] "a gift from the king is terrible (in its consequences) and . . . that gift appears sweet like honey but is like poison (i.e., deadly in its effects)" (Kane 1962–1975, 4: 549; see Parry 1980, 89).

Rules of Gift Societies and Religion

By means of a gift one acknowledges the social status of another person and vice versa, which is called reciprocity. For modern societies this seems to be an enigma (Godelier 1996) for it does not follow the rules of modern monetary economy (Wees 1998; Benavides 2005). Gifts play a role in modern societies as well. Characteristically gifts (in contrast to money) seek more than an exchange of economic interests. Thorstein Veblen explained non-rational behavior in modern societies like conspicuous consumption and status symbols (1899). Not least by religious architecture and treasures, cities and institutions proudly presented and present their economic power and their sense for aesthetics, the sublime, and for the hereafter, beyond daily needs and satisfaction. At the same time, they thus engage the local economy and attract tourists/pilgrims (Stausberg 2011). That means that reciprocity in religious logic has both mundane and supra-mundane aims and effects, with material losses offset by putative otherworldly returns (Gladigow 1995; 2004).

To understand the difference between social bonding by gifts and money exchange, prostitution offers an example. Under most circumstances, when a client pays prostitutes for their services, no further obligation arises. Love, however, can create a bond between two individuals, producing obligations, gift exchanges, and signs of appreciation. The ongoing chain of exchanges is not paid and repaid in a closely calculated manner, as it is the case in market exchange. Signs of appreciation are given in different modes: giving birth to a child might be answered with flowers and a kiss, a necklace with sex, the partner's success in job with a holiday trip. In a similar way reciprocity functions in (pre-modern) gift societies, where no state institutions structure social groups. Especially in the relations between the poor and powerless and the wealthy and powerful it is not so much friendship, but patronage that matters. Poor people bring often small gifts, to which the powerful seldom respond, yet they offer a big gift on important days—as when the poor man's daughter marries, when he needs help in a law court, or when he asks for intervention in a financial crisis. This is one mode of generalized (or indefinite) reciprocity. And, according to this model, the relation of men to god may find an adequate description. Many times participants bring their gifts to god, believing that, when help is needed, god will intervene.

---

[2] Citing an email from Engler. Thanks also to him for providing these citations and for sharing parts of his forthcoming book.

And if he does not? An example for the third issue of reciprocity, negative reciprocity (Auffarth 1991, 162f., 188f., *potlatch* 399), is told in a famous myth. The Greek poet Hesiod (seventh century BCE) sets sacrifice in opposition to the god's reciprocity. In difference to concepts of god as identical with goodness, as Plato and monotheistic concepts maintain, Greek gods are suspicious and jealous. Hesiod presents them "in the beginning" in near intercourse with men; there was no sharp dividing border between humans and god. By parting the meal unequally—the bones, etc. for the gods, the edible portions for men—Prometheus offers a deceptive sacrifice: a toxic gift. Zeus looks through the unequal distribution, he acknowledges the ritual nevertheless, but reacts in negative reciprocity by another toxic gift in return. Zeus sends back an *anti-doron* to Prometheus's brother Epimetheus: he sends an attractive woman, endowed with lovely appearance, together with a jar. She is called Pandora in a double meaning of the words *pan* (every) *dora* (gifts): Hesiod explains the name both in a passive and in an active meaning. Pandora is gifted (passively) with gifts from every goddess and god. Pandora gives (actively) lavishly whatever is stored in the jar; and these are negative gifts of the gods to mankind: diseases, infirmity, death. Just one thing remains in the jar, the *elpis*—hope. By closing the jar Pandora saved the 'hope' in the jar. The 'hope' can be interpreted that it is not vain hope as yet another evil, but that Pandora did not give out the necessary seeds, yet saved them for the coming year (Hesiod, *Works and Days* 57–105; Auffarth 2015, following Wolfgang Rösler). Wives fulfill a duty which keeps the family and household in continuity and which cannot be fulfilled by men, like saving the seeds, carrying children.

Conclusion

For a long time the study of religion was fascinated by sacrifice as the central ritual of religions' archaic style, in contrast to which modern religion has allegedly superseded ritual violence and vain repetition. The history of religions served here as an apology for Christianity, because it dismissed sacrifice. But around 1900 this view was reversed: under a small humanistic gloss, the old rituals and irrational behavior continued to be seen as central to religion. Focusing on just one ritual, reduced to bloody sacrifice, religion became the source and resource of violence. The study of religion can avoid this impasse by (1) a rich description of ritual in its cultural context, (2) sharpening the differences instead of the similarities of a given anthropological fact, and (3) considering the perspective that—if one regards sacrifice in the systematic matrix of other rituals—sacrifice is a special form of material gifts, which, in order to be handed over to the god, have to be transformed or substituted. The addressee can also be substituted, so that almsgiving for the poor or instituting a foundation for education becomes the equivalent to a gift to god. In difference to other forms of exchange and communication, giving gifts follows other rules, which are best studied in archaic gift societies (where giving gifts is a 'total' fact), but one can still observe it in modern societies as well. Religion is a part of modern life. Laying out conspicuous wealth, religious institutions present their claim to be important players in society (documented by gifts they received by many members of the society), especially by setting higher values in society that are not functional for daily needs.

GLOSSARY

Communication with god(s) communication with gods is imagined in the form of verbal salutatory addresses, prayers, hymns, etc. and/or transfer of material gifts (offerings, sacrifices). God's response is imagined as generalized (sometimes negative) reciprocity in time delay and the imagination of a re-gift.

Gift society societies which are structured not by state power and the market-value of things but rather by communicative acts to appreciate the social status of a person, especially by giving and receiving gifts.

Reciprocity giving and accepting gifts are mutual activities. Responding to a gift means both the appreciation of the social place of the person, from which one accepted the gift, and one's own social (or religious) status. The re-gift will differ in terms of time delayed and economic value. And there are three modes of response: direct, generalized (or indefinite), and negative reciprocity.

Sacrifice/offerings whereas sacrifice was regarded as a form of religion in an earlier stage of mankind, superseded by the modern form of religion practiced more inside the individual, in a study of religion-approach it is but one special form of offerings/gifts. One part is transmitted to god, the other one, as a rule, is distributed to the family, friends, and community partaking at the ritual. Other offerings are assigned to the property of the god, which in quality and quantity appreciates the social status of the god and his/her servants (in god's perspective) and (in human perspective) representatives.

REFERENCES

Algazi, Gadi. 2003. "Doing Things with Gifts." In *Negotiating the Gift: Pre-modern Figurations of Exchange*, edited by Gadi Algazi, Valentin Groebner, and Bernhard Jussen. Göttingen: Vandenhoeck & Ruprecht, 9–28.

Algazi, Gadi, Valentin Groebner, and Bernhard Jussen, eds. 2003. *Negotiating the Gift: Pre-modern Figurations of Exchange*. Göttingen: Vandenhoeck & Ruprecht.

Angenendt, Arnold. 2005. "Sühne durch Blut." In *Liturgie im Mittelalter*. Münster: LIT, 191–225.

Angenendt, Arnold. 2011. *Die Revolution des geistigen Opfers: Blut—Sündenbock—Eucharistie*. Freiburg im Breisgau: Herder.

Angenendt, Arnold. 2013. *Offertorium: Das mittelalterliche Meßopfer*. Münster: Aschendorff.

Arens, William. 1979. *The Man-Eating Myth: Anthropology and Anthropophagy*. New York: Oxford University Press.

Assmann, Jan 1997. *Moses the Egyptian: The Memory of Egypt in Western Monotheism*. Cambridge, MS: Harvard University Press.

Auffarth, Christoph. 1991. *Der drohende Untergang: 'Schöpfung' in Mythos und Ritual im Alten Orient und in Griechenland am Beispiel der Odyssee und des Ezchielbuches*. Berlin and New York: de Gruyter.

Auffarth, Christoph. 1994. "Der Opferstreik: Ein altorientalisches 'Motiv' bei Aristophanes und im homerischen Hymnus." *Grazer Beiträge* 20: 59–86.

Auffarth, Christoph. 2005. "How to Sacrifice Correctly—Without a Manual?" In *Greek Sacrificial Ritual: Olympian and Chthonian*, edited by Robin Hägg and Brita Alroth. Stockholm: Paul Forlag Astroms, 11–21.

Auffarth, Christoph. 2008. "Teure Ideologie—billige Praxis: Die 'kleinen' Opfer in der römischen Kaiserzeit." In *Transformations in Sacrificial Practices: From Antiquity to Modern Times*, edited by Evtychia Stavrianopoulou, Axel Michaels, and Claus Ambos. Münster: LIT, 147–170.

Auffarth, Christoph. 2012a. "Christliche Festkultur und kulturelle Identität im Wandel: Der Judensonntag." In *Christliches Fest und kulturelle Identität Europas*, edited by Benedikt Kranemann and Thomas Sternberg. Münster: Aschendorff, 30–47.

Auffarth, Christoph. 2012b. "Antike Konzepte von Heilig und Heiligkeit: Eine religionswissenschaftliche Perspektive." In *Communio Sanctorum: Heilige, Heiliges und Heiligkeit in spätantiken Religionskulturen*, edited by Peter Gemeinhardt and Katharina Heyden. Berlin and New York: de Gruyter, 1–33.

Auffarth, Christoph. 2012c. "Le rite sacrificiel antique: la longue durée et la fin du sacrifice." *Kernos* 25: 297–303.

Auffarth, Christoph. 2015. "Pandora: Vorsicht vor Gottes Freigiebigkeit! Ein religionswissenschaftlicher Vergleich kultureller Werte." In *Die Gabe*, edited by Veronika Hoffmann. Freiburg: Alber.

Barchiesi, Alessandro and Jörg Rüpke, eds. 2004. *Rituals in Ink*. Stuttgart: Steiner.

Benavides, Gustavo. 2005. "Economy." In *Critical Terms for the Study of Buddhism*, edited by Donald S. Lopez, Jr. Chicago, IL: University of Chicago Press, 77–102.

Bendlin, Andreas. 2006. "Anstelle der anderen sterben: Zur Bedeutungsvielfalt eines Modells in der griechischen und römischen Religion." In *Stellvertretung*, edited by J. Christine Janowski, Bernd Janowski, and Hans P. Lichtenberger. Neukirchen-Vluyn: Neukirchener, 9–41.

Bremmer, Jan. 2001. "Sacrificing a Child in Ancient Greece: The Case of Iphigeneia." In *The Sacrifice of Isaac: The Aqedah, Genesis 22 and Its Interpretations*, edited by Ed Noort and Eibert J. C. Tigchelaar. Leiden: Brill, 21–43.

Bremmer, Jan, ed. 2007. *The Strange World of Human Sacrifice*. Leuven: Peeters.

Bugenhagen, Johannes. 2013. *Historia des lydendes und der upstandinge unses Heren Jesu Christi, uth den veer Evangelisten*. Barth 1586. Critical edition by Anneliese Bieber-Wallmann in *Bugenhagen: Reformatorische Schriften* 1(1). Göttingen: Vandenhoeck & Ruprecht, 80–605. Original edition, 1524.

Burkert, Walter 1972. *Homo necans: Interpretationen altgriechischer Opferriten und Mythen*. Berlin: de Gruyter.

Cancik-Lindemaier, Hildegard. 1991. "Opfersprache. Religionswissenschaftliche und religionsgeschichtliche Bemerkungen." In *Schrift der Flammen: Opfermythen und Weiblichkeitsentwürfe im 20. Jahrhundert*, edited by Gudrun Kohn-Waechte. Berlin: Orlanda, 38–56.

Despland, Michel. 2009. *Le recul du sacrifice: Quatre siècles de polémiques françaises*. Québec: Presses de l'Université Laval.

Douglas, Mary. 1966. *Purity and Danger: An Analysis of Concepts of Pollution and Taboo*. London: Routledge & Kegan Paul.

Eitrem, Samson. 1915. *Opferritus und Voropfer der Griechen und Römer*. Kristiania: Dybwad.

Ekroth, Gunnel. 2002. *The Sacrificial Rituals of Greek Hero-Cults in the Archaic to the Early Hellenistic Periods*. Liège: Centre International d'Étude de la Religion Grecque Antique.

Ekroth, Gunnel. 2005. "Blood on the Altars? On the Treatment of Blood at Greek Sacrifices and the Iconographical Evidence." *Antike Kunst* 48: 9–29.

Ekroth, Gunnel. 2009. "Thighs or Tails? The Osteological Evidence as a Source for Greek Ritual Norms." In *La norme en matière religieuse en Grèce ancienne*, edited by Pierre Brulé. Liège: Centre International d'Étude de la Religion Grecque Antique, 125–152.

Ekroth, Gunnel 2011. "Meat for the Gods." In *Nourir les dieux. Sacrifice et représentation*, edited by Vinciane Pirenne-Delforge and Francesca Prescendi. Liège: Presses Universitaires Liège, 15–41.

Engler, Steven. Forthcoming. *Theorizing 'Religious': Agency, Order and Time in Early Modern Charity*. Göttingen: Vandenhoeck & Ruprecht.

Girard, René. 1972. *La violence et le sacré*. Paris: Grasset.

Gladigow, Burkhard. 1971. "Ovids Rechtfertigung der blutigen Opfer: Interpretationen zu Ovid. *fasti* I 335–456." *Der Altsprachliche Unterricht* 14: 3:5–23.

Gladigow, Burkhard. 1984. "Die Teilung des Opfers: Zur Interpretation von Opfern in vor-und frühgeschichtlichen Epochen." *Frühmittelalterliche Studien* 18: 19–43.

Gladigow, Burkhard. 1986. "*Homo publice necans*. Kulturelle Bedingungen kollektiven Tötens." *Saeculum* 37: 150–165.

Gladigow, Burkhard et al. 1995. "Religionsökonomie—Zur Einführung in eine Subdisziplin der Religionswissenschaft." In *Lokale Religionsgeschichte*, edited by Hans G. Kippenberg and Brigitte Luchesi. Marburg: Diagonal, 253–258.

Gladigow, Burkhard. 2000. "Opfer und komplexe Kulturen." In *Opfer*, edited by Bernd Janowski and Michael Welker. Frankfurt am Main: Suhrkamp, 86–107.

Gladigow, Burkhard. 2004. "Bilanzierungen des Lebens über den Tod hinaus." In *Tod, Jenseits und Identität: Perspektiven einer kulturwissenschaftlichen Thanatologie*, edited by Jan Assmann and Rolf Trauzettel. Freiburg: Alber, 90–109.

Gladigow, Burkhard. 2008. "Opferkritik, Opferverbote und propagandistische Opfer." In *Transformations in Sacrificial Practices: From Antiquity to Modern Times*, edited by Evtychia Stavrianopoulou, Axel Michaels, and Claus Ambos. Münster: LIT, 263–288.

Godelier, Maurice. 1996. *L'énigme du don*. Paris: Fayard.

Gouldner, Alvin W. 1973a. "The Importance of Something for Nothing." In *For Sociology: Renewal and Critique in Sociology Today*. New York: Basic Books, 260–299. Original edition, 1960.

Gouldner, Alvin W. 1973b. "The Norm of Reciprocity." In *For Sociology: Renewal and Critique in Sociology Today*. New York: Basic Books, 226–259. Original edition, 1960.

Hauck, Karl. 1950. "Rituelle Speisegemeinschaft im 11. und 12. Jahrhundert." *Studium Generale* 3: 611–621.

Heim, Maria. 2004. *Theories of the Gift in South Asia: Hindu, Buddhist, and Jain Reflections on Dāna*. New York and London: Routledge.

Kane, Pandurang V. 1962–1975. *History of Dharmashastra*. 5 vols. Poona: Bhandarkar Oriental Research Institute.

Maier, Bernhard. 2009. *William Robertson Smith: His Life, His Work, and His Times*. Tübingen: Mohr Siebeck.

Maistre, Joseph de. 1821. *Les Soirées de Saint-Pétersbourg, au entretiens sur le gouvernement temporel de la providence: suivis d'un traité sur les sacrifices*. Paris: Librairie grecque, latine et française.

Mauss, Marcel. 1924. "Essai sur le don: Forme et raison de l'échange dans les sociétés archaïques." *L'Année Sociologique* NS 1: 30–186.

Naiden, Fred S. 2013. *Smoke Signals for the Gods: Ancient Greek Sacrifice from the Archaic through Roman Periods*. Oxford: Oxford University Press.

Pan, David. 2012. *Sacrifice in the Modern World: On the Particularity and Generality of Nazi Myth*. Evanston, IL: Northwestern University Press.

Parry, Jonathan. 1980. "Ghosts, Greed and Sin: The Occupational Identity of the Benares Funeral Priests." *Man* NS 15(1): 88–111.

Parry, Jonathan and Maurice Bloch, eds. 1989. *Money and the Morality of Exchange*. Cambridge and New York: Cambridge University Press.

Robbins, Jill. 1998. "Sacrifice." In *Critical Terms for Religious Studies*, edited by Mark C. Taylor. Chicago, IL: University of Chicago Press, 285–297.

Rüpke, Jörg, ed. 2013. *The Individual in the Religions of the Ancient Mediterranean*. Oxford: Oxford University Press.

Sahlins, Marshall. 2004. "On the Sociology of Primitive Exchange." In *Stone Age Economics*. London and New York: Routledge, 185–275. Original edition, 1965.

Silber, Ilana F. 1995. *Virtuosity, Charisma, and Social Order: A Comparative Sociological Study of Monasticism in Theravada Buddhism and Medieval Catholicism*. Cambridge: Cambridge University Press.

Smith, Jonathan Z. 2004. "The Domestication of Sacrifice." In *Relating Religion: Essays in the Study of Religion*. Chicago, IL: University of Chicago Press, 145–159.

Stausberg, Michael. 2011. *Religion and Tourism: Crossroads, Destinations, and Encounters*. London: Routledge.

Steiner, Franz Berman. 1956. *Taboo*. London: Cohen and West.

Stengel, Paul. 1910. *Opferbräuche der Griechen*. Leipzig: Teubner.

Straten. Folkert T. van. 1995. *Hierà kalá: Images of Animal Sacrifice in Archaic and Classical Greece*. Leiden: Brill.

Strenski, Ivan. 1993. "At Home with Girard." In *Religion in Relation: Method, Application and Moral Location*. Columbia, SC: University of South Carolina Press, 202–216.

Stroumsa, Guy G. 2005/2010. *La fin du sacrifice: Les mutations religieuses de l'antiquité tardive*. Paris: PUF.

ThesCRA. 2004–2006. *Thesaurus Cultus et Rituum Antiquorum*, vols. 1–5. Los Angeles: Getty.

ThesCRA. 2011–2014. *Thesaurus Cultus et Rituum Antiquorum*, vols. 6–9, Index. Los Angeles: Getty.

Veblen, Thorstein. 1899. *The Theory of the Leisure Class*. New York: Macmillan.

Versnel, Henk. 2005. "Making Sense of Jesus' Death: The Pagan Contribution." In *Deutungen des Todes Jesu im Neuen Testament*, edited by Jörg Frey and Jens Schröter. Tübingen: Mohr Siebeck, 213–294.

Wagner-Hasel, Beate. 2000. *Der Stoff der Gaben: Kultur und Politik des Schenkens und Tauschens im archaischen Griechenland*. Frankfurt am Main: Campus.

Wees, Hans van. 1998. "The Law of Gratitude: Reciprocity in Anthropological Theory." In *Reciprocity in Ancient Greece*, edited by Christopher Gill, Norman Postlethwaite, and Richard Seaford. Oxford: Oxford University Press, 13–49.

Weijert, Rolf et al., eds. 2011. *Living Memoria: Studies in Medieval and Early Modern Memorial Culture in Honour of Truus van Bueren*. Hilversum: Verloren.

White, Charles S. J. 2005. "Gift Giving." In *Encyclopedia of Religion*, edited by Lindsay Jones. New York: Macmillan Reference, vol. 5, 3479–3486.

Yelle, Robert A. 2013. *Semiotics of Religion: Signs of the Sacred in History*. London: Bloomsbury.

FURTHER READING

Algazi 2003 [*Systematic evaluation of the concept of gift exceeding the distinction 'archaic'–modern societies by an historian of medieval cultures.*]

Burkert 1972 [*The classical historical and philological study on Greek sacrifice regarding anthropological and psychoanalytical theories.*]

Mauss 1924 [*The classic meta-study on the gift in 'archaic' societies of the French sociologist without own field experience. He analyzes Malinowski's descriptions of a small island society. In this case there is no elaborated concept of religion with god, priest, temple. This study is used, far beyond its original scope, as anthropologically valid in general.*]

Wagner-Hasel, Beate. 2003. "Egoistic Exchange and Altruistic Gift: On the Roots of Marcel Mauss' Theory of Gift." In *Negotiating the Gift: Pre-modern Figurations of Exchange*, edited by Gadi Algazi, Valentin Groebner, and Bernhard Jussen. Göttingen: Vandenhoeck & Ruprecht, 141–171. [*As an historian of ancient civilizations W.-H. analyzes differentiated societies and modes of reciprocity (in her monograph Stoff der Gaben 2000); in her analysis of ancient economies in general she includes gift economy theories.*]

CHAPTER 37

....

GODS

....

GUSTAVO BENAVIDES

CHAPTER SUMMARY

....

- Gods are agents believed to be largely free from the physical, psychological, and moral constraints that limit the agency of humans.
- Their deeds defy reason, that incomprehensibility contributing to the gods' majesty as well as to the authority of those who are regarded as the intermediaries between the gods and ordinary mortals.
- Divine qualities can be understood as produced by the projection of intensified human characteristics upon imaginary beings, by means of two mutually reinforcing, if contradictory processes: on the one hand, the desire to leave behind the limitations that afflict us and, on the other, the inescapable tendency to conceive the world as if it were populated by beings analogous to us.

GODS AND SACREDNESS

....

Classical definitions of religion have generally been built either around concepts such as sacredness or around imaginary beings known as gods and spirits. An example of the former is Émile Durkheim's, which is based upon the distinction between secular and sacred things (1897–1898), while the latter can be traced back to Edward Tylor, who proposed as "a minimum definition of Religion, the belief in Spiritual Beings" (1871, 383). Besides being quoted in countless discussions of religion, Tylor's definition is echoed by more recent authors who, although critical of Tylor in some respects, incorporate 'non-human entities,' 'non-human alters,' 'non-human agencies,' and 'superhuman beings' in their definitions (see Stausberg/Gardiner, "Definition," this volume). Limiting ourselves to theories of religion proposed by Anglophone anthropologists in the mid-twentieth century (see Stausberg/Engler, "Theories of Religion," this volume, for contemporary theories), we find that Raymond Firth understands religion "as a concern of man in society with basic human ends and standards of value, seen in relation to non-human entities or powers" (1959, 131). Robert Horton in turn writes that "religion can be looked upon as an extension of the field of people's social relationships beyond the confines of purely human society . . . this extension must be one in which human beings see themselves in a dependent position vis-à-vis their non-human alters . . ." 1993 [1960], 31–32). Agreeing with Horton, Jack Goody writes, "We may say then that religious beliefs are present when non-human agencies are propitiated on the human model. Religious activities include, of course, not only acts of propitiation but all behavior which has reference to the existence of these agencies" (1961, 157–158). Finally, Melford Spiro defines religion as "an institution consisting of culturally patterned interaction with culturally postulated superhuman beings" (1966, 96 = 1987, 197).

Despite Durkheim's claim that the distinction between sacred and profane things is frequently independent from any idea of god (1897–1898, 16), and in spite of non-theistic understandings of ritual efficacy in India, supernatural agents and sacredness tend to be intimately related, as gods inhabit and in many ways constitute the realms that, while apart from the ordinary world, serve to regulate it. This has been recognized by historians of religion as well as by theorists who approach religion from a cognitive perspective. Thus Walter Burkert places gods as the guarantors of absolute truth (1996, 172), whereas for Thomas Lawson and Robert McCauley, "the ritual's *efficacy* depends upon the cooperation of . . . superhuman agents. All religious rituals ultimately enlist superhuman agents" (1990, 125; cf. 95). The terminology itself used to refer to the entities with which we are concerned in this chapter marks their separation from the ordinary realm, since the prefix "super" in "supernatural being" or in "supernatural" *tout court* points to the non-ordinary, that is, sacred nature of the beings known as gods and spirits, just as the "non-" in "non-human," found in some of the definitions of religion just quoted, refers to their otherness—relative as that otherness may be, as we shall see in what follows. Moreover, the fact that gods are approached with awe, being generally considered to be above the moral norms that regulate human behavior, places them in the domain that Rudolf Otto identified as the "numinous," i.e. the sacred minus its moral and rational components (1971 [1917], 6). As we shall see later on, such amoral sacredness can be identified across cultures, as demonstrated by the characteristics of the Japanese *kami* and the New Guinea *dema*, which can refer to supernatural beings as well as to uncommon qualities that elicit awe.

ON THE NATURE OF THE GODS

Who, then, are these non-humans on whom humans depend and whom they feel the duty to propitiate? Despite their multifariousness—which goes from immateriality to human- or animal-like corporeality, from auspiciousness to ominousness, from being the incarnation of health and beauty to that of disease and death, from purposeful to gratuitous behavior, from genocidal ferocity to boundless compassion, from asceticism to polymorphous lust, from male to female to androgynous, gods being conceived in many cases as embodying a *coincidentia oppositorum*—they are to be understood, first of all, as agents believed to be largely, but not fully, free from the physical, psychological, and moral constraints that limit the agency of humans. Gods are able to create and destroy, although it should be noted that being a creator is not a precondition for being a god. They can punish and reward for reasons that remain unfathomable to mere humans, that very incomprehensibility contributing to the god's majesty as well as to the authority of those who are regarded as the intermediaries between the gods and ordinary mortals. Gods move unencumbered by the laws of physics. They know what remains unknowable to humans, including that which has not yet happened, omniscience being a recurrent characteristic of deities. Cognitive and evolutionary theorists have in fact explored the manner in which the very nature of the gods violates our cognitive expectations, as well as the role played by the belief in divine omniscience in the evolution of cooperation and morality in general.[1]

The divine characteristics just mentioned, centered on the gods' might, should not cause us to forget that throughout history gods have been imagined with features that frequently collide with the tacit theological expectations nurtured by contemporary monotheistic religions, especially by the versions of Christianity that prevail in the Western world, which are built around a benign god, believed to be incapable of doing anything objectionable. Traditionally, gods have demanded offerings, especially food, as if they were subject to need. An early example is the feast of Lugalbanda, during which the Sumerian gods An, Enlil, Enki, and Ninhursaŋ partake of "dark beer, strong drink, white beer, wine, drinks pleasing the palate," and also of the "meat of the brown goats and roasted dark livers" (Vanstiphout 2009, 23); a contemporary example involves the animal sacrifices offered to Durgā, Kālī, Śītalā Devī, Māriyamman, Bhairava, and Narasiṁha, Hindu deities considered as fierce, violent, and "hot" (Fuller 2004, 85). These offerings create a relation of interdependence between gods and humans, which allows the latter to threaten the gods with withholding their oblations, as was done by Muršili II (r. 1321–1295 BC), and as was recognized by Ea, the Hittite god of wisdom, who warns Kumarbi that if he annihilates mankind, there will remain nobody to feed the

---

[1] For examples of genocidal violence ordered by a god there is no need to go beyond the Old Testament: Numbers 25:1–15, 31:1–20; Deuteronomy 2:30–35, 3:6–7, 7:2–6, 13:12–18, 20:12–18; Joshua 6:17–27; 7:20–26; 8:1–2, 22–29; 10:11–14, 28–42; 11:10–15; Judges 18:10–12, 27; 1 Samuel 15; 22:19; 2 Kings 15:16; Psalms 105:26–36; Jeremiah 43:11–12 (but see also the following in the New Testament: Matthew 10:34; Mark 5:1–20, 11:12–25; Luke 12:49–53, 14:23, 22:35–38); on a god (Śiva), who is ascetic and lustful: Doniger [O'Flaherty] 1973; on a god (medieval Krishna) who is just lustful: Miller 1977; Siegel 1978; on the polymorphous sexuality of a god (Zeus): Buffière 1980, 351–366; on divine androgyny: Baumann 1955; on gods as *coincidentiae oppositorum*: Hernández Catalá 1972; on the counterintuitive characteristics of gods: Boyer 1994; 2001; Pyysiäinen 2001; on divine motion: West 2007, 152–153; on divine omniscience: Pettazzoni 1955; on omniscience and morality: Roes/Raymond 2003; Johnson/Krüger 2004; Johnson 2005; Bering/Johnson 2005.

gods with offerings (Güterbock 1997, 44; Haas 1994, 36). The same interdependence—which is not paid enough attention to in the definitions of religion proposed by Horton and Goody quoted earlier—can be seen at work in China, where a statue of a god—which is not merely the representation of a divinity (Delahaye 1983)—may be exposed in the sun in order to force the god to cause rain to fall (Cohen 1978), and also in medieval, early modern, and contemporary Christendom, much as the practice of threatening saints with punishment or, even worse, actually punishing them, may be theologically incorrect (Trexler 1972, 26–28; Geary 1979; Graziano 2007, 59).

An important type of interaction is the one that exists between a god and his antagonist (see Biezais 1983; Stoyanov 2000). In the case of the Zoroastrian tradition, as it was systematized after the Islamic conquest of Iran, the interaction involves the opposition between Ohrmazd and Ahriman, which will result in Ohrmazd's final victory (Stausberg 2002a, 325–338; 2002b, 102–105). However, as shown by the exchanges between Mardānfarrox, son of Farrux i Ohrmazddād, the Zoroastrian author of the mid-ninth-century *Doubt-Dispelling Exposition* (*Škand-Gumānīg Wizār*), and Mihrāyar ī Mahmadān, (ch. 2–4 = tr. Menasce 1945, 33–61), to the latter, possibly a Muslim, such antagonism appears rather as cooperation, as demonstrated by Mihrāyar's claim that "If Ohrmazd and Ahriman have created [the Sphere and the stars] by mutual agreement, it is then evident that Ohrmazd is the accomplice and associate of Ahriman concerning the sins and evils that come from the Sphere" (ch. 4, 6 = Menasce 1945, 51, 6). While Mardānfarrox devotes the remainder of the chapter to establish that the Creator "does not afflict, nor torture nor punish his own creatures" (ch. 4, 102 = Menasce 1945, 59, 102)—in other words, does not cooperate with Ahriman—the cooperation is explicit in the case of the biblical Satan, who collaborates with Yahweh, tormenting Job (Job 1:6–12, 2:1–7) and accusing Joshua (Zechariah 3:1). The existence of a divinity in charge of the dark aspects of life relieves the good god from the taint of evil, an insoluble problem in the case of a monotheistic religion such as Christianity, which stresses both the omnipotence and the goodness of the divinity. Richer in narrative possibilities is the dualistic solution found in vast areas of the world, in which a trickster—frequently a coyote, fox, or crow—seeking to thwart the deeds of the creator god, ends up becoming his collaborator in fashioning the world in which we live. Indeed, taking into account Iranian developments analogous to the ones referred to earlier, Ugo Bianchi has asked whether the dualistic elements found in Eastern European folklore and in Finnish and Altaic mythologies, among others, are the survival of Iranian, Manichaean, and Bogomil dualisms, or whether the latter have emerged in a dualistic *humus* that stretches from northern Eurasia to North America (1958, 8, 26–27; 1978, 63–156).

In general, adversaries such as Ahriman and the Christian devil are exceptions in a landscape populated by divinities who encompass positive and negative characteristics. The best-known living examples are Śiva and Durgā, whose fearsome aspects are personified as Bhairava (iconography in Kramrisch 1981, 31–39) and Kālī, the latter being also worshiped as an independent deity (McDermott/Kripal 2003). Of the multitude of divinities who were givers of life and of death, mention must be made of the Aztec *teotl*, a

Nahua term usually translated as 'god.' Fernando Cervantes claims that such translation is misleading, since "its glyph is the figure of the sun, which conveys a sense of vastness and awesomeness, but also one of difficulty and danger" (1994, 41). Cervantes's criticism might be justified if the term 'god' were to be reserved for the deities of Christianity and Islam, but it is not if one considers that the majority of the supernatural beings referred to in this essay encompass awesomeness and its counterpart awfulness, both of which derive from 'awe,' a term that is part of the semantic field of terror, fear, and horror.[2] In fact, theological speculation about the unfathomable character of the deeds of the god of the Christians is merely an attempt to subsume the awfulness of some of that god's actions under the awesomeness of his freedom. Equally unjustified in light of some of the processes of deification studied in this essay is Claude-François Baudez's claim that the Maya of the classic period (250–950) did not have gods, so that, for instance, even god K, whose name appears in the monuments of the classic period, is but the personification of lightning, the other so-called 'gods' being personifications of various aspects of cosmic forces (2002, 268, 359, 375; cf. Rivera 2006, 219–251).

In the context of the divine omnipotence, assumed by the followers of monotheistic religions, it must be remembered that most ancient Egyptian gods were neither omnipotent nor immortal (Baines 2000, 26), that being also true of the Hittite divinities (Wilhelm 2002, 65)—in fact, omnipotence and polytheism are incompatible. Gods are dangerous, vengeful, jealous, easy to take offense, and ever ready to demand reparation: the entire edifice of Christian theology, for instance, is based on a primordial offense for which humans cannot atone, that unpaid debt having led to a divine intervention which generates an even more unpayable debt. Although placed far above humans, the gods themselves are subject to ranking, which in the Mesopotamian myth of Atramhasīs, for example, causes the lower gods—Igigi—to rebel against the high ranking ones—Anunnaku—who had forced them to engage in back-breaking labor (Tablet I, 1–181, tr. Lambert/Millard 1999, 43–53). Gods of similar rank engage in competitions with each other, whether in the Homeric poems or in the mythologies of Vishnu and Shiva. Gods move down in status, as happened in India to Brahma, an important god at the time of the Buddha, but now with barely a temple devoted to him; or up, as is currently happening with the monkey-god Hanuman, also in India. Gods become *dei otiosi*—that is, divinities no longer concerned with the world (Eliade 1970, 52–55)—who make space, sometimes reluctantly, for young energetic divinities such as the Babylonian Marduk. Gods are also brought back to life, as is happening now, as some Europeans are trying to revive the pantheons obliterated by the triumph of Christianity or, more generally, are promoting the virtues of polytheism (Augé 2015), all of this as the survival of European Christian monotheism itself seems to be threatened by the increasingly assertive presence of Islamic monotheism.

---

[2] See Linguistics Research Center—Indo-European Lexicon—Pokorny Master PIE Etyma, 7–8: agh-, agh-(lo-). <http://www.utexas.edu/cola/centers/lrc/ielex/PokornyMaster-X.html>.

THE PRODUCTION OF DIVINITY

Divine qualities can be understood as being produced by the projection of intensified human characteristics upon imaginary beings, along the lines proposed by Xenophanes in the sixth century BCE, Hume (1992 [1757]), Feuerbach (1841),[3] Marx (1844), and, more recently, Ernst Topitsch (1958, 1973).[4] God concepts, then, emerge as the result of two mutually reinforcing, if contradictory, processes: on the one hand, the desire to leave behind the limitations that afflict us and, on the other, the tendency—almost inescapable—to conceive the world as if it were populated by beings analogous to us, with human-like bodies, appetites, and minds; hence the tendency to generate anthropomorphic divinities—as visible in ancient Mesopotamia, the ancient Mediterranean world and classical Greece, as in contemporary India[5]—much as those divine bodies, appetites, and minds may require to be transfigured to ensure that they are not identical to ours—or, in the language of cognitivists, to achieve the optimal degree of counterintuitiveness. The same applies to our tendency not just to detect agency where it is actually found, but to sense it everywhere, ultimately generating the supernatural agents that populate religions (Guthrie 1993). Scott Atran maintains that god concepts have been produced by an "encompassing *evolutionary program for avoiding and tracking predators and prey*" (2002, 78; cf. 59–63; original emphasis), an understanding that has the advantage of grounding religion in the struggle for survival. Important as avoiding predators and tracking prey is, however, one must also consider, among other things, the effects that the kind of prey being tracked has on the kind of gods that the human predators and potential prey are likely to generate (Benavides 2010a). In addition, one must ask why animals, which, like early (and some modern) humans, are also prey and predators, and who have an agency detector that is even more active than that of humans, have not generated superhuman agents or religion or complex human-like cultures. One must consider, furthermore, events that have no connection with hunting, such as the meteorological phenomena, which, processed through the filter of anthropomorphism and intentionality, gave rise to the

---

[3] Nesselrath (2009, 21) points out that Feuerbach's assertion about man having made god in his image was anticipated by Georg Christoph Lichtenberg, the eighteenth-century physicist and author of aphorisms that remained unpublished during his lifetime: "Gott schuf den Menschen nach seinem Bilde, das heißt vermutlich der Mensch schuf Gott nach dem seinigen" (Sudelbücher C 201, 1773, ed. Promies 1986, 261): "God created man in his own image, meaning presumably that man created God in his own [image]."

[4] It can be said in this regard that cognitive and evolutionary approaches to religion constitute the working out of the insights found in Hume's, Feuerbach's, and Marx's work, much as the latter's views are usually reduced in a caricaturesque manner (even by serious scholars: see, for example, Burkert 1996, 13n51: 191) to the "religion-as-opium" sentence in Marx's *Critique of Hegel's Philosophy of Right*. It is no less regrettable that, with few exceptions, scholars of religion have ignored Ernst Topitsch's work.

[5] See Ornan 2009; Kiechle 1970; Koch 1956; Nesselrath 2009. The cognitive predispositions and ideological pressures that lead to divine anthropomorphism are studied in Benavides 1995, where further references can be found.

storm gods of the ancient Near East. In Ugarit, for example, a region in which, instead of depending on irrigation, agriculture was subject to the uncertainty of rainfall and storms, that relative unpredictability brought forth the storm god Baal (Loretz 2002, 85; overview in Green 2004).

These examples force us to consider that the main source of god representations may have to do with a human peculiarity that, although connected to hunting and being hunted, is more encompassing, this peculiarity being the precondition for the tendency to personify, among other things, natural phenomena and celestial objects, endowing them not just with human form, agency, and in some cases with omniscience, but above all with the capacity to have a theory of mind, that is to say, the ability to recognize others as being able to recognize one as able to recognize them—potentially ad infinitum, but in reality limited to a few levels of recursiveness. The ability to engage in meta-cognition, generating meta-representations—that is to say, concepts about concepts, second-order representations—involves above all being able to recognize the other as an intentional being like oneself, an ability that is one of the sources of the belief in divine omniscience, since omniscience is but the aggrandizement of a basic human capacity. Related to this is the ability to engage in mental time traveling—i.e. the capability to imagine future scenarios based on the memory of past ones—which contributes to one's survival. At the most elementary level, then, conceptions of god require the implicit or explicit postulation of the identity between human and divine minds. The "Instructions to Priests and Temple Officials," a Hittite text composed before the fourteenth century BCE, is instructive in this regard. Describing the manner in which masters and gods punish the servants who anger them, the text states: "(Are) the mind of man and god somehow different? No! In this which (is concerned)? No! The mind (is) one and the same" (§ 1, tr. McMahon 1997, 217).

That the capacity to recognize others as intentional agents is present in very young children has been studied in detail by psychologists, who have shown that children pay special attention to objects and shapes that seem to act in a purposeful manner, children being in fact predisposed to see reality in teleological terms. Present in young children is also the tendency to engage in mental time travel and to see the world in terms of the opposition between essence and appearance, a disposition that is combined with a tendency to perceive reality in dualistic terms.[6] This cluster of predispositions generates spiritual or quasi-spiritual entities—gods, spirits, ghosts, ancestors—endowed with a theory of mind, believed to act in a manner that oscillates between purposefulness and arbitrariness in a world that is itself assumed to function in a teleological manner. But it must be remembered that personification and related characteristics constitute but one of the strands that generate religion, the other being the desire to leave behind

---

[6] What follows is a sample of the literature on the topics listed in this and the previous paragraph. On religion and theory of mind: Bering 2011; on meta-cognition and meta-representations: Sperber 2000; Terrace/Metcalfe 2005; on recursiveness: Bering/Johnson 2005; Voland 2007; on teleology: Kelemen 1999; 2004; on mental time traveling: Suddendorf 2006; Suddendorf/Addis/Corballis 2009; on essentialism: Gelman 2003; on dualism: Astuti 2001; Bloom 2004.

the limitations that afflict us in a world defined by death, disease, and scarcity, the latter being a hardship that—despite the divinities' occasional mortality and their dependence on sacrificial offerings—does not seem to affect the gods in the same manner. This brings us to a human peculiarity whose role in the generation of religion, including the bringing forth of gods, has not received the attention it deserves, namely labor. That is a most strange neglect, for while it is through labor that humans have sought to defeat that which does not afflict the gods, namely scarcity, it is by fantasizing about a world free from death and disease, but also from the servitude of labor, that humans have generated beings free from those limitations.

It must be noted in this context that although gods are generally regarded as not being subject to the servitude of work, the burden of labor must have been such after the appearance of the early states in the ancient Near East, that even the gods were believed to be subject to it. In the second millennium BCE Atramhasīs myth, for example, the high ranking gods create humans "to bear the yoke . . . to carry the toil of the gods" (Tablet I, 9–12, tr. Lambert/Millard 1999, 55–57; see also von Soden 1969, 415 = 1989, 149; Bottéro/Kramer 1989, 535, 537; further discussion in Benavides 2000b). It is indeed the case that it is while working that humans act like the gods, since working requires the exercise of capacities at which the gods excel, such as engaging in meta-cognition and mental time traveling. It is significant in this regard that in the Atramhasīs myth humans are created by mixing clay with the blood of Wê-ila, a god who had 'ṭēmu'—translated as "personality" (Lambert/Millard 1999, 59), "*esprit*" (Bottéro/Kramer 1989, 537), *Verstand* ("understanding": von Soden 1973, 352 = 1985, 168), or, more specifically, *Planungsfähigkeit* ("the capacity to plan": von Soden 1979, 11 = 1989, 239),[7] a capacity that presupposes meta-cognition and mental time traveling. The difference between gods and humans is that whereas gods tend to exercise their cognition without limitation and act in a gratuitous manner in a realm of abundance, human beings act purposefully, generate meta-representations, and engage in mental time travel in order to cope with the affliction of being subject to need in a world of scarcity. To sum up: the capacity to generate meta-representations about being subject to future need is the precondition for labor; the interplay between labor and need contributes, in turn, to the intensification of meta-cognition and purposeful activity; and it is this intensification, coupled with the desire to escape labor, scarcity and disease, that generates the beings who excel at gratuitous knowing and doing (Benavides 2000b; 2009; 2010b; 2013).

---

[7] Among the meanings of *ṭēmu* listed in *The Assyrian Dictionary* (Chicago, IL: The Oriental Institute, vol. 19, Ṭ, 2006, 85–97), the following are relevant in this context: 2. order, command, instructions; 3. decision, deliberation, (divine) counsel, will, discretion, initiative; 4. plan, intention; 5 (a). reason, intelligence (90–95).

AMONG THE GODS

Approached from a cultural evolutionary perspective, divine representations can be seen to vary, so that the divinities of hunter-gatherers—trickster, master of the animals—differ from the gods of chiefdoms and, even more so, from those who constitute the pantheons of ancient Near Eastern societies. In general, the dissolution of kinship-based arrangements which characterize hunter-gatherer societies, leads to increased social complexity, stratification, and extraction of surplus on the part of elites. That complexity and extraction of surplus have their counterpart and their validation at the supernatural level. Thus the ruler's right to demand obedience and goods from his subjects presupposes divine protection and even divine kinship, but that right also requires the ruler's abasement in front of the gods. This self-humiliation reached its climax in pre-conquest Mesoamerica, particularly among the Maya, where the intensity and frequency of rituals that involved self-inflicted pain went hand in hand with social rank, so that rulers inflicted pain upon themselves to a greater degree than the nobles, who in turn engaged in more painful practices than the ordinary people.[8]

The developments just mentioned became intensified at the political and supernatural levels as the result of the emergence of agriculture in the Fertile Crescent, as increased agricultural productivity led to a population expansion that in turn resulted in the emergence of states. The early states that appeared in the ancient Near East generated pantheons whose gods demanded and consumed sacrificial offerings, just as elites extracted and consumed the fruits of their subjects' labor—a parallel that has led a scholar of Hittite religion to refer to the "pampered life of the gods" (Beckman 2005, 369). Given the role of agriculture in the development of states and pantheons, it is not unjustified to refer to the birth of the gods as going hand in hand with the birth of agriculture, as is done by Jacques Cauvin (1997). However, Cauvin's thesis that the mental shifts that led to the appearance of the gods preceded the appearance of agriculture must be regarded with the utmost skepticism.

A celestial god is the divinity that is likely to come to mind when the word "god" is used, as shown by the first few words of a popular Christian prayer that goes back to the gospels of Matthew (6:9–13) and Luke (11:2–4): "Our Father which art in heaven ..." Indeed, terms such as *dios, dio, dieu*, but also 'divine', go back to proto Indo-European *deiwos* (from the root *dei-*: shine), meaning 'luminous', 'celestial', as opposed to night and also to humans (Lat. *homōs*), who are earthly (Benveniste 1969, 180; Gamkrelidze/Ivanov 1995, I, 396, 693; Sergent 1995, 323; West 2007, 120, 124). That celestial nature is shared by ancient Near Eastern gods such as the Mesopotamian ones, whose names

---

[8] On the divinities of hunter-gatherers: Pettazzoni 1957, 114–129; Guenther 1999; on polytheism in general: Brelich 2007; on the differentiation of gods from their domains: Benavides 2000a, 299; on conceptions of god, including divine arbitrariness: Gladigow 1975; 1979; 1993; on the ruler's omniscience: Pettazzoni 1955, 71–73, 167; on Maya and Aztec rulers' autosacrifice: Baudez 2002, 219–225; 2012, 51, 67, 86–91; Rivera Dorado 2006, 119–120.

are preceded by a sign that originally meant "star" (Krebernik 2002, 34). As one would expect, the relation between Mesopotamian celestial gods and actual celestial bodies was ambiguous, for in some cases gods were regarded as celestial bodies, while in others celestial bodies were regarded as images, manifestations, and/or personifications of gods (Rochberg 2009; 2011). Such oscillation is not surprising since it is not uncommon that an aspect of nature such as the sky be also regarded as a supernatural realm, as shown by German *Himmel*, French *ciel*, and Spanish and Italian *cielo*. If we move beyond European languages, we find that in ancient Turkish and Mongol *tängri* (*tngri*) refers both to the sky and to the supreme god (Roux 1956; Heissig 1970, 350–364), the same being true of Chinese *Tian* (*T'ien*) since the Zhou dynasty (Eichhorn 1973, 29–31; 1975), and perhaps also of Maya Itzam Na in the early sixteenth century (Baudez 2002, 362).

Regarding the relations among gods, we encounter a range of scenarios, most of which will appear as strange to anyone who lives in a culture defined by monotheism. The most common, before the appearance of religions built around a single god, involved understanding alien divinities in terms of those worshiped by one's people. The best known cases are the *interpretatio graeca*, which goes back to Herodotus, and the *interpretatio romana*, that is to say, the practice of seeking Greek or Roman equivalents for alien divinities, a procedure also attested elsewhere, for example in ancient Anatolia (Wilhelm 2002, 170) and in Mesoamerica (Rivera Dorado 2006, 251). A parallel practice, known as syncretism (Benavides 2001), involved merging gods or elements from various divinities. On the other hand, the relative alienness of the divinity was presupposed in the case of the Roman *evocatio*, which consisted in the attempt to entice the gods of one of Rome's enemies to desert their own people, thus facilitating Rome's victory (Le Gall 1976). In this case, there was no doubt about the alienness of the divinity in question, but at the same time there was no attempt to deny the legitimacy of that divinity. All of that changed with the emergence of monotheism, as other divinities began to be regarded first as inferior, then as demonic, and finally as non-existent.[9] When dealing with this type of religion it must be noted that although about half of the world population professes to believe in a single god, exclusive monotheism has been the exception in the history of religions. In fact, even religions regarded as monotheistic have a tendency to multiply the objects of devotion, and although theologians insist that the various objects of worship—gods, saints, prophets, angels—and the manner in which they are approached are radically different, ordinary devotees tend to approach the objects of their devotion in a manner that is frequently unencumbered by theological correctness. For example, in Israelite religion, generally regarded as the epitome of monotheism, the worship of a single god in the postexilic period went hand in hand with the belief in intermediary beings such as angels and demons (Koch 1994). In the case of Christianity, whatever agreement may have been reached by bishops in the fourth century concerning the nature of their deity, the term

---

[9] Due to lack of space, no attempt will be made to discuss the phenomenon of monotheism, including the emergence of Israelite monotheism. See Pettazzoni 1946 as well as the contributions found in Porter 2000; Krebernik/Oorschot 2002; Pongratz-Leisten 2011, the last of which includes critiques of Pettazzoni and Assmann 2003.

"God" is generally used by ordinary Christians to refer to the first person of the trinity, while the second person of the said trinity is generally referred to as "the son of God" in a manner that has Arian overtones. Be that as it may, the status of Jesus has fluctuated over the centuries, going from being considered by Ignatius of Antioch, in the first century, as subordinate to the father, to being regarded by Justin, in the second, as sharing the same being with the father, to the belief that Jesus was adopted by God as his son, 'adoptionism' having survived well into the medieval period (overview in Hurtado 2003). The status of Mary is no less complex, since the mother of Jesus, while never having lost her human condition, is said to be present in heaven in body and soul, just as her divine son is believed to be. Her subordinate status is marked by the belief that while Jesus ascended to heaven on his own, Mary was lifted to her heavenly abode. That subordinate position is, however, disregarded in practice, as shown, for example, by Italian Renaissance paintings that depict Mary as the *Madonna della misericordia*, not just towering over both Jesus and God the father, but also stopping them from punishing humans for their sins (Marshall 1994, 518), thus demonstrating her superiority in the eyes of ordinary Christians. Mary's pre-eminent position is equally apparent in the late medieval rituals developed around her in cities such as Florence and Siena (Trexler 1972; 1973), not to mention the omnipresence of her street shrines in Italian cities, especially in Tuscany.

In the case of Islam, its uncompromising monotheism is shown not just by claims about the oneness (*tawhid*) of its god, found in the Qur'an, but even more so by the explicit condemnation of the Christian doctrine of the incarnation, found in the same book—for example: "And they say, 'the All-merciful has taken unto himself a son.' You have indeed advanced something hideous" (19:88–89, tr. Arberry); and even more explicitly: "Say: 'He is God, One, God, the Everlasting Refuge, who has not begotten, and has not been begotten, and equal to Him is not any one" (112:1–4, tr. Arberry). On the other hand, it is precisely speculation about the uncreated nature of the Qur'an, and even more so, devotion to Mohammad (Schimmel 1981), regarded as a perfect man (Schaeder 1925, 239) who serves as an intermediary between Allah and ordinary humans, that show how difficult it is to function in a strict monotheistic fashion. It should be pointed out in this context that violent protests against the desecrations of Mohammad and the Qur'an that have occurred recently in Denmark and France, show the exalted status of the sacred book and the messenger, both of which have ancient Near Eastern roots (see Widengren 1950; 1955), just as the concept of the perfect man has. The surprise that those violent protests elicited in the West shows the extent to which notions of divinity and sacredness as well as of its counterparts, profanation and blasphemy, seem to have disappeared from Western Christendom (see Benavides 2007).

If exclusive monotheism is difficult to uphold, building a religion on non-theistic foundations requires an extraordinary conceptual effort, which, as demonstrated by the history of Buddhism, is condemned to failure. Already at the time of the Buddha, we find that the enlightened one was the object of veneration, a practice that increased immediately after his death (Bareau 1974), when, apparently with his previous approval, his relics became the object of worship (Waldschmidt 1961). Later on, Buddhas and Bodhisattvas were worshiped, along with personifications of virtues, such as *Prajñāpāramitā* (Perfection of Wisdom), all of them having become indistinguishable from traditional Indian divinities. It is true that these divinities were not regarded as creators, but it must be kept in mind that being a creator is not the precondition for being a god. In Daoism the situation is no less complex in that already in the *Daodejing* the Dao is presented as that which cannot be named (ch. 1), but also as the mother of all things (ch. 1, 42, 51). Later developments expand the process of anthropomorphization and divinization; for example, in the *Scripture of the Inner Explanations of the Three Heavens*, a fifth-century text, the Dao gives birth to the Elder of the Way and its Power, an anthropomorphized Dao; after a number of further births, three pneumas give birth to the Dark and Wondrous Jade Maiden, who in turn gives birth to the divinized Laozi in a manner that resembles the birth of the Buddha (tr. Bokenkamp 1997, 207–208; cf. Kohn 1998, 15–18, 239–242). These brief examples may suffice to remind us that, against widespread misconceptions regarding South and East Asian religions, as soon as one ventures beyond the canonical texts—and in some cases already in those texts themselves—one finds that founders, as much as cosmic principles, tend to be transformed into gods.

Unstable Boundaries

If the borderlines among gods as well as among monotheisms and polytheisms are uncertain, the boundaries among god, human, and nature are equally permeable. The best-known breaching of boundaries involves a god who "formed man from the dust of the earth and breathed into his nostrils the breath of life; and the man became a living being" (Genesis 2:7). Older and more physical than the biblical account is the one found in the already mentioned myth of Atramhasīs, according to which the god Wê-ila, who had the capacity to plan, "they [the great Annunaki] slaughtered in their assembly. From his flesh and blood [the goddess] Nintu mixed clay . . . After she had mixed that clay she summoned the Annunaki, the great gods. The Igigi, the great gods, spat upon the clay" (I, 223–226, 231–234 = tr. Lambert/Millard 1999, 59; Bottéro/Kramer 1989, 538). Even more carnal are the stories about gods who copulate and occasionally beget semi-divine offspring with humans, such as the ones that involve Zeus. Moving from Greek mythology to ritual, the permeability between the human and divine realms can be seen when a ruler was sacrificed to, honored, proclaimed, and ultimately recognized as a god (Versnel 2011, 486). Better known is the deification of Roman emperors, which began in 42 BCE, when the senate granted posthumously the title of *Divus Iulius* to Julius Caesar. But just as the boundaries between the human and the divine are permeable, so are the boundaries between belief and skepticism. It may be salutary in this regard to remember that, as death drew near, Emperor Vespasian (r. 69–79) is reported to have said "Woe's me. Methinks I am turning into a god,"[10] an ironic comment that presupposes a metacognitive exercise concerning the concepts of divinity and humanity.

---

[10] *"Vae," inquit, "puto deus fio"*: Suetonius, *Lives of the Caesars*, VIII, 23, 4, tr. J. C. Rolfe, 1914 (Loeb Classical Library), II, 318.

Regarding the permeability between nature and divinity in China, we may refer to the god of the soil, defined by Chavannes as "the personification of the energies that reside in the soil" (1910, 437). In terms of the relation between humans and divinity, we find that since the late fourth century BCE, in the circles that produced the "Neiye" (inner cultivation) chapter of the *Guanzi* it was believed that the cultivation of *qi* led to attaining the power of spirits (Puett 2002, 115–117; text in Roth 1999). More recently, and lasting till the nineteenth century, a person could become the object of cult, eventually being regarded as a divinity, as a result of an out of the ordinary, untimely death. That is what happened to Chen Jinggu, known as Lady Linshui, born either in 766 or, according to legendary sources in 904. She is said to have died of a hemorrhage after having to abort her fetus in order to be able to perform a shamanic ritual to save the Min kingdom from a severe drought (Baptandier 1996, 110). More generally, divinization could also be the fate of a young woman who had killed herself to protect her virtue, for she could be believed to have become a vengeful ghost (*ligui*) who would need to be ritually appeased, that appeasement turning into reverence, then to official recognition, and ultimately to divinization (Yu 2012, 105–114). Violent and untimely death is also a prerequisite for deification in folk Hinduism, the violence of the death and the suffering of the victims rather than their innocence being the determining factor in the transformation of humans into divinities (Blackburn 1985, 260; cf. Knipe 1989; Coccari 1989). In contemporary Latin America, on the other hand, where deification as such is not possible, it is "tragic death in its broadest sense—including violent, accidental, sudden, painful, youthful, and unjust deaths" that generates folk saints (Graziano 2007, 15).

The unstable boundaries between human and divine spheres as well as among object, quality, and agent can also be seen when one examines terms such as *kami*, *dema*, and *waka*. The uncertainty concerning what *kami* refers to is exemplified by a statement by the renowned eighteenth-century Shinto scholar Motoori Norinaga: "I do not understand the meaning of the term *kami*." Motoori, however, goes on to say that "*kami* signifies, in the first place, the deities of heaven and earth that appear in the ancient records and also the spirits of the shrines where they are worshiped," and then he adds that "It is hardly necessary to say that it includes human beings. It also includes such objects as birds, beasts, trees, plants, seas, mountains and so forth." Especially significant is a passage that reminds one of Otto's numinous: "In ancient usage, anything whatsoever which was outside the ordinary, which possessed superior power, or which was awe-inspiring was called *kami*" (Motoori, *Norinaga Zenshū*, Tokyo, 1901, vol. 1, 150–152, quoted in Holtom 1938, 23). Moving from the Japanese islands to Australasia, we find parallels between the *kami* and the New Guinea *dema* insofar as both are considered as beings and as qualities. Jan van Baal describes the *dema* as "beings who lived in the mythical era . . . [who] usually . . . take the form of human beings, but sometimes . . . change into animals or appear predominantly in animal shape" (1966, 179). As happened with the *kami*, "there is a certain correlation between *dema* and the uncommon," for in some cases "the term dema refers to a quality rather than to a specific mythical being. Extraordinarily big trees or animals may be called dema-trees or

-animals even when there is no specific reference to a mythical ancestor" (185), the word dema itself not being used lightly or carelessly, but rather "surrounded with awe and mystery" (178). Equally ambiguous is the meaning of the Andean term *waka* (*huaca, guaca*), which is used to refer to mummies, graves, cemeteries, sanctuaries, oracles, idols, and especially to mountain summits, which according to some Spanish chroniclers and "extirpators of idolatries," such as the early seventeenth-century Jesuit Arriaga, were venerated as gods (1621, ch. 5 = ed. Urbano 1999, 56–62; see also Besom 2009, 65; for Mesopotamian parallels: Porter 2009a, 169–171). As shown in Guaman Poma de Ayala's almost contemporary insider's account, *El primer nueva corónica i buen gobierno, wakas* interacted with the Inka rulers and were offered sacrifices (c.1615, 261–273 = ed. Murra/Adorno 1992, 234–247); blood was particularly valued, especially human blood, which was offered to the most important *wakas* on special occasions (Benson 2001, 2).

SACREDNESS AND DIVINE AGENCY

Returning to the connection between sacredness and agency discussed at the beginning of this chapter, it is clear that although also used to refer to objects that elicit awe, *kami, dema*, and *waka* are associated with agents, especially supernatural ones. In this they have something in common with the Polynesian term *mana*, which according to R. H. Codrington, who introduced it to the vocabulary of anthropology in the late nineteenth century, "though itself impersonal, is always connected with some person who directs it" (1891, 119). However, due to Codrington's emphasis on *mana*'s impersonal nature, *mana*'s connection with an agent, which he himself had mentioned, was disregarded, with the result that the term was used to refer to a presumed predeistic stage of religion. In this context, scholars of Roman religion such as Hendrik Wagenvoort (1980, 223–256) interpreted the term *numen* as an impersonal force analogous to *mana*. Against this view Georges Dumézil has argued, with his usual forcefulness, that rather than being understood as an impersonal force, *numen* had been understood for centuries by the Romans as *numen dei*, that is, as *numen* of a god and as the expression of a god's will (1974, 46–47). In an analogous manner, Roger Keesing has shown that in the languages of Oceania *mana* functions as a stative verb rather than as a noun, so that things and human enterprises and efforts are *mana* (1984, 138). In Tikopia *mana* (*manu*) is an attribute of chiefs and of spirit mediums, derived from the mediums' relation to spirits (Firth 1967b, 194); it is also understood as that which is added to human efforts to ensure success (Firth 1967a, 468). Therefore, rather than being impersonal forces or substances, both in ancient Rome and in mid-twentieth-century Polynesia, *mana* and *numen* are attached to the will or to the deeds of agents, whether human or divine.

Conclusion

> Inquire of me as to the being and nature of god, and I shall follow the example of Simonides, who having the same question put to him by the great Hiero, requested a day's grace for consideration; next day, when Hiero repeated the question, he asked for two days, and so went on several times multiplying the number of days by two; and when Hiero in surprise asked why he did so, he replied, "Because the longer I deliberate the more obscure the matter seems to me."[11]

Thus Cotta, one of the characters in Cicero's *On the Nature of the Gods.* Twenty-five centuries after Simonides and almost twenty-one after *De natura deorum,* one may be tempted to share the Greek poet's pessimism; but as the preceding pages have attempted to show, the conceptual fog that surrounds the frequently luminous beings labeled as gods can be pierced if one focuses on the unresolvable tension between the gratuitousness and the deliberateness of their deeds; between their neediness and their self-sufficiency; between their human-like nature and their otherness; between their omniscience and the realization that, as the Hittite text referred to earlier states, their minds cannot but be like ours; between their being our transfiguration and our caricature.

Glossary

Anthropomorphization the transformation of a natural object or process into a human-like being.

Divinization the transformation of a human being into a god.

Gods agents said to be largely free from the physical, psychological, and moral constraints that limit the agency of humans, but who are in fact believed to function in ways analogous to those of ordinary human beings.

Meta-representation a thought about a thought, representation, or concept.

Monotheism the worship of one god, who in some rare cases is believed to be the only existing divinity; more common is monolatry or henotheism, the worship of one god, while recognizing the existence of others.

Pantheon "all the gods": the group—in some cases, the family—of gods worshiped by a community.

---

[11] *Roges me quid aut quale sit deus, auctore utar Simonide, de quo cum quaesivisset hoc idem tyrannus Hiero, deliberandi sibi unum diem postulavit; cum idem ex eo postridie quaereret, biduum petivit; cum saepius duplicaret numerum dierum admiransque Hiero requireret cur ita faceret, 'Quia quanto diutius considero,' inquit, 'tanto mihi res videtur obscurior.'* Cicero, *De natura deorum* I, 22; translation by H. Rackham, 1933 (Loeb Classical Library), 58.

Polytheism the worship of a number of gods, generally arranged in a hierarchical manner, who are in charge of various but overlapping aspects of reality.

REFERENCES

Arberry, Arthur. 1955. *The Koran Interpreted*, translated by Arthur J. Arberry. New York: Macmillan.

Arriaga, Pablo Joseph. 1999. *La Extirpación de la Idolatría en el Pirú*. Estudio preliminar y notas de Henrique Urbano. Cuzco: Centro de Estudios Regionales Andinos "Bartolomé de las Casas." Original edition, 1621.

Assmann, Jan. 2003. *Die Mosaische Unterscheidung oder der Preis des Monotheismus*. Munich and Vienna: Carl Hanser.

Astuti, Rita. 2001. "Are We All Natural Dualists? A Cognitive Developmental Approach." *Journal of the Royal Anthropological Institute* 7: 429–447. doi: 10.1111/1467-9655.00071

Atran, Scott. 2002. *In Gods We Trust: The Evolutionary Landscape of Religion*. Oxford and New York: Oxford University Press.

Augé, Marc. 2015. "Contre le dogmatisme, faisons l'éloge de la résistance païenne." *Le Monde*, December 26, 2015. <http://is.gd/q49iWE>, accessed February 2, 2016.

Baal, Jan van. 1966. *Dema: Description and Analysis of Marind-Anim Culture (South New Guinea)*. The Hague: Martinus Nijhoff.

Baines, John. 2000. "Egyptian Deities in Context: Multiplicity, Unity and the Problem of Change." In *One God or Many? Concepts of Divinity in the Ancient World*, edited by Barbara Nevling Porter. Casco Bay Assyriological Institute, 9–78.

Baptandier, Brigitte. 1996. "The Lady Linshui: How a Woman Became a Goddess." In *Unruly Gods: Divinity and Society in China*, edited by Meir Shahar and Robert P. Weller. Honolulu: University of Hawai'i Press, 105–149.

Bareau, André. 1974. "Le Parinirvāna du Bouddha et la naissance de la religion bouddhique." *Bulletin de l'École Française d'Extrême Orient* 61: 275–299.

Baudez, Claude-François. 2002. *Une histoire de la religion des Mayas: Du panthéisme au panthéon*. Paris: Albin Michel.

Baudez, Claude-François. 2012. *La douleur rédemptrice: L'autosacrifice précolombien*. Paris: Riveneuve.

Baumann, Hermann. 1955. *Das doppelte Geschlecht: Ethnologische Studien zur Bisexualität in Ritus und Mythos*. Berlin: Dietrich Reimer.

Beckman, Gary. 2005. "How Religion Was Done." In *A Companion to the Ancient Near East*, edited by Daniel C. Snell. Oxford: Blackwell, 366–376.

Benavides, Gustavo. 1995. "Cognitive and Ideological Aspects of Divine Anthropomorphism." *Religion* 25(1): 9–22. doi: 10.1006/reli.1995.0002

Benavides, Gustavo. 2000a. "Stratification." In *Guide to the Study of Religion*, edited by Willi Braun and Russell T. McCutcheon. London and New York: Cassell, 297–313.

Benavides, Gustavo 2000b. "Towards a Natural History of Religion." *Religion* 30(3): 229–244. doi: 10.1006/reli.2000.0268

Benavides, Gustavo. 2001. "Power, Intelligibility and the Boundaries of Religions." *Historical Reflections/Réflexions historiques* 27(3): 481–498.

Benavides, Gustavo. 2007. "Islam and European Identity, from the *Mozarabic Chronicle* to the *Jyllands-Posten* Cartoons." *Bulletin of the Council of Societies for the Study of Religion* 36(4): 94–97.

Benavides, Gustavo. 2009. "Religion, at the Intersection." *Historia Religionum* 1: 21–31.

Benavides, Gustavo. 2010a. "Monotheism, or the Paradoxes of Agency." In *Le Monothéisme: diversité, exclusivisme ou dialogue?* edited by Charles Guittard. Paris: Société Ernest Renan—Société française d'histoire des religions, 33–43.

Benavides, Gustavo. 2010b. "On the Production of Religious Configurations." *Method and Theory in the Study of Religion* 22: 239–253. doi: 10.1163/157006810X531030

Benavides, Gustavo. 2013. "Le metarappresentazioni, il lavoro e l'insorgere della religione." *Studi e Materiali di Storia delle Religioni* 79: 609–624.

Benson, Elizabeth. 2001. "Why Sacrifice?" In *Ritual Sacrifice in Ancient Peru*, edited by Elizabeth Benson and Anita Cook. Austin: University of Texas Press, 1–20.

Benveniste, Émile 1969. *Le vocabulaire des institutions indo-européens*. Vol. 2: *Pouvoir, droit, religion*. Paris: Minuit.

Bering, Jesse. 2011. *The Belief Instinct: The Psychology of Souls, Destiny, and the Meaning of Life*. New York: Norton.

Bering, Jesse and Dominic Johnson. 2005. "'O Lord ... You Perceive My Thoughts from Afar': Recursiveness and the Evolution of Supernatural Agency." *Journal of Cognition and Culture* 5(1–2): 118–142. doi: 10.1163/1568537054068679

Besom, Thomas. 2009. *Of Summits and Sacrifice: An Ethnohistoric Study of Inka Religious Practices*. Austin: University of Texas Press.

Bianchi, Ugo. 1958. *Il dualismo religioso: Saggio storico ed etnologico*. Rome: "L'Erma" di Bretschneider.

Bianchi, Ugo, 1978. *Selected Essays on Gnosticism, Dualism and Mysteriosophy*. Leiden: Brill.

Biezais, Haralds. 1983. "Der Gegengott als Grundelement religiöser Strukturen." *Saeculum* 34: 280–291. doi: 10.7788/saeculum.1983.34.34.280

Blackburn, Stuart H. 1985. "Death and Deification: Folk Cults in Hinduism." *History of Religions* 24(3): 255–274.

Bloom, Paul. 2004. *Descartes' Baby: How the Science of Child Development Explains What Makes Us Human*. New York: Basic Books.

Bokenkamp, Sephen. 1997. *Early Daoist Scriptures*. Berkeley: University of California Press.

Bottéro, Jean and Samuel Noah Kramer. 1989. *Lorsque les dieux faisaient l'homme: Mythologie mésopotamienne*. Paris: Gallimard.

Boyer, Pascal. 1994. *The Naturalness of Religious Ideas: A Cognitive Theory of Religion*. Berkeley: University of California Press.

Boyer, Pascal. 2001. *Religion Explained: The Evolutionary Origins of Religious Thought*. New York: Basic Books.

Brelich, Angelo. 2007. *Il politeismo*. Rome: Editori Riuniti.

Buffière, Félix. 1980. *Eros adolescent: La pédérastie dans la Grèce antique*. Paris: Les Belles Lettres.

Burkert, Walter. 1996. *Creation of the Sacred: Tracks of Biology in Early Religions*. Cambridge, MA: Harvard University Press.

Cauvin, Jacques. 1997. *Naissance des divinités, Naissance de l'agriculture: La Révolution des symboles au Néolitique*, 2nd edition. Paris: Flammarion. Original edition, 1994.

Cervantes, Fernando. 1994. *The Devil in the New World: The Impact of Diabolism in New Spain*. New Haven, CT: Yale University Press.

Chavannes, Edouard. 1910. *Le T'ai chan. Essai de monographie d'un culte chinoise. Appendice: Le dieu du sol dans la Chine antique*. Paris: Ernest Leroux.

Coccari, Diane M. 1989. "The Bir Babas of Banaras and the Deified Dead." In *Criminal Gods and Demon Devotees: Essays on the Guardians of Popular Hinduism*, edited by Alf Hiltebeitel. Albany: State University of New York Press, 251–269.

Codrington, R. H. 1891. *The Melanesians: Studies in Their Anthropology and Folk-Lore.* Oxford: Clarendon Press.

Cohen, Alvin P. 1978. "Coercing the Rain Deities in Ancient China." *History of Religions* 17(3–4): 244–265. doi: 10.1086/462793

Delahaye, Hubert. 1983. "Les antécédentes magiques des statues chinoises." *Revue d'esthétique* 5: 45–53.

Doniger [O'Flaherty], Wendy. 1973. *Asceticism and Eroticism in the Mythology of Siva.* London: Oxford University Press.

Dumézil, Georges. 1974. *La Religion romaine archaïque, avec un appendice sur la religion des Etrusques,* 2nd edition. Paris: Payot. Original edition, 1966.

Durkheim, Émile. 1897–1898. "De la définition des phénomènes religieux." *L'Année sociologique* 2: 1–28.

Eichhorn, Werner. 1973. *Die Religionen Chinas.* Stuttgart: Kohlhammer.

Eichhorn, Werner. 1975. "Der 'Name Gottes' in den religiösen Strömungen des alten China." In *Der Name Gottes,* edited by Heinrich von Stietencron. Düsseldorf: Patmos, 66–74.

Eliade, Mircea. 1970. *Traité d'histoire des religions,* 2nd edition. Paris: Payot. Original edition, 1949.

Feuerbach, Ludwig. 1841. *Das Wesen des Christentums.* Leipzig: Otto Wigand = Stuttgart: Reclam, 1994.

Firth, Raymond. 1959. "Problem and Assumption in the Anthropological Study of Religion." *Journal of the Royal Anthropological Society of Great Britain and Ireland* 89: 129–148.

Firth, Raymond. 1967a. *The Work of the Gods in Tikopia.* London: Athlone Press.

Firth, Raymond. 1967b. *Tikopia Ritual and Belief.* London: George Allen & Unwin.

Fuller, C. J. 2004. *The Camphor Flame: Popular Hinduism and Society in India,* 2nd edition. Princeton, NJ: Princeton University Press. Original edition, 1992.

Gamkrelidze, Thomas and Vjačeslav Ivanov. 1995. *Indo-European and the Indo-Europeans: A Reconstruction and Historical Analysis of a Proto-Language and a Proto-Culture I–II.* Berlin: Mouton de Gruyter.

Geary, Patrick J. 1979. "La coercition des saints dans la pratique religieuse médiévale." In *La culture populaire au moyen âge,* edited by Pierre Boglioni. Québec: Univers, 145–161.

Gelman, Susan. 2003. *The Essential Child: Origins of Essentialism in Everyday Thought:* Oxford and New York: Oxford University Press.

Gladigow, Burkhard. 1975. "Götternamen und Name Gottes: Allgemeine religionswissenschaftliche Aspekte." In *Der Name Gottes,* edited by Heinrich von Stietencron. Düsseldorf: Patmos, 13–22.

Gladigow, Burkhard. 1979. "Der Sinn der Götter: Zum kognitiven Potential der persönlichen Gottesvorstellung." In *Gottesvorstellung und Gesellschaftsentwicklung,* edited by Peter Eicher. Munich: Kösel, 41–62.

Gladigow, Burkhard. 1993. "Gottesvorstellungen." In *Handbuch religionswissenschaftlicher Grundbegriffe,* edited by Hubert Cancik, Burkhard Gladigow, and Karl-Heinz Kohl. Stuttgart, Berlin, and Köln: Kohlhammer, III, 32–49.

Goody, Jack. 1961. "Religion and Ritual: The Definitional Problem." *British Journal of Sociology* 12(2): 142–164. doi: 10.2307/586928

Graziano, Frank. 2007. *Cultures of Devotion: Folk Saints of Spanish America.* Oxford and New York: Oxford University Press.

Green, Alberto R. W. 2004. *The Storm-God in the Ancient Near East.* Winona Lake, IN: Eisenbrauns.

Guaman Poma de Ayala, Don Phelipe. *c.*1615. *El primer nueva corónica y buen gobierno.* Edición crítica de John V. Murra and Rolena Adorno, 3rd edition. México, DF: Siglo veintiuno, 1992. Original edition, 1980.

Guenther, Mathias. 1999. *Tricksters and Trancers: Bushman Religion and Society.* Bloomington: Indiana University Press.

Güterbock, Hans Gustav. 1997. "The Hittite Version of the Hurrian Kumarbi Myth: Oriental Forerunners of Hesiod." *American Journal of Archaeology* 52(1): 123–134. Original edition, 1948.

Guthrie, Stewart Elliott. 1993. *Faces in the Clouds: A New Theory of Religion.* New York and Oxford: Oxford University Press.

Haas, Volkert. 1994. *Geschichte der hethitischen Religion.* Leiden: Brill.

Heissig, Walther. 1970. "Die Religionen der Mongolei." In *Die Religionen Tibets und der Mongolei.* Stuttgart: Kohlhammer, 293–428.

Hernández Catalá, Vicente. 1972. *La expresión de lo divino en las religiones no cristianas.* Madrid: Biblioteca de Autores Cristianos.

Hiltebeitel, Alf, ed. 1989. *Criminal Gods and Demon Devotees: Essays on the Guardians of Popular Hinduism.* Albany: State University of New York Press.

Holtom, D. C. 1938. *The National Faith of Japan: A Study in Modern Shinto.* London: Kegan Paul.

Horton, Robin. 1993. "A Definition of Religion and Its Uses." In *Patterns of Thought in Africa and the West.* Cambridge: Cambridge University Press, 19–49, 390–391. Original edition, 1960.

Hume, David. 1992. *Writings on Religion.* La Salle: Open Court. Original edition, 1757.

Hurtado, Larry W. 2003. *Lord Jesus Christ: Devotion to Jesus in Earliest Christianity.* Grand Rapids, MI: William B. Eerdmans.

Johnson, Dominic. 2005. "God's Punishment and Public Goods: A Test of the Supernatural Punishment Hypothesis in 186 World Cultures." *Human Nature* 16(4): 410–446. doi.org/10.1558/poth.2004.5.2.159

Johnson, Dominic and Oliver Krüger. 2004. "The Good of Wrath: Supernatural Punishment and the Evolution of Cooperation." *Political Theology* 5(2): 159–176.

Keesing, Roger. 1984. "Rethinking 'Mana.'" *Journal of Anthropological Research* 40: 137–156.

Kelemen, Deborah. 1999. "Belief about Purpose: On the Origins of Teleological Thought." In *The Descent of Mind: Psychological Perspectives on Hominid Evolution*, edited by Michael Corballis and Stephen Lea. Oxford: Oxford University Press, 278–294.

Kelemen, Deborah. 2004. "Are Children 'Intuitive Theists'? Reasoning about Purpose and Design in Nature." *Psychological Science* 15(5): 295–301. doi: 10.1111/j.0956-7976.2004.00672.x

Kiechle, Franz K. 1970. "Götterdarstellung durch Menschen in den altmediterranen Religionen." *Historia. Zeitschrift für Alte Geschichte* 19: 259–271.

Knipe, David M. 1989. "Night of the Growing Dead: The Cult of Vīrabhadra in Coastal Andhra." In *Criminal Gods and Demon Devotees: Essays on the Guardians of Popular Hinduism*, edited by Alf Hiltebeitel. Albany: State University of New York Press, 123–156.

Koch, Carl. 1956. "Vom Wirkungsgeheimnis des menschengestaltigen Gottes." In *Aus dem Bildungsgut der Antike* I, edited by Friedrich Hörmann. Munich: Bayerischer Schulbuch-Verlag, 61–110 = Carl Koch, *Religio. Studien zu Kult und Glauben der Römer.* Nürnberg: Verlag Hans Carl, 1960, 205–252.

Koch, Klaus. 1994. "Monotheismus und Angelologie." In *Ein Gott allein? JHWH-Verehrung und biblischer Monotheismus im Kontext der israelitischen und altorientalischen*

Religionsgeschichte, edited by Walter Dietrich and Martin A. Klopfenstein. Freiburg, Schweiz: Universitätsverlag/Göttingen: Vandenhoeck & Ruprecht, 565–581.

Kohn, Livia. 1998. *God of the Dao: Lord Lao in History and Myth*. Ann Arbor: Center for Chinese Studies, University of Michigan.

Kramrisch, Stella. 1981. *Manifestations of Shiva*. Philadelphia: Philadelphia Museum of Art.

Krebernik, Manfred. 2002. "Vielzahl und Einheit im altmesopotamischen Pantheon." In *Polytheismus und Monotheismus in den Religionen des Vorderen Orients*, edited by Manfred Krebernik and Jürgen van Oorschot. Münster: Ugarit, 33–51.

Krebernik, Manfred and Jürgen van Oorschot, eds. 2002. *Polytheismus und Monotheismus in den Religionen des Vorderen Orients*. Münster: Ugarit.

Lambert, W. G. and A. R. Millard. 1969. *Atra-hasīs: The Babylonian Story of the Flood*. Oxford: Clarendon Press = Winona Lake, IN: Eisenbrauns, 1999.

Lawson, Thomas and Robert McCauley. 1990. *Rethinking Religion: Connecting Religion and Culture*. Cambridge: Cambridge University Press.

Le Gall, Joel. 1976. "Evocatio." In *Mélanges offerts à Jacques Heurgon: L'Italie Préromaine et la Rome Républicaine I*. Rome: École française de Rome/Palais Farnèse, 519–524.

Lichtenberg, Georg Christoph. 1986. *Schriften und Briefe I—Sudelbücher I*, edited by Wolfgang Promies. Munich: Carl Hanser.

Loretz, Oswald. 2002. "Die Einzigkeit eines Gottes im Polytheismus von Ugarit. Zur Levante als Ursprungsort des biblischen Monotheismus." In *Polytheismus und Monotheismus in den Religionen des Vorderen Orients*, edited by Manfred Krebernik and Jürgen van Oorschot. Münster: Ugarit, 71–89.

McDermott, Rachel Fell, and Jeffrey J. Kripal, eds. 2003. *Encountering Kālī: In the Margins, at the Center, in the West*. Berkeley: University of California Press.

McMahon, Gregory. 1997. "Instructions to Priests and Temple Officials (1.83)." In *The Context of Scripture*, edited by William W. Hallo and K. Lawson Younger. Leiden: Brill, vol. 1, 217–221.

Marshall, Louise. 1994. "Manipulating the Sacred: Image and Plague in Renaissance Italy." *Renaissance Quarterly* 47(3): 485–532. doi: 10.2307/2863019

Marx, Karl. 1844. *Zur Kritik der Hegelschen Rechtsphilosophie*. Reprinted in Karl Marx, *Frühe Schriften I*, edited by H.-J. Lieber and P. Furth. Darmstadt: Wissenschaftliche Buchgesellschaft, 1981, 488–505.

Menasce, Pierre Jean de. 1945. *Une apologétique mazdéenne du IXe siècle, Škand-Gumānī Vičār, la solution décisive des doutes*. Fribourg en Suisse: Librairie de l'Université.

Miller, Barbara Stoler. 1977. *Jayadeva's Gītagovinda: Love Song of the Dark Lord*. Edited and translated. New York: Columbia University Press.

Nesselrath, Heinz-Günther. 2009. "Die Griechen und ihre Götter." In *Götterbilder Gottesbilder Weltbilder: Polytheismus und Monotheismus in der Welt der Antike II: Griechenland und Rom, Judentum, Christentum und Islam*, edited by Reinhard Gregor Kratz and Hermann Spieckermann, 3rd edition Tübingen: Mohr Siebeck, 21–44. Original edition, 2006.

Ornan, Tallay. 2009. "In the Likeness of Man: Reflections on the Anthropocentric Perceptions of the Divine in Mesopotamian Art." In *What is a God? Anthropomorphic and Non-Anthropomorphic Aspects of Deity in Ancient Mesopotamia*, edited by Barbara Nevling Porter. Winona Lake, IN: Eisenbrauns, 93–151.

Otto, Rudolf. 1971. *Das Heilige: Über das Irrationale in der Idee des Göttlichen und sein Verhältnis zum Rationalen*, Munich: Beck. Original edition, 1917.

Pettazzoni, Raffaele. 1946. *Saggi di storia delle religioni e di mitologia*. Rome: Edizioni Italiane = Naples: Loffredo, edited by Giovanni Casadio, 2013.

Pettazzoni, Raffaele. 1955. *L'onniscienza di Dio*. Turin: Einaudi.

Pettazzoni, Raffaele. 1957. *L'essere supremo nelle religioni primitive*. Turin: Einaudi.

Pongratz-Leisten, Beate, ed. 2011. *Reconsidering the Concept of Revolutionary Monotheism*. Winona Lake, IN: Eisenbrauns.

Porter, Barbara Nevling, ed. 2000. *One God or Many? Concepts of Divinity in the Ancient World*. Casco Bay Assyriological Institute.

Porter, Barbara Nevling. 2009a. "Blessings from a Crown, Offerings to a Drum: Were there Non-Anthropomorphic Deities in Ancient Mesopotamia?" In *What is a God? Anthropomorphic and Non-Anthropomorphic Aspects of Deity in Ancient Mesopotamia*, edited by Barbara Nevling Porter. Winona Lake, IN: Eisenbrauns, 153–194.

Porter, Barbara Nevling, ed. 2009b. *What is a God? Anthropomorphic and Non-Anthropomorphic Aspects of Deity in Ancient Mesopotamia*. Winona Lake, IN: Eisenbrauns.

Puett, Michael. 2002. *To Become a God: Cosmology, Sacrifice, and Self-Divinization in Early China*. Cambridge, MA: Harvard University Asia Center.

Pyysiäinen, Ilkka. 2001. *How Religion works: Towards a New Cognitive Science of Religion*. Leiden: Brill.

Rivera Dorado, Miguel. 2006. *El pensamiento religioso de los antiguos mayas*. Madrid: Editorial Trotta.

Rochberg, Francesca. 2009. "'The Stars their Likenesses': Perspectives on the Relation between Celestial Bodies and Gods in Ancient Mesopotamia." In *What is a God? Anthropomorphic and Non-Anthropomorphic Aspects of Deity in Ancient Mesopotamia*, edited by Barbara Nevling Porter. Winona Lake, IN: Eisenbrauns, 41–91.

Rochberg, Francesca. 2011. "The Heavens and the Gods in Ancient Mesopotamia: The View from a Polytheistic Cosmology." In *Reconsidering the Concept of Revolutionary Monotheism*, edited by Beate Pongratz-Leisten. Winona Lake, IN: Eisenbrauns, 117–136.

Roes, Frans and Michel Raymond. 2003. "Belief in Moralizing Gods." *Evolution and Human Behavior* 24(2): 126–135. doi:10.1016/S1090-5138(02)00134-4

Roth, Harold. 1999. *Original Tao: Inward Training (nei-yeh) and the Foundations of Taoist Mysticism*. New York: Columbia University Press.

Roux, Jean-Paul. 1956. "Tängri. Essai sur le ciel-dieux des peoples altaïques." *Revue de l'histoire des religions* 149(1): 49–82. doi:10.3406/rhr.1956.7087

Schaeder, Hans Heinrich. 1925. "Die islamische Lehre vom Vollkommenen Menschen, ihre Herkunft und ihre dichterische Gestaltung." *Zeitschrift der Deutschen Morgenländischen Gesellschaft* 79: 192–268.

Schimmel, Annemarie. 1981. *Und Muhammad ist Sein Prophet: Die Verehrung des Propheten in der islamischen Frömmigkeit*. Munich: Eugen Diederichs.

Sergent, Bernard. 1995. *Les Indo-Européens: Histoire, langues, mythes*. Paris: Payot.

Shahar, Meir and Robert P. Weller, eds. 1996. *Unruly Gods: Divinity and Society in China*. Honolulu: University of Hawai'i Press.

Siegel, Lee. 1978. *Sacred and Profane Dimensions of Love in Indian Traditions as Exemplified in the* Gītagovinda *of Jayadeva*. Delhi: Oxford University Press.

Sperber, Dan, ed. 2000. *Metarepresentations: A Multidisciplinary Perspective*. Oxford and New York: Oxford University Press.

Spiro, Melford. 1966. "Religion: Problems of Definition and Explanation." In *Anthropological Approaches to the Study of Religion*, edited by Michael Banton. London: Tavistock,

85–126 = Melford E. Spiro. 1987. *Culture and Human Nature.* Chicago, IL: University of Chicago Press, 187–222.

Stausberg, Michael. 2002a. *Die Religion Zarathushtras: Geschichte—Gegenwart—Rituale I.* Stuttgart, Berlin, and Köln: Kohlhammer.

Stausberg, Michael. 2002b. "Monotheismus, Polytheismus und Dualismus im Alten Iran." In *Polytheismus und Monotheismus in den Religionen des Vorderen Orients*, edited by Manfred Krebernik and Jürgen van Oorschot. Münster: Ugarit, 91–111.

Stietencron, Heinrich von, ed. 1973. *Der Name Gottes.* Düsseldorf: Patmos.

Stoyanov, Yuri. 2000. *The Other God: Dualist Religions from Antiquity to the Cathar Heresy.* New Haven, CT: Yale University Press.

Suddendorf, Thomas. 2006. "Foresight and Evolution of the Human Mind." *Science* 312(5776): 1006–1007. doi: 10.1126/science.1129217

Suddendorf, Thomas, Donna Rose Addis, and Michael C. Corballis. 2009. "Mental Time Traveling and the Shaping of the Human Mind." *Philosophical Transactions of the Royal Society B* 364(1521): 1317–1324. doi:10.1098/rstb.2008.0301

Terrace, Herbert and Janet Metcalfe, eds. 2005. *The Missing Link in Cognition: Origins of Self-Reflective Consciousness.* Oxford and New York: Oxford University Press.

Topitsch, Ernst. 1958. *Vom Ursprung und Ende der Metaphysik: Eine Studie zur Weltanschauungskritik.* Vienna: Springer.

Topitsch, Ernst. 1973. *Gottwerdung und Revolution: Beiträge zur Weltanschauungsanalyse und Ideologiekritik.* Pullach bei München: Verlag Dokumentation.

Trexler, Richard. 1972. "Florentine Religious Experience: The Sacred Image." *Studies in the Renaissance* 19: 7–41. doi: 10.2307/2857086.

Trexler, Richard. 1973. "Ritual Behavior in Renaissance Florence: The Setting." *Medievalia et humanistica* 4: 125–144.

Tylor, Edward. 1871. *Primitive Culture: Researches into the Development of Mythology, Philosophy, Religion, Art, and Custom*, 2 vols. London: John Murray.

Vanstiphout, Herman. 2009. "Die Geschöpfe des Prometheus, or How and Why Did the Sumerians Create their Gods?" In *What is a God? Anthropomorphic and Non-Anthropomorphic Aspects of Deity in Ancient Mesopotamia*, edited by Barbara Nevling Porter. Winona Lake, IN: Eisenbrauns, 15–40.

Versnel, H. S. 2011 *Coping with the Gods: Wayward Readings in Greek Theology.* Leiden: Brill.

Voland, Eckart. 2007. "Wir erkennen uns als den anderen ähnlich: Die biologische Evolution der Freiheitsintuition." *Deutsche Zeitschrift für Philosophie* 55: 739–749.

von Soden, Wolfram. 1969. "'Als die Götter (auch noch) Mensch waren.' Einige Grundgedanken des altbabylonischen Atramhasīs-Mythos." *Orientalia* 38: 415–432 = W. von Soden 1989, 147–164.

von Soden, Wolfram. 1973. "Der Mensch bescheidet sich nicht: Überlegungen zu Schöpfungserzählungen in Babylonien und Israel." In *Symbolicae Biblicae et Mesopotamicae Francisco Mario Teodoro de Liagre Böhl dedicatae*, edited by M. A. Beek, A. A. Kampman, C. Nijland, and J. Ryckmans. Leiden: Brill, 349–358 = W. von Soden. 1985. *Bibel und Alter Orient. Altorientalische Beiträge zum Alten Testament.* Berlin and New York: de Gruyter, 165–173.

von Soden, Wolfram. 1979. "Konflikte und ihre Bewältigung in babylonischen Schöpfungs— und Fluterzählungen, mit einer Teilübersetzung des Atramhasīs-Mythos." *Mitteilungen der Deutschen Orient-Gesellschaft* 111: 1–33 = W. von Soden 1989, 229–261.

von Soden, Wolfram. 1989. *Aus Sprache, Geschichte und Religion Babyloniens. Gesammelte Aufsätze*. Neapel: Istituto Universitario Orientale, Dipartimento di Studi Asiatici.

Wagenvoort, Hendrik. 1980. *Pietas: Selected Studies in Roman Religion*. Leiden: Brill.

Waldschmidt, Ernst. 1961. "Der Buddha preist die Verehrungswürdigkeit seiner Reliquien." *Nachrichten der Akademie der Wissenschaften, Philologisch-historische Klasse* 11. Göttingen: Vandenhoeck & Ruprecht, 75–385 = Ernst Waldschmidt, *Von Ceylon bis Turfan. Schriften zur Geschichte, Literatur, Religion und Kunst des indischen Kulturraumes*. Göttingen: Vandenhoeck & Ruprecht, 1967, 417–427.

West, M. L. 2007. *Indo-European Poetry and Myth*. Oxford and New York: Oxford University Press.

Widengren, Geo. 1950. *The Ascension of the Apostle and the Heavenly Book (King and Saviour III)*. Uppsala and Leipzig: A. B. Lundequistska Bokhandeln/Otto Harrassowitz.

Widengren, Geo. 1955. *Muḥammad, the Apostle of God, and his Ascension (King and Saviour V)*. Uppsala and Wiesbaden: A. B. Lundequistska Bokhandeln/Otto Harrassowitz.

Wilhelm, Gernot. 2002. "'Gleichsetzungstheologie', 'Synkretismus' und 'Gottesspaltungen' im Polytheismus Altanatoliens." In *Polytheismus und Monotheismus in den Religionen des Vorderen Orients*, edited by Manfred Krebernik and Jürgen van Oorschot. Münster: Ugarit, 53–70.

Yu, Jimmy. 2012. *Sanctity and Self-Inflicted Violence in Chinese Religions, 1500–1700*. Oxford and New York: Oxford University Press.

FURTHER READING

Atran 2002 [*Based on ethnographic research and using an anthropological/evolutionary perspective, this is one of the most insightful treatments of the phenomenon of religion available.*]

Brelich 2007 [*Originally delivered in 1957–1958, the lectures propose a comprehensive view of the phenomenon of polytheism, backed by references to a number of religious traditions.*]

Burkert 1996 [*Combines vast historical knowledge of Near Eastern and Mediterranean religions and a theoretical approach informed by evolutionary theory.*]

Hiltebeitel 1989 [*Analogous to Shahar and Weller's edited volume on unruly Chinese gods (1996), this one also deals with gods who violate traditional morality and with the frequently violent events that lead to deification.*]

Krebernik/van Oorschot 2002 [*An exploration of the polytheistic milieu out of which monotheistic tendencies emerged; at the same time, an attempt to rethink the simple antithesis between monotheism and polytheism.*]

Pongratz-Leisten 2011 [*A valuable, if somewhat hypercritical, examination of the thesis that monotheism arose as a reaction to polytheism. Unlike most work by historians, it includes some overdue references to research in cognition.*]

Porter 2000 [*An exploration of divine unity vs. divine multiplicity in the ancient Near East and Greece.*]

Porter 2009b [*A study of the pervasiveness of anthropomorphic representations of the divine in ancient Mesopotamia, including the presence of human features in non-anthropomorphic representations; attention is also paid to non-anthropomorphic representations.*]

Shahar/Weller 1996 [*Moves beyond the understanding of Chinese gods as bureaucrats and of the pantheon as a reflection of the social order, showing that some gods deviated from social norms, were rebellious and represented marginal groups.*]

CHAPTER 38

INITIATIONS AND TRANSITIONS

HENRIK BOGDAN

CHAPTER SUMMARY

- Initiations and transitions can be found in all known cultures, both historically and geographically.
- When ritualized, initiations and transitions can be analyzed as rites of passage.
- The ritualized use of secrecy is frequently encountered in this type of ritual, especially in those that are connected to closed or secret societies, but it is not so much the content as the function of secrecy which is of importance.
- The experience of undergoing a ritual of initiation is often seen as non-communicable, and that is one of the reasons why initiation is often veiled in secrecy.

PRELIMINARY REMARKS AND OVERVIEW

In his classical work, *Lectures on the Religion of Semites*, William Robertson Smith contemptuously remarked that "there is an extensive class of rites prevalent among savage and barbarous peoples in which blood-shedding forms part of an initiatory ceremony, by which youths, at or after the age of puberty, are admitted to the status of man, and to a full share in the social privileges and sacra of the community" (1889, 304). Smith went on to state, "Among wholly barbarous races these initiation ceremonies have a very great importance, and are often extremely repulsive in character" (1889, 310). Smith was discussing a very well-known type of ritual, puberty rites, which mark the transition from child to adult, and which (minus the blood-shedding) can be found in all known societies even to this day, contrary to Smith's assertion that it is in particular 'barbarous' people that practice such rituals.

Puberty rites are often seen by scholars as a member of a larger family of rites, rites of transition, or rites of passage. More often than not, rites of transition are also understood as rites of initiation, that is, as ritualized acts that mark entry into a new social setting (such as adolescence in the case of puberty rites). As will be discussed in this chapter, scholars—ever since the days of early pioneering works such as Heinrich Schurtz's *Altersklassen und Männerbünde* (1902) and Hutton Webster's *Primitive Secret Societies* (1908)—have tended to divide initiations into two groups: puberty rites and initiations into secret societies.

The range of phenomena covered by the terms 'initiations' and 'transitions' is vast, and it stretches both across cultures and throughout historical periods: confirmation in Christian churches and denominations; Bar and Mat Mitzvah in Judaism; first menstruation, such as the South Indian *Sevapuneru* or *Turmeric* ceremonies; weddings; Sweet Sixteen in the United States; Walkabout in Australia; the rituals connected to the Islamic *hajj*; initiation into secret societies, such as tantric groups in Hinduism and Buddhism, initiatic societies such as Freemasonry, and new religious movements such as the modern Witchcraft movement (as created by Gerald Gardner in the 1950s); just to mention a few.

The topic of this chapter, initiations and transitions, can thus be seen as two interlinked types of ritualized behavior, which share the basic common object of marking an event that leads to a new social and psychological state. This chapter will begin with a discussion of the ritual of the first degree of Freemasonry, that of Entered Apprentice, as a case study of a widely practiced rite of initiation. The academic study of Freemasonry has in recent years been established as a multidisciplinary field of research (see Bogdan/Snoek 2014), and, given the central role that rituals of initiation have within Freemasonry, this particular case study will be used as an example of how rituals of initiation can be approached from an analytical perspective. The case study will be followed by a brief discussion of the most significant classical approaches to the study of rites of initiation and transition. In the following sections, some key issues in the more recent study of initiations and transitions will be discussed.

Before we can begin with our case study, however, a word or two needs to be said about the delimitations of the chapter. Rites of initiation and transition can, of course, be studied from the broader perspectives of ritual studies, but I have deliberately refrained from more general approaches to the study of rituals (see Michaels/Sax, "Performance," this volume) and limited myself to issues that deal with initiations and transitions specifically.

THE ENTERED APPRENTICE RITUAL
OF FREEMASONRY: A CASE STUDY

Freemasonry is the oldest and largest initiatory society in the West not dependent on a religious institution. Although officially founded in London in 1717 by four existing lodges, Freemasonry can be identified at least from 1600, when parts of the medieval stonemasonry guilds had transformed into non-operative lodges in both Scotland and England (Snoek/Bogdan 2014). The transition from operative to non-operative or gentleman masonry appears to have developed independently in Scotland and England, but similar developments can also be seen in other parts of Europe. The most conspicuous—and for our present purposes relevant—characteristic of Freemasonry is its use of rituals of initiation. These rituals can be divided into two main groups, the so-called three Craft degrees (Entered Apprentice, Fellow Craft, and Master Mason), which date from the 1720s and remain the basic rituals to this day, and the so-called high or additional degrees which differ from system to system. Masonic rituals can further be divided into three classes from an analytical perspective: initiation, emblematic, and investiture rituals (Snoek 1987). According to Jan A. M. Snoek, the clearest examples of masonic initiation rituals are the degrees of Entered Apprentice, Master Mason, and the French Rose Croix, understood by Snoek as rituals of passage *sensu* van Gennep (see section "Rites of passage"), "which express a confrontation, or even identification, with a divinity" (Snoek 2014, 321).

The Ritual

The ritual of the first degree of Freemasonry, that of Entered Apprentice, begins with an opening ceremony during which the candidate is not present.[1] Instead, the candidate is placed alone in a separate room, the Dark Room, which by masons is often interpreted as the realm of death, an interpretation which is further strengthened by 'emblems of life and death' placed upon the desk in front of the candidate, such as a burning candle, salt, bread, water, and a skull. The candidate is prepared by the Terrible Brother, who represents death, for the initiation by having parts of his clothes removed (usually the left knee and left breast is bared), and all metals or valuables are removed. The object of the opening ceremony, which takes place when the candidate is being prepared is on the one hand to make sure that all present persons are at least Entered Apprentices and that the room is guarded against outsiders, and on the other hand to 'place' the ritual

---

[1] The description of the Entered Apprentice ritual is based on Snoek 2014, although I have deliberately left out many details in the ritual that have changed over time. For further discussions on the development of masonic rituals of initiation, see Bogdan 2007; Carr 1971; Knoop/Jones/Hamer 1945; 1963. For a standard masonic and widely used version of the ritual, see Emulation Lodge 1976.

in its mythological setting, and thereby to transform the room into a sacred space (see Chidester, "Space," this volume).

The candidate is led, blindfolded, to the entrance of the lodge room to which he is admitted after being interrogated by the main officer, the Master of the Chair, who represents the Great Architect of the Universe, i.e. God. The candidate then circumambulates the lodge room three times, an element of the ritual which during the eighteenth century was often performed in the manner of an ordeal, during which the candidate was deliberately disoriented and frightened. The circumambulation leads the candidate around the so-called Tracing Board, a large image placed on the floor in the center of the lodge room on which the *sacra*, or central symbols of the degree are depicted (in Freemasonry the central symbols are either taken from medieval stone masonry, such as the square and the compass, the white apron, and gloves, or from the Bible, such as the Temple of Solomon with its two pillars Jachin and Boaz). The climax of the ritual occurs when the candidate kneels in front of an altar, taking an oath never to divulge the secrets that have been imparted to him. Significantly, it is by taking the oath that the candidate is made into an Entered Apprentice. He is then led back to the tracing board where the blindfold is removed and he is exposed to the so-called Great Lights of Freemasonry: i.e. the Bible, square, and compasses. The candidate has now transitioned from a profane ('outside the temple') to an initiated state of being. Or to put it in the words of Snoek, "Just as his being blindfolded symbolized his death as a 'profane,' this seeing of the 'Great Lights' of Freemasonry implies the rebirth of the candidate as a Freemason. Essentially, he here symbolically sees God from face to face, a confrontation with the divinity, which forms the culmination rite of the initiation" (Snoek 2014, 324). ("Culmination rite" refers to the part of the ritual of initiation that can be seen as the culmination or climax, at which the initiate is considered to have been transformed from one state of being to another.)

The remainder of the ritual emphasizes the incorporation of the candidate into the new state, by dressing him in the regalia of the degree (apron and gloves), and by instructing him in the esoteric knowledge, consisting of the traditional secrets and an explanation of the tracing board. The lodge is then ritually closed (i.e. the ritual formally ends and the room is once again transformed into a profane space), and one of the Wardens exclaims: "Brethren, in the name of the Great Architect of the Universe, and by command of the Worshipful Master, I close the Lodge." Lastly, the newly made Entered Apprentice takes part in a ritual meal, which further integrates him into the new social group of which he is now a member.

The Components of a Masonic Ritual of Initiation

The ritual of Entered Apprentice not only marks the admittance of the candidate into the Order of Freemasonry, but it also contains the basic components of which the great majority of all later masonic rituals are composed, and, by extension, the rituals of all those organizations which are derived from or inspired by the masonic system of initiation. These components include (1) the *opening* of the lodge during which the candidate is not present, (2) *admission* into the lodge at which the candidate answers a number of questions, (3) *circumambulations* around the lodge, often symbolic of an ordeal, (4) *obligations* never to divulge the secrets of the degree (often a sign, grip or handclasp, and word), but also certain ethical rules which the candidate swears to observe, (5) formal *admission* into the degree, (6) *instruction* in the traditional secrets of the degree (signs, passwords, etc.), but also in the Order's particular teachings, (7) the giving of *visible tokens*, such as gloves or apron, sometimes also a new name, title, or motto, (8) *closing* of the lodge, during which the candidate is present (Bogdan 2007, 51).

RITES OF PASSAGE

Arnold van Gennep's (1873–1957) book *Les Rites de Passage* (1909), stands out as one of the few scholarly works in the field of religious studies that continues to be of relevance from a theoretical perspective, over a century after its first publication. In this work, van Gennep focused on various kinds of transitional rites that marked the passing from one state of being (or status) into another: so-called rites of passage. In addition to the ritualization of recurrent events such as the phases of the moon and the seasonal changes, van Gennep analyzed the ritualization of life-crises such as pregnancy, childbirth, and the reaching of puberty, marriage, and death.

Van Gennep argued that rites of passage have a common structural denominator: they mark the transition from an old state to a new one by a three-phased scheme. First, there is a *separation* from the old social position or state of being. This separation is often expressed by symbolic ritualistic acts such as removing the candidates from their parents in cases of puberty rites, or through the cutting of hair or removal of clothes. Second, there is the *marginal* (or threshold) state in which the candidate finds her- or himself between the old and the new states. This is usually considered to be the most significant phase of a rite of passage, in which the actual transition or transformation is believed to occur. Third, *aggregation* or incorporation into the new state, in which the candidate assumes the new identity and re-enters the society. These three phases are composed respectively of rites of separation, rites of transition, and rites of incorporation. Van Gennep's structural theory of rites of passage can be seen as the most influential theoretical approach to the study of transition and initiation, especially after the translation of *Les Rites de Passage* into English in 1960.

BETWIXT AND BETWEEN: LIMINALITY AND TRANSFORMATION

The most striking aspect of a rite of passage—and the one that has attracted the most scholarly attention—is the antinomian (*anti*—against, *nomos*—law) nature of many of the ritualized acts. To put it simply, during a rite of initiation the officers and the candidate(s) act and behave in ways that challenge or transgress the perceived norms of society, but which are accepted in the specific setting of the ritual. The antinomian aspects of these rites are symbolic, in the sense that their significance is contingent upon their position within the ritual context, yet at the same time they both challenge and confirm the norms outside of the specific ritual context (see section "Anti-structures"). For example, the marriage ritual in most cultures—which marks the transition from one state of being (single) to another state (married)—traditionally includes the use of special clothes that mark the extraordinary nature of the event. It would thus be seen as perfectly normal to wear an elaborate white wedding dress at one's wedding, but wearing a wedding dress while, say, going to work, would be seen as breaking the norms of accepted behavior. A more obvious example would be the practice of women flashing or baring their breasts at Mardi Gras at New Orleans in exchange for beads. This controversial tradition, which goes back to the 1970s, illustrates the apparent antinomian or liminal character of a specific ritual setting (in this case, a carnival). While the exposure of breasts or other private body parts is in the United States legally prohibited as 'indecent exposure,' this practice appears to be tolerated (even if not legally allowed) within the ritual setting of the Mardi Gras. Paradoxically, the antinomian nature of these rites is regulated by new sets of rules: again, to use the example of the marriage ritual, it would usually be seen as improper if another person than the one being married wore a wedding dress. In the case of the Entered Apprentice ritual discussed above, the candidate is not only blindfolded and dressed in a peculiar way (left knee and left breast exposed), but the whole ritual as such—with ordeals in the form of circumambulations, the swearing of oaths, the symbolic clothes worn by the officers, the ritualized language, etc.—has the effect of making the event into something that goes beyond the 'normal' state of being.

One of the scholars that paid special attention to the seemingly antinomian nature of rites of passage is the cultural anthropologist Victor Turner (1920–1983), who focused on the marginal (or *liminal* as he preferred to call it) phase of van Gennep's rites of passage. In the article "Betwixt and Between: The Liminal Period in Rites of Passage" (1964), and his influential book *The Ritual Process* (1995 [1969]) he analyzed initiation in the form of the puberty rites and the curative cults of the Ndembu of Northern Rhodesia (today the Ndembu are to be found in Angola, the Democratic Republic of Congo, and Zambia). Turner argued that it is during the liminal phase, when the candidate is 'betwixt and between' the old and the new states, that the most decisive part of the initiation takes place. It is during this phase that the candidate receives the 'gnosis,' or sacred knowledge, which is believed to transform the candidate's innermost being, to turn him or her into a new being.

As mentioned, liminality is connected to an abnormal state, which falls outside structured society. It is a state where 'normality' is turned upside-down. In the case of the Ndembu puberty rites which Turner studied, the candidates are usually acting in a passive or humble manner. They have to obey their instructors during the period of the ritual, and "accept arbitrary punishment without complaint," and they tend to "develop an intense comradeship and egalitarianism" apart from the ordinary societal bonds

(Turner 1995, 95). According to Turner, the candidate must separate from his or her old state of being so that the new knowledge that is being transmitted during the liminal period can change the *persona* of the candidate, and thereby to *replace* the candidate's former knowledge. Here, we see clear parallels to what is believed to occur during the Entered Apprentice ritual.

Anti-Structures

Liminality is not, however, exclusively connected with the second phase of a *rite de passage*. The term can also be applied to other phenomena which in one way or another either fall outside the societal structure or even form the basis of an 'anti-structure'. Turner enumerates such diverse phenomena as "subjugated autochthones, small nations, court jesters, holy mendicants, good Samaritans, millenarian movements, 'dharma bums', matrilaterality in patrilineal systems, patrilaterality in matrilineal systems, and monastic orders" (Turner 1995, 125).

The primary function of these liminal phenomena is to maintain and strengthen the social structure(s) by forming an anti-structure. The liminal persons or principles indirectly set the standards for the normal or structured society. That which is not liminal is normal, and therefore part of the structured sphere of society. A ritual of initiation or transition thus operates on different levels, as it were. First, there is the stated object of the ritual which works on an individual level, e.g. transforming the boy into a man in the case of a male puberty rite. This 'transformation' is believed to be caused primarily through an internalization of the *sacra* (esoteric teaching and symbols) encountered during the liminal phase of the ritual. Second, there is the collective level in which relatives and other members of the society treat the person that has gone through the initiation differently according to his or her new status. Third, on the societal level, the anti-structure that emerges during the liminal phase strengthens the norms and rules of society. It is frequently argued that when rites of passage lose their significance in a given society—as they arguably are doing in the West—it causes many people to question their identity ("When do I become an adult?"), yet we can also see that just as new traditions emerge (see Hammer, "Tradition and Innovation," this volume), new forms of rites of passage are constructed (cf. Grimes 2000; Mahdi/Christopher/Meade 1996).

CLASSIFICATIONS OF INITIATION

One of the major scholarly concerns has been to classify "initiation." The word itself, "initiate," derives from the Latin *initiare* and literary means "to begin or to originate" and the two most frequent usages of the word are to admit new members into a society or club and to teach fundamentals of something to someone. This literal approach might appear clear enough, but when confronted with the wide range of ritualized practices that in one way or another mark the admittance into a new social setting, the usefulness of the term becomes questionable. Instead, as Fritz Graf has argued in connection with ancient Greek religion, initiation as an explanatory paradigm needs to be specific rather than general, in order to be useful (2003). The preferred way among scholars to understand the specificity of initiation has been to classify initiation into different categories.

As mentioned at the outset of this chapter, early pioneers such as Heinrich Schurtz and Hutton Webster classified initiations into puberty rites and initiations into secret societies. Although these two basic categories remain the most used even to this day, further divisions soon appeared. James Frazer (1854–1941)—who in his *Golden Bough* claimed that initiation is the central mystery of 'primitive society'—thought that religious practices such as initiation rites contained magical elements that had survived from the, so-called, primitive magical phase of human evolution. To Frazer, initiation should be divided into three groups: initiation into adult status of boys and girls, initiation into secret societies or cults, and induction into ancient cults such as the Eleusinian mysteries.

Van Gennep shared Frazer's division of initiations into three groups, but he further divided Frazer's third group into a several of subgroups: ordination of a priest or magician; enthroning of a king; and consecration of monks, nuns, and sacred prostitutes. In addition to these groups and subgroups, van Gennep also discussed admission into six different social groups, namely totem groups; fraternities; religious brotherhoods; classes, castes, and professions; Christianity, Islam and the ancient mysteries; and passage from one religion to another. Obviously, admission to the social groups discussed by van Gennep raises a number of problems, such as the apparent omission of Judaism, Islam, and Buddhism, etc., though, in defense of van Gennep, one should perhaps point out that the discussion is more reflective of his own research interests than an attempt to elaborate a complete classification.

The Impact of Mircea Eliade

The most influential (in terms of its impact on the research of other scholars) classification of initiation is the one proposed by Mircea Eliade in his work *Rites and Symbols of Initiation* (1958) and further promoted in the *Encyclopaedia of Religion* (1987). According to Eliade, initiations can be divided into three different categories. The first category consists of rites of initiation that are connected to the passing from childhood to adolescence. The second category of initiations consists of admissions into secret or closed societies. These initiations are usually made on a voluntary basis, as opposed to the initiations of the first category that almost exclusively are an integral part of a society which leaves little room for personal objections. Usually the candidates cannot apply for membership in a secret society, but are instead invited to join by the society itself. There are various ways of determining whether a person is qualified to join a secret society. For instance, the right to become a member of a Dancing Society, a secret society in some North American indigenous traditions, is often hereditary (Eliade 1994, 69). The third and final group of initiations is that of the heroic and shamanic initiations. The shamanic initiation is, according to Eliade, connected to an ecstatic state that must be achieved and acknowledged by other shamans in order for the candidate to be recognized as a shaman (Eliade 1994, 84).

SECRECY AND INITIATION

The ritualized use of secrecy is an intrinsic part of many forms of rituals of initiation. For example, the obligation never to divulge the secrets of the particular degree in question is one of the components of a masonic ritual of initiation. One of the earliest manuscripts of a masonic initiation, *The Chetwode Crawley Ms.* (*c.*1700), states that the first point of a person who has received the "Mason Word," is to "conceal" the word, under "no less pain than the Cutting of the throat." Consequently, many scholars have focused on the function of secrecy in so-called secret societies. Georg Simmel is often invoked as a pioneer of the notion of the 'empty secret': the sociological form and function of secrecy are independent of its content, and can operate even in the absence of actual secrets (Simmel 1906). Similarly, based on the study of American Freemasonry, Hugh B. Urban (2001) argues that secrecy and the masonic hierarchical initiations were not only means to acquiring status, but more importantly that the layers of secrecy also served to re-code and legitimate that status. In this context it is helpful to view the use of secrecy in Freemasonry as 'symbolic capital' along the lines of Pierre Bourdieu: i.e. the resources accessible to an individual on the basis of honor, status, or recognition, that serve as value within a specific cultural setting (Bourdieu 1984; see also von Stuckrad 2010).

To Urban, secrecy is a discourse that can be used to support or undermine a given social or political arrangement, and it is thus ultimately a strategy connected to power and status. Even though the content of masonic secrets may differ from those of other secret societies or groups, such as Sufi orders, Jewish kabbalah, and the hierarchy of elders among the Australian Aborigines, the function remains the same. Or to use Urban's own words: "Now, the specific *content* of the secrecy in all these various esoteric traditions will no doubt be radically different and determined by their particular historical, political, and social contexts. However . . . *the forms and strategies* through which secrecy operates . . . may well turn out to be strikingly similar across cultures and throughout historical periods' (Urban 2001, 22, emphasis in original). The specific function of secrecy from a sociological perspective, then, can be described as a means to legitimacy and authority, the latter of which can be used to uphold or challenge the norms and values of the surrounding society.

The use of secrecy by initiatic societies is closely connected to their self-image, and secrecy can thus be understood as a significant marker of identity, firmly linked to the construction of tradition, legitimacy, and authority. The masonic tradition, for instance, and its rituals of initiation are often interpreted and presented as a 'secret tradition,' and masons often see themselves as the custodians and transmitters of this secret tradition.

In a certain sense it is the secrecy itself that constitutes the message of secret societies, rather than the content of the secret, as pointed out by Urban. The idea that the veil
constitutes the message is significant for the understanding of masonic rituals of initiation since it explains how the rituals are often interpreted from an emic perspective. It
is often claimed that the secrets of Freemasonry and similar orders are inexpressible,
despite the fact that the rituals themselves have been revealed to the public. In other
words, the purpose of the secrecy is not so much a matter of keeping the rituals secret as
to keep that which is inexpressible secret. As argued by scholars such as Snoek, the secret
of a Western esoteric ritual of initiation is, simply put, the experience of undergoing
the ritual, an experience which is non-communicable.[2] The experience of undergoing
a ritual of initiation is similar to that of a mystical experience, and one characteristic of
mystical experience is the difficulty in expressing and describing it verbally. Or to put it
in the words of Snoek:

> The secret concerned, however, is nothing unethical, but just the experience of going
> through the ritual of the first degree, which turns one into an Entered Apprentice
> Freemason. Like any other experience, this cannot be communicated to someone
> else in any other way than letting that person go through it as well, which will turn
> him automatically into a Freemason too. So, this is the kind of secret which cannot be
> divulged. (Snoek 2010, 39)

What we are dealing with here, then, is a particular discourse on the experience of
undergoing a masonic ritual of initiation: it is claimed that only those masons that have
gone through the ritual share the 'same' experience, and that this experience is 'impossible' to share with those that have not gone through the same ritual.

EXPERIENCE AND INITIATION

The non-communication of the experiential aspect of the initiation can, furthermore,
be seen as connected to Western esotericism as understood by scholars such as Wouter
J. Hanegraaff and Kocku von Stuckrad, i.e. as discourses on claims to absolute knowledge, or *gnosis*. According to Hanegraaff, Western esotericism is characterized by an
emphasis on *gnosis*, rather than on rationality or the reliance on religious authority, and
this *gnosis* should be understood as a revelatory experience that leads to an encounter
with one's true self as well as with the divine aspect of existence (Hanegraaff 2004, 510).
The various degrees in a given esoteric initiatory system can thus be interpreted as an

---

[2] This should be compared with Antoine Faivre's statement: "Esoteric transmission cannot, so it
seems, unveil secrets. Rather, it is the noncommunication of what is not transmissible that constitutes
the secret" (Faivre 1999, 167). The reader is referred to Faivre's article in question for a full discussion of
concealment and secrecy in Western esotericism.

internalization of the esoteric form of thought in the sense that the degrees ritually correspond to the stages in a transmutative process leading to the realization of *gnosis*—the non-communicable experience of the self and union with the godhead.

Finally, a word or two needs to be said about emic understandings of initiation as experience. While it remains a contested issue to access religious experiences (see Martin, "Experience," this volume), there is a large body of literature by practitioners that claims that initiation is an inner process, an experience, which has to all intents and purposes been ignored by scholars focusing on initiations and transitions. These experiences are, furthermore, not arbitrary, but can be understood as stipulated by tradition-specific discourses. Two examples will suffice. First, we have *diksa* or initiation in the tantric tradition. Historically, *diksa* can be divided into two groups. On the one hand there is the formal induction into a tantric secret school or sect and, on the other, the inner spiritual initiation which is linked to secret spiritual practices restricted to the members of a tantric sect. The initiatic experience is expressed as the raising of the *kundalini* serpent, whereby the *cakras* are activated. This, in its turn, bestows *siddhis* or allegedly supernatural powers on the adept (Silburn 1988). Second, one frequently encounters in the literature of contemporary occultism the notion of initiation as an inner process, often patterned upon the kabbalistic Tree of Life. More often than not, this notion is based on the teachings of the British occultist order The Hermetic Order of the Golden Dawn, and perhaps to a larger extent, on the writings of Aleister Crowley (1875–1947). In terms of the latter, it is in particular the experiences known as the "Knowledge and Conversation of the Holy Guardian Angel," and the "Crossing of the Abyss" that stand out (these are usually interpreted as getting in contact with one's higher self, and as the transcending of the illusion of duality).[3] The significant aspect about these emic understandings of initiation is the emphasis on the inner or experiential dimension of initiation. With the notable exception of literature on shamanism, scholarly literature on initiations has tended to focus on initiation in its outer, ritualistic form or on the sociological implications of initiation, whereas emic accounts of the supposedly inner processes still remain an understudied field of research.

Concluding Remarks

Initiations and transitions are central topics in the study of religion, and many of the most influential scholars in the field have devoted themselves to the phenomena. As far as we know, in every culture and every religion throughout history, men and women have ritualized the transitions that we, as human beings, go through from birth, via puberty and marriage, to death. Similarly, the ritualization of initiation (e.g. into secret societies or specific religious offices) appears to be universal. It is striking that the structure of

---

[3] For a discussion on Crowley and experiential or initiatic knowledge, see Owen 2012; Pasi 2012.

the ritualization of transitions, understood as rites of passage *sensu* van Gennep, parallels that of the ritualization of initiation into closed societies, such as the Order of Freemasons discussed in this chapter. Initiation and transition, in their ritualized forms, are thus often studied as two interlinked phenomena, if not as two aspects of one and the same phenomenon. Moreover, the fact that initiations and transitions are often connected to the use of secrecy, is telling as to the importance attributed to this type of ritualized behavior from a social perspective. However, the use of secrecy poses challenges to the scholar when attempting to study this type of ritual in that the sources are often deliberately obscure and non-revealing for non-initiates. This is captured in a wonderful way in the perhaps most well-known and influential of all literary accounts of an initiation, Apuleius's *Metamorphoses*, or *The Golden Ass*, usually credited as the only ancient Roman novel to have survived. The climax of the story occurs at the moment when Lucius, as newly-made initiate, describes what his initiation into the mysteries of Isis and Osiris actually consisted of: "See, I have told you things which, though you have heard them, you still must know nothing about. I will therefore relate only as much as may, without committing a sin, be imparted to the understanding of the uninitiate' (Reid 1987, 170).

GLOSSARY

Freemasonry an initiatory society officially founded in London in 1717, although its roots go back to the Medieval Stone Masons' Guilds in England and Scotland. Although there exist today a wide range of masonic organizations, in its basic form Freemasonry consists of the three so-called Craft degrees: Entered Apprentice, Fellow Craft, and Master Mason.

Gnosis in the field of Western esotericism, gnosis refers to claims to absolute or experiential knowledge that often is interpreted as salvific or transformative.

Puberty rites performative acts (rituals) that mark the transition from the social state of being of a boy or a girl, to that of a man or a woman.

Secret societies organizations that are characterized by a ritualistic use of secrecy, often in connection with the performance of rituals of initiation, i.e. rituals that mark the admittance of a candidate, and the various degrees or levels, of the organization in question.

REFERENCES

Bogdan, Henrik. 2007. *Western Esotericism and Rituals of Initiation*. Albany: State University of New York Press.

Bogdan, Henrik and Jan A. M. Snoek, eds. 2014. *Handbook of Freemasonry*. Leiden: Brill.

Bourdieu, Pierre. 1984. *Distinction: A Social Critique of the Judgement of Taste*. Cambridge, MA: Harvard University Press.

Carr, Harry. 1971. *The Early French Exposures*. London: The Quatuor Coronati Lodge No. 2076.

Dodd, David B. and Christopher A. Faraone, eds. 2003. *Initiation in Ancient Greek Rituals and Narratives: New Critical Perspectives*. London: Routledge.

Eliade, Mircea. 1994. *Rites and Symbols of Initiation: The Mysteries of Birth and Rebirth*. Dallas: Spring Publications. Original edition, 1958.

Emulation Lodge of Improvement. 1976. *Emulation Ritual*, 5th edition. London: Lewis Masonic.

Faivre, Antoine. 1999. "The Notions of Concealment and Secrecy in Modern Esoteric Currents since the Renaissance." In *Rending the Veil: Concealment and Secrecy in the History of Religions*, edited by Elliot R. Wolfson. New York and London: Seven Bridges Press, 155–176.

Graf, Fritz. 2003. "Initiation: A Concept with a Troubled History." In *Initiation in Ancient Greek Rituals and Narratives: New Critical Perspectives*, edited by David B. Dodd and Christopher A. Faraone. London: Routledge, 3–24.

Grimes, Ronald L. 1995. *Marrying & Burying: Rites of Passage in a Man's Life*. Boulder, CO: Westview Press.

Grimes, Ronald L. 2000. *Deeply into the Bone: Re-Inventing Rites of Passage*. Berkeley: University of California Press.

Hanegraaff, Wouter J. 2004. "The Study of Western Esotericism: *New Approaches to Christian and Secular Culture*", in *New Approaches to the Study of Religion*, Vol. 1: *Regional, Critical, and Historical Approaches*, edited by Peter Antes, Armin W. Geertz and Randi R. Warne. Berlin and New York: Walter de Gruyter, 489–519.

Knoop, Douglas, G. P. Jones, and Douglas Hamer. 1945. *Early Masonic Pamphlets*. Manchester: Manchester University Press.

Knoop, Douglas, G. P. Jones, and Douglas Hamer. 1963. *The Early Masonic Catechisms*. Manchester: Manchester University Press.

Mahdi, Louise Carus, Nancy Geyer Christopher, and Michael Meade, eds. 1996. *Crossroads: The Quest for Contemporary Rites of Passage*. Chicago, IL: Open Court.

Owen, Alex. 2012. "The Sorcerer and His Apprentice: Aleister Crowley and the Magical Exploration of Edwardian Subjectivity." In *Aleister Crowley and Western Esotericism*, edited by Henrik Bogdan and Martin P. Starr. New York: Oxford University Press, 15–52.

Pasi, Marco. 2012. "Varieties of Magical Experience: Aleister Crowley's Views on Occult Practice." In *Aleister Crowley and Western Esotericism*, edited by Henrik Bogdan and Martin P. Starr. New York: Oxford University Press, 53–88.

Reid, Patrick V., ed. 1987. *Readings in Western Religious Thought: The Ancient World*. Mahwah, NJ: Paulist Press.

Schurtz, Heinrich. 1902. *Altersklassen und Männerbünde: Eine Darstellung der Grundformen der Gesellschaft*. Berlin: Georg Reimer.

Silburn, Lilian. 1988. *Kundalini: Energy of the Depths*. Albany: State University of New York Press.

Simmel, George. 1906. "The Sociology of Secrecy and of Secret Societies." *American Journal of Sociology* 11(4): 441–498.

Smith, William Robertson. 1889. *Lectures on the Religion of the Semites*. Edinburgh: A. & C. Black.

Snoek, Jan A. M. 2010. "The Allusive Method." In *Mots et signes de reconnaissance. Congrès maçonnique 28-11-2009-30 ans GLRB*, edited by Kris Thys. Brussels: Grande Loge Régulière de Belgique, 57–73.

Snoek, Jan A. M. 2014. "Masonic Rituals of Initiation." In *Handbook of Freemasonry*, edited by Henrik Bogdan and Jan A. M. Snoek. Leiden: Brill, 321–327.

Snoek, Jan A. M. and Henrik Bogdan. 2014. "The History of Freemasonry: An Overview." In *Handbook of Freemasonry*, edited by Henrik Bogdan and Jan A. M. Snoek. Leiden: Brill, 13–32.

Stuckrad, Kocku von. 2010. "Secrecy as Social Capital." In *Constructing Tradition: Means and Myths of Transmission in Western Esotericism*, edited by Andreas B. Kilcher. Leiden: Brill, 239–252.

Turner, Victor. 1964. "Betwixt and Between: The Liminal Period in *Rites of Passage*." In *Proceedings of the American Ethnological Society for 1964*. Seattle: University of Washington Press, 4–20.

Urban, Hugh B. 2001. "The Adornment of Silence: Secrecy and Symbolic Power in American Freemasonry." *Journal of Religion & Society* 3: 1–29.

Webster, Hutton. 1908. *Primitive Secret Societies: A Study in Early Politics and Religion*. New York: Macmillan.

FURTHER READING

Bremmer, Jan N. 2014. *Initiation into the Mysteries of the Ancient World*. Berlin: de Gruyter. [*An impressive and detailed discussion of the Ancient mysteries, such as the Eleusinian and Orphic-Bacchic mysteries.*]

Fontaine, Jean La. 1985. *Initiation: Ritual Drama and Secret Knowledge Across the World*. Harmondsworth: Penguin Books. [*A basic, comparative overview of rituals of initiation from various parts of the world.*]

Gennep, Arnold van. 1960. *The Rites of Passage*. Chicago, IL: University of Chicago Press. Original edition, 1909. [*Classical study of initiations and transitions in which the three phases of rites of passage was first presented.*]

Grimes 2000 [*In-depth analysis of a wide range of rites of passage.*]

Holm, Jean and John Bowker, eds. 1994. *Rites of Passage*. London: Pinter Publishers. [*Good overview of life-crisis rites (birth, initiation, marriage, and death) in the major world religions.*]

Snoek, Jan A. M. 1987. *Initiations: A Methodological Approach to the Application of Classification and Definition Theory in the Study of Rituals*. Pijnacker: Dutch Efficiency Bureau. [*An often-overlooked important theoretical study of rituals of initiation.*]

Turner, Victor. 1995. *The Ritual Process: Structure and Anti-Structure*. New York: Aldine de Gruyter. [*A classic study on the liminal phase of rites of passage.*]

CHAPTER 39

PRIESTS, PROPHETS, SORCERERS

MANFRED HUTTER

CHAPTER SUMMARY

- Most definitions of 'priests,' 'prophets,' or 'sorcerers' are rooted in biblical traditions and thus Eurocentric.
- Prophecy is not a universal phenomenon in the history of religions. Prophets have their best-attested 'specimen' in the Hebrew Bible, but prophecy is a phenomenon which originated in Ancient Syria. 'Prophets' attested in later periods or other areas of the history of religions are derived from the biblical and/or Qur'ānic tradition.
- Biblical and Qur'ānic tradition prophecy is characterized by the prophet as a bringer of a divine message (in written form); but from a more general perspective prophecy is—first of all—a mantic (divination) technique.
- As ritual and religious specialists and those able to communicate with superhumans/the 'divine,' 'priests' are the guardians and 'safe-keepers' of tradition, thus gaining—especially in premodern societies—high social prestige and an elite status. They tend to build a relatively closed social group, maintaining prestige and power, by means of a so-called 'Amtscharisma' (charisma of office).
- 'Sorcerery' and 'magic' are concepts developed by priestly hierarchies to marginalize other ritualists.
- Processes of democratization in modern societies and conflicting interests between religious and mundane knowledge are an aspect of criticizing priests, especially those who either technically or morally cannot fulfill the expectations of 'lay' persons in the society.

THE PROBLEM OF TERMINOLOGY:
PRIEST, PROPHET, AND SORCERER

From the perspective of common sense, it is not difficult to give an everyday explanation to the three terms in question: a priest is a person related to the cult; a prophet is a person bringing some divine knowledge (about future things) to people; and a sorcerer is somebody whose actions are 'outside' of religion and are potentially harmful. While such definitions may be widespread in European culture, they have two related weaknesses: (a) they are deeply rooted in the biblical-Christian tradition, and (b) they are Eurocentric. This makes it problematic to transfer such definitions to a global world of religion, and therefore it is necessary to look for a broader definition. As three types of religious specialists, the terms overlap in part because a priest can also exercise some prophetic functions, and the mantic competence of such prophets can also be shared by sorcerers. A sharp distinction between the three terms is inherited from the biblical background, which constructs exclusive differences not found in the history of religions more generally.

Prophets: Their Background in the History of Syria

Let us start with the 'prophet,' whose core functions are more limited than those of the 'priest' or the 'sorcerer.' The prototypes of 'prophets' are the biblical prophets and their Qur'ānic counterparts, despite differences in the theological interpretation of 'prophets' in Judaism, Christianity, Islam, and to some degree also in the Bahā'ī faith. In European tradition a prophet has often been taken as a person who can foresee the future. This interpretation is problematic, based in part on the Greek rendering, *prophētēs*, of the Hebrew word *nabi*,' and also on Christian theology which interpreted biblical prophets as those in the Hebrew Bible (the 'Old' Testament) who predicted the coming of the Messiah or (Jesus) Christ. But a closer look at the biblical tradition shows that (a) passages in the Hebrew Bible referring to the Messiah are limited, and the term 'prophets' in the Hebrew Bible—compared to other passages—refers even less to the Messiah, and that (b) the main function of the Biblical *nabi'* can be defined as the person who has been called by the deity to present a divine message on behalf of the god to humans (cf. e.g. Heiler 1979, 395–402; Sheppard/Herbrechtsmeier 2005). This interpretation also fits well to the Greek rendering *pro-phētēs*, who is—in public—a speaker in front of people or a speaker interpreting the divine will. So the concern of the prophet is not telling the future, but bringing knowledge about divine (or other) secrets. This makes the prophet a religious specialist comparable to other diviners engaged in mantic (cf. e.g. the Babylonian *bāru*) who interprets divine secrets by the means of extispicy (i.e. divination using animal entrails; Schneider 2011, 83–84; Durand 2008, 411–413; Cancik-Kirschbaum 2003, 46–47).

Prophets' relationship to literary texts also reflects biblical evidence and thus should not be generalized. In historical perspective, biblical prophets characterized by their written message are restricted to times of political crises in Ancient Israel: the time of the breakdown and capture of the Kingdom of Samaria/Israel by the Assyrians in 722 BCE; the devastation of Jerusalem and the deportation of a good number of inhabitants of the small kingdom of Judah by the Babylonians in 586 BCE; and the time of revival after the Babylonian exile in the last quarter of the sixth century BCE. Besides these prophets, there are 'non-literary' prophets mentioned in the Bible, among them famous ones like Samuel, Elijah, or Elisha but also prophetesses like Deborah (Judges 4) or Huldah (2 Kings 22:14ff.).

Setting aside scripturality as central to prophecy, 'biblical' prophets can be situated within the broader scope of prophecy in the Ancient Near East. Prophets and prophetesses are mentioned in many Old Babylonian letters from Mari on the Euphrates (in modern Syria) during the eighteenth century BCE (Henshaw 1994, 156–162; Durand 2008, 433–451; Schneider 2011, 85–88). Terms like *muḫḫûm* (fem. *muḫḫûtum*) "the ecstatic" or *āpilum* (fem. *āpiltum*) "the one who gives an answer" indicate their function: these prophets were—like some of their biblical counterparts—experts in the field of mantic, revealing hidden (divine) things to humans, either in an ecstatic state through vision or by oracular techniques. The phenomenon of prophets can also be found in Middle Syria along the Euphrates during the thirteenth century BCE, among Aramaeans in the early first millennium, during a short span of time in the seventh century BCE in the Neo-Assyrian Empire, and in the single case of the 'seer' Balaam, whose "prophetic activity" is documented by an inscription found in Deir ʿAlla (in the south of modern Jordan), with a reference to him also preserved in the Hebrew Bible (Numbers 22–24). Weighing these sources—including the biblical texts—one has to conclude that prophecy in the history of religion is first of all a type of religious practice which originated in Greater Syria (including Palestine), as there are good reasons to believe that Neo-Assyrian prophecy was also inspired by this Syrian practice (Schneider 2011, 87–88).

By bringing a message—attributed in origin to a deity—to the public, prophets are in close interaction with society, either in affirmative or questioning ways: hence prophets can be closely connected to kings and politicians, working as 'political' advisors for the political success of the ruler. From the theological point of view, the canonical Hebrew Bible tends to dismiss prophets siding with the king as 'false prophets,' set over against the 'true' prophets who engage themselves against social injustice or against oppression of the poor. This theological stance is not well based in history, as even the Hebrew Bible admits that, for example, Nathan and Isaiah are 'true' prophets, despite their close ties to the royal court in Jerusalem. So even if the judgment is not shared by all sources—that prophets who are engaged at the court and in the royal cult (in Israel as well as in other kingdoms) are not 'real' prophets (cf. the critical point of view in e.g. Micah 3:11 and

Jeremiah 2:8, 26)—one has to admit that prophets were considered inferior to priests, who were engaged in performing rituals, sacrifices, and festivals on behalf of the community's well-being. To perform their tasks, prophets also had their own social organizations (cf. e.g. 1 Kings 20:35; 1 Kings 2:1ff.; 1 Sam 19:18ff.), and the lines between prophets and 'priests' were never insurmountable, as with Jeremiah and Ezekiel, both born into priestly families. But prophethood is never heritable. One becomes a prophet by vocation or through god's direct interference. Therefore—as far as we know—the social background of prophets is distributed among milieus other than priestly families, e.g. herdsmen or members of the administrative staff.

'Later' Prophets—Ongoing Traditions of the Syrian Origin

To these Ancient Oriental traditions of prophecy, the prophets of the Qur'ān can be added (Rubin 2004). The *nabī'* (plural: *nabīyūn, anbiyā'*) is a person who—according to the Qur'ān—conveys to the people belief in the 'true' god. Among lists of prophets in the Qur'ān (e.g. Sūrah 4:163; 6:83–89; 37:37–148; 38:15–48) we find prophets of the biblical tradition, but it is noteworthy that those biblical prophets who—according to Jewish and, even more so, Christian tradition—are characterized by their prophecy in written form do not have a central position in the Qur'ānic lists of prophets. Besides them, further prophets like Šuʿaib, Hūd, and Sālih are mentioned in the Qur'ān (e.g. Sūrah 7:65–85). Among the characteristics of prophecy in the Qur'ān is that the prophets bring a (revealed) book from god and their task is to warn people of god's judgment, in part by revealing god's verdict for those who do not listen to and accept the divine message (e.g. Sūrah 89:6–14). In sum, prophets in the Qur'ān are characterized as bringers of a divine revelation, but we have little information from the Qur'ān about their social or political-historical involvement. But, given that Mohammad is the focal point of prophecy in the Qur'ān and was also highly engaged in politics, one can assume that Qur'ānic prophets were involved in politics (and rulership). But—at least partly contrary to the earlier traditions—the Qur'ān seems to separate this theological concept of prophecy from mantic in general, as the *kāhin*, the pre-Islamic specialist for oracles and omens (Stewart 2006, 78f.), is never taken as a 'prophet' in the Qur'ān.

Judging from the terminology and the religio-historical observations on prophets, we can suggest the following general definition: prophecy is a non-heritable mantic technique, using oracles, ecstasy, visions, auditions, or dreams to communicate with the deities in order to reveal divine plans or messages to their society. The biblical texts (and following from it, also the Qur'ān) reduce this broader approach to prophecy to the transmission of the 'divine word' (cf. Hebrews 1:1: god has 'spoken' through his prophets). Later religious traditions (e.g. the 'New Prophecy' at the margins of Christianity in Asia Minor in the second and third centuries; Joseph Smith as the founding 'prophet' of the Church of Jesus Christ of Latter Day Saints; 'prophets' as founders of various African Independent Churches; Bahā'u'llāh as founding 'prophet' of the Bahā'ī Faith) all continue the biblical and Qur'ānic restricted function of a prophet as revealer of the divine 'word.' This is surely an important aspect of the prophet, but not the only one. For better terminological clarity, one can say that 'prophecy' in a narrow sense should be characterized as a mantic technique, originating in Ancient Syria, which became 'canonized' by the Bible and the Qur'ān through stressing the prophet's task of revealing the 'divine word.' In this sense, this phenomenon is a special technique of human–divine communication, distinguishable from the term 'mantic,' which is widely spread in the history of religion.

Priests—The Main Specialists in Performing and Preserving 'Religion'

A very general, common-sense definition of 'priests' might be the following: a priest or a priestess is an expert in cultic practices, and he or she is able to establish and/or maintain relations to superhuman beings. This expertise is primarily a task of representatives of the family and/or the social or political community. However, processes of establishing and specializing a 'priesthood' very often led in the history of religion to a social group of priests, differentiating them as religious specialists from the larger community of 'lay persons.' The task of mediating between humans and 'superhumans' (or deities) overlaps to some extent with that of the prophets; similarly, so-called 'sorcerers' and 'mantic specialists' cannot be sharply separated from priests. It is the priests or the 'sorcerers' who can communicate in these ritual processes with the gods: by performing public festivals or rituals—e.g. healing, appeasing, or invoking the gods, solving inter-human problems (with the help of the gods), the latter now often solved by psychotherapists or psychologists—on behalf of the society and the well-being of the community, in order to please the gods and strengthen shared values and worldviews. Therefore—on the theoretical (and phenomenological) level—a sharp differentiation between priests and 'sorcerers' is untenable, as they share a core function, that of ritual performers (Weber 1972, 260; Heiler 1979, 375–376; Wach 1948, 365 [1951, 416]). This is a valid observation if one accepts that the distinction or opposition between 'religion' and 'magic' is a result of Christian theology and ancient Roman law, but not if 'religion' and 'magic' are taken as substantially identical (Biezais 1978; Schneider 2011, 113–116). Of course, religion can be used for destructive purposes, and priests—like any other religious specialist—can act in a negative way, producing what might be called—in modern terms—'bad religion' or 'black magic.' But such misuse does not support constructing an artificial difference between religion (with 'priests') and magic (with 'sorcerers'). In this sense, Friedrich Heiler's observation is partly correct: actions performed by (or to be precise: in most cases only assigned to) so-called 'sorcerers' can be compared to priestly actions (1979, 372; cf. also Wach 1948, 362–363 [1951, 413]; James 1955, 13–14; Weber 1972, 259–260). But Heiler is not right in arguing that a priest interacts with a 'personalized superhuman' (divinity) while a sorcerer interacts with 'impersonal powers' only. Heiler's distinction reflects a (Christian) ideological dualism between religion and magic, which should be abandoned in the study of religions (for the problems of defining magic see Otto/Stausberg 2013).

Let me problematize this distinction with an example: Roman Catholic 'priests' (in the European Middle Ages) were often engaged (officially by the church) for (now out-of-date) exorcisms to 'heal' a person whose physical or mental incapacity was attributed to the power of the devil or of demons. The priest counteracted this demonic mischief by prayers, by invoking god (or Jesus or Catholic saints), and by using holy water or incense for the symbolic purification of the 'ritual client' for whom he performed such an exorcism. If we look back to the Old Babylonian period in central Mesopotamia, we can find the following scenario. The exorcist treats the sick ritual client, whose sickness is imagined to be the result of demons overpowering him. He does this by reciting prayers, by invoking the Babylonian gods (very often Ea who was thought to be the most suitable god in such cases) and by performing symbolic acts of purification, using holy water or burning spices and incense to chase the demons out of the body of the ritual client. From a comparative perspective there are no differences that would support concluding that the one specialist is a 'priest' and the other a 'sorcerer'. Both perform a (healing) ritual based on their given belief system and using symbols from this system, and both handle the client in similar ways. Therefore, either the Catholic priest is also a 'sorcerer' and the Babylonian 'sorcerer' or exorcist is also a priest, or we should discard the distinction, defining 'priest' broadly in terms of an ability to perform rituals—based on their belief system—for the good of an individual or their community. Thus 'sorcerers' cannot be taken as a special category of types of religious specialists, as the category is only constructed by theologians of a religion in order to marginalize or even eliminate competing ritualists and their practices.

Priests as Social Elites

The performance of rituals has an important function for any society, and priests—as the specialists for such tasks—are the main keepers of learned or sacred traditions. Thus their ability is not restricted to ritual performance: they become scholars, administrators, or even judges—as keepers of tradition—and they establish rules of conduct for the society, including developing administrative duties (partly also for subalterns) based on ritual knowledge. It is thus not surprising that priesthood goes hand in hand with competence in teaching and transmitting religious knowledge. However, teaching is not the primary characteristic of a priest (Wach 1948, 366 [1951, 417–418]; Heiler 1979, 403), and therefore, for example, Muslim ʿulamā' (who preserve and transmit knowledge) or Protestant preachers (who offer religious 'education') are not to be counted as priests, if they only are concerned with teaching. Vedic (or Brahman) priests are good examples, as they are specialists in performing rituals who also know (and teach) the mantras necessary for performing the rituals or ceremonies. Similarly one can mention the *daoshi*, Daoist religious authorities with special knowledge connected to the *dao* and the ritual skills to put the *dao* in effect in the world, on behalf of both the living and of the dead (Kirkland 2008, 326).

With this authority of 'ritualistic' and 'religious' knowledge, priests were a leading social group in premodern societies, building a social elite that gains power in all fields of daily life, including political and economic power. In order to keep this power as elites, priests made use of their influence and power to organize and administer religion, developing those traits most suitable to keep their leading position in society. On the theoretical level this leads to a situation in which kings (or rulers) in premodern societies can act as priests or become incorporated into the 'priesthood.' Some traditions and cultures take it for granted that the ruler acts by the 'grace' or the 'will' of the gods, which means that their rule cannot exist independently from the priestly elites who define religious teachings and administer religion. Therefore a ruler 'by the grace of god' can only be a ruler who rules according to religion (defined and performed by the priestly elites). This kind of dominance of priestly elites also leads to another consequence, namely that such a 'priesthood' is necessarily differentiated from the non-priestly common people (lay persons), because priests in many societies can be considered to be the ones who have all relevant knowledge of the society as, for example, the *daoshi* "represent Daoist culture on a professional basis" (cf. Reiter 1998, vii). As a consequence, lay persons are often considered less competent in or lacking knowledge of religion—at least from the point of view of the priests. Further, members of the laity can be outcast from the community based on a verdict by priests—for example, for being a heretic or a 'sorcerer' and culpable for questioning the priests' prerogatives or (parts of) their practice or doctrines. With this in mind, one should be skeptical about talking of the *pater familias* as the priest in the private cult at home: performing rites for private religious practice partly matches the ritual activities of the priests, but as an individual or private religious practice—performed on behalf of all the family—it does not make the *pater familias* a priest, as his work is not relevant for the society as a whole. The elite status of priests also leads us back once more to the prophets mentioned earlier. Prophets are surely 'religious specialists' with a high level of competence—but they can be criticized by 'priests' because prophets (generally) are not part of the priestly elites (Wach 1948, 361 [1951, 411]). Therefore priests as holders and transmitters of religious knowledge try to minimize the role of prophets (as seen in the conflicts described in the Hebrew Bible), while at the same time, prophets can challenge the authority of the priests.

This leads to a final aspect of a characterization of 'priests': granted different "types of religious authority" (Wach 1948, 331 [1951, 375]), one can say that priests are the central type, not just a type on a par with others (like prophets, shamans, mystics, etc.). Priests are the central religious 'elites,' and several features maintain this extraordinary status. Different practices serve this purpose in various religions: sometimes priesthood is, for example, strictly hereditary or sometimes it allows for initiation into the priests' (elite) community—thus changing one's social status and becoming part of the new social group, the 'priests'; in extreme cases this social change might even lead to a break with former family bonds. Both ways of becoming a priest exist in the history of religions, and they can also be combined with each other: in cases when priesthood is hereditary, only those members of a priestly family who are initiated will practice. The priests' dominance can be further fostered by special lifestyle requirements like diets, restrictions in social contacts, dress codes, or celibacy. The resulting lifestyle differentiates the priestly community from 'regular' society, as an elite group—claiming religious knowledge for the group as an institution, though individual priests are unlikely to possess all this knowledge—thus combining the activities of ritual performance and teaching/preserving tradition.

Sorcerers

As noted earlier, the distinction between 'priests' and 'sorcerers' presumes an ideological dichotomy between religion and magic. A sorcerer cannot be described or defined independently: he or she engages in the same ritual practices and possesses the same knowledge as a priest and makes use of it for his or her society. When we look at the differentiation between 'black' and 'white' magic, the sorcerer is the one who practices 'black' magic against the society or individuals—as characterized by the religious elite. But the ones who practice the same things on behalf of the society—again as characterized by the same religious elite—are doing 'white' magic, which is not distinguished from the religious and ritual tasks performed by these elites (cf. e.g. Schneider 2011, 113f.; Henshaw 1994, 135–151). Thus, 'sorcerer' cannot be taken as a category existing independently in religion: it is a category constructed (or imagined) by the priests qua religious elites. Or, conversely, priests and sorcerers are two sides of the same coin.

POWER AND PRESTIGE OF RELIGIOUS SPECIALISTS

'Religious specialists'—in this chapter taken partly as an umbrella term for prophets, priests, and 'sorcerers'—can gain power and prestige because of their birth, their 'initiation,' their 'vocation' which constitute their status as priests, or their religious actions, for example by keeping purity or dietary regulations or practicing some kind of asceticism like celibacy (Hutter 2004; Olson 2011, 42–48—both with further literature). That the 'right of birth' is an important aspect of giving power to priests can be seen in priestly groups which are closed societies: for example, the Levites in Hebrew religion, the priesthood by birth in Zoroastrianism, or Brahmans in Hindu traditions. The hereditary side of priesthood is still reflected in name-giving, when we find modern family names derived from priestly terms: for example, among Jews, Kohen, Cohen, or Kuhn from Hebrew *kohen* (priest) and Katz from Hebrew *kohen zadiq* (the righteous priest); among Arab Christians (mainly in Lebanon) Khoury from Arabic *khūrī* ([Christian] priest); and, among Zoroastrians, Dastur or Dastoor from the priestly title *dastur* in

New Persian (developed from Middle Persian *dastwar*). Hereditary priesthood leads to a closed society or in-group, a status that can also be attained by initiation into priesthood in some traditions. But in such cases we also find the idea of being 'born' into this group, as initiation into priesthood is often seen as a 'new birth': although the priests in the group are not siblings, they are 'brothers.'

Creating Power by Seniority and Special Status

Such 'family bonds' lead to another important concept related to issues of power and prestige, i.e. seniority, which is the etymologically basic meaning of the English word 'priest,' deriving from Greek *presbyter* 'the elder.' In relation to power, seniority does not mean biological age, but 'social age,' which is based either on experience, hierarchical rank, and/or the date of membership (Hutter 2013, 291–292). Thus 'priestly competence' is also closely connected to the development of hierarchies among religious specialists. The idea of seniority (and hierarchy depending thereupon) is an argument supporting the use of the term 'priest' as a generic term, despite the word's deep roots in Christian tradition. Recognizing the Greek origin of the word, this term serves better than others for characterizing religious experts in a broad sense. Terms like Latin *sacerdos* "the one who acts as agent for the holy," Hebrew *kohen* "the one who stands [in front of god]," or Sanskrit *brahman* "the one who interacts (with) *brahman*" are all restricted to only a limited aspects of the functions of 'priest' as a religious specialist.

Seniority and 'family' bonds are also the basics for hierarchies among priestly groups. Of course, hierarchical orders differ from religion to religion, and they are also intertwined with the priest's competence in ritualistic or religious knowledge. Also within a given religion, such hierarchies are open to development and changes, but they can never disappear totally. To give just one example: Philip Kreyenbroek (2013, 195–234)—in several studies—has shown how Zoroastrian priestly hierarchy developed over the centuries, fusing or changing different functions: especially noteworthy is the differentiation between the *hērbed* and the *hāwišt* in the early Islamic times, the former being the 'learned' priest and the latter the one who knows to perform rituals but has little knowledge of teaching and theology. But Kreyenbroek also mentions that the different sources cannot fully be harmonized with each other, as sometimes one gets the impression that a *hērbed* is of lower rank than other learned priests like the *rad* or *dastwar*. Generalizing this, one can say that the priests make a highly stratified group within a society and that they try to maintain their prestige and their distance from 'lay persons' as common people (cf. the relationship of the English word "lay[-person]" to Greek *laos* "[common] people"). Practices of abstinence, of special lifestyle (including clear regulations about, for example, sexuality, food, 'behavior' to avoid 'impurity'), but also of keeping (or sometimes hiding) religious knowledge from common people, are important techniques for maintaining this distance and constructing the power of the religious specialists, insofar as they are seen to have a monopoly on access to religious salvation. Thus perceived competence in—and a monopoly on—the transmission and performance of rituals on behalf of the community constitutes and maintains their social status (e.g. Hindu Brahmans). But this also renders priests ambivalent: they are both held in high esteem and feared by the rest of the society because of their power; and, as a corollary, priests who are feared can be labeled 'sorcerers' by marginalized or oppositional groups in a society dominated by priestly elites.

Power by Keeping and Managing Authority

Power and prestige of priests are also connected with their authority, which they receive generally by their office, a mode of authority that Max Weber labeled *Amtscharisma* ("charisma of office") (1972, 674–675; cf. Wach 1948, 337–338 [1951, 382–383]). Priests, as guardians of knowledge, claim to have access to so-called 'holy scripture/books', the origin of which is often attributed to a divine revelation (perhaps given to prophets), making them in principle unquestionable. As long as priests can keep a monopoly on mastering, teaching, and transmitting such scriptures, their authority is difficult to challenge. The fact that particular priests might have limited knowledge or teaching skills generally does not lead to a decline of priestly authority because of their *Amtscharisma*.

As a practical consequence of the ambivalence of priestly power and prestige, the relation between religious specialists and political or social leaders—both the ruling class and opposition groups—can be one of either friction or mutual support. Such leaders (in 'worldly affairs') try to make use of priests as persons who can manage or provide 'salvation' to others. Therefore, in the history of religions, we often find a close intermingling of priestly and political activities: court priests, royal Brahmans, or royal chaplains are well known from history (James 1955, 105–144 [1957, 117–161]; Oxtoby 2005, 7397–7398). Conversely, in premodern cultures the king often acted in various priestly ways, leading to the idea of a 'sacred king'. Sometimes the crown prince (and even other members of the royal family) could—at least for a (symbolic) period—be initiated as priest at an important sanctuary in order to gain high status, which would later prove helpful. Convergence between religious and political specialists sometimes results in priestly hierarchies being neatly arranged along the lines of political hierarchies: e.g. with one 'high priest' as there is only one ruler in the country, with a priestly leader corresponding to the political leader in every province or district, and with this parallel extending all the way to very local entities.

CRITICISM OR LOSS OF POWER AND 'DEMOCRATIZING' OF FUNCTIONS

Priests are generally esteemed in their societies, but they are also open to criticism on different grounds: e.g. due to lack of charismatic authority—whether based on heredity, kinship, or office—to technical failure in the performance of ritual, or to moral weakness. The hereditary kind of priesthood is especially liable to the latter critique: sons—occasionally daughters—of priests may conduct their ritual work in a manner that is seen by their clients to be perfunctory or otherwise unsatisfactory. This can be extended to a critique of the entire priestly structure, based on the view that inheritance hinders the most qualified and fittest from becoming ritual specialists, while less competent persons keep their position without merits. The stronger the separation between the in-group of ritual specialists and lay people, the stronger the potential conflicts that may arise. In those cases where certain tasks are restricted to male practitioners, gender-based criticism can also emerge. The general dynamic of such critiques is to push for 'democratizing' processes that make these religious functions open to a broader range of candidates, independent of birth or gender.

Ritual specialists are firmly embedded in tradition, which helps to maintain their authority. Nevertheless religions are always affected by social changes. Such changes can also provoke new problems, mainly in cases where 'priestly' and 'mundane' knowledge drift away from each other (James 1955, 243–245 [1957, 276–278]; Oxtoby 2005, 7398–7399). When the 'profane' teacher takes responsibility for providing education or propagating the values of a given society, this task of the priest gets lost—if the religious professionals cannot keep up with this modern challenge. Similarly, other areas of religious and ritual competence—e.g. using rituals to reconcile members of the society with each other, to integrate people into their social environment, or to heal—are appropriated by different professions in societies that manifest a growing division of labor: e.g. psychologists, doctors, and scientists. So-called secularization and/or new forms of individual religious practice lead to the decline of the authority of religious (and ritual) specialists. While secularization in general tends to marginalize religion in a society, individualized religious practices may no longer require such specialists, as all their functions and competences are covered by everybody in his or her individual religious life—in a sort of secular 'priesthood of all believers.' Where religious traditions cannot cope with such changes, a decline in the authority, acceptance, and power of religious professionals is the inevitable result.

Conclusion

Religious and social changes are challenging the traditional roles of religious specialists. 'Priest' is best taken as a general and very broad term for a person serving a community as the primary specialist transmitting religious knowledge, establishing the relationship between individuals or the society as a whole and superhuman beings ('gods'—by performing rituals on behalf of the society and for the pleasure of the superhumans), and communicating with the superhumans to transmit their wishes to the people. In this light, 'prophets,' insofar as their role is limited to conveying the gods' messages to people, can be seen as a subgroup of priests, sometimes in tension with them. But generally prophets, whose communicative role is relatively limited among religions, also perform other tasks similar to those of priests and sorcerers insofar as they are involved in teaching or ritualistic divination practices. The knowledge held by these various religious specialists is important to societies. Thus their involvement in politics—whether cooperative or oppositional—is seen as valuable or even essential, as long as the 'priestly knowledge' is seen as useful and (partly) supplementary to the 'mundane knowledge' for the society's benefit. 'Priest'—despite the term's roots in Mediterranean and mainly Christian traditions—is the best umbrella term in a typology of terms of religious authorities, while other terms—e.g. shaman, guru, preacher, prophet—cover restricted aspects of those also found in 'priests.' At the same time, the specialist qualities, e.g. of a shaman or a preacher, do not in themselves constitute or define them as priests. The definition of priests, prophets, or sorcerers cannot be based on arguments taken from one religion only: it is necessary to take account of the social setting of such religious specialists.

GLOSSARY

Priest a person who is an expert in the practices of a cult and who is able to establish relations with superhuman/divine beings. As such, the priest becomes the expert and 'guardian' of religious traditions.

Prophecy a mantic technique, using oracles, ecstasy, visions, auditions, or dreams to communicate with superhuman/divine beings.

Prophet a person who can communicate with superhuman/divine beings to reveal their plans or messages to society.

Religion and magic the dichotomy between ('good') religion and ('bad' or 'black') magic is the result of theological constructions established by the superior group of 'religious and ritual specialists' who defend their status as 'priests' by marginalizing and even eliminating other groups of specialists as 'sorcerers' who do 'magic.'

Sorcerer a person whose experience, ritual skills, and religious knowledge are the same as those of a priest. Based on an artificial dichotomy between 'religion' and 'magic,' these persons can be disparaged by competing priests defending their own power and prestige.

REFERENCES

Biezais, Haralds. 1978. *Von der Wesensidentität der Religion und Magie*. Åbo: Åbo Akademie.

Cancik-Kirschbaum, Eva. 2003. "Prophetismus und Divination: Ein Blick auf die keilinschriftlichen Quellen." In *Propheten in Mari, Assyrien und Israel*, edited by Matthias Köckert and Martti Nissinen. Göttingen: Vandenhoeck & Ruprecht, 33–53.

Durand, Jean-Marie. 2008. "La religion amorrite en Syrie à l'époque des archives de Mari." In *Mythologie et religion des Sémites occidentaux. 1: Ébla, Mari*, edited by Gregorio del Olmo Lete. Louvain: Peeters, 161–716

Heiler, Friedrich. 1979. *Erscheinungsformen und Wesen der Religion*, 2nd edition. Stuttgart: Kohlhammer. Original edition, 1961.

Henshaw, Richard A. 1994. *Female and Male: The Cultic Personnel—The Bible and the Rest of the Ancient Near East*. Allison Park, PA: Pickwick Publications.

Hutter, Manfred. 2004. "Zölibat. I. Religionsgeschichtlich." In *Theologische Realenzyklopädie* 36, edited by Gerhard Krause et al. Berlin: de Gruyter, 720–722.

Hutter, Manfred. 2013. "Die Sorge für die Älteren." In *Altern in den Religionen*, edited by Karl Baier and Franz Winter. Vienna: Lit-Verlag, 281–302.

James, Edward O. 1955. *The Nature and Function of Priesthood: A Comparative and Anthropological Study*. London: Thames & Hudson.

Kirkland, Russell. 2008. "Daoshi." In *The Encyclopedia of Taoism*, 2 vols., edited by Fabrizio Pregadio. London: Routledge, I, 326–329.

Kreyenbroek, Philip G. 2013. *Teachers and Teachings in the Good Religion: Opera Minora on Zoroastrianism*, edited by Kianoosh Rezania. Wiesbaden: Harrassowitz.

Olson, Carl. 2011. *Religious Studies: The Key Concepts*. London: Routledge.

Otto, Bernd-Christian and Michael Stausberg, eds. 2013. *Defining Magic: A Reader*. Sheffield: Equinox Publishing.

Oxtoby, William G. 2005. "Priesthood: An Overview." In *Encyclopedia of Religion*, edited by Lindsay Jones, 2nd edition. Detroit: Macmillan Reference, vol. 11, 7394–7399.

Reiter, Florian. 1998. *The Aspiration and Standards of Taoist Priests in the Early T'ang Period*. Wiesbaden: Harrassowitz.

Rubin, Uri. 2004. "Prophets and Prophethood." In *Encyclopaedia of the Qur'ān*, edited by Jane Mammen McAuliffe. Leiden: Brill, vol. 4, 289–307.

Sabourin, Leopold. 1973. *Priesthood: A Comparative Study*. Leiden: Brill.

Schneider, Tammi J. 2011. *An Introduction to Ancient Mesopotamian Religion*. Grand Rapids, MI: Eerdmans Publishing.

Sheppard, Gerald T. and William E. Herbrechtsmeier. 2005. "Prophecy: An Overview." In *Encyclopedia of Religion*, edited by Lindsay Jones, 2nd edition. Detroit: Macmillan Reference, vol. 11, 7423–7429.

Stewart, Devin J. 2006. "Soothsayer." In *Encyclopaedia of the Qur'ān*, edited by Jane Mammen McAuliffe. Leiden: Brill, vol. 5, 78–80.

Wach, Joachim. 1948. *Sociology of Religion*. Chicago, IL: University of Chicago Press. (German: *Religionssoziologie*, translated by Helmut Schoeck. Tübingen: J. C. B. Mohr, 1951.)

Weber, Max. 1972. *Wirtschaft und Gesellschaft: Grundriss der verstehenden Soziologie*, 5th revised edition, arranged by Johannes Winckelmann. Tübingen: J. C. B. Mohr. Original edition, 1022.

FURTHER READING

Biezais 1978 [*A useful study of the relationship between religion and magic; given the overlap of both areas, the difference between 'priests' and 'sorcerers' becomes artificial.*]

Heiler 1979 [*As comparative studies in priesthood and prophecy are rather limited, this classical study focusing on the 'phenomenology' of religion remains a helpful tool for studying concepts and types of religious 'functionaries.'*]

James 1955 [*A classical study of priesthood. Though partly dated, this (like Sabourin 1973) remains a valuable book-length study of this topic.*]

Sabourin 1973 [*Despite its focus on Christianity, the book remains a valuable overview of priesthood.*]

Wach 1948 [*This remains an important study for comparing different religious 'functionaries,' especially the section about "types of religious authorities."*]

CHAPTER 40

....

PURITY

....

HUGH B. URBAN

CHAPTER SUMMARY

....

- Purity is an extremely varied and heterogeneous religious ideal that lies at the critical intersection between the individual physical body, the social body, and the cosmos as a whole.
- At once a material and a spiritual ideal, purity overlaps partially with but far exceeds modern notions of cleanliness or hygiene—indeed, it may in some cases even contradict the latter.
- One can distinguish five different forms of purity, each in this chapter illustrated by one primary example: physical purity, social purity, mental purity, sexual purity, and the ritual use of impurity.
- There is a variety of contemporary theoretical approaches to purity, drawn from psychology, cognitive science, cultural anthropology, gender studies, and comparative religions.

Concepts of purity and pollution can be found in virtually every culture and religious tradition, ancient or modern, and often play a critical role in the construction of religious worldviews, ritual practices, and social boundaries. While some of the most elaborate and theologically sophisticated ideas of purity can be found in traditions such as Jewish law (*halakhah*), Islamic law (*shari'ah*), or Zoroastrian sacred texts (such as the *Videvdad*), they also run throughout virtually all indigenous cultures and continue to inform popular culture even in twenty-first century America (Douglas 2002; Urban 2000; Preston 2005; Ortner 2013; DeRogatis 2014).

Notions of purity range from the cleanliness of the individual body, to relations between bodies (such as sharing food and sexual intercourse), to the integrity of the social group, to performance of rituals aimed at dispelling impurity, to internalized states of 'mental purity' achieved through meditation and asceticism. Ritual acts of purification may pertain specifically to individual bodies—such as Muslims performing *wudu* or washing parts of the body in preparation for prayer—or they may pertain to the collective body of the entire human race or the cosmos—such as Shinto rites of purification that are performed periodically to resacralize the world as a whole (Preston 2005, 7504). In many cases, contact with something considered to be physically polluting (such as a corpse or sexual fluids) renders one impure; yet in other cases, contact with things considered sacred (such as handling the parchment of the Sefer Torah, or Torah scroll used for prayer in a Jewish synagogue), may also render one ritually impure. Moreover, purity in a religious sense typically has only a partial overlap with 'cleanliness' or 'hygiene' in a modern medical or scientific sense. For most Hindus, for example, the River Ganga has long been regarded as the holiest water on earth and the ultimate source of ritual purification; yet in the twenty-first century context of heavily populated, polluted, and industrialized India, this river could scarcely be considered 'clean' in a merely physical sense (Ortner 2013).

The concept of purity, in this sense, lies at the complex intersection between multiple levels of reality. As a critical node at which the individual body (microcosm), the social body or community (mesocosm), and the universe (macrocosm) all intersect, rites of purification help forge a series of "triangular links among the individual, the cosmos and the social structure" (Preston 2005, 7503). For the sake of this brief chapter, I will focus on five key forms of purity, each illustrated by one or two specific examples. These are: (1) physical purity, as understood in early Islamic jurisprudence; (2) social purity, as understood in classical Hindu texts on religious duty or *dharma*; (3) mental purity, as understood in early Buddhist literature; (4) sexual purity, as discussed in contemporary evangelical Christian literature; and (5) the power of impurity, as utilized in South Asian Tantra and other esoteric traditions. To conclude, I will discuss a few of the major theoretical approaches to understanding purity and impurity today.

Pure Bodies: Pollution, Cleanliness, and the Physical Body in Early Islam

Purity tends to center first and foremost on the human body, with its various substances, orifices, and physical boundaries. In the Hebrew Bible, for example, concepts of impurity (*tumah*) and purity (*taharah*) focus heavily on bodily states and conditions such as the human corpse, menstruation, childbirth, sexual intercourse, and certain kinds of disease (Macoby 2009). While we could mention many examples here, one of the most sophisticated discussions of physical purity was developed in early Sunni Islam. According to one key saying of the Prophet Mohammad, "purity [*tahara*] is half of faith" (Maghen 2005, 13). While it is surely an exaggeration to say that "no other religion has given such importance to prescribed purity as Islam" (Bakhtiar 1996, 3), ritual purification does play a central role in the quotidian life of all practicing Muslims. As an essential precondition to prayer, purification is a duty of every Muslim throughout the day, achieved through lesser and greater ablutions, or *wudu* and *ghusl* (Maghen 2005, 13; Bouhdiba 1985).

Much of this concern with purity focuses specifically on the human body and its various activities, products, and effluences. Statements about the Prophet's own bodily fluids are a ubiquitous presence across the pages of *hadith* (the sayings of the Prophet) and *fiqh* (interpretation of Islamic law), and even the menstrual blood of his wives is regularly discussed (Maghen 2005, 13). Various classic works of Islamic law recount the Prophet's vomiting, defecation, urination, and sexual intercourse, as well as his subsequent bathing to exit the state of impurity (Maghen 2005, 10–11). In some accounts, we even see the Prophet's state of impurity directly juxtaposed with his need for purification in order to perform ritual prayer, as for example in this narrative collected in the "book of bathing" (*ghusl*) by Muhammad al-Bhukari:

> Prayers were announced and the rows were straightened, and the Messenger of God came in [to the mosque to lead the service]. And when he stood up at his place of prayer he suddenly remembered that he was sexually impure. "Stay in your places," he ordered us, and he ran home and performed *ghusl*, and came back with his head dripping wet. Then he called out "God is Great!" and we prayed together with him. (Maghen 2005, 30)

For some scholars, this intense concern with purity and this focus on sexual purification has been viewed as a tension between the material and spiritual domains of existence in Islam (Bouhdiba 1985). However, as other authors such as Ze'ev Maghen persuasively argue, the concern with purity in early Islam is better understood not as a conflict but rather as an attempt to reconcile fleshly with spiritual existence and to see the two domains as complementary and equally laudatory aspects of the same human condition: "The defiling 'events' and purifying ablutions combine to create a two-way portal, as it were, though which the believer passes many times daily between a condition appropriate to the bodily and a condition appropriate to the disembodied … between the sensual human and the psychic divine" (Maghen 2005, 32).

Obviously, Muslim attitudes toward purity and impurity have developed in many various forms over the last 1,400 years and have been interpreted in widely divergent ways in different schools of Islamic law in different historical and cultural contexts. Nonetheless, the purity of the individual body and its fitness for the spiritual life remains a central concern in contemporary Islam, from the most progressive reformist movements to the most conservative Salafist movements in the twenty-first century (Mahmood 2011; Gauvain 2014).

Pure Communities: Purity, Pollution, and Caste in Classical Hindu Literature

Purity is typically not just a matter of the individual body but is also often intimately tied to the social body and to relations between groups and communities. Perhaps the clearest example of the relationship between 'purity' and 'community' is classical Hinduism, which reflects an unusually complex understanding of purity (*shaucha, shuddha*), impurity (*ashaucha, ashuddha*), and social class and caste (*varna* and *jati*). As Gavin Flood notes, "[t]here is ... a deeper level of pollution which is a property of the body and differentiates one social group from another. The polarity of purity and pollution organizes Hindu social space" (1996, 57; see Dumont 1981).

Today, of course, there is much debate as to how rigid the rules of caste and purity were in premodern India. As scholars such as Nicholas Dirks have argued, the caste system as we think of it today—as a monolithic, rigid, and unchanging hierarchy—is largely the result of European Orientalist scholarship of the nineteenth and twentieth centuries. In precolonial India, Dirks suggests, caste was a far more diverse and fluid system that was intimately tied not only to notions of purity but also to regional communities, kinship groups, factional parties, and political affiliations that varied dramatically from one region and one historical period to another (2001, 13). Nonetheless, the classical Hindu texts on social duty and religious life (the *dharma sutras* and *dharma shastras*) do lay out an extremely complex and well-developed—even if idealized and never practically realized—theory of purity, impurity, and social hierarchy.

Perhaps the best known of these *dharma* texts is the *Laws of Manu* or *Manavadharmashastra* (hereafter *Manu*), which was composed some time between the second century BCE and third century CE. As in Islamic legal discourse, *Manu* devotes great attention to the purity and impurity of the physical body, its openings, and its various emissions. Thus: "All orifices above the navel are ritually clean; those below are ritually unclean, as are the foul substances that shed from the body" (these latter include oil, semen, blood, bone marrow, urine, excrement, snot, and so on; Olivelle 2004, 145).

However, the *dharma* literature also applies these bodily concepts of purity and impurity to the larger structure of the 'social body' and to the hierarchy of classes and castes. According to the cosmology in *Manu* (which continues a cosmogonic narrative going back to the *Rig Veda*, the oldest part of the foundational Hindu scriptures or *Vedas*), the Lord and Creator fashioned the four social classes out of the parts of his own body: "he produced from his mouth, arms, thighs, and feet the Brahmin, the Kshatriya, the Vaishya, and the Shudra" or the priest, king, producer, and servant classes (Olivelle 2004, 6–7). In the *dharma* literature, the structure of the four *varnas* is described as a hierarchy of relative purity and impurity, with the Brahmins or priests as the most pure at the top of the social organism and the Shudras or servants at the bottom as least pure. Beneath the Shudras there are still more impure groups, the various 'untouchables' who handle particularly polluting substances such as corpses, garbage, or dead animal flesh (Doniger 2009, 285). Finally, in addition to the four social classes, there are also a huge number of *jatis* or occupational 'castes,' which *Manu* roughly maps onto the hierarchy of the *varnas*, and which are similarly ordered according to a logic of relative purity and impurity. And all of these are in turn closely tied to the physicality of the social body itself: "The caste of any individual is inalienable; it is a property of the body and cannot be removed" (Flood 1996, 59; Dumont 1981).

The boundaries between the classes and castes are maintained by strict rules of commensality and marriage. *Manu* and other texts contain elaborate guidelines concerning who can share food and water with whom, who can marry whom, and the various negative results that proceed from violating these rules (Olivelle 2004, 135). In fact, on specific ritual occasions, not only is sharing food with Brahmins forbidden but even watching Brahmins while they eat is a potential source of impurity: "[An outcaste], a pig, a cock, a dog, a menstruating woman, or a eunuch should not look at the Brahmins while they are eating"; and should they do so, the ceremony will go wrong (Olivelle 2004, 120).

Proper marriage relations within social classes are an even more central concern for *Manu*, which enumerates in detail the negative results that follow from marriages that run against the grain of social hierarchy. Indeed, improper sexual relations between social classes are said to be the cause of the lowest untouchable or outcaste groups. For example, the offspring of a Shudra father and a Brahmin mother is the Chandala, who is "the worst of all men," and so impure that his mere touch pollutes (Olivelle 2004, 208, 989). Therefore, a long list of punishments follows for those who have sexual relations in violation of class boundaries, ranging from loss of property and freedom to loss of physical body parts, depending on the specific classes involved: "When a Shudra has sex with a guarded or unguarded woman of a twice-born class, he loses a limb and all his possessions. A Vaishya is imprisoned and all his property is confiscated; and a Kshatriya is fined 1000 and his head is shaved using urine" (Olivelle 2004, 187).

Finally, not only are the social classes distinguished by relative purity and by relations of food and marriage; they are still further distinguished by their respective processes of purification, that is, by the period of time required to regain a state of purity and by the means of purification. For example, following the death of a relative, "A Brahmin is purified in ten days, a Kshatriya in twelve, a Vaishya in fifteen, a Shudra in a month"; meanwhile, "a Brahmin is purified by touching water, a Kshatriya his conveyance, a Vaishya his goad or reins, and a Shudra his staff" (Olivelle 2004, 142–143).

Of course, texts such as *Manu* provide just one example of the social construction of purity, and these ideas of purity have developed in myriad complex ways over the millennia of Hindu traditions in South Asia. Moreover, the very concepts of purity, pollution, and untouchability have been challenged, rethought, reworked, and sometimes rejected altogether by Gandhi, Ambedkar, and various other reformers in the modern era. Nonetheless, the role of purity in the understanding of social relations continues to inform most Hindu communities to this day (see Milner 1994; Mendelsohn 1998; Flood 1996, 261).

Pure Minds: Interior, Moral, and Mental Defilement and Internal Means of Purification

The concept of purity is not limited to the physical and social bodies; in many traditions it is also internalized, as it were, to the inner realm of consciousness and mental or spiritual states. For example, early Christians maintained some basic concepts of purity such as baptism, foot washing, and the priest's washing of hands before the Eucharist; yet, for the most part, early Christians were unconcerned with the complex dietary restrictions of Jewish practice and the elaborate rules of *halakhah*. As David Brakke suggests in his detailed history of early Christian literature, "it was precisely the Christian community's lack of such purity concerns that was seen as a mark of Christian difference from neighboring Jews" (1995, 433). And yet, early Christian monks were still deeply concerned with 'purity of the soul,' achieved through ascetic discipline. As such, Brakke notes, there was a general trend in early Christian discussions away from a very literal concept of impurity "toward a greater interiorization of impurity at two levels, the individual's body of the male and the collective body of the Church" (1995, 458; Brakke 2006).

However, perhaps the most elaborate example of this 'internalized' concept of purity was developed in early Buddhism. Most Buddhist traditions do, of course, contain some beliefs regarding physical purity and pollution such as not allowing women to circumambulate stupas or the belief that a menstruating woman will pollute a temple or shrine (Ortner 2013; Faure 2003). For the most part, however, early Buddhism rejects the elaborate laws of purity, pollution, class, and commensality of the Hindu tradition and instead focuses on the processes of mental and moral purification, aimed less at outward impurity than on the inner defilements of thought (Harvey 2012, 15, 73).

One of the most important early works on Theravada Buddhist practice is the *Path of Purification* (*Visuddhimagga*) by the fifth-century Indian monk, Buddhaghosa. Purification or *visuddhi* in Buddhaghosa's text refers primarily to Nibbana (Nirvana) itself, and the path of purification is simply the practical means of achieving that state. Quoting the *Dhammapada*, Buddhaghosa describes this path as first and foremost a method of seeing all mental formations (*samskaras* or *sankharas*, meaning all mental habits, thoughts, opinions, and prejudices) as without permanent existence:

> Formations are all impermanent:
> When he sees this with understanding
> He turns away from all that is ill.
> This is the path to purity. (Buddhaghosa 2010, 71)

Likewise, the notion of impurity is itself largely internalized. For Buddhaghosa, the primary concern is not bodily impurity; indeed, he utterly rejects the idea that different social classes are marked by different degrees of physical purity, since all bodies, in his view, are equally 'defiled.' They are *all* impermanent, mortal, and subject to the same processes of deterioration and decay: "there is no distinction between a king's body and an outcaste's body in so far as impure stinking nauseating repulsiveness is concerned" (Buddhaghosa 2010, 183). Rather, the defilements (*kilesas* or *kleshas*) are mental states or negative psychological tendencies that cloud the mind and result in unwholesome actions, namely: "greed, hate, delusion, conceit, false view, uncertainty, stiffness [of mind], agitation, consciencelessness, and shamelessness" (Buddhaghosa 2010, 713; Harvey 2012, 73).

As such, purification refers not to external acts such as bathing or any of the means described in *Manu*. Indeed, Buddhaghosa explicitly rejects the ideal of the Hindu

Brahmin who "leads the life of [outward] purity" by merely fulfilling vows and under-taking asceticism; for if he is still egotistically attached to his outward purity and takes satisfaction it, he remains bound to the realm of suffering (2010, 49). In contrast, the Buddhist path of moral and mental purification has nothing to do with class, caste, or outward markers of physical purity. Thus, he quotes the Buddha's words in the *Majjhima Nikaya*,

> By deeds, vision, and righteousness,
> by virtue, the sublimest life—
> By these are mortals purified
> And not by lineage or wealth. (Buddhaghosa 2010, 7)

Buddhaghosa's internalized understanding of purification is, of course, just one of many in the vast diverse body of Buddhist traditions; and other forms of Buddhism do also focus on the more 'external' aspects of impurity, such as women, sexuality, and blood (Faure 2003). Yet with its sophisticated reflection on the mind and mental states, early Buddhism developed some of the most elaborate discussions of purity and defile-ment as interior rather than simply exterior states of being.

PURE DESIRES: SEXUALITY, IMPURITY, AND CHASTITY

Discussions of purity in many traditions often devote special attention to sexual desire and sexual pollution. As Paul Ricoeur put it in his classic work, *The Symbolism of Evil*, "the inflation of the sexual is characteristic of the whole system of defilement, so that an indissoluble complicity between sexuality and defilement seems to have been formed from time immemorial" (1986 [1960], 28). The focus on sexual purity can be seen throughout Jewish, Muslim, and Hindu legal texts, which have quite specific rec-ommendations for sexual relations and means of cleansing the body following sexual emissions or contact (Bouhdiba 1985; Feinstein 2014). Yet the concern with sexual purity is by no means simply an archaic relic of ancient texts or distant traditional cultures; rather, it is very much a vital issue for many groups such as conservative Christians in the contemporary United States.

As Amy DeRogatis suggests in her work on *Saving Sex* (2014), the concern with sex-ual purity runs throughout American Evangelical culture, giving rise to a vast body of guidebooks, magazines, websites, blogs, and podcasts on the importance of chas-tity and saving sex for heterosexual marriage and procreation alone. Thus, in popular texts such as S. Dawn Chandler's *The Purity Movement*, sexual purity is described as one of the most important aspects of the Christian life, precisely because sexual sin has such profound and wide-reaching consequences for the individual body as the temple of God: "Sexual sin is different from every other kind of sin because the act affects the heart, soul, mind and the body. Not every sin is like this. In 1 Corinthians 6:18, Paul states that we must run away from sexual sin. No other sin clearly affects the body as this one does, for sexual immorality is a sin against your body—don't you know that your body is the temple of the Holy Spirit?" (Chandler 2014, 65; see Mally 2006, 185).

Purity for these Evangelical authors is thus not simply a matter of the flesh but a kind of deep inner 'radiance' or 'illumination' that emanates from within. Purity is a deep inner quality of chastity, abstinence, and sexual wholesomeness that prepares the young woman to become a 'princess' awaiting her ideal 'princely' match (Bishop 2000; Mally 2006): "True purity is evident all over the body. To attain it, young women must be pure in all respects, not just their bodies but also their minds and hearts . . . When young women follow [the] purity path the real beauty of a true princess shines through as she waits for her eternal prince" (DeRogatis 2014, 24).

Ultimately, sexual purity is understood to be not simply a matter of personal salvation but a much larger concern that affects the whole of society: "in the Evangelical world-view sexual sins impact everyone . . . A person's sexual misdeed has individual, communal and eternal consequences. Those who fall into sexual sin and impurity . . . jeopardize their own salvation, the salvation of future children, and souls waiting to be brought to Christ. Sexual sins—masturbation, premarital sex, adultery, and same-sex acts, and more—imperil . . . the salvation of the world" (DeRogatis 2014, 3).

Indeed, the modern Christian purity literature also includes a number of 'deliverance manuals' that aim to help to expel the demonic forces that enter the body through sexual sin. In texts such as Terry Weir's *Holy Sex: God's Purpose and Plan for our Sex* (1999), the physical body itself becomes an arena for the battle between good and evil, often played out in sexual terms: "the human body can either be filled with the Holy Spirit or defiled by demonic residents" (DeRogatis 2014, 74). In terms that strongly recall early Christian monastic literature (Brakke 2006), the body thus becomes the site of intense *spiritual warfare*, waged with the pure weapons of prayer, confession, and Scripture against the defiling demonic forces of sexual temptation (Weir 1999).

In sum, the Evangelical literature on sexuality, desire, and chastity provides ample evidence that the concern with purity is by no means a relic of the premodern past but is indeed alive and well in the contemporary world.

THE POWER OF THE IMPURE: PURITY, POLLUTION, AND TRANSGRESSION IN ESOTERIC RITUAL

If purity is a central concern for most religious traditions and a key means of ensuring the integrity of the individual and social body, that does not necessarily mean that its opposite—impurity—is an absolute evil to be denied or destroyed. On the contrary, purity and impurity are often understood to be dialectical and interdependent categories—like the spiritual and physical aspects of the human in the example of Islam (discussed earlier) or like the periods of ritual anti-structure and 'carnivalesque' behavior that accompany many religious festivals (the hedonistic chaos Mardi Gras immediately before the fast of Lent, the celebration of 'topsy-turvy' rituals such as Holi in Hinduism). As Mary Douglas observes in her classic anthropological study, *Purity and Danger*, the impure spaces that lie outside the established social order also embody tremendous *power*—the dangerous but fecund power inherent in the universe itself. This is a power that can also be tapped into and harnessed by ritual means: "The danger risked by boundary transgression is power. Those vulnerable margins and those attacking forces which threaten to destroy good order represent the powers inhering the cosmos. Ritual which can harness these for good is harnessing power indeed" (2002 [1966], 199; Urban 2000).

Perhaps the clearest example of this ritual use of boundary transgression and the 'power of the impure' is found in South Asian Tantric traditions. A movement that spread through the Hindu and Buddhist communities from roughly the fifth century CE onward, Tantra makes frequent use of symbols, substances, and practices that are considered extremely impure by conventional social and religious standards. In the Hindu Tantric schools, the most famous example of this ritual use of transgression is the 'five M's' (*pancha-makara*), or five things that begin with the phoneme *ma* in Sanskrit, namely: *mamsa* (meat), *madya* (wine), *matsya* (fish), *mudra* (a term of some debate that may refer either to parched grain or to specific gestures and postures used in yogic practice), and *maithuna* (sexual union; see Urban 2010, 102–123; Flood 1996, 189–197; Sanderson 1985; White 2003).

The last of these, *maithuna* or sexual union, often involves explicit use of impurity. According to many Hindu Tantric texts, the intercourse should also be performed in a deliberately transgressive manner—for example, in violation of class relations (such as sex between a high and a low class partner), in the 'reverse' position (the woman on top), and in some cases with a menstruating woman (Urban 2010, 110). Sexual union here is not primarily a matter of sensual pleasure. Rather, according to the oldest forms of the Tantric ritual, the aim is actually to collect the sexual emissions from the male and female partners, which are then consumed orally as a sacramental meal (White 2003; Urban 2010, 110–113).

Ultimately, the goal of this systematic boundary transgression is precisely to tap into and harness the tremendous power that flows through the universe. In Hindu Tantra, this power is *shakti*, the divine energy of the Goddess (Shakti or Devi), which permeates and sustains the cosmos, the social order, and the human body alike. As the impure, dangerous, and yet creative 'remainders' overflow the boundaries of the human body, the sexual fluids are seen as particularly potent embodiments of this divine energy. When ritually consecrated and consumed, they are said to be transformed from a terrible source of pollution into the ultimate source of both material power and spiritual liberation (Urban 2010; White 2003). As Alexis Sanderson notes in his classic study of purity and power in Kashmir, the Tantric traditions offered a radical ideal of empowerment, precisely through their rejection of orthodox notions of purity and their embrace of transgressive substances that lay outside of the dominant social and religious order: "This inhibition, which preserved that path of purity and barred his entrance into the path of power, was to be obliterated through the experience of a violent, duality-devouring expansion of consciousness beyond the narrow confines of orthodox control into the domain of excluded possibilities by gratifying with wine, meat and . . . caste-free intercourse" (1985, 199).

While South Asian Tantra may provide the clearest example of the 'power of the impure,' similar uses of impurity and transgression can be seen in various other esoteric traditions. Modern occultism and magic in the British, American, and European traditions also often draws upon the power of impure substances, including sexual fluids, blood, and other bodily 'leftovers' as a source of supernatural power and spiritual liberation (Urban 2000; 2005).

Pure Speculation: Modern Theories of Purity and Pollution

There is a large body of theoretical literature that has attempted to explain the concepts of purity from a range of psychological, sociological, evolutionary, and materialist approaches. One of the earliest views expressed by authors such as Sigmund Freud is that the concept of impurity and the widespread practice of purification rituals reflect a kind of 'obsessional neurosis.' Ritual concerns with purity are, in effect, comparable to the compulsive washing of hands and other neurotic behaviors (Freud 1989, 67; see Boyer 2002, 238–239).

However, most later anthropological literature has attempted to understand the concepts of purity and pollution within their local religious and cultural contexts. Perhaps the most important work on the concepts of pollution and taboo remains the classic work of Mary Douglas, *Purity and Danger*, first published in 1966. As Douglas suggests, dirt or impurity is best understood as "matter out of place," that is, what falls outside of a given cultural and religious classificatory system: "Uncleanness or dirt is that which must not be included if a pattern is to be maintained" (2002, 50). As such, rites of purification are neither neurotic nor marginal to religious life; rather, they are central to the maintenance of symbolic order and cultural meaning: "rituals of purity and impurity create unity in experience. So far from being aberrations from the central project of religion, they are positive contributions to atonement. By their means, symbolic patters are worked out and publicly displayed. Within these patterns disparate experience is given meaning" (2002, 3). Moreover, Douglas suggests, these concepts of purity and pollution are by no means relics of a 'primitive' religious mind of the past but are very much still with us in 'modern' societies.

More recently, some scholars have also tried to explain the concepts of purity and pollution from the perspectives of cognitive science and evolutionary theory. As Pascal Boyer argues, the ideas of pollution surrounding objects such as corpses can be explained largely as a result of our evolution as a species and the ways in which human cognition operates. The impulse to avoid contact with dead bodies and to cleanse ourselves after such contact has probably served a useful role in our survival as a species, even if we aren't always very clear about why we do so: "For evolutionary reasons humans may be rather good at detecting definite sources of contamination yet remain very vague in their explicit reasons for avoiding them" (2002, 215).

Finally, other scholars have viewed the concepts of purity and impurity as primarily a matter of power, in both a material and symbolic sense. As Bruce Lincoln suggests in his analysis of the Hindu class system described in the Vedas, the classifications of purity and impurity reinforce a clear social hierarchy with the Brahmans (the authors of the Vedas) at the top and commoners at the bottom, while simultaneously 'naturalizing' this hierarchy by making it appear to be inscribed into the very fabric of the universe (and so very difficult to challenge): "More than legitimate, arbitrary social hierarchies are thus represented as if given by nature, and agitation against their inequities . . . is made to seem but the raving of lunatics" (2014, 141).

Others have examined the close association between femininity and impurity (for example, in the taboos surrounding menstrual blood), arguing that this is largely a means of controlling and subordinating female bodies. As Julie Marcus suggests in her study of gender and hierarchy in Turkey (1992), the primary function of Islam's elaborate purity codes is to control women by reproducing and naturalizing gender hierarchies. However, as more recent authors such as Richard Gauvain suggest, purity is by no means always or solely about control and domination. Rather, as he argues in his study of contemporary Salafi Islam in Egypt, women can also in some cases achieve a form of agency and "religious empowerment" through their active embrace of purity rules (2014, 259; see Mahmood 2011, 112).

In sum, it would seem most accurate to say that purity cannot be reduced to any single religious function—whether it be a psychological need or an evolutionary by-product, a mechanism of domination, or a means of empowerment. Rather, much like sexuality in Michel Foucault's classic analysis, purity is more like a linchpin that lies at the intersection of many different interests, conflicts, and negotiations, and thus the nodal point for a "great number of maneuvers" and "varied strategies" (1990, 103). As the intersection between the individual body, the social body, and the cosmos, purity is very much this sort of crucial node or linchpin connecting multiple levels of existence.

GLOSSARY

Dharma religious and social duty, law.
Ghusl full body washing, greater ablution.
Halakhah collective body of Jewish law based on written and oral Torah.

Impurity a state of religious uncleanliness and/or contact with spiritually polluting substances, which may or may not overlap with modern secular ideas of hygiene.

Purity a state of religious cleanliness and freedom from pollution, which may or may not overlap with modern secular ideas of hygiene.

Shari'ah Islamic law, based on the Qur'an and *hadith.*

Shaucha purity, cleanliness.

Shuddha pure, clean, bright.

Tahara(h) purity.

Transgression the violation of conventional rules of purity, sometimes done intentionally and with an aim of unleashing sources of physical, social, and cosmic power.

Varna social class.

Visuddhi purification, holiness.

REFERENCES

Bakhtiar, Laleh. 1996. *Encyclopedia of Islamic Law: A Comparison of the Major Schools.* Chicago, IL: Kazi Publications.

Bishop, Jennie. 2000. *The Princess and the Kiss: A Story of God's Gift of Purity.* Anderson, IN: Warner Press.

Bouhdiba, Abdelwahab. 1985. *Sexuality in Islam.* Boston, MA: Routledge & Kegan Paul.

Boyer, Pascal. 2002. *Religion Explained: The Evolutionary Origins of Religious Thought.* New York: Basic Books.

Brakke, David. 1995. "The Problematization of Nocturnal Emissions in Early Christian Syria, Egypt and Gaul." *Journal of Early Christian Studies* 3(4): 419–460.

Brakke, David. 2006. *Demons and the Making of the Monk: Spiritual Combat in Early Christianity.* Cambridge, MA: Harvard University Press.

Buddhaghosa, Bhadantacariya. 2010. *The Path of Purification: Visuddhimagga.* Translated by Bhikkhu Nanamoli. Kandy, Sri Lanka: Buddhist Publication Society.

Chandler, S. Dawn. 2014. *The Purity Movement.* S. Dawn Chandler [self-published].

DeRogatis, Amy. 2014. *Sexuality and Salvation in American Evangelicalism.* New York: Oxford University Press.

Dirks, Nicholas B. 2001. *Castes of Mind: Colonialism and the Making of Modern India.* Princeton, NJ: Princeton University Press.

Doniger, Wendy. 2009. *The Hindus: An Alternative History.* New York: Penguin.

Douglas, Mary. 2002. *Purity and Danger: An Analysis of Concepts of Pollution and Taboo.* New York: Routledge. Original edition, 1966.

Dumont, Louis. 1981. *Homo Hierarchicus: The Caste System and its Implications.* Chicago, IL: University of Chicago Press.

Faure, Bernard. 2003. *The Power of Denial: Buddhism, Purity and Gender.* Princeton, NJ: Princeton University Press.

Feinstein, Eve Lavavi. 2014. *Sexual Pollution in the Hebrew Bible.* New York: Oxford University Press.

Flood, Gavin. 1996. *An Introduction to Hinduism.* Cambridge: Cambridge University Press.

Foucault, Michel. 1990. *The History of Sexuality, Volume I: Introduction.* New York: Penguin.

Freud, Sigmund. 1989. *The Future of an Illusion.* New York: W. W. Norton.

Gauvain, Richard. 2014. *Salafi Ritual Purity: In the Presence of God.* New York: Routledge.

Harvey, Peter. 2012. *An Introduction to Buddhism: Teachings, History and Practice*. Cambridge: Cambridge University Press.

Lincoln, Bruce. 2014. *Discourse and the Construction of Society: Comparative Studies in Myth, Ritual, and Classification*. New York: Oxford University Press.

Macoby, Hyram. 2009. *Ritual and Morality: The Ritual Purity System and its Place in Judaism*. Cambridge: Cambridge University Press.

Maghen, Ze'ev. 2005. *Virtues of the Flesh: Passion and Purity in Early Islamic Jurisprudence*. Leiden: Brill.

Mahmood, Saba. 2011. *The Politics of Piety: The Islamic Revival and the Feminist Subject*. Princeton, NJ: Princeton University Press.

Mally, Sarah. 2006. *Before You Meet Prince Charming: A Guide to Radiant Purity*. Marion, IA: Tomorrow's Forefathers.

Marcus, Julie. 1992. *A World of Difference: Islam and Gender Hierarchy in Turkey*. London: Zed Books.

Mendelsohn, Oliver. 1998. *The Untouchables: Subordination, Poverty and the State in Modern India*. New York: Cambridge University Press.

Milner Jr., Murray. 1994. *Status and Sacredness: A General Theory of Status Relations and an Analysis of Indian Culture*. New York: Oxford University Press.

Olivelle, Patrick, trans. 2004. *Manu's Code of Law: A Critical Edition of the Manava-Dharmashastra*. New York: Oxford University Press.

Ortner, Sherry B. 2013. "Purification Rite." *Encyclopedia Britannica*. <http://www.britannica.com/EBchecked/topic/483975/purification-rite>.

Preston, James. 2005. "Purification: An Overview." In *The Encyclopedia of Religion*, edited by Lindsay Jones. New York: Thomson Gale, vol. 11: 7503–7511.

Ricoeur, Paul. 1986. *The Symbolism of Evil*, translated by Emerson Buchanan. Boston, MA: Beacon Press. Original edition, 1960.

Sanderson, Alexis. 1985. "Purity and Power among the Brahmins of Kashmir." In *The Category of the Person*, edited by Michael Carrithers, Steven Collins, and Steven Lukes. New York: Cambridge University Press, 190–216.

Urban, Hugh B. 2000. "The Power of the Impure: Transgression, Violence and Secrecy in Shakta Bengali Tantra and Modern Western Magic." *Numen* 50(3): 269–308.

Urban, Hugh B. 2005. *Magia Sexualis: Sex, Magic and Liberation in Modern Western Esotericism*. Berkeley, CA: University of California Press.

Urban, Hugh B. 2010. *The Power of Tantra: Religion, Sexuality, and the Politics of South Asian Studies*. London: I. B. Tauris.

Weir, Terry. 1999. *Holy Sex: God's Purpose and Plan for Sex*. Dallas, TX: Cuington Press.

White, David Gordon. 2003. *Kiss of the Yogini: "Tantric Sex" in its South Asian Contexts*. Chicago, IL: University of Chicago Press.

FURTHER READING

Bouhdiba 1985 [*A good starting point for understanding purity and sexuality in Islam. However, it should be complemented with later, more nuanced works such as Ze'ev Maghen's work on purity in early Islamic jurisprudence.*]

Douglas 2002 [1966] [*A classic anthropological study of the categories of purity, pollution, and taboo, and it remains a must-read text for any work on these topics.*]

Dumont 1981 [*Though outdated and suffering from some of the legacies of Orientalism, this remains an important starting point for the understanding of class, caste, and purity in India. It should be supplemented with other recent works, such as Nicholas Dirks's Castes of Mind.*]

Ortner 2013 [*A very useful anthropological overview covering many different cultures and practices.*]

Ricoeur 1986 [*A profound philosophical reflection on the ideas of impurity, defilement, sin, and guilt.*]

Sanderson 1985 [*One of the best studies of the ritual use of impurity in the Tantric tradition, which has inspired many works by later scholars, such as David Gordon White (2003), Hugh B. Urban (2000, 2010), and others.*]

CHAPTER 41

··

SALVATION

··

GAVIN FLOOD

Chapter Summary

- As a general category, salvation entails overcoming the human limitations of material causation, suffering, and death. Despite its emergence within Christianity, it can include concepts in other religions that claim to promote human flourishing and the transcendence of mortality as a goal.
- Salvation is linked to eschatology.
- Salvation in Christianity has its origin in Judaism, in sacrifice during the Second Temple period.
- An example of broader cross-cultural usage is provided by salvation as liberation in Hinduism, in relation to earlier Vedic sacrifice, and in light of the variety of conceptions of liberation.
- Salvation has strengths and weaknesses as a category of comparison: it draws attention to broad similarities, but it retains an irreducibly specific character in relation to Christianity.

The idea that human beings can be rescued from the defective condition they are in or transcend the limitations of material causation and death is a theme found across religions. Although the category 'salvation' developed in the context of Christian theology linked to the idea of Jesus Christ as a 'savior,' it has come to be used as a fundamental category defining religion in general. Arguably all religions have a doctrine of salvation or soteriology that claim that the human condition of death and suffering can be overcome. Doctrines of salvation in religions present accounts of how humans can flourish, which means how they can achieve or be restored to a state of completion or wholeness. Yet there is great variation as to how this is understood and achieved and great variation in the analysis of how the limiting human condition came about in the first place. The idea of salvation in the history of religions has translated into political action and regimes of governance and law that have sought to articulate this idea.

Salvation in different religions entails a trichotomy of related concepts: grace, the idea that salvation occurs less through human effort and more due to a higher power; effort, the idea that salvation occurs through human effort to overcome ignorance and/or sin; and ritual, the idea that certain practices or sequences of action have an automatic efficacy independent of human or divine intention. For religions, or subgroups within a given religion, that emphasize grace—the blessing or favor of a higher power—human beings have an essentially receptive role; whereas for those that emphasize effort and technique, humans have an active role in a journey along a structured path toward salvation. We see an emphasis on grace in Judaism, Christianity, and Islam, for example, as well as in some forms of Hinduism and even in Buddhism. Although Buddhist teaching eschews the idea of a transcendent, unchanging god, its Pure Land form—developed particularly in China and Japan—claims that salvation comes through the power of the Buddha Amitābha or Amida. This is effectively a theistic tradition: repeat the name of Amitābha and he will meet you at death to take you to the pure land out of his compassion for suffering humanity. Overtly theistic religions tend to emphasize grace or compassion in salvation. Some traditions such as Gnosticism claim that the dispelling of ignorance comes about through a saving cognition or knowledge (gnosis) that conveys humans from a world of darkness to a world of light. If human effort is important in salvation, then this takes the form of leading a good life and cultivating moral virtues as well as practices such as prayer and meditation understood as methods in transcending ignorance and/or sin. In Christianity there is a debate about whether 'works' that entail human effort lead to salvation or grace and a similar discussion is found in other religions. Distinct from this axis of grace vs. human efforts is another: individual vs. collective: in Judaism, Christianity, and Islam, salvation has been linked to a political vision of the human future, whereas in other traditions, such as Hinduism, salvation has been conceptualized in a more individualistic manner, in which particular persons achieve liberation without broader political consequences.

The Abrahamic religions, Judaism, Christianity, and Islam, generally understand salvation either in terms of the perfection of this world at the end of history, when a savior figure or Messiah appears, or in terms of individual perfection in another, non-material world or heaven reached after death. This also holds true of Zoroastrianism. Religions originating in India such as Buddhism, Hinduism, and Jainism understand salvation as liberation from the cycle of rebirth and as redemption from the acts committed in former lives, either achieved in this life or after the death of the body. The term 'liberation' translates a number of Sanskrit words (see section "Salvation in Hinduism") and, although we can take it to be equivalent to salvation, the two concepts do not directly map onto each other. Liberation is a less theologically loaded term that potentially could replace salvation as a more appropriate category for the study of religions, although 'liberation' is also problematic in that the English word connotes a political struggle for freedom from oppression not necessarily entailed by its use as an analogue to salvation.

As there are variations in how salvation is understood, so there are varied ideas about who can attain it and how it can be attained. Several religions have specialists—e.g. monks and nuns, ascetics, and mendicants—who forgo normal life to seek salvation and prepare themselves for it. The salvific goal of these religious virtuosi often stands in contrast with the aims of the majority who seek not so much the 'other-worldly' goal of salvation, to use Weber's phrase, but the more mundane objectives of "health, wealth, and long life" (Weber 1991 [1946], 277). What we mean by salvation is therefore closely linked to what we mean by religion. In the contemporary secularized context of the West, salvation might be understood in terms of developing well-being and health. This chapter offers a general account of salvation and then presents two examples from the histories of Christianity and Hinduism.

Theories of Salvation

Salvation is a noun related to the verb "to save." It has the everyday use in English of an action that rescues a person from a more-or-less perilous situation: e.g. saving someone from drowning, or saving time or trouble. The use of the verb in Christianity is a metaphorical extension of this literal meaning to indicate a transformation from a condition of sin and suffering—that can be metaphorically expressed as drowning—to a state of grace or contentment achieved in the future and conceptualized in Abrahamic religions, Zoroastrianism, and Pure Land Buddhism as 'heaven' or a heaven equivalent. Salvation is a transition from the human condition of suffering and death to its antithesis, a condition believed to transcend death.

Religion and Salvation

In contrast to skeptical views about the category 'religion,' other scholars have understood salvation to be central to it. Martin Riesebrodt argues for the universality of religion, not as a concept but as a set of social practices, and offers a substantive definition of religion as practices "of establishing contact with superhuman powers" (Riesebrodt 2010, 13). Such contact involves the idea of salvation, although Riesebrodt has little to say about the category of 'salvation' per se. Religions hold out the promise of averting misfortune and ultimately of salvation. This promise of salvation, which remains constant, needs to be distinguished from the functions of religion—e.g. group belonging—that vary in particular historical and cultural instances. Promise and function can also be distinguished from 'religiousness' or the individual appropriation of religion. But what is important about religion is the *promise* of salvation, as arrived at through religious practices (Stausberg 2009, 274).

The idea that salvation is linked to the repeated practices of religion is compelling. It is not so much what people believe or think but what they do that defines their identity within a particular religious tradition. Such action mediates between human and superhuman powers in averting misfortune and assuring final salvation, conceptualized minimally as the cessation of suffering, or as peace, or a state of happiness abiding in a heavenly realm. Many scholars have emphasized the importance of action. Staal argues for the independence of the ritual domain quite distinct from doctrine and belief (1988); Bowker has spoken about religions as systems of 'somatic exploration' (1987); and I have emphasized religious action as mediating the human encounter with mystery (2013). Max Weber most influentially drew our attention to the importance of religious action and religion as interest in salvation expressed through social action, namely religious practices, particularly asceticism (Weber 1991 [1946]). All of these approaches show us that, if we try to understand religion primarily in terms of belief or worldview, we can find no unifying features, but if we understand religions as ways of being in the world, as systems of practice, then we find cultural forms that are shared and orientated toward salvation.

There are a variety of practices geared to the goals of averting misfortune and offering salvation. On the one hand we have popular practices of averting misfortune through protective prayers or repeating protective utterances, while on the other we have more extreme kinds of asceticism and meditation practiced by religious virtuosi intent upon final salvation rather than worldly prosperity. Weber gives a list of different possibilities of redemption, including freedom from political servitude, freedom from the material body, freedom from evil and the servitude of sin, or freedom from rebirth, and the system of compensation of the acts of former births (Weber 1991 [1946], 80–81). What these different conceptions have in common is that salvation creates a meaningful cosmos for humans to dwell in. Salvation brings the apparent absurdity of death into the realm of human meaning and becomes the motivation for the transformation of the world. As Weber has argued, the other-worldly asceticism of Christianity in the service of disciplining the mind and body in readiness for salvation becomes a this-worldly asceticism with primarily Calvinistic Protestantism and transforms the public realm through the development of capitalism. Thus, on this view, salvation is not simply an ideal to be realized in a different world but has direct impact on this world and on people's behavior. Religious ideas of salvation impact upon the economic and social realm and, according to Weber, contributed to the rise of capitalism and thereby the global economic system we have today. In this sense salvation has had a direct impact upon contemporary world politics. Despite commonalities, salvation has specific meaning in particular religions. By way of illustration let us take as examples Christianity and Hinduism.

SALVATION IN CHRISTIANITY

Salvation has been the central concern of Christianity throughout its history, but its meaning has varied in different periods and according to different sources. On the one hand we have salvation as referring to the saving grace that God bestows on believers symbolized through the ceremony of baptism; on the other we have the idea of salvation as a future event that occurs after the return of the savior Jesus Christ, accompanied by a divine judgment that separates the saved from the damned. These views are not incompatible. To understand the Christian view of salvation we need to see its origin in Judaism in the ideas of the Messiah and of sacrifice, both of which come to form an integral whole in the Christian understanding of salvation. The Hebrew term *mashiach*, the anointed one, denoted a king who would return to restore order and justice to the world. Translated into Greek as *christos*, it came to be associated by early Christian communities with the person of Jesus and his message and life, as read back into the Hebrew Scriptures that became, from the Christian perspective, the Old Testament. This Messiah figure was identified with Jesus from an early period in Christian history and became central in its idea of salvation. Christ was also identified with the sacrifice into whom went all the sins of the world, not only those of the local community.

Rather than awaiting a future Messiah, Christians understood that Jesus Christ had already brought salvation (Davies 1997, 103). This is a significant shift from the Jewish attitude for the early Christians who, after Jesus's death, believed that he had fulfilled the earlier prophecies about the Messiah. Jesus saves humanity from sin, a quality of guilt that all human beings have inherited from Adam, the first human. The majority view in all Christian theologies is that this original sin was paid for or neutralized by the sacrifice of Christ on the cross: Christ is God incarnate and through his sacrificial death original sin is transferred to him and so removed from the human community. His subsequent resurrection bears witness to the new life beyond death that he thereby establishes.

All modern theologies must deal with and reinterpret salvation as the central doctrine of Christianity, and all theologies must maintain an economy of salvation that takes into account the fallen nature of humankind and God's saving grace through the death and resurrection of Christ. Thus, for example, the Protestant theologian Wolfhart Pannenberg (1928–2014) combines a philosophical account of history derived from Hegel with a Christian account of salvation. History is God's self-revelation through time. Sin is a quality that all humans inherit, a "motivational structure that precedes and underlies individual decisions" (Pannenberg 1985, 119) and so distorts the will. The fall is thus repeated in each individual life, and to overcome this humanity needs the saving grace of Christ.

From this brief sketch we see that salvation in Christianity is accompanied by a specific set of related concepts. We have to be saved from something and that is 'sin,' understood as a distortion of the will and rectified by the sacrificial death and resurrection of Christ. Salvation therefore has a future orientation and a view of history as a meaningful enterprise that moves toward a salvific telos. By contrast we can see major differences in understanding what salvation can mean through an examination of Hinduism.

SALVATION IN HINDUISM

In Hinduism salvation means liberation from the cycle of reincarnation that is a condition of suffering. A number of Sanskrit terms could be used as equivalents to "salvation."

Among them the most important are *mokṣa* from a verbal root *muc*, which means "to release" or "to free" (as an animal might be freed from a trap). *Nirvāṇa* is used, particularly in Buddhism, with the primary designation being "blowing out," that is, blowing out the fires of greed, hate, and delusion. The term *kaivalya*, "solitude," from the word *kevala*, "alone," is used in Jainism and the Hindu philosophy called Sāṃkhya, to denote the idea of salvation as the soul's achieving isolation from the world (and from other souls). All of these terms are translated into English as "liberation" to indicate the shared conception that the person is freed from repeated rebirths. For Hinduism and Jainism this means that the soul (*ātman*) is reincarnated over and over again in human, animal, and divine bodies depending upon its actions (*karma*), whereas for Buddhism there is a process of rebirth but without the idea of an unchanging essence occupying different bodies. Every act has an effect that might come to fruition in future lives and the ultimate goal of life is salvation from this endless cycle.

Beyond this basic structure liberation is understood in various ways by different Hindu traditions. While there are numerous views of what liberation is, they boil down to three fundamental positions. Firstly, non-dualist traditions, such as Advaita Vedānta, understand liberation to be the direct cognition during this life that the self is identical to the absolute. Secondly, theistic traditions, such as those of Vishnu, regard liberation to be the soul directly experiencing God at the end of life. Thirdly, what we might call isolationist traditions, such as Śaiva Siddhānta and Sāṃkhya, regard liberation to be the isolation of the soul from contact with matter, as occurs at the end of life.

The idea of liberation came to be associated with the idea of sacrifice. The religion of the Vedas is a religion of sacrifice par excellence. Sacrifice was regarded as an obligation on the highest social group, the Brahmins, who performed elaborate sacrifices for paying patrons where the sacrificial victim was regarded as a substitute or symbol for the patron and a way of purifying the patron of sin (*pāpa*) (Doniger 2014, 208). In the course of time the goal of sacrifice was reframed in more general terms and related to a broader range of practices focused on salvation or liberation, although the sacrificial religion continued. The later layers of the Veda, the Upaniṣads composed from around 800 BCE, speak of the true sacrifice being that of the self to the absolute: the sacrifice is internalized and in a sense its deeper meaning of self-sacrifice recognized. Liberation of the self that becomes the dominant ideology of the later tradition may have grown out of the sacrificial logic of the earlier tradition. We see in Hinduism the trichotomy of grace, self-effort, and ritual playing out through history. The distinctiveness of ritual's potential contribution to salvation is illustrated by Vedic sacrifice, which has ritual efficacy regardless of human intention in contrast to human effort in yoga and grace in the religions of Vishnu.

In contemporary Hinduism, liberation from the cycle of reincarnation is still an important ideal. While most Hindus will be more concerned with everyday interests such as worldly success, some will focus on liberation. There are still strong traditions of male and female world renouncers; yoga is popular among the Indian middle class; and devotion to particular gurus is an important feature of the religious landscape in India and the West. Yoga, originating in a technology to achieve salvation through stilling the mind, has become a multi-million dollar global industry focused on health and well-being rather than the traditional goal of liberation. We see here how salvation as human flourishing understood as well-being or even fitness, has been transformed in the contemporary world. Rather than an 'other-worldly' salvation—the traditional goal of Yoga as a system of philosophy being the isolation of the soul from matter—we now have a 'this-worldly' salvation of well-being in community. What might even be called a world-negating set of practices and ideology has become transformed into a world-affirming set of bodily regimes to promote well-being; salvation comes to reflect a broader set of cultural values in the West.

Comparing Salvations

From these accounts of salvation in Christianity and Hinduism we can begin to draw out a broader understanding of the place of salvation in religions and in contemporary Western culture. In Christianity and Hinduism, the idea of salvation is historically rooted in sacrifice: there is an affinity in sacrifice with salvation in that the sacrificial patron or community is transformed through that practice. Salvation is a kind of purification, and similarly salvation across religions can be understood as a moral purification of the self, which is also a healing of the human condition. In Abrahamic religions the idea of salvation has been associated with particular political regimes regarded as generating social forms conducive to the common good and reception of salvation at the end of history. Before the relegation of religion (specifically Christianity) to the private realm in the West, the ideal of salvation informed governance from the king as analogue to the deity. In contemporary terms—with the emptying of churches in northern Europe and much of North America—there is a weakened sense of salvation in the generic term "spirituality" that designates vague sets of practices and ideas to promote human flourishing in a secularized world (see Streib/Klein, "Religion and Spirituality," this volume). While the harder sense of salvation is perhaps restricted to traditional religions whose origins are in the distant past, a softer sense of salvation is relevant to contemporary Western cultures in the promotion of 'spiritual' values that seek to affirm meaning in life beyond the satisfaction of basic human needs.

Histories of salvation or liberation are distinct to particular traditions although there are commonalities and there is a salvationist affinity in sacrifice. So long as humans are unable to surmount the difficulties that they face, especially "the vulnerability and mortality of our bodies" (Riesebrodt 2010, 183), religions will continue with the promise of salvation. The function of salvation in the history of religions has united communities in a common goal and for a shared purpose; but it has also divided communities over its nature, how it can be achieved, and how it is translated into contemporary, religious politics—salvation can be a destructive ideal when violence serves it. In the contemporary world we thus have inherited traditional theories of salvation from religions whose origins lay in the premodern period, along with the development of analogues to the idea of salvation in secular spirituality. Contemporary religious politics draw on the symbols of salvation of their own traditions and on ideas about the end of our current world and the formation of a new world governed by particular political regimes. This clearly shows that the idea of salvation is not merely restricted to those within religious traditions but impacts populations on a global scale. Religious fundamentalisms in Christianity and Islam, for example, take the idea of salvation seriously and literally, translating a salvific ideology into political action.

GLOSSARY

Economy of salvation the Christian doctrine of God's plan for salvation.

Grace the free favor or blessing of God, often the forgiveness of sins. The doctrine is maintained by a number of theistic religions and a very similar doctrine is maintained in Pure Land Buddhism.

Justification in Christianity the doctrine that God removes guilt and sin through the saving power of Christ.

Liberation a term used to denote salvation in the religions of India where it indicates freedom from the cycle of reincarnation.

Sin the idea in Abrahamic religions that human beings possess a particular quality due to disobeying God's will. In Christianity original sin is an inherited distortion from Adam, the first man.

Soteriology the doctrine of salvation explicitly or implicitly maintained by religions.

REFERENCES

Bowker, John. 1987. *Licensed Insanities: Religions and Belief in God in the Contemporary World.* London: Darton, Longman & Todd.

Campbell, Jonathan. 1997. "Messianic Hope in Second Temple Judaism." In *The Coming Deliverer: Millennial Themes in World Religions*, edited by Fiona Bowie. Cardiff: University of Wales Press, 77–101.

Collins, Steven. 1998. *Nirvana and Other Buddhist Felicities.* Cambridge: Cambridge University Press.

Davies, D. P. 1997. "Eschatological Hope in the Early Christian Community: New Testament Perspectives." In *The Coming Deliverer: Millennial Themes in World Religions*, edited by Fiona Bowie. Cardiff: University of Wales Press, 102–118.

Doniger, Wendy. 2014. *On Hinduism.* Oxford: Oxford University Press.

Dundas, Paul. 1992. *The Jains.* London: Routledge.

Fitzgerald, Timothy. 2000. *The Ideology of Religious Studies.* Oxford: Oxford University Press.

Flood, Gavin. 2013. *The Importance of Religion: Meaning and Action in Our Strange World.* Oxford: Wiley-Blackwell.

MacCulloch, Diarmaid. 2009. *A History of Christianity.* London: Penguin.

Mandair, Arvind-Pal S. 2013. *Sikhism: A Guide for the Perplexed.* New York: Bloomsbury.

Pannenberg, Wolfhart. 1985. *Anthropology in Theological Perspective*. London and New York: T. & T. Clark.

Riesebrodt, Martin. 2010. *The Promise of Salvation: A Theory of Religion*. Chicago, IL: University of Chicago Press.

Staal, Frits. 1988. *Rules Without Meaning: Ritual, Mantras, and the Human Sciences*. New York and Bern: Peter Lang.

Stausberg, Michael. 2009. "Interventionist Practices and the Promises of Religion: On Martin Riesebrodt, *Cultus Und Heilsversprechen* (2007)." In *Contemporary Theories of Religion: A Critical Companion*, edited by Michael Stausberg. London and New York: Routledge, 264–282.

Weber, Max. 1991. *From Max Weber: Essays in Sociology*, edited by H. H. Gerth and C. Wright Mills. London: Routledge. Original edition, 1946.

FURTHER READING

Bowie, Fiona, ed. 1997. *The Coming Deliverer: Millennial Themes in World Religions*. Cardiff: University of Wales Press. [*This series of essays presents examples from different religions of the idea of a future savior. The volume as a whole presents the view that millennialism is a common theme found in religions.*]

Hall, T. William. 1978. "Paths to Salvation." In *Introduction to the Study of Religion*, edited by T. William Hall. San Francisco, CA: Harper & Row. [*Hall argues that salvation is the common structure of world religions. It entails a number of elements that show that it is a fundamental category shared not only by Judaic religions but by Indo-Asian ones as well.*]

Riesebrodt 2010 [*In this important book Riesebrodt offers a definition of religion that entails the idea of salvation. This is discussed in the context of debates about the viability of the category 'religion.'*]

Stausberg 2009 [*This article presents an excellent overview of Riesebrodt's thesis and offers a critical evaluation of it.*]

Watson, Alex, Dominic Goodall, and S. L. P. Anjaneya Sarma. 2013. *An Inquiry into the Nature of Liberation*. Pondichéry: Institut Française de Pondichéry. [*This is a translation and critically edited text of a Śaiva Siddhānta theologian, Rāmakaṇṭha, who presents different Hindu, Jain, and Buddhist views of salvation in order to refute them.*]

PART VI

PROCESSES

CHAPTER 42

....

DIFFERENTIATION

....

STEVE BRUCE

CHAPTER SUMMARY

....

- Differentiation plays a major part in most explanations of secularization.
- Social differentiation—social division resulting primarily from the division of labor in modernizing nations—is normally secularizing due to the fragmentation of overarching religious institutions into competing sects and denominations.
- This is correlated with increased religious pluralism, which is generally secularizing, due to decreasing dogmatism.
- Functional (or structural) differentiation—the increasing autonomy of activities into clearly distinguishable systems driven by their own values—has an important implication for religion: as religion becomes separated off as a discrete subsystem, it loses power and influence. The creation of secular alternatives leads to a decline in the popularity of recourse to religion.
- Claims that modernization is characterized by de-differentiation—as advanced by rational-choice theory/supply-side approaches—are unconvincing.

Differentiation is primarily of interest to students of religion because it is a key element in the explanation of secularization.[1] Although there are still arguments about whether and to what extent religion has declined in power, popularity, and prestige in the United States, there is no doubt that other Western societies have become obviously more secular as they have become wealthier, more urban, more industrialized, more culturally diverse, and more democratic. The theory of secularization postulates a non-accidental and non-tautological link between modernization (a complex set of processes that is far from uniform across nations and regions) and a decline in religion's popularity and power. Note that modernization here refers primarily to the linked series of changes in

---

[1] Due to health concerns, Steve Bruce was unable to revise his initial draft. Summary, further readings, and glossary have been added by Steven Engler.

Western societies from the late eighteenth century. It is not supposed that the Western past forms a template which the rest of the world must follow (Bruce 2011, 177–201). Not surprisingly, given the complexity of modernization, there are many explanations of secularization, but differentiation plays a major part in most (granted that there are multiple modernities and divergent processes of differentiation). Although they are intertwined, for the purposes of explanation we can distinguish social and functional differentiation.

SOCIAL DIFFERENTIATION

Precisely how social differentiation occurs varies considerably from society to society— and it is more prominent in modern Western societies—but the basic idea is simple. The growth of industrial production and the division of labor it entails, and the shift from rural to urban living, creates significant social divisions. It also encourages a basic egalitarianism: an ideological emphasis on human equality. In societies—such as England in the Middle Ages—which are built on the open and honest acceptance of unchanging social statuses, people of very different stations in life can live side-by-side because the proximity of people of lower status does not embarrass or threaten the upper orders. The coincidence of greater egalitarianism and deep social division encourages greater class avoidance. A good example can be seen in the architecture of Edinburgh. Until the 1760s the Old Town was socially mixed with the tall tenement buildings housing people of diverse social statuses on different floors. When overcrowding forced a radical expansion of the city, the creation of the 'New Town'—an area of elegant, architect-designed houses—allowed the upper and middle classes to separate themselves from the lower orders (except, of course, for their live-in servants). As Karl Marx noted, the novelty of capitalism was not the creation of social divisions but the bringing together of large numbers of like-situated people (see Day, "Marxism," this volume). Different living conditions and life chances encouraged people to alter the dominant religious tradition in ways which suited their material circumstances. In Catholic and Lutheran Protestant cultures, such variation was limited by the singularity of the church's structures. In radically reformed Protestant cultures, the rejection of the priesthood and the hierarchical church allowed factionalism and schism. England, for example, saw the proliferation of alternatives to the state church. The aristocracy and major landowners, whose interests gave them good reason to see this world as a pyramid (with themselves at its apex), expected their religion to take the same shape. They continued to support a hierarchical church and the small tenants and peasants they controlled did likewise. The minor gentry, large farmers with security of tenure, skilled craftsmen of the town and cities, and the skilled working class were more likely than the peasantry to think well of themselves. Financial independence allowed independence of mind and that led to the creation of schismatic movements which stressed the equality of all believers: Independents and Baptists in the seventeenth century, Methodists in the eighteenth. The class correlates of such sects could be quite fine. The County Durham villages that were hastily thrown up around collieries in the late nineteenth century often had a small but clear difference in quality of housing. Management and skilled colliery workers occupied larger and better-built houses than the ordinary pitmen. And their brand of Methodism reflected that class divide. The Wesleyan Methodist chapel (more staid in its worship; less puritanical in its ethics) was on the posh side of the village: the Primitive Methodist chapel (enthusiastic and evangelical) was on the rough side.

Social differentiation is normally secularizing because, as we will see in the following, the fragmentation of a single overarching church into a series of competing sects and denominations reinforces the consequences of functional differentiation. It also has a strong independent effect in undermining the plausibility of religion by making clear its human origins. When there was a single church that spoke with a single voice, it was easy to believe that it was the voice of God; when there are a variety of alternatives, at least some of them must be false, and this allows the possibility that all of them are false. (This holds primarily in the case of Western monotheistic traditions; East Asia offers important cases where attitudes to religious pluralism are more flexible.) As Peter Berger (1980) notes, even for the committed believer, a context of religious pluralism is radically different to one of religious homogeneity because, despite the many strategies for avoiding it, it will periodically become obvious that we have chosen God and not the other way round. (Of course, Berger later modified his position to suggest that pluralism undermines 'taken-for-granted' religion but not religion per se [Berger et al. 2001, 194]).

Of itself pluralism need not be secularizing. If it arises from the conquest of alien territory or immigration and thus allows the carriers of alternative beliefs to be dismissed as of no account, its effects on the dominant religion may be negligible. But when it results from social differentiation within a society, such dismissal becomes more difficult and the natural consequence (once the state has given up trying to enforce religious conformity) is a gradual reduction of dogmatism. People become more tolerant of religious deviation and this is reflected in the evolution of many sects into denominations. Differences with others can be managed in two ways. The faith can be watered down by creating a distinction between what is essential and what is peripheral. So the things on which we disagree get shifted into the peripheral category. The difficulty with this is that, as the diversity that one has to accommodate increases (and increasingly includes religious indifference), the peripheral gets larger and the core smaller until one is left with such banalities as "All nice people will go to heaven." The second strategy is relativism. This is the ethos of what is variously called New Age, alternative, contemporary, or holistic spirituality. It supposes that competing ideas can simultaneously be true because there is a variety of truths—there is what is true for you and there is what is true for me and they need not be the same thing—that are reconciled only at the highest level of abstraction: everything is part of the same cosmic consciousness.

These methods of adjusting to diversity make perfect 'socio-logic' sense in that they allow some continued adherence to a particular faith while reducing the need for conflict with those with different allegiances but they are secularizing because they seriously weaken the transmission of religion from one generation to the next. To the extent that parents allow that there is more than one way to heaven and that we are all God's children, they lose the key driver to indoctrinate their children in any particular faith and, from the child's point of view, all faiths lack plausibility. This is particularly the case with mixed marriages. Even if parents agree to raise their children in one faith, church, denomination, or sect, that one parent belongs to another makes it difficult to associate virtue with religious identification.

Functional or Structural Differentiation

There is a second meaning to differentiation. As societies become wealthier and larger they become more complex and more functionally differentiated. Activities which were once subsumed become autonomous and clearly distinguishable as systems driven by their own values. The economy and the polity are two obvious such systems. The notion first appeared in sociology in the writings of Adam Smith and Adam Ferguson on the division of labor, but perhaps more significant was the development of the microscope which allowed for the observation of single-celled organisms and thus their comparison with more complex micro-organisms. That contrast provided a popular metaphor for comparing societies. As Herbert Spencer put it, differentiation was the transition from "an indefinite incoherent homogeneity to a definite coherent heterogeneity" (1898, 584). In Émile Durkheim's comparisons of primitive and modern societies, differentiation was the key difference in his two forms of social solidarity: mechanical and organic solidarity (1964 [1893]). The Australian aboriginal societies (which served for Durkheim as a model of what all societies used to be like) hung together because everyone was much the same: there was little specialization and all people occupied the same lifeworld. In contrast, modern societies are highly complex with a great deal of occupational specialization and internal functional differentiation and they hang together because the very different parts depend on each other and are integrated at a high level through a common culture and the social organization of the state. The point can be readily seen in a musical metaphor. Mechanical solidarity is singing in *unison*: everyone sings the same tune. Organic solidarity is singing in *harmony*: the overall effect is created by groups singing different things that only sound euphonious when sung together.

The idea of differentiation as decomposition was most thoroughly established in sociology by Talcott Parsons who assumed it in his elaborate systems theory (1961). In a nutshell, social systems have a tendency to respond to the increased complexity of their environments by generating functionally more specialized subsystems. As a small firm expands, it finds that its secretariat can no longer handle both the amount and the changing nature of its growing workload. So a marketing department is created, professional accountants are hired for its finance department, and so on. There are alternatives to this internal decomposition view. Niklas Luhmann's view of modernization accepts the Parsonian notion of decomposition but augments it with the possibility of the creation of entirely new systems (Luhmann 1977). The example commonly given to illustrate Luhmann's divergence from Parsons is sport, a clearly differentiated realm of society which owes its origins to at least three very different activities each with its own long and complex history: athletics, gymnastics, and the dog and horse-related sports of the aristocracy.

The difference between these two views of functional differentiation need not concern us because the consequences for religion are much the same. As it loses functions, religion loses power and influence; the number of occasions on which people engage in acts of religious communication (e.g. prayer and rituals) and the casual everyday contact with religious culture are reduced. In becoming separated off as a discrete subsystem, religion loses address.

The details differ with region, society, and confession but the Christian church in the Middle Ages was central to the operation of society. Its senior officials were often key figures in government (Cardinal Wolsey in England in the 1520s, Cardinal Richelieu in France in the 1630s). Its junior officials were often the only literate people in any parish. Its abbeys and monasteries kept historical and administrative records. Insofar as any medieval society provided education, health, and welfare, it was generally religious provision. The church also claimed the right to discipline the citizenry, not just about their church life, but about social mores more generally.

Exactly how the church lost its central position in Europe and North America varies from nation to nation. In France, its marginalization was abrupt: punished by the Revolutionaries for its support of the ancient regime. In the United Kingdom, the displacement of religion and the creation of a secular state occurred in a very different way. It is in the nature of Reformed Protestantism that it accidentally encourages factionalism and schism. As the religious culture became more diverse it became ever less credible for important social matters such as education to be left in the hands of the state church. Scotland offers a very clear example. Through the eighteenth and nineteenth centuries, sectarian alternatives to the Church of Scotland proliferated so that at one point, in addition to the Scottish Episcopal Church, there were six Presbyterian alternatives to the state church. By the end of the nineteenth century there were also imports of almost every sect originated in England: Baptist, Brethren, Independent. Although many of the Presbyterian sects were originally in favor of imposed religion (they just did not think the Church of Scotland was what should be imposed), the fact that the dissidents had to be self-financing encouraged a shift to thinking of religion as a voluntary choice. From the point of view of the individual Seceder or Baptist, that meant freedom from Church of Scotland discipline and taxation. From the point of view of the state, fragmentation meant that an effective national system of education (and health and social welfare) would have to be based on secular provision.

In Britain the separation of church and state was gradual, inconsistent, and clumsy. In the United States, the need to draft a constitution for a new state meant a clear resolution: there would, in Jefferson's words, be a "wall of separation" between church and state. Where a people shared a single religion (and especially if that single religion became part of a national identity that had to be defended from external aggressors of a different religion or none), the church could retain important social functions: the Catholic Church in Ireland and Poland are examples. But even there secular encroachment can be seen. The Catholic Church was funded by the state to provide education and welfare (those functions which could be seen as an extension of the family) but its influence over the economy waned.

Although France, Britain, and the United States got there by rather different routes, the notion that the individual should be free to choose a religion without loss of citizen rights was sufficiently well established by the end of the nineteenth century that societies which had avoided the revolutionary upheaval of France and lacked the religious diversity of Britain or the North American colonies nonetheless embraced it and the Lutheran Scandinavian countries gradually weakened the position of the Lutheran state churches.

LOSS OF ADDRESS

Though proving the case is difficult, it seems beyond question that modernization, differentiation, and secularization are causally related. Although there may have been small revivals of religious interest along the way, all now highly differentiated societies are also considerably less religious than they were two hundred years ago.

An illustration of the difficulty of distinguishing the separate cause of secularization can be seen in the shifting prestige and power of medicine and religion. In traditional societies religion and medicine are often inseparable. As they became analytically distinguishable, they often remained conjoined because at least in rural areas the clergy were the best educated people. The great Puritan Divine Richard Baxter (1615–1691) was also a physician. John Wesley, the founder of Methodism, was also the author of a popular medical text: *Primitive Physic or An Easy and Natural Method of Curing Most Diseases* (1747). His prescriptions carried weight not just because he was an educated man who had read other medical texts but because he was widely regarded as spiritual. Now only the fringes of religion—New Agers employing Amerindian cures, Jehovah's Witnesses rejecting blood transfusion in favor of prayer, US television evangelists claiming that HIV/AIDS is divine punishment for homosexuality—practice or reject medicine. The mainstream—primarily political response—can be seen in the Church of England's response to HIV/AIDS: it recommended that the government invest more in scientific research.

That religion no longer offers cures has reduced its status relative to secular science and medicine; the change is visible in the decline of clergy salaries relative to those of secular professionals. It could be explained by effectiveness: science (especially in its offspring technology) works better. Praying that one's sheep will not get worm infestation is nowhere near as reliable as chemical dipping. But it can also be explained by differentiation. We no longer expect religious officials to be expert in a wide range of secular knowledge and look instead to more specialized groups of professionals.

We see social and functional differentiation combining in the churches' loss of a role in social control. In the eighteenth century, the clergy of the Church of Scotland and the Puritans of New England claimed the right to monitor social behavior and to punish people for crime and deviance. As more and more people dissented from the dominant religion, such claims became increasingly hollow and power irreversibly shifted to the secular state. Here the marginalization of religion carries a subtle but clear signal about relative importance: we have to obey the state; we do not have to obey any church.

In considering exactly how some particular role was lost by the churches, it is often difficult to distinguish relative effectiveness (that is, rational grounds for choosing secular over religious provision) and more contingent issues of social power but, whatever the specific local levers of change, there is one uniform consequence: people have ever less contact with religious officials and religious culture. Committed believers may compensate for the church's declining intrusion in many aspects of life by attending its services more often but the effect of the marginalization of religion can be seen in the decline in the number of such committed believers.

In the Parsonian view, differentiation was always associated with an increase in efficiency. One could suppose that as religion loses its non-core activities and becomes an autonomous subsystem, it becomes better at being religious (in a context-specific sense) and thus more attractive. There is certainly plenty of evidence that congregations of the state Church of Scotland were generally relieved when the 1872 Education Act removed from them the obligation to fund and manage schools. However, there is no evidence that they become more popular as a result of being able to concentrate on their core business and the general historical association is uncontentious. The creation of secular alternatives to the secular activities of the churches in Western societies correlates with a decline in their popularity.

Bringing together the consequences of social and functional differentiation, we can summarize by saying that the religious freedom of the modern Western society forces us to choose our religion in a context where the reasons for choosing any over none are getting fewer. Hence differentiation causes secularization.

De-differentiation?

Much of the above could have been written without any reference to social theory; it is observably the case that religion has become marginalized over the last two hundred years as more specialized institutions have taken over many of its functions in many modern Western societies. The importance of the sociological gloss is to argue that such changes were not accidental: that, to the extent that any social change is inevitable, they were bound to happen because differentiation is a necessary element of modernization. For example, it is difficult to see how medical science could have developed had religious institutions retained control over education or how democracy could have developed so long as the polity was beholden to the dominant religion. If differentiation is indeed a necessary element of modernization, its reversal would be either a surprise or a challenge to secularization theory. From the 1980s, as part of a general 'postmodern' critique of the social sciences, there was a brief flourish of talk of 'de-differentiation' in the sense of a return of religious beliefs and values to prominence in the operations of the non-religious subsystems of societies. There were a variety of examples offered. Paul Heelas (1999) argued that the promotion of New Age spirituality as a psychological technology for advancement in the world of work showed a breaking down of the barriers between systems. The New Christian Right (NCR) in the United States was presented as proof that religion had returned to the public square. The same case was made with regard to Islam in the West.

None of these cases is convincing. That some corporations flirted with yoga, meditation, and the like in their management training tells us no more than that, in fields where it is unclear what works best, businesses will try anything that might increase productivity. It was a brief flirtation and it made no difference to their basic functioning or to the fundamental logic of capitalism. When the Findhorn Foundation (Europe's oldest center for New Age spirituality) announced that it was offering training programs for major corporations, there was no doubt who had sold out. While the growth of the NCR and its later incorporation as a ginger group within the Republican party might at first sight seem like an example of de-differentiation, it is worth noting that the NCR played by the rules of secular politics: it encouraged voters to register, it used primaries to influence candidate selection, it fought elections, it promoted legislation, and it tried to influence public policy through the courts. And it accepted the results of those contests. Furthermore, it framed its agenda in secular terms. It did not oppose abortion, homosexuality, and divorce on the grounds that God said these were bad. It instead argued that abortion infringed the right to life of the unborn child, and that homosexuality and divorce weakened the family which was the most effective way of promoting social goods. That is, it was not theocratic. It did not argue that the will of God trumped the votes of citizens. Such theocrats can now be found in the West but this is not the result of any de-differentiation; it is a consequence of migration of people from less differentiated societies. That British Muslims wanted to have novelist Salman Rushdie murdered for blasphemy and forced him into hiding for a decade from 1989 tells us a lot about the societies from which they came. But the progress of that dispute tells us more about the modern West: instead of extending the existing blasphemy laws to protect Islam, the British state in 2008 abolished the common law offenses of blasphemy and blasphemous libel. Although most Western societies have extended to Islam the privileges it accords Christianity (providing chaplains for prisons and the armed services, for example), they have not wavered in their rejection of theocracy.

The Supply-Side Alternative

In the 1980s the above logic was challenged by the expansion into sociology of principles of free market economies associated with the Chicago economist Gary Becker. Rodney

Stark and associates argued that far from being secularizing, religious diversity or pluralism was associated with a growth in popular religiosity (Young 1997). Differences
in religious involvement across time and space were not to be explained by changes in
'demand' for religion but by differences in supply. All people are basically religious; what
explains why, for example, the United States had a higher church-going rate in the 1960s
than most Western European societies, are features of the religious marketplace. For a
wide variety of reasons religious monopolies are less effective than free and competitive
markets. Two examples will give a flavor of the approach. One concerns clergy motivation. If clergy are paid from taxation irrespective of the size of their congregations, they
will have no incentive to recruit. Indeed, their rational interest will lead them to prefer
smaller to larger congregations: less work for the same salary. The second concerns satisfaction of diverse preferences. Social differentiation has created populations with very
different preferences. If there is only a single church (whether it is a legally established
state church as in the Scandinavian countries or simply a hegemonic church as with the
Catholic Church in France), the many people who will find it unsatisfactory for whatever reason will lose interest in religion. If there are lots of competing churches, sects,
and denominations, more people will find something that suits them.

Although both of these propositions (like much of the supply-side approach) initially sound plausible, they do not stand up to close inspection. Many state churches
had internal systems that did reward clergy for being popular and even where they did
not it seems unlikely that many clergy would prefer less work to greater popularity. By
the same logic tenured university lecturers should try to be bad teachers so that fewer
students enrolled for their classes. I know of very few academics who think and behave
like that. Like the clergy, they are driven by a commitment to their subject. And the
idea that diversity encourages greater religiosity by better meeting a range of preferences
supposes that people seek their religion in the same way they seek their next automo-
bile: that they see their religious life as an opportunity for maximizing utility. Yet religious commitment is unlike car purchase in too many ways to completely list here. It
is rarely chosen but is instead, like language, given at birth; though, like language, it is
subject to learning and socialization. That few people treat religion as a realm for utility-
maximization is readily explained by its key features. Religions cannot be compared by
reward because, until death, we cannot know which one, if any, is correct. They cannot
be compared by cost because there is no neutral pricing system. Possible transfer is difficult for most believers even to contemplate because most religions socialize their adherents in such a manner that other faiths are not seen as utility-maximizing opportunities.
Car drivers have preferences but they are rarely exclusivist. I drive a Ford but am happy
to recognize a Volvo as a possible alternative. Someone who is a committed Quaker is
very unlikely to view Catholicism as a viable alternative. (Of course, this can vary within
a narrow range of options: e.g. Protestants and Catholics sometimes see each other as
viable alternatives, for example in countries like the Netherlands or Germany.)

As well as being open to many logical challenges, the supply-side approach patently
fails the tests of comparison over space and time. The most religious societies (e.g.
Poland) are those that have a single near-monopoly faith. With the exception of the

United States, the most diverse societies are also the least religious. And however religiously diverse any Western society is now, it is more diverse now than it was a century or two centuries ago and as it has become more diverse, so church-going has declined.

CONCLUSION

Differentiation is an important concept in the social sciences. The two varieties discussed here—social and functional—are important elements of a larger package of changes that constitute modernization and that are historically linked with an obvious decline in the power, popularity, and prestige of religion. It is possible to describe the marginalization of religion and the expansion of secular provision of roles which the churches once performed without any reference to social theory. The importance of the notion of differentiation (and its association with other aspects of modernization such as increasing egalitarianism and individualism) is that it assumes that such changes were not contingent. That is, they could not have easily been otherwise without important changes to other parts of the package. Indeed, we can go so far as to say that modernization would have been impossible without differentiation, and that differentiation in both forms is almost inevitably secularizing.

GLOSSARY

Differentiation a key aspect of modernization with two related dimensions. Social differentiation occurs as the division of labor, in part, leads to significant social divisions and, in religious terms, the fragmentation of a single overarching church into a series of competing sects and denominations. Functional or structural differentiation occurs, for Parsons, as social systems respond to the increased complexity of their environments by generating functionally more specialized subsystems or, for Luhmann, as activities which were once subsumed become autonomous and clearly distinguishable as systems driven by their own values.

Modernization primarily, a linked series of changes in Western societies that began or accelerated from the late eighteenth century, e.g. increasing functional and social differentiation, occupational specialization, egalitarianism, individualism, and religious diversity. Secondarily, comparable processes in other regions of the world that share some but not necessarily all of these characteristics.

Secularization a historical decline in the functions, prestige, power, and influence of religion, involving such factors as the separation of church and state, declining participation in acts of religious communication (e.g. rituals), and reduction of casual everyday contact with religious culture. It occurs as religion is separated off as a discrete subsystem through processes of modernization.

References

Berger, Peter L. 1967. *The Sacred Canopy: Elements of a Sociological Theory of Religion.* New York: Doubleday.

Berger, Peter L. 1980. *The Heretical Imperative: Contemporary Possibilities of Religious Affirmation.* London: Collins.

Berger, Peter L., Linda Woodhead, Paul Heelas, and David Martin. 2001. *Peter Berger and the Study of Religion.* London and New York: Routledge.

Bruce, Steve. 1999. *Choice and Religion: A Critique of Rational Choice.* Oxford: Oxford University Press.

Bruce, Steve. 2011. *Secularization.* Oxford: Oxford University Press.

Durkheim, Émile. 1964. *The Division of Labor in Society.* Glencoe, IL: Free Press. Original edition, 1893.

Heelas, Paul. 1999. "Prosperity and the New Age Movement." In *New Religious Movements: Challenge and Response,* edited by Bryan R. Wilson and J. Jamie Cresswell. London and New York: Routledge, 49–77.

Luhmann, Niklas. 1977. "The Differentiation of Society." *Canadian Journal of Sociology* 2(1): 29–53.

Parsons, Talcott. 1961. "An Outline of the Social System." In *Theories of Society: Foundations of Modern Sociological Theory,* edited by Talcott Parsons, Edward Shils, Kaspar D. Naegele, and Jesse R. Pitts. Glencoe, IL: Free Press, 30–79.

Spencer, Herbert. 1898. *First Principles.* New York: D. Appleton & Co.

Young, Lawrence A. 1997. *Rational Choice Theory and Religion.* New York: Routledge.

Further Reading

Beyer, Peter. 2006. *Religions in Global Society.* London and New York: Routledge. [*Drawing on Luhmann's systems-theory, Beyer defines religion as a communication system rooted in a binary distinction between blessed and cursed. This differentiates religion from other systems of communication and allows for a nuanced discussion of religious differentiation in terms of distinct 'programs,' i.e. "patterns through which communications that constitute each religion refer to each other and thus achieve the closure or identity of the religion" (88).*]

Bruce 2011 [*A concise defense of secularization theory, engaging with critics and drawing on recent empirical data. The book argues that individualism, religious diversity, and other aspects of modernization undermine the power, prestige, and popularity of religion.*]

Petzke, Martin. 2015. "Religious Differentiation and World Culture: On the Complementary Relationship of Systems Theory and Neo-Institutionalism." In *From Globalization to World Society: Neo-Institutional and Systems-Theoretical Perspectives,* edited by Boris Holzer, Fatima Kastner, and Tobias Werron. London and New York: Routledge, 148–176. [*Engaging critically with Luhmann and Beyer, Petzke sets out a theoretical frame for analyzing religious differentiation: "neo-institutionalist accounts of world-cultural ontologies should be combined with systems-theoretical sensibilities for autonomous logics when analyzing the globalization of specific spheres" (169).*]

CHAPTER 43

··

THE DISINTEGRATION AND DEATH OF RELIGIONS

··

ALBERT DE JONG

CHAPTER SUMMARY

- The question of how religions disappear, how they disintegrate and die, has been avoided by most students of religion, either because of a perceived lack of interest, or because the notion as such is rejected in favor of a search for continuities.
- A responsible study of religions must keep the question of religion death firmly in focus.
- Such a focus requires the courage to claim (heuristic) distinctiveness for particular formations—without such a claim, no credible statements on 'existence,' 'continuity,' or 'disappearance' are possible.
- Rich sources of theoretical reflection are available from the comparable fields of the study of institutions, and especially of linguistics ('language death').

The question of how religions die has only rarely been the subject of theoretical, or even historical, interest among students of religion. Not one single-authored monograph has ever been devoted to the subject. The only book-length treatment of the phenomenon of 'religion death' is Zinser (1986), a collection of individual case studies (not all of them entirely relevant) prefaced by a very important more general article by Carsten Colpe. In 2000, Gary Lease proposed a program of "natural histories of religions," which would include a distinct focus on their death. The importance of this contribution is the clarity with which he proposed, succinctly, the importance of tracking developments (including disappearance) in order to establish identity: "And without identity, there is not intelligibility" (Lease 2000, 109). By far the most important contributions to the field have been made by Joel Robbins, in two path-breaking articles (Robbins 2007; 2014), in which he has adequately defined what seems to be the chief theoretical obstacle. Robbins characterizes anthropology as a "science of continuity," with little to no interest in questions of how traditions, practices, or indeed entire systems disappear. He allows a minor role for this question to historians, but even though there exists a huge bibliography on subjects like the Christianization of Europe (or the Americas) and the Islamization of the Middle East, virtually none of this literature is written from the perspective of—or with an interest in—the religions destroyed, marginalized, and displaced by these processes. The same applies, *mutatis mutandis*, to the enormous literature on secularization, most of which is concerned with the disappearance of 'religion' as such, and not with the disappearance of concrete religions (which is, it seems, seen merely as an example of the wider process). And yet, knowledge of the difference between the two is widely spread both within and outside the academy: it is not just that there seems to be a trend of de-institutionalization rather than disappearance of religion, but there is good evidence for the fact that *certain forms* of institutionalized religion are more susceptible to processes of secularization, are more threatened in their existence, than others. In the contemporary West, for example, obvious examples of declining religions are liberal Protestant Christianity, Christian Science, and Theosophy.

In the absence of a rich theoretical literature to engage with, this chapter can merely scratch the surface of the subject. It will do so in two distinct ways: first, by referencing theoretical perspectives from two fields that are intimately connected with the study of religion in distinct aspects: the study of institutions, and linguistics. Both fields have struggled with questions similar to that of the breakdown of concrete religious formations, and both fields have explicitly managed to thematize the temptation to develop into 'sciences of continuity.' Religions are, of course, partly institutions themselves, and partly systems of communication (see Krech, "Communication," this volume). They therefore share essential features with institutions and with languages, but they cannot be reduced to either of those, nor to both of them combined. After these attempts to learn from neighboring fields, the remainder of this chapter will be devoted to the question of whether the insights from these fields can be used in the study of religion.

THE NEW INSTITUTIONALISM

Ours is a world of institutions and organizations. The work of political scientists, sociologists, and economists tends to be dominated, therefore, by questions about these institutions. In this work, there is a permanent negotiation between the urge to see institutions as relatively stable formations, and the knowledge that real stability can never be achieved, and should not be seen as a desirable goal. This urge is both a social reality—societies claim to be in need of 'stable institutions'—and a theoretical premise: most theory is based on an assumption of permanence rather than one of transience. This assumption has been questioned by representatives of what has come to be called the 'new institutionalism' (Powell/DiMaggio 1991; Lecours 2005). These scholars' work remains rooted in the 'old' institutionalism of Weber and Durkheim—founding fathers of sociology as well as of the study of religion—but it attempts to integrate, into a view of the 'inner workings' of institutions, a more processual and multi-layered approach (see Seele/Zapf, "Economics," this volume). Questions of the decay and disappearance of institutions are, therefore, very much in focus, especially among those scholars who take a *longue durée* perspective on institutional developments. Particularly relevant to students of religion is their insight into the dynamics of institutional change. One of the leading theorists in this field (foreshadowing Joel Robbins in this) notes:

> New institutionalists are more comfortable in explaining continuity rather than change because the logic of their approach focuses on institutional reproduction rather than transformation. New institutionalists argue that institutions embody the societal situation prevailing at the time of their birth because, once created, they have autonomy from society and their development follows a largely independent pattern. Moreover, institutions tend to generate 'positive feedback' of 'increasing returns' which act as mechanisms of reproduction. As a result, institutions adapt imperfectly and with much delay to whatever occurs in society, and they resist change. (Lecours 2005, 11–12)

These insights are important precisely because they locate the drive for continuity in the system itself, but also predict that it inevitably contains the seeds for its ultimate destruction, or disappearance. Much work on institutional change has tended to focus on so-called 'exogenous' shocks—wars, societal breakdown, financial meltdown—but the more interesting perspectives are those that foreground 'endogenous' factors: the difference in speed of social and institutional developments (or adaptations), the inner urge to protect the institution even in situations where it can no longer truly meet societal needs, and the tendency to what is called 'convergence' or 'isomorphism.' This latter phenomenon points at the theoretical position that institutions have a tendency to resemble (or imitate) each other in their inner workings, regardless of their real contexts or settings. "Institutions can, therefore, survive even if they engender sub-optimal outcomes" (Lecours 2005, 13). A point can be reached, however, when an institution can no longer survive but faces either abolishment or change to such an extent that the question whether it is still recognizable as the 'same' institution becomes acute.

LANGUAGE DEATH

Similar questions have been asked with regard to language maintenance, language attrition, and language death. The subject of 'language death' has indeed developed into one of the central subjects in the field of linguistics (Brenzinger 1992; Janse/Tol 2003), as well as one of the more reliable sources of research money for that field. Unlike students of religion, linguists have long insisted on the fact that the numerical strength of languages (i.e. the question of how many people actually speak a particular language) has little to no theoretical relevance for the great project of understanding and studying language as a phenomenon. This has given great urgency to the task of documenting (describing) as many languages as possible, which in turn has led to a lively interest in the question of how languages disappear.

When a language dies, its speakers do not stop communicating: they begin to communicate in a different language. A crucial stage in this language shift is in the transfer of primary languages to the next generation. People may have a close emotional bond with the language they have learnt from their parents, but they may experience this primary language as socially inconvenient, or as not allowing them to express whatever they would like to communicate with the desired degree of clarity (see Piirainen/Sherris 2015, focusing on metaphors). The first observation sometimes leads to the decision to raise one's children in a different, socially more promising, language. The second may lead to extensive borrowings from other languages, or to a situational shift, where the choice of language is dictated by considerations of practical use. Since most humans are multilingual, or at the very least operate in multilingual contexts, such shifts are ubiquitous, and can be assumed to have been an important aspect of the development of languages throughout human history.

Languages have always developed, and will even develop in those (rare) contexts where contact with speakers of other languages is uncommon. In order to get a grasp of such 'internally driven' developments, linguists can divide languages over various stages, as well as over various dialects to mark geographical or social distinctiveness. Thus, Old Persian, Middle Persian, and New Persian are considered three different languages—with hugely different structural features—but they are genetically linked: Middle Persian developed out of Old Persian, and New Persian is the living descendant of Middle Persian. Between Old Persian and Middle Persian, we can witness the collapse of the inherited system of inflection, and the rise of new verbal and nominal morphologies and syntactic patterns to compensate for the loss of cases and tenses. Something similar can be observed in the transition from Middle Persian to New Persian. For our subject, this means that Old Persian and Middle Persian can be considered 'dead languages' in the sense that they no longer have living speakers, but these speakers did not switch languages: the languages developed into each other. Such long-term changes can only be traced in languages that are served by a diachronically rich body of (written) evidence, which is true for only a tiny number of the world's languages. In such situations, it is usually the case that every datable source shows an 'in-between' stage of the slow process of language development. It is important to distinguish this process from the other types of language change or language shift, which are more strongly conditioned by social developments.

Language Diversity

Linguists estimate that there are currently 7,000 living languages in the world, more than half of which are considered seriously endangered. They have devised a system of threat analysis, classifying languages along a scale running from 'extinct' through 'moribund' to several levels of 'endangerment' and, finally, 'safe.' In light of current knowledge of language death and a written record going back some 5,000 years, it is reasonable to assume that the total number of languages that have existed in human history would run into the tens, or even hundreds, of thousands (Evans/Levinson 2009). These have been classified in many different language families on the basis of shared characteristics. Some of these language families are represented only by a single language ('isolate'), others by very many; yet others, however, escape such classification altogether. This is particularly true of the so-called 'creole' languages, which have developed in situations of intense, socially unequal, language contact (Thomason/Kaufman 1991).

Theorizing Language Change

What makes it possible to recognize, and theorize, language diversity, language change, and as a consequence language death, is the fact that languages can be described and analyzed (on multiple levels) on the basis of recognizable, and broadly shared, criteria: phonology (sounds), morphology (forms), syntax (organization), semantics (meaning), and pragmatics (use). While the question whether there are linguistic universals is still hotly debated among specialists (Evans/Levinson 2009, with following discussion), linguists can agree on these five domains as all playing a role in the construction of linguistic systems of communication (although the first category, that of sounds, is largely irrelevant to sign languages). This has given the field the necessary instruments to reach a higher level of testable hypotheses than is (believed to be) possible for most other human cultural formations. For the purpose of the present chapter, it makes it possible for linguists to establish the very fact of language death (interpreted as the absence of living speakers), and to hypothesize likely scenarios of linguistic change which, in combination, may contribute to the disappearance of a particular language.

There are three phenomena that have been particularly fruitful for such an analysis (although they are the subject of controversy among linguists). These are relexification (the replacement of [items of] the vocabulary from the inherited language by items of the vocabulary of another), reanalysis (a shift in understanding, and consequent use, of morphological or syntactic patterning), and dialect leveling (convergence of regional or social linguistic variation toward a socially more powerful linguistic form). All three are common in all languages, but they may differ greatly in intensity or pervasiveness. The first and the third can only exist in situations of language contact; the second usually does, but is theoretically ambiguous in that it can also occur as a purely internal phenomenon.

What this yields is a multitude of different scenarios of language change (and development). Such scenarios can only be observed if linguists are bold enough to assume, heuristically, 'standard' forms of particular languages. Theoretically, all individuals speak their own particular variety of a language (a so-called 'idiolect'), but there are observable, and testable, boundaries in practical use: some people are capable of understanding them, others are not. In cases where understanding is no longer possible, a secondary medium of communication must be resorted to, and in those situations where this happens frequently, mixed languages are most likely to come into being. These serve a practical function (communication), but they can become so frequent in use that they slowly develop into primary languages, pushing out earlier systems of communication. This is also possible in the case of socially dominant languages, whose use can be enforced, or which can be considered socially or economically desirable. As a result of either of these situations, the active use of subordinate languages shrinks and the innate capabilities of languages to adapt to new situations (e.g. to express new phenomena) slowly but unceasingly give way to patterns of borrowing and reanalysis. These processes generally escalate in the transmission of languages to the next generation, and they have been greatly impacted by the rise of nation states with national languages, and by the use of such national languages in education (Spolsky 2012).

Patterns of Language Erosion

To summarize these findings, it may be useful to point to a few of the observable patterns in language death. These range from the most extreme and immediate cases of genocide, or extinction of linguistic communities, to the slower, and more interesting, patterns of language erosion described earlier. They can, therefore, be divided (as in the case of institutions) between 'exogenous' and 'endogenous' factors. Externally produced language death has occurred multiple times throughout recorded history (and in untold numbers for languages that have never been recorded), in situations of war, genocide, conquest, and epidemics, which have caused whole communities to perish, with their languages (and, incidentally, religions).

The rise of multi-ethnic imperial structures in antiquity yields the first real evidence for language policy (Clackson 2015). Empires used official and administrative languages, which were generally in the hands of specialists in writing ('scribes' and 'clerks'), setting examples that were followed all the way down the imperial bureaucracies. Since these were highly specialized written mediums of communication they did not in all cases spell the death of actually spoken languages (e.g. Greek wiped out most of the languages spoken in Anatolia, but Old Persian did not wipe out any local language that we know of). The fate of the many languages usually included in such imperial structures seems to have depended, therefore, on the speed with which the official language was adapted in other domains of society. Where this happened quickly or pervasively, the local languages would be set on a path of attrition—or of convergence toward the socially dominant variety of the language. Where this did not happen, for example because official languages remained restricted in use (as was the case with Old Persian), the promise of enduring linguistic diversity tends to be greater.

An in-between situation is the case of migration, with the resulting rise of diasporic communities that constitute linguistic minorities. These may preserve their own language to protect their distinctiveness, but they may also yield to the social pressure to adopt the dominant language, or become part of the larger process of the rise of mixed languages—and the concomitant disappearance of the languages they brought with them. Religion often plays a role in these processes. It is especially among religious diasporic communities that languages of place have been preserved: this is true of Yiddish among Ashkenazi Jews, of Pennsylvania Dutch among the Amish, of Sarnami Hindi among the Surinamese Hindustanis, etc. Our task, however, is to determine if such observable patterns of linguistic change can help us understand the phenomenon of the disappearance of concrete, recognizable, religions—whether, that is, there are developments in the sphere of religion that would resemble the dynamics of linguistic change.

Religion Death and Disappearance

Many religions that are known to have existed have actually disappeared. Religion death, in this context, can be defined as the process resulting in the absence of believers or practitioners. The religions of the ancient Greeks, Mesopotamians, Elamites, Egyptians, and numerous other ancient societies have suffered this fate. We know about them because there is an abundance of evidence interpreted as religious for all these societies: texts, figurative art, ritual objects, buildings, cult statues, etc. (Salzman/Adler 2013). In the four cases mentioned, the evidence stretches over very long periods of time—thousands of years for Mesopotamia, Elam, and Egypt—allowing scholars to register the same kind of internal developments that linguists note in the evolution of languages: there is an almost constant pattern of the appearance and disappearance of gods, rituals, priesthoods, festivals, and temples. Since these religions do not thematize their own existence *as religions* (but do thematize the history of particular places, statues, rituals, priesthoods, etc.), they owe their scholarly existence to the privilege that modern (and premodern) scholars have attached to 'place,' 'people,' and 'language.' They have been constructed (as is evident from their names) as 'ethno-specific' religions and there are roughly two scenarios for their disappearance: the first would be the disappearance of the people bearing the religion, or of the political formations that underpinned them. This would be applicable, for example, to ancient Hurrian, Hittite, and Elamite religion: it is not just that the gods and temples and priests of Hittites and Elamites are lost from sight; the Hittite and Elamite states disappear from the record, together with the Hittite and Elamite languages, and peoples. This scenario does not preclude the possibility that elements from these religions lived on in the religions that replaced them. It is widely believed, for example, that some of the great goddesses of Hellenistic Anatolia (such as the goddess Ma of the two cities named Comana) ultimately go back to Hittite deities, but their actually attested cult is part of a different religion.

Switching Religion

The second scenario is much more common for these historically traceable religions: it is a scenario of switching religion ('conversion'). Greeks and Romans did not disappear as such, but gradually adopted a new religion (Christianity) and lost (or shed) their old, ethno-specific, ones. Since they occupied a uniquely densely documented part of the world and have played a highly important role in the construction of (later) European identities, and since their religions were the main examples of a type of religion ('paganism') against which the newly forming Christian religion defined itself, this process is uniquely well documented, both textually and materially, and served by a very rich body of scholarly work. Both the documentation and the scholarly work, however, are shockingly one-sided. The focus is so heavily tilted toward the eventual outcome (conversion), that the mechanisms of religious change run the risk of being lost from sight. This has resulted in the widespread conviction that the traditional religions that were (to be) replaced by Christianity were somehow doomed to fail, ossified beyond repair, or that they had never been genuinely borne by conviction, but 'merely' by tradition or social pressure (e.g. Stark 2006). This type of reasoning tantalizingly replicates (and may actually be a source of) current interpretations of the phenomenon of secularization.

Scholars unsatisfied with such overt expressions of a history of salvation have tended to focus not so much on what was lost, but on how much of the former religion(s) actually survived in the new one. This has resulted in a generally recognizable unwillingness among some historians to deal with what was substantially new, or rather with repeated attempts to 'unmask' purported novelties as adaptations of pre-existing patterns of thought and action (Flint 1991; MacMullen 1991). Key terms for this perspective are the opposition between 'indigenous' and 'imported' and the 'syncretism' that followed from their collision (see Johnson, "Syncretism and Hybridization," this volume).

Many of the observations made by historians from either perspective are actually likely to be historically plausible: the old religions of Europe were replaced by Christianity, and it is indeed possible that patterns of thought and/or action found their way into the new religion (see, however, Frankfurter 2013, for a critical perspective). The problem is that these observations are not carried by any recognizable theoretical orientation or interest. Instead, they are largely carried by ideological convictions—the superiority of Christianity on the one hand, its fundamental intolerance on the other—and these convictions govern much of the interpretation. What makes matters worse is that it is likely that the narrative of the Christianization of Europe, in view of its foundational importance for the construction of Western culture, has been the (implicit or explicit) model applied to most other historical processes of the spread and conquest of religious systems: the interest in the ways in which the traditional religions of the Arabian peninsula, or the pre-Islamic Turkic religions disappeared is very meager compared to the intense interest in the rise of Islam and the Arab conquests that brought these changes about. The consequences of the spread of Buddhism for the religious worlds it entered have never been explored, but scholars have largely reproduced the Buddhist notion that Buddhism incorporated the local deities, or have subjected them to the laws of karma (see section "Inclusion in a larger political or social order"). The most widely respected history of Zoroastrianism (Boyce 1975) squarely pits Zoroaster the prophet against Iranian 'pagans' and uses these pagans only when an explanation is needed for a perceived laxity in following the prophet's vision.

Two observations are necessary here. The first is that there is an obvious lack of evidence for a radically different perspective. Religions that disappear become silent: the voices of believers are lost, and most often lost forever. This is true even for modern cases of religion death, from both possible ends of a very large continuum: when a religion has died with the death of all (or the last) of its believers, sources of information immediately disappear. When a religion has died because its believers have moved on to another religious identity (or claim to have abandoned religion altogether), or in a process of integrating their religion into a larger whole, it is their current frame of reference that clearly informs their representation of the former.

The second point is that a focus on the disappearance of religion foregrounds another huge theoretical difficulty for students of religion: the problem of the demarcation, or identification, of separate 'religions.' Knowing what disappears obviously demands knowledge of what was there to begin with. But here, the basic questions to be asked—when is a system different enough to qualify as a separate religion, and who has the right to establish, or work with, such difference—have largely been evaded. There are very good reasons for this hesitance, but it has led the study of religion into a systemic crisis, from which it has been unable to extract itself. One of the main obstacles in this regard seems to be an insufficient recognition of the crucial distinction between two basic types of religion: those that are grounded in other social formations; and those that have transformed (themselves) into a separate social formation that in principle *denies* the importance of previously existing social forms for the maintenance of relations with postulated beings, realities, and processes: i.e. communities that *have* a religion ('community religions'), and communities that *are* a religion ('religious communities') (Platvoet 1996).

Modeling Religious Change

One of the ways of dealing with this would be to use the evidence gathered and the theories designed by specialists in institutions and in languages and see if they help us understand similar dynamics in the case of religions. There is one dramatic difference especially between natural languages and religions: new religions come into being much more easily than new languages, because they can be (and have, in fact, been) designed or generated. Scholars have tended to underestimate the crucial transformation of the rise of religions that actively denied the importance of birth or place, that made it possible to *opt* to join another community, but made that choice dependent upon a *rejection* of earlier, inherited, patterns of thought and behavior. What students of religion can learn from the study of institutions is precisely the dynamics of this transformation: how 'organized religions' were generated; how they, as institutions, developed the instruments that could assure them a continuing existence even in periods of rapid social (and physical) change; and, finally, how they could fail and therefore vanish. A good example may be the case of Manichaeism, a religion that was self-consciously designed in third-century Mesopotamia, spread very rapidly from Spain to China, but eventually disappeared altogether, seemingly by first integrating with, and then dissolving into, Christianity, Islam, and Buddhism (Lieu 1992). The common narrative about the disappearance of Manichaeism is that it was rooted out of existence: Manichaeans were perceived as 'heretics' by Christians and Muslims and their presence was not tolerated in societies dominated by these religions. Christian and Muslim sources show great signs of concern over the fact that Manichaeans had entered their religious communities, and sought to 'pervert' them from the inside. This has most often been taken as a fantasy, but the scenario itself is not at all unlikely. It seems to be plausible, at least, that in situations of intense control, Manichaeans made the decision to work within the currently existing institutional settings, and attempted to maintain their systems of beliefs and practices within these settings, and dissolved slowly but unstoppably because of that choice (see Russell 1997, for a twentieth-century example). There is no hard evidence for this, but there is no hard evidence for the violent scenario of the disappearance of Manichaeism either. Not long ago, Australian scholars found what they believe to be the last remaining Manichaean sanctuary in existence, in a rural part of China: it was a Buddhist shrine, whose Manichaeanness was only evident from the inscription on the chief image of the Buddha ('of Light'), and possibly from minor details in its iconography (Lieu 2012). This find strongly supports a scenario for the disappearance of Manichaeism in terms of a process of gradual dissolution or dilution.

Some steps of such processes may more aptly be understood by bringing linguistic theories and analysis into focus. Community religions are the oldest, and most durable, form of religion attested. Originally, all religions were community religions, and since their development depends on the development of the societies of which they were a part, they can be predicted to have developed under the same kind of social, technological, and physical constraints that governed the development of the languages spoken by these societies, and of the societies themselves. Unknown numbers of these religions, but surely running into the tens of thousands, must once have existed. Unlike the languages that came with them, they have only rarely been seen as worthy of note as individual formations. Instead, they have generally been treated as representatives of a 'class' of religions, and this class itself has been interpreted as having been conditioned by environmental, technological, and social constraints. Almost all of them have died out together with the societies to which they belonged, and it is only with the concomitant rise of anthropology and intense missionary activity in the nineteenth century that they have begun to be recorded and explored. Some of them have disappeared as the result of community extinction—quickly in the shape of genocide and expulsion, but mainly more slowly through epidemics, political and social marginalization, or the destruction of their environment. Most have died out as the result of the chief reason for these developments, i.e. various (independent) processes of rapid territorial expansion of others (Platvoet 1996). This explains why this type of religion (and also the most impressive linguistic diversity) has only survived into the twentieth century in parts of the world that were geographically and politically marginal or isolated (rain forests, island nations, circumpolar areas, deserts, high mountains). In more central, open, and desirable parts of the world, these community religions were forced into contact with others, and this contact produced a number of different types of response, especially when these others brought with them religions of the second type, or social and political systems that depended heavily on ritual or religious behavior. The former confrontation—with strongly defined religious communities—is the standard case of the expansion of Christianity and of Islam, and of the European and Muslim colonial expansions; the latter case—inclusion in a ritually determined social or political order—is more clearly in evidence for the expansion of Buddhism and of Hinduism, and for Roman provincial religion.

Inclusion in a Larger Political or Social Order

If we start with the latter scenario, the first response (which is similar to lexical borrowing) that can be traced could be labeled as selective *mimesis*. The inclusion of Gaul, Germania, and Britain into the Roman Empire not only led to the migration of Romans to these parts of the world, importing their own gods, festivals, and holy places, but also to the adoption of temples, votive reliefs, and types of ritual for local gods who were often identified by their local name and through being identified with (perceived) Roman counterparts (Derks 1998). Interestingly, some of these types of mimetic adaptation disappeared with the Romans, while the religions of the areas themselves survived in what is believed to be their older forms, disappearing only with the next 'Roman' novelty: Christianity.

The phenomenon of Sanskritization has been suggested by the Indian sociologist Srinivas as an explanation of the gradual expansion of Hinduism into all or most parts of India (Srinivas 1952; Charsley 1998). He observed that communities could improve their status within the huge social structure of India by imitating the behavior of those who were higher up in that system. Key elements of this process were the adoption of vegetarianism, abandoning the consumption of alcohol, and Sanskritizing the gods and the rituals of the community. The relative 'openness' of Roman religion and Hinduism (both representatives of the broad category of 'community religions') made this behavior possible and rewarding.

This is also true of similar developments in the Buddhist world, which have been observed over vast territories of Asia. Buddhism acted chiefly as a superstructure that could live together with, and absorb, a wide variety of local expressions of religion. It sponsored the rise of 'nativist' religions, i.e. religions that thematized their 'belonging' to a particular community or area, which organized or defined themselves as 'indigenous,' and in competition, or coequal, with Buddhism (the best-known examples are Tibetan Bön and Japanese Shinto; Blezer/Teeuwen 2013). Any willingness to interpret these developments as examples of the death or attrition of religions depends on the level of confidence scholars would have in identifying the earlier religions that came into contact with the newer ones as stable or actually existing—and 'transformed' beyond recognition in this type of contact. The linguistic concepts of a *lingua franca* or a *koine* would seem to be adequate models to apply in these cases: these were systems of communication used for practical purposes, that did not immediately cause the primary languages to disappear, but in many cases increasingly restricted their social (and economic) use, and impacted their development (Niehoff-Panagiotidis 1994).

Inclusion in a New Religious Order

A wholly different range of responses came about with the territorial (and numerical) expansion of Christianity and Islam. This expansion was, in both cases, accompanied by what can only be described as a mass extinction of religions. Although it took an extensive period of time, Christianity eventually made extinct all religions of Europe, and most religions of the Near East west of the Euphrates, with the sole exception of Judaism. Likewise, Islam removed much of Christianity, most of Zoroastrianism (all of it in Central Asia), and all of whatever had remained of the community religions of the Near and Middle East, with the exception of those of the Jews, Samaritans, and Mandaeans. The dynamics of these periods of mass extinction—to be followed by the even greater onslaught on community religions with the European colonial expansion—were quite different in both religions, because they were driven by very distinct basic assumptions about the role of religion in their territories. These can be explained in historical terms. Christianity arose in competition with Judaism, from which it had sprung, and with various community religions, which it saw, and treated, as a single 'type' of religion: 'paganism' or 'idolatry.' The former was framed as eclipsed by Christianity, but the latter was framed as false and therefore, ultimately, unlawful. Islam, by contrast, arose largely in competition with Judaism, Christianity, Manichaeism, and Zoroastrianism, and it expanded its territory long before its religion had fully crystallized. While being equally convinced of the possession of superior, and ultimate, truth, Muslims did not judge the desirability of the presence of 'unbelievers' in their realm on the question of truthfulness, but on the question of admissibility: there was room in the house of Islam for Jews, Christians, the mysterious Sabians, and Zoroastrians (but not for the other religions, which were equally treated as belonging to a [legal] category: idolaters or polytheists; Friedmann 2003). While it is true to say that both the Christian and the Muslim worlds were always to a certain extent multi-religious societies, this situation had a *de facto* expression in the case of Christianity, but a *de iure* dimension in the case of Islam.

Diversity and Stability in European Christianity

Both religions sprawled out, moreover, in a bewildering variety of competing interpretations of the religion, which European Christianity sought—in vain—to quell, and which the Muslim world attempted to ignore. As a result, European Christianity was torn asunder institutionally in an ongoing process of fragmentation: from the 'Great Schism' of 1054, which established an unhealed rift between 'East' and 'West,' through the rise of independent churches in the high middle ages (Lollards, Waldenses, Cathars,

Hussites, etc.) to the more lasting effects of the Protestant Reformations and the genesis of various, indeed thousands, of fully institutionalized Christian communities. In spite of this high level of institutionalization, most scholars hesitate to study, or interpret, these communities as constituting separate religions. Because of their high level of institutionalization, however, change—including disappearance—is richly documented for them: many of these communities have disappeared, and many more are likely to disappear in the near future. The Muggletonians died out in 1979 (Lamont 2006), when their last member died. The number of Shakers in North America (Taysom 2010) has been reduced to less than five, the Russian Skoptsy (Engelstein 2003)—who still numbered in the tens of thousands in the beginning of the twentieth century—have disappeared altogether, and many similar Christian communities—especially those (like the ones listed) that are grouped around (currently) unusual patterns of communal organization, sexual abstinence, or radical transformations of the body—seem to be moribund.

Diversity and Stability in the World of Islam

Religious diversity increased almost constantly in the Islamic world, partly in a much less institutionalized way (with the rise of multiple schools of thought and of law), but remarkably also with the genesis of new religious identities that frame themselves as not (fully) belonging to the tradition of Islam (Druze, Yezidis, Bahá'ís). This seems to have been a continuing process in the history of Islam, with many more of such movements (such as the Hurufis) that somehow failed to survive. It is only in the twentieth century that the differences between Christian Europe and the Muslim world have begun to turn into their opposites: Europe is becoming increasingly diverse in religious terms (including a large and growing group of people who have abandoned [organized] religion altogether), and the Middle East is quickly losing its previous high level of diversity. Some of this loss was, once again, caused by genocide (Armenian and Assyrian Christians in Turkey) and expulsion (or semi-voluntary migration, such as the Yezidis of Turkey, or the Karaites worldwide), but in many other cases there are other factors at work. This is also true of the rise of secularism in Europe: some of it was produced as part of state-imposed atheism, but much of it is the result of different choices made by people themselves.

Patterns of Change

These historical pathways can be represented in various ways: there are quite distinct patterns of religious development, and the insights from linguistics can be of great help here. Although there are instances of destruction—of communities, of religious specialists and leaders, of sacred objects, buildings, and texts, stories and memories—these cover only a part of the process of the death of religions in any period. In most cases, a scenario similar to that of language death is much more plausible: people can become convinced of the greater advantage, usefulness, or possibilities of expressing emotions, of other religions.

They can, in other words, be coerced into abandoning their former traditions, but they can also be seduced to do so, or they can slowly inscribe themselves into another religious tradition or community. Much more violence has been exerted to sponsor a change of religion than one of language, but this is a difference of degree, not of substance. Very often, moreover, the two go together: the suppression of the Sami languages and of the Sami religions in Northern Scandinavia are almost inextricable; the burning of the drums that were used in Sami rituals seems to have aimed at suppressing both the community religions of the Sami and the language that played an equally central role in the maintenance of their distinctive culture. The most infamous episode of religious extinction in medieval history, the destruction of the 'Cathars' (or rather, the Church of Good Christians, unmistakably part of Christianity, but differently institutionalized; Lambert 1998), elicited a double response: some of them chose to die for their religion, others chose to accept Catholicism; the two processes together led to the death of the community.

Crypto-Religions

There is a well-attested in-between situation in such circumstances: that of crypto-religions, where people adopt the politically dominant religion, but privately attempt to remain true to their earlier religion, creating a (communal) distinction between 'outward' appearance and 'inner' conviction. However, these strategies are notoriously unstable; and they have, in many cases, been 'resolved' either through people reverting to their old religion when this became possible, or through the gradual dilution of their distinctiveness over time (as in the case of Manichaeism discussed earlier). This phenomenon is generally known from historical situations of violence and persecution: the conversion of the Jews of Kashan and Mashhad (Moreen 1987; Patai 1997), and, of course, of the Jews and Muslims on the Iberian peninsula (Ingram 2009–2012). But as a strategy for (temporary) survival, it is in fact much more commonly attested, especially in the context of the Middle East through the much-disputed phenomenon of *taqiyya* or religious dissimulation. Because of this wider attestation, it is theoretically interesting. It is similar to those situations where active language policy attempted to eradicate linguistic diversity, forcing primary languages into the realm of the private. The success of the maintenance of a distinct religion or language in such contexts depends to a large extent on marriage and on decisions about children. It is only in strictly endogamous communities that this kind of distinct identity has had a chance of survival—and it is not strange, therefore, that all religious minorities in the Middle East, including many of those that see themselves as belonging to (a very broad definition of) Islam, are strictly endogamous.

Realignment

One of the patterns of development that resembles the linguistic phenomenon of relexification is very much in evidence among some of these minorities. The Syrian Alavis have attempted repeatedly, and with success, in the twentieth century to be recognized as Twelver-Shi'i Muslims (Müller 2009, 194–199). Facing the widespread belief among Sunni Arabs that they were not, in fact, Muslims at all, many of their leaders have publicly declared, for example, their unwavering faith in the Qur'an, and have produced numerous histories of their community that bring it into full alignment with Twelver-Shi'ism (Firro 2005). Since they do not share much information about their religion with outsiders, it is difficult to estimate how pervasive this attempt at re-identification has in fact been, but if they would continue their attempts to participate in the Shi'i world, this impact is unlikely to be trifling. The territorial division of the Druze community across Muslim, Jewish, and Christian lands (Syria, Lebanon, Jordan, Israel, and a large diaspora community in the Americas and Australia) shows itself in quite different levels of fore-grounding Islam in their self-representation (Müller 2009, 282–290; Armanet 2011). Both the Turkish Alevis and the Kurdish Ahl-e Haqq are divided over the question how much they belong to Islam: a small section of the Alevi community in diaspora now claims to be wholly distinct from Islam (Olsson 1998), and a much larger section of the Ahl-e Haqq community claims the same (Mir-Hosseini 1996); and so, of course, do all Yezidis.

The rise of diasporic communities of all these movements (and of almost all Mandaeans), partly through voluntary migration, largely under duress, has caused these problems to escalate: the confrontation, in Western countries, with the question 'who' or 'what' the members of these communities are manifests itself in a veritable crisis of identity, and in a general inability to transmit the religion to a next generation. There are important processes similar to the linguistic phenomenon of 'reanalysis' going on here, with communities being forced, for the first time, to represent their religion in propositional terms (see especially Kreyenbroek 2009).

Convergence

The phenomenon of dialect leveling in religious terms would probably be most associated with officially guided movements of reconciliation between churches (in the ecumenical movement), but it seems to be a much more pervasive phenomenon. The establishment of the state of Israel has generated a huge process of flattening of distinctions between the intensely localized interpretations of Judaism, and liturgical usages, in the formerly diasporic Jewish communities. This process has, in turn, been exported to the remaining diasporic communities themselves. The dogmatic and ritual distinctions between the Calvinist churches of various European countries are melting away, in view of the common threats of secularization on the one hand, and the rise of Evangelical Christianity on the other.

Research Ethics and Advocacy

Not a single student of religion has ever attempted to establish how many religions there currently are in the world, let alone how many have existed historically (Strenski

2003, 169). No one, it seems, sees the point of this—the number would change considerably each week, at any rate, in view of the rise of new religious movements—and no one would be brave enough to decide, and publish, how religions are to be counted. Similarly, very few specialists seem to be interested in the question of which religions are 'safe' and which are 'threatened' or 'moribund' or 'extinct.' The only ones who cannot escape an interest in this question are those who specialize in religions that seem to be seriously endangered. In order to assess endangerment, however, we need some theory regarding likely processes of religious attrition and of religion death. Historical evidence is problematic because of large gaps in our documentation; contemporary evidence is problematic, because it produces difficult questions of research ethics. Although most scholars will agree that they have a responsibility for advocacy in the most extreme cases of persecution (such as that of the Yezidis, or of the Muslim Rohingya of Myanmar), engaging with endangered communities that are not directly persecuted is a much more delicate matter. Academics working with such communities have a real impact on their development, whether they want to or not (De Jong 2008), but they must engage with the community, or they would have no information to work with. In this area, linguists are actually divided (Sallabank 2013): some have been actively attempting to revive or keep alive the languages they recorded, whereas others refuse to do this and attempt to withdraw wholly to the role of observer. The combination of problematic sources for historians, scholarly reticence about the identity of religions or religious communities (the fear of 'essentialism'), and difficulties in research ethics among scholars with living communities seems to have been partly responsible for the evasion of the subject of religion death. What we need, therefore, are careful case-studies and a broad discussion of possible patterns of development—and the courage to claim certain types of religion to be 'distinctive' and others to be 'extinct.' The late Robert Bellah summarized his *magnum opus* in the slogan 'Nothing is ever lost' (Bellah 2011, 267). He was wrong: religions die around us every day, but we still lack the instruments, and the courage, to establish what caused them to disappear.

GLOSSARY

Convergence the phenomenon of shedding or reinterpreting distinctive elements of a religion in order to harmonize that religion with others. This gradual loss of distinctiveness is less actively sought than that labeled as *realignment*.

Realignment the phenomenon of redescribing and reinterpreting a religion to make it fit the parameters of a socially or politically dominant formulation of (a) religion. Compared to *convergence*, realignment is a more actively pursued strategy

Religion death can refer both to the process that leads toward the disappearance of a particular religion and to the end result of that process: the absence of living believers or practitioners.

Religious erosion (or attrition) this label identifies various steps in the process of religion death marked by individuals or communities gradually abandoning, or replacing, elements of their religious lives, or of their religion altogether.

Selective mimesis the adoption, for use within the own community, of elements from other religions by imitating (or adopting) elements of practice and belief without registering conflict or change.

REFERENCES

Armanet, Eléonore. 2011. *Le ferment et la grâce: Une ethnographie du sacré chez les Druzes d'Israël*. Toulouse: Presses Universitaires du Mirail.

Bellah, Robert N. 2011. *Religion in Human Evolution: From the Paleolithic to the Axial Age*. Cambridge MA and London: Belknap Press of Harvard University Press.

Blezer, Henk and Mark Teeuwen, eds. 2013. *Challenging Paradigms: Buddhism and Nativism—Framing Identity Discourse in Buddhist Environments*. Leiden: Brill.

Boyce, Mary. 1975. *A History of Zoroastrianism I: The Early Period*. Leiden: Brill.

Brenzinger, Matthias, ed. 1992. *Language Death: Factual and Theoretical Explanations with Special Reference to East Africa*. Berlin and New York: Mouton de Gruyter.

Charsley, Simon. 1998. "Sanskritization: The Career of an Anthropological Theory." *Contributions to Indian Sociology* 32(2): 527–549. doi: 10.1177/006996679803200216

Clackson, James. 2015. *Language and Society in the Greek and Roman Worlds*. Cambridge: Cambridge University Press

Colpe, Carsten. 1986. "Was bedeutet 'Untergang einer Religion'?" In *Der Untergang von Religionen*, edited by Hartmut Zinser. Berlin: Dietrich Reimer Verlag, 9–33.

De Jong, Albert. 2008. "Historians of Religion as Agents of Religious Change." In *The Study of Religion and the Training of Muslim Clergy in Europe: Academic and Religious Freedom in the 21st Century*, edited by Willem B. Drees and Pieter Sjoerd van Koningsveld. Leiden: Leiden University Press, 195–218.

Derks, Ton. 1998. *Gods, Temples and Ritual Practices: The Transformation of Religious Ideas and Values in Roman Gaul*. Amsterdam: Amsterdam University Press.

Engelstein, Laura. 2003. *Castration and the Heavenly Kingdom: A Russian Folktale*. Ithaca, NY: Cornell University Press.

Evans, Nicholas and Stephen C. Levinson. 2009. "The Myth of Language Universals: Language Diversity and its Importance for Cognitive Science." *Behavioral and Brain Sciences* 32(5): 429–492. doi: 10.1017/S0140525X0999094X

Firro, Kais M. 2005. "The 'Alawis in Modern Syria: From Nusayriya to Islam via 'Alawiya." *Der Islam* 82: 1–31.

Flint, Valerie. 1991. *The Rise of Magic in Early Medieval Europe*. Princeton, NJ: Princeton University Press.

Frankfurter, David. 2013. "Amente Demons and Christian Syncretism." *Archiv für Religionsgeschichte* 14(1): 83–101. doi: 10.1515/arege-2012-0006

Friedmann, Yohanan. 2003. *Tolerance and Coercion in Islam: Interfaith Relations in the Muslim Tradition*. Cambridge: Cambridge University Press.

Ingram, Kevin, ed. 2009–2012. *The Conversos and Moriscos in Late Medieval Spain and Beyond*, 2 vols. Leiden: Brill.

Janse, Mark and Sijmen Tol, eds. 2003. *Language Death and Language Maintenance: Theoretical, Practical and Descriptive Approaches*. Amsterdam and Philadelphia: John Benjamins.

Kreyenbroek, Philip G. 2009. *Yezidism in Europe: Different Generations Speak About their Religion*. Wiesbaden: Harrassowitz.

Lambert, Malcolm. 1998. *The Cathars*. Oxford: Blackwell.

Lamont, William. 2006. *Last Witnesses: The Muggletonian History, 1652–1979*. Aldershot: Ashgate.

Lease, Gary. 2000. "Follow the Genes: Religion as a Survival Strategy." In *Secular Theories on Religion: Current Perspectives*, edited by Tim Jensen and Mikael Rothstein. Copenhagen: Museum Tusculanum Press, 107–116.

Lecours, André, ed. 2005. *New Institutionalism: Theory and Analysis*. Toronto: University of Toronto Press.

Lieu, Samuel N. C. 1992. *Manichaeism in the Later Roman Empire and Medieval China*. Tübingen: Mohr Siebeck.

Lieu, Samuel N. C., ed. 2012. *Medieval Christian and Manichaean Remains from Quanzhou (Zayton)*. Turnhout: Brepols.

MacMullen, Ramsay. 1991. *Christianity and Paganism in the Fourth to Eighth Centuries*. New Haven, CT: Yale University Press.

Mir-Hosseini, Ziba. 1996. "Faith, Ritual and Culture among the Ahl-e Haqq." In *Kurdish Culture and Identity*, edited by Philip Kreyenbroek and Christine Allison. London: Zed Books, 111–134.

Moreen, Vera Basch. 1987. *Iranian Jewry's Hour of Peril and Heroism: A Study of Babai ibn Lutf's Chronicle (1617–1662)*. New York: American Academy for Jewish Research.

Müller, Hannelore. 2009. *Religionen im Nahen Osten 1: Irak, Jordanien, Syrien, Libanon*. Wiesbaden: Harrassowitz.

Niehoff-Panagiotidis, Johannis. 1994. *Koine und Diglossie*. Wiesbaden: Harrassowitz.

Olsson, Tord, ed. 1998. *Alevi Identity: Cultural, Religious, and Social Perspectives*. Richmond: Curzon.

Patai, Raphael. 1997. *Jadid al-Islam: The Jewish "New Muslims" of Meshhed*. Detroit: Wayne State University Press.

Piirainen, Elisabeth and Ari Sherris, eds. 2015. *Language Endangerment: Disappearing Metaphors and Shifting Conceptualizations*. Amsterdam and Philadelphia: John Benjamins.

Platvoet, Jan. 1996. "The Religions of Africa in their Historical Order." In *The Study of Religions in Africa: Past, Present and Prospects*, edited by Jan Platvoet, James Cox, and Jacob Olupona. Cambridge: Roots and Branches, 46–102.

Powell, Walter W. and Paul J. DiMaggio. 1991. *The New Institutionalism in Organizational Analysis*. Chicago, IL: University of Chicago Press.

Robbins, Joel. 2007. "Continuity Thinking and the Problem of Christian Culture: Belief, Time and the Anthropology of Christianity." *Current Anthropology* 48(1): 5–38. doi: 10.1086/508690

Robbins, Joel. 2014. "How do Religions End? Theorizing Religious Traditions from the Point of View of How They Disappear." *Cambridge Anthropology* 32(2): 2–25. doi: 10.3167/ca.2014.320202

Russell, James R. 1997. "The Last of the Paulicians." *Hask hayagitakan taregirk'* 7–8 [1995–1996]: 33–47 (reprinted in James R. Russell, *Iranian and Armenian Studies*. Cambridge, MA: Harvard University Press, 2005, 677–692).

Sallabank, Julia. 2013. *Attitudes to Endangered Languages: Identities and Policies*. Cambridge: Cambridge University Press.

Salzman, Michele and William Adler, eds. 2013. *The Cambridge History of Religions in the Ancient World*, 2 vols. Cambridge: Cambridge University Press.

Spolsky, Bernard. 2012. *The Cambridge Handbook of Language Policy*. Cambridge: Cambridge University Press.

Srinivas, Mysore Narasimhachar. 1952. *Religion and Society among the Coorgs of South India*. Oxford: Clarendon Press.

Stark, Rodney. 2006. *Cities of God: The Real Story of How Christianity Became an Urban Movement and Conquered Rome*. San Francisco: Harper San Francisco.

Strenski, Ivan. 2003. "Why it is Better to Know Some of the Questions than All of the Answers." *Method & Theory in the Study of Religion* 15(2): 169–186. doi: 0.1163/157006803765218236

Taysom, Stephen C. 2010. *Shakers, Mormons, and Religious Worlds: Conflicting Visions, Contested Boundaries*. Bloomington: Indiana University Press.

Thomason, Sarah Grey and Terrence Kaufman. 1991. *Language Contact, Creolization, and Genetic Linguistics*. Berkeley: University of California Press.

Zinser, Hartmut, ed. 1986. *Der Untergang von Religionen*. Berlin: Reimer.

Further Reading

Colpe 1986 [*Characteristically impenetrable, but very inspiring* vue d'ensemble *of the many problems that inhere in thinking about the death of religion/s.*]

Robbins 2014 [*Indispensable anthropological reflection on the end of religions, the reconstruction of the past from the point of view of newly acquired religious identities, and the role of physical destruction of the material aspects of religion in these processes.*]

Zinser 1986 [*The only volume on 'religion death' in existence; the result of a workshop organized by the German Association for the Study of Religion (DVRW).*]

CHAPTER 44

....

EXPANSION

....

ASONZEH UKAH

Chapter Summary

....

- Religion connects peoples and cultures by crossing boundaries and adapting to cultures.
- Religions expand through four major processes: (i) missionary enterprise, (ii) migration, (iii) imperial/military conquest, and (iv) revivals.
- Migration is central to contemporary religious transformation and expansion.
- By crossing boundaries and adapting new cultures and lifestyles, religious organizations change doctrinally and organizationally.

Religions expand primarily, but not exclusively, through mission activities or enterprise. Mission—a term with an explicit Christian connotation—is conceptualized as having four related functions: the dissemination or transmission of the faith, expansion of the Kingdom of God, the conversion of the unconverted, and the constitution of new communities of faith or believers (Pillay 2010, 14). As American sociologist Rodney Stark (2007, 349) demonstrates, every religion begins small, attracting followership first among a small circle of family members before expanding further afield by drawing in 'friends and associates.' Every organization, whether religious or not, seeks self-perpetuation in time and space and strives to expand beyond the inaugural circle of family, friends, and associates to non-friends, non-associates, and strangers. Expansion determines whether or not a religious group survives.

The survival of religious organizations involves, among other important factors, a two-pronged process of expansion. Religious expansion may involve the outward geographical spread of influence and membership; it may also involve an expansion of structures, duties, doctrines, and rituals—its promises and capabilities—to attend to the human or existential concerns and challenges of its members or those it seeks to recruit into its fold. In some historical instances, religious expansion has dialectically incorporated dynamics in which the attempt to spread outward has also occasioned the expansion of its internal resources and structures, as well as the modification of doctrines and practices, in order to embrace and accommodate new social contexts. As systems of meaning-making, religions have a systemic way of changing while maintaining some core elements that anchor them to a firm historical base.

This chapter focuses on how religions expand geographically through migration, mobility, and mission, and on what implications these dynamics have for the future of religion in the context of globalization processes. Religious expansion—through migration and mission—is too complex, complicated, multifaceted, and diverse for a single theory to explain. In this sense, the triangulation of theories may provide a better explanatory force than a single narrative. Empirical evidence is needed to illustrate the expansion of specific religious organizations and to buttress specific theory about religious expansion (Arango 2000).

Migration, mobility, and religious mission appear to be intrinsically connected. While 'migration' and 'mission' are clear, 'movement' (more aptly characterized as mobility) is nebulous, involving a diversity of networking processes or even commercial and social connectivity. Religious leaders or preachers move/travel from one community to another preaching, teaching, and building up communities, but not settling down in a single location. Religious migration and mobilities generate a multiplication of religious communities as instantiation of ideas and practices (see Ukah 2005a). Ulrich Berner (2005, 45) describes how Greek religion spread outward, not through missionary enterprise but through the efforts of migrants who founded the ancient city of Olbia in the seventh century BCE; "for it is the culture and traditional religion of Greece which has given them their identity." As this historical instance indicates, even before the invention of 'mission' and 'missionaries' during the early Christian Church period, religious doctrines and practices had spread from one place to another through 'unofficial' carriers, migrants, and travelers. Similarly, the expansion and flourishing of Islam in West Africa was not through peripatetic Muslim preachers carrying out *da'wa* (invitation to the faith or proselytizing through preaching and sermons), but through itinerant traders and merchants seeking a common denominator with their clients and mobilizing their faith in the context of commercial transactions. As global migration has expanded and intensified—from 75 million in 1960 to 190 million in 2005 (Awumbila/Manuh 2009, 104) and 232 million in 2013—there are marked global religious resurgences and diversifications in the public sphere (UN 2013, 1; IOM 2015, 2). The same processes responsible for accelerated global interconnectivity (see Vásquez/Garbin, "Globalization," this volume)—such as the movement of goods, persons, media, and finances—are also at the roots of the increasing expansion of religious movements and organizations.

Migration forces are driven by many factors; these factors determine the two broad classifications, namely, voluntary and involuntary or forced migration. Voluntary migration may be caused by economic reasons such as jobs, education, or the search for better living conditions, while forced migration may be because of war, environmental problems, economic depression, and/or political oppression. Migration is complex and dynamic; it often defies clear-cut categorization into categories such as labor migrants, regular/irregular migrants, refugees, and asylum seekers. The number of internal migrants is 740 million, more than three times that of international migrants (IOM 2015).Whatever the causes of migration, it has real consequences on the religious ecology of many societies today. African migrants were estimated at 25 million in 2005; with the intensification of globalization pressures and economic crises of the last decade, this figure would have risen to about 35 million in 2015 (Awumbila/Manuh 2009, 104–105). Like globalization processes, migration processes are movements that transgress national or cultural boundaries. New religious movements have inevitably ridden on the tidal waves unleashed by globalization processes; as Margit Marburg and Armin Geertz (2008, 11) argue, "No religion ... is without local roots, and, equally, no religion is separate from global developments." Similarly, no religion that survives over a long period of time is without migration of some sort.

Migration is central to the survival of religious organizations and ideas. Religion plays into migration dynamics as a meaning-making and survival strategy for many migrants who often reconfigure their traveling experiences in religious terms and metaphors. Religion provides people with the symbolic resources for making sense of these processes in which they are caught up. Some migrants with Christian backgrounds mine biblical narratives and concepts such as 'exile' and 'living in Egypt' to make sense of their experiences away from home. For example, a Nigerian migrant in Durban, South Africa, who uses a different name from her original one, justifies it by saying: "I cannot use my real name while in exile" (field notes, Durban, South Africa, May 2011). Living a fraught existence in South Africa—as many migrants do since the escalation of Afrophobic resentment in the country—is framed as exile along the lines of "how can we sing the Lord's song in a strange land" (Ps 134:4). Religion knits together a purpose for their journey and suffering. Migration presents a pattern of religious expansion within a continent like Africa—with a large population of internal migrants—as well as from Africa to elsewhere in the world, especially to Western Europe, North America, and Asia. From the last quarter of the twentieth century, African migrants have been in the forefront of establishing religious organizations wherever they have settled either within the continent or outside (Ukah 2010; Ludwig/Asamoah-Gyadu 2011).

The relationship between migration and religious expansion complicates, or rather destabilizes, certain classifications of religions. In the academic study of religion/s, there is a distinction, that stands in tension with current events, between migrating, and therefore, missionizing religions, on the one hand, and non-migrating and therefore, non-missionizing religions, on the other hand. The former type is sometimes called 'world religions' while the latter is called 'indigenous' or 'ethno-religion.' This distinction is obsolete and contradicted by the global expansion of various religious traditions (e.g. African traditional religions) which are now practiced all over the Afro-Atlantic world as well as in Europe (Olupona/Rey 2008). Because these hitherto 'indigenous-' or 'ethno-religions' have crossed boundaries and oceans, finding viable new homes and massive followership in far-flung places of the world, their status has dramatically changed, and so should their classification.[1] Spatial expansion transforms the self-understanding and self-presentation of religions.

RELIGION AS CROSSING

Thomas Tweed suggests that "movement and relation" are core aspects of religion (2006, 77). Movement and relations carry a notion of place and flows of peoples and cultures. These ingredients of religion are especially important today, with ongoing religious resurgence and with increasing public awareness of different religious traditions. This is why Tweed (2006, 54) defines religions as "confluences of organic-cultural flows that intensify joy and confront suffering by drawing on human and suprahuman forces to make homes and cross boundaries." Such a definition is particularly pertinent today when there is an ongoing crisis of migration in many parts of the world, which inevitably carries important implications for religions. While many scholars emphasize the doctrinal, ritual, or salvific aspects of religion (Riesebrodt 2009), Tweed's book concretizes the material aspects of religion as activities engaged in by humans in place, time, and space. Religion survives through its capacity to cross boundaries and to inspire movement from one place and culture to another. The focus on religion as movement, flow, and relation underlines that religious behaviors are an embodied and embedded exercise that create possibilities for new relationships with both human and non-human powers on multiple levels as well as new communities that embody religious ideas, practices, and cultures. Religion as movement is purposive and expansionary.

Throughout recorded history, religions have expanded through four major processes, namely, (i) missionary enterprise, (ii) migration processes, (iii) imperial/military conquest, and (iv) revivals. The word 'revival' as used by Christian missionaries, specifically Pentecostals, means the practice of consolidating the Christian message or invigorating the (Christian) community. It implies, however, a rekindling of faith and zeal where these seem to have become weak, dull, or dampened and attenuated by contaminating influences. Revival also means strengthening and maintaining religious communities through the incorporation of new members and expansion of practices or congregations. Revival produces religious zeal and communal energy, revitalizes religious community practices, and nurtures missionary inspiration. This is its evangelistic meaning for many practicing Pentecostal Christians. In this sense, there is a close relationship between 'missionary enterprise' (establishment or founding of religious communities) and 'revival' (maintaining and strengthening faith communities through increased spiritual zeal and energy). Religious revival, as a project of spiritual reawakening, takes

---

[1] Judaism is often classified as a 'world religion' even when it is not missionizing and has less than 15 million adherents globally. It has also not succeeded in recruiting membership from African communities, the Beta Israel communities in Ethiopia notwithstanding (on the arbitrariness of the concept of 'world religion,' see Chidester 2003).

place within any religious tradition, for example, within Christianity, African indigenous religions, or Islam. It restructures and expands a religious tradition or movement
by increasing the rate or levels of observance and spiritual fervor. There is a complex
and dynamic as well as intrinsic relationship between religion and migration, or the
spread and expansion of new or novel religious behaviors and ideas from one locality
to another. Religious practice and expansion are spatial practices, some of which entail
religious actors creating new homes or sites of practices away from home. Religious
expansion inevitably embraces and problematizes the politics of location: the tension
between home and (a new) home away from home. Investigating religion as a form
of cultural flow requires also the exploration of cultures other than that (or those) in
which a particular religion was founded. Missionary enterprise, migration, and religious revival are contemporary ways through which religions expand. (Military conquest as a means of expanding the geographical spread of a religion is most unlikely in
the contemporary world. However, the strategies of the Islamic State [and Boko Haram
in West Africa] in its apocalyptic war and use of violence as a spectacle for conversion
comes dangerously close to religious expansion through violence and military conquest
[Celso 2015; Hall 2009].) These processes indicate cultural and social mediations that
transmit religious ideas, institutions, practices, and rituals from one place to another.
As Tweed underscores, globally successful religions are those that have crossed boundaries, built new homes away from home, and created new and functional institutions
in the new territories. They are those that have mobilized the most "kinetics of itiner-
ancy," generating multiple crossings: terrestrial, corporeal, and cosmic (Tweed 2006,
123). Contemporary times are characterized by rapid flux and confounding, even confusing, transformations; this situation compels religious actors and practices to be constantly on the move, literally and metaphorically. Migration drives a diversified religious
ecology, vibrant economic enterprises, as well as population increase in the migrants'
new home. Importantly, migrants tend to have more children than members of their
host societies, resulting in religious growth when the children are raised in and adhere
to their parents' traditions. This is particularly the case for migrants moving from the
South to the North, for example, Nigerians in the United Kingdom (see Ukah 2009).
These multifaceted consequences of migration further accelerate religious expansion on
a large scale, transforming social life and networks in the host society.

The following sections of this chapter examine how religious groups embrace terrestrial and corporeal crossings by detailing migrant religious organizations from the
majority world (the South) to the minority world (the North). Every major religious
tradition is experiencing what might be termed global resurgence. Two examples will
be drawn, one from Islam, and the other from Christianity, each using different sets
of strategies to expand its membership and influence across borders. Transnational
Islamic movements are key players in global revival and expansion of Islam, particularly in Europe and Africa. Similarly, Pentecostal-charismatic Christianity has captured scholarly interests as the fastest expanding strand of Christianity, perhaps the
fastest expanding "religion in the history of the world" (Jacobsen 2011, 51). Pentecostal
Christianity's expansion is multifaceted: it has restructured the religious landscape in

Africa, Asia (East and South), and Latin America; it is also reshaping the practice of religion in Western societies where migrants are the new missionaries exercising their 'mission mandate' as believers to reintroduce a new kind of Christianity to old Christian societies.

MARKET-DRIVEN EVANGELISM

Although Berner (2005, 43) is right in observing that "we are not used to speaking of missionaries as migrating people," it is plausible to consider missionaries as migrants with a religious message and purpose. Similarly, migrants have frequently become *de facto* missionaries, eager to spread their religious convictions and culture from their home countries to their new home or point of destination. For both missionaries and migrants, their mode of life is defined by movement. European migratory processes of the fifteenth century were the beginning of the introduction of Christianity to many parts of the world hitherto unchristianized. Apart from northern Africa and the Horn of Africa—where Coptic and Orthodox Christianities existed prior to this time—the rest of (so-called sub-Saharan) Africa was first exposed to the Christian message from this period onwards. This is also the case in Eastern Europe and the Middle East where Orthodox Christianity maintains a strong foothold that cannot be attributed to the European expansionary movement of the fifteenth and sixteenth centuries (Daughrity 2013, 42–59).

Europeans who pioneered these processes were primarily economic migrants and travelers—in search of trade and commodity goods or new sea routes—who were accompanied by a support staff of Christian personnel (Kalu 2012). The movement of Europeans outward to different parts of the world brought about the expansion of Christianity. Similarly, as noted above, the expansion of Islam consistently followed the trading routes of the ancient world, either across the Sahara Desert to West Africa or across the seas from the Middle East to East Africa (Tayob 1999; Mvumbi 2008, 110–127; Aslan 2011).

For Christianity and Islam, processes of expansion tend to mix both religious/missionary and economic motifs in an almost equal measure. Missionaries "cross geographical, religious, and social frontiers in order to win others" to a religious cause (Pillay 2010, 7). From a Judeo-Christian perspective, missionaries are central to the spread of the message—of the sovereign rule of Yahweh or salvation through the redemptive work of Jesus Christ (see Stark 2006). The expansion of the sovereignty of God implies building new communities of faith, a process that has spatial and territorial consequences.

Besides the key concept of the 'sovereignty of God' as a primary motive for missionary enterprise, some scholars have argued that certain human needs drive religious expansion. The German sociologist Max Weber (2011 [1905]) argues in his *Protestant Ethic* thesis that the puritan work ethic accounts for the expansion of Calvinism and, indirectly, the evolution of Western capitalism. According to Weber's argument, the

Protestant work ethic inspired a strong and diligent devotion to work as a service to God and an emphasis on wealth as a sign of God's blessing. Further, some scholars point to material profit from the perspectives of individuals, as well as institutions, as a driver of religious expansion (Ekelund/Hebert/Tollison 2006). In the twenty-first century, however, it is difficult to sustain an either/or argument for the role of spiritual or economic motifs in the expansion of religion. This is particularly the case when migrants morph into missionaries and when individuals or small groups of persons, rather than huge philanthropic organizations (as was the case in the eighteenth and nineteenth centuries), fund missionary enterprise. More importantly, certain religious organizations, such as Pentecostal groups, have merged the market and profit paradigms with spiritual and missionary zeal to account for their popular appeal and success—i.e. expansion— in terms of a market-driven evangelism model. A market-driven evangelism paradigm emphasizes the appropriation of business or neoliberal models, such as new methods of reaching the unconverted, quantification of outcomes, new packages and programs to appeal and attract those outside the Christian fold, as well as the mobilization of competitive and profit-making strategies to expand evangelism (Warren 1995; Gilley 2002; Miller 2002). In an era of seemingly inescapable neoliberal expansion, religion expands fastest when it is welded to business. As Micklethwait and Wooldridge (2009, 173) argue, changes in the modern entertainment industry and urban lifestyle pressure 'the God business' to innovate. The new paradigm of religious organizations—those organized according to business models—have found acceptance among a wide variety of religious start-ups and actors who are now in the forefront of a new wave of "religion on the move" (Adogame/Shobana 2013). An important aspect of the 'religion on the move' wave is how it is wedded not just to migration patterns and networks, but also to media penetration—particularly television and the Internet—and to neoliberal market dynamics, which is bolstered by the view that "religion flourishes best where it operates in a world of free choice" and in a free market (Micklethwait/Wooldridge 2009, 373). Prosperity Pentecostalism, for example, has flourished globally through intense media production and dissemination (Thomas/Lee 2012; Heuser 2015). In parts of Africa, a new form of 'Pentecostal Islam' is emerging which borrows from methods of Pentecostal self-presentation and strategies of expansion to further its cause of forestalling Muslims from joining Pentecostal groups and also expanding its influence among Muslim communities.

ITINERANT MUSLIM PREACHERS: *TABLĪGHĪ JAMĀ'AT*

In the twentieth and early twenty-first centuries, Islam has become the fastest expanding religion in Europe. The engine of this spread has been Muslim brotherhoods (such as the Qadiriyya, the Tijaniyyah, Mourides, and the Layene) and the migration of Muslims from former European colonies, particularly from northern and west-ern Africa, the Middle East, and South Asia. Some Muslim associations, such as the Jamāʾat Izalatul Bidʾa Wa Iqamatis Sunna (The Society of Eradication of Innovation and Re-establishment of the Sunna, Izala, for short) and Tablīghī Jamāʾat (The Society for the Spreading of the Faith) have been spearheading the expansion of Islam from their homelands or places of establishment to other territories. The Izala, a Sunni movement, was founded in Jos, Nigeria, in 1978, by a former chaplain in the Nigerian military, Sheikh Ismaila Idris (1937–2000). Its primary purpose was to combat Sufi groups and their practices in the country by urging Muslims to return "to the 'right' path of Islam based on the Qurʾān, *sunna* (Arab.: traditions of the Prophet), and *as-salaf as-ṣāliḥ* (Arab.: pious predecessors)" (Amara 2014, 126). The Izala has spread to all the countries of West Africa where its members preach against 'innovations' (*bida*) among Muslim communities, build mosques, produce media materials (books, pamphlets, and CDs and DVDs of sermons), and more importantly, build educational institutions as a strategy for the transmission of doctrines from one generation to another. By moderating its earlier aggressive doctrinal disputes and violent sectar-ian clashes with Sufi groups in northern Nigeria, and embarking on massive transre-gional educational projects, the Izala society found acceptance among West African Muslims. It has a large number of institutions and membership in countries like Cameroon, Chad, Niger, and Togo. The establishing of mosques and educational insti-tutions is Izalaʾs key expansionary strategy. By founding nursery, primary, secondary, vocational, and higher Islamic schools and by insisting on the education of women, the Izala recruited large numbers of young people who became the group's foot sol-diers, carrying its doctrines and influence across borders and societies. The schools also become projects and structures of renewal and consolidation that give it access and acceptance as well as networks with other Islamic establishments in other coun-tries such as Mali and Senegal (Amara 2011). The group is still expanding its activities in Central and Eastern Africa where it is a major player in Islamic education, particu-larly among the poor and the campaign for establishing sharia law among Muslim communities. Its transborder expansion and successes, however, are less spectacular than that of Tablīghī Jamāʾat.

Founded in colonial India in 1927 by Muhammad Ilyas al-Kandhlawi (1885–1944), the Tablīghī Jamāʾat is today a transnational Muslim organization found in almost all countries where Islam is practiced. Its key purpose exemplifies religious expansion by revival, that is, the spiritual transformation of those who are already Muslims, rather than the proselytization of non-Muslims. It is a lay movement headed by ordinary, com-mitted Muslims. Its purpose is to reform Islamic practice from below, to respond to deteriorating Muslim observances or lax moral conduct within Muslim communities. While *daʾwa*, meaning "call" or "invitation," is the practice of proselytization directed toward non-Muslims and Muslims alike, to the members of Tablīghī Jamāʾat, *daʾwa* is focused on the intensification of religious practice such as observance of prayers among local Muslim communities. The mission of the group is to call/invite Muslims to God and so to revive or intensify Islamic conduct and community. Religious expansion in this context is a deepening of faith among Muslims, making them serve as exemplary witnesses to both believers and non-believers alike. Individual character building through the invitation of other Muslims to "the world of practical Islam in which egalitarianism, spiritual salvation and change are within the reach of all" is the hallmark of Tablīghī Jamāʿat (Wario/Amara 2013, 168). The group prioritizes the jihad of the heart over the jihad of the sword and bases its activities on six principles, namely, (i) article of faith (*shahada*); (ii) five daily ritual prayers (*salat*); (iii) knowledge (*ilm*) and remembrance of God (*dhikr*); (iv) respect for every Muslim (*ikram-I Muslim*); (v) emendation of intention and sincerity (*ikhlas-i niyat*), and (vi) spare time (*tafriq-i waqt*) (Wario 2012a, 79).

Its spread throughout the South Asian subcontinent occurred from the middle of the 1940s following the partition of India, and again following the founding of Bangladesh in the early 1970s. It founded the largest mosque in Europe in London in the late 1970s (having spread to England two decades earlier), and from there expanded to different parts of Europe, such as Germany and Russia. It is arguably the fastest spreading Islamic movement in sub-Saharan Africa, found in Nigeria, Tanzania, Kenya, and South Africa among other African countries (Mfumbusa 2014, 246–247). Its expansion to and in Africa started in the 1950s and continues until present times where it has grown and adapted to local contexts.

The rapid expansion of the group follows its focus within the Muslim community and, according to Wario (2012a, 78), "its apolitical stand, its focus on individual and collective re-spiritualization, its ability to mobilize ordinary Muslims as active preachers." More significantly, its rapid growth hinges on a strategy of "religious mobility and border crossing" which builds on the sixth principle of *tafriq-i waqt*, spare time. The most important growth strategy is its grassroots base system of *khuruj fi sabillilah* (going out for the sake of God). This system involves volunteers dedicating time and resources to travel away from home for varying durations, such "as 3 days, 10 days, 40 days, 4 months and even a year. Members are expected to set aside at least 3 days every month, 40 days every year and 4 months in a lifetime for the sole purpose of missionary journeys" (Wario 2012a, 80). Similar to the Pentecostal Christians who believe that the key duty of the born-again person is to spread the message of salvation and convert others to Christianity, members of Tablīghī Jamāʿat insist that the duty of inviting Muslims to the Islamic faith is not the preserve of the clergy, but the duty of every Muslim on behalf of the Muslim *Umma*. Because every Muslim is called to preach, women are also proselytizers, "implementers of the *da'wa* ethos at home by socializing the children and managing her home in an Islamic manner" (Wario/Amara 2013, 170). The democratization of missionary work through self-sponsored travels empowers many ordinary Muslims to cross boundaries, carrying with them a religious message and zeal. In addition to the group's apolitical stance and focus on revival and purification of belief and practice within Muslim communities, the force of lay and self-sponsoring volunteer preachers accounts for its successful expansion to far-flung parts of the (Islamic) world (Wario 2012b).

MAKING DISCIPLES OF ALL
NATIONS: PENTECOSTAL GLOBAL EXPANSION

Pentecostalism is the fastest expanding global religion, having more followers in the global South than in other parts of the world (Cox 2001 [1995]; Martin 2002; Westerlund 2009). The expansion and appeal of Pentecostalism provide strong empirical evidence in the investigation of patterns and dynamics of religious expansion and of the relationship between expansion, movement, migration, and mission. Pentecostalism provides Christians from the southern hemisphere with a unique interpretation and relationship with the Judeo-Christian scriptures which privileges mission as the fundamental duty of a 'reborn' Christian (Jenkins 2006). Doctrinally, Pentecostalism as a global missionary religion privileges conversion drive as the key duty of the saved believer (Anderson 2007; Bergunder 2008). In practice, however, with the increase in the popularity of the prosperity gospel, many African and Latin American Pentecostal preachers teach their followers that financial giving is more important than believing or spreading the good news (Hackett 1995; Oyedepo 1997; 2008, 517–526; Ukah 2013, 52–56).

There are two broad ways of considering the relationship between migration and religion. One way is to examine religious organizations founded in one part of the southern hemisphere that have migrated and taken root in a different part of the same southern hemisphere but also the northern hemisphere. An example would be the Universal Church of the Kingdom of God (UCKG)—originally founded in 1977 by Edir Macedo in a poor suburb of Rio de Janeiro, Brazil—with its numerous congregations in Africa (South Africa, Lesotho, and Nigeria, among others). Within two decades of its founding, it transformed into a transnational religious organization, present in 96 countries (Freston 2005; Van Wyk 2014). The UCKG has a systematic method of penetrating African countries. It first surveys the practices of other churches, identifies levels of developments and needs among the general population, and thereafter designs its services and rituals targeting that local situation. In so doing, the UCKG creates and occupies a religious niche that is difficult to dislodge or occupy by other competing churches. Paying attention to the underbelly of the African worldview is significant in positioning its services as an important element in the achievement of salvation. Although not without accusations and controversies about selling prayers and healing and racism against local clergy, the expansion of UCKG, especially in non-Lusophone Africa, is remarkable. The first African congregation of UCKG was founded in 1992 in Johannesburg; the church currently has congregations in more than forty countries of Africa. This exemplifies a South–South religious migration cum expansion model.

On a similar but smaller scale, in cities throughout Africa, large Pentecostal congregations are being founded by African migrants, and these are, in many respects, in the forefront of restructuring the religious texture of their host communities. The Congolese in South Africa have established massive congregations in large cities such as Johannesburg, Durban, and Cape Town (Nzayabino 2010). Nigeria is popularly framed, particularly by the Evangelical community, as the Pentecostal capital of the world and the global epicenter of Christian evangelism, and by implication as a nation specially chosen by God for the purpose of reconverting people to God for the end-time. (Managing historical time, the social imagination of time and focus on the eschaton—end of time—are aspects of the drive for the expansion of mission among Nigerian Pentecostal-Charismatic Christians.)

Nigerian-founded churches dominate the Pentecostal landscape of South Africa; the largest black Pentecostal congregation in the country is a migrant congregation, The Believers' LoveWorld, better known as Christ Embassy Ministries, established in 1989 by the Nigerian miracle-healing pastor, Chris Oyakhilome (born December 7, 1961). Christ Embassy, with more than 150 congregations in South Africa, is very popular and attractive particularly to young people, who constitute about 78 percent of the congregants. The most popular Pentecostal pastor in South Africa is the controversial Nigerian healer Temitope Balogun Joshua (born 1963), who has a massive following—though with a single congregation in the country, in Bellville in Cape Town. His followers throng his healing church—The Synagogue of All Nations Church, founded in 1987 in Lagos—in search of miracles. These religious organizations, spreading outwards from Lagos, are influencing and spreading new urban religiosity far from their sites of founding. This type of religiosity responds to the anxieties and concerns of urban life such as loneliness and anonymity in the midst of a crowd, scarcity in the midst of plenty, anomie and alienation, and infrastructural challenges particularly in the health sector. Migrant religious organizations, while targeting the larger society in which they exist, provide coping, survival, and integrative strategies for the migrant communities; they also constitute competitive or negotiation strategies for scarce and highly valued resources (respect, visibility, livelihood) in an increasingly fraught, often openly hostile, socio-economic and political environment such as South Africa. The presence of African migrants in South Africa has decisively transformed and revitalized the religious field and ecology of the country, introducing new ways of being religious and doing religion in contemporary times, and challenging the dominant narratives of the local religious communities (Echtler/Ukah 2015).

In addition to the South–South religious expansion dynamic, various religious organizations expand along a South–North axis. These are organizations founded in the global South—a term that refers to Africa, Asia, and Latin America—which have expanded their spheres of influence to the Northern hemisphere. This model of religious expansion is sometimes called the 'reverse mission' (Ukah 2009) or 'reverse flow' of mission. According to Ogbu Kalu (2011, 29), reverse flow generally describes "the religion of immigrants that reshape northern religious landscapes . . . [I]mmigrants come with a more conservative theology and practice, insist on using their languages and cultural expressions, prefer to import their own priests and challenge the authority of traditional hierarchy." African migrants to the West (i.e. Western Europe, North America, and Australia/New Zealand) have decisively and irreversibly transformed their host societies through a new model of missionary expansion, one that is not supported or funded by state power or large philanthropic or missionary societies but democratized in such a way as to almost destabilize the traditional notions of 'missionary enterprise' (Hanciles 2008). This process is not uniform, of course. For example, the influence of immigrant churches in Europe is unevenly distributed. While they may not have achieved social prominence in some parts of Europe such as Norway, they have arguably become a force to be reckoned with in the gradual and steady transformation of such countries as Ireland (Ugba 2009) and Germany (Quaas 2011).

Arguably, the most important, fastest-growing, and farthest-spread religious organization from the global South to other parts of the globe is a Pentecostal organization from Nigeria called the Redeemed Christian Church of God (RCCG) (Premack 2014; Wariboko 2014, 29–31). In August 2015, the RCCG reported having congregations in 188 countries out of the 193 sovereign countries in the world. (In addition to the 193 sovereign states which are part of the United Nations, there are two UN observer states, the Vatican and the Palestinian Authority, adding up to 195 countries in the UN.) The RCCG was an organization that embraced expansionary strategies late in its history. Its mode of expansion has correlated with increased outmigration of Nigerians starting from the implementation of Structural Adjustment Program during the military government of Ibrahim Babangida in 1986. The downsizing of the functions and services of the state compelled many educated Nigerians to leave the country in search of better conditions of living and work. Wherever they settled, they also founded a church from home. Global expansion along the model of the Coca-Cola company defines the RCCG's self-understanding and has brought the church fame, recognition, and wealth; expectedly, it has also spun "a rhetoric of grandiose claims that exaggerate [its] actual impact abroad" (Premack 2014, 215). The RCCG explicitly imitates the successful strategy of the Coca-Cola company by breaking up large congregations into smaller units, and forcing these units to aggressively recruit membership and build up the congregation (only to be broken down into smaller congregations once again). As part of its mission statement, the RCCG aims "to plant churches within five minutes' walking distance in every city and town of developing countries; and within five minutes' driving distance in every city and town of developed countries" (Ukah 2008, 48).

"Missions" for the RCCG is multifaceted: it means sending out trained members as missionaries to other parts of the world to found congregations. Further, immigrants founding congregations where they settle constitutes another missionary strategy. Additionally, the church focuses on proselytizing the very wealthy in order to use their resources (wealth, influence, social position, networks) to penetrate different strata of any society such as the corporate and political spheres in Nigeria and elsewhere. A special organization founded by the leader of the church, Enoch Adejare Adeboye, called Christ the Redeemer's Friend Universal (CRFU) is responsible for recruiting only the very rich in any society and mobilizing their resources (ostensibly) for missionary objectives (Ukah 2008, 125–127). Cumulatively, these strategies have made the RCCG a locomotive of global Pentecostal expansion in the twenty-first century. According to one of its senior officials, "Missions contributed immensely to the expansion of RCCG in taking the gospel across the world. . . . It has infused energy to the church because it helps the vision [of the church] to spread like wild fire". . . . The church believes in evangelism, [as] the vehicle of progress to propel the actualization of this vision" (Odesola 2012, 39).

The above strategies illustrate the place of religious expansion and its dynamic in the structure and relevance of religious organizations in contemporary times. Expansion spreads the message and 'vision' of an organization, infuses it with energy, and enlarges its scope of influence, thereby actualizing or materializing and defining its progress. The 'vision' of the RCCG as mentioned in the preceding quote was articulated about 2005 by its leader, Enoch Adeboye, and states thus:

1. To make [enter] heaven.
2. To take as many people with us.
3. To have a member of RCCG in every family of all nations.
4. To accomplish No. 1 above, holiness will be our lifestyle.
5. To accomplish No. 2 and 3 above, we will plant churches within five minutes' walking distance in every city and town of developing countries and within five minutes' driving distance in every city and town of developed countries.

    We will pursue these objectives until every Nation in the world is reached for the Lord Jesus Christ. (<https://trccg.org/rccg/who-we-are/mission-and-vision//>, accessed February 3, 2016)

The RCCG epitomizes the triumphalist evangelical narrative about Nigeria as the powerhouse of global Pentecostal expansion. To have a member of the church in every family in the world is not merely an ambitious, global project; it is clearly a world-dominating, territorial agenda. What requires scrutiny is how the RCCG has created a dense transnational network of churches, businesses, and worship sites (including prayer camps and religious cities) in a bid to demonstrate its global expansion and ambition. The church has expanded through three principal means. The first is the simplest: breaking large congregations into smaller ones. If a congregation is composed of more than a hundred worshipers, it splits into smaller congregations; each begins the process of growing its membership again through active membership drive or proselytism. Active proselytism for the RCCG has been by reaffiliating members from mainly other Christian churches, a process that effectively means fishing fished fishes. The second method of growth is through larger congregations, called 'mother parishes,' sponsoring the establishment of new congregations, called 'daughter parishes.' The third is through a wealthy parish sponsoring—by financial support—missionaries in a foreign territory to proselytize and establish parishes. These wealthy congregations in Lagos or London or Texas are challenged by the church leadership to compete among themselves in sponsoring and founding congregations outside Nigeria or the countries they are located. During its annual convention every August, statistics are released about the churches that have out-performed others and these are given national recognition in the form of 'Mission Award.' In addition to these methods, the church has taken over some other smaller independent churches in the same way that stronger businesses force hostile mergers. There have been instances in which some independent church founders or owners have thought that their ambition would be better realized if they brought their organizations under the administrative and organizational resources and oversight of the RCCG. In such situations, they become a parish of the RCCG.

CONCLUSION

In contemporary times, religious organizations such as the Izala, Tablīghī Jamāʿat, the RCCG, and the UCKG have expanded through three out of the four identified pathways: missionary engagement, migration, and revival. The Izala and the Tablīghī Jamāʿat are principally Muslim revivalist movements focused on purifying, strengthening, and deepening Islamic faith within Muslim communities, and through that, building missionary zeal for outward expansion. They have done this through stressing core doctrines and ritual practices of Islam, liberalizing preaching and education to include women, and building mosques and education facilities as structures of Islamic knowledge production and transmission. Peripatetic preaching, cross-border travels, and volunteerism play important roles in their methods of expansion and appeal. In addition to reproduction and fertility within faith communities, expansion through mobility and recruitment guarantees the social survival of religious organizations.

There are many dimensions and perspectives on religious expansion, including geographical, organizational, and doctrinal. As an organization expands its geographical spread and crosses borders, it inevitably settles in new locations, and in so doing, restructures religious landscapes in more or less significant ways. Further, the expansion of religious ideas and practices into new territories interacts with the cultures and lifestyles of its host societies and inevitably modifies or adapts its doctrines. As the settling religion alters its host environment, so also is it altered by its present circumstances and challenges. In contemporary times, it is possible for religious ideas and practices to cross borders and exert influence on a population far from their site of origin, through the use of media technologies. However, historically, the most potent strategies of expansion have been through migration, trade, and mission. As the history and practices of the RCCG demonstrate, religious expansion has occurred fastest in the current era of intense migratory processes, as exacerbated by globalization and its economic consequences both negative and positive. Through expansion, a religious community re-evaluates its relevance in the present context in which it exists and refashions its evangelistic and competitive strategies. As religions witness and embrace expansion as a method of remaining relevant, charisma—the influence and power of individual religious leaders—also expands to non-religious spheres, particularly political and economic.

Evangelical entrepreneurship is key in understanding Pentecostal methods of expansion, particularly into economically affluent societies. Religious expansion is motivated by many factors; the primary outcomes are structural changes that play out in the social, political, economic, and cultural spheres. Some have charged that religious expansion breeds intolerance and conflict. There is some truth to this, because conversion presupposes the offering of a better alternative: economic uplift, better social networks, salvation, escaping persecution, finding a spouse, doctrinal and ritual satisfaction or enrichment. Those who espouse the idea that they have been divinely mandated to bring others to a new religious vision and truth often feel "stronger," possessing "more force," and can, therefore, become intolerant (Durkheim 2008 [1912], 416), and sometimes violently so. However, not all forms of religious expansion through mission and migration take this pathway. An important irony, with respect to the RCCG and its global expansionary adventures in the contemporary world, is that Africans, whose traditions and cultures did not include religious conversion, are pioneering what may amount to one of the fastest and most widespread conversion drives known in the history of religions.

GLOSSARY

Migration encapsulates the dynamics of mobility, the process and experience of moving from one's place of birth or home country to another society or country for a variety of reasons, some voluntary, others forced or involuntary, either temporarily or permanently.

Mission the process of incorporating persons who are not part of a religion into the worldview and lifestyle of a particular religion. In a broader sense, mission may also mean addressing the spiritual needs of those who already belong to a religious tradition in order to nourish, intensify, and deepen their faith.

Pentecostalism a protean strand within Christianity that emphasizes embodied spiritual experience such as speaking in tongues, the indwelling of the Holy Spirit, and the exercise of the gifts of the Holy Spirit such as miracles of healing, prophecy, and strong orality and lay participation.

(Religious) expansion outward movement of religious organizations and cultures from a center, usually the site of its founding, to the periphery, which may in time become a new center. Expansion may be progressive or serial. Christian expansion is serial rather than progressive (some societies that once were Christian are no longer so, while others are just becoming christianized).

Reverse mission the process by which immigrants from former mission fields in the global South become missionaries to the peoples of the global North, introducing their own form of Christianity and building religious organizations to sustain this enterprise.

REFERENCES

Adogame, Afe and Shobana Shankar, eds. 2013. *Religion on the Move! New Dynamics of Religious Expansion in a Globalizing World*. Leiden: Brill.

Amara, Ben Ramzi. 2011. "The Izala Movement in Nigeria: Its Split, Relationship to Sufis and Perception of Shari'a Re-Implementation." PhD dissertation, Bayreuth International Graduate School of African Studies, University of Bayreuth, Germany.

Amara, Ben Ramzi. 2014. "'We Introduced Shari'a': The Izala Movement in Nigeria as Initiator of Shari'a—Reimplementation in the North of the Country: Some Reflections." In *Shari'a in*

Africa Today: Reactions and Responses, edited by John A. Chesworth and Franz Kogelmann. Leiden: Brill, 125–145.

Anderson, Allan. 2007. *Spreading Fires: The Missionary Nature of Early Pentecostalism*. Maryknoll, NY: Orbis Books.

Arango, Joaquín. 2000. "Explaining Migration: A Critical Review." *International Social Science Journal* 52(165): 283–296. doi: 10.1111/1468-2451.00259

Aslan, Reza. 2011. *No god but God: The Origins, Evolutions, and Future of Islam*. New York: Random House. Original edition, 2005.

Awumbila, Mariama and Takyiwaa Manuh. 2009. "Migration and Development in Sub-Saharan Africa." In *Knowledge on the Move: Emerging Agendas for Development-Oriented Research*, edited by Henk Molenaar, Louk Box, and Rutger Engelhard. Leiden: International Development Publications, 104–112.

Bergunder, Michael. 2008. *The South Indian Pentecostal Movement in the Twentieth Century*. Grand Rapids, MI: Eerdmans.

Berner, Ulrich. 2005. "Mission and Migration in the Roman Empire." In *Religion in the Context of African Migration*, edited by Afe Adogame and Cordula Weissköppel. Bayreuth: Eckhard Breitinger, 43–56.

Celso, Anthony N. 2015. "The Islamic State and Boko Haram: Fifth Wave Jihadist Terror Groups." *Orbis* 59(2): 249–268. doi:10.1016/j.orbis.2015.02.010

Chidester, David. 2003. "Global Citizenship, Cultural Citizenship and World Religions in Religion Education." In *International Perspectives on Citizenship, Education and Religious Diversity*, edited by Robert Jackson. London: Routledge, 28–45.

Cox, Harvey. 2001. *Fire from Heaven: The Rise of Pentecostal Spirituality and the Reshaping of Religion in the Twenty-First Century*. Cambridge, MA: Da Capo Press. Original edition, 1995.

Daughrity, Dyron. 2013. "Ignoring the East: Correcting a Serious Flaw in World Christianity Scholarship." In *Religion on the Move! New Dynamics of Religious Expansion in a Globalizing World*, edited by Afe Adogame and Shobana Shankar. Leiden: Brill, 42–59.

Durkheim, Émile. 2008. *The Elementary Forms of the Religious Life*. Translated by Joseph Ward Swain. Mineola, NY: Dover. Original edition, 1912.

Echtler, Magnus and Asonzeh Ukah, eds. 2015. *Bourdieu in Africa: Exploring the Dynamics of the Religious Fields*. Leiden: Brill.

Ekelund, Robert, Robert Hebert, and Robert Tollison. 2006. *The Marketplace of Christianity*. Cambridge, MA: MIT Press.

Freston, Paul. 2005. "The Universal Church of the Kingdom of God: A Brazilian Church Finds Success in Southern Africa." *Journal of Religion in Africa* 35(1): 33–65. doi: 10.1163/1570066052995816

Gilley, Grey. 2002. *This Little Church Went to Market*. Benin City: Gospel Vision Publication.

Hackett, Rosalind I. J. 1995. "The Prosperity Gospel in West Africa." In *Religion and the Transformations of Capitalism*, edited by Richard H. Roberts. New York: Routledge, 200–214.

Hall, John R. 2009. *Apocalypse: From Antiquity to the Empire of Modernity*. Cambridge: Polity Press.

Hanciles, Jehu J. 2008. *Beyond Christendom: Globalization, African Migrants, and the Transformation of the West*. Maryknoll, NY: Orbis Books.

Heuser, Andreas, ed. 2015. *Pastures of Plenty: Tracing Religio-Scapes of Prosperity Gospel in Africa and Beyond*. Frankfurt am Main: Peter Lang.

International Organization for Migration (IOM). 2015. *World Migration Report 2015: Migrants and Cities: New Partnerships to Manage Mobility*. Geneva: IOM.

Jacobsen, Douglas. 2011. *The World's Christians: Who They Are, Where They Are, and How They Got There*. Chichester: Wiley-Blackwell.

Jenkins, Philip. 2006. *The New Face of Christianity: Believing the Bible in the Global South*. Oxford: Oxford University Press.

Kalu, Ogbu. 2011. "The Anatomy of Reverse Flow in African Christianity: Pentecostalism and Immigrant African Christianity." In *African Christian Presence in the West: New Immigrant Congregations and Transnational Networks in North Africa and Europe*, edited by Frieder Ludwig and J. Kwabena Asamoah-Gyadu. Trenton, NJ: Africa World Press, 29–54.

Kalu, Ogbu. 2012. "West African Christianity: Padres, Pastors, Prophets, and Pentecostals." In *Introducing World Christianity*, edited by Charles E. Farhadian. Chichester: Wiley-Blackwell, 36–50.

Ludwig, Frieder and J. Kwabena Asamoah-Gyadu, eds. 2011. *African Christian Presence in the West: New Immigrant Congregations and Transnational Networks in North Africa and Europe*. Trenton, NJ: Africa World Press.

Marburg, Margit and Armin Geertz. 2008. "New Religions and Globalization: An Introduction." In *New Religions and Globalization: Empirical, Theoretical and Methodological Perspectives*, edited by Armin Geertz, Margit Warburg, and Dorthe Refslund Christensen. Aarhus: Aarhus University Press, 9–19.

Martin, David. 2002. *Pentecostalism: The World their Parish*. Oxford: Blackwell.

Mfumbusa, Bernardin. 2014. "'Chaos will Never Have a Chance': Shari'a Debates and Tolerance in a Provincial Tanzanian Town." In *Shari'a in Africa Today: Reactions and Responses*, edited by John A. Chesworth and Franz Kogelmann. Leiden: Brill, 241–258.

Micklethwait, John and Adrian Wooldridge. 2009. *God Is Back: How the Global Revival of Faith Is Changing the World*. New York: Penguin.

Miller, Kent D. 2002. "Competitive Strategies of Religious Organizations." *Strategic Management Journal* 23(5): 435–456. doi: 10.1002/smj.234

Mvumbi, Frederic Ntedika. 2008. *Journey into Islam: An Attempt to Awaken Christians in Africa*. Johannesburg: Paulines Publications Africa.

Nzayabino, Vedaste. 2010. "The Role of Refugee-Established Churches in Integrating Forced Migrants: A Study of Word of Life Assembly in Yeoville, Johannesburg." *HTS Teologiese Studies/Theological Studies* 66(1): 1–9. doi: 10.4102/hts.v66i1.290

Odesola, Johnson O. 2012. "60 Years of RCCG in Missions . . . the Way Forward." *Missions' Focus: A Quarterly Publication of RCCG Central Missions Board* 6(0712): 38–43.

Olupona, Jacob K. and Terry Rey. 2008. *Òrìsà Devotion as World Religion: The Globalization of Yorùbá Religious Culture*. Madison, WI: University of Wisconsin Press.

Oyedepo, David O. 1997. *Understanding Financial Prosperity*. Lagos: Dominion Publishing House.

Oyedepo, David O. 2008. *Pillars of Destiny: Exploring the Secrets of an Ever-Winning Life*. Lagos: Dominion Publishing House.

Pillay, Jerry. 2010. "Theological Foundations of Mission." In *Mission Continues: Global Impulses for the 21st Century*, edited by Claudia Währisch-Oblau and Fidon Mwombeki. Oxford: Regnum Books International, 7–17.

Premack, Laura. 2014. "'The Coca-Cola of Churches Arrives': Nigeria's Redeemed Christian Church of God in Brazil." In *The Public Face of African Religious Movements in Diaspora: Imagining the Religious 'Other'*, edited by Afe Adogame. Farnham: Ashgate, 215–231.

Quaas, Anna D. 2011. *Transnationale Pfingstkirchen: Christ Apostolic Church und Redeemed Christian Church of God*. Frankfurt am Main: Verlag Otto Lembert.

Riesebrodt, Martin. 2009. *The Promise of Salvation: A Theory of Religion.*Translated by Steven Rendall. Chicago, IL: University of Chicago Press.

Stark, Rodney. 2006. *Cities of God: The Real Story of How Christianity Became an Urban Movement and Conquered Rome.* New York: HarperOne.

Stark, Rodney. 2007. *Discovering God: The Origins of the Great Religions and the Evolution of Belief.* New York: HarperOne.

Tayob, Abdulkader. 1999. *Islam: A Short Introduction.* Oxford: Oneworld Publications.

Thomas, Pradip Ninan and Philip Lee, eds. 2012. *Global and Local Televangelism.* New York: Palgrave Macmillan.

Tweed, Thomas A. 2006. *Crossing and Dwelling: A Theory of Religion.* Cambridge, MA: Harvard University Press.

Ugba, Abel. 2009. *Shades of Belonging: African Pentecostals in Twenty-First Century Ireland.* Trenton, NJ: African World Press.

Ukah, Asonzeh. 2005a. "Mobilities, Migration and Multiplication: The Expansion of the Religious Field of the Redeemed Christian Church of God (RCCG), Nigeria." In *Religion in the Context of African Migration Studies*, edited by Afe Adogame and Cordula Weissköppel. Bayreuth: Theilmann & Breitinger, 317–341.

Ukah, Asonzeh. 2005b. "Globalisation of Pentecostalism in Africa: Evidence from the Redeemed Christian Church of God," *IFRA Ibadan Special Research Issue* 1: 93–112.

Ukah, Asonzeh. 2008. *A New Paradigm of Pentecostal Power: The Redeemed Christian Church of God in Nigeria.* New Jersey and Asmara: Africa World Press/Red Sea Press.

Ukah, Asonzeh. 2009. "Reverse Mission or Asylum Christianity? African Christian Churches in Britain." In *Africans and the Politics of Popular Cultures*, edited by Toyin Falola and Augustine Agwuele. Rochester, NY: University of Rochester Press, 104–132.

Ukah, Asonzeh. 2010. "God@eBay: Nigerian Churches in South Africa." In *Creativity and Change in Nigerian Christianity*, edited by David O. Ogungbile and Akintunde E. Akinade. Lagos: Malthouse Publishing Limited, 333–348.

Ukah, Asonzeh. 2013. "Born-Again Muslims: The Ambivalence of Pentecostal Response to Islam in Nigeria." In *Fractured Spectrum: Perspectives in Christian–Muslim Relations in Nigeria*, edited by Akintunde E. Akinade. New York: Peter Lang, 43–62.

United Nations (UN). 2013. *International Migration Report 2013.* New York: UN Department of Economic and Social Affairs, Population Division.

Van Wyk, Ilana. 2014. *The Universal Church of the Kingdom of God in South Africa: A Church of Strangers.* Cambridge: Cambridge University Press.

Wariboko, Nimi. 2014. *Nigerian Pentecostalism.* Rochester, NY: University of Rochester Press.

Wario, Halkano Abdi. 2012a. "Stock Taking in a Transnational Islamic movement: Accounting for the Growth of Tablīghī Jamāʿat in Kenya", *BIGSAS Works: Bayreuth African Studies Working Papers* 9 (2): 78–101.

Wario, Halkano Abdi. 2012b. "Networking the Nomads: A Study of Tablīghī Jamāʿat among the Borana of Northern Kenya." PhD dissertation, Bayreuth International Graduate School of African Studies, University of Bayreuth, Germany.

Wario, Halkano Abdi and Ramzi Ben Amara 2013. "Door to Door Daʿaw in Africa: Dynamics of Proselytization in Yan Izala and Tablīghī Jamāʿat." In *Religion on the Move! New Dynamics of Religious Expansion in a Globalizing World*, edited by Afe Adogame and Shobana Shankar. Leiden: Brill, 159–177.

Warren, Rick. 1995. *The Purpose Driven Church: Growth without Compromising Your Message and Mission.* Grand Rapids, MI: Zondervan.

Weber, Max. 2011. *The Protestant Ethic and the Spirit of Capitalism*. Translated by Stephen Kalberg. Oxford: Oxford University Press. Original edition, 1905.

Westerlund, David, ed. 2009. *Global Pentecostalism: Encounters with Other Religious Traditions*. London: I. B. Tauris.

FURTHER READING

Kalu 2011 [*This essay maps out the contours of immigrant religious activities in Western societies and identifies certain indices to measure and evaluate the character of what constitutes 'reverse mission'.*]

Olupona/Rey 2008 [*This book examines the changing character of an indigenous African religion as it expands from its original location in Yorubaland, in southwest Nigeria to the Afro-Atlantic world. The book interrogates the concept of 'world religion' that excludes such religions as Orisha worship that has achieved what the authors argue is a global presence.*]

Ukah 2008 [*Examines the history and processes of social and doctrinal transformations of a little-known Aladura church in Nigeria into a global Pentecostal empire in the twenty-first century.*]

Van Wyk 2014 [*Presents the fascinating expansion and interpretation of a Brazilian Neo-Pentecostal church in Durban, South Africa, and the cultural elements that gives the church its wildfire appeal among ordinary people.*]

CHAPTER 45

GLOBALIZATION

MANUEL A. VÁSQUEZ AND DAVID GARBIN

CHAPTER SUMMARY

- Trans-local religious dynamics, linked for instance to trade and missionary networks, are not new and originated before the consolidation of the modern international system.
- Some of the 'command centers' in the contemporary global religious field have already been central in the spread of age-old 'World' Religions. Others are emerging in the 'global South,' in countries such as Brazil, Nigeria, and Ghana.
- The interplay of globalization, migration, and religion has been dramatically intensified by rapid innovations in transportation and computer-mediated communications.
- Migrants, minorities, and diasporas are key actors of the globalization of religion and are integral to the contemporary expansion of globe-spanning religious networks associated with Islam, Hinduism, and (primarily Pentecostal and Charismatic) Christianities.
- While the economic dimensions of religion are central, the dynamics of global religious fields cannot be reduced to those of the capitalist world system, with a clear center and periphery. Religious flows and networks are multi-directional, requiring interdisciplinary and multi-sited approaches.

TWO VIGNETTES

The Temple of Solomon of the Brazilian Igreja Universal do Reino de Deus ([Neo-Pentecostal] Universal Church of the Kingdom of God—UCKG) rises majestically over the bustling district of Brás in the center of São Paulo, the second largest city in Latin

America. Built at a cost of over US$300 million, the eighteen-story building is a replica of the original temple in Jerusalem as imagined by the church, complete with soaring ornate columns, elaborate gardens and water fountains, and imposing gold-plated doors. The UCKG went as far as spending more than $8 million to bring stones from Israel to build the temple, stones that, in the words of Edir Macedo, the church's founder, directly witnessed Jesus's life and ministry (Romero 2014).

When asked about why he built the Solomon's Temple, Macedo articulates a geo-spiritual pastoral project that places Brazil at the center of a vast "globally integrated network," which inverts the country's peripheral place in the capitalist world system, in effect, mirroring Brazil's standing as one of the BRICS—i.e. one of five major emerging economies, Brazil, Russia, India, China, and South Africa (Mafra et al., 2013; on Brazil's role in the new global religious economy, see Rocha/Vásquez 2014). Making reference to Joseph's dream in the Hebrew Bible that foretold how his brothers would eventually bow before him after having cast him out and sold him as a slave, Macedo declared that he foresees "all religions and nations of the world bowing down [*estarão se curvando*] before Solomon's Temple."[1] Macedo has also stated that he would like Solomon's Temple to overshadow the famous Christ at Corcovado in Rio de Janeiro as the image that the world has of Brazil.

The UCKG is also known for its very public exorcisms of evil spirits that it holds responsible for the everyday tribulations of urban Brazilians. These exorcisms often circulate widely on YouTube and are often used by UCKG missionaries abroad to demonstrate the church's efficacy not only in carrying out the Great Commission, Jesus's call to make disciples of all nations, but also in fulfilling the church's injunction to potential adherents to "stop suffering" (*pare de sofrir*), as the church's motto states. In places like Mozambique and Angola, these videos are deployed to demonstrate the UCKG's efficacy in fighting *feitiçaria*, "witchcraft" (Van de Kamp 2013). Until recently, these exorcisms were beamed globally by Rede Record, now the second most popular television network in Brazil, owned since 1990 by Edir Macedo. These images of spiritual warfare are a key dimension of what anthropologist Simon Coleman (2000) has called a global Charismatic culture, which includes the construction of disciplined subjects not only through the expert use of the latest developments in communication technologies, but also through booming entertainment (music, most prominently) and self-help (books and tapes) industries.

---

[1] Here Macedo is making reference to Genesis 37:8–9. "Then his brothers said to him [Joseph], 'Are you actually going to reign over us? Or are you really going to rule over us?' So they hated him even more for his dreams and for his words. Now he had still another dream, and related it to his brothers, and said, 'Lo, I have had still another dream; and behold, the sun and the moon and eleven stars were bowing down to me.' He related it to his father and to his brothers; and his father rebuked him and said to him, 'What is this dream that you have had? Shall I and your mother and your brothers actually come to bow ourselves down before you to the ground?'" The report prepared by Rede Record on the inauguration of Solomon's Temple repeatedly pointed to the presence of delegations from Africa and Latin America, representing a gathering of all the tribes of Israel. See <http://is.gd/BNE7aP>.

Spiritual warfare, however, is now a global phenomenon that has transcended Christian Charismatic referents. Circulating among the YouTube exorcism clips is a widely popular one of a 'witch doctor' *catcheur* ("wrestler") who challenges an Evangelical pastor in Kinshasa. The staged fight ends with 'Luck Mistique,' the catcheur, confronting the pastor with a smoking *fétiche*, whereupon the Pentecostal preacher falls flat on his back (<http://is.gd/cz41Tu>). Under Luck Mistique's control, the pastor then proceeds to eat pages of the Bible and to wash them down, for good measure, with a large bottle of cheap beer, as the crowd cheers on the defeat of the *faux pasteur* ("fake pastor"). This video shows that spiritual combat has now become a global religious spectacle staged and disseminated by multiple actors operating in multiple locations and scales. Of course spiritual warfare is an old phenomenon. However, Meyer (1999) and others have shown how, in Africa, witchcraft and use of *fétiches*, etc. have been 'translated' into Pentecostal idioms, as part of a global—yet local and intimate—struggle between good and evil forces in postcolonial times (see also Geschiere 2013).

The second vignette takes us to London—Stratford (East London) to be more precise. Stratford, in the 'superdiverse' borough of Newham (Vertovec 2007), was the recent host of the 2012 Olympic Games, a global mega-event promoting another kind of universal and ritualized sacredness hinging on the quasi-religious function and moral project of so-called 'Olympic values' (see Cusack, "Sports," this volume). The Games provided an immeasurable opportunity for London and for a range of other local, national, and international stakeholders, corporations, public, and private bodies to capitalize on the global mass appeal of such a mega-event. The 2012 Games had a major impact on this formerly industrial zone of the 'Global City.' The construction of the Olympic Park and its associated transport infrastructures transformed this part of London into one of the largest urban regeneration sites in Europe.

Adjacent to the Olympic Park, the presence of another local actor, the Islamic group Tablighi Jamaat (TJ), has also had an impact on the discursive construction of place and Otherness in global and multicultural context. The TJ were embroiled in a conflict over the development of what became pejoratively known as 'the Olympic mega-mosque,' intended to replace a complex of prefabricated buildings as TJ's main place of worship in London. From its modest origin as a localized Islamic revivalist and reformist movement in colonial India, the TJ has gradually acquired a transnational scope, mainly through the mobility and migration of its members and affiliates. Traveling to "convey" (*tabligh*) the Islamic message is still considered a prime component of this global missionary work. Tablighis (exclusively males) go to *silla* (spiritual retreat) and attend *ishtima* (large religious gatherings) across Britain and abroad and many regularly visit the large *markaz* in Dewsbury, where the European headquarters of the TJ are located. While this transnational Islamic movement rejects any form of involvement in political affairs, the controversy surrounding the initial plan for the new mosque in Stratford has forced the TJ to be more visible and to respond to political and media pressure on both local and national levels.

The TJ can be seen as global religious movement, relying on a loose polycentric organization, and shaped by the global forces of migration, diasporization, or transnational mobility networks (e.g. old and new trade routes). However, each local context constitutes a space of 'friction'; a "friction [which] inflects historical trajectories, enabling, excluding, and particularizing" as Tsing (2005, 6) argues. The local is both shaping and shaped by the global, and the deployment of modes of interaction with and within different—religious or and non-religious—publics cannot be understood without accounting for processes of translation, hybridization, and adaption—even if religious discourses of purification and authenticity tend to be hegemonic. The global/local dialectics can perhaps be best framed through a micro/macro politics of 'scale.' While for Tablighis the experience of faith is constructed as a retreat from the *dunya* (the "world"), it relies on a nexus connecting different socio-spatial scales: the disciplined and reformed body, the localized territories of Islamic piety interaction, socialization and differentiation; and the globalized sphere of Islamic universalism (*ummah*) and traveling missions "in the way of God" (*nafr*).

These two vignettes illustrate the complex interplay between religion and globalization, throwing into relief the multifarious processes and actors involved in this interaction, including the roles that transnational migrants, religious entrepreneurs, and pilgrims/tourists, as well as global media, play in the creation, circulation, and consumption of religious images, narratives, and practices. The vignettes also demonstrate how contemporary capitalism and mass consumer culture are redefining notions of space and time, foregrounding the urban as a staging place for the sacred and heightening the tension between dynamics of boundary-making in the search for purity and boundary-crossing, as part of widespread hybridization and transculturation within and among religions. This chapter offers a panoramic view of these processes and the scholarly literature that has addressed them.

UNDERSTANDING GLOBALIZATION

Mobility has been an enduring and widespread feature of human history. However, not all forms of mobility can be characterized as globalization, at least as we understand it today. In the most general terms, globalization is "the widening, deepening and speeding up of worldwide interconnectedness in all aspects of contemporary social life, from the cultural to the criminal, the financial to the spiritual" (Held et al. 1999, 2). As such, there have been many prominent examples of trans-local movement and exchange in early human history, such as the Silk Road, which emerged in some shape or form during the Han dynasty (226 BCE to 220 CE), or the Mongol Empire in the thirteenth century that extended from Korea to the gates of Vienna. Nevertheless, true global interconnectedness only starts with the rise of what sociologist Immanuel Wallerstein (1974) calls the modern capitalist world system in the sixteenth century, as the Spanish and Portuguese empires established intercontinental routes in which slaves, colonists, raw materials, coins, and commodities circulated. At this point, we can refer to an "expansive globalization . . . defined more by its reach and impact than the velocity of the flows" (Held et al. 1999, 23).

Globalization gathered considerable momentum following the Industrial Revolution and the age of free trade in the 1800s, which was only temporarily curtailed by World War I and the Great Depression. During this period we witnessed the emergence of a 'thick globalization,' in which global networks and flows attained "high intensity, high velocity and high impact propensity across all the domains or facets of social life from the economic to the cultural" (Held et al. 1999, 21). In the context of the inventions of new transportation technologies, such as the steam locomotive, the car, and the telegraph, this period was marked by pervasive migration: between 1850 and 1914, close to 4 percent of the world's population—60–70 million people—left their countries of origin (Osterhammel/Petersson 2005).

The advent of thick globalization inaugurated an ongoing process of "time–space compression" (Harvey 1989), in which technological innovations have increasingly sped up the pace of life, "obliterating space through time," with space appearing "to shrink to a 'global village' of telecommunications and a 'spaceship earth' of economic and ecological interdependencies . . . as time horizons shorten to the point where the present is all there is" (Harvey 1989, 240). According to Harvey, time–space compression accelerated dramatically in the late 1960s, as the economies of scale that characterized the postwar Fordist–Keynesian regime of production gave way to flexible production systems based on decentered transnational networks. Because this flexible production regime is knowledge-intensive, based on the rapid circulation of information and culture, alongside capital, the transition has also ushered in important changes in cultural and religious fields. In this context, religions have become part of a 'postmodern condition,' providing symbols, images, narratives, practices, and identities—from Lakota sweat lodges, Santería drumming, and Ayahuasca-based shamanism to Yoga, Reiki healing, and Wicca Sabbats—that are combined in new hybrid formations. As the case of the New Age Movement shows, often these new formations are commodified, entering a thriving therapeutic, self-help industry that plays a key role in "making the human sacred," as Hexam and Poewe (1997) put it. Alternatively, religions may become part of the "society of the spectacle" (Debord 1994), as the architectural monumentality of the two vignettes with which we started shows. Or religions may also serve to cope with the cultural whiplash produced by globalization's time–space compression by redrawing and reinforcing cognitive maps built on dualistic cosmologies which set the believer against an evil, corrupt, secular world or against other religions in increasingly pluralistic contexts. The rapid global expansion of Neo-Pentecostalism, such as the one advanced by the Universal Church of the Kingdom of God, and rectificationist Islam, like the Tablighi Jamaat, illustrate this dynamic.

While Harvey's neo-Marxist account of cultural dimensions of globalization—as a postmodern sensibility 'mimetic' of structural changes in contemporary capitalism—is in many ways compelling, it is, in the end, too one-sided to capture the multiple processes at play. Anthropologist Arjun Appadurai has suggested that the "new global cultural economy has to be seen as a complex, disjunctive order" that confounds "even the most complex and flexible theories of global development that have come out of the Marxist tradition" (1996, 32, 33). He proposes, instead, a framework to explore the divergences and convergences among five global cultural flows or 'scapes,' that is, "fluid, irregular landscapes" that are "deeply perspectival constructs, inflected by the historical, linguistic, and political situatedness of different sorts of actors: nation-states, multinational, diasporic communities, as well as subnational groupings and movements (whether religious, political, or economic), and even intimate face-to-face groups, such as villages, neighborhoods, and families" (1996, 33). Among these flows are ethnoscapes, referring not only to the transnational movement of immigrants and refugees, but also of tourists, entrepreneurs, and missionaries; financescapes, the global circulation of capital at blinding speeds; technoscapes, the emergence and movement of new communication, information, and transportation technologies; mediascapes, the expansive "distribution of the electronic capabilities to produce and disseminate" (1996, 35) culture in the forms of "image-centered, narrative-based accounts of strips of reality" (1996, 35); and ideoscapes, notions such as human rights, citizenship, civil society, and democracy that have become widespread.

Despite the fact that Appadurai acknowledges that religious actors are actively engaged in the process global work of imagination, he does not consider religion a distinct scape. Drawing from her work on Haitian Vodou in Haiti and the United States, Elizabeth McAlister (1998, 156) suggests the term 'religioscapes' to characterize "the religious maps (and attendant theologies) of diasporic communities who are also in global flow and flux." Thomas Tweed goes even further, suggesting a 'hydrodynamic' theory that sees the 'sacroscapes' of religions as "confluences of organic-cultural flows that intensify joy and confront suffering by drawing on human and suprahuman forces to make homes and cross boundaries" (2006, 54).

Tweed's theory goes a long way toward de-territorializing religion by not assuming that it has an essence tied to a particular place or people. However, it is not without its limitations. Vásquez (2008) has argued that overreliance on aquatic metaphors to understand how religion operates in the global context leads to an excessive anti-structuralism, which elides widespread dynamics of closure, exclusion, containment, friction, and surveillance (Cunningham 2004; Tsing 2005). In order to understand not only the processes of de-territorialization that accompany globalization, but also those of re-territorialization, as well as to capture the persistence and even exacerbation of old power asymmetries and the creation of new ones, Vásquez suggests critiquing and augmenting Tweed's analysis with metaphors of relationality such as networks and fields (2011, 292–307).

RELIGION AND GLOBALIZATION: KEY PROCESSES, ACTORS, AND MEDIA

Early work on religion and globalization took a macro perspective. Roland Robertson (1991, 215–216; 1992, 27), for example, focused on the contributions of religion to the intensification of international interdependence (internationalization) and the global spread of shared notions of humanity (humanization), the person (individualization), and modern society (societalization). These processes generate a dialectical interplay between "particularization of the universal" and "universalization of the particular" (1992, 130), which Robertson argued was most saliently expressed through the concept of 'glocalization,' or global localization, the dynamic through which ideas, symbols, practices, and goods, which are unmoored from their original local referents and circulate globally, are creatively adapted to new local conditions as they are 'consumed' by situated social actors (Robertson 1995). In the study of religion, the concept of glocalization has been used by Vásquez and Marquardt (2003) to argue from an approach that foregrounds the pervasiveness and generativity of hybridity in religious discourses and practices over against traditional perspectives that see the public presence and vitality of religion as declining (the secularization thesis) or that stress religious competition among self-contained traditions within pluralistic religious fields.

For his part, Peter Beyer (1994; 2006), another pioneer in the study of religion and globalization, has drawn from sociologist Niklas Luhmann's systems theory, to point to how the emergence of the category of religion and of the system of world religions, was central to the process of globalization. Here, Beyer offers an important complement and corrective to Immanuel Wallerstein's theory of the world capitalist system, which underplays the role of ideas and values in the process of globalization.

More recent work on religion and globalization has tended to take ethnographic and case studies approaches, which focus primarily on specific actors and vectors.

Transnational Religious Networks, Fields, and Regimes

In a context of globalization, the diversification in immigration flows has radically altered the racial, ethnic, and religious landscape of societies of settlement. Steven Vertovec (2007) speaks of "super-diversity" to describe the highly variegated social formations that are emerging, particularly in global cities such as New York and London, out of the complex interplay of multiple variables such as country of origin, migration channel, legal status, etc. Moreover, immigrants today, in contrast to those in the past who were expected to leave behind their countries of origin and assimilate into the societies of settlement, have the means to be "simultaneously embedded." To describe this phenomenon, Linda Basch, Nina Glick Schiller, and Cristina Szanton Blanc (1994) use the term 'transnationalism,' denoting "the processes by which immigrants forge and sustain multi-stranded social relations that link together societies of origin and settlement" (1994, 7). 'Transmigrants'—immigrants engaged in multiple social relations spanning national borders—"live their lives across international borders" through the articulation in everyday life of "multiple interlocking networks of social relations through which ideas, practices, and resources are unequally exchanged, organized, and transformed" (Levitt/Glick Schiller 2004, 1009).

At the micro, everyday life level, transnational religious networks play crucial roles throughout the process of migration and settlement, allowing migrants keep in touch with their places of origin through 'social remittances' (Levitt 2001). In her study of unauthorized immigration from Latin America to the United States, sociologist Jacqueline Hagan found that "religion permeates the entirety of the migration experience, from decision making and departure through the dangerous undocumented journey from their home communities north to the United States" (2008, 7). Here religion acts as a transnational vehicle, serves as moral guide, 'companion,' and spiritual support, and also operates as a sanctuary and advocate for the rights of immigrants in 'host societies.'

At the institutional level, Peggy Levitt has identified at least three types of transnational religious organizations. "Extended transnational religious organizations" basically "broaden and deepen a global religious system that is already powerful and legitimate" (2004, 6). Thus, a central concern among this type of organization is the maintenance of orthodoxy, which given the scale that these networks often have, can seldom be fully achieved. This is why the concept of glocalization is particularly relevant to characterize the production, circulation, and performance of religious phenomena in these organizations. The prime example of an extended transnational religious organization is the Catholic Church, which is sustained by the complex interactions among the Vatican, global religious orders, regional and national episcopal bodies, as well as local parishes, all held together by networks and flows operating at multiple scales and by a universalizing doctrine.

Despite the centralized and hierarchical institutional morphology of the transnational Catholic regime—following Robertson's notion of religious glocalization—Catholicism's universalizing doctrine assumes myriad local expressions as a result of widespread processes of hybridization with indigenous traditions. The creative cross-fertilization of Catholicism in the Americas with Native American traditions such as shamanism and animism and African-based practices of divination and spirit incorporation offers a good example of the dynamics of glocalization for extended transnational religious organizations. Moreover, transnational movements such as Liberation Theology and the Catholic Charismatic Renewal, which often travel through immigrants, as the case of Latinos in the United States shows, introduce centripetal and centrifugal dynamics that revitalize the Church, enabling it to 'broaden and deepen' its global reach.

According to Levitt (2004, 8–11), "negotiated transnational religious organizations" constitute a second type of transnational institutional morphology, presenting a more flexible and decentralized morphology. Thus, in contrast to extended transnational religious networks in which authority and resources are more centralized, even if always contested, the various interconnected nodes in the more flexible organizations must negotiate "with respect to authority, organization, and ritual. There is generally no one leader or administrative hierarchy to set policy and dictate how things are done. A more diverse, diluted set of partnerships emerges that are malleable and shift over time" (Levitt 2004, 10).

The best examples here would be many independent Pentecostal churches from countries such as Nigeria, Ghana, Brazil, and the Philippines that have set up churches in various host countries that minister transnationally to fellow immigrants, assisting them, as we saw, through the immigration and settlement process (see Ukah, "Expansion," this volume). In light of the tension between social disembedding and time–space compression in contemporary globalization, the loose connections within these negotiated transnational networks give them a comparative advantage over extended transnational organizations like the Catholic Church: they are more nimble, portable, and responsive, capable of creative adaptation to changing environments and media. No wonder, then, that Latin American and African Pentecostal churches are spearheading a process of 'reverse missionizing,' in which countries to which Christian missionaries were once sent, now send missionaries back to former missionary nations in Europe and North America. Reverse missionizing is part and parcel of the dramatic shift in Christianity's center of gravity to the global South (Jenkins 2011; Ukah, "Expansion," this volume).

In Levitt's typology, the third type of transnational religious networks are "recreated organizations" formed by "groups with guidance from home-country leaders" (2004, 11) which seek to replicate local practices, beliefs, and modes of organization abroad. According to Levitt, movements such as the Swaminarayanan or Swadhyaya Parivar, which "strongly reinforce members' ties with their home country [in this case India] often at the expense of receiving-country social integration," fit this model (2004, 3). While these movements do represent a kind of "long distance nationalism," they often reimagine the nation in utopian terms. The nation becomes the source of universal ethical and metaphysical teachings that dovetail with New Age notions of self-improvement and personal spiritual quests, allowing non-immigrants that join these transnational movements.

Levitt recognizes that these three categories hardly exhaust the multiple ways in which transnational religious networks operate. She has called for "a more systematic study of how the various constituent elements in these networks, including formal structural ties at the local, regional, and national levels, informal ties between leaders and members, labor power and resource exchanges, funding, and programmatic coordination" are combined and operate (2004, 15).

Diasporic Religions and Religious Diasporas

Since the concept of transnationalism presupposes the nation state, it can only be applied to cross-boundary processes that emerged after the Peace of Westphalia ended the Thirty-Years War in 1648, establishing autonomous nations, with religion serving as one of the criteria for demarcation. In other words, trans-local dynamics that originated before the consolidation of the modern international system but that continue to have an effect in contemporary globalization cannot be rigorously characterized by the concept of transnationalism. As an alternative, some scholars have advanced the notion of diaspora. In its most general sense, diaspora refers to dispersed populations, deriving from *diaspeirein*, a Greek term which literally means "to scatter the seeds." In the ancient Mediterranean world, the term designated the spread of Hellenistic culture through conquest, colonization, immigration, and mercantile networks. There is, however, a narrower definition of diaspora modeled after the paradigmatic Jewish experience of exile in Babylon following the destruction of the Second Temple in Jerusalem. According to this more restricted definition, diasporas would be self-conscious groups which have been forcefully displaced from an original homeland to more than one host land and which—unable to return and not fully accepted in the new contexts of settlement—have maintained cultural, linguistic, and spiritual connections with their place of origin through idealized memories and utopian visions of the homeland (Safran 1991, 83–84).

Given the fact that many dispersed populations exhibit strong elements of diasporic consciousness while not fully conforming to this ideal type, Clifford suggests that we take a more flexible definition of diaspora, which explores ambivalence, contestation, and the waxing and waning of "diasporism, depending on changing possibilities— obstacles, openings, antagonisms, and connections—in their host countries and transnationally" (Clifford 1994, 306).

Both transnationalism and diaspora point to the immigrant experience of 'bifocality' or 'multifocality,' challenging the traditional assumption that migration always entails assimilation to the receiving country's hegemonic culture and the loss of the sending country's way of life. The concepts of transnationalism and diaspora characterize different dynamics of mobility. Whereas transnationalism refers to simultaneity across present-day localities, such that decisions taken in the society of settlement have an impact in the society of origin and vice versa, the notion of diaspora also operates trans-temporally, joining multiple spaces through a work of imagination and memory that links past, present, and future.

A seminal work on religion and diaspora is Tweed's ethnography of Cuban-Americans in Miami, who came to the United States in successive waves following the Cuban revolution in 1959. Unable to return to Cuba, they, among other things, built in Miami a shrine to Our Lady of Charity, the country's patroness. This shrine has a series of architectural features that incorporate Cuban history and landscape, but in a way that imagines a mythical Cuba before the revolution and a utopian Cuba liberated from communist rule. Tweed argues that diasporic religion operates through three spatio-temporal configurations or 'chronotopes': the locative, the translocative, and the supralocative. The locative refers to the diasporic group's work in building a new home through the transposition of imagined landscapes and the materialization of memories associated with the homeland, from which it has been forcibly exiled and to which it cannot return. The translocative points to "the tendency among first- and second-generation migrants to symbolically move between homeland and new land" (Tweed 1997, 95). Finally, the supralocative involves vertical connections with the cosmos or with religious utopias (spaces that transcend all places) that may call for the overturning of the existing fallen or iniquitous order.

In his work on Garifuna shamans in Honduras and New York, Paul C. Johnson (2007) elaborates further on Tweed's insights, showing that religion does not link just societies of origin and settlement; it often involves "multiple diasporic horizons" (7) that orient groups in relation to manifold locations in trajectories of migration that are not always unilinear. While Johnson returns to the paradigmatic example of the Jewish diaspora, which is marked by a "repeated experience of rediasporization" (Boyarin/Boyarin 2002, 11), he adds an important distinction in the ways in which religion, migration, and globalization are linked by the diasporic experience. He defines 'diasporic religions' as "the collected practices of dislocated social groups whose affiliation is not primarily or essentially based on religion but whose acts, locutions, and sentiments toward the distant homeland are mediated by, and articulated through, a religious culture" (Johnson 2007, 258). This definition would fit the Garifuna as well as the Cuban diaspora that Tweed has studied. In contrast, Johnson refers to 'religious diasporas' "to denote the extensions in space of a group whose most salient reference is religious identity rather than ethnic, racial, linguistic, or any other social bond and whose process of dispersion is a direct consequence of that affiliation" (258). Such a characterization would apply to the Puritans emigrating from England and Scotland to North America or the Mormons living in Mexico or elsewhere. While both diasporic religion and religious diasporas are implicated in the current processes of globalization, more research needs to be done on religion's specific contributions to global dynamics. Arguably, Brazilian neo-Pentecostalism, like the Universal Church of the Kingdom of God, can be said to be not only a diasporic religion, in the sense that it is carried by dispersed Brazilian immigrants and religious entrepreneurs, but also a religious diaspora, since these religious actors see themselves above all as members of the church of the elect, as demonstrated by their baptism in the Holy Spirit and the charismas associated with it. Moreover, their global professions of faith fulfill the Great Commission, Jesus Christ's call to apostles to "make disciples of all nations."

Media and Virtuality

Appadurai argues that one of the key sources of the de- and re-territorialization of culture has to do with the widening "distribution of the electronic capabilities to produce and disseminate information" (1993, 35). The interplay of globalization, migration, and religion has been dramatically intensified by rapid innovations in computer-mediated communications (CMCs), particularly expansion of the Internet and, more recently, the rise of social media such as Facebook, Twitter, and YouTube. Some scholars have argued that CMCs challenge the 'metaphysics of presence' (i.e. the privileging of physical presence and face-to-face interactions as authenticity) and the distinction between virtuality and reality. Baudrillard (1994) suggests that CMCs are now capable of producing the 'hyper-real,' that is, experiences that are more intense, more vivid, and more all-consuming and all-encompassing than the 'real.'

This capacity to generate a virtual world, perhaps even a hyper-real one, has enormous consequences for religion. For one thing, it means that authentic and authoritative religious experience is no longer the monopoly of elites dwelling in a particular place which is claimed to be a sacred center (e.g. Rome). Now, many people skilled in the use of electronic media are in principle able to invent traditions and generate a religious following, if they can generate sufficient charisma. This 'decentering' of authority leads Brenda Brasher (2001, 25) to argue that cyberspace represents the "ultimate diaspora," which by "materializing a perpetual presence . . . offers the ideal public space for a people without history."

Brasher (2001, 6) sees this electronic diasporization and 'virtualization of community' as a positive development. On the ground, among migrants, reality is far more complex. To begin with, there is a divide between those who have easy access to the new media and those that do not, which is affected by factors such as class, race, gender, and immigrant status, and which renders the impact of CMCs uneven. For instance, the spread of the Hindutva movement has been spearheaded by successful Indian entrepreneurs, doctors, software engineers, and journalists turned freelance scholars in diaspora, who have the financial resources, time, and technological competence to combine ethnic and religious primordialism (i.e. the recovery of an imagined ancestral land and a unified Hindu people with a glorious myth of origins) with de-territorialized cyberspaces. In contrast, when unauthorized Latino migrants in the United States organized massive demonstrations in 2005, demanding a comprehensive immigration reform, they relied for their mobilizations on Spanish-radio hosts and TV news anchors, who, in between salsa shows and popular telenovela (soap opera) broadcasts, encouraged listeners and viewers to take to the streets (Vásquez 2008). In yet another case, Hirschkind (2001) describes how the circulation of sermons in cassettes has produced an 'ethical soundscape,' a transnational oral culture among Muslims in Egypt and beyond. In other words, it is too simplistic to think that new media take over all aspects of everyday life. We need to look more carefully at the actual relationships among religion, CMCs, and mobility in particular places in order to draw conclusions which take account of diversity.

In many cases, CMCs do not in fact render physical presence irrelevant or erase the importance of locality under a flood of free-floating signifiers. Rather, CMCs and physical presence often sustain a relationship of reciprocal influencing, with the Internet serving to make locality and material things more significant by beaming them globally through a process of 'global localization.' This was the case with an apparition of the Virgin Mary on the windows of a bank building in Clearwater, Florida, which quickly made the national and international news, attracting not only pilgrims from throughout the area, but tourists from Europe and Australia vacationing in nearby Orlando (Vásquez/Marquardt 2000).

The complex relation between reality and virtuality is also illustrated by the proliferation of cyber-rituals and cyber-pilgrimages. While, as Scheifinger (2013, 126) observes, "online *puja* is a valid and efficacious form of ritual" among Hindus, in the diaspora these electronic performances become part of the work of imagination that memorializes and enacts the migrants' embodied, multi-sensory experiences with sacred landscapes, objects, traditions, and incarnate deities and territorialized spirits in the homeland.

Heidi Campbell has suggested the term 'digital religion' to characterize "the technological and cultural space that is evoked when we talk about how online and offline religious spheres have become blended and integrated. We can think of digital religion as a bridge that connects and extends online religious practices and spaces with offline religious contexts, and vice versa" (2013, 3–4). Campbell's notion can also help us make sense of the often paradoxical ways in which CMCs, religion, globalization, and migration interact to produce hybrid identities, practices, and spaces (see also Krüger, "Media," this volume).

Conclusion

Anthropologist Thomas Csordas identifies four vectors of "transnational transcendence": migration, mobility, mediatization, and missionization (2009, 5–6). These modalities roughly correspond to the key processes, media, and actors behind the contemporary globalization that we have characterized. These vectors can be isolated for analytical purposes, but, on the ground, they often interact with each other, alternatively reinforcing each other or generating borderlands.

The interaction of these modalities produces both homogenization and cultural heterogeneity and transculturation. On the one hand, religious globalization may involve McDonaldization, i.e. the one-directional spread of made-in-the-US religion as a complement to American geopolitical hegemony and pre-eminence in financial and media networks, as the United States continues to be a seminal node in global 'spirit industries' (Ritzer 1996; Endres 2010). The quintessential example here is some versions of the gospel of health and wealth. On the other hand, in the interplay of religion, migration, and globalization, emerging national and local actors across the globe are increasingly developing alternative religious styles, services, entrepreneurial strategies, distribution networks, and markets. The result has been the articulation of a polycentric cartography of religious globalization with multiple key nodes of religious production, circulation, and consumption. Offutt (2015, 24), for example, refers to "New Centers of Evangelicalism (NCEs)" in Latin America and Africa, "shar[ing] the globe with their preexisting Western Centers of Evangelicalism (WCEs)" and exchanging resources with the latter, particularly through a growing and diverse entrepreneurial class.

Saskia Sassen (1998) has noted that, despite all the talk that globalization has made the world flat, the contemporary global scene is marked by deepening inequalities. In particular, global cities such as New York, London, and Tokyo have become heavily networked 'command centers' in the global economy where financial and corporate services are concentrated and where innovation in knowledge-based industries takes place, a concentration that is also accompanied by growing inequalities within these cities. The uneven spatial configuration of the global economic system dovetails to some extent with the new geography of global religious production. As crossroads to the world, topoi where immigrants, business people, tourists, and cultural cosmopolitans interact, global cities in the North are indeed incubators of great religious creativity (Orsi 1999). The salience of the global city as a spiritual battleground (Garbin 2013) or an amplifying node for the performance of religious geopolitical visions explains the controversy around the Tablighi Jamaat mosque, with which we started this chapter.

However, while the logics of late capitalism may go a long way toward explaining the new cartographies of the sacred, the dynamics of the global religious field cannot be reduced to those of the world capitalist system, with a clear center and periphery. The religious field has its own variegated architecture and spatial logics. Some of the 'command centers' in the new global religious economy—such New Delhi and Mumbai in India and Beijing and Shanghai in China—have already been central in the production and spread of age-old 'World' Religions such as Hinduism, Buddhism, Confucianism, and Taoism.

Others nodes such as São Paulo, Rio de Janeiro, and Salvador in Brazil, Lagos and Ibadan in Nigeria, Accra in Ghana, Kinshasa in the Democratic Republic of the Congo, and Johannesburg in South Africa, although always connected in a subaltern position to the world capitalist system through slavery, colonialism, and the African diaspora, have only recently begun to play a leading role in religious globalization. These nodes highlight the proliferation of multi-directional and multi-scalar religious flows and networks, going not only from 'North' to 'South' but also in the opposite direction, as immigrants and religious entrepreneurs reverse-missionize, exorcize demons, summon ancestor spirits, or clean karmic residues in the metropole, while in the process contributing to religious diversity and vitality in places like London, Paris, Amsterdam, New York, or Atlanta, despite the pressures of secular (late) modernity. Thus, in order to understand the ongoing entwinement of religion and globalization, the study of religion will have to be not only interdisciplinary but also multi-sited, strategically mapping out established as well as emergent flows, networks, and fields in the polycentric cartography of religious globalization.[2]

GLOSSARY

Diaspora from *diaspeirein*, a Greek term which literally means "to scatter the seeds." Often used to refer to self-conscious groups which have been forcibly displaced from an original homeland to more than one host land and which—unable to return and not fully accepted in the new contexts of settlement—have maintained cultural, linguistic, and spiritual connections with their place of origin through idealized memories and utopian visions of the homeland.

---

[2] For examples of this type of approach, see Coleman/Von Hellermann (2011) and Marcus (1995) and the special issue of *Global Networks* (2014) edited by Josh DeWind and Manuel Vásquez.

Globalization "The widening, deepening and speeding up of worldwide interconnectedness in all aspects of contemporary social life, from the cultural to the criminal, the financial to the spiritual" (Held et al. 1999, 2).

Glocalization global localization, the dynamic through which ideas, symbols, practices, and goods—unmoored from their original local referents and circulating globally—are creatively adapted to new local conditions as they are 'consumed' by situated social actors.

Hybridization the emergence of new (religious) identities, practices, theologies, symbols, artifacts, spaces, and institutions out of the combination of (religious) traditions that have become de-territorialized from their traditional local referents.

McDonaldization a process of homogenization driven by the one-directional spread of made-in-the-US religion and culture as a complement to American geopolitical hegemony and pre-eminence in financial and media networks.

Polycentric global cartography of the sacred the new irregular global religious space which includes multiple nodes of religious creativity and multi-directional flows and networks of religious production.

Transnationalism the processes whereby individuals on the move build and sustain widespread relations across national borders, building social networks and fields that span more than one nation, including nations of origin and settlement.

REFERENCES

Appadurai, Arjun. 1996. *Modernity at Large: Cultural Dimensions of Globalization.* Minneapolis: University of Minnesota Press.

Basch, Linda, Nina Glick Schiller, and Christina Szanton Blanc. 1994. *Nations Unbound: Transnational Migration, Postcolonial Predicaments, and the Deterritorialized Nation-State.* Langhorne, PA: Gordon and Breach.

Baudrillard, Jean. 1994. *Simulacra and Simulation.* Ann Arbor: University of Michigan Press.

Beyer, Peter. 1994. *Religion and Globalisation.* London: Sage.

Beyer, Peter. 2006. *Religions in Global Society.* London: Routledge.

Boyarin, Jonathan and Daniel Boyarin. 2002. *The Powers of Diaspora: Two Essays on the Relevance of Jewish Culture.* Berkeley: University of California Press.

Brasher, Brenda. 2001. *Give Me That On-Line Religion.* San Francisco, CA: Jossey-Bass.

Campbell, Heidi. 2013. "Introduction: The Rise of the Study of Digital Religion." In *Digital Religion: Understanding Religious Practice in New Media Worlds*, edited by Heidi Campbell. New York: Routledge, 1–22.

Chesnut, Andrew R. 1997. *Born Again in Brazil: The Pentecostal Boom and the Pathogens of Poverty.* New Brunswick, NJ: Rutgers University Press.

Clifford, James. 1994. "Diasporas." *Cultural Anthropology* 9(3): 302–338.

Coleman, Simon. 2000. *The Globalisation of Charismatic Christianity: Spreading the Gospel of Prosperity.* Cambridge: Cambridge University Press.

Coleman, Simon and Pauline von Hellermann. 2011. *Multi-Sited Ethnography: Problems and Possibilities in the Translocation of Research Methods.* London: Routledge.

Csordas, Thomas. 2009. "Introduction: Modalities of Transnational Transcendence." In *Transnational Transcendence: Essays on Religion and Globalization*, edited by Thomas Csordas. Berkeley: University of California Press, 1–29.

Cunningham, Hillary. 2004. "Nations Rebound? Crossing Orders in a Gated Globe." *Identities: Global Studies in Culture and Power* 11(3): 329–350. doi: 10.1080/10702890490493527

Debord, Guy. 1994. *The Society of the Spectacle*. New York: Zone Books.

Endres, Kirsten. 2010. "'Trading in Spirits'? Transnational Flows, Entrepreneurship, and Commodifications in Vietnamese Spirit Mediumship." In *Traveling Spirits: Migrants, Markets, and Mobilities*, edited by Gertrud Hüwelmeier and Kristine Krause. Oxford and New York: Routledge, 118–132.

Garbin, David. 2013. "Visibility and Invisibility of Migrant Faith in the City: Diaspora Religion and the Politics of Emplacement of Afro-Christian Churches." *Journal of Ethnic and Migration Studies* 39(5): 677–696. doi: 10.1080/1369183X.2013.756658

Geschiere, Peter. 2013. *Witchcraft, Intimacy and Trust: Africa in Comparison*. Chicago, IL: University of Chicago Press.

Hagan, Jacqueline. 2008. *Migration Miracle: Faith, Hope, and Meaning on the Undocumented Journey*. Cambridge, MA: Harvard University Press.

Harvey, David. 1989. *The Condition of Postmodernity: An Enquiry into the Origins of Cultural Change*. Cambridge, MA: Blackwell.

Held, David, Anthony McGrew, David Goldblatt, and Jonathan Perraton. 1999. *Global Transformations: Politics, Economics and Culture*. Stanford, CA: Stanford University Press.

Hexam, Irving and Karla Poewe. 1997. *New Religions as Global Cultures: Making the Human Sacred*. Boulder, CO: Westview Press.

Hirschkind, Charles. 2001. "Civic Virtue and Religious Reason: An Islamic Counterpublic." *Cultural Anthropology* 16(1): 3–34. doi: 10.1525/can.2001.16.1.3

Jenkins, Philip. 2011. *The Next Christendom: The Coming of Global Christianity*. New York: Oxford University Press.

Johnson, Paul C. 2007. *Diaspora Conversions: Black Carib Religion and the Recovery of Africa*. Berkeley: University of California Press.

Levitt, Peggy. 2001. *Transnational Villagers*. Berkeley: University of California Press.

Levitt, Peggy. 2004. "Redefining the Boundaries of Belonging: The Institutional Character of Transnational Religious Life." *Sociology of Religion* 65(1): 1–18. doi: 10.2307/3712504

Levitt, Peggy and Nina Glick Schiller. 2004. "Conceptualizing Simultaneity: A Transnational Social Field Perspective on Society." *International Migration Review* 38(3): 1002–1039. doi: 10.1111/j.1747-7379.2004.tb00227.xd

McAlister, Elizabeth. 1998. "The Madonna of 115th Street Revisited: Vodou and Haitian Catholicism in the Age of Transnationalism." In *Gatherings in Diaspora: Religious Communities and the New Migration*, edited by Stephen Warner and Judith Wittner. Philadelphia, PA: Temple University Press, 123–160.

Mafra, Clara, Claudia Swatowiski, and Camila Sampaio. 2013. "Edir Macedo's Pastoral Project: A Globally Integrated Pentecostal Network." In *The Diaspora of Brazilian Religions*, edited by Cristina Rocha and Manuel A. Vásquez. Leiden: Brill, 45–67.

Marcus, George. 1995. "Ethnography in/of the World System: The Emergence of Multi-Sited Ethnography." *Annual Review of Anthropology* 24: 95–117.

Meyer, Birgit. 1999. *Translating the Devil: Religion and Modernity among the Ewe in Ghana*. Edinburgh: Edinburgh University Press.

Offutt, Stephen. 2015. *New Centers of Global Evangelicalism in Latin America and Africa*. Cambridge: Cambridge University Press.

Orsi, Robert. 1999. "Crossing the City Line." In *Gods of the City: Religion and the American Urban Landscape*, edited by Robert Orsi. Indianapolis: Indiana University Press, 1–77.

Osterhammel, Jürgen and Niels P. Petersson. 2005. *Globalization: A Short History*. Princeton, NJ: Princeton University Press.

Ritzer, George. 1996. *The McDonaldization of Society*. Thousand Oaks, CA: Pine Forge Press.

Robertson, Roland. 1991. "Globalization, Modernization, and Postmodernization: The Ambiguous Position of Religion." In *Religion and Social Order*, edited by Roland Robertson and W. R. Garrett. New York: Paragon House, 281–291.

Robertson, Roland. 1992. *Globalisation: Social Theory and Global Culture*. London: Sage.

Robertson, Roland. 1995. "Glocalization: Time-Space and Homogeneity-Heterogeneity." In *Global Modernities*, edited by Mike Featherstone, Scott Lash, and Roland Robertson. London: Sage, 25–44.

Rocha, Cristina and Manuel A. Vásquez, eds. 2014. *The Diaspora of Brazilian Religions*. Leiden: Brill.

Romero, Simon. 2014. "Temple in Brazil Appeals to a Surge in Evangelicals." *The New York Times*, July 24.

Safran, William. 1991. "Diasporas in Modern Societies: Myths of Homeland and Return." *Diaspora* 1(1): 83–99.

Sassen, Saskia. 1998. *Globalization and its Discontents: Essays on the New Mobility of People and Money*. New York: New Press.

Sassen, Saskia. 2000. "Digital Networks and the State: Some Governance Questions." *Theory, Culture & Society* 17(4): 19–33. doi: 10.1177/02632760022051293

Scheifinger, Heinz. 2013. "Hindu Worship Online and Offline." In *Digital Religion: Understanding Religious Practice in New Media Worlds*, edited by Heidi Campbell. New York: Routledge, 121–127.

Tsing, Anna L. 2005. *Friction: An Ethnography of Global Connection*. Princeton, NJ: Princeton University Press.

Tweed, Thomas. 1997. *Our Lady of the Exile: Diasporic Religion at a Catholic Shrine in Miami*. New York: Oxford University Press.

Tweed, Thomas. 2006. *Crossing and Dwelling: A Theory of Religion*. Cambridge, MA: Harvard University Press.

Van de Kamp, Linda. 2013. "South–South Transnational Spaces of Conquest: Afro-Brazilian Pentecostalism, *Feitiçaria* and the Reproductive Domain in Urban Mozambique." *Exchange* 42(4): 343–365. doi: 10.1163/1572543X-12341284

Van Wyk, Ilana. 2014. *The Universal Church of the Kingdom of God in South Africa: A Church of Strangers*. Cambridge: Cambridge University Press.

Vásquez, Manuel A. 2008. "Studying Religion in Motion: A Networks Approach." *Method and Theory in the Study of Religion* 20(2): 151–184. doi: 10.1163/157006808X283570

Vásquez, Manuel A. 2011. *More than Belief: A Materialist Theory of Religion*. New York: Oxford University Press.

Vásquez, Manuel A. and Marie F. Marquardt. 2000. "Globalizing the Rainbow Madonna: Old-Time Religion in the Present Age." *Theory, Culture & Society* 17(4): 119–143. doi: 10.1177/0263276002251347

Vásquez, Manuel A. and Marie F. Marquardt. 2003. *Globalizing the Sacred: Religion across the Americas*. New Brunswick, NJ: Rutgers University Press.

Vertovec, Steven. 2007. "Super-Diversity." <http://www.mmg.mpg.de/research/all-projects/super-diversity/>, accessed February 18, 2014.

Wallerstein, Immanuel. 1974. *The Modern World System*. New York: Academic Press.

FURTHER READING

Beyer 1994 [*A seminal examination of the emergence and dynamics of religious social systems in a context of globalization, using case studies ranging from the Christian Right in the United States and Liberation Theology in Latin America to the Islamic Revolution in Iran and religious environmentalism.*]

Global Networks 2014. "Special Issue: The Religious Lives of Migrant Minorities—A Multi-Sited and Transnational Perspective" 14(3): 251–400. [*A collection of articles on Christians, Muslims, Hindus, and Buddhists, who live as minorities and transnational migrants in three urban contexts (London, Johannesburg, Kajang-Kuala Lumpur) and whose different national regimes for governing migrant and religious diversity have been shaped historically by the British Empire and its legacy. It offers a good illustration of the pay-offs and challenges of the multi-sited comparative study of religion and globalization.*]

Robertson 1992 [*One of the earliest systematic treatments of globalization, stressing the roles of religion. It develops key concepts such as internationalization, societalization, individualization, humanization, and glocalization.*]

Vásquez/Marquardt 2003 [*Explores the interplay of globalization, religion, and migration drawing through case studies in Latin America and among US Latinos in different urban contexts.*]

CHAPTER 46

....

INDIVIDUALIZATION
AND PRIVATIZATION

....

JÖRG RÜPKE

Chapter Summary

....

- Recent discussions of the individualization and privatization of religion have been advanced by Thomas Luckmann's notion of invisible religion.
- The debate about individualization and privatization of religion has risen as a function of and in critical engagement with theories of secularization and modernization.
- These concepts do not refer only to phenomena in the Western industrial and post-industrial world; they have relevance for conceptualizing religion far beyond.
- Processes of individualization are key to important developments in the history of religion.
- Processes of individualization can paradoxically lead to institutionalization and the establishment of institutionally sanctioned norms, which limit individual choice or castigate deviant religious behavior; this in turn has the potential to provoke further individualization.

Religion changes, even if some are not ready to admit this.[1] Change can be constituted by new agents and new events and can be regarded as contingent and narrated as such. Change can also be analyzed as a sequence of changes in time and as a result of time, that is to say, as a 'process,' as underlined by the words ending in "-ization" in the title. A process can be classified as continuous or as temporary, as repeated or unique, or as

[1] Work on this chapter has been helped by discussion in the Kolleg-Forschergruppe 'Religious individualisation in historical perspective' at the Max Weber Center, Erfurt, financed by the German Science Foundation (DFG, FOR 1013). I am particularly grateful to Martin Fuchs, Erfurt, to whom I owe the references regarding *bhakti*.

reversible or irreversible (as is illustrated by other chapters in this volume). Progress was regarded as irreversible in much nineteenth- and twentieth-century research; monotheism was seen either as a primordial phenomenon that soon declined or as an irresistible trend in the history of religion. A process looks very different when regarded as a contemporary development rather than as a historical and comparative phenomenon. Diagnosis of one's own time tends to stress uniqueness and the acceleration of change. A comparative perspective is more able to take account of large variations. 'Privatization' and 'individualization' take on very different aspects if used as tools of cultural criticism or historical research. Concepts are products of history, but might be useful far beyond their origins. Thus, I will start by historically locating the concept of privatization.

Privatization of Religion: A Theory of the 1960s

By the 1960s industrialization and the spread of welfare, socialism, and democratization, along with de-colonization and the arms race, were seen as hallmarks of the period and perspectives for the future. What was the place of religion? It is important to look beyond Europe. In the wake of postcolonialism—1960 was a prodigal year for the African continent due to the sheer number of states founded—members of elites approached religion as important for the continuity of collective identities and cultural pride. This holds true not only for Africa. Hindu nationalists, for instance, founded the *Vishva Hindu Parishad*, a "world council of Hindus" in 1964 (Jaffrelot 2007). However, the Western academic discipline of Sociology still adhered to the paradigm of secularization, developed in the formative period of the discipline, according to which modernization and rationalization would leave less and less space for the phenomena and functions of religion (critically reviewed by Joas 2012).

Thomas Luckmann, to whom we owe the concept of 'privatization of religion,' was born in Slovenia in 1927, studied at Vienna, and taught at the New School of Social Research in New York. He participated in empirical research in Germany, where he taught sociology from 1967 onwards. His contributions are above all theoretical, but his experience of the very different role, activities, and social bases of Christian churches in Europe and the United States were vital for his thinking and for his book on the problems of religion in modern society (thus the title of the original German edition in 1963). It became famous in its English version as *The Invisible Religion* (Luckmann 1967) and was later republished in an enlarged version in German (Luckmann 1991).

Invisible Religion

An evolutionary perspective on religion within the framework of Talcott Parsons's theory of social differentiation leads to the paradox that religion is, on the one hand, defined by its ensuring individuals' integration into society. On the other hand, at least in Europe, religion had developed very special institutional forms, i.e. churches, which are part of the process of differentiation and which could offer little or no guidance for many areas of social action. One might suppose on theoretical grounds that the 'sacred cosmos,' as formulated by institutionalized religious reflection ('theology'), is the perfect blueprint of an individual's ultimate meaning, thus enabling his or her full integration into society. This flies in the face of the empirical evidence (Luckmann 1991, 119). The fact that an individual is able to act effectively within the many different and independent organizations of modern life proves to be increasingly irrelevant for that person's identity (139), traditional dogmatized churches being no exception. Personal identity has become a private matter. Meaning as produced by the existing plurality of institutionalized religions is on offer and might or might not be utilized by individuals in their private formation of ultimate meanings for the 'great' transcendences they face. Whereas, according to Luckmann, the 'smaller' transcendences beyond daily routine are dealt with by concepts like 'personal' or 'self-fulfillment,' and the 'intermediate' transcendences are reflected in concepts like 'nation' or 'humanity,' the 'great' transcendences are those countered by a 'holy cosmos' of specifically religious concepts.

Institutionalized religion is thus either the (functional) remainder of rather peripheral and premodern groups (dominantly in Europe) or the result of the new and voluntary, less specialized forms of religious action (143). According to Luckmann there is no comprehensive symbolic system organized as Church that embraces all *and* ensures their integration into society.

Given these conditions, privatization of religion has two dimensions. It refers to a private activity and it concerns solving problems mostly situated in the private sphere outside of the internal rationalities of large institutions. In that sphere, many small and secondary institutions try to offer religious ideas as commodities, competing in an open market (147) (see Koch, "Economy," this volume). Why are they successful? Even subjective experiences need communicative reconstruction (171). However, such communication need not be qualified as 'religious' by subjects as they are by observers. Still fulfilling the *function* of religion, i.e. integrating the intersubjectively constituted individual into society in order to allow him or her to act as a full member of society, these constructions of ultimate realities are no longer visible *as* religion, they are 'invisible religion.'

Luckmann's book merits this (summary) retelling because it was the foundational text for a large field of empirical research, even if the phenomenological breadth of his functional definition of religion (see Stausberg/Gardiner, "Definition," this volume) has drawn some criticism. 'Privatization' extended the search for religious action and beliefs well beyond membership and participation in religious institutions. The notion of 'spirituality' follows Luckmann's lead in definitively transcending 'church sociology' without giving up substantialist definitions of religion. It has come to characterize large areas of religious identities (e.g. Knoblauch 1999, 189–202; Woodhead/Heelas 2000; van der Veer 2008; Wilcox 2013), and it has come to serve as the most important counter-argument against the diagnosis of secularization (Aupers/Houtman 2008). Individual 'bricolage,' spiritual self-empowerment in New Age figures of thought (Bochinger 1994; Hanegraaff

2000; Woodhead 2009, 319–338), biographical production of meaning in narrating con-version (Oksanen 1994; more generally Somers 1994), or fragmented episodes of pil-grimage and tourism (see Bauman 1996, 25; Stausberg 2010, 28–29) and the sacralization of the self (Dawson 2006; see also Joas 2013)—all illustrate such privatization.

INDIVIDUALIZATION: AN ELEMENT OF A THEORY OF MODERNITY

Looking at empirical data in the early 1960s, Luckmann pointed to the growth of American churched religion. For Europe, too, recent studies have pointed to the fact that a lot of prototypical privatized religious action happens within the wider framework of religious affiliations or that it tends to build networks (Bochinger/Engelbrecht/Gebhardt 2009; Wilke 2013). And yet, most of these modifications remain truthful to the dominant sociological narrative of modernization theory. Here, 'individualization' is regarded as a characteristic feature of the modern age far beyond religion: a de-traditionalization of individual behavior. This is one of the dominant associations of 'modernity' even in popularized sociological discourse, usually—and unlike Luckmann—losing sight for example of the paradoxical rise of mass culture as a concomitant mode of integration. Even if there are differences in the importance of the notion in individual sociological theories of modernity, individualization takes a firm place within all classical sociologi-cal accounts (Kippele 1998). In these theories, religion is negatively related to the pro-cess of individualization. With the exception of a few thinkers—who reflected upon a specific function of religion for the constitution of the individual in society like Georg Simmel (1858–1918) (1968) and later Luckmann—religion, taken as the epitome of tra-ditional acting, is held, as a consequence of secularization, to have fallen prey to those processes characterized by individualization.

Narratives about Religion and Individualization

From a study-of-religion perspective, it is worthwhile venturing a closer look at the nar-ratives of historical processes, which were thought to form the basis for the equation of individualization and modernity. These narratives take quite different forms. In his famous study of the Italian Renaissance, Jacob Burkhardt (1818–1897) (1860, 141) claimed that interest in subjectivity rose considerably from the end of the thirteenth century onwards. A space of critical distance toward traditional society by means of new ground-breaking philosophical, aesthetic, linguistic, institutional, and also religious alternatives was formulated and practiced in this period (e.g. Martin 2004). If Renaissance pagan-ism was not merely an aesthetic form but also a religious alternative (which remains controversial, see Stausberg 2009) a tradition of religious individualization can be identified which would be enlarged by late-medieval practices of religious piety (*devotio moderna*). Later in the early sixteenth century, the Reformation made religion the object of individual choice, thus creating space for the individual. When in the Renaissance the dominating Aristotelian and Scholastic paradigms came under scrutiny, the Reformation again questioned a dominant, that is, Catholic, religious tradition. Now, however, the mainstream was not only supplanted by intellectual and artistic enterprises, but even openly resisted.

European Prejudices

The European focus of these narratives and the resulting self-image is strengthened by a view beyond the Euro-Mediterranean world. Louis Dumont (1911–1998), a French anthropologist of India, identified Indian tendencies toward individualization in the phenomenon of ascetic renunciation. Dumont supposed that in traditional societies individualism could only appear in clear opposition to society (1986, 26); societies composed of self-oriented individualists are a modern phenomenon. Historically, the individualism identified by Dumont was the opting out of society by somebody who replaced any interest in this-worldly society by an extra-worldly orientation (a *sannyasin*). However, Dumont thought Indian individualism to have remained ineffective in the long run since it did not come to the same theocratic radicalization of social order witnessed by Europe, where, in a first phase, the religious authorities of the church and the pope were made superior to the more worldly powers of the emperor and the nobles and where, in a second phase, religious freedom of the individual was established in the institutionalized shape of a post-theocratic society itself. In Dumont, one of the most influential thinkers on modern India, the story ends as we know it—in the exceptionalism of Western modernity—but he offered at least hypotheses on a more complex early phase.

Careful analyses like this or the earlier ones by Max Weber (1864–1920) on non-Western rationality (1921; 1996) were easily silenced by the Orientalist stereotype of Asian despotism and collective protagonists like the 'castes' dominating the imagination (Said 1978; Assayag/Lardinois/Vidal 2001; Robinson 2004). Individualization was seen as a prerogative of a unique Western Modernity. This led so far as to insinuate that certain non-European, contemporary, but so-called premodern cultures lack even the possibility of formulating any opposition of interests between 'themselves' and 'society.' Such extreme 'dividualism' has been successfully criticized by anthropologists (e.g. Spiro 1993). Recent work on the religion of premodern and pre-Christian Mediterranean antiquity, usually characterized as 'collective,' has produced similar results. Extensive ancient discussions about religious deviance and attempts to legally standardize religious behavior attest to the perception and acceptance of an extensive religious individuality practiced in quite different forms (Rüpke 2011).

A COMPARATIVE VIEW ON PROCESSES
OF INDIVIDUALIZATION

Meanwhile it appears that such phenomena can be critically reviewed outside a 'Western world' that claims to distinguish itself from others by virtue of the self-description 'modern.' This critique takes either the form of pointing to the historical nonsense of such claims of singularity or the form of a counter-stereotype, elevating Eastern collectivity over supposed Western individuality (e.g. Asad 1973; 1983), taken to combine philosophical notions of an autonomous subject, legally guaranteed and socially supported by corresponding options.

Criticizing Stereotypes of Unique Western Individualization

The conceptual linking of the modern age and religious individuality has obstructed the study of comparable phenomena in earlier periods, so that a focus on individuality has played only a limited role in the examination of the dynamics of religion in history. Here I will give just two examples. For Mediterranean antiquity, the concept of '*polis* religion' or 'civic religion' identifies the shared religious practices of a political unit and their functions as being the whole, or at least the only significant sector, of religion. The variety and changeability of individual religious actions and their profound influence on those rituals called 'public' by the elite has been disregarded. This allows modern research to underline the collective and fundamentally different character of premodern societies (see Rüpke 2007, 5–38; Kindt 2012, 12–35 for criticism). Likewise the stereotype of the religious unity of medieval Europe (see Borgolte 2001 for criticism) is just the reverse of the self-description of modern societies implied in the secularization thesis. The diagnosis of modern privatization and individualization and the ascription of a public and collective character to premodern and non-Western religion reinforce each other.

Such observations and criticism cannot overlook the fact that religious individuality is distributed unevenly. This holds true even in situations characterized by processes of individualization based on, or transforming, religion. In identifying the Renaissance as a turning point, Burkhardt recognized the existence of some isolated dissenters already in the preceding period of the twelfth and thirteenth centuries. However, what made a difference in the fourteenth century and constituted individualization as a process was not only an intellectual like Francesco Petrarca (1304–1374), but the large number of people interested both in objective processes of technical and economic matters and in the subjectivity of human agents. But mere numbers do not provide a scale for assessing this phenomenon. One needs to more precisely identify the extent and forms within a local society. Even in a 'modern' and 'Western' society, the acclaimed form of 'individuality' might turn out to be very partial.

An examination of contemporary religion in the United States has shown that 'individuality' is not simply a characteristic of 'modern' religion, as is claimed for the privatization of religion. 'Individuality,' as a framework of interpretation and a form of behavior, is primarily located among mobile members of the white middle class. For them 'individuality' is confirmed by their own commitment and its social consequences (Madsen 2009, 1279–1282). This emic concept of 'individuality' is not an arbitrary option within the range of possible privatized sacred *cosmoi*; rather it is a concept developed by a specific group, and which carries a hegemonic character. It is a way of life that is dominant in the eyes of the entire society (Madsen 2009, 1279–1282). Historically as well as sociologically, there is an important consequence to this. Certain religious traditions might have (or develop) practices (or anthropological and theological reflections) that could foster individuality. The institutionalization of such tendencies, however, and its conceptualization as 'individuality' is a matter of historical contexts and social location; it is contingent.

From such a perspective, there is no fundamental difference between 'Western' and 'non-Western.' For India, *bhakti* offers a comparable constellation. The narrative and theological framework of the propagation of an individual and even loving relationship between a human and a god—Vishnu and Shiva being particularly popular, wherever the addressee was regarded as personalized (instead of abstract, *nirguna*)— proved to be a reservoir that led and leads to processes of individualization of very different forms. These are different in terms of the media employed and the longevity of the process (Eck/Mallison 1991). They could serve as a medium of expression, for instance in giving a voice to women in the form of religious poetry and thus constituting a self (Chakravarty 1989; Craddock 2007). Its inbuilt distancing from the world as it is and simultaneous opening toward divine and human others could serve as political tool and basis for political movements, which aim at gaining recognition (Fuchs 2001; Omvedt 2008).

Delineating Individualization

Contrary to the dominant view of individualization as a unilinear and coherent process, the perspective from the history of religion reveals diverse, temporary, and discontinuous processes. The usual claim of uniqueness, unity, and irreversibility of individualization is not the result of empirical findings, but is in itself part and parcel of a self-description that finds a scientific expression in modernization theory. For historical analysis, it is useful to differentiate between the concepts of 'individual' and of 'individuality,' of 'individuation' (the biographical process of acquiring a full member's role in a society; see Musschenga 2001, 5 for these terms) and 'individualization' (the social structural process of institutional or discursive changes allotting more space for individuality). Elsewhere I have proposed differentiating types of individuality, in order to enable a closer look at phenomena and their contexts, a typology that will be introduced and developed further in the following (Rüpke 2013a). A more general reflection is necessary first.

What kind of phenomena does the concept of individualization embrace? What kind of family resemblance does it produce? First and foremost it includes the notion of de-traditionalization. This is a temporary process, in which a certain field of individual action is less and less determined by traditional norms handed down by family and the larger social context. Options open up; choices can and need to be made. On the part of the individual, this development is reflected in changes in 'individuation'—the process of a gradual full integration into society and the development of self-reflection and of a notion of individual identity. Socialization is the parallel biographical process of being integrated into ever-larger social contexts. The individual's appropriation of social roles and traditions—more specifically religious roles and traditions—and the development of individual identity go hand in hand. I know how to act in society and I act strategically, being self-aware, not necessarily selfish. Religious individuation for instance does not imply the individual's wish to be different. Quite to the contrary, in many historical circumstances being different was not a value-informing individuation. Dignity and honor were such values, along with notions of competition, being better than others in certain respects, or even being perfect. Religious practices might be among fields of competition, for instance in sponsorship and charity, in displays of a cultured taste, or in intensive relationships with a deity. Being able to make meaningful religious experiences is conceptualized as part of becoming an adult in some discourses.

De-traditionalization and individualization entail institutional developments: options are declared legitimate; voluntary associations help to realize certain options; writing, as is suggested by *bhakti* or *Sufi* poetry, helps to develop notions of individuality; inscriptions on stone, wood, or websites might help to express it on a larger social scale. The rights of the individual are legally protected against society's demands, culminating in the formulation of individual human rights. As we have seen for the American white middle classes, individuality takes on a normative character: you have to be 'an individual.'

TYPES OF INDIVIDUALITY

Against the backdrop of the complex notion of individualization used in sociological discourse, it is necessary to develop sharper instruments for historical inquiries. Instead of asking which *degree* of individuality had been achieved it seems to be more useful to inquire into the *forms* of individuality supported by concepts, practices, or institutions that are important for processes of individualization. Elsewhere I differentiate five types of individuality (Rüpke 2013a) that could inform the detailed description and typological differentiation of any long-term processes that might be addressed as individualization (or its opposite, de-individualization). They are here presented in a modified form, namely: pragmatic, moral, competitive, expressive, and reflective individuality. The types are neither mutually exclusive nor necessarily manifested conjointly.

Pragmatic individuality—the fact that people are forced by circumstances to act on their own instead of simply following established norms or commands—points to situations of dis-embeddedness, due to temporary or permanent rupture of social bonds (as in the case of migrants, travelers, survivors) or to a sharp division of labor. Such a situation was experienced by the large number of migrants in ancient Mediterranean societies. This situation led to the fixation (usually at least partly an invention) of traditions carried on by the migrants or to the invention of traditions in the form of different cults, religious services offered by small entrepreneurs, and hence the exercise of choice on the part of their clients on a much larger scale than previously known (Scheidel 2003 for demography; Noy 2000; Rüpke 2014, 35–52). But we need not confine the argument to antiquity. In present-day Korea, for example, processes of de-traditionalization, typical of 'second modernity' (Beck/Beck-Gernsheim 2002), have led to 'pragmatic individuality' among females, trapped and overburdened in families (Kyung-Sup/Min-Young 2010), and one might hypothesize about consequences for religious behavior. Usually, such developments are not reflected by most practitioners. Prior religious practices and beliefs did not prepare people for the consequences of such migrations and ruptures. Rare exceptions to that are written or memorized instructions for post-mortal traveling (Colpe/Habermehl 1996), exemplified by Orphic gold lamellae accompanying the dead (de Jáuregui 2011; Faraone 2011).

Moral individuality involves the ascription of responsibility to persons for their own behavior, e.g. concepts of sin and punishment as well as law. The very idea of personhood is related to this ascription of responsibility from its ancient—Greek and Roman—roots onwards (Gill 1988; Cancik 2002). Standing in contrast to the concept of privatization, guidelines for individual behavior in antiquity were not developed by autonomous individuals but were the moral norms formulated by others and included judgments about social obligations, often to the point of negating individuality. Specific duties rather than universal rights were stressed. And yet, an obligation for the individual to participate in rituals in person instead of just relying on a community to hold the ritual can be seen as indicative of such a moral religious individuality that transcends mere bans ('taboos'). Such social obligations can entail specifically religious consequences. In several instances people claim that their close personal relationship with a deity forced them to take over standards of behavior that were in conflict with societal standards, as is illustrated by the phenomenon of asceticism or even martyrdom in ancient Judaism and Christianity or by Dalit-movements (among the 'Untouchables') in contemporary India which are based on *bhakti* and are striving to gain recognition (see Rüpke/Spickermann 2012 for further examples).

Martyrdom or, on a larger scale, monasticism also exemplify *competitive individuality*. This refers to the wish to be distinct, often, for instance in aristocratic societies, combined with a struggle for recognition and superiority, which typically establishes norms toward which other social groups would orient themselves. Individuals should strive to become exemplary. The life of such distinct personalities would be narrated as example, thus adding a further incentive for the individual endeavor. The aim is not individual difference but perfection in fulfilling a social or religious role, whether as female Roman priest, Christian martyr, or male rabbinic Jew (Fonrobert 2013), yet fulfillment remains a personal feat. Individual differences would be sharply noticed by close contemporary observers, but evaluated against a discursively constructed common ethos that would stress the commonwealth. In difference to privatized or 'implicit religion' (for the development of the concept see Bailey 1990; 2009) visibility of performance is important and can be perpetuated in material form. Donations in the form of votives or the founding of temples and churches in Southern India or medieval European cities could result (Appadurai/Appadurai Breckenridge 1976; Jaritz 1980; Schleif 1990).

Expressive individuality was at the heart of Robert Bellah and his team's investigations of American individualism (Bellah 1985). People felt legitimized and encouraged to present a very specific image of themselves, to express their 'individuality' in material and behavioral form. This goes clearly beyond just striving to be better in fulfilling social norms, but rather was based on a perceived social expectation to be individual. It could also be a part of private and situational, rather than coherent, 'sacred cosmoi,' which are created by the very individual and by diverse appropriation (to speak with Certeau 1984) of institutionalized religious traditions. American anthropologist Meredith McGuire (2008) has delineated everyday religious life on such a basis, but demonstrative forms of renunciation or mysticism are known from Indian, West Asian, or European medieval examples. One might count 'visionary individuality' as a form of this, too, even if the semantics of visionaries usually stresses the external source of their sometimes far-reaching claims and thus gain a substantial reflective element (Rüpke 2013b).

Finally, *reflective individuality* demands the formation of an individualistic discourse, an individualist ideology so to speak. Again, such reflections on the self or individual human nature (for example in the Stoic figure of *oikeiosis*, according to which each person should learn about and adapt to his or her physical and social nature [Engberg-Pedersen 1990; Trapp 2007, 109–114]) could be informed by normative concepts of social roles, usually produced by and adapted to elites. Such concepts of the self can further be combined with different concepts like 'soul' (frequently employed in antiquity, Bremmer 2002) or 'inner person.' Again, imagined communication with the divine or the presence of the divine in or for oneself could be of great importance in religiously stabilizing such subjective individuality, and its expression could lead to visible processes of individualization, institutionalized for instance in practices of confession or spiritual care.

Paradoxes: Individualization and De-individualization

Evidently, different types of individuality relate to different types of processes and contexts of changes that are referred to as individualization. Pragmatic individuality is only rarely accompanied by a growing tradition of reflexivity, the latter being the typical standard for acknowledging the existence of a process of individualization in modernization theory. Competitive individuality presupposes a (even if minority) social environment of shared values, at least indirectly questioned by expressive individuality. Without the support of individual choices by institutionalized practices or beliefs or even full-grown organizations, explicit religion might become implicit religion, visible religion invisible religion, and vice versa. Processes of individualization in their different forms are in principle reversible (even if sometimes self-stabilizing), potentially following or being followed by processes of de-individualization.

This relationship is, however, even more complicated. Periods and regions that are characterized by a variety of individualization processes were also seedbeds of religious traditions, even religious organizations. Let me give a few examples before I unpack the seemingly paradoxical constellation. Mediterranean Late Antiquity was the birthplace of what has been called the first autobiography, Augustine of Hippo's *Confessions* at the end of the fourth century, and of monastic and ascetic *virtuosi* in the preceding century. At the same time, Augustine was the powerful head of the Catholic 'church' of Carthage, fighting the widespread Donatist movements. Many ascetics and hermits grouped together as cenobites in monasteries. Their 'fathers', the abbots, started to write monastic rules (as stressed by later historiography). Elaborated in South Asia and beginning in the Puranic period (roughly the third century CE), the idea of the loving relationship to a god (*bhakti*), quickly led to the formation of religions of *sampradayas*, of sects, focusing the religious practices on specific deities. The European Reformation of the early sixteenth century propagated individual belief and a personal salvation, which is dependent on God's grace, not on ritual services provided by the Christian Church. At the same time different theologies and alliances organized themselves in structures that were not only of an ecclesiastical nature but also went hand in hand with the establishment of the territorial state. New Religious Movements and New Age spirituality manifest a wide differentiation of worldviews and religious practices, but they are not only indicators of individual options and choices made. At the same time they attest to loose and tight networks, practices of bonding, or even sanctioning disloyalty.

These observations can be generalized. Individual behavior that might be judged deviant, or at least non-conformist, from the point of view of the majority or the religious mainstream, is precarious and threatened. As a consequence, it is safeguarded and institutionalized in the form of minority groups (which can become a majority). From here the paradox takes its point of departure. A bundle of factors and motifs lead to the increasing boundedness of those who group together to preserve their choice and to defend their deviant religious individuality. In order to define their boundaries, groups ('sects' developing into 'churches') dogmatize their norms and denounce outsiders as well as exclude internally deviant members. Systematization of belief and the attempt to gain political support produce rigidity or compromises that turn away other members. Professional leaders judge the power of their institution by its influence on the behavior of people who regard themselves as members of that organization or who are ascribed membership therein. The conviction or practice safeguarded by the institution might be rigidly enforced among its members. By the fourth century CE, Christian bishops had achieved juridical power, granted by the Roman emperor; 'heretics,' 'followers' of (just another) sect had been banned earlier, but could now be reprimanded with the help of political and juridical authorities. Manichaeans and heretics had to fear for their careers and even their lives. In short, individualization processes culminate in the formation of sharply differentiated 'religions' (Rüpke 2010), even if the question of what constitutes a separate entity might have been disputed. Whether Mohammad's Islam was just a new heresy or an independent 'religion' of its own was discussed by Christian observers far into the Middle Ages.

In Europe, a comparable process can be observed in the early modern period. Down into the eighteenth century, processes of confessionalization—the development of different 'confessions' (Roman Catholic, Lutheran, Reformed), of sharp group boundaries, and of formalized standards of belief and behavior—assured the internalization of specific denominational norms, leading to lasting habits, social and economic behaviors, and intellectual orientations. However, few were in a position to choose their confession. Despite the existence of religious plurality from a bird's eye view, the exercise of choice was severely restricted for any historical individual. In many instances, this stimulated internal differentiation within groups rather than a costly switching of allegiances.

To sum up: as has been observed for and criticized with regard to the concept of 'privatization of religion,' processes of religious individualization are frequently paradoxical processes. As a concept for initializing research, 'individualization' like 'privatization' offers a focus, a lens for observing processes that have been neglected due to a conviction on part of many scholars of the 'Western' world, namely that individuality is tied to the notion of modernity. Removing this prejudice opens up a fruitful field of comparative research. Discarding the nexus of individualization and modernity means dropping the idea of a transhistorical process with a concomitant shift to the study of particulars in broader contexts. Historical evidence as sketched briefly above, and not least the relationship of privatization and de-privatization in the 1960s, encourages us to pay attention to the entanglement of processes of individualization and de-individualization.

GLOSSARY

Individuality a Western self-stereotype seen as a philosophical notion of an autonomous subject, legally guaranteed and socially supported by corresponding options for individual action and a corresponding ideology of obligation to present oneself as somebody choosing among available options, even in matters religious.

Individualization the de-traditionalization of individual behavior, often, but as shown here, wrongly claimed to be part of modernization.

Individuation the biographical process of acquiring a full member's role in a society.

Privatization (of religion) transferring religious activities from the public into the private realm and/or focusing religious activities on private problems.

References

Appadurai, Arjun and Carol Appadurai Breckenridge. 1976. "The South Indian Temple: Authority, Honour and Redistribution." *Contributions to Indian Sociology* NS 10(2): 187–211.

Asad, Talal, ed. 1973. *Anthropology & the Colonial Encounter*. London: Ithaca Press.

Asad, Talal. 1983. "Anthropological Conceptions of Religion: Reflections on Geertz." *Man* NS 18(2): 237–259.

Assayag, Jackie, Roland Lardinois, and Denis Vidal. 2001. *Orientalism and Anthropology: From Max Müller to Louis Dumont*, 2nd edition. Pondichéry: Institut Français de Pondichéry.

Aupers, Stef and Dick Houtman. 2008. "The Sacralization of the Self: Relocating the Sacred on the Ruins of Traditions." In *Religion: Beyond a Concept*, edited by Hent de Vries. New York: Fordham University Press, 798–812.

Bailey, Edward. 1990. "Implicit Religion: A Bibliographical Introduction." *Social Compass* 37(4): 499–509. doi: 10.1177/003776890037004007

Bailey, Edward. 2009. "Implicit Religion." In *The Oxford Handbook of the Sociology of Religion*, edited by Peter B. Clarke. Oxford: Oxford University Press, 801–816.

Bauman, Zygmunt. 1996. "From Pilgrim to Tourist—or a Short History of Identity." In *Questions of Cultural Identity*, edited by Stuart Hall and Paul Du Gay. London and Thousand Oaks, CA: Sage, 18–36.

Beck, Ulrich and Elisabeth Beck-Gernsheim. 2002. *Individualization: Institutionalized Individualism and Its Social and Political Consequences*. London: Sage.

Bellah, Robert N. 1985. *Habits of the Heart: Individualism and Commitment in American Life*. Berkeley, CA: University of California Press.

Bochinger, Christoph. 1994. *'New Age' und moderne Religion: Religionswissenschaftliche Analysen*. Gütersloh: Kaiser.

Bochinger, Christoph, Martin Engelbrecht, and Winfried Gebhardt, eds. 2009. *Die unsichtbare Religion in der sichtbaren Religion—Formen spiritueller Orientierung in der religiösen Gegenwartskultur*. Stuttgart: Kohlhammer.

Borgolte, Michael, ed. 2001. *Unaufhebbare Pluralität der Kulturen? Zur Dekonstruktion und Konstruktion des mittelalterlichen Europa*. Munich: Oldenbourg.

Bremmer, Jan N. 2002. *The Rise and Fall of the Afterlife*. London: Routledge.

Burckhardt, Jacob. 1860. *Die Cultur der Renaissance in Italien*. Basel: Schweighauser.

Cancik, Hubert. 2002. "'Dignity of Man' and 'Persona' in Stoic Anthropology: Some Remarks on Cicero, *De Officiis* I 105–107." In *The Concept of Human Dignity in Human Rights Discourse*, edited by David Kretzmer and Eckart Klein. The Hague: Kluwer Law International, 19–39.

Certeau, Michel de. 1984. *The Practice of Everyday Life*. Berkeley: University of California Press.

Chakravarty, Uma. 1989. "The World of the Bhaktin in South Indian Traditions: The Body and Beyond." *Manushi* 50–52: 18–29.

Colpe, Carsten and Peter Habermehl. 1996. "Jenseitsreise (Reise Durch Das Jenseits)." *Realenzyklopädie für Antike und Christentum* 17: 490–543.

Craddock, Elaine. 2007. "The Anatomy of Devotion: The Life and Poetry of Karaikkal Ammaiyar." In *Beyond the Circle: Women's Rituals, Women's Lives in Hindu Traditions*, edited by Tracy Pintchman. New York: Oxford University Press, 131–148.

Dawson, Lorne L. 2006. "Privatisation, Globalisation, and Religious Innovation: Giddens' Theory of Modernity and the Refutation of Secularisation Theory." In *Theorising

Religion: Classical and Contemporary Debates, edited by James A. Beckford and John Walliss. Aldershot: Ashgate, 105–119.

de Jáuregui, Miguel Herrero. 2011. "Dialogues of Immortality from the *Iliad* to the Gold Leaves." In *The 'Orphic' Gold Tablets and Greek Religion: Further Along the Path*, edited by Radcliffe G. Edmonds. Cambridge: Cambridge University Press, 270–290.

Dumont, Louis. 1986. *Essays on Individualism: Modern Ideology in Anthropological Perspective*, Chicago, IL: University of Chicago Press.

Eck, Diana L. and Françoise Mallison, eds. 1991. *Devotion Divine: Bhakti Traditions from the Regions of India. Studies in Honor of Charlotte Vaudeville*, Groningen/Paris: Egbert Forsten/ École Française d'Extrême Orient.

Engberg-Pedersen, Troels. 1990. *The Stoic Theory of Oikeiosis: Moral Development and Social Interaction in Early Stoic Philosophy*. Aarhus: Aarhus University Press.

Faraone, Christopher A. 2011. "Rushing into Milk: New Perspectives on the Gold Tablets." In *The 'Orphic' Gold Tablets and Greek Religion: Further Along the Path*, edited by Radcliffe G. Edmonds. Cambridge: Cambridge University Press, 308–309.

Fonrobert, Charlotte Elisheva. 2013. "'Humanity Was Created as an Individual': Synechdocal Individuality in the Mishnah as a Jewish Response to Romanization." In *The Individual in the Religions of the Ancient Mediterranean*, edited by Jörg Rüpke. Oxford: Oxford University Press, 489–521.

Fuchs, Martin. 1988. *Theorie und Verfremdung: Max Weber, Louis Dumont und die Analyse der Indischen Gesellschaft*, Frankfurt am Main: Peter Lang.

Fuchs, Martin. 2001. "A Religion for Civil Society? Ambedkar's Buddhism, the Dalit Issue and the Imagination of Emergent Possibilities." In *Charisma and Canon: Essays on the Religious History of the Indian Subcontinent*, edited by Vasudha Dalmia, Angelika Malinar, and Martin Christof. New Delhi: Oxford University Press, 250–273.

Gill, Christopher. 1988. "Personhood and Personality: The Four-Personae Theory in Cicero, *De Officiis* I." *Oxford Studies in Ancient Philosophy* 6: 169–199.

Hanegraaff, Wouter J. 2000. "New Age Religion and Secularization." *Numen* 47(3): 288–312. doi: 10.1163/156852700511568

Jaffrelot, Christophe, ed. 2007. *Hindu Nationalism: A Reader*. Princeton, NJ: Princeton University Press.

Jaritz, Gerhard. 1980. "Seelenheil und Sachkultur: Gedanken zur Beziehung Mensch— Objekt im späten Mittelalter." *Europäische Sachkultur des Mittelalters: Gedenkschrift aus Anlaß des zehnjährigen Bestehens des Instituts für mittelalterliche Realienkunde Österreichs*. Vienna: Verlag der Österreichischen Akademie der Wissenschaften, 57–81.

Joas, Hans. 2012. "Gefährliche Prozessbegriffe: Eine Warnung vor der Rede von Differenzierung, Rationalisierung und Modernisierung." In *Umstrittene Säkularisierung: Soziologische und historische Analysen zur Differenzierung von Religion und Politik*, edited by Karl Gabriel, Christel Gärtner, and Detlef Pollack. Berlin: Berlin University Press, 603–622.

Joas, Hans. 2013. *The Sacredness of the Person: A New Genealogy of Human Rights*. Washington, DC: Georgetown University Press.

Joas, Hans and Jörg Rüpke, eds. 2013. *Bericht über die erste Förderperiode der Kolleg-Forschergruppe 'Religiöse Individualisierung in Historischer Perspektive' (2008–2012)*. Erfurt: Max-Weber-Kolleg.

Kindt, Julia. 2012. *Rethinking Greek Religion*. Cambridge: Cambridge University Press.

Kippele, Flavia. 1998. *Was heißt Individualisierung? Die Antworten der soziologischen Klassiker.* Opladen: Westdeutscher Verlag.

Knoblauch, Hubert. 1999. *Religionssoziologie.* Berlin: de Gruyter.

Kyung-Sup, Chang and Song Min-Young. 2010. "The Stranded Individualizer under Compressed Modernity: South Korean Women in Individualization without Individualism." *British Journal of Sociology* 61(3): 539–564. doi: 10.1111/j.1468-4446.2010.01325.x

Luckmann, Thomas. 1967. *The Invisible Religion: The Problem of Religion in Modern Society.* New York: Macmillan.

Luckmann, Thomas. 1991. *Die unsichtbare Religion.* Frankfurt am Main: Suhrkamp.

McGuire, Meredith B. 2008. *Lived Religion: Faith and Practice in Everyday Life.* Oxford: Oxford University Press.

Madsen, Richard. 2009. "The Archipelago of Faith: Religious Individualism and Faith Community in America Today." *American Journal of Sociology* 114(5): 1263–1301. doi: 10.1086/595946

Martin, John Jeffries. 2004. *Myths of Renaissance Individualism.* Basingstoke: Palgrave Macmillan.

Musschenga, Albert W. 2001. "The Many Faces of Individualism." In *The Many Faces of Individualism*, edited by Anton von Harskamp and Albert W. Musschenga. Leuven: Peeters, 3–23.

Noy, David. 2000. *Foreigners at Rome: Citizens and Strangers.* London: Duckworth.

Oksanen, Antti. 1994. *Religious Conversion: A Meta-Analytical Study.* Bromley: Chartwell-Bratt.

Omvedt, Gail. 2008. *Seeking Begumpura: The Social Vision of Anticaste Intellectuals.* New Delhi: Navayana.

Robinson, Rowena, ed. 2004. *Sociology of Religion in India.* New Delhi: Sage.

Rüpke, Jörg. 2007. *Religion of the Romans.* Translated by Richard Gordon. Cambridge: Polity Press.

Rüpke, Jörg. 2010. "Hellenistic and Roman Empires and Euro-Mediterranean Religion." *Journal of Religion in Europe* 3(2): 197–214. doi: 10.1163/187489210X501509

Rüpke, Jörg. 2011. *Aberglauben oder Individualität? Religiöse Abweichung im Römischen Reich.* Tübingen: Mohr Siebeck.

Rüpke, Jörg. 2013a. "Introduction: Individualization and Individuation as Concepts for Historical Research." In *The Individual in the Religions of the Ancient Mediterranean*, edited by Jörg Rüpke. Oxford: Oxford University Press, 3–28.

Rüpke, Jörg. 2013b. "Two Cities and One Self: Transformations of Jerusalem and Reflexive Individuality in the Shepherd of Hermas." In *Religious Dimensions of the Self in the Second Century CE*, edited by Jörg Rüpke and Greg Woolf. Tübingen: Mohr Siebeck, 49–65.

Rüpke, Jörg. 2014. *From Jupiter to Christ: On the History of Religion in the Roman Imperial Period.* Translated by David M. B. Richardson. Oxford: Oxford University Press.

Rüpke, Jörg and Wolfgang Spickermann, eds. 2012. *Reflections on Religious Individuality: Greco-Roman and Judaeo-Christian Texts and Practices.* Berlin: de Gruyter.

Said, Edward W. 1978. *Orientalism.* New York: Pantheon Books.

Scheidel, Walter. 2003. "Germs for Rome." In *Rome the Cosmopolis*, edited by Catherine Edwards and Greg Woolf. Cambridge: Cambridge University Press, 158–176.

Schleif, Corine. 1990. *Donatio et memoria: Stifter, Stiftungen und Motivationen an Beispielen aus der Lorenzkirche in Nürnberg.* Munich: Deutscher Kunstverlag.

Simmel, Georg. 1968. *Soziologie: Untersuchungen über die Formen der Vergesellschaftung.* Berlin: Duncker & Humblot.

Somers, Margaret R. 1994. "The Narrative Constitution of Identity: A Relational and Network Approach." *Theory and Society* 23(5): 605–649. doi: 10.1007/BF00992905

Spiro, Melford E. 1993. "Is the Western Conception of the Self 'Peculiar' within the Context of the World Cultures?" *Ethos* 21(2): 107–153.

Stausberg, Michael. 2009. "Renaissancen: Vermittlungsformen des Paganen." In *Europäische Religionsgeschichte: Ein mehrfacher Pluralismus*, edited by Hans G. Kippenberg, Jörg Rüpke, and Kocku von Stuckrad. Göttingen: Vandenhoeck & Ruprecht, 695–722.

Stausberg, Michael. 2010. *Religion and Tourism: Crossroads, Destinations and Encounters.* London: Routledge.

Trapp, Michael. 2007. *Philosophy in the Roman Empire: Ethics, Politics and Society.* Aldershot: Ashgate.

van der Veer, Peter. 2008. "Spirituality in Modern Society." In *Religion: Beyond a Concept*, edited by Hent de Vries. New York: Fordham University Press, 789–798.

Weber, Max. 1921. *Gesammelte Aufsätze zur Religionssoziologie 2: Hinduismus und Buddhismus.* Tübingen: Mohr.

Weber, Max. 1996. *Gesamtausgabe I, 20: Die Wirtschaftsethik der Weltreligionen: Hinduismus und Buddhismus 1916–1920.* Tübingen: Mohr.

Wilcox, Melissa M., ed. 2013. *Religion in Today's World: Global Issues, Sociological Perspectives.* New York: Routledge.

Wilke, Annette. 2013. "Säkularisierung oder Individualisierung von Religion? Theorien und empirische Befunde." *Zeitschrift für Religionswissenschaft* 21(1): 29–76.

Woodhead, Linda, ed. 2009. *Religions in the Modern World: Traditions and Transformations.* London: Routledge.

Woodhead, Linda and Paul Heelas, eds. 2000. *Religion in Modern Times: An Interpretive Anthology.* Oxford: Blackwell.

FURTHER READING

Aupers, Stef, ed. 2010. *Religions of Modernity: Relocating the Sacred to the Self and the Digital.* Leiden: Brill. [*This remains one of few introductions to the sociology of religion that takes a global view. The discussion of privatization and individualization is not simply reduced to the modernization and secularization paradigms.*]

Fuchs, Martin and Jörg Rüpke (guest editors). 2015. *Religious Individualization in Historical Perspective = Religion* 45(3) (2015). [*The contributions to this volume introduce and illustrate processes of individualization by examples taken from the history of religion of the ancient Mediterranean, early modern Europe, and ancient as well as modern India.*]

Schnettler, Bernt. 2006. *Thomas Luckmann.* Konstanz: UVK. [*This is a good introduction to Luckmann. For the latter's sociology of religion in particular see 111–120.*]

Wilke 2013 [*Wilke offers a broad review and critical discussion of recent applications of the concept of individualization within a framework of modernization theory.*]

CHAPTER 47

....

TRADITION
AND INNOVATION

....

OLAV HAMMER

CHAPTER SUMMARY

....

- All religions change gradually over time. Although tradition and innovation used to be seen as opposites, it is now generally recognized that there is a close connection between the two.
- Examples of how religious narratives and actions are transmitted over time illustrate some mechanisms by which a historical tradition arises. These in particular include cognitively based mechanisms, e.g. ways by which cultural transmission from one person to another or across generations is linked to particularities of human memory.
- A range of mechanisms, from the work of religious entrepreneurs to structural factors, introduce innovative practices into these traditions.
- Although innovation is ubiquitous, theological elites will often deny that any significant change has taken place, and accuse their ideological opponents of being excessively innovative.

A CASE STUDY: LUCIA DAY

....

Throughout most of Scandinavia, and especially in Sweden, December 13 or Lucia Day is an occasion of ritual celebration of the imminent return of sunlight in the darkest

period of the year.[1] In schools, day care centers, hospitals, in many workplaces and public venues, on national television, and elsewhere, boys and girls walk in procession holding candles. One girl is selected as Lucia, and her role is to walk first in the procession,
wearing a crown of candles, or in these safety-conscious times, more likely electrical
simulacra. Special songs are sung, most commonly one called 'Santa Lucia.' The event is
celebrated in especially grand style in the capital, Stockholm, where 'the Swedish Lucia'
is crowned and a Lucia concert is held in the city's most spectacular venue.

The celebration is so much part of Swedish national identity that emigrants in various localities around the world attempt to arrange Lucia processions. Conversely, when
Nobel laureates who attend the festivities associated with the award on December 10
are treated with a Lucia procession on the eve of their departure from the capital on the
13th of the month, the Swedish press regularly delights in relating how puzzled these
foreigners were with the event. To the surprise of some Swedes, Italian Nobel Prize win-
ner Dario Fo appeared to be much less mystified than other visitors from abroad: as the
Swedish boys and girls began to intone the Lucia song, Dario Fo joined in—singing in
Italian.

It requires only a modicum of detective work to find out why Dario Fo felt that the
tune was familiar: it turns out that the supposedly arch-Swedish song is in fact an adaptation of a melody from Napoli, with no connection at all to December 13. The lyrics
were freely reworked into Swedish and adapted to the celebrations on Lucia Day because
of a striking coincidence: the Neapolitan version contains a sentimental reference
to Santa Lucia, which in the Italian song is not the name of a light-bearing saint, but a
district on the waterfront of Napoli. Not only does the song have a little-known background, much of the modern Lucia tradition, it turns out, was created within the space
of a few years around the turn of the twentieth century, and received a major boost when
it was publicized by a Stockholm newspaper in 1927. A variety of older and more locally
based Lucia traditions also exist, or at least existed until they were replaced by the pan-
Swedish procession. Although less than a century has passed since the modern celebration swept the country, nearly all historical recollection of these older regional customs
has faded. In 2004, Swedish national television chose to replace the usual Lucia broadcast with a program where such older customs were presented. As a result, the network
received numerous complaints from viewers who felt that a tradition dear to them had
been disrupted.

The modern version of Lucia Day will no doubt continue to be celebrated for a long
time to come, thanks to this massive popular support. But sentiment alone cannot

---

[1] Basic information on the historical background of the Lucia Day celebration is taken from Bringéus
1999, 110–119. Contemporary events are summarized from information available at <http://www.
sanktalucia.se and naturenshus.wordpress.com/2009/12/13/luciafirandet/>, accessed August 12, 2014.

mobilize the resources necessary to host and broadcast the largest-scale performances of the ritual, or to produce the ritual paraphernalia needed to carry out the procession. The role of national television has already been noted. The major Stockholm celebration is sponsored by *Året Runt*, the country's most widely sold weekly periodical, and arranged in collaboration with a company called Swedish Traditional Events. On a commercially more modest scale, costumes, crowns with electrical lights, and other accessories can be purchased in any department store once the Lucia season approaches.

The place in contemporary Scandinavian culture of the Lucia custom illustrates some of the topics to be covered in this chapter. Over the span of a few years, a cultural innovation was created by a small number of individuals. This innovation was presumably perceived as something new and unfamiliar in the first few years of its existence, but soon became to be seen as old, venerable, and in some vague and unspecified way handed down from earlier generations. The historical facts thus became obscured behind this nebulous appeal to an undefined link to ancient customs. Following Hobsbawm and Ranger's celebrated work (1992), we might call Lucia Day an invented tradition. But the story doesn't end there. Although we may trace the Lucia celebration to the early twentieth century, and can even pinpoint the date when the Stockholm daily newspaper covered an event that it itself had arranged, the Lucia procession has become a tradition in another and probably more familiar sense of the word. For the better part of a century, children have been socialized into the culturally correct way to dress for the occasion, how to walk, what words to sing, and so forth. What was at one point constructed or invented is now an entrenched part of Swedish culture.

The Topic and Structure of this Chapter

The Lucia Day tradition illustrates the interconnected historical phases that are typical of the trajectory of most viable cultural elements: an innovation arises; it is consolidated by receiving a legitimating warrant; and it then becomes part of the cultural repertoire that is passed on to younger members of the society. Yet, in older scholarship these three phases were generally studied as distinct phenomena, even as opposites. Classical sociological approaches, for instance, tended to understand tradition as a set of practices transmitted from generation to generation, as opposed to the innovative products of creative individuals. The everyday or dictionary use of the word, as well as its etymology (Latin for "something handed down"), reinforce this impression that tradition implies venerable age. This basic sense of the word may seem to be merely descriptive, as a way of marking a particular custom as older than a vaguely defined cut-off point, but 'tradition' comes with a heavy normative baggage as well. In the study of religions, for instance, quite a few scholars have distinguished traditions that were in some sense 'authentic' from those that were 'invented,' with the effect that religions with a shaky connection to a documentable past were until fairly recently bracketed out as unworthy of serious study. Although all religions were at some point in time new, an academic field, the study of New Religious Movements, arose largely as a response to public concerns about the emergence of an entire cohort of unfamiliar religions in the 1960s and 1970s. More recently, New Age phenomena have become the focus of scholarly attention, after similarly languishing in academic limbo as inventions too recent to merit being taken seriously.

The double topic of this chapter, tradition and emergence, signals an awareness that this differential treatment is normative and unwarranted. In recent years, this awareness has become a common feature of academic writing on religion (Engler/Grieve 2005; Hammer/Lewis 2007; Engler forthcoming). Nonetheless, it is possible for analytical and terminological purposes to study each phase in the process of emergence, consolidation, and transmission separately. After a brief survey of some of the classical approaches that saw a radical dichotomy between innovation and tradition, this chapter proceeds to look at a number of factors that lead to a tradition in the sense of a successful transmission of religious elements from one generation to the next. It then briefly passes on to the question of how an appeal to tradition can function as a legitimating claim. In the section that follows, some basic mechanisms for the emergence of religious innovations are considered. Finally, the chapter, again very briefly, notes the role of tradition and innovation in religious polemics, i.e. the widespread practice of accusing one's ideological foes of being excessively innovative and disregarding tradition.

Some Classical Approaches to Tradition

The academic study of tradition and emergence is rooted in an older discourse that saw tradition and its counterpart (typically, the modern way of life) as utterly distinct and attached value judgments to both. Tradition could be seen either as something inherently positive, often (inspired by the thought of Johann Gottfried von Herder, 1744–1803, and his successors in the Romantic period) in a somewhat nostalgic vein as the true expression of a people, or (in particular after the Enlightenment) as a shackle from which 'we moderns' needed to free ourselves. Tradition was often described as the passing on, from generation to generation, of a set of customs and values, ensuring continuity and conformity across generations. Some societies, typically small-scale and tribal or locally based peasant societies, were said to be especially prone to this kind of unreflecting transmitting of past traditions, whereas others, in particular Western nation states, were dynamic. As one of the founding fathers of anthropology theorized, wherever elements of traditional thinking subsisted into modern and putatively more advanced societies, these were mere 'survivals' from earlier cultural stages (Taylor 1871).

Building on such historical precursors, classical twentieth-century sociological theories up to the 1950s and 1960s continued to regard traditional and modern societies as radically different modes of existence. Traditional societies, in this perspective, are local, whereas we are globally oriented; they are collectivist, while we have an individualistic focus; their societies are largely homogeneous, whereas ours are highly differentiated; their mode of existence is static, passed on virtually unchanged generation after generation, while we are engulfed in a perpetual maelstrom of dynamic change; they look back on an exemplary historical past, while we orient ourselves toward the future.

By the mid-to-late 1960s, something had begun to change. Although still dichotomous, Claude Lévi-Strauss's distinction between hot and cold societies introduced an important corrective (Lévi-Strauss 1966, 233). Here changeless tradition is pushed back to a much earlier stage, before social stratification, castes, and endogamy enter the picture. On this view, only very small hunter-gatherer societies with an egalitarian ethos live largely untouched by historical change. Class-like or hierarchical modes of organization will, even in tribal societies, introduce a mechanism for cultural transformation. Social mobility from one class or social stratum to another will typically depend on possessing, displaying, and distributing prestige goods. These items are often brought in from an external source, which means that novelties enter the society via trade with outsiders, marriage with members of other groups, or warfare. Rituals and myths come to surround these prestige items, and in this way the local religion is affected by change even among most tribal peoples.

An apt example concerns the indigenous ethnic groups of the Canadian west coast, people who in pre-contact times were hunter-gatherers, but were thanks to the very generous ecological niche in which they lived able to develop a complex system of social stratification and a rich ritual life. Every element of their religious tradition was owned by one clan or another, and high-ranking individuals could gain access to each other's religious heritage by arranging large gift-giving festivals. The Kwakwaka'wakw of the Vancouver Island area (formerly also known as the Kwakiutl, after the name of one of their local groups) were particularly well known for their ritual displays. Lavish feasts performed during the winter months linked powerful families to various spirit beings, a link that was essential for maintaining and building social status.[2] The distribution of wealth was accompanied by ritual dances, during which men from aristocratic clans impersonated their ancestral spirits. The central role that these rituals played in Kwakwaka'wakw culture can be gauged from the fact that they are still carried out in modified form in an otherwise strongly acculturated society (Cranmer Webster 1991). Yet, scholars have analyzed the key role played by such rituals as the result of massive cultural changes in the mid-nineteenth century. In earlier times, warfare and headhunting had been privileged ways to acquire status. Once warfare was no longer possible, not least because of the presence of the 'white' Canadian authorities, gift-giving rituals took over its role (Codere 1950).

---

[2] The winter ceremonials were extraordinarily complex and involved practically every aspect of Kwakwaka'wakw life; see Goldman 1975, esp. 86–121 for an interpretation.

Discussions of tradition over the following years increasingly stressed the close relationship between continuity and change. Thus, a classic treatment of tradition (Shils
1981, 13) sees tradition as something that can be literally *traditum*, i.e. handed down
across generations (such as the Greek text of the *Iliad*, which scribes attempted to preserve intact over the centuries), but can also constitute a more loosely connected 'chain
of transmitted variants' (e.g. the Platonic tradition, a number of individual philosophers
and schools who disagreed on many issues but saw themselves as faithfully preserving
the insights of their founder Plato).

Shils also notes briefly (1981, 14) that the degree of variation may be perceived very
differently by adherents and outsiders, and that adherents will be prone to focus on continuity where outsiders perceive change. The classical sociological theory that explains
this discrepancy is the work of Max Weber. His seminal contribution was the recognition that the label 'tradition' can be a claim, strategically deployed as a way to make
specific cultural traits legitimate (Weber 1947, 341–358). Writers who followed his lead,
especially beginning in the 1970s and 1980s, no longer used the terms 'traditional' and
'modern' as mere descriptive labels for specific social formations, but increasingly
saw them as ideological constructions. Thus, Eisenstadt (1973, 151–156) distinguished
between tradition (a custom that people follow because they perceive it as being
unproblematically given) and traditionalism (a conscious decision to follow a putatively
ancient custom, and an ideology that opposes change). Conversely, 'modern' began to
be seen not only as a descriptive label for certain social patterns, but was unmasked as
an often self-congratulatory term by which the West designated a universal goal toward
which, it was felt, other societies should strive.

TRADITION AS THE TRANSMISSION
OF CULTURE

Although the insight that tradition and emergence are closely linked seems to have reap-
peared remarkably late in scholarly thinking, it is, in one of its guises, an ancient one. In
chapter 23 of his *Life of Theseus*, the Greek writer Plutarch raised the question whether a
ship where every single plank over time has been exchanged for a new one still remains
the same ship. In the domain of religion, the simile is quite apt. As generations pass,
old myths are interpreted in new ways, rituals fall out of use while new ones are created, institutions adapt to changing times, and doctrines that are perceived as quaint
or irrelevant are tacitly dropped. The net effect is that what a church-going twenty-first
century Christian of any particular denomination, for example, sees as a self-evident
understanding of Christianity would have seemed utterly strange to his or her ancestors.
Yet innovation is not an instant and wholesale process. Not all planks are removed at
once, i.e. some concepts and practices are indeed transmitted across generations. Some
models of how successful historical transmission takes place are briefly summarized in
the following paragraphs.

Cultural Memory

Especially since the late 1970s and early 1980s, numerous scholars have charted the ways in which societies collectively remember the past (see Olick/Vinitzky-Seroussi/Levy 2011 for a survey of the field, with numerous excerpts from the scholarly literature on the topic). Just as individual people create narratives about who they are, based on memories of crucial events in their life histories, societies metaphorically have a cultural or collective memory. And just as the memory of an individual is a reconstruction of the past and not just a straightforward account of what happened, this shared view of the past highlights some events, marginalizes or suppresses others, provides a master narrative in the light of which the past is understood, and ensures that the collective vision of the past endures by using texts, historical sites, images, shared rituals, and so forth. If a society collectively remembers itself as valiantly overcoming its foes in a series of patriotic wars, this collective memory can be shaped and reinforced by means of schoolbooks, speeches, national holidays, flags, medals, photographs, museums, and monuments.

Epidemiology of Representations

Speaking of societies remembering, or of a cultural or collective memory is, of course, a metaphor. A concept such as 'our nation has a glorious past' may be part of the narrative shared by most members of a given society, being in that sense part of its collective memory, but the concept needs to be stored in the individual memories of countless people and transmitted successfully from person to person by specific psychological mechanisms. Our understanding of those mechanisms is still in its infancy, but a significant early attempt to understand how such social micro-processes of cultural transmission take place was formulated by French anthropologist Dan Sperber, who gave his theory the equally metaphoric name "the epidemiology of representations" (Sperber 1985). Just as diseases are transmitted from one host to another, ideas that are sufficiently catchy will also be transmitted until most of the population has accepted them. The process of transmission is also one of transformation: we do not just passively copy the information we receive, but adapt it to our own interests. Again, we find that passing on a religious tradition and allowing something novel to emerge are two sides of the same coin.

Cognitive Approaches

Sperber's approach raises a crucial question: what makes ideas 'catchy'? In recent years, scholars have devised several models to explain successful cultural transmission based on the fundamental insight that the characteristics of the human mind play a crucial role. A theological doctrine or a sequence of ritual actions that is dull or hard to remember will stand less chance of surviving the passage of time than competitors with more appealing traits. The literature on such cognitively based theories of transmission has expanded significantly in the last two decades, and only a couple of such theories can be mentioned here.

Pascal Boyer (1994; 2001) has drawn attention to an attention-grabbing feature of narratives that are successfully transmitted. Our minds engage in a constant task of sorting impressions into neat categories. For example, from a very early age, we distinguish objects from living beings: our intuitions tell us that the former only move or act when budged by an external force, whereas the latter have a volition and power of motion of their own. A successful narrative, Boyer suggests, is one that contains a minimally counterintuitive element, for instance telling of a seemingly inert object (a statue) that has a striking characteristic normally associated with a living being (it weeps). Without any counterintuitive element, the story seems pointless. Presumably, no religion declares that everything is precisely as it seems to the intuitive cognition of everyday observers. With too many counterintuitive elements, the story also loses its potential, for instance by having a plot that is too unwieldy or incredible (a narrative about a statue that weeps vinaigrette dressing every other Wednesday seems ill-suited for a religion that is meant to be taken seriously).

A different track is taken by Harvey Whitehouse, who proposes (2000; 2004a) that religious practices and concepts are transmitted by one of two fundamentally different modes: the imagistic and the doctrinal. His 'modes of religiosity' theory is based on the observation that there are two distinct forms of memory with divergent properties that profoundly influence the way in which religious elements are passed on from one person to another.

Episodic memory stores recollections of single, salient events. In the domain of religion, a typical case would be the painful ordeals youngsters in many societies are subjected to as part of rituals of initiation. Semantic memory, by contrast, allows us to recall general knowledge, procedures, and routines. Characteristic examples are theological postulates and ritual actions that are internalized in the course of a monastic education or a school curriculum. The two types of memory function very differently, and religions that are based largely on the one or the other will also display quite divergent features. Doctrinal religiosity (the type that is stored in semantic memory) is fundamental in traditions where the sheer amount of material that one is expected to memorize may be very large, the specifics are often hard to learn and easy to forget. In order for a tradition to form, occasions for memorizing the material need to be organized, and the bulk of doctrinal knowledge can be so great that only a few members of the community can be expected to master it and function as the prime keepers of the religious tradition. By contrast, imagistic religiosity, i.e. the type that is characterized by striking experiences that will be distinctly remembered, forges strong bonds between those who have taken part in the experience, but generates few theories about the meaning of the experience. In societies where imagistic religiosity predominates, what gets passed on from one generation to the next is the form such rituals take and the social organization necessary to perform them.

There are also doctrines and rituals transmitted by means that have too little 'content' to fit the category of doctrinal religiosity, but are also too emotionally low-key to serve as examples of the imagistic mode. Scholars of religion with a cognitive science approach (Boyer 2001; Whitehouse 2004b) therefore suggest that these can be explained in terms of cognitive optimality, i.e. that some concepts are in themselves easier to memorize or feel more natural than others. There are numerous ways in which cognitive optimality affects religious concepts and makes them more prone to survive over time. Anthropomorphism, for instance, is pervasive in religions, because it feels natural for humans to assume that the gods are also human-like: they have feelings, thoughts, and desires that resemble those of humans, and even look like us (Guthrie 1993). Anthropomorphic understandings of the gods are more likely to become part of a tradition that survives the passage of time than abstract concepts that are cognitively unnatural and therefore hard to remember.

Tradition as a Claim and a Mode of Authority

As noted earlier, religious elements that are demonstrably recent can also be imbued with an aura of venerable age. Tradition in this sense affirms social bonds, provides ties back to a putative past, and legitimates practices. Most religions are characterized by this recourse to tradition, no matter what the historical records may reveal. Innovations in theology, scriptural exegesis, ritual behavior, and so forth are made legitimate by being anchored in the exemplary past. In the formative period of Sunni Islam, for instance, this appeal to tradition was ubiquitous: once a precedent was found in a hadith (or, as skeptical scholars of Islam have maintained, an appropriate hadith had been fabricated), a practice was deemed acceptable, and the charge of introducing a nefarious innovation could be defused. Even the very distaste for innovation, characteristic of an age when a fluid Islamic religion was being more sharply defined, could be projected back to the opinion of the prophet by invoking a famous hadith: 'the most evil affairs are . . . innovations, and every innovation is an error' (*Muslim* 1885).

The key role played by often spurious traditions is attested to by the fact that various Muslim communities could diverge on numerous points of doctrine and practice, and support their own claims with apparently impeccable references to the past. Whether controversies dealt with matters of ritual purity, allowable foodstuffs, details of the ritual prayers, political succession, or any number of other issues, tradition seemingly supported all sides of the conflict (Burton 1994).

Mechanisms of Emergence

At this point of the discussion, we seem to be faced with a puzzling fact. On the one hand, social and cognitive mechanisms ensure that successful cultural transmission across generations is possible. In the most extreme cases, e.g. the Vedic rituals documented by Frits Staal (Staal et al. 1983), the minutiae of ritual action seem to have been passed on unaltered over several centuries. On the other, strategic appeals to tradition have a powerful rhetorical appeal. If the force of tradition in both senses of the word is so strong, what makes the emergence of something new nevertheless such a ubiquitous phenomenon? The facts of religious innovation are often complex and messy, and a mere catalogue would be endless. With the major caveat that the different ways in which novelties emerge in a religion tend to coexist and interact, I here suggest three ideal types of innovation-producing mechanisms. The first has to do with the lifecycle of religious movements. Some scholars (such as William Bainbridge and Rodney Stark) propose that religious groups, like organisms, have cycles of birth, maturity, stagnation, reform or schism, decay and stagnation, and for most, death. The second concerns the introduction of novelties created by religious entrepreneurs of various kinds, including prophets, reformists, leaders of new religions, successful authors of religious literature, and so forth. Finally, the third type could be called structural, i.e. innovations that arise as adaptations to other cultural changes.

LIFECYCLE FACTORS

Emergent religions can be classified in a small number of categories, each of which seems to follow roughly the same pattern of development over time. Stark and Bainbridge (1985) have developed a theory of how such developments take place in a seemingly endless round of emergence, decline, and new emergence of religious movements. Schismatic movements, for instance, typically arise when a faction within a larger body feels that the spiritual insights or the emotional fervor of the movement in its earlier phase have now been lost (Stark/Bainbridge 1985, 99–125, building on the work of H. Richard Niebuhr). The breakaway group denounces the parent organization with much sound and fury, and re-establishes what it sees as these original ideals, usually following the day-to-day directives of a charismatic leader. As the splinter group grows and as its membership ages, the level of commitment will sink, leadership loses its charisma and becomes bureaucratic, and the movement begins to feel stagnant to some members, who form the nucleus of the next schismatic faction. The vast number of sects within Protestant Christianity can in part be explained as a result of this *perpetuum mobile* of religious emergence.

ENTREPRENEURIAL FACTORS

The entrepreneur was defined by economist Joseph Schumpeter (cf. Schumpeter 2011) as a person who disrupts an otherwise relatively stable market by introducing new products. Innovators and entrepreneurs are, in this perspective, two distinct roles: whereas an innovator can invent something new, what defines successful entrepreneurs is their skill in undermining the status quo of the market. The same goes for the domain of religion: innovators can attempt to create new rituals or propose new doctrines, but most such novelties are picked up by only a few other people. It is when religious entrepreneurs back such innovations that there is a substantial impact on the religious landscape (acknowledging that the innovator and entrepreneur can on occasion be the same person).

Some entrepreneurs were political and military leaders. Buddhism would conceivably never have become a major religion if it were not for the political support given to it after King Ashoka (304–232 BCE) converted, and used his power to spread the teachings of an obscure reformist movement based in northeast India over much of South Asia. The same goes for Christianity, which might have remained just one of many religions of the Roman Empire if it hadn't been promoted with exceptional zeal by rulers such as Constantine (272/273–337) and Theodosius (347–395).

Other entrepreneurs have the practical skills necessary for launching new forms of religion: writing books, lecturing, organizing groups of devotees, and managing the affairs of these devotees. Yet others change the religious landscape thanks to their charisma, another of the many fundamental concepts due to the work of Max Weber (1947, 358–363). Charismatic individuals can gain acceptance for their novel practices and ideas by virtue of the extraordinary personal qualities displayed by or attributed to them. The Mormon prophet Joseph Smith came from an utterly humble background, had no political clout and only a modest level of education when he began his religious career, but he nevertheless managed to convince people to accept the messages he purportedly transmitted from a transcendent source and thus became the founding figure of one of the most successful new religions.

It should be kept in mind that religious change is the result of historically contingent factors, and that entrepreneurs do not always fall into any of the neat categories identified in the standard literature on religion. The reader will recall that some of the most important people in promoting the modern Lucia celebration were the (now utterly forgotten) editor at the daily newspaper *Stockholms Dagblad*, who in 1927 decided that it would make excellent commercial sense for the newspaper to organize and promote a procession in Stockholm, and the equally anonymous people who run the magazine *Året Runt* and the company Swedish Traditional Events.

STRUCTURAL FACTORS

The very category of 'religion', and the decision to use it to label some phenomena but not others, is constituted by the linguistic habits by which scholars as well as ordinary language users divide up the world. Religious people tell myths, carry out rituals, and manufacture religious material culture, but this in turn requires that the myths be made available through various media, that the specialists who know the minutiae of how

rituals should be performed can set aside time to cultivate this expertise by withdraw-
ing from more immediately productive work, and that the norms and laws of the society
make it possible to allocate resources, educate the specialists, and allow adherents of the
religion to practice it. Religion, as defined narrowly (e.g. as practices and concepts that
ultimately refer to a culturally defined suprahuman dimension), is thus in any society
inextricably linked to other sectors of society, such as the economy, the legal system,
media, and education. As a few examples will illustrate, changes in any of these sectors
will have effects on the religion.

The Effect of Changing Social Norms and Legal Systems

The last century has seen major changes in gender roles and gender relations in the
Western world, from the introduction of voting rights for women in the decades around
1900 to an increasingly equal participation in the labor market in the post-World War II
epoch. In the world of religion, women have also taken on increasingly central roles. In
the nineteenth century, this was in particular the case in emergent religious movements
such as Spiritualism and Theosophy. In the twentieth century many mainline Protestant
churches also began to give women a more prominent role, and today many Lutheran
churches ordain women as priests and bishops.

   An increasing acceptance in many countries of other sexual orientations than heterosexual has resulted in the ordination of openly gay individuals in denominations such as
the Church of Sweden and some Anglican/Episcopal churches (albeit, in the latter case,
with considerable controversy in its wake) and of the creation of church rituals for same-
sex marriages in countries such as Denmark. In countries where homosexuality is by
now generally accepted, such innovative religious practices typically generate polemics
for some years, but finally become so established that those who remain opposed come
to be viewed as an embattled minority.

Religion and New Technologies

The form and content of religion have throughout history been profoundly affected by
technological developments. The emergence of written records led to radical changes in
the way religious rituals and doctrines were formulated and transmitted from one generation to the next. In orally based cultures, religion depends on human memory, and
given that memory is not always a faithful record of past events, such religions are often
very malleable. Once myths and historical events have been fixed in writing, a much
more stable record is available, and new ways emerge that ensure that the religion can
change and adapt. For instance, a set of sacred texts can be seen as unchangeable and
sacrosanct, but commentaries change the way these sacred texts are understood.

   The invention of the printing press added new methods of spreading religious innovations over large distances. When texts were copied by hand, books could be both

expensive and rare. The new technology made it possible to reproduce any particular book in thousands of copies. Printing became progressively cheaper, and in the seventeenth and eighteenth centuries, religious dissenters and Enlightenment skeptics could reach literate elites all over Europe and North America. The process accelerated even further throughout the nineteenth century, when religious publications became affordable to the masses and literacy increased. A wide variety of new religious currents from that period, such as Mormonism, Spiritualism, Christian Science, and Theosophy, could compete for adherents by producing voluminous bodies of literature at low cost. Our own age has radicalized the trend even further, and the cost efficiency of printing and distribution technologies is such that religious (or 'spiritual') books can be printed in millions of copies and reach audiences worldwide.

Finally, more recent media technologies such as television and the Internet continue to affect the form and content of religion. Television has allowed a variety of religious phenomena, from Christian Evangelicalism to Spiritualism, to reach large audiences. The Internet provides a platform where anybody with even quite modest resources can spread their messages. Contacts via e-mail, Twitter, Facebook, online discussion groups, and so forth can provide the opportunity even for very small religious movements to reach out to sympathetic audiences around the world.

The Spread of Global Religions

Many emergent religious phenomena are the result of contacts with other religions and other societies. Numerous peoples have undergone complete shifts in religion as a result of such interactions. The various ethnic groups of Europe once had local gods that were worshiped in locally based rituals. Monks and missionaries introduced Christianity, with the result that Celtic, Norse, or Slavic myths and gods are mentioned in history books as vestiges of the past, and the rituals that were once performed to propitiate or honor them are only imperfectly known today, whereas Christian myths about the Christian god are familiar to many, and rituals centering on the Christian deity are performed all over the world. In similar fashion, Islam has spread from its historical core area in the Middle East to become a numerically very significant religion over a vast area from Senegal in the west to Indonesia and the southern Philippines in the east, partially or wholly replacing indigenous religions. Such global contacts have taken many forms, including the work of missionaries, the circulation of texts, trade, and military aggression.

The spread of Christianity, Islam, or other powerful, global religions does not mean that the imported gods, myth, or rituals are exact copies of those of the missionaries. The products of globalization are often adapted to local contexts, a process for which sociologist Roland Robertson (1992) coined the word *glocalization*. Religious glocalization implies that, for example, African Christianity or African Islam will be different from European forms of Christianity or Islam as practiced in a country in the Middle East. Some independent African churches, for instance, rejected monogamy as a foreign imposition and felt that their own form of Christianity could accept the locally well-established polygamous family structure. Others could stress such elements as material prosperity, exorcism, or faith healing, elements that are certainly found also in European and American churches from where missionaries to Africa came, but which were placed on center stage in their new settings.[3] In this way, new forms of the major religions emerge.

The Transmission of Religious Texts

Mission and direct contacts with other ethnic groups are thus some of the most dominant forces behind the emergence of a new religious landscape. However, new religious phenomena also emerge when texts spread to new parts of the globe. The literati of the Middle Ages gained access to a new set of philosophical concepts when ancient Greek documents began to be translated and commented upon in the eleventh to thirteenth centuries. The Aristotelian corpus, in particular, changed the face of Christian intellectual culture. A much later and more popular example of how the spread of texts can lead to the emergence of new religious trends is the role played by American spiritual and self-help books in forming the contemporary religious landscape. Books such as the channeled text *A Course in Miracles*, James Redfield's *The Celestine Prophecy*, or the book series *Conversations with God* written by Neale Donald Walsch are translated into a host of European languages and shape popular religion all over Europe without any concomitant influx of American New Age gurus.

Such contacts with new texts can produce far more profound changes in the religion of the recipients than just the emergence of new ideas. Typically, the introduction in a short period of time of many new texts gives rise to new categories of religious experts. The new texts are often written in a previously unfamiliar language, which calls for a cohort of translators who are able to transform a Greek or Arabic text into Latin, or a Sanskrit scripture into Chinese or Tibetan. Such translations can at times be nearly undecipherable for the less learned, and commentators will come forward to provide the necessary guidance. Anybody who has attempted to penetrate the dense prose of Aristotle's *Metaphysics*, or Nagarjuna's utterly cryptic treatise on the Root Verses on the Middle Way (or *Madhyamakakarika*) will soon become aware of why such texts could never reach their new audiences without copious explanatory notes. Yet other specialists will study the contents of such books, discuss their 'true' meaning, and harmonize them with other texts that they understand to be fundamental to their religion. Via such processes, new intellectual cultures—scholastic and monastic—emerged in places as far apart as the medieval West and Buddhist Tibet.

[3] For information on glocalized religion in Africa, see Clarke 2012 and the literature cited there.

Trade, Pilgrimage, and Tourism

For one religion to adopt elements from another requires neither mission nor an advanced literate culture. The everyday contacts between people traveling to each other's territories for such purposes as trade have transformed religions throughout human history. Just as people exchange material goods, religious knowledge is traded, the right to perform rituals is transferred to others, and religious objects are passed on. Even in the premodern world, where most people never ventured far beyond the borders of their own ethnic group, religious artifacts could be given from one person to the next along trade routes spanning entire continents. An archaeological excavation on the Swedish island of Helgö, in the Stockholm region, identified the remains of an Iron Age settlement, i.e. a site occupied before the Viking age when warriors from Scandinavia swept across much of Europe and ventured across the Atlantic. Even in this early period, trade was international. Coins minted in Ravenna, Rome, Byzantium, and the Arab world testify to the importance of Helgö as a northern outpost in these trade routes. Among the many finds from this site, a Buddha figure manufactured in the Swat Valley of what is today northern Pakistan is striking evidence of how religious objects could be transported over vast distances.

Trade and travel have increased exponentially in modern times. Immigration has brought Muslims, Hindus, Sikhs, and Buddhists to Europe and North America, and tourism has allowed many Westerners to visit famous religious sites across the world. Modern attitudes to travel and to religion have led to forms of contact that hover between religious quest, entertainment, tourism, and the wish to take up a physical challenge: modern pilgrimages. In 2012, nearly 200,000 people, many of whom had no intention of performing a Christian ritual, walked along the popular pilgrimage route of Santiago de Compostela in the border regions between France and Spain.[4]

Military Intervention

As the history of encounters between small-scale societies and powerful aggressors has repeatedly demonstrated, the demographic disaster that often results from such encounters will have a decisive impact on religion and produce massive change. If the population decreases drastically, it can be impossible to maintain all details of the rites and myths in the collective memory, and it can become too onerous for the remaining adherents of the religion to mobilize the necessary resources to perform collective rituals. Indigenous peoples around the world have created condensed versions of their religious traditions in order to adapt to the effects of warfare, epidemics, and major socio-economic changes. The Kwakwaka'wakw, referred to earlier, were severely

---

[4] The figure is taken from statistics available on caminodesantiago.me (accessed August 12, 2014). On religious tourism, see Stausberg 2011.

affected by the contact with 'white' Canadian society: their population was drastically reduced by disease, prestige objects that were vital to their religious life were confiscated by the authorities, draconic legal measures were adopted to prevent them from performing their rituals, and missionaries were intent on converting them to various Christian denominations. Today, Kwakwaka'wakw dances and gift-giving festivals are still performed, but in versions that differ dramatically from those documented just a century ago (Cranmer Webster 1991).

Many societies have, when faced with such massive cultural change, created new religions that attempt in very diverse ways to overcome the problems they are facing. Some attempt to revive the glories of the past, others await the imminent end of history, yet others follow religious and political leaders who try to overthrow their foreign oppressors, or attempt by ritual means to transfer the power of the foreign intruders into the hands of the local population (Wilson 1973). Thus, the so-called cargo cults found in parts of Melanesia focus on bringing prosperity to the locals by staging rituals where such emblems of foreign wealth as American flags and simulacra of US military aircraft and uniforms are used.

Styles of Innovation and Tradition

One typology of New Religious Movements classifies them into historically connected families: new religions belonging to, for example, a Lutheran family, a Pentecostal family, an Adventist family, a Magick family, a Middle Eastern family with roots in Judaism, a Pagan family, and so forth (cf. Melton 2009; Partridge 2004). Although presumably introduced as merely a useful heuristic, substantive similarities between various religions in any particular family make this classificatory method into a valuable analytic tool. Shared origins tend to translate into shared characteristics, and these similarities not only concern the doctrines and practices of various religions but also similar styles of handling tradition and emergence. A few brief examples can illustrate this phenomenon.

Many religions within the Protestant family show how references to a canonical text allow for a complex interplay of tradition and innovation. On the one hand, the existence of a sacred scripture provides a link to the past. On the other, there are mechanisms that provide a creative re-reading of scripture. Some measure of innovation can be introduced by suggesting that parts of the canon have been mistranslated. The Jehovah's Witnesses, for instance, base some of their doctrinal innovations on the claim that their own rendition of the Bible, the *New World Translation*, rectifies errors in other versions of the biblical text.

A more common mode of balancing tradition and innovation within the Protestant family of religions is by producing commentaries and exegeses of the canonical text. By presenting one's ideas as merely interpretations of scriptural passages, one can keep tradition (the canon of scripture) intact while at the same time allowing for the introduction of large-scale innovation (the commentary/interpretation ekes out meanings from the canonical text that have not been seen previously). Each particular group within the Protestant family of religions constitutes an interpretative community (Fish 1980) for whom a particular interpretation of the canon is valid. The interpretative freedom can be so great that the canonical text ultimately becomes a Rorschach blot upon which such interpretations are projected. The Swedish seer Emanuel Swedenborg (1688–1772) was convinced that the words of the text of Genesis were mere externals that hid an internal meaning, and that the external and internal senses bear only the faintest resemblance to each other (Benz 2002, 351–352). Whereas an 'external' reading of the first chapter of Genesis might lead readers to believe that the text presents a cosmogony, and that the result of the first of six creative days according to this myth was the existence of heaven and earth, Swedenborg explains (*Arcana Coelestia* §§ 6–13, 17) that the internal message of these passages is a description of the spiritual regeneration of the human being through six stages, that 'heaven' means internal man, and 'earth' signifies external man before regeneration.

Other families of religions base their blends of tradition and innovation on references to an exemplary past. The sayings and deeds of its founder in the formative golden age provide the basis for doctrines and ways of acting. Innovative practices can be justified by renegotiating the community's understanding of what, precisely, happened in the past: what historical records are authentic, how should the behavior of the ancient luminaries be understood, and so on. As we have seen, in various understandings of Islam the formative age of the tradition is a primary legitimating factor. In particular, the life of the prophet Muhammad is mined for information allowing innovators to suggest, for example, that 'Islam really is' a liberal or conservative, feminist or patriarchal, politically radical or socially conservative religion. During the rule of Egypt's socialist president Nasser, Muhammad was declared to be the world's first socialist, while Moroccan feminist author Fatima Mernissi concluded that the Prophet was a feminist whose message had been distorted into the patriarchal ideology that one finds in much of the Islamic world (cf. Khalidi 2009).

Yet other families of religions suggest that correct doctrines and practices arise from the continued contact with transcendent sources of information. In particular, a Theosophical family of religions carries on the claim of founding figure Helena Blavatsky (1831–1891) to have been in touch with a group of beings endowed with suprahuman wisdom (the Masters). Numerous currents in the wake of Theosophy claim that their founders continued to receive guidance from these Masters, and that seeming innovations were actually the result of new revelations from the same source, or from other members of the same hierarchy of beings. Theosophically inspired religions in America, such as the I AM movement and the Summit Lighthouse group, incorporated much of the lore disseminated by Blavatsky, but added numerous innovations. These were, however, not presented as strictly speaking innovative doctrines, but as perennial wisdom received from a Master by the name of Saint Germain, who was particularly responsible for the spiritual destiny of America (Rudbøg 2013; Abravanel 2013).

Whereas all of the above attempt to emphasize tradition at the expense of innovation, some religions in the modern world wholeheartedly embrace the idea that their founders discovered something entirely new. Although such an insistence on novelty and innovation is rather uncommon, Scientology serves as an example of a religion that builds its bid for legitimacy on change at the expense of tradition, suggesting that its founder L. Ron Hubbard discovered truths that surpassed anything that had been known before. This, of course, merely fixes the life of the founder as the point of departure for a new tradition: the Church of Scientology is so committed to maintaining the purity of Hubbard's 'technology' that it will go to extraordinary lengths to protect his legacy by litigation and other means.[5]

COMBATING INNOVATORS
AND PROTECTING ORTHODOXY

This chapter has argued that one of the most common ways of handling innovation effectively denies that change has taken place. Theological elites that define orthodoxy will be particularly insistent on denying that their concepts and practices are recent inventions. They are conversely often eager to accuse others of undue innovation, and tend to produce what one might call second-order reflection about why such departures from a purported tradition arise, and what to do about excessive innovators. Quite a few religious communities have translated such theories about the undesirability of innovation into aggressive politics of repression against 'heretics.' A few examples can illustrate this fear of novelty.

Strikingly, Islamic vocabulary can use the very word for innovation, *bid`ah*, as a way to denote a perceived divergence from correct practice or belief. Anything that runs counter to what can be found in the Qur'an or traced back to prophetic precedent is considered a malignant innovation. The Qur'an itself needed to be commented upon to be fully comprehensible, and this commentarial activity should according to one influential line of thought also rely on tradition and prophetic precedent in order to avoid the risk of innovating (McAuliffe 2006, 196–198). Careful linguistic analysis, it is suggested, increases one's assurance of clinging wherever possible to the literal meaning of the divine text (cf. Gleave 2012).

Christian historical writers of the first centuries CE created a picture of early Christianity as one true teaching traceable back to its founding figures, constantly under threat from purveyors of falsehood who deviated from this original truth. That this portrait of Christian origins is unhistorical has been increasingly accepted ever since Walter Bauer published his seminal work *Rechtgläubigkeit und Ketzerei im ältesten Christentum* in 1934 (translated as *Orthodoxy and Heresy in Earliest Christianity*). Bauer argued that

---

[5] Scientology's tendency to use legal means against perceived enemies is documented in much of the literature on the movement; a recent monograph that devotes considerable space to this issue is Urban 2011.

Christianity in the formative age took on many shapes, and that the very division into 'orthodoxy' and 'deviance' was the result of a long process. Not least, orthodoxy is the result of constant efforts to enforce religious hegemony. Wherever Christian churches have wielded power, the strategy of accusing others of introducing heretical changes into the pure tradition has been a mighty tool in the hands of any church that claimed to possess a true understanding of Christianity. It is all the more remarkable that innovation has been rampant throughout Christian history, even in times when the consequences of being declared a heretic could be dire.

Conclusion

To summarize, two concepts that could seem like each other's opposites are in fact inextricably interwoven. Most religions see themselves as passing on a historical legacy, and this self-presentation has caught on to such an extent that the phrase 'religious tradition' is commonly used as a synonym for religion. More realistically, a religion is like Theseus's ship in Plutarch's parable: as individual bits and pieces get replaced over time, the practices and doctrines of a religious community are constantly being shaped both by the transmission of existing material and by the emergence of innovations.

Glossary

Cultural transmission the passing on from one person, group, or generation to another of a cultural element.

Emergence the appearance of a new religious element (a myth, ritual, type of religious object, etc.).

Invented tradition a custom that was deliberately created at some point in time but has become generally perceived as ancient.

Tradition a pattern of action that is widely perceived as having deep historical roots.

References

Abravanel, Michael. 2013. "The Summit Lighthouse: Its Worldview and Theosophical Heritage." In *Handbook of the Theosophical Current*, edited by Olav Hammer and Mikael Rothstein. Leiden and Boston: Brill, 173–191.

Bauer, Walter. 1934. *Rechtgläubigkeit und Ketzerei im ältesten Christentum*. Tübingen: Mohr.

Benz, Ernst. 2002. *Emanuel Swedenborg: Visionary Savant in the Age of Reason*. West Chester, PA: Swedenborg Foundation.

Boyer, Pascal. 1994. *The Naturalness of Religious Ideas: A Cognitive Theory of Religion*. Berkeley: University of California Press.

Boyer, Pascal. 2001. *Religion Explained: The Evolutionary Origins of Religious Thought*. New York: Basic Books.

Bringéus, Nils-Arvid. 1999. *Årets festdagar*. Stockholm: Carlssons.

Burton, John. 1994. *An Introduction to the Hadith*. Edinburgh: Edinburgh University Press.

Clarke, Peter B. 2012. "New Religious Movements in Sub-Saharan Africa." In *The Cambridge Companion to New Religious Movements*, edited by Olav Hammer and Mikael Rothstein. Cambridge: Cambridge University Press, 303–319.

Codere, Helen. 1950. *Fighting with Property: A Study of Kwakiutl Potlatching and Warfare*. New York: American Ethnological Society.

Cranmer Webster, Gloria. 1991. "The Contemporary Potlatch." In *Chiefly Feasts: The Enduring Kwakiutl Potlatch*, edited by Aldona Jonaitis. New York: American Museum of Natural History, 227–248.

Eisenstadt, S. N. 1973. *Tradition, Change and Modernity*. New York: John Wiley & Sons.

Engler, Steven. Forthcoming. "The Concept of Tradition." In *The Blackwell Companion to Religious Diversity*, edited by Kevin Schilbrack. Oxford: Wiley-Blackwell.

Engler, Steven and Gregory P. Grieve, eds. 2005. *Historicizing "Tradition" in the Study of Religion*. Berlin and New York: de Gruyter.

Fish, Stanley. 1980. *Is There a Text in this Class? The Authority of Interpretive Communities*. Cambridge, MA: Harvard University Press.

Gleave, Robert. 2012. *Islam and Literalism: Literal Meaning and Interpretation in Islamic Legal Theory*. Edinburgh: Edinburgh University Press.

Goldman, Irving. 1975. *The Mouth of Heaven: An Introduction to Kwakiutl Religious Thought*. New York: John Wiley & Sons.

Guthrie, Stewart. 1993. *Faces in the Clouds: A New Theory of Religion*. Oxford: Oxford University Press.

Hammer, Olav and James R. Lewis, eds. 2007. *The Invention of Sacred Tradition*. Cambridge: Cambridge University Press.

Hobsbawm, Eric and Terence Ranger. 1992. *The Invention of Tradition*. Cambridge: Canto.

Khalidi, Tarif. 2009. *Images of Muhammad: Narratives of the Prophet in Islam across the Centuries*. New York: Doubleday.

Lévi-Strauss, Claude. 1966. *La pensée sauvage*. Paris: Presses Universitaires de France.

McAuliffe, Jane Dammen. 2006. "The Task and Traditions of Interpretation." In *The Cambridge Companion to the Qur'an*, edited by Jane Dammen McAuliffe. Cambridge: Cambridge University Press, 181–209.

Melton, J. Gordon. 2009. *Encyclopedia of American Religions*, 8th edition. Detroit: Gale.

Olick, Jeffrey K., Vered Vinitzky-Seroussi, and Daniel Levy, eds. 2011. *The Collective Memory Reader*. Oxford: Oxford University Press.

Partridge, Christopher. 2004. *Encyclopedia of New Religions: New Religious Movements, Sects and Alternative Spiritualities*. Oxford: Lion.

Rolandson, Robert. 1992. *Globalization: Social Theory and Global Culture*. London: Sage.

Rudbøg, Tim. 2013. "The I AM Activity." In *Handbook of the Theosophical Current*, edited by Olav Hammer and Mikael Rothstein. Leiden and Boston: Brill, 151–172.

Schumpeter, Joseph. 2011. *The Entrepreneur: Classic Texts by Joseph A. Schumpeter*. Stanford, CA: Stanford University Press.

Shils, Edward. 1981. *Tradition*. Chicago, IL: University of Chicago Press.

Sperber, Dan. 1985. "Anthropology and Psychology: Towards an Epidemiology of Representations." *Man* 20(1): 73–89. doi: 10.2307/2802222

Staal, Frits, C. V. Somayajipad, M. Itti Ravi Nambudiri, and Adelaide De Menil. 1983. *Agni: The Vedic Ritual of the Fire Altar*. Berkeley, CA: Asian Humanities Press.

Stark, Rodney and William Sims Bainbridge. 1985. *The Future of Religion: Secularization, Revival, and Cult Formation*. Berkeley: University of California Press.

Stausberg, Michael. 2011. *Religion and Tourism: Crossroads, Destinations and Encounters*. London and New York: Routledge.

Taylor, Edward B. 1871. *Primitive Culture*. New York: J. P. Putnam's Sons.

Urban, Hugh B. 2011. *The Church of Scientology: A History of a New Religion*. Princeton, NJ: Princeton University Press.

Weber, Max. 1947. *The Theory of Social and Economic Organization*. Glencoe, IL: Free Press.

Whitehouse, Harvey. 2000. *Arguments and Icons: Divergent Modes of Religiosity*. Oxford: Oxford University Press.

Whitehouse, Harvey. 2004a. *Modes of Religiosity: A Cognitive Theory of Religious Transmission*. Walnut Creek, CA: AltaMira.

Whitehouse, Harvey. 2004b. "Toward a Comparative Anthropology of Religion." In *Ritual and Memory: Toward a Comparative Anthropology of Religion*, edited by Harvey Whitehouse and James Laidlaw. Walnut Creek, CA: AltaMira, 187–205.

Wilson, Bryan. 1973. *Magic and the Millennium*. London: Heinemann.

Further Reading

Boyer 1994 [*A basic introduction to the cognitive mechanisms that allow for the successful transmission of a religious tradition.*]

Eisenstadt 1973 [*Classic essays on the sociology of tradition and cultural change.*]

Engler/Grieve 2005 [*A seminal selection of case studies illustrating the many strategic uses of 'tradition' in the domain of religion.*]

Engler forthcoming [*A useful summary of the state of the art on the connection between tradition and change.*]

Hobsbawm/Ranger 1992 [*A modern classic showing how and why many supposedly ancient customs were created quite recently.*]

Olick/Vinitzky-Seroussi/Levy 2011 [*A reader with numerous classical and recent excerpts on the study of 'collective memory.'*]

Shils 1981 [*A key reference from the formative age of the sociological study of tradition.*]

Whitehouse 2004a [*A study that links the transmission of religious elements to the specific characteristics of human memory.*]

CHAPTER 48

OBJECTIFICATION AND COMMODIFICATION

JEREMY CARRETTE

CHAPTER SUMMARY

- Objectification and commodification are challenging and disturbing processes, seen in the treatment of women and the extension of the market.
- Commoditization and commodification are different. The former changes an object into something saleable and the latter seeks to make and exploit a non-object as saleable.
- Kantian ethical thought, Marxism, and feminist theory all identified aspects of the inhumane processes of objectification and/or commodification.
- Religious traditions can both facilitate and provide resistance to objectification and commodification.
- Objects and commodities can be part of the material culture of religion, but there is a complex ethical concern when these processes extend to profit motivations or are applied to non-objects, such as persons.
- Studies of Western and Asian traditions reveal many ambiguities in relation to objects and commodities, but much of this reflects a confusion between commoditization and commodification.
- Academic concepts, such as 'religion,' can be seen as forms of objectification and commodification.

Mapping the Terms:
Definition and Meaning

Objectification and commodification are some of the most subtle and challenging processes in social life, manifesting in disturbing ways in the history of slavery and prostitution, and extending into the increasing marketization of all aspects of human relations and knowledge in the twenty-first century. They are processes of thinking and acting that seek to transform the world into objects and commodities ('things') for control, exchange, and wealth. They form part of what is known as 'reification,' that is a process of transforming bodies, practices, ideas, and social relations into 'things,' into manageable forms, for utility, controlled use, and domination. Although a Marxist lexicon of critical thinking has had a strong influence on these ideas, they have a wider use in terms of social and cultural analysis, philosophy, and studies of cognition. The processes are related to structures of thought/consciousness, social attitudes, political and economic power, and ethical concerns about social relations. They reflect forms of relation between subject (persons) and object (materiality) and the desire to make one into the other. However, there is a distinction between commoditization (making objects into commodities) and commodification (making persons, values, or ideas into commodities). The latter often entails objectification (the process of making of something into an object). Objectification and commodification are, therefore, closely related.

In this chapter I will map the complex development of the terms objectification and commodification since the eighteenth century, separating out many confusing aspects of the language and showing their use in feminist and critical theory. I will then explore how these processes are transforming 'religious' ideas, persons, and practices into 'things' across a wide variety of traditions and contexts, something that increases in the world of global capitalism. My overall aim is to show that the terms reflect distinct cognitive and social processes that arise from desire, control, and power. They refer to processes of thinking and acting that seek to make the world static and controllable for the desires of a dominant person or group. They are thus embedded deep within the psychological, social, and political worlds.

From 'Objects' and 'Commodity'
to Objectification and
Commodification

The terms objectification and commodification have been predominantly deployed in the study of religion for the analysis of the social world since the nineteenth century, but have increased in their intensity and social relevance through feminist theory (as in, for example, the objectification of women's bodies) from the 1970s and in the critique of the neoliberal economic shaping of the world (as, for example, in the marketization of social life) from the 1980s. The study of religion has a long and ambivalent interest in the nature of objects and things, has intermittently reflected on how objectification and commodification are part of patriarchy and capitalism, but has insufficiently understood how its own processes of analysis and forms of study are determined by objectification and commodification in the knowledge economy (see later discussion). There has been a strong—and highly problematic—de-politicization of these terms in studies of material culture and economic anthropology and little understanding of their effects on the processes of thought and the analysis of thought (in, for example, cognitive theory). These terms in this sense cross both philosophical and empirical domains of study. As a result, working through the language and meaning of these terms is complex and highly charged, because it demands taking a normative position on the nature of these processes and their social relevance.

Significantly, Karl Marx does not deploy the terms commodification and objectification as such, only the related forms of 'commodity' and 'objects.' However, the shaping of these terms as *processes* (the -*ification* of the terms) can be seen to be a feature of late twentieth- and twenty-first-century society (post-1970s), insofar as feminist theory and the analysis of global capitalism increased awareness of the intensity and power of these processes and the way more and more areas of social life are turned into objects and commodities (areas of life that are not normally deemed objects or commodities). This is an important shift from Marx, because it extends his concern about the denigration of 'labor' (working people) to a concern about all areas of life that are turned from non-economic to economic identities, i.e. into saleable forms.

Confusing Objects: Commodity, Commoditization, and Commodification

In neoliberal capitalist society (that is the social world following the deregulation of world markets in the 1980s), there is a move to a situation where everything has the potential to be turned into a question of wealth production rather than other systems of value, such that homes become financial assets rather than places to live, education becomes skill investment rather than learning, research becomes business innovation rather than insight or wisdom, and relationships become financial agreements rather than forms of intimacy. It is the increased turning of personal and social life into objects or commodities that results in the theoretical need for terms that represent distinct mutating processes of the late capitalistic world. The increased turning of non-object religious forms—which were not previously objects or commodities—into objects and commodities is the concern of this chapter. This is significant, because there are objects and commodities in cultural/religious traditions that may legitimately be objects and commodities, but the process of turning something that is not an object into an object or commodity raises a key ethical concern.

Here we need to make an important distinction that is cause for a lot of confusion in the discussion of commodity and object in the study of religion. It is a confusion that touches existing debates between economic and anthropological definitions of commodity (see Haugeraud/Stone/Little 2000, 7–9), but demands greater separation from these concerns. It is the distinction between objects that are ethically legitimated to become commodities and those realities that are ethically seen as distinct from objects (such as persons, values, ideas, spirits, gods). The distinction is confused, because of the tradition of devaluing objects in the spirit/matter dualism of the study of religion (see Vásquez 2011). However, since Malinowski (2014 [1922]) and Mauss (2002 [1950]) examined the *kula* ring and gift exchange in the Trobriand Islands, the symbolic and economic aspect of objects is much debated (see Taussig 1980; Appadurai 1986; Kopytoff 1986). These debates have touched a number of important problems: first, the problem of pre-capitalistic societies and objects outside commodity exchange (e.g. Taussig's rethinking of commodity in peasant societies in Columbia and Bolivia); second, the biography of objects and the way objects become and lose their status as commodities (e.g. Kopytoff's ideas of commoditization); and, third, the importance of the social value of objects in everyday life (e.g. Appadurai's discussion of the social life of things).

A central aim of anthropological thinking has been to highlight and explore the signification and codes that surround objects and to recover the religious value of materiality or objects (see, for example, Srinivas 2010). This latter set of debates has resulted in important developments—to some extent responding to consumer trends—to explore religion and materiality (Morgan 2010; Houtman/Meyer 2012; Fleming and Mann 2014; see Morgan, "Materiality," this volume). These aspects of culture are part of the longer recognition of the place of objects and things within life as valid parts of social reality and meaning. The renewed interest in materiality and social objects is to some extent a corrective against Protestant reactions against "scandalous materiality" (Houtman/Meyer 2012, 14) and, as Fleming and Mann (2014, 3–6) indicate, the colonial attitude toward Asian traditions was to see the material culture as "a sign of cultural inferiority." These studies show how the discipline of the study of religion has shaped traditions of idolatry, totemism, and animism as inferior and primitive in the text-based scriptural and belief priorities of Protestant-shaped studies of religion (see Keane 2007). However, the economic category of 'commoditization' and the discussion of materiality and objects are not the primary focus of the processes of objectification and commodification.

In order to separate the present discussion from these very interesting debates around objects and commodity, it is important to underline that although there is a relation to discussions of commodity and commoditization, objectification and commodification are distinct processes insofar as they represent the process of making something into an object or commodity when it is not socially classified or ethically legitimated as an object or commodity. Objectification and commodification raise ethical concerns or "anxieties," as Timothy Bewes (2002, xiv–xv) usefully argues in his study, *Reification*.

They cause unease with, or a refusal of, the 'thingitude' of modern (capitalistic) life. Commodification and objectification refer to dehumanizing processes, though we might add that in wider environmentalist and animal rights discourse this understanding is not just related to 'dehumanization,' but the treating of any life form (non-object) as an object for exploitation, use, and sale.

INHUMANE PROCESSES: FROM KANT AND MARX TO FEMINISM

Although the terms objectification and commodification emerge predominantly in twentieth-century critical theory, their related forms of 'object' and 'commodity' have longer salience in philosophy and political theory. As feminist theorists have underlined, Kant's 1784–85 lectures on "Moral Philosophy" in Königsberg explored the problem of sexual impulses and the making of someone into an "object of appetite" (see Kant 1997; Papadaki 2007). Kant believed that where sexual appetite set aside a person's humanity it turned them into 'a thing.' However, as a person the human being cannot be a 'thing' and become property (Kant 1997, 156). This rejection of objectification in Kantian sexual ethics related to all forms of relationship and applied to both issues of prostitution and masturbation, both of which were seen to reflect a loss of personhood by making bodies merely things for pleasure (including one's own body). For Kant the sexual appetite could only be managed within marriage, because the object of desire was contained within a wider contractual understanding and value of personhood. These concerns about objectification carry aspects of the Christian attitude to sex within marriage and reflect distinctive features of freedom and choice in moral discourse as well as the emerging Western sense of individual rights being potentially undermined by property and possession, which becomes the distinctive feature of Marxist thinking when related to the economic ideas of commodity. It also underlines how commodification and objectification are related in important ways.

Marx (1995 [1867], 11) begins his major work, *Capital*, with a critical analysis of "commodity," because "wealth" in the "capitalist mode of production" is the "accumulation of commodities." Marx defines the commodity as "an object outside us, a thing that by its properties satisfies human wants of some sort or another." The notion is linked to wants and satisfactions and is thus importantly part of the "desire" human beings hold for things (objects). The commodity is "an object outside us" and is open to use. Objects are of use-value—that is they have value because of their use ("an object of utility")—and these uses are established by "convention" (culture). It is the combination of the "physical or natural form" (natural object) and the "value" form (social attitude) that make something a commodity, but the value is established socially through the "exchange" or social relation; what Marx refers to as "the riddle presented by money" (the "money form").

In Marx's discussion, the element that is lost or denied in the use-value and the exchange-value of a thing is the value of labor (people) and thus, by implication, there is a process through which persons and the environment are turned into 'things' for wealth production or satisfaction of wants and desires. Objects become commodities for Marx because of the labor, but this is not shown in the exchange. Borrowing from religious fetishism, Marx argues commodities assume the status of "independent beings endowed with life." Insofar as commodities are separated from the labor, the commodity is a fetish object (that is one endowed with a hidden social value). Marx relates the notion of the fetish to commodity when an object assumes greater importance and meaning, but Marx also saw that the commodity is "abounding in metaphysical subtleties and theological niceties" (Marx 1995, 42).

In summary, commodities hide social values and power relations in the social world and the process of commodification demonstrates the power of those values and relations in society to enforce commodity value on things which are not normally objects for commodification, i.e. labor and the human body. Objects become the social value to the extent that social life and scientific analysis take on the nature of commodities rather than "their actual historical development" and, in turn, there is an 'alienation' from hidden labor-time, which is enforced by the interval of time between labor and exchange. As Postone (1993, 200–202) indicates—exploring time as a dependent and independent variable in relation to Marx's ideas of labor—it sets up a divisive system of "concrete labor" ("sorts of time that are functions of events") alongside "abstract labor" (time "independent of events"), which allows the domination and creates alienating forms of social relation. In turn, time itself becomes a commodity (Postone 1993, 215).

THE DANGERS OF OBJECTIFICATION: PSYCHOSIS, PORNOGRAPHY, AND THE HOLOCAUST

Critical thinking in social theory and feminism extended the discussion of Kant and Marx in various ways. Georg Lukács developed his ideas about commodity and object in *History and Class Consciousness*, with his idea of 'reification' (the making of something into an object). For Lukács (1971, 197) reification is the "necessary, immediate purpose of every person living in capitalist society." Recognizing the importance of Marx beginning his work with the idea of commodity, Lukács sought to consider both the objective social relation alongside the subjective state of alienation in his thinking about commodity and reification. Importantly, linking both objective and subjective features, Lukács (1971, 92) understood the connection between commodity and object to consciousness and objective knowledge. He extended Kant's idea of the 'thing-in-itself' (the problem of knowing) and Marx's commodity (objects of exchange) to show how "rational objectification conceals above all the immediate—qualitative and material—character of things." What counts as objective knowledge was part of the processes of reification and in this way Lukács opened up the cognitive problem of 'things' and the way 'things' are made in the relation of subject to object. Responding to Lukács, Theodor Adorno (2005, 231) developed the same link between thought and object, viewing objectification as a form of 'psychosis.' This relation establishes the key link between objectification and commodification as attitudes or ways of thinking (cognition).

Bridging both Kantian and Marxist critique and linking objectification and commodification, feminist writers such as Andrea Dworkin (1989; 1974) and Catharine Mackinnon (1987) have shown how pornography presents women as sex objects and commodities. As Dworkin (1989, 21) states: "In the realm of money, sex and women are the same commodity." It reveals the close correspondence between the two processes of objectification and commodification, the relation between making somebody into a thing and its salability; hence Lukács's linking of the two as the aims of capitalist society. The link between making women property and their objectification is deeply enmeshed in historical processes of patriarchy and misogyny. These aspects of violence in objectification are identified in John Rector's (2014) insightful exploration of objectification as a psychological process. He examines the spectrum of emotional responses from indifference, through emotional hardening to dehumanization, which result in the capacity for violence and human evil, as in the processes of objectification in the Holocaust (racial bodies as disposable things). The nature of objectification as a cognitive process is significant, even to the point of making thought and cognition an 'object,' which shows how scientific practice, as Lukács understood, can be part of objectification and commodification (see Carrette 2007).

TYPES OF OBJECTIFICATION

Recognizing the complexity of objectification as a process, Martha Nussbaum explored the idea of a range of positions within objectification. Nussbaum (1995, 257) attempts to extend the nature of objectification to seven different forms: instrumentality (treating as a tool), denial of autonomy (treating as lacking autonomy), inertness (treating as lacking agency), fungibility (treating as interchangeable), violability (treating as permissible to smash), ownership (treating as saleable), and denial of subjectivity (treating as lacking experience and feelings). This extension of objectification attempts to widen its scope to positive and negative forms. According to Nussbaum, some forms of objectification, such as instrumentality, denial of autonomy, violability, and denial of subjectivity are always morally wrong, but other forms may be contextually specific in terms of their moral significance. Nussbaum indicates that there may be temporary forms of objectification in romantic love, which echoes Kant's containment of objectification within a relation of wider appreciation of personhood. The central issue in feminist readings of objectification, as Papadaki (2007, 341) discusses, is the problem of 'inequality' in objectification. This raises key issues related to gender and objectification, as becomes manifest in Earl Jackson's (1995) consideration of the male subject in gay pornography. There is a challenge to male domination when the male is made into a passive object of the powerful male gaze of same-sex desire. These tensions reflect the socially specific nature of the ways women's bodies are the focus of objectification and the market extension of bodies as objects of consumption that increase with the circulation of pornography on the Internet.

All these aspects of objectification and commodification illustrate, as we indicated earlier, that, in the study of religion, these processes reflect moral and ethical concerns or anxieties about the way we transform life into objects and commodities for purposes of desire, power, and control. Commodities relate to objects, but not all forms of reality are objects or commodities. All these processes have significant implications for the understanding and reading of religion. The way this shapes religion is the concern of the next section.

RELIGION AS A FACILITATOR OF OBJECTIFICATION AND COMMODIFICATION

If, as we have shown, objectification and commodification are processes of treating a non-object as an object for use, sale, and/or exploitation, then we can approach the literature on religion and commodification with a sharper lens of inquiry. We move beyond a simple consideration of the place of commodity and object within different cultural systems to a specific exploration of those points where 'anxieties' of reification (making non-objects into objects) emerge. In this sense, social, cultural, and religious traditions assert values about the boundary between subject (persons) and objects (things), but through various forms of influence these orders are transgressed. These forms of influence can range from interpersonal cognitive reactions to complex social mechanisms, such as patriarchy, capitalism, or fascism.

Not surprisingly, the notions of objectification and commodification emerge most poignantly in discussions of women and religion and of the marketization of religion and are always related to issues of power. The literature on the intersection of patriarchy and religion is extensive and is considered in depth elsewhere (see Gross 1996). However, we might note, for example, Parentelli (1996, 31) revealing the plight of Catholic women in poverty in Latin America—considered as "'objects' with assigned roles" to service the Vatican hierarchy—as one instance of patriarchy. But equally, we might consider Shehabuddin's (2008,18) discussion of Muslim women in Bangladesh to show that women also have the power of 'resistance' to becoming 'objects' by deploying their religious understanding in specific social action and developmental programs. Nonetheless, the economic disempowerment of women, as Vandana Shiva (1996,

67) indicates, increases the objectification of women as "raw materials" for "[m]an's production of commodities." Objectification of women in religion shapes and supports patriarchal expectations and norms (such as male domination, leadership, and gendered labor division), but it also manifests in more extreme situations, such as temple prostitution (devadasi) in parts of Southern India (Vijaisri 2004). The position of women in religion is often an index of the levels of objectification and commodification (both sexual and economic) at work in social systems.

Prostitution is one of the direct forms of overlap between the processes of objectification and commodification. It is the place where the denial of personhood and commodity exchange are manifest. However, religious symbols and images also become objectified and commodified by exploiting women's bodies. This can be seen in two instances, among many: first, in the use of images of Eve in contemporary advertising (Edwards 2012) and, second, in the Western reception of tantra (Urban 2003). Katie Edwards's insightful study *Admen and Eve* shows how post-feminist advertising (objectifying women for empowerment, fame, and money) uses images of Eve to sell everything from cars to perfume and from restaurants to hair products. As Edwards (2012, 89) indicates, the media industry uses religious images and objectified female sexuality to foster ambitions: "The Eve image often functions as a vehicle, not just for already famous actresses, models and pop stars to connect their persona with the cultural myth of Eve, but for those 'wannabe' celebrity females wishing to become famous through their sexuality." There is here a convergence of objectification and commodification—the hallmarks of capitalism.

In a similar blend of objectification and commodification of women and religion, Hugh Urban's study of tantra shows the shifting imagination of tantra from its archaic etymological root in weaving to forms of secrecy and—eventually—to its reception in the Western marketing context, where it has become "exaggerated and, ultimately, commercialized—celebrated as the sexiest, most tantalizing offering of the exotic Orient" (Urban 2003, 10). Urban (2003, 236) sees a commodification of tantra emerging in Osho-Rajneesh's version of the tradition, which embraced the wider "commodification of sex" in the West, which in turn resulted in the "commodification of ecstasy." Here we see how non-objects (persons, sex, and ecstasy) are made into objects for economic gain and power, not least using women and the exotic East as objects to sell, amongst other things, perfumes, marketed on the basis of a social imaginary of ecstasy, tantra, or the kama sutra.

If objectification is reflective of patriarchy, commodification is reflective of capitalism, but one serves and intensifies the other; insofar as the increased creation or production of objects (or the increase of non-object forms treated as if they were objects) increases the potential saleable nature, market and commodification of the objects in question. With the rise of neoliberal capitalism, the concern with objectification and commodification in religion increased and scholars likewise shifted their focus to the commodification of knowledge about religious things.

THE MARKET OF RELIGIOUS OBJECTS

The notion of 'selling' religion was reframed under neoliberal capitalism in an extension of the market to all areas of life, and it is here that the notion of commodification of religion took its sharpest focus. The extension of market ideals meant that—in the logic of capitalism—the more objects/commodities, the more extensive the exchange and potential profit, a process intensified, according to David Lyon (2000), through the technology of the Internet. In his book *Jesus in Disneyland*, Lyon suggested that the limitless boundaries of the market opened a new world of religious commodification: "In a deregulated marketplace, where cultural commodification practices proliferate, the sacred symbols of religious communication circulate unpredictably, promiscuously" (Lyon 2000, 71). This 'unpredictable' element registers anxiety about the transgression of boundaries around objects and commodities within society. Some objects/commodities can be viewed as part of traditional material cultures of religion (such as icons, relics, bibles, prayer cards, scapulars, rosaries). They are seen to support religious life. However, as the commodity culture extends to a wider range of commercial objects—beyond those deemed as integrated—it becomes more 'promiscuous' (with postcards, mugs, pens, jewelry and T-shirts). Once the domain of objects/commodities stretches beyond that of integrated objects, in a logic subordinated to the maximization of profits, it becomes even more precarious and extends to the commodification of human relations (viewing religious subjects as commercial resources). It is this boundary and its ethical negotiation that scholars of religion interrogate.

The extent of 'selling' emerges in relation to evangelicals in Wade Clark Roof's (1999) *Spiritual Market Place*, in relation to Catholicism in Vincent Miller's (2007) *Consuming Religion* and in relation to spirituality in Carrette and King's (2005) *Selling Spirituality*. We find in all these works a negotiation of a moral limit. These scholars sought to describe the changing nature of religion in a world of intensive commodification and market power and some sought to mark out the perceived moral transgression. Was there a limit to commodization? And where do we find commodification in religion? What is at stake in these texts is the boundary between commodit*ization* (religious objects and materials becoming commodities) and commod*ification* (non-things, such as persons and religious values becoming commodities/objects for profit); the former perceived as legitimate and the latter a transgression. As R. Laurence Moore acknowledged in his study of American Christianity: "the very importance of the phenomenon of commodification, its capacity to fixate our attention, requires us to stop for a moment and remind ourselves that religion is much else besides a commodity" (Moore 1994, 272).

ASIAN OBJECTS: BETWEEN
COMMODITIZATION AND COMMODIFICATION

As Tulasi Srinivas (2010, 283) rightly confirms, commodification is related to globalization, and the rethinking of the place of objects and commodities in interrelated worlds and diverse geopolitical situations raises specific religious and cultural issues; such that global capitalism is embedded in different ways, even as it operates on similar objectifying and commodifying processes. The diversity of cultural contexts also creates different boundaries between commoditization and commodification of religious objects. One area we see this emerge is in recent examinations of the Asian context (see Kitiarsa 2008; Srinivas 2010; Sinha 2011). In an insightful collection of studies examining diverse Asian contexts and religious traditions, Kitiarsa's study reveals the rich, ambiguous, and complex ways commodification emerges around religious practices: from festivals (Cohen), tourist pilgrimages (Askew), and the 'merit-making' industry (Kitiarsa) in Thailand to blessings in Malaysia and China (DeBernardi). Here the tensions between commoditization and commodification become evident. In the context of Vietnam, for example, Salemink (2008, 167) shows—in relation to spirit mediumship and the goddess tradition—how the issue extends beyond objects to "performance as spectacle to be consumed." It raises questions about the ambiguous boundary between traditional rituals and religious tourism and whether it therefore forms legitimate commoditization or unethical commodification.

The distinction between commoditization and commodification is not entirely transparent. In her study of the Sathya Sai movement, for example, Srinivas (2010) examines the complex trade in souvenirs and devotee objects and the specific 'coding and inscription' of objects. She makes a distinction between 'ephemera' (bought objects) and 'sacra' (sacred gifts), which have a magical quality in their closeness to Sai Baba; not unlike medieval relics believed to be close to Christ or the apostles: "since Sai divinity cannot be defined as distinctly other to humanity or material worlds, the relationship between human, object and divinity in the Sai movement is shaded and ambiguous, leading to the object being possibly seen as sublime" (Srinivas 2010, 321). The divine/material ontology is an important part of commoditization, and it redraws the commodification boundary insofar as there is a legitimate making of something into an object. In this sense, we might suggest that religious objects can go through commoditization without facing the moral problem of commodification.

Furthermore, for other scholars there is a clear acknowledgment of value in 'commoditization' (though they often use the word "commodification"), as seen in Sinha's discussion of the 'merchandizing' of Hinduism as a positive rather than negative term, insofar as commodities "feed back into the realm of religious practices" (Sinha 2011, 185). The legitimating rationale of 'feed back' is one based on objects that are seen to be integrated into the religious life as opposed to commoditized objects that are merely established for the sake of maximizing profit. However, while commoditization enables us to see how at times objects, materiality, and commodities can be valued, it also raises ethical concerns about the means of production and exploitation of labor in the creation of the objects, such that (so-called) legitimate commoditization can conceal a hidden objectification of human labor.

Conclusion: Knowledge and 'Religion' as an Object

In this chapter I have sought to make a clear distinction between commoditization and commodification in order to show that the principal concern of objectification and commodification as 'processes' relates to an ethical anxiety about non-object forms (such as persons, ideas, and practices) being made into objects or commodities. My argument has been that objectification and commodification are processes of imagining and relating to the world that arise from a desire to control. Above all, objectification and commodification are processes that hold a moral anxiety about the dehumanization of world in the face of dominant and oppressive modes of thinking and acting. They hold within themselves a sense of loss and distortion and pertain to undermining of basic rights, social equality, and personhood.

The extension of objectification and commodification is such that they are also related to knowledge production in the study of religion as well as wider forms of social reality. The creation of ideas as objects—as things—is one that goes to the heart of thought and imagination and it therefore relates to debates about the category of 'religion' and the way it is made into an object for colonial domination and educational consumption (see Fitzgerald 2000; King 1999). In this sense, scholarly works and textbooks, like perfumes, can become forms of objectification and commodification through the construction and packaging of ideas (like 'Hinduism,' 'religion,' and 'mysticism') for sale in the commercialized publication market. It raises important questions about the reach and extent of objectification and commodification and the importance of critical reflection in the use and exploitation of concepts. There is also the question of how far we make 'thought' an object, as in forms of cognitive psychology that create 'thought' as a thing (see Carrette 2007, 163–203). What becomes clear from these wider considerations of knowledge and objectivity is the depth of ethical concern that objectification and commodification entail. The reach of global capitalism and patriarchy make these processes ever central for the study of religion. They draw attention to the human ability to cognitively relate to the world as objects and commodities and the way this raises the moral stakes of these processes for the future of humanity and personal welfare.

GLOSSARY

Commodification the process through which non-objects (such as persons, values, and practices) are perceived, treated, and valued as commodities or saleable objects.

Commoditization a term from business theory referring to the historical and contextual process through which objects become commodities at any given point in time, implying that objects can gain and lose the status of a commodity in a specific cultural moment and context.

Exchange-value the value of an object in the economic process of exchange.

Fetish commodity Marx's idea that an object carries a greater meaning through the social relation than its physical status alone.

Objectification the process through which persons, values, or ideas are perceived, treated, and valued as objects or things.

Pornography the visual objectification and commodification of bodies for sexual pleasure, exploitation, and power.

Reification the process through which something is made into an object or a thing.

Use-value the value of an object for human use.

REFERENCES

Adorno, Theodor. 2005. *Minima Moralia: Reflections on Damaged Life*. London: Verso. Original edition, 1951.

Appadurai, Arjun, ed. 1986. *The Social Life of Things: Commodities in Cultural Perspective*. Cambridge: Cambridge University Press.

Bewes, Timothy. 2002. *Reification, or The Anxiety of Late Capitalism*. London: Verso.

Carrette, Jeremy. 2007. *Religion and Critical Psychology: Religious Experience in the Knowledge Economy*. London: Routledge.

Carrette, Jeremy and Richard King. 2005. *Selling Spirituality: The Silent Takeover of Religion*. London: Routledge.

Dworkin, Andrea. 1974. *Woman Hating*. New York: Dutton.

Dworkin, Andrea. 1989. *Pornography: Men Possessing Women*. New York: Dutton.

Edwards, Katie B. 2012. Admen and Eve: *The Bible in Contemporary Advertising*. Sheffield: Sheffield Phoenix Press.

Fitzgerald, Timothy. 2000. *The Ideology of Religious Studies*. New York and Oxford: Oxford University Press.

Fleming, Benjamin and Richard Mann, eds. 2014. *Material Culture and Asian Religions: Text, Image, Object*. New York: Routledge.

Haugerud, Angelique, Priscilla Stone, and Peter Little. 2000. *Commodities and Globalization: Anthropological Perspectives*. Oxford: Rowman & Littlefield.

Houtman, Dick and Birgit Meyer. 2012. *Religion and the Question of Materiality*. New York: Fordham University Press.

Gross, Rita. 1996. *Feminism and Religion: An Introduction*. New York: Beacon Press.

Kant, Immanuel. 1997. *Lectures on Ethics*. Translated by Louis Infield. New York: Harper & Row. Original lecture, 1784–1785.

Kant, Immanuel. 1998. *Groundwork of the Metaphysics of Morals*. Translated by Mary Gregor. Cambridge: Cambridge University Press. Original edition, 1785.

Keane, Webb. 2007. *Christian Moderns: Freedom and Fetish in the Mission Encounter.* Berkeley: University of California Press.

King, Richard. 1999. *Orientalism and Religion: Postcolonial Theory, India and 'The Mystic East'.* London: Routledge.

Kitiarsa, Pattana, ed. 2008. *Religious Commodifications in Asia.* New York: Routledge.

Kopytoff, Igor. 1986. "The Cultural Biography of Things: Commoditization as Process." In *The Social Life of Things: Commodities in Cultural Perspective*, edited by Arjun Appadurai. Cambridge: Cambridge University Press, 64–93.

Lukács, Georg. 1971. *History and Class Consciousness.* Translated by Rodney Livingtone. London: Merlin Press. Original edition, 1923.

Lyon, David. 2000. *Jesus in Disneyland: Religion in Postmodern Times.* Cambridge: Polity Press.

MacKinnon, Catharine. 1987. *Feminism Unmodified.* Cambridge, MA: Harvard University Press.

Malinowski, Bronislaw. 2014. *Argonauts of the Western Pacific.* London: Routledge. Original edition, 1922.

Marx, Karl. 1995. *Capital: An Abridged Edition.* Translated by Samuel Moore, Edward Aveling, and David McLellan. Oxford: Oxford University Press. Original edition, 1867.

Mauss, Marcel. 2002. *The Gift.* Translated by W. D. Halls. London: Routledge. Original edition, 1950.

Miller, Vincent. 2007. *Consuming Religion: Christian Faith and Practice in a Consumer Culture.* New York: Continuum.

Moore, R. Laurence. 1994. *Selling God: American Religion in the Marketplace of Culture.* New York and Oxford: Oxford University Press.

Morgan, David, ed. 2010. *Religion and Material Culture: The Matter of Belief.* London: Routledge.

Nussbaum, Martha. 1995. "Objectification." *Philosophy and Public Affairs* 24(4): 249–291.

Papadaki, Evangelia. 2007. "Sexual Objectification: From Kant to Contemporary Feminism." *Contemporary Political Theory* 6(3): 330–348. doi: 10.1057/palgrave.cpt.9300282

Parentelli, Gladys. 1996. "Latin America's Poor Women: Inherent Guardians of Life." In *Women Healing Earth: Third World Women on Ecology, Feminism and Religion*, edited by Rosemary Radford Ruether. Maryknoll, NY: Orbis Books, 29–38.

Postone, Moishe. 1993. *Time, Labor, and Social Domination.* Cambridge: Cambridge University Press.

Rector, John. 2014. *The Objectification Spectrum: Understanding and Transcending our Diminishment and Dehumanization of Others.* Oxford: Oxford University Press.

Salemink, Oscar. 2008. "Spirits of Consumption and the Capitalist Ethic in Vietnam." In *Religious Commodifications in Asia*, edited by Pattana Kitiarsa. New York: Routledge, 147–168.

Shehabuddin, Elora. 2008. *Reshaping the Holy: Democracy, Development and Muslim Women in Bangladesh.* New York: Columbia University Press.

Shiva, Vandana. 1996 "Let Us Survive: Women, Ecology and Development". In *Women Healing Earth: Third World Women on Ecology, Feminism and Religion*, edited by Rosemary Radford Ruether. Maryknoll, NY: Orbis Books, 65–73.

Sinha, Vineeta. 2011. *Religion and Commodification: 'Merchandizing' Diasporic Hinduism.* New York: Routledge.

Srinivas, Tulasi. 2010. *Wings of Faith: Rethinking Globalization and Religious Pluralism Through the Sathya Sai Movement.* New York: Columbia University Press.

Taussig, Michael. 1980. *The Devil and Commodity Fetishism in South America*. Chapel Hill: University of North Carolina Press.

Urban, Hugh B. 2003. *Tantra: Sex, Secrecy, Politics, and Power in the Study of Religion*. Berkeley, CA: University of California Press.

Vásquez, Manuel. 2011. *More Than Belief: A Materialist Theory of Religion*. Oxford: Oxford University Press.

Vijaisri, Priyadashini. 2004. *Recasting the Devadasi: Patterns of Sacred Prostitution in Colonial South India*. New Delhi: Kanishka Publishers.

FURTHER READING

Carrette/King 2005 [*A critical discussion of the late-capitalist drive for profit and how this has extended to include all aspects of human life, including spirituality.*]

Kitiarsa 2008 [*A useful collection of essays examining the diverse ways religious traditions across Asia face aspects of commodification. It reveals both the positive and negative interactions of capitalism, materiality, and religion.*]

Marx 1995 [1867] [*This offers Marx's classic analysis of capitalism, the means of production, and the exploitation of labor. It examines the nature and form of commodity and is foundational for understanding processes of commodification.*]

Nussbaum 1995 [*This is a foundational essay in thinking about the nature and complexity of objectification, its definition and ambiguities.*]

Rector 2014 [*An insightful psychological discussion of the ways the processes of objectification create dehumanization.*]

....

CHAPTER 49

SYNCRETISM AND HYBRIDIZATION

....

PAUL CHRISTOPHER JOHNSON

CHAPTER SUMMARY

....

- There is a wide range of terms of religious mixture including syncretism and hybridization but also terms like creolization, transculturation, and métissage.
- These competing terms of mixture possess different genealogies and impinge on 'religion' differently, such that they should not be simply interchanged or arbitrarily applied.
- Terms of religious mixture have been unevenly deployed. Brazil and Japan, for example, have often been studied as examples of syncretism. Theories of mixture are entwined with, and help to constitute certain religious geographies or 'worlds.'
- Despite calls for the removal of 'syncretism' and other terms of mixture from the scholarly lexicon, they are as vibrant and widely used as ever, even enjoying a renaissance via other fields like Science and Technology Studies. Recent revivals of terms of mixture in adjacent fields offer potential new applications in the study of religion.

From Herodotus's *Histories*—which related Zeus to Ammon, Apollo to Horus, and Hephaistos to Ptah—to Sir Thomas Roe's early seventeeth-century description of the sadly "mingled" Islam he saw on the island of Molalia near Madagascar (1905 [1625], 451), travelers and philosophers have long taken note of religions' fuzzy boundaries and permeability. Even religious 'rigorists' are "latitudinarians of coalition, whom we may call *syncretists*," wrote Kant in 1793 (1960, 18). Yet it was only in the last century that the vocabulary of mixture was systematically extended, coming to include not only the old words like syncretism but also new words like hybridity, creolization, métissage, transculturation, and more. This proliferation can be seen as itself a historical product of a place vividly described by Michel Foucault: "nineteenth-century Europe: the land of interminglings and bastardy, the period of the 'man-of-mixture'" (1984, 92). With the phrase, "man-of-mixture," Foucault referenced both the empirical coupling that colonial ventures produced and the specter of the decline of Europe, but also the nineteenth-century study of evolutionism. To counter the 'interminglings' and the decline they might cause, Europeans created their own imagined purity, whether in race or religion, by discovering bastards and illegitimately-born religions everywhere on colonial shores. So effective was this venture that even the study of such 'mixed' religions was suspect in the academy, hence the general scholarly disinterest, for example, in Caribbean religions prior to *circa* 1980 (Trouillot 1992). Wrote Paul Gilroy, "from the viewpoint of ethnic absolutism, this [creolization, métissage, mestizaje, hybridity] would be a litany of pollution and impurity" (Gilroy 1993, 2). The fantasy of purity gained force in proportion to fears of dangerous social mixture produced by conquests, the slave trade, colonialism, migration, exile, and diaspora, among many historical sources. Over the past several decades, in part as a postcolonial critique, the occidental fantasy of 'pure religion' has itself become suspect, and the concept of mixture has become a standard requisite for thinking about religion in general. Ever since that shift, scholars have again been obliged to consider different models of religious 'interminglings,' and the affordances and liabilities of each.

This is no easy task, since the mix-list only continues to expand, with additions like 'combinative' (Grapard 2002; Albanese 2012), or 'recombinant culturology' (Strathern 1996), not to mention earlier words still on the menu for recuperation like Van der Leeuw's preferred term, "transposition" (*Verschiebung*) (1963, 610). These words seek to name an alternative to other logically possible outcomes of religious encounter, which must include at least conversion, rejection, and adjacency. In ideal-typical terms, 'conversion' connotes the complete adoption by one individual or group of another's tradition. Adjacency or parallelism, by contrast, describes a situation in which two or more traditions dwell side-by-side but with little or no mutual influence or interpenetration. Roger Bastide named this logical possibility "mosaic syncretism," using the metaphor of a collage composed of multiple bounded pieces (1972, 69, 82, 88). There are multiple forms of potential 'synthesis,' which Michael Pye described as the (however provisional) conclusion of a process of encounter between traditions. 'Syncretism,' by contrast connotes in his terminology an open-ended, ongoing debate between live options (Pye 1994).

It seems clear that we should locate the syncretic process as one among multiple possible outcomes of complex interreligious encounters. Scholars apply terms like hybridization or syncretization in order to 'cut' into interreligious encounters and freeze a moment for analytical purposes (Strathern 1996, 522). The term one selects may set up the analytical cut in a particular way, yet the words are mostly applied carelessly, and in lamentably uniform ways. Syncretism is used indistinguishably from creolization, and the hybrid much like the transcultural. This flattening does not serve us well, and we can profit from restoring at least modest specificity to each entry (Stewart 2007, 6).

To begin a project of redress, this chapter will first plot the field of terms within which syncretism and analogous mix-terms signify. The second section briefly rehearses genealogies; the third considers the main criticisms of the word syncretism; the fourth section offers examples of two religious traditions studied *as* syncretic, from Brazil and Japan; and the final section considers revivals and recommendations for future applications of syncretism and hybridization.

Plotting the Semantic Field

In order to answer the question: what are the possible uses of syncretism or hybridization? we should first locate them within a field of alternatives. Here I present several of the most common terms.

Mestizaje/Mestiçagem/Métissage

This set has been especially used to describe processes of racial mixture. The cluster is encumbered by ideological liabilities, especially in Latin America, where it has been variously invoked as a lament and call-to-arms to racially purify the nation or, as in twentieth-century Mexico and Brazil, a glorified and mostly specious claim of post-racial national distinction (e.g. Vasconcelos 1925; Freyre 2003 [1933]). The rubric gained little traction in the study of religion. Noteworthy for our purposes, however, was James Scott's use of *métis* as a form of knowledge: Scott nominated as 'Métis' the knowledge forms that are mixed and contingent, local and practical, fragmentary, implicit, permeable, open-ended, and learned in practice, over against 'Techne,' standardized scientific knowledge that claims its own universal status (1998, 309–341). The reason I call attention to Scott's intervention is that what he called 'Métis' knowledge is not infrequently also 'religious' knowledge, a rapport with the world acquired in tacit ritual practice.

Hybridity

This word expanded dramatically over the course of the nineteenth century, carried on discursive currents of biology, breeding, evolution, and race. Hybridity bridged and linked plant morphology, animal husbandry, and discourses of race and nationalism. Only later in its career was it applied to questions of culture, including religious cultures (e.g. Young 1995; Engler 2015). I first encountered references to 'human hybridity' in print after 1865, and to 'cultural hybridity' not before 1934, and accelerating in usage only decades thereafter.

Among the term's most celebrated mid-twentieth-century applicants was Mikhail Bakhtin, who used 'hybridization' as a keyword for describing how novelistic discourse works: "What is a hybridization? It is a mixture of two social languages within the limits of a single utterance, an encounter, within the arena of an utterance, between two different linguistic consciousnesses, separated from one another by an epoch, by social differentiation or by some other factor" (Bakhtin 1981, 359). Useful for our purposes is Bakhtin's distinction between intentional or conscious hybridity versus unconscious, everyday linguistic hybridizations. This has value for students of religion because it reminds us to distinguish the deliberate efforts toward combining parts of various religious traditions from unintentional or unconscious borrowing or interpenetration (see also Kamstra 1967, 9). Scholars of religion should also pay attention to Bakhtin's notion of *parodia sacra*, those hybrids that blend so-called vulgar and sacred words or modes of speech (Bakhtin 1981, 77).

In the decades after Bakhtin, scholars from multiple disciplines leveraged hybridity to critique the idea and ideal of purity whatsoever—moving from the question of textual purity to social domains—and thereby expose and defuse the power of 'purity' as an ideological artifact, whether nationalist, racialist, ethnic, or religious. This was a powerful postcolonial intervention (Bhabha 1994; García-Canclini 1995). "Places of hybridity," wrote Bhabha, "[are] . . . where the construction of a political subject that is new, *neither one nor the other*, properly alienates our political expectations" (1994, 37; emphasis added). Here the phrase, "neither one nor the other" referred to established political positions such as 'right' and 'left.' Bhabha proposed that hybridity could shift the very idea and practice of politics by lifting it out of its entrenched names and parties. Moreover, he argued, positing hybridity as a value could destabilize colonial symbols (e.g. flags, names of streets, monuments) whose force was premised on their capacity to convey ethnic, racial, or national purity. Take, for example, the many monuments and memorials devoted to British magnates like Cecil Rhodes, or Afrikaner leaders like Paul Kruger, that still impose their presence on cityscapes of South Africa.

In a similarly critical vein, Néstor García Canclini used hybridity to analyze the mixing and exchange between previously distinct classes of 'high culture' and 'popular' or mass culture. And for Serge Gruzinski, hybridity aptly describes the interpenetration of temporal frames in cities like Hong Kong or Mexico City, where the simultaneous presence of the symbols of past and present introduces a "double time frame" and, in a sense, an experience of double consciousness, especially for indigenous residents of metropolitan centers (2002, 207).

These interdisciplinary interventions made hybridity productive by drawing religion into conversation with postcolonial studies, cultural studies, and other fields. Yet if hybridity is and was frequently applied to anti-colonial and emancipatory causes, the word also carries risks. Pnina Werbner (2001) decried "interruptive hybridity" (149) perceived as demeaning for indigenous groups for whom the persuasive impression of boundedness and unchanging tradition are politically crucial. Werbner argued that these groups have their own, indigenous forms of transgressive critique and revision, and are harmed rather than helped by scholars from outside informing them of their hybridity.

In recent work on religion, Steven Engler reworked the term to generate the complex phrase "hybridity of *refraction*." This refers to the way in which social boundaries that are activated and reworked within a system of religious beliefs and practices reflect, refract, and combine with homologous boundaries present in a given society (Engler 2009,

23). In other words, Engler's hybrid describes the ways ritual frames become linked to other social frames—socio-economic, cultural, ethno-religious, gender. Engler pushes scholars of religion to consider how power acquired in religious contexts is inflected by broader social notions of gender, race, or class, or resists them; and how religious power works or fails when carried outside a specifically 'religious' frame of action.

Finally, Bruno Latour and his many disciples have used hybridity to dethrone the alleged purity of human agency as distinct from the agency of other animals and things (1993; 2010). Latour describes, for example, the 'hybrid' of man and cigarette where it is unclear which one is in control (2010, 55). Latour is important for the study of religion because he calls attention to materials and environments, and the ways religious ideas, discourses, practices, and communities are co-constituted by the things and procedures they use, complicating notions of religious agency with a concern for how things, and not only persons, wield agency. Even more radically, Latour's idea of hybridity pushes us to even consider the question of whether and to what degree 'religion' is a uniquely human event, or rather a way of perceiving agency that may be shared with other kinds of beings (cf. Kohn 2013, 41).

Creolization

Criollo or creole came from the Portuguese *criado*, meaning to be "created," in the sense of being raised or bred. In the first uses of the term, creole communities were those born and bred in the New World; thus in the sixteenth century the term denoted white Europeans born in the Americas as distinguished from *peninsulares* or other European-born metropolitans. Its first connotation was of purity, not mixture (Stewart 2007, 5). Benedict Anderson (1983) famously wrote of "creole nationalisms," and their ideological flipside, "creole racisms," as those born in the Americas were soon accused of being of mixed blood compared with the European-born; that is, of being hybrids. Anderson used the actual term 'hybrid' only once, in relation to the linguistic conjunction 'Indochine'; and he did not use processual terms like creolization or hybridization, which seem to have arrived only in the 1990s. Beginning in the eighteenth century, *creoles* were peoples of partly African descent raised in slave colonies of the Americas, differentiated from the African continent itself, or *negros 'da costa'* (Portuguese).

In the twentieth century, creolization began to be used by linguistics to describe the formation of 'creolized languages' (Palmié 2006; 2007). Leonard Bloomfield's foundational 1933 linguistics essay, "Intimate Borrowing," described linguistic creolization:

> a subject group gives up its native language in favor of a jargon. This happens especially when the subject group is made up of persons from different speech-communities, who can communicate among themselves only by means of the jargon. This was the case, presumably, among Negro slaves in many parts of America. When the jargon has become the only language of the subject group, it is a creolized language. (1965, 473–474)

Just as in linguistics the study of creole languages has become fundamental to learning about language-building whatsoever, so too in religion the study of creolization and creole religions has turned out to be crucial to understanding the making of 'religious tradition,' moving putative mixtures and their study from the margins of theoretical reflection to its very center. The idea is that every religion begins as a relatively improvised jargon drawn from multiple sources, just like new languages. As such, the key question of origins has shifted away from "Where did it come from?" to "Why, from among the infinite bits of information that cross awareness, are certain things, words, persons, practices selected, remembered, recalled, authorized, and established as *a religion*?" From linguistics, then, by analogy to creole languages (Mintz 2008, 257), the word was applied to cultures: "[C]reole cultures like creole languages are those which draw in some way on two or more historical sources, often originally widely different" (Hannerz 1987, 552). Sidney Mintz, a foundational figure in the study of creole cultures of the Caribbean, made clear that creolization referred to something new being born, not just mimesis of extant societies whether European or African: "I mean that creolization was not primarily about mixing cultures; it was about building new institutions." (Mintz 2008, 258).

Creolization has most often referred to cultures formed through and in colonial situations (Khan 2007) blending, for example, European languages and practices with South Asian or African ones. Though some scholars have expanded creolization to refer to global processes (Hannerz 1987), others continue to insist on its historic and geographic specificity to the Caribbean (e.g. Mintz 2010, 189–190). Important for students of religion is Mintz's principle that a 'creole religion' is less a selective replication than a new creation, a new religion generated from the challenge of two traditions to forge a new working 'language.' Language is key to the creolization paradigm.

Transculturation

Transculturation was also an intellectual product of the Caribbean, a neologism that first appeared in Fernando Ortiz's *Cuban Counterpoint: Tobacco and Sugar* (first published in 1940) as a modification of the then-fashionable term, *acculturation*. Ortiz used transculturation alongside syncretism, sometimes in the same paragraph and in more or less interchangeable ways (1995, 98).

Transculturation nuanced acculturation by insisting that even cultural losses, and the responses to loss, continued to inform the experience of a new territory and generate new practices both among the colonized and the colonizers. This latter point—the ways metropolitan modes of representation are transformed in 'contact zones' of the periphery—became a central theme of Mary Louise Pratt's *Imperial Eyes: Travel Writing and Transculturation* (1992), the work that brought transculturation into common usage across disciplines, at least for anglophones. Roger Bastide had used 'transculturation' in 1945, in a private letter to Arthur Ramos (Document 31, Archivo Arthur Ramos, Biblioteca Nacional do Brasil, Rio de Janeiro). Yet to my knowledge Bastide never used the word in print, thus he should not be seen as a primary primogeniture. Like métissage, transculturation has gained less traction than hybridization, creolization, or syncretism among scholars of religion.

Syncretism

"Syncretism still?," one is tempted to ask. Yet in publications on religion, syncretism dominates the rival terms named above (Engler 2009). The word's etymology and early history are well documented (e.g. Rudolph 2004; Martin 1983; 2001). The Greek word syncretism derives from Plutarch's *Moralia*, appearing in the essay "On Brotherly Love": "[the Cretans] often quarreled with and warred against each other, made up their differences and united when outside enemies attacked; and this it was which they called 'syncretism'" (1939, 314). In that original appearance, the word held a positive valence as a tactic or strategy (Shaw/Stewart 1994, 3).

Syncretism was applied in early Christianity to describe the mixture and alliance between Hellenistic and Christian ideas and practices, but it shifted to describe the process of conversions to Christianity, acquiring a pejorative connotation when applied to new Christians considered to be overly Hellenized. In the early Renaissance, Erasmus drew on Plutarch's description of the Cretan proverb, and brought the term into Latin usage by 1517 (Erasmus 1982, 60). For Erasmus it again denoted an alliance drawn between enemies in opposition to a common foe, but Erasmus like Zwingli makes reference to factions of rival Christians in Western Europe's wars of religion, bitter enemies who nevertheless join military forces in their thirst for vengeance over religious rivals.

Between 1600 and 1650 a key shift in meaning occurred from the positive sense of strategic alliance to the negative sense of improper or dangerous mixture. The shift revolved around the debate about writings of Stephan Georg (1586–1656), a Lutheran theologian and professor from Helmstedt who endeavored to find common ground with Catholics during the Thirty Years War based on a few core tenets. He was accused by his rivals of being 'syncretist,' his followers were called Syncretists, and their campaign took the title of the Syncretistic Controversy (c.1645–1686). In 1648 Johann Konrad Dannhauer's work *Mysterium syncretismi* compared Lutheranism to an eye that cannot stand a particle of dust, and Protestantism and Catholicism to chemicals that cannot combine (Herzog et al. 1911, 219; Rudolph 2004, 69–70). After this juncture, syncretism consistently was used as an accusation against the practice of illegitimate forms of Christianity. Important to note is that after 1650, syncretism was rarely a self-selected descriptor, but rather usually one applied to a group by critical outsiders, though Kurt Rudolph has documented occasional Christian and Hindu thinkers who embraced the moniker as a positive value (2004, 73).

During the nineteenth century, syncretism was used in an expanded sense as a comparative adjective applied to religions. Predictably, the term oscillated between positive uses, as a description of cosmopolitan exchange, and negative ones, as religions considered shallow, fickle, and insubstantial. Since the second half of the nineteenth century, syncretism has been used as an etic term of comparative analysis as well as an emic term used by religious actors themselves, either to criticize rivals within their own tradition, or other traditions perceived as competitors. For a century after 1870, it existed on two tracks—one of religious practice, and one of the academic study of religion. Oscillations between 'positive' and critical significations of syncretism continued to the present. The negative accusations we are already familiar with. In the positive vein, syncretism was sometimes invoked to signal cosmopolitanism and ecumenical religious exchange; and late nineteenth-century movements like Theosophy and early twentieth-century religions like Umbanda in Brazil, and other progenitors of the so-called 'New Age', took pride in adaptive 'mixing', cutting against the usual grain of religions' claims to unchanging tradition (Kraft 2002; Sansi 2007; Engler 2009).

Terms of Religious Mixture as an Assemblage

When we compare the terms for mixture, *syncretism* has mostly been applied to religions, often to skewer traditions perceived as incoherent and lacking depth. *Hybridity* has mostly been applied to organisms—to plants, animals, and questions of breeding and 'race'. More recently, mostly due to the influence of Latour and the rise of Science and Technology Studies (STS), it has become the pre-eminent word used in descriptions of techno-organic blends, or the mutual interpenetrations of scientific methods, religious hermeneutics, and the material and cultural ecologies within which 'science' or 'religion' are produced. *Creolization*, meanwhile, is the standard term linguists apply to early forms of language-formation as forged alongside more established languages, even above the protests of some like Mintz who see creolization as specific to societies formed under plantation slavery that generated cultures and languages independent of the master-class. In short, syncretism's primary domain was ritual; hybridity's was biology; creolization's was language. The decision to foreground one or another of these terms in the study of religion may depend on how one intends to situate a given interpretation. To some degree these intertwined terms of mixture are now interchangeable, or at least they are often used that way. Yet because each term was embedded in a different genealogy, each proffers different theoretical affordances. I do not have space to explore this idea further here, but we should presume that analyzing a given religious tradition as a process of 'syncretization' suggests different possibilities than analyzing it in terms of 'hybridity'. Analyzing a tradition as a 'hybrid' may have different implications than thinking of it through the prism of 'creolization'. Regional tendencies may also affect which term is preferred: *the melting pot* is a common image, for example, in North America but not elsewhere; *mestizaje* is frequent in Latin America but less so elsewhere; and *creolization* is most local and 'at home' in the Caribbean (Khan 2004, 165).

Etymologies and historical tendencies of usage do not determine definition or meaning, however, and a transculturation of academic disciplines, so to say, is underway. Whereas syncretism was traditionally the province of scholars of religion, it crossed into social scientific and now even history of science uses. Roland Barthes, for example, used the phrase 'planned syncretism' to describe how the bourgeois class merged its interests into nationalism and, with this masking ('ex-nominating'), transformed its own class interests into the 'natural' order of things (Barthes 1982, 126). Meanwhile 'hybridity' is now frequently wielded as a tool in the study of religion. Moreover, the very framing of 'the human' or 'the world' that once undergirded applications of both terms has been troubled. For example, what is the nature of human beings in whom religions or other cultural forms are being 'mixed'? Where do these assemblages reside—in memory, in the brain, in the bodily repertory, in emotion, in language? The increasing technological participation in human systems and shifting knowledge about humanness have reanimated syncretism and hybridity as key words of the scholarly lexicon.

Dual Points of Entry

Syncretism entered scholarly discourse on religion through the two distinct paths, the study of religion and of anthropology. In the study of religion, early Christianity and the Hellenic world are the root cases. For anthropology the root case was Afro-Brazilian religions and, by extension, Afro-American religions in general. In the study of religion, William Robertson Smith, in the first lecture of his *Religion of the Semites* (1894), referred to the period of religious syncretism, "when different faiths and worships began to react on one another, and produce new and complex forms of religion" (15). Joachim Wach also broached the topic, and was critical of the part scholars played in generating shallow syncretisms:

> Since the end of the initial phase in which the contact was established between scholars of different nations and faiths, it has become ever more manifest that the vague syncretism characterizing some of the gatherings of those of different faiths around the turn of the last century cannot fulfill the demands of the newly awakened religious consciousness nor stand the scrutiny of a strong constructive philosophical interest. (1999, 492)

In the anthropology of religion, Roger Bastide, among others, credited Raimundo Nina Rodrigues, the first ethnographer of Afro-Brazilian religions, with the notion. To be precise, though he described phenomena that later were studied as 'syncretic'—the juxtaposition in practice of Catholic saints and West African deities called *orixás*—Nina Rodrigues never actually used the word syncretism, though he did invoke métissage (for example, in a letter to the criminal psychiatrist M. A. Lacassagne in Lyon, on November 16, 1899 [Fonds Lacassagne, MS 5255, Feuillets 87–90]). Rather, Marcel Mauss used it in his short review of Nina Rodrigues's book, published in *L'année sociologique* in 1901–1902. In fact Mauss used 'syncretism' in multiple reviews he drafted for *L'année sociologique* in the late 1890s and early 1900s. In my reading, the Brazilian scholar Arthur Ramos acquired the word from reading Mauss's review of Nina Rodrigues. Melville Herskovits in turn began to invoke 'syncretism' after his 1936 presentation in Bahia, Brazil, and he credited Ramos with its first usage in relation to Afro-Brazilian religions

(Herskovits 1958, xxxvi). It was from Herskovits that 'syncretism' entered the twentieth-century anthropological lexicon (Apter 1991).[1]

CRITICISMS

Though the usage of syncretism expanded during the twentieth century, the term was on multiple occasions nearly banished. The main problem was that *all* traditions emerge from a confluence of multiple streams and are in that sense syncretic. If everything is syncretic, critics wrote, than the word serves no purpose, since it fails to classify or distinguish anything. "Every religion," noted Wach in 1924, "has its own previous history and is to a certain extent a 'syncretism'" (86). Van der Leeuw echoed this in 1933, and Robert Baird administered the *coup de grâce* in 1971: "to say that 'Christianity' or the 'mystery religions' or 'Hinduism' are syncretistic is not to say anything that distinguishes them from anything else [and] is merely equivalent to admitting that each has a history and can be studied historically' (146). Syncretism, as the process of religious change and exchange, is simply part and parcel of being in history whatsoever. There are no religions that have not formed as a result of historical encounters.

Second and equally damning, after the postcolonial turn of the 1960s, syncretism was considered as an exercise of power by which Christianity and its European apologists had long delegitimized and marginalized other traditions. As Gustavo Benavides put it, "The concept of syncretism can be regarded . . . as fulfilling now the same role fulfilled in previous centuries by witchcraft, for just as in earlier centuries clerics could define Andean transformations of European Christianity as illegitimate and dangerous, in the twentieth century anthropologists, some of them still acting as missionaries, would define it as perhaps colorful, but nevertheless, illegitimate" (1995, 37).[2]

---

[1] Herskovits was not overly invested in the word syncretism, however, as indicated in a letter he wrote to Roger Bastide on September 1, 1950: "It is gratifying to know that you agree with my position basically in these matters. As concerns the matter of communal labor, I do not think that there is any real difference of opinion between us. I also feel that there is no essential difference in the matter of the synchretisms [sic] on which you comment. My own feeling about these matters is that problem is more important than terminology, and if you feel that 'convergence' is the proper word to use for the phenomenon, it is quite all right with me." IMEC (Institut Memoires de l'Edition Contemporaraine), Fonds Roger Bastide BST2.N1-02.05.

[2] Sydney Greenfield (1998) argued for the need to see the political context of Boas and Herskovits, namely their use of "syncretism" as part of a program for thinking about assimilation in order to oppose the crisis of United States racism, the rise of the Ku Klux Klan, and other dangers.

CASE STUDIES: BRAZIL AND JAPAN

Afro-Brazilian Religions

Multiple Afro-Brazilian religions—Macumba, Quimbanda, Umbanda, Candomblé, even Espiritismo—form a coherent system organized around a "syncretic dynamic" (Hess 1992, 151). Candomblé in particular, like other religions of the African diaspora, was cast by Arthur Ramos and many others as a tradition of 'syncretism.' Borrowing from Ramos, Herskovits (1937; 1958) noted the nominal Catholicism of Africans. He suggested that Catholicism was mostly a superficies that overlay a deeper and more authentic African religious identity (cf. Pérez y Mena 1995, 140).[3] Roger Bastide traced such subterfuge to the historical moment when "whites had to be given the impression that members of the 'nations' were good Catholics" (Bastide 1978, 272), though he later argued that the Catholic saints became as effective at evoking real religious sentiments for Africans as the orixás. Due to a process of forced conversion, at least in external forms like baptism and calendrical adherence to saints' days, to the Roman Catholic Church, enslaved Africans learned to classify orixás in relation to iconically matched Catholic saints: Saint Lazarus with Obaluaê, the feared orixá of disease, Our Lady of the Conception with Yemanjá, the motherly water orixá, and so on. The syncretism of Catholic saints and African gods was not always opposed by ecclesiastical authorities, moreover, but rather was sometimes viewed as a positive step on the path toward conversion to Catholicism.

In this scholarly syncretic script, African religions were pure and authentic before becoming diluted by Brazilian Catholicism. This position was most stridently presented by the revered Candomblé priestess Mother Stella since 1983, who pressed contemporary devotees of Candomblé to renounce the Catholic saints and purify the true African tradition, since devotion to the saints was a contingency of the simulated 'conversions' required under slavery but not in the present (Azevedo dos Santos 1995).

Many Candomblé *terreiros* (temples and their grounds), though, insisted that the Catholic saints are part of 'the tradition,' and that to abandon them would be to reject their houses' ancestry. Practitioners say that orixás and saints, while similar and often matched, are not identical. Pérez y Mena (1995) suggested for the Puerto Rican context that they serve different areas of need: the saints responding to heaven and the afterlife, the orixás responding to immediate worldly needs. Judith Gleason (2000, 268), writing of Afro-Cuban practice, roughly echoed this position: the Catholic saints are austere and patient listeners located in iconic images; they neither dance nor wish for sacrificial

---

[3] This is not generally the case with Herskovits's language of reciprocal influence, "reconciliation", "correspondence," and "synthesis," terms which do not of necessity connote a hierarchic order in the meeting of cultures (Herskovits 1958, 16–17).

offerings beyond flowers and candles. The orixás, by contrast, dance and are always 'hungry.'

Saints and orixás were 'syncretically' combined in Candomblé practice but not utterly fused. They were combined in part as a strategic discursive 'switch' enabling initiates to effectively communicate with multiple audiences, a skill crucial to Candomblé's survival.

Japan

Like Brazil, Japan has long been interpreted through the prism of syncretism (e.g. Kamstra 1967; Pye 1994; 2013). As Allan G. Grapard (1992) described, Shinto and Buddhist practices and sites were thoroughly intertwined for most of Japanese history. The Kasuga Shrine ('Shinto') and the Kofukuji Temple ('Buddhist') together comprised a 'combinatory' ritual multiplex in the city of Nara, which grew up to serve the needs of this syncretic cultic center. In fact, Grapard notes, 'Shinto' itself emerged as a confluence of Confucianism, Taoism, and shamanic practices. From the eighth century forward, *kami*—spirits of nature and ancestral lineages—of the Kasuga Shrine, and *buddhas* and *boddhisatvas* of the Kofukuji Temple have been closely associated with one another in Nara. Together the kami, buddhas, and boddhisatvas wove a ritual repertory that related people to a specific place, time, and lineage. Today as 1,000 years ago, Buddhist monks chant scriptures before the kamis' shrine (Grapard 1992, 7, 73; cf. Pye 1994, 223–229). This is not surprising, since most Buddhist temples in Japan were built right next to kami shrines or sacred sites, reflecting the ways Buddhism entered Japan via a close association and engagement with Shinto and its aesthetics and practices. From the ninth century at least, certain kami have been also regarded as Buddhist boddhisatvas and vice versa, beginning with the kami of war and warriors called Hachiman (Grapard 1992, 79–80), much revered by the Samurai.

The associations between kami and buddhas/boddhisatvas were not random but followed structured rules—linguistic, socio-political, and material. Among Grapard's key points is that combinatory associations were and are not haphazard but rather structured and historically specific. Therefore the combinatory form carries within it an historical archive, however opaque, including an archive of power. This particular syncretic assemblage, for example, expressed and fortified the political legitimacy of the Fujiwara house (51) and later the imperial lineage (61).

With the arrival of the Meiji Restoration in 1868, Shinto was mandated to purify itself of Buddhism, regarded as politically suspect, but under this duress the Buddhist priests of the Kojukuji Temple simply donned new robes and moved to the nearby building to become Shinto priests of Kasuga Shrine (250). Grapard makes another key intervention here, showing how discrete 'religions' are produced through the labor of purification and the exercise of power. This abrupt effort to carefully distinguish Shinto from Buddhism was the exception not the rule in Japanese history; by far the more common pattern was of fluid borrowing and exchange. As in the case of Candomblé in Brazil, 'anti-syncretic' purification attempts are uncommon and usually generated by specific leaders motivated by specific ideological aims such as the burnishing of African or Japanese authenticity through "syncretic re-archaization" hearkening back to a time "before contamination" (Naficy 1993, 20).

REVIVALS AND RECOMMENDATIONS

Given the serious criticism levied above, do syncretism, hybridity, and other terms of mixture have a future? Yes, they do. As Charles Stewart argued, we can agree that everything is mixed without conceding that all religions are mixtures in just the same way (Stewart 2011, 52–53; Pye 1994, 220). What significant distinctions can be drawn between and among *kinds* of mixtures?

First, we should distinguish intentional syncretic acts and movements as a form of religious *practice* from the generic processes of borrowing that characterize all traditions, and all cultural forms. For example, Siv Ellen Kraft described the "hypersyncretic" discourses in Theosophy (2002, 150), a tradition that proudly and overtly borrowed from Hindu and Buddhist traditions, among others.

Second, we should pay attention to the specific forms, processes, and sites of combination—why *that* particular kami was associated with *that* particular boddhisatva, or *that* particular saint with *that* specific orixá. Terms of mixture begin with, and depart from, terms of wholeness and vice versa. This parsing calls into being a map of what can be divided and then recombined. Syncretism or hybridity require 'worlds' of parallel entities that can or could be juxtaposed or joined. We don't usually imagine or posit the creole, hybrid, or syncretic possibilities of, say, dogs and planets, or Augustinian theodicy and snow tires, because such entities occupy different worlds. We should treat the syncretic form as an historical archive worth investigating, since syncretic associations specify the viable possibilities of exchange. By paying attention to a given tradition's syncretic habits we learn about the worlds they make and dwell in.

Third, we can take note of the *rate* of syncretizing events and the temporal lumpiness of history and history-making. Perhaps the emergence of the Hellenistic world and the birth of Rastafari in Jamaica both could be described as entailing 'syncretic' processes, but the former was a project shaped over centuries, while the latter erupted rapidly after 1930 as Garveyism's messages were calibrated with the crowning of a new Ethiopian king, Haile Selassie. The difference in the speed of syncretic process calls for interpretation and a reckoning of difference.

Fourth, we should attend to the *politics* of syncretism. For example, as Emerson Giumbelli (1997) showed, the putative permeability of certain religions of Brazil compared to others was a key part of their relative legitimacy and the degree of police surveillance they received. Aisha Khan (2004) described the political import to Trinidad of being a 'callaloo nation' where Indo- and Afro-Trini religious practices are freely mixed, but also how certain syncretic processes, or the resistance to them, were politically marked, while others were not. Khan shows how Trinidad's ideals of democratic plural-ism were and are cast, within Trini political discourse, as a result of cultural (including religious) creolization. In the ancient world, syncretic Hellenism was a project of Alexander the Great's conquests. And in the present, as Luther Martin (2000) argued, 'syncretism' often advances the same crypto-theological projects as 'comparative religion', leveling differences between traditions to generate comforting similarity, for specific reasons of power. We must ask, which groups are invested in syncretic events and moments, and to which ends?

Fifth, we should remain cognizant of *scholarly* syncretisms and hybrids, that is, the ways in which scholarship about religion becomes entwined with communities of practice to generate new hybrid forms and new versions of purity or authenticity (Martin 2000; Capone 2010). A classic example in this genre is Donald Lopez's *Prisoners of Shangri-La*, which detailed the production of 'Tibetan Buddhism' via the mediations of Western religious sympathizers (1999).

Sixth, future scholars of religion should apply syncretism or hybridity not only to inter-religious mixes but rather also to the study of how religion is enmeshed with and co-produced in and through domains other than 'religion' narrowly conceived, like language, the material world, the body, and technologies of mediation. We should ask how the *appearance* of coherence and totality is achieved, given that 'religions' are clusters of intersecting but mostly non-coherent networks—communication media, theologies, buildings, aesthetic values, ritual techniques, and more. This will require our ability to clearly answer the question of what syncretism or hybridity is claimed to combine in a given project. The old idea was that a syncretic religion blended two different traditions. More recent iterations propose the blending of human and non-human forms of agency, or the blending of domains like social networking and friendship, or religion and advertising. The hybridity that scholars now often seek to interpret is more likely between previously disparate domains of human action, or of analysis, not between allegedly distinct races, or religions.

Seventh and finally, students of religion must be precise about where, at what level, and in what idiom, the alleged mixing—whether cast as hybridization, syncretism, or creolization—occurs (Leopold/Jensen 2004, 5–6), whether it is primarily linguistic, cognitive, visual, or otherwise sensorial; whether located at the level of social networks, or political mobilization, or the ritual production of power. The possibilities are mani-fold. The key is to be clear about syncretism or hybridity's value for a given research objective, and about the empirical parameters called into play to perceive it.

GLOSSARY

Creolization from the Portuguese *criar* and *criollo* meaning 'to be raised' or 'one raised' (in a given place), creolization names the process of something created in one place as it becomes 'native' or indigenous to another, different site. Creolization has held special import for describing adaptations of languages to situations of combination in a newly occupied space.

Hybridity this word long was applied to the grafts of one plant onto another, or the cross-breeding of animals previously regarded as distinct. More recently it has been used to describe cultural intersections of codes that were previously separate, and reconsiderations of 'the human' now understood to be dependent on its technical or digital extensions, as a cyborg.

Syncretism originally a Greek word, syncretism became the preferred term for putative mixtures between two or more religious traditions. Often applied in polemics against religions considered less pure or original than others, it has been criticized as holding dubious analytical value since all traditions were born of multiple sources and are thus 'mixed.'

Transculturation coined by the Cuban scholar Fernando Ortiz in 1940, transculturation was invoked as an alternative to acculturation. The word suggested that even in situations of domination like slavery, the dominated group does not merely adapt itself to the master class and its ways; rather the dominant are equally infiltrated and influenced by the practices of the subject group. In Ortiz's example, Spanish Cuba was Africanized every bit as much as Africans and Afro-Cubans were hispanized and catholicized.

References

Albanese, Catherine. 2012. *America: Religions and Religion*, 5th edition. Belmont, CA: Wadsworth. First edition 1981.

Anderson, Benedict. 1983. *Imagined Communities: Reflections on the Origin and Spread of Nationalism*. London: Verso.

Apter, Andrew. 1991. "Herskovits's Heritage: Rethinking Syncretism in the African Diaspora." *Diaspora: A Journal of Transnational Studies* 1(3): 235–260.

Azevedo dos Santos, Maria Stella de. 1995. *Meu tempo é agora*. Curitiba: CENTHRU.

Baird, Robert D. 1971. *Category Formation and the History of Religions*. The Hague: Mouton.

Bakhtin, Mikhail. 1981. *The Dialogic Imagination*. Translated by C. Emerson and M. Holquist. Austin: University of Texas Press.

Barthes, Roland. 1982. "Myth Today." In *A Barthes Reader*, edited by Susan Sontag. New York: Macmillan, 93–149.

Bastide, Roger. 1972. *African Civilisations in the New World*. New York: Harper Torchbooks.

Bastide, Roger. 1978. *African Religions in Brazil*. Baltimore, MD: Johns Hopkins University Press.

Benavides, Gustavo. 1995. "Syncretism and Legitimacy in Latin American Religions." In *Enigmatic Powers: Syncretism with African and Indigenous Peoples' Religions Among Latinos*, edited by Anthony M. Stevens-Arroyo and Andres I. Pérez y Mena. New York: Bildner Center, 19–47.

Bhabha, Homi. 1994. *The Location of Culture*. London: Routledge.

Bloomfield, Leonard. 1965. *Language*. New York: Holt, Rinehart and Winston.

Capone, Stefania. 2010. *Searching for Africa in Brazil*. Durham, NC: Duke University Press.

Engler, Steven. 2009. "Umbanda and Hybridity." *Numen* 56(5): 545–577.

Engler, Steven. 2015. "Hybridity." In *Vocabulary for the Study of Religion*, edited by Robert A. Segal and Kocku von Stuckrad. Leiden and Boston: Brill, vol. 2, 212–216.

Erasmus, Desiderius. 1982. *Adages*, vol. 2. Toronto: University of Toronto Press.

Foucault, Michel. 1984. *The Foucault Reader*. New York: Pantheon.

Freyre, Gilberto. 2003. *Casa grande e senzala*. Recife: Fundação Gilberto Freyre. Original edition, 1933.

García Canclini, Nestor. 1995. *Hybrid Cultures: Strategies for Entering and Leaving Modernity*. Translated by Christopher L. Chiappari and Silvia L. López. Minneapolis and London: University of Minnesota Press.

Gilroy, Paul. 1993. *The Black Atlantic*. Cambridge, MA: Harvard University Press.

Giumbelli, Emerson. 1997. *O cuidado dos mortos: uma história da condenação e legitimação do Espiritismo*. Rio de Janeiro: Arquivo Nacional.

Gleason, Judith. 2000. "Oya in the Company of Saints." *Journal of the American Academy of Religion* 68(2): 265–291. doi: 10.1093/jaarel/68.2.265

Grapard, Allan G. 1992. *The Protocol of the Gods: A Study of the Kasuga Cult in Japanese History*. Berkeley: University of California Press.

Greenfield, Sidney M. 1998. "Recasting Syncretism . . . Again: Theories and Concepts in Anthropology and Afro-American Studies in the Light of Changing Social Agendas." In *New Trends and Developments in African Religions*. Edited by Peter B. Clarke. Westport, CT: Greenwood Press, 1–16.

Greenfield, Sidney and A. F. Droogers. 2001. *Reinventing Religions: Syncretism and Transformation in Africa and the Americas*. Lanham, MD: Rowman & Littlefield.

Gruzinski, Serge. 2002. *The Mestizo Mind*. Translated by Deke Dusinberre. New York and London: Routledge.

Hannerz, Ulf. 1987. "The World in Creolisation." *Africa: Journal of the International African Institute* 57(4): 546–559.

Hannerz, Ulf. 1996. *Transnational Connections*. London: Routledge.

Herskovits, Melville J. 1937. "African Gods and Catholic Saints in New World Negro Belief." *American Anthropologist* 39(4): 635–643.

Herskovits, Melville. 1958. *The Myth of the Negro Past*. Boston, MA: Beacon Press. Original edition, 1941.

Herzog, J. J., Philip Schaff, Albert Hauck, Samuel Macauley Jackson, Charles Colebrook Sherman. 1908–1914. *The New Schaff–Herzog Encyclopedia of Religious Knowledge*. New York and London: Funk and Wagnalls Company.

Hess, David J. 1992. *Spirits and Scientists: Ideology, Spiritism, and Brazilian Culture*. University Park, PA: Pennsylvania State University Press.

Kamstra, J. H. 1967. *Encounter or Syncretism: The Initial Growth of Japanese Buddhism*. Leiden: Brill.

Kant, Immanuel. 1960. *Religion Within the Limits of Reason Alone*. London: Harper Torchbooks.

Khan, Aisha. 2004. "Sacred Subversions? Syncretic Creoles, the Indo-Caribbean, and 'Cultures-in-Between.'" *Radical History Review* 89 (Spring): 165–184.

Khan, Aisha. 2007. "Good to Think? Creolization, Optimism, and Agency." *Current Anthropology* 48(5): 653–673. doi: 10.1086/522318

Kohn, Eduardo. 2013. *How Forests Think: Toward an Anthropology Beyond the Human*. Berkeley: University of California Press.

Kraft, Siv Ellen. 2002. "'To Mix or Not to Mix': Syncretism/AntiSyncretism in the History of Theosophy." *Numen* 49(2): 142–177.

Latour, Bruno. 1993. *We Have Never Been Modern*. Translated by Catherine Porter. Cambridge, MA: Harvard University Press.

Latour, Bruno. 2010. *On the Modern Cult of the Factish Gods*. Durham, NC: Duke University Press.

Leopold, Anita Maria and Jeppe Sinding Jensen, eds. 2004. *Syncretism in Religion.* London: Equinox.

Lopez, Donald S. 1999. *Prisoners of Shangri-La: Tibetan Buddhism and the West.* Chicago, IL: University of Chicago Press.

Martin, Luther H. 1983. "Why Cecropian Minerva?" *Numen* 30(2): 131–145. doi: 10.1163/156852783X00023

Martin, Luther H. 2000. "Of Religious Syncretism, Comparative Religion, and Spiritual Quests." *Method & Theory in the Study of Religion* 12(1): 277–286. doi: 10.1163/157006800X00184

Martin, Luther H. 2001. "To Use 'Syncretism' or Not to Use 'Syncretism': That is the Question." *Historical Reflections/Réflexions Historiques* 27(3): 389–400.

Mintz, Sidney. 2008. "Creolization and Hispanic Exceptionalism." *Review* 31(3): 251–265.

Mintz, Sidney. 2010. *Three Ancient Colonies: Caribbean Themes and Variations.* Cambridge, MA: Harvard University Press.

Naficy, Hamid. 1993. *The Making of Exile Cultures: Iranian Television in Los Angeles.* Minneapolis: University of Minnesota Press.

Nina Rodrigues, Raimundo. 2006. *O animismo fetichista dos negros baianos.* Rio de Janeiro: Biblioteca Nacional. Original edition, 1896–1897.

Ortiz, Fernando. 1995. *Cuban Counterpoint: Tobacco and Sugar.* Durham, NC: Duke University Press. Original edition, 1940.

Palmié, Stephan. 2006. "Creolization and Its Discontents." *Annual Review of Anthropology* 35: 433–456. doi: 10.1146/annurev.anthro.35.081705.123149

Palmié, Stephan. 2007. 'Is There a Muddle in the Middle? "Creolization" in African Americanist History and Anthropology.' In *In Creolization: History, Ethnography, Theory*, edited by Charles Stewart. Walnut Creek, CA: Left Coast Press, 178–200.

Pérez y Mena, Andres I. 1995. "Puerto Rican Spiritism as a Transfeature of Afro-Latin Religion." In *Enigmatic Powers: Syncretism with African and Indigenous Peoples' Religions Among Latinos*, edited by Anthony M. Stevens-Arroyo and Andres I. Pérez y Mena. New York: Bildner Center, 137–158.

Plutarch. 1939. *Moralia, Volume VI. De fraterno amore.* Translated by W. C. Helmbold. Cambridge, MA: Harvard University Press.

Pratt, Mary Louise. 1992. *Imperial Eyes: Travel Writing and Transculturation.* London: Routledge.

Pye, Michael. 1994. "Syncretism versus Synthesis." *Method & Theory in the Study of Religion* 6(3): 217–229.

Pye, Michael. 2013. *Strategies in the Study of Religions*, 2 vols. Berlin and Boston, MA: de Gruyter.

Rudolph, Kurt. 2004. "Syncretism: From Theological Invective to a Concept in the Study of Religion." In *Syncretism in Religion: A Reader*, edited by Jeppe Sinding Jensen and Anita Maria Leopold. London: Equinox, 68–85.

Sansi, Roger. 2007. *Fetishes and Monuments: Afro-Brazilian Art and Culture in the 20th Century.* Oxford and New York: Berghahn.

Scott, James C. 1998. *Seeing Like a State.* New Haven, CT: Yale University Press.

Smith, William Robertson. 1894. *Lectures on the Religion of the Semites.* London: A. & C. Black.

Stewart, Charles. 2007. "Creolization: History, Ethnography, Theory." In *Creolization: History, Ethnography, Theory*, edited by Charles Stewart. Walnut Creek, CA: Left Coast Press, 1–25.

Stewart, Charles. 2011. "Creolization, Hybridity, Syncretism, Mixture." *Portuguese Studies* 27(1): 48–55. doi: 10.5699/portstudies.27.1.0048

Strathern, Marilyn. 1996. "Cutting the Network." *Journal of the Royal Anthropological Institute* 2(3): 517–535. doi: 10.2307/3034901

Trouillot, Michel-Rolph. 1992. "The Caribbean Region: An Open Frontier in Anthropological Theory." *Annual Review of Anthropology* 21: 19–42.

Van der Leeuw, Gerardus. 1963. *Religion in Essence and Manifestation: A Study in Phenomenology, Vol. 2.* Translated by J. E. Turner. New York: Harper & Row. Original edition, 1933.

Vasconcelos, José. 1925. *La Raza Cósmica.* Madrid: Agencia Mundial de Libreria.

Wach, Joachim. 1924. *Religionswissenschaft: Prolegomena zu ihrer wissenschaftstheoretischen Grundlegung.* Leipzig: J. C. Hinrichs'sche Buchhandlung.

Wach, Joachim. 1999. "On Comparative Studies in Religion." In *Classical Approaches to the Study of Religion,* edited by Jacques Waardenburg. New York: de Gruyter, 491–498.

Werbner, Pnina. 2001. "The Limits of Cultural Hybridity: On Ritual Monsters, Poetic Licence and Contested Postcolonial Purifications." *Journal of the Royal Anthropological Institute* 7(1): 133–152.

Young, J. C. 1995. *Colonial Desire: Hybridity in Theory, Culture and Race.* London: Routledge.

FURTHER READING

Apter 1991 [*A key essay for understanding syncretism's lineage coming out of the anthropology of religion and the central role of Melville Herskovits in bringing the term into common usage in twentieth-century scholarship.*]

Benavides 1995 [*One of the clearest and incisive essays on the politics of religious syncretism, benefiting from Benavides's typically extensive reading.*]

Leopold/Jensen 2004 [*The best single volume of essays on religious syncretism, a compilation of many of the classic genealogies and most astute contemporary interpretations of the syncretism concept. The volume includes key essays by Robert Baird, Kurt Rudolph, Michael Pye, Roger Bastide, André Droogers, Luther H. Martin, and many others.*]

Stewart, Charles and Rosalind Shaw. 1994. *Syncretism/Anti-Syncretism: The Politics of Religious Synthesis.* London and New York: Routledge. [*Excellent edited volume on anthropological interpretations of the actual practice of religious syncretism and, crucially, the resistance to it, in various parts of the world.*]

PART VII

THE DISCIPLINE

CHAPTER 50

HISTORY

MICHAEL STAUSBERG

CHAPTER SUMMARY

- As an academic discipline, the history of the study of religion\s is embedded in the wider field of religious studies and in institutional and societal developments.
- Disciplinary history is often self-justificatory; different narratives emphasize continuity or discontinuity and engage tropes of progress or nostalgia.
- A historical perspective on doing scholarship is inherent in academic work and is strengthened by reflexive and contextualizing modes of inquiry.
- From the last quarter of the nineteenth century to the first quarter of the twentieth, the discipline emerged in Western Europe, the United States, and Japan (and to some extent in China) in an international network of scholarly interaction.
- A new wave of institutional growth and expansion occurred from the 1960s onwards, in the context of a worldwide expansion of tertiary education.
- The development of journals evidences accelerated growth and diversification of publication activities.

FIELD AND DISCIPLINE: RELIGIOUS STUDIES AND THE STUDY OF RELIGION\S

Writing a history of the study of religion\s requires making choices—beginning with the question of which and whose histories one is to write. There are two main perspectives: writing the history of religious studies in a broad sense or the history of the study of religion\s in a narrow sense. Religious studies as a field, as understood in this chapter, is a relatively amorphous area of academic work that covers all sorts of studies of religious phenomena undertaken by scholars from a variety of academic disciplines, whereas the study of religion\s as a discipline addresses one institutionally distinct segment of this field. A history of 'religious studies' is discursive and topical, whereas a history of the study of religion\s is the history of an academic discipline that distinguishes its mode of operation from other forms of studying religion. Yet, these histories are interrelated. First, insofar as the study of religion\s draws on and ideally has an impact on other disciplines, the history of the discipline is anchored in the history of the field of religious studies. Second, developments in philosophy, for example, and trends in intellectual history eventually find a resonance in religious studies and the study of religion\s. Third, academics who self-identify as scholars of religion continue to have appointments in other departments.

A history of the discipline of the study of religion\s is set in three broader contexts: intellectual, institutional, and societal. Throughout its history the study of religion\s has relied heavily on importing data, methods, and theories from other disciplines and has emulated models of other disciplines such anthropology, history, linguistics, philology, the social sciences, or theology. Only very occasionally, if at all, has the study of religion\s sung a leading voice in the chorus of disciplines. Since the university has predominantly been organized by disciplines, in the form of programs, chairs, and departments, the history of a discipline is also embedded in the history of universities and education. In turn, disciplines, fields, and universities are part of wider cultural, economical, and societal processes. Given that changes, developments, and turns in the intellectual history of the discipline are discussed in the various chapters of this *Handbook*, the present chapter will focus mainly on the institutional aspects and the historiography of the discipline. (This chapter will not discuss the related histories of anthropology, philosophy, psychology, and sociology of religion and of theologies or other relevant neighboring and overlapping disciplines.)

Disciplines

Disciplines are regimes of knowledge production and transmission (see Engler/Stausberg 2011 for more on disciplines and the study of religion\s as a discipline). They are discursive, intellectual, organizational, and social entities engineered by processes of exclusion and inclusion with regard to what is negotiated and established to be the legitimate subjects, objects, and forms of disciplinary knowledge. These processes are not entirely explicit and formalized, so that entrance and socialization into disciplines—typically mediated by supervision—amount to developing a sense of their respective codes of communication and tacit rules. Disciplinary knowledge production is qualified by fit as much as by truth: what is treated as acceptable or solid in one discipline may not be appreciated, or less so, in another. Interdisciplinary work is scholarship that counts as acceptable in two or more disciplines. Disciplinary standards of knowledge are malleable and contextual: they are subject to ongoing negotiations and vary according to time, space, and circumstances—what is taken for granted at one place and at one time may not be so, less so, or differently so elsewhere, previously, or in the future, and under different circumstances. A history of a discipline needs to analyze changes in these modes of knowledge production and transmission. Knowledge is produced, disseminated, digested, and contested by people. Starting from a variety of relationships (e.g. between the teachers or supervisors and their students, among groups of teachers or of students, the collegium, authors and referees, writers and their critics, bloggers and their readers and commentators) disciplines operate as social processes, networks, groups, or communities of communication with different degrees of active and constructive cooperation. Creating, developing, and sustaining a discipline amounts to creating, developing, and sustaining institutional spaces that allow these social processes of communication to unfold. Main institutional spaces of disciplinary communication include chairs, departments, and programs, departmental seminars, conferences, professional associations, periodicals (journals and book series), and reference works (introductory textbooks and handbooks, lexica and encyclopedias, collections of sources). A full-blown discipline requires these to be in place and operative. A history of a discipline analyzes their respective developments. This chapter can only select some among these threads.

DISCIPLINARY HISTORIES IN THE STUDY OF RELIGION\s

The appearance of histories of a discipline can be read as a sign of the respective discipline having reached a certain degree of maturity or of its experiencing dramatic change or a sense of crisis. The first histories of the study of religion\s were published in the early twentieth century in several modern Western languages (Stausberg 2007, 305). Compared to that of major disciplines, the current literature on the history of the study of religions\s is relatively limited, even though the bibliography may appear rich on some specific issues. Most of the work has been done by scholars of religion\s rather than by historians or historians of science (exceptions include Reuben 1996; Wheeler-Barclay 2010). Few scholars of religion\s can be said to have the history of the field or the discipline as their main scholarly occupation. Accordingly, many publications in this area have a piecemeal character. There are few, if any, sustained long-term projects or programs devoted to the history of the discipline or the field.[1] Many publications are occasional in nature since they result from centenaries or similar celebrations. Reflecting the relative marginality of the discipline, the study of religion\s is not included in most publications that review the history of the (social) sciences.

---

[1] Since 2002, the annual meetings of the American Academy of Religion have 'Cultural History of the Study of Religion' as a program unit. Its current statement of purpose reads: "This group is devoted to historical inquiry into the social and cultural contexts of the study of religion and into the constructions of 'religion' as an object of scholarly inquiry." <http://papers.aarweb.org/content/cultural-history-study-religion-group>.

Literature Review

Eric Sharpe's *Comparative Religion: A History*, first published in 1975 (second edition 1986, followed by several reprints), remains the standard book-length account of the discipline's intellectual and institutional history. Even though the subtitle of Walter H. Capps's book *Religious Studies* (1995) speaks of "the making of a discipline," the book surveys intellectual not institutional history. Hans Kippenberg's *Discovery of Religion in the Modern Age* (2001, original German edition 1997) is not concerned with disciplinary history. Instead, he reads nineteenth- and early twentieth-century scholars of religion as theorists of modernity: their work reflected on modernity's often ignored and neglected dimensions that could not be subsumed under the narrative of progress. Kippenberg's account stops before World War II and his discussion is limited to European (and a few American) scholars.

Much continues to be written on religious studies in Victorian England (e.g. Wheeler-Barclay 2010; Chidester 2014) and the emergence of the discipline of the study of religion\s (e.g. Molendijk 2005). The previously neglected trajectory of the discipline during fascism and the Nazi period has attracted some attention (e.g. Heinrich 2002; Junginger 2008). Few publications look at the last 25 to 50 years (e.g. Alles 2009), unless occasioned by specific circumstances such as crises and conflicts or as surveys of contemporary scholarship. Extant work deals almost exclusively with specific countries only. Examples are too many to be listed here. Comparative studies (e.g. Engler 2006 on Brazil and Canada) and single-authored surveys covering several countries (e.g. Stausberg 2008; 2009a; 2010 on Western Europe and Bœspflug 2010 on Francophone Europe) are rare; mostly such work is commissioned for specific publications (e.g. Alles 2008; Bubík/Hoffmann 2015).

Relatively much has been written on some foundational figures, including biographies (e.g. van den Bosch [2002] on Friedrich Max Müller, Maier [2009] on William Robertson Smith, Sharpe [1990] and Lange [2011] on Nathan Söderblom).[2] Correspondences between scholars are edited and studied (e.g. Maier 2012; Spineto 1994 on Mircea Eliade and Raffaele Pettazzoni; Buckley 2012 on Lady E. S. Drower's scholarly correspondence; Accorinti 2014 on Pettazzoni and Herbert Jennings Rose). Mircea Eliade has been a subject of study in his own right for decades, with a group of specialists and an immense bibliography comprising contributions from different disciplines. In Italy, vast bibliographies have grown around Raffaele Pettazzoni and Ernesto de Martino. Studies on Pettazzoni have in recent years been published in some of the leading international journals (Rennie 2013; Severino 2015). Scholars such as Eliade, Henri Corbin, Gershom Scholem, Antoine Faivre, and others are being studied as part of the history of scholarship on the one hand and the history of discourses or intellectual or religious tendencies such as Western esotericism on the other (e.g. Hanegraaff 2012). There are some studies that critically review key categories in the study of religion\s—in

---

[2] See also the Key Thinkers in the Study of Religion book series (Routledge).

addition to the category of religion itself, there are partial studies on the category 'world religion' (Masuzawa 2005), 'primitive/indigenous religion' (Cox 2007); and volumes in the series Critical Categories in the Study of Religion edited by Russell McCutcheon give important glimpses, even if not full histories, of the trajectories of major categories.

This reflects the increasing critical reflexivity of the discipline, which has come to realize that scholars and scholarship are among the things we study. This realization comes in several forms. To begin with, there are the ideological agendas of scholars and scholarship (see Strenski 2004 for a critical review). The entanglement of the study of religion\s as an academic enterprise with colonialism has been studied with increasing degrees of sophistication (Chidester 2014). In Japan, the early development of the study of religion fell into the period of imperialist expansion; and scholars of religion undertook ethnographic studies with an understanding that their work would serve the country's colonial agenda (Fujiwara 2008, 198; Josephson 2012, 247).

Critique

Extremist right-wing political ideologies or unforced cooperation of scholars with totalitarian political regimes, in particular fascism or Nazism, has been a subject of intense debate, in particular in the case of Eliade. By contrast, scholars' support of extreme left-wing political ideologies such as communism has not faced the same sort of critique and moral outrage. While some find that, even if a scholar is compromised politically, her or his work may still be of value, others do not seem to endorse such a dividing line; similar debates are found in other disciplines—think of the debates on Heidegger.

Some scholars of religion have evidently been motivated to enter this line of academic business out of religious, anti-religious, esoteric, or spiritual interests or curiosity. People's worldviews, attitudes, and values motivate them in their life, including their academic work—sometimes explicitly, sometimes implicitly. One influential line of scholarship has insisted on the religious premises of the discipline. Where scholarship of religion was championed by religious liberals, these scholars' concept of religion would typically reflect their specific and historically contingent religious convictions; the same, of course, is the case with scholars who endorse other religious views. Unmasking such preconceptions is part of the necessary labor of critical purification, but the consequences of such entanglements and the possibility, prospects, and desirability of their elimination, acknowledgment, or affirmation remain a matter of dispute.

Modernity

Kippenberg (2001) and Krech (2002) have analyzed the emerging study of religion\s as a mode of reflection and intellectual response to modernization. Scholars and some religious groups alike have constructed modernity and modernization in antagonistic terms. In this way, scholarship of religion administers the 'other' of modern society. On this view, scholars of religion are keepers of the realm of the 'other', be it the abyss underneath the surface of modern life, alternative Western traditions and cosmologies, or non-Western cultures and lifeworlds.

It has also become increasingly clear that scholars are not only observers but also actors; as soon as our views of religion or of specific religions are public they can become subject to various sorts of appropriations or criticism in religious discourses as much as in discourses about religion. While there still are relatively few activists or advocates among scholars of religion (Stausberg 2014), even purist historians of religions can nonetheless become agents of religious change (de Jong 2008). The thick walls that have seemed at times to separate scholars and their 'objects' of inquiry have been torn down, or at least have become much thinner and more fragile.

The Historical and Contextual Nature of Scholarship

An interest in the history of scholarship is to some extent inherent in the pursuit of research, insofar as all research seeks to advance knowledge and therefore constructs its own narrative of scientific progress; in practice, research always requires a review of previous research. The intellectual history of the study of religion\s is something like such a literature review writ large and reflects (on) this essential historicity of scholarship. There are different degrees and strategies of continuity and discontinuity at play: in a sequential model, research deliberately follows established parameters, which the revolutionary model seeks to overcome. The latter model may seem to enjoy a greater prestige in a post-Kuhnian world, where truly relevant knowledge is often held to require a 'change of paradigm'; the premium put on 'innovation' in the economy of knowledge might also reflect changes in the economy at large.

Attention to disciplinary and academic history also comes as a result of historicizing and contextualizing approaches in the discipline: as much as we analyze religious phenomena in historical contexts, we will have to reflexively historicize and contextualize our own ambitions. Now that more scholars of religion are interested in lived, ordinary or vernacular religion, in the performance of religion, and in material religion, scholars of religion should presumably also look at these aspects of disciplinary history: at the ordinariness of disciplinary practice, the performance of meetings and publishing, and the kind of materials and things engaged by scholars in our work.

It is difficult to see how we as scholars could perceive our work as meaningful and engaging if we were not able to convince ourselves that we—as individuals, as a group of peers, or as a community of discourse—are making a genuine contribution, be it only by becoming aware of the problems at hand. Even if the intellectual history of the study of religion\s were written as a gargantuan history of error and failure, one would still either express the hope of overcoming previous failures to provide a truly scientific, objective, and unbiased vision or resign oneself to one's fate and play the role of the ironist, perhaps wedded to an ultra-skeptic epistemology and a philosophy of science that regards scholarship primarily as literature. Academic self-preservation—endemic to disciplines as they try to secure their survival—might restrain one from making such a self-destructive plea, but this would hardly convince administrators, policy-makers, and research funding agencies of the viability of the discipline. Instead, histories of scholarship typically function as projects of legitimation and self-justification.

Points of Departure

Writing the history of something requires marking a starting point. One kind of narrative emphasizes innovation, another continuity, in particular by seeking to identify precursors. The earliest twentieth-century historians of the discipline have followed its traces back in time (in particular Pinard de la Boullaye 1922). In books appearing at the beginning of the twenty-first century, the Swiss historian of religion Philippe Borgeaud (2004) recalled the comparative practice of ancient Mediterranean authors from Herodotus onwards and the Israeli historian of religion Guy Stroumsa (2010) argued that the early modern discovery of religions in Asia, the Near East, and the Americas resulted during the seventeenth century in the emergence of a new field of studies of comparative religion, which was mainly practiced by relatively open-minded Christians, and which came to stipulate the existence of religion and religious rituals as universal phenomena. One crucial difference from the modern academic study of religion\s was the absence of the term 'religion.' Against the tendency of regarding the comparative and historical study of religion as a distinctive feature of Europe, scholars have pointed at some 120 works of refutations, descriptions, and inventories written by learned Islamic historians and theologians in Arabic and later in Persian from the seventh to the seventeenth centuries CE (e.g. Brodeur 2008, 78–87). In Indic intellectual history different schools of thought are discussed comparatively. In Buddhist East Asia some learned scholars provided comparative discussions of different teachings, albeit mostly with an apologetic agenda: in the eighteenth century the Japanese thinker Nakatomo Tominaga (1715–1746) advanced "a detached or objective approach to religions" (Fujiwara 2008, 194), but without, it seems, a term for 'religions' (Josephson 2011).

ESTABLISHING THE DISCIPLINE

In addition to the emergence of 'religion' as a key concept for the formation of some segment of social reality, the decisive point of departure for the modern academic study of religion\s was the establishment and spread of the early nineteenth-century German model of the relatively independent and generously funded research university with its three axes of research, teaching, and adult socialization. However, in addition to history, philology, and philosophy at German universities, religion was (and still is) studied in the form of confessional theology, and to some extent theology has remained something of a point of reference for—or even a powerful and potentially threatening though sometimes also allied 'other' of—the study of religion\s. On an international scale, the study of religion\s emerged institutionally in three forms: (1) as an additional dimension of theological research, typically as a historical extension, for example with a view to the religious and historical context of the Bible and early Christianity or to contemporary competitors; (2) as a transformation of theology (e.g. its de-confessionalization); (3) as an independent endeavor.

Continental Europe

The early and lasting establishment of the study of religion\s in the Netherlands can serve as an example of the second variety. Ministers in the Dutch Reformed Church were trained in state-run universities, even though state and church had become separated by the constitution in 1848, but this was increasingly deemed problematic. As a result, the Higher Education Act of 1876 decreed a de-confessionalization of Dutch faculties (divisions) of theology; as a side-effect of this transformation, history of religions and philosophy of religion were introduced as new additional subjects (Moldendijk 2005, 71–79), and the first chairs in history of religions were established in Leiden and Amsterdam in 1877.

France is an example of the third option. Here, faculties of theology were not transformed but disbanded in 1885 and, on their ruins, the fifth section of the École Pratique des Hautes Études (EPHE) was erected in 1886. Instead of a single chair, this institution started on the scale of a whole division. Of its ten initial chairs, half were devoted to the study of Christianity and one each to the religions of India, Egypt, Greece/Rome, the Far East, and the Western Semites. In 1888, a chair for the religions of the 'non-civilized peoples' was added. The number of chairs has gradually continued to increase and the fifth section of the EPHE remains one of the leading institutions in research on a variety of religions in the world. Yet, while the model of the single chair at least partially casts the chair holder in the role of a generalist or representative of a discipline, the model of the division operates more like an assembly of specialists without a systematic or theoretical center of gravitation. Outside the EPHE, however, the study of religion\s has not found fertile ground in France. Italy is an example of a country where the closure of the state-run faculties of theologies, in 1873, was not replaced by the introduction of a new, non-confessional study of religion\s. Here, the discipline was lastingly established only forty years later, in 1923, in the early period of Mussolini's rule, at the university of Rome. In several European countries one finds chairs and courses in the study of religion\s both within faculties of theology and in other divisions (often in small independent departments).

In several cases, chairs and courses have coexisted inside and outside divisions of theology at the same universities. In Denmark (Copenhagen), the first position was located in the division of philosophy, whereas one finds examples for both institutional locations in Sweden (Uppsala and Lund: theology; Stockholm: philosophy) and in Germany (Leipzig and Berlin: theology; Bonn: philosophy).

Britain

A vibrant scholarly debate on religion unfolded in Victorian Britain. The prolific and versatile German-born and -educated scholar of Indian languages Friedrich Max Müller, who had come to England in 1846 to work on his translation of the Rig Veda, is commonly considered a founding father of the discipline of the study of religion\s. In his *Autobiography* he recollects that having studied "at a German university . . . the historical study of Christianity was to me as familiar as the study of Roman history"; it studied "the limits of our knowledge" (Müller 1901, 193). He expresses his surprise, upon coming to Oxford, that "these excellent and really learned men were much more deeply interested in purely ecclesiastical questions, in the validity of Anglican order, in the wearing of either gown or surplices in the pulpit, in the question of candlestick and genuflections" (194). Müller wrote his programmatic *Essays on the Science of Religion*, published as the first volume of his *Chips from a German Workshop* in 1867, and four lectures *On the Science of Religion* from 1870 (published 1873). Müller, who was something like a celebrity scholar residing in the imperial center of Oxford (where he, however, was not always unanimously embraced), acted as an entrepreneurial intellectual empire builder. Müller sought to establish a trinity of sciences comprising language, myth, and religion. Playing on his immense network of academic contacts, one of his lasting achievements is the fifty-volume set of *Sacred Books of the East* (SBE) published by Oxford University Press (Girardot 2002; Sun 2013, 60–66). The SBE provided the nascent discipline with a reference corpus of relevant source materials. Yet, Müller, who eventually obtained a chair in comparative philology, never held a chair in comparative religion, nor was such a position created at Cambridge or Oxford.

That step was first taken by the University of Manchester in 1904, but within the Faculty of Theology. This location prevented the anti-religious anthropologist James George Frazer, if we are to believe a letter of his, from accepting the potential offer of accepting that chair. Instead, the chair went to his friend, the scholar of Buddhism Thomas William Rhys Davids (Sharpe 1980), who had collaborated with Müller on the *Sacred Books of the East* project. At that time, however, the former coherence and prominence of the academic debate on religion in Britain had already disintegrated (Wheeler-Barclay 2010, 247), and neither Rhys Davids nor any of his successors had a significant impact on the public debate on religion or the shaping of the discipline.

United States of America

In the United States of America, the field was introduced toward the end of the nineteenth century by people from a variety of educational and religious backgrounds, research interests, and scholarly identities. Early chairs in the field carried names such as Comparative Theology (Boston University, 1873), History and Philosophy of Religion (Cornell University, 1891), or Comparative Religion (New York University, 1890). Scholars shared a Christian outlook and none of these chairs would pave the way to the establishment of the discipline of the study of religion\s. Morris Jastrow, Jr., who had studied with Cornelius Tiele in Leiden, the Netherlands, was one of the most energetic advocates for the new discipline; he was the author of an early influential textbook (*The Study of Religion*, 1901) and editor of several handbooks. Yet, like Müller, Jastrow, who was a specialist in ancient Mesopotamian religions, never held a chair in the study of religion\s, serving as a professor of Semitics at the University of Pennsylvania (Shepard 1991). In 1895, he initiated "The American Lectures on the History of Religions" series for a consortium of East coast universities, where Rhys Davids was the first lecturer (Chidester 2014, 289).

At the University of Chicago, incorporated in 1890, a Department of Comparative Religion was started in 1892, not in the Divinity School, but in the Faculties of Arts, Literature, and Science; it was only in the 1940s that it became part of the Divinity School (Cherry 1995, 81). At the Harvard Divinity School, history of religions obtained departmental status in 1902 (Shepard 1991, 50–51, 59). Both departments were unsuccessful in terms of attracting students and doctoral candidates from outside theology. In the United States, and elsewhere, academic opportunities were very few (Shepard 1991, 65; Reuben 1996, 113). The first professors mainly worked on topics related to the Bible and its contexts. According to Robert S. Shepard, the study of religion\s did not grow into an independent discipline but remained "an ancillary field of Christian theology" (Shepard 1991, 119), surviving as "an acceptable, and often desirable, component of a theological education" (128) that did not make much of an intellectual contribution to the university (Reuben 1996).

Japan

An early institutionalization of the study of religion\s took place in Japan, where the University of Tokyo, which followed the modern Western model, was founded in 1877. At the same time, as part of societal reform, a modern concept and word for 'religion' (*shūkyō*) was created (Josephson 2012). Anesaki Masaharu, who for a time studied in Germany, was the co-founder of a first Japanese Association for Comparative Religion in 1896; in 1898, he gave his inaugural lecture, and in 1905 he was appointed to the first professorship and the first department was created at the University of Tokyo (Fujiwara 2008, 196; Josephson 2012, 248). Chairs were also established at four other Japanese universities (Isomae 2014, 201). Anesaki, who "was both a person of religion and a scholar of religion" (Isomae 2014, 197), had a nationalist and religious agenda and held some government-related posts; he was also active in international peace activities (Isomae 2014, 147) and, on behalf of the government, he helped to arrange a meeting of representatives of different religions (Hayashi 2011, 9).

The Japanese Association for Religious Studies was founded in 1930, and scholars of religion contributed to an intellectual defense against Marxist tendencies. At the time, there were departments or programs of religion at eighteen universities (Fujiwara 2008, 200). In addition to the non-confessional (albeit pro-religious) study of religion\s, the new discipline of Buddhist Studies emerged, focusing on textual and doctrinal matters. Buddhist priests also worked at departments for the study of religion\s at Buddhist universities (Fujiwara 2008, 200–201). During the Japanese occupation of Korea, the study of religion\s was also introduced at Kyeonosong Imperial University, where a first professor was appointed in 1927.

China

At the turn of the twentieth century China experienced a period of turbulent cultural and political change. (The following account is based on Meyer in preparation; see also Meyer 2015.) As in Japan, and reflecting the Japanese *shūkyō*, a new Chinese concept and word for 'religion' (*zongjiao*) slowly emerged in the early twentieth century; as in Japan, this word eventually prevailed over alternative ones. Via Japan, Western terms such as 'animism,' 'fetishism,' 'idolatry,' and 'magic' reached China even before the study of religion\s was institutionalized as an academic project. Just as the status of Shinto as a religion was a matter of dispute in Japan, so also was the status of Confucianism in China. Following intense public debates on the topic of religion, calls for a scientific and critical study of religion\s were put forward by leading intellectuals in the early 1920s. In 1923 a course on general history of religions was taught by Jiang Shaouyan at Peking University. Jiang had studied at the University of Chicago and translated the introductory textbook *The Birth and Growth of Religion* (1923) by George Foot Moore, the holder of the first chair at Harvard, into Chinese in 1926; but, unable to find an academic position in this field, Jiang shifted his academic work toward anthropology.

As a rudimentary discipline, the study of religion\s found a home from the mid-1920s at several Christian colleges and universities, where Western missionaries and their Chinese successors had already taught courses in comparative religion or history of religions, while non-Christian institutions did not implement its institutionalization. In 1925, in conjunction with the anti-Christian movement, the government decreed that all private, foreign-financed colleges and universities had to seek state approval. The relevant regulations decreed that religious courses should not be among the required subjects and that the institution should not aim at the propagation of religion. As a result, colleges and universities started to reorganize their departmental structure and teaching so that departments of religion (rather than of theology) and a variety of courses about religions emerged at some universities, mainly Yenching (Beijing), Lingnan (Hong Kong), and Cheeloo (Shandong) (Meyer 2015, 59–60). At state-run universities, no similar development took place. Before 1925 teaching faculty were mainly Chinese, but there were no ready-made jobs for students who graduated from study of religion\s programs. The reorganization of tertiary education in 1952 resulted in the closure of the few existing departments and programs (Meyer forthcoming).

Networks

The emergence of the study of religion\s functioned from early on as an international network of a relatively limited group of scholars. Textbooks or handbooks were written, some of which went through different editions and some of which were translated; journals and works of reference were published. The exchange was greatly facilitated by academic tourism. People traveled to study at other places and to attend a series of international conferences. After a series of congresses that were dominated or accompanied by religious agendas—such as the World Parliament of Religions in Chicago (1893) and the Science of Religion Congress in Stockholm (1897), where scholars of the nascent discipline participated along with spokespersons of different religions—a first exclusively academic international congress in the study of religion\s took place in 1900 in Paris, occasioned, like the event in Chicago, by the Universal Exposition. Further international congresses, all held in Western Europe, followed, in 1904 (Basel), Oxford (1908), and Leiden (1912). In the interwar period, only two congresses were held, one in Lund (1929), the other in Brussels (1935).

POST-WORLD WAR II

After the war, the cycle of international congresses on the history of religions was re-established and placed on a more regular basis, mainly coordinated by a newly founded scholarly organization, the International Association for the History of Religions, which seeks to promote the academic study of religion on an increasingly global level. In tune with the general expansion of tertiary education, since the 1960/70s, the study of religion\s has seen a new era of expansion.

The International Association for the History of Religions (IAHR) and the Quinquennial International Congresses

The first post-World War II congress took place in Amsterdam (1950). At this conference, a world body for the study of religion\s was founded, which later adopted the name International Association for the History of Religions (IAHR). Article 1 of its constitution defines its scope as "the promotion of the academic study of religion through the international collaboration of all scholars whose research has bearing on the subject." However, the mandate of the organization is defined in negative terms: "The IAHR is not a forum for confessional, apologetical, or other similar concerns" (<http://www.iahr.dk/constitution.php>). Article 2 speaks about "holding quinquennial congresses" as its most prominent means of achieving its mission: since 1950 international congresses have been held every fifth year.

During the subsequent quarter of a century, Western Europe remained the center of gravity (Rome 1955; Marburg 1960; Stockholm 1970; Lancaster 1975), but the circuit then became increasingly global, occasionally also spreading toward Africa, Asia, and Central America (Tokyo 1958 [an extraordinary congress]; Claremont 1965; Winnipeg 1980; Sydney 1985; Mexico City 1995; Durham 2000; Tokyo 2005; Toronto 2010), with only two further congresses held in Europe (Rome 1990; Erfurt 2015). Over the decades, the number of attendees has not significantly increased. Apart from the congresses at Mexico City and Tokyo—the latter counting some 2,000 participants—none of these events attracted more than some 600 scholars, illustrating the relatively restricted demography of the discipline (figures based on Wiebe 2015); the 2015 congress at Erfurt, however, had 1,296 participants (65 percent from Europe).

The founding of the IAHR has stimulated the establishment of an increasing number of affiliated national and some regional member organizations. As of 2014, all presidents and general secretaries of the IAHR have been Europeans (by residence or birth and education). However, American scholars expressed some dissatisfaction with the European dominance in the association in the mid-1960s (Wiebe 2015). At present, close to half of the member associations are European, their number having further increased after the fall of the Iron Curtain. (The European Association for the Study of Religion [EASR], founded and affiliated with the IAHR in 2000, has emerged as an increasingly visible player, mainly by arranging annual meetings that have expanded from a meeting of the executive board and some associates to full-fledged international conferences.) Since the late 1980s, the then leadership of the IAHR made a more concerted attempt to emphasize the organization's global or 'intercultural' mission. Reviewing the history of the congresses not only provides insights into the increased internationalization of the discipline, but also some turning points and developments in its intellectual history. One turning point, in retrospective, was the Marburg congress (1960), where a younger but later dominant group of scholars articulated a resistance to religious (or religionist) models in and purposes of the study of religion\s (Sharpe 1997, 276–278; Stausberg 2008, 315; Jensen 2010, 69–71).

Western Europe and Australasia

The 1960s and 1970s gave a new impetus to the study of religion\s. To begin with, this was the period when contemporary mass universities took shape. The expansion of the university sector resulted in a period of growth for the study of religion\s (Stausberg 2008, 314). In England, where the discipline had never obtained a foothold in the classical universities and had not prospered much, it benefited from the founding of new universities: new and innovative departments were started at the new university of Lancaster (1967) and the Open University (1971). In Italy, the number of positions expanded in the 1960s. In the Netherlands, apart from the expansion of the university sector, theology underwent a substantial change, whereby in the early 1970s there occurred "a silent and quiet transformation of faculties of theology into faculties for the science of religions"

(Wiegers 2002, 25). In Scotland, some pioneering efforts to establish Religious Studies outside Schools of Divinity were undertaken during the 1970s and 1980s, but these were reversed after the dramatic cuts in university funding that affected British universities during the mid-1980s (Cox/Sutcliffe 2006).

Similar growth also occurred outside of Western Europe. In Australia and New Zealand, courses, programs, and positions started emerging out of philosophy and divinity from the 1960s. From the 1970s, positions, chairs, and departments were established; the discipline continued to grow but "remained relatively small overall" (Franzman 2008, 225).

East Asia

Beyond the Anglosphere, in Korea, after independence from Japan, a department of religious studies was established at the new Seoul National University in 1946. Initially, the Japanese influence remained strong, but eventually Korean scholars oriented themselves toward the West. In 1969, a Korean Association for the History of Religions was formed by scholars of different religions who, in addition to Seoul National University, were mostly teaching at universities founded by religious communities. In 1984 a department of theology was to be established at Sogang University, an institution founded by the Jesuits. Since the Ministry of Education would not allow for a department of theology at a university, it was framed as 'religious studies.' In addition, since the 1980s departments were founded first at some Christian, then at Buddhist and Confucian universities, and in this century also at universities affiliated to New Religious Movements (Guanghu/Chin-hong/Chang-yick 2008, 180–181). In Japan, according to Isomae Jun'ichi, the dissolution of State Shinto, the principle of separation of religion and the state, and the migration of religion into the private realm resulted in a loss of societal significance of the study of religion\s compared to the prewar period. Accordingly few new courses and departments were established (Isomae 2014, 207–208), but Tsukuba University, a new national university established in 1973, developed into a new "center of religious studies" (Fujiwara 2008, 210).

In the People's Republic of China, political developments hampered the expansion of tertiary education as the Cultural Revolution disrupted academic life, including the Institute of World Religions (IWR) that was established in 1964 in Beijing. Once academic institutions were reopened in 1978, the IWR reassumed its work. Now under the aegis of the Chinese Academy of Social Sciences, the IWR produced a plethora of publications. The former director of the institute for many years advanced an orthodox Marxist approach to religion (Seiwert 1989, 130, note 4). Since the late 1970s some further research institutes such as provincial academies of social sciences with institutes of religion were established; from the late 1980s onwards, a new series of departments were founded (Guanghu/Chin-hong/Chang-yick 2008, 126–167).

Africa

In Africa, the process of decolonization has led to the emergence of independent universities systems, which, nevertheless, have inherited certain legacies from the academic cultures of the former colonial powers. Accordingly, given the limited spread of the study of religion\s at French universities (with the exception of the fifth section of the EPHE), the discipline did not develop at universities in Francophone Africa. In Nigeria, an Anglophone country, religious studies was taught since the founding at the University of Ibadan; in 1950, the former director of religious broadcasting for the BBC (James Welch) became the first chair (Cox 2007, 17). In Nigeria and other Anglophone countries such as Zimbabwe, Uganda, and Ghana, some departments of divinity or theology mutated into religious studies or philosophy and religion departments in the 1960s, and new departments were founded. This development took place in relatively wealthy countries during relatively prosperous periods, such as Nigeria from the 1960s to the early 1980s (Platvoet 1989, 113, 118). Platvoet (1996) has chronicled the development by which African theologians, scholars of religion\s, and others have assumed the role of subjects in analyzing African religions and their histories—in addition to Africa being the object of study for European and American scholars. British scholars such as Andrew Walls and Geoffrey Parrinder worked at African departments during the early period (and before returning to Britain); in addition they had been active as missionaries (Stausberg 2008, 315–316).

Economic limitations and political instability have repeatedly threatened the viability of academic life in Africa, including the study of religion\s. There have also been library and publication scarcities, not to mention a brain drain of talented African scholars (Chitando 2008, 113). Even in relatively stable economical circumstances, not only in Africa, student enrollment depends to some extent on available employment opportunities. For Nigeria, where courses on one or several religions are taught at around half of the country's some 100 universities, Oyeronke Olademo (2011) reports that the low number of students and the high rate of unemployment among former students were matters of grave concern, and that some universities have taken steps to revise their programs accordingly. She also mentions the persistence of a low number of female faculty and expresses the need to distinguish the study of religion\s more carefully from confessional approaches; the teaching of religion is also embedded in religious patterns of behavior, for example by students praying before lectures or being expected to follow certain dress codes (Olademo 2011). At the University of Zambia, "Religious Studies as opposed to Theology" has been taught, since 1985, as "an academic, open approach to the study of religion whereas Theology normally assumes religious commitment" (Carmody 2007, 26); yet, even though it regards itself in opposition to theology, the openness of this approach implies "spiritual" dimensions and aims to provide students with "holistic" and "transformative" experiences (31).

In South Africa, a department of religious studies was established at the University of Cape Town in 1967, and the discipline is now taught at several universities. At some, like Cape Town, it is independent from theology. The journal *Religion in Southern Africa* was published from 1980 to 1987 and was then replaced by the *Journal for the Study of Religion* (1988ff.). Michel Clasquin (2005) describes the late 1980s and early 1990s as a period of unprecedented growth (followed by some later decline). Nevertheless, as in many other countries (on most continents), the discipline is only taught at a minority of universities and, even where it is present, it is a small and marginal subject. In 1979 the Association for the Study of Religion in Southern Africa (based in but not restricted to South Africa) was established, which was then instrumental in founding the continent-wide African Association for the Study of Religion in 1992.

North America

In the United States, the massive expansion of tertiary education was largely a product of the Cold War. The shock of the Soviet launch of the Sputnik in 1957 was taken as evidence that the United States was being outperformed in science, education, and technology. This spurred an unprecedented wave of investments in academic research, which accelerated in the early 1960s and strengthened the global supremacy of the American research university. For religious studies, Russell McCutcheon and William Arnal have shown how enterprising and entrepreneurial scholars could secure significant grants and that the field "in its many guises was well represented among the ranks of National Defense Fellows" (Arnal/McCutcheon 2013, 81).

During the same period, however, the parameters of religious studies in America changed fundamentally as a result of a new interpretation of the First Amendment by the Supreme Court. In particular, the *Abington School District v. Schempp* ruling from 1963 was a landmark decision which regarded as permissible only such 'objective', 'neutral' approaches to religious studies that analyzed religious documents for their historic and artistic qualities but not for their religious message; it allowed for teaching about religion, but not religious teaching. This pushed religious studies in publicly funded institutions in a non-religious or 'secular' direction (Engler 2006, 454).

In the same year (1963), the National Association of Bible Instructors (founded in 1909) proposed a name change, and the association was incorporated under the name American Academy of Religion (AAR) in 1964. The AAR has remained closely associated with the Society of Biblical Literature (SBL). The name change, however, did not signify a complete reversal of the type of work done by scholars, but at best opened the door for gradual change. Ray Hart (1979, 510) recalls how at an annual meeting of the AAR in the mid-1960s "sixteen papers were read . . . fifteen of them in biblical studies." Religious approaches have never disappeared from the AAR (Wiebe 2006).

At the conference of the IAHR held at Claremont in 1965, tensions surfaced between American and Europeans. In his opening address the general secretary of the IAHR, the Dutch scholar C. Jouko Bleeker (1968, 8–9), affirmed a transcendentalist view of the origin of religion, but at the same time felt compelled to remind his audience of a "sharp borderline" to ecumenical initiatives and emphasized the commitment to "purely scientific research" (4). His North American counterpart, Wilfred Cantwell Smith, expressed a contrasting view on the aims of the discipline; for him, through "Comparative Religion . . . man is striving to become conscious of himself in his fragmented relation to transcendence" (1968, 72). It was only with the founding of the North American Association for the Study of Religion (NAASR) in 1985 that the firmly non-religious study of religion assumed an organizational framework in the United States.

There are also academic organizations that focus on social science approaches to religious studies: the Religious Research Association (RRA, founded in 1944/1951, current name adopted in 1959) and the Society for the Scientific Study of Religion (founded in 1949/1950, current name adopted in 1956). Both were founded on the initiative mainly of Protestant theologians who were eager to engage with social science research (see Moberg 2000 for the history of these organizations). Both associations publish journals: the RRA publishes the *Review of Religious Research* (1959ff) and the SSSR publishes the *Journal for the Scientific Study of Religion* (1961ff), which has the highest bibliometric ranking of all religious studies journals; more than 80 percent of its published articles are written by American scholars (Engler 2014).

Probably because of its more encompassing and open policy and its strategy to position itself as the default home for Religious Studies in the United States, the AAR has been a success story. In 1966, it established the *Journal of the American Academy of Religion* (JAAR)—the IAHR had launched its journal *Numen* in 1954 and NAASR started *Method & Theory in the Study of Religion* in 1989. Like the AAR itself, its journal operates more like a religious studies publication (inclusive of theology). In the period 1970–1976, JAAR did not publish a single article that its then editor classified as "academic study of religion"; the majority was history of Christianity, philosophy of religion, and theology (Hart 1979, 513). The membership base of the AAR has risen over the years to some 9,000 (in 2014), and its annual meetings are attended by around half that number (some 4,500 in 2014), which make these meetings by far the most important social arena for academic interaction. By comparison, in 2014 the North American Association for the Study of Religion (NAASR), which represents the study of religion\s in a narrower sense, had less than 100 members, and it does not arrange independent meetings, holding a handful of panels concurrently with the annual meetings of the AAR. Compared to the annual AAR meetings, the quinquennial IAHR world congresses are also minor affairs. The membership bases of the other member associations and societies of the IAHR—the AAR became a member of the IAHR in 2010—are relatively small; in 2014, the British Association for the Study of Religion (BASR), for example, had some 250 members, the German Association (DVRW) some 360, and the Korean Association for the History of Religion some 400.

By the end of the 1960s, some form of religious studies was offered at most four-year colleges in the United States. Most religiously affiliated schools had such programs, but also "half of the private, nondenominational schools and a third of the state schools. In the latter the increase was most dramatic in the late 1960s and early 1970s" (Remus/

Lusby/Tober 1988, 1658). "In 1970, nineteen universities in North America were offering doctorates in religion without any reliance on theological school faculties" (Cherry 1995, 89). Canada followed on the heels of these developments, albeit with a slight delay (Engler 2006, 454). For Canada, Coward (2014, 13) refers to the years from 1966–1976 as "the Golden Decade" that "saw the shift from the theological, mainly Bible-based study of religion, to a comparative, interdisciplinary approach"; many programs were created and "by 1976 any Canadian university that did not have a religious studies undergraduate program was considered to be behind the times" (Coward 2014, 13). Some departments were from the beginning conceived as non-Christian programs, while others evolved from Christian contexts (Coward 2014, 37). Canada established its own corporation and, since 1971, publishes a national journal (*SR: Studies in Religion/Sciences religieuses*, which replaced *The Canadian Journal of Theology*, founded in 1955) (Coward 2014, 5).

In addition to political and legal factors—consider that immigration laws had recently been changed, facilitating immigration of non-Europeans—cultural and religious changes played into the hands of the emerging discipline: the tempering of Western civilizational triumphalism and an ideology of superiority and the countercultural movement and its interest in alternative ways of life and ideologies. Many new departments and programs have been created since the 1960s, though divinity schools, where the discipline had already been taught, remained prominent.

The University of Chicago, where the study of religion\s was eventually transferred to the Divinity School, remained especially renowned. It managed to hire several academic luminaries and some charismatic personalities (such as Eliade and Jonathan Z. Smith). It also secured its intellectual impact through its joint venture with the University of Chicago Press, which since 1961/1962 has published the journal *History of Religions*, whose editors from the time of its founding editor (Eliade), have been professors at the Divinity School.

CONSOLIDATION AND ONGOING MARGINALITY

On an international scale, by the 1970s, the study of religion\s had reached a steady institutional basis, which was further developed in the following decades. In some countries, this development was driven by increased student enrollment. In Scandinavia and Germany, for example, the subject became more popular in the 1980s and 1990s, sometimes outperforming theology in terms of student numbers (but not in terms of academic positions). In Central and Eastern Europe, the discipline was put on the academic map by the fall of the Iron Curtain and the demise of atheist state ideologies (Bubík/Hoffmann 2015), and it benefited from the political changes in China. Nevertheless, in most countries where the discipline is by now recognized, it tends to remain rather marginal; it is far from present at all universities, not even at all top universities. Even where it is found, it is usually not among the most strategically important programs or departments, despite the fact that 9/11 and other political events have given expertise on religion a certain urgency.

Yet, there are many countries and regions in which the study of religion\s remains quasi-absent as an academic discipline. In countries dominated by Islam, the discipline is typically not established at universities, perhaps because it is only operative when it studies all instances of the category 'religion' according to the same principles of academic scrutiny, which can be perceived as a critical relativization and methodological or even metaphysical egalitarianism that could risk spilling over to other spheres of social and political life. By contrast, in countries with a Muslim majority population and state ideologies that do not emphasize Islam, openings toward establishing the study of religion\s have emerged: e.g. in Turkey and Indonesia. Yet, even in the Islamic Republic of Iran some departments of comparative religion have been established in faculties of theology at state universities, and there is a faculty of comparative religion at the private University of Religions and Denominations in Qom.

Turning to the non-Islamic Middle East, in Israel the study of religion\s flourished for several decades at the Hebrew University of Jerusalem, but not at other universities or colleges. Even though much relevant research continues to be conducted by Israeli scholars, the discipline has lost its foothold at the Hebrew University after the chair holder (Guy Stroumsa) accepted a position in Britain and was not replaced. In Beirut, Lebanon, a Faculty of Religious Sciences was established in the year 2000 at the Université de Saint-Joseph, a Jesuit institution. The name of this division is quite accurate since the programs and research conducted at this faculty seem to have a religious orientation, so that we are dealing with *religious* sciences—or theology.

India is another important country where the study of religion\s has not established a bridgehead, even though it remains a vibrant 'object' of study. Relevant religion-related academic research is done in a variety of settings and there even is a national IAHR member association; yet, some departments and programs notwithstanding, as an academic discipline the study of religion\s remains largely absent at universities and centers of research (see Narayanan 2015 for a discussion). Moreover, American Hindus and right-wing Hindu nationalists in India have repeatedly criticized, and sometimes even threatened, American scholars of Hinduism.

In addition to Central, Western, and South Asia, the discipline has not achieved much of a foothold in Central and Latin America. In Brazil, however, several doctoral programs have emerged, journals and a handbook have been published, and there is an IAHR member association (Engler 2006).

Intellectual Limitations

In a self-critical mode one might add that the institutional marginality of the discipline corresponds to its intellectual mediocrity. I see little diffusion of specific issues in study of religion\s to other disciplines; the study of religion\s has mostly been at the receiving end of inter- or transdisciplinary innovations. Developments such as the linguistic, performative, literary, postcolonial, spatial, translational, discursive, iconic, material, or sonic turns in the humanities and/or social sciences had long been explored by other disciplines before they had an impact on the study-of-religion\s; the same can be said about actor-network theory, cognitive science, or evolutionary theory, which are often applied to religion in creative ways, but generally not by scholars trained in the study of religion\s. Theories of religion are relatively rarely advanced by scholars of religion (Stausberg 2009b; 2010), and, while the discipline has reveled in meta-theoretical and meta-methodological reflections, research methods have still not reached the level of sophistication found in several other disciplines (Stausberg/Engler 2011). Even though this *Handbook* may show progress on many fronts and even though solid work continues to be published on many religions, there is little reason for collective self-congratulation.

Contextual Factors

The development of the discipline depends on a variety of societal, economic, and political developments, some of which were mentioned in this chapter. Changes in educational policies such as the so-called Bologna process in Europe have implications for the course of the discipline (Stausberg 2011). Another important factor is the existence (or not) and the scope of 'religion' as a subject of primary and secondary education and the potential involvement of the study of religion\s in teacher training—where this is the case, the discipline often (but not always) has a relatively solid institutional grounding. Especially in North America, but also in Britain, religious benefactors have started funding positions in the study of their respective religious traditions such as Hinduism, Sikhism, and Zoroastrianism (but also Catholicism and Christianity). In the case of Sikhism, conflicts between scholars holding these positions and Sikh groups have occurred.

Modes of or possibilities for research sponsorship are decisive for the progress of the discipline. In Britain, larger projects in the study of religion\s have been funded only in the past decade, and in Germany three universities (Bochum, Erfurt, and Leipzig) have considerably up-scaled their involvement in the discipline thanks to major grants. Internationally, the John Templeton Foundation (established 1987), for example, made projects focusing on certain types of questions viable. Given that such 'big' questions are typically not posed by contemporary study-of-religion\s scholars, scholars from other disciplines have been in a better position to benefit from this opportunity.

Patterns of Progress

Most work in the study of religion\s is done in specific geographical, historical, or tradition-related fields of research. There are few generalists: scholars are mainly scholars of region A, period B, and/or religion C. Some work on two or three fields, but only few virtuosos master more corpora of sources and historical contexts. Progress in these fields follows the ordinary logic of scientific progress. Occasionally, innovation takes the form of drawing on imported approaches: poststructural, feminist, critical, cognitive, material, spatial, and other approaches can be and have been engaged with in any subfield of study. Additionally, perspectives such as 'lived' or 'everyday' religion have almost unlimited ranges of application (see Tweed 2015 for a critical discussion).

The still-so-called world religions are taught and studied in undergraduate programs all over the globe. It is also typical that each country or continent has a preference for its respective indigenous religious cultures and heritages: ancient Mediterranean religions are studied all across in Europe, old Norse and Sami religions are studied most intensely in Scandinavia, African scholars work on African religious traditions, Chinese scholars on Confucianism and Daoism, Koreans on indigenous shamanism, Japanese colleagues on Japanese religious traditions, and American scholars on Native Americans. In addition, Brazilians study Brazilian religions (but leave the study of indigenous traditions to anthropologists), Europeans study religion in European history, Americans study American religion, etc. Moreover, contemporary cultural and religious history brings groups, movements, and phenomena into the scholarly limelight: e.g. East Asian scholars, for example in Japan and South Korea, have intensively studied New Religious Movements. Thus, religious developments to some extent naturally steer the history of scholarship, but other disciplines are often faster in providing benchmark work (take Pentecostalism for example, where sociologists, anthropologists, and theologians have taken the initiative). Because of some extraordinary circumstances, the study of Western Esotericism is one of the few exceptions where scholars trained in the study of religion\s have taken the lead (Stausberg 2013).

Given the immensity of possible, and potentially interesting, data for the study of religion\s, there is an endless range of potential areas for empirical research. Journal editors are regularly faced with the situation that there are only two, three, or at most a handful of scholars who could potentially act as expert referees for a submission; likewise, there is a limited range of readership for such articles, if accepted for publication. As knowledge grows, increasing specialization in research appears to be endemic to academic progress. In nostalgic narratives this might be framed as fragmentation, while more optimist accounts would interpret this as increased diversity, specialization, or even sophistication. Of course, other aspects of the disciplinary practice, in particular teaching and supervision, provide counterbalances to overspecialization.

Journal History

The trend toward diversification in the study of religion\s can be documented by looking at the history of academic journals. There are two main types of journals: generalist journals that impose no restrictions in terms of types of materials or approach within the boundaries of the discipline; and specialist ones, which define their agenda in terms of specific (sub)fields of research. Generalist journals range along a spectrum from the more national to the more international by way of circulation and origin of authors. The IAHR has its own generalist journal (*Numen*), which is highly international, while many national associations have their separate generalist journals, which are often primarily targeted at national audiences and mainly receive submissions from their countries of origin. International outreach is also a matter of language: journals with international ambitions will nowadays seek to publish predominantly, even if not exclusively, in English. An example of this hegemony of English can be traced in the history of *Numen*. Between 1995 and 2013, excluding book reviews, *Numen* published some 300 articles as well as obituaries, conference reports, country reports, editorials, notes, and review articles. Almost all of these papers were in English—with the exception of seven in French and six in German. By contrast, in the first three years (1954–1956) of that journal, more non-English pieces were published than in the last eighteen years: fourteen in German, eleven in French, and three in Italian. Yet, the use of English alone does not make a generalist journal international. The previously mentioned *Journal for the Study of Religion*, for example, published by the Association for the Study of Religion in Southern Africa, appears not to be widely known outside of Africa. Probably the only non-English generalist journal with an international outreach, mainly in Francophone regions, is the *Revue de l'histoire des religions* (RHR), which is also the discipline's oldest periodical, published continuously since 1880. In terms of bibliometrics, however, its international impact is low (h-index: 1 according to Google Scholar; by comparison, *Numen* has an h-index of 7 (retrieved September 22, 2014).

Turning to specialist publications (leaving aside religion-related journals in the social sciences and in the philosophy of religion or related fields such as science and religion), while there were some earlier specialist journals that were discontinued, two region-specific journals started publishing in the 1960s: *Contemporary Religions in Japan* (1960ff.), published in Japan, which later changed its name to *Japanese Journal of Religious Studies* (1974ff.), and the *Journal of Religion in Africa* (1967ff.). With the exception of *Religion Today* (1984ff.), since 1995 known as the *Journal of Contemporary Religion*, the construction of niches in terms of specialized journals started in the 1990s and accelerated in the middle of the past decade. Consider the following list for specific religious traditions and regions, arranged chronologically:

- *Journal of Islamic Studies* (1990ff.)
- *Islam and Christian–Muslim Relations* (1990ff.)
- *International Journal of Hindu Studies* (1997ff.)
- *Annual Review of Islam in Africa* (1998ff.)
- *The Journal of Southern Religion* (1998ff.)
- *Contemporary Buddhism* (2000)
- *Aries: Journal for the Study of Western Esotericism* (2001ff.)
- *Comparative Islamic Studies* (2005ff.)
- *Sikh Formations* (2005ff.)
- *Religions of South Asia* (2007ff.)
- *Journal of Hindu Studies* (2008ff.)

- *Journal of Religion in Europe* (2008ff.)
- *Journal of Global Buddhism* (2010ff.)
- *Journal of Korean Religions* (2010ff.)
- *Journal of Religion in Japan* (2012ff.)
- *Religious Studies in Japan* (2012)

In addition, in the same period several journals have appeared that have a thematic focus:

- *Religion and the Arts* (1996ff.)
- *Implicit Religion* (1998ff.)
- *Fieldwork in Religion* (2005ff.)
- *Material Religion* (2005ff.)
- *Journal for the Study of Religion, Nature and Culture* (2007ff. [formerly *Ecotheology*])
- *Relegere: Studies in Religion and Reception* (2011ff.).

There are clusters of journals for some fields, such as spirituality studies, which are only loosely connected to the study of religion\s, and religion and law, where scholars of religion\s are a minority of editors and contributors. Similarly, there now are two journals dedicated to the cognitive and evolutionary study of religions (*Religion, Brain, & Behavior* [2011ff.] and *Journal for the Cognitive Science of Religion* [2013ff.]). A new journal makes a case for engaging critical theories in the study of religion\s (*Critical Research in Religion* [2013ff.]). This growth of niche publication outlets—seen from a disciplinary perspective—reflects the emergence and stabilization of fields of study. However, it also reflects the eagerness of publishers to invest in (and profit from) new journals. The increased importance of journal publication has swept over from the natural sciences into the humanities and social sciences. Given that publication is a key currency on the academic market, publishers must not be neglected as factors and actors in the shaping of the discipline, seeing as they still control the majority of publication outlets. The impact of the recent emergence of inter- or transdisciplinary Open Access journals on the discipline remains to be seen.

Even generalist journals have continued to grow. In addition to a growing number of journals, established journals such as *Numen* and *JAAR* have increased their numbers of published issues and pages; until 1998, for example, *Numen* had three annual issues, while the journal is now up to six issues per year. Until the end of the 1980s the number of generalist journals was relatively small; here is the list of the earlier ones that are still being published:

- *Revue de l'histoire des religions* (1880ff.)
- *Studi e Materiali di Storia delle Religioni* (1925ff. [with some interruptions]/Italy)
- *Numen* (1954ff.)
- *Journal of Religious History* (1960ff. [predominantly a church history journal])
- *History of Religions* (1961ff.)
- *Temenos* (1965ff./Scandinavia)

- *Journal of the American Academy of Religion* (1966)
- *Religion* (1971ff./initially British)
- *Studies in Religion/Sciences Religieuses* (1971ff. [bilingual, Canadian; also publishes theology])

These remain flagship journals in the discipline, among which *Religion* "has the largest number of often-cited articles" (Engler 2014, 213). In the past twenty-five years, however, more than ten new generalist journals publishing in English, French, and German have been launched:

- *Method & Theory in the Study of Religion* (1989ff./linked with the NAASR)
- *Religiologiques* (1990ff./French)
- *Zeitschrift für Religionswissenschaft* (1993ff.; journal of the German Association for the Study of Religion)
- *Diskus* (1993–1996; 2006ff./OA journal of the British Association for the Study of Religion)
- *Marburg Journal of Religion* (1996ff./OA, relatively few articles published)
- *Archiv für Religionsgeschichte* (1999ff.)
- *Culture and Religion* (2000ff.)
- *Archævs* (2001ff./multilingual, published from Romania)
- *Asdiwal* (2006ff./mainly French, published from Geneva)
- *Religion Compass* (2007ff./review articles)
- *Historia religionum* (2009ff./published from Italy)
- *Approaching Religion* (2011ff./OA/published from Finland)
- *Journal for the Academic Study of Religion* (2013ff., formerly *Australian Religion Studies Review*, the journal of the Australian Association for the Study of Religion)

In addition, there are several relatively young journals in other languages (e.g. in Portuguese, Danish, and Norwegian). The proliferation of journals may be read as evidence for the increasing growth and consolidation of the discipline and its publication activities. From the other chapters published in this *Handbook*, readers will be able to decide for themselves whether work is moving in the right directions—whatever they might consider these to be.

GLOSSARY

Discipline a distinct segment of an academic field comprising processes of boundary making, an academic/social community of scholars, institutional structures such as chairs, departments, and associations, platforms of communication such as journals, and modes of transmission and recognition such as programs of study and degrees.

Field a relatively amorphous area of academic work that covers a given subject matter, broadly understood, e.g. 'religion,' and that is undertaken by scholars from a variety of academic disciplines such as the study of religion\s.

References

Accorinti, Domenico. 2014. *Raffaele Pettazzoni and Herbert Jennings Rose, Correspondence 1927–1958. The Long Friendship between the Author and the Translator of the All-Knowing God. With an Appendix of Documents.* Leiden and Boston: Brill.

Alles, Gregory D., ed. 2008. *Religious Studies: A Global View.* London and New York: Routledge.

Alles, Gregory D. 2009. "The Study of Religions: The Last 50 Years." In *The Routledge Companion to the Study of Religion*, 2nd edition, edited by John R. Hinnells. London and New York: Routledge, 39–55.

Arnal, William E. and Russell T. McCutcheon. 2013. *The Sacred Is the Profane: The Political Nature of "Religion."* Oxford and New York: Oxford University Press.

Bleeker, C. Jouco. 1968. "The Opening Address." In *Proceedings of the XIth International Congress of the International Association for the History of Religions. I: The Impact of Modern Culture on Traditional Religions.* Leiden: Brill, 3–12.

Boespflug, François. 2010. "The History of Religions and Francophone Research in Europe: Main Disciplinary Trends in Switzerland, France, Belgium and Luxemburg." *Religion* 40(4): 259–270. doi: 10.1016/j.religion.2010.07.003

Borgeaud, Philippe. 2004. *Aux Origines de l'histoire des Religions.* Paris: Seuil.

Brodeur, Patrice. 2008. "North Africa and West Asia." In *Religious Studies: A Global View*, edited by Gregory D. Alles. London and New York: Routledge, 75–101.

Bubík, Tomáš and Henryk Hoffmann, eds. 2015. *Studying Religions with the Iron Curtain Closed and Opened: The Academic Study of Religion in Eastern Europe.* Leiden and Boston: Brill.

Buckley, Jorunn Jacobsen. 2012. *Lady E. S. Drower's Scholarly Correspondence: An Intrepid English Autodidact in Iraq.* Leiden and Boston: Brill.

Capps, Walter H. 1995. *Religious Studies: The Making of a Discipline.* Minneapolis, MN: Fortress Press.

Carmody, Brendan. 2007. "The Nature and Role of Religious Studies at the University of Zambia: 1985–2005." *British Journal of Religious Education* 30(1): 25–35. doi: 10.1080/01416200701711683

Cherry, Conrad. 1995. *Hurrying toward Zion: Universities, Divinity Schools, and American Protestantism.* Bloomington: Indiana University Press.

Chidester, David. 2014. *Empire of Religion: Imperialism and Comparative Religion.* Chicago and London: University of Chicago Press.

Chitando, Ezra. 2008. "Sub-Saharan Africa." In *Religious Studies: A Global View*, edited by Gregory D. Alles. London and New York: Routledge, 102–125.

Clasquin, Michel. 2005. "Religious Studies in South(ern) Africa: An Overview." *Journal for the Study of Religion* 18(2): 5–22.

Coward, Harold. 2014. *Fifty Years of Religious Studies in Canada: A Personal Retrospective.* Waterloo, ON: Wilfrid Laurier University Press.

Cox, James L. 2007. *From Primitive to Indigenous: The Academic Study of Indigenous Religions.* Aldershot and Burlington, VT: Ashgate.

Cox, James L. and Steve Sutcliffe. 2006. "Religious Studies in Scotland: A Persistent Tension with Divinity." *Religion* 36(1): 1–28. doi: 10.1016/j.religion.2005.12.001

de Jong, Albert. 2008. "Historians of Religion as Agents of Religious Change." In *The Study of Religion and the Training of Muslim Clergy in Europe: Academic and Religious Freedom in the 21st Century*, edited by Willem B. Drees and Pieter Sjoerd van Koningsveld. Leiden: Leiden University Press, 195–218.

Engler, Steven. 2006. "Religious Studies in Canada and Brazil: Pro-Pluralism and Anti-Theology in Context." *Studies in Religion/Sciences religieuses* 35(3–4): 447–473. doi: 10.1177/000842980603500306

Engler, Steven. 2014. "Bibliometrics and the Study of Religion\s." *Religion* 44(2): 193–219. doi: 10.1080/0048721X.2014.893680

Engler, Steven and Michael Stausberg. 2011. "Introductory Essay. Crisis and Creativity: Opportunities and Threats in the Global Study of Religion/s." *Religion* 41(2): 127–143. doi: 10.1080/0048721X.2011.591209

Franzmann, Majella. 2008. "Australia, New Zealand and the Pacific Islands." In *Religious Studies: A Global View*, edited by Gregory D. Alles. London and New York: Routledge, 218–241.

Fujiwara, Satoko. 2008. "Japan." In *Religious Studies: A Global View*, edited by Gregory D. Alles. London and New York: Routledge, 191–217.

Girardot, N. J. 2002. "Max Müller's *Sacred Books* and the Nineteenth-Century Production of the Comparative Science of Religion." *History of Religions* 41(3): 213–250.

Guanghu, He, Chung Chin-hong, and Lee Chang-yick. 2008. "Continental East Asia." In *Religious Studies: A Global View*, edited by Gregory D. Alles. London and New York: Routledge, 159–190.

Hanegraaff, Wouter J. 2012. *Esotericism and the Academy: Rejected Knowledge in Western Culture*. Cambridge: Cambridge University Press.

Hart, Ray L. 1979. "JAAR in the Seventies: Unconcluding Unscientific Postface." *Journal of the American Academy of Religion* 47(4): 509–516. doi: 10.1093/jaarel/XLVII.4.509

Hayashi, Makoto. 2011. "Religious Studies in Japan: A Historical Perspective." *Pantheon: religionistický časopis* 6(1): 4–14.

Heinrich, Fritz. 2002. *Die Deutsche Religionswissenschaft und der Nationalsozialismus: Eine ideologiekritische und wissenschaftsgeschichtliche Untersuchung*. Petersberg: Imhof.

Isomae, Jun'ichi. 2014. *Religious Discourse in Modern Japan: Religion, State, and Shintō*. Leiden: Brill.

Jensen, Tim. 2010. "The EASR within (the World Scenario of) the IAHR: Observations and Reflections." *Historia Religionum* 2: 61–90.

Josephson, Jason Ānanda. 2011. "The Invention of Japanese Religions." *Religion Compass* 5(10): 589–597. doi: 10.1111/j.1749-8171.2011.00307.x

Josephson, Jason Ananda. 2012. *The Invention of Religion in Japan*. Chicago, IL and London: University of Chicago Press.

Junginger, Horst, ed. 2008. *The Study of Religion under the Impact of Fascism*. Leiden: Brill.

Kippenberg, Hans G. 2001. *Discovering Religious History in the Modern Age*. Translated by Barbara Harshav. Princeton, NJ: Princeton University Press.

Krech, Volkhard. 2002. *Wissenschaft und Religion: Studien Zur Geschichte der Religionsforschung in Deutschland 1871–1933*. Tübingen: J. C. B. Mohr (Paul Siebeck).

Lange, Dietz. 2011. *Nathan Söderblom und seine Zeit*. Göttingen: Vandenhoeck & Ruprecht.

Maier, Bernhard. 2009. *William Robertson Smith: His Life, His Work and His Times*. Tübingen: Mohr Siebeck.

Maier, Bernhard. 2012. "Habent Sua Fata Libelli: Thoughts on an Early Parody of Max Müller and Other Classics in Comparative Religious Studies." *Religion* 42(4): 495–519. doi: 10.1080/0048721X.2012.681979

Masuzawa, Tomoko. 2005. *The Invention of World Religions, or, How European Universalism Was Preserved in the Language of Pluralism*. Chicago, IL and London: University of Chicago Press.

Meyer, Christian. 2015. "The Emergence of 'Religious Studies' (*Zongjiaoxue*) in Late Imperial and Republican China, 1890–1949." *Numen* 62(1): 40–75. doi: 10.1163/15685276-12341355

Meyer, Christian. In preparation. *Die chinesische 'Entdeckung' der Religionsgeschichte*. Göttingen: Vandenhoeck & Ruprecht.

Moberg, David O. 2000. "Refining the Nature and Purpose of Research on Religion: Competing Goals in the Early Years (1944–1973) of the RRA and SSSR." *Journal for the Scientific Study of Religion* 39(4): 401–421. doi: 10.1111/j.1468-5906.2000.tb00003.x

Molendijk, Arie L. 2005. *The Emergence of the Science of Religion in the Netherlands*. Leiden and Boston, MA: Brill.

Müller, Friedrich Max. 1901. *My Autobiography: A Fragment*. New York: C. Scribner's Sons.

Narayanan, Vasudha. 2015. "The History of the Academic Study of Religion in Universities, Centers, and Institutes in India." *Numen* 62(1): 7–39. doi:10.1163/15685276-12341354

Olademo, Oyeronke. 2011. "A Critical Appraisal of Recent Trends in the Teaching of Religious Studies in Nigerian Universities." *Religion* 41(2): 169–174. doi: 10.1080/0048721X.2011.579790

Pinard de la Boullaye, Henry. 1922. *L'étude comparée des Religions*. Paris: G. Beauchesne.

Platvoet, Jan G. 1989. "The Institutional Environment of the Study of Religion South of the Sahara." In *Marburg Revisited: Institutions and Strategies in the Study of Religion*, edited by Michael Pye. Marburg: Diagonal, 107–126.

Platvoet, Jan. 1996. "From Object to Subject: A History of the Study of the Religions of Africa." In *The Study of Religions in Africa: Past, Present and Prospect*, edited by Jan Platvoet, James Cox, and Jacob Olupona. Cambridge: Roots and Branches, 105–138.

Remus, Harold E., F. Stanley Lusby, and Linda M. Tober. 1988. "Religion as Academic Discipline." In *Encyclopedia of the American Religious Experience: Studies of Traditions and Movements. Volume III*, edited by Charles H. Lippy and Peter W. Williams. New York: Charles Scribner's Sons, 1653–1669.

Rennie, Bryan. 2013. "Raffaele Pettazzoni from the Perspective of the Anglophone Academy." *Numen* 60(5–6): 649–675. doi: 10.1163/15685276-12341298

Reuben, Julie A. 1996. *The Making of the Modern University: Intellectual Transformation and the Marginalization of Morality*. Chicago, IL and London: University of Chicago Press.

Seiwert, Hubert. 1989. "The Institutional Context of the History of Religions in China." In *Marburg Revisited: Institutions and Strategies in the Study of Religion*, edited by Michael Pye. Marburg: Diagonal, 127–141.

Severino, Valerio Salvatore. 2015. "For a Secular Return to the Sacred: Raffaele Pettazzoni's Last Statement on the Name of the Science of Religions." *Religion* 45(1): 1–23. doi: 10.1080/0048721X.2014.918060

Sharpe, Eric J. 1980. "Comparative Religion at the University of Manchester, 1904–1979." *Bulletin of the John Rylands University Library of Manchester* 63(1): 144–170.

Sharpe, Eric J. 1990. *Nathan Söderblom and the Study of Religion*. Chapel Hill: University of North Carolina Press.

Sharpe, Eric J. 1997. *Comparative Religion: A History*. Chicago and La Salle, IL: Open Court. Original edition, 1975.

Shepard, Robert Stephen. 1991. *God's People in the Ivory Tower: Religion in the Early American University*. Brooklyn, NY: Carlson Pub.

Smith, Jonathan Z. 2001. "A Twice-Told Tale: The History of the History of Religions' History." *Numen* 48(2): 131–146. doi:10.2307/3270496

Smith, Wilfred Cantwell. 1968. "Traditional Religions and Modern Culture" ' In *Proceedings of the XIth International Congress of the International Association for the History of Religions. I: The Impact of Modern Culture on Traditional Religions*, 55–72. Leiden: Brill.

Spineto, Natale, ed. 1994. *Mircea Eliade/Raffaele Pettazzoni: L'histoire des Religions a-t-elle un sens? Correspondence 1926–1959*. Paris: Les Éditions du Cerf.

Spineto, Natale. 2010. "Religioni. Studi Storici-Comparativi." In *Dizionario del sapere storico-religioso del Novecento II*, edited by Alberto Melloni. Bologna: Il Mulino, 1256–1317.

Stausberg, Michael. 2007. "The Study of Religion(s) in Western Europe (I): Prehistory and History until World War II." *Religion* 37(4): 294–318. doi: 10.1016/j.religion.2007.10.001

Stausberg, Michael. 2008. "The Study of Religion(s) in Western Europe (II): Institutional Developments after World War II." *Religion* 38(4): 305–318. doi: 10.1016/j.religion.2008.08.008

Stausberg, Michael. 2009a. "The Study of Religion(s) in Western Europe (III): Further Developments after World War II." *Religion* 39(3): 261–282. doi: 10.1016/j.religion.2009.06.001

Stausberg, Michael, ed. 2009b. *Contemporary Theories of Religion: A Critical Companion.* London and New York: Routledge.

Stausberg, Michael. 2010. "Prospects in Theories of Religion." *Method & Theory in the Study of Religion* 22(4): 223–238. doi: doi:10.1163/157006810X531021

Stausberg, Michael. 2011. "The Bologna Process and the Study of Religion/s in (Western) Europe." *Religion* 41(2): 187–207. doi: 10.1080/0048721X.2011.586259

Stausberg, Michael. 2013. "What Is *It* All About? Some Reflections on Wouter Hanegraaff's *Esotericism and the Academy*." *Religion* 43(2): 219–230. doi: 10.1080/0048721X.2013.767612

Stausberg, Michael. 2014. "Advocacy in the Study of Religion/s." *Religion* 44(2): 220–232. doi: 10.1080/0048721X.2014.892248

Stausberg, Michael and Steven Engler, ed. 2011. *The Routledge Handbook of Research Methods in the Study of Religion.* London: Routledge.

Strenski, Ivan. 2004. "Ideological Critique in the Study of Religion: Real Thinkers, Real Contexts and a Little Humility." In *New Approaches to the Study of Religion. Volume 2: Textual, Comparative, Sociological, and Cognitive Approaches*, edited by Peter Antes, Armin W. Geertz, and Randi R. Warne. Berlin and New York: de Gruyter, 271–293.

Stroumsa, Guy G. 2010. *A New Science: The Discovery of Religion in the Age of Reason.* Cambridge, MA and London: Harvard University Press.

Sun, Anna Xiao Dong. 2013. *Confucianism as a World Religion: Contested Histories and Contemporary Realities.* Princeton, NJ and Oxford: Princeton University Press.

Tweed, Thomas A. 2015. "After the Quotidian Turn: Interpretive Categories and Scholarly Trajectories in the Study of Religion since the 1960s." *The Journal of Religion* 95(3): 361–385. doi: 10.1086/681112

van den Bosch, Lourens P. 2002. *Friedrich Max Müller: A Life Devoted to the Humanities.* Leiden and Boston, MA: Brill.

Wheeler-Barclay, Marjorie. 2010. *The Science of Religion in Britain, 1860–1915.* Charlottesville and London: University of Virginia Press.

Wiebe, Donald. 2006. "An Eternal Return All over Again: The Religious Conversation Endures." *Journal of the American Academy of Religion* 74(3): 674–696. doi: 10.1093/jaarel/lfj091

Wiebe, Donald. 2015. "Memory, Text, and Interpretation: A Critical Appreciation of Iahr International Congresses—1975 to 2010." In *NVMEN, the Academic Study of Religion and the IAHR*, edited by Tim Jensen and Armin Geertz. Leiden: Brill, 245–274.

Wiegers, Gerard. 2002. "Introduction. The Science of Religion: Its Social Functions and Applications in a Changing World." In *Modern Societies & the Science of Religions: Studies in Honour of Lammert Leertouwer*, edited by Gerard Wiegers. Leiden: Brill, 17–38.

FURTHER READING

Alles 2008 [*A collection of chapters covering all regions of the world; it envisions a discipline that "is a global enterprise" (2).*]

Bubík/Hoffmann 2015 [*Essays on the trajectories of the study of religion/s in the Czech Republic, Estonia, Hungary, Latvia, Poland, Russia, Slovakia, and the Ukraine.*]

Coward 2014 [*Reflections on the history of the study of religion/s in Canada by a senior Canadian scholar.*]

Smith 2001 [*More concerned with the prehistory of the discipline, the author distinguishes between two major historiographical strategies of narrating the history of religious studies, which he calls the exceptionalist and the assimilationist, the former emphasizing its distinctiveness, the latter its equivalence with other human sciences.*]

Spineto 2010 [*A book-length up-to-date treatment of the intellectual and institutional history of the discipline from a highly international and critical perspective.*]

The Encyclopedia of Religion. 2005. Edited by Lindsay Jones. Detroit: Macmillan Reference. [*This reference work has several relevant entries, see especially "Study of Religion" as well as numerous entries on individual scholars.*]

CHAPTER 51

··

RELEVANCE

··

THOMAS A. TWEED

CHAPTER SUMMARY

···

- The liberal arts are relevant because they preserve subjectivity, are socially useful, contribute to happiness, contribute to democracy, and are intrinsically valuable.
- The study of religion is relevant because it advances knowledge, enriches individuals, and improves society.
- Assessing the value and relevance of the study of religion requires acknowledging guiding values, considering local contexts, and recognizing multiple goods.

The need for this entry, which considers the relevance of the academic study of religion, emerges from the sense that someone thinks the subject is not worthwhile. If you have managed to get to the end of this *Handbook*, the value of the study of religion might not be in question for you. However, since the 1990s, and with renewed vigor since the late 2000s, it has been challenged, including by those who fund and administer higher education (Engler/Stausberg 2011, 128; Lease 1995, 301). So it is useful to reconsider the central question: Why study religion? But that inquiry is part of a wider debate about the value of many subjects in the liberal arts curriculum that do not seem to have direct economic utility, so it might help to recall some of the defenses scholars in the arts, humanities, and social sciences have offered. Scholars of religion have crafted their own arguments for the relevance for their subject, and I classify and assess those defenses. I conclude by proposing how we might refine the arguments by emphasizing that judgments about relevance always are made in particular contexts and for particular ends.

Defending the Relevance of the Liberal Arts

Proponents of the academic study of religion are not the only members of the Academy who have felt obliged to answer charges about their field's irrelevance. Almost all scholars who do not specialize in engineering, medicine, law, or business have felt the pressures. In an age when fewer students are majoring in the liberal arts and many stakeholders around the world expect institutions of higher education to perform like other institutions, especially corporations, critics have appealed to a narrow notion of utility as they wonder aloud why anyone should study a variety of subjects in the arts, humanities, and social sciences ("Overview of Findings"; Teichler 2007, 20; Nussbaum 2010, 1–11). Of course, charges of irrelevance have come from within colleges and universities, as when marginalized students in the United States have called for greater representation in the curriculum and Muslim scholars in Singapore have dismissed Western humanities and social sciences as 'irrelevant' and advocated 'indigenous' models and methods (Alatas 1995, 124–125). However, in most parts of the world, including Western Europe and North America, the most strident criticism has come from beyond the university gates, and those doubters have insisted on greater 'accountability' for programs and greater 'employability' for students (Stausberg 2011, 205; Nussbaum 2010, 2).

Scholars in diverse fields have come to the defense. Consider, for example, the arguments defending the value of the humanities. A professor of literature at Oxford, Helen Small, has identified five basic types of arguments (2013, 3–7): (1) unlike the natural and social sciences, the humanities' interpretative methods preserve "an indispensible element of subjectivity"; (2) despite charges to the contrary, "the humanities are useful to society"; (3) these humanistic fields of study "have a contribution to make to our individual and collective happiness"; (4) because the humanities cultivate skills in reflection and argument, "democracy needs us"; (5) setting aside all consideration of their instrumental value, some suggest that "the humanities matter for their own sake."

Defending the Relevance of the Study of Religion

Those who promote the academic study of religion have made similar arguments, though their defenses have taken slightly different forms, partly because advocates claim that religion plays a distinctive role in posing ultimate questions and shaping global cultures, even if most acknowledge the role of literature in stimulating imagination and philosophy in sharpening reasoning. Some appeal to the utility argument and suggest either that religious practice is adaptive for the individual or that knowledge about religion is crucial for carrying out their role-specific duties in a variety of occupations, from physicians and social workers to legislators and diplomats. So the scholarly literature includes everything from studies of the positive effects of religious commitment for bi-polar patients (Mitchell/Romans 2003) and the elderly (Johnson 1995) to the role of religious literacy in improving international relations (Sheikh 2012) and the effectiveness of 'faith-based diplomacy' in building peace (Johnston 2003). In a similar way, some scholars in the liberal arts also trumpet the study of religion's relevance, including philosopher Martha Nussbaum (2010, 83), who claims that "crucial to the success of democracies in our world is the understanding of the world's many religious traditions."

Religion scholars have offered defenses that identify varied private and public goods, including similar appeals to the utility of their subject for democratic citizenship (Alles 2011, 221). But, as ongoing scholarly debates and conflicting organizational mission statements indicate, religion scholars disagree among themselves about what constitutes the 'academic' study of religion, even if most concur that the undergraduate major is "intercultural, comparative, and multidisciplinary" (Taves 2011, 289; Führding 2009; "The Religion Major" 2007).

This is not the place to recount all the debates about the boundaries of the 'academic' study of religion: divergent views of the relation between theology and religious studies as well as disagreements between those who favor either 'interpretation' or 'explanation' as the primary aim. It is important to note, however, that some of those differences manifest themselves in the mission statements, by laws, and constitutions of the major scholarly organizations for the study of religion around the world. Engler (2006) offers a helpful comparison of the Canadian and Brazilian cases, and to get some sense of the broader continuities and discontinuities you might follow the links to the Members and Affiliates at the International Association for the History of Religions' (IAHR) web page and compare those official statements (<http://www.iahr.dk/associations.php>). Note, for example, that the official statements of the African Association for the Study of Religions (AASR), the Japanese Association for Religious Studies (JARS), and the European Association for the Study of Religions (EASR) simply say that they are dedicated to the 'academic' study of religion but do not map the boundaries more precisely than that. Some organizations explicitly exclude theological approaches, as with the IAHR's declaration that it "is not a forum for confessional, apologetical, or other similar concerns," and the Dutch Association for the Study of Religion's (NGG) statement indicates that it represents an academic field "distinct from Christian theology" and one that "analyzes the history and the contemporary forms of religion from a non-confessional and critical perspective." Other professional groups make a point to include theologians, as with the Australian Association for the Study of Religion (AASR), the Canadian Society for the Study of Religion (CSSR), and the American Academy of Religion (AAR). Each mentions 'theology' or, as with the AAR, uses similar language. Consider the AAR's mission statement: "Within a context of free inquiry and critical examination, the Academy welcomes all disciplined reflection on religion—both from within and outside of communities of belief and practice . . . ."

Some identify the study of religion with the humanities; others with the social sciences. And some suggest it "straddles" the two (Engler/Stausberg 2011, 135). Still others urge "increased collaboration" with the natural sciences (Taves 2011, 288). Some religion specialists include theology as well as approaches that aim for "interpretation" (Hinnells 2005, 5, 13–14), while others reserve the label 'academic' only for methods that seek to 'explain' religious practice in terms of psychological, sociological, or economic forces (Wiebe 1998; Lease 1995; Alles 2008, 5–7; Berner 2011, 155–156).

Yet there are some continuities. Religion specialists have made several types of arguments for their field's relevance, usually combining more than one of these defenses. They have suggested that the study of religion (1) advances knowledge, (2) enriches individuals, and (3) improves society.

The first sort of argument takes at least two forms. Repeating one prominent defense of the humanities and refusing to imagine such intellectual activity as a means to some other end, some scholars suggest that the academic study of religion should be valued not only for instrumental reasons but also 'for its own sake' (Hinnells 2005, 8, 19; Engler/Stausberg 2011, 139). When specialists worry only about the subject's contemporary relevance, those who favor this intrinsic-value argument warn, it can lead to a preoccupation with the here and now at the expense of interacting with other cultures and learning about the past (Freiberger 2013). Keeping the focus within the campus walls, others note that the study of religion makes important contributions to other academic fields. One German scholar combines both arguments, for example, suggesting that studying the religions of the world is worthwhile "for its own sake as a treasure house of accumulated knowledge of great importance," but also because it is "a functional help to other disciplines," including law, science, medicine, communication, and business (Antes 2002, 42, 52; see also Tweed 1998; Engler/Stausberg 2011, 138).

A second cluster of arguments focuses on what such pursuits do for the individual. These arguments, which resonate with defenses that point to 'happiness' as an outcome of humanistic study, have both faith-based and secular versions, with proponents suggesting, for example, that the study of religion "helps us formulate our own religious belief or philosophy of life" (Livingston 2009, 13). This approach has drawn stringent criticisms (McCutcheon 2011, xii), but in its most widely accepted form it suggests that the study of religion leads to "the enrichment of life" (Alles 2011, 221). It is enriching because religious traditions propose answers to the most important questions about human existence, and reflecting on those can provide "meaning, purpose, and comfort" (Jacobsen/Jacobsen 2008, 12; Livingston 2009, 13). Studying religions also yields transforming moral benefits: encountering other ways of being human inculcates satisfying and praiseworthy habits of thinking, feeling, and acting. It cultivates virtues. The academic study of religion is "intrinsically deprovincializing" (Alles 2011, 221); it increases students' empathy, tolerance, and openness (Hinnells 2005, 9, 15).

These personal enrichments, some suggest, also advance the collective good, and another cluster of defenses for religion's place in the curriculum points to the ways it impacts the public arena. The study of religion can help to reduce the 'bigotry' that leads to conflict and violence, some propose (e.g. Alles 2011, 222). And many celebrate spiritually inspired peacemakers around the globe, from Mahatma Gandhi to Martin Luther King (e.g. Hinnells/King 2007, 1), though most scholars readily acknowledge that religion also has been one of the "forces for destruction" in many global conflicts (Hinnells 2005, 6, 19), including in Northern Ireland, Kashmir, the Balkans, the Sudan, and the Middle East. Some scholars have challenged the representational pattern of associating religion and violence because it enacts mistaken Western presuppositions and "does violence to the cultures and civilizations of the non-Western world" (King 2007, 252; see also Tweed 2008; Jerryson 2010, 3). Still, a number of religion scholars have agreed with philosopher Kwame Anthony Appiah's (2006, 137–151) suggestion that the social good requires vigilance about religion's role in producing violence, including among faith-based 'counter-cosmopolitans' across the globe who advocate a narrow sectarianism (Juergensmeyer 2000; Lincoln 2003; Kippenberg 2008).

The study of religion has a role to play, they suggest, in broadening that narrowed sectarian vision. That broadening begins with respectful and responsible comparison. Many defenses of the comparative study of religion rest on an assumption first announced by one of the field's nineteenth-century founders, Friedrich Max Müller (Hinnells 2005, 14; Müller 1870, 4–5)—"he who knows one, knows none"—and specialists emphasize the utility of "empathetic understanding of other cultures" for making sense of the past and comprehending the present (Hinnells 2005, 6; Tweed 2000, 36; Tweed 2014, 5). "Whether one is religious or not," one British scholar has proposed, "the study of religions is key to understanding other cultures; religions have been powerful forces throughout history in any country, sometimes working for the good and sometimes working to destroy," Therefore, he continues, "scholars who have left religions out of their pictures when writing about various societies, be they Hindus in Britain or Muslims in America, are excluding a key element from their study" since "it is essential to know the values, ideals, and priorities of those from another culture or religion with whom one comes into contact" (Hinnells 2005, 19). In other words, this line of argument suggests, the study of religion helps to create the conditions for democratic citizenship, social justice, and peace-building (Alles 2011, 221; Tweed 2006, 180; Livingston 2009, 12; Juergensmeyer 2000, 243). It is not only good for the academy and the individual; it improves collective well-being.

Refining the Arguments

These arguments for the relevance of the study of religion—it advances knowledge, enriches individuals, and improves society—all have merit, but scholars might refine them, if they hope to be more persuasive in conversations with detractors. Three minor refinements might help.

Acknowledging Guiding Values

First, it can help if scholars explicitly identify their own values, and not just those of their interlocutors (Tweed 2006, 13–33; Engler 2006, 449–452). Some defenders of the study of religion have offered "personal pieces" that are quite explicit, even autobiographical (Hinnells 2005, 6). More often, however, there is a baffling omission: scholars are quite clear about their opponents' condemnable values but somewhat murkier about their own laudable ones. So scholars should declare their guiding values, though this does not mean that disclosure will settle debates or that arguments about religion's intrinsic value—'for its own sake'—are always most persuasive. Clearly, that is not the case. In fact, my experience as a university administrator and a professional organization leader suggests that the opposite usually holds true. Insisting that some things are just worthwhile can have little effect. Administrators and funders deliberating about the fate of an endangered program most often think in utilitarian terms. They want to measure the benefits that will result from the costs. Yet, and this is my point here, eventually the appeals to utility come to an end, as the philosopher John Dewey (1916, 282) suggested in *Democracy and Education*: "Some goods are not good *for* anything; they are just goods. Any other notion leads to an absurdity. For we cannot stop asking the question about instrumental good, one whose value lies in its being good *for* something, unless there is something that is intrinsically good, good for itself" (see also Cahn 1988, xi–xii). In other words, defenders of religion's relevance might find themselves needing to appeal to instrumental arguments, but making sure that everyone in the conversation self-consciously articulates their own working presuppositions and deepest values can advance the conversation, even if this only reveals the extent of the disagreement.

For example, in my various professional roles, I have made all those arguments for the study of religion's relevance at one time or another; but, since I have urged scholars to acknowledge their values, I should note that I care most about advancing social justice and building lasting peace. Those are my deepest values. Further, I believe, as William James proposed, that humans have a certain imaginative and moral incapacity, "the blindness with which we all are afflicted in regard to the feelings of creatures and people different from ourselves" (James 1962, 259). To correct that 'blindness,' in the classroom I try to cultivate empathy, the ability to understand others, by making the familiar strange and making the strange familiar (Tweed 2006, 180). I do so in the hope that interpersonal understanding allows us to act compassionately, to feel with others as we work in a spirit of receptive generosity—being able to receive as well as give—to bring about more fair and peaceful ways of being in the world (Tweed 2009, 456). My experience in the classroom for more than a quarter century has convinced me that the comparative study of religion can help in producing that personal transformation which, in turn, contributes to the collective good. But an administrator might respond by suggesting that she is less interested in peace and justice, or, more likely, that those aims cannot be her guiding motives for curricular decisions. Her role-specific obligations, as she sees them, might lead that university official to insist that other values—efficiency, accountability, or employability—are higher goods. At that point, we might not be able to work out our differences in a way that leads to greater support for the study of religion, but at least we know more about the rules of the game we are playing as we contend for limited resources.

Considering Local Context

The current rules of the game in most universities around the world demand that scholars talk about the study of religion's relevance in terms of its instrumental value. That makes sense, since the meaning of the term *relevance* suggests a relative and not an absolute good. As the entry in the *Oxford English Dictionary* defines it, relevance must be assessed in terms of something's "relation to the matter at hand" or pertinence "to a specified thing". So to make a case for the study of religion's relevance is to suggest it is pertinent in a particular context for a particular purpose. It is always relevant *to* someone and *for* something. Even arguments about the value of the field for its own sake would be more persuasive in some settings than others. So context matters. Defenses should be "context-sensitive" (Engler/Stausberg 2011, 139), and they should be assessed in terms of their "contextual utility" (Tweed 2006, 165–166; see also Dewey 1988, 240). The problem is that advocates have tended to offer decontextualized arguments that presume some general state of affairs; however, actual negotiations about curricular relevance are enacted in varied cultural settings and institutional frameworks.

Pointing to his own German institution, Bayreuth University, Ulrich Berner has suggested that just as scholars of comparative religion have been sensitive to contextualize all claims about traditions, the study of religion must be 'contextualized' too (Berner 2011, 154–155). At Bayreuth, a university with a cultural studies focus on Music Theater Studies in a town famous for its Richard Wagner music festival, contextualization has meant reimagining the religion major as an interdisciplinary specialization in *Kulturwissenschaft mit Schwerpunkt Religion*, or Cultural Studies with a Focus on Religion (Berner 2011, 150). Whether or not that curricular innovation proves successful, it is noteworthy that the faculty reframed arguments for religion's relevance in terms of the cultural setting and institutional context. Specialists there can propose that their program advances knowledge by contributing to other fields of study, while it also yields social benefits by relating educational efforts to local cultural concerns, even local economic realities. Students majoring in that cultural studies program in religion might seek knowledge for its own sake. They might also find themselves being more informed global citizens. Yet defenders of the program's relevance have a better chance of being heard—at least if the faculty has understood administrators' values—if they emphasize this contextual fit.

That rhetorical and curricular strategy might not work in all contexts, however, just as no single argument will prove effective everywhere. Consider, for example, educational institutions that enjoy prominence in petroleum engineering, institutions where the study of religion defenders work in different cultural landscapes and contend with other situated interests—such as, say, the University of Calgary, the University of Qatar, or the University of Lagos. In the same way, the intrinsic-value argument might be received more warmly in religiously affiliated private schools, though in such contexts the comparative and cross-disciplinary emphasis of religious studies might be seen as a threat to faith formation, a prized educational outcome. In religiously plural nations with a state church, government-funded universities, and relatively few citizens attending worship services—for example, England or Norway—arguments that center on the curriculum's spiritual rewards might elicit fewer enthusiastic responses, while defenses that emphasize cross-cultural literacy's political and economic advantages might work better. The persuasiveness of the 'democracy needs us' argument also presumes certain political conditions: if funders and administrators do not cherish democratic principles and informed citizens, then advocates for the study of religion will have a much harder time convincing anyone with that approach. Arguments that highlight the study of religion's contributions to the humanities might have more impact in liberal arts colleges, like Swarthmore, than they might in universities with a special focus on science and engineering, such as MIT. We could multiple the examples. The point? Differences persist and context matters even if the academic study of religion has become "a global enterprise" ' (Alles 2008, 2) and surveys of students and faculty in North America and Europe indicate some agreement about the shared commitment to cross-cultural analysis (Taves 2011, 288–289; Führding 2009; "The Religion Major" 2008). Institutional context and social setting determine, to some extent, which relevance arguments might yield the best results and which good might be most widely valued among the local conversation partners.

Recognizing Multiple Goods

That means—and this is a third and final way scholars might refine their arguments for relevance—religion specialists should resist the temptation to narrow their focus to a single value or a sole purpose. It is important to keep in mind that the study of religion might yield many goods, and awareness of the variety of institutional practices and cultural niches "calls into question the view that there can or should be just one answer to questions of the value of the discipline" (Engler/Stausberg 2011, 139). There are, I have tried to suggest, a number of cogent arguments for the relevance of the academic study of religion, whether that enterprise is imagined narrowly or broadly, and scholars should agilely employ those arguments that seem most contextually useful for promoting the subject in the academy and beyond the campus walls.

Glossary

Humanities one of the clusters of disciplines, or areas of knowledge, that constitute a liberal arts education. The meaning and scope of the humanities has changed over time and has varied across regions, but many educators today would take it to include the disciplines that study literature, languages, history, philosophy, and religion.

Liberal arts the diverse areas of study deemed necessary to provide students the broad knowledge and diverse skills required for enhancing well-being and participating in civic life, as opposed to a narrower curricular focus on a single vocational specialization. The areas of study deemed optimal have changed over time and varied across cultures, but many educators today would suggest a liberal arts education involves familiarity with the arts, humanities, social sciences, and natural sciences.

Relevance the value of something for a particular person and a particular task in a particular context. In turn, claims about the relevance of the study or religion tend to insist on its intrinsic value or, more commonly, suggest it is worthwhile because it advances knowledge, enriches individuals, or improves society.

Values judgments about the worth of something. That worth might be seen as intrinsic (for its own sake) or instrumental (for the sake of something else). Further, values can be of different kinds—epistemic values (about truth), moral values (about good), or aesthetic values (about beauty). All value judgments, however, have implications for claims about how we ought to think and act. In that sense we can speak of guiding values.

References

Alatas, Syed Farid. 1995. "The Theme of 'Relevance' in Third World Human Sciences." *Singapore Journal of Tropical Geography* 16(2): 123–140.

Alles, Gregory D., ed. 2008. *Religious Studies: A Global View*. London: Routledge.

Alles, Gregory D. 2011. "What (Kind of) Good Is Religious Studies?" *Religion* 41(2): 217–223. doi: 10.1080/0048721X.2011.579786

Antes, Peter. 2002. "Why Should People Study History of Religions?" In *Themes and Problems of the History of Religions in Contemporary Europe: Proceedings of the International Seminar, Messina, March 30–31, 2001*, edited by Giulia Sfameni Gasparro. Consenza: L. Giordano, 41–52.

Appiah, Kwame Anthony. 2006. *Cosmopolitanism: Ethics in a World of Strangers*. New York: W. W. Norton.

Berner, Ulrich. 2011. "Contextualization of Religious Studies and of Religious Phenomena." *Religion* 41(2): 149–157. doi: 10.1080/0048721X.2011.579787

Cahn, Steven M. 1988. "Introduction." In *John Dewey: The Later Works, 1925–1953*. Vol. 13, edited by Jo Ann Boydston. Carbondale: Southern Illinois University Press, ix–xviii.

Dewey, John. 1916. *Democracy and Education*. New York: Macmillan.

Dewey, John. 1988. *Theory of Valuation*. In *John Dewey: The Later Works, 1925–1953*. Vol. 13, edited by Jo Ann Boydston. Carbondale: Southern Illinois University Press, 191–251.

Engler, Steven. 2006. "Religious Studies in Canada and Brazil: Pro-Pluralism and Anti-Theology in Context." *Studies in Religion/Sciences Religieuses* 35(3–4): 447–473. doi: 10.1177/000842980603500306

Engler, Steven and Michael Stausberg. 2011. "Introductory Essay: Crisis and Creativity: Opportunities and Threats in the Global Study of Religion/s." *Religion* 41(2): 127–143. doi: 10.1080/0048721X.2011.591209

Freiberger, Oliver. 2013. "Die deutsche Religionswissenschaft im transnationalen Fachdiskurs." *Zeitschrift für Religionswissenschaft* 21(1): 1–28. doi: 10.1515/zfr-2013-000

Führding, Steffen. 2009. *Warum Religionswissenschaft? Eine empirische Studie über die Gründe, Religionswissenschaft zu studieren*. Marburg: Diagonal.

Hinnells, John R. 2005. "Why Study Religions?" In *The Routledge Companion to the Study of Religion*, edited by John R. Hinnells. London: Routledge, 5–20.

Hinnells, John R. and Richard King, eds. 2007. *Religion and Violence in South Asia: Theory and Practice*. London: Routledge.

Jacobsen, Douglas and Rhonda Hustedt Jacobsen, eds. 2008. *The American University in a Postsecular Age*. New York: Oxford University Press.

James, William. 1962. "On a Certain Blindness in Human Beings." In *Essays on Faith and Morals: William James*, edited by Ralph Barton Perry. Cleveland, OH: Meridian, 259–284.

Jerryson, Michael. 2010. "Introduction." In *Buddhist Warfare*, edited by Michael K. Jerryson and Mark Juergensmeyer. New York: Oxford University Press, 3–16.

Johnson, Timothy R. 1995. "The Significance of Religion for Aging Well." *American Behavioral Scientist* 39(2): 186–208.

Johnston, Douglas, ed. 2003. *Faith-Based Diplomacy: Trumping Realpolitik*. New York: Oxford University Press.

Juergensmeyer, Mark. 2000. *Terror in the Mind of God: The Global Rise of Religious Violence*, 2nd edition. Berkeley: University of California Press.

King, Richard. 2007. "The Association of 'Religion' with Violence: Reflections on a Modern Trope." In *Religion and Violence in South Asia: Theory and Practice*, edited by John R. Hinnells and Richard King. London: Routledge, 226–257.

Kippenberg, Hans G. 2008. *Gewalt als Gottesdienst: Religionskriege im Zeitalter der Globalisierung*. Munich: C. H. Beck.

Lease, Gary. 1995. "Foreword." *Method and Theory in the Study of Religion* 7(4): 299–303.

Lincoln, Bruce. 2003. *Holy Terrors: Thinking about Religion after September 11*. Chicago, IL: University of Chicago Press.

Livingston, James C. 2009. *Anatomy of the Sacred: An Introduction to Religion*, 5th edition. Upper Saddle River, NJ: Pearson.

McCutcheon, Russell. 2011. *Critics Not Caretakers: Redescribing the Public Study of Religion*. Albany: State University of New York Press.

Mitchell, Logan and Sarah Romans. 2003. "Spiritual Beliefs in Bipolar Affective Disorder: Their Relevance for Illness Management." *Journal of Affective Disorders* 75(3): 247–257. doi: 10.1016/S0165-0327(02)00055-1

Müller, F. Max. 1870. *Introduction to the Science of Religion*. London: Spottiswoode.

Nussbaum, Martha C. 2010. *Not for Profit: Why Democracy Needs the Humanities*. Princeton, NJ: Princeton University Press.

"Overview of Findings from the 2012–13 Humanities Departmental Survey." Humanities Indicators: A Project of the American Academy of Arts and Sciences. Available at: <http://www.humanitiesindicators.org/content/indicatordoc.aspx?i=458>, accessed October 10, 2014.

"Relevance, n." 2014. *OED Online*. Oxford: Oxford University Press. Last accessed June 27, 2014.

"The Religion Major and Liberal Education—A White Paper." 2007. American Academy of Religion—Teagle Working Group. *Religious Studies News* 23(4): 21–24. Available at: <https://www.aarweb.org/about/teagleaar-white-paper>, accessed October 10, 2014.

Sheikh, Mona Kanwal. 2012. "How Does Religion Matter? Pathways to Religion in International Relations." *Review of International Studies* 38(2): 365–392. doi: 10.1017/S026021051100057X

Small, Helen. 2013. *The Value of the Humanities*. Oxford: Oxford University Press.

Stausberg, Michael. 2011. "The Bologna Process and the Study of Religion/s in (Western) Europe." *Religion* 41(2): 187–207. doi: 10.1080/0048721X.2011.586259

Taves, Ann. 2011. "2010 Presidential Address: 'Religion' in the Humanities and the Humanities in the University." *Journal of the American Academy of Religion* 79(2): 287–314. doi: 10.1093/jaarel/lfr004

Teichler, Ulrich. 2007. *Higher Education Systems: Conceptual Frameworks, Comparative Perspectives, Empirical Findings.* Rotterdam: Sense.

Tweed, Thomas A. 1998. "Religion and Healing: Cultivating a Respectful Ambivalence." *North Carolina Medical Journal* 59(3): 186–187.

Tweed, Thomas A. 2000. Contribution to a Forum on "Why Is Religion Important?" *Ideas* 7(2): 36.

Tweed, Thomas A. 2006. *Crossing and Dwelling: A Theory of Religion.* Cambridge, MA: Harvard University Press.

Tweed, Thomas A. 2008. "Why Are Buddhists So Nice? Media Representations of Buddhism and Islam in the United States since 1945." *Material Religion* 4(1): 91–93. doi: 10.2752/175183408X288168

Tweed, Thomas A. 2009. "Crabs, Crustaceans, Crabiness, and Outrage: A Response." *Journal of the American Academy of Religion* 77(2): 445–459. doi: 10.1093/jaarel/lfp034

Tweed, Thomas A. 2014. "'Following the Flows: Diversity, Santa Fe, and Method in Religious Studies." In *Understanding Religious Pluralism: Perspectives from Religious Studies and Theology*, edited by Peter C. Phan and Jonathan S. Ray. Eugene, OR: Pickwick, 1–19.

Wiebe, Donald. 1988. "Why the Academic Study of Religion? Motive and Method in the Study of Religion." *Religious Studies* 24(4): 403–413.

Further Reading

Alles 2011 [*Identifying two related movements in higher education—the tendency to emphasize education's utility for employment and the inclination to apply administrative models from business—the author argues that those contemporary patterns are unhelpful for both the study of religions and for "the society at large."*]

Antes 2002 [*Focusing on the German context, this essay helpfully distinguishes two arguments for the importance of the study of religion: its utility to other disciplines and its value as a deposit of accumulated knowledge.*]

Engler/Stausberg 2011 [*Especially useful for its cross-cultural perspective, this is an excellent overview of the challenges faced by the academic study of religion "in light of economic and political pressures."*]

Hinnells 2005 [*This wide-ranging essay takes on the central question—why both believers and non-believers might find the study of religion valuable—as the author identifies many of the usual arguments for the relevance of the academic study of religion.*]

Nussbaum 2011 [*A helpful overview and impassioned call for the relevance of the humanities in higher education.*]

Index of Names

Abbreviations: *n* refers to footnote. A page number with an unnumbered '*n*' indicates that references are found both in the text and in a footnote on that same page.

Index of Subjects

Abbreviations: f refers to figure; *n* refers to footnote; *t* refers to table. A page number with an unnumbered '*n*' or '*t*' indicates that references are found both in the text and in a footnote or table on that same page.

Page numbers in italics indicate chapters, or significant portions thereof, dedicated to the index term.

Page numbers in bold indicate definitions of index terms in chapter glossaries.

Printed in the USA/Agawam, MA
May 3, 2024

865425.016